SYMPOSION 2022

ÖSTERREICHISCHE AKADEMIE DER WISSENSCHAFTEN
PHILOSOPHISCH-HISTORISCHE KLASSE
ÖSTERREICHISCHES ARCHÄOLOGISCHES INSTITUT
ABTEILUNG ALTERTUMSWISSENSCHAFTEN

AKTEN DER GESELLSCHAFT FÜR GRIECHISCHE UND HELLENISTISCHE RECHTSGESCHICHTE

begründet von HANS JULIUS WOLFF

HERAUSGEGEBEN VON

ATHINA DIMOPOULOU
MARTIN DREHER
MICHELE FARAGUNA
KAJA HARTER-UIBOPUU
ADRIAAN LANNI

Band 29

SYMPOSION 2022

Vorträge zur
griechischen und hellenistischen Rechtsgeschichte
(Gmunden, 22.–24 August 2022)

herausgegeben von

Philipp Scheibelreiter

VERLAG DER
ÖSTERREICHISCHEN
AKADEMIE DER
WISSENSCHAFTEN

Diese Publikation wurde unterstützt durch
das Land Öberösterreich und die Universität Wien.

mit Unterstützung von
Kultur ober österreich

universität wien

Herausgeber der
Akten der Gesellschaft für griechische und hellenistische Rechtsgeschichte
seit 1975:
1 (1975) – 4 (1983) H. J. Wolff
5 (1989) – 12 (1998) A. Biscardi, J. Mélèze Modrzejewski, G. Thür
13 (2001) – 19 (2007) E. Cantarella, J. Mélèze Modrzejewski, G. Thür
20 (2008) – 26 (2017) E. Cantarella, M. Gagarin, J. Mélèze Modrzejewski, G. Thür
27 (2018) E. Cantarella, M. Gagarin, G. Thür, J. Velissaropoulos
28 (2021) A. Dimopoulou, M. Dreher, M. Faraguna, K. Harter-Uibopuu, A. Lanni

ISBN 978-3-7001-9564-1

Satz: Susanne Lorenz, Wien
Druck und Bindung: Prime Rate, Budapest
https://epub.oeaw.ac.at/9564-1
https://verlag.oeaw.ac.at
MADE IN EUROPE

Angenommen durch die Publikationskommission der philosophisch-historischen Klasse
der Österreichischen Akademie der Wissenschaften:

Diese Publikation wurde einem anonymen, internationalen
Begutachtungsverfahren unterzogen.
Peer Review ist ein wesentlicher Bestandteil des Evaluationsprozesses des Verlages der Österreichischen Akademie der Wissenschaften. Bevor ein Buch zur Veröffentlichung angenommen werden kann, wird es von internationalen Fachleuten bewertet und muss schließlich von der Publikationskommission der Österreichischen Akademie der Wissenschaften genehmigt werden.

Bibliografische Information der Deutschen Nationalbibliothek
Die Deutsche Nationalbibliothek verzeichnet diese Publikation
in der Deutschen Nationalbibliografie;
detaillierte bibliografische Daten sind im Internet über http://dnb.dnb.de abrufbar.

Die verwendete Papiersorte in dieser Publikation ist DIN EN ISO 9706 zertifiziert und
erfüllt die Voraussetzung für eine dauerhafte Archivierung von schriftlichem Kulturgut.

INHALT

VORWORT

I. Von 21.–25. August 2022 fand das für den nahezu gleichen Zeitraum des Jahres 2021 geplante „23. Symposion für Griechische und Hellenistische Rechtgeschichte" in Gmunden am Traunsee statt. Trotz der pandemiebedingten Verschiebung konnte das für 2021 geplante Programm abgehalten werden, und die 28 Beiträge – zwei Respondentinnen hatten leider ihre Teilnahme absagen müssen – finden sich nun in diesem Band vereint.

Wie beim Symposion üblich, gab es keine thematischen Vorgaben. Dennoch lassen sich inhaltliche Blöcke bilden, welche hier kurz vorgestellt werden sollen:

Einen ersten, dem **archaischen Recht** gewidmeten Schwerpunkt bilden die Beiträge von Athina Dimopoulou (Athen), welche das 2016 in Phaleron gehobene Massengrab und darin gefunden Skelette aus dem 7. Jh. v. Chr. in einen rechtshistorischen Kontext setzt. Bernhard Palme (Wien) überlegt in seinem *responsum*, inwiefern dieser Befund auch Auswirkungen auf die Trittyen-Verfassung Athens gezeitigt haben könnte. Thematisch anknüpfend hat es Werner Riess (Hamburg) unternommen, das drakontische Gesetz über die unvorsätzliche Tötung und insbesondere die darin getroffene Kompetenzverteilung neu zu bewerten, was Winfried Schmitz (Bonn) in seinem *responsum* etwa für Epheten und Areopagiten vertieft.

Ein zweiter Block widmet sich unterschiedlichen Aspekten und Funktionen der **Gesetze**: Martin Dreher (Magdeburg) stellt die Frage nach der Geltungsdauer athenischer Gesetze, wofür Lene Rubinstein (London) in ihrem *responsum* epigraphische Evidenz des nichtathenischen Griechenland miteinbezieht. Die Ergebnisse von Bob Wallace (Evanston) zur Frage der Funktion von νόμοι bei Thukydides macht Mirko Canevaro (Edinburgh) für eine verfassungstheoretische Perspektive nutzbar. Den im Gesetz Nikophons niedergelegten Bestimmungen zum athenischen Marktrecht, deren Analyse sich Mariagrazia Rizzi (Mailand) verschrieben hat, stellt Adele Scafuro (Providence) auch Ergebnisse der 2021 erfolgten Neuedition des Münzgesetzes des Epikrates gegenüber. Anna Magnetto (Pisa) vergleicht das Gesandtschaftsrecht der platonischen Gesetze mit den dieses betreffenden Bestimmungen des positiven Rechts. Kaja Harter-Uibopuu (Hamburg) vertieft in ihrem *responsum* dazu wichtige, auch verfahrensrechtliche Fragen.

Dem Recht von **Gortyn** nähern sich die Referenten in einer dritten thematischen Einheit auf unterschiedliche Weise: Während David Lewis (Edinburgh) mögliche Kategorien des *status servitutis* für das Recht Kretas untersucht, wozu Alberto Maffi (Mailand) auch wichtige, dem familienrechtlichen Kontext zuzuweisende Probleme ausleuchtet, greift Stephen Todd (Manchester) kein Thema des materiellen Rechts auf, sondern erörtert die Rezeption und erste Edition der kretischen Inschrift(en), welche er – wie auch sein Respondent Ilias Arnaoutoglou (Athen) mit weiteren Beispielen – in den Kontext der Wissenschaftsgeschichte und Methode juristischer Gräzistik stellt.

Fragestellungen zum griechischen **Vermögensprivatrecht** als dem viertem Block lassen sich drei Beiträge zuordnen: Sophia Aneziri (Athen) erörtert die Problematik einer dogmatischen Erfassung und begrifflichen Eingrenzung griechischer Stiftungen. Andreas Victor Walser (Zürich) geht anhand der Mehrfachverpfändung der alten Streifrage nach, ob das griechische Pfandrecht dem Verfalls- oder Verkaufsprinzip verpflichtet ist. Die hier aufbereiteten literarischen und epigraphischen Quellen korrespondieren mit dem bei Thomas Kruse (Wien) analysierten, papyrologischen Material. Der griechische Kaufvertrag steht im Mittelpunkt der Untersuchung von Carlos Sánchez Moreno-Ellart (Valencia), welcher sich anhand einer Szene aus Charitons „Kallirhoe" mit den Komponenten Kaufpreiszahlung und Eigentumserwerb auseinandersetzt. Dem für den Rechtserwerb womöglich konstitutiven Element dieser Passage, der καταγραφή, nähert sich Respondent Patrick Sänger (Münster) an.

Der **juristischen Papyrologie**, einer fünften thematischen Einheit, sind die Beiträge von José Luis Alonso (Zürich) zum ἄγραφος γάμος, worauf Gerhard Thür (Wien) respondiert hat, und die Überlegungen von Uri Yiftach (Tel Aviv) zur Romanisierung des griechischen Privatrechts gewidmet, deren Spuren er anhand eines Belegs zur *stipulatio* folgt. Das *responsum* von Éva Jakab (Budapest) belegt geradezu paradigmatisch, welchen wichtigen Beitrag die antike Komparatistik für das Verständnis römischer wie griechischer Rechtskultur leisten kann.

Hier schließt der sechste Themenkomplex an, der mit **Interdependenzen zwischen griechischem und römischen Recht** betitelt werden kann: Während Christel Müller (Paris) den Wurzeln der τριγονία, welche in einer *epistula* Marc Aurels genannt ist, bis ins Athen des 5. Jhs. v. Chr. nachspürt, macht Kostas Buraselis (Athen) einen neuen Vorschlag zur Ergänzung des Edikts von Kaiser Caracalla aus 212 n. Chr., der *Constitutio Antoniniana.* Lina Girdaynite (Edinburgh) setzt sich in ihrem *responsum* mit dem Forschungsstand zur hierzu auseinander.

II. Die Entscheidung, das Symposion in Gmunden abzuhalten, war zum einen deswegen gefallen, weil Gmunden die idealen Voraussetzungen dafür bietet: Der Stadtgemeinde und den örtlichen Kooperationspartnern sei herzlich für ihre unkomplizierte und stets lösungsorientierte Hilfe sowie die so gastliche Aufnahme gedankt, insbesonders Herrn Stadtamtsdirektor Dr. Heimo Pseiner und Frau Dr. Andrea Holly (Universität Salzburg). Das Seeschloss Ort bot, im Schatten der „schlafenden Griechin", einen inspirierenden und höchst repräsentativen Rahmen für das Symposion. Aber auch lokalhistorische Gesichtspunkte haben den Ausschlag dafür gegeben, zum Symposion 2022 an den von den Römern als *lacus felix* bezeichneten Traunsee zu laden:

Als aus militärischen Gründen der Provinzstatthalter von *Noricum* nach den Markomannenkriegen (um 180 n. Chr.) seinen Sitz nach *Lauriacum* (heute Lorch bei Enns) verlegt hatte und das nun bereits zur *colonia* erhobene *Ovilava* (Wels) zum Verwaltungssitz der Provinz geworden war, schlug sich die politische Aufwertung des nördlichen *Noricum* auch in der Alltagskultur nieder[1] – römische Villen der provinzialen Oberschicht lassen sich etwa am nahegelegenen Attersee nachweisen: Lokale Berühmtheit erlangte auch das Pfauenmosaik aus einer *villa urbana* italischen Stils in Weyeregg[2]. Doch auch am Traunsee selbst sind römische Gutshöfe bezeugt, etwa in der Nachbargemeinde Gmundens, in Altmünster, in dessen spätgotischen Pfarrkirche ein Grabstein gefunden wurde, der auf einen *vicus* verweist[3]. Geza Alföldy interpretiert diesen als „a large-scale farming establishment" in Altmünster aus dem späten 2. Jh. n. Chr.[4]. Die Region um Gmunden selbst könnte also wohlhabenden Familien aus *Iuvavum* (Salzburg) und *Ovilava* als Sitz ihrer Sommerresidenzen gedient haben.

Ein zweiter lokalhistorischer Bezugspunkt betrifft die Kongressstadt Gmunden: So fand hier vom 2. bis zum 5. September 1951 „unter glänzender Beteiligung"[5] der 8. Deutsche Rechtshistorikertag statt. Veranstalter war auch schon damals die „Rechts- und Staatswissenschaftliche Fakultät" der Universität Wien. Unter den Vortragenden fanden sich neben Max Kaser[6], Salvatore Riccobono[7] und Helmut Coing[8] auch Artur Steinwenter, der zum „Problem der Kontinuität zwischen mittelalterlichen und antiken Rechtsordnungen"[9] referiert hat, diese Frage „tief fundiert von der antikrechtlichen Seite aufgerollt" und dabei „die Rechtsentwicklung Ägyptens" berücksichtigt haben soll[10]. Für ein antikrechtliches Symposion in Gmunden lassen sich also Kontinuitäten nicht nur konstruieren, sondern auch aufzeigen.

III. Für die Durchführung der Tagung von 2022 gilt mein Dank allen Teilnehmerinnen und Teilnehmern sowie und vor allem meinen unermüdlichen und stets gut gelaunten Mitarbeiterinnen und Mitarbeitern: Katharina Fiegl, Julia Rauscher, Michael Binder und Stefan Schmatzberger. Für die großzügige Unterstützung zur Finanzierung der Tagung sowie der Edition und Drucklegung der Tagungsakten ist der Österreichischen Akademie der Wissenschaften und hier auch namentlich dem Österreichischen Archäologischen Institut sowie der Universität Wien und dem

---

1 Haider (1987) 22.
2 Vgl. dazu Morton (1956) 132-133.
3 CIL III[2] 5622, vgl. dazu Morton (1956) 138 und vor allem Winkler (2000).
4 Alföldy (1974) 74; zur Datierung vgl. Winkler (2000) 40.
5 Fischer (1952) 557.
6 Publiziert in: Kaser (1952).
7 Publiziert in: Riccobono (1952).
8 Publiziert in: Coing (1954).
9 Steinwenter (1961).
10 So Niederländer (1952) 551.

Land Oberösterreich zu danken. Für umfassende Unterstützung und Motivation, für Beratung und Hilfe sowohl in wissenschaftlichen als auch organisatorischen Fragen schulde ich Gerhard Thür (Wien) größten Dank. Ebenso gebührt mein Dank den Herausgeberinnen und Herausgebern der „Akten für griechische und hellenistische Rechtsgeschichte“, Athina Dimopoulou (Athen), Martin Dreher (Magdeburg), Michele Faraguna (Mailand), Adriaan Lanni (Harvard) und Kaja Harter-Uibopuu (Hamburg). Im Namen aller Autorinnen und Autoren bin ich den Gutachterinnen und Gutachtern für wertvolle Hinweise und ihre Kritik auf das Äußerste verbunden. Redaktion und Lektorat lagen in den kompetenten Händen von Frau Susanne Lorenz (Wien), ohne deren Expertise dieser Band nicht und nicht so rasch hätte fertiggestellt werden können.

Wien, 26. Juni 2023 Philipp Scheibelreiter

LITERATUR

Alföldy (1974): G. Alföldy, *Noricum*, London – Boston 1974.

Coing (1954): H. Coing, Die Anwendung des Corpus Iuris in den Consilien des Bartolus, in: Studi in memoria di Paolo Koschaker, „L’Europa e il diritto romano“, vol. 2, Milano 1954, 71–98.

Fischer (1952): H. Fischer, Bericht über die Rechtshistorikertagung 1951, in: ZRG-GA 69 (1952) 557–558.

Haider (1987): S. Haider, Geschichte Oberösterreichs, Wien 1987.

Kaser (1952): M. Kaser, Zum heutigen Stand der Interpolationenforschung, ZRG-RA 69 (1952) 60–101.

Morton (1956): F. Morton, Salzkammergut. Die Vorgeschichte einer berühmten Landschaft, Hallstatt 1956.

Niederländer (1952): H. Niederländer, Bericht über den Rechtshistorikertag 1951 in Gmunden am Traunsee (Österreich), in: ZRG-RA 69 (1952) 549–556.

Riccobono (1952): S. Riccobono, Problemi vecchi, compiti nuovi, ZRG-RA 69 (1952) 1–4.

Steinwenter (1961): A. Steinwenter, Zum Problem der Kontinuität zwischen mittelalterlichen und antiken Rechtsordnungen, IVRA 2 (1961) 15–42.

Winkler (2000): G. Winkler, Der römische Grabstein von Altmünster, JbOÖM 145/1 (2000) 37–45.

ATHINA DIMOPOULOU (ATHEN)

BIAIOΘANATOI IN THE PHALERON CEMETERY MASS GRAVE: IN SEARCH OF THE HISTORICAL AND LEGAL CONTEXT

Abstract: The paper examines the archaeological find of 79 corpses of captives bearing signs of execution, discovered in 2015-6, in the archaic cemetery of Pharelon bay, in Athens.The meaning of ἀποτυμπανισμός as a means of execution of the death penalty is re-examined. A possible connexion of the find with Kylon's conspiracy, the famous story of the Κυλώνειον ἄγος is argued, by examining the find in view of the narratives of later sources.

Keywords: Δεσμώται, death penalty, Kylon's conspiracy, asebeia, pollution.

The cemetery of Phaleron, on the shores of Athens, is one of the most extended and significant necropoleis in Attica during the Archaic Period. The Phaleron Bay was the first harbor of Athens,[1] in an area laying outside the boundaries and walls of Athens. The sandy and soft ground near the beach, in a marshy and brackish area which could not be cultivated, built or otherwise exploited, has been consistently used as a burial ground over a long period. In the excavated part of the cemetery, which is estimated to correspond to just 1/10 of its total surface,[2] a total of 2115 burials have been discovered in excavations under the supervision of the Ephorate of Antiquities of Piraeus and Islands,[3] dating from the 8th to the 4th century BC, but mainly from the Archaic period. A great part of the cemetery remains still unexcavated. Many different forms of burials have been found, with the majority being pit graves in the sand, but also pot burials, funeral pyres and cist and tile graves.[4]

The Phaleron cemetery is unique in Greece in terms of the large number of burials of βιαιοθάνατοι, people who had suffered a violent death, that have been

---

1 Phaleron was the port of Athens until 493/2, till Themistocles had the idea of transferring it to Piraeus, Pausanias, 1.1.2. The port continued to be used, being at a short distance (4 km) from the south city gates, see Chryssoulaki 2019.

2 Chryssoulaki–Pappas 2021.

3 I am grateful to Dr. Stella Chryssoulaki, Ephor of the Ephorate of Antiquities of West Attika, Piraeus and Islands and Mr. Ioannis Pappas, Archaeologist, and member of her excavation team, for their remarks, information and materials provided for this paper, for the opinions expressed in which or for possible omissions, they share no responsibility.

4 Animal burials, including 18 horses, were also found.

unearthed to this day,[5] often referred to by the archaeologists as the D-group from the initial of the Greek word δεσμώται.[6] It is the only cemetery in Attika with βιαιοθάνατοι burials, making it the possible location where those condemned to the death sentence were buried. In total, 187 skeletons dating from the last quarter of the 8th to the 4th century BC, representing close to 18% of the total number of burials found so far, bear signs of having suffered a violent death or execution. The βιαιοθάνατοι are found in all the excavated area of the Phaleron cemetery, throughout its periods of use (archaic and classical times). All of the violently killed skeletons, whose sex could be identified, were males. Among the anthropological and taphonomic indications of a violent death are the presence of shackles made from iron, indications of ties of perishable material, prone[7] or kneeling body positioning of the corpses, *perimortem* trauma, including crushed skulls and bones, feet mutilations, and lack of the usual burial rites. Simple plaque σήματα marked some of the burials as βιαιοθάνατοι.[8]

The 187 βιαιοθάνατοι were found in both individual and mass burials. Mass burials date from the 7th to the 4th century BC, consisting in 15 to 18 group burials, counting each from 3 and up to 79 individuals (the most recent find). These βαιοθάνατοι attest to the frequency of mass executions, allow to explore methods of execution of the death penalty, and, to a second extent, questions related to the formation of the Athenian state, the resort to state violence and to speculate on the identities of the captives and their possible crimes.

In the area of the Faliron Delta, in 1911 and 1915 respectively, the archaeologists Kourouniotis[9] and Pelekidis brought to light graves of the Late Geometric and Early Archaic periods in a dense arrangement.[10] The first πολυάνδριον of 18 βιαιοθάνατοι in the Phaleron cemetery was identified in 1915 by Stratis Pelekides.[11] The skeletons were found each with five shackles attached around their necks, on their wrists, and feet, including some wood remains of the wooden plank, called τύμπανον, on which their bodies had been attached. The find created a sensation at the time in Athenian society, raising popular curiosity, attracting wide publicity, and even royal visits (by members of the then royal family of Greece) to the site. The brutality of the execution raised reactions and gave rise to different interpretations, which may have been influenced by predominant historical perceptions at the time on Athenian

5 Chryssoulaki 2017; 2019; 2020; 2022.

6 Prevedorou – Buikstra 2019.

7 Skeletons buried face down are interpreted as an act of perpetual punishment, not allowing the persons executed eternal rest, or as a magical practice aiming to protect the *demios* from reprisals, Chryssoulaki 2017.

8 Only the βιαιοθάνατοι of the Phaleron cemetery had σήματα in unmarked plaques. Some were buried over older burials, but none above. This indicates the σήματα were meant to designate these burials as places to be avoided for future funerals, Chryssoulaki 2017.

9 Kourouniotis 1911.

10 On the history of the excavations since 1863 and up to 2020, see Pappas 2022.

11 Pelekidis 1916, 45–64; Keramopoulos 1923.

civilization. Pelekides was the first to suffer the consequences of this controversial find. In spite of him doing for the first time an exemplary interdisciplinary research including analysis of the shackles and of the skulls of the skeletons[12] by Koumaris, and a first publication of the find,[13] he was removed from his post in Athens. The skeleton finds were published by his supervisor, Keramopoulos, in his book on ἀποτυμπανισμός, where he collected the relevant sources and subsequent Greek folklore tradition.[14] He established the theory that the ἀποτυμπανισμός was death by crucifixion, by tying of the condemned on a wooden plank, so that death may come from hunger, thirst, suffocation, exposure to the elements and to be devoured by vultures. His hypothesis was that the condemned individuals were pirates, executed close to the Phaleron shore for making an example out of them. To this date, however, this mass burial that was the first to be unearthed, missing any pottery, has not been securely dated and the pirates hypothesis cannot be confirmed. Ever since, a great number of βιαιοθάνατοι have been discovered in the same cemetery, many of which do not include evidence of having been exposed on wooden planks.

In 2015–2016, during rescue archaeological excavations at the construction site of the Stavros Niarchos Foundation Cultural Center (SNFCC) in Phaleron, led by the Ephorate of Antiquities of West Attica, Piraeus and Islands, under the Ephor Dr. Stella Chryssoulaki, several new mass graves of βιαιοθάνατοι were found. One such grave contained 16 captives, their hands tied behind their back, thrown in a trench, along with a ceramic ritual basin for the offering of some funerary rites (preliminary dating around 530–480 B.C).[15] The most impressive find though was a mass grave found in 2016 in the periphery of the Phaleron cemetery, not far from the 2015 find, consisting of 78 skeletons, lined up in three trenches, found at the same layer as the current sea level, 0.70–1.05 m from the surface of the ancient sandy layer of earth. Their study has made the object of a multidisciplinary project, in collaboration of the Ephorate of Antiquities of Piraeus and the Islands, the Swedish Institute of Athens and the American School of Classical Studies at Athens,[16] the finds of which have only partially been published to this date.

Resuming the main finds of the anthropological field documentation of the skeletons undertaken by the Swedish Institute of Athens and Dr. Anne Ingvarsson and Ylva Bäckström (2019), the western, first row (Row 1) consisted of 47 bound individuals divided in two groups. The main group had 39 individuals in a row, carefully laid the one next to the other in supine position. The majority had their arms positioned over their heads. Iron shackles were found on the wrist of 32, one had traces of iron under the right knee, 3 lying in prone position could have been tied together, while among the 15 without shackles their arm position indicates they

---

12 Chryssoulaki 2020.
13 Pelekidis 1916.
14 Pelekidis 1916, 13–64; Keramopoulos 1923.
15 Chryssoulaki 2019.
16 Buikstra 2020.

may have been tied at the time of burial. The executed were not totally deprived of passage rites, two οἰνοχόαι having been found on the corpse, at the northern and southern part of Row 1, allowing to date the burial between the 2nd and 3rd quarter of the 7th century BC. The second group of the first row consists of 7 skeletons with their hands tied behind their backs (without metal shackles), in a different posture than the rest: most in a lateral position with their limbs bent at right angles. They seem to have been deposited later than the rest, although it cannot be determined whether they were associated with the same event, nor the timespan between the depositions. The middle row (Row 2), buried in the same level as the first row, consisted of 16 individuals with their arms tied behind their backs, without metal shackles. In contrast to Row 1, they seem to have been haphazardly deposited. The different orientation of Rows 1 and 2 suggest they were deposited on different occasions, but probably close in time. The eastern row (Row 3) consists of another 16 skeletons buried in a pit, with their arms tied with iron bonds around their wrists. Their body position indicates they were executed in situ, probably from a standing position, and thrown in, after falling, almost like dominoes.[17] The relation and period between the three row depositions has not been determined, since there is no stratigraphic information available. The simultaneous burial of the three rows of the 79 captives in total cannot be positively confirmed, although proximity in the time of burial cannot be excluded.

The preliminary field observations and analysis of the remains show that all skeletons whose sex can be identified belonged to males. Age-wise, the individuals assigned to an age group were mostly young (74%), among which 6 juvenile (12–19 years, 7.6%), 33 young adult (20–34 years, 41.8%), 13 middle adults (35–49 years, 16.4%), and one old male (50+, 1.3%). Twenty-six, whose age could not be assigned to an age group, were assigned among the adults, although older individuals may have been among them. Most of them are without signs of active disease and with a generally good oral health status, being in a good shape, having been well fed and exercised, which may assign them to upper class individuals, although they seem to have suffered from dehydration and violent beating close to their death.[18]

Numerous breaks and skeletal trauma were observed.[19] *Perimortem* fractures were identified in 14 cases and possible *perimortem* fractures in 25 cases, including skull fractures.[20] These fractures include mandibular fractures, often caused by blows to the chin through violence, depressed comminuted fractures to the cranium, often the result of interpersonal violence, although other causes cannot be excluded. The form and location of the cranial fractures may indicate that many among the

17 Invgarsson – Bäckström 2019, 74.

18 Chryssoulaki 2019. Bone analysis has shown that some of the skeletons belonged to individuals who had carried out strenuous activities, such as soldiers, Ingvarsson – Bäckström 2019, 60.

19 Ingvarsson – Bäckström 2019, 57.

20 Ingvarsson – Bäckström 2019, 58.

captives were executed in situ, when kneeling (perhaps in front of a trench) or lying down, with a blow from a blunt object like a club.[21] The initial rapport concludes that (Ingvarsson – Bäckström 2019, 75): "*The scenario surrounding the depositions of the individuals in the mass graves at Phaleron is largely obscure and cannot be elucidated through the osteological field observation. However, it seems likely that the individuals died within a short period of time, some of them more or less simultaneously. Why and where the individuals were killed is a matter of conjecture; the observations from the field documentation neither validate, nor disprove the hypothesis that these individuals were the captives and victims of the so-called 'Kylonian conspiracy'. A hypothetical scenario is that a majority of the captives, probably in poor physical condition, e.g. starved, dehydrated, and beaten but otherwise in good general health, were brought to Phaleron in shackles, some of them plausibly tied to a frame with ropes, as suggested by their positions. The individuals may have been pushed to the ground, some of them perhaps kneeling, before fatal blows/punches to the head of the individuals not already dead were inflicted before the bodies were covered.*"

Although there is no certain way of determining either the identity of the deceased, or their connection to any historical even, the two *oinochoae* found by the lower limbs of two of the individuals of this row, which are tentatively dated between the 2nd and 3rd quarter of the 7th century B.C., allow for a dating of the first row of the captives around the time traditionally assigned in the sources to the attempted seizure of power by Kylon, known in the sources as the Κυλώνειον ἄγος.[22]

The period starting with the Kylon events, in the third quarter of the 7th century, and ending with the establishment of democracy under Kleisthenes in the 5th century, is a period characterized in Athens by prolonged στάσις, intensive internal strife. Milestones such as Drakon's and Solon's reforms, Peisistratus' and his sons' tyrannies, and the Alcmeonids' lasting impact on Athenian politics make it a period of gestation of the democratic constitution of Athens, of the first written legal norms and of the foundation of the Athenian state on the rule of law.[23] The Phaleron burials offer valuable evidence regarding the beginnings of this process in the 7th century, on what may be a basically legal event (the execution of a large number of individuals), for a period about which later literary traditions are confused, uncertain and often manipulated. This archaeological data will be a precious complement to our knowledge of the period, which will put to the test the textual record, but also mainstream ideas about Athens' state identity in the 7th century. As Robin Osborne has pointed out in a lecture at the British School at Athens focusing

---

[21] Invgarsson – Bäckström 2019, 75, Bérard – Castex 2021.

[22] Chryssoulaki – Pappas, 2021. Radiocarbon analyses (C14) were conducted in selected burials, and the results are expected to be published.

[23] Morris 1987, 16–17.

on the find of the mass grave in Phaleron,[24] the importance of the find is what it tells us about archaic Athens. The great number of the people buried in a common grave is per se a parameter that requires explication in view of the strong impact of their death at the society of the time. Although estimation of population numbers in antiquity is notoriously difficult and uncertain, in view of the lack of statistical data, the sheer number of the captives executed simultaneously (assuming they were free Athenians and considering their corresponding family members) must have represented a significant percentage of the Athenian population at the time, signifying that this was an extraordinary event for Archaic Athens.

Where the Phaleron mass grave burials the result of executions?[25] The skeletons analysis will provide more answers in the future on this point. However, the presence of several cranium *perimortem* fractures at the temple area makes it very likely that a certain number among the dead were killed, or given the coup de grace, by a τύμπανον, a blow by a club on the head. It is to be noted that the 70 skeletons recently excavated, contrary to the find of 19 skeletons published by Pelekides (1916) and Keramopoulos (1923), bear no traces of wood attached to the shackles and no indication that the bodies were exposed to wooden planks prior to their death. These of the third row seem to have been executed in situ and fallen in the pit.

The Phaleron δεσμώται find allows us to question the *communis opinio*, established since Keramopoulos' book on ἀποτυμπανισμός, according to which ἀποτυμπανισμός as the prevalent method of execution of the death penalty in ancient Athens consisted in the condemned being fastened on a board (τύμπανον) and left to die a long and agonizing death, though thirst, hunger and being devoured by animals.[26] Before Keramopoulos' study, ἀποτυμπανισμός was considered to consist in the crushing of the skull by the τύμπανον, a wooden club.[27] Keramopoulos brought forth a number of references in the sources referring to the τύμπανον as a means of execution following a court sentence,[28] including the

---

24 Osborne 2021 thinks the story about killing supplicants on the Acropolis or the altars of the Σεμναὶ θεαί on the Areopagos does not fit well with the mass execution at Phaleron. However, exactly because a very significant number of men appear to have been executed all together, within the same time-frame Kylon's affair is assigned in the sources, the find, a missing part in the puzzle of a period with no contemporary written sources, once fully investigated, as may help us better understand state organization in early Athens.

25 Supported by Thür 2018.

26 Keramopoulos 1923; Gernet 1924; Thür 1991; Todd 2000; Velissaropoulou 1984; Cantarella 1991; Hall 1996.

27 Youni 1998, 48.

28 On an indirect reference to the fact that the ἀποτυμπανισμός brought instant death, see Aristotle, *Rhetoric* 2.6, where he describes how the tragic poet Antiphon, when he was about to be clubbed to death (μέλλων ἀποτυμπανίζεσθαι) by order of the tyrant Dionysius, seeing that those who were to die with him covered their faces as they

grammarians' and scholiasts' definitions thereof. In all relevant testimonies though, the meaning of τύμπανον is this of a wooden club used as a weapon incurring wounds or killing.[29] The meaning of ἀποτυμπανίζειν even in Plutarch (*De Stoicorum repugnantiis* 1049.D, *De sollertia animalium* 968.E, *Pericles* 28.2, *De superstitione* 169.F–170A) and the lexicographers (Pseudo-Zonaras, *Lexicon*: s.v. Τυμπανίζεται) is clearly this of beating with a club, although Keramopoulos assumed Plutarch may have not known the correct meaning of the word because the application of roman law may have changed things.[30]

The torture of being hanged from a plank is indeed mentioned in the sources (Herodotus, 7.33, ζώοντα πρὸς σανίδα διεπασσάλευσαν, 9.120, σανίδα προσπασσαλεύσαντες ἐνεκρέμασαν). However, in these instances the word ἀποτυμπανισμός is not used. In the scenes from Aristophane's *Thesmophoriazousai* (930–946; 1001–1055; 1107–1110; 1121–1125; 1165–1171; 1203–1209) describing how Mnesilochos is tied onto a board by a Scythian archer after trying to pass in a festival as a woman (and therefore being guilty of ἀσέβεια), the term ἀποτυμπανισμός is also missing, although it is mentioned that he was hung to die (l. 938, ἀποθανουμένῳ) and left to become dinner for the crows (l. 1028–9, κρεμάσας κόραξι δεῖπνον). Herodotus mentions that "Ἀθηναῖοι κατέδησαν τὴν ἐπὶ θανάτῳ" the collaborators of the Spartan King Cleomenes, when he seized the Acropolis in support of Isagoras, after they forced Kleisthenes to exile as ἐναγὴς due to the killing of the Kylonians.

However, the torture of being hang from a plank and left to die on the one hand, and ἀποτυμπανισμός on the other, do not seem to be one and the same thing. In the passage of Plutarch's life of *Pericles* (28), it is mentioned that the harsh punishment reserved for the trierarchs of the Samians was to expose them on a plank for ten days into the marketplace of Miletus and then, after they had suffered, to kill them by crashing their heads with clubs. Keramopoulos assumed that the ἀποτυμπανισμός/ἀποτυμπανίζειν was named after the plank on which the bodies were exposed and left to die and that the grammarians got the wrong sense by accepting the τύμπανον as the club through which the convicted were killed.[31]

---

passed through the gates, said, "Why cover your faces? Is it because you are afraid that one of the crowd should see you tomorrow?".

29 In Aristotle (*A.C.* 45.6) is told the story of Lysimachus, convicted without trial to the death sentence by the Boule, who, as he already sat awaiting death, was saved by Eumelides who argued that no citizen should be executed without trial by a court, was acquitted and nick-named "ὁ ἀπὸ τοῦ τυμπάνου". The references to ἀποτυμπανισμός in Lysias 13.56, 13.67, speak about putting to death. In Demosthenes 8.61, 9.61, 19.137, the word has the meaning of hitting on the head or executing.

30 Keramopoulos 1923, 22.

31 Followed by Gernet 1924; Velissaropoulou 1984; Cantarella 1991; Cantarella 2004; Mélèze Modrzejewski 2008; Hall 1996; Cirio 2015; Foxhall–Lewis 1996, 79–90; Allen 2000, 200 argues that the punishment of being fastened on a wooden plank did not always lead to death. For a list of known cases of *apotympanismos* see Hansen 1976, 122–43.

Balamoshev, in an article published in 2011,[32] based on references to ἀποτυμπανισμός in the papyri[33] which have the meaning of severely assaulting and beating with a club, has contested[34] that the word refers to execution by exposure on a plank, although he attributes this to a semantic evolution of the term in Hellenistic times. I think he is right in the interpretation of the meaning of the term in the papyri, and that this was not a semantic evolution, but the original meaning of the term. Keramopoulos, based on the find of the 19 skeletons who had been attached to planks prior to their death, has identified ἀποτυμπανισμός as this ordeal and went further by arguing that this was the standard method of execution of the death penalty. However, a close look at the sources (e.g. Pollux, *Onomasticon* 8.70–71), shows that ἀποτυμπανισμός' primary meaning was death by clubbing in the head[35] and that exposure on a plank was a torture inflicted –only in some cases– prior to death, as an aggravated form of execution or pre-execution punishment. It was reserved to certain hideous crimes (including treason or sacrilege), and in cases where the condemned were to be made an example, such as in the myth of Prometheus, guilty of the theft of fire, or the Samian trierarchs executed by Pericles. In the last case (Plutarch, *Pericles* 28) it is mentioned that the captives "σανίσι προσδήσας ἐφ' ἡμέρας δέκα κακῶς ἤδη διακειμένους προσέταξεν ἀνελεῖν, ξύλοις τὰς κεφαλὰς συγκόψαντας". The hanging from the plank was a torture prior to the final execution by clubbing on their head. This attachment to a wooden plank took different forms,[36] called πεντεσύριγγον ξύλον (Aristophanes, *Equites* 1049) bearing five holes for the neck, hands, and feet, or ποδοκάκκη, attaching the feet (Lysias 1.10; Dem., 24.105). Attachment to wood, other than a means to avoid escaping of captives, is mentioned as an additional πρόστιμον according to a law attributed to Solon, punishing thieves, those who maltreated their parents and fleeing the army (Lysias, 1.16), a penalty adjudicated by the Heliaia at anyone's request.

Depending on the circumstances and the nature of the crime, not all convicts sentenced to the death penalty in Athens must have suffered the long and agonizing ordeal or being attached on a plank and left to die, but may have been executed swiftly, by a blow on their head, according to the original meaning of ἀποτυμπανισμός. The Phaleron βιαιοθάνατοι, bearing no shackles around the neck and no sign of wood to which they may have been attached, may have been victims of such instant executions.

---

32 Balamoshev 2011.

33 *Enteux.* 86, dated to 221 BC, Mich. inv. 6979 (=*SB* XX 15001), *UPZ* I 119 (156 BC); *Oxy.* XV 1798 (late second c. A.D.).

34 Refuting Mélèze Modrzejewski 2008.

35 Pollux defines ἀποτυμπανίζειν as one of the methods of inflicting the death penalty and τύμπανον as one of the *demios'* instruments: ὁ δὲ παραλαμβάνων τοὺς ἀναιρουμένους καλεῖται δήμιος, δημόκοινος, ὁ πρὸς τῷ ὀρύγματι ὁ ἐπὶ τῷ ὀρύγματι· καὶ τὰ ἐργαλεῖα αὐτοῦ ξίφος, βρόχος, τύμπανον, φάρμακον, κώνειον.

36 Herodotus 9.37, 6.75, Aristophanes, Equites 367, Demosthenes 18.129; cf. Acta Apostolorum 16.24, OGI 483.181 (Pergamum, 2nd c. A.D.).

It is therefore certain that the wooden club was a real weapon, used to administer the death sentence by the holders of power. Hence the κορυνηφόροι, the bodyguards latter given to Peisistratus (Herodotus, 1.59), who assisted him in seizing the Acropolis in view of becoming tyrant, were not only bearing a symbolic tool, as it has been argued,[37] but an actual weapon used in state executions, synonymous with the power to administer corporal punishment (later, the *fasces* of the Roman magistrates *cum imperium* serving a similar purpose, Plutarch, *Romulus* 26.3).

The presence of many corpses in the same grave indicates an abnormal and simultaneous mortality. Regarding the question whether these were state executions,[38] the large number of the βιαιοθάνατοι, both individual and in groups,[39] the evidence of the corpses having been attached to a wooden plank in one group burial, the presence of shackles,[40] and the body alignment of skeletons showing that several captives were executed *in situ* and thrown in the pit at once, makes this the only plausible explanation. The way the bodies fell into the trench seems an exact illustration of Pollux' description of the *demios* (*Onomasticon* 8.70–71), the executioner acting in the name of all the demos, called also "ὁ πρὸς τῷ ὀρύγματι, ὁ ἐπὶ τῷ ὀρύγματι", the one in front of, or upon the trench. Even individual βιαιοθάνατοι, if they were victims of murder or vendettas, would have had proper burials by their family members. The shackles show the captives were arrested, tied, and brought (probably on foot) to be killed in situ, and not casualties in an armed strife, killed in a violent clash. Having ready access to iron shackles in large numbers points out to a state authority rather than a private force. Mass executions require some degree of organization and legitimation, that no private citizen (not even a member of a γένος of Eupatridai) could possibly have and freely exercise against anyone, especially against his fellow-citizens, including guards and δήμιοι able to execute several people within a short time-frame, the attendance of some form of public authority supervising and rendering possible the execution against popular or families' violent reactions, without incurring the risk of immediate reprisals from family members of the deceased, resulting in a bloodbath. This of course does not mean that the executions were justified or dispensed via due process, just that they were not private, but public affairs. The Phaleron mass

37 As argued by Boardman, 1972.

38 Information on actual executions in Athens imposed as a death penalty concerns mainly κακοῦργοι, including thieves and burglars, caught in the act, who were brought before the Eleven and executed right away in they confessed the crime. They were brought to trial if they denied committing the act and, if found guilty, were executed. Another category were traitors. Citizens accused of other crimes subject to the death penalty had the option to go into voluntary exile after the first of the two speeches allowed to the defense. On these see Hansen, 1976, 121 sqq.; Cohen 1983, 52–61.

39 On Athenians burying their dead one by one see Plutarch, *Solon* 10.3.

40 The term δεσμώτης designates a prisoner who has been attached, sometimes before or in view of execution, Thucydides 4.41.1, Herodotus 3.143.

graves offer evidence that state executions, as expressions of the state's monopoly of legitimate deadly force, existed long before Solon, attesting the existence of an early state structure for Athens in the 7th century, that had a system of retribution and execution of the death penalty, applied to a large scale. All of which presuppose a system of state authority capable of carrying out the killing and the burial of several individuals at once, and, possibly, a system of justice in place. Which would bring earlier the date of existence both of the death penalty in Athens[41] and of a complex and sophisticated state apparatus, entitled to use legitimate violence against its members, at a date anterior to Solon.

Who were the captives? The existence of *perimortem* fractures, especially on the cranes, and the presence of two adolescents, makes it unlikely the captives were victims of warfare, even if an arrowhead in the chest of a skeleton indicates armed resistance has taken place before their capture. Other possible candidates could be criminals, slaves or pirates. In view of the number of the larger burials, criminals such as burglars could not have acted in such large groups. As for slaves, the bone analysis could furnish useful information, but finds such as rings and a knife make this unlikely. Pirates are a possibility, although the evidence of some basic rites of passage, attested by the two *oinochoae* containing libation liquids, proves that a minimum of respect was shown for the victims, which is not compatible with the execution of κακοῦργοι. As Robin Osborne has remarked, it is highly unlikely either that the recent discovery of the Phaleron mass burial were prisoners of war, which in preclassical times were considered too valuable, in terms of possibility of exchange or ransom, to be put to death. The number of the 40 people of the first raw, belonging to the same young age group (including two adolescents), combined with the existence of rites of passage as attested by the two *oinochoae*, makes the hypothesis that these were executed citizens a plausible one. Since, thanks to these *oinochoae*, the burial can be dated in the 7th c., events assigned to this century in the sources can be assessed in the attempt to establish the circumstances of their death.[42] This burial would constitute the earliest dated mass execution known for Athens, for a period where the narratives of the latter sources on the Kylonian affair, not based on any contemporary written evidence but on oral traditions recorded at a latter date, do offer an image of Athens divided by στάσις, although the exact nature, unfolding and dating of the events remain uncertain and have made the subject of many speculations by modern historians.

The notorious Kylonian affair and sacrilege, which can dated at some point between the years 636–624,[43] is one of the oldest stories told about early Athens

41 Contra Thür 1990, on Drakon not knowing the death penalty. On the death penalty see Velissaropoulou 1984, on the relevant sources and the rich bibliography see Phillips 2013.

42 Bérard – Castex 2021 13, argue in favor of the possible identification of the plotters led by Kylon.

43 Kylon's Olympic victory at the 35th Olympiad (640/39) and the tradition that the events took place before Drakon's reforms allow for a date between 636–624. Gagarin 1981b,

whose historicity is generally acknowledged.[44] This earliest certain "constitutional" event in Athenian history had also the strongest and longest impact on Athenian political life, both internally, paving the way to democratic reforms, but also affecting Athens' foreign relations, being widely known in Greece and brought up by the city's enemies.[45] Oral stories and remembrances of an event that had cast its shadow over the city and affected many leading families circulated widely in Athens, slightly changing the narrative from generation to generation.[46] Variations of the same story are given by Herodotus (5.71), Thucydides (1.126), Plutarch (*Solon,* 12.1–9), Aristotle,[47] the Scholia to Aristophanes' *Knights* (445) and some references to Kylon by Pausanias. Although later projections of dominant ideas and ideologies in the interpretation of events of the city's past are not to be excluded, the common denominators of the narratives are an attempt to establish tyranny by a local aristocrat benefitting from foreign support, the killing of the supplicants by the city's authorities, the ongoing στάσις involving the city's Eupatrid families and popular factions, the trial and punishment of the authors of the sacrilege and the purification of the city, events that unfolded over two centuries, leading from archaic to classical Athens.

Kylon, an Athenian noble and Olympic victor of the δίαυλος (footrace) at the 35th Olympiad (640–39), son-in-law of the tyrant of Megara Theagenes,[48] after misunderstanding a Delphic Oracle as to correct timing, instructing him to conquer the Akropolis "during the greatest celebration of Zeus",[49] attempted a coup in

---

74, n. 18 argues against the attempt by Lévy 1978, to date Kylon's affair to the mid-590's. See also Phillips 2008, 35.

44 Thomas 1989, 273.

45 Both Herodotus' and Thucydides' narratives on the Kylonian sacrilege are digressions, explaining the persistence of the charge of pollution against the Alcmeonids, as brought in the 6th c. against Kleisthenes and in the 5th against Pericles. Herodotus is explaining why Cleomenes of Sparta demanded the banishment of Kleisthenes during his struggle with Isagoras, and Thucydides why the Lacedaemonians asked for the expulsion of Pericles, one of the reasons leading to the Peloponnesian war.

46 On a discussion of the traditions connected to Kylon, see Thomas 1989, 144–54; 261–81; Moulinier 1946, 182–202; Jacoby 1949, 366–7; Rhodes 1981, 79–84; Hornblower 1996, 202–10.

47 The preserved part of the *Constitution of the Athenians* begins with the trial of the Alcmeonids following the Kylonian sacrilege, cf. Heraclides Lembus, *Epit. 2.*

48 Such alliances were common among aristocratic families, see Gernet 1981, 298. The homonymous grandson of the Alcmeonid Megacles would marry Agariste, the daughter of the tyrant Cleisthenes of Sicyon, Herodotus 6.130–31.

49 As explained by Thucydides, 1.126, the coup took place during Zeus Meilichios festival. According to Jameson 1965, Zeus Meilichios was a prominent deity of purification, which made the attempted coup especially impious and put the plotters religiously on the wrong. The archons could have argued that the killing of Kylon's supporters was a response to an impious act, which may explain the ambiguity with which the curse was regarded later. On this see Hornblower 1997, 202.

Athens during the Olympic celebrations, in view of becoming a tyrant, supported by a small group of elite Athenians and by a force given by his father-in-law.[50] Although no source gives us the name of Kylon's γένος, he was considered a member of the Athenian elite, described as εὐγενής τὲ καὶ δυνατός by Thucydides (1.126.3). His Athenian supporters are described by Herodotus as ἑταίροι of the same age (5.71.1) and by Thucydides as "friends" (1.126.6). The strong impact of their death[51] and the fact that, a generation after the event, their families claimed and obtained justice against the Alcmeonids, while the στάσις continued for many years to come, shows that they counted among the leading Athenian families.

Kylon and his supporters seized the Acropolis[52] in view of establishing a tyranny, but they were trapped inside and sieged. Thucydides (1.124.7) is the only source that gives details on popular support of the siege, saying that a large number of Athenians (πανδημεὶ)[53] rushed from the fields to help in the blockade. However, the siege taking a long time, many left, authorizing the nine archons with plenary powers to arrange everything according to their good judgment (Thucydides 1.124.8). The besieged suffered from want of food and water, some even dying of hunger (Thucydides 1.124.9). According to Herodotus (5.71.3), the archons were "οἱ πρυτάνιες τῶν ναυκράρων, οἵ περ ἔνεμον τότε τὰς Ἀθήνας",[54] while according to Thucydides they were the nine archons. Thucydides is the only source stressing the people's authorization to the archons to act at will, as plenipotentiary, using the latter term αὐτοκράτορες, which seems an attempt to justify that they acted within their powers and with some legitimacy.[55] The name of the archon in charge of the siege, the Alcmeonid Megacles I, is deliberately omitted by Herodotus and

---

50 Thucydides 1.126.5. Kylon's connection to Megara, through his father-in-law, an opulent city at the time, which would be engaged in a long and bitter dispute with Athens over the control of Salamis, may signify that this was an attempt by the tyrant of Megara to extend his influence over Athens.

51 On the impact of the death of an individual varying according to the deceased's position within society, see Morris 1987, 31.

52 On why Kylon, latter Peisistratus and the Spartan King Kleomenes (in support of Kleisthenes' rival Isagoras) attempted to seize the Acropolis, perhaps because there lay the headquarters of government at the time, where the city's *prytaneion* lay, see Rosivach 2008. The relocation of the *prytaneion* in the agora may have taken place after Kleisthenes' reform, as a way to avoid also similar precedents.

53 Forsdyke 2005, 81–82, doubts the massive resistance to Cylon and thinks that if the Athenians did participate in it, they may have been prompted by the presence of Megarian troops.

54 This reference by Herodotus has been seen as an attempt to divert the blame from the Alcmeonids, something rejected by Rhodes 1981, 82.

55 Such an authorization, supposing some form of popular vote in an assembly, even if spontaneous, seems ill-suited to the conditions of a siege. Thucydides, who is sympathetic to Pericles, may be pointing out to the popular support enjoyed by the Alcmeonids in Athens.

Thucydides, but provided by Aristotle and Plutarch.[56] In the aftermath of the event, the family accursed will be only the Alcmeonids, which gives Megacles a role of leader in putting down the coup-d'état.

The Kylionians were persuaded to leave the protection of the sanctuary after being promised they would not suffer capital punishment. Plutarch (*Solon* 12.1) says that the archon Megacles persuaded those besieged to come down from the Acropolis to submit to trial. Herodotus mentions they would be held liable except to execution (5.71.1, ὑπεγγύους πλὴν θανάτου). Those charged with the duty of keeping guard, seeing the supplicants dying of hunger in the sanctuary (implying therefore they initially acted to avoid the altar's pollution),[57] on the condition that they would do them no harm (Thucydides 1.124.11, ἐφ' ᾧ μηδὲν κακὸν ποιήσουσιν), took them away and killed them (ἀπαγαγόντες ἀπέκτειναν). These references imply the existence in Athens of a court of law and some sort of legal procedure[58] before the time of Drakon,[59] Solon and Peisistratus, that could judge the crimes of which Kylon and his followers were guilty, which were punishable by death.[60]

The promises given to the besieged were not kept. Thucydides says that some who, as they passed by, took refuge at the altars of the Σεμναὶ θεαὶ (the Erinyes or Eumenides),[61] were despatched on the spot (Thucydides 1.124.11), while the rest were taken away to be killed (ἀπαγαγόντες ἀπέκτειναν). Plutarch embellishes the narration with the broken thread story,[62] tied on the goddesses' statue and deployed

56 On the possibility of him being the eponymous archon see Develin 1989, 30–31.

57 According to the Greek ἔθος, pollution would come from death within a temple, cf. the decree, of Augustan age, on the restoration of sanctuaries in Attica, IG II2 1035, l. 10–11: ἐπεὶ δὲ πάτριόν ἐστιν ἐν μηδενὶ τῶν τεμενῶν μήτ' ἐντίκτειν μὴτ' ἐναπο||[θνήσκειν.

58 Gagarin 1981a.

59 In this paper the discussion of the possible relation of Kylon's affair and Drakon's law on homicide has been omitted due to space limitations and will make to object of a future publication.

60 In the *Scholia in Aristophanem* one of the explanations given on the word ἀλιτηρίων (those who offend the Goddess) is that Kylon, in his attempt to become a tyrant, was caught stealing the sanctuary of Athena (ἐλήφθη δὲ συλῶν τὸ ἱερὸν τῆς Ἀθηνᾶς). Such a crime would constitute sacrilege, in combination with treason in view of Kylon's support by Megarian forces, conspiracy (Plutarch, *Solon* 12.1, uses the word συνωμόται) and attempt to establish a tyranny (Herodotus, 5.71, Κύλων…ἐπὶ τυραννίδι ἐκόμησε, Thucydides 1.126.3, κατέλαβε τὴν ἀκρόπολιν ὡς ἐπὶ τυραννίδι). In the *Scholia in Aristophanem* it is mentioned (455) that "οἱ συγκατακλεισθέντες τῷ Κύλωνι ἐν τῇ ἀκροπόλει εἰς τὴν κρίσιν κατέβησαν ἐν Ἀρείῳ πάγῳ". According to Aristotle (*A.C.* 3.6), the Areopagos was responsible before the time of Drakon for keeping the laws and punished transgressors with corporal punishments.

61 For this identification see Lloyd-Jones 1989.

62 Gould 1973, 78. The story only found on Plutarch, on a thread being tied to the base of Athena's statue, regardless of its historicity, preserves an essential element in the ritual of supplication and of the importance of physical contact with the altar or statue of the divinity.

on the way down, the critical breaking of which took place at the altars of the Furies,[63] upon which Megacles and his fellow-archons rushed to seize the supplicants and they were slain on the spot (Plutarch, *Solon* 12.2), while the rest were executed outside (καὶ τοὺς μὲν ἔξω κατέλευσαν), ἔξω probably meaning outside the sacred area.[64] The assumption that they were stoned to death by the mass, adopted by many modern scholars, is nowhere to be found in the sources. Herodotus attributes this killing to the Alcmeonids as instigators (5.71.2), Thucydides to the nine archons, who were ever since "called accursed and guilty against the goddess, they and their descendants" (1.124.1), although he avoids naming directly the Alcmeonids. Plutarch adds that only those were spared who made supplication to the wives of the archons (*Solon* 12.2), and that the archons were called polluted and were held in execration (ἐκ τούτου δὲ κληθέντες ἐναγεῖς ἐμισοῦντο).

As a first remark, a close look at the sources shows that, even if the above narratives contain different variations of the same story, none is incompatible with a possible execution of the captives and their burial in Phaleron. The sources point out that while some of Kylon's supporters were killed on the spot, on the altars, others were lifted and taken away to be killed (Thucydides 1.126, Plut. *Sol.* 12.1). The verbs used point out to killing by dagger for those on the altars (ἀπεσφάγησαν) but do not specify the mode of execution of the rest (ἀπέκτειναν, κατέλευσαν). It is insinuated that the rest were taken away to be killed (ἀπαγαγόντες ἀπέκτειναν, τοὺς μὲν ἔξω κατέλευσαν). Given that the victims of this failed coup d'état –the historicity of which is not contested– must have been buried in Athenian soil, Phaleron, the most important of the archaic cemeteries of Athens, and the only one attesting a great number of βιαιοθάνατοι, remains the most probable place for their execution and burial. An execution of the main group of captives outside the center of Athens is probable. Although the killing of those among Kylon's supporters, who sought sanctuary by sitting on the altars, could have happened in the heat of the moment, during their resistance to arrest, the execution of the rest –which must have counted a considerable number of captives– once they had descended from the Acropolis, could hardly have been done without some kind of process. Rather than the archons having them killed in cold blood at the end of their descent, they could have had the captives attached with shackles to avoid their escape and carried away to be executed, out of sight of their families, to the place where they would be immediately buried. At the order of Megacles, to avoid further spreading pollution in the heart of Athens, they could have been brought to the Phaleron shore, which lays at just a one-hour distance on foot (ca 5 km) from the Acropolis, along with the corpses of their comrades who had already perished by famine or were killed on

[63] Wallace 1989, 24; Lang, 1967.

[64] Harris-Cline 1999, based on a different interpretation on the location of the old agora of Athens, close to Tripodon street, argues for a different exit route of the Kylonians, not from the Propylea western side entrace of the Acropolis, but from the north-eastern side of the Acropolis.

the altars. Such an arrest and transfer to their place of execution would even allow some time for the supplication mentioned by Plutarch to the archon's wives. The soft sandy shores of the Phaleron graveyard, permitting to easily dig a drench for many corpses at once, but far enough from Athens to avoid spreading the miasma at the city's core, would be a suitable execution and burial place for the victims of the attempted coup. Other elements that make possible an identification of the skeletons of the first row of captives with the Kylonians are the young age of the group; the presence of the two *oinochoae* attesting the bare minimum of the funeral rites for those who must have been members of the Athenian nobility; the lying of the dead bodies the one next to the other, in the same direction. The number of the 40 skeletons found in the first row is also not far from the number of 50 guards, with the help of which Peisistratus would latter seize the Acropolis, establish a tyranny, and hold power briefly in 560/559 (Plutarch, *Solon* 30).

Thucydides is the only source mentioning that Kylon and his brother escaped the siege and fled the city. However, the sacrilege of the killing of the supplicants was linked forever to Kylon's own name (Κυλώνειον), while we have no reference to him as a survivor in the aftermath of the events. According to Herodotus (5.71.1–2), Kylon was among the supplicants to Athenas' statue lifted by the archons at the guarantee they would not be executed, who were killed at the order of the Alcmeonids. The historian Aristodemos (*FGrH* 104 F 2, writing in the 2nd century A.D., who confuses Megacles with Perikles), says that Kylon was killed on his way down from the Acropolis. Aristotle (*A.C.* 1.28), also seems to mention Kylon was killed along with his supporters. The mention of Kylon's escape could be an attempt by Thucydides to exonerate the Alcmeonids (and Pericles as the target of relevant Spartan allegations) of his death. Escaping from the Acropolis under siege, under the nose of their own collaborators, would be close to impossible. If Thucydides was right, Kylon's and his brother's lives may have been spared due to his family ties with Megara's tyrant Theagenes. It is more likely though that Kylon was among the supplicants killed, as attested by an indirect piece of evidence given by the geographer Pausanias. As Thucydides (1.126.1–12) explains, two centuries later, in 432, the Spartans –raising a war of propaganda before the actual outbreak of the Peloponnesian war– sent an embassy to Athens, asking the Athenians to "drive out" (ἐλαύνειν) the curse (ἄγος) of the goddess, a reference to the curse placed on the Alcmeonids (which Thucydides does not name) for the Kylonian affair,[65] clearly targeting Pericles, whom they hoped to get rid of or discredit.[66] The Athenians counter-demanded that the Spartans should drive out the curse of Taenarum and of Athena of the Brazen House, alluding to the murder of some helot suppliants at the altar of Poseidon at Taenarum and the death by starvation of the commander

65 Although the accusation according to Plutarch brought the opposite effect of reinforcing his popular support, *Pericles* 33.1.

66 On this incident, see Marr 1998, Hornblower 1997, 202–203.

Pausanias, walled by the Spartans in the temple of Athena. The Spartans, following a Delphic oracle, dedicated to the offended gods two bronze statues of Pausanias, as an antidote to the ἄγος related to the sacrilege of his starvation to death (Thucydides 1.134.4). Pausanias the geographer (1.17.29) mentions that he saw on the Acropolis a bronze statue of Kylon, noting that he does not understand why they dedicated a statue to an attempted tyrant. This statue could not have dated from before the Persian wars, in view of the complete destruction of the Acropolis and all dedications by the Persians when they seized the city before the naval battle of Salamis in 480. Athens' purification of the pollution linked to Kylon's affair followed the instructions of a Delphic oracle (Diogenes Laertius 1.10.109). Like the two bronze statues of the supplicant Pausanias dedicated by the Spartans to Athena, Kylon's statue could have been dedicated by the Athenians to Athena, as a restitution of his image.[67] Kylon's seizure of the Acropolis had, after all, also followed a Delphic oracle, even if he misinterpreted the god's instructions as it is mentioned by Thucydides (1.124.4), therefore a dedication of his statue would be most appropriate if he had been killed as a supplicant to Athena. A precinct called the Κυλώνειον (Polemon, *Schol. Soph.* O.C. 489) may have also been dedicated outside the main entrance to the Acropolis, perhaps at the place of death of the supplicants.

Plutarch (*Solon* 12.2–3) describes an on-going στάσις among the survivors of the coup and the descendants of Megacles, dividing Athens into two factions, [68] until Solon persuaded the Alcmeonids to submit to trial by their peers (ἔπεισε τοὺς ἐναγεῖς λεγομένους δίκην ὑποσχεῖν καὶ κριθῆναι). The trial of the Alcmeonids is perhaps the first historical trial attested for Athens. The court consisted of 300 jurors selected ἀριστίνδην, Myron of Phlya acting as prosecutor, who may have been related to the victims.[69] The delayed punishment of the Alcmeonids may be explained because at the time of the sacrilege and for one generation afterwards they had been too powerful to be held accountable.[70] Why and how did Solon convince the most powerful family to be tried by their peers (the number of jurors showing that most members of the aristocratic γένη of Athens at the time stood as jurors) and to face perpetual exile, especially if they enjoyed strong popular support? Perhaps it was a result of a major compromise, to avoid on-going bloodshed in the

---

67 Jameson 1965, 167–170.

68 Phillips 2008, 36–49 denies the existence of a "horizontal στάσις" between members of the aristocracy in the late 7th c. and argues in favor of a "vertical στάσις" between the nobility and the people. However, seeing the στάσις as either horizontal or vertical is over-compartmentalizing a social strife in which both elements were included.

69 The identity of the persecutor in this trial could link Kylon to the Lycomidae γένος of Athens. Themistocles, who belonged to the same γένος according to Plutarch (*Themistocles* 1), would later be indicted for treason by the Alcmeonid Leobotes of Agraule, perhaps in an on-going legal feud among descendants of the two families, see Botsford 1897, Humphreys 2018, I, 650.

70 Anderson 2005.

city. On the one hand, the pollution connected to the sacrilege required both a legal and a sacral catharsis.[71] On the other hand, the Alcmeonids would have argued that their ancestor Megacles had protected the city from tyranny and subdued a *stasis* and potential submission of Athens to Megara. If the old θέσμια and πάτρια recorded latter in the Athenian tyranny law, cited in the *A.C.* 16.10 (*if any people establish a tyranny or if any one assists in establishing a tyranny, he shall be outlawed [atimon], both he and his family*) already formed part of Athens' oral law at the time Kylon's supporters' killing,[72] the Alcmeonids would have claimed their forefathers had acted in defense of public interest. The middle solution devised by Solon could be that the Alcmeonids would be tried on the accusation of sacrilege and suffer exile (a most comfortable exile, as all evidence shows), while the city would be cleansed by pollution by appeal to the best religious expert. And as a countermeasure, Solon may have passed the law attributed to him, considered strange by many scholiasts, ancient and modern alike, penalizing citizen's neutrality in case of *stasis* (Aristotle, *A.C.* 8.5).[73] Under the light of this measure, in retrospect, Megacles' and the other archons' reaction to Kylon's attempt to establish a tyranny would have been justified, only the killing of the supplicants was not. Acknowledging this could be a political trade, to counterbalance a trial whose outcome would be highly politicized and would be used against the Alcmeonids for generations to come.

The crime of which the Alcmeonids could have been accused was not homicide per se (vicarious and transmissible liability of family members for homicide is unknown in ancient Greek law),[74] but something bigger, affecting the community as a whole and this was their sacrilege as ἐναγεὶς. The crime for which the Alcmeonids were put to trial and convicted was not simply homicide, but impiety (ἀσέβεια),[75] which was punished through fining, perpetual exile, confiscation of property or death. According to Thucydides (1.126.11), the perpetrators of the sacrilege and their descendants

---

71 On the concept of pollution see Harris 2015.

72 Gagarin 1981a, 72 suggests that the original *thesmion* was recorded before Drako by the Thesmothetai and that Solon later incorporated it as part of his revised tyranny law. The fact that Kylon took arms to seize the Acropolis and him and his followers negotiated against the death penalty, argues in favor of such a *thesmion* pre-existing their coup. However, contrary to Gagarin's hypothesis, a trial of the followers of Kylon or their descendant is not mentioned in the sources, only their killing. Contra, Ostwald 1955, argues the *thesmion* against tyranny cannot antedate Drako on the basis of such a law requiring some previous experience of attempted tyranny, which was this of Kylon.

73 On further sources, bibliography, and the controversial nature of this measure, see Leão – Rhodes 2015, 59–66.

74 On responsibility of family members being restricted to cases of treason or sacrilege, as in the case of the Miletus inscription against tyrants, Syll.[3] 58, see Velissaropoulou 1991.

75 Glotz 1904, 480. See also X. Hell. 1.7.22; Demosthenes 24.7; Lysias 1.24, 45, 78, 91; Aeschines 3.252.

were considered "ἐναγεῖς καὶ ἀλιτήριοι τῆς θεοῦ", [76] accursed and guilty against the goddess.[77] The term ἐναγὴς, always connected to religious ideas, was used for those who had committed sacrilege against a god,[78] but also, interesting enough in view of the Alcmeonid's broken promise to the supplicants, of those who had violated an oath,[79] and of those guilty of the killing of suppliants.[80] Generally applied to persons considered accursed, it was used to describe the condition of the Alcmeonids after the killing of the Kylonians, as persons who had committed sacrilege and broken their promise to the supplicants, subject to the abhorrence of men and the enmity of gods. The term ἀλιτήριος, one of the strongest terms denoting a religious offender,[81] according to Suidas (s.v.), has the meaning of ἀνόσιος, ὁ ἐνεχόμενος μιάσματι καὶ ἐξημαρτηκὼς εἰς θεούς. It is also referred to by Andocides[82] and Lysias[83] as someone who has committed sacrilege against the gods, while the same term is used to characterize those who have committed serious crimes against the state[84] or against Greece.[85] It is a condition subjective to a specific deity (ἀλιτήριος τῆς θεοῦ) which, like a genetic defect in today's terms, is considered to be passed from generation to generation, a man being born ἀλιτήριος without having committed any fault of his own, but inheriting the sin of his forefathers.[86] The Alcmeonid's conviction made them guilty of a crime against a divine entity (Athena), a place (the altars) and the city of Athens, of which Athena was the protector.

The curse itself would not have automatic political consequences, the punishment of the accursed being the gods' responsibility. But it served as an instrument for propaganda and for bringing the Alcmeonids to trial for the corresponding civil offense, perhaps a combination of ἱεροσυλία (sacrilege) and a general charge of ἀσέβεια (impiety),[87] crimes of religious nature, in their earliest forms. Ἱεροσυλία, the most serious offense against the gods, carried the death penalty,[88] confiscation of property and prohibition of burial within the borders of Attica,[89] which corresponds to the "penalty" imposed on the deceased perpetrators of the Kylonians' homicide

---

76 Herodotus 5.71–72; Thucydides 1.126; Plutarchus, *Solon* 12.1; 13.1.

77 On the inherited sin of the Alcmeonids see Gagné 2013, 204 sqq. On the role of Delphi in the affair and on some religious authority, probably Delphi, declaring the Alcmeonids ἐναγεῖς καὶ ἀλιτήριοι τῆς θεοῦ, see Forrest 1954, 39–42.

78 Aeschines 3.108, 3.117.

79 Aeschines 3.110, 3.121, 3.122.

80 Thucydides 1.139 on the Lacedaemonians murdering some suppliants.

81 Parker 1983, 270.

82 Andocides, 1.51.

83 Lysias 6.52, 6.53.

84 Aeschines 3.131, Demosthenes 18.159.

85 Aeschines 3.131, 3.157, Dinarchus 1.77.

86 Gagné 2013, 309–310.

87 Forrest 1954, 39–42. On these crimes see Eidinow 2015.

88 Xenophon, *Memorabilia* 1.2.62; Isokrates 20.6.

89 Xenophon, *Hellenica* 1.7.22; See Garland 1984.

on the altars (Thucydides 1.126: τῶν τεθνεώτων τὰ ὀστᾶ ἀνελόντες ἐξέβαλον). Ἀσέβεια was an all-comprising offense, the definition of which even in latter Attic law is uncertain, which may have covered any offense against established religious custom.[90] Homicide and the consecration of shrines are mentioned in the sources as being understood, according to ancestral traditions, to automatically incur ἀσέβεια.[91] Although ἀσέβεια as a technical term in Attic law appears in the 6th century, the condemnation and exile of the Alcmeonids as ἐναγεὶς may attest that this category of offense existed much earlier than the 5th century, when it finally took the form of the γραφή ἀσεβείας.

The supplicants enjoyed inviolability, sharing the sacredness of the altars,[92] abiding to the ancient social and religious institution of ἱκετεία, known through both the mythological tradition and historical record.[93] The ritual act of supplication was addressed to both gods and human beings (in the case of the Kylonians to Athena and the archons' wives), and included physical contact with parts of the body which had a peculiar sanctity, or sacred objects such as altars of statues of gods. An "abandoned" act of supplication, in which physical contact with the person or place of supplication was lost or broken, lost its binding force and left the person exposed. The act of ἱκετεία, already present in Homer, will later develop into the institution of ἀσυλία. The version of the story of Kylon given by Plutarch,[94] about the breaking of the rope (αὐτομάτως ... ραγείσης) connecting the supplicants with the goddesses' statue, may reflect an argument put forward to exonerate Megacles and his descendants of the crime of sacrilege, in view of the loss of status of the supplicants as ἱκέται (ὡς τῆς θεοῦ τὴν ἱκεσίαν ἀπολεγομένης). For as long as contact with the sacred space was unbroken, the supplicants remained under the protection of the goddess. Reason why, all versions of the story insist both on the physical contact of the supplicants with the altars[95] and on this contact being broken by the archons on the promise of their lives would be spared.[96] The archons, by persuading the supplicants to voluntarily abandon the divine protection, showed treachery, doubled by sacrilege when they did order the execution of those who took refuge on the altars of the Furies. Breaking the rules of supplication was a shocking act of ἀσέβεια.[97]

---

[90] Humphreys 1984, 188; Garland 1984, 79.

[91] Eidinow 2015, with references on the sources. Lysias 2.7.

[92] Parker 1983, 182–183. The protection of the divinity was transmitted through the contact with the statue or altar, hence the story by Plutarch of the thread attached to the altar. See Gould 1973, 82–85.

[93] Gould 1973.

[94] Plutarch, *Solon* 12.1.

[95] Herodotus 5.71; Thucydides, 1.126.10l; Aristotle, *Athenian Constitution* 1.28; Plutarch, *Solon* 12.1.

[96] Herodotus 5.71; Thucydides 1.126.11; Plutarch, *Solon* 12.1.

[97] Herodotus 1.157–60, narrates the story of the Lydian Paktyes, who took refuge as an ἱκέτης in Kyme. Apollo's verdict when asked about his surrender is that such an act would constitute the crime of ἀσέβεια.

In the different versions of the story combined, ἱκεσία appears at three different levels, places and instances, on the way that brought the supplicants from the top of the Acropolis down to its foothill: first on the altar at the Acropolis, then, on their way down, by clinging to the altars of the Furies and finally, for those arrested, before the archons' wives. This last reference, only included in Plutarch's narrative, which insinuates a process during which some of the captives' lives were spared, may not be totally unhistorical.[98] It may be an indirect reference to at least one archon's wife for which an institutional role is known, the archon basileus' wife, *basilinna*, who held important religious functions.[99] According to Aristotle, in Athens' constitution before Drakon the basileus was the oldest among all offices, who also had the power to give final judgement in lawsuits and not merely conduct preliminary inquiries,[100] and later introduced homicide trials at the Areopagus.[101] Although we have no direct evidence on this, this reference by Plutarch may insinuate that the fate of those among the captives who had not perished on the way down from the Acropolis, was decided by the Archons, who sentenced them to death and sent them to be executed (some being spared through their last ἱκεσία to the wives), something which presupposes an already organized form of jurisdiction in archaic Athens.

The Kylonian curse often served as a pretext for political revenge against the Alcmeonids and for recurring requests to have them (re)expelled from the city, after their initial exile. Thucydides (1.126.12) mentions two exiles,[102] but notes that *"their descendants are still in the city."* Despite of their condemnation to perpetual exile (ἀειφυγία), in ca. 561/0, Lycurgus, head of the Boutad family, allowed the Alcmeonids to return to Athens in exchange of their support in overthrowing Peisistratus. Their second period of exile followed the Alcmeonids' defeat by Peisistratus at Pallene in ca. 546/5, for a period close to twenty years (up to 526, before Kleisthenes assumed the archonship in 525/4). Important archaeological remains from Anavyssos (ancient Anaflystos) and Sounion (including monumental Kouroi) associated with their family, dating from this period, suggest this area of Attika was their base of operations. This would assume that as exiles they did not leave the Attic peninsula altogether but were free to stay in marginal areas which

---

98 The women's' presence could also be understood in view of the sensational event that must have been the arrest of the followers of the prestigious and good-looking (κάλλιστος in the words of Pausanias) Olympic victor Kylon and some of the fine Athenian youths, after many days of siege.

99 Garland 1984.

100 Aristotle, *Athenian Constitution* 3.2.

101 Aristotle, *Athenian Constitution* 57.4

102 The first expulsion of the Alcmeonids can be dated to the period shortly before Solon's reforms. The Alcmeonids returned by about 590, since Alkmeon, son of the Megacles involved in the Kylon affair, commanded the Athenian forces in the First Sacred War, see Plutarch, Solon 11.2. The second expulsion mentioned by Thucydides occurred in 508/7, Herodotus 5.70.2.

may not have properly belonged to the Athenian polis at the time. The exception of the amnesty given by Solon (Plutarch, *Solon* 19) possibly did not apply to them, having been judged by an extraordinary court for ἀσέβεια. The Alcmeonids, throughout their different periods of exile, were able to cultivate high-profile political alliances,[103] maintained their wealth (which was not confiscated nor auctioned, allowing them to even finance the building of Apollo's temple in Delphi from Parian marble, Herodotus, 5.62), many held the highest offices in Athens[104] and extended their popular influence, emerging after their exile as leaders of the "party" of the παράλια (coast) areas of Attika.[105]

The diffusion of the Alcmeonids' association with impurity as a reason for their expulsion from Athens's political scene must have been initially spread by the Peisistratids,[106] in the context of the antagonism among the Eupatrid families. The trial and conviction of the Alcmeonids confirmed their status as ἐναγεῖς and the pollution resulting from the supplicants' homicide.[107] It is therefore not strange that then, already many years after the tragic events,[108] this judicial confirmation was linked in popular belief[109] to supernatural phenomena such as pestilence (Diogenes Laertius, 1.110). According to Plutarch (*Solon* 12.3), "*the city was also visited with superstitious fears and strange appearances, and the seers declared that their sacrifices indicated pollutions and defilements which demanded expiation*". The purification of Athens by the Cretan seer Epimenides (Aristotle, *A.C.* 1.28) was a process aimed to both appease the spirits of vengeance (Furies) and the public opinion. The city's purification (necessary in every instance of homicide, to limit the effects of pollution) may have followed some divinatory process through sacrifices and be mandated by diviners (Plutarch, *Solon*, 12.3). It is noteworthy that

---

103 Peisistratus (around 556/5) married for political reasons an Alcmaeonid daughter, although he avoided normal intercourse with her to avoid having children who would carry the curse (Herodotus 1.61.1). When her father Megacles found out, their alliance suffered. Megacles was chosen himself as son-in-law of the tyrant of Sicyon Kleisthenes, among the best suitors in Greece.

104 The late 5th c. inscription listing archons from the 6th c. contains the names of aristocrats from the Alcmaeonid family (SEG 28.19, 33.23).

105 Anderson 2003, 24–34. Regarding the throwing of the bones of the Alcmeonids beyond the border mentioned by Plutarch, Anderson (n. 36 226) thinks this may be an anachronistic assumption based on knowledge of later practice. See also Hall 2006, 248.

106 Gagné 2013, 207–8.

107 On pollution linked to homicide, see Arnaoutoglou 2000; Harris 2015. On the process of purification following homicide as preserved in the laws of Selinous and Cyrene, see Salvo 2012, with bibliography.

108 Contra, Duplouy 2019 argues for a latter dating Kylon's affair and purification, right before Solon's archonship.

109 Regarding this popular belief, cf. among the questions asked to the Dodona oracle, if harsh winter was the result of someone's pollution, SEG XIX 427: ἐπερωτῶντι Δωδωναῖοι τὸν | Δία καὶ τὰν Διώναν ἦ δι' ἀνθρώ|που τινὸς ἀκαθαρτίαν ὁ θεὸς | τὸν χείμωνα παρέχει.

a foreigner, Epimenides of Phaestus[110] brough to this purpose from Crete[111] was asked to perform the rites that would allow appeasement, in collaboration with Athens' own reformer Solon.[112] No mention to Epimenides is found in Herodotus and Thucydides' reports of the Kylonian affair, only in Aristotle and Plutarch, while other strange stories make him a mystical semi-legendary figure[113] of seer and miracle-worker,[114] counted among the Seven Sages (Diogenes Laertius 1.42). Plutarch (*Solon* 12.4–5) states that "*on coming to Athens he made Solon his friend, assisted him in many ways, and paved the way for his legislation*," citing examples of rules he established regarding mourning and funeral sacrifices. [115] He goes on, "*Most important of all, by sundry rites of propitiation and purification, and by sacred foundations, he hallowed and consecrated the city, and brought it to be observant of justice and more easily inclined to unanimity*." Regardless of the historicity of the figure of Epimenides, both the importance given to the purification process and his association with Solon's upcoming reforms, signal that a higher, religious legitimization, in the figure of a foreign sage, was thought to have been instrumental and necessary in order to achieve katharsis and reach concord in Athens, after a long civil conflict that lasted over several generations. Epimenides is credited with reforming both the cult practices (εὐσταλεῖς ἐποίησε τὰς ἱερουργίας) and the funeral ceremonies (τὰ πένθη), practices targeted also by Solon's legislation, both of which are strongly connected with the antagonism between the Eupatridai, the great families of Attika controlling local cults and using funerals as means of ostentatious display. Epimenides, by reforming Athenian

[110] Vernant 1962, 70, considers Epimenides the "very model of the inspired shaman or theios aner" who appeared at a moment of crisis, when the Greeks were beginning to question their old system of values.

[111] The man sent to escort him, Νικίας Νικηράτου, mentioned by Diogenes Laertius (1.10.109), bears the same name as the general of the Peloponnesian war, a man reputed as religious and who had performed the second Athenian purification of Delos. Duplouy 2019, argues on some topicality of the tale in late 5th c. Athens, when the city was suffering from the great plague and thinks the story about Epimenides shows how mythography was used as a means to mediate social action and to record history in Classical Greece. The involvement of a seer in Greek politics of the 6th and 5th centuries also questions the popular notion that rational thinking had by then overcome superstition and magical mediation in the rule of the Classical city.

[112] On purification from murder, the role of the Delphic Oracle and the special purifying priests, *kathartai*, promising relief in cases of epidemic and civil discords, of which Epimenides was the most famous, see Burkert 1985, 77.

[113] West 1983, 45 sqq., thinks the story about Epimenides's purification may not be historical fact and may be confusing elements related to the Bouphonia ritual which took place on the Acropolis.

[114] Plato, *Leges* 1. 642D–E. Plato mentions he visited Athens ten years before the Persian Wars, a century later than the purification after the Kylonian sacrilege under Solon.

[115] On a possible connection between Epimenides with Delphi, in view of the relations between Delphi and Crete, see Forrest 1954, 39–42.

mourning practices, allowed for Solon's funerary legislation, including the limitation of luxury in burials and the prohibition of insulting the deceased – another possible reason for cultivating passions an hatred among the Athenians.

The actions ascribed to Epimenides[116] (κατοργιάσας – a form of initiation, καθοσιώσας-consecration, in the sense of ὅσιος as correct religious and political behavior), through "ἱλασμοῖς τισι καὶ καθαρμοῖς καὶ ἱδρύσεσι" (appeasement, purifications and reorganizations of the sacred space, sanctuaries, altars and statues), resulting in the perpetual commemoration of the atonement through the erection of monuments and cults, is presented as a profound religious transformation,[117] through which "τὴν πόλιν ὑπήκοον τοῦ δικαίου καὶ μᾶλλον εὐπειθῆ πρὸς ὁμόνοιαν κατέστησε".[118] Most noteworthy, Epimenides' religious reforms are believed to have paved the way to Solon's reforms (τῷ Σόλωνι χρησάμενος φίλῳ πολλὰ προσυπειργάσατο καὶ προωδοποίησεν αὐτῷ τῆς νομοθεσίας). The ἄγος related to the sacrilege is considered responsible for the long division (στάσις) opposing Athenian factions, as if the prolonged state of civil turmoil (τὸ δὲ Κυλώνειον ἄγος ἤδη μὲν ἐκ πολλοῦ διετάραττε τὴν πόλιν) and the hatred dividing the citizens could only explained in supernatural terms, as the effect of a curse related to an ancestral fault, requiring a religious as well as legal solution.

According to Diogenes Laertius (*Lives of Eminent Philosophers,* 1.10.109–110) who is describing in detail the purification process, the city was purified following a Pythian oracle, during the 47th Olympiad, which dates the process at the time of Solon. He mentions that Epimenides' rites of purification included καθαρμοὶ and an ἐξίλασις: black and white sheep he brought to the Areopagus and instructed those who followed them to offer a sacrifice[119] to the local divinity where they lay down, reason for which, Laertius adds, anonymous altars are found to his day in different demes of Athens (one of which was perhaps seen by the Apostle Paul many centuries later, as stated in his discourse to the Areopagus, *Acts of the Apostles* 17. 22–23). Laertius adds a story about the human sacrifice of Kratinos and Ktesibios, which was specifically signaled as the means to deliver the city from the scourge. This "notorious" (διαβόητα) incident is also commented by Athenaeus (*Deipnosophistae,* 13.78), reporting from his source Neanthes of

---

116 On the importance of this purification, see Gagné 2013, 313–325.

117 In connection to the religious aspect of the sacrilege, a new γένος may have been created in the late 7th c., the Hesychidai, to whom the cult of the *Semnai* at the Areiopagos, as it had been re-organized by Epimenides, was entrusted. It is noteworthy that the Eupatridai were excluded from its rituals, see Polemon, *Schol. Soph. O.C.* 489. It has been suggested that the Hesychidai's name may have derived from their neutrality in the conflict between the Eupatrid families surrounding the Kylonian conspiracy and subsequent accusations of impiety and homicide, Humphreys 2018, 650; Thomas 1989, 291.

118 Gagné 2013, 317–318.

119 Purification often took the form of a sacrifice and purification of a shrine with animal blood. Its purpose was to restore the broken unity of the city, Parker 1983, 10, 23.

Cyzicus (late 3rd century BC), who mentions that when Epimenides was purifying Attica by human blood (Ἐπιμενίδου καθαίροντος τὴν Ἀττικὴν ἀνθρωπείῳ αἵματι διά τινα μύση παλαιά), the beautiful Kratinos volunteered to sacrifice himself for his country, whereby his lover Apollodorus also died. Laertius notes that this story is fiction created by Polemo Periegites.[120] This story of the offer of blood for the blood of the supplicants slaughtered on the altar of the Erinyes, if not true, may be understood as a symbolic substitution, on behalf of the city of Athens, of a victim satisfying the right of revenge of the relatives of the victims for the intentional killing of the supplicants.

Epimenides' intervention under Solon, a story not present in Herodotus and Thucydides, but dominant in versions circulating from Aristotle onwards, shows that Kylon's sacrilege and its resolution came to be seen something akin to democratic Athens' foundation myth, the ancient conflict giving ground for a profound transformation of the city. Following also Kleisthenes' radical democratic reforms, close to two centuries after Kylon's affair, Aeschylus' tragedy *Eumenides* (175) presented in 458, narrating the story of Orestes, a killer tinted by miasma, his affliction by the Furies, his trial following his refuge at Delphi, his acquittal by the Areopagos and the Furies' appeasement and transformation to Eumenides, bears strong resemblances to the Alcmeonids' story as ἐναγεὶς.[121] Several verses of the tragedy seem to allude to episodes of the Kylonian saga, at a time when the insult of ἐναγεὶς was still directed in Athens against the prominent Alcmeonids of the time by their political opponents. The accusation addressed against their descendants up to two centuries later, attests to the instrumentalization of an accusation of impurity for political reasons, as carriers of the hereditary sin of being "ἐναγεῖς καὶ ἀλιτήριοι τῆς θεοῦ",[122] transmitted from generation to generation.[123] The μίασμα connected to the killings, expulsed through Epimenides' purification, was to "wake up" at later instances, at the request of political opponents, as an excuse for curbing the Alcmeonid's influence as leaders of a popular faction.[124] The epithet ἀλειτηρός is directed in elegiac verses against Xanthippos, Pericles' father, on an ostracon, referring to his marriage to Agariste, of the accursed family of the Alcmeonids.[125] Also, against his brother-in-law Megacles, mentioned as both ἀλειτηρός Κυλόνε<ο>ς in *ostraca* found in

[120] Similar human sacrifices as means of purification of an ancient crime are found in Herodotus, 7.197.

[121] Mazzarino 1960, 119–22; Samons 1998–9. On the rapport between the two stories, see Gagné 2013, 320.

[122] On these terminologies see Hatch 1908, Chantraine – Masson 1954, Rudhardt 1958, 41–48, Parker 1983, 5–12.

[123] On the inherited sin of the Alcmeonids see Gagné 2013, 204 sqq.

[124] Parker 1983, 16 sqq.

[125] Raubitschek 1947.

Kerameikos.[126] In Aristophanes' *Knights* (445–450), the sausage-seller (ἀλλαντοπώλης) impersonating Alcibiades, an Alcmeonid on the side of his mother, is accused by Kleon of being one of the ἀλιτηρίων (of the family of the sinners against the goddess), to which he replies "your grandfather was one of the bodyguards of the tyrant Hippias", showing that the accusation of impiety had become part of common political slander, apt also to produce laughter more than to be taken seriously.[127]

In conclusion, although there can be no certainty as to the identity of the Phaleron captives, nor any direct link to the Kylonian conspiracy, the combination of preliminary finds and the political context of στάσις shaking Athens over a long period, in the turn of the 7th and through the 6th century, make it plausible that the δεσμῶται were victims of state execution, possibly for an offense against the state. Solon's law on amnesty (Plutarch, *Solon* 19) explicitly excepting those exiled as condemned ἐπὶ φόνῳ ἢ σφαγαῖσιν ἢ ἐπὶ τυραννίδι, signals that such events had been current in Athens. In view of the dating allowed by the two *oinochoae*, in the 7th century, if these victims are not the Kylonians, they should correspond to some other bloody incident of early Athenian history unknown in the sources.[128] The skeletons found could thus be among the first victims of civil unrest in Athens. The number of victims attest to the importance of loss of lives in terms of numbers and the proportional involvement of factions in στάσις. The antagonism among the Eupatridae, combined with the social discontent and need for reform, in the 5th century, dictated the institutional changes of Kleisthenes. The social re-engineering it entailed made Athens develop into a democratic polis, one in which no faction linked to a particular family or people from one area of Attika could easily take over another, and impose their rule over the rest. Instability due to elite rivalries gave way to a form of government where the new institution of ostracism reserved to the people the right to expel prominent figures. Paradoxically, democracy, the only form of government founded on the rule of the people, can also be seen as an act of self-preservation for the Athenian elite, whose members have often suffered decimations and exiles by their peers. Seen in its entirety and its unforeseen consequences over several generations, the Kylonian conspiracy was a defining moment for Athenian history, the effects of which make it the initial stage of development of Athens into a democratic polis. A long and often violent and painful process, some victims of which may lay among the βιαιοθάνατοι buried at the Phaleron bay.

adimopoul@law.uoa.gr

126 Siewert 2002, 104–6; Duplouy 2006, 93–94.

127 Vickers 2020.

128 The possible identification of the victims with the Kylonians is consistent with the traditional dating of the event before the end of the 7th c. and would contradict the theory by Lévy 1978 and Giuliani 1999, that the event should be downdated to the early 6th c., immediately before Solon's archonship (594–3).

BIBLIOGRAPHY

Allen, D. 2000. The World of Prometheus. The Politics of Punishing in Democratic Athens. Princeton.

Anderson, G. 2003. The Athenian Experiment: Building an Imagined Political Community in Ancient Attica, 508–490 BC, Ann Arbor.

Anderson, G. 2005. "Before Turannoi Were Tyrants: Rethinking a Chapter of Early Greek History", Classical Antiquity, 24.2, 173–220.

Arnaoutoglou, I. 1993, "Pollution in the Athenian homicide law", RIDA 40, 109–137.

Balamoshev, C. 2011. "ΑΠΟΤΥΜΠΑΝΙΣΜΟΣ: Just death by exposing on the plank?", Journal of Juristic Papyrology, XLII, 15–33.

Bérard R.-M. – Castex D. 2021. "Epidemics and Wars: Comparative Archaeology and Anthropology of Ancient Greek Mass Burials", Athens Journal of History - Volume 7, Issue 4, 295–318, available at https://doi.org/10.30958/ajhis.7-4-3 doi=10.30958/ajhis.7-4-3, accessed July 8th, 2022.

Boardman, J. 1972. "Herakles, Peisistratos, and Sons", Revue archéologique, 57–72.

Botsford, G.W. 1897. "The Trial of the Alcmeonidae and the Cleisthenean Constitutional Reforms", Harvard Studies in Classical Philology, 1897, Vol. 8, p 1–22.

Buikstra, E. 2020, "The Birth of Democracy in Ancient Athens: A Bioarchaeological Perspective, American School of Classical Studies in Athens", online lecture, June 16, 2020, available at: https://www.ascsa.edu.gr/news/newsDetails/webinar-the-birth-of-democracy-in-ancient-athens-live-from-the-lab, accessed July 8th, 2022.

Burkert, W. 1985. Greek Religion, Oxford.

Cantarella, E. 1991. I supplizi capitali in Grecia e a Roma, Milan.

Cantarella, E. 2004. "Controlling passions or establishing the rule of the law? The functions of punishment in ancient Greece", Punishment – Society 6, 429–36. (= Cantarella, Diritto e società), 391–400.

Chantraine, P. – Masson, O. 1954. " Sur quelques termes du vocabulaire religieux des Grecs: la valeur du mot agos et de ses dérivés ", Sprachgeschichte und Wortbedeutung, Festschrift Albert Debrunner , Bern, 85–107.

Chryssoulaki, S. 2017. "The Archaic Cemetery at the Phaleron Delta" [in Greek], Lecture, Acropolis Museum 20.01.2017, https://www.blod.gr/lectures/to-arhaiko-nekrotafeio-sto-delta-falirou/ accessed July 8th, 2022.

Chryssoulaki, S. 2018. "Δέλτα Φαλήρου. Νεκρόπολη Φαλήρου", Archaeologikon Deltion, 68 (B1), 89–92.

Chryssoulaki, S. 2019. "The Excavations at Phaleron Cemetery 2012–2017: An introduction", in C. Graml, A. Doronzio, V. Capozzoli (Eds.), Rethinking Athens before the Persian wars. Proceedings of the international workshop at the Ludwig-Maximilians-Universität München (Munich, 23rd–24th February 2017) (Münchner Studien zur Alten Welt, 17), München, 103–14.

Chryssoulaki, S. 2020. "Ομαδικό πορτρέτο με ένα νεκρό", The Art of Crime, No. 8, 132–141 (= online journal: https://theartofcrime.gr/ομαδικό-πορτραίτο-με-ένα-νεκρό/, last accessed June 19th 2023).

Chryssoulaki, S. – Pappas, I. 2021. "The shackled men of Phaleron: A 3D-model of a mass grave found in the Phaleron Delta Cemetery. A collaboration between the Ephorate of Antiquities of Piraeus and the Islands and the Swedish Institute at Athens", online publication, published 2021–09–09, available at https://www.sia.gr/en/articles.php?tid=520#-ftnref7 , accessed July 8th, 2022.

Chryssoulaki, S. 2022. "Κραυγές και ψίθυροι: Οι αποκλίνουσες ταφές του Φαληρικού νεκροταφείου", in S. Chryssoulaki, I. Pappas et al., ΦΑΛΗΡΟΘΕΝ, ανάμεσα σε δύο κόσμους, Αρχαιολογικό Μουσείο Πειραιά, Athens 2022, 26–31.

Cirio, A.M. 2015, "L'ἀποτυμπανισμός e une singolare pluralità di interpretazioni.", SemRom, IV, 187–212.

Cohen, D. 1983. Theft in Athenian law, München.

Demoulin, H. 1901. Epiménide de Crète. Brussels. Repr. 1979. New York.

Develin, R. 1989. Athenian Officials 684–321 B. C., Cambridge.

Ducrey, 1999. Le traitement des prisonniers de guerre dans la Grèce antique dès origines à la conquête romaine, Paris.

Duplouy, A. 2006. Le prestige des élites. Recherches sur les modes de reconnaissance sociale en Grèce entre les Xe et le Ve siècles avant J.-C., Paris, 93–94.

Duplouy, A. 2019. "Epimenides the Cretan: A History of Athens (6th–5th c. BC)." CHS Research Bulletin 7, http://nrs.harvard.edu/urn-3:hlnc.essay:DuplouyA.Epimenides-the-Cretan.2019. Accessed July 10, 2022.

Eidinow, E. 2015. 'Ancient Greek Religion: "Embedded" . . . and Embodied', in C. Taylor and K. Vlassopoulos, eds. Communities and Networks in the Ancient Greek World, Oxford, 54–79.

Ellis, J.R. – G.R. Stanton, 1968. "Factional Conflict and Solon's Reforms", Phoenix 22, 95–110.

Forrest, G. 1956. "The First Sacred War", BCH 80, 33–52.

Forsdyke, S. 2005. Exile, Ostracism, and Democracy: The Politics of Expulsion in Ancient Greece, Princeton.

Foxhall, I. –Lewis, A.D.E. 1996. Greek Law in Its Political Setting: Justifications Not Justice, Oxford.

Gagarin, M. 1981a. Drakon and Early Athenian Homicide Law, New Haven, CT.

Gagarin, M. 1981b. "The Thesmothetai and the Earliest Athenian Tyranny Law", Transactions of the American Philological Association (1974–2014), Vol. 111, 71–77.

Gagarin, M. 1986. Early Greek Law, Berkeley.

Gagarin, M. 2005. "The Unity of Greek Law", in Gagarin, M. – D. Cohen (eds.) 2005. Cambridge Companion to Ancient Greek Law, Cambridge, 29–40.

Gagarin, M. 2008. Writing Greek Law, Cambridge.

Gagné, R. 2013. Ancestral Fault in Ancient Greece, Cambridge.

Garland, R.S.J. 1984. "Religious Authority in Archaic and Classical Athens", The Annual of the British School at Athens, Vol. 79, 75–123.

Gernet, L. 1924. "Sur l'exécution capitale : à propos d'un ouvrage récent", REG 37, 261–293.

Gernet, L. 1981. "Marriages of Tyrants", The Anthropology of Ancient Greece, Baltimore.

Ghinatti, F. 1970. I gruppi politici ateniesi fino alle guerre persiane, Roma.

Giuliani, A. 1999. "Il sacrilegio ciloniano : tradizioni e cronologia.", Aevum 73, 21–42.

Glotz, G. 1904. La solidarité de la famille dans le droit criminel en Grèce, Paris.

Gould, J. P. 1973 "Hiketeia", JHS 93, 74–103.

Hall, D. 1996. "Even the dogs have Erinyes: Sanctions in Athenian practice and thinking", L. Foxall – A. D. E. Lewis (eds.), Greek Law in Its Political Setting: Justifications Not Justice, Oxford 1996, 73–90.

Hall, J.M. 2006. History of the Archaic Greek World, ca. 1200–479 BCE, Massachusetts.

Hansen, M. H. 1976. Apagoge, endeixis and ephegesis against kakourgoi, atimoi and pheugontes: A study in the administration of justice in the fourth century BC, Odense.

Harris-Cline, D. 1999. "Archaic Athens and the Topography of the Kylon Affair", ABSA 94, 309–320.

Harris, E.M. 2015. "The Family, the Community and Murder: The Role of Pollution in Athenian Homicide Law", in C. Ando – J. Rüpke (eds), Public and Private in Ancient Mediterranean Law and Religion, Berlin–Munich–Boston 2015, 11–35.

Harrisson, A.R.W. 1961. "Drakon's ΠΡΩΤΟΣ ΑΞΟΝ", The Classical Quarterly, N.S. V. 11.1, 3–5.

Hatch, W. H. 1908. "The Use of ἀλιτήριος, ἀλιτρός, ἀραῖος, ἐναγής, ἐνθύμιος, παλαμναῖος and προστρόπαιος: a Study in Greek Lexicography", HSCP 19, 157–86.

Hignett, C. 1952. A History of the Athenian Constitution to the End of the Fifth Century BC, Oxford, 87.

Hornblower, S. 1996. A Commentary on Thucydides, V. II: Books IV–V.24, Oxford.

Hornblower S. 1997. A Commentary on Thucydides, V.I, Books I–III, Oxford.

Hughes, D.D. 1991. Human Sacrifice in Ancient Greece, London – New York.

Humphreys, S.C. 2018. Kinship in Ancient Athens: An Anthropological Analysis (2 vols.). Oxford; New York, 2018, I.

Invgarsson, A. – Bäckström, Y. 2019. 'Bioarchaeological field analysis of human remains from the mass graves at Phaleron, Greece. With an introduction by Stella Chryssoulaki and an appendix by Anna Linderholm, Anna Kjellström, Vendela Kempe Lagerholm, and Maja Krzewińska', OpAthRom 12, 7–158.

Jacoby, F. 1949. Atthis. The Local Chronicles of Ancient Athens, Oxford.

Jameson, M. 1965. "Notes on the Sacrificial Calendar from Erchia", BCH 89, 154–172.

Keramopoulos, A.D. 1923. Ο Αποτυμπανισμός. Συμβολή αρχαιολογική εις την ιστορίαν του ποινικού δικαίου και την λαογραφία (Βιβλιοθήκη της εν Αθήναις Αρχαιολογικής Εταιρείας, 22), Athens.

Koumaris, I. 1915. Κρανιολογικαί παρατηρήσεις επί των εν κοινώ τάφω κλοιοφόρων σκελετών του Παλαιού Φαλήρου, Athens.
Kourouniotis, K. 1911. 'Εξ Αττικής. Ανασκαφαί Παλαιού Φαλήρου', AEphem 50, 246–251.
Lang, M. 1967. "Kylonian conspiracy", CP 62, 243–249.
Leão, D. – Rhodes, J. 2015. The Laws of Solon, A New Edition with Introduction, Translation and Commentary, London, New York.
Lévy, E. 1978. "Notes sur la chronologie athenienne au VI siècle", Historia, 27, 513–521.
Lloyd-Jones, H. 1989. "Les Erinyes dans la tragédie grecque", REG 102, 1989, 1–9.
Marr, J. 1998. " What Did the Athenians Demand in 432 B. C.?", Phoenix, Spring – Summer, Vol. 52, No. 1/2, 120–124.
Mazzarino, S. 1960. "Incontro con le Eumenidi. Gli Eupatridi, Eschile e Pericle", Orpheus 7, 119–22,
Mélèze Modrzejewski, J. 2008. "L'apotympanismos", Symposion 2007, Vienna, 229–245.
Morris, I. 1987. Burial and Ancient Society: The rise of the Greek city-state, Cambridge.
Moulinier, L. 1946. "La nature et la date du crime des Alcméonides", REA 48, 182–202.
Osborne, R. 2021. "Archaeology and the rewriting of early Athenian history", Virtual Annual Open Lecture of the British School at Athens, 09.02.2021, https://www.bsa.ac.uk/videos/robin-osborne-archaeology-and-the-rewriting-of-early-athenian-history/, accessed July 8th, 2022.
Ostwald, M. 1955. "The Athenian Legislation against Tyranny and Subversion", Transactions and Proceedings of the American Philological Association, 86, 103–128.
Pappas, I. 2022. "1863–2020: Ανασκόπηση της έρευνας στο νεκροταφείο του Δέλτα Φαλήρου", in S. Chryssoulaki, I. Pappas et al., ΦΑΛΗΡΟΘΕΝ, ανάμεσα σε δύο κόσμους, Αρχαιολογικό Μουσείο Πειραιά, Athens 2022, 18–23.
Parker, R. 1983. Miasma. Pollution and purification in early Greek religion, Oxford.
Pelekidis, E. 1916. "Ανασκαφή Φαλήρου", AD 2, 13–64.
Phillips, D.D. 2008. Avengers of Blood. Homicide in Athenian Law and Custom from Draco to Demosthenes (Historia Einzelschriften 202), Stuttgart.
Phillips, D.D. 2013. Law of ancient Athens, Ann Arbor.
Prevedorou, E.–A. – Buikstra, J.-E. 2019. 'Bioarchaeological practice and the curation of human skeletal remains in a Greek context: The Phaleron Cemetery', Advances in Archaeological Practice 7, 60–67.
Raubitschek, A.E. 1947. "The Ostracism of Xanthippos", AJA 51, 257–262.
Rhodes, J. 1981. A Commentary on the Aristotelian Athenaion Politeia, Oxford, 79–84.
Rosivach, V.J. 2008. "Why Seize the Acropolis?", Historia: Zeitschrift für Alte Geschichte, Bd. 57, H. 2, 125–133.
Rudhardt, J. 1958. Notions fondamentales de la pensée religieuse et actes constitutifs du culte dans la Grèce classique, Paris.
Salvo, I. 2012. "A note on the ritual norms of purification after homicide at Selinous and Cyrene", Dike 15, 125–157.
Samons, L.J. 1998–9. Aeschylus, the Alcmeonids and the reform of the Areopagos', CJ, 94, 221–33.

Siewert, 2002. Ostrakismos-Testimonien, vol. i: Die Zeugnisse antiker Autoren, der Inschriften und Ostraka über das athenische Scherbengericht aus vorhellenistischer Zeit (487–322 v. Chr.), Stuttgart.

Sinn, U. "Greek Sanctuaries as Places of Refuge"" in N. Marinatos and R. Hagg (eds.), Greek Sanctuaries: New Approaches, London, 1993, 88–109.

Thomas, R. 1989. Oral Tradition and Written Record in Classical Athens, Cambridge.

Thür, G. 1990. "Die Todesstrafe im Blutprozess Athens (Zum dikazein in IG I3 104, 11–13; Dem. 23, 22; Aristot., AP 57, 4)", Journal of Juristic Papyrology 20, 143–156.

Thür, G. 1991. "The Jurisdiction of the Areopagus in Homicide Cases", in Symposion 1990, Köln, 53–72.

Thür, G. 2002. "Gesetzeskodizes im archaischen und klassischen Athen" in: Mélanges en l'honneur D. Dimakis (n. 6), 631–640.

Thür, G. 2014. "Rationality and Irrationality in the Ancient Greek Law of Procedure", in: R. Van den Berg – G. Van Niekerk – Pichonnaz – Thomas – D. Kleyn – F. Lucrezi – J. Mutton (eds.), Meditationes de iure e historia: Essays in honour of Laurens Winkel, Unisa, 916–924.

Thür, G. 2018. "New Light on Draco and the Cylonian Sacrilege" in: W. Riess (Hg.), Colloquia Attica, Stuttgart 2018, 28–35.

Todd, S. C. 2000. "How to execute people in fourth-century Athens" in: Law and social status, 31–51.

Todd, S.C. 2017. "Death and religion in Athenian law: identifying pollution?" in: Symposion 2015, 325–64.

Velissaropoulou, I. 1984. "Η ποινή του θανάτου", Αρχαιολογία 11, 36–44.

Velissaropoulou, I. 1991. "Nepoinei tethnanai", Symposion 1990, 93–105.

Vernant, J. 1962. Les origines de la pensée grecque. Paris.

Vickers, M. 2020. "Thucydides and Aristophanes", in E. Poláčková – J. Čechvala – D. Čadková – A. Sarkissian et al. (eds), Jubilate et bibite ad honorem Jan Bažant (Studie k antice a její recepci v evropské kultuře), Prague, 107–132.

Wallace, R.W. 1989. The Areopagus Council to 307 BC, Baltimore, MD.

West, M.L. 1983.The Orphic Poems, Oxford.

Youni, M. 1998. ΑΤΙΜΟΣ ΕΣΤΩ ΑΤΙΜΟΣ ΤΕΘΝΑΤΩ, Συμβολή στη μελέτη της ποινής ατιμίας και της θέσης εκτός νόμου στο αττικό δίκαιο. Θεσσαλονίκη.

BERNHARD PALME (WIEN)

KYLONISCHER FREVEL UND MASSENEXEKUTION MIT ODER OHNE URTEIL: ANTWORT AUF ATHINA DIMOPOULOU

Als eines der frühesten fassbaren Ereignisse der athenischen Geschichte haben der Kylonische Frevel und seine langhin wirkenden Konsequenzen für die aristokratische Familie der Alkmeoniden immer wieder die altertumswissenschaftliche Forschung beschäftigt. Über die Grundannahme, dass die u.a. von Herodot, Thukydides, Aristoteles und Plutarch erzählte Geschichte eine echte historische Begebenheit war, herrscht weithin Einigkeit: In (bewusster?) Missdeutung eines delphischen Orakelspruches hat Kylon, Exponenten einer anderen aristokratischen Familie, um 636–632 v. Chr. (oder 628–624) die Akropolis besetzt und damit einen Staatsstreich versucht. Nach Belagerung und Aushungern der Aufständischen hat der amtsführende Archon Megakles aus dem Haus der Alkmeoniden unter Bruch des zugesicherten freien Abzuges sowie Missachtung des Asylrechtes die Tötung der Aufständischen veranlasst und damit einen Frevel gegen die Götter begangen, der als Makel auf ihm und seinen Nachkommen lastete[1]. Viele Einzelheiten der Geschichte sind umstritten – wie es kaum anders sein kann, wenn die frühesten historiographischen Nachrichten erst ca. zweihundert Jahre nach den Ereignissen niedergeschrieben wurden. Neben Fragen zur Datierung, zum Zusammenhang mit der Gesetzgebung Drakons und den Regelungen Solons, zu den politischen Implikationen (blutige Stasis, Exil der Alkmeoniden, propagandistische Ausnutzung gegen die Alkmeoniden bis in die Zeit des Peloponnesischen Krieges) und den religionsgeschichtlichen Aspekten (Asyl, Frevel, kultische Reinigung) sind auch rechtshistorische Fragestellungen wiederholt und zuweilen kontrovers diskutiert worden: Blutgerichtsbarkeit und Exekutionsgewalt im archaischen Athen, Asylrecht, Exil, Amtsgewalt und richterliche Befugnisse der Archonten[2].

Athina Dimopoulou rollt mit neuer, archäologischer Evidenz die rechtshistorischen Fragen wieder auf. Der Anstoß kam durch aufsehenerregende Funde in der Nekropole von Phaleron, wo mindestens 187 Skelette des späten 8. Jh. bis 4. Jh. v. Chr. Verletzungen aufweisen, die auf Exekutionen deuten. Besonderes Aufsehen

---

1 Thuk. I 126, 11: ἀπὸ τούτου ἐναγεῖς καὶ ἀλιτήριοι τῆς θεοῦ ἐκεῖνοί τε ἐκαλοῦντο καὶ τὸ γένος τὸ ἀπ' ἐκείνων.

2 Die älteren Forschungen werden von A. Dimopoulou sorgfältig diskutiert und finden sich in ihren Fußnoten dokumentiert.

hat ein Massengrab am Rande des Friedhofes mit 79 Skeletten erregt, die in drei Reihen angeordnet waren, wobei die der ersten beiden Reihen sorgfältig neben einander gelegt wurden, während jene der dritten Reihe offenbar an dieser Stelle hingerichtet wurden und ungeordnet in die Grube fielen. Zwei Grabbeigaben – Oinochoai, die um 675–624 und 650–625 v. Chr. zu datieren sind – lassen einen chronologischen Bezug zum Kylonischen Frevel zu, so dass angesichts der großen Zahl gleichzeitig Hingerichteter die Vermutung im Raume steht, es könnte sich um die Anhänger Kylons handeln.

Ausgehend von diesem sorgfältig dokumentierten Fund analysiert Dimopoulou sowohl die archäologischen Befunde als auch die mit dem Kylonischen Frevel verbundenen rechts- und religionshistorischen Aspekte. Es darf schon vorweg gesagt werden, dass die mit großer methodischer Vorsicht und ausgezeichneter Sachkenntnis vorgetragenen Beobachtungen kaum Angriffspunkte für kritische Einwände oder Ergänzungen bieten. So weist Dimopoulou darauf hin, dass der Bezug des Massengrabes auf die Opfer des Kylonischen Frevels zwar wahrscheinlich, aber nicht einwandfrei beweisbar ist. Für die rechtshistorischen Fragen bleibt dies letztlich auch nebensächlich, denn falls die Hingerichteten nicht Kylons Anhänger sind, dann sind es die Opfer einer anderen, ähnlich gewalttätigen Eskalation einer *stasis*, derer es – wie Dimopoulou zu Recht betont – im archaischen Athen viele gab. Man könnte sogar argumentieren, dass die 79 Hingerichteten noch krasser den hohen Blutzoll unter den Athenern und insbesondere den konkurrierenden aristokratischen Familien zeigen, wenn sie *nicht* auf den prominenten Kylonischen Frevel zu beziehen sind, sondern auf ein anderes, uns unbekanntes politisches Ereignis, das die historiographischen Quellen nicht einmal der Erwähnung wert fanden.

Vielleicht lässt sich ein Detail des archäologischen Befundes aber doch als ein weiteres Indiz für einen Zusammenhang mit dem Kylonischen Frevel deuten: Die 47 Skelette der ersten Reihe liegen geordnet neben einander und hatten zu einem erheblichen Teil eiserne Fesseln, während die 16 Skelette der zweiten Reihe ungeordnet daneben liegen und die Hände mit organischen Materialien (Seile, Lederriemen) auf den Rücken gebunden hatten. In den sorgsam Bestatteten der ersten Reihe könnte man die vornehmen Anhänger des Kylon sehen, während die Toten der zweiten Reihe wegen der erniedrigenden Art der Fesselung (Hände auf dem Rücken) und der unsorgfältigen Anordnung einfache Bürger gewesen sein könnten. In scharfem Kontrast zu diesen Bestattungen hat man die 16 Toten der dritten Reihe nach ihrer Exekution an Ort und Stelle einfach in den vorbereiteten Graben gestoßen. Es handelt sich demnach um eine dritte Gruppe von Männern, die keine Bestattung erhielten: Man hat sich nicht einmal die Mühe gemacht, die Körper dieser Hingerichteten gerade zu legen, sondern die Leichen achtlos verscharrt, so wie sie bei der Exekution gefallen sind. Darf man in ihnen vielleicht jene bei

Thukydides[3] bezeugten Männer sehen, die Theagenes, der Tyrann von Megara, seinem Schwiegersohn Kylon als zusätzliche Streitkraft (δύναμις) geschickt hatte und die als Nicht-Athener keiner Bestattung würdig erschienen?

Ausgehend von dem archäologischen Befund, der bei zahlreichen Skeletten einen Keulenschlag auf den Kopf als Todesursache zeigt, greift Dimopoulou nochmals die alte Streitfrage auf, welche Art von Hinrichtung der ἀποτυμπανισμός gewesen sei. Nach penibler Sichtung der literarischen Quellen kommt sie – vollkommen überzeugend – zu dem Schluss, dass damit die Tötung durch Schlag mit der Keule (τύμπανον) auf den Kopf gemeint ist, nicht die qualvolle Tortur durch Bindung an ein Brett, wie A. D. Keramopoulos (und die meisten Forscher nach ihm) auf schmalerer Quellenbasis gedacht hatte[4].

Für die Rechtsgeschichte im engeren Sinn stehen freilich andere Aspekte der Episode im Vordergrund, und Dimopoulou bespricht sie systematisch: Zum einen der Umstand, dass die Ereignisse bereits gegen Ende des 7. Jh. v. Chr. eine staatlich-jurisdiktionelle Struktur in Athen voraussetzen, die Todesurteile auch in großer Zahl fällen und exekutieren konnte. Die Ausdrucksweise bei Herodot V 71 und Thukydides I 126 impliziert, wie schon Michael Gagarin gesehen hat[5], dass in Athen schon damals – also vor Drakon, Solon und Peisistratos – ein Gerichtshof und ein Verfahren bestanden haben, die für Vergehen wie jene des Kylon die Todesstrafe verhängen konnten. Zum anderen ist der zeitliche Konnex zwischen Kylons gescheitertem Staatsstreich von 636–632 (oder 628–624) v. Chr. und Drakons Gesetz von 621/0 v. Chr. mit seiner Unterscheidung zwischen vorsätzlicher und unbeabsichtigter Tötung sowie dem Verweis der jeweiligen Straffälle an spezialisierte Gerichtshöfe zwar nicht zu übersehen, aber schwer zu deuten. Vielfach hat man angenommen, dass Drakons Gesetzgebung eine unmittelbare Reaktion auf den Kylonischen Frevel war[6] oder eigens als Rahmen für den Prozess gegen die Alkmeoniden geschaffen wurde[7], der allerdings erst unter Solon um 594 v. Chr. anzusetzen ist. Beides lässt sich, wie Dimopoulou deutlich sieht, weder beweisen noch ausschließen.

Eine konzise rechtshistorische Auswertung wird – wie Dimopoulous Studie neuerlich zeigt – dadurch erschwert, dass die uns vorliegenden Quellen leicht abweichende Varianten der Ereignisse erzählen: Herodot V 71 erwähnt, dass die Prytaneis der Naukraroi (damals die Staatsoberhäupter Athens) die Schutzflehenden von den Götterstatuen fortgerissen und getötet haben. Nach

3 Thuk. I 126, 5: ὁ δὲ παρά τε τοῦ Θεαγένους δύναμιν λαβὼν καὶ τοὺς φίλους ἀναπείσας, ἐπειδὴ ἐπῆλθεν Ὀλύμπια τὰ ἐν Πελοποννήσῳ, κατέλαβε τὴν ἀκρόπολιν ὡς ἐπὶ τυραννίδι, κτλ. Über das weitere Schicksal der megarischen Unterstützer des Kylon schweigen die schriftlichen Quellen.

4 Keramopoulos 1923.

5 Gagarin 1981.

6 Vor allem Stroud 1968, bes. Vol. I, 72 und Humphreys 1991, 17–45, bes. 20–22.

7 Thür 2018, 27–35.

Thukydides I 126, 9–11 wurden die halb verhungerten Schutzflehenden von jenen Athenern, welche die neun Archonten zu ihrer Bewachung abkommandiert hatten, vom Altar weggezerrt und getötet; einige Schutzflehende, die es weiter geschafft haben, wurden beim Altar der Erinnyen niedergemacht. Bei Plutarch, *Solon* 12, 1–2 verspricht der Archon Megakles den Anhängern des Kylon freien Abzug und einen Prozess (δίκη). Die Abziehenden halten durch einen Faden zusätzlich den Kontakt zur Statue (und dem Asylschutz) der Göttin. Als der Faden abreißt, werden sie von Megakles und den anderen Archonten auf der Stelle getötet. Einige, die sich zum Altar der Erinnyen flüchten konnten, werden dort umgebracht. Einige (wenige) Schutzflehende wenden sich an die Frauen der Archonten (vielleicht nur die Frau des *archon basileus*, die *basilinna*) und werden zunächst verschont. Dies könnte die Bemerkung des Aristoteles (*Athenaion politeia* III 2 und LVII 4) bestätigen, wonach der *archon basileus* vor Drakons Gesetzgebung die Befugnis hatte, Urteile zu fällen (und nicht nur Voruntersuchungen durchzuführen) sowie Mordfälle vor den Areopag zu bringen. In keiner der Darstellungen ist jedoch ausdrücklich von einem Prozess oder auch nur einem 'standrechtlichen' Urteil die Rede[8]. Die meisten Anhänger des Kylon wurden sofort, sogar am Altar der Athena und der Erinnyen getötet. Allenfalls könnten diejenigen, die zunächst bei der *basilinna* Zuflucht gefunden hatten, später zum Tode verurteilt worden sein; doch auch dies wird nirgends explizit gesagt. Über das Gericht, Ort und Zeit eines Prozesses kann allenfalls spekuliert werden. Der archäologische Befund der Nekropole von Phaleron ist mit diesen – freilich durchwegs späteren – schriftlichen Nachrichten nicht leicht in Deckung zu bringen, denn er zeigt ja eine Exekution in Phaleron, die in keiner der Erzählvarianten begegnet; im Gegenteil: Herodot, Thukydides und Plutarch geben zu verstehen, dass zumindest die meisten Aufständischen auf oder nahe bei der Akropolis getötet wurden[9].

So schattenhaft die Hinrichtung – oder sofortige Tötung ohne vorhergehendes Urteil? – von Anhängern Kylons bleibt, so konkret ist der Prozess gegen die Alkmeoniden um 594 v. Chr., der gewissermaßen als Spätfolge des Frevels anzusehen ist. Wegen der anhaltenden Unruhen zwischen den Nachkommen des Megakles (denen der Frevel wie eine Erbsünde anhing) und den überlebenden Komplizen des Kylon (die

---

8 Plutarch, *Solon* 12, 1 erwähnt zwar, dass Megakles die Aufständischen unter dem Vorwand, dass ihnen ein Prozess gemacht würde, überredet hatte, das Asyl zu verlassen (ἐξ οὗ τοὺς συνωμότας τοῦ Κύλωνος ἱκετεύοντας τὴν θεὸν Μεγακλῆς ὁ ἄρχων ἐπὶ δίκῃ κατελθεῖν ἔπεισεν); die nachfolgende Schilderung der Ereignisse macht jedoch klar, dass die Aufständischen beim Verlassen des Asyls ermordet wurden und der versprochene Prozess eben nicht stattfand.

9 Dimopoulou (bei Anm. 61–64) sieht in der Formulierung bei Thuk. I 126, 11 ἀπαγαγόντες ἀπέκτειναν einen Hinweis darauf, dass „the main group of captives" abgeführt wurden, um in Phaleron hingerichtet zu werden. Ihr Argument, dass die Exekution (und eine vorangehende Verurteilung?) eher im entfernten Phaleron als im Zentrum Athens, unter den Augen der Familien der Verurteilten, stattgefunden haben wird, ist zwar plausibel; das ἀπαγεῖν kann aber ebenso gut bloß das Wegführen aus dem Asylbereich bedeuten.

sich auf den Orakelspruch zur Besetzung der Akropolis berufen konnten und den Alkmeoniden grobe Verletzung des Asylrechtes vorwarfen), überredete Solon die Alkmeoniden, sich einem Gerichtsverfahren zu stellen – um durch juristische und sakrale Katharsis die frevelhafte Schuld abzuschütteln. In diesem frühesten uns überlieferten Gerichtsverfahren, das wir allerdings erst aus Aristoteles, *Athenaion politeia* I 28 und Plutarch, *Solon* 12, 2–13,1 kennen, werden die Alkmeoniden zu immerwährendem Exil (ἀειφυγία) verurteilt, aus dem sie dann doch mehrfach zurückkehren: um 590 (da Megakles' Sohn Alkmeon die athenischen Truppen im Ersten Heiligen Krieg kommandierte), 561/9 unter Lykurgos, und, nach neuerlichem Exil unter Peisistratos, ca. 526, bevor Kleisthenes 525/4 das Archontat erlangte.

Nach Plutarchs Beschreibung – über 700 Jahre nach dem Prozess entstanden – sieht Dimopoulou einen außerordentlichen Gerichtshof agieren, der mit 300 vereidigten Richtern aus den vornehmen Familien (wie in Drakons Ordnung) besetzt war. Die Klage gegen die Alkmeoniden, so vermutet Dimopoulou, wird nicht auf Mord gelautet haben, sondern auf Gottlosigkeit (ἀσέβεια) oder/und Sakrileg (ἱεροσυλία). Dies ist schon deshalb überzeugend, weil zwischen dem Frevel und dem Prozess bereits eine Generation liegt. Eine Klage wegen Mord hätte nur Megakles selbst und die anderen Archonten treffen können, eine wegen Asebeia hingegen auch deren Nachkommen. Die Archonten hatten sich gegenüber den Göttern doppelt schuldig gemacht, indem sie die Schutzflehenden entweder überredet hatten, den göttlichen Schutz und das sakrale Gelände zu verlassen, oder aber im Glauben gelassen hatten, sie könnten sich in einem Gerichtsverfahren rechtfertigen (und allenfalls ins Exil gehen); aber als der Faden zum Götterbild abriss, wurden alle umgebracht, sogar diejenigen, die sich zum Altar der Erinnyen geflüchtet hatten – ein besonders schweres Vergehen gegen die Götter. Im Prozess gegen die Alkmeoniden ging es nicht um die institutionelle Frage, ob Megakles und die Archonten die Befugnis hatten, gegen die Umstürzler vorzugehen, oder ob die Todesstrafe gerechtfertigt war; es ging ausschließlich um die sakralen Vergehen, die demnach schon als Kategorie von Delikten bestanden, lange bevor im 5. Jh. die Form der γραφὴ ἀσεβείας installiert wurde.

Aufhorchen lässt der (wahrscheinliche) Aufenthaltsort der Alkmeoniden während der langen Jahre ihrer Verbannungen: Hier eröffnen Dimopoulous Hinweise auf archäologische Funde in Anavyssos (dem antiken Anaphlystos) und Sounion aus dem 6. Jh. v. Chr., die aufgrund verschiedener Indizien mit den Alkmeoniden in Verbindung gebracht werden, einen weiteren interessanten Ansatzpunkt: sie deuten darauf hin, dass der Süden Attikas die Machtbasis der Alkmeoniden gewesen ist. Möglicherweise haben sie während ihres Exils also Attika gar nicht verlassen, sondern haben sich nur in den Süden der Halbinsel zurückgezogen, der vielleicht (noch) nicht als Staatsgebiet der Polis Athen im engeren Sinne zählte? Vergleichbare regionale Machtbasen in verschiedenen Teilen Attikas darf man auch bei anderen aristokratischen Häusern des archaischen Athen annehmen, was zur Folge hätte, dass bei fortdauernden Rivalitäten unter den vornehmen Familien auch Spannungen zwischen den verschiedenen Regionen Attikas entstehen konnten. Könnte der Versuch, solchen Spannungen entgegenzuwirken, eine weitere Intention der Kleisthenischen Trittyen-Ordnung gewesen sein – neben der Logistik militärischer Mobilisierung, die Peter Siewert herausgestrichen hat[10]? Wäre es denkbar, dass das ausgefeilte und komplizierte Konzept des Kleisthenes zur Zusammensetzung der Trittyen auch das Ziel verfolgte, regionale Machtkonzentrationen durch massierten aristokratischen Grundbesitz aufzubrechen und durch eine neue Strukturierung Attikas zu ersetzen? Dies könnte erklären, weshalb für uns (ohne Kenntnis der Grundherrschaften) die Ratio hinter mancher Trittys nach wie vor rätselhaft bleibt; das würde aber auch besagen, dass Kleisthenes mit seiner Reform die Machtbasis seines eigenen Hauses zugunsten der Neugestaltung Attikas hintan gestellt hat[11].

bernhard.palme@univie.ac.at

BIBLIOGRAPHIE

Gagarin 1981: M. Gagarin, *Drakon and Early Athenian Homicide Law*, New Haven, CT 1981.

Humphreys 1991: S. C. Humphreys, *A Historical Approach to Drakon's Law of Homicide*, Symposion 1990, Köln 1991, 17–45.

Keramopoulos 1923: A. D. Keramopoulos, Ο Αποτυμπανισμός. Συμβολή αρχαιολογική εις την ιστορίαν του ποινικού δικαίου και την λαογραφία (Βιβλιοθήκη της εν Αθήναις Αρχαιολογικής Εταιρίας 22), Αθήναι 1923.

Siewert 1982: P. Siewert, *Die Trittyen Attikas und die Heeresreform des Kleisthenes* (Vestigia 33), München 1982.

Stanton 1984: G. R. Stanton, *The Trittyes of Kleisthenes*, Chiron 24 (1994) 161–208.

Stroud 1968: R. S. Stroud, *Dracon's Law on Homicide*, Berkeley, CA 1968.

Thür 2018: G. Thür, *New Light on Draco and the Cylonian Sacrilege*, in: W. Riess (Hg.), *Colloquia Attica: Neuere Forschungen zu Archaik, zum athenischen Recht und zur Magie*, Stuttgart 2018, 27–35.

Traill 1986: J. S. Traill, *Demos and trittys. Epigraphical and topographical studies in the organization of Attica*, Toronto 1986.

[10] Siewert 1982: Organisation entlang der „Zentralwege" nach Athen; dem gegenüber hat Traill 1986, stärker die geographischen Aspekte betont; Stanton 1994 in Hinblick auf die Rolle in den demokratischen Institutionen die Bevölkerungszahlen.

[11] Stanton hatte hingegen die gegenteilige Intention vermutet: „compact trittyes for the family of Kleisthenes" (1994, S. 207)

WERNER RIESS (HAMBURG)

DRAKON DER VERSÖHNER: EINE NEUDEUTUNG DES DRAKONTISCHEN TÖTUNGSGESETZES VOR DEM ZEITGENÖSSISCHEN GESELLSCHAFTSPOLITISCHEN HINTERGRUND*

Abstract: Drakon regelte in seinem Tötungsgesetz nicht nur die Anwendung der Rache, sondern nahm auch eine erste Machtverteilung zwischen „Regierung" und „Jurisdiktion" bei Kapitalverbrechen vor, wobei letztere von niedrigen Amtsinhabern bzw. Nicht-Magistraten (Epheten) ausgeübt wurde. Die Einbeziehung weiter Kreise der Bevölkerung in die Aburteilung von Tötungsdelikten hatte das Austarieren sozialer und politischer Kräfteverhältnisse und damit Pazifizierung zum Ziel.

Keywords: Drakon, Areopag, Epheten, *basileis*, *gerontes*

1. Einleitung

Die Interpretation des drakontischen Gesetzes zur unvorsätzlichen Tötung stellt die Forschung bis heute vor große Probleme. Ziel dieses Beitrags ist nicht, einige ungelöste Fragen einer Lösung näher zu bringen, sondern drei Aspekte näher zu beleuchten, die noch nicht genügend Aufmerksamkeit in der Forschung gefunden haben. Dabei ist Grundlage der Untersuchung der drei Themen eine teilweise Neuübersetzung des Gesetzes ins Deutsche, die sich aus den Forschungen Gerhard Thürs, die unser Verständnis des Textes in den letzten Jahren bedeutend erweitert haben, zwanglos ergibt. Auf dieser Wissensbasis gilt es zum einen, das Verhältnis zwischen den *basileis* und den Epheten zu vertiefen, zum anderen muss weiter über die *aidesis*, die Aussöhnung, nachgedacht werden. Hierbei geht es nicht um die notorisch schwierige Frage, ob nur bei der unvorsätzlichen Tötung die *aidesis* möglich war, sondern inwieweit sich die Einbindung der Verwandten bei der *aidesis* von derjenigen bei der Strafverfolgung unterschied und wie ein „staatliches" Organ bei der Aussöhnung mitwirkte, nicht jedoch bei der Verfolgung

* Mein herzlicher Dank gilt Martin Dreher, mit dem ich seit Jahren über „drakonische Fragen" diskutieren kann und der eine erste Version des Vortrags gelesen und mit kritischen Anmerkungen und Nachfragen bereichert hat, Winfried Schmitz, der mir großzügig das Manuskript seiner Neuedition der Gesetze Drakons und Solons zukommen ließ, Gregor Weber für die Kommentierung der Endversion, Justine Diemke für die stete Gesprächsbereitschaft, wichtige Hinweise v.a. in Fragen der Archäologie und Korrektur der Endversion sowie Johannes Christopher Held für Hilfe bei der Literaturbeschaffung. Für alle Irrtümer und Fehldeutungen bin alleine ich verantwortlich.

des Täters. In einem dritten Schritt soll einmal mehr demonstriert werden, dass sich das drakontische Gesetz mit hoher Wahrscheinlichkeit auf den sog. Kylonischen Frevel inklusive seiner Vorgeschichte wie seiner Folgen bezieht[1], indem drei Rückbezüge aufgezeigt werden. Schließlich werden die anhand des Textes gewonnen Befunde in den größeren Kontext von in der Sozialanthropologie und Politikethnologie verwendeten Modellen gestellt, um die Gesellschaft zur Zeit Drakons an ihrem Übergang von vorstaatlichen Verhältnissen zu beginnender Staatlichkeit näher zu charakterisieren. Durch diese größere historische Kontextualisierung des drakontischen Gesetzes soll die Engführung einiger Diskussionen aufgebrochen werden, wie etwa die Frage nach der vermeintlich exakten Bezugnahme des Gesetzes auf den Putsch Kylons. Vor diesem Hintergrund einer Verbindung von Rechtsgeschichte und Sozialanthropologie ergibt sich als Fazit eine zum Teil neue Bewertung Drakons und seines Gesetzes vor dem zeitgenössischen Hintergrund: Der archaische Gesetzgeber kann durchaus als Diallaktes und Aisymnetes gelten und gewinnt damit Anschluss an Solon, dessen Vorläufer er war, auch und gerade in seinen Bemühungen um Ausgleich und Versöhnung.

Betont werden muss, dass es in diesem Beitrag um das Funktionieren der drakontischen Regelungen nur in der archaischen Zeit gehen kann. Die Verhältnisse des 5. und 4. Jhs. v. Chr. bleiben ausgeklammert. Manches muss spekulativ bleiben, denn viele Fragen und Probleme können mangels Quellen nicht sicher gelöst werden, so dass über Plausibilitäten kaum hinauszukommen ist.

2. Neuübersetzung zentraler Passagen des drakontischen Gesetzes ins Deutsche

Seit langem tragen die Überlegungen Gerhard Thürs zu einem besseren Verständnis des komplizierten Textes des drakontischen Gesetzes bei. Vor allem die Zeilen 11–13 stellen die Forschung vor große Herausforderungen, denn die dort für die Tätigkeit der *basileis* und der Epheten verwendeten Verben können nicht die spätere Bedeutung des klassischen Griechisch haben. Übersetzte man das *dikazein* der *basileis* mit „urteilen“, würde sich ihre Tätigkeit nicht von derjenigen der Epheten unterscheiden, denn das *diagnonai* der Epheten ist in jedem Fall mit „urteilen“ in Form einer Abstimmung zu übersetzen. Die Handlung der *basileis* ist zeitlich derjenigen der Epheten vorgelagert. In der griechischen Literatur werden *basileis* immer wieder auch mit Eiden und Schwüren in Verbindung gebracht. Sie sind für die Durchsetzung der *dike* verantwortlich (*dik-azein*), die bekanntlich von Zeus kommt[2]. Die *basileis* sind also die Garanten der von Zeus gesetzten Ordnung[3].

---

[1] In der Fülle der Sekundärliteratur zu diesem Thema kommt Humphreys 1991, 21f. meiner Ansicht am nächsten, indem sie einen engen Bezug des drakontischen Gesetzes zum Kylonischen Frevel annimmt, es aber auch in einem größeren soziopolitischen Kontext verortet. Auch Gagarin 2008, 102 leugnet einen eventuellen Bezug zum Kylonischen Frevel nicht, nimmt aber an, dass es nach dem Coup zu weiteren Tötungen gekommen sei, die einer grundsätzlichen Klärung bedurften.

[2] Dike ist eine Jungfrau, Tochter des Zeus (Hes., *Erg.* 256).

Dennoch werden sie in den literarischen Quellen, wo sie das Szepter tragen[4], eher als Schiedsrichter denn als Richter, also in einer eher schwachen Funktion dargestellt[5]. In mehreren Aufsätzen, die in diesem Kontext nicht referiert zu werden brauchen, plädiert Thür dafür, die Aufgabe der *basileis* in der Formulierung von zwei sich widersprechenden prozessinitiierenden bzw. prozessstrukturierenden Reinigungseiden zu sehen, die sie dann den Streitparteien auferlegten[6]. Anders als in anderen Rechtskulturen[7] ist an dieser Stelle aber nicht von prozessbeendenden Eiden die Rede, engl. *ordeal*, sondern von Eiden, die den Prozess einleiten und strukturieren. Deshalb stehen die *basileis* im Text *vor* den Epheten. Wer gute, d.h. wohl situationsadäquate Eide formulieren kann, genießt in der Gemeinschaft

---

3 Nach Hes., *Theog.* 80–97 kommen gerechte *basileis* von Zeus, auf dessen Gnade auch ihre Stellung beruht (vgl. auch Hom., *Il.* 1,279; 2,98.196f.). Ihr Segen wird von den Göttern verliehen (Hom., *Od.* 19,108ff.). Das Recht, d.h. die Göttin *dike*, folgt ihnen. Im Gegenzug kommt es ihnen zu, die göttlichen Satzungen zu bewahren (Hom., *Il.* 1,237ff.; 9,98; *Od.* 11,184ff.). Für weitere jurisdiktionelle Tätigkeiten der *basileis* vgl. Hom., *Il.* 23,485; 16,542; *Od.* 3,244.

4 Auch das Szepter ist ihnen von Zeus gegeben: Hom., *Il.* 1,279; 9,98f. „Szeptertragend" ist bei Homer ein Epitheton für die *basileis*: Hom., *Il.* 2,86.101.206.265 (Odysseus schlägt Thersites mit dem Szepter); 9,38; 18,556f.; Hom., *Od.* 5,9; 8,41.47. Aber auch die *gerontes* können Szepter tragen, so Nestor in *Od.* 3,412. Er versteht sich von allen Sterblichen am besten auf das Richten, *Od.* 3,244: Νέστορ', ἐπεὶ περὶ οἶδε δίκας ἠδὲ φρόνιν ἄλλων.

5 Ihre Macht ist durch soziale Konventionen begrenzt: Thuk. 1,13; Aristot., *Pol.* 3,1285b; Dion. Hal. 5,74. Aristot., *Pol.* 3,1285b listet ihre Pflichten im Krieg, bei den Opfern, also im sakralen Bereich, sowie in der Rechtsprechung. Ich danke Justine Diemke für den Hinweis, dass der homerische Hymnos an Demeter Könige kennt, die das Recht/die Gesetze ver/behandeln (*Hom. h.* 2,215: θεμιστοπόλων βασιλήων; 473: θεμιστοπόλοις βασιλεῦσι). Spätestens als der *archon polemarchos* eingeführt wurde, verblieben den *basileis* nur noch religiöse Aufgaben und, wie wir im drakontischen Gesetz sehen, begrenzte Befugnisse in der Rechtsprechung. Dreher 2019b betont, dass bereits in archaischer Zeit *basileis* im griechischen Kulturraum keine absolute vererbbare Macht hatten, sondern als Funktionäre der *poleis* zu verstehen sind.

6 Thür 1990, 150f.; 1996, 71; 2007 (mit Diskussion von Parallelen im Alten Orient). Thür 2014 unterscheidet die Irrationalität der beiden Reinigungseide vom rationalen Abstimmungsverfahren der Epheten. Das drakontische Recht zeige also den Übergang von Irrationalität zu mehr Rationalität; Thür 2015, 145; Thür 2018, 32f. Die passivische Formulierung *katadikasthentes* in Solons Amnestiegesetz (Plut., *Sol.* 19,4) spricht nicht gegen diese Bedeutung. Zum einen kann Solon das *dikazein* im drakontischen Gesetz schon anders verstanden haben, zum anderen kann durchaus passivisch übersetzt werden, „denen Eide auferlegt worden waren" bzw. „die der Verfahrenshoheit der *basileis* unterworfen worden waren". Sealey 1994, 119 lehnt sich z.T. an Thür an, bleibt aber zweideutig, ob es sich beim *dikazein* um die Formulierung von Eiden oder einer Frage handelte, welche die Epheten zu entscheiden hatten.

7 Thür 2015, 173 betont, dass der doppelte Parteieneid keine Vorbilder im Alten Orient hatte.

höchstes Ansehen[8]. Wenn nun aber die *basileis* Eide aufsetzen und sie den Gerichtsparteien auferlegen, dies ist wohl die Wortbedeutung von *dikazein* (wörtlich, „dem von Zeus gegebenen Recht Geltung verschaffen“), heißt dies, dass die Epheten darüber abstimmen (auf die Abstimmung weist auch die ungerade Zahl 51 hin), wer die Eide wahrheitsgetreu geschworen hat[9]. Die Epheten fällen also das Urteil, nicht die *basileis*[10]. Die Entscheidungsträger im Text sind ausschließlich die Epheten, die viermal durch Abstimmung richten und damit ein Urteil fällen[11]. Drakon hat also in Athen das Richten bei der Blutgerichtsbarkeit formalisiert, und zwar in der Hand der andernorts nicht belegten Epheten[12].

---

8 Dies ist insbesondere dann der Fall, wenn die *basileis* milde sind, was der Gemeinschaft Glück und Wohlstand beschert, vgl. dazu etwa Hom., *Od.* 2,230f.; 19,106–114; Hes., *Theog.* 80–97.

9 Streit wird durch Schwur beendet: Hom., *Il.* 3,97–110; 23,602–611. Ulf – Kistler 2020, 95: Konfliktparteien versöhnen sich durch gegenseitigen Schwur: Hom., *Od.* 24, 529–548. Auch Ruschenbusch 1960, 144 geht davon aus, dass bei Tötung die Tatfrage durch die *diomosia* geklärt wurde. Die drakontischen Eide könnten durchaus Vorläufer der klassischen *diomosia* gewesen sein. Thür 1996, 71; 2014, 921f.; 2015, 167, 170 bezeichnet denn auch die gegensätzlichen Eide als *diomosiai.*

10 Von der älteren Forschung kommt Wecklein 1873, 16 Thür am nächsten. Für Wecklein nehmen die *basileis* die gerichtliche Untersuchung vor, die Epheten urteilen. Nach Carlier 1984, 349 verkünden die *basileis* das Urteil. Die Reihenfolge im Text lässt diesen Schluss jedoch nicht zu. Mirhady 2008, 19–22 weist im *dikazein* den *basileis* eine andere Aufgabe zu, die formale Feststellung, dass ein Tötungsdelikt erfolgt sei. Die Proklamation des *basileus* sei ungefähr zeitgleich mit derjenigen der Angehörigen erfolgt; beide Ankündigungen hatten zum Ziel, die Stadt vor einer Verschmutzung zu warnen. Dieses *dikazein* der *basileis* richtete sich sogar gegen unbekannte Täter, Tiere und Objekte, die einen Tod verursacht hatten. Die Epheten urteilten (*diagnonai*) dann in einem zweiten Schritt (sofern es zu einem Verfahren kam) über die Willensrichtung (ebd. 21f.). Auch bei dieser Rekonstruktion sind meine untenstehenden Hypothesen einer frühen Gewaltenteilung gültig. Eine zu Mirhady gegensätzliche Hypothese schlägt Pepe 2012, 30–40, 77 vor: Die *basileis* hätten über den Vorsatz geurteilt, die Epheten nur darüber, ob jemand getötet hatte oder nicht, ebd. 77: „… i *basileis*, qualora si debba giudicare, *dikazein*, se il soggetto sia *aitios*, colpevole di un'azione volontaria a seguito della quale egli abbia ucciso di sua mano o istigato a uccidere; gli efeti, per i casi nei quali invece non si debba valutare l'intenzione ma soltanto stabilire se il soggetto sia o non sia omicida, attività indicata da *diagignosko*…“ Die Reihenfolge erscheint wie bei Carlier seltsam. Soweit ich sehe, wurde diese Hypothese bislang nicht in der Forschung aufgegriffen.

11 Die Epheten erscheinen sechsmal im Gesetzestext, viermal urteilen sie durch Abstimmung (Z. 13, 17, 29, 35). Das Verb hierfür ist konsistent *diagignoskein/diagnonai.* Einmal wählen sie Phratriemitglieder nach ihrer Bestheit/Güte aus (*haireomai*, Z. 19), einmal überführen sie Täter der oder erkennen auf unvorsätzliche(n) Tötung (*haliskomai*, Z. 26).

12 Cantarella 1976, 123–126 betont zu Recht, dass die Tatsache, dass erst ein Urteil eines Gremiums die Ausübung der Blutrache durch Verwandte legitimierte, einen entscheidenden Schritt in der Rechtsentwicklung darstellt. Zur Fernhaltung eines potentiellen Täters von öffentlichen Räumen vgl. Salvo 2012.

Nach Klärung der Tätigkeiten der beiden Gremien hat Thür 2014 und 2018 eine wichtige Ergänzung der Lücke in Zeile 12 vorgeschlagen, in der Platz für 17 Buchstaben besteht. Diese Konjektur beruht auf einer alten Manuskriptüberlieferung der sechsten Rede Antiphons (6, 16–17)[13]. Es geht darum, dass zwei Szenarien für die unvorsätzliche Tötung aufgespannt werden, zum einen die Möglichkeit, dass der Täter selbst die Hand erhoben, also eigenhändig getötet hat, zum anderen die Alternative, dass er einen Auftrag oder einen Befehl gegeben hat[14], in dessen Folge jemand zu Tode kam. Auch diese Bedeutung von *bouleuein*, die von der klassischen Bedeutung abweicht, hat Thür in der Vergangenheit in mehreren Aufsätzen herausgearbeitet[15]. Die Passage ist am besten auf die Umstände des Kylonischen Frevels zu beziehen. Die Kylonier, Putschisten, hatten um 632 v. Chr. Zuflucht an heiligen Stätten gesucht und waren von dort weggezerrt und z. T. erschlagen worden[16]. Zur Rechenschaft zu ziehen sind aber nicht nur die Totschläger (die, die selbst die Hand erhoben haben), sondern auch diejenigen, die den Zugriff auf die Kylonier befohlen hatten. Sie haben zwar nicht selbst getötet, aber die Tötung der Feinde beim Zugriff, im Handgemenge durch ihre Anhänger billigend, wenn nicht sogar zustimmend in Kauf genommen. Es handelte sich also nicht um einen direkten Tötungsauftrag, sondern um eine Anordnung mit Todesfolge. Auch diese Auftraggeber müssen sich nun also verantworten. Soweit Gerhard Thür.

Je nachdem, welches Niveau an Staatlichkeit man für die Zeit Drakons annehmen möchte, bieten sich für *pheugein* verschiedene Übersetzungen an. „Fliehen" setzt das geringste Maß an Staatlichkeit voraus[17], „stand trial"[18] das höchste. „In die

---

[13] Thür 2014, 923; 2018, 34.

[14] Thür versteht unter *bouleuein* im Wesentlichen die Verantwortlichkeit für eine indirekte Tötung. „Auftrag" ist also nur eine Möglichkeit der Übersetzung.

[15] Jüngst Thür 2018, 30.

[16] Vgl. Hdt. 5,70f.; Thuk. 1,126,3–12; Plut., *Sol.* 12,1–9; *Ath. pol.* 1; Herakl. Pont., *Ath. pol.* Fr. 4; schol. Aristoph., *Equ.* 445 (443 Dindorf). Zur Datierung vgl. Dorn – Schmitz – Shahin 2023, 73 mit weiterer Literatur. An dieser Stelle sei ein caveat formuliert: Die in diesem Beitrag zitierten Belege aus Dorn – Schmitz – Shahin 2023 beziehen sich auf die Druckfahnen, die mir Winfried Schmitz freundlicherweise im November 2022 zukommen ließ. Geringfügige Abweichungen in der endgültigen Druckfassung sind möglich. Rönnbergs (2021) grobe Datierung des Kylonischen Frevels und der Gesetzgebung Drakons auf die zweite Hälfte des 7. Jhs. (z.B. 2021, 34, 37) ist in ihrem Skeptizismus gegenüber allen literarischen Quellen nicht zielführend.

[17] Ruschenbusch 1960, 147 und Dorn – Schmitz – Shahin 2023, 147 übersetzen mit „fliehen" (vor der Blutfehde).

[18] So Phillips 2008, 50f.; 2013, 53 in seiner Quellensammlung, ebenso Mirhady 2008, 17 und Pepe 2012, 22–28. „Sich einem Gerichtsverfahren stellen" oder „angeklagt werden" setzt bereits ein hohes Maß an Staatlichkeit voraus, das wir in keinem anderen Bereich Athens in drakontischer Zeit nachvollziehen können.

Verbannung gehen“[19] umschreibt eine mittlere Ausbildung der Staatlichkeit, wofür ich mich, Thür folgend, entscheide[20].
Mit der plausiblen Klärung der Begrifflichkeiten und der höchst gelungenen, kontext-spezifischen Konjektur Thürs bietet sich eine Neuübersetzung zentraler Passagen des Textes ins Deutsche an (s. Appendix).

3. Aufgabenverteilung zwischen *basileis* und Epheten – erste Gewaltenteilung auf zwei Ebenen

a) basileis – Epheten

Die Aufgabenteilung zwischen *basileis* und Epheten sowie die ihr zugrunde-liegenden Gründe, wurden, soweit ich sehe, in der Forschung noch nicht aus-reichend thematisiert. In keiner anderen Quelle zur Gerichtsbarkeit der archaischen Zeit ist von zwei Gremien die Rede. Bei Hesiod werden *basileis* generalisierend im Plural als Richter genannt[21], aber insbesondere aus der berühmten Passage in der Theogonie geht hervor, dass jeweils ein Einzelrichter entscheidet. Bei Homer urteilen in der Schildszene die *gerontes*[22], die Älteren[23], womöglich bilden sie einen Ältestenrat. Im 23. Buch der Ilias ruft Menelaos bei den Wettkampfspielen für den gefallenen Patroklos Anführer und Ratgeber an, die *dikazein* sollen (573f.: „Hört denn also, ihr, der Argeier Berater und Führer, Richtet nun zwischen uns beiden gerecht und keinem zuliebe …“). Menelaos selbst will dann aber auch *dikazein* (579: „Oder ich selber fälle den Spruch, …“)[24].

Epheten sind außerhalb Athens unbekannt. Der seit langem vertretenen Forschungsmeinung ist zuzustimmen, dass es sich bei den athenischen *basileis* um den *archon basileus* und die vier *phylobasileis* gehandelt haben wird, also um die jeweiligen Amtsinhaber[25].

---

[19] So m.E. zurecht Thür 2015, 159. Osborne – Rhodes 2017, 507 übersetzen mit „he shall be exiled“.

[20] Ulf – Kistler 2020, 94f. mit weiteren Beispielen, wo *pheugein* „in die Verbannung gehen“ heißt.

[21] Hes., *Erg.* 35–39; 262–264.

[22] Hom., *Il.* 18,501–507.

[23] Auch dies ist umstritten. Manche meinen, dass das umstehende Volk durch die Intensität des Beifalls das Verfahren entscheiden würde, andere, dass der *histor* der Entscheider sei. Für Westbrook 1992, 74f. ist das Volk hier die Versammlung der Notabeln (eines Dorfes), 75: „the community as a legal entity represented by a body of notables.“ Zu den *gerontes* in der Schildszene vgl. Wirbelauer 1996, 165–168.

[24] Hom., *Il.* 23,573f.: ἀλλ' ἄγετ' Ἀργείων ἡγήτορες ἠδὲ μέδοντες ἐς μέσον ἀμφοτέροισι δικάσσατε, μὴ δ' ἐπ' ἀρωγῇ. Hom., *Il.* 23,579: εἰ δ' ἄγ' ἐγὼν αὐτὸς δικάσω, […]. Zu den zwei *dikazein* schreibt Thür 1996, 66: „the two *dikazein* in this text seem to harmonize best if we assume that the other leaders formulated oaths too, as Menelaos did. An oath according to the *dikazein* sworn by one of the litigants would have settled the dispute.“

[25] So vertreten z.B. von Welwei 1992, 140; Gagarin 2000, 570–572; Thür 2014, 921; 2015, 161; Dreher 2019a. Vgl. die ältere Literatur, dem zustimmend, zitiert bei Rönnberg 2021, 39, FN 223 sowie bei Dorn – Schmitz – Shahin 2023, 112, FN 79, 80.

Die andere relevante Meinung hat angenommen, hier handele es sich um den gegenwärtigen und alle zukünftigen *archontes basileis*[26], also um einen kollektiven Plural, was grammatikalisch möglich ist.

Da ich davon ausgehe, dass Drakon exakt und juristisch formulierte, hätte er in letzterem Falle wohl den Singular benutzt. Es gibt ein weiteres Indiz, das für den *archon basileus* und die vier *phylobasileis* spricht: In der *Ath. pol.* heißt es (57, 4), dass noch im 4. Jh. diese fünf gemeinsam über unbekannte Täter, Gegenstände und Tiere urteilen[27], die einen Tod verursachten. Es handelt sich also um einen jurisdiktionellen Atavismus; diese fünf Personen sind in klassischer Zeit auf quasi religiös-zeremonielle Funktionen beschränkt, aber sie tagen immer noch im Prytaneion, dem alten Regierungssitz der Polis. Wir dürfen also mit einiger Sicherheit davon ausgehen, dass Drakon mit den *basileis* den amtierenden *archon basileus* und die vier amtierenden *phylobasileis* meint.

Dass diese *basileis* Ämter bekleideten, ist zum einen daraus ersichtlich, dass die uns überlieferte Archontenliste 683/2 v. Chr. beginnt (und mindestens der *archon basileus* im drakontischen Gesetz gemeint sein muss)[28], und zum anderen die *basileis* nicht näher charakterisiert werden. Es war jedem klar, um welchen genau definierten Personenkreis es sich handelte. Hätte es sich bei den *basileis* lediglich um „die Gruppe der vorstaatlichen Siedlungsvorsteher im homerischen Sinne, also [um die] an persönlichem Prestige reichsten Personen“, wie Rönnberg annimmt, oder um die Priester der Tempel gehandelt, an denen die Täter Zuflucht

---

26 So vertreten z.B. von Philippi 1874, 236, 239; Lange 1874, 226, 228–230; Stroud 1968, 45–47, dezidiert Carlier 1984, 350, neuerdings wieder von Dorn – Schmitz – Shahin 2023, 114f. Vgl. die ältere Literatur, diese Hypothese vertretend, zitiert bei Rönnberg 2021, 39, FN 224 sowie bei Dorn – Schmitz – Shahin 2023, 112, FN 79, 80. Gagarin 2000, 570–572 widerlegt diese Annahme unter Einbeziehung inschriftlicher Parallelquellen und Aufarbeitung der älteren Literatur zu diesem Thema.

27 Vgl. dazu Kahrstedt 1937, 22. Stroud 1993, 214–221 schreibt *Ath. pol.* 57 hohe historische Authentizität zu, denn Aristoteles habe alle ihm zur Verfügung stehenden Quellen benutzt und selbstverständlich auch die Stele mit dem drakontischen Totschlagsgesetz gelesen.

28 Aristoteles folgend wird man sich die Entstehung des Archontats wohl sukzessive vorstellen müssen. Das älteste Amt des *basileus* wurde nie abgeschafft, aber es wurde durch das Hinzufügen weiterer Ämter geschwächt. Auf das Jahr 683/2 datiert die Überlieferung des ersten *archon* (*eponymos*), der nur ein Jahresamt bekleidete und den *basileus* als Oberbeamten ablöste. *Ath. pol.* 3,1–3 setzt diesen *archon eponymos* in der Chronologie an die dritte Stelle. Angeblich wurde dem *basileus* zunächst der *archon polemarchos* beigefügt, erst dann folgte der *archon eponymos*. Die sechs Thesmotheten wurden erst eingeführt, als die anderen Funktionen schon alle Jahresämter waren (*Ath. pol.* 3,4). Es ist darauf hinzuweisen, dass die *Athenaion Politeia* bzgl. der Zeit vor Solon keine validen Informationen liefert. Thukydides (1,126,8) setzt die Thesmotheten beim Kylonischen Frevel bereits voraus. Für Rönnberg 2021, 60 ist die Archontenliste unhistorisch, da eine spätere Rekonstruktion.

suchten, wie Schmitz früher meinte[29], hätte ihre Bestellung im Gesetz näher erläutert werden müssen, ähnlich der Erwähnung des Auswahlmodus bei den zehn Phratriemitgliedern, die man gelegentlich bei der *aidesis* brauchte. Mit einer bedeutungsoffenen Formulierung einer nicht näher definierten Gruppe von Eliteangehörigen Funktionen in der Blutgerichtsbarkeit anzuvertrauen, hätte sicher zu erneuten Rivalitäten innerhalb der Führungsriege geführt.

Basileis und Epheten entstammen sicher denselben Oberschichten, doch wird man annehmen dürfen, dass die Epheten[30], welche die Urteile fällten, älter und erfahrener als die *basileis* waren[31]. Die *basileis* agieren kraft ihres Amtes, sie leisten die juristische Arbeit der Eidformulierung, auch wenn sie möglicherweise stark ritualisiert war; die Epheten könnten gewesene *basileis* (oder andere Amtsinhaber) gewesen sein. Erinnern wir uns, dass in der homerischen Schildszene (*Il.* 18, 490–526) die *gerontes* „urteilen" (18, 501–506, 506: *dikazein*), die Älteren. Sie halten die Stäbe und „urteilen" einer nach dem anderen. Sie werden nicht als *basileis* bezeichnet; sie sind eindeutig aufgrund ihres Alters und ihrer hohen sozialen Stellung herausgehoben[32]. Sie verfügen über mehr Lebenserfahrung und damit wohl auch „juristische" Kenntnisse. Da wir die homerische Sozialstruktur wohl *mutatis mutandis* auch für das archaische Athen annehmen dürfen, entsprechen wohl diese homerischen *gerontes* ungefähr den Epheten im drakontischen Gesetz, die vielleicht vormalige *basileis* waren, die sich zuerst im Formulieren von Eiden geübt hatten, bevor ihnen das Fällen von Urteilen anvertraut wurde. Es erscheint also plausibel, dass die Epheten aufgrund ihres Alters – sie mussten nach einer Notiz

---

29 Rönnberg 2021, 39, ähnlich 61. Ähnlich Flament 2009, 122–132 und Schmitz 2001, 24–30; 2018, 42f. (revidiert Dorn – Schmitz – Shahin 2023, 112, FN 80 nach der Kritik von Dreher 2019a). Auch Sealey 1994, 117f. geht von *basileis* als Privatpersonen aus.

30 In Aischyl., *Pers.* 79 erscheinen die Epheten in ihrer Funktion als Befehlshaber.

31 Forchhammer 1876, 469 erkennt richtig, dass die Epheten höherrangig als die *basileis* waren; auch ist ihm zuzustimmen, dass die Epheten schon vor Drakon existierten, allerdings irrt er in der Annahme, dass Drakon die Epheten nach Würde wählbar gemacht (diese Hypothese fußt wohl auf dem Missverständnis von Pollux 8, 125, nach dem die Epheten *aristinden* zu bestimmen waren, also in Analogie zu den Phratriemitgliedern, und von Drakon eingeführt wurden. Selbst wenn die Epheten nach Würde bestimmbar waren, dann wohl eher durch ihre *peers* und nicht durch Volkswahl, wie Forchhammer ohne Belege postuliert) und damit ein Aufbrechen der Elitenherrschaft intendiert habe (ebd. 470). Wie unten deutlich wird, ging es Drakon gerade um Versöhnung innerhalb der und zwischen den gesellschaftlichen Schichten.

32 Bei Homer kooperieren *basileis* und *gerontes* eng; der *basileus* bespricht öffentliche Angelegenheiten mit den *gerontes* beim gemeinsamen Mahl (Hom., *Il.* 9,70; 22,119; *Od.* 7,189; 8,42; 21,21) und bringt die vorbesprochenen Dinge dann vor die Volksversammlung. Vor Gericht sind die Funktionen von *basileis* und *gerontes* bei Homer für uns kaum zu trennen, vgl. oben FN 4. Es scheint, als ob Drakon für Athen differenziert und eine Aufteilung von Funktionen für *basileis* einerseits und *gerontes* andererseits in Gestalt der Epheten vornimmt.

des Photios über 50 Jahre alt sein[33] –, ihrer größeren Lebenserfahrung und auch als „Rechtsexperten“ in Athen für die Aburteilung von Tötungsdelikten verantwortlich waren. Ludwig Lange führt etliche Belege dafür an, dass die Epheten im Grunde *gerontes*, also Ältere waren[34].

Eine weitere Überlegung bzw. Spekulation Langes legt nahe, dass die Epheten ehemalige Amtsinhaber gewesen sein könnten. Der alte Adelsrat, bzw. nennen wir ihn besser den Rat der sozialen Eliten, den Lange als *he boule tes Areiou pagou* bezeichnet, mag aus 60 Mitgliedern bestanden haben, d.h. 15 aus jeder Phyle. Aus ihrer Mitte wurden neun Archonten bestimmt, die restlichen 51, die Epheten, hatten wohl schon Ämter bekleidet, sie waren ja älter. Neun Personen des Rates dienen also als aktive Magistrate, 51 sind nicht mehr aktiv, sie sind ehemalige Magistrate, die hohes Ansehen genießen. Lange erklärt jedoch nicht, wie die Zahl 60 stabil gehalten werden konnte.

Warum aber verteilt Drakon die Kompetenzen? Sowohl die *basileis* als auch die Epheten hätten jeweils die Aufgabe der Eidesformulierung sowie der Urteilssprechung übernehmen können. Diese Aufgabenteilung, die es ja andernorts nicht gibt, beschränkt die Machtbefugnisse beider Gruppen. Aus Hesiod (auch bei Homer, *Il.* 18, 508: Belohnung für besten Spruch) wissen wir, dass Richter, die situationsadäquate Eide formulieren konnten, hoch geachtet waren (s. oben) und von beiden Parteien als eine Art Entlohnung reich beschenkt wurden[35]. Offenbar gab es Missbrauch, wurden Geschenke schon vor Prozessbeginn von den Richtern erwartet und verband sich mit der Höhe der Geschenke sehr wohl die Hoffnung auf einen Sieg vor Gericht. Hesiod spricht in diesem Zusammenhang von „Geschenke fressenden“[36], d.h. korrupten Richtern (*basileis*), die nicht etwa der Dike zum Sieg verhelfen, sondern „krumme Urteile sprechen“ und damit die herkömmlichen Normen verletzen. Damit sind sie mitverantwortlich für die *dysnomia*, die sich in manchen Städten ausbreitet. Genau diesen Missstand will Drakon offenbar beseitigen[37]. Diejenigen, welche die Eide formulieren, richten nicht; diejenigen, die richten, haben die Eide nicht formuliert. Für Bestechung und Amtsmissbrauch gab es damit weniger Raum, zumal die Epheten, die richteten, ja nicht mehr in einem Amt,

---

33 Phot. Suid. s.v. (S 3876, 3877). Betont von Kahrstedt 1937, 13.

34 Vgl. Lange 1874, 200.

35 Hes., *Theog.* 80–97: *Basileis* müssen auch in schwierigen Situationen gerechte Urteile fällen. Dann werden sie wie ein Gott geachtet und die Gemeinde blüht, vgl. dazu Ulf – Kistler 2020, 72. Demos und *basileis* waren aufeinander bezogen. Wenn *basileis* im Sinne des Demos erfolgreich handelten, konnten ihnen materielle Ausgaben durchaus von diesem erstattet werden (Ulf – Kistler 2020, 81, 83). Vgl. zu den für die Richter fälligen Geschenken etwa Hom., *Il.* 1,230; 9,155.

36 Hes., *Erg.* 35–39; 262–264. Vgl. aber auch schon früher zur Habsucht der Richter Hom., *Il.* 1,231; 16,387; *Od.* 4,690–695. Geradezu kritisch werden Richter gesehen, die eben nicht milde wie Odysseus sind, sondern mit Willkür herrschen (*Od.* 2, 230–233).

37 Vgl. Ulf – Kistler 2020, 76. Nach Hesiod beachten die *basileis* in der friedlichen Stadt das Recht, die *dike*; genau das will Drakon sicherstellen.

sondern, wie ich meine, älter und erfahrener als die *basileis* waren. Die Aufgabenteilung hat also primär zum Zweck, die Urteilssuche von der Urteilsfällung zu trennen und damit beide Handlungen vor Missbrauch und Korruption zu schützen.

Was bedeutet diese Trennung von Urteilssuche und Urteilsfällung? Ganz sicher geht es um die Verhinderung von Machtmissbrauch. Amtsinhaber mit recht geringen Funktionen richten nicht, sondern formulieren Eide. Die, die richten, haben gar keine Amtsgewalt und damit keine Macht mehr. Dies scheint eine direkte Reaktion auf die Krisen der Archaik gewesen zu sein. Macht übersetzt sich in Athen nun nicht mehr in politische Gerichtsurteile. Gerichtsurteile ihrerseits übersetzen sich nicht (mehr) in Machtgewinn, denn die Epheten werden oftmals zu alt gewesen sein, um weitere Ämter zu bekleiden.

Ich möchte betonen, dass aufgrund der Verwendung zweier unterschiedlicher Verben (*dikazein* vs. *diagnonai*) von zwei verschiedenen Tätigkeiten und damit von einer Aufgabenteilung zwischen den *basileis* und den *Epheten* ausgegangen werden muss, unabhängig davon, ob man die Aufgabe der *basileis* in der Formulierung und dem Auferlegen von Eiden sehen mag oder nicht. Die folgenden Hypothesen beruhen also lediglich auf der Tatsache einer Aufgabenteilung, nicht auf dem Spezifikum der Frage nach den Eiden.

b) Weitere Archonten und Amtsträger – Blutgerichtsbarkeit

Schauen wir uns das Personal genauer an, dann verstärkt sich dieser Eindruck einer frühen Gewaltenteilung noch: Die einzigen, die Drakon in die Rechtsprechung nicht einbezieht, sind der mächtige *archon eponymos*, der *archon polemarchos* sowie die sechs Thesmotheten, wenn es sie schon gab (laut Thukydides 1, 126, 8 gab es sie schon[38]). Sie sind mächtig genug, regieren, setzen Gesetze auf, sie sind eventuell Mitglieder des Rats, sie müssen nicht auch noch richterlich tätig werden. Und bedeutsamer: Sie sind als Amtsinhaber mit Machtbefugnissen ausgestattet; genau diese Leute sollten nach Meinung Drakons nicht richten!

Drakon lässt also nur den altehrwürdigen *archon basileus*, der fast keine Macht mehr und eigentlich nur noch zeremonielle Bedeutung hat[39], aus kultischen Gründen in der Funktion des Vorsitzes bei einem Blutgericht bestehen. Die *phylobasileis* haben auf Polis-Ebene wenig Einfluss. Und die 51 Epheten waren

---

[38] Dorn – Schmitz – Shahin 2023, 164, v.a. FN 244 (mit Verweis auf *Ath. pol.* 52,1) sind bereit, ein hohes Alter der Thesmotheten anzunehmen.

[39] Nach Drews 1983, 130f. gab es in der griechischen Welt schon sehr früh keinen König mehr in unserem Sinne, sondern lediglich kleinere Anführer, die mit einem Rat und einer Versammlung gemeinsam regierten. Schon im 8. Jh. bildeten sich langsam staatliche Strukturen aus, Ämter bildeten sich. Eine Gemeinschaft von Bürgern wählte, politische Rechte wurden nach Vermögen abgestuft, Rat und Ämter wurden von einer *ruling class* besetzt. Gleichzeitig mit Drews lehnte Dreher schon in seiner Dissertation (1983) ein frühes staatliches Königtum ab und hat seine Argumentation zuletzt in Dreher 2019b bekräftigt.

keine Amtsträger mehr, d.h. Drakon hat die Jurisdiktion insgesamt streng von den aktiven und mächtigen Amtsinhabern getrennt. Die Mächtigen, d.h. die Regierungsfähigen, sind also im Gericht ausgebremst, ihnen wird der Einfluss über die Gerichte entzogen bzw. verwehrt. Die Missstände, die Hesiod (allerdings für Böotien) beklagt, sollen in Athen nicht mehr möglich sein.

Es ist also eine erste Aufgaben- und damit Machtverteilung nicht nur innerhalb der Jurisdiktion, zwischen *basileis* und Epheten, sondern auf einer höheren Ebene eine weitere Art von früher Gewaltenteilung festzustellen: Auf der einen Seite aktive Magistrate, die politische Tätigkeiten ausführen (*eponymos*, *polemarchos*, Thesmotheten), auf der anderen Seite eine Jurisdiktion, die mit beinahe machtlosen Amtsinhabern (*archon basileus*, *phylobasileis*) bemannt ist und den alten Epheten, die machtlos waren, entweder weil sie keine Magistratur mehr bekleideten oder noch nie ein Amt innehatten, sie also zum Zeitpunkt des Richtens keine Amtsinhaber (mehr) waren.

Schaubild: Machtverteilung in Athen unter Drakon

Oberschichten (= Eupatriden?)

Jurisdiktion		Regierung
Urteilsuche	Rechtsprechung	
Archon basileus 4 Phylobasileis (Ämter mit wenig Macht: zeremonielle Funktion bzw. keine Funktionen auf Polisebene)	51 Epheten (ohne Amtsgewalt)	*Archon Eponymos* *Archon Polemarchos* 6 Thesmotheten (politisch aktive und mächtige Amtsinhaber)

Kehren wir zum Gesetzestext zurück: Im Gesetz Drakons urteilen nur und ausschließlich die Epheten, nicht die *basileis*. Auch bei der Aussöhnung spielen die *basileis* nicht die geringste Rolle. Ihre Funktion ist also im Vergleich zu derjenigen der Epheten kleiner und eng umrissen. Thür geht davon aus, dass die Eide formelhaft[40], aber doch situationsbezogen waren. Die Befugnisse der *basileis* sind also spätestens ab Drakon beschränkt, sie werden in der Ausübung ihrer Funktion von den Epheten „überwacht". Allzu streng wird man sich dieses Gegengewicht durch Standesgenossen freilich nicht vorstellen dürfen, denn Drakon intendierte nicht,

[40] Thür 2015, 168.

einen Keil zwischen die Eliten zu treiben, sondern es ging ihm wohl um ein Austarieren der Machtverhältnisse, d.h. um Verteilung der Macht zwischen den führenden Familien Athens und damit letztlich auch um Pazifizierung[41]. Dieser Machtausgleich führte in Folge zu einer gesellschaftlichen Balance, zumindest innerhalb der Oberschichten. Und dadurch, dass Kompetenzen auf mehrere Schultern verteilt wurden (durch den Einbezug der *phylobasileis*), konnten weite Kreise der Eliten einbezogen werden, kam es also zu einer gestiegenen Partizipation unter den Führungseliten bei wichtigen Strafverfahren, womit dem Ehrgeiz vieler vornehmer Männer Rechnung getragen wurde. Die Einbindung der Ambitionen vieler Angehöriger der Eliten trug wesentlich zur Befriedung Athens und zur weiteren Ausbildung staatlicher Strukturen bei.

4. Das Verhältnis zwischen Epheten und Areopag (drei mögliche Szenarien)

Notorisch umstritten und mangels Quellen nicht mit Sicherheit eruierbar ist das Verhältnis der Epheten zum Areopag. Über Plausibilitäten wird man auch in nächster Zeit nicht hinauskommen, doch erscheinen folgende Hypothesen, z. T. den Überlegungen Robert Wallaces folgend, mindestens bedenkenswert. Zwei mögliche Szenarien sollen hier vorgestellt werden, gefolgt von einer eigenen Hypothese, die auf den Ergebnissen jüngster archäologischer Befunde auf der sogenannten „Alten Agora“ fußt.

Szenario 1: Wenn die Epheten ein höheres Lebensalter als die *basileis* hatten und damit gewesene Amtsträger waren, könnten sie Vorläufer der späteren Areopagiten gewesen sein. Die Epheten bildeten[42] oder waren Mitglieder eines alten Rats der Eliten, der sich gewöhnlicherweise im Prytaneion auf der Agora traf, dem ursprünglichen Amtssitz des *archon basileus*, den später der *archon eponymos* einnahm[43]. Seit 683/2 v. Chr. ist die Archontenliste belegt. Die Archonten werden wohl von den Ratsmitgliedern aus ihrer gesellschaftlichen Schicht gewählt[44] oder anderweitig bestimmt worden sein. Nach Ablauf ihres Amtes gehörten sie dem Rat an[45]; ob dies auch für die *phylobasileis* galt, ist unklar[46], zumindest hören wir

41 Gagarin 2000, 573 erkennt richtig, dass die *basileis* und die Epheten zwei Gremien sind, dass diese Konstruktion zum ersten Mal im griechischen Bereich vorkommt und dass die beiden Gremien kooperieren sollen.

42 Wallace 1989, etwa 12, 16, 22 identifiziert die Epheten als Areopagiten.

43 Wallace 1989, 25. Zu den Amtslokalen der führenden Magistrate vgl. Kahrstedt 1936, 297f.

44 So zumindest *Ath. pol.* 8,2 (wahrscheinlich unhistorisch); vgl. Aristot., *Pol.* 1273b35ff. Nach Aristoteles wurden öffentliche Wahlen ab Solon etabliert (*Pol.* 1274a15–16). Nach Ledl 1914 und Wallace 1989, 46 ist die *Ath. pol.* für die drakontische Zeit keine zuverlässige Quelle, erst ab Solon werden die Informationen glaubwürdiger.

45 *Ath. pol.* 3,6. Allerdings könnte dies eine Erfindung auf Basis von 8,4 und 23,1 sein, vgl. dazu Wallace 1989, 41f., 44f. und Braun 1998, 37. Smith 1927, 62f. nimmt genau diese Reihenfolge an, Wahl der Archonten durch den Rat aus der Schicht der Eliten, nach Ablauf ihrer Amtszeit gehörten sie dem Rat an.

davon nichts[47]. Nur wenn ein Urteil über Tötungsdelikte anstand, traf sich der Rat oder einige seiner Mitglieder (wie diese 51 Männer bestimmt wurden, entzieht sich unserer Kenntnis[48]) aus mythischen Gründen am Nordostabhang des Areshügels, an den heiligen Stätten der *semnai theai* (Erinyen)[49]. Während Wallace davon ausgeht, dass die Epheten dort mindestens ab Drakon über Mord urteilten[50], ist es heute *communis opinio* der Forschung, dass die vorsätzliche Tötung keiner Regelung bedurfte, da in diesem Fall nach wie vor die Blutrache galt. Wallace nimmt an, Drakon habe auch die Einrichtung der weiteren Gerichtshöfe, die sich mit verschiedenen Arten der unvorsätzlichen Tötung beschäftigen, vorgenommen (wofür es in dem uns erhaltenen Text keinen Beleg gibt)[51]. Nach Wallace trafen sich

---

46 Wallace 1989, 33 geht davon aus, dass *basileus* und *phylobasileis* dem ursprünglichen elitären Rat angehörten.

47 Generell scheint erst Solon die neun Magistrate zu einem Kollegium zusammengeschlossen haben (*Ath. pol.* 3,5; Diog. Laert. 1,58). Thukydides setzt bei seinem Bericht über den Kylonischen Frevel (1,126,8) voraus, dass die sechs Thesmotheten bereits zu den neun Archonten gehörten. *Ath. pol.* 3,4 datiert die Einführung der Thesmotheten in die Zeit, als die Archonten schon Jahresbeamte waren, d.h. nach 683/2 v. Chr.

48 Vgl. oben FN 31. Nach Pollux 8,125 waren die Epheten an fünf Gerichtshöfen tätig. Vgl. dazu Wallace 1989, 35, 232, Anm. 42.

49 Wallace 1989, 9, 215–218, so schon Wecklein 1873, 19. Wann der Kult an diesem Schrein eingerichtet wurde und damit die Totschlagsprozesse begannen, ist unklar, vgl. dazu Wallace 1989, 236, Anm. 93 zu den Quellen, v.a. Plut., *Sol.* 12; *Thes.* 27; Thuk. 1,126; Paus. 7,25,2. Wallace nimmt an (ebd. 31), dass Totschlagsprozesse um 700 v. Chr. begannen, wenn Täter sich zum Schrein der *semnai* flüchteten, auf alle Fälle jedoch vor 682 v. Chr., als der eponyme Archon den *basileus* verdrängte. Hätten die Prozesse nach 682 begonnen, wäre der *archon eponymos* der Vorsitzende bei Totschlagsprozessen gewesen (ebd. 30f.; Wallace folgend Braun 1998, 29). Ulf – Kistler 2020, 120f. beschreiben Heiligtümer als Orte der Kommunikation und gehen von multidimensionalen Begegnungen in sakralen Räumen aus. Bezeichnenderweise werden die *semnai* von alters her mit Eiden in Verbindung gebracht, was die Thesen Thürs zur Bedeutung der Eide bei Totschlagsprozessen stützt.

50 Z.B. Wallace 1989, 8. Er ist der Meinung, dass *nach* Drakon die Epheten über alle Arten der Tötung urteilten (z. B. ebd. 13–20), auch über die vorsätzliche, die auf dem Areopag verhandelt wurde. Wilamowitz, Arist. II 199 ist der Meinung, dass *ursprünglich* der Areopag über alle Arten von Tötungen urteilte (so auch Wallace 1989, 20, der Epheten und Areopag gleichsetzt). Nach Wilamowitz habe Drakon durch die Einführung der Epheten den Areopag entlastet bzw. in seiner Macht beschränkt. Vgl. dagegen Harrison, Law II 41 und Wallace 1989, 19.

51 Wallace 1989, 8f. mit den zugehörigen Gottheiten; vgl. aber ebd. 231, Anm. 27, etwas abgeschwächt, Drakon habe zwar verschiedene unvorsätzliche Tötungsarten unterschieden (basierend auf Demosth. 20,158), aber noch nicht unbedingt die weiteren Gerichtshöfe geschaffen. Wieder anders ebd. 19: Drakon habe die Gerichtshöfe nicht *ex nihilo* geschaffen, sie hätten schon als Schreine bestanden, zu denen die der Tötung Beschuldigten geflohen seien. Diese Hypothese wurde in jüngster Zeit von Schmitz (2001, 2018) wieder aufgegriffen. Aus den archaischen Schwurstätten, an denen die Beschuldigten die prozessinitiierenden Eide schworen, hätten sich die Gerichtshöfe der

also die Epheten ab Drakon am Palladion, Delphinion, im Phreatto und Prytaneion zum Aburteilen unvorsätzlicher Tötungsfälle und auf dem Areshügel zur Behandlung vorsätzlicher Tötung[52]. Da die Epheten also noch nicht permanent mit dem Hügel verbunden waren, ihr normaler Treffpunkt blieb ja weiterhin das Prytaneion auf der Agora[53], braucht Drakon den Areopag auch nicht zu erwähnen. Diese Hypothese würde erklären, warum nach Plutarch viele ältere Quellen Solon die Gründung des Areopags zuschreiben[54]. Solon mag die Epheten mit mehr Aufgaben betraut haben (Plut., *Sol.* 19,2: Aufseher über alles und Hüter der Gesetze [*nomophylakia*]; vgl. *Ath. pol.* 3,6 zur Zeit vor Solon und ähnlich 8,4 in Bezug auf Solon; die erste Stelle ist in ihrer Historizität höchst problematisch) oder aber (auch) festgelegt haben, dass der Areopag sich nun aus allen gewesenen Archonten zusammensetzte[55]. Damit hätte Solon also einen fester umrissenen Rat der Eliten auf dem

klassischen Zeit entwickelt. Dreher (2019a) lehnt diese Hypothese ab, da für die klassischen Gerichtshöfe keine aitiologischen Mythen bekannt seien, doch Braun 1998, 19, Anm. 39 listet die wichtigsten Quellen zu den aitiologischen Mythen der Gerichtshöfe, Köhler 1872 jene zum Areopag. Drehers Einwand mündet in einer Aporie: Die Herkunft der klassischen Gerichtsstätten bleibt damit ungeklärt. Ulf – Kistler 2020, 78 weisen darauf hin, dass in griechischen Städten die Streitschlichtung eigentlich auf der Agora stattfand, so auch in der homerischen Schildszene. In Drakons Gesetz ist denn auch von Schwurgerichtstätten nicht die Rede. Das Auferlegen der Eide und ihr Beschwören könnten also auch auf der Agora stattgefunden haben, ähnlich wie die Mordproklamation. In allen anderen griechischen Quellen wird auf der Agora gerichtet. Wenn die Epheten sich also aus mythischen Gründen an einer heiligen Stätte versammelten, und dies scheint doch gesichert zu sein, scheinen sie in der griechischen Welt eher eine Ausnahme gebildet zu haben.

52 Wallace 1989, 19f., der stark Philippi 1874 folgt. Ähnlich Wecklein 1873, 20f.

53 Für Wecklein 1873, 31 hatte der Staatsrat seinen Sitz im Prytaneion. Dort wurden auch Fälle des Versuches der Etablierung einer Tyrannis verhandelt (Wallace 1989, 24–28, dezidiert 28, ebenso schon Lange 1874, 247–263 und neuerdings Braun 1998, 28), allerdings von den Magistraten, genauer den Archonten der Stadt, die nicht mit den Epheten identisch zu sein brauchen. Noch in klassischer Zeit wurden Prozesse gegen unbekannte Täter, Tiere und Gegenstände, die einen Tod verursachten, im Prytaneion verhandelt (*Ath. pol.* 57,4; Demosth. 23,76; Pollux 8,120; Paus. 1,28,11; vgl. Demosth. 43, 57). Der sakrale Charakter dieses Ortes blieb also als eine Art Atavismus erhalten. Es ist bemerkenswert, dass in klassischer Zeit der *archon basileus* und die vier *phylobasileis* dort immer noch zu Gericht sitzen (Wallace 1989, 25). Damit ist die Identität der *basileis* im drakontischen Gesetz geklärt (s. die Diskussion oben FN 25–28). Wallace ist korrekt (ebd. 26), wenn er feststellt, dass die Präsenz von *basileus* und *phylobasileis* in allen Totschlagsprozessen nötig war. Ebd. 27: „This passage shows that in Drakon's lawcode, the *phylobasileis* did sit with the *basileus* in the Palladion court. And if we grant them this court, they surely sat in the other homicide courts as well."

54 Plut., *Sol* 19; Aristot., *Pol.* 1273b35–1274a5. Vgl. dazu Wallace 1989, 35–37.

55 Für letztere Variante argumentiert Wallace 1989, 18. Solon habe dieses nun leicht anders zusammengesetzte Gremium mit der vorsätzlichen Tötung betraut.

Areopag konstituiert, der vorher dort nur als Gericht diente[56]. Die Epheten wären demnach direkte Vorläufer der späteren Areopagiten gewesen.

Szenario 2: Insbesondere wenn es den Areopag als Elitenrat zu Drakons Zeit schon gegeben haben sollte, muss er nicht unbedingt etwas mit der Bestellung der Epheten zu tun gehabt haben. Der *archon basileus* und die vier *phylobasileis* kommen unter dem summarischen Terminus *basileis* im Gesetz vor. Wie wir gesehen haben, sind die 51 Epheten wahrscheinlich ehemalige *basileis*, genossen also den gleichen Rang und waren nur älter als ihre Standesgenossen, die die Eide formulierten. Soweit wir wissen, gelangten (schon vor Drakons Zeit) aber nur gewesene Archonten in den Areopag[57], also nur der *archon basileus*[58], nicht etwa die *phylobasileis*. Wenn sich also die Epheten aus den gewesenen *basileis* speisten, konnten nicht alle von ihnen in das edle Gremium gelangen, sondern nur ein Fünftel, d.h. die ehemaligen *archontes basileis*. Andererseits gelangten der *archon eponymos*, der *archon polemarchos* und vielleicht auch schon die Thesmotheten nach ihrer Amtsführung in den Areopag, ohne vorher als *basileis* gedient zu haben. Dies würde bedeuten, dass Epheten und Areopagiten nur teilidentisch waren. Wenn es ferner stimmt, dass ab Drakon die waffenfähigen Männer die neun Archonten (und vielleicht auch die *phylobasileis*?) wählten[59] und damit auch die Zusammensetzung der Epheten z.T. bestimmten, dann hatte der Areopag selbst mit der Auswahl der Epheten unter Umständen nichts oder nur wenig zu tun. Er war ein etwas anders zusammengesetztes, noch exklusiveres Gremium. Drakon hätte dann die Rechtsprechung bei Totschlagsfällen durch die Einbeziehung der Phylenoberhäupter auf eine breitere Basis gestellt, die über den Kreis derjenigen Regimentsfähigen, aus denen die Archonten zu wählen waren, hinausreichte. Auf Basis sozialanthropologischer Überlegungen werden wir sehen, dass auch dieses Szenario einiges für sich hat. Die logische Konsequenz muss also lauten, dass es entweder in drakontischer Zeit noch keinen Areopag bzw. noch keinen Rat gab, was unwahrscheinlich ist, oder aber er ein exklusiver „Adelsrat" war, der mit Totschlagsfällen nur bedingt zu tun hatte. Er wurde mit der Verhandlung vorsätzlicher Tötung erst betraut, als diese, wohl ab Solon, in das Gerichtswesen mit einbezogen wurde[60]. Wie sich die Epheten nach Gründung des Areopags oder nach der Betrauung des

---

[56] Wecklein 1873, 20f. und ihm folgend Wallace betonen immer wieder, dass die Epheten nur als Gericht auf dem Areopag tagten, nicht etwa als „Staatsrat". Zum gänzlich unwahrscheinlichen Szenario eines Rates, dessen Funktion ausschließlich auf die Blutgerichtsbarkeit beschränkt war, vgl. unten FN 74, 76.

[57] Sofern man der *Ath. pol.* 3,6 hier in der Chronologie folgen möchte. Nach Wallace 1989, 15 (basierend auf Plut., *Sol.* 19,1) ist das spätestens ab Solon der Fall.

[58] Der *basileus* bleibt in klassischer Zeit der Vorsitzende bei allen Totschlagsprozessen (z. B. *Ath. pol.* 57,3–5).

[59] *Ath. pol.* 4,2 im Widerspruch zu *Ath. pol.* 8,2 (wahrscheinlich unhistorisch, weil späterer Zusatz), wo der Areopag die jährlichen Magistrate auswählt. Vgl. dazu Wallace 1989, 43f. Öffentliche Wahlen ab Solon: Aristot., *Pol.* 1274.

[60] So wiederholt Schmitz, z.B. 2018, 44; Dorn – Schmitz – Shahin 2023, 174.

Areopags mit der vorsätzlichen Tötung zum Areopag verhielten, lässt sich nicht sagen. Entweder wurden sie Teil des Areopags oder blieben eine gesonderte Körperschaft, über die wir nicht viel wissen, außer, dass sie für alle Arten der unvorsätzlichen Tötung zuständig blieb.

Szenario 3 ist ebenfalls nicht beweisbar, halte ich jedoch für am wahrscheinlichsten: Das Zentrum des archaischen Athen inklusive des Prytaneion befand sich nordöstlich der Akropolis, auf der sogenannten Alten Agora, was Harris-Cline aufgrund neuerer Grabungen plausibel macht[61]. Der Abstieg der Kylonier vom alten Athena-Tempel war somit kürzer und ist daher wahrscheinlicher als ihr Abgang nach Westen über den Abhang, an dem später die Propylaen errichtet werden sollten. Die Überlegungen von Harris-Cline können hier nicht *in toto* referiert werden, aber wenn ein alter Rat der Eliten im Prytaneion auf dieser archaischen Agora tagte, spielte der Areshügel in dieser frühen Zeit noch überhaupt keine Rolle, konnte also im drakontischen Gesetz gar nicht erwähnt werden[62]. Die sog. „Eupatriden" bestimmten in welcher Art auch immer die Archonten (keine Volkswahl[63]) oder der Rat der Eliten erwählte aus seiner Mitte die Archonten[64]. Im ersteren Fall bildeten die gewesenen Archonten einen exklusiven Rat der Älteren (*boule geronton*)[65]. Gegen Lange halte ich dieses Szenario, bei dem die aktiven

---

[61] Harris–Cline 1999 *passim*. Doronzio 2018, 210 lehnt die Existenz einer Alten Agora an einer anderen Stelle als der klassischen Agora ab. Es sei also nicht zu einer Verlegung des Bürgerzentrums gekommen. Sie geht für das Ende des 8. und das beginnende 7. Jh. aufgrund des Auflassens von Gräbern und Werkstätten, der Verschüttung von Brunnen sowie zunehmender Kultaktivitäten auf dem Gelände der späteren Agora davon aus, dass hier in einer kollektiven Entscheidung bewusst eine Freifläche für die Konstituierung eines öffentlichen Versammlungsplatzes geschaffen wurde, auf dem junge Krieger kultische Festmähler abhielten (ebd. 201f., 206, 209–211, 285, 289, 291). Doch gerade der von Doronzio 2018, 202 präsentierte Befund, dass ab dem dritten Viertel des 7. Jhs. eine tiefgreifende Umstrukturierung stattfand, die auf der uns bekannten Agora keinen Raum mehr für handwerkliche Tätigkeiten ließ und zu vermehrten Kultaktivitäten führte, schließt zumindest die Annahme nicht aus, dass es durch die Aufgabe einer älteren Agora zu einem verstärkten und beschleunigten Ausbau der späteren klassischen Agora gekommen sein kann.

[62] Ruschenbusch 1960, 135 betont, dass der Areopag zur Zeit Drakons kein Blutgericht war.

[63] Eine Volkswahl nimmt Kahrstedt 1937, 15 an, wäre jedoch in dieser frühen Zeit, die ganz von den sozialen Eliten bestimmt war, ein Anachronismus.

[64] So Lange 1874, 208f. Möglich ist auch, dass vor Solon der Rat der Eliten zwar nicht aus seinen Reihen, aber aus den Eupatriden die Archonten auswählte, so Wade-Gery 1931, 10f. auf Basis der allerdings unzuverlässigen Stelle *Ath. pol.* 8,2 und Smith 1927, 62f. Meister 2020, 275–294 kritisiert Wade-Gery und dekonstruiert die Existenz einer festgefügten „adeligen Kaste" der Eupatriden. Das Reüssieren in verschiedenen Konkurrenzfeldern verlieh Prestige und eine herausgehobene soziale Stellung, die immer prekär war.

[65] Wade-Gery 1931, 10f. sieht zwar richtig, dass die Archonten erst nach ihrer Amtszeit dem Rat angehörten und dass bis Solon alle Archonten und Ratsmitglieder zu den höchsten gesellschaftlichen Schichten zählten. Aber dass Theseus den Areopag als permanenten Königsrat begründet habe, gehört ins Reich der Mythologie (so ebd. 8).

Archonten noch nicht dem Rat angehörten, für plausibler. Ein Rat bestehend aus 51 Epheten und neun amtierenden Archonten, wie Lange ihn annimmt, hätte sich mit einer Gesamtmitgliederzahl von 60 u.U. beim Fällen von Urteilen in Pattsituationen befunden. Und wie hätte die Mitgliederzahl von 60 stabil gehalten werden können? Die oben angestellten Überlegungen einer frühen „Gewaltenteilung" legen es auch nahe, dass auf beiden Ebenen der Aufgabenteilung (Urteilssuche und Rechtsprechung innerhalb der Jurisdiktion sowie Jurisdiktion vs. „Regierung"), aktive „Politiker" von Ratsmitgliedern (vormalige Magistrate) geschieden wurden. M.E. wurden also aus den Reihen des Rats, dem die aktiven Archonten (noch) nicht angehörten und dessen Mitgliederzahl wir nicht kennen, die jedoch höher als 51 gewesen sein muss[66], auf welche Weise auch immer Epheten bestimmt, die bereits vor Drakon[67] entweder auf der Agora oder an Schwurgerichtsstätten (oder unterschiedlich je nach Falltypen) über Mord- und Totschlagsfälle urteilten, ohne zwischen Vorsatz und Nicht-Vorsatz zu differenzieren[68]. Drakon explizierte nun aufgrund der vorangegangenen und gegenwärtigen Unruhen, dass die Epheten auch (*kai ean*) für die unvorsätzliche Tötung zuständig sind[69]. Nörr und Schmitz folgend

---

[66] Die Gleichsetzung von Areopagiten und Epheten, die vor Solon bestanden habe, die Braun 1998, 20f., Philippi 1874, 213–215, 233, Kahrstedt 1937, 15 und Wallace folgend, vornimmt, ist unterkomplex. Wie hätte der Rat seine Zahl stabil auf 51 halten können? M.E. können Epheten und Rat nicht völlig identisch sein, d.h. die Epheten müssen vielmehr Teil eines größeren Rats gewesen sein.

[67] Nach Carawan 1998, 133 führte Drakon die Epheten ein. Hierfür gibt es keinen Beleg. Richtig wohl Philippi 1874, 203, 214 und Lange 1874, 194, nach denen die Epheten schon vor Drakon existierten, er sie also nicht einsetzte. Dies sei ein Missverständnis von Pollux. Auch für Lipsius 1905–15, 121 existierten die Epheten bereits vor Drakon.

[68] Aufgrund des Wortlauts des Gesetzes geht Thür 2015, 160, 167, 169f. davon aus, dass auch Drakon nicht über die Willensrichtung urteilen ließ, also über den Vorsatz oder den Nicht-Vorsatz, sondern nur darüber, ob unmittelbar (mit eigener Hand) oder mittelbar (im Auftrag) getötet wurde. Nur bei der *aidesis* habe die Frage nach dem Vorsatz eine Rolle gespielt. In Zeile 11 jedoch ist der Nicht-Vorsatz eindeutig erwähnt: καὶ ἐὰμ μὲ 'κ {^{26}ἐκ}^{26} [π]ρονοί[α]ς [...].

[69] Vgl. Nörr 1983 *passim*. Demnach war also der Areopag tatsächlich zur Zeit Drakons noch nicht mit Mord betraut. Daher nimmt Drakon dem Areopag auch die Blutgerichtsbarkeit nicht zugunsten der Epheten weg, wie Wecklein 1873, 9f. fälschlicherweise meint. Richtig erklärt Wecklein (ebd. 17f.) jedoch die Bedeutung des „protos axon" als die solonische Zählweise. Möglicherweise gingen den Regelungen zur unvorsätzlichen Tötung, die uns erhalten ist, im drakontischen Text Regelungen zur vorsätzlichen Tötung voraus (so Ruschenbusch 1960, 129–131, 143f.), die jedoch nicht mehr abgeschrieben wurden, weil sie durch die solonischen Regelungen obsolet geworden waren. Nach Westbrook 2008 ging der erhaltenen Regelung eine Satzung zum „unintentional wounding" voraus. Drakon habe überhaupt einen ganzen „law code" erlassen. Dies erscheint unwahrscheinlich, da sich hiervon keine Kunde in der literarischen Überlieferung erhalten hat. Carey 2013 betont jedoch, dass sowohl in materieller als auch in prozeduraler Hinsicht Drakons Gesetzgebungstätigkeit stärker weiter wirkte als dies die Athener der klassischen Zeit bemerkten oder zuzugeben bereit

bin ich der Meinung, dass die Epheten, wie auch vor Drakon, implizit auch über die vorsätzliche Tötung urteilten[70]. Wurde die Behauptung des Täters, er habe unvorsätzlich getötet, von den Epheten zurückgewiesen, also von den Epheten die Vorsätzlichkeit festgestellt, wurde der Mörder den Verwandten zur Vollstreckung der Blutrache übergeben[71]. Ob die Schwurgerichtsstätten schon vor-drakontisch sind oder von Drakon geschaffen oder erst nach ihm eingeführt wurden, lässt sich nicht mehr feststellen. Drakon erwähnt sie in seinem Gesetz nicht, doch spricht eine Kombination der Hypothesen von Thür und Schmitz dafür, dass die Eide in der Tat an bestimmten Kultstätten vorgenommen wurden, die, weil allgemein bekannt, im Gesetz nicht erwähnt zu werden brauchten[72].

Durch den Kylonischen Frevel war die Alte Agora gerade um den Bereich der Schreine für die *semnai theai* und das Prytaneion herum so verschmutzt, dass man die gesamte Agora nach Westen umzog, inklusive der Altäre der Rachegöttinnen, die eine neue Heimstatt in den Höhlen bzw. Spalten am Nordabhang des Areshügels fanden. Dieser Umzug, in dessen Zusammenhang die Stadt wohl vom Kreter Epimenides gereinigt wurde, fand zwischen der Zeit Drakons und Solons statt[73], in der die Epheten bei ihren Urteilen und wohl auch der Rat als Ganzes bei politischen Beratungen gelegentlich schon auf dem Hügel zusammenkamen[74]. Solon mag nun

---

waren. Solon habe womöglich den drakontischen Text nur ediert und ergänzt, nicht aber annulliert.

70 Ähnlich Braun 1998, 25–27.

71 Dieses Modell setzt voraus, dass nach Loomis 1972 nur zwischen vorsätzlich (*ek pronoias* und *hekon* identisch) und nicht vorsätzlich (*me ek pronoias* und *akon* identisch) unterschieden wurde. Dem widersprechen jedoch z. B. Wallace, Cantarella und Pepe aus unterschiedlichen Perspektiven: Für Wallace 1989, 98–100 gehen die Fälle *ek pronoias* (premeditated) an den Areopag, die *hekousios*–Fälle an andere Gerichtshöfe. Cantarella 1976, 105–11; 126f. unterscheidet drei Arten der schuldhaften Tötung: Nur die Tötung *ek pronoias* (in etwa dt. Vorsatz) sei *volontario*. Die beiden Kategorien *me ek pronoias* (in etwa dt. unvorsätzlich) und *akousios* (auf dt. in etwa unrechtmäßig) seien von einem absteigenden Vorsatz charakterisiert und beide *involontario*. Porrello 2008, 156f. schließt sich dieser Ansicht an. Pepe 2008 *passim*, 2009/10 *passim* und 2012, 87–128 sieht den Hauptunterschied zwischen *ek pronoias* (premediation) und *akousios*, der Tötung ohne Absicht, die einen sehr weiten Bedeutungsumfang gehabt habe, inklusive Tötung im Affekt oder durch kausale Mechanismen, die zu einem Tod führten.

72 Schon Wecklein 1873, 18 nimmt an, dass unterschiedliche Gerichtshöfe lange vor Drakon existierten, sie für ihn also selbstverständlich waren. Sealey 1983 geht intensiv auf die fünf klassischen Gerichtshöfe ein und legt eindringlich dar, wie schwierig die Datierung ihrer Entstehungsgeschichte ist.

73 Dorn – Schmitz – Shahin 2023, 69, 78 datieren diese Reinigung, belegt bei Plut., *Sol.* 12,6–9, im Zusammenhang mit Solons Wirken (596–593 v. Chr.).

74 Anders als Wecklein und Wallace gehe ich nicht davon aus, dass der alte Rat der Eliten nur jurisdiktionelle Kompetenzen hatte, sehr wohl aber trifft es zu, dass Solon den neu konstituierten Areopag mit wohl zusätzlichen und dezidiert politischen Funktionen betraute (ähnlich Wecklein 1873, 22). Sanctis 1896, 40f. sieht dagegen das Wirken Solons als sehr beschränkt an: Ein alter Königsrat habe sich zu einem Tribunal für

die physische Präsenz des alten Elitenrats auf dem Areopag bestätigt und ihm in Abgrenzung vom neu gegründeten Rat der Vierhundert feste Kompetenzen als Aufseher über die Gesetze, Sitten und Gebräuche sowie die Magistrate (*nomophylakia*[75]) zugewiesen haben, womit er ihn in gewisser Weise „gründete"[76]. Deutlich greifen wir also einen Prozess der Institutionalisierung und damit eines Anwachsens von Staatlichkeit[77]. Und da Solon den Gerichtszwang für vorsätzliche Tötung einführte und somit den Mord durch die Einführung der staatlichen Hinrichtung in seine Regelungen miteinbezog[78], wies er die Aburteilung der vorsätzlichen Tötung (*ek pronoias*) explizit dem auf dem Areshügel neu konstituierten Rat in seiner Gänze zu[79], während die Epheten, da man auf sie und ihren durch Drakon genau definierten Aufgabenbereich aus Ehrerbietung gegenüber dem alten Gesetzgeber nicht verzichten wollte, nun auf die Aburteilung unvorsätzlicher Tötungsfälle begrenzt wurden[80]. Diese Verfahren nahmen die Epheten, wie von alters her üblich, bis in klassische Zeit an den gewohnten Schwurgerichtstätten vor[81], die sich allmählich zu Gerichtshöfen entwickelten bzw. unter Solon als solche konsolidiert wurden[82].

Totschlagsfälle entwickelt, also nach und nach Kompetenzen verloren. Solon habe also nur eine Entwicklung sanktioniert.

75 *Ath. pol.* 8,4 scheint bzgl. dieser Information glaubwürdig zu sein, so Wallace 1989, 44f. und Braun 1998, 40. Vgl. auch *Ath. pol.* 25,2.

76 In anderer Nuancierung Wallace 1989, 8–10, 55–64 und ihm folgend Braun 1998, 38f., nach denen die Epheten sich vor Solon zur Aburteilung vorsätzlicher Tötungsfälle auf dem Areopag getroffen hätten. Diesem „Rat" wären jedoch keine weiteren Funktionen außerhalb der Blutgerichtsbarkeit zugekommen (so auch Wallace 1989, 6f.; Braun 1998, 30, 37), was in Anbetracht des Fehlens eines anderen Rates als historisch unwahrscheinlich gelten kann (s. oben FN 56, 74). Auch für Dorn – Schmitz – Shahin 2023, 149 ist Solon der eigentliche Begründer des Areopags.

77 Rönnberg 2021, z.B. 61, 63f., 259 sieht erste Anzeichen eines Institutionalisierungsprozesses am Ende des 7. Jhs., eine deutliche Zunahme an Staatlichkeit dann allerdings erst in der ersten Hälfte des 6. Jhs.

78 Nach Thür 1990 kannte Drakon zwar noch nicht die Todesstrafe, aber sehr wohl die Tötung des Bannbrüchigen, die somit eine Etappe hin zur staatlichen Todesstrafe darstellte.

79 So schon Kahrstedt 1937, 17; Wecklein 1873, 21.

80 Dorn – Schmitz – Shahin 2023, 149. Nach Carawan 1991 bildeten die Epheten auch im 4. Jh. keinen heliastischen Gerichtshof, sondern einen Unter-Ausschuss des Areopags. Sie richteten nach wie vor am Delphinion und Palladion. Dieses recht konservative System muss im 4. Jh. seltsam angemutet haben, aber dadurch, dass alle Areopagiten Archonten gewesen waren, verfügten die Epheten über große Erfahrung, gerade auch in prozeduralen Dingen. Gagliardi 2012 weicht in vielerlei Hinsicht von dieser *communis opinio* ab.

81 Interessanterweise sieht Rönnberg 2021, 260 Heiligtümer bereits im 8. und 7. Jh. v. Chr. als „identitätsstiftende Interaktionsorte", an denen „innerelitäre Konkurrenz" um die „Verstetigung gesellschaftlicher Vorrangstellungen" zugenommen habe. Diese Hypothese bestätigt die Funktion von Schwurgerichtsstätten im Zusammenhang mit den drakontischen Regelungen: Diese heiligen Orte wurden durch die Beurteilung von

Trotz der vielen Unwägbarkeiten lässt sich so viel sagen: Drakon geht es sowohl bei der Aufgabenteilung zwischen *basileis* und Epheten als auch bei der Bestimmung des Verhältnisses zwischen Epheten und Areopag, wie auch immer es ausgesehen haben mag, um ein Austarieren von Kräfteverhältnissen. Das Erreichen einer Balance, d.h. eines soziopolitischen Ausgleichs unter den Führungsschichten sollte durch eine möglichst breite Partizipation der führenden Männer zumindest an der Aufarbeitung von Totschlagsfällen bewerkstelligt werden. Damit verband Drakon wohl die Hoffnung, dass die Ambitionen der Elitenangehörigen auf diesem Weg wenigstens teilweise saturiert würden.

5. Die Rolle der *aidesis*

a) Neuerung durch Beteiligung eines „staatlichen" Organs (Z. 16–19)

Drakons Bemühen um Ausgleich und Kompromiss sieht man deutlich auch bei seinen Regelungen zur *aidesis*, zur Aussöhnung zwischen dem Täter und der Familie des Opfers. Sie folgt unmittelbar nach der Regelung der unvorsätzlichen Tötung, also noch *vor* den Regelungen zur Strafverfolgung. Diese Gewichtung wurde in der Forschung bislang, soweit ich sehe, nur von Michael Gagarin, Sally Humphreys und neuerdings David Mirhady explizit betont[83]. Zudem ist der meiste Raum in dem uns erhaltenen Gesetz (Z. 13–20) der Aussöhnung gewidmet. Im Mittelpunkt der hier vorliegenden Betrachtungen steht nicht die vieldiskutierte Frage, in welchen Fällen es überhaupt zu einer Aussöhnung kommen konnte (ich folge der bestechenden Argumentation von Heitsch, dass sie nur bei unvorsätzlicher Tötung möglich war[84]), sondern Drakons Bemühen, sowohl die Interessen der Familie des Opfers als auch die des unvorsätzlichen Täters zu wahren. Ziel war

---

Totschlagsfällen zu Kristallisationspunkten der Aushandlung von Machtbeziehungen in der Hoffnung, innerelitäre Konkurrenzsituationen zu entschärfen.

82 Zu Solon als Schöpfer der Gerichtshöfe vgl. Dorn – Schmitz – Shahin 2023, 102, 121f. mit Verweis auf die Quellen, welche die Systematisierung der Schwurgerichtsstätten als Gerichtshöfe durch Solon belegen (Demosth. 23,62–81; Aristot., *Pol.* 4,16 (1300b13–30); *Ath. pol.* 57,3–4; Paus. 1,28,5–11; Pollux 8,117–120).

83 Gagarin 1981, 53f.; 1986, 88; Humphreys 1991, 23f.; Mirhady 2008, 24.

84 Heitsch 1984, 17f., 22. Folgende Varianten sind möglich: Lipsius (1905–15, 604) geht davon aus, dass die Aussöhnung mit den Verwandten bei vorsätzlicher Tötung nicht möglich war, es sei denn der Getötete konnte noch vor seinem Tod dem Täter Vergebung gewähren. Nach Schmitz 2001, 27 und Dorn – Schmitz – Shahin 2023, 139 sei das Exil bei vorsätzlicher Tötung lebenslang, ohne die Möglichkeit der Aussöhnung gewesen. Anders Ruschenbusch (1960, 138) und neuerdings Pepe (2012, 28, 71–78) sowie Thür (2015, 160), nach denen die Versöhnung auch bei der vorsätzlichen Tötung möglich war (rein von der Textgestaltung her ist dies möglich), wobei Ruschenbusch eine zeitliche Differenzierung vornimmt: In drakontischer Zeit konnte die Aussöhnung auch bei Vorsatz erfolgen, im 4. Jh. nicht mehr. Die Regelung des 4. Jhs. würde also eine Einschränkung der Aussöhnungsmöglichkeit darstellen. Dies wiederum würde bedeuten, dass Drakon die Aussöhnung wichtiger war als den Gesetzgebern im 4. Jh., was meine unten vorgestellte These von Drakon als einem Versöhner bekräftigen würde.

wieder das Streben nach Kompromissen mit dem Ziel der Befriedung der Gesellschaft. Spätestens mit dem gescheiterten Putsch Kylons 632 v. Chr. war die Konkurrenz unter den Eliten außer Kontrolle geraten und in bürgerkriegsähnliche Auseinandersetzungen eskaliert[85]. Diese blutigen Kämpfe müssen sich bis in die Zeit Drakons fortgesetzt haben. Ein Achten auf gesamtgesellschaftliche Interessen war nicht mehr gegeben, vielmehr drohte diese Gesellschaft auseinanderzubrechen und im Chaos zu versinken. Drakons Maßnahme, auch die unvorsätzliche Tötung einem rechtlichen Verfahren zu unterwerfen, war ein erster, wichtiger Schritt zur Pazifizierung, weitere sollten unter Solon folgen. Die von den Intellektuellen der Zeit formulierte Norm, auf alle zu achten, ist, wie ich meine, im drakontischen Gesetz mustergültig umgesetzt. Ein Schlüssel zum Verständnis dieser Intention liegt in der näheren Betrachtung der zur Strafverfolgung und zur *aidesis* Berechtigten. Die beiden Gruppen von Verwandten des Opfers werden leicht anders definiert, die Unterschiede sind jedoch signifikant: Bei Verfolgung eines Tötungsfalles kündigen die Verwandten des Opfers bis einschließlich Vettern und Vetternsöhne Rache auf der Agora an. Wichtig ist, dass bei der Aufzählung der Mitglieder dieser strafverfolgenden Gruppe die Schwiegersöhne und Schwiegerväter und sogar Phratriemitglieder inkludiert sind. Der Kreis wird zwar weit gezogen, die Tötung soll auf alle Fälle gesühnt werden, bleibt aber streng begrenzt auf die (weitere) Familie. Die Epheten spielen in diesem Kontext keine Rolle; es gibt definitiv, übrigens auch in klassischer Zeit, keine staatliche Strafverfolgung. Die Epheten werden auch dann nicht aktiv, wenn keine männlichen Familienmitglieder mehr am Leben sein sollten. Dieser Fall galt als unwahrscheinlich bzw. für den Fall, dass eine Familie aufgrund von Blutracheakten ausgelöscht worden war, wurden die Schwiegersöhne und Schwiegerväter mobilisiert, also alle männlichen Kräfte in der weiteren Familie inklusive der Phratrie[86].

Die zur *aidesis* Berechtigten werden nun leicht anders definiert. Wieder sind in erster Linie die männlichen Angehörigen bis zu den Vettern und den Vetternsöhnen angesprochen, doch die Schwiegerväter und Schwiegersöhne sind nun *nicht* inkludiert. Drakon hält also den Kreis der zur *aidesis* Berechtigten kleiner, damit sie mit höherer Wahrscheinlichkeit zustande kommt. Vergessen wir nicht, dass jeder einzelne Angehörige ein Vetorecht hatte. Je mehr Männer also nach Gewährung der *aidesis* gefragt wurden, desto höher war die Wahrscheinlichkeit, dass sie nicht gelang[87]. Im Unterschied zur Strafverfolgung kommt es nun zu einer erstaunlichen Regelung, einer wirklichen Neuerung, da ein formales, „staatliches" Organ in Gestalt der Epheten eingebunden wird (Z. 16–19). Wenn Vater, Brüder, Söhne und alle männlichen Verwandten einschließlich der Vettern und Vetternsöhne tot sind, möchte Drakon immer noch sicherstellen, dass eine Rückkehr der Exilierten möglich ist. In diesem

[85] Vgl. Ulf – Kistler 2020, 89 zur Gewalt.

[86] Zur Solidarität der Familie im drakontischen Gesetz, vgl. Glotz 1904, 299–324.

[87] Heitsch 1984, 10 betont zu Recht, dass die *aidesis* an hohe Hürden gebunden war. Die Entscheidung über das Gewähren von Gnade musste einstimmig fallen.

Fall beschäftigen sich die Epheten mit der zur Debatte stehenden Tötung. Nur wenn sie auf unvorsätzliche Tötung befunden haben bzw. vielleicht sogar zum ersten Mal darüber urteilten, bestimmten sie nach Würdigkeit, wörtlich „Bestheit" (*aristinden*), zehn Phratriemitglieder[88], die über die Gewährung der *aidesis* beraten sollten. Die Epheten verweisen die Angelegenheit also an den Kultverband, in dem der Verstorbene Mitglied war[89]. Die Phratriemitglieder werden also nicht von sich aus tätig, wie bei der Strafverfolgung, sondern erst im Auftrag der Epheten, da diese zunächst die Unvorsätzlichkeit der Tötung und somit die Vorbedingung für die Aussöhnung feststellen müssen. Und noch ein Unterschied ergibt sich zur Strafverfolgung. War dort die Zahl der Phratriemitglieder, die tätig werden konnten, unbegrenzt, weil Drakon die Strafverfolgung sicherstellen wollte, so wird jetzt der Kreis der zur *aidesis* Berechtigten auf zehn Mitglieder begrenzt, um somit leichter einen Konsens herbeiführen zu können.

b) Neuerung durch Rückwirkungsklausel (Z. 19–20)

Dadurch, dass die Regelung auch rückwirkend galt (Rückwirkungsklausel Z. 19–20), d.h. wer wegen unvorsätzlicher Tötung im Exil lebte, konnte auf Versöhnung und Rückkehr hoffen[90], kann bei allem Zugeständnis an die berechtigte und notwendige Strafverfolgung durch die Angehörigen die Möglichkeit der Aussöhnung als ein zentrales, wenn nicht *das* zentrale Anliegen Drakons gelten. Hierfür spricht auch seine hervorgehobene Platzierung zu Beginn des Gesetzes, *vor* den Regelungen zur Strafverfolgung. Die retrospektive Versöhnungsleistung zeitigt eine wichtige Folge: Der Ausgleich wirkte zeitlich eben zurück und damit auch zwischen den Generationen. Fehden, die sich oftmals über mehrere Generationen hingezogen und sicher einen hohen Blutzoll gefordert hatten, konnten so *ad acta* gelegt werden. Wieder sehen wir Drakons Bemühen um Ausgleich, einen Kompromiss zwischen den Familien der Opfer und den Tätern, wobei die Betonung eher auf den Möglichkeiten zur Aussöhnung zwischen den Familien als auf den Rachemöglichkeiten lag. Die Möglichkeit der Versöhnung war Drakon dabei so wichtig, dass er dafür in Gestalt der Epheten sogar ein „staatliches" Organ für Ausnahmefälle betraute.

6. Rückbezug zum Kylonischen Frevel und die darauf folgenden Wirren

a) Definition der unvorsätzlichen Tötung (Konjektur Thürs von Z. 12)

Wenn wir Drakons Leistung primär in seiner Versöhnungsarbeit und seinem Bemühen um Ausgleich und Pazifizierung sehen, müssen wir diese Gesetzgebungs-

---

[88] Hignett 1952, 117 schlussfolgert daraus zu Recht, dass Phratrien also nicht nur aristokratische Mitglieder hatten.

[89] Während für Dorn – Schmitz – Shahin 2023, 154f. Phratriemitglieder „Angehörige fiktiver verwandtschaftlicher bzw. dörflicher Vereinigungen" sind, betont Rönnberg 2021, 57, 59f. ihren geographischen Charakter als „lokale Siedlungsgemeinschaften" (60).

[90] Den Innovationscharakter der Rückwirkungsklausel betonen Dorn – Schmitz – Shahin 2023, 142 (mit älterer Literatur).

arbeit in unruhigen Zeiten, ja gesellschaftlichen Verwerfungen verorten, die nicht erst um 620 v. Chr. plötzlich ausbrachen. Der Kylonische Frevel, der traditionell auf 632 v. Chr. datiert wird, wird dabei überwiegend von der deutschsprachigen Forschung als Referenzpunkt gesehen, während anglophone Gelehrte diesen Zusammenhang nicht unbedingt herstellen wollen, da der zeitliche Abstand zwischen Kylons Putschversuch und der drakontischen Regelung zu groß sei[91]. Dabei muss sich Drakons Gesetzesprojekt nicht nur spezifisch auf den Vorfall beziehen, der ca. 12 Jahre zurücklag, sondern auf ihn inklusive seiner Vorläufer sowie blutigen Langzeitfolgen, die noch zur Zeit Drakons Athen erschüttert haben müssen[92]. Am prononciertesten plädiert Gerhard Thür für einen eindeutigen Bezug des Gesetzes auf den Kylonischen Frevel[93]. Im Folgenden möchte ich diese Überlegungen mit weiteren Argumenten untermauern, aber auch betonen, dass die Regelung über den engen Bezug auf den Kylonischen Frevel hinausging.

Die Konjektur Thürs in Zeile 12 spricht eigentlich für sich und soll hier nur kurz referiert werden. Während des Kylonischen Coups hatten sich die Putschisten an Altäre geklammert, um ihr Leben zu retten. Die Alkmaioniden, allen voran wohl Megakles, der im Jahre 632/1 Archon gewesen zu sein scheint[94], gaben die Order, diese Menschen zu ergreifen (oder sogar gleich zu töten). Diese werden sich beim Zugriff gewehrt haben; in den Handgemengen muss es Todesopfer gegeben haben. Die Familien der Opfer strengten sicher die Blutrache an, einmal gegen die Gefolgsleute der Alkmaioniden, die als ihre Schergen aktiv waren, also selbst die Hand vielleicht auch im Affekt ohne Tötungsabsicht erhoben hatten, als auch gegen die Alkmaioniden selbst, die den Auftrag zur Ergreifung der Putschisten erteilt und dabei den Tod der Festzunehmenden zumindest billigend in Kauf genommen hatten[95]. Es verwundert nicht, dass Megakles in Folge ins Exil ging. Solche Szenarien sind natürlich auch bei vorhergehenden und nachfolgenden Blutrachezyklen anzu-

---

91 Für Rönnberg 2021, 34 ist der Bezug zwischen dem Putsch Kylons und der drakontischen Regelung allein schon aufgrund der nicht genauen Datierbarkeit beider Ereignisse nicht herzustellen. Rönnberg geht sogar weit, den Putsch lediglich auf die vor-solonische Zeit zu datieren (ibid.).

92 Die Massengräber von „Hingerichteten“ (via *apotympanismos*?) im Phaleron, die auf das 7. Jh. datiert werden, deuten darauf hin, dass ganze Familien (Clans?) regelhaft dezimiert wurden. Ingvarsson – Bäckström 2019 behandeln die Grabung von 2016. Allerdings gab es schon 1916 einen ähnlichen Fund, den Young 1942 mit dem Zeugnis der Vasen verband. Das Areal wurde offenbar über einen längeren Zeitraum für die Bestattung „Hingerichteter“ benutzt. Weitere Funde sind daher zu erwarten. Ich danke Justine Diemke herzlich für diese Hinweise. In diesem Kontext ist auf den Beitrag von Athina Dimopoulou in diesem Band zu verweisen.

93 Z.B. Thür 2018 *passim*. Einen starken Situationsbezug stellen auch Dorn – Schmitz – Shahin 2023, 108 her. Gagarin 2008, 102 betont eher die langfristigen Folgen, die zum drakontischen Gesetz geführt hätten.

94 Vgl. dazu Develin 1989, 30f.

95 Natürlich ist nicht auszuschließen, dass die Alkmaioniden auch eigenhändig getötet haben.

nehmen, in denen Clanoberhäupter an jüngere Clanmitglieder Strafaktionen gegen verfeindete Familien in Auftrag gegeben haben werden.

b) Rückwirkungsklausel (Z. 19–20)

Auch die Rückwirkungsklausel bezieht sich auf Vergangenes, das Jahre zurückliegen kann (Z. 19–20: „Auch diejenigen, welche fr]üh[e]|[20]r eine Töt[ung begangen hab]en, [sollen unter] die[se Satzung fallen“[96]). Diese Klausel ist sowohl positiv wie negativ gemeint: Positiv ist, dass auch diejenigen, die aufgrund einer unvorsätzlichen Tötung ins Exil gegangen sind, nun eine Chance auf Aussöhnung und damit Rückkehr haben (s. oben). Negativ ist, dass sich jetzt auch rückwirkend Täter verantworten müssen, selbst wenn sie „nur“ unvorsätzlich getötet haben und deshalb zu Hause geblieben sind. Auch sie werden nun zur Rechenschaft gezogen (*kai ean*…). Kombiniert man diese Rückwirkungsklausel mit den Überlegungen von Heitsch zur *aidesis*, die nur bei unvorsätzlicher Tötung anwendbar war, so bestand eine der Neuerungen nun darin, dass Mörder (also vorsätzliche Täter) auch rückwirkend von der Rückkehr ausgeschlossen waren[97]. Bis zum drakontischen Gesetz war offenbar ungeregelt, wer verfolgen und begnadigen durfte, auch war unklar, welcher Totschläger oder Mörder unter welchen Umständen zurückkehren durfte. Es herrschte also (nach unserem Verständnis) große Rechtsunsicherheit, daher nun die ausführlichen Regelungen. Möglicherweise waren auch vorsätzliche Täter in den Genuss der Aussöhnung gekommen, was fortan unterbunden wird.

c) Recht auf Selbstverteidigung (Z. 33–38, v.a. 37f.)

Und schließlich ist noch der letzte erhaltene Satz auf Axon 1 in Anschlag zu bringen: Z. 37f.: „Auch wenn (jemand) einen, der mit Gewalt und unrechtmäßig wegträgt oder wegführt, sofort bei der Abwehr tötet, dann soll er (der Getötete) bußlos getötet sein.“[98] Ab jetzt ist also die Selbstverteidigung in Fällen erlaubt[99], die u.a. auch der Situation beim Putschversuch zu entsprechen scheinen. Wer unrechtmäßig ergriffen wird[100], darf sich bis zur Tötung des Angreifers hin wehren.

Sowohl die Definition der unvorsätzlichen Tötung als auch die Rückwirkungsklausel sowie das Recht zur Selbstverteidigung beziehen sich m.E. nicht nur auf den Kylonischen Frevel, sondern auch auf die blutigen Auseinandersetzungen, die ihm vorausgingen und folgten. Drakon will also Aussöhnung und Pazifizierung

---

[96] καὶ *h*οι δὲ πρ]ότε[ρ] / ον κτέ[ν]α[ντ]ε[ς ἐν] το̂[ιδε το̂ι θεσμο̂ι ἐνεχέσθον.

[97] Heitsch 1984, 19f.

[98] κ̣α̣[ὶ ἐὰν φέροντα ἒ ἄγοντα βίαι ἀδίκος εὐθὺς] ἀ̣μυνόμενος κτέ[ν]ει, ν̣[εποινὲ τεθνάναι [. . .].

[99] Vgl. das Überblicksschema zur Gliederung des drakontischen Gesetzes bei Dorn – Schmitz – Shahin 2023, 94.

[100] Bzw. wer unrechtmäßig gepfändet wird. Dorn – Schmitz – Shahin 2023, 169f. weisen darauf hin, dass *pherein* das Wegtragen beweglicher Gegenstände meint, *agein* das Wegführen von Menschen und Tieren. Gemeint ist also ein gewaltsamer, unrechtmäßiger Zugriff eines Gläubigers auf einen Schuldner, der von diesem straffrei abgewehrt werden kann.

über Gerechtigkeit herstellen und das heißt, über rational nachvollziehbare Verfahrenswege[101]. Bislang hatte man bei Tötungen offenbar nicht zwischen Vorsatz und Nicht-Vorsatz differenziert. Dies hatte zu schwerwiegenden Problemen geführt. Drakon weitet nun die Straftatbestände aus, sogar auf die Auftraggeber eines Zugriffs, um den Familien der Opfer weitgehende Strafverfolgungsmöglichkeiten zu geben. Noch in klassischer Zeit wird die *bouleusis*, dann in der Bedeutung der Planung oder Veranlassung einer Tötung, mit der Tötung selbst gleichgesetzt.

7. Die Sicht der Sozialwissenschaften – Leistung Drakons liegt in der Integration von

a) Erster Ebene (Archonten, Epheten = Eupatriden?) durch Aufgabenteilung

Politikethnologie und Sozialanthropologie haben in den letzten Jahrzehnten Modelle entworfen, mit denen vorstaatliche Gesellschaften in ihren sozialen und politischen Strukturen analysiert werden können. Insbesondere Archäologen machen sich diese Modelle zu Nutze, um ihre Befunde in größere Kontexte einordnen zu können. Grundsätzlich beziehen sich diese sozialwissenschaftlichen Theorien auf vorstaatliche Verhältnisse. Wer also für das Athen des 7. Jhs. v. Chr. bereits frühe staatliche Strukturen annehmen möchte, wird die Anwendung sozialwissenschaftlicher Theorien auf die Zeit Drakons für wenig hilfreich halten. Für Martin Dreher, beispielsweise, geht Athen den Schritt in die Staatlichkeit schon um 700 v. Chr. Menschen, so Dreher, treffen zu bestimmten Zeiten konkrete Entscheidungen, wie etwa die Einführung des Archontats als einjähriges Amt spätestens 683/2 v. Chr. Die Staatswerdung sei also nicht etwa ein Fluidum, sondern eine bewusst herbeigeführte Entscheidung[102]. Dagegen betrachten die Sozialanthropologen und, ihnen folgend, manche Archäologen, wie Maximilian Rönnberg, die Staatswerdung als einen fluiden Prozess, der sich über Jahrzehnte, wenn nicht Jahrhunderte hinzog. Die Wahrheit liegt wohl irgendwo dazwischen. In Athen wird es immer wieder Schritte hin zur Staatlichkeit gegeben haben. Die vielleicht sukzessive Einführung des Archontats, das drakontische Gesetz und später die Reformen Solons sind mit Sicherheit als solche Schritte zu definieren[103]. In welchem Maße Athen nun im 7. Jh. v. Chr., respektive zur Zeit Drakons, „staatlich" war, lässt sich kaum mehr bemessen. Von frühen, rudimentären oder proto-staatlichen

---

[101] Gagarin 2008, 103 sieht das drakontische Gesetz als überwiegend zukunftsorientiert, es sei Drakon nicht um die Vergangenheit gegangen. M.E. spricht Drakons Interesse an Versöhnung, gerade auch über die Rückwirkungsklausel, gegen diese Hypothese.

[102] Dreher 2021, 126–129.

[103] Die völlige Dekonstruktion Solons durch eine zu geringe Beachtung der literarischen Evidenz durch Rönnberg 2021, z.B. 55f., 64, 259 (die Reformen seien spätere Fiktion, welche der mythischen Gestalt Solons zugeschrieben worden seien) führt in die Aporie.

Strukturen wird man ab den 680ern sicher ausgehen dürfen[104]. Der Prozess der Staatswerdung, der ja parallel zur Polisgenese abläuft, hatte sich sicher in drakontischer Zeit bereits beschleunigt und verdichtet[105]. Doch allein die Tatsache, dass die Blutrache von Drakon nicht etwa abgeschafft, sondern nur kanalisiert wurde, spricht schon gegen ein hohes Niveau an Staatlichkeit[106]. Aus diesem Grund bin ich der Meinung, dass die Begrifflichkeit der Sozialanthropologie sehr wohl auch noch auf die Verhältnisse des 7. Jhs. fruchtbar angewandt werden kann, und uns Befunde der Politikethnologie zu neuen Erkenntnissen auch in Bezug auf die Gesellschaft zur Zeit Drakons und seiner Intentionen führen.

Ab 700 v. Chr. gibt es in vielen griechischen Städten eine Agora und damit eine kritische Öffentlichkeit[107], die dort über gemeinsame Belange diskutiert, in unserer Terminologie also in Grenzen politisch aktiv ist. In Athen hatten um diese Zeit mit Sicherheit schon gesellschaftliche Ausdifferenzierungsprozesse stattgefunden. Athen war keine Dorfgesellschaft mehr, sondern eine komplexe, weil gegliederte big men-Gesellschaft am Übergang zum Chiefdom[108]. Die Anthropologie schlägt nun drei in einer gewissen Hierarchie zueinander stehende gesellschaftliche Instanzen vor:

---

[104] Nach Harris 1989, 234 sind drei Bedingungen für Staatenbildung wesentlich, Bevölkerungswachstum, ein intensiver Bodenausbau sowie ein begrenzter Lebensraum. Die ersten beiden Kriterien treffen sicher auf Attika im 7. Jh. v. Chr. zu.

[105] Rönnberg 2021, 259 nimmt einen solchen Verdichtungsprozess erst ab dem 6. Jh. v. Chr. an. Er leugnet auch (ebd. 262) eine „politische Zusammengehörigkeit“ Attikas vor dem 6. Jh. Diese habe erst Peisistratos in Ansätzen herbeigeführt. Soweit wir jedoch wissen, waren die Regelungen Drakons nicht nur Athen-spezifisch gemeint, sondern galten für ganz Attika, weswegen zumindest in Umrissen von einem politischen Zusammengehörigkeitsgefühl der Bewohner Attikas am Ende des 7. Jhs. ausgegangen werden kann. Sicher wird auch gerade das drakontische Gesetz zu dieser verstärkten politischen Integration beigetragen haben. Ganz in diesem Sinne erkennt auch Gagarin 2008, 104f. im Gesetz Drakons einen großen Sinn für Attika als politische Einheit. Doronzio 2018, 283 sieht in den auf der Akropolis im 7. Jh. durchgeführten Kulthandlungen eine Selbstrepräsentation aller Bewohner Attikas.

[106] Legt man anthropologische Kriterien, wie die Ausbildung einer Bürokratie, die Etablierung eines Militärapparats und die Institutionalisierung einer Staatsreligion, für die Ausbildung des archaischen Staates zugrunde (so Johnson – Earle ^{2}2000, 328f.), wird eine exakte zeitliche Bestimmung der Staatsentstehung quasi unmöglich. Eine Bürokratie darf man bei der Umsetzung der hochkomplexen kleisthenischen Phylenreform voraussetzen. Die militärische Organisation blieb die gesamte klassische Zeit hindurch an die Phylenstruktur gebunden und damit relativ gering ausgeprägt. Die athenische „polis religion“ erfuhr unter den Peisistratiden wesentliche Impulse, die zu einer „Staatsreligion“ führten. Die Staatswerdung Athens verlief also uneinheitlich in Schüben und, gemessen an den anthropologischen Definitionsmerkmalen, phasenverschoben.

[107] In der homerischen Schildszene ist die Agora ausdrücklich als Versammlungsort genannt (Hom., *Il.* 18,497). Vgl. oben FN 61.

[108] Ein „simple chiefdom“ zeichnet sich nach Johnson – Earle ^{2}2000, 279f. durch eine Institutionalisierung politischer Hierarchien sowie eine gewisse Zentralisierung und

Die erste, oberste Instanz sind wenige Inhaber herausgehobener Machtpositionen, im Falle Athens also die Archonten und später die Areopagiten, die sich aus den ehemaligen Archonten rekrutierten. Auch die Epheten gehören in diese Kategorie[109]. Die Anthropologie legt ebenfalls die Existenz eines Ältestenrates für Athen nahe[110]. Ob man diese Männer, die bereits Amtsinhaber sind, noch als big men bzw. chiefs[111] bezeichnen möchte, sei jedem Interpreten überlassen, zumindest verhalten sie sich ähnlich wie big men bzw. chiefs und ringen untereinander, wie etwa Kylon und Megakles, um eine übergeordnete Führungsposition, welche die Anthropologie als chiefdom bezeichnet, die Alte Geschichte traditionellerweise als Tyrannis[112].

b) Zweiter Ebene: *phylobasileis* (auch Elitenangehörige), Oberhäupter der Phratrien (*aristinden* zu bestimmen)
Die zweite Instanz wird von den weiteren Eliten gebildet, etwa den *phylobasileis* und den Oberhäuptern der Phratrien sowie allen Mitgliedern der durch Besitz bestimmten Oberschicht, die nicht im Rat sind. Wie wir gesehen haben, überschneiden sich in Athen erste und zweite Instanz bzw. lassen sich für uns nicht mehr klar trennen (die *phylobasileis* gehören auch den Oberschichten an).

c) Dritter Ebene: Phratrien, *demos*
Die dritte Instanz wird vom einfachen Volk gebildet, das sich von den Eliten geführten Kultverbänden, den Phratrien, zuordnet. Diese dritte Instanz ist also in

Kontrolle der Wirtschaft aus. Während das erste Phänomen in Form des Archontats deutlich greifbar ist, fehlen uns für den zweiten Aspekt die Quellen.

109 Es ist klar, dass Archonten und *basileis* bereits institutionalisierte Ämter sind, wir uns also bereits in einem frühen Stadium der Staatlichkeit befinden. Dennoch sollen hier, aus heuristischen Gründen, Modelle der Sozialanthropologie Anwendung finden. Angesichts der Tatsache, dass sich viele Amtsinhaber noch vorstaatlich verhielten, erscheint mir diese Anwendung gerechtfertigt.

110 Vgl. Ulf 2015, Sp. 878. Die Ältesten im Rat sind Anführer von Clans und Stämmen.

111 Ein Chief hat genügend institutionalisierte Kontrolle über die politische und ökonomische Organisation seines Gemeinwesens, so dass er die Führung auf einen kleinen Kreis der Gesellschaft beschränken kann (Johnson – Earle ^{2}2000, 302).

112 Diese Vereinbarkeit, wenn nicht Gleichsetzung, legen Ulf 2015, Sp. 878 und Kohl ^{3}2012, 62 nahe, der ein „chiefdom“ als permanent, festumrissen und erblich beschreibt. Ein Gewaltmonopol sei dafür nicht erforderlich (ebd. 64). Noch im klassischen Athen war ein Gewaltmonopol von Seiten des Staates nicht mehr als „wishful thinking“ intellektueller Kreise (vgl. Riess 2012, 391f.). Johnson – Earle ^{2}2000, 301 beschreiben ein „complex chiefdom“ als wesentlich stärker integriert als eine big men-Gesellschaft. Die Führung sei auf lokaler wie regionaler Ebene institutionalisiert. Die Gründe für eine zentralisierte Gesellschaft lägen im Bedürfnis nach mehr Risikomanagement, effizienterer Kriegsführung, gestiegener technologischer Komplexität sowie im zunehmenden Handel, was zu zentralem Management und zentraler Kontrolle führe. Für die Peisistratidenherrschaft lassen sich diese Grundzüge des „complex chiefdoms“ (bis auf die gestiegene technologische Komplexität) nachvollziehen.

Athen der *demos*, dessen Zusammenkünfte auf der Agora stattfinden. Archäologisch ist die spätere klassische Agora in Athen schon früh belegt[113]; womöglich lag eine noch ältere, Archaische Agora nordöstlich der Akropolis. Wir müssen also bereits früh eine etwas politisierte Öffentlichkeit von Bürgern, die Anteil an den Angelegenheiten, welche die Gemeinschaft betreffen, nehmen will, voraussetzen.

Was liegt näher als anzunehmen, dass weite Kreise der big men (1. Ebene) Einfluss auf die Rechtsprechung nehmen wollten und auch nahmen? Sicher verfolgten die Clanchefs der führenden Familien gerade in den unruhigen Zeiten vor und nach dem Kylonischen Putschversuch ihre eigenen Interessen. Die Kompetenzen werden oftmals unklar gewesen sein, Machtkämpfe allein schon um das Prärogativ des Richtens werden stattgefunden haben. Und die, die sich schließlich durchsetzten und richten durften, fällten sicher oft Urteile *pro domo*, d.h. im Sinne ihrer eigenen Anhängerschaft, was andere Gesellschaftsmitglieder als grobe Ungerechtigkeit empfunden haben werden. Auch juristisch gesehen muss Chaos geherrscht haben. Drakon legt nun jenseits der innovativen Regelung der unvorsätzlichen Tötung auch Verfahrensweisen fest, er definiert Kompetenzen und führt eine erste Gewaltenteilung, oder besser Machtverteilung ein. Die Oberschichten werden gestärkt, nur die erste (*archon basileus,* Epheten) und z.T. zweite gesellschaftliche Instanz (*phylobasileis*) werden mit der Rechtsfindung und -sprechung in Tötungsfällen betraut. Doch wird eine Art milde Selbstkontrolle eingebaut: Die Urteilssuche liegt bei Amtsinhabern, denen nur (noch) eine sehr begrenzte Amtsgewalt zukommt, der Urteilsspruch bei gewesenen Magistraten oder solchen, die eben zum Zeitpunkt eines Urteils gar kein Amt bekleideten (Epheten). Drakon kann diese Aufgabentrennung nur vornehmen, weil Athen bereits über Ämter verfügt. Bezeichnend ist, dass er damit die Rechtsprechung auf eine breite aristokratische Basis stellt: Durch die Berücksichtigung der *phylobasileis* bindet er also die Eliten über den Ältestenrat hinausgehend in die Rechtsprechung ein und schafft damit viel jurisdiktionelle Partizipation unter den Führungseliten sowie eine Repräsentation, eine gewisse Mitsprache der Phylen. Damit ist klar, dass Drakon – anthropologisch gesprochen – die erste und zweite gesellschaftliche Instanz in die Aburteilung von Tötungsdelikten einbindet. Viele führenden Familienoberhäupter, nicht nur die Archonten (sondern auch die *phylobasileis*), sollten am Rechtsprechungsprozess beteiligt werden, um die bürgerkriegsartigen Auseinandersetzungen zu beenden und weitere *staseis* zu verhindern. Die Familien der Opfer, die oftmals der dritten Instanz angehört haben werden, sind über die Regelungen zur Strafverfolgung und *aidesis* intensiv eingebunden, bis hin zu den einfachen Phratriemitgliedern (dritte Instanz). Gerade die von einer Tötung betroffenen Familien wurden also gehört.

---

[113] Schon Camp 2010, 15 datiert, ähnlich wie Doronzio 2018, die Agora auf vorsolonische Zeit (ab dem beginnenden 7. Jh.). Ab Solon zeichne sich dann die klassische Agora als Zentrum der Stadt ab. Vgl. oben FN 61 und 107.

Damit war die Rechtsprechung zumindest in Tötungsangelegenheiten auf eine denkbar breite gesellschaftliche Basis gestellt[114].

Was heißt das konkret? Drakon legt Wert darauf, dass die erste (Archonten, Epheten) und zweite gesellschaftliche Instanz (*phylobasileis*), die ja teilidentisch sind (alles Angehörige der sozialen Eliten), sich nicht bekriegen, sondern kooperieren. Schon in den homerischen Epen geht es um Kommunikation und Aushandlungsprozesse. Der *demos* lehnt gewaltbereite Führer ab, die nur ihre eigenen Interessen verfolgen und sich bereichern[115]. Genau in diesem Sinne schränkt Drakon die Funktion der *basileis* leicht ein, indem er die eigentliche Rechtsprechung den nicht mehr politisch aktiven Mitgliedern der Oberschichten anvertraut. Die Verhältnisse in Athen sind also komplexer als selbst in einer ausdifferenzierten big men-Gesellschaft; die drakontische Gesellschaft weist damit eindeutig ausgeprägte Züge einer frühen Staatlichkeit auf[116]. Dennoch lehren uns die Konzepte der Sozialanthropologie und der Politikethnologie in Verbindung mit althistorischen Einsichten zur fortgeschrittenen Staatlichkeit um 620 v. Chr., dass Drakon in diesem Umfeld die Machtkämpfe nicht nur zwischen führenden Familien, sondern genauer zwischen führenden Familien, deren Angehörige schon zum Teil Magistrate sind, zu mildern sucht. Durch Kommunikation und sorgsames Austarieren von Interessen verteilt Drakon also soziopolitischen Einfluss über die Zuweisung juristischer Befugnisse auf mehrere Schultern in der Hoffnung, bürgerkriegsähnliche Auseinandersetzungen, hervorgerufen durch innerelitäre Konkurrenz, zu beenden. Bei der Aussöhnung wirkt sogar ein „staatliches" Organ in Form der Epheten gelegentlich mit. Obwohl die unteren Schichten an der Rechtsprechung nicht partizipierten, waren sie über die Regelungen zur Strafverfolgung und *aidesis* in den Sozialverband fest eingebunden, so dass die Intention der Aussöhnung und Pazifizierung selbstverständlich auch sie umfasste.

8. Fazit: Drakon der Versöhner vor dem Hintergrund der athenischen Staatswerdung

Die Archäologie hat die *longue durée* einer sukzessiven Staatswerdung erfolgreich und überzeugend herausgearbeitet. Dennoch finden sich innerhalb dieser allmählichen Entwicklung auch Phasen des beschleunigten Wandels, ja sogar gewisse Sprünge, die uns die literarische Evidenz sehr wohl erlaubt, mit historischen Ereignissen und

---

114 Hawke 2011 sieht die archaische Gesetzgebung Athens ganz situativ, es sei um die Festlegung neuer Regeln für das Austragen innerelitärer Konkurrenz gegangen und damit gerade auch um Machtverteilung, bündig ebd. 197: „THE WRITTEN LAWS OF EARLY GREECE constituted a response by the ruling elites of the early *poleis* to the anxieties and challenges created by the transformations of the eighth and early seventh centuries, as they attempted to work out how to compete for power and prestige but at the same time prevent anyone from gaining overwhelming advantages through the accumulation and concentration of resources."

115 Ulf – Kistler 2020, 96.

116 Pace Rönnberg, s. oben FN 105.

Personen in Verbindung zu bringen, die als so wichtig und wegweisend begriffen wurden, dass sie ihren Niederschlag in den literarischen Quellen gefunden haben. Die institutionelle Verdichtung ging zwar graduell vonstatten, aber wir können sie früher greifen als Rönnberg annimmt, nämlich schon in der ersten Hälfte des 7. Jhs. v. Chr. Ob man nun die Archontenliste ab 683/2 v. Chr. als historisch ansehen möchte oder nicht, klar ist, dass zur Zeit Drakons bereits ein gewisses Amtsverständnis vorhanden war. Die *basileis* erfüllen für eine bestimmte Zeit gewisse Funktionen. Die Epheten waren Teil einer sozialen Elite, die mit der Aburteilung von unvorsätzlichen Tötungen betraut wurde. Und, sofern wir nicht unsere gesamte literarische Überlieferung in Frage stellen wollen, gab es weitere „Ämter", vielleicht besser Funktionen, die von Männern für eine bestimmte Zeit ausgeübt wurden. Durch das einmalige Dokument des drakontischen Gesetzes erkennen wir, dass ein Gesetzgeber situationsspezifisch in eine höchst komplexe soziale und politische Konfliktlage eingegriffen und Neuerungen durchgeführt hat. Eine Zweiteilung in der Jurisdiktion z.B. ist andernorts nicht belegt. Auch die Reformen Solons können in ihrer Gänze unmöglich spätere Zuschreibungen an eine mythische Figur gewesen sein. Es ist hier nicht der Ort, auf die Historizität unserer Überlieferung zu Solon einzugehen, doch dass wir eine Kontinuitätslinie von Drakon zu Solon ziehen können (s. unten), macht das Wirken des Letzteren historisch höchst plausibel. Gerade die allmähliche institutionelle Verdichtung, welche die „Staatswerdung" Athens über Jahrzehnte, wenn nicht Jahrhunderte, darstellt, wurde immer wieder durch das Wirken Einzelner befeuert, denen für einen befristeten Zeitraum außergewöhnliche Vollmachten zugestanden wurden. In einer kleinräumigen, relativ egalitären Gesellschaft, in der innerelitäre Konkurrenzkämpfe nicht nur blutig ausgetragen, sondern Machtverhältnisse durchaus auf vielfältige Weise ausgehandelt wurden, kam diplomatischem Geschick, rhetorischen Fähigkeiten sowie einer hohen sozialen Position wie moralischen Wertigkeit eine herausragende Bedeutung zu. Nur Männern, die zumindest zu Beginn ihrer Reformtätigkeit von einem breiten gesellschaftlichen Konsens und einem großen Vertrauensvorschuss getragen wurden, vertraute man umfassende Kompetenzen an, mit denen sie die betreffenden Gemeinschaften aus tiefen Krisen herausführen sollten.

Dadurch, dass vor diesem Hintergrund Drakon in seinem Gesetzgebungsverfahren die Kommunikation priorisierte[117], erscheint er eher als Versöhner denn als strenger Gesetzgeber, wie ihn die spätere antike Überlieferung gerne darstellt. Auf drei wichtigen Ebenen ist ein großer Ausgleich intendiert, ein Kompromiss:

1. Bei der Trennung von Urteilssuche und Urteilsfällung durch die Aufgabenteilung zwischen *basileis* und Epheten, welche die führenden Familien Athens einbindet und damit ein hohes Maß an jurisdiktioneller Partizipation der Eliten sicherstellt. Gleichzeitig stellte die Rechtsprechung durch Nicht-

[117] Vgl. Ulf – Kistler 2020, 92.

Magistrate ein Zugeständnis an den *demos* dar, der korrupte und parteiische Richter mit Machtbefugnissen beklagte. Dass die Probleme damit nicht gelöst waren, zeigt das Reformwerk Solons eine Generation nach Drakon.

2. Bei dem Versuch einer Aussöhnung zwischen den Familien, bei der in gelegentlichen Fällen der „Staat" mithilft, um sie auch dann zu ermöglichen, wenn es keine männlichen Verwandten mehr gab[118]. Die *aidesis* kann als das zentrale Element des Gesetzes gelten. Je nach gesellschaftlicher Herkunft von Täter und Opfer wirkte sie sowohl vertikal als auch horizontal befriedend in die Gesellschaft hinein.

3. Bei der Frage der Rückbezüglichkeit und damit dem Problem, wer eigentlich als Täter galt und zur Rechenschaft gezogen werden sollte. Die Definition der auch zu ahndenden unvorsätzlichen Tötung, die Rückwirkungsklausel sowie das Recht zur Selbstverteidigung beziehen sich nicht nur auf den Kylonischen Frevel und seine gewaltträchtigen Vorläufer und Folgen, sondern dienen auch zum Austarieren der Interessen zwischen Opferfamilien und unvorsätzlichen Tätern, die z. T. im Exil lebten.

Insgesamt handelt es sich also – die sozialwissenschaftliche Sichtweise bestätigt diesen Befund – um einen rechtlichen, gesellschaftlichen und damit auch politischen Ausgleich zwischen verfeindeten Familien, und zwar zwischen sozial hoch stehenden und auf der sozialen Skala niedriger angesiedelten und auch und v.a. zwischen Familien, die sich auf gleicher sozialer Stufe befanden. Durch die Integration der drei gesellschaftlichen Ebenen in der Regelung der Blutschuld vermittelte Drakon also in vertikalen wie horizontalen *staseis* und verhinderte in einer spezifischen Situation das Auseinanderbrechen der athenischen Gesellschaft und ihr Versinken im Chaos. Damit ist Drakons Gesetz nicht nur als Regelung der Blutrache anzusehen, sondern als sehr viel mehr, als Versuch einer auch rückwirkend wirksamen gesellschaftlichen Versöhnung und Pazifizierung. Damit kann Drakon mit Fug und Recht auch unter die *diallaktai* und *aisymnetai* der archaischen Zeit gezählt werden und damit auch als Vorläufer Solons gelten[119].

werner.riess@uni-hamburg.de

[118] Ich folge der Argumentation Tulins 1996, dass selbst in klassischer Zeit praktisch nur Angehörige des Opfers Anklage wegen Tötung erheben konnten. Umso mehr muss dies für die archaische Zeit gegolten haben, in der von einem geringeren Grad an politischer und jurisdiktioneller Institutionalisierung ausgegangen werden darf.

[119] Develin 1989, 31 bezeichnet Drakon für das Jahr 621/20 als Thesmothet, gesteht aber zu, dass es sich nicht um das Amt eines der sechs Thesmotheten gehandelt haben muss, sondern dass Drakon durchaus eine Sonderposition bekleidet haben könnte. Ähnlich Hignett 1952, 307.

APPENDIX

Neuübersetzung ausgewählter Passagen des drakontischen Gesetzes ins Deutsche

Textausgaben und Übersetzungen:
IG I[3] 104; IG I[2] 115; Syll. I[3] 111; M/L 86; Tod I[2] 87; HGIÜ I 145; F 5a (Leão – Rhodes 2015); F 2 (Dorn – Schmitz – Shahin 2023); Osborne – Rhodes 2017, nr. 183 A; Stroud 1968, 5-7; Gagarin 1981, xiv-xvi; Gagarin 1986, 87.

Der deutsche Text folgt im Wesentlichen Dorn – Schmitz – Shahin 2023, 136f. Die Neuübersetzung von W. Riess bezieht sich auf die im Griechischen fett und im Deutschen kursiv gesetzten Passagen. Abweichende Übersetzungen dieser Stellen finden sich in den Fußnoten 121–124.

προ̂τος ἄχσον.
καὶ ἐὰμ μὲ ᾽κ {[26]ἐκ}[26] [π]ρονοί[α]ς [κ]τ[ένει τίς τινα, φεύγ]ε[ν· **δ]ι-**
κάζεν δὲ τὸς βασιλέας αἴτ̣ιο[ν] φόν̣[ο] ἒ[**ναι ἒ χεῖρα ἀράμενον**[120]] ἒ [β]ολ-
εύσαντα· **τὸς δὲ ἐφέτας διαγν[ο̂]ν̣[α]ι̣**. [αἰδέσασθαι δ᾽ ἐὰμ μὲν πατὲ]ρ ἒ-
ι ἒ ἀδελφὸ[ς] ἒ *h*υε̂ς, *h*άπαντ[α]ς, ἒ τὸν κ̣ο[λύοντα κρατε̂ν· ἐὰν δὲ μὲ] *h*̣οῦ- τοι ο̂σι̣, μέχρ᾽ ἀνεφ[σι]ότετος καὶ̣ [ἀνεφσιο̂, ἐὰν *h*άπαντες αἰδέσ]α̣σ-
θαι ἐθέλοσι, τὸν κο[λύ]οντ̣α [κ]ρα[τε̂ν· ἐὰν δὲ τούτον μεδὲ *h*ε̂ς ε̂ι, κτ]έ-
νει δὲ ἄκο[ν], **γνο̂σι** δὲ ***h*οι̣ [πε]ντ[έκοντα καὶ *h*ε̂ς *h*οι ἐφέται** ἄκοντ]α̣
κτε̂ναι, ἐσέσ̱θ[ο]ν δὲ *h*̣[οι φ]ρ[άτορες ἐὰν ἐθέλοσι δέκα· τούτος δ]ὲ *h*̣ο̣-
ι πεντέκο[ν]τ[α καὶ] *h*ε̂ς ἀρ̣[ι]στ̣[ίνδεν *h*αιρέσθον. καὶ *h*οι δὲ πρ]ότε[ρ]-
ον κτέ[ν]α[ντ]ε[ς ἐν] το̂[ιδε το̂ι θεσμο̂ι ἐνεχέσθον. προειπε̂ν δ]ὲ το̂ι κ-
τέν̣α̣ν̣[τι ἐν ἀ]γορ̣[âι μέχρ᾽ ἀνεφσιότετος καὶ ἀνεφσιο̂· συνδιόκ]εν
δὲ [κ]ἀνεφσ[ιὸς καὶ ἀνεφσιο̂ν παῖδας καὶ γαμβρὸς καὶ πενθερὸ]ς κ-
αὶ φρ̣[ά]τ[ο]ρ̣[ας . . . . .36. . . . .] αἴτι-
ος [ε̂ι] φό[νο . . . . . . .26. . . . . .τὸς πεντέκοντ]α καὶ̣
*h*ένα . . . . 42. φόνο
*h*έλ̣οσ[ι . . . . 35. . . . . ἐὰν δ]έ [τ]ις τ-
ὸ[ν ἀν]δ̣ρ̣[οφόνον κτένει ἒ αἴτιος ε̂ι φόνο, ἀπεχόμενον ἀγορâ]ς ἐφο-
ρί[α]ς κ̣[α]ὶ [ἄθλον καὶ *h*ιερο̂ν Ἀμφικτυονικο̂ν, *h*όσπερ τὸν Ἀθεν]αῖον κ̣-
[τένα]ν̣[τα, ἐν τοῖς αὐτοῖς ἐνέχεσθαι· **διαγιγνόσκεν δὲ τὸς] ἐ[φ]έτα[ς]**
. Ε̣. . . . . 39. . . . . τ̣ει ἐμεδ̣-
[απε̂ι . . . . 41. . . . .]ΟΝΑΤ.

120 Z. 12 Ergänzung G. Thür 2018, 34 (= 2014, 923).

. . . . .45. . . . . .Α̣Ν̣Α̣. .
Ν̣[. . . . . .39. . . . . ἄρχον]τ̣α χερ̣-
ο͡ν̣ ἀ[δίκον . . . . .30. . . . . χερ]ο͡ν ἀδίκον κ-
τέ[νει . .7. . .]Σ̣[. . . . . 19. . . . .**διαγιγνόσκ]εν̣ δὲ τὸς ἐ-**
[φέτ]ας . . . . .36. . . . . .ΕΙΣΕ ἐλεύθ-
ε[ρ]ος ε̣͡ι̣. κ̣α̣[ὶ ἐὰν φέροντα ἒ ἄγοντα βίαι ἀδίκος εὐθὺς] ἀ̣μυνόμενο-
ς κτέ[ν]ει, ν̣[εποινὲ τεθνάναι . . . . . .19. . . . .]Σ̣ΕΧΟΝΤΟΒ.
ΙΑΝ. .Λ̣[. . . . . .35. . . . . .τ]ὲν ἀ̣πόστα̣-
σιν ΤΟ. . . . . .37. . . . . .ΕΣ δεκατ͡ε̣-

Übersetzung Dorn – Schmitz – Shahin 2023, 136f. mit Abweichungen durch Riess, kursiv gesetzt (2023):

|[10] Erster Axon: | Auch wenn jemand einen anderen nicht aus Vorsatz tötet, soll er *verbannt werden.* | *Die Basileis sollen (prozessinitiierende) Eide (formulieren und) auferlegen: Er ist verantwortlich für eine (unvorsätzliche) Tötung, sei es, dass er [die Hand selbst erhoben hat] oder (eine Maßnahme) angeordnet hat (, die einen Tod verursachte). Die Epheten sollen das Urteil durch Abstimmung fällen*[121]. Sich (mit dem Täter) aussöhnen sollen, wenn der Vater (noch) lebt oder der Bruder oder die Söhne, alle zusammen; andernfalls soll derjenige obsiegen, der (die Aussöhnung) verweigert. Wenn diese nicht (mehr) |15 leben, dann die bis hin zur Vetternschaft, und zwar bis zum Vetter, wenn alle sich aussöhnen wollen; andernfalls soll der obsiegen, der (die Aussöhnung) verweigert. Wenn aber auch von diesen nicht einer (mehr) lebt und er (der Täter) ohne (feste) Absicht (ákōn) getötet hat und die Einundfünfzig, die ephétai, *durch Abstimmung das Urteil gefällt haben*[122] (gnṓnai), dass er ohne (feste) Absicht (ákōn) getötet hat, dann sollen ihn die phrátores wieder (in das Land) einlassen, wenn zehn es wollen. Diese sollen die Einundfünfzig ihrer Würdigkeit nach (aristíndēn) wählen. Und auch diejenigen, die früher |20 getötet haben, sollen unter diese Satzung (thesmós) fallen. Dem, der getötet hat, sollen (die Verfolgung) in der agorá ankündigen (proeipeín) (die

[121] Dorn – Schmitz – Shahin 2023, 136: fliehen (= außer Landes gehen). Richten (*dikázein*) sollen die *basileís* den an der Tötung Schuldigen, der entweder [mit eigener Hand] oder dies beschließend (= veranlassend) getötet hat, die *ephétai* sollen entscheiden (*diagnónai*).
HGIÜ I 145: nicht vorsätzlich get[ötet hat, soll er verbannt werden]. | Für des Mordes schuldig sollen erklären (so auf Englisch auch Wallace 1989, 26 und auch Osborne – Rhodes 2017, S. 507) die Basileis [den, der die Tat selbst ausgeführt hat oder (?) dazu] angestiftet hat; die Epheten (= „Zulasser“) sollen abstimmen.
Thür 2002, 634: Selbst wenn jemand einen nicht mit Absicht getötet hat, soll er verbannt sein. Die Könige sollen anordnen (daß der Kläger schwört, der Verklagte) sei schuldig der Tötung, entweder „mit der Hand, die er geregt hat“ oder „durch Ratschlag“.
Thür 2018, 34: The basileis are to impose the oaths: *He is responsible for killing* (alternatively) either *by having raised a hand* (himself) or *by having ordered* (a measure causing death).

[122] Dorn – Schmitz – Shahin 2023, 136: darauf erkannt haben (= HGIÜ I 145).

Verwandten des Opfers) bis hin zur Vetternschaft, und zwar bis zum Vetter. An der Verfolgung teilnehmen (syndiókein) sollen auch Vettern und Vetternsöhne, Schwiegersöhne, Schwiegerväter und phrátores. … schuldig ist an der Tötung ... die Einund|25fünfzig ... [wenn sie einen] der Tötung |26–29 überführt haben ... Wenn jemand den Täter (androphónos) (eigenhändig) tötet oder an dessen Tötung Schuld trägt, obwohl er sich von agoraí ephóriai, von Wettkämpfen und Festen der Amphiktyonen fernhielt, so soll er unter dieselben Bestimmungen fallen, wie wenn er einen Athener getötet hätte. *Abstimmen und urteilen*[123] (diagignṓskein) aber sollen die ephétai. … auf heimischem Boden ... |33–38 ... (wer einen, der) unrechtmäßig Hand anzulegen begonnen hat, ... (jemand) einen, der unrechtmäßig Hand (angelegt hat), tötet, (so soll der bußlos getötet sein) ... *Abstimmen und urteilen*[124] (diagignṓskein) aber sollen die ephétai ... ein Freier ist. Auch wenn (jemand) einen, der mit Gewalt und unrechtmäßig wegträgt oder wegführt, sofort bei der Abwehr tötet, dann soll er (der Getötete) bußlos getötet sein … *(17 Zeilen weitgehend unlesbar)*|

VERWENDETE LITERATUR

BRAUN, M., Die „Eumeniden“ des Aischylos und der Areopag, Tübingen 1998.

BRODERSEN, K. – GÜNTHER, W. – SCHMITT, H., Historische Griechische Inschriften in Übersetzung. Band I: Die archaische und klassische Zeit, Darmstadt 1992 (= HGIÜ I).

CAMP, J., The Athenian Agora. Site Guide, Princeton/NJ 2010.

CANTARELLA, E., Studi sull'omicidio in diritto greco e romano, Milano 1976.

CARAWAN, E. M., Ephetai and Athenian Courts for Homicide in the Age of the Orators, in: CPh 86, 1991, 1–16.

CARAWAN, E. M., Rhetoric and the Law of Draco, Oxford 1998.

CAREY, C., In Search of Drakon, in: CCJ 59, 2013, 29–51.

CARLIER, P., La royauté en Grèce avant Alexandre, Strasbourg 1984.

DEVELIN, R., Athenian Officials 684–321 B. C., Cambridge 1989.

DORN, A. – SCHMITZ, W. – SHAHIN, T., Leges Draconis et Solonis (LegDrSol). Eine neue Edition der Gesetze Drakons und Solons mit Übersetzungen und historischer Einordnung, Stuttgart 2023.

DORONZIO, A., Athen im 7. Jh. v. Chr. Räume und Funde der frühen Polis, Berlin 2018.

DREHER M., Sophistik und Polisentwicklung. Die sophistischen Staatstheorien des fünften Jahrhunderts v. Chr. und ihr Bezug auf Entstehung und Wesen des griechischen, vorranging athenischen Staates, Frankfurt/M. 1983.

DREHER, M., Hikesie, Asylie und das Tötungsgesetz Drakons, in: L. GAGLIARDI – L. PEPE (Eds.), DIKE. Studi in onore di Alberto Maffi, Milano 2019a, 87–103.

[123] Dorn – Schmitz – Shahin 2023, 137: entscheiden; HGIÜ I 145: abstimmen.

[124] Dorn – Schmitz – Shahin 2023, 137: entscheiden; HGIÜ I 145: abstimmen.

DREHER, M., Il re nella Grecia antica, in: R. FIORI (Ed.), Re e popolo. Istituzioni archaiche tra storia e comparazione, Göttingen 2019b, 117–138.

DREHER, M., Staat und Individuum in der griechischen Polis bis zur klassischen Zeit, in: W. RIESS (Ed.), Colloquia Attica II. Neuere Forschungen zu Athen im 5. Jh. v. Chr., Stuttgart 2021, 119–142.

DREWS, R., Basileus. The Evidence for Kingship in Geometric Greece, New Haven 1983.

FLAMENT, C., IG I³ 104 et les basileis de Dracon. Réflections sur l'organisation sociale, politique et militaire de l'Athènes préclisthénienne, in: LEC 77, 2009, 115–132.

FORCHHAMMER, P., Die Epheten und der Areopag, in: *Philologus* 34, 1876, 465–473.

GAGARIN, M., Drakon and Early Athenian Homicide Law, New Haven 1981.

GAGARIN, M., Early Greek Law, Berkeley – Los Angeles 1986.

GAGARIN, M., The basileus in Athenian Homicide Law, in: P. FLENSTED-JENSEN – T. HEINE NIELSEN – L. RUBINSTEIN (Eds.), Polis & Politics: Studies in Ancient Greek History Presented to Mogens Hansen on His Sixtieth Birthday, August 20, 2000, Copenhagen 2000, 569–579.

GAGARIN, M., Writing Greek Law, Cambridge 2008.

GAGLIARDI, L., Ruolo e competenze degli efeti da Draconte all'età degli oratori, in: Dike 15, 2012, 33–71.

GLOTZ, G., La solidarité de la famille dans le droit criminelle en Grèce, Paris 1904 (New York 1973).

HARRIS, M., Kulturanthropologie. Ein Lehrbuch, Frankfurt/M. – New York 1989.

HARRISON, A., The Law of Athens. Volume II: Procedure, Oxford 1971 (Second Edition, Foreword and Bibliography by D. M. MacDowell, London 1998).

HARRIS-CLINE, D., Archaic Athens and the Topography of the Kylon Affair, in: ABSA 94, 1999, 309–320.

HAWKE, J., Writing Authority. Elite Competition and Written Law in Early Greece, DeKalb/Il. 2011.

HEITSCH, E., Aidesis im attischen Strafrecht, Wiesbaden 1984.

HIGNETT, C., A History of the Athenian Constitution to the End of the Fifth Century BC, Oxford 1952.

HUMPHREYS, S., A Historical Approach to Drakon's Law on Homicide, in: M. GAGARIN (Ed.), Symposion 1990, Köln 1991, 17–45.

INGVARSSON, A. – BÄCKSTRÖM, Y., Bioarchaeological Field Analysis of Human Remains from the Mass Graves at Phaleron, Greece, in: Opuscula 12, 2019, 7–158.

JOHNSON, A. – EARLE, T., The Evolution of Human Societies. From Foraging Group to Agrarian State, Stanford ²2000.

KAHRSTEDT, U., Untersuchungen zur Magistratur in Athen, Stuttgart 1936 (repr. Aalen 1969).

KAHRSTEDT, U., Untersuchungen zu athenischen Behörden, in: Klio 30, 1937, 10–33 = Zur griechischen Rechtsgeschichte, Darmstadt 1968, 197–223.

KÖHLER, U., Der Areopag in Athen, in: Hermes 6, 1872, 92–112.

KOHL, K.-H., Ethnologie – die Wissenschaft vom kulturell Fremden. Eine Einführung, München [3]2012.

LANGE, L., Die Epheten und der Areopag vor Solon, in: Abh. d. philol.-hist. Classe d. kgl. Sächs. Gesellsch. d. Wiss. 7, Leipzig 1874, 187–264.

LEÃO, D. – RHODES, P., The Laws of Solon. A New Edition with Introduction, Translation and Commentary, London – New York 2015.

LEDL, A., Studien zur älteren athenischen Verfassungsgeschichte, Heidelberg 1914.

LIPSIUS, J. H., Das attische Recht und Rechtsverfahren, Leipzig 1905–1915.

LOOMIS, W., The Nature of Premeditation in Athenian Homicide Law, in: JHS 92, 1972, 86–95.

MEIGGS, R. – LEWIS, D., A Selection of Greek Historical Inscriptions to the End of the Fifth Century BC, Oxford 1969, rev. 1988 (= M/L).

MEISTER, J., ‚Adel' und gesellschaftliche Differenzierung im archaischen und frühklassischen Griechenland, Stuttgart 2020.

MIRHADY, D., Drakonian Procedure, in: C. COOPER (Ed.), Epigraphy and the Greek Historian, Toronto – Buffalo – London 2008, 15–30.

NÖRR, D., Zum Mordtatbestand bei Drakon, in: Studi in onore di Arnaldo Biscardi, Bd. 4, Milano 1983, 631–655.

OSBORNE, R. – RHODES, P. J., Greek Historical Inscriptions 478–404 BC, Oxford 2017.

PEPE, L., Osservazioni su *phonos akousios* e *phonos dikaios* nell'Atene del V e IV secolo a.C., in: Dike 11, 2008, 139–166.

PEPE, L., Osservazioni sulla „pronoia" in tema di omicidio, in: Dike 12/13, 2009/10, 69–90.

PEPE, L., Phonos: l'omicidio da Draconte all'età degli oratori, Milano 2012.

PHILIPPI, A., Der Areopag und die Epheten, Berlin 1874.

PHILLIPS, D., Avengers of Blood. Homicide in Athenian Law and Custom from Draco to Demosthenes, Stuttgart 2008.

PHILLIPS, D., The Law of Ancient Athens, Ann Arbor 2013.

PORRELLO, M. S., Omicidio tra vendetta e punizione, in: D & Q 8, 2008, 139–165.

RIESS, W., Performing Interpersonal Violence. Court, Curse, and Comedy in Fourth-Century BCE Athens, Berlin – New York 2012.

RÖNNBERG, M., Athen und Attika vom 11. bis zum frühen 6. Jh. v. Chr. Siedlungsgeschichte, politische Institutionalisierungs- und gesellschaftliche Formierungsprozesse, Rahden/Westf. 2021.

RUSCHENBUSCH, E., ΦΟΝΟΣ: Zum Recht Drakons und seiner Bedeutung für das Werden des athenischen Staates, in: Historia 9, 1960, 129–154.

SALVO, I., *Eirgesthai agoras*: l'allontanamento degli omicidi dallo spazio pubblico, in: C. AMPOLO (Ed.), Sicilia Occidentale. Studi, rassegne, ricerche, Pisa 2012, 319–323.

SANCTIS, G. D., L'Amnistia di Solone e le origine dell'Areopago, in: Saggi storico-critici, fasc. 1, Roma 1896, 21–41.

SCHMITZ, W., „Drakonische Strafen". Die Revision der Gesetze Drakons durch Solon und die Blutrache in Athen, in: Klio 83, 2001, 7–38.

SCHMITZ, W., Das Gesetz Drakons über die Tötung in der neueren Forschung, in: W. RIESS (Ed.), Colloquia Attica: Neuere Forschungen zur Archaik, zum athenischen Recht und zur Magie, Stuttgart 2018, 37–59.

SEALEY, R., The Athenian Courts for Homicide, in: CPh 78, 1983, 275–296.

SEALEY, R., The Justice of the Greeks, Ann Arbor 1994.

SMITH, G., The Jurisdiction of the Areopagus, in: CP 22, 1927, 61–79.

STROUD, R. S., Drakon's Law on Homicide, Berkeley – Los Angeles 1968.

STROUD, R.S., Aristotle and Athenian Homicide, in: M. PIÉRART (Ed.), Aristote et Athènes – Aristotle and Athens, Paris 1993, 203–221.

THÜR, G., Die Todesstrafe im Blutprozess Athens (Zum dikazein in IG I3 104, 11–13; Dem. 23, 22; Aristot., AP 57, 4), in: Journal of Juristic Papyrology 20, 1990, 143–156.

THÜR, G., Oaths and Dispute Settlement in Ancient Greek Law, in: L. Foxhall – A. D. E. Lewis (Eds.), Greek Law in its Political Setting – Justification not Justice, Oxford 1996, 57–72.

THÜR, G., Der Reinigungseid im archaischen griechischen Rechtsstreit und seine Parallelen im Alten Orient, in: R. ROLLINGER – H. BARTA (Eds.), Rechtsgeschichte und Interkulturalität. Zum Verhältnis des östlichen Mittelmeerraums und ‚Europas' im Altertum, Marburg 2007, 179–196.

THÜR, G., Rationality and Irrationality in the Ancient Greek Law of Procedure, in: R. VAN DEN BERGH – G. VAN NIEKERK – P. PICHONNAZ – P. THOMAS – D. KLEYN – F. LUCREZI – J. MUTTON (Eds.), Meditationes de iure e historia: Essays in honour of Laurens Winkel, Unisa 2014, 916–924.

THÜR, G., Prozesseide im Gesetz Drakons und ihr Nachleben im klassischen Athen, in: H. BARTA – M. LANG – R. ROLLINGER (Eds.), Prozessrecht und Eid. Recht und Rechtsfindung in antiken Kulturen I. ,Wiesbaden 2015, 153–178.

THÜR, G., New Light on Draco and the Cylonian Sacrilege, in: W. RIESS (Ed.), Colloquia Attica: Neuere Forschungen zur Archaik, zum athenischen Recht und zur Magie, Stuttgart 2018, 27–35.

TOD, M., A Selection of Greek Historical Inscriptions I: To the End of the Fifth Century, Oxford ^{2}1946 (= Tod I^{2}).

TULIN, A., Dike phonou: the Right of Prosecution and Attic Homicide Procedure, Stuttgart 1996.

ULF, C., Gesellschaft und Herrschaft, in: A.-M. WITTKE (Ed.), Frühgeschichte der Mittelmeerkulturen. Historisch–archäologisches Handbuch, Stuttgart – Weimar 2015, Sp. 853–888.

ULF, C. – KISTLER, E., Die Entstehung Griechenlands, Berlin – Boston 2020.

WADE-GERY, H., Eupatridai, Archons, and Areopagus, in: CQ 25, 1931, 1–11, 77–89 = EGH 86–115.

WALLACE, R. W., The Areopagos Council, to 307 B.C., Baltimore 1989.

WECKLEIN, N., Der Areopag, die Epheten und die Naukraren, in: Sitz. Bayer. Akad. Wiss. 1873, 1–48.

WELWEI, K.-W., Athen. Vom neolithischen Siedlungsplatz zur archaischen Großpolis, Darmstadt 1992.

WESTBROOK, R., The Trial Scene in the Iliad, in: HSCPh 94, 1992, 53–76.

WESTBROOK, R., Drakon's Homicide Law, in: E. HARRIS – G. THÜR (Eds.), Symposion 2007, Wien 2008, 3–16.

WILAMOWITZ-MOELLENDORFF, U. VON, Aristoteles und Athen, 2 Bde., Berlin 1893.

WIRBELAUER, E., Der Schild des Achilleus (Il. 18, 478–609). Überlegungen zur inneren Struktur und zum Aufbau der ‚Stadt im Frieden', in: H.-J. GEHRKE – A. MÖLLER (Eds.), Vergangenheit und Lebenswelt: Soziale Kommunikation, Traditionsbildung und historisches Bewußtsein, Tübingen 1996, 143–178.

YOUNG, R., Graves from the Phaleron Cemetery, in: AJA 46, 1942, 23–57.

WINFRIED SCHMITZ (BONN)

DRAKONS GESETZ ÜBER DIE TÖTUNG, SOLONS AMNESTIEGESETZ UND DIE ENTSTEHUNG DES AREOPAGS: ANTWORT AUF WERNER RIESS

In einem 2016 erschienenen Beitrag über rechtlich zulässige Eigenmacht im Falle eines tätlichen Angriffs, wie sie in Drakons Gesetz geregelt war, forderte Edward M. Harris: „A new edition of the inscription is urgently needed“.[1] Werner Riess hat in seinem Beitrag das Gesetz Drakons über die Tötung erneut einer grundlegenden Revision unterzogen und einen neuen Interpretations- und Übersetzungsvorschlag sowie eine historische Kontextualisierung unterbreitet. Seinen Ausführungen über die Aussöhnung (*aídesis*) stimme ich weitestgehend zu, ebenso wie seiner Annahme, dass das Gesetz in unmittelbarem Zusammenhang mit den bürgerkriegsartigen Wirren in den 630er Jahren steht. Dies gilt auch für die von Gerhard Thür vorgeschlagene und von Werner Riess übernommene Ergänzung der Inschrift in Zeile 12 zur eigenhändigen Tötung, für die Unterscheidung von eigenhändiger und auf Anordnung vollzogener Tötung und für Werner Riess' Einbettung der veränderten Verfahrensregeln in die Ausgestaltung von Institutionen in Athen in archaischer Zeit.[2]

Konzentrieren möchte ich mich in meiner Stellungnahme auf das so genannte Amnestiegesetz Solons, das direkt auf die Urteile unmittelbar nach dem Tyrannisversuch Kylons, infolge der rechtlichen Neuregelung Drakons sowie des Schlichtungsversuchs Solons Bezug nimmt:

> ὁ δὲ τρισκαιδέκατος ἄξων τοῦ Σόλωνος τὸν ὄγδοον ἔχει τῶν νόμων οὕτως αὐτοῖς ὀνόμασι γεγραμμένον· „ἀτίμων· ὅσοι ἄτιμοι ἦσαν πρὶν ἢ Σόλωνα

---

1 Die berechtigte Tötung bei tätlichem Angriff ist geregelt in IG I^3 104 Z. 33–35. Harris (2016) 216, vgl. 215: „This study shows that we urgently need a new edition of *IG* I^3 104, one that accurately reports what can be seen on the stone without any mistaken preconceptions about what is to be found there.“ In der neuen Edition der Gesetze Drakons und Solons (LegDrSol) sind der Satzung Drakons nur diejenigen literarisch überlieferten Zitate zugewiesen, die sich vom Ablauf des Verfahrens her in das Gesetz einfügen lassen (F 2–18 LegDrSol).

2 Die von Antiphon in or. 6,16 f. verwendete Formulierung (ἐγὼ δὲ μὴ ἀποκτεῖναι, μήτε χειρὶ ἀράμενος μὴτε βουλεύσας) lässt sich in die Lücke in IG I^3 104, Z. 12 (δ]ι|κάζεν δὲ τὸς βασιλέας αἴτ̣ιο[ν] φόν̣[ο] E[.........^{17}........]E [β]ολ|εύσαντα) einfügen: αἴτ̣ιο[ν] φόν̣[ο] ἐ̑[ναι ἒ χειρὶ ἀράμενον] ἒ [β]ολ|εύσαντα.

ἄρξαι ἐπιτίμους εἶναι, πλὴν ὅσοι ἐξ Ἀρείου πάγου ἢ ὅσοι ἐκ τῶν ἐφετῶν ἢ ἐκ πρυτανείου καταδικασθέντες ὑπὸ τῶν βασιλέων ἐπὶ φόνῳ ἢ σφαγαῖσιν ἢ ἐπὶ τυραννίδι ἔφευγον, ὅτε ὁ θεσμὸς ἐφάνη ὅδε".

Der dreizehnte *áxōn* Solons hat als achtes der Gesetze folgendes mit diesen Worten verzeichnet: „Über die Ehrlosen (*átimoi*): Diejenigen, die ehrlos (*átimoi*) waren, bevor Solon als Archont im Amt war, sollen wieder ehrbar (*epítimoi*) sein, mit Ausnahme derjenigen, die vom Areopag, oder derjenigen, die von den *ephétai* oder vom *prytaneíon* – abgeurteilt (*katadikasthéntes*) von/unter den *basileís* wegen Tötung oder Abschlachtens oder wegen Errichtung einer Tyrannis – [aus Attika] verbannt waren (*épheugon*), als diese Satzung (*thesmós*) erlassen wurde".[3]

Da Plutarch das Gesetz ausdrücklich wortwörtlich zitiert und der Gesetzestext selbst auf das Archontat Solons verweist, ist ein hohes Maß an Glaubwürdigkeit vorauszusetzen, und dies bestätigen Formulierung und Inhalt des Gesetzes. Hervorzuheben ist, dass es ein Gesetz „Über die Ehrlosen" ist, also vermutlich in den Kontext rechtlicher Bestimmungen gehört, die den Zugang zu politischen Ämtern sowie die Teilnahme an Volksversammlung und Gerichten regelten.[4] Zunächst werden Personen, die bis zum Archontat Solons „ehrlos" (*átimoi*) waren, wieder zu „Ehrbaren" (*epítimoi*) erklärt. Es waren dies Personen, die Schädigungen verursacht hatten, sei es aufgrund mutwilliger Handlungen, Vergehen oder Vertragsverletzungen, sei es aufgrund nicht zurückgezahlter Schulden. Als solche unterlagen sie der Noxalhaftung und mussten – genauso wie es das frühe römische Recht vorsah – an den Geschädigten übergeben werden, wenn sich der Geschädigte nicht mit einer Entschädigung für den erlittenen Schaden zufriedengab.[5] Der Geschädigte hatte die Möglichkeit, die ihm übergebene Person für sich arbeiten zu lassen oder sie in die Sklaverei nach auswärts zu verkaufen. Genau diese beiden Optionen nennt Solon selbst in einer seiner Elegien, in der er das Schicksal derjenigen Athener beklagt, die zu Recht oder gegen das Recht in die Sklaverei verkauft worden waren, die, um einem solchen Schicksal zu entgehen, aus Attika geflohen waren oder die an Ort und Stelle – also in Attika – schmachvolle Abhängigkeit (*doulíē*) erduldeten und den Launen ihrer Herren (*despótai*) ausgesetzt waren.[6] Mit seiner *seisáchtheia* hob Solon vermutlich nicht die Schulden selbst, wohl aber die bestehenden – und oft wohl schon lange bestehenden – Abhängigkeitsverhältnisse, die aus der Übergabe der Person infolge der

3 Plut. Solon 19,4.

4 Daher ist die Bestimmung als F 50–52 (S. 367–372) in der neuen Edition der solonischen Gesetze in den Kontext der Gesetze über die Amtsträger gestellt.

5 Dazu ausführlich Schmitz (2022) mit weiterer Literatur.

6 Solon *fr.* 36 West, 30 Gentili/Prato Z. 8–15, vgl. *fr.* 4 West, 3 Gentili/Prato Z. 23–25 (F 102 LegDrSol). Der Sachverhalt ist in Plut. Solon 13,4–5 sachlich korrekt wiedergegeben (offenbar unmittelbar oder mittelbar über einen Atthidographen auf Solon selbst zurückgehend), missverständlich hingegen in Ath. pol. 2,2.

Noxalhaftung resultierten, auf, so dass die den Geschädigten Übergebenen aus deren Gewalt entlassen werden mussten und wieder Personen eigenen Rechts, demnach wieder *epítimoi*, „Ehrbare“, waren.[7]

Der darauf folgende Gesetzestext (alle Ehrlosen sollen wieder ehrbar sein) „mit Ausnahme derjenigen, die vom Areopag, oder derjenigen, die von den *ephétai* oder vom *prytaneíon* – abgeurteilt von/unter den *basileís* wegen Tötung oder Abschlachtens oder wegen Errichtung einer Tyrannis – [aus Attika] verbannt waren (*épheugon*), als diese Satzung (*thesmós*) erlassen wurde“, hat zu kontroversen Diskussionen geführt. Dabei geht es insbesondere darum, welcher der drei Gerichtshöfe über welches der genannten Delikte entschieden habe, ob dabei eine Art Chiasmus vorliegt.[8] Die wahrscheinlichste Lösung scheint mir jedoch darin zu liegen, dass die Aufzählung der Gerichtshöfe in chronologischer Abfolge zu lesen ist: Ausgenommen von der Amnestie und damit von der politischen Teilhabe, ja sogar von der Rückkehr nach Attika sollten nach Solons gesetzlicher Festlegung diejenigen sein, die vor ganz kurzer Zeit erst von dem von Solon neu geschaffenen Areopag verurteilt worden waren, außerdem diejenigen, die in den Jahren nach 621 von den Epheten auf Grundlage des drakontischen Gesetzes, und auch diejenigen, die unmittelbar nach dem Tyrannisversuch Kylons in den Jahren nach 636 oder 632 vom Prytaneion verurteilt worden waren.[9]

Eine solche (umgekehrt) chronologische Anordnung eines ursprünglich im Prytaneion abgehaltenen Gerichts, eines anschließend von Drakon eingerichteten neuen Gerichtshofs von einundfünfzig Epheten und eines schlussendlich von Solon geschaffenen Gerichtshofs am *áreios págos*, am Fuß des der Akropolis gegenüber gelegenen „blanken Felsens“ (es ist nicht der ‚Hügel des Ares‘), folgt dabei der Darstellung Plutarchs über die Ereignisse nach dem Tyrannisversuch Kylons. Sein Bericht setzt unvermittelt damit ein, dass um 600 der Kylonfluch Athen immer noch und schon lange Zeit in Aufruhr gehalten habe: Der Alkmeonide Megakles sei es gewesen, der damals (636 oder 632) die Mitverschworenen Kylons überredet habe, von der Akropolis herabzukommen und sich einem Gerichtsverfahren zu stellen.[10] Die um die Episode herumgesponnene Geschichte, die auf der Akropolis Belagerten, die sich als Schutzflehende zum Altar der Athena begeben hätten, hätten einen Faden an das Bild der Göttin gebunden und so eine Verbindung zum Sakralen bewahrt, spiegelt spätere Kontroversen um die Frage, ob die Tötung berechtigt war oder nicht. Als der Faden beim Herabsteigen von der Akropolis „von selbst“ (αὐτομάτως) riss, hätten Megakles und die Mitarchonten die Kylonanhänger

7 Zu zurückhaltend diesbezüglich scheinen mir Leão/Rhodes (2015) 36 zu sein.

8 Leão/Rhodes (2015) 36: „It is best to read this passage as chiastic, with the Areopagus concerned with tyranny (…) and the *ephetai* and the *prytaneion* with homicide and wounding“.

9 Unbefriedigend bleibt die Erklärung von Leão/Rhodes (2015) 36 zur Frage, welches Delikt das Prytaneion mit Atimie bestraft habe.

10 Plut. Solon 12,1: ἐπὶ δίκῃ κατελθεῖν.

ergriffen, weil die Göttin Athena den Schutzflehenden doch offensichtlich die *hikesía* entzogen hätte. Einige der sich außerhalb der heiligen Stätte Aufhaltenden wurden ergriffen und zum Tode durch Steinigung verurteilt, andere, die sich in diesem Tumult wiederum an Altäre – diesmal an die Altäre der Semnai am Fuß des *áreios págos* – geflüchtet hatten, an den Altären „abgeschlachtet" (ἀπεσφάγησαν).[11] In den folgenden Jahren hätten die überlebenden Anhänger Kylons aber erneut an Macht gewonnen – so fährt Plutarch fort – und in ständigem Zwist mit den Anhängern des Megakles gelegen. Die starke politische Polarisierung und der erbittert geführte Konkurrenzkampf fanden also kein Ende. Solon sei es schließlich „zusammen mit den vornehmsten Athenern" gelungen, die an der Tötung der Kylonanhänger Schuldigen dazu zu bewegen, sich einem Gericht aus dreihundert herausragenden Bürgern zu stellen. Myron von Phlya habe die Anklage geführt, und die Angeklagten seien verurteilt worden. Die noch lebenden hätten das Land verlassen, die Leichname der bereits verstorbenen Schuldigen seien aus den Gräbern geholt und über die Grenzen geworfen worden.[12]

Die Mitverschworenen Kylons hatten die Akropolis verlassen, sollten sich einem Verfahren vor Gericht stellen. Ich verbinde dies mit den unmittelbar nach dem Tyrannisversuch vom Prytaneion Verurteilten, wie sie im Amnestiegesetz genannt sind.[13] Wenn in den Jahren danach gemäß Plutarch die Kylonanhänger wieder mächtiger geworden waren, so lässt sich dies mit Drakons Gesetz über die Tötung in Verbindung bringen, das vorsah, dass sich diejenigen, die eine Tötung begangen hatten, sei es eigenhändig, sei es durch Anweisung, vor einem nun größeren Gerichtshof von einundfünfzig Männern zu verantworten hatten.[14] Offenbar hatten die überlebenden Anhänger Kylons so weit Oberwasser bekommen, dass durchgesetzt werden konnte, die an der Tötung Schuldigen müssten sich für ihre Tat vor einem Gericht verantworten, auch wenn sie in der Absicht gehandelt hatten, eine Tyrannis zu verhindern. Werner Riess geht auf die Bezeichnung „Epheten" nicht ein, betont lediglich, dass ein solches Gericht sonst nicht belegt sei. Aber lässt sich die Bezeichnung nicht in Verbindung mit dem Verfahren der *éphesis* bringen, also einer Appellation? Denn die einundfünfzig Epheten sollten erneut über die

---

11 Plut. Solon 12,1; vgl. Schol. Aristoph. equ. 445a: λίθοις αὐτοὺς ἔβαλλον οἱ Ἀθηναῖοι. Nach Plut. Solon 12,1 seien nur diejenigen verschont worden, die sich als Schutzflehende an die Frauen der Archonten gewandt hatten. Die Episode mit dem gerissenen Faden hat auch Aristodemos, ein Historiker unbekannter Zeit, aufgegriffen (FgrH 104 F 2). Vgl. Scheer (2000) 174 f. mit Verweis auf die Parallele bei den Ephesiern (Hdt. 1,26).

12 Plut. Solon 12,2–4 (ἀριστίνδην); 13,1.

13 Das Gericht im Prytaneion blieb ungeachtet des Gesetzes Drakons über die Tötung und der Neuregelungen Solons für Tötungen zuständig, bei denen ein unbekannter Täter, ein Tier oder ein Gegenstand einen Menschen getötet hatte (LegDrSol F 32; die Quellenbelege zum Prytaneion sind zusammengestellt in Wycherley [1957] 166–174 Nr. 541–571; Boegehold [1995] 148–150).

14 IG I^3 104 Z. 11–13 (LegDrSol F 2).

Tötungsdelikte im Zusammenhang mit dem Tyrannisversuch Kylons entscheiden.[15] Obwohl durch Drakons Gesetz die Zahl der über das Urteil Entscheidenden von einigen wenigen im Prytaneion auf einundfünfzig erhöht worden war, trat in Athen keine Ruhe ein. So sah sich Solon gezwungen, diejenigen, denen die Schuld an den Tötungen gegeben wurde, dazu zu bringen, sich einem Gericht aus dreihundert Athenern zu stellen, in einer Art erneuter *éphesis*.[16] Meiner Ansicht nach war dies die Geburtsstunde des Areopags, denn es wird kein Zufall sein, dass dieser Gerichtshof am Fuß des *áreios págos* zusammentrat, also unmittelbar an der Stelle, an denen die Belagerer die Kylonanhänger an den Altären der Semnai „abgeschlachtet hatten" (ἀπεσφάγησαν).[17] Mit der Verurteilung, der Verbannung und der Verfluchung der Täter trat endlich Ruhe ein – und Solon nahm dies zum Anlass, so möchte ich behaupten, das erneut vergrößerte Gericht als Gerichtshof für Tötungen und Tyrannisversuche auf Dauer zu stellen, indem er die Form der Klage, die *eisangelía*, regelte.[18] Für die Tatsache, dass das von Solon einberufene Gericht auf den immer noch schwelenden Konflikt um den Tyrannisversuch Kylons und die Tötung seiner Anhänger bezogen war, spricht, dass Plutarch angibt, die *noch lebenden* Angeklagten hätten nach der Verurteilung das Land verlassen müssen, die Leichname *der bereits verstorbenen Schuldigen* wären aus den Gräbern geholt und über die Grenzen geworfen worden. Es waren also bereits etliche Jahre zwischen den Taten und dem von Solon eingerichteten Verfahren vergangen.

Plutarch selbst verweist darauf, dass „die meisten Autoren" angeben, Solon habe den Areopag eingerichtet, und in der Tat spreche die Satzung Drakons nirgends von Areopagiten.[19] Auch im Zusammenhang mit dem Tyrannisversuch Kylons ist der Areopag in keiner Quelle belegt. Plutarch wendet indes ein, dass Solons Amnestiegesetz die vom Areopag verurteilten Täter von einer Amnestie ausnahm, was doch eine frühere Entstehung des Areopags belege. Doch Plutarchs Schlussfolgerung ist keineswegs zwingend, wenn man davon ausgeht, dass Solon erst wenige Jahre vor seiner Gesetzgebung erstmals ein Gericht von 300 Athenern eingesetzt hat.[20]

---

15 Zur *éphesis* LegDrSol F 65; Pelloso (2016); Dreher (2016).

16 Plut. Solon 12,2–4.

17 Vgl. dazu auch Valdéz Guía (2022) 294.

18 LegDrSol F 44 (Aristot. Ath. pol. 8,4; Plut. Comparatio Solonis et Poplicolae 25(2),4).

19 Plut. Solon 19,3.

20 Von der Einrichtung des Areopags durch Solon geht auch Cicero (de off. 1,22 [75]) aus. In der *Athenaion politeia* (3,6; 8,2 und 8,4; vgl. 4,4) und in Aristoteles' *Politik* (2,12, 1273b 35–1274a 7) wird von einem höheren Alter des Areopags ausgegangen. Robert Wallace hat überzeugend nachgewiesen, dass die Aussagen in Ath. pol. 3,6 auf Grundlage von Ath. pol. 8,4 in frühere Zeit zurückprojiziert seien und Aristoteles deswegen von einer früheren Entstehung ausgehe, weil im späten 4. Jh. der Areopag als Institution einer vordemokratischen Ordnung galt, die sich mit dem vermeintlichen Begründer der Demokratie, Solon, nicht vereinbaren lasse (Wallace [2014] insbes. 202 f.). Er plädiert dafür, dass erst Solon dem Areopag wichtige politische Funktionen gab,

Eine sukzessive Einsetzung von Gerichtshöfen mit jeweils höherer Zahl von Urteilenden, durch die die Akzeptanz der Urteile erhöht werden sollte, lässt sich zudem aus einem Fragment des Androtion und Philochoros ableiten:[21]

> „Man muss verstehen, dass es nicht jedem – wie ich vorher schon gesagt habe – möglich war, dem Rat auf dem Areopag anzugehören, sondern nur denen unter den Athenern, die durch Geburt (*génos*), Reichtum (*ploútos*) und Lebensführung (*bíos chrēstós*) hervorragten; und die, die auf solche Weise hervorstachen, berieten gewöhnlich im Areopagrat. Aus den neun in Athen ins Amt eingesetzten Archonten nämlich sollen die Areopagiten als Richter (*dikastaí*) zusammentreten, wie Androtion im zweiten [Buch] der *Athenischen Geschichten* (*Atthides*) sagt. Später bestand der Rat vom Areopag aus mehr Personen, dies sind die aus hervorragenden Männern bestehenden Einundfünfzig, ausschließlich aus Eupatriden, wie wir [bereits] gesagt haben, die sich durch Reichtum (*ploútos*) und anständige Lebensführung (*bíos sṓphrōn*) auszeichneten, wie Philochoros im dritten [Buch] seiner *Athenischen Geschichten* (*Atthides*) berichtet."

Androtions und Philochoros' Äußerungen sind wahrscheinlich auf die Entstehung des Areopags zu beziehen, genauer gesagt auf eine Entwicklung, die zur Einrichtung des Areopags als Gerichtshof führte: zunächst die neun Archonten, dann die einundfünfzig Epheten, schließlich der Areopag.

Das hier entworfene Modell lässt sich in mehreren Thesen zusammenfassen. Erstens: Das Amnestiegesetz Solons nimmt mit seinen Ausnahmen unmittelbar Bezug auf frühere Rechtsverfahren: Denn wie in Drakons Satzung ist im Amnestiegesetz von *basileís* im Plural die Rede; die Angeklagten waren „von/unter den *basileís* abgeurteilt worden" (καταδικασθέντες ὑπὸ τῶν βασιλέων) – womit auf das δ]ι|κάζεν δὲ τὸς βασιλέας in der Inschrift verwiesen ist –,[22] und die Abgeurteilten waren durch das vom Areopag, dem Ephetengericht oder dem Prytaneion ausge-

---

er als Institution aber bereits bestand: „I argued that before Solon the Areopagos was primarily a site especially for homicide trials, at a shrine of the Semnai, as most ancient sources and (before 1891) most scholars thought" (ebd. 203).

21 Androtion FgrH 324 F 4a und Philochoros FgrH 328 F 20b (aus: Maximus Confessor, Prolog des Kommentars zu Ps.-Dionysius Areopagita [Migne, Patrologia Graeca 4 p. 16]). Erwähnt ist der Areopag auch in Androtion FgrH 324 F 3 und Philochoros FgrH 328 F 20a.

22 Vgl. IG I³ 104 Z. 11–13: δ]ι|κάζεν δὲ τὸς βασιλέας αἴτ̣ιο[ν] φόν̣[ο] ἒ[ναι ἒ χειρὶ ἀράμενον] ἒ [β]ολ|εύσαντα· τὸς δὲ ἐφέτας διαγν[ο̃]ν̣[α]ι̣. Hinsichtlich des ungewöhnlichen Plurals *basileís* in IG I³ 104 sei auch auf den Rat von *basileís* in Mytilene verwiesen (Theophrast, *Über die Verträge* – Περὶ συμβολαίων bei Stob. flor. 44,20 [IV 2,20 Hense/Wachsmuth]; fr. 97 Wimmer): Einige Gesetzgeber hätten bei einem Kauf angeordnet, dass er unter Heroldsruf und mehrere Tage vorher zu erfolgen habe, andere, dass er vor einer Behörde (*archḗ*) geschehe, z. B. Pittakos „vor den *basileís* und dem *prýtanis*". Die *basileís* bildeten offenbar einen Rat unter Leitung eines Vorstehers. Zu den *basilē̃es* in den Epen Hesiods Tandy (2018) 52 f. (zu Threophrast über Pittakos und Plut. quaest. Graec. [mor. 291f–292a] ebd. 53 mit Anm. 19).

sprochenen Urteil aus Attika verbannt worden. Erst das Prytaneion, dann die Epheten, schließlich der Areopag urteilten über „Tötung (*phónos*), Abschlachtung [an den Altären] (*sphagaí*) und *tyrannís*“. Dies bedeutet zweitens, dass erst durch Drakons Satzung ein Ephetengericht eingerichtet wurde, wobei die Epheten wahrscheinlich aus vornehmen Athenern ausgewählt waren, und schließlich Solon die Zahl der Urteilenden noch einmal deutlich erhöht und das Verfahren gegen die Megaklesanhänger zum Anlass genommen hat, am Fuß des *áreios págos*, unmittelbar neben dem Heiligtum der Semnai, einen *ständigen* Gerichtshof zu etablieren. Der Areopag war kein beratender Adelsrat, sondern stets „nur“ ein Gerichtshof, der zunächst über Tyrannis und das Abschlachten der Kylonanhänger an den Altären, bald danach auch über die Prüfung von Kandidaten für ein Amt sowie über Amtsvergehen urteilte.[23] Da er Rechenschaft von den Amtsträgern verlangen konnte, war der Areopagrat „Wächter über die *politeía*“.[24]

Ich stimme mit Werner Riess darin überein, dass es Drakon und Solon vor allem um eine breitere Fundierung und höhere Akzeptanz von Gerichtsurteilen ging, die das konfliktträchtige und oft gewaltsame Agieren von Aristokraten in die Schranken weisen sollten. Da Megakles und seine Mitarchonten unmittelbar in die Tötung und „Abschlachtung“ der Kylonanhänger involviert waren, konnte ein Gericht aus neun Archonten schlechterdings nicht über deren Schuld befinden. Drakon setzte daher einundfünfzig Epheten und die *basileís* als die Eide formulierenden, aber wohl auch das Verfahren leitenden und vielleicht auch das Urteil verkündenden Verantwortlichen ein. Solon ging diesen Weg mit der Einrichtung des Areopags, also einer erneuten Vergrößerung der Zahl der Urteilenden, noch einen Schritt weiter. In diesem Licht gesehen waren Drakon und Solon zweifelsohne „Aussöhner“ (*diallaktaí*) und „Schlichter“ (*aisymnē̃tai*).

Ausgehend von der hier vorgelegten Rekonstruktion der Ereignisse, die zur Entstehung des Areopags geführt haben, kann eine weitere Hypothese angeschlossen werden, nämlich ob nicht der Areopag aus der Ratsversammlung, der *boulḗ*, gebildet wurde. Wenn das Volksgericht ((*h*)*ēliaía*), das ebenfalls von Solon eingerichtet worden sein soll, mit der Volksversammlung identisch war, wie vielfach angenommen wird, so könnte dies in analoger Form auch für den Rat gelten. So wie das Volk als *ekklēsía* oder – was für die Zeit Solons angemessener scheint – als *agorá* eine beschließende politische, als (*h*)*ēliaía* hingegen eine rechtsprechende Institution war, so könnte die *boulḗ* als beratende politische und pro-

[23] Da häufig nicht eindeutig zu entscheiden war, ob eine mächtige Gruppe von Adeligen tatsächlich eine Tyrannis errichten wollte oder nicht, hat Solon Abstimmungen darüber dem neu errichteten Rat am *áreios págos* übertragen und die Areopagiten durch das Stasisgesetz verpflichtet, mit einem Votum an der Abstimmung teilzunehmen (dazu LegDrSol F 46; Schmitz [2013]; vgl. auch Grote [2017]). Zur Prüfung der Amtsfähigkeit und zur Rechenschaftspflicht siehe LegDrSol F 48–59.

[24] Aristot. Ath. pol. 8,4; Plut. Solon 19,2: ἐπίσκοπος πάντων καὶ φύλαξ τῶν νόμων. Vgl. Ath. pol. 4,4.

bouleutische Institution im Ratsgebäude auf der Agora, als rechtsprechende Institution hingegen am Fuß des *áreios págos* (und in religiöser Funktion nach den Mysterienfeiern im Eleusinion[25]) zusammengetreten sein.[26]

Wenn Solon den nach wie vor schwelenden Konflikt und den gegen die Anhängerschaft des Megakles gerichteten Vorwurf eines schweren sakralen Vergehens durch ein erneut vergrößertes Gericht entscheiden lassen wollte, lag es nahe, statt der einundfünfzig Epheten die gesamte Ratsversammlung (eventuell mit Ausnahme der Mitglieder jener Phyle, der die Megaklesanhänger angehörten) als urteilende Instanz einzusetzen, die zu diesem Zweck nicht auf der Agora, dem üblichen Ort ihrer Zusammenkunft, sondern neben dem Heiligtum der Semnai als Ort des Geschehens zusammentreten sollte. Dies würde erklären, warum der Areopag als Gerichtshof den Namen „der Rat der Areopagiten" oder „der Rat vom Areopag" (ἡ τῶν Ἀρεοπαγιτῶν βουλή oder ἡ ἐξ Ἀρείου πάγου βουλή)[27] trug und warum der Rat der 400 für die Zeit Solons nur sehr selten und dann in unmittelbarem Zusammenhang mit dem Areopag genannt wird.[28] Dafür dass die Mitglieder des Rats der 400 und des Areopags in archaischer Zeit identisch waren, könnte schließlich der Eid ein Indiz sein, der in Demosth. or. 24,144–148 als Ratseid auszugsweise überliefert ist.[29] Weil der von Demosthenes dem Gesetzgeber Solon zugeschriebene „Ratseid" (*hórkos bouleutikós*) sich auch auf Rechtsverfahren bezieht, auf Anzeige, Abführung und die Stellung von Bürgen aus derselben Schatzungsklasse, auf die Fesselung „in das Holz", auf Landesverrat und die Auflösung der Verfassung, ist gut vorstellbar, dass der Eid von den Bouleuten geschworen werden musste, die im Rat der Vierhundert als politische und im Areopag als urteilende Instanz tätig waren.[30] Mit der Entmachtung des Areopags

---

[25] Andok. 1,111 (LegDrSol F 86).

[26] Vgl. Leão/Rhodes (2015) 39. Stephen Todd geht davon aus, dass es sich bei der *(h)ēliaía* um eine Volksversammlung in Ausübung rechtsprechender Tätigkeit handelt (Todd [2007] 680); Raphael Sealey hingegen sieht in der *(h)ēliaía* einen speziellen Gerichtshof (1983). Die Teilnahme an der *(h)ēliaía* war indes an ein Alter von 30 Jahren gebunden. Zur Frage, ob es bereits in der Zeit Solons einen probouleutischen Rat gegeben hat, Valdéz Guía (2022) 294 mit Anm. 1. Zur Bezeichnung *agorá* für die Volksversammlung im archaischen Athen LegDrSol F 91b (Lykurg, Leokr. 5 und fr. 77 Conomis; Aischin. leg. 148) und S. 356 f.

[27] In der Form ἡ ἐξ Ἀρείου πάγου βουλή häufig bei den attischen Rednern und Plutarch (z. B. Solon 19,3; 19,5; 22,3), in der Form ἡ τῶν Ἀρεοπαγιτῶν βουλὴ in Aristot. Ath. pol. 3,6; 8,4 und 26,1.

[28] Aristot. Ath. pol. 8,4; Plut. Solon 19; vgl. 25,2. Darüber hinaus ist der Rat in Diog. Laert. 1,49 (in der Zeit des Peisistratos) und im Konflikt zwischen Isagoras und Kleisthenes (Hdt. 5,72,2; Aristot. Ath. pol. 20,3) genannt.

[29] Auch Miriam A. Valdéz Guía zieht den Bouleuteneid als Indiz heran, setzt aber nicht den Areopag mit dem Rat der Vierhundert gleich, sondern die *(h)ēliaía* ([2022] bes. 297 f.).

[30] Deshalb enthielt der Eid die Klausel, die bestehenden Gesetze zu wahren (Plut. Solon 25,3; Xen. mem. 1,1,18) und als Ratsmitglied dem Volk der Athener am besten Rat zu

werden diese Kompetenzen (mit Ausnahme der Urteile über Tötungsdelikte) an den von Kleisthenes 508/7 v. Chr. ganz neu zusammengesetzten Rat der Fünfhundert übergegangen sein, bis auch dessen Kompetenz zu strafen später eingeschränkt wurde. Der Eid wurde wahrscheinlich in entsprechender Weise angepasst.[31]

winfried.schmitz@uni-bonn.de

LITERATUR

LegDrSol –Winfried Schmitz (unter Mitarbeit von Anja Dorn und Tino Shahin), Leges Draconis et Solonis (LegDrSol). Eine neue Edition der Gesetze Drakons und Solons mit Übersetzung und historischer Einordnung, 2 Bde. (Historia Einzelschriften 270), Stuttgart 2023.

Boegehold (1995): Alan L. Boegehold, The Lawcourts at Athens. Sites, Buildings, Equipment, Procedure, and Testimonia (The Athenian Agora 28), Princeton N.J. 1995, 148–150.

Dreher (2016): Martin Dreher, Jenseits von Berufung und Überweisung. Antwort auf Carlo Pelloso, in: Symposion 2015. Vorträge zur griechischen und hellenistischen Rechtsgeschichte (Coimbra, 1.–4. September 2015), hrsg. von Delfim F. Leão, Gerhard Thür, Wien 2016, 49–53.

Grote (2017): Oliver Grote, Das Stasisgesetz des Solon – ein Gesetz für die ganze Polis, in: MH 74 (2017) 129–143.

Harris (2016): Edward M. Harris, The Nature of Self-Defense in Draco's Homicide Law: The Restauration of *IG* I^3 104, Lines 33–35, in: Hyperboreus 22 (2016) 203–216.

Leão/Rhodes (2015): Delfim F. Leão & P. J. Rhodes, The Laws of Solon. A New Edition with Introduction, Translation and Commentary, London – New York 2015.

---

geben (Lys. 31,1; Ps.-Demosth. or. 59,4; dazu Rhodes 1972, 195), aber auch die Klausel, keinen Bürger zu binden, wenn er Bürgen stellt, mit Ausnahme derer, die Hoch- und Landesverrat begangen oder öffentliche Gelder unterschlagen hatten. In Aristot. Ath. pol. 1 ist belegt, dass in dem auf Veranlassung Myrons durchgeführten Rechtsverfahren gegen diejenigen, die sich der Tötung und des „Abschlachtens" der Kylonanhänger schuldig gemacht hatten, die dreihundert zu Richtern bestimmten Athener einen Eid abgelegt hätten. In Antiph. 5,17 führt der Angeklagte in einem Tötungsprozess an, er sei entgegen den Gesetzen gefesselt worden; es sei ihm nicht gestattet worden, drei Bürgen zu stellen, wie das Gesetz es zulasse.

31 Delfim F. Leão und P. J. Rhodes gehen davon aus, dass der Rat der Fünfhundert erst mit den Reformen des Ephialtes jurisdiktionelle Kompetenzen erhalten habe. Wenn nach Ath. pol. 45,1 der Rat bereits „früher die Befugnis hatte, Geldstrafen zu verhängen, Personen in Fesseln zu legen und zu töten", sei dies ein sachlicher Fehler (Rhodes [1972] 194; Leão/Rhodes [2015] 156); vgl. Rhodes (1972) 190–199; dagegen Valdéz Guía (2022) 299–301.

Pelloso (2016): Carlo Pelloso, Ἔφεσις εἰς τὸ δικαστήριον. Remarks and Speculations on the Legal Nature of the Solonian Reform, in: Symposion 2015. Vorträge zur griechischen und hellenistischen Rechtsgeschichte (Coimbra, 1.–4. September 2015), hrsg. von Delfim F. Leão, Gerhard Thür, Wien 2016, 33–48.

Rhodes (1972): P. J. Rhodes, The Athenian Boule, Oxford 1972 (^{2}1985).

Scheer (2000): Tanja Scheer, Die Gottheit und ihr Bild. Untersuchungen zur Funktion griechischer Kultbilder in Religion und Politik, München 2000.

Schmitz (2013): Winfried Schmitz, Den politischen Konflikt durch Abstimmung entscheiden. Solons Stasisgesetz und die Mehrheitsentscheidung im Areopag, in: Egon Flaig (Hrsg.), Genesis und Dynamiken der Mehrheitsentscheidung, München 2013, 79–99.

Schmitz (2022): Winfried Schmitz, Led away into slave-like dependency. Noxal liability in archaic Athens and Solon's *seisáchtheia*, in: AncSoc 52 (2022) 1–33.

Sealey (1983): Raphael Sealey, The Athenian Courts for Homicide, in: CPh 78 (1983) 294–296.

Tandy (2018): David W. Tandy, In Hesiod's World, in: A. Loney & S. Scully (Hrsg.), Oxford Handbook of Hesiod, Oxford 2018, 43–60.

Todd (2007): Stephen C. Todd, A Commentary on Lysias, Speeches 1–11, Oxford 2007.

Valdés Guía (2022): Miriam A. Valdés Guía, The Solonian Council of 400 and the *Heliaea* in Light of *IG* I^{3} 105, in: Hormos. Ricerche di Storia Antica n.s. 14 (2022) 293–306.

Wallace (2014): Robert Wallace, Greek Oligarchy, and the pre-Solonian Areopagos Council in [Aristotle] *Ath. Pol.* 2.2–8.4, in: Polis 31 (2014) 191–205.

Wycherley (1957): R. E. Wycherley, Literary and Epigraphical Testimonia (The Athenian Agora 3), Princeton N.J. 1957.

MARTIN DREHER (MAGDEBURG)

WANN UND WIE WURDEN ALTGRIECHISCHE GESETZE UNGÜLTIG?

Abstract: Anhand von Material überwiegend aus der archaischen und klassischen Zeit werden folgende Themenbereiche behandelt: Die Unveränderlichkeit der Gesetze (I), Die Veränderbarkeit der Gesetze (II), Die (aktive) Außerkraftsetzung von Gesetzen (III), Das (passive) Außerkrafttreten von Gesetzen (IV), Die Formen des Geltungswegfalls (V).

Schlagwörter: Nomothesie; Aufhebung, Annullierung, Zerstörung, Obsoletwerden von Gesetzen.

Die Entstehung von Gesetzen, ihre Konzeption, ihre Formen und ihre Verabschiedung durch gesetzgebende Gremien haben für alle historischen Zeiträume ein reges Forschungsinteresse gefunden. Das Gegenteil gilt für die hier aufgeworfene Frage, auf welche Weise Gesetze ihr Ende gefunden haben, also ungültig wurden.[1] Das relativ geringe wissenschaftliche Interesse an diesem Thema erstreckt sich ebenfalls auf alle historischen Zeiträume, einschließlich der Gegenwart, und mag verschiedene Gründe haben, nicht zuletzt die Einstellung, dass man sich mit Vorschriften, die wegfallen, nicht näher befassen muss, und dass ein solcher Wegfall, als *fait accompli*, ein relativ banaler Vorgang ist, den man nicht weiter aufschlüsseln muss. Für die Zeit der griechischen Poleis, auf die wir uns hier konzentrieren, kommt der Umstand hinzu, dass auch die Zeitgenossen kaum Nachrichten über das Ungültigwerden von Gesetzen hinterlassen haben, sicherlich auch deshalb, weil ihnen die entsprechenden Vorgänge selbstverständlich erschienen und daher kaum thematisiert wurden.

Diese Quellenlage spiegelt sich verständlicherweise in der modernen Forschung wider, die sich ebenfalls intensiv mit dem Zustandekommen der politisch bedeutsamen Gesetzgebung beschäftigt, aber das Ende von deren Geltungsdauer allenfalls

[1] Die schriftliche Ausarbeitung des Vortrags konnte wegen Überlänge nicht vollständig in diesen Tagungsband aufgenommen werden. Eine ausführliche Version ist daher in der Zeitschrift Dike 25, 2002, 7–76 unter dem Titel: „Das Ungültigwerden von Gesetzen in den griechischen Poleis“ erschienen. Die vorliegende Version hingegen bleibt trotz einiger Erweiterungen insgesamt enger am mündlichen Vortrag. Alle Daten beziehen sich, sofern nicht anders angegeben, auf die Zeit vor Christus.

in Nebenbemerkungen anspricht, es jedoch meines Wissens kaum jemals als eigenständiges Thema behandelt hat.[2]

Aus Gründen des Umfangs beschränkt sich die vorliegende Studie auf die Kategorie der Gesetze, zieht in seltenen Fällen auch die in mancher Hinsicht ähnlichen Dekrete heran, lässt jedoch weitere Rechtsvorschriften wie etwa Kultregelungen einzelner Heiligtümer ausser Acht.[3] Die soeben vorausgesetzte Unterscheidung zwischen Gesetzen (*nomoi*) und Dekreten (*psephismata*) haben die Athener am Ende des 5. Jahrhunderts v. Chr. getroffen, indem sie Gesetze als überpersönliche, allgemeine und dauerhaft geltende staatliche Vorschriften von Einzel-Vorschriften unterschieden, die auf eine konkrete Situation oder einen konkret benannten Adressaten bezogen sind und mit dem Ende dieser Situation nichtig werden. Nur die Vorschriften der erstgenannten Kategorie, die allgemeinen Normen, sollen hier ‚Gesetze' genannt werden, obwohl der Begriff sowohl in der heutigen Sprache als auch in der entsprechenden griechischen Terminologie meist weniger präzise verwendet wird.[4] Denn die bekannten griechischen Termini *nomos*, *thesmos* und *psephisma* werden in vielen Zusammenhängen bedeutungsgleich verwendet und können daher grundsätzlich mit ‚Gesetz' übersetzt werden. Nicht berücksichtigt werden auch die sogenannten ‚ungeschriebenen' (*agraphoi*) oder ‚göttlichen' Gesetze, da sie nicht dem Bereich des staatlichen Rechts angehören. Das Quellenmaterial wird weitgehend der archaischen und der klassischen Epoche (7. bis 4. Jahrhundert v. Chr.) und nur ausnahmsweise der hellenistischen Zeit, in der sich die politischen Rahmenbedingungen geändert haben, entnommen.

---

2 Thematisch einschlägig, aber sehr überblicksartig ist Dimopoulou 2014. Einige Gesichtspunkte thematisiert Camassa 2011, beschränkt sich aber meist auf die Vorstellung von Quellenbeispielen. Am meisten zu dem Thema beigetragen hat bisher Mirko Canevaro, an dessen Publikationen ich daher in vieler Hinsicht anknüpfe. Ich danke ihm und Michele Faraguna sehr für die Zusendung einschlägiger Publikationen, sowie Alberto Maffi, Andreas Mehl und Gerhard Thür für gute Ratschläge bei der Festlegung des Themas. Hinweise auf zeitgenössisches Recht verdanke ich Meinrad Dreher, Lorenzo Gagliardi und Thomas Langheinrich.

3 Die „invalidity" und „invalidation" mehrerer Kategorien von Rechtsvorschriften, vor allem aber privater Rechtsakte behandelt Dimopoulou 2014.

4 Vgl. z. B. Rhodes 1987, 7. Das Corpus „Inschriftliche Gesetzestexte der frühen griechischen Polis" von R. Koerner befasst sich nicht ausdrücklich mit der Definition des Gesetzesbegriffs, vielleicht weil es dem Verfasser einfach nicht mehr vergönnt war, das Werk selbst herauszugeben und mit einer entsprechenden Einleitung zu versehen. In Kommentaren zu einzelnen Dokumenten wird jedoch als Kriterium für ein Gesetz das Bestehen einer überpersönlichen Regelung angedeutet, z. B. S. 129. Dennoch zeigt Koerners Auswahl der Texte, die vom Herausgeber K. Hallof unverändert übernommen wurde, dass Koerner den Begriff sehr breit auslegte und darunter eher so etwas wie ‚allgemeine Rechtsvorschriften' zu verstehen schien. Das führte unter anderem dazu, dass er solche Vorschriften aus den Dokumenten herauslöste und in seine Sammlung aufnahm. Diese enthält daher Dokumente aller Kategorien, auch solcher, die nicht zu Gesetzen und Dekreten zählen und deshalb in diesem Beitrag nicht behandelt werden.

Die Ausführungen zu dem gewählten Thema stellen die Ausgangsfrage in einen etwas grösseren Kontext, indem vor der engeren Thematik in zwei, im folgenden nur angedeuteten Abschnitten ein Einblick gegeben werden soll, wie die Griechen grundsätzlich zu Veränderungen ihrer Gesetze standen. Einerseits priesen sie die Unveränderlichkeit ihrer Gesetze (Abschnitt I), andererseits trugen sie auch deren Veränderbarkeit Rechnung (Abschnitt II). Im Anschluss daran wird das Ungültigwerden von Gesetzen in weitere zwei Abschnitte aufgeteilt, nämlich die (aktiv betriebene) Ausserkraftsetzung (Abschnitt III) und das (passive) Ausserkrafttreten (Abschnitt IV). In welchen Formen sich der Geltungswegfall von Gesetzen vollzog, wird im letzten, fünften Abschnitt betrachtet (Abschnitt V).

I Die Unveränderlichkeit der Gesetze

Ebenso wenig wie in der modernen Gesetzgebung findet sich in der hier betrachteten Zeit der griechischen Poleis ein Gesetz, das explizit das Ende seiner eigenen Geltungsdauer festlegen würde.[5] Im Gegenteil wird der gesamte Gesetzesbestand einer Polis oft als altüberkommen, ehrwürdig, ja sogar ewig und unveränderlich angesehen.[6] Man schrieb die Einführung dieser Gesetze hochverehrten, manchmal legendären Gesetzgebern zu, die zudem listenreiche Massnahmen zum Schutz vor Gesetzesänderungen getroffen hätten. So sollen sowohl Solon in Athen als auch Lykurg in Sparta nach dem Ende ihrer Gesetzgebungstätigkeit ihre Heimatstadt verlassen und angeordnet haben, dass in ihrer Abwesenheit keine Gesetzesänderungen stattfinden dürfen.[7] Noch in späterer Zeit rühmte man ein Gesetz des Zaleukos oder des Charondas, beides berühmte archaische Gesetzgeber, welches festlegte, „dass derjenige, welcher eine Gesetzesänderung vorschlagen wollte, seinen Nacken in eine Schlinge stecken und darin verharren müsse, bis das Volk über die Gesetzesänderung beschlossen habe; und wenn die Volksversammlung das später geschriebene (Gesetz) annehme, sei der Antragsteller zu befreien, wenn jedoch die Änderung verworfen werde, müsse die Schlinge zugezogen werden und der Mann auf der Stelle sterben.“[8]

Während diese Form der Abschreckung gegen Gesetzesänderungen und -neuerungen allzu grausam und daher legendenhaft anmutet, liegen aus der Zeit, in der unsere Überlieferung zuverlässiger ist, zahlreiche inschriftliche Zeugnisse für

---

5 Zur Gegenwart vgl. Baumeister 1996, 272; ähnlich Winkler 1995, 201; wenige Ausnahmen nennt von Münch 2000, 4. Zur Relativierung der Feststellung über die Antike vgl. die Antwort von Rubinstein auf diesen Beitrag.

6 Vgl. z. B. Boegehold 1997; Thomas 2005, 58. In der Literatur wird verschiedentlich auf die Parallele zur altorientalischen Gesetzgebung hingewiesen, z. B. Camassa 1994, 97ff.; Canevaro 2015, 2ff.

7 Zu Solon Aristot. *Ath. pol.* 7,2; Plut. *Sol.* 25,1. Zu Lykurg Plut. *Lyk.* 29,1ff.

8 So Diod. 12,17,2; weitere Versionen bei Dem. 24,139ff.; Polyb. 12, 16, 6–8.

sogenannte Bestandsklauseln vor, englisch entrenchment clauses, die jegliche Änderung oder Aufhebung des beschlossenen Textes mit Sanktionen bedrohen.[9]

II Die Veränderbarkeit der Gesetze

ist die andere Seite der Medaille. Denn auch die Griechen waren sich darüber bewusst, dass die Unveränderlichkeit ihrer Gesetze aufgrund sich ändernder Umstände, neuer politischer Konstellationen oder zwingender Notwendigkeiten nicht bedingungslos durchgehalten werden konnte. Alle Maßnahmen zum Schutz gegen Gesetzesänderungen implizieren ja bereits die Möglichkeit, dass es zu solchen Änderungen kommen kann. Schon in dem oben referierten sogenannten Revisionsgesetz des Zaleukos oder des Charondas wird durchaus die Möglichkeit eingeräumt, neue Gesetze zu beschließen, nur dass die Sanktion für mögliche Antragsteller bei einem Scheitern drastisch hoch ist.

Auch viele Bestandsklauseln sind nicht als absolute Änderungsverbote konzipiert, sondern begnügen sich damit, mehr oder weniger hohe Hürden für Änderungsmaßnahmen zu errichten. Eine sehr frühe Verfahrensvorschrift, datiert um 500 v. Chr., zur Änderung von Bestimmungen über das Heiligtum in Olympia ist uns aus Elis erhalten: „Von den Gesetzen (γραφέον), die sich auf das Heiligtum beziehen, möge man Verbesserungen durch Streichungen und Zusätze zusammen mit dem Rat der 500 und dem versammelten *damos* beschließen, wobei die Änderungen ohne die Gefahr der Gesetzwidrigkeit (vorgebracht werden sollen). Verändern darf man beim dritten Mal durch Zusatz oder Streichung."[10] Die Eleer gingen also davon aus, dass Änderungen ihrer Bestimmungen nötig werden könnten und akzeptierten sie, sofern sie zu Verbesserungen führten. Diese Möglichkeit galt sicher nicht nur für Gesetze im oben definierten Sinn, sondern umfasste alle Bestimmungen, die schriftlich vorlagen (γραφέον) und von den höchsten politischen Gremien der Polis, Bule und Ekklesia, erlassen worden waren.[11] Dass diese Gremien die gesetzgebenden waren, dürfen wir daraus schließen, dass sie es sind, denen unser Text die Beschlusskompetenz über zukünftige Änderungen zuweist. Beide Gremien hatten sogar, wenn der Text so zu

---

9 IG IV 506 = Koerner 29, Z. 1–4 = Nomima I 100 (Argos Mitte 6. Jh.); IG IX 1^2 3, 609 = ML 13 = Koerner 47 = Nomima I 44, Z. 9–14 (Naupaktos ca. 500); IG V 2, 262 = Koerner 34 = IPArk 8 (mit Anm. 24 S.86), Z. 23 (Mantineia ca. 460?); ML 30 = Koerner 78 = Nomima I 104, Z. 35–41 (Teos um 470); IvOl 16 = Koerner 44 = Nomima I 56, Z. 17–19 (Skillous ca. 450/425); IG V 2, 433 = IPArk 30, Z. 13–15 (Megalopolis 2. H. 2. Jh.). Zur Funktion dieser Bestandsklauseln vgl. grundlegend Lewis 1997; ferner z. B. Harris 2006, 23–25; Dimopoulou 2014, 256ff.; Esu 2021, 158f.

10 IvO 7 = Koerner 43 = Nomima I 109, Z. 3–5 (Übersetzung Koerner). Vgl. Gagarin 2008, 61f.

11 Nicht von dieser Regelung betroffen sind also eher alltägliche Vorschriften, wie sie etwa von einer Priesterschaft über Verhaltensweisen in deren Heiligtum angeordnet wurden.

verstehen ist, dreimal über jeden Änderungsantrag abzustimmen, wodurch leichtfertige Beschlüsse verhindert werden sollten.[12]

Neben solchen Verfahrensvorschriften sind es auch tatsächlich durchgeführte Gesetzesänderungen, die uns eine gewisse gesetzgeberische Flexibilität der griechischen Staaten bezeugen. So sollen bereits die frühesten athenischen Gesetze, die Drakon zugeschrieben wurden, nach etwa eineinviertel Jahrhunderten in größerem Umfang außer Kraft gesetzt worden sein, wie die aristotelische *Athenaion politeia* in Kapitel 7,1 festhält: „Eine Verfassung richtete er (sc. Solon) ein und erließ andere Gesetze; die Gesetze Drakons verwendete man nicht mehr, außer denjenigen über Tötung".[13] In welchem Umfang oder ob überhaupt weitere Gesetze unter dem Namen Drakons vorhanden waren, ist in der Forschung umstritten,[14] aber dass überhaupt Gesetze im vorsolonischen Athen existierten, wird man kaum bezweifeln können.[15] Wenn dem so war, hat Solon sie durch seine eigenen Gesetze ersetzt, und das heißt nichts anderes, als dass die vorsolonischen Gesetze außer dem Tötungsgesetz in Solons Neuordnung des ganzen Staatswesens ausdrücklich außer Kraft gesetzt wurden. Plutarch hat das so verstanden und entsprechend deutlich, mit dem Verb ἀναιρεῖσθαι ausgedrückt .[16] Eine weitere umfassende Gesetzesrevision wurde in Athen 410 v. Chr.nach dem Sturz der vierhundert Oligarchen in Angriff genommen und 403/2 nach der Herrschaft der Dreißig weitergeführt. Ebenso wie in der solonischen Zeit waren es insbesondere Krisen- und Umbruchsituationen, in denen grundlegende Neukonzeptionen des Gesetzesbestandes notwendig wurden.

Aus unseren ersten beiden Abschnitten wird folgendes deutlich: Die griechischen Poleis haben ihre Gesetze „im Prinzip" für unveränderlich und ewig

---

12 So auch IvO ad loc. und Koerner, S. 125f. Andere Interpreten verstehen die Klausel so, dass jede getilgte oder eingefügte Gesetzesbestimmung höchstens dreimal geändert werden könne, so Gagarin 2008, 62. Aber wie soll eine getilgte Bestimmung noch mehrfach geändert werden können? Und gerade wenn Änderungen in größeren zeitlichen Abständen erfolgten, erforderte die entsprechende Dokumentation einen kaum vorstellbaren Dokumentationsaufwand.

13 Πολιτείαν δὲ κατέστησε καὶ νόμους ἔθηκεν ἄλλους, τοῖς δὲ Δράκοντος θεσμοῖς ἐπαύσαντο χρώμενοι πλὴν τῶν φονικῶν.

14 Dazu Rhodes 1981, 110f., mit einigen Literaturverweisen. Rhodes selbst stellt sich auf die Seite derer, die weitere drakontische Gesetze für historisch halten.

15 So auch z. B. Sickinger 1999, 17, der wie viele andere davon ausgeht, dass die Thesmotheten *thesmia* aufgezeichnet hätten.

16 Plut. *Sol.* 17,1: Πρῶτον μὲν οὖν τοὺς Δράκοντος νόμους ἀνεῖλε πλὴν τῶν φονικῶν ἅπαντας, ... Terminologisch könnte man die Formulierung in *Ath. pol.* 7,1 ἐπαύσαντο χρώμενοι als stillschweigende Nichtbeachtung der früheren Gesetze auffassen. Wie jedoch weitere Stellen zeigen, meint das Verb χρῆσθαι nicht nur die faktische Verwendung von Gesetzen, sondern deren normative Geltung: so noch *Ath. pol.* 7,1: ὤμοσαν χρήσεσθαι πάντες (nunmehr die solonischen Gesetze); vgl. And. 1,83. Die ausdrückliche Aufhebung der drakontischen (und späterer) Gesetze bestreitet u. a. Camassa 2011, 126f. mit Verweis auf G. Glotz.

erklärt. Dass das eher ein Ideal als eine unumstößliche Richtschnur war, muss den Griechen bewusst gewesen sein, denn sie haben sich in der Praxis immer wieder neue Gesetze gegeben[17] und dabei auch frühere ersetzt, und sie haben manchmal sogar Verfahrensweisen für Gesetzesänderungen festgelegt. Die Vorstellung von der Unabänderlichkeit der Gesetze ist aber deshalb keineswegs ein reines Ideal geblieben, sondern hat durchaus konkrete Auswirkungen auf die Praxis gehabt. Denn erstens schrieb man neuen Gesetzen ein hohes Alter und die Autorschaft legendärer Gesetzgeber zu, zweitens war man bestrebt, dem Ideal durch möglichst wenige und seltene Gesetzgebungstätigkeit nahezukommen[18] und drittens und vor allem sicherte man die bestehenden Gesetze zu diesem Zweck gegen Änderungen ab und erschwerte die Einführung neuer Gesetze.

III Die Außerkraftsetzung von Gesetzen

In einigen Gesetzestexten wird ein Datum für ihr Inkrafttreten festgelegt, meist der Beginn eines Amtsjahres.[19] Wenn, wie in den allermeisten Fällen, keine solche Bestimmung getroffen wurde, ist davon auszugehen, und so wird es in einem von Demosthenes referierten Gesetz für Athen ausdrücklich festgelegt, dass ein Gesetz am Tag seiner Beschlussfassung in Kraft trat.[20] Umgekehrt legt kein Gesetz fest, zu welchem Datum oder nach welcher Frist es außer Kraft treten würde. Das ist übrigens auch in der heutigen Gesetzgebung kaum jemals der Fall.[21] Aber explizit außer Kraft gesetzt werden konnten Gesetze durchaus. Die verschiedenen Vorgehensweisen sollen im folgenden in vier Punkten systematisiert werden, in die auch die schon bisher genannten Verfahren aufgenommen werden.

1. Eine erste Form von Außerkraftsetzung besteht darin, den Gesamtbestand oder einen zusammenhängenden Teilbestand der Gesetze einer Polis für ungültig zu erklären. Für die Aufhebung fast des gesamten athenischen Gesetzesbestandes steht

---

17 In ähnlichen Worten hat Camassa 2011, 122, das Verhältnis auf den Punkt gebracht: „Ideologia dell'inalterabilità e pratica del mutamento delle leggi". Er verknüpft dieses Verhältnis vielleicht allzu eng mit dem für ihn zentralen Faktor der Schriftlichkeit der Gesetze.

18 Das gilt besonders für die archaische Zeit. Aber auch in der klassischen Zeit finden sich entsprechende Reflexe, wenn die in der Tat gerade in Athen stark intensivierte Gesetzgebung als unkontrolliert und ausufernd kritisiert wird, vgl. z. B. Dem. 20,91: „Denn damals (sc. zu Solons Zeit) … verwendete man die gültigen Gesetze und gab keine neuen. Aber seit bestimmte Politiker an die Macht kamen und es erreichten, dass sie Gesetze erlassen konnten, wann immer und wie immer sie wollten, gibt es so viele widersprüchliche Gesetze …".

19 Vgl. etwa ML 83 = Koerner 70, Z. 6.

20 Dem. 24,43: κελεύει γὰρ ἕκαστον ἀφ' ἧς ἡμέρας ἐτέθη κύριον εἶναι, πλὴν εἴ τῳ χρόνος προσγέγραπται, … .

21 Vgl. Baumeister 1996, 272. Dazu und zur möglichen befristeten Geltung von Gesetzen in den griechischen Poleis sowie die sogenannten *sunset clauses* vgl. jetzt die Antwort auf diesen Beitrag von Lene Rubinstein im vorliegenden Band.

die bereits oben zitierte Nachricht der aristotelischen *Athenaion politeia* (7,1), dass im Zuge der solonischen Reformen die Gesetze Drakons mit Ausnahme der Tötungsgesetze außer Kraft gesetzt worden seien. Stattdessen erließ Solon eine ganze Reihe von neuen Gesetzen.[22] Für die Aufhebung eines kleineren Teilbestandes von Gesetzen verweise ich auf die Maßnahme der Dreißig während ihrer oligarchischen Herrschaft in Athen im Jahr 404/3. Wiederum in der *Athenaion politeia* heißt es (35,2): „Die Gesetze des Ephialtes und des Archestratos über die Areopagiten entfernten sie vom Areshügel;“.[23] Es waren also diejenigen Gesetze betroffen, die, wie sich aus *Ath. pol.* 25,2 und 27,1 ergibt, Kompetenzen des Areopags auf die demokratischen Institutionen Bule, Ekklesia und Dikasterien übertragen hatten.

Beide genannten Sammel-Aufhebungen sind Ausnahmen, die jeweils in außergewöhnlichen Umbruchsituationen Athens stattgefunden haben. Wie also sah es mit der Aufhebung einzelner Gesetze in „normalen“, friedlichen Zeiten aus?

2. Die bewusste und ausdrückliche Aufhebung eines vollständigen Gesetzes ist in der archaischen und klassischen Zeit kaum bezeugt. Lediglich zwei Regelungen können meines Erachtens dafür angeführt werden: Zum einen ermöglicht ein Gesetz der Opuntier (erstes Viertel 5. Jh.), es selbst „durch die Mehrheit der Tausend Opuntier und die Mehrheit der naupaktischen Siedler“ aufzuheben. Zum anderen erlaubt ein Sakralgesetz des attischen Demos Paiania, seine Vorschriften bei Anwesenheit von (mindestens) 100 Demoten (erneut) zur Abstimmung zu stellen – wobei wir annehmen müssen, dass diese Vorschriften auch widerrufen werden konnten.[24]

Die weiteren Indizien für die hier behandelte Maßnahme sind hingegen mehr oder weniger indirekter Natur und können nur kurz angesprochen werden.

a) Ebenso wie Dekrete, von denen wir es positiv wissen, muss die athenische Ekklesia im 5. Jahrhundert befugt gewesen sein, auch Gesetze mit einfacher Mehrheit aufzuheben, da zwischen beiden Beschlussformen erst nach 403 v. Chr. unterschieden wurde. Diese Möglichkeit müssen wir wohl für die meisten griechischen Poleis gleichermaßen annehmen.

b) Im Rahmen der oligarchischen Umstürze und der Wiederherstellung einer demokratischen Verfassung kam es in Athen mehrfach zur Aufhebung von Gesetzen. Nach der Herrschaft der Vierhundert mussten bei der athenischen Gesetzesüberprüfung ab 410/09 alle Gesetze der Volksversammlung zur Entscheidung darüber vorgelegt werden, ob diese Gesetze weiterhin gültig sein sollten. Die Forschung hat zu Recht angenommen, dass dabei auch Gesetze nicht bestätigt und damit aufgehoben wurden, wenn sie als widersprüchlich zu anderen, überholt oder

---

[22] Aristot. *Ath. pol.* 7,1; Plut. *Sol.* 17,1.

[23] καὶ τούς τ' Ἐφιάλτου καὶ Ἀρχεστράτου νόμους τοὺς περὶ τῶν Ἀρεοπαγιτῶν καθεῖλον ἐξ Ἀρείου πάγου, ... , vgl. Rhodes 1981 ad locum.

[24] IG IX 1^2 3, 718 = Koerner Nr. 49, Z. 38–41; IG I^3 250 = Koerner Nr.18, Z. 11–12.

sonstwie nicht nützlich beurteilt wurden.[25] 404/3 beseitigten die oligarchischen Dreißig einige demokratische Gesetze, wie oben erwähnt; genannt wird in der *Ath. pol.* (35,2) auch die Abschaffung einer solonischen Einzelbestimmung im Testiergesetz. Nach der Beseitigung des oligarchischen Regimes 403 wurde die demokratische Gesetzesüberprüfung wiederaufgenommen und bis 399 fortgesetzt.

c) Auch im 4. Jahrhundert waren die Athener bestrebt, ihre Gesetze durch Überprüfungsverfahren möglichst widerspruchsfrei zu halten. Nach einer Aussage des Aischines (3,38–40) waren die Thesmotheten zu einer jährlichen Überprüfung der Gesetze verpflichtet. Deren aktive Rolle ist seit langem bezweifelt worden, und Carawan hat jüngst sehr ansprechend vorgeschlagen, dass die Thesmotheten nur auf Initiative von einzelnen Bürgern aktiv werden sollten.[26] In beiden Fällen bestand jedenfalls die Möglichkeit, ein beliebiges, auch älteres Gesetz wegen Widersprüchlichkeit mit anderen bestehenden Gesetzen aus dem Bestand zu tilgen.

d) Ein in der demosthenischen Rede gegen Timokrates zitiertes Gesetz besagt, dass ein Gesetz nur von den Nomotheten aufgehoben werden dürfe, und nur, wenn stattdessen ein neues Gesetz eingebracht werde (Dem. 24,33). Die Echtheit des Dokuments ist umstritten, aber seine Übereinstimmung mit anderen demosthenischen Aussagen ist von Maffi gegen Canevaro verteidigt worden.[27] Während dieses Vorgehen den Normalfall einer Nomothesie beschreibt, deutet eine andere Demosthenes-Stelle möglicherweise an, dass die Nomotheten auch nur zur Aufhebung eines bestehenden Gesetzes eingesetzt werden konnten, ohne ein neues Gesetz zu beschließen. In seiner dritten Olynthischen Rede (Dem. 3,10–13) nennt der Redner nämlich als Bedingung für einen Antrag zur Kriegsfinanzierung, dass vorher zwei bestehende Gesetze aufgehoben werden müßten.[28] Ein eigenes, ausdrückliches Verfahren zur Aufhebung von Gesetzen entwickelten die Athener jedoch nicht.

e) Allerdings führten sie nach 403 eine Klage gegen neu beantragte Gesetze ein, wenn diese unzweckmäßig oder schädlich sein sollten, die γραφὴ νόμον μὴ ἐπιτήδειον θεῖναι.[29] Gegen die traditionelle Forschungsmeinung ist, in Kürze schon von Hans-Julius Wolff, dann wieder ausführlicher von Canevaro, überzeugend

---

[25] Lys. 30,2.25; IG I[3] 104 = ML 86 (Tötungsgesetz Drakons), Z. 5–6. Vgl. etwa Bleicken 1995, 591; Canevaro 2015, 26; Canevaro – Harris 2012, 112 mit A. 76 und 124.

[26] Carawan 2020, 28f.

[27] Canevaro 2013, 157, dagegen Maffi 2018, 135f., ohne auszuschließen, dass das Dokument eine spätere Einfügung sein könne.

[28] MacDowell 1975, 72 akzeptiert die Stelle als Beleg dafür, dass ein Gesetz jederzeit durch die Nomotheten aufgehoben werden konnte. Maffi 2018, 125, 133f. bleibt hingegen vorsichtig und belässt es dabei, dass ein solches Vorgehen grundsätzlich nicht vorgesehen sei.

[29] Die bisherigen Behandlungen dieser Klage, z. B. Lipsius 1905, 385–387; Wolff 1970, 28ff.; Hansen 1974, 44; Harris 2018, 109ff., sind oft inkonsistent und zumindest in Teilen überholt, gerade durch die Erkenntnisse von Mirko Canevaro. Dieser hat jedoch keine zusammenhängende Darstellung des Themas vorgelegt.

dargelegt worden, dass die Klage auch erhoben werden konnte, ohne dass ein neues Gesetz an seiner Stelle vorgeschlagen werden musste.[30] Über die Klage wurde von einem Dikasterion entschieden, wobei das neue Gesetz entweder bestätigt oder verworfen wurde.[31] Die demosthenischen Reden 20, Gegen Leptines, und 24, Gegen Timokrates, sind höchstwahrscheinlich genau solche Klagen gegen ein schädliches Gesetz. Vor Einführung der *graphe nomon me epitedeion theinai* konnte im 5. Jahrhundert mit dem Pendant der *graphe paranomon* gegen gesetzwidrige Volksbeschlüsse geklagt werden, bei denen, wie oben erläutert, zwischen Dekreten und Gesetzen nicht unterschieden wurde.[32]

Als Fazit zu diesem Punkt ist zu konstatieren, dass die griechischen Poleis konkrete Regelungen am ehesten zur Verhinderung neuer Gesetze aufstellten. Die Aufhebung bereits länger bestehender Gesetze war wohl ebenfalls grundsätzlich möglich, wurde aber in der Praxis kaum wahrgenommen, nicht zuletzt, weil das Ideal von deren Unveränderlichkeit die Menschen von Aufhebungs-Initiativen abgehalten haben dürfte.

3. Eine andere Perspektive liegt einem Verfahren zugrunde, das die athenische Gesetzgebung nach der Wiederherstellung der Demokratie 403/2 auf eine neue Basis stellte, die Nomothesie. Im Unterschied zu den bisher betrachteten Möglichkeiten der Gesetzesannullierung hatte die Nomothesie den vorrangigen Zweck, neue gesetzliche Vorschriften demokratisch legitimiert einführen zu können. Für unseren Zusammenhang ist jedoch bedeutsam, dass das Verfahren vorschreibt, dass vor der Verabschiedung eines neuen Gesetzes durch die Nomotheten alle bisher bestehenden widersprechenden Gesetz aufgehoben werden müßten.[33] Nach Canevaro mußte der Antragsteller des neuen Gesetzes dazu eine Klage, wiederum die *graphe nomon me epitedeion theinai*, erheben und ein Dikasterion konnte die beklagten Gesetze, die durch eigens gewählte *synegoroi* verteidigt wurden, aufheben. Wahrscheinlicher erscheint mir jedoch die traditionelle Annahme, nach der für die Aufhebung widersprechender Gesetze die Nomotheten selbst zuständig waren.[34]

---

30 Wolff 1970, 35f., Canevaro 2016, 43ff. 55.

31 Aristot. *Ath. pol.* 59,2.

32 Eine konkrete Klage ist aber erstmals für das Jahr 415 bezeugt: And. 117. 22. Vgl. Wolff 1970, 15ff. 47f.; MacDowell 1962, 76f. Klagen gegen ein Gesetz im engeren Sinn sind aus dem 5. Jahrhundert nicht überliefert.

33 Zentraler Beleg ist die Aussage bei Dem. 24,34: οὐκ ἐᾷ τοῖς ὑπάρχουσι νόμοις ἐναντίον εἰσφέρειν, ἐὰν μὴ λύσῃ τὸν πρότερον κείμενον. „(Das Gesetz) lässt nicht zu, dass (ein Gesetz) eingeführt wird, welches den geltenden Gesetzen widerspricht, außer wenn das vorher in Kraft befindliche Gesetz aufgehoben wird.“ Vgl. ebd. § 32; Dem. 20, 93.

34 Vgl. Canevaro 2016, 40ff.; die *communis opinio* verteidigt Maffi 2018, 128. 134; vgl. auch o. 2 d).

4. Auch *Teile* von Gesetzen konnten außer Kraft gesetzt werden,[35] und zwar entweder als ersatzlose Streichung oder als Änderung eines Gesetzesbestandteils. Beide Vorgehensweisen sind in einem Gesetz aus Olympia von ca. 500 v. Chr. vorgesehen, das bereits oben zitiert wurde.[36]

Belege für die tatsächliche Umsetzung von Streichungen oder Änderungen von Gesetzesteilen finden sich allerdings selten, obwohl gerade technische Anpassungen zum Beispiel an neue Währungen, an neue Kalender oder an neue Ämter und Gremien zu erwarten wären. Interessant sind jedoch mehrere Passagen im „Codex" von Gortyn, unter deren Text Spuren von weitgehend ausgemeißelter vorheriger Beschriftung sichtbar sind.[37] Wenn der getilgte Text bereits zu dem Gesetzeskonvolut gehörte, was nicht mehr feststellbar ist, dann hat es sich um eine Änderung innerhalb dieser Gesetzessammlung gehandelt. Leider können wir auch nicht wissen, ob der neue Text mit dem ausradierten in einer inhaltlichen Beziehung stand. War das nicht der Fall, dann könnte der getilgte Text ersatzlos gestrichen worden und mit einem davon unabhängigen Text überschrieben worden sein. Gab es den Zusammenhang, dann würde es sich um eine Änderung handeln, also um die Ersetzung einer Bestimmung durch eine neue, die in einem einzigen Beschluss erfolgt ist. Davies sieht dahinter sogar einen kontinuierlichen Verbesserungsprozess, den als Dekodifizierung bezeichnet, wobei er die Änderungen und Zusätze als Konsequenzen aus konkreten Gerichtsverfahren versteht.[38] Auf Bronzeplatten, die oft für Gesetzesaufzeichnungen verwendet wurden, waren solche Überschreibungen allerdings kaum möglich. Alternativ konnten Änderungen und Zusätze an ein bestehendes Gesetz angefügt oder nachträglich aufgestellt werden, wie bei einem *diorthema* auf hellenistischen Papyri.[39]

IV Das Außerkrafttreten von Gesetzen

Konnten Gesetze auch ohne einen Aufhebungsbeschluss außer Kraft treten? In der Forschung ist, ohne dass darüber genauer reflektiert wird, nicht selten davon die Rede, dass Gesetze obsolet werden, veraltet sind, nicht mehr beachtet werden, in

---

[35] Nach Boffo 2021, 587 war die Änderung von einzelnen Gesetzesbestimmungen der Normalfall gegenüber der Revision eines Gesetzesbestandes oder ganzer Einzelgesetze.

[36] IvO 7 = Koerner 43, Z. 3–5, s.o. mit A. 10.

[37] Freundlicher Hinweis von Michele Faraguna; vgl. Faraguna 2011, 10 der John K. Davies 1996, 51f. folgt und auf IC IV 43. 47. 48 verweist. Er selbst scheint eher an eine Art von Obsolet-Werden als an Aufhebungsbeschlüsse zu denken („testi di legge che con tutta evidenza non erano considerati più in vigore"), so auch Faraguna 2021, 121.

[38] Davies 1996, 52. Dabei bleibt noch offen, warum die Regelung in IC IV 81, die durch IC IV 75 ersetzt worden sein müsste, nicht ihrerseits getilgt wurde, wie einige andere Passagen. Bei Dekreten kamen Anpassungen und Änderungen offenbar häufiger vor, vgl. Faraguna 2021, 225f. Die verschiedenen grundsätzlichen Möglichkeiten der Texttilgung und Wiederbeschriftung werden genannt von Culasso Gastaldi 2014a, 1–3.

[39] Boffo in Boffo – Faraguna 2021, 561–2 mit Verweis auf L. Robert. Zu *nomographia* und *diorthosis* im Hellenismus vgl. Sickinger 2008, 109f. und Rubinstein 2008, 113f.

Vergessenheit geraten oder in *abusus* verfallen.[40] Dafür steht die aus dem kanonischen Recht stammende Regel *cessante ratione legis cessat lex ipsa* („wenn der Grund für ein Gesetz wegfällt, fällt auch das Gesetz selbst weg“). Auch nach heute gängiger Lehre besitzt eine Norm keine Geltung mehr, „wenn sie für geänderte Verhältnisse durch keinen vernünftigen Zweck mehr getragen wird“.[41] Rechtstheoretisch ist der Grundsatz jedoch nicht unumstritten.

Würden wir also etwa das drakontische Tötungsgesetz als in klassischer Zeit veraltet und unanwendbar bezeichnen, wenn wir nur die ursprünglichen *axones* und nicht die Wiederabschrift aus dem Jahr 409/8 v. Chr. als Beweis für seine fortdauernde Gültigkeit besäßen? Waren die kretischen Gesetze aus dem 6. Jahrhundert mit den dort genannten Ämtern und Gremien auch im 5. und 4. Jahrhundert v. Chr., auch in demokratischen Verfassungen, noch in Kraft? Wie lange inschriftlich überlieferte Gesetze gültig waren, können wir kaum je wissen, da uns unbekannt bleibt, bis wann der Textträger öffentlich aufgestellt war. Einen klaren inschriftlichen Beleg dafür, dass ein archaisches Gesetz ohne einen ausdrücklichen Aufhebungsbeschluss obsolet oder ungültig geworden ist, haben wir, soweit ich sehe, nicht.

Bezüglich der literarischen Überlieferung ist vor allem das Beispiel Sparta interessant. Im Rahmen seiner innovativen Überlegungen zum frühen Sparta hat Winfried Schmitz unter anderem die These entwickelt, die meisten Gesetze Lykurgs hätten nur für die freigelassenen Heloten in Messenien nach dessen Eroberung gegolten, „mithin nur für einige Jahre, allenfalls Jahrzehnte nach dem Messenischen Krieg.“[42] Wodurch die Gesetze ungültig geworden sein sollen, sagt Schmitz nicht. Im Widerspruch zu der zitierten Aussage meint Schmitz dann, dass man sich später, im klassischen Sparta, wieder auf diese, im kulturellen Gedächtnis gebliebenen Gesetze im Bedarfsfall habe berufen können, wobei in Vergessenheit geraten sei, dass sie ursprünglich nur für eine bestimmte Bevölkerungsgruppe gegolten hätten. Aus mehreren Gründen kann ich dieser These von Schmitz nicht folgen;[43] vielmehr sollte man weiterhin davon ausgehen, dass – außer der sogenannten großen Rhetra – ein guter Teil dieser von Xenophon und Plutarch beschriebenen Regeln als fiktiv anzusehen ist, und die übrigen keine Gesetz im formalen Sinn, sondern Sitten und Gebräuche waren, die sich im Lauf der Zeit herausgebildet und selbst nicht alle dauerhaft Bestand hatten.

---

40 Vgl. etwa MacDowell 1975, 65; Rhodes 1987, 8; Bleicken 1995, 217; Sickinger 1999, 21.33.194; ders. 2008, 99f.

41 So Baumeister, 1996, 50 (vgl. 43–54). S. 291 verweist er auf eine entsprechende Stellungnahme des deutschen Bundesverwaltungsgerichts. Baumeister selbst hingegen (S. 43.308) vertritt die Gegenposition, dass also also eine Norm weiterhin gültig und rechtlich wirksam, nur eben nicht anwendbar sei.

42 Schmitz 2018, 132; ders. 2021, 162f.

43 S. dazu Dreher 2021 und nunmehr meine Ausführungen im ausführlicheren Beitrag für die Zeitschrift Dike (s. o. A. 1)

Es ist also abschließend festzuhalten, dass das Obsolet-Werden eines Gesetzes im Sinne eines Geltungswegfalls für die griechische Rechtsgeschichte nicht nachweisbar – allerdings auch nicht positiv auszuschließen – ist. Wenn auch die *rechtliche* Wirksamkeit auf diese Weise nicht unbedingt endet, ist in einzelnen Fällen zu vermuten, dass die *faktische* Wirksamkeit aufhörte, indem Gesetze „außer Gebrauch kamen", obwohl sie formal noch in Kraft waren. Die aristotelische *Athenaion politeia* nennt als eine der Verfassungsbestimmungen Solons – die sicher als Gesetze zu denken sind –, dass Angehörige der Thetenklasse kein Amt übernehmen durften. „Deshalb wird auch heute noch keiner, der als Kandidat bei der Auslosung eines Amtes gefragt wird, welcher Klasse er angehöre, die Klasse der Theten angeben" (*Ath. pol.* 7,4). Offenbar war also zur Abfassungszeit der Schrift allgemein akzeptiert, dass ein wahrscheinlich noch bestehendes Gesetz einfach ignoriert wurde.[44] Dieser Befund lässt sich allerdings nicht dahingehend verallgemeinern, dass alte Gesetze leichthin als überholt betrachtet worden wären. Für einen solchen Vorgang ist schon das Kriterium nicht eindeutig bestimmbar. Denn wieviel Zeit muss vergangen sein, damit man von einem veralteten Gesetz sprechen kann? Und vergessen wir nicht, dass für die Griechen das hohe Alter eines Gesetzes dessen Autorität im allgemeinen noch gesteigert hat.

V Die Formen des Geltungswegfalls

Hier ist vor allem die Begrifflichkeit der Quellen in den Blick zu nehmen.[45] Ein Gesetz „gültig machen", in Kraft setzen heißt im allgemeinen κύριον ποεῖν, ein Gesetzen ungültig machen, aufheben, dementsprechend ἄκυρον ποεῖν. Diese Wortgruppe wird vornehmlich in literarischen Texten, namentlich von den athenischen Rednern verwendet,[46] aber oft ist in ihren Texten die Aufhebung von Gesetzen mit dem Verbum λύειν ausgedrückt,[47] das wiederum auch inschriftlich vorkommt.[48] Ein dritter Begriff aus der literarischen Überlieferung ist ἀναιρεῖν, mit dem ebenfalls die Aufhebung von Gesetzen bezeichnet wird.[49] Inschriftlich wiederum wird auch ἀφαιρεῖσθαι verwendet.

[44] Vgl. Rhodes 1981, 146: „Apparantly by the time of A. P. the law which excluded the thetes from all offices had not been repealed but had become a dead letter". So auch Blösel 2014, 73f., gegen Schmitz und andere, nach denen der Ausschluss der Theten von den höheren Ämtern zwischenzeitlich rechtsförmig aufgehoben wurde. Wallace 2012, 120, verweist auf ein weiteres, möglicherweise später nicht mehr beachtetes Gesetz.

[45] Vollständigkeit kann aber nicht angestrebt werden. Diese ist auch bei Rhodes 2019 nicht gegeben, der gleichwohl weitere Beispiele aufführt, auch aus anderen Dokumenten als Gesetzen und Dekreten.

[46] Z.B. And. 1,103; Dem. 20,139; 24,42f.; Aisch. 3,38; Is. 1,21.

[47] Dem. 3,10; 24,33. καταλύειν ist bei Aristot. *Ath. pol.* 35,2 für die Aufhebung von solonischen *thesmoi* durch die Dreißig verwendet.

[48] IG I^3 46 = ML 49, Z.20–25. ἀφαιρεῖσθαι meint auch bei And. 2,24 die Annullierung eines Psephismas. Die mediale Form des Verbs hat die gleiche Bedeutung wie die aktivische.

[49] Aisch. 3,39.40.

In den bisher herangezogenen Zusammenhängen findet die *Form* der Gesetzesaufhebung entweder keine Erwähnung, oder es werden nur die zuständigen Gremien genannt, die das Gesetz per Beschluss aufheben können oder sollen. In anderen Zusammenhängen jedoch beziehen sich teils dieselben, teils ähnliche Verben, wie das Kompositum καθαιρεῖν, auf die *materielle* Vernichtung des betroffenen Dokuments.[50] Damit ist in erster Linie die Zerstörung des Textträgers gemeint, auf dem die Gesetze öffentlich aufgestellt waren. Ein Terminus kann sich auch spezifisch auf metallene Textträger beziehen, etwa wenn dessen Einschmelzen unter Strafe gestellt wird.[51]

Eine frühere, auf Kahrstedt zurückgehende Forschungsmeinung, dass die inschriftlich aufgestellten Dokumente mit der physischen Zerstörung ihrer Träger oder zumindest ihrer Texte ihre Gültigkeit verloren hätten, wurde meines Erachtens spätestens durch die Darlegungen von Michele Faraguna und James Sickinger zum griechischen Archivwesen widerlegt.[52] Die Zerstörung der inschriftlich aufgestellten Gesetze war in erster Linie ein symbolischer Akt, die Manifestation einer vorausgehenden Willensbildung. Das ergibt sich als Umkehrschluss auch aus dem Zeitpunkt der Gültigwerdung von Gesetzen, die eben nicht mit ihrer inschriftlichen Aufzeichnung zusammenfällt. Denn wie von Demosthenes (24,43) formuliert, „treten Gesetze in Kraft, wenn sie verabschiedet werden, nicht wenn sie inschriftlich aufgestellt werden". Entsprechend endet ein Gesetz auch nicht automatisch und allein durch die Entfernung seiner Inschrift.[53]

Wenn aber die Zerstörung der inschriftlichen Kopie nur die öffentlich sichtbare Manifestation der beabsichtigten Gesetzesannullierung ist, so müssen wir uns schließlich noch fragen, was mit den originalen, in Archiven aufbewahrten Dokumenten auf Holz oder Papyrus geschah, wenn ein Gesetz ungültig wurde. Die erste Möglichkeit besteht darin, dass sie wie die inschriftlichen Kopien einfach physisch vernichtet wurden. Dafür könnte sprechen, dass Andokides die Existenz eines Volksbeschlusses behauptet, nach dem alle Psephismata über *atimoi* vernichtet werden sollten, „sowohl sie selbst als auch jegliche Abschrift, wo auch immer sie sich befindet".[54] Dagegen spricht, dass verschiedene politische Beschlüsse nach der

---

[50] And. 1,103; Aristot. *Ath. pol.* 35,2; Philoch. FGrHist 328 F 55; RO 25, Z. 55–56.

[51] So die Formulierung ἐὰν .. συγχέοι („wenn jemand … einschmilzt") in IG IV 506 = Koerner 29, Z. 1–2, aus Argos, 6. Jahrhundert.

[52] Vgl. Sickinger 1999, 64ff. mit weiteren Verweisen; Faraguna 2011, 13; ders. 2015, 4; ders. 2017, 24ff. 207–218. MacDowell 1978, 45 behauptet zwar, dass die auf Holz oder Stein aufgestellten Gesetze „were not merely copies of the laws; they were the laws themselves, the official texts", räumt aber ein, dass wahrscheinlich jeder Archon „may have had an official set of copies of the laws relevant to his office". Nach Rhodes 2019, 146, bildeten nicht die Inschriften, sondern die Papyri in den Archiven die Originale.

[53] Ein größeres Gewicht wird den Stelen als Textträgern beigemessen von Culasso Gastaldi 2014b.

[54] And. 1,76: ἐξαλεῖψαι πάντα τὰ ψηφίσματα, καὶ αὐτὰ καὶ εἴ πού τι ἀντίγραφον ἦν, ... Das Verb muss hier wohl die physische Vernichtung der Dokumente bezeichnen, da etwaige

mutwilligen oder naturbedingten Zerstörung ihrer Inschriftenkopien wieder aufgezeichnet worden sind, was nur mithilfe von Papyrus-Originalen geschehen sein konnte. Auch ist in einer Passage bei Aischines (3,38–40) glaubhaft die Möglichkeit erwähnt, dass sich zwischen den gültigen auch ungültige Gesetze befinden könnten, die man ausfindig machen solle. Auch wenn wir oben daran gezweifelt haben, dass das die Aufgabe der Thesmotheten war, konnte man, wer auch immer, die Ungültigkeit nur daran erkennen, und das ist die zweite, wahrscheinlichere Möglichkeit, dass auf dem Papyrus, oder auf der Holztafel, in Athen durch den Sekretär der Bule beziehungsweise den Staatssklaven im Metroon, ein Vermerk über die Annullierung des Gesetzes angebracht worden war.[55] So blieb der Zugriff auf frühere Gesetze weiterhin möglich und ihr Inhalt konnte bei Bedarf zur Kenntnis genommen werden. Wenn man zumindest tendenziell, auch in der außerathenischen Welt, so verfuhr, dann nicht zuletzt deswegen, weil die Griechen damit ein weiteres Mal ihren großen Respekt vor den „ererbten" Gesetzen bezeugten und dem Ideal von deren dauerhaftem Bestand huldigten, mit dem wir unsere Betrachtungen begonnen haben – auch wenn der Respekt in diesem Fall, wie wir nüchtern konstatieren möchten, „lebenden Leichen" galt.

martin.dreher@ovgu.de

LITERATURVERZEICHNIS

Baumeister, P. 1996: *Das Rechtswidrigwerden von Normen. Eine rechtsdogmatische Untersuchung zu den Grenzen der Wirksamkeit und Anwendbarkeit von Normen – Probleme des Spannungsverhältnisses von Recht und Zeit*, Berlin (Diss. Mannheim 1994).

Bleicken, J. 1995: *Die athenische Demokratie*, 4. Aufl., Paderborn u.a.

Blösel, W. 2014: Zensusgrenzen für die Ämterbekleidung im klassischen Griechenland, in: W. Blösel u.a. (Hrsg.), *Grenzen politischer Partizipation im klassischen Griechenland*, Stuttgart, 71–93.

Kopien nicht im metaphorischen Sinn aufgehoben werden können. Vgl. dazu MacDowell 1962, 113.

55 Nach Boffo in Boffo – Faraguna 2021, 584 musste ein annulliertes Gesetz „in teoria" (nach welcher Doktrin?) physisch vernichtet werden. In der Praxis jedoch sei man verschiedene Wege gegangen und habe das Original manchmal im Archiv belassen, vielleicht an einem besonderen Ort, „in una forma di deposito" (S. 586). Waren nur Teile eines Gesetzes von der Aufhebung betroffen, so kann sich Boffo auch „un semplice segno di cancelleria" in den hellenistischen Archiven vorstellen. Warum aber sollte eine solche Markierung nicht auch an annullierten vollständigen Gesetzen angebracht worden sein?

Boegehold, A.L. 1997: Resistance to Change in the Law at Athens, in: J. Ober – C. Hedrick (Hrsg.), *Demokratia. A Conversation on Democracies, Ancient and Modern*, Princeton, 203–214.

Boffo, L. 2021: Parte seconda – L'età ellenistica, in: L. Boffo – M. Faraguna (Hrsg.), *Le poleis e i loro archivi. Studi su pratiche documentarie, istituzioni e società nell'antichità greca*, Trieste, 370–750.

Camassa, G. 1994: Verschriftung und Veränderung der Gesetze, in: H.-J. Gehrke (Hrsg.), *Rechtskodifizierung und soziale Normen im interkulturellen Vergleich*, Tübingen, 97–111.

Camassa, G. 2011: *Scrittura e mutamento delle leggi nel mondo antico. Dal Vicino Oriente alla Grecia di età arcaica e classica*, Roma.

Canevaro, M. 2013: Nomothesia in Classical Athens: what sources should we believe?, Classical Quarterly 63, 139–60.

Canevaro, M. 2015 (online publication): Making and Changing Laws in Ancient Athens, in: E.M. Harris – M. Canevaro (Hrsg.), *The Oxford Handbook of Ancient Greek Law* (print edition forthcoming), Oxford, 1–50.

Canevaro, M. 2016: The Procedure of Demosthenes' *Against Leptines*: How to Repeal (and Replace) an Existing Law, Journal of Hellenic Studies 136, 39–58.

Canevaro, M. – Harris, E.M. 2012: The Documents in Andocides' On the Mysteries, Classical Quarterly 62, 98–129.

Canevaro, M. – Harris, E.M. 2016/17: The Authenticity of the Documents at Andocides' *On the Mysteries* 77–79 and 83–84, Dike 19/20, 9–49.

Carawan, E. 2020: *Control of the Laws in the Ancient Democracy at Athens*, Baltimore.

Culasso Gastaldi, E. 2014a: "To Destroy the Stele": Epigraphic Reinscription and Historical Revision in Athens, AIO Papers no. 2 (Transl. by C. Dickman-Wilkes; italienischer Originaltext Cahiers Glotz 14, 2003, 241–262).

Culasso Gastaldi, E. 2014b: "To Destroy the Stele", "To Remain Faithful to the Stele": Epigraphic Texts as Guarantee of Political Decision, AIO Papers no. 3 (Transl. by C. Dickman-Wilkes; italienischer Originaltext in: A. Tamis u.a. (Hrsg.), *Philathenaios. Studies in Honour of M.J. Osborne*, Athen 2010, 139–155).

Davies, J.K. 1996: Deconstructing Gortyn: When is a Code a Code?, in: L. Foxhall – A.D.E. Lewis (Hrsg.), *Greek Law in its Political Setting. Justifications not Justice*, Oxford, 33–56.

Dimopoulou, A. 2014: Ἄκυρον ἔστω: Legal Invalidity in Greek Inscriptions, in: M. Gagarin – A. Lanni (Hrsg.), *Symposion 2013*, Wien, 249–275.

Dreher, M. 2021: Die Gesetze Lykurgs und die spartanischen Parthenier. Antwort auf Winfried Schmitz, in: K. Harter-Uibopuu – W. Riess (Hrsg.), *Symposion 2019*, Wien, 175–184.

Dreher, M. 2022: Das Ungültigwerden von Gesetzen in den griechischen Poleis, Dike 25, 7–76.

Esu, A. 2021: *Adeia* in Fifth-Century Athens, Journal of Hellenic Studies 141, 153–178.

Faraguna, M. 2011: Legislazione e scrittura nella Grecia arcaica e classica, Zeitschrift für Papyrologie und Epigraphik 177, 1–20.

Faraguna, M. 2015 (online publication), Archives, Documents, and Legal Practices in the Greek Polis, in: E.M. Harris – M. Canevaro (Hrsg.), *The Oxford Handbook of Ancient Greek Law* (print edition forthcoming), Oxford, 1–20.

Faraguna, M. 2017: Documents, Public Information and the Historian: Perspectives on Fifth-Century Athens, Historika 7, 23–52.

Faraguna, M. 2021: Parte prima – Dall'età arcaica al iv secolo, in: L. Boffo – M. Faraguna (Hrsg.), *Le poleis e i loro archivi. Studi su pratiche documentarie, istituzioni e società nell'antichità greca*, Trieste, 61–367.

Gagarin, M. 2008: *Writing Greek Law*, Cambridge.

Hansen, M.H. 1974: *The Sovereignty of the People's Court in Athens in the Fourth Century B. C. and the Public Action against Unconstitutional Proposals*, Odense.

Harris, E.M. 2006: *Democracy and the Rule of Law in Classical Athens: Essays on Law, Society, and Politics*, Cambridge.

Harris, E. 2018: *Demosthenes, Speeches 23–26*, translated with introduction and notes by E. Harris, Austin.

Hölkeskamp, K.-J. 1999: *Schiedsrichter, Gesetzgeber und Gesetzgebung im archaischen Griechenland*, Stuttgart.

IPArk = Thür, G. – Taueber, H. 1994: *Prozessrechtliche Inschriften der griechischen Poleis: Arkadien*, Wien.

Kahrstedt, U. 1968: Untersuchungen zu athenischen Behörden. II. Die Nomotheten und die Legislative in Athen, in: E. Berneker, *Zur griechischen Rechtsgeschichte*, Darmstadt 1968, 223–262 (ND; Original in: Klio 31, 1938, 1–32).

Koerner = *Inschriftliche Gesetzestexte der frühen griechischen Polis*, aus dem Nachlaß von R. Koerner herausgegeben von K. Hallof, Köln u.a. 1993.

Lewis, D.M. 1997: Entrenchment-Clauses in Attic Decrees, in: D.M. Lewis, *Selected Papers in Greek and Near Eastern History*, ed. by P.J. Rhodes, Cambridge, 136–149.

Lipsius, J.H. 1905: *Das Attische Recht und Rechtsverfahren*, 3 Bde., Leipzig.

Maffi, A. 2018: Rezension von M. Canevaro, *Demostene, Contro Leptine. Introduzione, Traduzione e Commento storico*, Berlin – Boston 2016, Dike 21, 120–137.

ML = Meiggs, R. – Lewis, D. (Hrsg.) 1988: *A Selection of Greek Historical Inscriptions to the End of the Fifth Century B. C.*, Oxford.

MacDowell, D.M. 1962: *Andokides. On the Mysteries, The text edited with introduction, commentary and appendixes*, Oxford.

MacDowell, D.M. 1975: Law-making at Athens in the fourth century B.C., Journal of Hellenic Studies 95, 62–77.

Münch, I. v. 2000: Die Zeit im Recht, Neue Juristische Wochenschrift Heft 1, 1–7.

Nomima I. II = van Effenterre, H. – Ruzé, F. (Hrsg.) 1994–1995: *Nomima. Recueil d'inscriptions politiques et juridiques de l'archaïsme grec*, I–II, Rome.

Rhodes, P.J. 1981: *A Commentary on the Aristotelian Athenaion Politeia*, Oxford (1993 mit select addenda zur Erstauflage).

Rhodes, P.J. 1987: Nomothesia in Classical Athens, in: A. Giuliani – N. Picardi (Hrsg.), *L'educazione giuridica* Vol. 5/2, Perugia, 5–26.

Rhodes, P.J. 2006: The Non-Literary Written Sources, in: K.H. Kinzl (Hrsg.), *A Companion to the Classical Greek World*, Malden – Oxford, 45–63.

Rhodes, P.J. 2019: Erasures in Greek Public Documents, in: A. Petrovic u.a. (Hrsg.), *The Materiality of Text-Placement, Perception, and Presence of Inscribed Texts in Classical Antiquity,* Leiden – Boston, 145–166.

RO = Rhodes, P.J. – Osborne, R. (Hrsg.) 2003: *Greek Historical Inscriptions 404–323 BC*, Oxford.

Rubinstein, L. 2008: Response to James P. Sickinger, in: E. Harris – G. Thür (Hrsg.), *Symposion 2007*, Wien, 113–124.

Schmitz, W. 2018: Lykurgs Gesetz über die Kinderzeugung und seine zweite und dritte Rhetra, Chiron 48, 107–141.

Schmitz, W. 2021: Die Rhetren des Lykurg und die Entstehung des spartanischen Kosmos, in: K. Harter-Uibopuu – W. Riess (Hrsg.), *Symposion 2019*, Wien, 155–174.

Sickinger, J.P. 1999: *Public Records and Archives in Classical Athens*, Chapel Hill – London.

Sickinger, J.P. 2008: Indeterminacy in Greek Law: Statutory Gaps and Conflicts, in: E. Harris – G. Thür (Hrsg.), *Symposion 2007*, Wien, 99–112.

Thomas, R. 2005: Writing, Law, and Written Law, in: M. Gagarin – D. Cohen (Hrsg.), *The Cambridge Companion to Ancient Greek Law*, Cambride, 41–60.

Todd, S.C. 1993: *The Shape of Athenian Law*, Oxford.

Thür, G. 1990: Die Todesstrafe im Blutprozeß Athens, The Journal of Juristic Papyrology 20, 143–156.

Wallace, R.W. 2012: When the Athenians Did Not Enforce Their Laws, in: B. Legras – G. Thür (Hrsg.), *Symposion 2011*, Wien, 115–125.

Winkler, G. 1995: *Zeit und Recht. Kritische Anmerkungen zur Zeitgebundenheit des Rechts und des Rechtsdenkens*, Wien – New York.

Wolff, H.J. 1970: *„Normenkontrolle" und Gesetzesbegriff in der attischen Demokratie*, Heidelberg.

LENE RUBINSTEIN (LONDON)

ABOLITION OF LAWS, CONSTITUTIONAL CHANGE, AND EMERGENCY LEGISLATION: RESPONSE TO MARTIN DREHER

As pointed out by Professor Dreher in his contribution to this volume, along with the expanded version of his paper,[1] the processes with which laws could be repealed is an area that has been relatively under-researched by Greek legal historians, compared to the processes with which laws could be introduced and ratified. This is especially true of the archaic and classical Greek world outside Athens. The issue has received more attention in research on archaic and classical Athens in connection with the abolition and replacement of Drakon's laws in the early 6th century, the reforms of 462 B.C.E. attributed to Ephialtes by the Aristotelian *Athenaion Politeia*,[2] and the episodes of regime change during the last decade of the fifth century. As for the repeal of legislation during periods of internal peace and stability, the scholarly debate has concentrated on the Athenian processes that are attested from the middle of the 350s to 323/2 B.C.E., the period for which the literary evidence is particularly rich.

The present response will focus mainly on the Greek world outside Athens and on the problems that are presented by the epigraphical evidence. Yet, classical Athens will figure in the discussion, too. Much of our reconstruction of Greek legal ideology, which often informs our interpretation of the inscriptions, depends to a significant degree on literary evidence that focusses on Classical Athens. An important question is how far it is safe to extrapolate from the Athenian example to other archaic and classical Greek communities.

The first section will draw attention to some of the limitations and opportunities presented by the epigraphical material currently available. Next, attention will turn to the phenomenon of temporary legislation as one of the ways in which Greek communities might respond to the legal repercussions of fundamental constitutional changes that almost inevitably would affect their administration of justice as well as their legislative procedures. Finally, my response will raise a more general question relating to the proposition that, for the Greeks in the archaic and classical periods, the constancy and immutability of their laws was a shared ideal, even if

1 Dreher (2023).

2 For a recent discussion of their historicity, see Zaccarini (2018).

tempered by the realisation that changing circumstances often called for changes to the community's legislation.

I. The epigraphical evidence for the amendment and abolition of laws.

It is not surprising that it is hard to identify epigraphical evidence for laws which had been repealed, let alone for the process with which the enactment in question had been rendered invalid. A law inscribed on stone obviously has a chance of survival into the 21st century, even after the law itself had been repealed and the published text taken down: the stone may have been broken into relatively large fragments or recycled almost intact as building material. Yet, in cases where legislation was repealed in connection with a radical regime change, more zealous destruction is likely to have been wrought upon the carrier of the text, not least if the legislation related specifically to political institutions and processes.[3] Laws inscribed on bronze could be melted down and thus vanish completely, but if the carrier had been defined as sacred property, the deterrent effect may have made it a preferable option to bury rather than destroy it. As argued by Faraguna and Boffo (2021: 584–587), texts of obsolete enactments may have been preserved in the community's archive even after a drastic change of government, but unless these were revalidated and republished on durable material at a later date or otherwise documented in our literary sources,[4] they will have left no trace in our record.

As noted by Professor Dreher, the many entrenchment clauses occurring in numerous enactment from communities across the Greek world permit the inference *e contrario* that changes and amendments to legislation were indeed envisaged as a possibility.[5] Some of the clauses contain very detailed prohibitions which offers a glimpse of the legislative processes in the community in question, as for example *SEG* 33: 275 from fifth-century Argos (lines 5–10):

> αἴ τ[ις] ἀτελέ τιθείε τὰ γράθματα τὰ [ἐ]ν τᾶι στάλα[ι] γεγραθμένα hό τε λέγον καὶ ho ἀϜρετεύον πασχ[έ]τ]ο hόσσα κα πολεμίονς ἐπάγον ...ατ..Χαλκιόν.

> If anyone renders the letters written on the stele ineffectual, then both the proposer and the presiding official shall suffer the same punishment as the one who invites in a hostile army (?).

Here the reference is clearly to an orderly legislative procedure in a collective decision-making forum, rather than to the unauthorised defacement or outright

---

3 See Faraguna and Boffo (2021: 584).

4 See *e.g.* the examples discussed in Faraguna and Boffo (2021: 226–227).

5 For a survey of 80 entrenchment clauses documented in the non-Athenian epigraphical record from the period between C7 and C2 B.C.E., see Rubinstein (2008: 116–119 with notes 10–17) complemented by the discussion in Harter-Uibopuu (2013).

destruction of the physical carrier of the text. It is likely that, had it not been for the express prohibition in the entrenchment clause, the amendment or even repeal of the enactment would have been entirely lawful, provided the correct procedure was followed.

Such entrenchment clauses are, however, quite few in number, considering the chronological and geographical span of the material predating the Roman period. Of the 80 documents in the survey mentioned above (n. 5), fewer than one in five contains regulations of a general, open-ended nature. By far the majority are measures applying to named individuals or specific groups (which in fourth-century Athens would almost certainly have been classified as decrees) or agreements, treaties or contracts regulating the relationship between two or more parties.[6]

As is well known, the distinction between different types of enactment was blurred in fifth-century Athens. It is probable that other archaic and classical Greek communities likewise did not distinguish clearly between laws and decrees in a hierarchy of norms, let alone differentiate the procedures required for their ratification, amendment and abolition. Even in the fourth century and later, it is difficult to tell if a given Greek community operated with a distinction similar to that made by the Athenians after 403/2 B.C.E., unless there is evidence that positively points in that direction. It is therefore not without risk to use the evidence of the entrenchment clauses as a basis for generalisations *e contrario* on procedures with which established *laws* (as distinguished from decrees) might under normal circumstances be amended or repealed altogether.

For the archaic and early classical period, the problems are compounded by the often ambiguous terminology used in the documents themselves, such as τὰ γράθματα in the Argive example above. Gagarin (2008: 110) notes that in the archaic period "terms like 'writing' (*graphos*, *grammata*) could be used without qualification to designate a written law". Yet the convention of committing treaties to writing is attested at an equally early stage, and it is sometimes difficult for us to tell the two genres apart. *IG* IX, 1^2 718, which regulates the relationship between the East Lokrians and their settlers at Naupaktos,[7] and which is mentioned by Professor Dreher in his discussion, is an example of how ambiguity in terminology could persist even as late as the fifth century. The enactment is referred to (l. 46) as

6 The documents pertaining to foundations (Stiftungen), most of them from C3 or later, belong in a grey area: the founders usually intended their foundations to be lasting and their regulation to be binding on the entire community. Some founders clearly endeavoured to frame their enactments in such a way as to approximate them to *nomoi* as far as possible. See Harter-Uibopuu (2013: 54–57).

7 For a discussion of the relationship between Opous and the rest of the East Lokrians, see Nielsen (2000).

a θέθμιον (rather than θεθμός), which is attested in the sense of 'agreement' in *IG* VII 3172 (C3 B.C.E.).[8]

This is important for the interpretation of lines 38–40 which forbid the cancellation of the enactment without the agreement of both parties.[9] If *IG* IX, 1^2 718 is approached as a treaty rather than a law, the provision may provide an early fifth-century parallel to the amendment clauses that are attested in several other treaties from the later fifth century onwards.[10] The interpretation of the text as a treaty also helps to explain the provision in lines 12-14. This specifies that a renewal by both parties of the sworn commitment to the alliance will be possible thirty years after the ratification of the present enactment.

A later example of an enactment which likewise is difficult to classify generically is *IK Sagalassos I*, 1. As noted by the editors,[11] the enactment is referred to in B 33–34 by the terms *homologiai* and *synthekai*,[12] and everything points to the conclusion that these agreements and treaty arrangement had a direct bearing on a concrete episode of *stasis*. Yet fr. A contains general regulations that appear indistinguishable from what the Athenians in the fourth century would have recognised as a genuine *nomos*. The generic complications are particularly pronounced, however, in B 31–32: *On theft. If anyone steals anything for which the penalty was previously three* mnai, *death shall now be the penalty to be imposed on the person who has been found guilty.*[13] Like the provisions in fr. A, this is a general future-oriented clause, and the editors suggest that the intention was eventually to incorporate it into Sagalassos' existing legislation. What must be noted here is that the provisional text included in the agreement was intended to override the *polis*' existing law. Yet it is also clear that the clause itself is phrased in such a way that its future interpretation and application would require access to the very text that it was intended to supersede, at least unless and until a thorough revision of the previous law *and of the amendment itself* had been completed.[14]

---

[8] The noun occurs only very rarely in the singular even in archaic and classical literary evidence, where it is usually translated as 'law' or 'custom': Aisch. *Agamemnon* 1564, Eur. *Troades* 267, Philochoros *FGrHist.* 328F5b.

[9] l. 39: ℎότι κα μὲ ἀνφοτάροις ⁝ δοκέει κτλ. Dreher (2023: 31) notes only one parallel in a document that appears to have been passed as a law, and which permits the abolition of the enactment in its entirety.

[10] See Fernandez Nieto (1983) and more recently Scheibelreiter (2013: 236). For a discussion of similar problems arising in connection with distinctions between treaties and decrees, see Mack (2013: 98–100).

[11] Eich, Eich and Eck (2018: 25).

[12] αἱ δὲ ὁμολογίαι καὶ αἱ συνθῆκαι ἐγένοντο ἐπὶ ἀρχόντων Μο[.]οιτου Μοασιος Ιδααδιος.

[13] περὶ κλοπῆς· ὃς ἂν κλέψηι τι οὗ πρότερον ἦσαν μναῖ τρε[ῖς] νῦν δ' ἔστω θάνατος ἡ ζημία ἐλενχθέντι·

[14] As noted by Eich, Eich and Eck (2018: 24–25), there is a probably substantial gap between frs. A and B. One possibility is that part of the missing text continued the general provisions in A (perhaps an existing *nomos* reproduced on the stone as a

Although Aristotle could characterise a *nomos* as a kind of *syntheke* (*Politics* 1280b1–10) and, conversely, refer to a *syntheke* as a *nomos idios* (*Rhetoric* 1376b7–11), a recurrent feature in especially the peace agreements attested for fifth-century Greece is that they are subject to renewal after a specified period of time, in some cases as long as a hundred years, sometimes fifty or thirty or even less.[15] In the case of the agreement between the Lokrians and the settlers at Naupaktos, it is difficult to tell if the agreement would automatically cease to be binding on the parties, unless there was a recommitment and a new exchange of oaths between the two sides. In other cases, however, it is clear that the agreement would expire, unless it was expressly renewed. That is, the agreement was furnished with a self-destruct mechanism, comparable to a modern 'sunset clause'.

II. Temporary legislation and constitutional change.

Sunset clauses, defined as "dispositions that determine the expiry of a law or regulation within a predetermined period",[16] are increasingly used in response to crisis situations, particularly in connection with the passing of legislation the contents of which is regarded as controversial, and which may require the suspension of other laws. Kouroutakis (2017) has provided an historical overview, which focusses primarily on the use of sunset clauses in mediaeval and early modern England, but the phenomenon is also known from other jurisdictions.[17]

Esù (2021) has recently argued that, in fifth-century Athens, a decision to grant *adeia* could serve to permit decree proposals to be made in the Assembly in contravention of entrenchment clauses in existing enactments, and that as a constitutional instrument *adeia* served similar purposes to those of modern emergency legislation. Yet, in other respects it differs significantly from the kind of temporary legislation that, until its expiry, has the same authority as the community's established laws, or which might even override them.

As noted by Professor Dreher, there is no surviving epigraphical example of a text which can be confidently classified by us as a *nomos*, but which at the same time included an explicit expiry date or other specific criteria that would automatically render the law invalid. Yet, there is evidence to suggest that the concept was not entirely alien to the Greeks in the classical period.[18] The first is the

---

complement to the covenants), which also contained the original clause on theft. See further Faraguna and Boffo (2021: 223–227) for parallels, but without the potential conflict between established legislation and stipulations agreed in the context of a treaty arrangement.

15 For examples see e.g. Scheibelreiter (2013: 158–159) and Wilker (2012a: 107–109) with references to previous discussions.

16 Kouroutakis and Ranchordás (2015: 51–52).

17 See *e.g.* Gusy (2018).

18 Kouroutakis (2017: 15) mentions as an early example Plato's suggestion (*Laws* 772B-C) that new legislation regulating sacrifices and dances should initially be subject to

evidence of *Ath. Pol.* 31, which purports to summarise a temporary constitution (ἐν δὲ τῷ παρόντι καιρῷ), intended to be replaced later by the 'constitution for the future' summarised in the preceding chapter, with the implication that the former was to lapse when the present emergency no longer applied. Its inclusion in the account of the *Ath. Pol.* shows, whatever its historical accuracy,[19] that the author expected his readers to find a temporary constitution plausible as a response to a severe emergency.

The second is the measure envisaged for the community created from the merger (*synoikismos*) of Teos and Lebedos.[20] Here, too, there is a distinction between legislation that is intended to be durable and legislation that is to apply during a period of transition, in this instance a year, until the legislative process has been completed.[21] The suggestion that the legislation of the larger community, Teos, should apply in the interim had been rejected by the smaller one, Lebedos;[22] instead the two communities agreed on a compromise, namely that the laws of Kos should be copied, imported, publicly displayed and enforced as a temporary measure.[23]

While the inscription itself may suggest that the Koan legislation was to be copied and conveyed on sealed papyrus or *deltoi*,[24] there is no indication of how the texts were to be displayed, let alone if they were to be inscribed onto durable material. Still, it seems highly unlikely that they were to be inscribed on stone, and a similar consideration applies also to other types of temporary legislation that was intended to be superseded entirely by laws that were intended to be permanent.

---

amendment for a period of ten years and be included among the laws as *akineta* only after that period has elapsed, but Plato does not explicitly say that the laws will automatically lapse, unless this final phase is completed. *IK Kyme* 12 and *SEG* 59: 1407 provide evidence for a similar two-stage process, but in these cases the decrees are designated as "valid for all time" (κύριον εἰς πάντα τὸν χρόνον), and there is no indication that the enactment will expire by a certain date, unless they are incorporated into the *polis' nomoi*. See further Faraguna and Boffo (2021: 557–560).

19 For a recent discussion, see Faraguna and Boffo (2021: 213–216).

20 Bencivenni (2003: 169–201) no. 7 (*RC* 3).

21 Bencivenni (2003: 169–201) no. 7 (*RC* 3), lines 44–55. See also Egetenmeier (2016/17: 179–181)

22 Contrast *e.g.* the merger of Helisson and Mantinea (*I. Ark*. 9, *RO* 14), where the existing laws of Mantinea are to apply in both communities. The concession to the Heliswassians that their laws are to be applied to transactions concluded before the merger is, as pointed out by Thür and Taeuber (1994: 107), a temporary measure. Note that, in practical terms, this requires an arrangement whereby the Heliswassian legislation would remain publicly accessible for a considerable period of time. For further discussion and comparison of the two mergers, see Mack (2013). For a settlement that is far less generous to the smaller party, see *IG* IX, 1^2 188 with Lasagni (2019: 141–147, esp. p. 145).

23 Bencivenni (2003: 169–201) no. 7, (*RC* 3) lines 55–66.

24 Faraguna and Boffo (2021: 556–557 with n. 3).

Thus, the fact that the epigraphical record has not (yet) produced any exact parallels to the arrangements for Teos and Lebedos does not permit the inference that the arrangements were eccentric, let alone unique. What may have made them unusual, however, was if the proposed *synoikismos* and the concomitant profound constitutional change had been the result of a peaceful agreement and internal consensus between and within the communities affected. This is impossible to tell. The context where temporary legislation was most likely to be adopted as a measure was in the wake of dramatic and violent regime change, and in particular when the regime that was overturned had been in place for a considerable period of time.

III. Unchanging legislation: a shared Greek ideal?

If we can trust Andokides (1.81), the Athenians did not need to look abroad for suitable legislation to see them through the transition from oligarchy to a democratic constitution in 403/2. The two factions were allegedly able to agree on a compromise that the legislation of Drakon and Solon would serve the purpose, until the legislative process had been completed.[25] The extent to which the Thirty had changed Athens' established legislation should not be underestimated: the wording in *Ath. Pol.* 35.2 suggests that it was not only the law on bequest that was tampered with, but that the legislative work (or vandalism) also extended to other statutes attributed to Solon.[26] As for the governments of the Four Hundred and the Five Thousand that succeeded them, it is extremely difficult to gauge the scale of their legislative reform programme, except in so far as it is likely to have encompassed amendment or wholesale abolition of any legislation relating directly to the functioning of key democratic institutions.

Yet, the fact that all of the three non-democratic regimes were shortlived may not only have simplified the subsequent process of removing any vestiges of their activities from Athenian legislation and restoring the latter to the *status quo ante* (except where there was broad agreement that changes would be desirable). In rhetorical terms, the fact that neither regime had had a chance to 'bed down' was almost certainly key to the Athenian success in creating a broad consensus that the previous oligarchic governments and the legislation passed by them were wholly illegitimate. That, too, may also greatly have facilitated the representation of the regime change back to democracy as an uncontroversial return to the Athenians' ancestral laws. Most important of all: the restoration of the democratic constitutions both in 410 and in 403/2 were processes that the Athenians themselves controlled, albeit with the acquiescence of the Spartans in 403/2. All of these, and perhaps particularly the third factor, are likely to have contributed to a broad Athenian consensus, repeatedly expressed in surviving Athenian oratory of all three genres,

---

25 δόξαντα δὲ ὑμῖν ταῦτα εἵλεσθε ἄνδρας εἴκοσι· τούτους δὲ ἐπιμελεῖσθαι τῆς πόλεως, ἕως ἄλλοι νόμοι τεθεῖεν· <u>τέως δὲ χρῆσθαι</u> τοῖς Σόλωνος νόμοις καὶ τοῖς Δράκοντος θεσμοῖς.

26 ὁμοίως δὲ τοῦτ' ἔδρων <u>καὶ ἐπὶ τῶν ἄλλων</u>.

that the laws should ideally remain unchanged and unchangeable, except when there was a compelling practical need for revision and innovation. In a world where *stasis* was a frequent and frightening experience for numerous communities, stable legislation could be taken as an indication also of stable relations within the community and as an indication that a balance between individuals and groups with diverging interests had been achieved.

Yet, an important question is how far it is safe to generalise from the Athenian example and to take it for granted that the adherence to unchanging legislation as an ideal was unconditional and universal across all Greek communities. Aristotle indicates in his *Politics* 1268b27–34 that there were at least some dissenting voices:

> For some people discuss whether it is harmful or beneficial to the poleis to change their ancestral laws, if there is a better alternative. For that reason, if indeed change is not beneficial, it is not easy to agree readily with the statement. For it is possible for some people to propose the abolition of laws or of a constitution as a collective benefit. Since we have now raised this point, it would be better to expand on it a little, for as we said, this is subject to discussion. And it is possible that change may appear to be better.[27]

Many Greek communities are known to have experienced more frequent crises and much deeper polarisation than the Athenians had had to endure. Many of them experienced oppressive regimes that could last for several generations, often propped up by military support from external hegemonic powers. Even the most stable legislation, embedded over many decades or even generations and claimed as 'ancestral' by its adherents, might be widely perceived to be not just undesirable but outright harmful by those who were opposed to the political order which it underpinned. Aristotle's indication that there were dissenting voices suggests that the evidence of especially the Attic Orators may reflect only part of the picture, and that we must be mindful of that in discussions which extend to the rest of the Greek world, and which endeavour to cover several centuries.

l.rubinstein@rhul.ac.at

BIBLIOGRAPHY

Bencivenni, A. (2003). *Progetti di reforme costituzionali nelle epigrafi greche dei secoli IV–II A.C.* Bologna: Lo Scarabeo Editrice.

Dimakis, P. [ed.] (1983). *Symposion 1979*. Cologne, Weimar and Vienna: Böhlau.

[27] ἀποροῦσι γάρ τινες πότερον βλαβερὸν ἢ συμφέρον ταῖς πόλεσι τὸ κινεῖν τοὺς πατρίους νόμους ἂν ᾖ τις ἄλλος βελτίων. διόπερ οὐ ῥᾴδιον τῷ λεχθέντι ταχὺ συγχωρεῖν, εἴπερ μὴ συμφέρει κινεῖν· ἐνδέχεται δ' εἰσηγεῖσθαί τινας νόμων λύσιν ἢ πολιτείας ὡς κοινὸν ἀγαθόν. ἐπεὶ δὲ πεποιήμεθα μνείαν, ἔτι μικρὰ περὶ αὐτοῦ διαστείλασθαι βέλτιον, ἔχει γάρ, ὥσπερ εἴπομεν, ἀπορίαν. καὶ δόξειεν ἂν βέλτιον εἶναι τὸ κινεῖν·

Dreher, M. (2023). "Das Ungültigwerden in Gesetzen in den griechischen Poleis" in *Dike* 25, 7–76.

Egetenmeier, P. (2016/17). "Prozessrechtliche Überlegungen zum geplanten *Synoikismos* zwischen Teos und Lebedos (RC 3)" in *Dike* 19/20, 167–198.

Eich, A., P. Eich, and W. Eck. (2018). *Die Inschriften von Sagalassos. Teil I. Inschriften griechischer Städte aus Kleinasien.* Bonn: Verlag Rudolf Habelt.

Esù, A. (2021). "*Adeia* in Fifth-Century Athens" in *Journal of Hellenic Studies* 141, 153–178.

Faraguna, M. and Boffo, L. (2021). *Le* poleis *e i loro archivi. Studi su pratiche documentarie, istituzioni e società nell'antichità greca.* Trieste: EUT Edizioni.

Fernandez Nieto, F. J. (1983). "Die Abänderungsklauseln in den griechischen Staatsverträgen der klassischen Zeit", in Dimakis, P. [ed.], *Symposion 1979*, 273–286.

Flensted-Jensen, P. [ed.] (2000). *Further Studies in the Ancient Greek Polis*, Stuttgart.

Gagarin, M. (2008). *Writing Greek Law*. Cambridge.

Gusy, C. (2018). "Ermächtigungsgesetzgebung in Deutschland zwischen Monarchie und Republik" in *Beiträge zur Rechtsgeschichte Österreichs* 8, 396–408.

Harris, E. M. and Thür, G. [eds.] *Symposion 2007*. Vienna: Verlag der österreichischen Akademie der Wissenschaften.

Harter-Uibopuu, K. (2013). "Bestandsklauseln und Abänderungsverbote: Der Schutz zweckgebundener Gelder in der späthellenistischen und kaiserzeitlichen Polis" in *Tyche* 28, 51–96.

Kouroutakis, A. (2017). *The Constitutional Value of Sunset Clauses. An Historical and Normative Analysis*. London: Routledge.

Kouroutakis, A. and S. Ranchordás. (2015). "Snoozing Democracy, De-Juridification, and Emergencies" in *Minnesota Journal of International Law* 25, 29–78.

Lasagni, C. (2019). *Le realtà locali nel mondo greco. Ricerche su poleis ed ethne della Grecia occidentale*. Alessandria: Edizioni dell' Orso.

Mack, W. (2013). "Communal Interests and Polis Identity under Negotiation: Documents Depicting Sympolities between Cities Great and Small" in *Topoi* 18, 87–113.

Nielsen, T. H. 2000. "Epiknemidian, Hypoknemidian and Opountian Lokrians. A Note on the Political Organisation of East Lokris in the Classical Period" in P. Flensted-Jensen, *Further Studies in the Ancient Greek Polis*, 91–120.

Rubinstein, L. 2008. "Response to James P. Sickinger", in Harris, E. M. and Thür, G. [eds.] *Symposion 2007*, 113–124.

Scheibelreiter, P. (2013). *Untersuchungen zur Vertragsrechtlichen Struktur des delisch-attischen Seebundes*. Vienna: Verlag der österreichischen Akademie der Wissenschaften.

Thür, G. and Taeuber, H. (1994). *Prozessrechtliche Inschriften der griechischen Poleis. Arkadien.* Vienna: Verlag der österreichischen Akademie der Wissenschaften.

Thomas, R. (2019). *Polis Histories, Collective Memories and the Greek World.* Oxford: Oxford University Press.

Wilker, J. (2012a). "War and Peace at the Beginning of the Fourth Century. The Emergence of the Koine Eirene" in J. Wilker (2012b), 92–117.

Wilker, J. (2012b). *Maintaining Peace and Interstate Stability in Archaic and Classical Greece.* Studien zur alte Geschichte 16. Mainz: Verlag Antike.

Zaccarini, M. (2018). "The Fate of a Lawgiver: the Invention of the Reforms of Ephialtes and the Patrios Politeia" in *Historia* 67, 495–512.

ROBERT W. WALLACE (EVANSTON, IL)

STATUTE *NOMOI* IN THUCYDIDES

Abstract: Especially in the 420s, elite Athenian anti-democrats developed arguments against statute laws, most conspicuously that laws conflict with nature. Thucydides, also an elite anti-democrat, attests five of these arguments, but condemns them, and condemns what he describes as Athens' moral decline. Yet he himself also provides major evidence that Athens suffered no such decline.

Keywords: Thucydides, laws, morality, Sophists, democracy

After centuries of unwavering support for statute laws,[1] invented by eighth-century Greeks to curtail elite judicial abuse,[2] at Athens during a dark intellectual period in the Peloponnesian War,[3] upper-class anti-democratic writers raised various objections against such laws.[4] A common claim was that Athens' democrats passed *nomoi* in

---

The following works are cited by author's name and date or section number: Hornblower 1987; Hornblower 1991, 1996, 2008; Lattimore 1998; Rhodes 1988. Unattributed translations are adapted from standard versions. Many thanks to Paul Cartledge for comments on this text.

1 See e.g. Solon's *nomophylakia*, [Arist.] *Ath. Pol.* 16.8 that Athens' tyrant Peisistratos was "willing to administer everything according to the *nomoi*," and Sparta's *nomos despotês* (Hdt. 1.65, 7.103–4). In addition to statute law, *nomoi* can mean (unwritten) customs (e.g., Thuc. 1.97.4), or (unwritten) international/universal Greek laws (e.g., Thuc. 1.41.1, 4.98.2), or songs (Thuc. 5.69.2, in Sparta). Cf. Sheet 1994, also on arbitration, and Scheibelreiter 2011, 155–159.

2 See my essay, Wallace 2016. Already ca. 700 Hesiod complained about elite judges' "bribe-swallowing" partiality.

3 See my essay, Wallace 2007a.

4 Earlier comments in Aeschylus' and Sophokles' plays do not necessarily criticize statute laws. In Aeschylus' *Oresteia* of 458, Athena warns the Athenians not to corrupt old laws with new laws (*Eum.* 690–695). This can be read as supporting current laws. In three early plays of the not very democratic aristocrat Sophokles, it is important to respect both gods' laws and civic *nomoi*. In *Ajax* (ca. 444 BC), Menelaus (1073, 1130–1132) and Agamemnon (1246–1269), both city officials, defend city laws but also gods' laws. In 1343–1344 Odysseus defends "the *nomoi* of the gods." In *Antigone* (442 BC) 454–455, Antigone denies that Kreon's edict is a law, calling it his proclamation (*kêrugma*). She says nothing against city laws. Champion of civic laws, *Antigone*'s Kreon concludes that he should have followed *tous kathestôtas nomous* (1113–1114), civic and gods' laws. In the play that Sophokles called *Oedipus* 865–870 (ca. 434), the gods' *nomoi* are important, but are not called superior to civic *nomoi*.

their own (not everybody's) interest. Usually dated to the Archidamian War (according to Marr and Rhodes, late summer 424 BC[5]), the "Old Oligarch" says,

> the demos do not wish *eunomia* (good government/laws) under which they themselves are slaves, they wish to be free and to rule. *Kakonomia* (bad government/laws) is of little concern to them. For what you consider *kakonomia*, from this the demos grows strong and is free. If you are seeking *eunomia*, you will first observe the cleverest men enacting *nomoi* in their own interest (1.8–9).

The "Old Oligarch's" general thesis is that although democracy has its problems, in Athens it was effective because the demos thereby could successfully pursue its own interests. In Aristophanes' *Clouds* (423 BC), some Athenian intellectuals also oppose laws. Its arch Sophist *Adikos Logos* ("Unjust Speech") claims that he "first conceived the notion of arguing against *nomoi* and *dikai*" (1039–1040), helping to date this development. Student of *Clouds'* Sokrates, Pheidippides rejoices "to look down on the established *nomoi*" (1400). Commonly dated to the mid-420s and defending laws, Euripides' *Hecuba* discusses *nomoi* in relation to gods' laws.[6] His *Suppliants*, ca. 424, links written laws with democracy (line 433). These major testimonia cluster around the mid-420s, a date that will also prove important for Thucydides. A Sophist of the later fifth century (Aristophanes' *Banqueters* of 427 supplies his first dated mention), Thrasymachus ("Brash-fighter") says in Plato's *Republic* (dramatic date ca. 421–412), "each ruling power passes laws with a view to its own advantage: a democracy passes democratic laws, a tyranny tyrannical ones," etc. (*Rep.* 338d, also 339c). This statement is consistent with Thrasymachus' immoral assertion in Plato, "the just is nothing other than the interest of the stronger" (*Rep.* 338c). Plato's Sokrates spends the rest of *Republic* I criticizing that assertion.[7]

Starting in the 420s, extant texts raise six specific objections against statute *nomoi*.[8]

1. From the 420s (*Clouds* of 423 supplies its first dated mention), *phusis* (nature) is sometimes judged superior to *nomos*. When *Clouds*' Pheidippides argues at length that it is perfectly fine to beat one's father and even one's mother, his father Strepsiades objects that "nowhere is it *nomos* that a father should be so treated." Pheidippides responds according to nature: "Consider chickens and those other animals, how they retaliate against their fathers. Aren't we animals, more or less, except that they don't propose decrees?" (1410–29). Anti-democratic and executed by Athens' democracy in 411, Antiphon (DK[6] = Pendrick fr. 44 [a] I) argued that the claims of *nomoi* are generally antithetical to those of human nature, and individuals' interests will best be served by following human nature when legal

---

[5] Marr – Rhodes 2008, e.g. on 2.15.

[6] See Fletcher 2012, 225–243, and Wohl 2015, 57–61, with reff.

[7] For another "might-makes-right" man, see Kallikles in Pl. *Gorg.* 483b–c, and also Pl. *Laws* 714b–d.

[8] For other details, see my essay, Wallace 2007b.

punishment can be avoided, especially given the inevitability of nature's reprisals if flouted. Thucydides praises Antiphon's intellectual brilliance (8.68), and his prose style was judged to resemble Antiphon's.[9] For *nomos/phusis* see also the sophist Hippias in Pl. *Prt.* 337c–d.

2. Laws are weak. For example, Antiphon (ibid. fr. 44a VI) complains that laws are not very helpful in aiding sufferers or stopping malefactors. In Eur. *Ion* 1045–47 (arguably 418–417 BC) the old servant proclaims, "when one seeks vengeance on one's enemies, no laws lie in the path" (cf. Hekabe in Eur. *Hecuba* 864–67).

3. For Hippias in anti-democratic Xenophon (*Mem.* 4.4.14), "laws cannot be thought of much account, since they are often rejected or amended."

4. The demos does not obey its own laws, as when it executed six generals as a group after the naval battle at Arginousai in 406.[10] [Arist.] *Ath. Pol.* 26.2 (see also 7.4) claims that after Ephialtes the demos no longer paid attention to laws, and after 403 the demos was *kurios* and did everything by decrees and the courts (ibid. 41.2). In *Pol.* 1291b14 Aristotle admits that in a democracy law may prevail at least in theory, but in a large state that is practically impossible. He regards as typical of extreme democracies that decrees prevail over laws and democrats do not adhere to the laws (*Pol.* 1292a4–37, cf. 1293a9–10, 30–34, 1298a28–33).

5. Virtue is advanced not by laws but by the habits of daily life: Isokr. *Areop.* 7.39–41.

6. A wise governing elite needs no laws, which are too simple and crude to be just, an argument of Plato's *Republic* (339a–340b against Thrasymachus) which includes no laws.

Statute *nomoi* in Thucydides

Thucydides' history stops in 411 but he was still writing in 399, if 2.100 sums up the career of Archelaus of Macedon who died that year (Hornblower 1987: 143). From 411 he worked hard at interlocking earlier episodes and themes including *nomos*, as we shall see. Himself upper-class and anti-democratic, what attitudes to statute *nomoi* are expressed in his history? In Thucydides such laws are mentioned almost always in the speeches. His statement that his speeches combine his views of what different speakers should say with the overall idea (*xumpasa gnômê*) of what they did say (1.22.1) readers of this essay will find consistent if, while retaining each speaker's major positions (for example, in favor of war), Thucydides largely wrote the speeches himself. One purpose was to reinforce for his readers his

[9] See e.g., Finley 1967, its index citing a dozen references to Antiphon; Dover 1973, 12 and reff.; Gagarin 2002, 44–45, quoting Hermogenes *On Style*: "I hear that many say that Thucydides was a student of Antiphon of Rhamnous" although "Thucydides is quite similar in style to the work *On Truth*," which Hermogenes thinks was written by the other Antiphon. Gagarin and others accept only one Antiphon.

[10] Xen. *Hell.* 1.7.12. Trying groups was illegal according to Xen. *Mem.* 12.1.18 and Pl. *Ap.* 32b, although this view has been challenged.

own interpretations and strengthen his work's credibility and coherence by having contemporary speakers echo his thoughts. As for Thucydides' values, he liked strong generals, including Brasidas, Hermokrates, and Perikles the leader of Athens' democracy. He disliked democracy, thinking it ignorant (e.g., 1.20 and 6.1), impetuous (see below on the demos's anger), fickle (e.g., 2.65.1–4, against Perikles), and easily deceived (e.g., 5.85).

Thucydides' first set of passages (a–d) on statute *nomoi* occurs before the war broke out, in speeches at a congress in Sparta in 432/1.

(a: 1.71.3) Unhappy with their ally Sparta which they thought was not being helpful, the oligarchic Corinthians say "it is necessary that as in *technê* [skill], what comes later always rules (*kratein*). In peacetime, Sparta's *akinêta nomima* ("unchanged institutions, laws, customs"[11]) are *arista*, but Athens was compelled to engage on many fronts and therefore needed to make much *epitechnêsis* (Hornblower on 1.71.3 = "reforms")." Here Thucydides has Sparta's major ally say positive things about Athens and the advantages (including *kratos* and victory) of changing *nomima,* as Athens sometimes did. This same contrast between innovative Athens and conservative Sparta they brilliantly develop in 1.70.

(b: 1.72–78) By chance at Sparta on other business, an Athenian embassy addresses this congress and justifies the growth of Athens' empire (*archê*), beginning with its major contributions to the Persian wars (1.73.2–74). We didn't acquire our power by force, our allies came to us [true enough] (1.75.1–2). We developed our empire because of fear, honor, and self-benefit; later it was too risky to let it go. You Spartans did the same in the Peloponnese, and if you become dominant in Greece the same will happen to you [as it did after 404, when many think this passage was written]. These words lead into the Athenians' observations about *nomos* and human nature (*phusis*), perhaps too early in 432/1 but not for the 420s (on dating, see below). It is neither "surprising nor alien to the human way to accept an empire when it was offered to us" (1.76.2). "All are entitled to win praise whenever they follow human nature (*anthrôpeia phusis*), by ruling others more justly than in accordance with their actual power" (1.76.3). Athens has shown moderation and fairness, *epieikeia* (1.76.4). In 1.77 the Athenians illustrate these qualities first by *nomoi* in their courts, which are the same for them as for others. Athenians and their allies equally obey Athens' impartial laws and do not abuse their power in court, although as a result they are thought to *philodikein*, "love litigation." Unlike others, Athenians don't use extra-legal force (*biazesthai*) but adjudicate (*dikazesthai*) (1.77.2). *Nomoi* have restrained Athens from unabashed aggrandizement. "You [Spartans] have *nomima* at home that are unmixed with those of others, while each one of you when going abroad uses neither your own

11 For the meaning of *nomima* (which may include statute laws), see Ostwald 1986, 102–105 (cited by Hornblower on 1.71.3). "The expressions *hoi nomoi*, *ta nomima*, and *ta tôn nomôn* are used interchangeably throughout Antiphon 44(a)": Pendrick 2002, 319.

[*nomima*] nor those which the rest of Greece observes." We do not break our treaties, but resolve our differences by *dikê* [justice/lawsuits] according to our agreements. We are willing to arbitrate (1.78.4).

Before the war, these Athenians present a positive picture of Athens using *nomoi* and *dikê*. By contrast, their comments on Sparta are mixed.

(c: 1.80–85). In a long speech atypical for a Spartan (and so inconsistent with their *nomima* [customs]?), King Archidamus, who was "thought to be intelligent [not anyway an official Spartan virtue] and self-controlled" [*sôphrôn*, a Greek upper-class virtue] (1.79.2), says that the Spartans "are educated too rudely to despise the *nomoi* and too well disciplined to disobey them" (1.84.3). However, the Athenians are ready to submit to arbitration, and it is not *nomimon* not to negotiate, as it would be against a wrongdoer (*adikounta*) (1.85.2). Here Archidamus calls the Athenians law-abiding and not wrongdoers, while the Spartans mostly follow their *nomoi* [the term he uses] because of their simple education and social discipline. Attitudes atypical for a Spartan.

(d: 1.86) Last in this first set of passages, the *ephor* Sthenelaidas, a people's elected official, rude and abrupt, says the Athenians were *agathoi* against Persia but are now *kakoi* to us. We must not seek redress by words [contrast Archidamus' long speech] or *dikai* [lawsuits: contrast the Athenians' *dikazesthai*], but speedily and with all our might. With the gods let us go against the wrongdoers (*adikountas*). [Archidamus had said the Athenians were not wrongdoers.] Sthenelaidas prevails in the assembly, but his Sparta also looks mixed, including on *dikai* (lawsuits or justice).

In the opening episode of the war at Plataia (2.1–7) the Plataians, Athens' allies, behave badly. Having promised to spare 180 captured Thebans, instead they massacre them (2.5–7). The Athenians seek to save the Thebans but in vain (2.5–6). In a trial in Book 3, Spartan judges will punish the Plataians for this offense although for selfish reasons (3.68.4), for which they too will be punished by defeat at Pylos.

So far, Thucydides has represented the Athenians as good in regard to *nomoi*. His second segment on *nomoi* includes two speeches, Perikles' Funeral Oration (430 BC) and Perikles' final speech (429), both written by Thucydides at later dates and divided by an account of the plague.

(e: 2.35–46) Funeral Orations were eulogies, especially for Athens' many military successes and democratic government.[12] By contrast, the Funeral Oration

---

[12] Many mostly fragmentary funeral orations for Athens' war dead include military history, whether legendary such as the Amazons' invasion of Attika, or historical including the battles of Marathon, Salamis, and Plataea, narratives from Athens' *Pentêkontaetia* (Lys. 2.48–53, Pl. *Men.* 241ff.), or events from the Peloponnesian war. Perikles delivered Athens' first known funeral oration in 439, after defeating its rebel ally Samos. According to Ion of Chios, a contemporary who knew him (Plut. *Per.* 28.4–7), Perikles said that in the Trojan War the Greeks needed ten years to conquer one

which Thucydides wrote for Perikles is a tissue of confusion and misrepresentation not least on *nomoi*, in part because Thucydides disliked democracy but liked Perikles. Many passages mix truths and falsehoods, often reflecting anti-democratic sentiment typical of Thucydides elsewhere.

Perikles' Oration begins, *hoi polloi*. Is this the democratic masses, as often in Thucydides? No, "the many speakers" whose funeral orations praise the man who added a speech to the *nomos* establishing this burial ceremony; but the ambiguity is deliberate. Perikles disagrees with these *polloi* and criticizes the speech part of this *nomos*. [An odd way to begin a eulogy, both points sound undemocratic, not least because Athenian speeches typically do not criticize Athens' *nomoi*.[13]] We should honor Athens' war-dead by deeds, not words [in 1.86 the Spartan Sthenelaidas said something similar], "when even the appearance of the truth is hardly assured, or which even those who know or are well-meaning might think inadequate compared with what they wish or know," while others feel envy (2.35.1–2). [Criticizing rhetoric seems again anti-democratic, and Perikles invites doubt about the truth of his own speech.] Still, he must follow the *nomos*. [Is his reluctance further anti-*nomos* sentiment?]

After his peculiar *prooimion* Perikles says it is "just" (*dikaion*, echoing his friends the Corcyreans' first word in 1.32) to begin by praising Athens' ancestors. However, he immediately retracks (as did the Corcyreans). The Athenians know all this "and I shall therefore pass it by" (1.36.1–4). He now turns directly to Athens' *nomoi,* which he says copy nobody (2.37.1). Athens is called a democracy because we live here in the interests not of the few but the majority. Yet even though according to the *nomoi* regarding private disputes [why this limitation?] there is equality [*to ison*] for all [in 1.77.1, 3 the Athenians at Sparta had said with no limitation that Athens' laws meant equality for all, *apo tou isou*], regarding popular esteem (*axiôsis*) individuals receive public preference according to their recognized achievement in some field, not by rotation [i.e. not by the lot, a democratic institution] but by *aretê* [a key aristocratic virtue]. [Except on the generalship, Perikles' aristocratic, anti-egalitarian sentiments against the democratic lot are mostly incorrect (so Rhodes 1988: 220).] Furthermore, should someone be poor but able to perform some service for the city, he is not prevented by insufficient public recognition (2.37.1). Poverty is no bar if a man can confer some benefit on the city. [This is democratic ideology but for Athens it is not very true. Thetes, the lowest economic class, were still excluded from office, and most politicians were wealthy

barbarian city, while in nine months he had conquered Ionia's most powerful city. The other fragments of Perikles' Samian oration also display a patriotic militarism. According to Aristotle, he said of Athens' young killed in that war, "the spring was taken from the year" (*Rhet.* 1365a32), while the Samians were like children who take their pap but go on crying (ibid. 1407a1, cf. Ar. *Cl.* 1001). According to Stesimbrotos (*ap.* Plut. *Per.* 8.9), he compared Athens' war dead to the gods.

13 See Thomas 1994.

(so Rhodes, ibid.).] In public, we live freely and "are not angry with our neighbor if he does something *kath' hêdonên*, according to pleasure" [a phrase always mistranslated, as far as I have seen.[14] Before Epicurus in the late fourth century, *hêdonê* was no virtue, including in Thucydides. For example, Archidamus said that the Spartans were not carried away by *hêdonê* (1.84.2); Thucydides says the demagogues after Perikles pandered to the demos's *hêdonai* (2.65.8, 10); in a clever paradox, Thucydides' chief demagogue (and rhetorician) Kleon rebukes the popular assembly for being "overcome by the *hêdonê* of listening, like the seated spectators of sophists more than deliberating about the city" (3.38.7).] As for our public lives, Perikles continues, we do not *paranomein,* "break the laws through fear [the Loeb translates "reverent fear"!] of the officials and the *nomoi,*" including unwritten laws (2.37.3). In *Symposion* 2001 I addressed these paradoxes, for example that the Athenians were told they were free to live as they wished but had to obey magistrates and laws.[15] *Antigone* of 442 champions unwritten laws (453–57), but, quoting Solon (F 30 West), the magistrate Kreon tells Antigone she must obey him (666–72: "the man whom the polis has put in place, him it is necessary to hear, even in small things, and whether right or wrong. There is no greater evil than anarchy"). Athens' democracy forbade citing unwritten laws (And.1.87). Following up on 2.39.1 ("we live in a relaxed way" [*aneimenôs*] in contrast to the Spartans, but "are nonetheless ready to face equal dangers"), in 2.39.4 Perikles says that "by taking our ease (*rathumia*) rather than by laborious training, our courage springs more from our way of life than from *nomoi*." Perikles again downplays *nomoi*, further anti-law sentiment. Many scholars have noted that no army can win without training.[16]

---

[14] See e.g. Smith (Loeb) "in the pursuits of everyday life"; Romilly (Budé) "agire à sa fantaisie"; Lattimore "does something so as to suit himself." Athens' democratic ideal was "living as anyone wishes" (ζῆν ὡς βούλεταί τις: e.g. Lys. 26.5, Arist. *Pol.* 1317b11–12), which courtroom (Lys. 10.3, 21.6, 25.33) and political enemies (Dem. 23.67, 25.20, 51.16) and anti-democrats perverted into "doing what you want," a tyrant's prerogative (first in Soph. *Aj.* 1081, ca. 444; see also Hdt. 3.80.3; Xen. *HG* 1.7.12; Pl. *Rep.* 557b), or in Thucydides (as here), "doing according to pleasure."

[15] Wallace 2005. On p. 147 I promised a future treatment of *nomoi*. Here is one part.

[16] In Perikles' so-called eulogy, various judgments seem perverse. For example, "Athens alone gives no occasion … to its subjects (*hupêkooi*) to question its title to rule by merit" (2.41.3: but Thucydides says its "subjects" hated Athens). "We have forced every sea and land to be the highway of our daring (*tolmê*) and everywhere, whether for evil or good, have left imperishable monuments behind us" (2.41.4). "There is justice (*dikaion*) in the claim that steadfastness in his country's battles should be as a cloak to cover a man's other imperfections, since the good has blotted out the bad, and his merit as a citizen more than outweighed his demerits as an individual" (2.42.3). On Athens' many athletic contests and festivals, Perikles calls these sources of relaxation without mentioning the gods (2.38.1), about whom both Perikles and Thucydides had doubts (Rhodes 1988: 221). Of Athens' women Perikles concludes, "Greatest will be her glory who is least talked of among men whether for good or bad" (2.45.2).

(f: 2.47–54) Thucydides further undercuts the Funeral Oration not with an anti-*logos* but an anti-*ergon,* the plague, contrasting Perikles' ambiguous comments on democratic Athens and *nomoi* with Thucydides' claims of legal, social and moral collapse during the plague years, 430–426. "As the bad [*kakon*] passed all bounds, people not knowing what would become of them became utterly careless of everything, whether sanctioned or permitted by the gods. All the *nomoi* about burial were thrown into confusion" [he describes several outrages] (2.52.3–4). "In other matters as well, Athens owed to the plague the beginnings of a state of unprecedented lawlessness (*anomia*). Everyone easily dared to act according to *hêdonê* which they had previously enjoyed only in secret... to spend their money on enjoyment... No one showed himself willing to abide by what was thought to be noble [*kalon*]; whatever was *hêdu*, pleasurable [the adjective of *hêdonê*] immediately... was considered *kalon* and good/useful [*chrêsimon*]. No fear of god or *nomos* of man restrained them... it seemed the same whether one worshipped the gods or not (2.53.4)... As for offenses against human law, no one expected to live long enough to be brought to trial" (2.53). Much of this is historically questionable, as I hope to show elsewhere (would people abandon worshipping the gods during a plague?), as is his similar contrast in Book 1 between the positive albeit qualified assessment of Athens' empire in the Athenian *logos* at Sparta (b: 1.72–78) and the many negative (and I believe unhistorical) *erga* of Athens' *Pentêkontaetia* shortly thereafter.

(g: 2.60–65) Perikles, to whom Thucydides attributes anti-democratic attitudes, delivers his last, somber speech, in which he says nothing about *nomoi,* invokes the possibility of Athens' destruction (2.64.2–3), and calls its empire "like a tyranny; to take it seems *adikon"* (unjust). Then, directly after Thucydides' anti-democratic eulogy of Perikles in 2.65 (Athens was "in name a democracy, in fact the rule of the first man"), in 2.65.8, 10 he writes that while Pericles did not need to "address the people *pros hêdonên,*" after his death by the plague Athens' demagogues "ended by committing even the conduct of city affairs to the *hêdonai* of the demos."

(h: 2.66–67) A final anti-*ergon* in this segment: after words now deeds. In two speechless paragraphs, Spartans kill Athenians and other sailors and Athenians kill Peloponnesians, all without trials, each side throwing the others' bodies into pits although the Peloponnesians "wished to say something [to the Athenians] in their defense" (no *logoi*). Positive interpretations of the Funeral Oration are again undercut. We remember the *ephor* Sthenelaidas: "We must not seek redress by means of legal procedures (*dikai*) or words, but speedily and with all our might." At the end of this second segment his words fit both Spartans and Athenians. So much for *dikaion* or obeying *nomoi,* by either side.

(3.2–19, 25–49) The Mytilenean episode of 428–427 is a third segment where *nomoi* play a significant role, as Thucydides' speakers display ever greater moral confusion although he presents rightly moral historical material inconsistent with it.

(i: 3.9–14) In 3.9, the first speech of this segment, the Mytileneans at Olympia seek to ally with the Spartans and their allies. "It is an established Greek *nomimon* to hold in *hêdonê"* [a bad word] those who revolt from previous alliances "in so far as they benefit from them" [= expediency, bad in Thucydides]; otherwise "they are considered traitors to their former friends [bad]. This assessment is not unjust (*adikos*) if those who revolt and those they revolt from are *isoi* in policy and loyalties, a match for each other in resources and power, and there is no *prophasis* (grounds or pretense) for revolting." However, the Mytileneans claim, they and the Athenians are not *isoi* or a match for each other, and they have a *prophasis*, even though the Athenians have honored them in peacetime [and also in war, before their revolt].

After this curious *prooimion*, again echoing the opening speech of Book 1 where the Corcyreans' first word at Athens is *dikaion* (1.32.1) but they talk mostly of expediency,[17] the Mytileneans say they will begin with *dikaion* and *aretê*, mostly by showing that the Athenians were dangerous and not to be trusted, having "enslaved" their other allies except us and the Chians and therefore likely to enslave us in the future. The Athenians are also afraid of our fleet. We did nothing wrong in revolting, although Athens always treated us "on an equal basis" (*apo tou isou*) (3.11–12). You in turn will benefit by depriving Athens of allied tribute and gaining a large navy (3.13: expediency). Concerning the justice of their revolt, the Mytileneans' arguments seem paradoxical. They admit that they had been treated on an equal basis by the Athenians, they had no *prophasis* for revolting but only fears for the future, and Sparta will profit by gaining resources and a powerful fleet. Are they then "traitors"? Although the Mytileneans begin by saying they will talk of justice and *aretê*, later they never mention those ideas. They close by invoking hope and Olympian Zeus "in whose temple we stand virtually as suppliants" (3.14.1). In Thucydides, hope and supplicating gods mostly fail (e.g., 3.81.2, 5.103.1).

Although Thucydides' portrait of these Mytileneans is pretty dreadful, the Spartans and their allies ally with them, but Sparta's allies were reluctant to fight (3.15) and Sparta mostly withdrew (3.16.2, 4, cf. 3.27.1, 29.1). Mytilene's demos had previously been disarmed, but as things were going badly for the *oligoi* (upper classes), the demos demanded weapons and immediately surrendered to the Athenians, provided a Mytilenean embassy could go to Athens and plead their case (3.27–28.1).

(j: 3.36–49) The Mytileneans arrive at Athens. What to do with them (3.36.1)? With no trial (cf. *dikazesthai*), on Kleon's proposal (3.36.6) "in anger" (3.36.2) the Athenians decide to kill the prisoners and all Mytilene's adult men and enslave the women and children, partly because the Mytileneans had long planned to revolt and had been an Athenian favorite, which are excusatory remarks, although Thucydides

[17] Macleod 1978 discusses the similarities between these speeches.

considered anger a common vice of democracy.[18] They immediately dispatched a boat to Mytilene with instructions "to put an end to the Mytileneans with all speed" [*kata tachos*] (3.36.3). That night, however, "most of the citizens" felt *metanoia,* "repentance" (LSJ[9], citing this passage) and wanted to reconsider the matter (3.36.5), not from democracy's fickleness (e.g., Corcyra 1.44.1), but from "the savagery and magnitude of destroying a whole city rather than those responsible."

In a second assembly the next day, "after various opinions were expressed by both sides," Kleon, "the most violent man at Athens and at that time by far the most powerful man with the demos, came forward and spoke" (3.36.6). Thucydides will have enjoyed having Athens' leading democrat (whom he despised, as a debased Perikles[19]) begin his speech by criticizing democracy as "incapable of ruling others," by changing its mind about Mytilene (Thucydides' Perikles often said he never changed his mind [e.g., 1.127.3, 1.140.1, 2.61.2]) and by yielding to compassion, "forgetting that your empire is a tyranny." (Thucydides' Perikles had said "it was like a tyranny" which it may have been "unjust" to take [2.63.2]. Thucydides implies that things are deteriorating, although Thucydides not Kleon composed this speech.) "The most terrible thing of all is that we will not stand firm over a thing that is decided, nor do we seem to know that a city employing worse but unmovable (*akinêtoi*) *nomoi* [in Book 1.71 the Corinthians at Sparta had praised Athens' laws as changeable, while Sparta's *nomima* are less usefully *akinêta*] is better than one that employs good *nomoi* that lack authority" (3.37.3). Thucydides also enjoyed having Kleon say that Athens' democracy had bad laws. As noted [n. 13], Rosalind Thomas shows that Athens' orators rarely criticized its *nomoi.* Kleon adds that intelligent people want to show that they are wiser (*sophôteroi)* than the laws, while the *phauloteroi* (the simpler sort) consider themselves more ignorant than the laws and less competent to criticize a good speaker, and so are impartial judges. Here Kleon echoes the Spartan king Archidamus in 1.84.3 that the Spartans are educated too rudely to despise the *nomoi.* He argues that executing Mytilene's men was both just and expedient (standard categories in Thucydides' speeches, but earlier speakers advocate one or the other). Kleon states that he is not changing his mind (3.38.1), and he attacks rhetoric as Perikles also did in the Funeral Oration, calling the demos a slave to every paradox (3.38.5), although he was a brilliant rhetorician. He says not to spare Mytilene's demos (3.39.6), although he was a democrat and knew Mytilene's demos was innocent. Kleon never gave this speech.

"After [Kleon], Diodotus son of Eukrates, who had also in the previous assembly spoken most strongly against putting the Mytileneans to death, came forward and spoke as follows" (3.41.1). He defends debate, which he does not call democratic. He then argues not for morality or justice but for expediency (bad in

---

[18] e.g., 2.11.7–8, 2.21.3–22.1, 2.59.3–60.1, 2.64.1, 2.65.1–3 here against Perikles.

[19] For reff., see Connor 1984, 79 n.1.

Thucydides), and for what is useful to Athens in the future regardless of Mytilene's guilt, because he says they are not in a court of law but making a political decision (3.44) and so can ignore *nomos* and justice. "By nature everyone, whether as an individual or in public life, does wrong, and there is no *nomos* that can keep people away from this" (3.45.3). "It is quite impossible, and naive, if someone thinks the strength of *nomoi,* or any other terror, forms some bulwark against human nature setting out eagerly to do something" (3.45.7). *Phusis* triumphs over *nomos.* He concludes that sparing the Mytileneans is in Athens' interest, and that Kleon's idea of combining justice and expediency is impossible (3.46–47).

Does this debate document Athens' further decline into moral chaos? For Thucydides that is its purpose, but as history his account raises three questions. First, although he says the Athenians' first decision was made in anger and they immediately dispatched a boat with instructions "to kill the Mytileneans with all speed" (3.36.3), he later says that this first boat "made no great haste, as going on so unwelcome (*allokotos*: LSJ[9]) an affair" (3.49.4): a contradiction. Second, Thucydides says that overnight "most of the demos" felt "repentance" about "the savagery and magnitude" of their earlier decision, and reopened the discussion. Although "various speakers spoke on either side of the question." Thucydides reproduces just two speeches, justifying his choice by claiming that they "most directly contradicted each other" (3.49.1) and that Diodotus "had also in the earlier assembly argued most forcefully not to kill the Mytileneans" (3.41). However, neither of these two speeches is affected by repentance, but Kleon by selfish cruelty and Diodotus by selfishness and lack of moral principle: another contradiction. Third, at the end of this episode Thucydides reveals the Athenians' and his own moral sense, when after reversing their condemnation (although not wanting to put the Athenians in too favorable a light, he says the vote was almost equal: 3.49.1), Athens' second ship was sent "at once in haste" and made all possible speed, rowing through the night with extra rations (which were provided by the Mytileneans!) and arriving just when the executions were being prepared. This second ship "saved Mytilene from being destroyed. So near had the Mytileneans come to danger" (3.49).

Did Diodotus give the speech that Thucydides attributes to him? I have just now argued that Kleon did not give the speech that Thucydides wrote to sabotage him, and as we shall see, probably nobody thinks that the Melian Dialogue was authentic. Thucydides tells us that most Athenians were unhappy at their initial condemnation and insisted on reopening the question. Rightly so, as Thucydides also records that Mytilene's revolt was the work of the upper classes and the demos had no part in it. That would indicate that the Athenians were still behaving morally, unlike the progressive decline that Thucydides attributes to them. Diodotus' speech is also immoral, representing the Athenians as not respecting justice but yielding to *phusis*. The tragedy of Thucydides' speeches is that, as he says in 1.22, they reflect Thucydides' views and therefore we don't know what

Assembly speakers actually said, either the Athenians' real reasons for sparing Mytilene, or the opinions of speakers he did not record.

Shortly afterwards in 427, the Plataians are tried before five Spartan judges for executing 180 Thebans at the start of the war. As this trial is international, the parties discuss not statute law but unwritten Greek customary law. The Plataians say their behavior was justified by a law established for everyone, of no attacking during peacetime or festivals, as the Thebans had done (3.56.2). Greek law says not to kill those who surrender with hands outstretched (3.58.3). The Thebans say the Plataians "acted unlawfully without having received provocation… They will suffer by a legal sentence… Defend, Spartans, the *nomos* of the Greeks which they have broken" (3.67.5–6). Both Plataians and Thebans (3.62–67) commend Greek law.

Yet the Spartans (including their leaders in Sparta) pull a fast one against Plataia in not wanting to capture it by force, lest it must be given back in a peace treaty (3.52). Also, the Spartans swore not to judge the Plataians "against justice," *para dikên* (3.52.2), but they immediately do so, "making no charge" (*katêgoria*) but asking each Plataian individually what good thing he has done to help Sparta or its allies (3.52.4). (We again remember Sthenelaidas, "not to seek redress by *dikai* [lawsuits] or words, but speedily and with all our might".) The Plataians protest, expecting a *dikê* "more suited to law," *nomimôtera* (3.53.1). However, the Spartan *dikastai* (ibid.) do not prove impartial, and the Plataians have nowhere to turn, and no idea they would be subject to capital punishment. "By taking your own immediate interest as the test of justice, you will prove yourselves to be not judges of the truth but respecters only of your advantage (*to xumpheron*)" (3.56.3).

The Thebans respond with a counter history of their quarrel with Plataia, stressing justice, law, and what they consider the Plataians' lawless behavior (3.61–67). In the Persian Wars, they state, Thebes was a *dunasteia* entirely opposite to laws. Afterwards "it accepted the laws" and fought Athens and the Plataians who willingly accepted Athens' alliance. 3.64.3: The Thebans say the Plataians were still under the rule of law when they helped the Athenians. 3.65.1: "You last complain that we lawlessly invaded your town at a time of peace and festival [a Hellenic law], but some of you invited us." 3.66.2: "Our men suffered by a kind of *nomos*… but those men who surrendered [= the 180], you butchered *paranomôs*." 3.67.1: "Thus the Spartans will *dikaiôs* condemn the [Plataian] prisoners," who for their lawless act will suffer lawful things.

Both Plataia and Thebes claim to be law-abiding and call the other side unlawful. But Thucydides considers Sparta's strategy to cheat the Plataians of their city unfair. Sparta's brief question to each Plataian, "what have you done for us?", was perverted laconism and "unjust"; at the end, the Spartans condemn and kill "200 or more" Plataians. Thucydides concludes that the Spartans were hostile to the Plataians because they wanted to please the Thebans, who might prove useful to them (3.68.4): that is, by expediency. In 2.66–67, during wartime, we saw that both

Spartans and Athenians behaved savagely. On the Mytileneans' arrival in Athens (3.25–50), the Athenians first in anger condemned all of them without trial (*dikê:* 3.36), but in the end were merciful. Against the Plataians (3.52–68) Sparta was self-serving and murderous.

At 3.70 Thucydides returns to Corcyra where the war began, and to Corcyra's brutal *stasis*, with sacrilege and disputes over proper conduct and law. "Death in every form ensued, and whatever horrors typically happen at such times, happened then" (3.70–81). 3.82–83 outlines similar developments around the Greek world, as "will happen while human nature is the same,.., for war is a teacher of violence" (3.82.2). "Factional associations were established not with the benefit of established laws, but by greed against the established laws, and pledges were not confirmed by divine law [which Thucydides' Perikles commended in the Funeral Oration, and anti-democratic Sophokles in *Antigone*] but together by common transgressions of the law" (3.82.6). Sparta and Athens had recently behaved badly. For Thucydides, now many others did also.

Statute *nomoi* are only of limited, non-thematic significance in the second half of Thucydides, presumably because Athens' debate over *nomoi*, heated in the 420s, had subsequently faded. The major exception — the culminating immorality — in Thucydides' history occurs in the Melian dialogue of 416, at the end of Book 5. Thucydides (5.85) tells that this dialogue was held not before the populace but only some magistrates and a select few, so people could speak without what the Athenians called "seductive arguments." It includes many familiar Thucydidean themes, beginning with the Athenians' condemnation of rhetoric and popular assemblies' capacity for being deceived (5.85). The Melians respond that because the Athenians have come as *kritai,* judges [compare the Spartans at Plataia], the result will be war if the Melians prevail because their cause is *dikaios*, while if they lose the result will be *douleia,* slavery (5.86). Athens has thus perverted both justice and legal procedure. The Athenian judges tell the Melians that *nomos*, here universal rather than statute law, has become *phusis* (i.e., they talk not of law or morality but brute fact). "According to our understanding, divinity, it would seem, and mankind, as has always been obvious, are under a necessary nature (*phusis*) to rule (*archein*) wherever they have *kratos*. Without being the ones who made this *nomos* or the first to use it, we took it up as one in existence, and will leave it behind to exist for all time, knowing that you and everyone else having the same power as we have, would do the same as we do." In response to the Melians' expectation for Spartan help, they repeat in 5.105.4 what the Athenians had said about the Spartans in 1.77.6: "The Spartans are entirely virtuous as concerns themselves and their own country's *nomima*," but concerning other people "they are most conspicuous in considering *kalon* (fair and noble) what is *hêdu* ("pleasurable," the adjective of *hêdonê)*, and what is expedient [*xumpheronta*] just." Except in the case of Archidamus and Brasidas, because Thucydides liked effective upper-class leaders, he has largely been hostile to Sparta throughout his book. Students of the Melian dialogue have too easily passed over 5.83, immediately preceding the dialogue, when the Spartans failed in an attack on Argos and therefore "attacked neighboring Hysiai, killing all the free men who fell into their hands," as the Athenians will do at Melos. Thucydides does not indicate that the Hysians had harmed the Spartans in any way. This contiguous episode (like h: 2.66–67) confirms Thucydides' judgment on what the Athenians at Melos think of Sparta, but typically he downplays it, focusing on the sins of Athens. Both the Athenians and the Spartans are violent, while the Athenians embrace as a universal *nomos* of nature that "the strong do what they can and the weak suffer what they must" (5.89). However, we are not to think that this is Thucydides' view of reality. Immediately after destroying the Melians, the Athenians invade Sicily, Thucydides says in order to conquer it (6.1 et al.), and are wiped out.

Conclusions: Thucydides and statute laws

As we saw at the start of this essay, from the 420s down through Thucydides' lifetime and thus encompassing the years when he wrote his history, elite anti-democratic Athenians raised five arguments against *nomoi*. (A sixth anti-*nomos* argument first occurs in Plato)

The first of these arguments is the superiority of *phusis* (nature) to law. The earliest attestation of this idea occurs in Antiphon, who may have been Thucydides' teacher and was executed by the democracy in 411. In Thucydides Book 1 (b: 1.72–78), the Athenians at Sparta acknowledge the importance of *phusis* but stress that they behave more justly, equitably, and in accordance with *nomoi* than they have to. Later in the Mytilenean debate (j: 3.36–49), Diodotus champions *phusis* over *nomos*, dismissing justice. His arguments prevail, although Thucydides gives evidence against the accuracy of this account. In the Melian dialogue, the Athenians flatly embrace the doctrine of might makes right, but directly afterwards they invade Sicily and are destroyed. Thucydides rejects the idea that *phusis* is superior to *nomos*, as people overstep.

A second, related argument against *nomoi* is that laws are weak, for example in helping sufferers or stopping malefactors. This argument also occurs in Antiphon, and again in the speech Thucydides gives Diodotus. "It is quite impossible, and naive, if someone thinks the strength of *nomoi,* or any other terror, forms some bulwark against human nature setting out eagerly to do something" (3.45.7).

Third, laws are evidently not of much account because they are often changed. At Sparta in 432/1 (a: 1.71.3), Thucydides has the Corinthians, Sparta's allies, praise Athens for changing its laws, unlike Spartan practice, because that is how to win. By contrast, in the Funeral Oration (e: 2.35) Perikles disapproves of adding a speech to the *nomos* that established the funeral ceremony. By contrast again, in the Mytilenean debate (j: 3.36–49) Kleon objects that "we do not seem to know that a city employing worse but unmovable (*akinêtoi*) *nomoi* is better than one that employs good *nomoi* that lack authority" (3.37.3). So, Athens' laws are not good but still must not be changed: an absurdity. He adds, also absurdly, that intelligent people [the elite] want to show they are wiser (*sophôteroi)* than the laws, while the *phauloteroi* (the simpler sort) consider themselves more ignorant than the laws and less competent to criticize a good speaker, and so are impartial judges.

Fourth, the demos does not always obey its own laws. In Thucydides, not obeying the laws occurred at Athens during the special circumstance of the plague, but then more seriously shortly afterward, in h: 2.66–67 just after Perikles' epitaph in 2.65, when both the Spartans and the Athenians kill people without trials. In 3.82–83, Thucydides claims that the whole Greek world now turned violent and lawless. In addition although less seriously, in 6.14.6 Nikias tells the President of the Prytaneis that he should not fear "undoing" (*luein*) the *nomoi* if he puts a question again to a vote, with so many fellow citizens also voting. Thucydides thinks Nikias was good, and did not generally want to undo the laws. Yet moral rot is spreading.

Finally, fifth, virtue is advanced not by laws but by the habits of daily life. This criticism may recur in Perikles' comment in the Funeral Oration (2.39.4) that in Athens military courage came not from laws but from its way of life (*tropoi*).

Did Thucydides accept these criticisms of statute laws? The preceding analysis shows that he did not accept the *nomos/phusis* argument that might makes right. Was changing laws bad, or imply that Athens' laws were bad? The Corinthians at Sparta ably defend the idea that changing laws to reflect changing times was good, and when Thucydides has his enemy Kleon say the opposite while at the same time calling Athens' laws bad and Athens' jurors ignorant and incompetent, it is evident that Thucydides did not reject changing laws. The fourth criticism of *nomoi*, that the demos does not always obey them, is primarily a criticism of the demos, not of *nomoi*. Thucydides often disparaged the demos.

When did Thucydides develop the themes of statute *nomoi* and *dikê* in his first four books? Outside of Thucydides, we found a focused interest in these themes in Athens during the years 425–423. Thucydides' speeches show a similar interest starting with the Athenians in Sparta in 432/1 and going down to 427. We may conclude that whenever he came to compose other parts of these books, he may well have developed his material on statute *nomoi* and *dikê* in the years 425–423 when these issues were of wide concern in Athens, and like others he lost interest in these topics afterwards. His similar arrangement of the points in these speeches also support both that he wrote these speeches and at the same time. The Athenians at Sparta in 1.72 begin with a series of introductory points followed by Athens' *nomoi*. So does Thucydides' Perikles in the Funeral Oration (*prooimion*, brief references to ancestors, and from 2.37.1 Athens' *nomoi*). In the Mytilenean debate, after echoing Perikles, Thucydides has Kleon criticize Athens' *nomoi* as inferior.

Thucydides has been considered a Realist, a Machiavellian, a political scientist, a medical analyst, and a historian, but mostly not a moralist. For two quotes of many, Paul Shorey called him "a cynic devoid of moral sensibility."[20] More recently, the political scientist Steven Forde has observed, "The general law that 'the strong do what they can and the weak suffer what they must' ... is the proposition that Thucydides' History as a whole supports."[21] On the contrary, Thucydides expresses horror over many episodes where innocents (or the Athenians following Melos) are destroyed. We have already considered his emotions over Mytilene (3.49), where the adjective "so unwelcome (*allokotos*)" for the mission of Athens' first ship (3.49.4) applies both to the crewmen and to Thucydides himself. Book 7.29–30 records the slaughter of an innocent population including women, children — also a boy's school — and "every other living thing they saw" by Thracian mercenary troops at Mykalessos, which Thucydides calls the greatest calamity ever visited on any city. In the larger histories of five *poleis,* Corcyra, Plataia, Sparta, Athens, and Syracuse, all of them destroyed through their own fault (although Thucydides stops before recounting the misfortunes of Syracuse), the age-old moral prescription prevails: if you behave badly you will be punished. Directly after the Athenians destroy Melos at the end of Book 5, their destruction in Sicily scholars rightly see as punishment for arrogant overreach. Afterwards, down through Book 8, the Athenians behave well, and the Spartans behave badly. As I have noted, already in Book 1 Thucydides alludes to Sparta's comeuppance after 404, the year when Athens lost the war.

Thucydides' theme of statute law is an important element of his moral stance. Adding bad laws, ignoring gods' laws, championing so-called nature over law ("the strong do what they can and the weak suffer as they must": 5.89), not following the law, and supporting Kleon's contradictory "just and expedient" verdict: those who follow bad or self-serving laws will suffer. Thucydides' horror at abusive conduct did not reflect Athens' moral deterioration, but Athens' greater moral sensitivity, most famously in Euripides' *Trojan Woman* of 415, defending innocent women and children, and by sparing the Mytileneans. In this same way, elite Athenians' complaints about democracy's legal inequities reflect Athenians' greater moral sensitivities, especially from the 420s. So far from being a political "realist," Thucydides shared the Athenians' heightened moral sense. So far from getting worse, concern against violence shows that the Athenians were getting better, ever more sensitive to misdeeds. Scholars misread Thucydides' expressions of horror as indicating a deterioration of character. They reflect the opposite.

rwallace@northwestern.edu

[20] Shorey 1893, 71.
[21] Forde 1992, 376.

BIBLIOGRAPHY

Connor 1984: W.R. Connor, *Thucydides* (Princeton 1984).

Dover 1973: K. J. Dover, *Thucydides* (*Greece and Rome* 1973).

Finley 1967: J. Finley, "The Origins of Thucydides' style," in *Three Essays on Thucydides* (Cambridge Mass. 1967) 55–117.

Fletcher 2012: J. Fletcher, "Law and spectacle in Euripides' *Hecuba*," in *Greek Drama* IV: *Texts, Contexts, Performance*, ed. D. Rosenbloom and J. Davidson (Liverpool 2012) 225–243.

Forde 1992: S. Forde, "Varieties of realism: Thucydides and Machiavelli," *The Journal of Politics* 54 (1992) 372–393.

Gagarin 2002: M. Gagarin, *Antiphon the Athenian. Oratory, Law, and Justice in the Age of the Sophists* (Austin 2002).

Hornblower 1987: Hornblower, S., *Thucydides* (Baltimore 1987).

Hornblower 1991, 1996, 2008: Hornblower, S., *A Commentary on Thucydides*, 3 vols. (Oxford 1991, 1996, 2008).

Lattimore, S., *Thucydides* (Hackett 1998).

MacLeod 1978: C.W. MacLeod, "Reason and necessity: Thucydides III 9–14, 37–48," *JHS* 98 (1978) 64–78.

Marr – Rhodes 2008: J. L. Marr and P. J. Rhodes, *The 'Old Oligarch': The Constitution of the Athenians attributed to Xenophon* (Oxford 2008).

Ostwald 1986: M. Ostwald, *From Popular Sovereignty to the Sovereignty of Law* (Berkeley and Los Angeles 1986).

Pendrick 2002: G. Pendrick, *Antiphon the Sophist. The Fragments* (Cambridge 2002).

Rhodes 1988: Rhodes, P., *Thucydides History* II (Aris and Phillips 1988).

Scheibelreiter 2011: Ph. Scheibelreiter, "Völkerrecht bei Thukydides. Rechtsquelle und völkerrechtliche Begrifflichkeit," in E. Baltrusch and Ch. Wendt, eds., *Ein Besitz für Immer? Geschichte, Polis und Völkerrecht bei Thukydides* (Baden-Baden 2011) 155–159.

Sheet 1994: G.A. Sheet, "Conceptualizing International Law in Thucydides," *AJP* 115 (1994) 51–73.

Shorey 1893: P. Shorey, "On the Implicit Ethics and Psychology of Thucydides," *TAPA* 24 (1893) 66–88.

Thomas 1994: R. Thomas, "Law and the lawgiver in the Athenian democracy," in R. G. Osborne and S. Hornblower, eds., *Ritual, Finance, Politics: Athenian Democratic Accounts Presented to David Lewis* (Oxford 1994) 119–133.

Wallace 2005: R.W. Wallace, "'Listening to' the *archai* in democratic Athens," *Symposion* 2001, ed. R. Wallace and M. Gagarin (Vienna 2005) 147–157.

Wallace 2007a: R.W. Wallace, "Plato's sophists, intellectual history after 450, and Sokrates," in L. J. Samons II, ed., *Cambridge Companion to the Age of Pericles* (Cambridge 2007) 224–234.

Wallace 2007b: R.W. Wallace, “Law’s enemies in ancient Athens,” in E. Cantarella, ed., *Symposion* 2005 (Vienna 2007) 183–196.

Wallace 2016: R.W. Wallace, “Equality, the *dêmos*, and law in archaic Greece,” *Symposion* XV, ed. D. Leão and G. Thür (Vienna 2016) 1–14.

Wohl 2015: V. Wohl, *Euripides and the Politics of Form* (Princeton 2015).

MIRKO CANEVARO (EDINBURGH)

LA SOVRANITÀ DELLA LEGGE COME CRITERIO DI GIUDIZIO COSTITUZIONALE – TRA DEMOCRAZIA E OLIGARCHIA: RISPOSTA A ROBERT WALLACE

Nelle prime pagine del suo contributo, Robert Wallace nota che una serie di argomentazioni contro la legge – contro le manifestazioni specifiche, poleiche, del diritto oggettivo – iniziarono ad emergere tra le élite ateniesi dopo il 458, "After centuries of unwavering support for statute laws". Procede poi a discutere le diverse forme che la critica alla legge assunse nei decenni successivi. Queste critiche, tuttavia, mi paiono emergere tutte da specifici circoli – vengono da sofisti e intellettuali, e sembrano avere pochissimo seguito nell'opinione pubblica e nelle opzioni ideologiche dominanti ad Atene (e oltre), che siano democratiche o oligarchiche.[1] Dopo questa premessa sulle forme della critica alla legge, Wallace raccoglie e analizza i passi nei quali Tucidide discute di legge e diritto oggettivo, sia in assoluto sia nelle specifiche incarnazioni che troviamo ad Atene, a Sparta e altrove. Le valutazioni di Tucidide paiono investire due questioni: se una data città sia più o meno caratterizzata dal rispetto delle leggi, e (più raramente) quale sia la qualità effettiva delle sue leggi. Le considerazioni di Wallace mi stimolano a tornare sulla questione (che ho toccato in passato)[2] della funzione dell'ideale della sovranità delle leggi ("rule of law") nel dibattito politico del V (e IV) secolo.[3] In quanto segue, cerco di tracciare (sommariamente) un abbozzo del dibattito all'interno del quale, credo, vanno situate le considerazioni di Tucidide, che offre nella sua opera tanto una rappresentazione quanto un commento a un certo stile di argomentazione, legato alla realtà delle opzioni ideologiche del suo tempo.

---

1 Il contesto è quello della critica allo *status quo* descritta da Ober 1998: 48 come 'rejectionist'.

2 Canevaro 2017.

3 Questa domanda è strettamente legata, e tuttavia non identica, a quella sulla natura dell'ordinamento giuridico ateniese in particolare – se cioè fosse conforme ai criteri del "rule of law". Gli interventi in questo dibattito sono numerosissimi, vd. per l'approccio a mio parere più produttivo Harris 2006; 2013, con anche Canevaro 2015; 2017; 2018; Pelloso 2017. Per la varietà delle posizioni vd. p.es. Osborne 1985; Ostwald 1986; Sealey 1987; Ober 1989; Todd 1993; Cohen 1995; Christ 1998; Lanni 2006; 2016; Gowder 2014; Carugati 2014; Carugati – Hadfield – Weingast 2015; Carugati – Calvert – Weingast 2021; Forsdyke 2018.

Il mio punto di partenza – lo stesso del contributo di Wallace – è "the unwavering support for statute law" che troviamo in gran parte delle fonti, ben oltre l'Arcaismo. Questo supporto non è generico – è caratterizzato nelle fonti come specificamente greco, centrale all'identità dei Greci e tratto distintivo che li contrappone al mondo monarchico e autocratico dei barbari. Questa opposizione ideale tra sovranità dell'individuo e sovranità della legge è ideologicamente centrale nel modo in cui la resistenza dei Greci ai Persiani viene concettualizzata al tempo delle Guerre Persiane, e nella riflessione successiva su quegli eventi.[4] L'esule spartano Demarato, come racconta Erodoto (7.104), spiega a Serse la differenza tra Greci e Persiani proprio in questi termini. Prima, afferma che il coraggio dei Greci si fonda sulla loro intelligenza e sulla forza della legge, e poi osserva (concentrandosi a questo punto specificamente sugli Spartani):[5]

> ἐλεύθεροι γὰρ ἐόντες οὐ πάντα ἐλεύθεροι εἰσί: ἔπεστι γάρ σφι δεσπότης νόμος, τὸν ὑποδειμαίνουσι πολλῷ ἔτι μᾶλλον ἢ οἱ σοὶ σέ. ποιεῦσι γῶν τὰ ἂν ἐκεῖνος ἀνώγῃ: ἀνώγει δὲ τὠυτὸ αἰεί, οὐκ ἐῶν φεύγειν οὐδὲν πλῆθος ἀνθρώπων ἐκ μάχης, ἀλλὰ μένοντας ἐν τῇ τάξι ἐπικρατέειν ἢ ἀπόλλυσθαι.
>
> Infatti, pur essendo liberi, non lo sono completamente: hanno un padrone, la legge, che temono molto più di quanto i tuoi uomini temano te; fanno dunque ciò che essa ordina: ed ordina sempre la stessa cosa: di non fuggire in battaglia neppure davanti a una folla di nemici, ma di restare al proprio posto e di vincere o morire. (Trad. Colonna-Bevilacqua)

Finché il nemico è il barbaro, troviamo nelle fonti un'opposizione binaria tra i Greci, caratterizzati dal rispetto per la legge (e da regimi fondati sulla sovranità della legge), e i barbari, caratterizzati dal dominio arbitrario di un uomo solo che risulta in *douleia* per tutti gli altri.[6] Nella cornice di questa opposizione binaria tra greci rispettosi della legge e barbari autocratici, le differenze costituzionali tra le città greche – nella distribuzione del potere politico e nella definizione dei confini della cittadinanza – sembrano marginali. Ateniesi e Spartani, in quanto Greci e non barbari, sono rispettosi delle leggi e vivono sotto costituzioni in cui sovrana è solo la legge e non uno o più individui.

Tutto questo cambiò progressivamente negli anni che seguirono alla vittoria greca nelle Guerre Persiane. Nei decenni a seguire, il mondo greco a poco a poco si

4 Per una discussione affascinante di come le Guerre Persiane divennero paradigmatiche nel discorso dell' "orientalismo", e particolarmente nella contrapposizione tra "rule of law" (greco) e oppressione (barbara), vd. Lianeri 2007. Sulla prima ricezione ed elaborazione memoriale delle Guerre Persiane vd. ora Proietti 2021.

5 Sul *nomos despotes* nel discorso di Demarato vd. ora Branscome 2013, 68–75 con bibliografia precedente.

6 Per l'estensione metaforica di *douleia* a caratterizzare rapporti politici di oppressione vd. Brock 2007; 2013: 109, 123, 157–8; Lewis 2018: 59–67.

divise in due aree di influenza, quella di Sparta e quella di Atene, con ripetuti conflitti militari, e il progressivo rafforzamento di un'opposizione ideologica e costituzionale.[7] Il regime spartano venne ad identificarsi come alfiere di un modello oligarchico che concentrava il potere nelle mani di una minoranza – *hoi oligoi* – mentre ad Atene tutti gli Ateniesi liberi (con Pericle, nati da due genitori ateniesi) erano politicamente eguali, con eguale accesso alle istituzioni di decisione politica, ai tribunali e alle magistrature.[8] Con l'intensificarsi di questa contrapposizione, ad essa venne ad accompagnarsi uno scontro ideologico senza quartiere sulla desiderabilità delle due opzioni costituzionali.[9] Alla fine del V secolo, questo scontro aveva spostato il baricentro del discorso politico-costituzionale greco dalla questione della similitudine dei regimi delle città greche (contrapposti al modello dei barbari) a quella delle loro differenze. Mentre la sovranità della legge ("rule of law") era un caposaldo ideologico condiviso nel contesto delle *poleis*, e dunque concentrarsi sulla sua importanza serviva ad evidenziare l'unità del modello costituzionale greco – come fattore anche identitario –, al contrario sottolineare le differenze tra democrazia ed oligarchia serviva a spostare lo scontro tra Atene e Sparta su un livello ideologico più alto, che coinvolgesse anche diverse "classi" e fazioni all'interno delle altre *poleis*. La mia tesi è che la centralità dell'ideale della sovranità della legge non perse, con questi sviluppi, alcuna della sua importanza e centralità. Al contrario, la "unanimity in support of the rule of law" divenne il metro di giudizio fondamentale nello scontro ideologico tra oligarchia e democrazia. Brian Tamanaha, un prominente teorico del diritto, ha osservato al riguardo del nostro mondo contemporaneo che "[t]he rule of law is an accepted measure worldwide of government legitimacy".[10] Lo stesso, a mio parere, avvenne nel mondo greco del V (e del IV) secolo: oligarchia e democrazia erano celebrate, difese, attaccate o condannate sulla base della loro aderenza (dichiarata e contestata) e compatibilità con l'ideale della sovranità delle leggi. Nel contesto di questa breve risposta, mi concentrerò su una manciata di testi che possano

[7] La fonte primaria è la Pentekontaetia di Tucidide. Rimando a Rhodes 2010: 14–76 per una trattazione sintetica ma precisa del periodo.

[8] Per la natura oligarchica del sistema decisionale spartano vd. Ste. Croix 1972: 124–51; Kennell 2010: 93–114; Esu 2018, con abbondante bibliografia. Per la diseguaglianza sociale, economica e politica a Sparta vd. Hodkinson 2000. Simonton 2017 mostra che lo sviluppo di regimi oligarchici – in quanto tali – è direttamente legato alla reazione alla diffusione del modello democratico. La contrapposizione costituzionale nasce da una contrapposizione ideale. Resto convinto, con de Ste. Croix 1954, che Atene fosse percepita come – e fosse in larga parte effettivamente – alfiere di regimi popolari intorno all'Egeo, nonostante le mie differenze rispetto all'analisi di Ste. Croix, vd. Canevaro – Lewis 2023.

[9] Per lo sviluppo di questa contrapposizione nel discorso ateniese sull'oligarchia vd. ora Caire 2016.

[10] Tamanaha 2004: 3.

illuminare queste dinamiche ideologiche, e in particolare su Tucidide e sullo Pseudo-Senofonte.

Il primo testo è la *Costituzione degli Ateniesi* dello Pseudo-Senofonte.[11] Questo testo è emblematico delle più ampie coordinate ideologiche e costituzionali in cui si manifestò il conflitto tra Sparta e Atene nel tardo V secolo, e rivela in modo chiaro (per quanto parziale) quali fossero, per i Greci (e per gli Ateniesi in particolare), le opzioni ideologiche disponibili. Esse si manifestavano – da un punto di vista oligarchico – in essenza come un'alternativa tra il governo dei "migliori" e quello dei "peggiori". Lo Pseudo-Senofonte introduce *demokratia* come un termine negativo, con *demos* indicante non il popolo in senso inclusivo (come totalità dei cittadini) ma piuttosto le classi basse, le masse, il popolino, in opposizione ai suoi leaders, caratterizzati – attraverso termini come *agathoi*, *aristoi*, *chrestoi* – come moralmente, fisicamente e intellettualmente superiori.[12] In contrasto, i membri del *demos* sono caratterizzati – attraverso termini come *kakoi* o *poneroi* – come moralmente, fisicamente e intellettualmente inferiori.[13] Ps.-Xen. *Ath. Pol.* 1.5–9 è emblematico di questo schema argomentativo e mostra che questa opposizione è nei fatti costruita in termini di aderenza (o meno) ai dettati della sovranità della legge. I "migliori" sono naturalmente più adatti a favorire la giustizia e a opporsi all'ingiustizia (*adikia*), mentre le masse sono caratterizzate da disordine (*ataxia*) e illegalità. Per lo Pseudo-Senofonte, l'*eunomia* (un ideale di buon governo caratterizzato dal rispetto della legge – caro tanto agli Ateniesi quanto agli Spartani) conduce naturalmente alla schiavitù del *demos*, mentre laddove il popolo (e cioè le masse popolari) è libero e forte, il regime è caratterizzato da *kakonomia*.[14] Per creare e preservare l'*eunomia*, è indispensabile che chi è più capace abbia il potere di legiferare, e che i "peggiori" siano sotto il fermo controllo dei "migliori" – senza poter sedere nel Consiglio o parlare nell'Assemblea. Ciò che colpisce di questo quadro è che nonostante l'obiettivo ideologico del trattato – un obiettivo figlio del nuovo contesto della contrapposizione tra Sparta e Atene (e tra oligarchia e democrazia): denigrare la *demokratia* – i presupposti e le coordinate fondamentali sottostanti sono ancora gli stesse che troviamo in Solone (fr. 4 West^2), in Tirteo

---

11 Rimando a Marr – Rhodes 2008 per una trattazione complessiva, e p.es. a Hornblower 2000, Faraguna 2011 e Ferrucci 2013 per studi e approcci di particolare valore.

12 Cf. Gomme 1956: 107–8: "*demokratia* can mean either simply majority rule in a state where all citizens have the vote... or the consistent domination of the state by the masses". Per diverse interpretazioni del significato primario di *demokratia* vd. p.es. Sealey 1974: 282, 292–5; Raaflaub 1983: 517–44; Ober 1989, 2008 e Canfora 2006: 8; Hansen 2008; Cammack 2019.

13 Per questi termini peggiorativi vd. Marr – Rhodes 2008: 24–6, 171–2, e più in dettaglio Cagnetta et al. 1977; Faraguna 2011: 85–87.

14 Questa è la prima attestazione di *eunomia* nel suo senso pieno di epoca classica – in riferimento al *nomos* come legge. Vd. Ostwald 1969: 82–85 e 94–95; Faraguna 2011: 89. Per l'accostamento tra *eunomia* e schiavitù del *demos* vd. Faraguna 2011: 89 (cfr. anche Plat. *Gorg.* 483c–484c, 490a–492c con Heftner 2003: 11–13).

(frr. 1–4 West^2) e, soprattutto, nelle opposizioni ideologiche del periodo delle Guerre Persiane. Il modello positivo è ancora l'*eunomia* e il suo contrario è la *kakonomia* – variante di *anomia* o *dysnomia*, come illegalità. La mossa ideologica dello Pseudo-Senofonte è di escludere la *demokratia* dall'orizzonte delle forme costituzionali compatibili con l'*eunomia*, e di caratterizzarla come una forma di potere arbitrario (simile alle autocrazie dei barbari). In *demokratia*, per lo Pseudo-Senofonte, non troviamo la sovranità delle leggi ("rule of law") ma quella degli uomini – dei "peggiori", per la precisione.

Nel nuovo contesto di tardo V secolo, con il mondo greco diviso politicamente, militarmente e costituzionalmente, il modello dell'*eunomia* non è più usato in senso identitario per unire i Greci e separarli dai non-Greci (e dai Persiani in particolare), ma non perde per questo la sua centralità. Diventa, per citare ancora Tamanaha, "the accepted measure [...] of government legitimacy" e, in quanto tale, è usato come base ideologica delle critiche incrociate che volano tra i due lati del nuovo discrimine costituzionale tra democrazia e oligarchia. Molti dei passi citati da Wallace nel suo contributo mi sembrano ricalcare questo schema argomentativo: non è l'ideale della sovranità della legge (e la sua desiderabilità) ad essere messo in discussione, ma piuttosto l'aderenza di questa o quella realtà costituzionale a quell'ideale. La tesi oligarchica è che la partecipazione stessa delle masse popolari al governo della *polis* sia per sua natura incompatibile con i requisiti della sovranità della legge – diventa potere delle masse al di sopra della sovranità della legge. La risposta democratica è che il *demos* è in realtà più ligio alle leggi degli *oligoi* che governano una città come Sparta. Questa è la linea tenuta dagli Ateniesi al congresso di Sparta del 432/1 (Thuc. 1.75): grazie al loro potere, alle loro risorse e alla loro ricchezza, gli Ateniesi potrebbero imporre a piacimento la loro volontà con la forza, ma scelgono invece di sottomettersi alle leggi, in termini paritari, persino nel contesto delle dispute con i loro alleati – tale è la loro reverenza per le leggi. Si noti che Archidamo, nella sua risposta (Thuc. 1.84–5), da un lato riconosce la pertinenza della difesa degli Ateniesi (e il suo valore), dall'altro tenta implicitamente di *battere* gli Ateniesi al loro stesso gioco, affermando che gli Spartani sono educati rudemente (*chalepos*) e per questo è loro impossibile disprezzare le leggi; e sono troppo disciplinati per poter disobbedire ai *nomoi*. Archidamo, insomma, risponde agli Ateniesi: pensate di essere ligi alle leggi? Noi siamo ben più ligi alle leggi di voi! La stessa dinamica è riprodotta anche nello scambio tra Plateesi e Tebani (Thuc. 3.61–7), dove entrambe le parti affermano con forza di avere agito secondo giustizia, sottolineano il loro impegno nel rispettare le leggi e sostengono che sia stata l'altra parte ad aver agito illegalmente (3.56.2; 58.3; 64.3; 65.1; 66.2; 67.1; 67.5–6) – e i Plateesi avevano già protestato (3.53) che il loro giudizio sarebbe dovuto avvenire attraverso una *dike* più in linea con la legge (*nomimotera*).

Vale la pena, a questo punto, di spendere qualche parola sull'Orazione Funebre periclea,[15] nel II libro di Tucidide. La mia tesi è che anche questo testo – spesso letto come prototipica difesa del modello democratico[16] – vada iscritto entro queste coordinate ideologiche e interpretato come una risposta implicitamente polemica al tipo di argomentazioni che abbiamo incontrato nello Pseudo-Senofonte.[17] Qui, mi pare, Tucidide offre una potente (e paradigmatica) difesa della democrazia che non si fonda né su un rifiuto né sul superamento dell'ideologia della sovranità della legge. Al contrario, il suo obiettivo è riscattare la *demokratia* da quelle critiche (di parte spartana e oligarchica) che ne negano la compatibilità con la sovranità della legge, al contempo ponendo in dubbio l'aderenza di Sparta a quel modello. Voglio concentrarmi su un particolare passo che pone in rilievo questa fondamentale mossa ideologica (Thuc. 2.37):

> χρώμεθα γὰρ πολιτείᾳ οὐ ζηλούσῃ τοὺς τῶν πέλας νόμους, παράδειγμα δὲ μᾶλλον αὐτοὶ ὄντες τισὶν ἢ μιμούμενοι ἑτέρους. καὶ ὄνομα μὲν διὰ τὸ μὴ ἐς ὀλίγους ἀλλ᾽ ἐς πλείονας οἰκεῖν δημοκρατία κέκληται: μέτεστι δὲ κατὰ μὲν τοὺς νόμους πρὸς τὰ ἴδια διάφορα πᾶσι τὸ ἴσον, κατὰ δὲ τὴν ἀξίωσιν, ὡς ἕκαστος ἔν τῳ εὐδοκιμεῖ, οὐκ ἀπὸ μέρους τὸ πλέον ἐς τὰ κοινὰ ἢ ἀπ᾽ ἀρετῆς προτιμᾶται, οὐδ᾽ αὖ κατὰ πενίαν, ἔχων γέ τι ἀγαθὸν δρᾶσαι τὴν πόλιν, ἀξιώματος ἀφανείᾳ κεκώλυται. [2] ἐλευθέρως δὲ τά τε πρὸς τὸ κοινὸν πολιτεύομεν καὶ ἐς τὴν πρὸς ἀλλήλους τῶν καθ᾽ ἡμέραν ἐπιτηδευμάτων ὑποψίαν, οὐ δι᾽ ὀργῆς τὸν πέλας, εἰ καθ᾽ ἡδονήν τι δρᾷ, ἔχοντες, οὐδὲ ἀζημίους μέν, λυπηρὰς δὲ τῇ ὄψει ἀχθηδόνας προστιθέμενοι. [3] ἀνεπαχθῶς δὲ τὰ ἴδια προσομιλοῦντες τὰ δημόσια διὰ δέος μάλιστα οὐ παρανομοῦμεν, τῶν τε αἰεὶ ἐν ἀρχῇ ὄντων ἀκροάσει καὶ τῶν νόμων, καὶ μάλιστα αὐτῶν ὅσοι τε ἐπ᾽ ὠφελίᾳ τῶν ἀδικουμένων κεῖνται καὶ ὅσοι ἄγραφοι ὄντες αἰσχύνην ὁμολογουμένην φέρουσιν.

> Abbiamo un sistema di governo che non emula le leggi dei vicini; ma siamo noi stessi un modello piuttosto che gli imitatori di altri. E quanto al nome, per il fatto che il potere non è nelle mani dei pochi, ma dei più, si chiama democrazia: secondo le leggi vi è per tutti l'eguaglianza per ciò che riguarda gli interessi privati; e quanto alla considerazione di cui si gode, ciascuno è preferito per le cariche pubbliche a seconda del campo nel quale si distingue, e non per la classe da cui proviene più che per il merito; d'altra parte, quanto alla povertà, se uno è in grado di far del bene alla città,

[15] Per i discorsi funebri vd. innanzitutto Loraux 1986 e, per alcune utili discussioni, p.es. Ziolkowski 1981; Thomas 1989: 196–237; Parker 1996: 131–41; Mills 1997: 58–78; Herrman 2009: 3–26; Low 2010; Shear 2013. La bibliografia sul discorso di Pericle è immensa, ma vd. almeno Hornblower 1987: 45–65; Harris 2006: 29–39; Bosworth 2000. Longo 2000 offre un buon commento all'orazione. Per l'oratoria del Pericle storico vd. Azoulay 2014: 40–51.

[16] Cfr. Canfora 2006: 7–35; Hansen 2008.

[17] Vd. Harris 2006: 29–39. per una lettura di questo testo come ideologicamente polemico.

non è impedito dall'oscurità della sua posizione sociale. Noi svolgiamo la nostra vita di cittadini liberamente, sia nei rapporti con lo stato, sia per ciò che riguarda i sospetti reciproci nelle attività di tutti i giorni: non siamo adirati col nostro vicino se fa qualcosa secondo il suo piacere, né infliggiamo molestie che, pur non facendo del male, sono tuttavia fastidiose alla vista. Mentre ci regoliamo nei nostri rapporti privati senza offendere, nella vita pubblica non ci comportiamo in modo illegale, soprattutto a causa della paura, perché diamo ascolto a coloro che di volta in volta sono in carica e alle leggi, specialmente quelle che sono stabilite per aiutare le vittime di ingiustizia e quelle che, senza essere scritte, portano a chi le viola una vergogna comunemente riconosciuta. (Trad. modificata da Donini)

Un primo punto degno di nota è che la discussione periclea del regime di Atene – in un paragrafo che è a buon diritto letto come una celebrazione della democrazia – non comincia con il *demos*, ma piuttosto con le leggi. È l'eccellenza delle leggi che è posta a fondamento dell'eccellenza della città. E in un contesto ideologico nel quale troviamo critiche della democrazia come quella dello Pseudo-Senofonte, che la caratterizzano come incompatibile con il governo della legge, cominciare la celebrazione – e la difesa – di Atene dalle sue leggi non sarà stato casuale. La *demokratia* come tale entra in gioco soltanto dopo questa prima focalizzazione sulla funzione fondamentale delle leggi: Pericle afferma esplicitamente che questa *politeia* fondata sulle leggi è una *demokratia.* Ed è una *demokratia* perché il governo della *polis* è nelle mani dei molti e non dei pochi.[18] Il bersaglio polemico – Sparta e il modello oligarchico più in generale – è evidente nel riferimento esplicito agli *oligoi.*[19] Pericle, dunque, caratterizza la *demokratia* non come un regime nel quale il *demos* ha sovranità assoluta, superiore anche a quella delle leggi, ma piuttosto come un regime fondato sulle leggi che in virtù delle leggi dà ai più (cioè alle masse) il controllo della *polis*. Questa difesa e celebrazione della democrazia è, per così dire, incorniciata dalle leggi, che non solo la precedono, ma la seguono: subito dopo l'affermazione dell'autorità dei più (che giustifica il nome *demokratia*) Pericle torna immediatamente alle leggi e afferma che le leggi sono garanzia di eguale trattamento per tutti. In questo modo, il nodo cruciale della compatibilità tra democrazia e sovranità della legge è affrontato incorniciando la difesa della *demokratia* tra due affermazioni della supremazia della legge sull'individuo, e dell'eguaglianza vigente tra gli Ateniesi come radicata nelle leggi. Il prosieguo del passo sviluppa questa stessa linea argomentativa, e Pericle afferma che il potere del *demos* (dei più) nell'amministrazione della *polis* non equivale ad una sovranità

[18] La mia interpretazione di διὰ τὸ μὴ ἐς ὀλίγους ἀλλ' ἐς πλείονας οἰκεῖν δημοκρατία segue quella di Harris 2006: 34–6 (con discussione delle diverse interpretazioni, contro l'idea che il governo sia qui detto da Tucidide "nell'interesse dei più" e non "sotto il controllo del più"; così anche Hansen 2008; *pace* p.es. Loraux 1986: 183; Ostwald 1986: 183; Rusten 1989: 145).

[19] Cf. anche Harris 2006: 34 per Sparta come contraltare polemico della descrizione periclea di Atene in questo passo; Hussey 1985: 123–29 per l'immagine del sistema valoriale spartano che troviamo nell'Orazione Funebre.

dell'uomo superiore a quella delle leggi – è invece iscritto nella sovranità delle leggi. La costituzione ateniese è poi celebrata e difesa anche nel modo in cui seleziona le cariche, aperte a tutti e scelte in base al valore di chi le dovrà ricoprire, e non sulla base di criteri ulteriori. Il bersaglio polemico è ancora una volta Sparta (e il modello oligarchico più in generale), e Pericle afferma qui che è ben possibile (*pace* lo Pseudo-Senofonte) preservare la sovranità della legge senza necessità alcuna di ridurre i poveri in una condizione di assoggettamento che si avvicina a quella della schiavitù. Non è un caso che quanto segue si volga alla questione della libertà, ma la libertà del *demos* non è qui affermata come licenza di fare ciò che si vuole, ma al contrario associata alla paura – delle autorità e, soprattutto, delle leggi – e alla vergogna che viene a chi non vi obbedisce.[20]

Ciò che troviamo in questi passi – in questo dialogo che ho un po' artificialmente instaurato tra lo Pseudo-Senofonte e l'Orazione Funebre del Pericle tucidideo – è un esempio a mio parere abbastanza tipico degli scambi e contrasti ideologici, che caratterizzarono il tardo V secolo, tra chi era convinto che i molti dovessero partecipare al governo della *polis* e chi credeva invece che dovessero essere esclusi in quanto indegni di potere politico. I posizionamenti ideologici, e i relativi dibattiti, tra forme costituzionali oligarchiche e democratiche non ridussero mai l'importanza e la centralità dell'ideale della sovranità della legge. Al contrario, il "rule of law" si affermò ancora più fortemente come ideale normativo: come criterio di giudizio fondamentale della legittimità di qualsiasi forma costituzionale. Una volta afferrata questa dimensione del dibattito ideologico dell'epoca, a me pare che molti dei riferimenti alla *legge* in Tucidide raccolti e discussi da Wallace nel suo contributo possano essere letti come tentativi brillanti di (di)mostrare come si articolasse questo dibattito *sul campo* – dimostrare, cioè, quali argomenti fossero effettivamente adottati dalle parti in causa – al contempo problematizzando entrambe le posizioni e rivelandone i presupposti (comuni) e i limiti. Se in certa letteratura sofistica dell'epoca è l'autorità della legge stessa ad essere messa in discussione, in Tucidide (come nello Pseudo-Senofonte e in tanti altri testi più direttamente politici) il problema non è l'autorità della legge, ma piuttosto quale forma costituzionale possa effettivamente dirsi fondata sul suo rispetto.

mirko.canevaro@ed.ac.uk

BIBLIOGRAPHY

Azoulay, V. (2014). *Pericles of Athens*. Princeton.

Bosworth, A.B. (2000). "The historical context of Thucydides' funeral oration", *JHS* 120: 1–16.

---

[20] Contro la nozione che la libertà democratica fosse mai concepita (in contesto democratico) come libertà di fare ciò che si vuole vd. ora (convincentemente) Filonik 2019.

Branscome, D. (2013). *Textual Rivals: Self-Presentation in Herodotus' 'Histories'*. Ann Arbor, MI.
Brock, R. (2007). "Figurative slavery in Greek thought", in A. Serghidou (a cura di). *Peur de l'esclave – Peur de l'esclavage en Méditerranée ancienne / Fear of Slaves – Fear of enslavement in the ancient Mediterranean (XXIXe colloque du GIREA, Rethymnon, 4–7 novembre 2004)*. Besançon: 217–224.
Brock, R. (2013). *Greek Political Imagery from Homer to Aristotle*. London.
Cagnetta, M., Petroccelli, C. e Zagaria, C. (1977). "χρήστος", *QS* 6: 155–172.
Caire, E. (2016). *Penser l'oligarchie à Athènes aux Ve et IVe siècles: Aspects d'une idéologie*. Paris.
Cammack, D. (2019) "The *demos* in *demokratia*", *CQ* 69: 42–61.
Canevaro, M. (2015). "Making and changing laws in ancient Athens", in E.M. Harris e M. Canevaro (a cura di). *Oxford Handbook of Ancient Greek Law*. Oxford.
Canevaro, M. (2017). "The Rule of Law as the Measure of Political Legitimacy in the Greek City States". *Hague Journal on the Rule of Law* 9: 211–36.
Canevaro M (2018). "Law and justice", in G. Martin (a cura di). *Oxford Handbook of Demosthenes*. Oxford. 73–85.
Canevaro, M. e Lewis, D.M. (2023). "Between 'The character of the Athenian Empire' and *The Origins of the Peloponnesian War* (and beyond): the popularity of the Athenian empire revisited", *Polis* 40.4.
Canfora, L. (2006). *Democracy in Europe: A History of an Ideology*. Oxford.
Carugati, F. (2014). "What is the rule of law good for? Democracy, development and the rule of law in Classical Athens", *Buffalo Law Review* 62: 119–56.
Carugati, F., Hadfield, G. e Weingast, B. (2015), "Building legal order in ancient Athens", *Journal of Legal Analysis* 7: 291–324.
Carugati, F., Calvert, R., Weingast, B. (2021). "Constitutional litigation in ancient Athens: judicial review by the people themselves", *Journal of Law, Economics, & Organization* 39, 1–26.
Christ, M.R. (1998). *The Litigious Athenian*. Baltimore.
Cohen, D. (1995). *Law, Violence, and Community in Classical Athens*. Cambridge.
Esu, A. (2018), "Divided power and oligarchy: deliberative procedures in ancient Sparta", *CQ* 67: 353–73.
Faraguna, M. (2011), "Lessico e argomenti politici nello scritto del « Vecchio Oligarca»", in F. Landucci e L. Prandi (a cura di). *L'*Athenaion politeia *rivisitata. Il punto su Pseudo-Senofonte*. Milano: 73–97.
Ferrucci, S. (2013). *La democrazia diseguale. Riflessioni sull'Atheneion politeia dello pseudo-Senofonte, I 1–9*. Pisa.
Filonik, J. (2019). "'Living as one wishes' in Athens: the (anti-)democratic polemics", *CPh* 114: 1–24.
Forsdyke, S. (2018). "Ancient and modern conceptions of the rule of law", in M. Canevaro, A. Erskine, B. Gray, J. Ober (a cura di). *Ancient Greek History and the Contemporary Social Sciences*. Edinburgh: 184–212.

Gomme, A.W. (1956). *A Historical Commentary on Thucydides, Volume II: The Ten Years' War (Books II–III)*. Oxford.

Gowder, P. (2014), "Democracy, solidarity, and the rule of law: lessons from Athens", *Buffalo Law Review* 62: 1–67.

Hansen, M.H. (2008). "Thucydides' description of democracy (2.37. 1) and the EU-convention of 2003", *GRBS* 48: 15–26.

Harris, E.M. (2006). *Democracy and the Rule of Law in Democratic Athens*. Cambridge.

Harris, E.M. (2013). *The Rule of Law in Action in Democratic Athens*. Oxford.

Heftner, H. (2003). "Oligarchen, *Mesoi*, Autokraten: Bemerkungen zur antidemokratischen Bewegung des späten 5. Jh. v. Chr. in Athen", *Chiron* 33: 1–41.

Herrman, J. (2009), *Hyperides: Funeral Oration*. Oxford.

Hodkinson, S. (2000). *Property and Wealth in Classical Sparta*. London.

Hornblower, S. (1987), *Thucydides*. Baltimore.

Hornblower, S. (2000). "The Old Oligarch (Pseudo-Xenophon's *Athenaion Politeia*) and Thucydides: a fourth-century date for the Old Oligarch?", in P. Flensted-Jensen, T.H. Nielsen, L. Rubinstein (a cura di). *Polis and politics: studies in ancient Greek history presented to Mogens Herman Hansen on his sixtieth birthday*. Copenhagen: 363–384.

Hussey, E. (1985). "Thucydidean history and Democritean theory", in P.A. Cartledge, F.D. Harvey (a cura di). Crux*: essays in Greek history presented to G.E.M. De Ste. Croix on His 75th Birthday*. Exeter: 118–38.

Kennell, N.N. (2010). *Spartans. A New History*. Oxford.

Lanni, A. (2006). *Law and Justice in the Courts of Classical Athens*. Cambridge.

Lanni, A. (2016). *Law and Order in Ancient Athens*. Cambridge.

Lewis, D.M. (2018). *Greek Slave Systems in their Eastern Mediterranean Context, c. 800–146 BC*. Oxford.

Lianeri, A. (2007). "The Persian Wars as the 'origin' of historiography: ancient and modern orientalism in George Grote's *History of Greece*", in E. Bridges, E. Hall, P.J. Rhodes (a cura di). *Cultural Responses to the Persian Wars: Antiquity to the Third Millennium*. Stuttgart: 331–355.

Longo, O. (2000), *Epitafio di Pericle per i caduti del primo anno di guerra (II, 34–47)*. Venezia.

Loraux, L. (1986). *The Invention of Athens: The Funeral Oration in the Classical City*. Cambridge, MA.

Low, L. (2010), "Commemoration of the war dead in classical Athens: remembering defeat and victory", in D.M. Pritchard (a cura di). *War, Democracy and Culture in Classical Athens*. Cambridge: 341–58.

Marr, J.L. e Rhodes, P.J. (2008). *The 'Old Oligarch': the constitution of the Athenians attributed to Xenophon*. Liverpool.

Mills, S. (1997), *Theseus, Tragedy and the Athenian Empire*. Oxford.

Ober, J. (1989). *Mass and Elite in Democratic Athens. Rhetoric, Ideology and the Power of the People*. Princeton.

Ober, J. (1998). *Political Dissent in Democratic Athens: Intellectual Critics of Popular Rule*. Princeton.

Ober, J. (2008), "The original meaning of 'democracy': capacity to do things, not majority rule", *Constellations* 15: 3–9.

Osborne, R.G. (1985). "Law in Action in Classical Athens", *JHS* 105: 40–58.

Ostwald, M. (1969). Nomos *and the Beginnings of the Athenian Democracy*. Oxford.

Ostwald, M. (1986). *From Popular Sovereignty to Sovereignty of the Law*. Berkeley.

Parker, R. (1996), *Athenian Religion: a History*. Oxford.

Pelloso, C. (2017). "*Nomos basileus* e potere giudicante nell'Atene del IV secolo a.C.", *RDE* 7: 1–28.

Proietti, G. (2021). *Prima di Erodoto. Aspetti della memoria delle Guerre persiane*. Stuttgart.

Raaflaub, K. (1983). "Democracy, oligarchy, and the concept of the 'free citizen' in late fifth-century Athens", *Political Theory* 11: 517–544.

Rhodes, P.J. (2010). *A History of the Classical Greek World. 478–323 B.C.* Malden².

Rusten, J.S. (1989). *Thucydides.* The Peloponnesian War. *Book II*. Cambridge.

Sealey, R. (1974). "The origins of *demokratia", CSCA* 6: 253–295.

Sealey, R. (1987). *The Athenian Republic: Democracy or Rule of Law?* University Park.

Simonton, M. (2017). *Classical Greek Oligarchy: A Political History*. Princeton.

Shear, J.L. (2013). "Their memories will never grow old: the politics of remembrance in the Athenian funeral orations", *CQ* 63: 511–536.

Ste. Croix, G.E.M. de (1954). "The character of the Athenian Empire", *Historia* 3: 1–41.

Ste. Croix, G.E.M. de (1972). *The Origins of the Peloponnesian War*. London.

Tamanaha, B. (2004). *On the Rule of Law: History, Politics, Theory*. Cambridge.

Thomas, R. (1989). *Oral Tradition and Written Record in Classical Athens*. Cambridge.

Todd, S.C. (1993). *The Shape of Athenian Law*. Oxford.

Ziolkowski, J. (1981), *Thucydides and the Tradition of Funeral Speech at Athens*. Salem.

MARIAGRAZIA RIZZI (MILANO)

AUTORITÀ DI MERCATO E CONTROLLO DELLA CIRCOLAZIONE MONETARIA IN SEG XXVI 72*

Abstract: Il contributo è volto all'analisi dei poteri e delle competenze degli *epimeletai tou emporiou*, dei *sitophylakes* e dei *syllogeis tou demou* menzionati nella legge ateniese sul saggio della moneta del 375/4 a.C. Dopo una breve indagine delle mansioni attribuite agli *epimeletai tou emporiou* e ai *sitophylakes*, nel *nomos* in linea con le funzioni di controllo delle attività di mercato generalmente spettanti a questi magistrati, l'attenzione sarà incentrata sui *syllogeis tou demou* ed in particolare sul rapporto tra queste autorità, *boule* e *dokimastai*, al fine di individuare alcune possibili ragioni alla base dell'attribuzione di competenze distanti rispetto a quelle ricavabili dalle altre testimonianze in materia.

Keywords: legge di Nicofonte, epimeletai tou emporiou, sitophylakes, sillogeis tou demou, boule, dokimastai.

1. Con il titolo *Droit et marché en Grèce ancienne. De la monnaie athénienne comme loi* Chr. Pébarthe presentava, nella relazione svolta al *Symposion* di Parigi del 2011 e nel contributo pubblicato all'interno dei relativi atti[1], una riflessione intorno al rapporto tra diritto, economia e regolamentazione della circolazione monetaria ricavabile dallo studio della legge di Nicofonte[2] del 375/4 a.C. Il titolo scelto

---

* Desidero esprimere il mio più profondo ringraziamento agli organizzatori del *Symposion*, in particolare al Prof. Philipp Scheibelreiter, per il gentile invito, nonché ai partecipanti al Convegno per le preziose osservazioni poste. Alcuni risultati della ricerca condotta sono stati esposti nella relazione *Autorità di mercato, schiavi pubblici e circolazione della moneta nell'Atene classica*, nell'ambito del Congresso *SIHDA* 2022, tenutosi a Bruxelles nel settembre 2022, e in occasione della lezione *Market Legislation in Athens through epigraphic sources*, svolta per le Cattedre dei Proff. Uri Yiftach e Ido Israelowich presso il Department of Classic, Faculty of Humanities, Tel Aviv University, nel gennaio 2023. Ringrazio di cuore per le interessanti suggestioni ricevute in occasione dei due incontri. Tutti gli errori presenti nel testo sono naturalmente da attribuire esclusivamente a me.

1 Pébarthe (2012), p. 237.

2 L'iscrizione, come noto, è stata portata in luce nel 1970 durante gli scavi americani dell'*agora* ed edita da Stroud nel 1974 unitamente ad un ricco commentario [Stroud (1974), p. 157–188]. Già due anni prima dell'*editio princeps* lo Studioso aveva presentato brevemente la nuova scoperta [Stroud (1972), p. 221]. Da allora la legge è stata oggetto di un numero considerevole di approfondimenti. Per uno sguardo bibliografico ai principali contributi in proposito mi sia permesso di rinviare a Rizzi (2020), p. 25 s. nt. 2 e 3, lavoro

dallo Studioso e il ragionamento sviluppato nel lavoro mostrano limpidamente quello che, a prescindere dai dubbi interpretativi ancora non dissolti in ordine a taluni aspetti della disciplina di fondo del *nomos*[3], costituisce un connubio inscindibile di questa preziosa iscrizione, insieme ad altre testimonianze epigrafiche di età classica ed ellenistica[4], ossia la predisposizione ad Atene (ma non solo) di una regolamentazione giuridica relativamente articolata volta a facilitare il commercio e a incoraggiare l'economia di mercato[5]. Nell'ambito di siffatta disciplina di carattere giuridico, tra i numerosi elementi di interesse contenuti nella legge di Nicofonte si intendono offrire in questa sede alcune riflessioni in ordine alle funzioni spettanti agli *epimeletai tou emporiou*, ai *sitophylakes* e soprattutto ai *syllogeis tou demou*, di cui il *nomos* fornisce una serie abbastanza ampia di informazioni, in parte volte a confermare i precedenti dati in nostro possesso, in parte introduttive di nuovi elementi di riflessione nella prospettiva degli interventi del potere pubblico e del ruolo delle diverse autorità nel controllo delle attività di mercato ad Atene.

2. Procedendo innanzitutto ad una breve presentazione del contenuto della legge, indugiando in particolare sulle porzioni dell'iscrizione di interesse, come vedremo, per il discorso qui condotto, dopo il prescritto[6] e l'ordine generale di accettare la moneta attica, se d'argento e con il *demosion charakter* (ll. 3–4), si prescrive che il *dokimastes*[7] dell'agora avrà il compito di effettuare ogni giorno tra i banchi il

---

nel quale (p. 25–40) sono affrontati alcuni temi ripresi e sottoposti ad ulteriore riflessione nel presente articolo. All'apparato bibliografico ivi indicato possono essere aggiunti Bitros – Economou – Kyriazis (2020); Economou – Kyriazis (2021), p. 7–8; Economou – Kyriazis – Kyriazis (2021), p. 5.

3 La discussione che ha impegnato ad oggi maggiormente la dottrina che si è occupata del *nomos* è sicuramente quella relativa all'interpretazione delle ll. 3–13, in particolare all'integrazione da fornire alla porzione finale della l. 9 e alla questione se la legge abbia introdotto un obbligo di accettazione della sola moneta ateniese d'argento escludendo dunque le monete argentate straniere con il simbolo della civetta o se anche queste ultime siano state ammesse nelle transazioni commerciali all'*agora* e al Pireo. Sul punto cfr. anche *infra* nt. 8

4 In quest'ottica si inserisce il progetto di ricerca dal titolo *Wirtschafts- und geldpolitikbezogene Regulierungsansätze im klassischen Athen*, finanziato dalla Fondazione von Humboldt e sviluppato presso il Leopold-Wenger-Institut e la Kommission für Alte Geschichte und Epigraphik des Deutschen Archäologischen Instituts München negli anni 2017–2022, dedicato tra l'altro proprio allo studio di questa iscrizione.

5 Tra le recenti prese di posizione a favore del ruolo di rilievo rivestito dal diritto con riguardo alla "expansion of markets and economic growth in Classical and Hellenistic Greece" si veda Harris (2020), *passim*.

6 Contenente l'indicazione dei *nomothetai*, la menzione dell'arconte e il nome del proponente (ll. 1–2).

7 Sugli schiavi pubblici ateniesi si rimanda, per tutti, al lavoro di Jacob (1928), *passim*, nonché al recente contributo di Ismard (2015), *passim* e in part. p. 136–140, con riguardo agli schiavi pubblici menzionati nella legge qui analizzata. Ivi riferimenti alla dottrina precedente che si è occupata di questa categoria di schiavi (il lavoro di Ismard è

controllo delle monete presentate, ad eccezione dei giorni in cui si trova impegnato nel *bouleuterion* a presenziare alla *chrematon katabole*; in quel caso la verifica dovrà essere effettuata al *bouleuterion* (ll. 4–8). Si individuano immediatamente dopo le conseguenze a seconda che quelle verificate siano monete straniere d'argento con lo stesso simbolo di quelle ateniesi, monete di bronzo argentato o piombo argentato o ancora monete false[8]. Mentre le monete d'argento dovranno essere restituite al loro proprietario[9], le monete in bronzo e piombo argentato, nonché le monete false dovranno essere ritirate, marcate, consacrate al Tempio della Madre degli Dei e depositate alla *boule* (ll. 8–13)[10].

Le linee successive sono dedicate alla previsione della punizione da infliggere al *dokimastes* che non sieda nel posto stabilito o non abbia eseguito le disposizioni della legge[11]; la comminazione di tali punizioni, consistente in cinquanta colpi di frusta[12], spetterà ai *syllogeis tou demou*:

SEG XXVI 72, ll. 13–16
ἐὰν δὲ μὴ καθῆτ[α]ι ὁ δοκι[μαστὴς]
ἢ μὴ δοκιμάζηι κατὰ τὸν νόμον, τυπ̣[τ]όντων [αὐτὸν ο]-
ἱ τõ δήμο συλλογῆς πεντήκοντα πληγὰς τ[ῆι μάστι]-
γι.

Seguono nel testo le sanzioni contro il venditore che non abbia accettato le monete d'argento ateniesi verificate dallo schiavo pubblico:

---

stato tradotto in inglese nel (2017)). In merito ai *dokimastai* menzionati nel *nomos* qui analizzato si veda, inoltre, in particolare Martin (1991), *passim*. Sugli schiavi pubblici ad Atene mi sia consentito rinviare a Silverio (2019), *passim*, del quale la sottoscritta ha curato riedizione, traduzione e aggiornamento bibliografico.

8 E' questo uno dei punti della legge su cui, come accennato nella precedente nt. 3, si è soffermata maggiormente la dottrina. Sulle diverse soluzioni offerte in merito all'integrazione dell'ultima porzione della l. 9 si vedano, tra i contributi più recenti, la sintesi e le osservazioni offerte da Psoma (2011), p. 28–36, nonché da Ellithorpe (2019), p. 64–66.

9 Secondo Stroud (1974), p. 169, 186, la restituzione di queste monete avrebbe comportato l'approvazione implicita delle stesse. La posizione di Stroud è stata seguita, tra gli altri, da Psoma (2011), p. 33–36; Pébarthe (2012), p. 254–256. Per altri autori, invece, la restituzione delle monete non avrebbe implicato la possibilità di utilizzarle nel mercato di Atene, ma i possessori avrebbero potuto cambiarle con la moneta d'argento ateniese. In questo senso si è espresso per primo Buttrey (1979), p. 39 s., seguito, tra gli altri, da Ober (2008); Kroll (2011), p. 19 e nt. 41.

10 Sul Metroon si veda, per tutti, Rhodes (1972), p. 30 nt. 6

11 Su cui cfr. *infra* nel testo.

12 Sull'uso della frusta nei confronti degli schiavi pubblici cfr., tra i contributi recenti, Rizzi (2017), p. 51–54, ove riferimenti bibliografici ulteriori.

SEG XXVI 72, ll. 16–26

ἐὰν δέ τις μὴ δέχηται τὸ ἀ̣[ρ]γ[ύρ]ιον ὅ τ[ι ἂν ὁ δοκι]-
μαστὴς δοκιμάστηι, στερέσθω ὧν ἂμ [π]ωλῆτ̣[αι ἐκείν]-
ηι τῆι ἡμέραι· φαίνειν δὲ τὰ μὲν ἐν [τ]ῶ̣ι σί̣[τωι πρὸς]
τὸς σιτοφύλακας, τὰ δὲ ἐν τῆι ἀγορᾶι κ[α]ὶ [ἐν τῶι ἄλ]-
λωι ἄστει πρὸς τοὺς τõ δήμο συλλογέ[ας], τὰ [δὲ ἐν τῶ]-
ι ἐμπορίωι καὶ τῶι Πει[ρ]αιεῖ πρὸς τοὺ[ς ἐπιμελητ]-
ὰς τοῦ ἐμπορίο πλὴν τὰ ἐν τῶι σίτωι, τὰ δὲ [ἐν τῶι σί]-
τωι πρὸς τοὺς σιτοφύλακας· τῶν δὲ φανθέ[ντων, ὁπό]-
σα μὲν ἂν ἦι ἐντὸς δέκα δραχμῶν, κύριοι ὄ[ντων οἱ ἄ]-
ρχοντες διαγιγνώσκειν, τὰ δὲ ὑπὲρ [δ]έ[κ]α [δραχμάς],
ἐσαγόντων ἐς τὸ δικαστήριον.

Dopo l'indicazione della punizione da infliggere al venditore, consistente nella confisca delle merci poste in vendita quel giorno[13], si specifica che il compratore dovrà ricorrere alla *phasis*[14], rivolgendosi ai *sitophylakes* nel caso di condotte illecite poste in essere nel mercato del grano, ai *syllogeis tou demou* per quelle poste nell'*agora* e nel resto della città e agli *epimeletai tou emporiou* per quelle realizzate al Pireo, ad eccezione di quelle relative al mercato del grano per le quali la competenza spetta ai *sitophylakes*. Laddove la controversia sia racchiusa entro il limite di valore di dieci dracme, saranno gli stessi *archontes* a giudicare, mentre nel caso in cui il valore sia superiore, la questione dovrà essere portata al *dikasterion*, dove *sitophylakes*, *syllogeis* e *epimeletai tou emporiou* avranno "a competency to preside over court"[15].

Nella porzione successiva vengono altresì individuate le sanzioni a carico dei magistrati che non abbiano effettuato i controlli secondo quanto stabilito dalla legge.

13 La confisca delle merci rappresenta a sua volta una forma di punizione ampiamente documentata nel mondo greco. Mi sia permesso ancora una volta rinviare a Rizzi (2017), p. 56–61. Nel caso in cui la condanna sia rivolta nei confronti di uno schiavo, questi subirà cinquanta colpi di frusta (ll. 30–32).

14 Sulle diverse interpretazioni in ordine alla natura e alla funzione della *phasis* si vedano, per tutti, Lipsius (1908), p. 309–316; Paoli (1930), p. 239; Harrison (1971), p. 218–221; Stumpf (1986), p. 35 s.; MacDowell (1991), *passim*; Wallace (2003), p. 168–181; Koch (2009), p. 277 e ntt. 116–119. In linea generale, la *phasis* è un'azione popolare esercitabile da qualsiasi cittadino. Stumpf (1986), p. 35 s., rileva in proposito che, a fronte di tale carattere generale, nel passaggio qui analizzato della legge di Nicofonte solo il compratore risulta legittimato nel caso di mancata accettazione da parte del venditore delle monete verificate dal *dokimastes*. In verità, è probabilmente più da seguire la diversa opinione di Koch (2009), p. 277 nt. 119, per il quale ciò non consente di escludere che "mehr oder weniger unbeteiligte Dritte sich der Sache mittels Phasis annahmen".

15 Scafuro (2006), p. 49. La procedura descritta nelle ll. 26–32 prevede in particolare che i *tesmothetai* dovranno assistere gli *archontes*, designando a sorte i membri del tribunale; nel caso in cui non lo facciano, dovranno pagare dieci dracme. Nell'ipotesi di condanna del venditore, il denunciante riceverà metà della somma.

Chiunque lo vorrà potrà presentare accusa alla *boule*, la quale avrà il potere di infliggere una punizione pecuniaria che potrà giungere verosimilmente fino a cinquecento dracme, oltre a sanzionare il magistrato con la cessazione dallo svolgimento della carica (ll. 32–36).

Seguono una serie ampia di prescrizioni dedicate allo schiavo pubblico collocato al Pireo. La *boule* avrà il compito di individuare uno schiavo tra quelli a disposizione, al fine dello svolgimento di siffatta mansione, nell'ipotesi in cui ne abbia uno adatto, oppure dovrà provvedere all'acquisto di uno schiavo idoneo, il cui prezzo sarà determinato dagli *apodektai* (ll. 36–41)[16]. Gli *epimeletai* dell'emporio dovranno di verificare che lo schiavo pubblico sieda vicino alla stele di Poseidone e applichi la legge conformemente a quanto previsto per il *dokimastes* dell'agora:

> *SEG* XXVI 72, ll. 41–44
> οἱ δὲ ἐπιμεληταὶ τοῦ ἐμπορίο ἐπιμελ̣έ[σ]θω[ν ὅπ]-
> ως ἂγ καθῆται πρὸς τῆι στήληι τοῦ Ποσειδῶνο[ς κα]-
> ὶ χρήσθων τῶι νόμωι καθάπερ περὶ τõ ἐν ἄστ[ει δοκ]-
> ιμαστõ εἴρηται κατὰ ταὐτά.

Spetterà dunque agli *epimeletai tou emporiou* procedere alla punizione, con cinquanta colpi di frusta, dello schiavo pubblico che violi gli obblighi lui spettanti, analogamente ai poteri spettanti al *syllogeis tou demou* nei confronti dello schiavo pubblico posizionato all'agora.

3. Diversi passaggi della legge, come veduto da questa prima presentazione, consentono di cogliere una serie preziosa di informazioni in merito alle competenze dei *syllogeis tou demou*, degli *epimeletai tou emporiou* e dei *sitophylakes*. Costoro hanno innanzitutto il compito di ricevere le accuse dei compratori contro i venditori che non accettino le monete verificate e di risolvere, entro i limiti di valore veduti, la relativa controversia. Ciascuna di queste autorità risulta a sua volta competente territorialmente in una specifica zona di mercato e/o per materia con riguardo a particolari tipologie di prodotti: i *syllogeis tou demou* all'*agora* e nel resto della città, gli *epimeletai tou emporiou* al Pireo, i *sitophylakes* al Pireo e all'*agora* per le controversie sorte in relazione al mercato del grano. *Syllogeis tou demou* e *epimeletai tou emporiou* sono altresì indicati come le autorità incaricate del controllo dell'operato dello schiavo pubblico posizionato rispettivamente all'agora e al Pireo, nonchè legittimate alla punizione dello stesso nel caso di condotte in violazione delle prescrizioni della legge.

---

16 Dalle successive ll. 49–53 si apprende che sia lo schiavo del Pireo che quello posizionato all'*agora* avrebbero ricevuto un salario, assegnato dagli *apodektai*.

Indugiando sulle singole figure, in termini generali si può affermare che le informazioni in nostro possesso concernenti le competenze degli *epimeletai tou emporiou* e dei *sitophylakes* si presentano relativamente ampie, nonchè concordi e conformi con quanto è dato leggere nel *nomos* di Nicofonte.

Nel limitarmi pertanto solo ad alcune esemplificazioni significative, con riguardo innanzitutto agli *epimeletai tou emporiou*[17] da Aristotele (*Ath. Pol.* 51.4)[18] apprendiamo che ad Atene operavano dieci *epimeletai tou emporiou*, con la funzione di controllare l'attività commerciale al Pireo e di costringere i commercianti a trasportare all'agorà di Atene, al *sitikon emporion*, due terzi del grano importato per mare.

Demostene, nell'orazione contro Lacrito[19], richiama il testo di una legge che stabiliva per i residenti ad Atene, cittadini o stranieri, pene severissime nel caso di trasporto del grano in porti diversi dal Pireo o nel caso di prestito di denaro per una nave che non avesse trasportato ad Atene grano o in generale le merci designate nell'accordo. Gli *epimeletai tou emporiou* sono individuati come i magistrati competenti a comminare la sanzione della confisca del denaro nell'ipotesi di violazione delle disposizioni della legge.

Nell'orazione di Dinarco contro Aristogitone[20] si fa riferimento allo svolgimento da parte di quest'ultimo della magistratura in discorso, con la precisazione della sua estrazione a sorte e della decisione da parte dei membri della commissione di esame di vietarne l'esercizio.

Ad un'epoca ancora più vicina alla data di pubblicazione della legge di Nicofonte, precisamente al 355 a.C., potrebbe essere il riferimento a questi magistrati all'interno di un passaggio dei *Poroi* di Senofonte[21], laddove si accetti

---

[17] Fonti letterarie: Arist. *Ath. Pol.* 51.4; Demosth. 35.50–51; 58.8,9,26; Lyc. Leocr. 27; Din. 2.10; Harpocr. e Suda.; ad esse bisogna aggiungere Xen. *Por.* 3.3. Fonti epigrafiche: *IG* II^2 1283, ll. 16–17 (anteriore alla metà del III a.C.); *IG* II^2 1013, 40, 47 (fine II/inizio I sec. a.C.); *IG* II^2 2336, ll. 74, 112, 178 (fine II/inizio I secolo a.C.).

[18] Arist. *Ath. Pol.* 51.4: ἐμπορίου δ' ἐπιμελητὰς δέκα κληροῦσιν· τούτοις δὲ προστέτακται τῶν τ' ἐμπορίων ἐπιμελεῖσθαι, καὶ τοῦ σίτου τοῦ καταπλέοντος εἰς τὸ σιτικὸν ἐμπόριον τὰ δύο μέρη τοὺς ἐμπόρους ἀναγκάζειν εἰς τὸ ἄστυ κομίζειν.

[19] Demosth. 35.51: ἀργύριον δὲ μὴ ἐξεῖναι ἐκδοῦναι Ἀθηναίων καὶ τῶν μετοίκων τῶν Ἀθήνησι μετοικούντων μηδενί, μηδὲ ὧν οὗτοι κύριοί εἰσιν, εἰς ναῦν ἥτις ἂν μὴ μέλλῃ ἄξειν σῖτον Ἀθήναζε, καὶ τἄλλα τὰ γεγραμμένα περὶ ἑκάστου αὐτῶν. ἐὰν δέ τις ἐκδῷ παρὰ ταῦτα, εἶναι τὴν φάσιν καὶ τὴν ἀπογραφὴν τοῦ ἀργυρίου πρὸς τοὺς ἐπιμελητάς, καθάπερ τῆς νεὼς καὶ τοῦ σίτου εἴρηται, κατὰ ταὐτά.

[20] Din. 2.10: καὶ ταῦθ', ὅπερ ἀρτίως εἶπον, τίς οὐκ οἶδε καταμαρτυρηθέντ' Ἀριστογείτονος, ὅτ' ἐμπορίου ἐπιμελητὴς λαχὼν ἀπεδοκιμάσθη ὑπὸ τῶν τότε δικαζόντων ἄρχειν ταύτην τὴν ἀρχήν;

[21] Xen. *Por.* 3.3: εἰ δὲ καὶ τῇ τοῦ ἐμπορίου ἀρχῇ ἆθλα προτιθείη τις ὅστις δικαιότατα καὶ τάχιστα διαιροίη τὰ ἀμφίλογα, ὡς μὴ ἀποκωλύεσται ἀποπλεῖν τὸν βουλόμενον, πολὺ ἂν καὶ διὰ ταῦτα πλείους τε καὶ ἥδιον ἐμπορεύοιντο.

l'identificazione tra gli *epimeletai tou emporiou* e l'*arche tou emporiou* ivi menzionata[22].

L'iscrizione di Nicofonte si colloca in maniera del tutto coerente all'interno di questo spettro di testimonianze, offrendo a sua volta un'importante conferma delle competenze degli *epimeletai tou emporiou* in ambito commerciale. Anzi, quella in discorso si pone come la testimonianza più risalente in materia[23], quantunque sia ragionevole ritenere che l'istituzione di questi magistrati sia stata antecedente all'emanazione della legge[24], non sussistendo elementi all'interno della stessa che consentano di pensare ad una creazione del tutto nuova.

Altrettanto numerose e in termini generali uniformi solo le informazioni concernenti i *sitophylakes*[25]. Si trattava di magistrati impegnati specificamente in funzioni di amministrazione e supervisione del mercato del grano, sia pubblico che privato. Originariamente, verosimilmente anche all'epoca dell'emanazione della legge di Nicofonte[26], operavano cinque *sitophylakes* al Pireo e cinque nel mercato del grano nell'agorà di Atene; successivamente, nel corso del IV secolo, il loro numero è incrementato a trentacinque[27], venti per l'agora di Atene e quindici per il Pireo[28].

Particolarmente significativa per il discorso condotto è la testimonianza fornita da Lisia nell'orazione *Contro i mercanti di grano*, del 386 a.C., collocabile dunque ad un'epoca di poco antecedente alla legge di Nicofonte. Ivi si fa riferimento all'acquisto di grano a seguito del consenso degli *archontes*, da identificarsi con i

22 Fondamentali, al riguardo, le osservazioni di Gauthier (1976), p. 80 s. Su tale identificazione si veda anche, tra gli autori più recenti, Maffi (2016), p. 203.

23 Il punto è stato messo in rilievo da Stroud (1974), p. 180 s., e accolto variamente in dottrina.

24 Si veda, per tutti, Stroud (1974), p. 180 s., ripreso, tra gli altri, da Gauthier (1981), p. 21 [2011, p. 210], per il quale "on ne sera guère téméraire en supposant que l'institution [degli *epimeletai tou emporiou* ndA] remonte au moins aux années 403–400".

25 Lys. 22.5–6,8–9 e 16; Demosth. 20.32; Arist. *Ath. Pol.* 51.3; Harpocr. s.v. σιτοφύλακες; Phot., s.v. σιτοφύλακες. Fonti epigrafiche *Hesperia* 3, 1934, 42 s.; *Hesperia* 6, 1937, 444–448, n.2; n. 7; n. 8; *Hesperia* 13, 1944, n. 8; *Hesperia* 30, 1961, 225 s., nm. 23–24. Su questi magistrati si vedano, rinviando soltanto ad alcuni tra i contributi più recenti e senza pretese di esaustività, Rhodes (1981), p. 577 s.; Gauthier 1981 (2011), p. 5–28 [193–219]; Figueira (1986), p. 150–152; Engels (2000), p. 99 s.; Rosivach (2000), in part. p. 46–51; Fantasia (2016), p. 31 s.

26 Cfr. Stumpf 1986, p. 28 nt. 17.

27 Arist. *Ath. Pol.* 51.3: ἦσαν δὲ καὶ σιτοφύλακες κληρωτοὶ <ι>, πέντε μὲν εἰς Πειραιέα, πέντε δ' εἰς ἄστυ, νῦν δ' εἴκοσι μὲν εἰς ἄστυ, πεντεκαίδεκα δ' εἰς Πειραιέα. οὗτοι δ' ἐπιμελοῦνται, πρῶτον μὲν ὅπως ὁ ἐν ἀγορᾷ σῖτος ἀργὸς ὤνιος ἔσται δικαίως, ἔπειθ' ὅπως οἵ τε μυλωθροὶ πρὸς τὰς τιμὰς τῶν κριθῶν τὰ ἄλφιτα πωλήσουσιν, καὶ οἱ ἀρτοπῶλαι πρὸς τὰς τιμὰς τῶν πυρῶν τοὺς ἄρτους, καὶ τὸν σταθμὸν ἄγοντας ὅσον ἂν οὗτοι τάξωσιν. ὁ γὰρ νόμος τούτους κελεύει τάττειν. La ragione di tale aumento deriva presumibilmente dalla grave carenza di grano degli anni 330–320 a.C.

28 Successivamente, nel III secolo, il numero di questi magistrati tornerà di nuovo ad essere di dieci, affiancati da due segretari: *Hesperia* 6, 1937, p. 444448, n. 2; *Hesperia* 13, 1944, p. 243 n. 2 e *Hesperia* 30, 1961, p. 225 s., n. 23.

sitophylakes (22.5–6)[29], e si ricava soprattutto come questi magistrati avessero la funzione di controllo del tragitto di questo prodotto, dagli *emporoi* ai *sitopolai*, dovendo verificare il rispetto delle norme volte a sventare manovre speculative dei dettaglianti, indicate nell'acquisto da parte dei *sitopolai* di più di cinquanta misure di grano dagli *emporoi* in una volta (22.6)[30], nonché ad evitare l'aumento del prezzo per più di un obolo per dracma (22.8–9)[31].

Conferme in ordine all'operatività e alle competenze dei *sitophylakes* nell'età successiva si ricavano innanzitutto dalla *Contro Leptine* di Demostene (del 355/354 a.C.)[32], nella quale si fa riferimento alla dichiarazione scritta fatta davanti a questi magistrati relativa al grano importato dal regno del Bosforo nella misura di 400.000 medimni[33].

Aristotele, a sua volta, menziona[34] i *sitophylakes*, accanto agli *astynomoi*, agli *agoranomoi* e ai *metronomoi*, indicando tra le funzioni quella di vegliare a che il grano in chicchi nell'agora sia messo in vendita al giusto prezzo[35], nonché che i mugnai vendano la farina d'orzo ad un prezzo proporzionato a quello dell'orzo in grani e che i fornai vendano i loro pani ad un prezzo proporzionato a quello del

---

29 Lys. 22.5–6: ἔγωγε: 'ἀπόκριναι δή μοι, εἰ ὁμολογεῖς πλείω σῖτον συμπρίασθαι πεντήκοντα φορμῶν, ὧν ὁ νόμος ἐξεῖναι κελεύει.' ἐγὼ τῶν ἀρχόντων κελευόντων συνεπριάμην. 6. ἐὰν μὲν τοίνυν ἀποδείξῃ, ὦ ἄνδρες δικασταί, ὡς ἔστι νόμος ὃς κελεύει τοὺς σιτοπώλας συνωνεῖσθαι τὸν σῖτον, ἐὰν οἱ ἄρχοντες κελεύωσιν, ἀποψηφίσασθε· εἰ δὲ μή, δίκαιον ὑμᾶς καταψηφίσασθαι. ἡμεις γὰρ ὑμῖν παρεσχόμεθα τὸν νόμον, ὃς ἀπραγορεύει μηδένα τῶν ἐν τῇ πόλει πλείω σῖτον πεντήκοντα φορμῶν συνωνεῖσθαι.

30 Cfr. nota precedente.

31 Lys. 22.8–9: ἐπειδὴ γὰρ οὗτοι τὴν αἰτίαν εἰς ἐκείνους ἀνέφερον, παρακαλέσαντες τοὺς ἄρχοντας ἠρωτῶμεν. καὶ οἱ μὲν δύο οὐδὲν ἔφασαν εἰδέναι τοῦ πράγματος, Ἄνυτος δ' ἔλεγεν ὡς τοῦ προτέρου χειμῶνος, ἐπειδὴ τίμιος ἦν ὁ σῖτος, τούτων ὑπερβαλλόντων ἀλλήλους καὶ πρὸς σφᾶς αὐτοὺς μαχομένων συμβουλεύσειεν αὐτοῖς παύσασθαι φιλονικοῦσιν, ἡγούμενος συμφέρειν ὑμῖν τοῖς παρὰ τούτων ὠνουμένοις ὡς ἀξιώτατον τούτους πρίασθαι· δεῖν γὰρ αὐτοὺς ὀβολῷ μόνον πωλεῖν τιμιώτερον. 9. ὡς τοίνυν οὐ συμπριαμένους καταθέσθαι ἐκέλευεν, ἀλλὰ μὴ ἀλλήλοις ἀντωνεῖσθαι συνεβούλευεν, αὐτὸν ὑμῖν Ἄνυτον μάρτυρα παρέξομαι.
Ancora, si ricava in termini generali la funzione di controllo del grano da parte di questi magistrati, a fronte della competenza generale di sorveglianza delle altre merci spettante agli *agoranomoi* (Lys. 22.16: οὕτω δὲ πάλαι περὶ τῆς τούτων πανουργίας καὶ κακονοίας ἡ πόλις ἔγνωκεν, ὥστ' ἐπὶ μὲν τοῖς ἄλλοις ὠνίοις ἅπασι τοὺς ἀγορανόμους φύλακας κατεστήσατε, ἐπὶ δὲ ταύτῃ μόνῃ τῇ τέχνῃ χωρὶς σιτοφύλακας ἀποκληροῦτε).

32 Demosth. 20.32: ἐκεῖνος πράττεται τοὺς παρ' αὐτοῦ σῖτον ἐξάγοντας τριακοστήν. αἱ τοίνυν παρ' ἐκείνου δεῦρ' ἀφικνούμεναι σίτου μιριάδες περὶ τετταράκοντ' εἰσί· καὶ τοῦτ' ἐκ τῆς παρὰ τοῖς σιτοφύλαξιν ἀπογραφῆς ἄν τις ἴδοι.

33 Su questo passaggio dell'orazione cfr., tra i contributi più recenti, Canevaro (2016), p. 252–254, ove richiami alla dottrina precedente.

34 Per il testo cfr. *supra* nt. 27.

35 E' questa l'interpretazione di δικαίως, all'interno dell'espressione ὁ ἐν ἀγορᾷ σῖτος ἀργὸς ὤνιος ἔσται δικαίως, proposta, tra gli altri, da Fantasia (2016), p. 31 s., in luogo della traduzione "in modo corretto, onestamente".

frumento e al peso corrispondente a quello che gli stessi *sitophylakes* hanno il dovere di fissare.

A prescindere in questa sede dall'ampiezza e dall'evoluzione delle competenze dei *sitophylakes* nel corso del tempo e dal rapporto tra siffatte competenze e quelle degli *epimeletai* (e degli *agoranomoi*) in relazione ai cereali[36], è evidente, in tutte le testimonianze vedute, il collegamento tra le funzioni di costoro e il controllo di attività commerciali concernenti questo prodotto, in ciò perfettamente in linea con le mansioni attribuite nella legge di Nicofonte.

4. Volgendo ora l'attenzione ai *syllogeis tou demou*[37], le notizie al riguardo nelle fonti a nostra disposizione si presentano per un verso non particolarmente numerose, per altro verso non prive di difficoltà interpretative, anche in rapporto con le informazioni ricavabili dal *nomos*.

I *syllogeis tou demou*, comitato della *boule*, forse designato per elezione[38], avevano innanzitutto la funzione di far confluire i cittadini nelle assemblee. In IG II^2 1749, la testimonianza concernente questa competenza cronologicamente più vicina a quella della legge di Nicofonte, è contenuto un elenco di pritani delle tribù Egeide, tra cui figurano i nomi di tre soggetti, Diodoro del demo di Gargetto, Timocrito del demo di Icaria, Tarria del demo di Erchia, lodati per essersi occupati "bene e con giustizia della *sulloge tou demou* e della distribuzione dei *symbola*"[39]. Il dato concernente queste funzioni, come posto in rilievo da Tuci[40], si può ritenere a sua volta confermato in testi epigrafici che si collocano tra il III e il II secolo a.C.[41].

Tali funzioni dei *syllogeis tou demou* sono ricordate anche nelle fonti letterarie. E' probabilmente a questi magistrati innanzitutto che fa riferimento Polluce in un passaggio dell'*Onomasticon* (8.104)[42]. Nel testo si afferma che sei lessiarchi, con l'aggiunta di trenta uomini, controllavano gli aventi diritto ad andare in assemblea e

---

[36] Per un'analisi di tale rapporto si veda Gauthier (1981), in part. p. 21–26 [(2011), p. 210–216].

[37] I contributi dedicati all'approfondimento delle funzioni di questi magistrati non sono particolarmente numerosi. Il lavoro certamente più significativo è l'articolo di Tuci (2007), p. 113–136, nel quale è presentata una rassegna completa delle testimonianze in materia. Si vedano altresì brevemente Muttelsee (1931), p. 1045 s.; Francotte (1964), p. 101–105; Rhodes (1972), p. 129 s.; Hansen (1984), p. 91 e nt. 459; Fantasia (2016), p. 46 nt.16, 47 nt. 25, cui *adde*, più recentemente, Humphreys (2018), p. 575 e nt. 102.

[38] Cfr. in particolare Tuci (2007), p. 117, il quale menziona in proposito IG II^2 1749, del 341/0 a C

[39] *IG* II^2 1749, ll. 75–76: … ἐπειδὴ καλῶς κ[αὶ δ]ικαίω[ς] | ἐπεμελήθησαν τῆς συλλογῆς τοῦ δήμου καὶ τῆς δ[ι]αδόσεως τῶν συμβόλων…

[40] Tuci (2007), p. 116.

[41] *IG* II^2 790; 848; 890; 902; 917; 920; 967; 977; 1004.

[42] Poll. *Onom.* 8.104: ληξίαρχοι ἕξ καθίσταντο τῶν πολιτῶν ἐγγεγραμμένων ἐν λευκώματι, καὶ τριάκοντα ἀνδρῶν αὐτοῖς προσαιρεθέντων τοὺς ἐκκλησιάζοντας ἐξήταζον καὶ τοὺς μὴ ἐκκλησιάζοντας ἐζημίουν καὶ σχοινίον μιλτώσαντες διὰ τῶν τοξοτῶν συνήλαυνον τοὺς ἐκ τῆς ἀγορᾶς εἰς τὴν ἐκκλησίαν.

punivano coloro che non vi avessero preso parte, precisando inoltre che, dopo aver intinto una corda nel *miltos*[43], per mezzo degli arcieri spingevano in assemblea quanti indugiassero nell'agorà. Nella voce *triakonta* di Esichio[44], a sua volta, si menziona la competenza dei trenta in ordine alla riunione del popolo in assemblea, con la specificazione della comminazione di multe contro i cittadini che non vi avessero preso parte, accanto al riferimento all'attribuzione di funzioni di carattere giudiziario, competenze da ritenere verosimilmente in relazione tra loro. Ancora, in un difficile lemma di Fozio[45] è ribadita la funzione di queste autorità di cura dell'assemblea insieme ai lessiarchi[46].

Accanto a siffatta competenza, in altre iscrizioni le funzioni dei *syllogeis* sono invece collegate all'ambito cultuale. Si tratta di *IG* II^2 1425 (370/69 e 368/7), *IG* II^2 2821 (351/0), *IG* II^2 1496 (334/333–331/0) e *IG* II^2 1257 (324/3 a.C.). Nella prima iscrizione, di pochi anni successiva alla legge di Nicofonte, all'interno dell'inventario del tesoro di Atena sono menzionati, tra gli altri, i *syllogeis tou demou* quali dedicatarii di corone[47]. In *IG* II^2 2821[48] si legge una dedica dei *syllogeis*, nella quale si precisa che erano stati coronati dal Consiglio e dal Popolo per la loro giustizia. In IG II^2 1496 queste autorità figurano, insieme ad altre, in relazione alle ricevute riguardanti le vendite di beni oggetto di sacrifici pubblici a Olimpia[49]. Alcuni anni dopo sono indicate con la funzione di compimento in qualità di *hieropoioi*, in nome dello stato, di sacrifici ad Atena e a Zeus Olimpio (*IG* II^2 1257)[50].

Talune delle testimonianze ora vedute consentono di individuare inoltre l'attribuzione, ai *syllogeis tou demou*, di poteri giudiziari. Polluce parrebbe menzionare il loro potere punitivo insieme a quello dei lessiarchi, in Esichio sono addirittura indicati come *dikastai*, con il potere di comminare multe ai cittadini che non si rechino all'assemblea, mentre in *IG* II^2 2821 si fa riferimento alla giustizia del loro operare.

---

43 Si trattava di una corda impregnata di rosso che macchiava le vesti e rendeva riconoscibili gli assenteisti.

44 Hesych., s.v. τριάκοντα· οὗτοι ἐχειροτονοῦντο δικασταὶ Ἀθήνησιν, οἵτινες ἐζημιοῦντο τοὺς μὴ παραγενομένους τῶν πολιτῶν εἰς ἐκκλησίαν.

45 Phot. s.v. τριάκοντα· πρῶτοι μὲν οἱ κατὰ πόλιν δικασταί· δεύτεροι οἱ κατὰ δήμους τριάκοντα, τῆς ἐκκλησίας ἐπιμελούμενοι μετὰ τῶν ληξιάρχων· οὕτως Φρύνιχος.

46 Per un'analisi dell'ambiguo contenuto del lemma di Fozio si rimanda a Tuci (2007), p. 114 s.

47 *IG* II^2 1425 ll. 126–27 (ἕτερος στέφανος παρὰ δήμο συλλογέων | τῶν ἐπὶ Δυσνικήτο, σταθμὸν...) e ll. 224–226 (ἕτερος στέφανος ὁ παρὰ {αν} δήμο | <σ>υλλογέων τῶν ἐπὶ Ναυσιγένους | ἄρχοντος, σταθμὸν...).

48 *IG.* II^2 2821 ll. 1–6: δήμου συλλογῆς [ἀ]νέ[θη]|καν οἱ ἐπὶ Θεέλλου ἄρχ[ον]|τος στεφανωθέντες | ὑπὸ τῆς βουλῆς καὶ τοῦ | δήμου δικαιοσύνης | ἕνε[κα]. sinistra in corona. ὁ δῆμος. dextra in corona. [ἡ β]ο[υ]λή.

49 *IG* II^2 1496, ll. 82–83: ἐξ Ὀλυμπείων παρὰ [τῶν τοῦ] | δήμου συλλογέων (ripetuto alle ll. 113–114).

50 *IG* II^2 1257A, ll. 6–7 (Atena); B, ll. 5–6 (Zeus Olimpio).

5. Se si pone un raffronto tra le mansioni relative ai *syllogeis tou demou* ora menzionate con quanto ricavabile dalla lettura delle su analizzate linee della legge di Nicofone, si dovrà dunque constatare che, ad esclusione dell'attribuzione di poteri punitivi in relazione alle funzioni loro attribuite, le mansioni indicate nel *nomos* "have no connection with their other attested duties", riprendendo le parole di Rhodes e Osborne[51]. D'altro canto, in considerazione delle vedute funzioni degli *epimeletai tou emporiou* e dei *sitophylakes* ci si attenderebbe di trovare menzionati nella legge, in luogo dei *syllogeis tou demou*, gli *agoranomoi*[52], i quali, come noto[53], avevano funzioni di sorveglianza della correttezza delle transazioni commerciali nell'agora[54].

Si pone dunque la necessità di cercare di comprendere le possibili ragioni a giustificazione della particolare menzione di queste autorità con le funzioni vedute all'interno dell'iscrizione[55].

Punto di partenza di questa riflessione può essere proprio il raffronto con le funzioni attribuite agli *agoranomoi*. Al riguardo, in via preliminare è sicuramente da escludere che all'epoca di emanazione della legge di Nicofonte gli *agoranomoi* non svolgessero alcuna funzione di controllo dell'agora e che tali mansioni fossero demandate ai *syllogeis tou demou*. Quantunque manchino testimonianze in ordine all'operare degli *agoranomoi* nel periodo specifico di emanazione della legge, è altrettanto indubbio come costoro fossero stati istituiti già precedentemente al 375/4 a.C.[56] e abbiano continuato a svolgere le proprie funzioni di controllo dell'agorà di Atene anche successivamente[57]. Sulla base di ciò, bisognerebbe pertanto rinvenire una ragione che avrebbe portato alla soppressione temporanea degli *agoranomoi* e all'istituzione, sempre temporanea, dei *syllogeis tou demou*.

---

51 Rhodes – Osborne (2003), p. 116.

52 Cfr. Fantasia (2016), p. 46 nt. 16.

53 La funzione generale di questi magistrati consiste nel mantenere nel mercato εὐταξία, κόσμος, εὐκοσμία (Arist. *Pol.* 6.8.1). Su siffatte mansioni ad Atene e in generale nelle città greche si vedano, tra i contributi più recenti, Migeotte (2005), *passim* [2015, *passim*]; Oliver (2012), *passim* (ove riferimenti bibliografici alla dottrina precedente), nonché in generale i diversi articoli contenuti nel volume a cura di Capdetrey – Hasenohr, nel quale è contenuto anche il lavoro da ultimo citato.

54 Arist. *Ath. Pol.* 51.1: κληροῦνται δὲ καὶ ἀγορανόμοι <ι'>, πέντε μὲν εἰς Πειραιέα, ε' δ' εἰς ἄστυ. τούτοις δὲ ὑπὸ τῶν νόμων προστέτακται τῶν ὠνίων ἐπιμελεῖσθαι πάντων, ὅπως καθαρὰ καὶ ἀκίβδηλα πωλήσεται.

55 La questione non è stata oggetto di particolare approfondimento in dottrina. Si vedano, per alcune brevi suggestioni, Stroud (1974), p. 178 s.; Stanley (1976), p. 199 s.; Figueira (1986), p. 544; Tuci (2007), in part. p. 119 s.; Fantasia (2016), p. 46 s. ntt. 16 e 25.

56 Si confrontino al riguardo le testimonianza degli Acarnesi di Aristofane (719–728), del 425 a.C., e delle Vespe (1406–1408), del 423 a.C.

57 Si veda il noto passaggio dell'*Ath. Pol.* 51.1–3, oltre a Alex. *Phraidr.* fr. 247; *IG* II^2 380; *Ag.* XVI 217 (254/244 a.C.). Per altre testimonianze successive cfr. Oliver 2012, p. 94–97.

Conseguentemente è da ritenere che i *syllogeis tou demou* abbiano operato accanto agli *agoranomoi* all'interno dell'agorà.

D'altro canto, dalle fonti emerge chiaramente come, insieme agli *agoranomoi*, fossero previsti anche altri magistrati per lo svolgimento di attività di controllo dei mercati. Aristotele ricorda i *metronomoi*, con il compito specifico di verifica dei pesi e delle misure[58], e gli stessi *sitophylakes*, sicuramente già istituiti all'epoca di emanazione della legge, come evidenziato nel § precedente, possono essere considerati come magistrati "speciali" operanti accanto agli *agoranomoi* e agli *epimeletai tou emporiou* al fine di supervisionare il mercato del grano nell'agora e al Pireo.

In dottrina si è avanzata l'ipotesi[59] secondo cui, verso la fine del V secolo a.C., il numero degli *agoranomoi* fosse solo di sei membri, distribuiti in numero eguale nell'agorà e al Pireo. Tale congettura è proposta tenendo conto di una testimonianza di Aristofane[60], in cui si legge che Diceopoli aveva istituito tre *agoranomoi* per la sua agorà. Prima del 348 a.C., poi, il numero degli *agoranomoi* sarebbe aumentato a dieci, come si ricaverebbe da un passaggio delle Leggi di Platone[61], morto proprio in quella data. Seguendo questa tesi, si potrebbe essere indotti a supporre che proprio in ragione del numero relativamente esiguo di *agoranomoi* si fosse giunti ad individuare i *syllogeis tou demou* come ulteriori autorità competenti per questioni legate al mercato e alle transazioni ivi effettuate, con particolare riguardo alla moneta utilizzata per le attività di compravendita.

6. Tuttavia, sia che si voglia seguire l'ipotesi da ultimo descritta in ordine al numero esiguo di *agoranomoi* all'epoca dell'emanazione della legge di Nicofonte, sia che invece si preferisca aderire alla tesi di coloro che ritengono le testimonianze ora vedute non conclusive nel senso della presenza di un numero così ridotto di magistrati dell'*agora* nell'epoca in discorso, sembra che l'indicazione all'interno della legge dei *syllogeis tou demou* con le funzioni vedute abbia alla sua base motivazioni specifiche e peculiari.

Riprendendo il contenuto della legge, è di tutta evidenza la specifica relazione tra la competenza dei *syllogeis tou demou* indicata nelle ll. 16 ss. e l'altra funzione fondamentale di questi magistrati contenuta nel testo, nelle linee precedenti, ossia il controllo e la punizione del *dokimastes* dell'*agora*.

Come veduto, laddove il venditore non avesse accettato la moneta verificata dallo schiavo pubblico, avrebbe mostrato di mettere in dubbio la correttezza dell'operazione di controllo effettuato o addirittura avrebbe operato in contrapposizione a quanto scaturito da siffatto controllo. Attribuendo la competenza suveduta ai

---

58 Parte della dottrina dubita che l'istituzione dei *metronomoi* possa collocarsi prima del 374 a.C. In particolare, si pone in questo senso Stanley (1979), p. 199. Contro tale congettura cfr., da ultimo, le osservazioni di Fantasia (2016), p. 47 nt. 25.

59 MacDowell (1971), p. 313 e, più ampiamente, Stanley (1979), p. 14.

60 Aristoph. *Ach.* 724.

61 Plat. *Leg.* 6.763e.

syllogeis tou demou si sarebbe avuta un'ottimizzazione nell'accertamento della singola situazione contestata e si sarebbe giunti più rapidamente alla soluzione della controversia. A fronte della condotta del venditore, i *syllogeis* avrebbero invero proceduto ad un controllo dell'operato dello schiavo pubblico. Ove questi effettivamente non avesse svolto correttamente la propria attività di verifica, sarebbe stato punito. Nell'evenienza in cui invece i *syllogeis tou demou* avessero accertato il corretto operare dello schiavo pubblico, avrebbero avuto elementi di rilievo per la valutazione a loro volta della condotta del venditore accusato di non aver accettato la moneta, con la possibilità di procedere eventualmente essi stessi alla comminazione della punizione prevista dalla legge oppure di rinviare la controversia al *dikasterion*[62].

Interessante può essere inoltre il raffronto con la testimonianza offerta da un decreto attico in materia di pesi e misure[63] della fine del II secolo a.C. (*IG* II^2 1013). Quivi, alle ll. 45–49[64], sono individuati, quali magistrati competenti a punire gli schiavi pubblici addetti ai pesi e alle misure pubblici, i *prytaneis* e lo *strategos epi ta opla* nella Skias, l'*epimeletes tou limenos* al Pireo, lo *hierophantes* e i preposti alla *panegyris* ad Eleusi. Pur trattandosi di una testimonianza più tarda rispetto alla legge di Nicofonte, appare significativa la presenza di diversi magistrati competenti alla punizione degli schiavi pubblici in connessione con i luoghi nei quali costoro svolgevano le proprie attività legate ai pesi e alle misure. Per altro verso, inoltre, è evidente la stretta relazione tra gli *epimeletai tou limenos* ivi menzionati con gli *epimeletai tou emporiou*, citati nella legge qui analizzata, ma altresì tra *prytaneis* e *syllogeis tou demou*, trattandosi, in entrambi i casi, di comitati della *boule*[65].

Dalla lettura dei suveduti passaggi del *nomos*, nonché dalla presentazione dei *syllogeis tou demou* del paragrafo precedente, emerge inoltre un collegamento tra queste autorità e la *boule* e tra la *boule* e i *dokimastai*. Nelle ll. 4–8 si specifica che il *dokimastes* dell'*agora* doveva prestare la propria opera di verifica delle monete tutti i giorni in uno specifico luogo, ad eccezione di quelli in cui era impegnato nel

---

[62] Analoghe osservazioni valgono per gli *epimeletai tou emporiou*, incaricati sia del controllo e dell'eventuale punizione dello schiavo pubblico del Pireo sia della punizione del venditore che non accetti le monete nei limiti di valore suindicati.

[63] Sul decreto mi permetto di rinviare al lavoro monografico Rizzi (2017), *passim*, cui *adde* Doyen (2016), p. 453–487; Rizzi (2018), p.185–198.

[64] *IG* II^2 1013, ll. 45–49: τ]ὸν μὲν ἐν τε[ῖ] Σ[κιάδι καθεστ]αμ[ένον | κολα]ζόντω[ν] ο[ἵ τε ἀεὶ] πρυτάνεις καὶ ὁ στρατη[γ]ὸς ὃς [ἂν ἦι] ὁ ἐπὶ [τὰ] ὅπλα μαστιγοῦντες καὶ κολ[άζ|οντ]ες κ̣ατὰ τ̣[ὴν] ἀξίαν τοῦ ἀδική[μα]τος, τὸν [δ]' ἐμ̣ Πε[ιραιεῖ] ὁ καθε̣σταμένος ἐπιμελη[τὴς τοῦ λιμέ|νο]ς, τὸν δ'ἐν Ἐλευσῖνι ὅ τε̣ ἱεροφάντ̣ης [καὶ οἱ κα]θ[εσ]ταμένο[ι] ἄ[ν]δ̣ρ̣ες καθ'ἕκαστον [τὸν ἐνιαυτὸν] | ἐπὶ τὴν πανήγυριν.

[65] Ancora, come veduto nel summenzionato Poll. VIII 104, nello svolgimento della loro attività di riunione del popolo in assemblea i *syllogeis tou demou* (e i lessiarchi) si avvalevano della preziosa collaborazione degli arcieri sciti, circostanza questa che potrebbe indurre a ipotizzare che i *syllogeis* avessero il compito di controllare e sovraintendere anche all'attività degli arcieri, almeno nel contesto in discorso.

bouleuterion a presenziare alla *chrematon katabole*[66]; in tal caso la verifica veniva svolta al *bouleuterion*. Subito dopo, alle ll. 11–13, si prescrive che le monete sequestrate dovevano essere consacrate al Tempio della Madre degli Dei e depositate alla *boule*[67]. Nella seconda parte della legge di Nicofonte, ancora, nell'ordinare la predisposizione di un *dokimastes* al Pireo, si indica la *boule* quale organo avente il compito di individuarne uno adatto tra quelli posseduti dalla città o di provvedere al suo acquisto nel caso in cui nessuno abbia le caratteristiche richieste[68].

Tutti i suddetti dati inducono a pensare che la *boule* rivestisse un certo ruolo nella sovraintendenza e gestione delle questioni disciplinate all'interno della legge, in particolare con riguardo agli schiavi pubblici. Tra di esse è plausibile supporre che rientrasse anche il controllo dell'operato del *dokimastes* operante all'agora, mansione quest'ultima che venne affidata a membri della *boule* stessa nella figura dei *syllogeis tou demou*, ai quali fu anche attributo il potere giudiziario collegato alle contestazioni sorte a seguito della verifica delle monete. In altri termini, le funzioni spettanti ai *syllogeis* sugli schiavi pubblici sembrano trovare giustificazione proprio in relazione al loro collegamento con la *boule*, quali mansioni specifiche attribuite a questo collegio in dipendenza delle attribuzioni ampie della *boule* concernenti gli schiavi pubblici addetti al controllo delle monete e alle operazioni di confisca delle monete vietate.

Quello che rimane incerto è se il potere attribuito ai *syllogeis tou demou* nei confronti del *dokimastes* dell'agora fosse preesistente e sia stato esteso alla competenza giudiziaria nella soluzione delle controversie sorte nel mercato entro i limiti veduti oppure se si sia trattato di una doppia attribuzione di competenza specificamente individuata legislativamente, attraverso il *nomos* di Nicofonte o attraverso una legge precedente riferita nella prima parte dell'iscrizione, ove si accolga l'ipotesi secondo cui il *nomos* del 375/4 avrebbe aggiunto alla disciplina preesistente le disposizioni relative allo schiavo pubblico al Pireo. Se alcuni indizi sembrano legittimare l'ipotesi che l'attività generale di verifica delle monete

---

66 *SEG* XXVI 72 ll. 4–8: ὁ δὲ] | δοκιμαστὴς ὁ δημόσιος καθήμενος με[ταξὺ τῶν τρ]|απεζῶν δοκιμαζέτω κατὰ ταῦτα ὅσαι ἡ[μέραι πλὴν] | ὅταν ἦ[ι] χρημάτωγ καταβολή, τότε δὲ ἐ[ν τῶι βολευτ]|ηρίωι.

67 Secondo l'interpretazione offerta da Stroud (1974), p. 166 e ripresa, tra gli altri, da Alessandrì (1984), p. 370 nt. 5, gli atti susseguenti alla verifica fatta dallo schiavo pubblico relativi alle monete straniere d'argento, a quelle di bronzo e piombo argentato, nonché a quelle false, segnatamente restituzione delle monete straniere di argento, sequestro delle monete argentate e false, la consacrazione alla dea Madre e il deposito alla *boule*, spetterebbero proprio al magistrato competente, dunque nel caso della verifica fatta dal *dokimastes* dell'*agora* ai *syllogeis*.

68 *SEG* XXVI 72 ll. 36–40. ὅ]|πως δ' ἂν ἦι καὶ ἐμ Πειραιεῖ δοκιμαστὴς [τοῖς ναυκ]|λήροις καὶ τοῖς ἐμπόροις καὶ τοῖς ἄλλο[ις πᾶσιν], | καταστησάτω ἡ βολὴ ἐκ τῶν δημοσίων ἐạ̀[ν -c.7- ὑπάρχηι] | ἢ ἐσπριάσθω…

affidata a schiavi pubblici potesse essere precedente al *nomos*[69], ciò non consente tuttavia di trarre conclusioni nella direzione di un eventuale controllo del loro operato già antecedentemente spettante ai *syllogeis*.

Pur se collegate con i poteri sullo schiavo pubblico dell'agora, sembrano comunque specificatamente dipendenti dalla regolamentazione che si legge nel *nomos* per un verso la competenza giudiziaria attribuita a questi magistrati nei confronti dei venditori che non accettino le monete verificate, estrinsecazione a sua volta di un potere giudiziario e punitivo già spettante a queste autorità, per altro verso la competenza a adire, con i *tesmothetai*, al *dikasterion* nel caso di controversia di valore superiore a dieci dracme, funzioni condivise con i *sitophylakes* e gli *epimeletai tou emporiou*.

Quanto al rapporto con le altre funzioni spettanti ai *syllogeis tou demou* testimoniate nelle fonti suvedute, le competenze contenute nella legge di Nicofonte non appaiono a ben vedere in contrasto con tali altre mansioni. L'analisi svolta nelle pagine precedenti ha mostrato un'autorità di un certo prestigio, come indicano le incombenze legate al radunarsi del popolo in assemblea e il ruolo significativo in ambito cultuale. Anche la verifica delle monete svolta dal *dokimastes* (insieme alla correlata punizione di coloro che avessero contestato siffatto controllo) costituiva a sua volta una funzione particolarmente delicata e rilevante, atteso che avrebbe determinato quali monete sarebbero state ammesse nel mercato e dunque quali avrebbero potuto essere utilizzate per le transazioni, quali monete sarebbero state restituite al compratore e quali, infine, sarebbero state confiscate. Non sorprende pertanto che tale attività fosse sottoposta al controllo di magistrati di un certo rilievo nella realtà ateniese. L'attribuzione di poteri giudiziari, a sua volta indicati anche nelle testimonianze suvedute, consentiva l'intervento punitivo di queste autorità sia nei confronti del *dokimastes*, sia, entro i limiti di valore visti, nei confronti dei venditori rei di non aver accettato la moneta verificata.

7. In sintesi, i *syllogeis tou demou*, nel 375/4 a.C., tra le altre funzioni di prestigio loro attribuite, sovraintendono all'attività di verifica delle monete in circolazione nell'*agora* nelle modalità e nei limiti che si leggono nella legge di Nicofonte, funzione comprensiva del controllo e dell'eventuale punizione del *dokimastes* dell'*agora*, della ricezione delle accuse poste dai compratori contro i venditori che abbiano rifiutato di accettare le monete verificate dallo schiavo pubblico nell'agorà e nel resto della città, della decisione della controversia entro determinati limiti di valore, nonché della presidenza delle cause portate al *dikasterion* a seguito di denuncia presentata agli stessi *syllogeis*. Le funzioni nei confronti degli schiavi

[69] Sul punto si veda da ultimo Ismard (2014), p. 738, che richiama gli inventari del 398/397 a.C. del tempio dell'Hekatompedon, sull'Acropoli, nei quali è menzionato il verificatore di stateri falsi, confiscati dalla *boule* e versati nel tesoro di Atena (IG II^2 1388 B ll. 61–62). Significativo appare anche in questa testimonianza il ruolo della *boule* in ordine all'operazione di confisca e di versamento al tesoro di Atena.

pubblici sembrano essere collegate e dipendenti dall'essere i *syllogeis* un comitato della *boule*, organo che appare rivestire nel *nomos* un ruolo di un certo rilievo in materia. A tali funzioni si collegano i poteri specifici attribuiti a queste autorità nei confronti del venditore che si rifiuti di accettare le monete verificate.

Attraverso l'attribuzione delle funzioni vedute, i *syllogeis tou demou* si affiancano di fatto agli *epimeletai tou emporiou* e ai *sitophylakes*, ma altresì agli *agoranomoi* e ai *metronomoi,* nelle attività di controllo delle operazioni commerciali svolte ad Atene[70]; in tale prospettiva si può altresì affermare che i *syllogeis tou demou,* analogamente alle altre autorità di mercato summenzionate, operano al fine di "implementing and enforcing the law", riprendendo le parole di Harris[71], ed in particolare, unitamente ai *sitophylakes* e agli *epimeletai tou emporiou,* rivestono un ruolo centrale al fine di garantire il rispetto delle prescrizioni relative alla corretta circolazione della moneta ad Atene nell'ambito dello svolgimento delle transazioni commerciali[72]. Anzi, seguendo l'ipotesi dell'attribuzione delle competenze dei *syllogeis* concernenti siffatto controllo come introdotta dalla legge del 375/4 o da una legge precedente riferita nella prima parte del testo, si dovrebbe ricavare uno specifico ruolo di particolare rilievo da parte del potere pubblico in ordine alla disciplina e alla regolamentazione delle attività di mercato, atteso che attraverso un intervento di tipo normativo si sarebbe provveduto all'attribuzione di funzioni

---

70 Il profilo in discorso è messo particolarmente in rilievo da Alessandrì (1984), *passim*, il quale, nel definire la legge di Nicofonte "un pacchetto di istruzioni per i magistrati che sono investiti a vario titolo di funzioni di polizia nell'agora, nel mercato del grano, nell'emporio e nel Pireo ed ai cui ordini opera il *dokimastes*" (p. 370), giunge addirittura a negare che essa possa essere definita come "una *silver currency law*", come invece denominata da Stroud nell'*editio princeps,* e generalmente indicata, pur con declinazioni particolari, dalla maggior parte degli studiosi che si sono occupati della legge. In realtà, pur ritenendo che il complesso delle disposizioni concernenti le competenze delle magistrature qui analizzate costituisca un punto centrale del *nomos*, si reputa che tali attribuzioni debbano essere lette e comprese proprio in funzione delle regole prescritte in materia di circolazione della moneta e che dunque, in tale prospettiva, denominazioni "legge sulla circolazione della moneta", "legge sulla monetazione d'argento" e simili siano del tutto corrette.

71 Harris (2007), p. 159.

72 Nella sua analisi volta a mettere in discussione la tesi di Hunter (1994), *passim*, secondo cui l'applicazione del diritto nell'Atene Classica sarebbe stata principalmente nelle mani di privati cittadini, Harris (2007) dedica la parte seconda delle sua argomentazioni a dimostrare come "in laws and decrees passed by the Athenian Assembly, the main responsibility for enforcing regulations is placed in the hands of public officials" (p. 160). All'interno di tale sezione Harris (2007), p. 161 s., analizza come primo esempio proprio il *nomos* di Nicofonte, sottolineando, accanto a quello delle autorità ivi menzionate, anche il ruolo degli schiavi pubblici, e rilevando come l'iniziativa privata abbia solo la funzione di consentire l'intervento delle autorità pubbliche, le quali provvederanno alla imposizione delle sanzioni previste.

speciali ad autorità preesistenti aventi mansioni distanti da quelle specificamente assegnate.

Resta la questione se i *syllogeis tou demou* possano essere indicati come "autorità straordinarie di mercato". Come veduto, le funzioni loro attribuite sembrano da vedere almeno in parte come un potere affidato alla *boule* ed implementato da parte di suoi organi, potere derivante a sua volta da una più ampia attribuzione al Consiglio della sovraintendenza e del coordinamento di alcuni profili significativi in ordine al controllo operato sugli schiavi pubblici. Mel conferimento delle specifiche competenze, anche punitive, vedute, tuttavia, i *syllogeis* si trovano ad operare insieme agli *epimeletai tou emporiou* e ai *sitophylakes* nelle attività di controllo della corretta circolazione della moneta. In base a ciò sembra si possa ritenere anche per i *syllogeis*, in un certo modo, la loro inclusione tra le autorità di mercato, pur tenendo conto delle peculiarità delle loro funzioni, legate alle circostanze che dovettero portare agli interventi in materia di circolazione monetaria che si leggono nel *nomos*.

mariagrazia.rizzi@unimib.it

BIBLIOGRAFIA

Alessandrì 1984: S. Alessandrì, *Il significato storico della legge di Nicofonte sul "dokimastes" monetario*, in *ASNP* 14.2, p. 369–393

Bitros – Economou – Kyriazis 2020: G.C. Bitros – E.M.L. Economou – N.C. Kyriazis, *Democracy and Money Lessons for Today from Athens in Classical Times*, London – New York

Buttrey 1979: T.V. Buttrey, *The Athenian Currency Law of 375/4 BC*, in O. Mørkholm – N. Waggoner (a cura di), *Greek Numismatics and Archaeology, Essays in Honor of Margaret Thompson*, Wetteren, p. 33–45

Canevaro 2016: M. Canevaro, *Demostene, Contro Leptine. Introduzione, Traduzione e Commento Storico*, Berlin – Boston

Doyen 2016 : C. Doyen, *Ex schedis Fourmonti. Le décret agoranomique athénien (CIG I 123 = IG II–III² 1013)*, in *Chiron* 46, p. 453–487

Economou – Kyariazis 2021: E.-M.L. Economou – N.A. Kyriazis, *Achieving Sustainable Financial Transactions under Regimes without a Central Bank – An Intertemporal Comparison*, in *Sustainability* 13, p. 1–13

Economou – Kyriazis – Kyriazis 2021: E.-M. L. Economou – N.C. Kyriazis – N.A. Kyriazis, *Money Decentralization under Direct Democracy Procedures. The Case of Classical Athens*, in *JRFM* 14, p. 1–17

Ellithorpe 2019: C.J. Ellithorpe, *Athenian Mercantilism: a new Approach to the Athenian Coinage Decree and the Law of Nicophon*, in *JAHA*. 6.3, p. 59–75

Engels 2000: J. Engels, *Das athenische Getreidesteuer-Gesetz des Agyrrhios und angebliche « sozialstaatliche » Ziele in den Maßnahmen zur Gedreideversorgung spätklassischer und hellenistischer Poleis*, in *ZPE* 132, p. 97–124

Fantasia 2016: U. Fantasia, *I cereali nell'antica Grecia e l'approvvigionamento granario dell'Atene classica*, in C. Bearzot (a cura di), *L'alimentazione tra Storia, Letteratura e Cultura nell'Antichità e nel Medioevo*, Milano, p. 7–39

Figueira 1986: T.J. Figueira, *Sitopolai and Sitophylakes in Lysias' «Against the Graindealers»*, in *Phoenix* 40, p. 149–171

Francotte 1964 : H. Francotte, *De la législation athénienne sur les distinctions honorifiques et spécialement des décrets des clérouchies athéniennes relatifs a cet objet*, ora in *Mélanges de droit public grec*, rist. an., Roma, p. 71–159

Gauthier 1976 : Ph. Gauthier, *Un commentaire historique des Poroi de Xénophon*, Paris

Gauthier 1981 [2011]: Ph. Gauthier, *De Lysias à Aristote (Ath. Pol. 51,4): le commerce du grain à Athènes et les fonctions des sitophylaques*, in *RHDE* 59, p. 5–28 (= D. Rousset (a cura di), *Études d'histoire et d'institutions grecques. Choix d'écrits*, Genève, p. 193–220)

Hansen 1984: M.H. Hansen, *Die athenische Volksversammlung im Zeitalter des Demosthenes*, Konstanz

Harris 2007: E. Harris, *Who enforced the Law in Classical Athens?*, in E. Cantarella (a cura di), *Symposion 2005*, Wien, p. 159–176

Harris 2020: E. Harris, *The Rule of Law and Economic Growth in Ancient Greece*, in E. Harris – M. Canevaro (a cura di), *The Oxford Handbook of Ancient Greek Law*, Oxford

Harrison 1971: A.R.W. Harrison, *The Law of Athens. II. Procedure*, Oxford

Humphreys 2018: S.C. Humphreys, *Kinship in Ancient Athens. An Antropological Analysis*, I, Oxford

Hunter 1994: V. Hunter, *Policing Athens. Social Control in the Attic Lawsuits, 420–320 B.C.*, Princeton

Ismard 2014 : P. Ismard, *Le simple corps de la cité. Les esclaves publics et la question de l'État grec*, in *HSS* 69, p. 723–751

Ismard 2015: P. Ismard, *La démocratie contre les experts. Les esclaves publics en Grèce ancienne*, Paris

Ismard 2017: P. Ismard, *Democracy's Slaves: A Political History of Ancient Greece*, trad. a cura di J.M. Todd, Cambridge – London

Jacob 1928 : O. Jacob, *Les esclaves publics à Athènes*, Paris

Koch 2000–2001 [2009]: Chr. Koch, *Reformbemühungen um Münzwesen und Währungssysteme in Griechenland*, in *BIDR*. 103–104, p. 247–291

Kroll 2011: J.H. Kroll, *Athenian Tetradrachm Coinage of the First Half to the Fourth Century BC*, in *RBN* 157, p. 3–26

Lipsius 1908: J.H. Lipsius, *Das Attische Recht und Rechtsverfahren, II*, Leipzig

MacDowell 1971: D.M. MacDowell (a cura di), *Aristophanes, Wasps*, Oxford

MacDowell 1991 [2017]: D.M. MacDowell, *The Athenian Procedure of Phasis*, in M. Gagarin (a cura di), *Symposion* 1990, Köln–Weimar–Wien, p. 187–198 (= I. Arnaoutoglou – K. Kapparis – D. Spatharas (a cura di), *Studies on Greek Law, Oratory and Comedy*, London, p. 159–170)

Maffi 2016: A. Maffi, *Riflessioni su dikai emporikai e prestito marittimo*, in D.F. Leão – G. Thür (a cura di), *Symposion* 2015, Wien, p. 199–208

Martin 1991: Th.R. Martin, *Silver Coins and Public Slaves in the Athenian Law of 375/4 BC*, in E.W. Metcalf (a cura di), *Mnemata: Papers in memory of Nancy M. Waggoner*, New York, p. 21–48

Migeotte 2005 (2015): L. Migeotte, *Les pouvoirs des agoranomes dans les cités grecques*, in R.W. Wallace – M. Gagarin (a cura di), *Symposion 2001*, Graz, p. 287–301 (= *Économie et finances publiques des cités grecques. II. Choix d'articles publiés de 2002 à 2014*, Lyon, p. 27–40)

Muttelsee 1931: M. Muttelsee, *s.v. Sullogeis*, in RE IV A 1, Stuttgart, p. 1044–1046

Ober 2008: J. Ober, *Democracy and Knowledge. Innovation and Learning in Classical Athens*, Princeton

Ober 2015: J. *Ober, Access, Fairness, and Transaction Costs. Nikophon's Law on Silver Coinage (Athens, 375/4 B.C.E)*, in D. Kehoe – D. Ratzan – U. Yiftach et alii (a cura di), *Law and Transaction Costs in the Ancient Economy*, Michigan, p. 51–79

Oliver 2012: G. Oliver, *The agoranomoi at Athens*, in L. Capdetrey – C. Hasenohr (a cura di), *Agoranomes et édiles. Institutions des marchés antiques*, Bordeaux, p. 81–100

Paoli 1930: U.E. Paoli, *Studi di diritto attico*, Firenze

Pébarthe 2012: Chr. Pébarthe, *Droit et marché en Grèce ancienne. De la monnaie athénienne comme loi*, in B. Legras – G. Thür (a cura di), *Symposion 2011*, Wien, p. 237–259

Psoma 2011: S. Psoma, *The Law of Nicophon (SEG 26 72) and Athenian Imitations*, in *RBN* 157, p. 27–36

Rhodes 1972: P.J. Rhodes, *The Athenian Boule*, Oxford

Rhodes 1981: P.J. Rhodes, *A Commentary on the Aristotelian Athenaion Politeia*, Oxford

Rhodes – Osborne 2003: P.J. Rhodes – R. Osborne, *Greek Historical Inscriptions 404–323 BC*, Oxford

Rizzi 2017: M. Rizzi, *Marktbezogene Gesetzgebung im späthellenistischen Athen: Der Volksbeschluss über Maße und Gewichte*, München

Rizzi 2018: M. Rizzi, *La "riscoperta" del decreto ateniese sui pesi e misure. Nuove notae*, in B. Biscotti (a cura di), *Kállistos Nómos. Scritti in onore di Alberto Maffi*, Milano, p. 185–198

Rizzi 2020: M. Rizzi, *Le funzioni dei syllogeis tou demou ad Atene nel IV secolo a.C. attraverso la testimonianza della legge di Nicofonte*, in QLSD 10, p. 25–40

Rosivach 2000: V.J. Rosivach, *Some Economic Aspects of the Fourth-Century Athenian Market in Grain*, in *Chiron* 30, p. 31–64

Scafuro 2006: A.C. Scafuro, *Magistrates with Hegemony in the Courts of Athens*, in H.-A. Rupprecht (a cura di), *Symposion 2003*, Köln – Weimar – Wien, p. 27–52

Silverio 2019: O. Silverio, *Ricerche sulla storia degli schiavi pubblici ateniesi*, a cura di M. Rizzi, Roma

Stanley 1976: Ph. Stanley, *Ancient Greek Market Regulations and Controls*, Dissertation, Berkeley

Stanley 1979: Ph. Stanley, *Agoranomoi and Metronomoi. Athenian Market Officials and Regulations*, in *AncW* 2, p. 13–19

Stroud 1972: R.S. Stroud, *A Law of the Athenian Nomothetai*, in *AJA.* 76, p. 221

Stroud 1974: R.S. Stroud, *An Athenian Law on Silver Coinage*, in *Hesperia* 43, p. 157–188

Stumpf 1986: G. Stumpf, *Ein athenisches Münzgesetz des 4. Jh. v. Chr.*, in *JNG* 36, p. 23–40

Tuci 2007: P.A. Tuci, *Polluce VIII 104 e i funzionari addetti al controllo della partecipazione assembleare*, in C. Bearzot – F. Landucci – G. Zecchini (a cura di), *L'Onomasticon di Giulio Polluce. Tra lessicografia e antiquaria*, Milano, p. 103–137

Wallace 2003: R.W. Wallace, *Phainein in Athenian Laws and Legal Procedures*, in G. Thür – F.J. Fernández Nieto (a cura di), *Symposion 1999*, Köln –Weimar – Wien, p. 167–181

ADELE C. SCAFURO (PROVIDENCE, RI)

FURTHER THOUGHTS ON THE *BOULĒ* AND *DOKIMASTĒS:* RESPONSE TO MARIAGRAZIA RIZZI[*]

Mariagrazia Rizzi prefaces her essay on Nikophon's law (*SEG* XXVI 72) with a look back to Christophe Pébarthe's essay *Droit et Marché en Grèce Ancienne* in *Symposion 2011*. Pébarthe had ended his rich discussion of legislation and the market with a brief and insightful analysis of that same law. It was found to be a definitive or at least a lasting solution to problems arising from the end of the Peloponnesian War; indeed, "elle ne peut donc être réduite à une réaffirmation de la décision des années 390, voire à une mesure d'urgence" (p. 253); especially in its acceptance of foreign currency, and with an understanding of the need for exchanges, "importations et exportations étant les deux faces d'une *autarkeia* bien comprise," the solution ensured not only prosperity for Athens but for other cities as well (p. 256).[1] Rizzi, after recalling Pébarthe's broad view of the law of 375/4 as one that facilitated trade and encouraged the market economy in Athens and elsewhere, takes up the law from a different perspective: she looks for the mechanisms of interventions from the public sphere and the role of public officials in controlling market activities. Accordingly, in the first part of her essay, she offers a meticulous study of the three magistracies (*sitophylakes*, *syllogeis tou dēmou*, *epimelētai tou emporiou*) involved in implementing and enforcing Nikophon's law, and in the second part, devises a nuanced construction of the *boulē's* involvement especially with the *syllogeis tou dēmou* and *dokimastēs*. In both parts of the essay, she looks for what may be considered new in the powers ascribed by the law to the three magistracies and especially to the *syllogeis tou dēmou.*[2]

---

* The author of this essay extends her thanks to Philipp Scheibelreiter for the invitation to participate in Symposion 2023 in Gmunden, Austria with its lovely scenery and illustrious traditions so ably presented by the organizer—and of course with the company of scholars so actively engaged in the study of ancient law.

1 Pébarthe 2012, 253–57.

2 Rizzi is a well-established expert in the study of this law and the later Athenian law on weights and measures (*IG* II^2 1013); see Rizzi 2017; 2018; 2020. Regarding *SEG* XXVI.72, she is able to encapsulate the major areas of scholarly debate on this important document in a very few notes and ably provides up to date bibliography. To her nn. 3 and 8, however, where she addresses problems posed by the text of the law, and especially the problem at the end of line 9, I add two important contributions by A.P. Matthaiou, an

Before offering a brief examination of Rizzi's arguments, I would like to comment on the timeliness of this study: in the last months of 2021, at least 8 months before Rizzi's presentation at the conference in Gmunden, M.B. Richardson published the long awaited *editio princeps* of Epikrates' law of 354/3 on the Athenian mint.[3] Obviously, there are strong reasons to compare the law about silver coinage enacted in 375/4 and the law on the mint enacted twenty years later. Legal historians in Europe and America have been studying this 'new' law since Richardson's 2021 publication—as well as trying to establish a firmer text (it is badly preserved) as a prelude to understanding its meaning.[4] Because of this conjunction of events, Richardson's publication of Epikrates' law in winter 2021 and Rizzi's re-examination of Nikophon's law in August 2022, I have been happy to take up Rizzi's essay, especially in the hope that it might provide some needed light on Epikrates' law. I shall return to this quest in my conclusions.

Rizzi's method in the first part of her study of Nikophon's law is to examine each magistracy by itself and to compare the tasks enjoined upon it in the law to tasks undertaken by the same magistracy in other attestations, both earlier and later, and mostly the latter. Briefly stated, the law assigns judicial and penal competencies to the *sitophylakes* for offences committed in the grain markets, to the *syllogeis tou dēmou* for offences committed by sellers in the Agora and in the rest of the city, and to the *epimelētai tou emporiou* for those in the emporion and in Piraeus—the offences in all three cases being rejection of the silver coinage approved by the *dokimastai.* Ron Stroud had determined in the *editio princeps* of 1974 that the judicial competencies of these three magistracies are attested for the first time in Nikophon's law. As for their *existence* before the law, i.e., regardless of those competencies, only one of the three, the *sitophylakes*, is certainly attested before 375/4—and that attestation appears in Lysias 22, perhaps in 386. The *epimelētai tou emporiou* have no previous attestation but are generally thought to have existed earlier, perhaps early in the fourth century;[5] they have considerable attestation later (e.g., *Ath. Pol.* 51.4; Dem. 35 *Lacr.* 50, ca. 351). The *syllogeis tou dēmou* are more problematic: while attested later in the fourth century with other tasks, they have no agreed upon date of origin—whether before or after the law of 375/4. Many, however, think they may have been functioning since the beginning of that century,

essay in *Γραμματεῖον* 2017, 6, 43–54 and a chapter in Ἔξι Ἀττικὲς ἐπιγραφὲς τοῦ 4ου αἰ. π.Χ., 2019, 75-95; in the latter, he has re-edited the law after autopsy with comments on certain phrases and restorations (esp. at the end of l. 9) and on the meaning of the law.

3 Richardson 2021, 685–746.

4 At the time of writing this reply, two essays have been published (and likely others, unknown to me); Matthaiou 2022 offers preliminary comments on the text of the new law based on autopsy; Harris 2022 bases an interpretation on the *ed. pr.* and on autopsy aided by Selene Psoma who sees two new letters leading to restorations for ll. 15–20. Matthaiou and Robert Pitt will be publishing a fully revised text soon.

5 For the association of these magistrates with those mentioned at Xen. *Por.* 3.3, Rizzi calls our attention to Gauthier 1976, 80 and more recently, Maffi 2016, 203.

basing their arguments partly on the notice in Pollux (8.104 s.v. Περὶ ληξιάρχων) and elsewhere in the lexicographers where the *syllogeis* are thought to be identifiable as a 'board of thirty' (though without the designation *syllogeis tou dēmou*);[6] this board, along with the six *lēxiarchoi*, convened the Assembly and examined those who were members, penalized those who were not, and, with the aid of the archers, drove stragglers from the Agora into the *ekklēsia*.[7] Other pieces of evidence more cogently suggest that the lexicographers' board of thirty was indeed a committee of the *boulē* and that three *syllogeis* were chosen from each tribe (*IG* II^3 4 76 = *IG* II^2 1749 of 341/0, see below).[8] Rizzi's exploration of the relationship of the *syllogeis* to the *boulē* is, I think, her most important contribution to the study of Nikophon's law. I shall return to it soon; I shall also propose supplementary support for that relationship by looking more closely at the *syllogeis tou dēmou* ('convenors of the *dēmos*') and *dokimastai* (the public slaves who served as the 'testers', 'approvers', 'verifiers') as they appear in this law and elsewhere, and I include a *dokimastēs* who appears in the new law on the Athenian mint.[9]

As noticed briefly already, the three magistracies (the *sitophylakes*, *syllogeis tou dēmou*, and *epimelētai tou emporiou*) were competent to decide denunciations (*phaseis*) of sellers for offences committed in the three locations of their jurisdictions (the grain markets, the Agora and the rest of the city, and the emporion of Piraeus, 18–23). They were authorized to decide on their own cases worth 10 drachmas or less against sellers, and, as for cases worth more, they were authorized to introduce them into a *dikastērion* and the *thesmothetai* were to allot the court upon request (23–28); if any of the denounced and convicted sellers were slaves, the three magistracies were to flog them with 50 lashes (29–30). Additionally, the *syllogeis tou dēmou* were authorized to punish the *dokimastēs*

6 Thus, e.g., Stroud 1974, 166, 176–77. This is a view which Rizzi will review in the course of her essay and expand: the *syllogeis tou dēmou* would appear to have summary judicial and penal competencies when they assist the *lēxiarchoi*; see nn. 7 and 20 infra.

7 Poll. *Onom.* 8.104: ληξίαρχοι ἓξ καθίσταντο τῶν πολιτῶν ἐγγεγραμμένων ἐν λευκώματι, καὶ τριάκοντα ἀνδρῶν αὐτοῖς προσαιρεθέντων τοὺς ἐκκλησιάζοντας ἐξήταζον καὶ τοὺς μὴ ἐκκλησιάζοντας ἐζημίουν καὶ σχοινίον μιλτώσαντες διὰ τῶν τοξοτῶν συνήλαυνον τοὺς ἐκ τῆς ἀγορᾶς εἰς τὴν ἐκκλησίαν. The words have been variously interpreted; nonetheless, 'the thirty' appear to have power to make decisions (on membership? on the right to collect pay for attendance?) and to fine offenders on the spot. Unfortunately, the lexicographic material does not permit us to identify the date when the *lēxiarchoi* and *syllogeis* were carrying out these tasks. Connection with the τοξόται promotes an early date: the (Scythian) archers are most often mentioned in Aristophanic comedies and scholia; but there is nothing secure here—the Aristophanic archers are assisted neither by *syllogeis* nor by a board of thirty. Other lexicographic notices, less reliable, include: Hesych., s.v. τριάκοντα· οὗτοι ἐχειροτονοῦντο δικασταὶ Ἀθήνησιν, οἵτινες ἐζημιοῦντο τοὺς μὴ παραγενομένους τῶν πολιτῶν εἰς ἐκκλησίαν. Phot. s.v. τριάκοντα is muddled.

8 Rhodes 1972, 21 and 129–30.

9 See Feyel 2003, a discussion of the semantic group *δόκιμος, δοκιμάζειν, and δοκιμασία*, is quite relevant here.

who worked in the Agora and occasionally in the *bouleutērion* (7–8), indeed, to flog him with 50 lashes, if he did not sit or did not approve the coins in accordance with the law (13–16). Rizzi suggests that the oversight of the *dokimastēs* by the *syllogeis tou dēmou* allowed for an efficient settlement of disputes; the *syllogeis* could easily check the conduct of the *dokimastēs* in the Agora and city environs and might quickly have all the information they needed for settling the case themselves or for requesting a *dikastērion*. Additionally, as Stroud had already seen in the *editio princeps* and as Rizzi concurs here, the *epimelētai* of the emporion must have been assigned a similar authority over the new *dokimastēs* of Piraeus: after all, the *epimelētai* were instructed by Nikophon's law to 'apply the law in the same way as has been stated in the case of the *dokimastēs* in the city' (ll. 41–44, Stroud 1974, 178).

To turn now more specifically to the *syllogeis tou dēmou* and to leave the *sitophylakes* and *epimelētai* of the emporion behind: Rizzi's examination of the *syllogeis* in Nikophon's law and in later literary and epigraphic sources will lead her to conclude that they were 'un'autorità di un certo prestigio'; that prestige, she maintains, is indicated in their functions, that is, their duties relevant to convening the assembly and performing cultic tasks, and relevant also to their own verification of the coins carried out by the *dokimastēs* and the punishment of those who contested his decision. Indeed, these 'prestige functions' are extended, in the end, to their competency to punish the *dokimastēs*, to decide disputes within certain limits, and to preside over the cases that went to court. Focus on the very first function listed here allows Rizzi to propose a continuity of their functions over time—that is, when the *syllogeis* acted alongside the *lēxiarchoi* (mentioned earlier) examining members, penalizing offenders, and driving stragglers into the Assembly.[10] Indeed, members of the *boulē*, and in particular, the *syllogeis tou dēmou*, appear to have the same kinds of powers (summary judgment and summary punishment) in 375/4 under Nikophon's law, though in a different sphere as they did earlier on—and these are, according to Rizzi, prestigious functions. Cultic activities, as already mentioned, also contribute to their prestige.[11] In this regard, we can perhaps give more emphasis to details in *IG* II^3 4 76 of 341/0 (= *Agora* Vol. 15 no. 38; *IG* II^2 1749), mentioned briefly by Rizzi in her essay. This is a dedication of the *prytaneis* of the tribe Aegeis in 341/0 after the *boulē* and *dēmos*

---

[10] See n. 7 *supra* for the text of Pollux 8.104. Rizzi (p. 155 n. 65, this volume) cautiously suggests that Poll. 8.104, by depicting the *syllogeis* as acting in collaboration with the archers, might allow the hypothesis that the "*syllogeis* avessero il compito di controllare e sovraintendere anche all'attività degli arcieri, almeno nel contesto in discorso". On the implications of such a hypothesis, see further n. 20 infra.

[11] I mention in the text only a few of the sources mentioned by Rizzi (*IG* II^2 1257; *IG* II^2 1425) and I do this to give more stress to particular features. The *syllogeis* are also attested as being responsible for the receipts from the sale of skins from public sacrifices at the Olympieia in 334/3–331/0 (*IG* II^2 1496, ll. 82–83, 113–14).

had crowned them for their *aretē* and *dikaiosynē*; it is a marble base, inscribed on three sides, with cuttings on top for a dedicatory statue that is not preserved—nonetheless, the object itself demonstrates its association with the religious realm.[12] The text includes a catalogue of all the members of the prytany listed by deme and displays four honorific decrees; one honors and names the three *syllogeis* of Aegeis (i.e., the tribe in prytany) who are praised for having dealt 'fairly and justly with the convening of the *dēmos* and the distribution of *symbola*' (ll. 75–79);[13] the names of the three men appeared earlier in the catalogue (ll. 5, 12, 26)—thereby supplying perhaps the best evidence for the *syllogeis* being a 'committee of the *boulē*' (three from each of the ten prytanies/tribes provide the board of thirty mentioned in the lexicographers). Moreover, two of the *syllogeis* on the same dedication of 341/0 propose separate honorary decrees for fellow *prytaneis*: the *syllogeus* Diodoros proposes praise for Aristophanes (90–91), the *prytanis* who had proposed the honors for the three *syllogeis* (78–82), and the *syllogeus* Tharrias proposes two decrees, one for the *tamias* of the tribe (74–77) and another for ten *hieropoioi* at Eleusis, including the *syllogeus* Timokritos (83–87). This is indeed a distinguished and active set of magistrates, both in the civic and religious realms. A later monument base (Schwenk 77; *IG* II^2 1257) of 324/3, meant to carry a votive offering to the Mother of the Gods and dedicated by the *syllogeis* under similar circumstances (a crowning by the *dēmos* for their *dikaiosynē*), contains the texts of two of their own decrees, praising their *archē* for carrying out, *inter alia*, the duties of a *hieropoios* for Athena in the first one and for Olympian Zeus in the second.[14] The first crowns for *syllogeis* appear in the inventories of the Treasurers of Athena in 370/69 and 368/7 (*IG* II^2 1425.126 and 225); Stroud had suggested that it may perhaps have been 'in partial recognition of competence in administering their new powers that the first honorary crowns for the *Syllogeis* appear shortly after Nikophon's law';[15] the point of interest here, however, is that those first attested crowns were preserved by the honorands as dedications to Athena.

Against this significant background (especially the earlier and later attestations of the *syllogeis* and the tasks enjoined in the law), Rizzi considers the reasons why the *syllogeis* were given their particular assignments in the law of 375/4, and here we come to her original contribution in what I have designated as the second part of

12 Photographs of the three sides appear in *IG* II^3 4 76, Tab. XVI–XVII.

13 The *symbola* refer to the 'tesserae civibus distributae ad μισθὸν ἐκκλησιαστικόν solvendum' (*IG* II^3 4 76, apud 79). Cf. the briefer but similar text of a dedication in 351/0, *IG* II^3 4 72 = *IG* II^2 2821).

14 This and other decrees of the *syllogeis* are discussed by Rhodes 1972, 129–130.

15 Stroud 1974, 178–179 with n. 83. It is unfortunate that these early crowns go without mention in Meritt's *Agora* Vol. XV, p. 7; he certainly recognized the 'exceptionality' of the award of crowns to the board in 351/0, 324/3, and possibly in 344/3 (via supplement).

the essay.[16] Comparison with a later Athenian law that deals with standard weights and measures (*IG* II^2 1013) allows Rizzi to take the first step. In that law (ll. 45–49), enacted at the end of the second century, the *epimelētai tou limenos* in Piraeus act similarly to the *epimelētai tou emporiou* (also in Piraeus) in the law of 375/4, and the *prytaneis* along with the hoplite general of the later law act similarly in the Agora to the *syllogeis tou dēmou* of the earlier law (also in the Agora designated 'Skias' in ll. 39, 65): all these magistrates are competent to punish public slaves, in the later law, they punish those assigned to handle public weights and measures, and in Nikophon's law, they punish those assigned to test silver coins. What draws Rizzi's attention most of all, however, is *not* that the *prytaneis* of the later law and the *syllogeis* of the earlier one are both situated in the Agora and competent to punish public slaves, but rather that both the *prytaneis* of *IG* II^2 1013 (*IE* 237) and the *syllogeis tou dēmou* of Nikophon's law are committees drawn from the *boulē*.[17] Rizzi sums up the significant connections between the *syllogeis* and the *boulē* and between the *boulē* and *dokimastai* evident throughout the law of 375/4 as follows:

1. In ll. 4–8, the *dokimastēs* is to test coins in the Agora 'every [day, except] whenever there is a cash payment; at that time, let him test in the *bouleutērion*' (trans. Stroud).[18]
2. In ll.11–13, the coins that are seized must be consecrated to the Mother of the Gods and deposited in the *boulē*.
3. In ll. 36–41, the *boulē* is to appoint a *dokimastēs* for Piraeus from the public slaves (ἐκ τῶν δημοσίων) or if there is none, then it must buy one and the *apodektai* are to allocate the funds.

---

16 I have omitted Rizzi's comparison of the sphere of activity of the *syllogeis* as articulated in the law of 375/4 with the similar activity of the *agoranomoi* (e.g., *Ath Pol* 51.1: κληροῦνται δὲ καὶ ἀγορανόμοι <ι'>, πέντε μὲν εἰς Πειραιέα, ε' δ' εἰς ἄστυ. τούτοις δὲ ὑπὸ τῶν νόμων προστέτακται τῶν ὠνίων ἐπιμελεῖσθαι πάντων, ὅπως καθαρὰ καὶ ἀκίβδηλα πωλῆται); she leaves the question open whether the *agoranomoi* were suppressed for a short period or operated alongside the *syllogeis tou dēmou* in the Agora. The evidence is not conclusive.

17 Rizzi's analogy appears to suggest that the *epimelētai* of the *emporion* are likewise a committee of the *boulē*; that is not implausible but there is no evidence for that connection; in *Ath Pol* 51.4, the *epimelētai* are 'allotted'.

18 Stroud 1974, 159; similarly, Rhodes – Osborne 2003, 113. The law expresses the exception this way (italicized): δοκιμαζέτω κατὰ ταῦτα ὅσαι ἡ[μέραι *πλὴν] ὅταν ἦ[ι] χρημάτωγ καταβολή, τότε δὲ ἐ[ν τῶι βολευτ]-ηρίωι*. Rizzi's articulation/interpretation is perhaps too vague. Surely the *dokimastēs* is to be understood as approving the coinage in which the payments are made. The translation of the δέ clause that follows the 'exception' assumes the insertion of a verb: 'except when there is a deposit of money, and then [he is to test] in *the bouleutērion*'. The *dokimastēs* even carries out his task before the *boulē*.

The *boulē* is central. Above all, because of their membership in the *boulē*, the *syllogeis tou dēmou* possess a judicial and penal competency that allowed them, perhaps even in the late fifth century, to assist the *lēxiarchoi* in examining and judging the membership of those attending Assemblies and in penalizing those on the spot who were not members. In 375/4, those competencies are extended to a new sphere: they may now punish a lawbreaking *dokimastēs* in the Agora with a lashing;[19] they have authority to adjudicate denunciations (*phaseis*) made in the Agora that concern less than ten drachmas and to preside over denunciations worth more in a *dikastērion*; and they oversee all the matters in which the *dokimastēs* is concerned. The law in 375/4, on Rizzi's interpretation, has extended these 'bouleutic-in-origin' competencies (e.g., their assistance to the *lēxiarchoi*) to the *syllogeis tou dēmou* because the tasks (entailing interventions in the Agora of Athens and the commercial activities transacted there) require a magistracy of recognized authoritative standing.[20] The *syllogeis tou dēmou*, prestigious by virtue of their membership in the *boulē*, enforce the law by their competencies, both by controlling the *dokimastēs*, and, by virtue of their judicial competency, facilitating trade and the circulation of acceptable currency. Indeed, the latter competency demonstrates how the law operates as more than a police action enacted in a time of crisis; it offers a jury decision under the hegemony of the *syllogeis tou dēmou* to those who think they have been wronged; public intervention by the judiciary allows commerce to flourish.

---

[19] Rizzi accepts that a *dokimastēs* may have functioned in the Agora before Nikophon's law and accepts Stroud's arguments (1974, 176–177) that Lakon may have been a *dokimastēs* in 398/7 ('the counterfeit staters sealed in a box παρὰ Λάκωνος', *IG* II^2 1388B 61–62), an argument carried further by Ismard 2017, 41. She leaves open the question regarding the identity of the magistrate in charge at that earlier time. In my view, Stroud's arguments (1974, 166–167) based on *SEG* XXVI 17.52–53 are persuasive for the existence of a *dokimastēs* in the Agora before Nikophon's law: "This seems clear from the phraseology of lines 4–8 and from the reference in lines 52–53 to his (unstated) salary which is to serve as a model for his counterpart [i.e, the *dokimastēs* in Peiraius]"; I am hesitant, however, about identifying Lakon as a *dokimastēs* in 398/7; likewise Rhodes – Osborne 2003, 119.

[20] Rizzi's discussion of the law on weights and measures (*IG* II^2 1013) suggests there may have been a lasting tradition, (a) starting from the 'board of thirty' who assisted the *lēxiarchoi* in dealing with those attending the Assembly (Pollux 8.104) and who might also have had the task of controlling and supervising the archers (see n. 10 *supra)*, and (b) continuing in the judicial and penal competencies of the *syllogeis tou dēmou* in the law of 375/4, and (c) extending to the law in the late second century. In the last two (b and c), the *syllogeis/prytaneis* oversee the *dokimastai*, and in the earliest attestation (a), Rizzi suggests hypothetically that 'the board of thirty' may have supervised the archers. Rizzi does not explicitly propose this evolutionary hypothesis but it hovers in her explicit comparisons. Accordingly, it would be useful to have an explicit discussion of the value and validity of these comparisons given their temporal range; they are indeed very interesting.

As I hope this summary of Rizzi's discussion shows, I am much in agreement with its presentation of the tasks and competencies of the *syllogeis tou dēmou*; nonetheless, I am troubled that all their functions turn out to be 'prestigious'—especially their judicial and penal competencies. Surely this cannot be right: literary and epigraphic sources widely attest the authority of magistrates to impose fines for numerous minor offences connected with their sphere of activity—and when those fines fall short of the offence, they are authorized to send the case to a *dikastērion*. Indeed, MacDowell, after citing numerous examples, states the obvious, that it was "not something exceptional, granted only to a few magistrates in particular circumstances," but was instead "a general principle that a man appointed to office was not only required to perform various functions but was also entitled to punish anyone who hindered him from performing them" (1978, 235).[21] Nonetheless, the office of the *syllogeis tou dēmou* was authoritative and therefore a 'prestigious' one (if we may define 'prestigious' this way)—but that is surely due, *not* to the functions it carried out (insofar as quite ordinary magistrates carried out those very same functions) but to its status as a committee of the *prytaneis*, and thus as a sub-committee of the *boulē*, itself a powerful 'magistracy' in Athens—indeed, as Hansen (1991, 255) remarks, 'much the most important board of magistrates'.[22] Particularly 'prestigious', then, by this definition, is any board appointed by the *boulē* from its own membership—and this includes the boards of ten *trieropoioi* (*Ath. Pol.* 46.1), ten *logistai* (for rendering accounts of magistrates each prytany, *Ath. Pol.* 48.3), sixteen *hieropoioi Eleusini (IG* II^2 1672.280)—and the thirty *syllogeis tou dēmou* (a board of the *boulē* by a surely correct inference from *IG* II^3 4 76 of 341/0, and trust in a late lexicographer).[23]

Accordingly, though I am not persuaded about 'prestige functions', I am much impressed with the connections Rizzi has found among *boulē, syllogeis tou dēmou*, and *dokimastēs*. To continue with the centrality of the *boulē*, surely Rizzi's most important point, some other links may be identified. A reminder of the three public slaves who operate in the Agora and Piraeus and whose tasks are elucidated in Rizzi's essay are the starting point. In the first two texts (i and ii) the slaves are designated *dokimastai* but in (iii), they are called *dēmosioi* but mentioned

21 MacDowell 1978, 235–237.

22 Hansen 1991, 247 and 255–265.

23 On the other hand, it may be more in line with Athenian thinking to consider their own honorary grid as indicating where and how 'prestige' was ascribed. Each year, a tribe in prytany was voted as winning the competition for being the best prytany in the *boulē*. The awards (though without a crown) may go back as far as Cleisthenes, but the first attested one (for winning such a competition) is dated to 408/7. That men allotted to the *boulē* would have the chance of winning such an award suggests that any *bouleutēs* may have been looked upon as standing a good chance of winning such an honor; prestige may have accrued to him merely by being in the running (similar to an Oscar nomination?). For discussion of the first such awards, see *Agora* Vol. 15, p. 2 and nos. 1 and 3–5; also Lambert 2018.

separatim in the 'punishing clauses', e.g., at l. 45, τ]ὸν μὲν ἐν τε[ῖ] σ[κιάδι καθεστ]αμ̣[ένον]; thus:

> (i) the *dokimastēs* in the Agora, under control of the *syllogeis*, is mentioned five times in Nikophon's law, at ll. 5, 13, 16–17, 43–44, and 53; (ii) the *dokimastēs* destined for Piraeus and to be selected by the *boulē* is mentioned twice in Nikophon's law, at ll. 37 and 50–51; (iii) the [slave] who handles weights and measures in Skias (i.e., the Agora) in *IG* II^2 1013 can be flogged by the *prytaneis* and the hoplite general (ll. 45–47).[24]

To these attestations, I add:

1. Public slaves named in bouleutic lists:

(a) *Agora* Vol. 15. 37 (343/2?), a scrappy four lines; in 1–3 the name of the secretary of the *dēmos* and *boulē* is followed by the title ὑπηρέτης and a slave name. (Here and in the entries below the names following ὑπηρέτης [or ὑπηρέται] have neither patronym nor deme and so are designated as 'slave names').

(b) *Agora* Vol. 15. 62, the 'great bouleutic list of 303/2'; this was first fully published by John Traill in 1968 and later incorporated into *Agora* Vol. 15 in 1974 with different line numbers (as followed here). A list of 8 names appears beneath the title ([ὑπηρέται τῆ]ς βουλῆς) on the first *stēlē*, col. V ll. 11–18. Especially noteworthy is their number.

(c) *Agora* Vol. 15. 72, the 'great bouleutic list of 281/0'; this, like the preceding list, was first fully published by John Traill in 1969 and then incorporated into *Agora* Vol. 15 with different line numbers. This has 5 slave names entered under different tribal contingents at ll. 5, 67, 83, 211, and 266.

2. Dokimastai in the naval records: (a) *IG* II^2 1604.56 of 377/6; (b) *IG* II^2 1612.149–50, 218–246 of 356/5. Also, *dēmosioi* who may have served as *dokimastai*: (c) *IG* II^2 1631.176–184, 184–199, and 350–401 (esp. 370–85) for the years 325/4 and 324/3; (d) *IG* II^2 1622.520–30 of 360/59.

In (a), the *dokimastēs* may be taking part in a rating of equipment (oars) for rowers (*dokimos* or *adokimos*).

In (b) the total expenses for the repair of fourteen hulls is said to have been registered and recorded by the *dokimastēs*; from this sum, ten percent is withdrawn (for an undisclosed recipient) and the rest is withdrawn for the naval architects hired by the city.[25]

---

[24] *IG* II^2 1013 (*IE* 237) 45–47: τ]ὸν μὲν ἐν τε[ῖ] σ[κιάδι καθεστ]αμ̣[ένον] [κολα]ζόντω[ν] ο[ἵ τε ἀεὶ] πρυτάνεις καὶ ὁ στρατη[γ]ὸς ὃς [ἂν ἦι] ὁ ἐπὶ [τὰ] ὅπλα μαστιγοῦντες καὶ κολ[ά]||[ζοντ]ες κ̣ατὰ τ̣[ὴν] ἀξίαν τοῦ ἀδική[μα]τος.

[25] Gabrielsen 2010, 137 and 143.

In (c), a public slave (named Opsigonos) is recorded in consecutive years and, while identified as working in the dockyards (ὁ ἐν τοῖς ν[εωρίοι]ς, 382), he might also have worked in the *bouleutērion*: in the first two passages, he deals with the records of the *boulē* concerning the original cost of equipment bought for trierarchs which the latter must now repay, and in the third, he works alongside the *tamias* and a general reporting the sum that must now be wiped out from Sopolis' debt.

In (d), an *epimelētēs* deposited a sum of money into the *bouleutērion* which had been incurred via a *diadikasia* against Theophanes Spoudiou.

3. *A dokimastēs in IG II² 1492: an inventory of Athena and the Other Gods, from 306–04.* At B 102 [δοκι]μαστά τάλ[α]ντα appears and at B 137 τὸ χρύσιον [ἐδ]οκίμασεν Σπο]υδ ---]; Stroud 1974, 166 reports and accepts Köhler's conjecture (1880, 279) that the man is a *dokimastēs* and a public slave.[26]

4. *A dokimastēs in Epikrates' Law of 354/3 (Agora I 7495, ed. pr. Hesperia 90, 2021, 685–746)*: The text of 32 lines is lacunose and difficult to interpret; in l. 13, two officials and a layman can be read in the genitive case connected by καί: the *dokimastēs*, *epistatēs*, and purchaser (τοῦ ἐωνημένου); what their combination signifies is unclear. In ll. 17–19, the *epistatai* are to compel 'the public slaves, the ones in the mint' to produce every day the products in a quantity left undefined. Different interpretations are possible but go beyond the scope of this essay. The important point to notice here is that a *dokimastēs* is explicitly mentioned (l. 13) and shortly afterwards, public slaves (l. 18) who are located in the mint. It would be safe to maintain that the *dokimastēs* is situated in the Agora and probably outside the mint, whereas the public slaves are working inside it.[27]

All these testimonies are important, but the first may be the most important of all; I add further brief considerations to Testimonies 2–4 and then return to Testimony 1.

The *dokimastēs* of Testimony 2a (*IG* II² 1604.56) probably rated equipment in the dockyards; the one who recorded the cost of repairs in 2b (*IG* II² 1612.149–50;

---

26 I exclude from consideration here the Lakon mentioned in n. 19 *supra* regarding "the counterfeit staters [seal]ed [in a box] by Lakon" that appears in the Hekatompedon inventories from 398/7 (*IG* II²1388. 61–2); Stroud 1974, 176–177 and n. 77, proposed that he may have been a public slave (possibly a *dokimastēs* of the *boulē*) who received the counterfeits before their consecration. Ismard 2017, 41 took this a step further: "the city's seal, entrusted to the slave, was required for the coins to be withdrawn from circulation". Ismard ibid. 147 n. 33 identifies another possible public slave who may have been in "charge of measuring and evaluating the cargos of wheat unloaded at Piraeus" and cites Dinarchus fr. 7 in particular. That there was such a public slave is quite plausible but Dinarchus' evidence is not very strong.

27 And. fr. 5: "Hyperbolus I blush to mention. His father, a branded slave, still works at the public mint; while he himself, being a foreigner and a barbarian makes lamps for a living". See Brun 1987, 187.

218–246) may have worked both in the dockyards and in the *bouleutērion* in conjunction with the *apodektai*. He will first have assessed the damage to the ships in the dockyards; in this instance, it appears that the city advanced the funds for repair (149–50).[28] When the repairs were completed, the *dokimastēs* subtracted 90% of the funds to pass on to the navy architects who had made the repairs (224–231). Since the trierarchs in this instance were required to reimburse the funds for repairs (241–46), most likely after a *diadikasia,* the *dokimastēs* might later have tested the coins when they were deposited with *the apodektai* in the *bouleutērion*—similar to the procedure followed by the *dokimastē*s in Nikophon's law (ll. 7–8; cf. *Ath. Pol.* 48.1).[29] In Testimonies 2c and 2d, the term *dokimastēs* does not appear; instead, a slave name or the title of another magistrate appears. In Testimony 2c (*IG* II^2 1631.176–184 and 184–99 and 350–401), Opsigonos (the public slave) may have acted similarly to the *dokimastēs* in 2b in a foreseeable phase of activity, when the payments owed by the trierarchs would be deposited in the *bouleutērion.*[30] In Testimony 2d (*IG* II^2 1622.520–30), no *dokimastēs* is mentioned; Rhodes, however, commenting on *Ath. Pol.* 48.1, cites this passage in the naval records and links it with the law of 375/4 at ll. 4–8 where the *dokimastēs* tests coins everyday 'between the tables' except when there is a deposit of money 'and then in the *bouleutērion*'.[31] Rhodes was surely right to infer the presence of a *dokimastēs* for the deposit. Stroud in the 1974 *ed. pr.* of Nikophon's law remarked, upon the first appearance of the *dokimastēs* in that text, 'Our *dokimastēs* is clearly to be distinguished from his homonym who appears in the Athenian naval lists, e.g., *IG* II^2 1604 line 56' (i.e., the *dokimastēs* who rates equipment).[32] Stroud is right that that public slave is not the same as the one in Nikophon's law—and he is also right in his implication that the public slaves in the other testimonies adduced here from the naval records are not the same, either. While the *dokimastai* in these texts might at some point serve as a verifier of coinage, they work under the *boule*'s oversight of naval matters;[33] the *dokimastēs* in Nikophon's law, on the other hand, works under the

---

[28] In tracking the activity of the *dokimastēs* in *IG* II^2 1612, 149–150 and 218–232, 241–246, I am following closely the scenario sketched by Gabrielsen 2010, 143; for a trierarch's liability in the fourth century, see ibid. 136–139. The determination of liability via a *diadikasia* is mentioned on pp. 138–139.

[29] This may be the scenario envisaged in *IG* II^2 1612.224–231: the *dokimastēs*, with cash [from the *apodektai*?] pays the naval architects who repaired the hulls.

[30] The passages cited under 2c refer to two different episodes and is too detailed to present here (the second one, about Sopolis, is quite well-known among legal historians; see also Gabrielsen 2010, 163–164). Opsigonos' participation is usually ignored; but Jacob's discussion is excellent (1928, 108–109) and concludes that his continuity of service over consecutive years 'permettait d'acquérir une competence incontestable.'

[31] Rhodes 1981, 558.

[32] Stroud 1974, 165 n. 23.

[33] *Ath Pol* 46.1: Ἐπιμελεῖται δὲ καὶ τῶν πεποιημένων τριήρων καὶ τῶν σκευῶν καὶ τῶν νεωσοίκων, καὶ ποιεῖται καινὰς τριήρεις ἢ τετρήρεις, ὁποτέρας ἂν ὁ δῆμος χειροτονήσῃ,

oversight of the *syllogeis tou dēmou* who in turn work under the oversight of the *boulē*. The central 'umbrella' organization is the *boulē*—but not all its spokes are precisely the same.

Testimony 3 is adduced to demonstrate another (likely) *dokimastēs* who may have verified the gold in *IG* II^2 1492.137 before it was consecrated; if these were coins, then he may have been a *dokimastēs* like the one in Nikophon's law; but if he were measuring weights (more likely), then he may have been a public slave (or *dokimastēs*) like those in *IG* II^2 1013 (who are called οἱ δημόσιοι) and probably under the control of the *boulē*—but there are too many 'ifs' for any certainty here.

Testimony 4 is the newest piece of evidence, from the recently published law on the mint. It is difficult to plug the *syllogeis tou dēmou* into this text; nonetheless, the *dokimastēs*—the one who appears in l.13 alongside the *epistatēs* and purchaser (τοῦ ἐωνημένου), is likely to work under the supervision of the *boulē*. His assignment may be quite similar to that of the *dokimastēs* in Nikophon's law: perhaps he inspects the weight and appearance of the newly minted coins and approves them for exchange and circulation. Then is the *dokimastēs* of the Agora in Nikophon's law and the one in Epikrates' law, ca. twenty years later, the same—or is Epikrates' *dokimastēs* more closely associated with the mint? The question is difficult to answer; nonetheless, a hint might be given in the penultimate provision of Nikophon's law. There, after the lawmakers enjoin that the *apodektai* are to allocate as much salary for the new *dokimastēs* in Piraeus as the they do for the one in the city (*SEG* XXVI 17. 52–53), they add, 'and as for the future, his payment is to be from the same source as it is for the mint workers' (53–55). The two spheres had been disambiguated in 375/4: in the future, the *dokimastēs* in Piraeus will not be paid from the same cash pot as used for the *dokimastēs* in the city (i.e., the one who works in the Agora); rather, the Piraeus *dokimastēs* will draw his pay from the cash pot used for οἱ ἀργυροκόποι. In l. 18 of Epikrates' law of 354/3, the latter workers are characterized as 'the *dēmosioi*, the ones in the silver mint'. The two spheres, the Agora where the *dokimastēs* of 375/4 operates, and the mint where the *dēmosioi* of 354/3 work, are distinct, by virtue of the cash pots from which they receive their pay. Possibly, the *dokimastēs* mentioned in Epikrates' law will also have drawn his pay from the 'cash pot' of the mint; if so (and this not certain by any means), he will certainly have been different from the *dokimastēs* of Nikophon's law who sat between the tables in the Agora.

Finally, we return to the first testimony—the bouleutic lists (1a–c): the number of names varies from text to text, and no text is preserved in entirety; both 1b and 1c are significant ('the great bouleutic lists')–but a difference must be noted: in the

---

καὶ σκεύη ταύταις καὶ νεωσοίκους· χειροτονεῖ δ' ἀρχιτέκτονας ὁ δῆμος ἐπὶ τὰς ναῦς. ἂν δὲ μὴ παραδῶσιν ἐξειργασμένα ταῦτα τῇ νέᾳ βουλῇ, τὴν δωρεὰν οὐκ ἔστιν αὐτοῖς λαβεῖν· ἐπὶ γὰρ τῆς ὕστερον βουλῆς λαμβάνουσιν. ποιεῖται δὲ τὰς τριήρεις, δέκα ἄνδρας ἐξ αὑτῆς ἑλομένη τριηροποιούς. See Rhodes 1981 *Comm.* ad loc.

list of 303, the list of 8 slave names appears directly beneath a title, [ὑπηρέται τῆ]ς βουλῆς (col. 5, ll. 8–18);[34] apparently, it is a later addition, in a different hand, and does not belong to the roster of Pandionis—the slaves belong to the *boulē* and not the tribe.[35] In the list of 281/0, slave names appear appended to the tribal rosters, each time with the term ὑπηρέτης directly preceding the name; there are five names in all, and only one name belongs to a given tribe; it is likely (but not certain—the lists are not entire) that these slaves belong to the tribe rather than the *boulē*. This difference makes the list of 303 very important: the *boulē* in 303 and perhaps in many other years had a reservoir of public slaves at its disposal; from it, the *boulē* could select one or another for a specific task, as suggested in the law of Nikophon in ll. 36–41, "so that there also be in Piraeus a *dokimastēs* for the shipowners and merchants and all the others, the *boulē* is to appoint one from its public slaves (καταστησάτω ἡ βολὴ ἐκ τῶν δημοσίων) . . . or else to buy one, and the receivers are to allocate the expense".[36] The *boulē* was a center for the dispersal of public slaves; if it lacked slaves of its own, it might buy them elsewhere—perhaps from a tribe; it would know its needs. It could also, as the last quoted lines show, turn a *demosios* into a *dokimastēs*.

To conclude: Mariagrazia Rizzi has given us a timely study of the magistrates in Nikophon's law of 375/4 with a meticulous study of earlier and later attestations of these figures. I say 'timely' because, as I mentioned at the start of my reply, Epikrate's law of 354/3 on the Athenian mint has been so recently published. Whenever a new piece of evidence is added to the huge patchwork of sources that illuminate Athenian law, we must not only study that brand new shiny text, we must also go back and re-evaluate and re-interpret the entire landscape. In my first foray here in thinking about the new law on the mint (which I have kept mostly in the background while writing this reply), I have re-studied the law on silver coinage through Rizzi's superb lens with its focus on magistracies; in the end, I focused primarily on *dokimastai*; I identified supplementary texts for further exploration of *dēmosioi* who may be *dokimastai* and noted the naval records and bouleutic lists as important quarries for exploring *dēmosioi* who may be *dokimastai*, for studying the transition of one into the other, and for thinking about their dispersal by the *boulē*. The latter institution, as Rizzi has shown over and over again, is absolutely central to the dispersal of authority and control—and commercial transaction—in Athens and elsewhere.

Adele_Scafuro@brown.edu

---

34 The same format appears in the scrappy Testimony 1a: *Agora* Vol. 15, 37.

35 Traill 1969, 4 gives the description of the appearance of the letters; p. 24 gives a larger picture, "these lines are notable as giving us the longest preserved list of Athenian public slaves."

36 *SEG* XXVI 72, 36–41: ὅ]-πως δ' ἂν ἦι καὶ ἐμ Πειραιεῖ δοκιμαστὴς [τοῖς ναυκ]-λήροις καὶ τοῖς ἐμπόροις καὶ τοῖς ἄλλο[ις πᾶσιν], καταστησάτω ἡ βολὴ ἐκ τῶν δημοσίων ἐὰ̣[ν . . c.7 . . |ἢ ἐσπριάσθω, τὴν δὲ τιμὴν οἱ ἀποδέκται [μεριζόντ]ων.

WORKS CITED

Agora Vol. 15: B. D. Merritt and J. Traill, 1974, *The Athenian Agora Vol. XV, Inscriptions, The Athenian Councillors*, Princeton.

Brun 1987: P. Brun, *Hyperbolos, la création d'une «légende noire»* in *Dialogues d'histoire ancienne* 13, p. 183–198.

Feyel 2003: Chr. Feyel, *À propos de loi de Nicophon. Remarques sur le sens de δόκιμος, δοκιμάζειν, δοκιμασία*, in *Revue de philologie, de littérature et d'histoire anciennes* 77, p. 37–65.

Gabrielsen 2010: V. Gabrielsen, *Financing the Athenian Fleet, Public Taxation and Social Relations*, Baltimore, Maryland.

Gauthier 1976: Ph. Gauthier, *Un commentaire historique des 'Poroi' de Xenophon*, Génève.

Hansen 1991: M.H. Hansen, *The Athenian Democray in the Age of Demost*henes, Oxford.

Harris 2022: E.M. Harris, *Notes on the New Law of Epicrates from the Athenian Agora*, in *ZPE* 222 (2022), p. 65–81.

Ismard 2017: P. Ismard, *Democracy's Slaves: A Political History of Ancient Greece*, trans. J.M. Todd, Cambridge – London.

Jacob 1928: O. Jacob, *Les esclaves publics à Athènes*, Paris.

Köhler 1880: U. Köhler, *Attische Schatzurkunde aus dem Ende des vierten Jahrhunderts*, in *Mittheilungen des Deutschen Archäologischen Institutes in Athen*, p. 268–283.

Lambert 2018: S.D. Lambert, *357/6 BC: A Significant Year in the Development of Athenian Honorific Practice*, in *AIO* (Attic Inscriptions Online), p. 1–7.

MacDowell 1978: D.M. MacDowell, *The Law in Classical Athens*, Ithaka, New York.

Maffi 2016: A. Maffi, *Riflessioni su dikai emporikai e prestito marittimo*, in D.F. Leão – G. Thür (eds.), *Symposion 2015*, Wien, p. 199–208

Matthaiou 2017: Α.Π. Ματθαιου, *Παρατηρήσεις εἰς ἐκδεδομένα Ἀττικὰ ψηφίσματα*, in *Γραμματεῖον* 6, p. 43–54.

Matthaiou 2019: Α.Π. Ματθαιου, *Ἕξι Ἀττικὲς ἐπιγραφὲς τοῦ 4ου αἰ. π.Χ.*, Athens.

Matthaiou 2022: Α.Π. Ματθαιου, *Ὀλίγα προκαταρκτικὰ σχόλια ἐπὶ τοῦ νόμου τοῦ Ἐπικράτους*, in *Γραμματεῖον* 11, p. 57–66.

Pébarthe 2012: Chr. Pébarthe, *Droit et marché en Grèce ancienne. De la monnaie athénienne comme loi*, in B. Legras – G. Thür (eds.), *Symposion 2011*, Wien, p. 237–259.

Rhodes 1972: P.J. Rhodes, *The Athenian Boule*, Oxford.

Rhodes 1981: P.J. Rhodes, *A Commentary on the Aristotelian Athenaion Politeia*, Oxford.

Rhodes – Osborne 2003: P.J. Rhodes – R. Osborne, *Greek Historical Inscriptions 404–323 BC*, Oxford.

Richardson 2021: M.B. Richardson, *The Law of Epikrates of 354/3 B.C.*, in *Hesperia* 90, p. 685–746.

Rizzi 2017: M. Rizzi, *Marktbezogene Gesetzgebung im späthellenistischen Athen: Der Volksbeschluss über Maße und Gewichte*, München.

Rizzi 2018: M. Rizzi, *La "riscoperta" del decreto ateniese sui pesi e misure. Nuove notae*, in B. Biscotti (ed.), Kállistos Nómos. *Scritti in onore di Alberto Maffi*, Milano, p. 185–198.

Rizzi 2020: M. Rizzi, *Le funzioni dei syllogeis tou demou ad Atene nel IV secolo a.C. attraverso la testimonianza della legge di Nicofonte*, in *QLSD* 10, p. 25–40.

Schwenk 1985: C.J. Schwenk, *Athens in the Age of Alexander, The Dated Laws and Decrees of 'The Lycurgan Era' 338–322 B.C.*, Chicago.

Stroud 1974: R.S. Stroud, *An Athenian Law on Silver Coinage*, in *Hesperia* 43, p. 157–188.

Traill 1968: J. Traill, *The Bouleutic List of 303/2 B.C.*, in *Hesperia* 37, p. 1–24.

Traill 1969: J. Traill, *The Bouleutic List of 281/0 B.C.*, in *Hesperia* 38, p. 459–494.

ANNA MAGNETTO (PISA)

LE LEGGI CIVICHE E GLI AMBASCIATORI NEL MONDO GRECO DI ETÀ CLASSICA ED ELLENISTICA

Abstract: The article addresses the issue of the relationship between the civic envoy and the law. Starting from Plato's thought, it identifies the perspective with which the legislator looked at the problem of diplomatic contact with the outside world and the measures the city had to put in place to regulate it. The second part of the work analyses the rules known in the Greek world relating to the various stages of the envoy's activity, from his appointment to the final account and possible honours.

Keywords: ambassador, diplomacy, envoy, law, Plato

1. Premessa: *status quaestionis* e obiettivi del presente lavoro

"Ambassadors and the law' è il titolo di un capitolo del libro di Derek Mosley *Envoys and Diplomacy in ancient Greece*, lo studio che più di ogni altro ha influenzato e ancora influenza le moderne conoscenze sulla diplomazia greca, a dispetto di una scelta cronologica che si limita all'età classica[1]. In poche pagine Mosley pone le prime questioni fondamentali sul tema – la *dokimasia* preliminare e il rendiconto alla fine dell'incarico – disegnando allo stesso tempo quello che è diventato il perimetro all'interno del quale indagare il rapporto fra l'inviato civico e la legge.

I medesimi temi sono affrontati nello splendido articolo *Presbeia* di Dietmar Kienast, comparso nello stesso anno 1973 nei supplementi della Pauly-Wissowa[2]. Ad oggi ancora poco utilizzato, il lavoro di Kienast rappresenta lo studio più completo sugli inviati delle *poleis* nel mondo greco-romano, segnalandosi per l'ampiezza cronologica – che abbraccia anche la prima età imperiale – e il disteso impiego delle fonti epigrafiche e papirologiche. Pur nei limiti imposti dalla natura del lavoro – una voce enciclopedica – l'analisi di Kienast offre indicazioni fondamentali per lo sviluppo di uno studio organico sulla figura dell'inviato civico.

Al di là del contributo presente nei due lavori indicati, manca ad oggi un'indagine sistematica sulle leggi alle quali era sottoposto il cittadino greco nel momento in cui ricopriva l'incarico di inviato civico, in tutte le fasi dell'incarico stesso: dalla nomina al rendiconto finale e ai suoi eventuali strascichi giudiziari,

---

1 Mosley 1973, pp. 39–42, capitolo VII.

2 Kienast 1973, con un'articolazione diversa dei temi di indagine.

agli onori che gli venivano tributati. L'obiettivo di questo lavoro è di presentare alcune prime osservazioni in tal senso.

Il punto di partenza sarà quanto ancora si coglie nelle fonti a livello di riflessione teorica sulla figura dell'inviato e più in generale sul tema della diplomazia civica (Platone, Aristotele, Enea Tattico). Si passerà quindi a quanto noto dalla realtà storica, prendendo in considerazione le informazioni disponibili in relazione a tutte le possibili tipologie di inviati civici (araldi, ambasciatori con incarichi squisitamente politici, *theoroi*, giudici stranieri) e abbracciando sia l'età classica che l'ellenismo (V–I sec. a.C.)[3]. Resteranno fuori dall'indagine, almeno per il momento, gli inviati dei sovrani e la diplomazia degli stati federali, se non per qualche breve accenno.

2. Magistratura o semplice incarico?

Il dato da cui partire è la definizione istituzionale dell'inviato greco. È opinione condivisa dalla critica che quella che l'inviato ricopriva fosse non un'ἀρχή, una 'magistratura', ma una ἐπιμέλεια, un incarico. I termini sono posti da un passo della *Politica*, in cui Aristotele afferma che «Non è facile neppure definire quali debbano essere chiamate magistrature. Poiché infatti la comunità politica necessita di molti funzionari, per questa ragione non bisogna considerare magistrati tutti coloro che sono eletti o sorteggiati: per esempio in primo luogo i sacerdoti (perché questa funzione deve essere considerata qualcosa di diverso dalle cariche politiche), e anche i coreghi, gli araldi e gli ambasciatori sono eletti» (*Pol.* 1299a 14–20: ἔστι δὲ οὐδὲ τοῦτο διορίσαι ῥᾴδιον, ποίας δεῖ καλεῖν ἀρχάς· πολλῶν γὰρ ἐπιστατῶν ἡ πολιτικὴ κοινωνία δεῖται, διόπερ <οὐ> πάντας οὔτε τοὺς αἱρετοὺς οὔτε τοὺς κληρωτοὺς ἄρχοντας θετέον, οἷον τοὺς ἱερεῖς πρῶτον (τοῦτο γὰρ ἕτερόν τι παρὰ τὰς πολιτικὰς ἀρχὰς θετέον)· ἔτι δὲ καὶ χορηγοὶ καὶ κήρυκες [δ'] αἱροῦνται καὶ πρεσβευταί). Poco più avanti concluderà che «per dirla semplicemente, vanno definite magistrature quelle a cui è affidato il compito di deliberare su questioni determinate, di decidere e di dare ordini, e soprattutto quest'ultimo: infatti il dare ordini è ciò che più caratterizza la funzione del magistrato» (*Pol.* 1299a 25–28: μάλιστα δ' ὡς ἁπλῶς εἰπεῖν ἀρχὰς λεκτέον ταύτας ὅσαις ἀποδέδοται βουλεύσασθαί τε περὶ τινῶν καὶ κρῖναι καὶ ἐπιτάξαι, καὶ μάλιστα τοῦτο· τὸ γὰρ ἐπιτάττειν ἀρχικώτερόν ἐστιν)[4]. Nella visione aristotelica dunque, gli ambasciatori, pur essendo eletti come molte magistrature cittadine e pur ricoprendo un incarico

---

[3] I temi affrontati in questo lavoro si inseriscono nell'ambito di un progetto di studio complessivo della diplomazia greca di età classica ed ellenistica portato avanti presso la Scuola Normale Superiore, che prevede anche la realizzazione di una prosopografia online a libero accesso di tutti gli inviati conosciuti nel mondo greco in età ellenistica. L'approccio che si intende seguire include appunto tutte le categorie di inviati; per questo aspetto cf. anche *infra* e nota 12.

[4] Su questo passaggio di Aristotele cf. il commento di M. Canevaro in Bertelli – Moggi 2014, 320–328.

pubblico, non sono da considerarsi dei veri e propri magistrati[5]. Ciò che definisce questi ultimi non risiede propriamente né nelle modalità di nomina e neppure nel campo in cui esercitano il loro mandato, quanto nelle prerogative e nell'autorità che detengono.

Va ribadito che la riflessione aristotelica non esprime un'opinione condivisa al tempo, né riflette necessariamente la prassi. Al contrario, come sottolinea Aristotele stesso, essa prende posizione all'interno di un dibattito contemporaneo ancora aperto sulla natura e la specificità delle *archai*[6]. Di questa discussione abbiamo traccia nell'oratoria, in Eschine e Demostene, dai cui passi traspare l'interesse specifico per una questione che aveva ripercussioni concrete sulla gestione e l'esito dei processi. Eschine, nella *Contro Ctesifonte*, pone con chiarezza i termini del dibattito: «Formuleranno, o Ateniesi, un'argomentazione diversa, opposta a quella appena espressa. (Diranno) che il ruolo svolto da uno eletto in base a un decreto non costituisce una magistratura, ma una sorta di sovrintendenza e di servizio; (affermeranno) che sono invece magistrature quelle che i tesmoteti attribuiscono per sorteggio nel Teseio e quelle che il popolo vota nelle assemblee indette a questo scopo: strateghi, ipparchi e le magistrature che seguono queste, mentre tutte le altre sono uffici assegnati per decreto» (3.13: λέξουσι δέ, ὦ ἄνδρες Ἀθηναῖοι, καὶ ἕτερόν τινα λόγον ὑπεναντίον τῷ ἀρτίως εἰρημένῳ, ὡς ἄρα, ὅσα τις αἱρετὸς ὢν πράττει κατὰ ψήφισμα, οὐκ ἔστι ταῦτα ἀρχή, ἀλλ' ἐπιμέλειά τις καὶ διακονία· ἀρχὰς δὲ φήσουσιν ἐκείνας εἶναι ἃς οἱ θεσμοθέται ἀποκληροῦσιν ἐν τῷ Θησείῳ, κἀκείνας ἃς ὁ δῆμος χειροτονεῖ ἐν ἀρχαιρεσίαις, στρατηγοὺς καὶ ἱππάρχους καὶ τὰς μετὰ τούτων ἀρχάς, τὰ δ' ἄλλα πάντα πραγματείας προστεταγμένας κατὰ ψήφισμα). Per sostenere la sua posizione (opposta a quella degli avversari), Eschine ricorda l'esistenza di una legge finalizzata, a suo dire, proprio a eliminare discorsi pretestuosi su cosa fosse una magistratura e cosa no: «Io citerò contro le loro argomentazioni una vostra legge, che voi avete stabilito per eliminare tali discorsi pretestuosi, nella quale è esplicitamente scritto «le magistrature elettive», comprendendole tutte in un unico termine e dicendo che sono magistrature tutte quelle che il popolo assegna per votazione, [...]» (3.14: ἐγὼ δὲ πρὸς τοὺς λόγους τοὺς τούτων νόμον ὑμέτερον παρέξομαι, ὃν ὑμεῖς ἐνομοθετήσατε λύσειν ἡγούμενοι τὰς τοιαύτας προφάσεις, ἐν ᾧ διαρρήδην γέγραπται, «τὰς χειροτονητάς», φησίν, «ἀρχάς», ἁπάσας ἑνὶ περιλαβὼν ὀνόματι, καὶ προσειπὼν ἀρχὰς ἁπάσας εἶναι ἃς ὁ

---

5 Aristotele menziona oltre agli ambasciatori anche gli araldi (κήρυκες). È plausibile che si faccia qui riferimento a agli araldi cittadini, a coloro che in varie fasi della vita della *polis* erano incaricati degli annunci, in assemblea o altrove, convocavano e scioglievano l'assemblea, leggevano documenti e iscrizioni (cf. Aeschin. 1.48; Aristoph. *Ach.* 42 sgg.) liste di debitori, di eredità e di ereditiere, al servizio di uno specifico magistrato o del Consiglio (cf. Canevaro in Bertelli – Moggi 2014, 326–327). In realtà il termine può indicare anche una figura che opera all'estero, che porta notizie, informazioni, ordini al di fuori della propria città. Non possiamo escludere che qui il riferimento sia più generale.

6 Arist. *Pol.* 4 1299a 29–30.

δῆμος χειροτονεῖ, [...]). E nell'orazione sui *Misfatti dell'ambasceria* ricorda come gli ambasciatori fossero di norma eletti dall'assemblea su proposta della *bule* (Aesch. 2.19).

Esisteva quindi in Atene una posizione, giuridicamente valida, perché fondata su una legge civica, che considerava magistrati tutti coloro che fossero eletti dall'assemblea per ricoprire un incarico pubblico. La definizione includeva dunque anche coloro che venivano designati per una durata di tempo limitata e per svolgere compiti specifici, come accadeva per gli inviati cittadini[7]. Vedremo più avanti come vi fossero obblighi di legge che accomunavano gli inviati alle *archai* 'vere e proprie', in particolare l'obbligo di sottostare alla *dokimasia* e alle *euthynai* (§ 5).

3. La riflessione teorica sugli inviati pubblici: le *Leggi* di Platone

a) I presupposti della norma di legge

Possiamo dunque essere ragionevolmente certi che per gli inviati valesse quanto accadeva per le altre magistrature o per gli altri incarichi pubblici: ogni città disponeva di una serie di leggi che definiva in dettaglio chi poteva accedervi, con quali modalità dovesse essere selezionato e come dovesse rispondere pubblicamente del suo operato. Abbiamo già ricordato la legge relativa alle magistrature menzionata da Eschine[8], ma una conferma ben più articolata dell'interesse che la riflessione politica e filosofica riservava ai temi della diplomazia e in particolare alla figura dell'inviato pubblico viene dal XII libro delle *Leggi* di Platone, in particolare 941a–b 1 e 949e 2–953e 4. Si tratta di passi noti alla critica, che li ha utilizzati sporadicamente per ricostruire singole norme relative all'inviato e alla sua attività. È interessante compiere qui un'operazione diversa e guardare alla riflessione platonica nel suo insieme. Da essa ricaviamo un'idea più generale sulla prospettiva con la quale il legislatore antico affrontava il tema dell'azione diplomatica, sugli elementi sui quali poteva ritenere opportuno intervenire per regolamentarla e sui principi in base ai quali lo faceva.

Il primo punto che emerge dal passo platonico mette nitidamente in chiaro i presupposti, tanto ovvi quanto fondamentali, per la costruzione della norma di legge.

Il primo è che per il filosofo/legislatore la questione degli inviati e del loro operare si pone nell'ambito di un tema molto più ampio e complesso, che è quello del contatto con l'esterno e dei suoi effetti sulla *polis*. Una volta stabilito che non solo il contatto con altre comunità è inevitabile, ma che deve essere accompagnato

---

[7] Interessante rilevare che in Platone la discussione riguarda anche il giudice, che è definito οὐκ ἄρχων (6 767a 5–9), anche se poi si ammette che, nei fatti, lo diventa e, nota il filosofo, non un magistrato di second'ordine, dal momento che ha il potere di giudicare le cause (cf. 876c, con riferimento alla *dokimasia* dei giudici stessi). Aristotele (*Pol.* 5 1275a 22–34) conia per giudici e per i partecipanti all'assemblea la definizione di «cariche senza vincoli temporali» (ἀόριστος ἀρχή).

[8] Le poche iscrizioni che conservano leggi relative a specifiche magistrature sono raccolte da Canevaro in Bertelli – Moggi 2014, 320–321.

da una buona reputazione (fondata sulla virtù), diventa necessario definire e quindi governare questo processo (949e 3–950d 6).

Il secondo presupposto è la definizione dei modi in cui tale contatto avviene, che sono necessariamente due: i viaggi dei cittadini verso altre città e regioni e l'accoglienza dello straniero che giunge in città (12 949e 4–6: περὶ ἀποδημίας ἑαυτῶν ἔξω τῆς χώρας καὶ ξένων ὑποδοχῆς ἄλλοθεν ἀνάγκη βεβουλεῦσθαι τί χρὴ δρᾶν). Al legislatore spetta il compito di offrire le deliberazioni migliori per entrambe le situazioni (cf. nuovamente 12 951d 4–6: ὧδε οὖν χρὴ ποιεῖν περὶ ἀποδημίας εἰς ἄλλας χώρας καὶ τόπους καὶ περὶ ὑποδοχῆς ξένων).

Il terzo presupposto riguarda l'ottica con cui il legislatore deve osservare questo processo, dalla quale dipenderà poi il contenuto della norma. Nel caso specifico la sua attenzione deve volgersi al problema generale della «mescolanza di città con le città» che «per natura mischia costumi di ogni tipo, dal momento che gli stranieri introducono l'uno all'altro innovazioni» (949e 7–950a 1: πέφυκεν δὲ ἡ πόλεων ἐπιμειξία πόλεσιν ἤθη κεραννύναι παντοδαπά, καινοτομίας ἀλλήλοις ἐμποιούντων ξένων ξένοις). Sono precisamente questa mescolanza e questo scambio che il legislatore deve governare in maniera accurata, nella consapevolezza che i suoi effetti non sono per tutte le città gli stessi. Per le città mal governate scambi e mescolanza non rappresentano un problema perché non potranno corrompere una costituzione già di per sé non ottimale. Molto diverso è il discorso per una città ben governata, dove il contatto può produrre un deterioramento delle buone leggi. Persino in questo caso, tuttavia, tale mescolanza può trasformarsi in una preziosa opportunità. Su questo aspetto torneremo più avanti.

b) L'oggetto della norma

La riflessione di Platone si addentra quindi progressivamente nell'analisi, individuando e chiarendo quali sono gli aspetti critici che si presentano nel caso di viaggi dei propri cittadini. Riferendosi alle città mal governate fa dire all'ateniese Clinia che «non fa nessuna differenza mescolarsi accogliendo tra loro stranieri e recandosi essi stessi nelle altre città, quando uno desideri andare all'estero, non importa dove e quando, sia egli giovane o vecchio» (950a 3–7: ταῖς δὲ πλείσταις πόλεσιν, ἅτε οὐδαμῶς εὐνομουμένοις, οὐδὲν διαφέρει φύρεσθαι δεχομένους τε αὐτοῖς ξένους καὶ αὐτοὺς εἰς τὰς ἄλλας ἐπικωμάζοντας πόλεις, ὅταν ἐπιθυμήσῃ τις ἀποδημίας ὁπηοῦν καὶ ὁπότε, εἴτε νέος εἴτε καὶ πρεσβύτερος ὤν). Nella seconda parte della frase sono delineati chiaramente i tre punti sui quali il legislatore è chiamato a intervenire per proteggere la comunità. Si tratta delle destinazioni dei viaggi, delle occasioni per le quali si va all'estero e dell'età a cui sia concesso farlo. L'indicazione è programmatica perché poco dopo Platone prenderà in esame esattamente questi punti.

La norma che regolamenta i viaggi all'estero è così formulata: «Prima di tutto sarà vietato uscire dalla frontiera per un viaggio all'esterno in qualsiasi luogo e modo a chi è più giovane di quarant'anni, e inoltre a nessuno sia lecito farlo privatamente, mentre sia lecito farlo in veste pubblica per gli araldi, per le ambascerie e ad alcuni viaggiatori d'ispezione» (12 950d 6–8: πρῶτον μὲν νεωτέρῳ ἐτῶν τετταράκοντα μὴ ἐξέστω ἀποδημῆσαι μηδαμῇ μηδαμῶς, ἔτι τε ἰδίᾳ μηδενί, δημοσίᾳ δ' ἔστω κήρυξιν ἢ πρεσβείαις ἢ καί τισι θεωροῖς).

Per comprendere l'affermazione è opportuno ricordare che per il filosofo la città ideale non dovrà esercitare il commercio ma vivere solo di attività agricole (12 949e 3–5); non esiste dunque l'ipotesi che il cittadino possa muoversi per scambi e traffici di natura economica. Gli unici movimenti consentiti sono due: quelli di natura militare, che Platone menziona subito dopo, e quelli per incarico pubblico, che ha definito prima δημοσίᾳ e che poco oltre, parlandone in relazione alle missioni militari, chiamerà ἐκδημίαι πολιτικαί. Le regole stabilite in questa sezione si riferiscono dunque solamente a quest'ultima categoria di viaggi all'estero.

Al netto dell'indicazione sull'età, per molti aspetti attesa e valorizzata ampiamente dalla critica[9], è interessante soffermarsi sulle tipologie di inviati e di missioni che sono raccolti sotto l'ampia definizione di incarico pubblico o viaggio per questioni inerenti la *polis*. Le categorie sono tre.

La prima è la missione compiuta dall'araldo (κῆρυξ), la figura che riceve, nel quadro delle attività diplomatiche, l'incarico relativamente più semplice, dal momento che il suo compito si limita alla trasmissione di un messaggio (o di un annuncio) e all'attesa di una eventuale risposta.

Subito dopo, con uno scarto linguistico, troviamo menzionata non la figura diplomatica, ma la classe generica delle «ambascerie» (πρεσβεῖαι). Sotto questo termine onnicomprensivo[10] si raccolgono tutte le possibili missioni pubbliche, incluse quelle che vengono ricordate in dettaglio subito dopo e che hanno un carattere più marcatamente sacrale: l'invio di delegazioni che partecipino ai sacrifici e alle gare in occasione delle grandi celebrazioni panelleniche (pitiche, olimpiche, istmiche e nemee)[11]. Le delegazioni inviate a questo scopo dovranno essere folte e composte dagli individui migliori, in modo che arrechino buona fama alla città in occasione di tali riunioni.

La forma scelta da Platone per indicare l'attività diplomatica della *polis* è indicativa di un dato apparentemente ovvio ma spesso non adeguatamente messo a frutto negli studi sulle relazioni internazionali. La missione diplomatica compiuta per incarico pubblico può svolgersi per le ragioni più diverse e coprire, anche simultaneamente, ambiti squisitamente politici, religiosi, economici. La legge antica non fa differenza sulla base dei contenuti della missione, ma norma inclusivamente

---

[9] Per una sintesi efficace cf. Piccirilli 2002, 28–31.

[10] Si può osservare che il termine πρεσβεία è lo stesso impiegato nelle iscrizioni attiche almeno fino ai primi decenni del IV sec. per indicare le delegazioni straniere (cf. *e.g. IG* I^3 11, 40, 61, 63, 89, 101, 105, 127, etc.); solo dopo si passerà al riferimento diretto ai *presbeis*, un uso che troviamo poi comune e generalizzato.

[11] Anche queste missioni hanno necessariamente carattere pubblico nella definizione platonica.

ogni tipo di incarico. Di conseguenza, l'approccio corretto per indagare l'inviato antico in tutti i suoi aspetti è quello che tiene conto di ogni possibile incarico di missione[12].

La terza tipologia di missioni pubbliche prese in esame da Platone individua una figura nuova, non ufficialmente presente nelle consuete tipologie di inviati attestate presso le città greche[13]. Si tratta di quelli che potremmo definire «gli osservatori» (θεωροί). Platone aveva già individuato il rischio di corruzione implicito in ogni contatto con l'esterno e riferendosi alle delegazioni inviate all'estero aveva scritto: «al ritorno in patria insegneranno ai giovani che tutte le norme relative alla costituzione sono inferiori alla nostra» (12 951a 2–3: ἐλθόντες δὲ οἴκαδε διδάξουσι τοὺς νέους ὅτι δεύτερα τὰ τῶν ἄλλων ἐστὶ νόμιμα τὰ περὶ τὰς πολιτείας). Nel compiere la sua missione all'estero l'inviato viene a contatto con l'assetto istituzionale (ma anche culturale e sociale) della comunità che lo riceve ed è naturalmente portato a osservare e a fare le sue valutazioni. Ed è inevitabile che, una volta rientrato in patria, le trasmetta ai suoi concittadini. Nell'ottica del filosofo la città ideale è già dotata delle istituzioni migliori e dunque il confronto non potrà che essere a suo vantaggio, ma in questo processo potrebbero emergere elementi utili anche alla città migliore. Non si tratta dunque solo di prevenire l'infiltrazione di elementi negativi, ma di individuare, acquisire e mettere a frutto eventuali esempi positivi. L'individuazione di tali elementi non è solo passiva, in occasione di normali missioni diplomatiche, ma si configura ora come scopo di un'iniziativa apposita e mirata, perché la ricerca e la conoscenza delle leggi e dei costumi migliori è garanzia e condizione indispensabile affinché il proprio stato e le proprie leggi permangano in una condizione ottimale.

L'ideazione di un'inedita tipologia di inviato per la città di Magnesia risponde al chiaro intento di controllare e governare al meglio anche questo aspetto delle interazioni con l'esterno, tanto delicato quanto percepito come essenziale. Le caratteristiche dei *theoroi* sono disegnate con cura, perché dovrà trattarsi di persone incorruttibili e in grado di condurre bene tale ricerca. E con altrettanta cura saranno stabilite le procedure sia di scelta che di resoconto al ritorno dall'incarico. Ci torneremo più avanti (paragrafo 4).

L'intuizione platonica di creare questa inedita tipologia di inviato e tutte le considerazioni che ad essa si associano sono di uno straordinario interesse, per almeno due ragioni. Esse offrono una prima riflessione teorica sul ruolo

12 È la prospettiva adottata da Poland 1885 e Kienast 1973, che tende però a quasi a scomparire nelle pubblicazioni più recenti a partire da Mosley 1973, il cui sguardo si concentra sulle missioni dal carattere più propriamente politico.

13 Uno scoliasta a Elio Aristide 172 offre per gli ἀγαθοεργοί spartani (menzionati da Hdt. 1.67) una definizione che li accomuna ai *theoroi* platonici (ἀγαθοεργοὶ δὲ καλοῦνται παρὰ Λακεδαιμονίοις πέντε τῶν ἱππέων, οἵτινες ἐξήρχοντο τοῦ βαθμοῦ, καὶ ἐσχόλαζον ἐπὶ γνώσει τῶν παρ' ἑτέροις νομίμων ἀγαθῶν); cf. tuttavia le riserve di Russel 1999, 118 nota 41.

dell'inviato pubblico nel processo di osmosi culturale fra le diverse città greche. In secondo luogo, e più nello specifico, lo sguardo di Platone è rivolto al tema delle leggi cittadine e al loro processo di conservazione e di miglioramento e in questo contesto si delinea il ruolo specifico dell'inviato come potenziale 'proponente' di leggi, sulla base della sua esperienza di viaggiatore.

La figura del *theoros* nel progetto platonico è quella di un viaggiatore che si muove su mandato pubblico con la missione di osservare le leggi delle altre comunità e di riferire in patria. Non siamo a conoscenza di un corrispettivo storico di questa tipologia di inviato, ma nella realtà della *polis* conosciamo figure che possono avere ricoperto concretamente questo ruolo, sia pure a partire da un mandato diverso. Si tratta dei giudici stranieri, una tipologia di inviato che per lungo tempo si è ritenuto fosse nata agli albori dell'età ellenistica[14], ma che oggi sappiamo con certezza essere già impiegata in piena età classica, come testimonia un documento da Olimpia recentemente pubblicato e databile alla prima metà del V sec.[15]

La prerogativa dei giudici stranieri era quella di recarsi in una città per risolvere una situazione processuale congestionata, a cui, per le più varie ragioni, i tribunali locali non erano temporaneamente in grado di fare fronte. La celebrazione dei processi avveniva secondo il codice di legge in vigore nella città che aveva richiesto l'intervento. Fin dal suo pionieristico articolo del 1973, Louis Robert sottolineava come questa pratica fosse destinata a favorire un confronto più puntuale fra i diversi sistemi legislativi e, contestualmente, a stimolare la nascita di una classe di persone 'esperte' nel settore. Questi individui, che avevano operato all'estero disponendo di potere e responsabilità, avrebbero condiviso in patria la loro esperienza e le loro riflessioni, generando, come effetto a lungo termine, un uniformarsi del diritto[16]. Le conclusioni sono probabilmente più applicabili all'età ellenistica, quando il fenomeno, documentato quasi esclusivamente dalle iscrizioni, si intensifica. Ma non possiamo escludere che anche questa pratica avesse influito sulla riflessione di Platone, che elabora un presupposto teorico esattamente sul tema del confronto fra le norme di diritto civico e della sua utilità – potremmo dire imprescindibilità – perché un buon codice di leggi si conservi tale nel tempo[17].

---

[14] Su queste figure cf. Robert 1973; gli studi di Crowther dal 1992 al 1999, 2006a, 2006b, 2007; Gauthier 1993 e 1994; Hamon 1999 e 2012; Scafuro 2014; Magnetto 2016.

[15] Cf. Hallof 2021, Minon 2021; l'ipotesi dell'impiego di giudici stranieri già nell'ambito della seconda lega delio-attica era formulata da Dreher 1995, 259–264; il ricorso a mediatori esterni per la soluzione di tensioni interne a Mileto è documentato da Hdt. 3.28 per una data precedente la rivolta ionica.

[16] Robert 1973, 778 (= *OMS* V, 150).

[17] La conoscenza di codici di legge diversi dal proprio è concretamente documentata dalla prima lettera di Antigono a Teo sul sinecismo con Lebedo. Nel testo il re approva la decisione congiunta delle due *poleis* di utilizzare le leggi di Cos come leggi temporanee della nuova *polis* (un anno), fino a quando non fosse pronto il *corpus* appositamente elaborato dai *nomographoi* (Welles, *RC* 3 ll. 55 sgg.; cf. Bencivenni 2003, 169–201).

4. Le norme sugli inviati nelle Leggi di Platone (e in Enea Tattico)

a) Il controllo della polis sui propri inviati

Sulla base dei presupposti teorici che abbiamo osservato, Platone elabora una serie di disposizioni che regolano nel concreto lo scambio diplomatico con le comunità esterne. In questo paragrafo vedremo nel dettaglio su quali punti il legislatore si sofferma, così da poter poi attuare un confronto con le norme di cui troviamo traccia nella documentazione letteraria ed epigrafica relativa alle *poleis* greche. Li esamineremo nella consapevolezza che la riflessione platonica non ha, per sua stessa dichiarazione[18], la pretesa di essere esaustiva e che rimangono dunque delle zone di indeterminatezza.

Un primo elemento che rientra nelle disposizioni di legge sono le caratteristiche richieste a coloro che saranno scelti come inviati e che appaiono diverse per gli araldi e gli ambasciatori rispetto ai *theoroi.* Tali caratteristiche riguardano in particolare l'età minima, l'aspetto fisico e la caratura morale con l'annessa reputazione.

Il requisito dell'età appare inferiore per i primi – quarant'anni – rispetto ai secondi, a cui ne sono richiesti almeno cinquanta[19]. Inoltre per i primi non viene fissato un limite massimo di età per ricoprire l'incarico, mentre per i secondi tale limite è stabilito a sessant'anni. La decisione è evidentemente connessa alla particolare delicatezza del compito affidato ai *theoroi*, la cui missione avrebbe avuto ripercussioni dirette sul sistema di leggi della *polis*. Non a caso si tratta dello stesso requisito necessario per ricoprire la carica di *nomophylax* (6 755a). L'età minima più avanzata è funzionale a garantire che l'inviato abbia sviluppato quelle caratteristiche di maturità ed esperienza che sono richieste per l'incarico e su cui torneremo subito. Il limite superiore fissato a sessant'anni pone invece qualche interrogativo. Farebbe infatti pensare alla volontà di escludere una fase della vita considerata in generale meno adatta all'impegno politico in tutte le sue forme[20], ma si osserva poi che Platone fissa a settant'anni lo stesso limite superiore per i *nomophylakes*. È dunque possibile che vi si assommassero anche considerazioni legate alla condizione fisica necessaria per i viaggi.

Per quanto riguarda l'attenzione alle caratteristiche fisiche e morali, Platone vi si sofferma solo in relazione alle delegazioni che verranno mandate ai grandi eventi religiosi panellenici e, ancora una volta, ai *theoroi.* In entrambi i casi i requisiti sono calibrati sulla base dello scopo della missione. Per le delegazioni destinate alle feste panelleniche si specifica che «andrà inviato, per quanto possibile, un numero alto di cittadini, i più belli e i migliori perché devono essere tali da creare un'ottima reputazione alla città durante le riunioni religiose e preparino una gloria almeno pari a quella che la città guadagnerà in guerra» (12 950e 2–951a 2 Πυθώδε τῷ

[18] Cf. Plat. *Leg.* 6 768b 6–8.

[19] Il limite è lo stesso fissato per i *nomophylakes* (6 755a 5–6) e per gli *euthynoi* (12 946a 2–3).

[20] Cf. ad es. Ar. *Pol.* 3 1275a 8–19 in cui i cittadini anziani sono definiti cittadini sfioriti e ormai incompleti, un passo da leggere alla luce di *Rh.* 2.13 e delle osservazioni di Fröhlich 2016.

Ἀπόλλωνι καὶ εἰς Ὀλυμπίαν τῷ Διὶ καὶ εἰς Νεμέαν καὶ εἰς Ἰσθμὸν χρὴ πέμπειν κοινωνοῦντας θυσιῶν τε καὶ ἀγώνων τούτοις τοῖς θεοῖς, πέμπειν δὲ εἰς δύναμιν ὅτι πλείστους ἅμα καὶ καλλίστους τε καὶ ἀρίστους, οἵτινες εὐδόκιμον τὴν πόλιν ἐν ἱεραῖς τε καὶ εἰρηνικαῖς συνουσίαις ποιήσουσι δοκεῖν, τοῖς περὶ τὸν πόλεμον ἀντίστροφον ἀποδιδόντες δόξης παρασκευήν). In questa occasione lo scopo della delegazione è fornire all'esterno una precisa immagine della *polis*, il criterio di scelta sarà dunque estetico, legato alla bella presenza, ma anche morale, legato alla condotta che i delegati dovranno tenere in pubblico. E il numero degli inviati dovrà essere alto, perché dimostri che quello è lo standard dei cittadini di cui la *polis* dispone. In un passo precedente (12 947a 1–4) Platone aveva stabilito che queste delegazioni fossero guidate da cittadini scelti fra i revisori (εὔθυνοι), magistrati «straordinari per ogni tipo di virtù» (12 945e 2–3), la cui presenza e il cui ruolo indicano chiaramente la caratura di queste missioni.

Per i *theoroi* il criterio individuato riguarda invece da un lato l'incorruttibilità (12 951c ἀδιάφθαρτος), dall'altro le conoscenze e l'esperienza maturati nell'impegno pubblico, sia in tempo di pace che nelle azioni militari, che devono essersi tradotti in un alto prestigio (12 951d: ἔτι δὲ τῶν εὐδοκίμων τά τε ἄλλα καὶ εἰς τὸν πόλεμον ἔστω γεγενημένος, «si sia segnalato fra gli uomini illustri nelle altre faccende e anche in quelle di guerra»). Si tratta dei presupposti necessari perché gli inviati siano in grado di condurre bene la ricerca (12 951c), confermando, attraverso il confronto con l'esterno, le buone leggi già vigenti in patria o integrandole qualora individuassero delle carenze.

A fronte di queste indicazioni si pone il problema – molto discusso anche in relazione all'inviato civico nella sua realtà storica (cf. § 5*a*) – dell'esistenza di una forma di verifica preliminare degli ambasciatori. La questione si lega, ancora una volta, alla definizione istituzionale del ruolo dell'inviato. Sappiamo che per Platone tutte le *archai* erano sottoposte a verifica[21], ma nessuna tipologia di ambasciatori (neppure i *theoroi*) viene menzionata nella sezione delle *Leggi* in cui si descrivono le istituzioni e le magistrature di Magnesia (6 751a–768e 3)[22]. Analogamente, a differenza di quanto accade per le magistrature e per i giudici, nelle *Leggi* non si parla mai di un esame preliminare (δοκιμασία) in riferimento agli inviati. Possiamo immaginare che, nel momento in cui si stabiliscono determinati requisiti per poter ricoprire i diversi incarichi, una verifica del loro possesso da parte dei candidati alle missioni fosse prevista e data per scontata. Al controllo sull'età, si doveva

[21] Plat. *Leg.* 6 754d 1–2; più in generale sul profilo civile e morale richiesto a coloro che si avviavano a ricoprire cariche pubbliche e alla loro famiglia, dall'infanzia al momento dell'elezione, cf. Plat. *Leg.* 6 751c 5–8.

[22] Un utilissimo prospetto è offerto da Reid 2020, che esprime riserve sulla natura di *archai* dei *theoroi*, pur includendoli nel suo esame delle magistrature civiche. Da osservare, in relazione al dibattito antico e moderno cui abbiamo fatto cenno sopra, che Reid include sotto la dicitura 'ambassadors' i soli *theoroi*, mentre non vi sono accenni a *kerukes* e *presbeutai*.

aggiungere un esame più accurato per i *theoroi*, alla luce dei criteri indicati in precedenza: la fama di incorruttibilità ma anche una reputazione di eccellenza sotto il profilo pubblico, civile e militare. Per questi ultimi è possibile – ma restiamo nel campo delle pure ipotesi, e per di più nel quadro di una costruzione ideale – che il compito spettasse agli stessi *nomophylakes*, dei quali si dice che dovevano fornire l'autorizzazione per il viaggio (12 951a 4–5: θεωροὺς δὲ ἄλλους ἐκπέμπειν χρεὼν τοιούσδε τινὰς τοὺς νομοφύλακας παρεμένους).

A queste osservazioni di Platone possiamo aggiungere una nota di carattere molto pratico che troviamo nel trattato di Enea Tattico in relazione ai viaggi all'estero di cittadini e ambasciatori. Il contesto è quello della città assediata e delle precauzioni da prendere in una situazione particolarmente delicata, ma riflette certamente una preoccupazione più generale. L'autore prescrive che nessuno, né cittadino né meteco lasci la città senza un documento di riconoscimento (ἄνευ συμβόλου)[23]. Il timore è evidentemente quello di uno scambio di identità che consenta l'infiltrazione di nemici all'interno della *polis*. La precauzione che Enea Tattico suggerisce riguardava certamente anche gli inviati pubblici.

Come ben attestato per la prassi civica (cf. § 5), anche per la *polis* platonica un secondo momento di verifica (*euthynai*) per chi aveva ricoperto un incarico pubblico si presentava al compimento del medesimo (6 761e 5–6)[24]. In relazione agli inviati su mandato civico, gli unici ai quali Platone dedica attenzione sono i *theoroi* al rientro dal loro viaggio di ispezione (952b 5–d 4). Essi dovranno presentarsi immediatamente al Consiglio dei custodi delle leggi e riferire le loro impressioni; i consiglieri valuteranno l'effetto del viaggio sul *theoros* e lo compenseranno con onori – da estendere anche a dopo la morte – se è tornato migliore di quando è partito. Qualora apparisse invece corrotto, verrebbe condannato a una vita ritirata, lontano da tutti, e sarebbe passibile di pena di morte se decidesse di interferire in questioni di legge o di educazione. Si tratta di una verifica in cui prevale il controllo sulle qualità morali dell'inviato e il cui esito, se negativo, porta di fatto a un allontanamento dalla società politica e civile.

Non vi sono viceversa riferimenti ai rendiconti di araldi e ambasciatori, ma il libro XII delle *Leggi* si apre con le disposizioni che riguardano possibili reati connessi con il ruolo di inviato o di araldo. L'elenco è dettagliato e puntuale e include tre violazioni molto precise: il compiere una falsa ambasceria fingendosi ambasciatore o araldo; il non trasmettere i veri messaggi per i quali uno è stato inviato, o il non trasmettere al proprio rientro le autentiche risposte restituite da

---

23 Aen. Tact. 10.8; cf. Lefèvre 2004.

24 La procedura di nomina dei revisori (εὔθυνοι) e di attuazione del rendiconto è poi descritta in 12 945b 3–948b 2. Per l'analisi della sequenza cf. Fröhlich 2004, 26–32, che sottolinea l'ampio spazio dedicato alla legislazione relativa agli *euthynoi* e in particolare alla loro nomina, così come il carattere 'morale' più che contabile che il filosofo attribuisce a questa verifica delle magistrature (p. 30).

amici o nemici presso i quali uno è stato inviato[25]. Troviamo qui, oltre a una delle prime menzioni del verbo παραπρεσβεύω, una riflessione compiuta, che identifica gli aspetti più specifici e qualificanti del ruolo diplomatico – la legittimità della missione, la fedeltà ai termini del mandato, l'attendibilità nel riferire le risposte ottenute –, quelli in relazione ai quali può essere definita e formalizzata una precisa responsabilità in campo giuridico. Una definizione che troverà eco in quella più famosa e assai più valorizzata che Demostene formula nell'orazione *Sulla falsa ambasceria*, su cui torneremo (§ 5*b*).

Altrettanto incisiva è la riflessione che accompagna l'elenco e spiega l'origine del reato. Si tratta di violazioni che vanno contro l'essenza stessa dell'incarico. La loro radice è individuata nella trasgressione a precisi ordini divini – ricondotti alle divinità di Hermes e Zeus, tradizionalmente associate agli ambasciatori –, a quello che potremmo definire un codice deontologico, che impegna l'inviato davanti alla divinità e, di riflesso, alla comunità. Su questa base legale si intenteranno cause contro di loro e si stabiliranno le pene da infliggere qualora siano ritenuti colpevoli. L'analisi dei casi documentati, come hanno messo in evidenza gli studi di Mosley e Kienast, mostrano che vi erano altri reati di cui un inviato poteva macchiarsi durante la missione e che appaiono in generale connessi all'attività politica, come la corruzione (cf. § 5*b*). Platone offre qui un'analisi puntuale e mirata che rispecchia lo sguardo del legislatore in relazione allo specifico ambito da regolamentare.

b) Il controllo della polis sugli inviati esterni

Oltre a elaborare leggi destinate a regolare l'attività degli inviati della propria *polis*, il legislatore, come annunciato, deve occuparsi dell'accoglienza di coloro che arrivano dall'esterno (12 952d 5–953e 4). Le tipologie di inviati presi in considerazione sono due. La prima abbraccia tutti gli inviati che si presentino in città per una questione di carattere pubblico (τὸν κατά τι δημόσιον ἐξ ἄλλης χώρας ἀφιγμένον). A costoro deve essere riservata un'accoglienza a spese dello stato (12 953b 5–7: ξένον ὑποδέχεσθαι χρὴ δημοσίᾳ) e li riceverà solo un numero ristretto di persone. Strateghi, ipparchi e tassiarchi prenderanno in carico le loro richieste mentre i

[25] 12 941a–b 1: ἐὰν ὥς πρεσβευτής τις ἢ κῆρυξ καταψευδόμενος τῆς πόλεως παραπρεσβεύηται πρός τινα πόλιν, ἢ πεμπόμενος μὴ τὰς οὔσας πρεσβείας ἐφ' αἷς πέμπεται ἀπαγγέλλῃ, ἢ πάλιν αὖ παρὰ τῶν πολεμίων ἢ καὶ φίλων μὴ τὰ παρ' ἐκείνων ὀρθῶς ἀποπρεσβεύσας γένηται φανερὸς ἢ κηρυκεύσας, γραφαὶ κατὰ τούτων ἔστων ὡς Ἑρμοῦ καὶ Διὸς ἀγγελίας καὶ ἐπιτάξεις παρὰ νόμον ἀσεβησάντων, τίμημα δὲ ὅτι χρὴ [941b] πάσχειν ἢ ἀποτίνειν, ἐὰν ὄφλῃ. «Qualora uno, fingendosi ambasciatore o messo della città, compia disonesta ambasceria in un'altra città, o, essendo inviato non riferisca le reali ambasciate per le quali viene mandato, o ancora non risulti riferire da parte dei nemici o anche di amici correttamente come ambasciatore o come araldo i loro messaggi, siano intentate azioni penali contro costoro, per aver violato empiamente contro la legge le ambasciate e gli ordini di Ermes e di Zeus e si stabilisca la pena che deve subire o pagare qualora sia riconosciuto colpevole».

pritani e colui presso il quale gli stranieri abbiano preso alloggio, si occuperanno di loro e delle loro esigenze durante la permanenza in città (12 953b 7–c 2: ὃν στρατηγοῖς τε καὶ ἱππάρχοις καὶ ταξιάρχοις ὑποδεκτέον ἐστὶν μόνοις, τήν τ' ἐπιμέλειαν τῶν τοιούτων μετὰ τῶν πρυτάνεων ποιητέον ἐκείνῳ παρ' ὅτῳ τις ἂν αὐτῶν τὴν κατάλυσιν ξενωθεὶς ποιήσηται μόνῳ). Questa affermazione completa quanto già detto in precedenza in merito ai compiti dei pritani, «guardie pronte, a turno, a incontrare chi viene da qualche altro luogo o dalla città stessa, sia che voglia portare una notizia, sia che voglia sapere qualcuna delle informazioni che conviene a una città dare in risposta ad altre città, e se è la città stessa a chiedere informazioni ad altre, è necessario renderli guardie pronte a ricevere le risposte[26]».

La norma platonica si configura in questo caso come un chiaro correttivo a quanto abitualmente accadeva nella vita pubblica, dove, al contrario, gli inviati cercavano il contatto diretto con le figure di spicco della politica locale, intrattenendo con loro relazioni personali e svolgendo anche informalmente la loro azione diplomatica[27]. I rischi di questa prassi, che poteva influire in maniera determinante sull'esito delle missioni e, nei casi estremi, giungere a minare gli equilibri interni di una città, sono percepiti negli stessi anni anche da Enea Tattico, che esorta a sorvegliare strettamente le delegazioni straniere. Non arriva a vietare loro il libero movimento in città, ma esorta a porre costantemente al loro fianco gli uomini più fidati della comunità, che li sorveglino per tutta la durata del soggiorno[28].

La seconda categoria di inviati – estremamente rara per ammissione dello stesso Platone – include eventuali ispettori che siano il corrispettivo dei *theoroi* di Magnesia. Su costoro è previsto un controllo preliminare dell'età – devono avere almeno cinquant'anni –, ma poi avranno facoltà di presentarsi liberamente alle porte «dei ricchi e dei saggi» e di essere ospitati presso il funzionario che si occupa di tutta l'educazione o presso uno dei cittadini più virtuosi della città, e, una volta ultimata la loro missione, ripartiranno onorati con onori convenienti[29].

---

[26] 6 758b 7–c 5: ἓν ἐφ' ἑνὶ παρέχειν αὐτοὺς φύλακας ἰόντι τέ τινί ποθεν ἄλλοθεν εἴτε καὶ ἐξ αὐτῆς τῆς πόλεως ἑτοίμως ἐπιτυχεῖν, ἄντε ἀγγέλλειν βούληταί τις ἐάν τ' αὖ πυνθάνεσθαί τι τῶν ὧν προσήκει πόλει πρὸς πόλεις ἄλλας ἀποκρίνεσθαί τε, καὶ ἐρωτήσασαν ἑτέρας, ἀποδέξασθαι τὰς ἀποκρίσεις.

[27] Cf. Feyel 2009, 210 e note 201 e 202.

[28] Aen. Tact. 10.11: ταῖς δὲ δημοσίαις ἀφικνουμέναις πρεσβείαις ἀπὸ πόλεων ἢ τυράννων ἢ στρατοπέδων οὐ χρὴ ἐν αὐτοῖς τὸν ἐθέλοντα διαλέγεσθαι, ἀλλ ἀεὶ παρεῖναί τινας τῶν πολιτῶν τοὺς πιστοτάτους, οἳ μετ αὐτῶν συνδιατελοῦσιν μέχρις ἂν ἐνδημῶσιν οἱ πρέσβεις. Cf. Russell 1999, 70 e nota 44.

[29] 12 953c2–d7: τέταρτος δέ, ἄν ποτέ τις ἀφίκηται, σπάνιος μέν, ἂν δ' οὖν ποτέ τις ἔλθῃ τῶν παρ' ἡμῖν θεωρῶν ἀντίστροφος ἐξ ἄλλης χώρας, πρῶτον μὲν ἔλαττον ἐτῶν μηδὲν πεντήκοντα γεγονὼς ἔστω, πρὸς τούτῳ δὲ ἀξιῶν τι καλὸν ἰδεῖν τῶν ἐν ταῖς ἄλλαις πόλεσιν διαφέρον ἐν καλλοναῖς ἢ καὶ δεῖξαί τι κατὰ ταὐτὰ ἄλλῃ πόλει. ἴτω μὲν νῦν πᾶς ἀκέλευστος ὁ τοιοῦτος ἐπὶ τὰς τῶν πλουσίων καὶ σοφῶν θύρας, τοιοῦτος ἕτερος αὐτὸς ὤν: ἐπὶ γὰρ τὴν τοῦ τῆς παιδείας ἐπιμελουμένου πάσης οἴκησιν ἴτω πιστεύων ἱκανῶς

I passi che abbiamo esaminato offrono una cornice teorica unica (anche perché complessiva) e una traccia di quella che doveva essere la riflessione del tempo sul ruolo degli inviati e soprattutto sugli aspetti delle missioni diplomatiche che la città regolava con le sue leggi (e quelli che avrebbe dovuto regolare). Le proposte platoniche rispecchiano le preoccupazioni che abbiamo visto al paragrafo precedente, e di conseguenza, pur certamente influenzate dalla realtà politica del tempo – in particolare quella attica –, non la riflettono se non in parte. Questo non toglie che esse rappresentino lo sfondo necessario sulla base del quale analizzare ciò che sappiamo delle leggi in vigore presso le singole comunità fra età classica ed ellenismo e la loro evoluzione.

5. Leggi civiche sugli ambasciatori: *dokimasia*, *euthynai*, viatico e onori

a) La *dokimasia*

Uno dei problemi più discussi in relazione alla nomina degli inviati e al loro ruolo di funzionari pubblici è, come abbiamo visto sopra (§ 2), l'esistenza di un esame preliminare come per tutte le magistrature. Le basi della questione si trovano già nello studio pionieristico di Poland[30], ma nel 1968 P. Briant, riaprì il dibattito nell'ambito di uno studio più generale volto a chiarire le dinamiche secondo cui venivano eletti gli ambasciatori ad Atene e, in particolare, il ruolo del Consiglio. Secondo Briant, dopo la ratifica del decreto in assemblea, il Consiglio procedeva alla scelta dei nominativi da sottoporre al nuovo voto e il primo compito era quello di rifiutare le candidature indegne. A sostegno dell'esistenza di una *dokimasia* riportava un passo di Lisia, in cui l'oratore accosta gli inviati a strateghi e ipparchi, due magistrature certamente sottoposte a scrutinio[31]. L'ipotesi nella sua interezza era vista con favorevole prudenza da Mosley[32], secondo il quale una *dokimasia* formale avrebbe potuto causare ritardi, mentre era più logico pensare a un breve esame preliminare dei candidati da parte della *bule*. L'ipotesi e la procedura indicata non convinsero viceversa Kienast, a cui va però il merito di aver introdotto nel dibattito due passi fondamentali tratti dalle orazioni che Demostene ed Eschine pronunciarono durante il processo del 343 a.C., relativo alla missione diplomatica del 348 a.C. presso Filippo II. In entrambi si fa chiara menzione di una verifica

εἶναι ξένος τῷ τοιούτῳ ξένῳ, ἢ τὴν τῶν νικηφόρων τινὸς ἐπ' ἀρετῇ, συνὼν δὲ τούτων τισὶν τὸ μὲν διδάξας, τὸ δὲ μαθὼν ἀπαλλαττέσθω, φίλος παρὰ φίλων δώροις καὶ τιμαῖς πρεπούσαις τιμηθείς.

30 Lo studio di riferimento sulla *dokimasia* è quello di Feyel 2009, cui va aggiunto Lefèvre 2010. Sulla *dokimasia* in relazione agli inviati pubblici cf. in part. Poland 1885, 53; Briant 1968; Kienast 1973, 526 e 543; Mosley 1973, 39; Feyel 2009, 209–212.

31 Lys. 26.20: τοιγάρτοι ἀντὶ τούτων αὐτοὺς ὁ δῆμος ταῖς μεγίσταις τιμαῖς τετίμηκεν, ἱππαρχεῖν καὶ στρατηγεῖν καὶ πρεσβεύειν ὑπὲρ αὐτῶν αἱρούμενοι· καὶ οὐδέποτε αὐτοῖς μετεμέλησεν. καὶ διὰ μέν γε τοὺς πολλὰ ἐξαμαρτόντας τὰς δοκιμασίας εἶναι ἐψηφίσαντο, κτλ.

32 Cf. Mosley 1973, 38 e 543.

preliminare (δοκιμάζειν) degli inviati, che va intesa in senso proprio e non figurato e che, secondo lo studioso tedesco, doveva tenersi davanti al tribunale eliastico, come per la maggior parte dei funzionari pubblici[33]. Non abbiamo elementi per chiarire i dettagli di una procedura che doveva essere troppo familiare all'uditorio perché i due oratori sentissero l'esigenza di soffermarvisi. Possiamo osservare, che, a dispetto delle perplessità di Kienast e considerate le esigenze che accompagnavano l'invio di una missione diplomatica, l'ipotesi di un controllo rapido dei candidati da parte del Consiglio prima del voto di nomina da parte dell'assemblea potrebbe non essere del tutto errata.

Per quanto riguarda i contenuti dell'esame preliminare, Demostene (19.338) si rivolge ai giudici con queste parole: «quando fate l'esame preliminare (δοκιμάζητε) di un araldo, dovete esaminare se ha una bella voce, ma se si tratta di un ambasciatore che pretende di occuparsi di questioni di interesse pubblico, (dovete valutare) se si tratta di un uomo giusto e abbia uno spirito improntato alla 'grandezza' come vostro rappresentante, ma anche uno spirito di eguaglianza nei vostri confronti. Così come (sono stato) io, che non ho mostrato rispetto verso Filippo, me ne ho mostrato verso i prigionieri e li ho salvati senza tirarmi indietro»[34]. Eschine, difendendosi dalle accuse di Demostene dirà: «precisai che non eravamo stati inviati dagli Ateniesi come loro delegati per parlare, in Macedonia, in difesa di noi stessi: un'indagine preliminare sulla nostra vita (ἐκ τοῦ βίου δεδοκιμασμένους) aveva già accertato in patria che eravamo degni (ἄξιοι) di rappresentare la città»[35].

Nelle parole di Demostene prevalgono l'intento autocelebrativo e il biasimo per chi aveva scelto Eschine, ambasciatore inadeguato e fautore di una pace miserevole, ma si colgono comunque alcuni principi generali che, secondo l'oratore, dovrebbero orientare la scelta degli inviati: senso di giustizia, capacità di visione in relazione alla patria, spirito civico e percezione di se stessi come parte di una comunità di eguali, nessuna soggezione di fronte ai potenti. L'impressione è che Demostene stia ponendo l'accento soprattutto su ciò che una *dokimasia*

---

33 Cf. Kienast 1973, 524 e 543, la cui menzione manca nella dicussione di Feyel 2009, incentrata sui due passi in questione. In merito alla nomina degli inviati Kienast predilige una procedura più snella, secondo cui il Consiglio interveniva una sola volta, con un *probuleuma* nel quale poteva essere indicato il numero degli ambasciatori, che sarebbero stati poi scelti direttamente in assemblea.

34 Dem. 19.338: μηδὲν ὑμεῖς ἀβέλτερον πάθητε, ἀλλὰ λογίζεσθ' ὅτι δεῖ κήρυκα μὲν ἂν δοκιμάζητε, εὔφωνον σκοπεῖν, πρεσβευτὴν δὲ καὶ τῶν κοινῶν ἀξιοῦντά τι πράττειν δίκαιον καὶ φρόνημ' ἔχονθ' ὑπὲρ μὲν ὑμῶν μέγα, πρὸς δ' ὑμᾶς ἴσον, ὥσπερ ἐγὼ Φίλιππον μὲν οὐκ ἐθαύμασα, τοὺς δ' αἰχμαλώτους ἐθαύμασα, ἔσωσα, οὐδὲν ὑπεστειλάμην.

35 Aesch. 2.113: λέγων ὅτι πέμψειαν ἡμᾶς Ἀθηναῖοι πρέσβεις οὐκ ἀπολογησομένους ἐν Μακεδονίᾳ περὶ ἡμῶν αὐτῶν, ἀλλ' οἴκοθεν ἐκ τοῦ βίου δεδοκιμασμένους ἀξίους τῆς πόλεως εἶναι.

avrebbe dovuto essere: un esame (anche) delle attitudini politiche dell'inviato[36]. Più asciutto e pragmatico Eschine, che parla di un esame sulla condotta di vita, richiamando soprattutto le doti morali.

D'altra parte è ancora Eschine, questa volta nella *contro Timarco* (19–20), a ricordare un divieto esplicito previsto dalla legislazione ateniese. Qualora un cittadino fosse divenuto per denaro l'amante di qualcuno, gli sarebbe stato vietato di ricoprire qualsiasi magistratura pubblica, in patria e fuori, sia sorteggiata sia eletta e dunque anche «di essere araldo e ambasciatore e di portare in tribunale degli ambasciatori», così come di parlare in Consiglio o in Assemblea. In caso di violazione rischiava di incorrere in una causa per prostituzione e in pene severe[37]. Ancora una volta vale il principio di una condotta irreprensibile per essere degni di rappresentare la città.

Sulla stessa linea e per molti aspetti ovvio è il divieto di scegliere come ambasciatore un cittadino colpito da ἀτιμία. Narra Diodoro che nel 322 a.C., sotto la pressione militare di Antipatro, il popolo ateniese chiese ripetutamente che fosse inviato Demade a trattare la pace. La missione fu possibile solo quando l'oratore e politico, che era stato privato dei diritti civili a seguito di una triplice condanna per illegalità, fu reintegrato nel suo pieno *status* di cittadino[38].

Per molti aspetti illuminante risulta infine un ultimo passo dell'orazione *Sull'ambasceria* di Eschine, che ci restituisce una delle immagini più nitide dell'ambasciatore ateniese nella sua qualità in primo luogo di cittadino, nei legami autentici e puri con la patria e con le sue leggi, quei legami che lo rendono degno della fiducia dei suoi pari e dunque della missione. «Noi abbiamo in patria» scrive Eschine «i nostri luoghi sacri, le tombe dei padri, abbiamo con voi quelle conversazioni e quelle relazioni di amicizia che si addicono a uomini liberi, le nostre nozze, i nostri parenti e i nostri figli sono legittimi, ed eravamo degni, ad Atene, della vostra fiducia (ἄξιοι τῆς ὑμετέρας πίστεως), altrimenti non ci avreste nominati; poi giungemmo in Macedonia e improvvisamente diventammo dei traditori»[39]. Un passo che riempie di contenuti quell'ἄξιος che Eschine aveva

---

[36] Cf. Feyel 2009, 211.

[37] Aesch. 1.19–20: 19. ἄν τις Ἀθηναίων, φησίν, ἑταιρήσῃ, μὴ ἐξέστω αὐτῷ τῶν ἐννέα ἀρχόντων γενέσθαι, ὅτι οἶμαι στεφανηφόρος ἡ ἀρχή, μηδ' ἱερωσύνην ἱερώσασθαι, ὡς οὐδὲ καθαρεύοντι τῷ σώματι, μηδὲ συνδικησάτω, φησί, τῷ δημοσίῳ, μηδὲ ἀρξάτω ἀρχὴν μηδεμίαν μηδέποτε, μήτ' ἔνδημον μήτε ὑπερόριον, μήτε κληρωτὴν μήτε χειροτονητήν· 20. μηδὲ κηρυκευσάτω, μηδὲ πρεσβευσάτω, μηδὲ τοὺς πρεσβεύσαντας κρινέτω, μηδὲ συκοφαντείτω μισθωθείς, μηδὲ γνώμην εἰπάτω μηδέποτε μήτε ἐν τῇ βουλῇ μήτε ἐν τῷ δήμῳ, μηδ' ἂν δεινότατος ᾖ λέγειν Ἀθηναίων. ἐὰν δέ τις παρὰ ταῦτα πράττῃ, γραφὰς ἑταιρήσεως πεποίηκε καὶ τὰ μέγιστα ἐπιτίμια ἐπέθηκεν.

[38] Diod. 18.18.1–2. Sull'episodio e sull'*atimia* inflitta a Demade cf. ora Amendola 2022, 194–196.

[39] Aesch. 2.23: ἡμεῖς δέ, οἷς ἱερὰ καὶ τάφοι προγόνων ὑπάρχουσιν ἐν τῇ πατρίδι, καὶ διατριβαὶ καὶ συνήθειαι μεθ' ὑμῶν ἐλευθέριοι, καὶ γάμοι κατὰ τοὺς νόμους καὶ κηδεσταὶ

appena pronunciato, e che non a caso riprende: è un filo costante nell'idea che l'oratore (e il politico) ha dell'ambasciatore idoneo al ruolo, e, in ultima analisi di ciò che rivendica essere stato lui stesso.

Questi passi consentono di ricostruire, almeno a grandi linee, i punti su cui verteva l'esame preliminare degli ambasciatori nell'Atene di IV secolo, a cui si accompagnava certamente la verifica sui limiti minimi di età – che sappiamo previsti non solo ad Atene –, e sui quali, come abbiamo visto, rifletteva anche Platone[40].

Come sottolineavamo all'inizio, mancano informazioni al di fuori di Atene, ma è interessante rilevare come il concetto chiave espresso da Eschine – essere valutati degni rappresentanti (ἄξιοι) della propria comunità –, sia destinato a diventare un elemento pressoché costante nella decretazione onorifica di età ellenistica, anche in riferimento agli ambasciatori[41]. Lo si incontra nei lunghi decreti biografici con i quali una città celebra le multiple benemerenze di un suo personaggio illustre[42] e lo si osserva nei decreti onorifici delle città che avevano ricevuto inviati con funzioni diverse. Si nota inoltre come il concetto venga progressivamente a coinvolgere sia la comunità che manda gli ambasciatori sia quella che li riceve, per cui l'inviato viene lodato sempre più spesso come 'degno di entrambe'. In alcuni casi il valore del nesso è precisato da apposite indicazioni, che possono riguardare sia la cura con cui gli argomenti sono stati riferiti e trattati davanti ai collegi magistratuali e/o alle assemblee popolari in relazione al mandato e ai decreti di cui gli inviati erano latori, sia le qualità mostrate durante il soggiorno[43]. Il decreto onorifico, che gli

---

καὶ τέκνα, Ἀθήνησι μὲν ἦμεν ἄξιοι τῆς ὑμετέρας πίστεως, οὐ γὰρ ἄν ποτε ἡμᾶς εἵλεσθε, ἐλθόντες δ' εἰς Μακεδονίαν ἐξαίφνης ἐγενόμεθα προδόται.

40 Sul requisito dell'età cf. le analisi di Kienast 1973, 527–528; Mosley 1973, 43–49; Piccirilli 2002, 28–31. Per quanto plausibile, non abbiamo indicazioni univoche sull'esistenza di un limite superiore di età e vi sono casi di inviati che intrapresero la missione anche in età avanzata (Polyb. 30.21. 1–2 ricorda il caso del rodio Theaidetos, emissario a Roma a oltre 80 anni; cf. Russell 1999, 65 nota 14).

41 L'espressione ἄξιος/ἀξίως τοῦ δήμου/τῆς πατρίδος o simili, per il suo carattere generico, è impiegata ad ampio spettro in riferimento a diverse figure pubbliche, lodate dalla propria o da altre comunità. Cf. a titolo puramente indicativo *IG* II³ 884, l. 10; *IG* IX.4 752, l. 8–9 (onori di Delo per un rodio); *I.Cret.* I XXII 5, decreto di Olunte per un *theoros* rodio, etc.

42 Cf. ad es. il decreto ateniese in onore di Callia di Sfetto, lodato, fra le altre benemerenze, per aver ricoperto il ruolo di *architheoros* ai Tolemaia ἐκ τῶν ἰδίων καλῶς καὶ ἀ[ξίω]ς τοῦ δ̣ήμου (*IG* II³ 911, ll. 61–62). Su questa categoria di documenti cf. nota 80.

43 Alcuni esempi: nel decreto con il quale il demos di Mileto stipula un accordo di *isopoliteia* con Mylasa, degli ambasciatori di Mylasa si dice che hanno condotto i loro discorsi ἀξίως τῶμ πόλεων ἀμφοτέρων (*Milet* I.3 146A, l. 10); analogamente nel decreto di Hermione in risposta a un'ambasceria di Asine finalizzata a rinnovare i legami di *syngeneia* si stabilisce di lodarli ἐπί τε τᾶι ἐνδαμίαι καὶ τ<ᾶι> ἀναστροφᾶ[ι ἇι π]επόηνται ἀξίως ἑκατέ[ραν τᾶν] πολίων (*IG* IV 679, ll 18–20); cf. inoltre *I.Erythrai* 507, ll. 27–28 (ἐπὶ τῶι διαλεγῆναι περὶ ἑκάστων μετὰ πάσης προθυμίας ἀξίως τῶν

inviati riportano in patria, diventa in questo modo una sorta di attestato che, da un lato conferma la bontà della scelta fatta dalla *polis*, dall'altro elogia i comportamenti dei quali, come vedremo, l'inviato era chiamato a rispondere in occasione del rendiconto. Il linguaggio diplomatico internazionale, nel suo evolversi e arricchirsi e – non meno importante – nel suo progressivo omologarsi, esplicita temi e principi che continuavano a guidare la scelta degli inviati, rivelandone non solo la persistenza all'interno delle singole comunità ma anche il carattere condiviso all'interno del mondo greco.

b) Il rientro in patria e il rendiconto (εὔθυναι)

Quello dell'inviato era, come abbiamo visto all'inizio, un incarico a tempo e con contenuti specifici, ma era accomunato alle magistrature (ἀρχαί) dall'obbligo di sottostare a un rendiconto. La procedura di controllo dei magistrati è documentata in maniera ineguale nel mondo greco, ma generalmente riconosciuta come ampiamente diffusa, perché garanzia di equilibrio e stabilità politica all'interno della *polis*[44]. In Atene, che ancora una volta conserva l'informazione più ricca e dettagliata, l'unica che consenta una ricostruzione coerente e completa, la procedura prevedeva due fasi: un primo controllo di natura finanziaria davanti ai *logistai* e al tribunale da essi presieduto e una seconda fase affidata agli *euthynoi*, che raccoglievano eventuali accuse da parte dei cittadini in merito alla condotta tenuta dal magistrato nel periodo di carica e le smistavano ai tribunali competenti in relazione alla natura privata o pubblica della causa[45].

Per quanto riguarda gli ambasciatori, le nostre conoscenze si fondano, ancora una volta, pressoché interamente sui discorsi pronunciati da Eschine e Demostene in occasione del processo del 343 a.C.[46]. Anche nel caso degli inviati, la ragione di una rendicontazione economica si giustificava per il fatto che agli ambasciatori era

---

πόλεων ἀμφοτέρων in riferimento a *theoroi* di Magnesia); *I.Magnesia* 101, ll. 20–21 (ἀπέστειλεν ἄνδρας καλοὺς καὶ ἀγαθο[ὺς] κ̣αὶ <ἀ>ξίους ἀμφοτέρων τῶν πόλεων, decreto dei Larbenoi in onore di giudici di Magnesia). Sul soggiorno dei giudici stranieri cf. Hamon 2012, 208 e nota 53 (con altri esempi)

[44] Lo studio di riferimento rimane Fröhlich 2004; cf. ora Faraguna 2021 con la bibliografia precedente.

[45] Cf. Ar. *Ath. pol.* 54.2 e 48.4–6; Poll. 8.46.

[46] Come nota Fröhlich 2004, 361, per il periodo successivo la documentazione non permette di sapere se gli ambasciatori fossero ancora sottoposti a rendicontazione, ma, a suo giudizio, non abbiamo ragione di dubitarne. Attestazioni ulteriori di quest'obbligo sono presenti nel lessico di Harp. s.v. εὔθυνοι (Λυσίας ἐν τῷ κατὰ Νικίδου, εἰ γνήσιος. εὔθυνοι ὄνομα ἀρχῆς παρ' Ἀθηναίοις. δέκα δὲ τὸν ἀριθμὸν ἦσαν ἄνδρες, παῤ οἷς ἐδίδοσαν οἱ πρεσβεύσαντες ἢ ἄρξαντες ἢ διοικήσαντές τι τῶν δημοσίων τὰς εὐθύνας. διείλεκται περὶ αὐτῶν Ἀριστοτέλης ἐν τῇ Ἀθηναίων πολιτείᾳ; cf. Canevaro nel suo commento ad Ar. *Pol.* 4 1299a p. 327) e in Poll. 8.45–46 (εὔθυνα δὲ κατὰ τῶν ἀρξάντων ἢ πρεσβευσάντων ἣν μὲν περὶ χρημάτων πρὸς τοὺς εὐθύνους καὶ λογιστάς (οἱ δ' ἦσαν δέκα), ἣν δὲ περὶ ἀδικημάτων πρὸς τοὺς δικαστάς. ἡ δ' εὔθυνα χρόνον εἶχεν ὡρισμένον, μεθ' ὃν οὐκέτ' ἐξῆν ἐγκαλεῖν. ἰδίως δὲ ἡ κατὰ τῶν πρεσβευτῶν γραφὴ παραπρεσβείας ἐλέγετο).

sempre affidata una somma di denaro, necessaria alla copertura delle spese di viaggio[47].

Se il rendiconto è in primo luogo una questione economica, la procedura nella sua interezza investiva in realtà tutto l'operato di un magistrato in generale e di un inviato in particolare. Ciò che ci si attendeva da un ambasciatore al suo rientro era non solo un rendiconto del denaro che aveva ricevuto, ma soprattutto un'assunzione di responsabilità politica e morale delle proprie azioni nei confronti dei cittadini[48]. Non a caso il suo primo obbligo era quello di presentarsi senza indugio davanti al Consiglio e poi all'assemblea per fornire un resoconto completo[49]. Questo è anche uno dei punti che Demostene elenca fra quelli sui quali la città doveva, a suo giudizio, chiedere conto agli inviati in relazione al loro operato (19.4: εἰ σκέψαισθε παρ' ὑμῖν αὐτοῖς, ὦ ἄνδρες δικασταί, καὶ λογίσαισθε τίνων προσήκει λόγον παρὰ πρεσβευτοῦ λαβεῖν). La lista ne include in tutto cinque: «Innanzitutto delle notizie riferite, in secondo luogo delle persuasioni generate in voi, in terzo luogo delle direttive che gli avete dato, poi dei tempi e, inoltre, se la corruzione sia estranea o meno alla realizzazione di tutto ciò» (19.4: πρῶτον μὲν τοίνυν ὧν ἀπήγγειλε, δεύτερον δ' ὧν ἔπεισε, τρίτον δ' ὧν προσετάξατ'αὐτῷ, μετὰ ταῦτα τῶν χρόνων, ἐφ' ἅπασι δὲ τούτοις, εἰ ἀδωροδοκήτως ἢ μὴ πάντα ταῦτα πέπρακται).

La valutazione di queste affermazioni necessita ovviamente di cautela, in primo luogo per la sede in cui sono pronunciate e poi per i diversi piani che vediamo evocati assieme. Vi sono elementi per i quali poteva essere pronunciato un giudizio su basi oggettive e altri che attengono alla sfera ben più complessa del giudizio politico. La loro inclusione è comunque rivelatrice del modo in cui il popolo di Atene guardava all'operato dei suoi ambasciatori e degli argomenti che potevano trovare accoglienza presso l'opinione pubblica.

Fra gli elementi evocati, il primo e il terzo trovano, come abbiamo visto, un parallelo nel passo delle *Leggi* di Platone (12 941a–b 1), che li evoca in ordine inverso. Entrambi questi reati, il non trasmettere correttamente le risposte del destinatario dell'ambasceria, e il venire meno al mandato ricevuto, erano evidentemente colpe che potevano essere dimostrate ricorrendo alle testimonianze dei colleghi di missione che avevano assistito ai colloqui[50].

---

[47] Cf. ancora Fröhlich 2004, 400.

[48] Sulla severità dei rendiconti e la scarsa riconoscenza degli Ateniesi cf. Aesch. 2.80.

[49] Aesch. 2.16 ricorda che l'attore Aristodemo, reduce dalla prima ambasceria a Filippo II non si curò di presentarsi subito a causa di alcuni impegni artistici connessi al suo lavoro e per questo molti Ateniesi si irritarono, al punto che Demostene, che era allora buleuta, dovette farlo richiamare ai suoi doveri.

[50] In questo senso l'invio di una delegazione composta da più persone consentiva un migliore controllo della *polis* sugli inviati; cf. Russel 1999, 65. La testimonianza dei colleghi di missione poteva, viceversa, essere determinante per un particolare tributo di onori, cf. *IG* II^3 844.

Il primo reato, come si premura di spiegare Demostene, poteva avere effetti drammatici per la comunità, perché il popolo delibera (βουλεύομαι) sulla base del rapporto che gli viene fatto dall'inviato e quindi sarà una decisione giusta e opportuna se il rapporto è affidabile e veritiero, sarà una delibera sbagliata se il rapporto non si attiene alla verità dei fatti (19.5). A questo l'oratore aggiunge un elemento ulteriore: il popolo guarda all'inviato come a colui che è in grado di fornire i consigli più fidati (τὰς συμβουλίας πιστοτέρας) perché ha conoscenza diretta dei fatti. Una considerazione che si salda con il secondo elemento di valutazione citato dall'oratore: le persuasioni che l'inviato genera nel popolo al suo ritorno, e che attengono chiaramente alla sfera molto più sfuggente della sua personale valutazione dei fatti e dell'influenza che esercita sui concittadini. Nella figura dell'inviato si fondono così responsabilità tecniche e responsabilità politiche, come è per molti aspetti logico attendersi per un incarico di natura fisiologicamente ibrida, spesso non a caso affidato a figure attive nel campo della vita pubblica[51].

Il passo platonico e ancor più le considerazioni di Demostene portano in primo piano il vincolo di fiducia come elemento caratterizzante del rapporto che lega la città ai suoi inviati. Un vincolo che è naturalmente sotteso a qualsiasi incarico pubblico, ma che diventa particolarmente sensibile quando tale incarico viene espletato all'estero, in contesti estremamente delicati come quelli che preparavano la conclusione di un trattato e in particolare di un trattato di pace, ma non solo. Anche in questo caso osserviamo come il tema della πίστις sia destinato ad affermarsi nella decretazione pubblica, con l'evoluzione del linguaggio e il diffondersi di quelle forme più distese e descrittive che sono proprie dell'età ellenistica avanzata[52]. E anche in questo caso, ben presto l'attestazione del rapporto di fiducia riguarderà non solo la città che ha scelto l'inviato, ma anche quella che lo ha ricevuto e ospitato[53].

Il terzo punto evocato da Demostene riguarda la fedeltà al mandato ricevuto. È un aspetto ben noto e indagato della diplomazia greca il fatto che l'inviato civico si muovesse su precise indicazioni espresse dalla comunità e contenute in un apposito

---

[51] Per un'analisi di questi aspetti rimando a un articolo in corso di preparazione.

[52] Cf. ad es. il decreto per Menas di Sesto del 130–120 a.C. (*I.Sestos* 1, ll. 10–12: πολλὰς μὲν πρεσβείας ἐπιτελ̣έ̣σ̣α̣ς̣ [π]ρ̣ὸ̣ς̣ τοὺς βασιλεῖς, ἐν αἷς πάντα τὰ συνφέροντα κατηργάσατο μετὰ τῶν συμπρεσβευτῶν τῶι δήμωι, τάς τ'ἐνχειρι[σ]θείσας ἑαυτῶι πίστεις ὁσίως διεφύλαξεν). Sul concetto cf. Faraguna 2012.

[53] La documentazione più ricca e interessante si riferisce ai giudici stranieri o a coloro che sono incaricati di richiederne l'invio e di scortarli (*dikastagogoi*). Cf. ad es. il decreto di Cos per il *dikastagogos* Theugenes inviato a Smirne a chiedere dei giudici (II metà del II sec., *IG* XII.4 59). Nel testo si sottolinea sia la fiducia del popolo di Cos verso il suo inviato (l. 25), sia la richiesta di giudici che godessero della fiducia degli Smirnei (ll. 11–13). In relazione a giudici stranieri cf. ad es. il decreto di Peparethos per giudici di Larisa (II sec. a.C., *SEG* 26 677, ll. 23–25 ἄνδρας καλοὺς καὶ ἀγαθοὺς τῶν τι[μωμένων παρ' αὐτοῖς κ]αὶ πιστευομένων, ἀξίους τῆς τε [ἑ]α[υτῶ]ν πατρ[ίδος καὶ τῆ]ς ἡμετέρας πόλεως).

decreto[54]. Il venir meno ai termini del mandato costituisce il presupposto, come sottolinea anche Platone, per un processo e Demostene evoca espressamente le disposizioni e i decreti della città a cui l'inviato deve uniformare la propria condotta (καὶ μὴν περὶ ὧν γε προσετάξατ' εἰπεῖν ἢ πρᾶξαι καὶ διαρρήδην ἐψηφίσασθε ποιῆσαι, προσήκει διῳκηκέναι). Si tratta di un principio che trova, ancora una volta, un riscontro puntuale nella documentazione epigrafica. Nel corso di tutta l'età ellenistica sono moltissimi i decreti di risposta a sollecitazioni diplomatiche, emanati da città di tutte le regioni del mondo greco, che si premurano di ricordare come gli inviati, comparsi al cospetto delle assemblee popolari, avessero agito conformemente ai decreti di cui erano latori (le formule più ricorrenti sono διαλέγειν ἀκολούθως τῶι ψαφίσματι / τοῖς ἐψηφισμένοις / τοῖς ἐν τοῖς γράμμασιν κατακεχωρισμένοις). Questa formulazione essenziale è poi sempre più spesso accompagnata da aggettivi che descrivono lo zelo, la cura e anche l'eloquenza impiegate nell'illustrare le richieste presentate dalle città di origine. Tutti questi documenti sono la prova di un sentire condiviso: dimostrano che, così come sappiamo per l'età classica, anche nelle *poleis* greche di età ellenistica ci si attendeva che il buon ambasciatore agisse in piena conformità con le istruzioni ricevute. Allo stesso tempo, ci si attendeva che una dichiarazione in questo senso nella propria decretazione di risposta, sarebbe stata apprezzata dalla città che aveva inviato l'ambasceria. In assenza di testimonianze dirette nelle fonti letterarie, la documentazione epigrafica conferma la persistenza e la diffusione di determinati principi a cui la condotta dell'inviato doveva uniformarsi e sulla base dei quali sarebbe stato giudicato al suo ritorno.

Fra gli altri due punti menzionati da Demostene è certamente il secondo, la corruzione, quello meglio noto e più discusso dalla critica e non merita dunque particolare approfondimento se non per porre in evidenza come non si tratti – lo sottolineava già Mosley – di un reato strettamente ascrivibile all'incarico di ambasciatore. Qualsiasi magistratura pubblica poteva essere soggetta a corruzione[55]. Può essere qui interessante rilevare che ci sono alcuni contesti diplomatici in cui il rischio era fisiologicamente alto. Mi riferisco non solo ad accordi di pace come quello su cui si affrontarono Eschine e Demostene, ma anche ai casi di arbitrato internazionale e di ricorso ai giudici stranieri. Per i primi la documentazione epigrafica ricorda che le parti in conflitto potevano imporre appositi giuramenti in particolare ai *dikastagogoi*, cioè a coloro che erano incaricati di recarsi presso la città designata a richiedere la corte arbitrale e poi di accompagnarla durante la sua permanenza nei luoghi contesi[56]. Una figura analoga

---

54 Cf. in particolare Mosley 1973, 21–29; Kienast 1973, 559–566.

55 Cf. Cuniberti 2014.

56 Cf. in particolare il caso di Halai e Boumeliteia (*FD* III 1362 e III 4 354; cf. Ager 1996, nr. 129) che conserva l'unico giuramento di cui disponiamo previsto per i *dikastagogoi* in contesto arbitrale (ll. 26–37). Fra gli impegni presi vi è anche quello a non corrompere i giudici.

operava anche nel caso dei giudici stranieri, e tre decreti rinvenuti a Cos in onore di *dikastagogoi* gettano luce su questi personaggi, che non solo erano inviati a richiedere i giudici, ma proseguivano il loro impegno in patria, assistendo i giudici stessi durante i processi, provvedendo alle loro necessità a proprie spese, e anche prevenendo tentativi di corruzione ai loro danni[57]. In entrambi i contesti era naturalmente previsto anche il giuramento della corte (degli arbitri e dei giudici stranieri) che si impegnava ad adempiere l'incarico con correttezza e secondo giustizia.

Un ultimo aspetto su cui merita soffermarsi rapidamente riguarda il primo capo di imputazione ricordato da Platone nelle *Leggi*: l'accusa di παραπρεσβεύειν/ παραπρεσβεύεσθαι. Al termine παραπρεσβεία è attribuito comunemente un valore generico, che può indicare varie tipologie di reato: corruzione, peculato, violazione delle istruzioni ricevute, in sintesi tutte le possibili imputazioni ricavabili dal passo di Demostene[58]. L'esame della casistica presente nelle fonti, relativamente abbondante, conferma questa interpretazione[59]. Nel testo platonico tuttavia si prefigura un reato diverso, distinto da quelli elencati subito dopo, che è quello di simulazione di ambasceria: si considera cioè il caso di un cittadino che si spacci per inviato senza esserlo[60]. Mancando qualsiasi ulteriore precisazione, non è chiaro se Platone pensasse a un cittadino che compiva una missione diplomatica senza avere il mandato per farlo, o se contemplasse, ad esempio, anche il caso di uno scambio di identità – un cittadino che si presenti con l'identità di un altro effettivamente incaricato di una missione. Un esempio utile a illustrare il primo caso è offerto da Senofonte, che ricorda l'iniziativa di cittadini di Fliunte recatisi a Sparta senza un mandato della loro città (μὴ πεμπούσης τῆς πόλεως) e per questo multati[61]. Platone pone il problema dal punto di vista interno alla *polis*, che, come nel caso di Fliunte, deve intervenire per punire un membro della sua comunità. È tuttavia evidente che il problema ha una portata più ampia, che riguarda in generale il movimento degli inviati e la loro 'riconoscibilità' da parte della città ricevente, come vedremo al § 6.

c) Spese di viaggio e onori per i propri inviati

Oltre alla legislazione che regolava la condotta degli inviati, esistevano norme civiche che stabilivano come gestire altri aspetti della missione diplomatica[62]. Fra

---

[57] Cf. *IG* XII.4 57–59, gli unici decreti di questo genere al momento noti; sulla figura di Theugenes e la fiducia in lui riposta dal *demos* di Cos cf. *supra* nota 53; sul carattere di liturgia assunto da questo ruolo cf. Hamon 2012.

[58] Cf. Mosley 1973, 40–41; Kienast 1973, 577–578; Piccirilli 2002, 40; Oranges 2021, 142 e nota 120; Bartzoka 2020.

[59] Indicativo in tal senso il passo di Polluce 8.46 (cf. nota 46).

[60] Plat. *Leg.* 12 941a–b 1: ἐὰν ὥς πρεσβευτής τις ἢ κῆρυξ καταψευδόμενος τῆς πόλεως παραπρεσβεύηται πρός τινα πόλιν, ἢ πεμπόμενος κτλ.

[61] Xen. *Hell.* 5.3.11.

[62] Cf. Kienast 1973, 574–577, par. 16; Mosley 1973, 74–77.

questi la somma di denaro da consegnare all'inviato per affrontare le spese previste per il viaggio e gli onori da conferire all'inviato stesso al suo ritorno, qualora la missione avesse avuto l'esito sperato.

Per quanto riguarda il primo aspetto, già l'esaustiva trattazione di Kienast[63] presentava le modalità secondo cui la *polis*, nelle diverse aree del mondo greco, disponeva il versamento agli inviati della somma di denaro necessaria a coprire le spese della missione, in genere calibrata sulla durata del viaggio[64]. Il versamento è disposto per decreto e la decisione sull'importo può essere demandata al popolo[65] o a funzionari locali[66]. Alcuni documenti conservano tuttavia anche un esplicito riferimento alla norma che regolava questo aspetto della missione diplomatica. Nel decreto di Smirne relativo alla *sympoliteia* con Magnesia al Sipylon (ca. 245 a.C.), si stabilisce che ai tre ambasciatori che andranno a negoziare i termini del trattato il tesoriere versi il viatico (μεθόδιον) stabilito per legge (τὸ ἐκ τοῦ [νόμου]) sulla base dei giorni che il popolo riterrà congrui (che saranno poi 5)[67]. In un decreto molto mutilo rinvenuto a Cos, in cui due città che restano anonime riconoscono l'*asylia* alla *polis* e al santuario (ca 242 a.C.), si legge ancora la menzione di un ἐφ]όδιον τὸ κατὰ τὸν νόμο̣ν (*IG* XII.4 228, l. 9); in un decreto di Abdera rinvenuto a Delfi (ca metà del III sec.) si parla di un πορεῖον ἔθ[ιμον che sarà corrisposto ai *theoroi* (*I.Thrake Aeg.* 4, l. 9). Infine, in un decreto emesso da una *polis* dorica che rimane anonima per il cattivo stato di conservazione della stele, si stabilisce che oltre al viatico, l'ambasciatore incaricato di recapitare a Messene gli onori decretati per dei giudici stranieri riceva anche una scorta «di legge» (II–I sec. a.C.)[68].

---

[63] Kienast 1973, 578–581.

[64] I termini impiegati, come mostra ancora Kienast, sono diversi: il più comune e diffuso, anche nelle fonti letterarie, è ἐφόδιον, a cui si affiancano, tramandati principalmente se non esclusivamente dalla documentazione epigrafica: ὅδιον (Magnesia); μεθόδιον (Cauno, Tralles e Smirne); πορεῖον (Delfi e Cos); σιτηρέσιον (Epidauro, Arcadia, Delfi, Priene); ὀψώνιον (Macedonia, Priene); l'espressione εἰς κομιδήν. Per uno studio più dettagliato su questi termini e sul loro impiego si rinvia a un lavoro in corso di preparazione.

[65] Cf. *I.Kaunos* 17, l. 44, decreto di Smirne per giudici stranieri di Kaunos, il contributo è per l'ambasciatore che comunicherà gli onori.

[66] Cf. *I.Erythrai* 5, ll. 23–28 (ca. 200 a.C.), decreto di Antiochea al Meandro per giudici di Smirne. Il viatico (σιτηρέσιον) per l'ambasciatore sarà fissato dai proedri. In un decreto di Taso per un lampsaceno (330–20 a.C.) l'*ephodion* per 30 giorni sarà pagato dagli oἱ ἐπὶ τῆς διοικήσει (*I.Thasos* III 106, ll. 36–38).

[67] *I.Smyrna* 573 I, ll. 31–32: τοῖς δὲ ἀποδειχθε[ῖ]σιμ πρεσβευταῖς δότω μεθόδιον Καλλῖνος ὁ ταμίας τὸ ἐκ τοῦ [νόμου] ἡμερῶν ὅσων ἂν ὁ δῆμος τάξηι ἀπὸ τῶν τῆς πόλεως προσόδων· ἡμέρα[ι] ἐτάγησαμ πέντε.

[68] *IG* V.1 1428, ll. 13–15: δόν̣[τω δὲ τοὶ – τῶι πρ]εσβευτεῖ καὶ ὀψώνιον ἐπὶ λόγο[ν – καὶ πο]μποὺς τοὺς ἐν τῶι νόμωι διασ[αφουμένους. La scorta è spesso prevista per ricondurre in patria in sicurezza i giudici stranieri (cf. Crowther 1999, 271–272; Hamon 2012, 209); nel caso specifico è evidente che la disposizione si riferiva nei fatti alla delegazione nel suo complesso.

Le indicazioni specifiche non sono moltissime, e non consentono di stabilire quando queste leggi cominciarono ad essere in uso. Possiamo solo dire che le menzioni più antiche di forme di salari o di rimborsi di questo genere cominciano a fare la loro comparsa nelle iscrizioni attiche nella seconda metà del V sec[69]. È possibile/probabile che già da allora tali norme (sotto forma di leggi o di appositi decreti) regolassero sia le votazioni del popolo in merito, sia la condotta dei funzionari o dei tesorieri preposti a versare le indennità.

Per quanto riguarda il secondo aspetto, gli onori, la questione si inserisce nel discorso molto più ampio e più complesso che riguarda il modo in cui la città ricompensa sia i suoi funzionari meritevoli, sia gli stranieri che abbiano acquisito benemerenze presso di lei. Un quadro generale che terremo sullo sfondo, cercando, più nello specifico, di individuare tracce di questa legislazione in riferimento agli inviati e al loro operato.

Nella testimonianza di Demostene e di Eschine troviamo chiara indicazione del fatto che ad Atene era consuetudine tributare agli inviati cittadini di ritorno dalla missione un decreto di lode pubblica, che poteva essere accompagnata da una corona, e invitarli al pasto al pritaneo[70]. Demostene definisce questa pratica come un νόμιμον ἔθος e precisa, con un voluto effetto retorico che doveva far risaltare l'eccezione riservata all'ambasceria in Macedonia, che tale consuetudine era in vigore da quando esisteva la città[71]. I decreti attici confermano la prassi dell'invito al pritaneo – sia per gli inviati cittadini sia per gli inviati stranieri – su base regolare, almeno a partire dall'ultimo terzo del V secolo, a volte accompagnata dall'onore della corona[72]. Ma un tale onore non era ristretto a questa categoria di

---

69 Il termine ἐφόδια è plausibilmente integrato nel decreto relativo a Colofone (*IG* I^3 37, l. 25, datato verso il 447/6 a.C. secondo Rhodes 2008, 501); di πορεῖαι per gli araldi si parla nel decreto del 425/5 relativo alla *taxis phorou* (*IG* I^3 71, l. 40).

70 Per la pratica dell'invito al pritaneo cf. in part. Osborne 1981.

71 Dem. 19.31 οὔτ' ἐπῄνεσε τούτους οὔτ' εἰς τὸ πρυτανεῖον ἠξίωσεν καλέσαι. καίτοι τοῦτ', ἀφ' οὗ γέγονεν ἡ πόλις, οὐδεὶς πώποτέ φησι παθεῖν οὐδένας πρέσβεις, οὐδὲ Τιμαγόραν, οὗ θάνατον κατεχειροτόνησεν ὁ δῆμος; e soprattutto 234: ἐγὼ καὶ πάλιν ἐν τῷ δήμῳ ταῖς ἐκκλησίαις, ἐν αἷς ἐμέλλετε βουλεύεσθαι περὶ τῆς εἰρήνης, οὐδενὸς οὔτε λόγου πω παρὰ τούτων οὔτ' ἀδικήματος ὄντος φανεροῦ, τὸ νόμιμον ἔθος ποιῶν, καὶ ἐπῄνεσα τούτους καὶ εἰς πρυτανεῖον ἐκάλεσα. Cf. Aesch. 2.46; 53 e 121. I decreti in onore di ambasciatori ateniesi menzionati nelle fonti letterarie sono raccolti da Liddel 2016, 341 nota 28; quelli conservati per via epigrafica sono discussi da Lambert 2012, 3–47, 208–14, 401–6.

72 Come ha mostrato Lambert 2012, 3 sgg. Atene cominciò a iscrivere regolarmente i decreti in onore dei suoi cittadini verso il 340 ca a.C. Le testimonianze più antiche di invito al pritaneo si riferiscono infatti a inviati esterni ricevuti in Atene. In riferimento a inviati cittadini, l'esempio più antico (salvo errore) è offerto dai decreti in onore di Samo, dove si tratta tuttavia degli inviati sami, naturalizzati, invitati al *deipnon* al pritaneo (Rhodes-Osborne, *GHI*, 2); seguono quindi *IG* II^2 102, ll. 8–10 e 14–16 (alleanza con Aminta di Macedonia, 370 a.C.; si lodano sia gli inviati di Aminta sia gli Ateniesi recatisi in Macedonia e si invitano al *deipnon* al pritaneo, nessuna menzione di

onorandi. Vi erano anche, come conferma Polluce (9.40), i benefattori civici, premiati con un invito singolo come gli inviati, e coloro che ricevevano invece il privilegio permanente della *sitesis*. Queste distinzioni, che ritroviamo operative nei decreti, suggeriscono l'esistenza di una legge complessiva che regolava l'attribuzione del privilegio a determinate persone in determinati periodi[73].

Allo stesso modo siamo a conoscenza di leggi che regolavano la concessione di altri onori, che riguardano soprattutto benefattori stranieri, e la cui menzione inizia a comparire nelle iscrizioni attiche nell'ultimo terzo del IV sec.[74]. L'esistenza di leggi di questo genere è certamente precedente, doveva riguardare tanto gli stranieri quanto i cittadini e fu soggetta a modifiche nel corso del tempo. Limitandoci al caso degli onori conferiti per ambascerie, come faceva notare già Kienast[75], l'allargamento degli scenari politici e la necessità di raggiungere destinatari lontani (i sovrani ellenistici o i loro funzionari, il senato romano), rese alcune missioni diplomatiche una questione complessa, dispendiosa e pericolosa[76]. La città si adattò alla nuova situazione, garantendo onori consoni, che fossero anche un incentivo per i cittadini a ricoprire l'incarico. La corona di foglie, l'onore più comune per una missione diplomatica, fu affiancata da concessioni di maggiore sostanza. Restando ad Atene, e limitandoci a pochi casi significativi, il decreto in onore di Fedro di Sfetto (259/8 a.C.), che riepiloga le molte azioni compiute dall'onorato a favore della comunità, fra cui un'ambasceria presso Tolemeo I per l'approvvigionamento di grano, prevede la concessione di una corona d'oro κατὰ τὸν νόμον[77]. Verso la fine del secolo un altro decreto onora Demainetos f. di Hermokles, del quale si ricordano molteplici onori (inclusivi della corona d'oro) accordati in precedenza per una serie di ambascerie condotte presso gli Etoli, ai quali si aggiungono un'ulteriore corona d'oro κατὰ τὸν νόμον e una statua bronzea, per benemerenze più recenti[78]. Decreti

una corona); *IG* II^2 107, ll. 32–33 (decreti per Mitilene, 369/8 e 368/7 a.C.); *IG* II^2 124, ll. 10–12 (relazioni con Caristo, Eretria, Calcide ed Estiea; 357/6 a.C.); *IG* II^3 398, ll. 11–12 (relazioni con gli Eubei, ca 348 a.C.). In questi casi sono presenti solo la lode e l'invito al Pritaneo. In *IG* II^3 295, ll. 42–43, relativo ai contatti con il satrapo Oronte (349/8 a.C.) per quanto mutilo, si riconosce il tributo della corona di foglie. Cf. anche Lambert 2012, 5 nota 5.

[73] Cf. Osborne 1981, 156; per la *sitesis* ad Atene in V sec. cf. Rivolta 2014.

[74] Cf. fra i primi casi, *IG* II^3 475 (conferimento di *prossenia*, 329–322 a.C., secondo Lambert 2006, 133 nota 77, il caso più antico di menzione della legge in una formula di concessione dell'*enktesis*); *IG* II^3 367 (decreto in onore di Eraclide di Salamina, incoronato con una corona d'oro del valore di 500 dracme, dichiarato prosseno ed evergete e accreditato del diritto di possesso di terra e casa in attica conformemente alla legge; 325/4 a.C.); *IG* II^3 379 (decreto per Apollonide di Sidone, incoronato con una corona d'oro del valore di 100 dracme, con il titolo di prosseno e di evergete e con il diritto di possedere terra e casa conformemente alla legge; ca 323/2 a.C.).

[75] Kienast 1973, 574–575.

[76] Cf. in particolare Habicht 2001, Gazzano 2006.

[77] *IG* II^3 985, l. 73.

[78] *I.Eleusis* 211, ll. 11–14 (cf. *IG* II^2 1304).

come questi lasciano intendere la presenza di norme che regolavano e calibravano la concessione di onori e privilegi in relazione ad azioni benemerite di livello e di durata diversa, spesso compiute da un individuo nell'arco di una vita[79].

Questo tipo di documenti, votati dalla *polis* in onore di propri cittadini, fanno la loro stabile comparsa in molte aree del mondo greco – secondo alcuni proprio sul modello ateniese – a partire dalla fine del IV secolo e la loro pubblicazione dura fino al I s. a.C. con modalità e concentrazioni diverse nelle varie regioni[80]. Fra le benemerenze maturate dal cittadino figurano spesso missioni plurime a vantaggio della patria, sia verso comunità confinanti, sia, con crescente frequenza, sovrani ellenistici e poi Roma. Fra le pieghe di questi testi è possibile cogliere riferimenti normativi che riguardano sia la concessione dei diversi onori, sia anche le modalità secondo cui dovevano essere richiesti, votati e pubblicati su pietra decreti di questo genere[81].

6. Ricevere e onorare gli inviati stranieri

Come abbiamo osservato analizzando la riflessione di Platone, la ricezione dello straniero entro le mura cittadine rappresentava sempre un rischio, almeno potenziale. Enea Tattico lo evidenzia molto chiaramente, sia pure partendo dalla delicata situazione di una *polis* sotto assedio, per la quale raccomanda un rigido controllo su chi entra e per tutto il tempo della permanenza (10.11).

Nella prassi quotidiana le delegazioni straniere trovavano all'estero l'accoglienza e il supporto dei prosseni della loro comunità[82] nell'attesa di venire ammesse al cospetto dei magistrati preposti a riceverle e poi delle assemblee cittadine. Il funzionamento generale di queste procedure è già stato ben analizzato[83], così come le modalità di controllo che potevano essere messe in atto dalle comunità[84]. In questa sede ci limiteremo dunque a mettere in luce gli aspetti normativi di questo processo.

---

79 Per una discussione recente sull'esistenza di una legge che regolasse la concessione delle cosiddette *megistai timai* nell'Atene ellenistica cf. Forster 2018, 91–95, che propende per una risposta negativa.

80 Lo studio di questi documenti è stato negli ultimi cinquant'anni oggetto di importanti lavori che ne hanno indagato i contenuti e la forma, esplorandone le implicazioni anche dal punto di vista dell'evoluzione sociale e politica delle comunità, del ruolo delle élite in età ellenistica e anche delle indicazioni che si possono trarre su possibili cesure nell'evoluzione stessa della *polis*. Cf. in particolare Gauthier 1985; Quass 1993 (con elenchi dettagliati delle fonti pp. 26–30); Forster 2018 che offre il primo studio onnicomprensivo interamente dedicato ai decreti onorari per propri cittadini. Per una raccolta completa cf. Forster 2018, 485–531.

81 Per questo aspetto cf. Quass 1999, 27 e nota 55.

82 Per queste figure cf. Mack 2015; cf. in generale Hennig 1997.

83 Cf. Mosley 1973, 78–80 e soprattutto Kienast 1973, 552–559; in relazione ai giudici stranieri cf. Hamon 2012.

84 Su questi aspetti cf. Russell 1999; Lefèvre 2004, che sottolinea i limiti dell'informazione disponibile.

La documentazione ateniese consente ad esempio di confermare che la ricezione degli inviati da parte del Consiglio era regolata da apposite leggi. Nel passo famoso della *Costituzione degli Ateniesi* in cui descrive il funzionamento dell'assemblea, Aristotele precisa che «le altre due assemblee [delle quattro previste per ogni pritania] sono dedicate agli affari restanti: durante queste assemblee le leggi prescrivono di occuparsi di tre questioni relative alle cose sacre, di tre questioni relative agli araldi e alle ambascerie e di tre questioni di rettitudine; talvolta se ne occupano anche senza voto preliminare. Gli araldi e gli ambasciatori si presentano dapprima ai pritani e chi porta epistole le consegna loro»[85]. Questo tipo di attenzione del legislatore per la gestione degli affari diplomatici è ricordato anche poco prima, quando si parla del colpo di stato oligarchico del 411 a.C. e si descrivono le proposte di riforma costituzionale. In quel caso si parla del Consiglio e la proposta prevedeva che araldi e ambasciatori fossero ricevuti dopo le questioni religiose, rispettivamente come secondi e come terzi, secondo un ordine stabilito dal sorteggio. Erano escluse le questioni relative alla guerra, che avrebbero invece avuto priorità[86].

La norma tuttavia non doveva essere rigidamente applicata: come faceva rilevare già Kienast[87], le iscrizioni mostrano che questioni diplomatiche potevano essere trattate anche nel corso delle altre sedute assembleari. È comunque evidente che la gestione degli affari diplomatici rivestiva grande importanza per le *poleis*, che integravano la legislazione con le disposizioni contenute negli accordi internazionali (cf. § 7) e in appositi decreti. Ancora a Kienast va il merito di avere introdotto quest'ultimo aspetto nella trattazione sugli inviati e di averne colto finalità e implicazioni. Il tema centrale era sicuramente quello dell'attesa a cui poteva essere sottoposta una delegazione giunta in città[88]. In questi casi si profilava non solo il rischio prodotto dalla prolungata presenza di stranieri, ma anche tensioni con la comunità d'origine, che poteva interpretare il protrarsi dei tempi come una manifestazione di disinteresse e dunque come uno sgarbo. È da leggersi in questa chiave l'inclusione della priorità di accesso al Consiglio e al popolo fra i privilegi e gli onori che potevano essere concessi a un singolo straniero o a una comunità. Questo privilegio compare per la prima volta nelle iscrizioni attiche poco dopo la

---

[85] Ar. *Ath. pol.* 43.6: αἱ δὲ δύο περὶ τῶν ἄλλων εἰσίν, ἐν αἷς κελεύουσιν οἱ νόμοι τρία μὲν ἱερῶν χρηματίζειν, τρία δὲ κήρυξιν καὶ πρεσβείαις, τρία δὲ ὁσίων. χρηματίζουσιν δ' ἐνίοτε καὶ ἄνευ προχειροτονίας. προσέρχονται δὲ καὶ οἱ κήρυκες καὶ οἱ πρέσβεις τοῖς πρυτάνεσιν πρῶτον, καὶ οἱ τὰς ἐπιστολὰς φέροντες τούτοις ἀποδιδόασι. Cf. Poll. 8.96 secondo cui araldi e ambasciatori erano ricevuti nel corso della quarta riunione.

[86] Cf. *Ath. pol.* 30.5.

[87] Kienast 1973, 554–555.

[88] La *Costituzione degli Ateniesi* dello Ps. Senofonte, forse esagerando, lamenta la lentezza generale nel disbrigo delle questioni da parte del Consiglio e dell'assemblea, per cui si potevano produrre attese perfino di un anno. Nel suo commento (p. 158) D. Lenfant ritiene, molto verisimilmente, che l''uomo che attende' di cui si parla sia uno straniero («ambassadeur ou autre»).

metà del V sec. in riferimento a privati[89], ma si trova poi, sia pure più raramente, anche in relazione a intere comunità[90].

Una volta sbrigato l'incarico per cui era stata inviata, qualunque esso fosse, la delegazione straniera riceveva abitualmente un tributo d'onore da parte della città ospite. Il decreto stabiliva almeno la lode e l'invito al pritaneo[91], ma poteva allargarsi alla concessione di onorificenze maggiori (corona) e di privilegi più significativi (titolo di prosseno e di evergete, diritto al possesso di terra e casa, esenzioni economiche, cittadinanza). Si tratta di onori che non riguardano solo gli inviati, ma che venivano concessi in generale a stranieri che si erano resi variamente benemeriti nei confronti della città[92]. L'aspetto per noi interessante è che, come abbiamo già rilevato nel caso di onori concessi dalla *polis* a suoi cittadini, anche nei decreti relativi agli stranieri compare, a partire dalla metà del IV sec., la menzione di leggi civiche che regolano tali concessioni. In Atene, come abbiamo visto, una legge regolava certamente l'attribuzione della corona aurea ed è più che probabile che la stessa norma fissasse le condizioni sia per i cittadini che per gli stranieri[93]. Sempre in Atene è nota anche una norma che regolava l'attribuzione del diritto al possesso di terra e casa[94]. Altre località del mondo greco confermano l'esistenza di norme analoghe[95] e nel caso di un decreto di Astipalea si

---

89 Il documento più antico a conservare una formulazione chiara è *IG* I^3 65 per un colofonio; cf. Henry 1983, 191–203 con analisi delle diverse formulazioni ed esempi; Lambert 2012, 93–183 per decreti compresi fra il 352/1 e il 322/1.

90 Fra i primi esempi: *IG* I^3 101, ll. 37–39 per Neapolis di Tracia (410/9 a.C.); II^2 1, ll. 72–73 per i Sami (403/2 a.C.; cf. Rhodes-Osborne, *GHI*, 2); II^2 107, ll. 15–16 per i Mitilenei (368/7 a.C.; cf. Rhodes-Osborne, *GHI*, 31)

91 La testimonianza più antica sembra essere offerta da un decreto ateniese per Colofone, molto frammentario in cui si riconosce l'invito al pritaneo per dei *theoroi* colofonî (*IG* I^3 43, ll. 21–22, ca 435–427; seguito dal trattato fra Atene e Segesta, con riferimento agli ambasciatori segestani (418/7 a.C.; *IG* I^3 11, ll. 14–15; cf. Rhodes-Osborne, *GHI*, 166; Erdas, in Ampolo-Erdas, *I.Segesta*, App. 2); *IG* I^3 63, ll. 7–9 in riferimento agli inviati di Aphyta.

92 Alla bibliografia citata sopra, nota 80, possiamo aggiungere Rubinstein 2009 sull'*ateleia*, Lenfant 2017 sui doni dei sovrani persiani agli ambasciatori greci, Cinalli 2015 sull'ospitalità; Marek 1984, 142–144 e Mack 2015 122–130 sul rapporto fra la *prossenia* e la legislazione locale.

93 Alcuni esempi senza pretesa di esaustività: *IG* II^3 912, ll. 54–61, decreto di Cremonide sull'alleanza con Sparta, 369/8 a.C.; *IG* II^2 495, ll. 20–21 del 303/2, decreto per Alkaios di Eno, funzionario di Demetrio; *IG* II^2 496, ll. 21–22 del 303/2 a.C., decreto per Solon di Bargylia, funzionario di Demetrio; *IG* II^3 1323, ll. 30 sgg., di poco posteriore al 175 a.C. (si decreta di incoronare Eumene II e la moglie χρυσ[ῶι] στεφάνωι ἀριστε<ί>ωι κατὰ τὸν νόμον, ll. 32–33).

94 Cf. *IG* II^3 475 del 329–22 a.C. (cf. *supra* nota 74); *IG* II^2 466, ll. 35 sgg. del 307/6 a.C. (gli inviati di Tenos, sono accreditati della corona di foglie, del titolo di prosseni ed evergeti e del diritto al possesso di terra e casa κατὰ τὸν νόμον, ll. 42–44).

95 Leggi che regolavano la concessione della corona sono note ad es. a Delo: *ID* 1497bis, ll. 10 11 (στεφανῶσαι χρυσῶι στεφάνωι ἀρισ[τε]ίωι κατὰ τὸν νόμον); a Tenos: *IG* XII.5

conserva anche una nota di procedura: la *bule* e il popolo decideranno con il loro voto, secondo la legge[96].

7. Una legge internazionale sugli inviati?

Abbiamo visto al paragrafo precedente come una città potesse concedere, spontaneamente e con propria autonoma decisione, ad un'altra il diritto di essere ricevuta per prima dal Consiglio e dall'assemblea, dopo il disbrigo delle questioni sacre. Questo privilegio rappresentava di fatto una norma che regolava l'attività degli inviati cittadini. Ad essa se ne poteva affiancare un'altra che troviamo invece nelle clausole dei trattati internazionali e che è dunque frutto di una decisione negoziata e congiunta. Anche in questo caso lo spunto viene dal lavoro di Kienast, che poneva in evidenza come due città potessero accordarsi anche sulle modalità da seguire per l'invio reciproco di delegazioni e sulle condizioni in cui queste ultime avrebbero operato. Tali disposizioni sarebbero rimaste in vigore per tutta la durata dell'accordo e avrebbero regolato le comunicazioni diplomatiche fra di loro, offrendo dunque un tessuto normativo.

Tucidide, illustrando i termini della tregua di un anno stipulata nel 423 a.C. fra Atene e Sparta, ricordava una clausola secondo cui araldi e ambasciatori inviati a discutere i termini della pace sarebbero stati protetti da un salvacondotto per tutta la durata della tregua[97]. Ma già nel decreto per Calcide (446/5 a.C.) Atene si impegnava a introdurre davanti al Consiglio e al popolo le delegazioni Calcidesi entro 10 giorni dal loro arrivo, almeno fino a quando Calcide fosse rimasta fedele e obbediente nei suoi confronti[98]. Nel trattato che sancisce il rinnovo della lega di Corinto sotto l'egida di Antigono Monoftalmo e Demetrio Poliorcete (302 a.C.), una clausola ancora ben conservata stabilisce il divieto di esercitare una rappresaglia sugli inviati che le *poleis* greche mandino presso il sinedrio della lega né su quelli che il sinedrio invii presso le singole *poleis*, così come di catturarli e

---

819 e 826; a Gortina: *IC* IV 222); a Cos *IG* XII.4 110 e 129 e un decreto di Taso per giudici di Cos stabilisce che l'inviato di Taso richieda che l'onore della corona concesso dalla sua patria sia proclamato in occasione delle celebrazioni stabilite dalla legge: *I. Thasos* III 18, ll. 9–12. Leggi sull'*ateleia* sono menzionate a Tenos (*IG* XII.7 229, l. 8); sui doni ospitali (*xenia*) a Taso 122 e a Priene (*I.Priene B–M* 118 e 119). Per una discussione sulle leggi relative alla *prossenia* cf. Marek 1984, 142–144 e Mack 2015, 122–130. Leggi analoghe erano presenti anche fra le norme comuni del *koinon* etolico che regolavano la concessione della *prossenia* e della politeia: *IG* IX.1² 4, 25 e 31 (*prossenia*); *IG* IX.1² 17 e 30 (*politeia*) e del *koinon* acarnano *IG* IX,1² 2:208 (*prossenia*).

96 *IG* XII.3 169, ll. 10–13: ἐπαινέσαι τε αὐτὸν καὶ διαψαφι[ξ]ασθαι τὰν βουλὰν καὶ τὰν ἐκλησίαν κατὰ τὸν νόμον, ἡ δοκεῖ αὐτὸν στεφανῶσαι θαλλοῦ στεφάνωι.

97 Thuc. 4.118.6: κήρυκι δὲ καὶ πρεσβείᾳ καὶ ἀκολούθοις, ὁπόσοις ἂν δοκῇ, περὶ καταλύσεως τοῦ πολέμου καὶ δικῶν ἐς Πελοπόννησον καὶ Ἀθήναζε σπονδὰς εἶναι ἰοῦσι καὶ ἀπιοῦσι καὶ κατὰ γῆν καὶ κατὰ θάλασσαν.

98 *IG* I³ 40, ll. 10–12; Osborne-Rhodes, *GHI*, 131, che mantiene la doppia possibilità di datazione, 446/4 o 424/3 a.C.; a favore della data più antica si pronuncia Rhodes 2008, 502.

tenerli in ostaggio. I magistrati cittadini dovranno impedire tali azioni in patria e i membri del sinedrio perseguiranno le violazioni[99]. Nel trattato concluso fra la città cretese di Eleutherna e Antigono Dosone (ca. 227–224 a.C.) si stabilisce che le delegazioni del re dovranno essere introdotte davanti all'assemblea entro dieci giorni, o comunque, in caso di impedimento, il prima possibile. Le questioni sollevate dal sovrano costituiranno il primo punto all'ordine del giorno e non sarà possibile passare oltre fino a quando gli inviati regi non avranno ricevuto risposta[100]. Nel trattato di *isopoliteia* fra Mileto e Milasa (215/4 a.C.), il decreto dei Milasei stabilisce l'accesso prioritario alla *bule* e all'assemblea per tutti i Milesî[101] e la stessa indicazione si trova in un decreto che rinnova uno scambio di privilegi fra Istiea e Sinope, in favore dei Sinopei (ca 232–220 a.C.)[102]. Una clausola del trattato di *isopoliteia* concluso fra Hierapytna e Priansos (ca. 205 a.C.) dispone che nel caso in cui una delegazione di ambasciatori abbia bisogno di un mezzo di trasporto, saranno i cosmi di Hierapytna a fornirlo ai Priansi e viceversa, in caso contrario pagheranno 10 stateri alla delegazione[103]. Un caso ancora differente è offerto dal trattato di *sympoliteia* fra le due *poleis* locresi di Hypnia e Myania (dopo il 189 a.C.), in cui si stabilisce che le ambascerie della nuova comunità saranno composte in proporzione da cittadini delle due *poleis* originarie[104].

Gli esempi mostrano il tipo di esigenze che potevano sollecitare l'inserimento di clausole di questo genere nei trattati. Fra tutte, una delle più interessanti è certamente quella presente nell'accordo multilaterale che sancisce il rinnovo – o la nuova nascita – della lega di Corinto sotto l'egida di Antigono Monoftalmo e del figlio Demetrio. Essa non solo pone una norma che riguarda una pluralità di soggetti politici, ma stabilisce anche il meccanismo di controllo e sanzione, affidato a un collegio di magistrati internazionali. Possiamo immaginare che situazioni e necessità analoghe fossero comuni in organismi come ad esempio le leghe e gli stati federali. Un tema che esula dal perimetro del presente lavoro e che potrà essere affrontato in altra sede.

8. Conclusioni

Queste prime considerazioni consentono di porre le basi per un quadro più sistematico del rapporto tra la funzione di inviato civico e le norme che ne regolavano lo svolgimento. Si possono individuare chiari elementi di una riflessione filosofica e politica sul ruolo dell'inviato e sul controllo che doveva accompagnarsi a questo incarico per la sicurezza e il benessere della città. L'indagine sulle fonti letterarie e soprattutto epigrafiche mette in luce l'esistenza di

[99] *Staatsverträge* III, 446, ll. 61–66; cf. Paganoni 2018.
[100] *Staatsverträge* III, 501, ll. 10–17.
[101] *Staatsverträge* III, 539, ll. 69–70; Saba 2020, nr. 6.
[102] *Staatsverträge* III, 563; il testo completo (molto lacunoso è in *IG* XII.9 1186).
[103] *Staatsverträge* IV, 605, ll. 30.33.
[104] *Staatsverträge* IV, 627, col II ll. 9–10.

tutta una serie di norme in molti casi non specificamente dedicate agli ambasciatori civici ma che comunque intervenivano nei vari momenti in cui un incarico diplomatico veniva deciso, espletato e quindi valutato nel suo svolgimento e nei suoi esiti per la comunità.

Si tratta di leggi che possono modificarsi nel tempo e che cogliamo grazie a importanti cambiamenti nelle modalità di comunicazione che la *polis* adotta, in particolare in età ellenistica, scegliendo forme di decretazione più ampie, che lasciano maggiore spazio a dettagli narrativi e procedurali. Si tratta di leggi civiche alle quali si affiancano (e si sovrappongono) nel tempo, almeno in diverse aree del mondo greco, leggi federali, che meritano un'analisi specifica. Così come sarebbe opportuno indagare, per quanto possibile, cosa cambia – o cosa permane – a livello normativo, nella comunicazione diplomatica con i sovrani ellenistici e con Roma.

anna.magnetto@sns.it

BIBLIOGRAFIA

Adcock – Mosley 1975: F. Adcock and D.J. Mosley, *Diplomacy in Ancient Greece*, London 1975.

Ager 1996: L. Ager, *Interstate Arbitrations in the Greek World 337–90 B.C.*, Berkeley – Los Angeles – London 1996.

Amendola 2022: *The Demades Papyrus (P.Berol. inv. 13045 = BKT VII 13–31). Introduction, Edition, Translation and Commentary*, Berlin 2022.

Bartzoka 2020: A. Bartzoka, *Désigner chez les orateurs attiques les discours des ambassadeurs «ratés»: vocabulaire et figures*, «Historika», 10 (2020), 57–84.

Bederman 2001: D.J. Bedermann, *International Law in Antiquity*, Cambridge 2001.

Bencivenni 2003, *Progetti di riforme costituzionali nelle epigrafi greche dei secoli IV–II a.C.*, Bologna 2003.

Bertelli – Moggi 2014: Aristotele, *La politica*, libro IV, a cura di L. Bertelli e M. Moggi, Roma 2014.

Briant 1968: P. Briant, *La Boulé et l'élection des ambassadeurs à Athènes au IVe siècle*, «REA» 70 (1968), 7–31.

Cinalli 2015: A. Cinalli, Τὰ ξένια. *La cerimonia di ospitalità cittadina*, Roma 2015.

Crowther 1992: Ch. Crowther, *The decline of Greek democracy*, «Journal of Ancient Civilizations» 7 (1992), 13–48.

Crowther 1993: Ch. Crowther, *Foreign Judges in Seleucid Cities*, «Journal of Ancient Civilizations» 8 (1993), 40–77.

Crowther 1994: Ch. Crowther, *Foreign Courts on Kalymna in the Third Century B.C.*, «Journal of Ancient Civilizations» 9 (1994), 33–55.

Crowther 1995: Ch. Crowther, *Iasos in the Second Century BC, III. Foreign Judges from Priene*, «BICS» 40 (1995), 91–136.

Crowther 1996: Ch. Crowther, *I. Priene 8 and the history of Priene in the Early Hellenistic Period*, «Chiron» 26 (1996), 195–250.

Crowther 1997: Ch. Crowther, *Inscriptions from the Sparta and Larissa Museums*, «ABSA» 92 (1997), 345–358.

Crowther 1999: Ch. Crowther, *Aus der Arbeit der ‚Inscriptiones Graecae' IV. Koan Decrees for Foreign Judges*, «Chiron» 29 (1999), 251–319.

Crowther 2006a: Ch. Crowther, *Foreign judges in Thessaly in the Hellenistic Period: A second century phenomenon?*, in *Inscriptions and History of Thessaly. New Evidence. Proceedings of the International Symposium in honor of the Professor Christian Habicht*, Volos 2006, 31–48.

Crowther 2006b: Ch. Crowther, *A Judicial Fragment from Chios*, in Χιακὸν Συμπόσιον εἰς μνήμην W. G. Forrest, Athènes 2006, 57–65.

Crowther 2007: Ch. Crowther, *Foreign Judges and Regional Variations in Hellenistic Asia Minor*, in H. Elton, G. Reger (ed.), *Regionalism in Hellenistic and Roman Asia Minor*, Bordeaux 2007, 53–60.

Crowther – Habicht – Hallof – Hallof 1998: Ch. Crowther, Chr. Habicht, L. et Kl. Hallof, *Aus der Arbeit der ‚Inscriptiones Graecae' I. Drei Dekrete aus Kos für dikastagogoi*, «Chiron» 28 (1998), 87–100.

Cuniberti 2014: G. Cuniberti, *Doni e favori illeciti: percezione e codificazione del reato di corruzione in Atene antica*, «Hormos» 6 (2014), 21–34.

Dreher 1995: M. Dreher, *Hegemon Und Symmachoi: Untersuchungen Zum Zweiten Athenischen Seebund*, Berlin 1995.

Faraguna 2012: M. Faraguna, Pistis *and* apistia: *Apsects of the Developments of Social and Economic Relations in Classical Greece,* «MedAnt» 15 (2012), 355–374.

Faraguna 2021: M. Faraguna, *Magistrates' Accountability and Epigraphic Documents: the Case of Accounts and Inventories*, K. Harter-Uibopuu – W. Riess (eds), *Symposion 2019*, Wien 2021, 229–253.

Feyel 2009: Ch. Feyel, Δοκιμασία. *La place et le rôle de l'examen préliminaire das les institutions des cités grecques*, Nancy 2009.

Forster 2018: F.R. Forster, *Die Polis im Wandel. Ehrendekrete für eigene Bürger im Kontext der hellenistischen Polisgesellschaft*, Göttingen 2018.

Fröhlich 2004: P. Fröhlich, *Les cités grecques et le contrôle des magistrats (IVe–Ier s. av. J.-C.)*, Genève – Paris, 2004.

Fröhlich 2016: P. Fröhlich, *La citoyenneté grecque entre Aristote et les modernes*, «CCGG» 27 (2016), 91–136.

Gauthier 1985: Ph. Gauthier, *Les cités grecques et leurs bienfaiteurs (IVe–Ier siècle avant J.–C): contribution à l'histoire des institutions*, Paris 1985.

Gauthier 1993: Ph. Gauthier, *Décrets d'Érétrie en l'honneur de juges étrangers*, «REG» 106 (1993), 589–598.

Gauthier 1994: Ph. Gauthier, *Les rois hellénistiques et les juges étrangers: à propos de décrets de Kimôlos et de Laodicée du Lykos*, «JS» 1994, 165–195 (=

Études d'histoire et d'institutions grecques. Choix d'écrits, Genève-Paris 2011, p. 113–144).

Gazzano 2006: F. Gazzano, *Ambasciatori greci in viaggio*, in M.G. Angeli Bertinelli and A. Donati (eds), *Le vie della storia. Migrazioni di popoli, viaggi di individui, circolazione di idee nel Mediterraneo antico*, Roma 2006, 103–125.

Gillett 2003: A. Gillett, *Envoys and Political Communication in the Late Antique West, 411–533*, Cambridge 2003.

Habicht 2001: Ch. Habicht, *Tod auf der Gesandtschaftsreise*, in «Studi Ellenistici» 13 (2001), 9–17.

Hallof 2021: K. Hallof, *Alte und neuen Inschriften aus Olympia III*, «Chiron» 51 (2021), 99–122.

Hamon 1999: P. Hamon, *Juges thasiens à Smyrne: I.Smyrna 582 complété*, «BCH», 123 (1999), 175–194.

Hamon 2012: P. Hamon, *Mander des juges dans la cité: notes sur l'organisation des missions judiciaires à l'époque hellénistique*, «CCGG» 23 (2012), 195–222.

Helly 1971: B. Helly, *Décrets de Démétrias pour des juges étrangers*, «BCH», 95 (1971), 544–559.

Hennig 1997: D. Hennig, *Die Beherbergung von 'Staatsgästen' in der hellenistischen Zeit*, «Chiron» 27 (1997), 355–368.

Henry 1983, A.S. Henry, *Honours and Privileges in Athenian Decrees*, Hildesheim 1983.

Kienast 1973: D. Kienast, s.v. *Presbeia*, *RE* Suppl. XIII 1973, 499–628.

Lambert 2006: S.D. Lambert, *Athenian State Laws and Decrees, 352/1–322/1. III Decrees Honouring Foreigners. A. Citizenship, Proxeny and Euergesy*, «ZPE» 158 (2006), 115–158.

Lambert 2012: *Inscribed Athenian Laws and Decrees 352/1–322/1 BC. Epigraphical Essays*, Leiden – Boston 2012.

Lefèvre 2004: F. Lefèvre, *Contrôle d'identité aux frontières dans les cités grecques. Le cas des entrepreneurs étrangers et assimilés*, in *La mobilité des personnes en Méditerranée de l'antiquité à l'époque moderne: procédures de contrôle et documents d'identification,* sous la direction de C. Moatti, Rome 2004, 99–125.

Lefèvre 2010: F. Lefèvre, *Le contrôle des compétences dans les cités grecques*, «JS» (2010), 3–16.

Lenfant 2017: D. Lenfant, *Liens personnels, pots-de-vin ou protocole ? Les dons du roi de Perse aux ambassadeurs grecs*, in G. Cuniberti (a cura di), *Dono, controdono e corruzione. Ricerche storiche e dialogo interdisciplinare*, a cura di Gianluca Cuniberti, Alessandria 2017, 41–69.

Liddel 2016: P. Liddel, *The Honorific Decrees of fourth–century Athens: Trends, Perceptions, Controversies*, in C. Tiersch (hg. v.), *Die Athenische Demokratie im 4. Jahrhundert: zwischen Modernisierung und Tradition*, Stuttgart 2016, 335–357.

Mack 2015: W. Mack, *Proxeny and Polis: Institutional Networks in the Ancient Greek World*, Oxford 2015.

Magnetto 2016: A. Magnetto, *Interstate Arbitration and Foreign Judges*, in Oxford Handbook of Ancient Greek Law. Publ. online 2016.

Marek 1984: Ch. Marek, *Die Proxenie*, Frankfurt am Main 1984.

Minon 2021: S. Minon, *La langue de la sentence des trois juges de Pellana: une* koina *diplomatique achéenne faiblement éleisée*, «Chiron» 51 (2021), 123–166.

Mosley 1973: D.J. Mosley, *Envoys and Diplomacy in Ancient Greece*, Stuttgart 1973.

Orange 2021: I. Orange, *Eythyna. I rendiconto dei magistrati nella democrazia ateniese (V–IV secolo a.C.)*, Milano 2021.

Osborne 1981: R. Osborne, *Entertainment in the Prytaneion at Athens*, «ZPE» 41 (1981) 153–170.

Paganoni 2018: E. Paganoni, *Trattato per la fondazione della lega di città e stati federali promossa da Antigono e Demetrio. Axon 128*, «Axon» 2 (2018) [edizione online]

Piccirilli 2002: L. Piccirilli, *L'invenzione della diplomazia nella Grecia antica*, Roma 2002.

Poland 1885: F. Poland, *De legationibus Graecorum publicis*, Lipsiae 1885.

Quass 1993: F. Quass, *Die Honoratiorenschicht in den Städten des griechischen Ostens. Untersuchungen zur politischen und sozialen Entwicklung in hellenistischer und römischer Zeit*, Stuttgart 1993.

Reid 2020: J. Reid, *The Offices of Magnesia*, «Polis» 37 (2020), 567–589.

Rhodes 2008: P.J. Rhodes, *After the Three–Bar "Sigma" Controversy: The History of Athenian Imperialism Reassessed*, «CQ» 58 (2008), 500–506.

Rivolta 2014: C. Rivolta, *Il decreto del pritaneo e la concessione della* sitesis *nel V secolo*, «Erga Logoi» 2 (2014), 79–91.

Robert 1973: L. Robert, *Les juges étrangers dans la cité grecque*, in *Xenion. Festschrift für Pan. J. Zepos*, Athènes 1973, 765–782 (= *Opera minora selecta*, V, 137–154 = *Choix d'écrits*, Paris 2007, 299–314).

Rubinstein 2009: *Ateleia grants and their enforcement in the Classical and early Hellenistic periods*, in L. Mitchell, L. Rubinstein (eds.), *Greek History and Epigraphy: Essays in honour of P. J. Rhodes*, Swansea 2009, 115–143.

Russell 1999: F.S. Russell, *Information Gathering in Classical Greece*, Ann Arbor 1999.

Rutherford 2013: *State Pilgrims and Sacred Observers in Ancient Greece. A Study of Theōriā and Theōroi*, Cambridge 2013.

Saba 2020: S. Saba, *Isopoliteia in hellenistic times*, Leiden – Boston 2020.

Scafuro 2014: A. Scafuro, *Decrees for foreign judges: judging conventions or epigraphic habits?*, in *Symposion 2013*, Wien 2014, 365–395.

KAJA HARTER-UIBOPUU (HAMBURG)

GESANDTE IN GEFAHR? ANTWORT AUF ANNA MAGNETTO*

Im vorliegenden Beitrag vermittelt Anna Magnetto einen ersten Eindruck aus ihrem groß angelegten Projekt zum Gesandtschaftswesen in der griechischen Antike. In diesem hat sie es sich zum Ziel gesetzt, neben umfassenden Studien zur Prosopo–graphie der klassischen und hellenistischen Zeit auch einen Überblick über die Gesetze und Vorschriften zu geben, die in literarischen und epigraphischen Quellen aus den griechischen Poleis erhalten sind. Dabei steht eine Verbindung zwischen theoretischen Überlegungen, wie sie etwa Platon in seinen Nomoi anstellt, und erhaltenen Regelungen zur Praxis im Mittelpunkt.[1]

Die Antwort soll am letzten Teil des Beitrages ansetzen, der sich mit den zwischenstaatlichen Beziehungen und der Frage nach „una legge internazionale sugli inviati“ beschäftigt. In aller Kürze – denn dieser Teil des Projekts soll erst zu einem späteren Zeitpunkt eine ausführliche Behandlung finden – stellt Magnetto vor, dass nicht nur eine Stadt intern Beschlüsse fassen konnte, die die Aufnahme und das Anhören fremder Gesandter zum Inhalt hatten, sondern dass auch in zwischenstaatlichen Abkommen derartige Fragen geregelt sein konnten. Bereits die erste Sammlung von Abkommen, die sie aufgenommen hat, zeigt, dass Fragen des privilegierten Zugangs zu Rats- und Volksversammlungen, die so prominent in den innerstaatlichen Rechten auftauchen, auch in den Übereinkommen angesprochen waren. Auch weitere Unterstützung, etwa durch die Stellung von Transportmöglichkeiten, wurde vereinbart.[2]

Am interessantesten scheint die Klausel, die sich im Gründungsakt des Korinthischen Bundes von 302 v. Chr. unter der Leitung von Antigonos I

* Der vorliegende Beitrag wurde durch die Deutsche Forschungsgemeinschaft (DFG) im Rahmen der Exzellenzstrategie des Bundes und der Länder – EXC 2176 „Understanding Written Artefacts: Material, Interaction and Transmission in Manuscript Cultures“, Projektnr. 390893796 gefördert. Die Forschung fand am Centre for the Study of Manuscript Cultures (CSMC) der Universität Hamburg statt.

1 Siehe dazu Magnetto 2023, ab Anm. 8.

2 Magnetto 2023, bei Anm. 97–104. Zum Transport: Isopolitievertrag zwischen Hierapytna und Priansos, ca 205 v. Chr., IC III iii 4, ll.30–33, mit Chaniotis 1996, 260–261.

Monophthalmos und Demetrios I Poliorketes findet.[3] Zwischen zwei Paragraphos-Strichen, die eines der Kennzeichen der umfangreichen Inschrift aus Epidauros sind, wird eine Regelung vorgestellt, die nicht nur klassische Gesandte betrifft, sondern wohl auch weitere Personengruppen, die im Auftrag ihrer Polis oder des gemeinsamen Synedrions unterwegs sind. Dazu zählen etwa Truppen auf dem Weg zum gemeinsamen Feldzug.

IG IV 1^2 68, Z.60–66[4]

— μὴ ἐ-
ξεῖνα[ι δὲ συλᾶν μήτε τοὺς παρὰ τῶν πόλεων πρ]εσβεύοντας π[ρὸς το]ὺς συνέ-
δρους [μήτε τοὺ]ς ἀποστελλομέ[νους ὑπὸ τῶν σ]υνέδρων μηδὲ τοὺς ἐπὶ τὴν κοι-
νὴν σ[τρατείαν] ἐκπεμπομένου[ς μήτε ἐξιόντ]ας ἐφ’ ἃ ἑκάστοις συντέτακται,
μήτ[ε καταπορε]υομένους ἐπὶ τὰ[ς πατρίδας] μηδὲ ἀνδροληπτεῖν μηδὲ κατεγ-
γυᾶ[ν ἐπὶ μηδεμ]ι[ᾶ]ι αἰτίαι· ἂν δέ τ[ις ταῦτα ποῆι, οἵ τ]ε ἄρχοντες οἱ ἐν ἑκάστηι τῶν
πό[λε]ων κ[ω]λυέτωσαν καὶ οἱ σύ[νεδροι ἐπικρινέτ]ωσαν. —

Z.61: παρὰ τῶν Ἑλλήνων(?) IG || Z.66: οἱ σύ[νεδροι δικαζέτ]ωσαν IG; οἱ σύ[νεδροι ἀποτεισάτ]ωσαν Peek

„Es ist nicht erlaubt, diejenigen zu pfänden, die von den Städten zu den *synedroi* abgesandt werden, noch diejenigen, die von den *synedroi* ausgesandt werden, noch diejenigen, die zu einem gemeinsamen Feldzug ausrücken, (und zwar) weder, wenn sie zu den ihnen befohlenen (Orten) ausziehen, noch wenn sie in die Heimatstädte zurückkehren; ebensowenig (ist es erlaubt), sie zu ergreifen oder als Bürgen festzunehmen wegen irgendeiner Forderung. Wenn aber jemand dieses tut, sollen die *archontes* in der jeweiligen Stadt es verhindern und die *synedroi* sollen (darüber) entscheiden.“

Verboten werden allerdings – wenn man den Ergänzungen in Z.61 Glauben schenkt – nicht allgemeine Übergriffe, sondern Pfandnahmen. Diese konnten dort vorgenommen werden, wo die städtische Gerichtsbarkeit in den Augen der Parteien versagte, v.a. im Rechtsverkehr zwischen Bürgern verschiedener Städte. Wenn man auf normalem Wege einen Schuldner nicht dazu bewegen konnte, Forderungen zu erfüllen, etwa weil er Bürger einer anderen Stadt war und sich einem Gerichtsverfahren nicht stellen konnte oder wollte, konnte man einen seiner Mitbürger ergreifen und dessen Besitz an sich nehmen. Natürlich musste das unter Einhaltung

3 Zu den prozessrechtlichen Vorschriften und den politischen Ordnungen in diesem Bund siehe Thür 2003 und Harter-Uibopuu 2003. Text und kritischer Apparat auch bei Paganoni 2018. Zum *boulomenos* und seinen möglichen athenischen Vorbildern vgl. nun Filias 2021.

4 Lesungen nach Thür 2003, 221.

bestimmter Vorschriften geschehen, die immer wieder in Staatsverträgen detailliert geregelt waren.[5] Dieses Vorgehen war nicht nur in der Antike weit verbreitet, sondern wurde auch im Mittelalter als probates Mittel wieder entdeckt, staatliche Justiz durch private Initiativen zu ergänzen. Reisende setzten sich also stets der Gefahr aus, Hab und Gut zu verlieren und sollten unter bestimmten Umständen davor geschützt werden. Dazu konnten einerseits bestimmte Orte oder Zeiten zu ‚a-syla' erklärt werden, andererseits konnten auch Personen oder Gruppen davor bewahrt werden.[6] Eines der Ziele des Hellenenbundes, der sich als Nachfolger des Korinthischen Bundes unter Philipp II verstand, war der friedliche Rechtsverkehr der Poleis und ihrer Bewohner untereinander. Es ist anzunehmen, dass Rechtsgewährungsverträge, wie etwa derjenige zwischen Sikyon/Demetrias und Stymphalos in seinem Umfeld entstanden und gefördert wurden. In diesen Rahmen ist das Verbot zu stellen.[7]

Wer nun eine unrechtmäßige Pfandnahme vornahm, sollte von den Amts–trägern der jeweiligen Stadt — gemeint ist wohl diejenige, in der die Tat geschah — daran gehindert werden. Hier setzt eine wichtige Änderung am Text (l.66) an, die von Gerhard Thür vorgeschlagen wurde: Die *synedroi* sollten nicht wie ursprünglich angenommen und ergänzt, die Tat weiterverfolgen oder vor Gericht bringen (δικάζειν), sondern eine Entscheidung über die Strafmaßnahmen der *archontes* treffen. Sie konnten diese im Rahmen einer Überprüfung bestätigen oder verwerfen (ἐπικρίνειν).[8] Zusätzlich zu den Pfandnahmen werden auch das Ergreifen der Person selbst (ἀνδροληπτεῖν), sowie das Festsetzen und zwangsweise als Bürgen Nehmen (κατεγγυᾶν), untersagt. Z.64–65 machen daher deutlich, dass die Ergänzung in Z.61 wohl richtig ist. Wichtig ist, hier festzuhalten, dass die Bundes–ordnung nicht primär die Fragen des Gesandtschaftswesens ins Auge fasst.[9] Das gemeinsame Heer, das von den griechischen Poleis aufgestellt werden musste, und dessen Mitglieder in der vorliegenden Klausel dezidiert erwähnt werden (Z.62–64) wird deutlich größer gewesen sein als die Gruppe der Abgesandten, seien sie nun Teilnehmer am Synedrion (Z.61–62) oder dessen Boten (Z.62). Hält man sich vor Augen, dass die Organisation des Bundes in Kriegszeiten für die beiden make–donischen Könige deutlich im Vordergrund stand, muss man eingestehen, dass wieder nur ein kleiner Fortschritt in Richtung des Schutzes von Gesandten durch zwischenstaatliche Übereinkünfte erzielt werden konnte. Im Mittelpunkt stand wiederum das Vermeiden von Rechtsstreitigkeiten über die Polis-Grenzen hinaus, in dem private Pfandnahmen und Festnahmen in allen

[5] Zum *sylan* immer noch: Bravo 1980, 735–747; Knäpper 2018, 32–38; zum vorliegenden Text Thür 2003, 231–232.

[6] Zur Entwicklung der territorialen Asylie nach den epigraphischen und literarischen Quellen v.a. Knäpper 2018. Dort 38–42 zur Asylie für Personen.

[7] Vgl. Thür 1995, 270.

[8] Thür 2003, 226–227.

[9] Harter-Uibopuu 2003, 331–337.

Formen bei Gelegenheiten, zu denen Bürger unterschiedlicher Staaten zusammenkamen, explizit verboten wurden. In diesen Kontext gehören auch Verträge, wie derjenige zwischen Stymphalos und Sikyon/Demetrias, die die Möglichkeiten gerichtlicher Beilegung aller denkbaren Streitfälle zwischen Bürgern und Nicht-Bürgern vorsehen und regeln. Zwar wird in Inschriften immer wieder davon gesprochen, dass Gesandten *asphaleia* verliehen werden soll. Ob es sich dabei aber um den Schutz vor dem hier angesprochenen *sylan* handelt, oder allgemein auf die persönliche Sicherheit von Reisenden abgezielt wird, lässt sich nicht immer entscheiden.[10]

Welche weiteren Gefahren konnten Gesandten drohen, wovor mussten sie beschützt werden? Welche Folgen waren zu erwarten, wenn sie verletzt oder getötet wurden? Der vorliegende Beitrag bietet nicht den Platz, diese Frage ausführlich behandeln zu können, im Folgenden können lediglich einige Quellen dazu kurz vorgestellt werden.[11] A. Magnetto zitiert in ihrem Beitrag den Waffenstillstand zwischen Athen und Sparta aus dem neunten Kriegsjahr (423 v. Chr.). Darin ist vorgesehen, dass Herolde, Gesandte und ihre Begleiter freies Geleit im Rahmen ihrer Missionen zur Auflösung des Krieges und in Streitfällen sowohl auf der Peloponnes als auch am Weg nach Athen haben sollten, sowohl zu Land als auch zu Wasser.[12] Dass dies vertraglich geregelt werden musste, lässt wohl darauf schließen, dass die beiden Gruppen ansonsten im Krieg den gleichen Gefahren unterlagen, wie ihre Mitbürger.

Eine interessante Passage enthält der sogenannte „Brief Philipps an die Athener“, der in einigen Manuskripten des demosthenischen Corpus überliefert ist.[13] Der makedonische König wirft den Athenern zunächst wiederholte Übergriffe auf Gesandte vor, so etwa den Herold Nikias oder den Gesandten Amphilochos (Dem. 12,2.3). Dabei erinnert er die Athener daran, dass dieses Vorgehen bei allen Griechen als *asebeia* qualifiziert werde:

Ps.-Dem.12, 4

(4) καίτοι τὸ παρανομεῖν εἰς κήρυκα καὶ πρέσβεις τοῖς ἄλλοις τε πᾶσιν ἀσεβὲς εἶναι δοκεῖ καὶ μάλισθ᾽ ὑμῖν· Μεγαρέων γοῦν Ἀνθεμόκριτον ἀνελόντων εἰς τοῦτ᾽ ἐλήλυθεν ὁ δῆμος ὥστε μυστηρίων μὲν εἶργον αὐτούς, ὑπομνήματα δὲ τῆς ἀδικίας ἔστησαν ἀνδριάντα πρὸ τῶν πυλῶν. καίτοι πῶς οὐ δεινόν, ἐφ᾽ οἷς παθόντες οὕτως ἐμισήσατε τοὺς δράσαντας, νῦν αὐτοὺς φαίνεσθαι ποιοῦντας;

---

[10] So etwa IG XII 7, 44, Z.7–9; IC III iii 3 C Z.14–16.

[11] Zu den Gefahren für Gesandte vgl. Kienast 1973, 571–573 und ausführlicher Habicht 2001.

[12] Thuk. 4,118,6: Magnetto 2023, Anm. 97.

[13] Der Brief wird inzwischen Anaximenes von Lampsakos zugeschrieben (FGrHist 72 F 41), Amendola 2022, 122 mit Anm. 457.

„Widerrechtliches Verhalten gegenüber einem Herold und Gesandten wird bei allen anderen für *asebeia* gehalten, und am meisten bei Euch: Als die Megarer damals Anthemokritos töteten, ging das Volk so weit, sie von den Mysterien auszuschließen und eine Statue als Erinnerung an das Unrecht vor den Toren aufzustellen. Wie könnt nun Ihr, die Ihr, als Ihr es erlittet, die Täter so hasstet, nun offensichtlich das Gleiche wie sie tun?"

Wenn auch nicht mit Sicherheit nachgewiesen werden kann, dass die Unverletz–lichkeit von Gesandten in allen griechischen Staaten als Recht angesehen wurde, gibt es doch Hinweise auf eine allgemeine Tradition.[14] Sie scheinen, ebenso wie Herolde, unter besonderem Schutz gestanden zu haben und als „privilegierte Fremde" behandelt worden zu sein. Damit verstieß ein Übergriff gegen sie auch gegen sakrale Vorschriften[15]

Ein Fall, in dem diese Nähe besonders deutlich wird, ist der Übergriff auf eine Gruppe von ephesischen *theoroi*, die nach Sardes gekommen waren, um Gewänder für die ephesische Artemis zu holen. Eine Inschrift aus Ephesos vom Ende des 4. Jh. v. Chr. bezieht sich auf die Vorkommnisse und enthält eine Liste von 44–46 Männern, die zum Tod verurteilt worden waren (Z.13–57).[16] Am Anfang steht knapp, was diesem Todesurteil voraus gegangen war:

I.Ephesos 2, Z.1–12

οἱ προήγοροι ὑπὲρ τῆς θεοῦ κατε[δι]-
κάσαντο θάνατογ κατὰ τὴμ προγρ[α]-
φὴν τῆς δίκης ταύτην· "ὅτι θεωρῶν

[14] Adcock – Mosley 1975, 122–127 vermag erst mit dem Auftreten Roms in Griechenland die Anfänge einer Theorie der Unverletzbarkeit von Gesandten zu sehen. Bedermans Verständnis der *asebeia* als ‚purely religious sanction' (Bederman 2001, 100) ist verfehlt. Vgl. zur *asebeia* Delli Pizzi 2011. Einen Überblick bietet nun Amendola 2022, 122–123, der auf eine Stelle im Demades-Papyrus (P.Berolin. inv.13045 G I, 25–27) verweist. Dort erwähnt Demades ein Gesetz (νόμος), das Gesandten Schutz garantiere. Dazu siehe unten bei Anm. 30.

[15] Zum grundsätzlichen Schutz von Fremden im Rahmen des Gastrechts Harter-Uibopuu 2021, 147–148. Habicht 2001, 10 zur möglichen Unterscheidung zwischen Gesandten und Herolden und der Frage, ob beiden die Unverletzlichkeit garantiert worden war. Siehe auch die Diskussion bei Adcock – Mosley 1975, 122–127 und Bederman 2001, 113–119.

[16] Erstpublikation des Steins bei Knibbe 1961, mit Umzeichnung und Erläuterung der Fundumstände. Er nimmt an, dass die Inschrift im Artemision aufgestellt war, bevor sie als Spolie im Prytaneion Verwendung fand (178 mit Anm. 2). In weiterer Folge wird der Text als I.Ephesos 2 ins Corpus aufgenommen (BE 1963, 211; BE 1966, 369; BE 1967, 498). Vgl. Wankel 1977 mit kurzen Anmerkungen zum terminus προγραφή (Z.2–3) und zum τίμημα (Z.11). Zur Datierung Robert 1967, 32–36. der überzeugend die Bürgerrechts–verleihung I.Ephesos 2010 mit den Vorfällen in Verbindung bringt. Er setzt beide Texte in die Zeit von 340–320 v. Chr. Mit guten Gründen spricht sich Walser 2008, 340–342, für die Zeit zwischen 315 und 300 v. Chr. aus.

ἀποσταλέντων ὑπὸ τῆς πόλεως ἐπ[ὶ]
χιτῶνας τῆι Ἀρτέμιδι κατὰ τὸν ν[ό]-
μον τὸμ πάτριογ, καὶ τῶν ἱερῶγ κα[ὶ]
τῶν θεωρῶν παραγενομένων εἰς Σ[άρ]-
δεις καὶ τὸ ἱερὸν τῆς Ἀρτέμιδος
τὸ ἱδρυμένον ὑπὸ Ἐφεσίων τά τε ἱ[ερὰ]
ἠσέβησαγ καὶ τοὺς θεωροὺς ὕβρι[σαν·]
τίμημα τῆς δίκης θάνατος."
κατεδικάσθη δὲ τῶνδε·

„Die *proegoroi* haben für die Göttin zum Tod verurteilt gemäß dieser schriftlichen Ankündigung des Verfahrens: (…),[17] da sie, nachdem *theoroi* von der Stadt wegen der Gewänder für Artemis nach dem väterlichen Gesetz ausgesandt worden waren und die Weihgaben und die Gesandten nach Sardes und in das Heiligtum der Artemis, das von den Ephesiern gegründet wurde, gekommen waren, Gaben entweihten und die Gesandten misshandelten. Strafantrag des Verfahrens: Tod.' Verurteilt wurden Folgende: *(44–46 Namen folgen)*"

Der Text bietet – so kurz er ist – immer noch einige Schwierigkeiten in der Rekonstruktion des Verfahrens und der Parteienrollen. Die Gruppe der Festgesandten, die wegen der Gewänder der Göttin nach Sardes gekommen waren (entweder um diese abzuholen, oder um sie zu deponieren) muss im Rahmen ihres Zuges überfallen worden sein. Dabei wird der Übergriff auf die Weihgaben im Text ἀσεβεῖν genannt, derjenige auf die *theoroi* ὑβρίζειν. Wie die beiden Taten gewichtet werden, ist nicht bekannt, das Ergebnis des Verfahrens war jedenfalls die Todesstrafe. Auch wenn die Inschrift selbst in Ephesos aufgestellt war, war der Tatort Sardes, das Ziel der *theoroi*. Wo aber hatte das Verfahren stattgefunden? Wenn man nicht davon ausgehen möchte, dass Sardes 44–46 Männer „ausgeliefert" hatte, muss das wohl in der lydischen Metropole gewesen sein. Die Publikation des Todesurteils in Ephesos wäre damit ein zufriedener Akt der Anerkennung der Reaktion der zuständigen Amts–träger und Gerichte in Sardes gewesen, und zugleich eine Warnung an alle anderen Griechen, die *theoroi* der ephesischen Artemis nicht zu belästigen.[18]

Das größte Rätsel aber ist wohl die Frage, wer die *proegoroi* waren, deren Tätigkeit in der Inschrift mit καταδικάζειν „verurteilen" angegeben wird (Z.1–2). Sie handelten jedenfalls für die Göttin, mag man nun den Einschub ὑπὲρ τῆς θεοῦ in Z.1 auf ihre Funktion als Amtsträger allgemein oder auf ihre Rolle in dem

---

17 Überzeugend Wankel 1977, 220, der hier ein Zitat aus der Klageschrift beginnen lässt.

18 R. Baladié teilte O. Masson in einem Brief eine weitgehend überzeugende Interpretation der Vorkommnisse mit und ging davon aus, dass der Prozess in Sardes stattgefunden hatte (Masson 1987, 228–229 mit Anm. 13). Ob in jedem Fall auch in Sardes eine entsprechende Inschrift aufgestellt war, wie Masson 1987, 229, vermutet, ist nicht mit Sicherheit anzunehmen.

speziellen Fall beziehen. Sie werden als ‚Rechtsvertreter' der Göttin interpretiert, zu deren Schutz sie das Todesurteil ausgesprochen hätten.[19] Dabei wird nicht immer deutlich, ob man sich hier Personen vorstellt, die Klage erhoben, oder die richteten.[20] Meines Erachtens muss man aber die beiden Rollen deutlich auseinanderhalten, das Verb καταδικάζειν lässt nur die zweite Interpretation zu. Ich sehe in den *proegoroi* also die Richter, die den Fall durch ein Urteil im Sinne des Klagebegehrens – wohl der Ephesier – entschieden und damit die Todesstrafe aussprachen.[21] Wer die Ephesier vertrat und Klage gegen die übergriffigen Sardier erhoben hatte, ist im Text nicht aufgenommen. In den Inschriften von Sardes ist kein Amt eines *proegoros* erhalten, weder unter den sakralen noch den zivilen Bereichen der Verwaltung. Jüngst hat David Sasseville argumentiert, dass der griechische Begriff προήγορος dem lydischen *šiwralm(i)-* entspräche und ebenso wie dieser einen Kultbeamten der Artemis in Ephesos und Sardes bezeichne. Auch in seinen Ausführungen wird die Rolle der *proegoroi*, die er als Ephesier sieht, nicht klar. Er übersetzt sowohl den griechischen als auch den lydischen Ausdruck mit ‚prosecutor', erläutert ihn aber einmal als ‚advocate' (132) und spricht an anderer Stelle davon, dass er ‚verurteile' (‚advocates of the goddess … in courts of law condemning impious offenders', 134). Dennoch denke ich, dass er den entscheidenden Beitrag zu einer Lösung leistet. Wenn man in den *proegoroi* in der Tat Kultbeamte der Artemis (allerdings in Sardes) sieht, wäre das Urteil nicht von einem städtischen Gremium von Richtern, sondern von Vertretern des Heiligtums und damit der Göttin ausgesprochen worden. Diese hätten für die Göttin ge–sprochen und sie vertreten, aber nicht als Partei im Verfahren.[22]

---

19 So Baladié bei Masson 1987, 228: ‚ce sont des magistrats d'Éphèse ou des citoyens de cette ville investis d'une fonction de défense des intérêts de la ville (ou de la déesse Artémis) dans un procès qui s'est déroulé à Sardes'. Diese Interpretation geht allerdings – ohne überzeugende Argumente oder Parallelen – davon aus, dass καταδικάζειν eben nicht ‚urteilen', sondern ‚ein Urteil erlangen' im Sinne einer erfolgreichen Vertretung der eigentlichen Klägerin bedeutet. Auch Knibbe 1961, 178–179, sieht in ihnen ein Gremium von Richtern, das er vorsichtig als Ausschuss der Boule identifiziert. Anzunehmenderweise – aber nicht ausgesprochen – denkt er dabei an die Boule von Ephesos und nimmt damit die ionische Stadt als Ort des Verfahrens an.

20 Delli Pizzi 2011, 70 übersetzt: “The defendants of the goddess condemned to death on the basis of the following lawsuit notice”, ohne im Weiteren zu erläutern, was genau er unter ‚defendant' versteht.

21 So auch Wankel in I.Ephesos 2, der übersetzt „Die Proegoren haben zugunsten (zum Schutz) der Göttin auf Todesstrafe erkannt“.

22 Als ‚Vertreter' der Göttin sind die *šiwralm(i)-* unter anderem in den Grabschutz involviert. Sasseville 2018, 129 Text (1). Auch die anderen dort angeführten Texte lassen sich unter der Voraussetzung verstehen, dass man sich von der Rolle als ‚Anwalt' einer Partei löst und von einer echten Vertretung in jeder Hinsicht ausgeht. Mit dieser Rekonstruktion lässt sich durchaus auch die Ehreninschrift I.Ephesos 2010 in Einklang bringen, in der einem Bürger von Sardes (so Robert 1967, 35) das Bürgerrecht von Ephesos verliehen wird, um ihm für seine Hilfe in einer Angelegenheit zu danken, in die die ephesischen *theoroi*

Jedenfalls kommen in dem in seinen Details immer noch rätselhaften Fall verschiedene sakrale Komponenten zusammen: Die Tat passierte möglicherweise im Heiligtum der Artemis. Die Täter vergriffen sich an den Weihgaben, damit also am Eigentum der Göttin. Nicht zuletzt standen wohl die *theoroi* unter göttlichem Schutz. Der Fall und seine Bereinigung — immerhin durch die Verurteilung einer großen Gruppe von über 40 Sardiern — muss für viel Aufmerksamkeit gesorgt haben.

Ein letztes Beispiel soll noch einmal verdeutlichen, wie eng Politik und Realität in der Frage des besonderen Status eines Gesandten beieinander lagen und wie sehr unsere Einschätzungen auf die historische Überlieferung angewiesen sind. An vielen literarischen Stellen lässt sich zeigen, dass der Mord an Gesandten als Unrecht angesehen wurde, so auch in der Schilderung des Todes von Demades, Demosthenes ewigem Gegner.[23] Diodor, Plutarch und Arrian überliefern, dass er gemeinsam mit seinem Sohn als Gesandter von Athen an den Hof des Antipatros nach Makedonien geschickt worden war, um über die Besatzung der Festung Munychia zu verhandeln.[24] In den Details unterscheiden sich die Berichte allerdings etwas: Während Plutarch am Ende der Vita des Demosthenes (31,4–6) sowie in der Vita des Phokion (30, 9–10) die Tatsache, dass Kassander den Athener eigenhändig tötet, als gerechte Strafe für dessen andauernden Verrat ansieht, schildert er doch auch einen rechtfertigenden Anlass. Kassander habe Kenntnis von einem Brief gehabt, den Demades dem Perdikkas geschickt habe, und in dem er nicht nur die Verein–barungen verriet, sondern den König auch lächerlich machte. Diodor erwähnt diese Briefe ebenfalls (18,48,1–4), es ist diesmal Antipatros, der davon Kenntnis erlangt. Dieser lässt den Athener, der deutlich als *presbeutes* seiner Stadt wegen der guten Kontakte zu den Makedonen charakterisiert wird, vor die entsprechenden Amtsträger bringen. Im Anschluss wird er gemeinsam mit seinem Sohn in ein Gefängnis geführt und schließlich hingerichtet. Im Vergleich zu Plutarch ist die Szene zurückhaltender und offizieller geschildert. Der Gesandtenstatus wird betont, nutzt dem verurteilten Demades aber nicht.

Der Bericht des Arrian (Fr. 1,14–15) ist allerdings nicht direkt, sondern nur in einem Auszug bei Photius erhalten. Dabei handelt es sich einerseits um die drastischste Darstellung des Todes, in der die Schuld ausschließlich bei Kassander liegt, während Antipatros kaum erwähnt wird. Andererseits kommt eine interessante Wendung vor:

---

verwickelt waren (Z.1) und in der es zu Untersuchungen von Straftaten (ἀδικήματα) gekommen war (Z.3–4, richtig bei Robert 1967, 33; I.Ephesos 2010 hat Z.4 ausgelassen).

23 Habicht 2001, 10–11. Allg. zu Demades: Marzi 1991; Dmitriev 2021, 1–9.

24 Demades war bereits zuvor immer wieder als Gesandter erfolgreich in Makedonien gewesen, etwa als er 336 v. Chr. nach der Niederschlagung des thebanischen Aufstandes Alexander III davon überzeugte, die antimakedonischen Politiker (unter ihnen Demosthenes) nicht ausliefern zu müssen. Dmitriev 2021, 1–2.

Deinarchos von Korinth tritt als Ankläger (κατήγορος) auf.[25] Auch in diesem Fall soll der Anschein erweckt werden, es habe sich nicht um einfachen Mord, sondern um eine gerechtfertigte Tötung gehandelt.[26] Davide Amendola untersucht die erhaltenen literarischen Quellen erneut und zieht zum Vergleich das Verfahren gegen Phokion heran, der in Athen ein knappes Jahr nach dem Tod des Demades verurteilt und hinge–richtet wurde. In diesem Fall hatte Polyperchon die athenischen Gesandten ausge–liefert und der athenischen Gerichtsbarkeit unterstellt, damit fanden sie nicht in der Fremde und während der Gesandtschaft, sondern zu Hause den Tod.[27]

Dies führt zur letzten Quelle: P.Berol. inv. 13045 (= BTK VII 13–31: 221–222). Erhalten sind 422 Zeilen in sieben Kolumnen einer Rolle, die in Abusir el-Melek 1904 gefunden worden war und 1923 der wissenschaftlichen Öffentlichkeit vorgelegt wurde. Neben einem Ver–gleich verschiedener Staatsformen findet sich ein Dialog zwischen Demades und Deinarchos von Korinth, in dessen Mittelpunkt der Verrat an Antipatros und Athen steht. Dieser ist die früheste Quelle zu den Ereignissen in Pella, er datiert nach Amendola an das Ende des 4. Jh.v.Chr.[28] Wenn auch nicht als gesichert gelten kann, dass die Beschreibungen die historische Realität abbilden, und der Text wohl deutlich den Versuch spiegelt, in Athen Phokion, Lykurg und Demosthenes als Demokraten und Vorbilder zu rehabilitieren,[29] enthalten einige Passagen doch interessante Details zu einem möglichen Verfahren und zur Frage, ob Diplomaten der Gerichtsbarkeit eines fremden Staates unterstellt werden können.

P.Berol. inv. 13045 C III Z.20–24:[30]

ᵛ κρινεῖ δὲ τίς ἡ-
μ]ᾶς; ᵛ (ΔΕΙ.) οὐθεὶς Μα[κ]εδόνων, ᵛ ἀλλ’ οἱ̣ μετ’ ἀδε̣[ί]ας̣
παρόντες πρέσβεις. ᵛ (ΔΗ.) Δείναρχε, κρ[ι]τὰς ποιε̣ῖ̣ς
ὧ̣ν ὁ φόβος̣ ἀφα[ι]ρε̣ῖ̣ται τὴν ψῆφον· ᵛ ὅ̣μω̣ς δ’ ἐκ̣-
π]ε̣μ̣πέτ̣ωσ̣αν. ᵛ

„(Demades): Wer soll über uns richten? (Deinarchos): Keiner der Makedonen, sondern hier anwesenden Gesandten, die Immunität haben. (Demades):

25 Arr. Fr. 1,14–15 = Phot. Bibl. 92 (70a).

26 Dmitriev 2021, 271–281 *passim* fasst die unterschiedlichen Traditionen zusammen, geht aber nicht auf den Status des Rhetors als athenischer Gesandter ein.

27 Nep. Phoc. 3,4; Diod. 18,66,3. Einleitend Amendola 2022, 113–114 mit einem Überblick über die bisherige Forschung.

28 Eine umfassende Beschreibung des Papyrus, seiner Erstpublikation und Forschungsgeschichte sowie der paläographischen Charakteristika ermöglicht D. Amendola eine Einordnung des Schriftstücks an das Ende des 2. Jh. v. Chr., Amendola 2022, 3–31 und 211.

29 Amendola 2022, 211.

30 Amendola 2022, 251–254 mit kritischem Apparat und 353–354..

Deinarchos, Du machst diejenigen zu Richtern, denen Furcht den Stimmstein nahm. Gleichwohl, sie sollen sie aussenden."

Zwar entsteht im Dialog zunächst der Eindruck, die beiden Angeklagten wären vor einer makedonischen Gerichtsversammlung gestanden, aber der Autor scheint gesehen zu haben, dass dies dem Gerechtigkeitsempfinden des athenischen Publikums, für das der Dialog wohl gedacht war, nicht entsprochen haben wird.[31] Durch die Einführung von athenischen Richtern, denen die Entscheidung über das Schicksal des Demades oblag, wurde aus dem Gesandtenmord der Fall eines *presbeutes*, der quasi in seiner eigenen Stadt vor Gericht gestellt worden war. Damit entsprachen die dem hier vorgestellten Ausschnitt folgenden Argumentationen des Deinarchos den üblichen Ausführungen der Gerichtsredner vor athenischen Geschworenen und das Urteil, das selbst nicht erhalten ist, aber an dem kein Zweifel besteht, wurde nachvollziehbar.[32] Auffallend ist allerdings, dass die späteren Quellen keine Kenntnis von der Beteiligung athenischer Gesandter als Richter haben. In jedem Fall zeigt der Dialog Denkmuster, die nicht nur die Zeitgenossen seines Autors beschäftigt hatten, sondern auch uns einen Einblick in das Gesandtschaftswesen geben können. Die sakrale Sphäre, die in den vorigen Beispielen deutlich wurde, spielt in keiner der Quellen zum Schicksal des Demades und seines Sohnes eine Rolle.

Es ist sicher ein lohnendes Unterfangen, sich in der weiten literarischen Überlieferung auf die Suche nach der Gefährdung von Gesandten, nach Übergriffen und nach deren möglicher Ahndung zu machen. Dies mag dabei helfen, zwischen sakralrechtlichen Vorstellungen, städtischen Ordnungen und zwischenstaatlichen Vereinbarungen den Status der Gesandten näher zu bestimmen.

kaja.harter@uni-hamburg.de

BIBLIOGRAPHIE

F. Adcock – D.J. Mosley, Diplomacy in Ancient Greece, London 1975

D. Amendola, The Demades Papyrus (P.Berol.Inv.13045). A New Text with Commentary, Sozomena 17, Berlin 2022

D.J. Bederman, Interntional Law in Antiquity, Cambridge 2001

[31] Umfassend analysiert Amendola 2022, 115–136, das Verfahren und versucht dabei, nicht aus der Perspektive des athenischen Rechts zu argumentieren, sondern literarische Quellen für das Gerichtswesen am makedonischen Königshof heranzuziehen. Dennoch bleiben in meinen Augen Zweifel daran bestehen, dass der Dialog den tatsächlichen Ablauf der Ereignisse widerspiegelt und nicht eine rhetorische Übung darstellt.

[32] Demades wird zum Ende des erhaltenen Texts dazu aufgefordert, sich auf den Tod vorzubereiten (G II 18–26). Er selbst scheint an diesem Ausgang des Prozesses nicht gezweifelt zu haben (vgl. C III 7–11).

B. Bravo, "Sulân". Représailles et justice privée contre des étrangers dans les cités grecques. ASNP 3a ser. 10. Scuola Normale di Pisa, Pisa 1980, S. 675–987

A. Chaniotis, Die Verträge zwischen kretischen Poleis in der hellenistischen Zeit, HABES 24, Stuttgart 1996

A. Delli Pizzi, Impiety in Epigraphic Evidence, Kernos 24 (2011), 59–76

S. Dmitriev, The Orator Demades. Classical Greece Reimagined through Rhetoric, Oxford 2021

D. Filias, *Ho boulomenos* in the legal procedure of the Hellenic League of 302 B.C. and Athenian influence on the prosecution systems of the Panhellenic Leagues, AHB 35.3–4 (2021) 125–149

P. Gauthier, Symbola. Les étrangers et la justice dans les cites grecques, Annales de l'Ést. Mémoire n. 42, Université de Nancy II, Nancy 1972

C. Habicht, Tod auf der Gesandtschaftsreise, in: B. Virgilio, Studi Ellenistici 13, Pisa 2001, 9–17

G.M.A. Hanfmann, The Sacrilege Inscription: The Ethnic, Linguistic, Social and Religious Situation at Sardis at the End of the Persian Era, Bulletin of the Asia Institute N.S. 1 (1987) 1–8

K. Harter-Uibopuu, Der Hellenenbund des Antigonos I Monophthalmos und des Demetrios Poliorketes, 302/1 v. Chr., in: G. Thür – F.J. Nieto (Hg.), Symposion 1999, Akten der Gesellschaft für griechische und hellenistische Rechtsgeschichte, Band 14, Köln – Weimar – Wien 2003, 315–337

K. Harter-Uibopuu, Fremde vor Gerichten der griechischen Städte, in: N. Grotkamp – A. Seelentag (Hg.), Konfliktlösung in der Antike, Handbuch zur Geschichte der Konfliktlösung in Europa 1, Berlin 2021, 147–156

D. Kienast, s.v. *presbeia*, RE Suppl. XIII 1973, 499–628

K. Knäpper, Hieros kai asylos. Territoriale Asylie im Hellenismus in ihrem historischen Kontext, Historia ES 250, Stuttgart 2018

D. Knibbe, Ein religiöser Frevel und seine Sühne. Ein Todesurteil hellenistischer Zeit aus Ephesos, JÖAI 46 (1961–63), 175–182

A. Magnetto, Le leggi civiche e gli ambasciatori nel mondo Greco die età classica ed ellenistica, in: P. Scheibelreiter, Symposion 2022. Akten der Gesellschaft für griechische und hellenistische Rechtsgeschichte, Band 29, Wien 2023, 179–212

M. Marzi, Demàde politico e oratore, Atene e Roma N.S. 36, 2–3 (1991) 70–83

O. Masson, L'inscription d'Éphèse relative aux condamnés à mort de Sardes (I.Ephesos 2), REG 100 (1987) 225–239

E. Paganoni, Treaty for the Foundation of the League of Cities and Federal States Promoted by Antigonus and Demetrius'. 2 | 2 | 2018 no. 2 (20 December 2018). doi:10.30687/axon/2532–6848/2018/02/012

L. Robert, Sur des inscriptions d'Éphèse, RPhil 41 (1967) 7–84

D. Sasseville, The Lydian word for 'prosecutor', Kadmos 57 (2018) 129–135

G. Thür, Zu den Hintergründen des „Rechtsgewährungsvertrags“ zwischen Stymphalos und Demetrias (IPArk 17), in: C. Schubert – K. Brodersen (Hg.), Rom und der griechische Osten. Festschrift für Hatto H. Schmitt zum 65. Geburtstag, Stuttgart 1995, 267–272

G. Thür, Prozessrechtliches in der Gründungsurkunde des Hellenenbundes (IG IV 1^2, 68, 302/1 v. Chr.), in: BIDR 39 (1997 [2003]) 219–232

A. V. Walser, Bauern und Zinsnehmer. Politik, Recht und Wirtschaft im frühhellenistischen Ephesos, Vestigia Band 59, München 2008

H. Wankel, Die Bekanntmachung des Todesurteils in der ephesischen Inschrift Inv. 1631, ZPE 24 (1977) 219–221

DAVID LEWIS (EDINBURGH)

DID SERFDOM EXIST IN CLASSICAL AND HELLENISTIC CRETE?*

Summary: This contribution engages in the longstanding debate over servile status in ancient Crete and asks whether secure evidence exists for a 'serf' status bound to the soil. It concludes in the negative though an analysis of the terms *dolos* and *woikeus* in Gortynian law, the literary sources for Cretan servile status, and several Hellenistic treaties.

Keywords: Crete, slavery, serfdom, Gortyn, epigraphy

In several recent studies I have argued against a longstanding view that two basic forms of dependency existed in Classical Greece: 'chattel' slavery (exemplified by the slave system of the Athenians), and serfdom (exemplified by Spartan Helotage, and also dependency in Crete, Thessaly, and Heraclea Pontica). My argument (based *imprimis* on contributions by other scholars, especially those of Jean Ducat, Stefan Link, and Nino Luraghi) is that both archetypes fit within the category of slavery.[1] This does not reduce the complexity of the picture – far from it, for significant variation existed at the regional level. Rather than two kinds of dependency, there were as many versions of slavery as there were city-states (and other non-*polis* forms of social organisation). The Greek world can therefore be envisaged as a patchwork of epichoric (i.e., local) slave systems, each differing from the next – some slightly, others profoundly, with Helotage (and its comparanda) differing so profoundly as to constitute something like a subcategory within the overall whole.[2]

* My thanks to Prof. Scheibelreiter and the committee for the invitation to speak at Gmunden, and to those present for a stimulating discussion; in particular, I thank my respondent Prof. Maffi as well as Profs. Thür and Müller for valuable suggestions, and especially Profs. Gagarin and Schmitz for a very constructive exchange – my disagreement with them in what follows in no way detracts from my admiration for their work, from which I have profited greatly. I also thank Mirko Canevaro and Edward Harris for reading the essay in draft and providing sage advice, and Selene Psoma for advice on Cretan coinage. References to inscriptions in *IC* IV follow Davies 2005 in printing the inscription number in **bold**, with columns (where relevant) in Roman numerals and lines in Arabic numerals.

1 Lewis 2018: 125–65, with references to other studies; Lewis forthcoming (a), (b), drawing on *inter alia* Ducat 1990, 1994; Link 1994, 2001; Luraghi 2002, 2003, 2009.

2 On epichoric slavery, see also Vlassopoulos 2021: 166–175.

Some, though, demur, and maintain that serfdom existed in Classical Greece.[3] This essay, accordingly, analyses the most promising evidence for solving the problem: the epigraphical (and, to a lesser extent literary) evidence pertaining to Crete, which remains overlooked in general treatments. The analysis will proceed in three phases. §I revisits Gortynian law and the *dolos–woikeus* debate, building on previous studies by adding new arguments for why these terms are best understood as effectively synonymous[4], and why *woikeus* means 'slave' not 'serf.' §II canvasses the meagre literary sources, critiquing their reliability and exploring how far their claims fit (or jar) with the inscriptions. §III turns to several Hellenistic Cretan treaties and argues that the servile vocabulary employed there makes better sense as referring to slavery, not serfdom.

I. Serfs in Gortynian law?

Key to the question about the existence (or not) of serfdom in Crete is the *dolos–woikeus* debate. The laws of Gortyn employ both words, and scholars have long debated whether they should be understood as synonyms for a single slave status or as terms for two distinct statuses, slave (*dolos*) and serf (*woikeus*).[5] My own view is that the former position is correct[6], and what follows surveys the reasons adduced so far in support of this position, adds several new ones, and critically evaluates the most erudite and robust recent defences of the contrary view, *viz.* those of Gagarin (2010), Bile (2019), and Schmitz (2022). The following twelve reasons support the view that both words are synonyms for a single slave status.

(I) As Lipsius pointed out in 1909, Attic Greek uses the words *doulos* and *oiketes* to refer to a single slave status. Since these are dialectical equivalents of the Gortynian *dolos* and *woikeus*, the obvious approach is to read the Gortynian terms in the same light.[7] We might also look for cognates of *woikeus* elsewhere to see whether these support a picture of slavery or serfdom. Some of the examples are

---

3 e.g., Forsdyke 2021: 41–47, but without detailed analysis of the Cretan material. The lynchpin of her argument about Helot status being vague and muddled to Classical Greeks is a misinterpretation of where Ephorus' wording ends at Str. 8.5.4 (= *BNJ* 70 F117; Forsdyke 2021: 43; also, Schmitz 2022: 122 n. 83). For the extent of Ephorus' wording see Hodkinson 2000: 117–118; Luraghi 2002: 244 n. 5.

4 Here and in what follows I use 'synonym' in its technical sense as referring to words whose semantic ranges overlap enough to allow their application to the same subject – the overlap need not be one of perfect, total eclipse. Thus, *doulos* and *oiketes* are synonyms in Attic Greek, despite certain differences of nuance: Lewis 2018: 295–305.

5 For an overview of the debate, see the admirably full notes of Gagarin 2010. In what follows I generally give the masculine forms for the sake of brevity; but NB the feminine forms *dola* and *woikea*. I follow the League of Nations definition of serfdom: Ste. Croix 1981: 135–136.

6 I will build on the most important contribution on the synonymy view, Link 2001.

7 Lipsius 1909: 398. The same spelling, δο̂λος, can be found in an inscription from fifth-century Laconia (*IG* V,1 1155), possibly applying to Helots, and even in 4th century Athens: *SEG* xxvi 72 line 30: ἐὰ̣ν δὲ δο̂λος ἦι ὁ πωλῶν ἢ δόλη…κτλ.

inconclusive.[8] But others emphatically show slavery. For example, Eumaeus in the *Odyssey* is called an *oikeus* (14.4, 63); he works in the country as a swineherd and is a slave who was kidnapped as a child and sold to Laertes (15.454–484). In Hellenistic Boeotia several of the so-called consecration-manumissions have the owner consecrating τὸν ϝίδιον ϝυκέταν, 'his own *wuketas*.'[9] Regardless of whether these inscriptions are understood as manumissions, gifts of persons to a god, or a mixture of both, these are clear examples of a cognate of the Gortynian *woikeus* meaning 'slave.' Of course, these parallels do not constitute proof positive, because words in a single given language may mean different things in different places where it is spoken – 'he's carrying a piece' means something different in Chicago than it does in Glasgow.[10] But the odds are heavily stacked in favour of a word denoting the same (or at least a similar) thing across multiple regions where a given language is spoken.

(II) J.K. Davies has rightly noted that the major point of doubt for scholars who reject the synonymy argument is this: why would a law code use two words for one status?[11] Yet we must recalibrate our assumptions on this point, for the Greeks habitually used numerous words for slaves, toggling between them with apparent ease and with a frequency that seems somewhat alien to us. Take, for example, Plato, *Resp.* IX.578e–579a:

> εἴ τις θεῶν ἄνδρα ἕνα, ὅτῳ ἔστιν ἀνδράποδα πεντήκοντα ἢ καὶ πλείω, ἄρας ἐκ τῆς πόλεως αὐτόν τε καὶ γυναῖκα καὶ παῖδας θείη εἰς ἐρημίαν μετὰ τῆς ἄλλης οὐσίας τε καὶ τῶν οἰκετῶν, ὅπου αὐτῷ μηδεὶς τῶν ἐλευθέρων μέλλοι βοηθήσειν, ἐν ποίῳ ἄν τινι καὶ ὁπόσῳ φόβῳ οἴει γενέσθαι αὐτὸν περί τε αὑτοῦ καὶ παίδων καὶ γυναικός, μὴ ἀπόλοιντο ὑπὸ τῶν οἰκετῶν; (...) Οὐκοῦν ἀναγκάζοιτο ἄν τινας ἤδη θωπεύειν αὐτῶν τῶν δούλων καὶ ὑπισχνεῖσθαι πολλὰ καὶ ἐλευθεροῦν οὐδὲν δεόμενος, καὶ κόλαξ αὐτὸς ἂν θεραπόντων ἀναφανείη;

8 *SIG*[3] 47 (= Tod no. 24, Naupaktos, *c.* 500 BC): an errant magistrate must have his μέρος confiscated μετὰ ϝοικιατᾶν. Here we have land and workers mentioned together – is this a case of serfdom, or just slaves and land being confiscated concurrently as happened to the Attic hermokopidai? *IG* v, 2 262 = *IPArk* 8 (Mantinea, 5th c BC): offenders must have their *khremata* and *woikiatai* confiscated, but with no specific mention of land. *SEG* xxvi 449 (Epidauros, 5th c BC): 'Κάλλιπος : hικέτας / Εὐκλος hυιὸς / τὸν 'Επιδαύριον / παρ' Ἀπόλλονος / Πυθίο Ἀργεῖος / ἀρχὸς καὶ Fοικιάται', 'Kallipos, son of Eukles, an Argive leader (or: magistrate) and his *woikiatai*, a suppliant of the Epidaurians from Apollo Pythios', (there is no mention of land here, but the inscription is generally mysterious). *Woikiatai* appear in the Dodona lamellae, again inconclusively: Meyer 2018.

9 Darmezin 1999 nos. 106, 109, 112, 118, 128, 130, 132. Other slave terms are used in this corpus; see Darmezin 1999: 207–210.

10 In the USA, this would mean 'he's carrying a gun'; in Glasgow, 'he's carrying a sandwich.'

11 Davies 2005: 316. *cf.* Schmitz 2022: 106: 'But we still need to explain why a legal text – which would surely strive for semantic precision – continually switches between *woikeús/woikéa* and *dólos/dóla.*' Bile 2019: 30 also assumes that a legal text must use technical language rather than everyday language.

> Suppose some god should catch up a man who has fifty or more slaves (*andrapoda*) and waft him with his wife and children away from the city and set him down with his other possessions and his slaves (*oiketai*) in a solitude where no free man could come to his rescue. What and how great would be his fear, do you suppose, lest he and his wife and children be destroyed by the slaves (*oiketai*)? (…) And would he not forthwith find it necessary to fawn upon some of the slaves (*douloi*) and make them many promises and emancipate them, though nothing would be further from his wish? And so he would turn out to be the flatterer of his own slaves (*therapontes*). (Tr. Shorey)

It is obvious that Plato's speaker is referring to a single group of slaves, but he uses no fewer than four different words for them, perhaps just to vary the diction. Or consider Thuc. 3.73: during the *stasis* in Corcyra, the democratic and oligarchic factions made overtures to the slaves. Thucydides initially calls them *douloi.* He then remarks that the mass of the slaves sided with the democrats – but here he calls them *oiketai.*[12] Nobody would suppose that Thucydides is referring to two different groups: the two terms are obviously used synonymously for just one group.

Legal texts show the same pattern. Lines 76–78 of the Hellenistic sacred law of Andania (*IG* v,1 1390) read: 'A free man (*eleutheros*), if he is condemned, must pay back double, but a *doulos* must be whipped and pay back double the theft, but for other offences the fine is 20 drachmas. If he does not pay immediately, the master must hand over the *oiketes* to the person damaged, for working off the debt' (tr. Gawlinski, adapted).[13] The two words are clearly synonyms here – the master of an errant *doulos* did not have to go back home to collect an *oiketes* and bring him to Andania to work off the debt: the *oiketes* in question *was* the *doulos*, and could be handed over directly. Similarly, *IG* xii,5 654 from Syros contains rules for punishing a *doulos* with a whipping and simultaneously fining his master (lines 1–6). If the master does not hand over his *oiketes* for punishment, the fine is doubled (lines 6–7). If we assume that the terms apply to different persons, we must conclude that some poor *oiketes* was dragged away from whatever he was doing to be whipped for the misdeed of his *doulos* colleague. Such an interpretation is obviously improbable – the words are synonyms.

Even Athens' laws contained multiple slave terms. A Solonian (or at least, archaic) law on damages quoted at Lysias 10.19 (= Solon, *Laws* fr. 34a Leão–Rhodes) uses the term *oikeus*, the same word (minus a digamma) as the Gortynian *woikeus*; the speaker goes on to explain the meaning of the genitive form οἰκῆος in

---

[12] τῇ δ' ὑστεραίᾳ ἠκροβολίσαντό τε ὀλίγα καὶ ἐς τοὺς ἀγροὺς περιέπεμπον ἀμφότεροι, τοὺς δούλους παρακαλοῦντές τε καὶ ἐλευθερίαν ὑπισχνούμενοι: καὶ τῷ μὲν δήμῳ τῶν οἰκετῶν τὸ πλῆθος παρεγένετο ξύμμαχον, τοῖς δ' ἑτέροις ἐκ τῆς ἠπείρου ἐπίκουροι ὀκτακόσιοι.

[13] καὶ ὁ μὲν ἐλεύθερος, ἂν κατακριθεῖ, ἀποτινέτω διπλοῦν, ὁ δὲ δοῦλος μαστιγούσθω καὶ ἀποτεισάτω διπλοῦν τὸ κλέμμα, τῶν δὲ ἄλλων ἀδικημάτων ἐπιτίμιον δραχμὰς εἴκοσι· ἂν δὲ μὴ ἐκτίνει παραχρῆμα, παραδότω ὁ κύριος τὸν οἰκέταν τῶι ἀδικηθέντι εἰς ἀπεργασίαν·

the Classical Attic familiar to the court: ‘τὸ δὲ οἰκῆος θεράποντος.’[14] A later law uses *oiketes* (*IG* ii^2 1013 = *I.Eleusis* 237, line 5). Yet Athens’ laws also used the term *doulos*. Nicophon’s law on silver coinage (*SEG* xxvi 72) mentions the possibility of a slave refusing to use official currency when buying and selling: ‘If the seller is a slave or a slave woman, let them be flogged with 50 lashes of the whip by the officials to whom each matter has been assigned’ (lines 30–32, tr. Lambert & Rhodes).[15] This law also uses the term *demosios* (public slave: line: 39), as does the recently published law on the mint (line 18).[16] A quotation from the *hybris* law at Aeschin. 1.17 shows that the inscribed enactment also used the term *doulos*.

If we lacked the rich literary evidence for Athens that we currently have, and instead possessed as substantial a corpus of its inscribed law as we do for Gortyn, we might equally be debating today whether Athens had serfs and slaves rather than just one slave status that could be referred to using multiple words.[17]

(III) Gortynian law uses multiple terms for single phenomena in other instances – nobody disputes the fact that the terms *eleutheros*, *poliatas*, and *dromeus* can be used to label individuals of citizen status (albeit with different nuances). Why therefore should the synonymy of *dolos* and *woikeus* seem improbable? Likewise, the provisions on rape in column II of the Great Code express the offence in more than one way: at line 3 we find κάρτει οἴπει, ‘mount forcibly’; at lines 11–12, κάρτει δαμάσαιτο, ‘forcibly overpower’; yet a study of the fines (see below, no. X) shows that the Gortynians were thinking of a single offence. And as for the fines – their consistency and logic (see no. X, below) only emerges clearly when one converts the staters into drachmas; the Great Code uses a mixture of both.[18] On the surface, one cannot disagree with J.K. Davies’ remark that this section of the Great Code is ‘rather a mess’.[19] But a remarkable logic and consistency lurks beneath the untidy veneer. At any rate, the point is that there are internal parallels within Gortyn’s laws for variant terminology applied to individual phenomena.

(IV) There is only one term for the master of a *dolos* or *woikeus*: *pastas*, a term that means ‘owner’, and which is derived from *paomai*, the equivalent of the Attic *ktaomai*. The unitary term for master, and its overtones of ownership, betoken a single status, one of slavery rather than serfdom.[20]

---

14 Some less secure examples where paraphrases of laws may match the language of the statute: Hyp. *Ath.* 15 (*andrapodon*) & 22 (*oiketes*); Aeschin. 3.44 (*oiketes*).

15 ἐ̣ὰ̣ν δὲ δο̂λος ἦι ὁ πωλῶν ἢ δόλη, ὑπ⟨α⟩ρχέτω̣ μ[ὲν αὐτῶι] τύπτεσθαι ΠΔ πληγὰς τῆι μάστιγι ὑπὸ [τῶν ἀρχόντω]ν οἷς ἕκαστα προστέτακται.

16 Richardson 2021. For improvements to this edition, see Harris 2022.

17 *Cf.* Vlassopoulos 2016 on the atypical fields of vision afforded by Athenian evidence.

18 Lotze 1959: 17; Gagarin 2010: 17.

19 Davies 1996: 40.

20 Lotze 1959: 19; Lévy 1997: 32.

(V) When the Great Code discusses individuals generally, it discusses them in terms of free persons (*eleutheroi*) and slaves (*doloi*); that is, two – not three – basic groups (e.g., **72** I 2, 4–5, 9, 15–16).[21]

(VI) One never finds a rule stating that 'if a *dolos* or *woikeus*' does a certain thing, then certain consequences will follow: one term or the other is used, but never both side-by-side in this manner. In other words, they are never set up as alternative groups in Gortyn's laws.[22]

(VII) The equivalence of *dolos* and *woikeus* is clearest from the provisions on sexual offences in column II of the Great Code, where the terms are used interchangeably. If we take them to be synonyms, what is produced is a logical and complete[23] list of rules. If we do not, we must conclude that the drafters of the Code produced a set of rules full of gaps.[24] Tables 1 and 2 below set out these two alternative views; gaps in the tables indicate gaps in coverage. NB the Swiss cheese of holes in table 2.

Table 1: Comprehensiveness of coverage, assuming that *dolos* and *woikeus* are synonyms

Rape provisions	**Covered?**	**Seduction provisions**	**Covered?**
Rape of free by free	Yes: II 1–5	Seduction of free by free	Yes: II 16–25
Rape of free by *dolos/woikeus*	Yes: II 5–7	Seduction of free by *dolos/woikeus*	Yes: II 27–8
Rape of *dolos/woikeus* by free	Yes: II 7–9	Seduction of *dolos/woikeus* by free	
Rape of *dolos/woikeus* by *dolos/woikeus*	Yes: II 9–10	Seduction of *dolos/woikeus* by *dolos/woikeus*	Yes: II 27–8

Table 2: Comprehensiveness of coverage, if *dolos* and *woikeus* relate to distinct statuses

Rape provisions	**Covered?**	**Seduction provisions**	**Covered?**
Rape of free by free	Yes: II 1–5	Seduction of free by free	Yes: II 16–25
Rape of free by *dolos*	Yes: II 5–7	Seduction of free by *dolos*	Yes: II 25–7
Rape of free by *woikeus*		Seduction of free by *woikeus*	
Rape of *dolos* by free		Seduction of *dolos* by free	
Rape of *woikeus* by free	Yes: II 7–9	Rape of *woikeus* by free	
Rape of *dolos* by *dolos*		Seduction of *dolos* by *dolos*	Yes: II 27–8
Rape of *dolos* by *woikeus*		Seduction of *dolos* by *woikeus*	
Rape of *woikeus* by *dolos*		Seduction of *woikeus* by *dolos*	
Rape of *woikeus* by *woikeus*	Yes: II 9–10	Seduction of *woikeus* by *woikeus*	

[21] Maffi 1997: 120–121; Davies 2005: 315; Bile 2019: 31–33.

[22] Gagarin 2010: 16–17.

[23] Lipsius 1909: 398; Lotze 1959: 17–18; Maffi 1997: 121; Lévy 1997: 31; Link 2001: 91–93; Davies 2005: 315. As Lotze 1959: 24 and Link 1994: 42–43 note, it is unsurprising that the seduction of a slave woman by a free man is not penalised – this is not an accidental gap in the law.

[24] Koerner 1993: 470; Davies 1996: 42.

As the tables illustrate clearly, to assume that the words *dolos* and *woikeus* denote distinct legal statuses requires the belief that the Gortynians omitted to write laws for the majority of possible combinations of offender and victim.

(VIII) The procedure to be followed when capturing a seducer (**72** II 28–45) assumes that *dolos* is a synonym of *woikeus* for the rules to work as a complete set.[25] These rules look first from the vantage point of the aggrieved husband, and secondly from that of the seducer. The aggrieved husband must declare to the relatives of the captured (free) seducer, before three witnesses, that he must be ransomed within five days (II 28–31). If the seducer is a *dolos*, then the aggrieved husband must make the declaration to the *dolos*' owner before two witnesses (II 32–3). The law then switches to the perspective of the man accused of seduction. If the seducer claims that he was tricked by the (free) husband, then the husband must swear (if the case is worth 50 staters or more) alongside four others (or with two others for an *apetairos*) that there was no trickery (II 36–42). If the seducer claims that he was tricked by the *woikeus* husband, then the *woikeus* husband must swear alongside his owner and one other that there was no trickery (II 42–5). Unless we suppose that *dolos* and *woikeus* are synonyms, we are forced to conclude that the Gortynians had an incomplete procedure.

(IX) If we take *dolos* as a synonym of *woikeus,* then there is a logical progression in the order in which the Great Code deals with cases of rape and cases of seduction, as table 3 illustrates.[26]

Table 3: parallelism in the order of laws on sexual offences

Order of rape provisions	**Order of seduction provisions**
1. Rape of free by free (II 1–5)	1. Seduction of free by free (II 16–25)
2. Rape of free by slave (II 5–7)	2. Seduction of free by slave (II 25–6)
3. Rape of slave by free (II 7–9)	3. Seduction of slave by free – omitted
4. Rape of slave by slave (II 9–10)	4. Seduction of slave by slave (II 27–8)

(X) The ratios of the fines related to these offences further cement the conclusion that we are dealing with two terms for one status. The principle is obvious from tables 4 and 5, where the proportions of the fines are internally consistent and logical if we proceed on the assumption that *dolos* and *woikeus* are synonyms denoting the same status.[27]

---

25 Lotze 1959: 18; Link 2001: 93–95; Gagarin 2010: 18.

26 Link 2001: 90–91.

27 Link 2001: 93; Davies 2005: 315. Tables are adapted from Gagarin 2010: 17, with staters converted into drachmas.

Table 4: If the slave is a victim, the penalty is 1/40th of that exacted were the victim a free person

Reference	Offence & offender	Victim	Fine (dr.)	Ratio
II 2–4	Rape by an *eleutheros*	*eleutheros*	200	Slave victim: 1/40th penalty
II 8–9	Rape by an *eleutheros*	*woikeus*	5	
II 5–7	Rape by a *dolos*	*eleutheros*	400	Slave victim: 1/40th penalty
II 9–10	Rape by a *woikeus*	*woikeus*	10	
II 25–6	Seduction by a *dolos*	*eleuthera*	400	Slave victim: 1/40th penalty
II 27–8	Seduction by a *dolos*	*dolos*	10	

Table 5: If the slave is the offender, twice the penalty is exacted than if the offender were a free person

Reference	Offence & victim	Offender	Fine (dr.)	Ratio
II 2–4	Rape of an *eleutheros*	*eleutheros*	200	Slave offender: incurs x 2 penalty
II 5–7	Rape of an *eleutheros*	*dolos*	400	
II 20–23	Seduction of an *eleuthera*	*eleutheros*	200	Slave offender: incurs x 2 penalty
II 25–6	Seduction of an *eleuthera*	*dolos*	400	
II 8–9	Rape of a *woikeus*	*eleutheros*	5	Slave offender: incurs x 2 penalty
II 9–10	Rape of a *woikeus*	*woikeus*	10	

Thus, in different situations where a slave is the victim of an offence, the penalty imposed is consistently 1/40th of the penalty imposed in otherwise identical situations where the victim is a free person. Likewise, in situations where the offender is a slave, twice the penalty is imposed as would be the case were the offender a free person. In other words, the penal law treats *dolos* and *woikeus* as identical, and the most economical solution is to assume that the two words apply to one status, rather than to two statuses that have somehow converged from the viewpoint of penal law.

(XI) As Lipsius pointed out, we can see from another law (**41** IV 6–16) that *woikeis* could normally be sold: 'The fugitive *woikeus* is not to be sold either when he has taken refuge in a temple or within a year of when he has run away. If the fugitive belongs to someone who is *kosmos*, he is not to be sold while he is *kosmos* nor within a year of when he has run away. But if he is sold before this time, let (the seller) be convicted' (tr. Gagarin, adapted).[28] If *woikeis* were inalienable serfs bound to the soil, then these rules would be otiose – they presume that *woikeis* could normally be sold, and impose a suspension of this right in particular circumstances.[29] Since we know from **72** VII 10–15 that *doloi* could be sold, the economical solution is that we have a single status subject to sale, *viz*. one of slavery.

[28] τὸν δὲ ϝοικέα τὸν ἐπιδιόμενον μὴ ἀποδόθθαι μήτε ναεύοντα μήτ' ἦ κ' ἀπέλθηι τô ἐνιαυτô. αἰ δέ κα κοσμίοντος ἦι ὀ ἐπιδιόμενος, μὴ ἀποδόθαι ἆς κα κοσμῆι μηδ' ἦ κ' ἀπέλθηι τô ἐνιαυτô. αἰ δέ κα πρὸ τô κρόνο ἀποδôται, νικήθθο·

[29] Lipsius 1909: 399; Maffi 1997: 120–121; Link 1994: 33–34; 44–45; Link 2001: 98; Davies 2005: 316; Dickey & Probert 2017: 62. Further discussion in Maffi 2003b: 20–21; Ismard 2019: 336–337.

(XII) The law on children born to divorced women (**72** III 44–IV 23) discusses both free women and slaves. Regarding the latter, we find rules about ownership of the child of a *woikea* recently divorced from her *woikeus* husband; these slave parents belong individually to different owners.[30] Several scenarios are unpacked where the rights of ownership over the child accrue either to the mother's owner or the father's owner (III 52–IV 8). The law then comes to the issue of child exposure (IV 8–17). If the child is free, a penalty of 50 staters is imposed (lines 11–13); but if the child is a *dolos*, the penalty is 25 staters (lines 13–14). Unless we are again to suppose that the law contains gaps, the obvious conclusion is that a *woikea* has given birth to a *dolos* – which is unsurprising if we treat the terms as synonyms, but requires complex speculation to resolve if one treats the words as relating to two separate statuses.[31]

The Counterargument

A different view is presented by Gagarin (2010), followed (though with some differences) by Schmitz (2022), whilst Bile (2019) argues along similar lines. All three studies are paragons of erudition and no small amount of ingenuity; my disagreement stems not primarily from the minutiae of interpretation of individual statutes, but from a more fundamental set of prior assumptions that drives their interpretations down a completely different path to my own, and necessarily produces disagreement at the level of detail.

Put simply, all three scholars approach the inscriptions with a traditional framework of the Cretan city as comprising a citizen group ruling over an indigenous population whose ancestors were enserfed *in situ* during some early conquest, to which a later influx of 'chattel' slaves was added. The inscriptions must be fitted into this framework; *woikeis* are therefore understood as the agrarian serf group, and *doloi* the urban chattel slaves.[32] Crucially, the framework is not itself derived from the inscriptions, but from elsewhere. Gagarin's framework is a minimal one: he does not base it explicitly on later literary sources, and indeed he has firmly sided with Perlman in viewing the literary sources for Crete as highly suspect.[33] For Gagarin, the framework simply seems to be the common-sense view – and a glance at recent historiography on the topic shows why, since this idea has been present in most of the key studies of the last century, creating a kind of anchoring effect that imparts to this framework an aura of common sense regardless of its particular merits.[34] Gagarin holds an further view that shapes his interpretation, namely that

---

30 Gagarin & Perlman 2016: 359.

31 Link 2001: 96; Gagarin 2010: 20. Further discussion in Lewis 2020: 84–5.

32 Gagarin 2010: 14–15; 31, and *passim*; Bile 2019: *passim*; Schmitz 2022: 102–103; 112; 117.

33 Perlman 1992 and 2005; *cf.* Gagarin & Perlman 2016: 1–2; Gagarin 2020.

34 On the idea of the *woikeis* originating in an early conquest, see e.g., Vinogradoff 1922: 208; Busolt & Swoboda 1926: 742–744; Kirsten 1942: 108–119; Van Effenterre 1948:

dolos and *woikeus* are applied in a manner reflecting spatial and occupational differences between the agrarian and urban servile populations. His analogy to justify this view is the word *oiketes* in Attic, which he translates as 'household servant.'[35] Since on this view *oiketai* are restricted to a particular space (the house), spatial connotations can be read into the Gortynian terms too. Schmitz's framework, on the other hand, owes partly to historiographical path-dependence, but mainly to a strongly held view of the reliability of the literary sources (see below, §II). Like Gagarin, he reads a spatial distinction into the terms *dolos* and *woikeus.* Unlike Gagarin, Schmitz avers that Gortyn's land was publicly owned and divided into *klaroi* (allotments), each citizen holding a *klaros* for life and being assigned publicly owned *woikeis* to farm it.[36] Bile holds a similar view.[37] Whether one takes the minimal framework of Gagarin or the maximal ones of Bile and Schmitz, the result is similar: Gortyn's laws must be interpreted consistently with the assumption of an enserfed rural labour force called *woikeis* later supplemented by imported chattel slaves called *doloi.*

How can the inscriptions be reconciled with this framework? Gagarin, Bile, and Schmitz make one key argument that allows them to avoid many of the improbabilities incurred by claiming that *dolos* and *woikeus* must always denote different statuses. They argue that *dolos* can be used in two senses: an inclusive, catch-all sense that embraces the two putative servile sub-groups of chattel-slave *doloi* and serf *woikeis*; and a narrow, exclusive sense that relates only to the chattel slaves.[38] This is the key that unlocks the option of eluding several of the objections outlined above; and it is not methodologically improbable *per se*, since the term *eleutheros* is used in two ways in the Great Code: inclusively to encompass all legally free persons (including *apetairoi*), and exclusively to encompass citizens alone (excluding *apetairoi*).[39] Thus, of the arguments for synonymy outlined above, argument V (that general statements in the laws divide Gortynian society into *eleutheroi* and *doloi*) can be reconciled with this approach by claiming that *doloi* must be used here expansively, including *woikeis*. Argument VII (that the rape and seduction laws are full of gaps unless one supposes synonymy) can be partly countered with the same argument – i.e. that the use of *dolos* in column II of the Great Code also covers *woikeis.*[40] Argument VIII (that the procedure relating to capture of a seducer is only complete on the assumption of synonymy) can partly be

---

93–96; Willetts 1955: 47; Lotze 1959: 5–6; Koerner 1993: 468. On *doloi* as a later wave of imported slaves, Willetts 1955: 52–56; 1967: 14; Lévy 1997: 41.

35 Gagarin 2010: 22–3.

36 Schmitz 2022: 116.

37 Bile 2019: 43–46.

38 Gagarin 2010: 18, 31, and *passim*; Bile 2019: 37–39; Schmitz 2022: 106–107. *Cf.* Lotze 1959: 17.

39 Seelentag 2015: 290–291.

40 Gagarin 2010: 17; Schmitz 2022: 106.

countered with the same argument, whilst argument XII (that the *dolos* born of a *woikea* assumes synonymy) can be wholly countered on this approach.

Yet this approach does not resolve several problems. First, it treats the synonymy argument as *prima facie* implausible, probably because it is incompatible with the aforementioned framework. Yet arguments I and II show that synonymous usage of multiple slave words is perfectly normal in other Greek societies, even in statutory law, and argument III shows that Gortynian law has its own internal parallels for synonymy.[41] Furthermore, arguments VII and VIII are not fully countered – there are still gaps in coverage where the laws mention *woikeis* alone. Bile's attempt to plug them requires another swerve: in all other circumstances, *woikeus* is used only for the rural serf, yet in the laws of column II it is used expansively to include the 'chattel' slave too.[42] So now both terms can be used narrowly or expansively, and one can pick (seemingly arbitrarily) between them to save the argument – this looks very much like special pleading. Furthermore, instead of the clear logical progression of topics noted in argument IX, we have instead a strange meandering, again with gaps.

Nor can their argument explain why one only finds either *dolos* or *woikeus* in individual rules and never both side-by-side (see argument VI, *supra*). Unless we suppose that *woikeis* and *doloi* (*qua* putatively separate social groups) never came into contact, and that the *woikeis* somehow left their payments at the margins of the city like Herodotus' Carthaginian merchants (4.196), there must have been many opportunities for these rural serfs and urban slaves to come into contact and conflict. One might reply that the expansive meaning of *dolos* would cover any such case; accordingly, we do not find the two terms treated as alternatives in the Great Code. But all three scholars believe that *woikeis* had special rights to marry and own property that *doloi* lacked, and the opportunities for conflict between the two groups must have generated some rules that considered the putatively superior rights of the *woikeus*, therefore making necessary an explicit distinction between the two groups. So, if Gagarin, Schmitz, and Bile are correct, we have a surprising silence to explain in the laws. If we accept the synonymy argument, these problems vanish.[43]

What is more, a certain amount of ingenious speculation is required to explain various aspects of the laws if one follows Gagarin, Bile, and Schmitz.[44] For example, the equivalence of the fines for *doloi* and *woikeis* (argument X) must be explained by positing an unattested historical process that led both groups to occupy a single

41 This can be paralleled in other areas of Greek law, e.g., real security: Harris 2013.

42 Bile 2019: 35–6.

43 Against the notion that *doloi*/*woikeis* had rights, Link 1994: 30–51; Lewis 2013; 2020.

44 Cf. Lotze 1959: 18: 'Die komplizierten Erklärungsversuche sind dagegen überflüssig, wenn wir synonymen Gebrauch von *dolos* und *woikeus* annehmen…'

level from the viewpoint of penal law.[45] If one accepts the synonymy view, there is no need to invent such a process. As for the law that implies that *woikeis* can normally be sold (**41** IV 6–17), highly ingenious solutions are needed to save the argument. Gagarin disassociates this law from the law on selling *doloi* (**72** VII 10–15) since the *dolos* is bought in the agora: 'If a *woikeus* could be sold, he would not be sold in the agora. This would make sense if *doloi*, some of whom would be new slaves captured in war or imported from abroad, were sold in the agora, but *woikeis*, as indigenous inhabitants, were only sold directly from one master to another, perhaps only as part of the land they lived on.'[46] A few pages later, he writes: 'There is no doubt that *doloi* could be sold (…), but if *woikeis* were attached to the land, it may not have been possible to sell them except with the land to which they belonged.'[47] He concludes: 'All in all, then, it seems likely that *woikeis* could be bought and sold. Perhaps they were most often sold along with the land, but in some circumstances a serf could perhaps be sold without land.'[48] All of this presumes much that is not found the laws themselves – the origin of the *woikeis*, their relationship to the land, the impossibility of selling them in the agora. Schmitz, on the other hand, prefers not to translate the aorist infinitive middle *apodoththai* (= Att. *apodosthai*) as 'sell' as other translators have done: 'it might be better understood in the sense of "to yield" or "to give up (i.e. into the authority of another person)"; this would have included the payment of compensation for the labor of the *woikeus*.'[49] Yet as Gagarin and Perlman rightly note, middle forms of *apodidomi* are more naturally translated as 'sell'; for the sense that Schmitz suggests, the active voice is more appropriate.[50] In fact, Gortyn's laws are quite clear in using *apodidomi* in the active voice to mean 'hand over' or 'give back', and in the middle voice to mean 'sell', so if Schmitz is right, we again have a mystery to explain: why did this law not use the (unambiguous) active voice?[51] The argument seems strained here to keep the *woikeus* bound to his *klaros*. Bile strains harder: the *woikeus* who can be sold, she avers, must have committed some grave offence; for him to be sold he must have been detached from his *klaros* and recategorized as a *dolos*.[52]

In short, to maintain this framework one must repeatedly explain *ignotum per ignotius*, and in most cases these ingenious solutions are only needed because of a

---

45 Lévy 1997: 41; Davies 2005: 316; Gagarin 2010: 31. This view sits uncomfortably with the idea that the *woikeis* had special rights. If they did, then surely the *woikeis* constituted a higher social stratum than the *doloi* and warranted better treatment in the penal law.

46 Gagarin 2010: 21–22.

47 Gagarin 2010: 25.

48 Gagarin 2010: 26.

49 Schmitz 2022: 111.

50 Gagarin & Perlman 2016: 298.

51 For active forms (meaning 'give back' or 'hand over'): *IC* IV **41** III 12–13; VI 14; **47A** 8–9; **72** I 27, 28, 34–5, 47; III 5, 33–4; VI 50; IX 45; X 19; XI 17; **78** 6–8. For middle forms (meaning 'sell'): **47B** 27; **72** V 49; VI 6, 10–11, 18–19, 34, 40–41; IX 5, 11; **80** 4.

52 Bile 2019: 41, following Willetts 1967: 15.

prior commitment to the hypothesis of rural serfs later supplemented by imported chattel slaves, identified as *woikeis* and *doloi* respectively. One wonders if all this ingenuity would have been necessary had there not been an old orthodoxy to defend.

II. Serfs in literary sources?

Since these approaches to the inscriptions are mandated by prior commitment to the aforementioned framework, it is now crucial that we determine whether this framework is warranted. We must also ask whether Gagarin's view that occupational or spatial connotations can be supposed for *woikeis* based on comparison with the Attic term *oiketes* is warranted. Let us consider the latter first, before turning to the more complex issue of the literary sources for Cretan dependency.

Gagarin's view of the meaning of *oiketes* as 'household servant' is based on the relevant gloss in LSJ[9], but even these colossi of classical scholarship were, at times, in error. *Pace* Liddell, Scott, and Jones, *oiketes* simply means 'slave', and differs from *doulos* insofar as it is almost always used concretely for legally enslaved individuals, whereas *doulos* is often also used metaphorically.[53] Despite the household element in the word's etymology, *oiketes* does not in practice mean 'domestic' or 'household' slave (or servant). Indeed, many rural slaves are labelled *oiketai*. Thucydides (8.40.2) writes that the Chians had more *oiketai* than any other *polis* except Lacedaemon, and that they were particularly troublesome because of their knowledge of the countryside – he is clearly talking about agricultural slaves. Aristophanes (*Pax* 1249) mentions figs as rations for *oiketai* working in the fields, and Lysias (7.19) writes of *oiketai* digging an olive stump out of a plot. In Menander's *Epitrepontes* (line 408), the slave Syros refers to himself as an *oiketes* – but he lives in the woods working as a charcoal burner. Likewise, Tibeios in the *Heros* is a former *oiketes* (line 22) who worked as a shepherd. Menander (fr. 560 Kock = fr. 783 K–A) even remarks that 'in matters of war a man must be preeminent, for farming is the work of an *oiketes*.'[54] And we find *oiketai* working in other non-domestic settings too: in a silver mine (Dem. 37.28–9); in a shoemaking shop (Aeschin. 1.97); one can even be found engaged in long-distance maritime trade over eight hundred miles as the crow flies from his master's house ([Dem.] 34.5) – hardly domestic labour! The point here is that there are no convincing analogies for limiting the terms *dolos* or *woikeus* to some particular occupation or physical space: the parallel, rather, suggests that these terms could be applied to slaves regardless of location or occupation.[55] Again, this allows us to explain the

---

[53] Lewis 2018: 295–305.

[54] ’Εν τοῖς πολεμίοις ὑπερέχειν τὸν ἄνδρα δεῖ· τὸ γὰρ γεωργεῖν ἔργον ἐστὶν οἰκέτου.

[55] Schmitz 2022: 112–13 (*cf.* 116) understands the *woikeus* living *epi korai*, 'in the countryside' at **72** IV 34–5 as a simple statement that *woikeis* live in the countryside. But if as he thinks *woikeis* generally lived in the countryside, then *epi korai* is otiose. As Lotze 1959: 16 points out (*cf.* Lévy 1997: 30), if *dolos* and *woikeus* are synonyms with no particular application

Gortynian rules economically, and to avoid trapping ourselves by reading spatial or occupational meanings into the words and then exercising ingenious speculation to explain why one or other term is used at this or that juncture.

Let us now turn to the literary sources for Cretan dependency. I will focus on the arguments of Bile and Schmitz as they are based on the same evidence that shaped the modern historiographical tradition from which Gagarin's framework is derived; the frameworks of all three scholars have therefore a common origin. Bile argues that 'Terre et *woikeus* relèvent donc de la communauté civique. Il y aurait ainsi deux sortes de terrains, les *klaroi* alloués par la cité aux citoyens et cultivés par le *woikeus*, et ceux, de moindre rentabilité, mis en vente par la cité et entretenus par un autre non-libre, le *dōlos* des LG' (*scil.* 'Lois de Gortyne').[56] Schmitz similarly argues that 'the *woikeis* were a dependent population group, subjugated originally in war and forced into a state of slave-like dependency.'[57] Furthermore,

> 'Land was not private property, but divided into land lots (*klaroi*) and farmed by the *woikeis* "living in the *chora*," who had to pay tribute to the citizens. These tributes made up a large part of the "revenues" (*chremata*) that, upon the death of a male or female citizen, were shared out between their sons and daughters. Each citizen of Gortyn was allotted a *klaros* over which, as *pastas*, they exercised the authority of a household head. This authority over the *klaros* was probably passed on down the generations, because the heir was entitled to the "revenue" or "produce." But a *klaros* was not property, and so – like the *woikeis* themselves – could not form part of an inheritance. Both land and *woikeis* were public property.'[58]

We must now ask two questions. First, is this view of publicly owned land parceled out in usufruct justified? Such a finding would be highly unusual: in a comprehensive study of landholding across the early Greek world, Zurbach found little evidence for public ownership of land divided into allotments to be held in usufruct by citizens.[59] (And is it just a coincidence that the evidence for such arrangements invariably comes from late literary sources?) Secondly, should we believe in a publicly owned labour force enserfed in some early war?

One early writer cited by Schmitz is Aristotle, who compares Crete to Sparta (*Pol.* 1271b41–1272a1): 'The Cretan organization (*taxis*) resembles that of Sparta. At Sparta the Helots do the farming; in Crete, the *perioikoi* do the farming.' In his

---

to space or occupation like *doulos* and *oiketes* in Attic, then *epi korai* has a limiting effect of referring to a slave living in a particular place; the same goes for the *endothidia dola* at **72** II 11 (on whom, Link 1994: 45–7). Thus, it is precisely because *dolos* and *woikeus* do *not* have spatial connotations that modifiers like these must be added when spatial issues warrant discussion. See further Dickey–Probert 2017.

56 Bile 2019: 45.

57 Schmitz 2022: 117.

58 Schmitz 2022: 116–117.

59 Zurbach 2017.

discussion of the Cretan mess groups (*Pol.* 1272a13–21) Aristotle notes that: 'From all of the crops and cattle produced from the public land, and from the tribute which the *perioikoi* bring, one part is earmarked for the gods and public use, the other for the *syssitia*, so that everyone is supported by the common funds: women, children, and men.' Aristotle should be a reliable source for his own time.[60] Even so, none of this shows a publicly owned workforce, or land wholly or mostly public and shared out among citizens to hold in usufruct. Aristotle simply mentions that some of the revenues for the messes came from cattle grazed on public land – this is unsurprising, as most *poleis* had public land that constituted a source of revenue, and we know of public land used for grazing from Gortynian epigraphy (**43**Ba).[61] Nothing forces us to accept a highly unusual situation where all the city's land was publicly owned, and I agree with Gagarin and Maffi, whose arguments are based on the inscriptions, that land at Gortyn was mainly held privately.[62] Nor is there any detail here about a publicly owned workforce – the comparison to Helotage suggests the opposite, as Aristotle uses Helots to illustrate a system of *private* property subject to a certain level of communal borrowing (*Pol.* 1263a35–7).[63] Nor does he say that the *perioikoi* worked on public land. The term *perioikoi* and reference to farming suggests that Cretan slaves were mainly active in agriculture, but this does not warrant a strict division between an agrarian servile group and an urban one – after all, in Sparta most Helots worked in the country, but others served in the urban houses of their masters, with no distinction of status.[64] As for the tributes (*phoroi*) of the *perioikoi*, these are easily viewed as the revenues produced from citizens' private land, cultivated by slaves.[65]

Things become more complicated when we come to an important passage from Athenaeus (*Deip.* VI.263e–264a):

> 'Aristophanes' student Callistratus (*BNJ* 348 F4) claims that people called the Mariandynoi *dorophoroi* ("gift-bearers") as a way of removing the sting of the term *oiketai*, as the Spartiates did in the case of the Helots, the Thessalians in the case of the penestai, and the Cretans in the case of the *klarotai*. The Cretans refer to urban slaves as *chrusonetoi*, and to those in the countryside who are native-born but have been enslaved in war as *amphamiotai*; they call them *klarotai* because they are distributed by lot. Ephorus says in Book III of the *Histories* (*BNJ* 70 F29): Cretans refer to their slaves as *klarotai* because of the lot cast for them. Certain festivals in Cydonia are considered theirs; free people do not enter the city during them, and

60 Link 2002; 2008; Seelentag 2015: 93–117.

61 Rousset 2013.

62 Maffi 2003a: 177–180; Gagarin 2010: 24–25; *cf.* Link 1994: 80–82.

63 Schmitz 2022: 122 n. 83 treats the Helots as publicly owned on Ephorus' authority, making the same error as Forsdyke in attributing Strabo's words to Ephorus: see note 3, *supra*. On Helotage as private slavery, Ducat 1990: 19–29; Hodkinson 2000: 113–117; Luraghi 2002: 228–233; Lewis 2018: 126–139.

64 Hodkinson 1997.

65 Lotze 1959: 10–11; Seelentag 2015: 417–430; Lewis 2018: 162–163.

> the slaves control everything and have the authority to whip free individuals. Sosicrates says in Book II of the *History of Crete* (*BNJ* 461 F4): The Cretans refer to public slaves as *mnoiai*; to slaves who belong to private individuals as *aphamiotai*; and to the subject population as *perioikoi*. Dosiadas too, in *Kretika* book IV (*BNJ* 458 F3), says similar things.' (tr. Olson, modified)

We are here in the world of Hellenistic intellectual agonism, viewed through the lens of Roman Imperial intellectual agonism, where Athenaeus' diners try to score points by showboating their knowledge of obscure trivia mentioned in earlier Greek writers.[66] As Diodorus (5.80.4) remarks, most ancient writers about Crete disagree with each other, a sobering claim confirmed by the passage in question.[67] Athenaeus begins with a reference to Callistratus, a 2nd c BC grammarian probably based at Alexandria, who makes an improbable claim about the rationale behind the names given to several slave populations.[68] We then find a firm distinction drawn between urban and rural slaves: the urban slaves are called *chrusonetoi*, and the rural slaves (who are local and enslaved in war) are called *amphamiotai*, an alternative term for which is *klarotai* because they are distributed by lot. This claim is obviously important for the view of Schmitz and Bile on an urban/rural divide; Schmitz attributes it to Callistratus.[69] Then we have a remark by another non-Cretan writer, Sosicrates (who probably came from Rhodes), that the Cretans have public slaves called *mnoia*, privately owned slaves called *aphamiotai*, and some other kind of dependant group called *perioikoi*.[70] Finally, we have the remark that Dosiadas (who probably was Cretan) says similar things. This passage is problematic in numerous respects.

First, it is not obvious that the second sentence does derive (as Schmitz claims) from Callistratus – Jacoby does not include it in *FGrH* 348 F4, nor does Jones in *BNJ* 348 F4; it more probably derives from Athenaeus himself.[71] Secondly, the term *chrusonetoi* is suspect because the Cretan cities issued silver (and bronze) coinage, rarely gold.[72] Thirdly, as Bile notes regarding the *a(m)phamiotai*, the suffix -ώτας is not found in the Cretan dialect and is suspect, at least in the form

---

66 On intellectual agonism, Gehrke 2015: 24.

67 See Link 2001: 103–110 on the fundamentally contradictory nature of the literary sources on Cretan dependency.

68 I write 'improbable' for two reasons: first, how could Callistratus have known? Secondly, the etymology of *heilos* (see Barnes in Luraghi 2009: 286–287) is obviously not a kindly euphemism but a humiliating term of domination, whilst the etymology of *klarotas* (see the appendix to this study) underscores something similar. On Callistratus, Jones 2011.

69 Schmitz 2022: 101–102; 121.

70 On Sosicrates, Bertelli 2009.

71 Lotze 1959: 6 and Link 2001: 104 attribute it to Athenaeus.

72 Le Rider 1966: 5–198 (silver); 221–267 (bronze); even the foreign coins found on Crete (Le Rider 1966: 315–320) are almost entirely silver and bronze. Nor are there any grounds to claim (as Schmitz does) that *chrusos* can be used as a generic term for money, like *arguros* and *argurion*.

that Athenaeus presents it.[73] Fourthly, Schmitz takes Dosiadas as writing the same thing as Sosicrates, except that the Greek says *ta paraplesia*, 'similar things' – so we should expect minor contradictions.[74] Furthermore, Aristotle and Sosicrates present contradictory views. For Aristotle, the *perioikoi* are the slaves of Crete, directly comparable to Sparta's Helots. For Sosicrates they are not slaves at all, but some other dependant group distinct from the public and private slaves.[75] Whereas Athenaeus writes that the native-born slaves are called *amphamiotai*, another writer that he cites elsewhere, Hermon, says that the native-born Cretan slaves are called *mnotai* (VI.267c). And where Athenaeus claims that the *aphamiotai* are also called *klarotai*, Sosicrates has these as a privately owned slave group, whilst a publicly owned slave group is called *mnoia*. The latter claim is improbable because we find the term *mnoia* used in the *skolion* of Hybrias, also preserved by Athenaeus (15.695f–696a = *PMG* 909). Here we find an elite warrior boasting that his prowess at arms secures him various privileges, including mastery over the *mnoia*. These are obviously his own slaves, and it is a sign of how tied in knots scholars can become through refusing to countenance that some of our evidence might be faulty that Sir Denys Page, accepting Sosicrates' claim, was forced to conclude that Hybrias was an ex-public slave who had become a citizen through military service and was boasting about his mastery over his former colleagues.[76]

Despite the contradictions and improbabilities, genuine knowledge of Crete lies behind some of the claims of this passage. For example, the word *apamia* does appear in Cretan inscriptions in reference to land, suggesting some genuine Cretan origin of the word *aphamiotai*, even if the word's form was warped by non-Cretan writers.[77] Likewise, the term *mnoia* is epigraphically attested in Crete, as is a phrase in Hybrias' *skolion*.[78] And we may accept the Cretan credentials of the (epigraphically unattested) term *klarotas* as it is discussed by Ephorus, who had detailed knowledge of Crete.[79]

Schmitz attempts to extract a consistent picture from this tangle, sidestepping Sosicrates' claim that the *aphamiotai* were privately owned, viewing them instead as publicly owned, accepting Athenaeus' claim that these were the equivalent of the

[73] Bile 2019: 43.
[74] Schmitz 2022: 121.
[75] Link 2001: 106–108.
[76] Page 1965: 64–65. Page does not explain why the song of an ex-slave social climber would have become a pan-Cretan 'hit' famous enough to find its way into Athenaeus' work. As Lotze 1959: 5 notes, 'Am natürlichsten wäre es doch, wenn er sich der Herrschaft über seine eigenen Leute, nicht der über Staatssklaven rühmte, zu denen er nicht in einem unmittelbaren Verhältnis steht.'
[77] Vagionakis 2020: 237–238; Bile 2019: 42–43.
[78] See §III, *infra*. *Cf.* **243** line 3 (πρόβλημα χροός) with Hybrias' πρόβλημα χρωτός; see Martínez Fernández 2006: 77.
[79] See Link 2002; 2008; Seelentag 2015: 93–117.

klarotai, and making them the equivalent of the Gortynian *woikeis*.[80] He furthermore connects the *klarotai* to a system of publicly owned *klaroi*. But perhaps it would be better to approach Athenaeus' passage with greater scepticism: what we have here is a collection of servile status words, some of which can be independently verified as Cretan, and which have been collected and systemised by non-Cretan writers in contradictory ways. There is simply no way to verify the claims about public versus private ownership, or rural versus urban slave groups, and we have seen above the tangle that emerges if one cherry-picks this passage to construct an interpretative framework and then forces the inscriptions to fit the framework. The danger of extracting a framework from this evidence is even more apparent if one looks at the recent debate over the accuracy of quotation and paraphrase in Athenaeus' work. When Athenaeus quotes or paraphrases texts that we have complete (e.g., works of Herodotus, Homer, Xenophon, Plato), he frequently errs, particularly in the paraphrases. For fragmentary authors whose original texts we cannot check to verify Athenaeus' citations, a circumspect approach is therefore needed.[81]

But even if, for the sake of argument, we accept Schmitz's claims, then where is the evidence for an early war of enserfment and the indivisible *klaroi* held in usufruct? The direct sources for Crete are rather scant, namely the remark by Athenaeus that the Cretans call natives enslaved in war *amphamiotai*. Yet there is no reference here to a specific war, never mind an early one; in a Cretan context there are rather a few wars from which to choose. Yet Schmitz's argument does not depend on a direct source for such an early war, but on the fact that Cretan dependants belong to a general category of Helot-like statuses, all of which supposedly originated in early wars of conquest.[82] Plato first compared Helotage to Thessalian and Herakleian forms of slavery, and Aristotle extended the comparison to Crete (Pl. *Leg.* 777b–d; Arist. *Pol.* 1330a25–33), but they did not make the comparison on the grounds of a special serf status *metaxy eleutheron kai doulon* or origins in mass conquest – they referred to these groups as *douloi*, and their criterion of comparison was that all these servile populations were monoglot and therefore a hazard from the perspective of management. Thus, we are not talking about a distinct group of systems defined by a set of consistent features, but a loose comparison based on just one shared trait: linguistic unity. And it is only relatively late in the tradition of Helot-comparison that ideas of non-slave status creep in.[83]

It is nonetheless true that various ancient writers accounted for the origins of e.g., the Helots and *penestai* in war; Schmitz considers these traditions as uncomplicatedly historical.[84] Regarding these traditions of early conquest, two points need to be made. First, as Luraghi has shown, not all ancient writers accounted for the origins

80 Schmitz 2022: 121.
81 Olson 2018, with reference to the wider debate.
82 Schmitz 2022: 123.
83 I discuss this further in Lewis, forthcoming (a).
84 Schmitz 2022: 99–104, esp. 104 n. 23.

of these groups in terms of conquest.[85] The earliest tradition on Helot origins (Antiochus *BNJ* 555 F13) views them not as conquered natives but as demoted Spartiates. For fourth century Spartans, the Messenian Helots were not the descendants of the Messenians of old, but slaves from here and there (Isoc. 6.28; 87–8). And [Aristotle] (fr. 586 Rose = fr. 603,1 Gigon) concurs regarding the Kallikyrioi of Syracuse: 'they were named from the fact that, though being of disparate origins, they came together in the same place, as Aristotle writes in his *Constitution of the Syracusans*; (they were) like the Helots among the Lacedaemonians, the *penestai* among the Thessalians, and the *klarotai* among the Cretans.'[86] If one thing is clear from this mysterious comment, it is that the Aristotelian *Constitution of the Syracusans* regarded the Kallikyrioi not as some aboriginal population enslaved *in situ*, but as having disparate origins (*pantodapoi*).[87]

Secondly, and more fundamentally, these conquest traditions are not credible historical sources: they are Just-So stories, aetiologies invented and passed down to account for the origins of the slave systems of these regions. We find no sign of these mass conquests in genuine archaic sources; they belong to the genre of politically inflected charter stories, part of what Gehrke calls 'intentional history.'[88] Comparative considerations further cement this conclusion, for as Luraghi notes, Orlando Patterson's wide-ranging survey of historical slave systems across the globe found only one example of a people successfully reduced to slavery *in situ* by incoming conquerors – Sparta's Helots, a fact that itself casts doubt on the Helot conquest tradition.[89] Thus it is hard to disagree with Luraghi's remark that 'the main reason for being sceptical of the modern *vulgata* on the origins of helotry concerns its inherent implausibility.'[90] As for state-owned *klaroi* allotted to the citizenry to hold in usufruct, one must leave Crete to find clear evidence, and proceed to Sparta and the 'Lycurgan' system of land tenure set out in Plu. *Lyc.* 8.3 & 16.1. The historicity of this system, however, has been demolished by Hodkinson: it is contradicted not only by an early, reliable source (Arist. *Pol.* 1271a15–b6), but by Plutarch himself, who presents a completely different reconstruction of Spartan land tenure in his *Life of Agis* (5.1–2). Public ownership of all land and Helots is a relic of the Spartan revolution of the late third century.[91]

---

85 Luraghi 2003.

86 ὠνομάσθησαν δ' ἀπὸ τοῦ εἰς ταὐτὸ συνελθεῖν παντοδαποὶ ὄντες, ὡς Ἀριστοτέλης ἐν Συρακοσίων πολιτείᾳ, ὅμοιοι τοῖς παρὰ Λακεδαιμονίοις εἵλωσι καὶ παρὰ Θεσσαλοῖς πενέσταις καὶ παρὰ Κρησὶ κλαρώταις. Ducat 1990: 33 omits from his quotation the text before ὡς, but notes that ὡς Ἀριστοτέλης ἐν Συρακοσίων πολιτείᾳ refers syntactically to the prior statement. Lotze 1959: 7 doubts the Aristotelian credentials of the comparison introduced by ὅμοιοι: „Der Vergleich scheint aber nicht mehr von ihm zustammen“.

87 As noted in van Wees 2022: 33.

88 Gehrke 2015.

89 Luraghi 2002: 237–238.

90 Luraghi 2002: 236.

91 Hodkinson 2000: 65–112; Kennell 2003.

Can epigraphical evidence save the argument? The only mention of the term *klaros* in Gortynian law occurs at **72** V 25–7. Here, after running through the pecking order of persons with a claim on the inheritance, the law considers a scenario where no descendants or collateral relatives exist or survive: 'And if there should be no claimants, those of the household who are the *klaros* are to have the property.'[92] Solutions to what *klaros* means in this very opaque and difficult rule have been admirably summarised by Mandalaki: (i) the family plot (but this is unlikely, as the phrase refers to heirs, and not to a category of the inheritance itself); (ii) dependant cultivators, i.e. the *woikeis* (but this is unlikely, as they could just have been named as such; anyhow, this would represent a surprising leapfrogging of citizens, freedmen and *apetairoi* up the status hierarchy); (iii) the *genos* of the deceased (but this is unlikely, as it is already accommodated in the prior lines); (iv) the neighbours; and (v) members of a larger military unit such as the Thessalian *kleros* (each of which provided forty cavalry and eighty foot soldiers for the Thessalian army).[93] To this set of solutions we must now add a variant of (ii), as Schmitz suggests a different understanding of the sentence's syntax, with *tas woikias* understood as an objective genitive going with *epiballontes*, 'And if there should be no claimants to the *woikia*, those who are the *klaros* are to have the property.'[94] Schmitz then suggests two categories of property: the *woikia* (comprising the yields of the *klaros* qua land-lot), and the rest of the property, with the *woikeis* becoming the recipients of the former. Here is not the place to attempt to crack this classic chestnut; rather, we may note that even on Schmitz's reconstruction, the *klaros* in the rule is not taken to be a plot of land but a group of prospective heirs. One must conjecture that they are being referred to metonymically because they work on a *klaros* to squeeze even an oblique reference to land out of the law.

To sum up so far: the framework that mandates the approach to the *dolos–woikeus* problem taken by Gagarin, Schmitz, and Bile does not derive from the inscriptions. It derives partly from literary sources on Crete, but mostly from a bricolage of late sources that describe the model Dorian conquering state, Sparta, and which is then generalised everywhere that had populations that were (at some point) compared to Helotage. If we reject this framework (as most historians of Sparta have done), then we can cut the Gordian knot of servile status in Gortyn's laws by taking the far more economical synonymy view sketched above (§I). If we adhere to the framework, we must perforce worsen the tangle.

None of this is to say that Cretan slavery was simply the same as slavery elsewhere – it evidently had distinctive traits. One feature that garnered comparison to Helotage was, as noted above, linguistic unity, which makes sense in terms of

---

[92] αἰ δὲ μὲ εἶεν ἐπιβάλλοντες, τᾶς ϝοικίας οἵτινές κ᾽ ἴοντι ὁ κλᾶρος, τούτονς ἔκεν τὰ κρέματα.
[93] Mandalaki 2000. Sensible discussion also in Lévy 1997: 37–39.
[94] Schmitz 2022: 119.

Crete's relatively low-volume foreign trade. We may expect therefore that slaves were mostly acquired via birth, local wars, and short-range piracy. And we may accept too a complex social organisation among the Gortynian slave population, where traditional family structures were crosscut by the entangled ownership rights of multiple masters.[95] This all fits rather well with Aristotle's claims that Crete's slaves mainly worked in farming and were afforded similar things to the free except for the right to bear arms and attend the gymnasium (*Pol.* 1264a20–2).[96] Thus I fully agree with Schmitz's claim that 'Mariandyni, *penestai*, helots and *klarotai* were dependent rural populations whose living conditions and form of life were fundamentally different from the slavery practised in classical Athens and many other Greek cities.'[97] As for the long-term development of Crete's slave system, a better approach than relying on late literary sources, nineteenth-century stage-theories about the evolution of landed property rights, or models of the Dorian conquest-state[98], might be to take Seelentag's 'epic perspective' and begin with Homer, viewing Archaic and Classical Cretan cities as outgrowths from the kind of society depicted in the epics.[99] In the *Odyssey* Eumaeus is described as an *oikeus* (14.4, 63) who works in the country herding animals, inhabits a small hut, and knows that had his master not been abroad, he would have rewarded him with a house, a plot of land, and a wife (14.61–7; 21.213–16; *cf.* 24.383–90). Even still, Eumaeus manages to accumulate enough possessions to buy his own slave, Mesaulius (14.449–52). Is this much different from the Gortynian *woikeus* who dwells in the country herding animals (**72** IV 33–6), who can marry a *woikea* (**72** III 40–4) and accumulate possessions? Seen in this light, Cretan slavery emerges as parochial and traditional, untransformed by the networks of long-distance trade that filled regions such as Attica with barbarian slaves from across the known world, exploited in a vast array of occupations.

III. Serfs in Hellenistic Treaties?

What of the Hellenistic era? The main recent article-length studies of Hellenistic Cretan forced labour are by Pałuchowski, but he shares the same view as many of the studies mentioned above that there must have been two systems of forced labour on Crete, *viz.* an older form of collective servitude and a newer form of chattel slavery.[100] The foregoing discussion should, I hope, cast doubt on the

---

95 Lotze 1959: 20–24; Lewis 2013, esp. 403–404; Vlassopoulos 2021: 171–172; Schmitz 2022: 108–109.

96 This claim is borne out in Gortyn's laws where rules on e.g., sexual offences, marriage, divorce, debt-bondage, etc. for slaves are modelled on the parallel provisions for the free, *mutatis mutandis*.

97 Schmitz 2022: 105.

98 As can be seen in dizzying profusion in e.g., Busolt & Swoboda 1926; Kirsten 1942.

99 See Seelentag 2015: 58–128. *Cf.* Lotze 1959: 20.

100 See Pałuchowski 2020, with references to his earlier studies.

security of this view. More immediately, we might note Chaniotis' entry at *SEG* li 1135 in relation to Link's 2001 article. Chaniotis summarises Link's view, states his disagreement, and then writes as follows: 'A new Hellenistic treaty, which will be published by B. Apostolakou, attests μνωΐα and οἰκετήια as two separate categories of dependent population, thus disproving L.'s views at least for the Hellenistic period; but until this text is published there is no point in critically reviewing L.'s discussion of the literary sources and the inscriptions on Cretan slavery.'

Apostolakou's edition has since been published (*SEG* lxiii 747), and we may now critically review Link's claims. It is an alliance between Hierapytna and Aptera from the late third century. After stating the establishment of an alliance (lines 5–6), the text then deals with a situation where the land of the Hierapytnians is invaded or annexed, or where attacks are mounted against harbours or islands or garrisons, ἢ μνωίαν̣ [φθείρηι (lines 6–9) – that is, the killing of the *mnoia* by some enemy. The same provisions apply if there is an invasion of the land of the Apterans, including attacks on their *mnoia* (lines 11–15). Yet there is no sign of οἰκετήια here.

Two other treaties of this sort employ similar formulae: *IC* I xvi 17 (Chaniotis, *Verträge* no. 37) and *SEG* xli 742 (Chaniotis, *Verträge* no. 38). The latter treaty, between Aptera and Eleutherna from the early second century, follows a similar format to *SEG* lxiii 747. Here we have the scenario of an invasion or annexation of Apteran land, but we quickly get into the square brackets, where we find (lines 8–9) the phrase: [ἢ φθείρηι κλάρος ἢ οἰκετήιαν] ἢ φρ̣ῴρ̣ι̣[α ἢ νάσος ἢ λιμένας καταλαμβάνηται ἢ πολεμῆι]. The counter-scenario, with an invasion or annexation of the land of the Eleuthernians, contains the same clause, similarly damaged and heavily restored (lines 13–15). Instead of the *mnoia* of *SEG* lxiii 747, we have the word *oiketeia* restored twice in this inscription. A glance at *Verträge* 37, line 16 shows that this restoration has a good parallel:

εἰ δέ τίς κ' ἐνβάλληι ἐς τὰ[ν]
[τῶν Ἐλευθερναίων χώρ]αν ἢ ἀποτάμνηται ἢ φρώρια ἢ λιμένα[ς]
[καταλαμβάνηι ἢ κλάρος φ]θείρηι ἢ οἰκετήιαν ἢ πολεμῆι, β[οα]θέτ[ω]
[ὁ Λάτιος ἀπροφασίστως] κατὰ γᾶν καὶ κατὰ θάλ[ασσαν παντὶ]
[σθένει, ὡσαύτως δὲ εἴ τίς κα ἐ]ς τὰν τῶν Λατίων χ[ώραν ἐνβάλληι]
[ἢ ἀποτάμνηται ἢ φρ]ώρια ἢ νάσος ἢ λι[μένας καταλαμβάνηι]
[ἢ κλάρος φθείρηι ἢ οἰκετήιαν, τ]ὰν ὀφει[λομέναν βοάθειαν]
[πεμπέτω ὁ Ἐλευθερναῖος κτλ. — — — — —]

If we accept the restoration, the Apterans referred to their slave population as *oiketeia* in *Verträge* 38 yet as *mnoia* in *SEG* lxiii 747. Must this mean that the Apterans had two different servile populations, as Chaniotis seems to suggest? Yet even assuming the correctness of the restoration *oiketeian* at *Verträge* 38, these can easily be explained as synonyms (see arguments I–II and VI, *supra*); if we assume that they relate to different groups, then we must suppose that each treaty omitted to protect one of these putative groups. *Pace* Chaniotis, Link's argument stands.

Were the *mnoia* and *oiketeia* in these treaties slaves or serfs? The linguistic parallels suggest slavery. The most obvious parallel for the use of an abstract noun in referring to the slave population is the Peace of Nicias, which obligates the Athenians to assist the Spartans if ἡ δουλεία revolts (Thuc. 5.23.3; *cf.* Pl. *Leg.* 776d; Arist. *Pol.* 1264a36). An inscription from Olbia (*SIG*^{3} 495) narrates an attack on its land and *oiketeia* (side B line 15) by barbarian tribes. A Hellenistic inscription from Magnesia (*SIG*^{3} 695B) makes provision for the annual festival of Artemis, where children shall be excused their lessons and the slave population (*oiketeia*) its tasks (lines 12–13). An almost identical clause mentioning *oiketeia* exists in an inscription from Hellenistic Kaïkos in Mysia regarding a festival of Demeter and Kore (*IMT Kaïkos* 818, lines 53–5).

But what about the term *klaros* sitting snugly next to these servile groups in *Verträge* 37 and 38, to be understood here as *<tos> klaros*, (i.e., *tous klerous* in Attic, an accusative plural); do we not have proof here of the attachment of *oiketeia* to land lots? Yet in both inscriptions the word is restored, and a search for the term *klaros* in Vagionakis' comprehensive collection of 600 Cretan institutional inscriptions turns up only **72** V 25–7 as a parallel; we have already seen that the equation of this *klaros* with a plot of land is improbable. Indeed, the complete absence of the word *klaros* meaning 'land-lot' from Crete's rich institutional epigraphy is rather remarkable given the centrality of *klaroi* to modern historical reconstructions of Cretan land tenure. The elaborate system of publicly owned *klaroi* that supposedly structured all Cretan cities turns out, as Link has noted, to be a chimera of modern research.[101] The restoration of *klaros* in *Verträge* 37 and 38 is not Chaniotis' fault; it is already there in *Inscriptiones Creticae* for *Verträge* 37, with the justificatory note *ad loc.* by Guarducci, 'praedia sorte divisa, ubi servi insidunt' ('farms divided by lot, on which slaves are settled').[102] Is not the whole problem of modern approaches to Cretan dependency perfectly captured here, where a reference to the servile population is inconceivable without mention of land allotments? The idea of serfdom has been around for so long in modern historiography that it can easily be restored into the gaps in our sources, either editorially or historically, based on apparently common-sense assumptions about what must have been the case derived from nineteenth-century certainties about Dorian invasions, state-controlled landholdings, and enserfed workers parcelled out to hold in usufruct and bound to the land. But if one chips away these modern historiographical and editorial accretions from the real evidence, serfs are nowhere to be found.

david.lewis@ed.ac.uk

[101] Link 2001: 109.

[102] The restoration *klaros* is not present in an earlier edition, *SGDI* IV pp. 1040–1.

APPENDIX: THE TERM κλαρώτας

Luraghi has rightly noted that the etymology of *klarotas* derives from the practice of dividing up war booty by lot – a *klarotas* is an 'allotted person'.[103] There is no need to limit this to some early war of conquest or to suppose that the *klarotas* must be bound to a land lot (*klaros*). War was a regular feature of Cretan life throughout its pre-Roman history.[104] Whereas elsewhere booty became the property of the state, the archaic custom of dividing booty by lot among warriors (e.g., Hom. *Od.* 39–42) persisted in Hellenistic Crete. For instance, *IC* III iii 4 (= Chaniotis, *Verträge* 28), an alliance between Hierapytna and Priansos, stipulates (lines 53–8) that 'if we should, gods willing, seize something good from our enemies, either if we campaign together or if the citizens of the two cities do it privately, by land or by sea, let them draw lots among themselves according to the number of men who came along; and they shall each bring a tithe to their own city.'[105] The respective *poleis* do get shares – each gets a tithe. But the bulk of the booty is divided by lot (λανχανόντων) according to the number of warriors participating in the expedition – each warrior therefore gets a private share of the booty, and this must often have included slaves. It could then be the case that *klarotas* always meant 'war captive.' Alternatively (and more probably, due to Ephorus' general application of the word to Cretan slaves), perhaps the term had its origin this way but subsequently became a general slave term, like Εἵλως (Helot) which also has military derivation from 'bound' captives, but was subsequently applied to all Helots, regardless of whether they were captured or born into slavery.[106] I remain agnostic on which of the two is correct; but only preconceived notions of serfdom require the *klarotas* to be bound to a plot of land.

BIBLIOGRAPHY

Bertelli, L. 2009. 'Sosikrates (461)', in I. Worthington (ed.), *Jacoby Online. Brill's New Jacoby, Part III*. Leiden.

Bile, M. 2019. '*Woikeus* et *dōlos* à Gortyne au Ve siècle', in L. Gagliardi & L. Pepe (eds.), *Dike. Essays on Greek Law in Honor of Alberto Maffi*. Milan: 29–47.

Busolt, G. & H. Swoboda. 1926. *Griechische Staatskunde. Zweite Hälfte*. Munich.

---

[103] Luraghi 2009: 267.

[104] See Lewis forthcoming (c), with reference to further studies.

[105] αἰ δέ τι θεῶν βωλομένων ἕλοιμεν ἀγαθὸν ἀπὸ τῶν πολεμίων, ἢ κοινᾶι ἐξοδούσαντες ἢ ἰδίαι τινὲς παρ' ἑκατέρων ἢ κατὰ γᾶν ἢ κατὰ θάλασσαν, λανχανόντων ἑκάτεροι κατὰ τὸς ἄνδρας τὸς ἕρποντας καὶ τὰς δεκάτας λαμβανόντων ἑκάτεροι ἐς τὰν ἰδίαν πόλιν.

[106] Barnes in Luraghi 2009: 286–287.

Chaniotis, A. 1996. *Die Verträge zwischen kretischen Poleis in der hellenistischen Zeit.* Stuttgart.

Darmezin, L. 1999. *Les Affranchissements par consécration en Béotie et dans le monde grec hellénistique.* Nancy.

Davies, J.K. 1996. 'Deconstructing Gortyn: when is a code a code?' in Foxhall, L. & A.D.E. Lewis (eds.) *Greek Law in its Political Setting.* Oxford: 33–56

Davies, J.K. 2005. 'The Gortyn laws' in Gagarin, M. & D. Cohen (eds.) *The Cambridge Companion to Ancient Greek Law.* Cambridge: 305–27.

Dickey, E. & P. Probert, 2015. 'Houses in which a serf living in the country does not reside: A reconsideration of Gortyn Laws column 4 lines 31–37', in A. Willi (ed.) *Sprachgeschichte und Epigraphik: Festgaben für Rudolf Wachter zum 60. Geburtstag.* Innsbruck: 57–81.

Ducat, J. 1990. *Les Hilotes.* Athens.

Ducat, J. 1994. *Les pénestes de Thessalie.* Besançon.

Forsdyke, S. 2021. *Slaves and Slavery in Ancient Greece.* Cambridge.

Gagarin, M. 2010. 'Serfs and slaves at Gortyn', *Zeitschrift der Savigny-Stiftung für Rechtsgeschichte, Romanistische Abteilung* 127: 14–31.

Gagarin, M. 2020. 'Cretan laws and the early polis', in Dimopoulou, A., Helmis, A. & D. Karambelas (eds.) ΙΟΥΛΙΑΝ ΒΕΛΙΣΣΑΡΟΠΟΥΛΟΥ ΕΠΑΙΝΕΣΑΙ. *Studies in Ancient Greek and Roman Law.* Athens: 97–109.

Gagarin, M. & P. Perlman. 2016. *The Laws of Ancient Crete c. 650–400 BCE.* Oxford.

Gehrke, H.-J. 2015. 'Greek representations of the past', in Foxhall, L., Gehrke, H.-J. & N. Luraghi (eds.) *Intentional History: Spinning Time in Ancient Greece.* Stuttgart: 15–34.

Harris, E.M. 2013. 'Finley's *Studies in Land and Credit* sixty years later', *DIKE* 16: 123–46.

Harris, E.M. 2022. 'Notes on the new law of Epicrates from the Athenian agora', *ZPE* 222: 65–81.

Hodkinson, S. 1997. 'Servile and free dependents of the Classical Spartan oikos', in M. Moggi & G. Cordiano (eds.) *Schiavi e Dipendenti nell'ambito dell'Oikos and della Familia.* Pisa: 45–71.

Hodkinson, S. 2000. *Property and Wealth in Classical Sparta.* Swansea.

Ismard, P. 2019. *La cité et ses esclaves.* Paris.

Jones, N.F. 2011. 'Kallistratos (348)', in I. Worthington (ed.), *Jacoby Online. Brill's New Jacoby, Part III.* Leiden.

Kennell, N. 2003. '*Agreste genus*: Helots in Hellenistic Laconia' in Luraghi, N. & S. Alcock (eds.) *Helots and their Masters in Laconia and Messenia.* Cambridge MA & London: 81–105.

Kirsten, E. 1942. *Das dorische Kreta. Die Insel Kreta im fünften und vierten Jahrhundert.* Würzburg.

Le Rider, G. 1966. *Monnaies crétoises du Ve au Ier siècle av. J.–C.* Paris.

Lévy, E. 1997. 'Libres et non-libres dans le Code de Gortyne' in Brule, P. & J. Oulhen (eds.) *Esclavage, guerre, economie en Grece ancienne: Hommages a Yvon Garlan.* Rennes: 25–41.

Koerner, R. 1993. *Inschriftliche Gesetzestexte der frühen griechischen Polis*. Cologne, Weimar & Vienna.

Lewis, D.M. 2013. 'Slave marriages in the laws of Gortyn: A matter of rights?' *Historia* 62.4: 390–416.

Lewis, D.M. 2018. Greek Slave Systems in their Eastern Mediterranean Context, c. 800–146 BC. Oxford.

Lewis, D.M. 2020. 'Legal knowledge in Gortyn: debt bondage and the liability of slaves in Gortynian law' in C. Ando & W.P. Sullivan (eds.) *The Discovery of the Fact*. Ann Arbor: 72–90.

Lewis, D.M. forthcoming (a). 'The local slave systems of ancient Greece' in Tandy, D.W. & S.D. Gartland (eds.) *Voiceless, Invisible, and Countless: The Experience of Subordinates in Greece, 800–300 BC.* Oxford; 155–83.

Lewis, D.M. forthcoming (b). Slavery and Ancient Greek Economic Development. Berlin.

Lewis, D.M. forthcoming (c). 'The Cretan way of war: status, violence and values from the Classical period to the Roman conquest', *JHS*

Link, S. 1994. *Das griechische Kreta. Untersuchungen zur seiner staatlichen und gesellschaftlichen Entwicklung vom 6. bis zum 4. Jahrhundert v. Chr*. Stuttgart.

Link, S. 2001. 'Dolos und Woikeus im Recht von Gortyn', *DIKE* 4: 87–112.

Link, S. 2002. '100 Städte, 100 Verfassungen? Einheitlichkeit und Vielfalt in den griechischen Städten Kretas', *Cretan Studies* 7, 149–175.

Link, S. 2008. 'Aristoteles, Ephoros und die "Kretische Verfassung"', *Gymnasium* 115, 469–479.

Lipsius, J.H. 1909. *Zum Recht von Gortyns.* Abhandlungen der sächsischen Gesellschaft der Wissenschaft, phil.-hist. Kl. XXVII no. 11. Leipzig: 393–410.

Lotze, D. 1959. *ΜΕΤΑΞΥ ΕΛΕΥΘΕΡΩΝ ΚΑΙ ΔΟΥΛΩΝ. Studien zur Rechtsstellung unfreier Landbevölkerungen in Griechenland bis zum 4. Jahrhundert v.Chr*. Berlin.

Luraghi, N. 2002. 'Helotic slavery reconsidered', in A. Powell & S. Hodkinson (eds.) *Sparta: Beyond the Mirage.* London: 229–250.

Luraghi, N. 2003. 'The imaginary conquest of the helots', in N. Luraghi and S. Alcock (eds.), *Helots and their Masters in Laconia and Messenia: Histories, Ideologies, Structures.* Cambridge, MA: 109–141.

Luraghi, N. 2009. 'The helots: comparative approaches, ancient and modern' in S. Hodkinson (ed.) *Sparta: Comparative Approaches.* Swansea: 261–304.

Maffi, A. 1997. *Il diritto di famiglia nel Codice di Gortina*. Milan.

Maffi, A. 2003a. 'Studi recenti sul Codice di Gortina', *DIKE* 6: 161–225.

Maffi, A. 2003b. 'L'asilo degli schiavi nel diritto di Gortina' in M. Dreher (ed.) *Das antike Asyl. Kultische Grundlagen, rechtliche Ausgestaltung und politische Funktion.* Cologne: 15–22.

Mandalaki, A. 2000. 'Ο κλᾶρος στὴ μεγάλη δωδεκάδελτο ἐπιγραφὴ τῆς Γόρτυνος', *Tekmeria* 5: 71–86.

Martínez Fernández, Á. 2006. *Epigramas Helenísticos de Creta.* Madrid.

Meyer, E. 2018. 'Slavery and paramonē in the Dodona lamellae', in L. Soueref (ed.), *Dodona: The Omen's Questions. New Approaches in the Oracular Tablets.* Ioannina: 151–57.

Olson, S.D. 2018. 'Athenaeus' "fragments" of non-fragmentary prose authors and their implications', *AJP* 139: 423–50.

Page, D.L. 1965. 'The song of Hybrias the Cretan', *PCPS* 11, 62–5.

Pałuchowski, A. 2020. 'Les formes de dépendance dans la Crète hellénistique: essai de classification dans le contexte socio-politique et économique de l'époque', in R. Cantilena & F. Carbone (eds.), *Monetary and Social Aspects of Hellenistic Crete.* Florence: 185–204.

Perlman, P. 1992. 'One hundred-citied Crete and the "Cretan ΠΟΛΙΤΕΙΑ"', *Classical Philology* 87, 193–205.

Perlman, P. 2005. 'Imagining Crete', in M.H. Hansen (ed.) *The Imaginary Polis.* Copenhagen: 282–334.

Richardson, M. 2021. 'The law of Epicrates of 354/3', *Hesperia* 90.4: 685–746.

Rousset, D. 2013. 'Sacred and public property in the Greek city', *JHS* 133: 113–133.

Schmitz, W. 2022. 'Dependent rural populations in archaic and classical Greece: free, slave, or between free and slave?' in Bischoff, J. & S. Conermann (eds.) *Slavery and Other Strong Forms of Asymmetrical Dependencies.* Berlin & Boston: 99–126.

Ste. Croix, G. E. M. de, 1981. *The Class Struggle in the Ancient Greek World.* London.

Seelentag, G. 2015. *Das archaische Kreta. Institutionalisierung im frühen Griechenland.* Berlin and Boston.

Vagionakis, I. 2020. Kretikai politeiai. Le istituzioni cretesi dal VII al I secolo a.C. Diss. Ca' Foscari, Venice.

Van Effenterre, H. 1948. La Crète et le monde grec de Platon a Polybe. Paris.

Van Wees, H. 2022. 'The archaic period', in S. von Reden (ed.) *The Cambridge Companion to the Ancient Greek Economy.* Cambridge: 29–48.

Vinogradoff, P. 1922. *Outlines of Historical Jurisprudence Vol. II: The Jurisprudence of the Greek City.* Oxford.

Vlassopoulos, K. 2016. 'Qui savons-nous vraiment de la société athénienne?' *Annales HSS* 71.3: 659–82.

Vlassopoulos, K. 2021. *Historicizing Ancient Slavery.* Edinburgh.

Willetts, R.F. 1955. *Aristocratic Society in Ancient Crete.* London.

Willetts, R.F. 1967. *The Law Code of Gortyn.* Berlin.

Zurbach, J. 2017. *Les hommes, la terre et la dette en Grèce, c. 1400–c. 500 a.C.* Bordeaux.

ALBERTO MAFFI (MILAN)

IL MATRIMONIO DEGLI SCHIAVI NEL CODICE DI GORTINA: RISPOSTA A D.M. LEWIS

Nella sua comunicazione Lewis afferma, nella scia di una cospicua schiera di interpreti del Codice di Gortina (= CdG), che *dolos* e *woikeus* nel CdG sono sinonimi e non designano due statuti diversi. Ammettiamo che gli argomenti messi in campo da Lewis siano convincenti. Non ne esaminerò qui nel dettaglio l'attendibilità, tenendo conto del fatto che gli argomenti sviluppati dall'opinione contraria sono stati da lui ben illustrati in un paragrafo della sua stessa comunicazione. Mi concentrerò invece sulla conseguenza che Lewis trae dalla sua presa di posizione: cioè che gli schiavi menzionati nel CdG, comunque denominati, sono 'slaves', non 'serfs'. Per valutare questa affermazione occorre naturalmente intendersi sul significato che 'slaves' e 'serfs' assumono quando si vuole descrivere la schiavitù nella Grecia antica. Per quanto riguarda la Gortina del CdG, Lewis ammette l'esistenza di "a complex social organisation among the Gortynian slave population, where traditional family structures were crosscut by the entangled ownership rights of multiple masters" (p. 16). E conclude (aderendo all'opinione recentemente espressa da Schmitz 2022) che 'Mariandyni, *penestai*, helots and *klarotai* were dependent rural populations whose living conditions and form of life were fundamentally different from the slavery practised in classical Athens and many other Greek cities.'[1] Ora, a parte il fatto che nel CdG (e nelle iscrizioni coeve) non ricorre il termine *klarotai*, sembra di capire che Lewis ascrive i *doloi/woikeis* a un tipo di schiavitù riconducibile al modello ilotico[2]. Un modello ilotico tuttavia diverso da quello costruito e tramandato dalla dottrina dominante, secondo cui, semplificando, gli Iloti spartani erano discendenti di popolazioni locali assoggettate dagli invasori *manu militari*, i cui componenti, ridotti a schiavi pubblici organizzati in gruppi familiari, coltivavano, in forza di una sorta di rapporto di mezzadria, le terre assegnate dalla polis a ciascun Spartiata. Secondo Lewis, invece, che si rifa qui alle tesi sviluppate negli ultimi due decenni soprattutto da Hodkinson e Luraghi, gli Iloti sarebbero sostanzialmente schiavi privati (ai cui padroni Spartiati sarebbero però imposte alcune limitazioni concernenti l'esercizio del loro diritto di proprietà);

---

[1] Ma l'adesione alle posizioni di Schmitz risulta ambigua, dato che, secondo quest'ultimo studioso, gli schiavi cretesi si inquadrano piuttosto nella categoria dei 'serfs'.

[2] Qui mi rifaccio, per esporre in modo più compiuto il suo pensiero, anche ai precedenti lavori di Lewis, 2013 e 2018 in particolare.

e il modello ilotico, che le fonti (in particolare Platone e Aristotele) ci presentano, sarebbe caratterizzato essenzialmente da un unico elemento che lo distingue dal modello caratteristico di un regime di schiavitù-merce, cioè dal fatto che i componenti di tali popolazioni parlano la stessa lingua. Secondo Lewis, quindi, la schiavitù cretese, quale ce la presenta in particolare il CdG, sarebbe riconducibile, almeno nelle linee essenziali, al modello ilotico riveduto e corretto secondo la tesi revisionistica a cui abbiamo accennato. Ora, proprio la principale caratteristica che, secondo Lewis, dovrebbe caratterizzare tale modello, cioè il fatto che gli schiavi in questione parlino la stessa lingua, è impossibile da accertare per Gortina. Lewis, invece, lo dà per scontato non solo per Sparta ma anche per Creta, e lo fa derivare dal fatto che queste poleis sarebbero tagliate fuori dal commercio internazionale, ivi compreso quindi il commercio di schiavi provenienti da terre lontane[3]. Come scrive Lewis (p. 16 della sua comunicazione), "We may expect therefore that slaves were acquired via birth, local wars, and short-range piracy". Per quanto riguarda in particolare quest'ultimo punto si può obiettare che i Cretesi erano conosciuti proprio per attività piratesche non certo limitate alle coste dell'isola, come dimostrano i trattati con Mileto del III sec. a.C.[4] Per di più nel CdG (col. VII 10–15) si parla di schiavi acquistati al mercato. Probabilmente si tratta di schiavi già presenti in città; tuttavia la norma dimostra che esisteva un mercato degli schiavi, verosimilmente alimentato proprio dalla pirateria, dunque un mercato che include anche schiavi-merce[5]. In Lewis 2018, p. 146, Lewis aveva già sostenuto che "Helotage was certainly different in many ways from the form of slavery found in Attica; not least, its linguistic uniformity implies major differences in structural organization and strategies of slave supply". Ma se per gli schiavi di Gortina l'argomento dell'uniformità linguistica, come abbiamo detto, non è dimostrabile, e se, come sostiene nella sua attuale comunicazione Lewis, non si tratta di popolazioni sottomesse dagli invasori dorici (p. 15), da dove derivano le loro "traditional family

---

[3] Così di recente anche Vlassopoulos 2021, p. 170: "Classical Sparta and Crete had limited engagement with Mediterranean markets and accordingly could not resort to the reproduction of their slave labourers through the market; consequently, their systems depended on the natural reproduction of the slaves, and this is the reason that slave families were encouraged". Ora, anche ammesso che, in particolare nel caso di Creta, questo scarso ricorso ai mercati sia vero, non si capisce perché il legislatore dovrebbe considerare matrimonio giuridicamente rilevante solo quello fra schiavi di padroni diversi, e non anche le unioni fra schiavi appartenenti allo stesso padrone. Torneremo più sotto sul punto.

[4] Schmitt 1969, n. 482

[5] Così già Maffi 1997, p. 120 n. 103, con la critica di Lewis 2013, p. 411 n. 69. Anche per quanto riguarda gli Spartani, se è vero che era vietato vendere i loro Iloti al di fuori dei confini, niente impedisce che essi potessero acquistare degli schiavi dall'esterno: Ducat, citato da Lewis 2018, p. 136 n. 48, lo nega, ma, a quanto pare, senza argomenti basati sulle fonti. Lewis 2013, p. 411 n. 69, scrive che "slaves from abroad were rarely bought-in to supplement the helot population", anche in questo caso senza citare fonti.

structures"? Per rispondere a questo interrogativo occorre secondo me tentare di comprendere il modo in cui, almeno per quanto si può capire dal CdG, si creano tali strutture familiari. Dal CdG emerge quello che, a mio parere, è un carattere peculiare all'organizzazione sociale di Gortina: il legislatore riconosce come unica modalità di riproduzione della popolazione schiavile il matrimonio fra schiavi appartenenti a padroni diversi[6]. Un matrimonio del genere è ignoto ad Atene[7], mentre per quanto riguarda Sparta non abbiamo nessun indizio testuale della sua esistenza (benché secondo me, proprio in forza dell'analogia con Gortina, questa modalità di riproduzione delle strutture familiari ilotiche non sia affatto da escludere[8]). I non molti commentatori del CdG che si sono interessati al fenomeno, fra cui lo stesso Lewis, considerano i matrimoni fra schiavi di padroni diversi come una forma di unione che coesiste con l'unione fra schiavo e schiava dello stesso padrone[9]. Nel suo articolo del 2013 Lewis aveva istituito un parallelo fra il CdG e la documentazione relativa agli schiavi neri americani: secondo gli studi degli specialisti della materia, i padroni concedevano volentieri ai loro schiavi la possibilità di scegliersi un

6 Lewis 2013, p 397 e n. 31, registra la mia opinione, ma a p. 414, esprime dubbi sull'eccezionalità della disciplina prevista dal CdG, facendo riferimento all'usanza licia descritta da Hdt 1.173 e a una norma contenuta nelle *Leggi* di Platone (XI 930 d–e). Ma dal passo di Erodoto non si desume con certezza che si tratti di un'unione fra una donna e uno schiavo altrui; quanto a Platone, non parla di matrimonio. In ogni caso tali passi non testimoniano l'esistenza di unioni schiavili esclusivamente esogamiche, come sono invece, a mio parere, quelle riconosciute dal CdG.

7 V. da ultimo Vlassopoulos 2021, p. 171.

8 Le trattazioni relative a Sparta, qualunque sia la valutazione dello status degli Iloti, parlano genericamente di una riproduzione interna: a titolo di esempio, Lombardo 1999, p. 142, parla di "autonomi processi di riproduzione"; Luraghi 2002, scrive a p. 241: "a selfreproducing group over generations". Sembrerebbe, quindi, che per tutti questi studiosi, le unioni di tipo matrimoniale fossero concluse per iniziativa delle famiglie degli Iloti stessi. Il che, alla luce dei dati del CdG, che fa dipendere le unioni dalla decisione dei padroni, non appare probabile.

9 Secondo Koerner 1993, p. 492, si può ritenere che i matrimoni fra schiavi di padroni diversi fossero frequenti; secondo Nomima II, p. 14, una *woikea* "pouvait ne pas avoir la même appartenance que son mari. Autrement dit elle s'était mariée hors de son *klaros*. Serait-ce l'indice d'une survivance d'exogamie?". Lewis, 2013, p. 403: "slaves could form unions with the slaves of other owners", da cui, in apparenza, "the right to marry slaves from other households"; e ancora Lewis 2018 p. 157: "Gortynian slaves –like their Homeric predecessors– certainly could form 'marriage' relationships, possess property, and have children; but the law was concerned with clarifying the property rights of slaveholders, particularly in complex scenarios where two slaves belonging to different owners might 'marry', entangling the property interests of the individual owners". Dal modo in cui quest'ultima affermazione è formulata (ed è poi ripresa, ma in modo secondo me meno chiaro, nell'attuale comunicazione), sembrerebbe che i padroni fossero messi di fronte al fatto compiuto dalle iniziative matrimoniali dei loro schiavi. Il testo del CdG mostra invece, secondo me in modo evidente, che l'iniziativa di dar luogo al matrimonio fra due determinati schiavi nasce ed è portata a compimento dall'accordo fra i rispettivi padroni.

partner fra gli schiavi di un altro padrone (c.d. "cross-plantation marriages") "in order to keep their slaves motivated, increase the slave stock, and maintain the benevolent and patriarchal image they wished to project" (Lewis 2013, p. 413). Sempre secondo Lewis (*ibid.*), ragionando per analogia, "the fact that the Code envisages the legal problems engendered by such unions hints at the role of slaves themselves in establishing them". Di conseguenza non è da escludere la possibilità che a Gortina "these unions were potentially quite common" (*ibid.*). È evidente che un simile modo di considerare il matrimonio fra schiavi di padroni diversi implica che fosse riconosciuto valido anche il matrimonio fra schiavo e schiava dello stesso padrone (così come era normalmente praticato nel Sud schiavistico degli Stati Uniti). In sé e per sé la possibilità per il padrone di combinare un'unione stabile fra i propri schiavi non doveva destare particolari difficoltà neanche a Gortina, così come ad Atene o in altre poleis. Ma se è vero, come io sostengo, che l'unica unione riconosciuta dal CdG è il matrimonio fra schiavi di padroni diversi, il figlio nato da un'unione fra schiavi dello stesso padrone avrebbe potuto essere rivendicato dal padrone del padre o dei fratelli della donna in base a col. IV 18–23[10]. Per evitare questa conseguenza, occorrerebbe che il legislatore riconoscesse l'esistenza di un regolare matrimonio fra schiavi appartenenti allo stesso padrone. Nel caso di unione fra schiavi appartenenti a padroni diversi, non vi è dubbio che il legislatore si riferisce a un matrimonio, non a un'unione informale (pur ignorando se il matrimonio fosse accompagnato da cerimonie pubbliche, se non altro doveva risultare quali fossero gli oggetti che accompagnavano la schiava e che avrebbero dovuto essere restituiti in caso di divorzio). Che si tratti di un matrimonio lo conferma prima di tutto l'uso dello stesso verbo (*opuio/opuiesthai*) usato per indicare il matrimonio dei liberi. E ancor più lo dimostrano le norme relative al divorzio (col. III 40–44) e alla presentazione del figlio nato dopo il divorzio (col. III 52 – IV 8): esse sono modellate su quelle riguardanti la coppia di liberi, e presuppongono necessariamente che gli schiavi interessati appartengano a padroni diversi e siano (stati) uniti in matrimonio. Viceversa, nel caso di schiavi appartenenti allo stesso padrone non avrebbe senso, né per il padrone né per gli schiavi interessati, distinguere fra matrimonio e unione informale. Ora, se parlando di *woikea me opuiomena* (di cui a col. IV 18–23) il legislatore si riferisse a una schiava non sposata con uno schiavo dello stesso padrone, occorrerebbe postulare che il legislatore distinguesse un regolare matrimonio da un'unione informale: soltanto nel secondo caso il neonato apparterrebbe al padrone del padre o dei fratelli della donna. Ma la maniera in cui sono formulate III 40–44 e III 52 – IV 8 ci impedisce di riferire queste norme a una separazione fra schiavi uniti in un'unione informale. Dunque quando il legislatore parla di 'schiava non sposata' si riferisce al

[10] Ne consegue, fra l'altro, che non sarebbe stato punibile uno schiavo altrui che si fosse reso *moichos* nei confronti di una schiava unita in un'unione apparentemente stabile con uno schiavo dello stesso padrone.

matrimonio che si conclude fra schiavi appartenenti a padroni diversi, non al matrimonio fra schiavi appartenenti al medesimo padrone, che non potrebbe essere distinto da un'unione informale. Il rasoio di Ockham ci impone dunque di interpretare la *woikea me opuiomena* di IV 18–19 come una schiava non sposata con uno schiavo altrui e non come una schiava non sposata con uno schiavo appartenente allo stesso padrone. È evidente, però, che questa conclusione riguarda soltanto una schiava che faceva già parte di una struttura familiare schiavile generata da un matrimonio conforme alla regola esogamica. *Quid iuris* se si fosse trattato di una schiava acquistata al mercato, quindi avulsa da una struttura di parentela? Una risposta coerente impone di riconoscere che se il padrone avesse creato, o comunque approvato, una relazione fra la schiava in questione e un proprio schiavo, avrebbe appunto dato luogo a un'unione informale fra gli schiavi coinvolti; e il figlio da essi generato sarebbe stato di sua proprietà. Tuttavia, stando alla *ratio legis* che propongo di riconoscere nelle norme del CdG relative al matrionio degli schiavi, si sarebbe trattato di un'unione che, a differenza di un matrimonio fra schiavi di padroni diversi, non avrebbe dato luogo alla formazione di un nucleo familiare; di conseguenza la distinzione fra padri e figli, tra fratelli e sorelle, da cui dipende l'applicazione di col. IV 18–23, non sarebbe stata giuridicamente rilevante. Per renderla rilevante la schiava acquistata al mercato avrebbe dovuto essere data in moglie a uno schiavo altrui. Si conferma così che il legislatore considera matrimonio solo l'unione fra schiavi appartenenti a padroni diversi[11].

Data la sua importanza, soffermiamoci ancora su col. IV 18–23. Come abbiamo anticipato, questo è l'unico punto della legislazione gortinia in cui sembra emergere una struttura familiare (nucleare) propria degli schiavi. Non è escluso, naturalmente, che padre e fratelli della *woikea* appartengano al padrone stesso della donna, oppure che la donna non abbia né padre né fratelli (ad es. perché sono premorti, e in tal caso l'esistenza di collaterali non rileva, o perché la donna è stata comprata al mercato degli schiavi, quindi al di fuori di un contesto familiare). Ma in questi casi l'attribuzione della proprietà sul neonato al padrone della *woikea* non richiede una esplicita previsione di legge. Il legislatore prospetta invece l'ipotesi più complessa, cioè che la donna faccia parte di un nucleo familiare, in cui il padre e i fratelli della donna appartengano a padroni diversi. Evidentemente si presuppone che in un momento iniziale vi sia stato un matrimonio fra schiavi di padroni diversi, a seguito del quale padre figli e figlie si trovavano in proprietà del medesimo soggetto (presumibilmente il padrone del padre); successivamente, però, o a seguito

---

[11] Non è il caso qui di allargare il discorso in chiave comparativa con la condizione degli schiavi in età moderna. Mi limito a ricordare che i 'Codes noirs' francesi (Taubira-Castaldo 2006), sia quello del 1685, sia quello del 1723, prevedevano matrimoni sia fra schiavi di padroni diversi sia fra schiavi dello stesso padrone. Ma la rilevanza attribuita a questi matrimoni dipendeva da un fattore religioso che è totalmente assente (almeno ragionando in termini cristiani) dalle unioni antiche (devo la conoscenza di questi testi a Monique Bile, che sentitamente ringrazio).

di vendita o di divisione ereditaria, i membri del nucleo familiare schiavile si sono dispersi venendo a cadere in proprietà di soggetti diversi. Non stupisce che il padrone della madre non venga menzionato: i figli appartengono al proprietario del padre secondo le regole del matrimonio virilocale fra schiavi (modellato sul matrimonio fra liberi), mentre la madre resta di proprietà del proprietario originario. Caso mai ci si sarebbe potuto aspettare la menzione dei proprietari delle sorelle della *woikea* in assenza di fratelli. Ma qui vengono menzionati solo coloro che, secondo il modello valido per i liberi, avrebbero avuto diritto a dare in moglie la rispettiva figlia e sorella (il che però non significa che sia il padrone del padre a combinare il matrimonio della figlia schiava appartenente ad altro padrone, come invece sostiene Schmitz 2022). L'attribuzione dei singoli membri della famiglia originaria a proprietari diversi implica necessariamente che alla persistenza dei legami di parentela non corrisponda una convivenza familiare: questa è infatti concepibile solo sotto lo stesso padrone[12]. Vediamo ora la questione dal punto di vista del padrone della schiava non sposata, e chiediamoci a che titolo avrebbe potuto rivendicare la proprietà del neonato. Dobbiamo partire dal presupposto che il padre del neonato sia noto (perché altrimenti si applicherà senz'altro col. IV 18–23). Potrebbe trattarsi di un compagno di schiavitù; ma in questo caso, per attribuire la proprietà al padrone dei due schiavi, dovremmo ammettere che il legislatore riconosca come matrimonio l'unione fra schiavi dello stesso padrone, ciò che, per le ragioni esposte sopra, abbiamo escluso. Potrebbe essere il padrone della donna; ma di un matrimonio di un libero con una schiava (per di più una schiava propria) non vi è traccia nel CdG. Potrebbe infine essere uno schiavo altrui, che abbia messo incinta la schiava senza averla regolarmente sposata; ma allora nessuno dei due padroni avrebbe interesse a far concludere la gravidanza, perché il neonato non apparterrebbe a nessuno dei due (in alternativa potrebbero accordarsi per far apparire il neonato figlio di un regolare matrimonio, sia pure tardivo rispetto al momento del concepimento; è forse anche per evitare questo escamotage che, in base alla legge, la *woikea* deve non solo partorire ma già risultare incinta –*kysaito*– nel momento in cui si verifica che non è sposata: col. IV 18).

Le considerazioni fin qui svolte suscitano un'ulteriore domanda: perché il legislatore considera così importante stabilire per legge a chi spetta il figlio di una coppia formata da schiavi di padroni diversi[13]? Non sarebbe stato più semplice nella

[12] A meno che lo stesso schiavo non sia in comproprietà di più soggetti, ipotesi che però, a mio parere, non è prevista nemmeno nel caso di col. IV 21–23: si veda Maffi 1997, p. 126 n. 113, la cui opinione è citata –erroneamente– e criticata in Gagarin – Perlman 2016, p. 161.

[13] Possiamo abbastanza verosimilmente, credo, sgombrare il campo da un'ipotesi ventilata da Vlassopoulos 2021, p. 141–142, secondo cui "…in situations where many households possessed one or two slaves, this would make more difficult…the formation of families and kinship groups…Nevertheless…even where households possessed one or two slaves, enslaved persons could create families with slaves belonging to different households". In realtà nel CdG non vi è nessun indizio probante che faccia pensare a una scarsità di questo

pratica quotidiana rimettere ai due padroni la decisione sull'appartenenza dell'eventuale futuro neonato? Se poi non si fossero messi d'accordo, ciascuno dei due avrebbe potuto cercare un terzo padrone più disponibile a stipulare un accordo soddisfacente per entrambi (specie se si tiene conto del fatto che probabilmente questo tipo di 'matrimoni' contemplava di fatto una clausola di reciprocità rivolta al futuro). Dobbiamo forse considerare le norme relative all'assegnazione della proprietà del neonato come norme derogabili di comune accordo da parte dei due padroni interessati, oppure dobbiamo ritenere che si trattasse di norme cogenti? A mio parere, ammesso che questa distinzione, elaborata nella teoria costituzionale romana, sia rilevante per il mondo greco, si tratta di norme cogenti: mi pare che ciò venga confermato sia dalla disciplina della mancata presentazione del neonato in col. III 52–IV 8 sia dalla regola assoluta di attribuzione del neonato nel caso della *woikea me opuiomene*. Infatti, benché col. IV 18–23 non preveda espressamente, per il padrone della *woikea*, l'obbligo di presentazione del neonato al padrone del padre o dei fratelli della donna, è lecito supporre che egli fosse tenuto per legge a presentarlo, per analogia con quanto era previsto per il figlio della *woikea* divorziata in col. III 52 – IV 8. Di conseguenza doveva anche essere consentito al padrone del padre o dei fratelli di non accogliere il neonato o, viceversa, di agire contro il padrone della *woikea me opuiomene* che non lo avesse presentato. Gli eventi che interessavano i membri della famiglia schiavile erano quindi tenuti sotto controllo dagli schiavi interessati e dai loro padroni. Alla luce di queste considerazioni è giustificato ribadire, prima di tutto, che la riproduzione della manodopera schiavile era riconosciuta dalla legge soltanto in forza di un matrimonio fra schiavi appartenenti a padroni diversi; in secondo luogo, che il legislatore imponeva alla famiglia schiavile l'osservanza del medesimo principio patrilineare che dominava il matrimonio fra liberi. Se dunque la schiava non sposata risulta inserita in una struttura familiare, la proprietà sullo schiavo neonato è attribuita in base a legami di parentela che prevalgono sul diritto di proprietà sulla schiava stessa[14]. È come se al legislatore premesse ricompattare, ove possibile, il nucleo familiare che atti di disposizione o vicende ereditarie dei proprietari (o l'attribuzione del neonato a uno dei due padroni in base a un accordo fra i 'consuoceri') rischiano di disperdere. Tuttavia il rimedio escogitato dal legislatore,

---

genere. Le regole in materia di processo di stato (col. I e col. X 25–32) inducono a supporre che vi fosse un numero talmente elevato di schiavi da renderne incerta l'appartenenza (come conferma, a mio parere, il *favor libertatis* stabilito in col. I 16–18). Così pure la norma relativa allo schiavo dato in pegno (IC IV 47) fa pensare che il padrone potesse privarsi dei servizi di uno schiavo senza che la sua situazione economica ne risentisse sensibilmente. E ancora: la norma che dà la preferenza al padrone dell'ex-marito in caso di nascita dopo il divorzio (III 52–55) presuppone che egli avesse a disposizione una schiava nutrice.

[14] Come è noto, il CdG non contiene alcuna regola riguardante la sorte del figlio della libera non sposata. Possiamo supporre, tuttavia, che la decisione se allevarlo o esporlo spettasse in primo luogo al padre della donna e, in caso di sua premorienza, ai fratelli.

cioè il matrimonio schiavile esogamico, non appare garanzia sufficiente[15]. Ne deriva una conseguenza che non possiamo ovviamente approfondire in questa sede. Quando si parla di popolazione dipendente rurale, quindi di una schiavitù di tipo ilotico (non importa se vecchia o nuova maniera), si pensa sempre a nuclei familiari investiti del compito di coltivare fondi (non importa se in proprietà pubblica o privata) e in grado di autoriprodursi. Ora, se l'analisi delle norme in materia di matrimonio degli schiavi, che abbiamo fin qui condotta, corrisponde alla *ratio legis* che informa il CdG, si direbbe che lo scopo perseguito dal legislatore sia proprio quello di contrastare il rischio, sempre più impellente, che venga meno il tradizionale nesso fra la coltivazione di un determinato fondo e l'integrità del nucleo familiare che è adibito a coltivarlo[16]. Dunque il legislatore tenterebbe di porre riparo a una situazione in cui la regolarità della riproduzione della famiglia schiavile adibita alla coltivazione dei fondi sta venendo meno o è già venuta meno. Questo non significa, però, che il matrimonio esogamico avesse come scopo esclusivamente la riproduzione della popolazione rurale dipendente: è da supporre che il legislatore intendesse far dipendere da matrimoni esogamici anche la riproduzione di schiavi adibiti a compiti diversi dalla coltivazione dei campi. Quindi tendenzialmente di tutti gli schiavi. Tuttavia, la possibilità di acquistare schiavi al mercato apriva una falla nel sistema. Come abbiamo visto, nel caso della schiava acquistata al mercato, che partoriva senza essere sposata, il neonato sarebbe appartenuto al padrone della donna perché non esistevano legami familiari con schiavi appartenenti ad altri padroni. È piuttosto evidente che una simile soluzione apriva la strada a un regime giuridico della schiavitù simile a quello che conosciamo per Atene. Si creano quindi le premesse per ammettere l'esistenza di una duplicità di figure schiavili. Se e in che misura il legislatore del CdG ne tenga conto è difficile dirlo: in ogni caso sostenere che *dolos* e *woikeus* sono dei meri sinonimi che designano una popolazione rurale dipendente, non riesce a rendere pienamente conto della complessità del quadro della schiavitù nella Gortina del Codice.

Due parole infine sulle origini della pretesa 'popolazione rurale dipendente'[17]. Lewis esclude che la popolazione rurale dipendente cretese, in particolare della Gortina del CdG, abbia le sue origini nella sottomissione di una popolazione sconfitta in guerra. Propone invece di ritrovarne le origini nel modello della schiavitù omerica, più specificamente incarnata nella figura emblematica di Eumeo, quale ci viene dipinta in Od. 14. 61–67 e in Od. 21. 213–216. Scrive Lewis: "In the Odyssey Eumaeus is an *oikeus* (14.4, 63), who works in the country herding animals, inhabits a small hut, and

---

15 È quanto riconosce, almeno indirettamente, lo stesso Lewis, quando scrive, come abbiamo visto, che le "traditional family structures were crosscut by the entangled ownership rights of multiple masters".

16 Che, per esempio, Hodkinson 2000, p. 119–120, postula per gli Iloti spartani.

17 L'unico (debole) indizio che la disciplina della schiavitù nel CdG riguardi una popolazione rurale dipendente lo si ricava da col. IV 31 ss.; e, come abbiamo visto, non è sufficiente a escludere che esistessero anche schiavi-merce.

knows that, had his master not been abroad, he would have rewarded him with a house, a plot of land, and a wife...Is this much different from the Gortynian *woikeus* who dwells in the country herding animals (72 IV 33–6), who can marry a *woikea* (72 III 40–44) and accumulate possessions?" (p. 16). A mio parere i termini di questo accostamento non sono congruenti. *Oikos*, *kleros* e moglie "richiesta da molti" per Eumeo sono ricompense per la dedizione manifestata nel servire il signore di Itaca (il quale, oltre tutto, è assente da vent'anni, il che rende ancora più anomala la comparazione con un *woikeus* gortinio): quindi tutto lascia pensare (come conferma d'altronde Od. 21. 213–216) che Eumeo si attenda, come ricompensa della sua fedeltà, la liberazione dalla schiavitù, rafforzata da una cospicua dotazione e da una moglie, che Odisseo richiederà per lui, come la richiederebbe per Telemaco (lo si desume da Od. 21. 214–216)[18]. Nel CdG IV 33–6 sono invece gli oggetti su cui si esercita la fatica del *woikeus* o gli strumenti necessari per portarla a buon fine (ivi compresa la moglie, che, nel modo in cui Eumeo se la prospetta non sarà certo una schiava, mentre lo è certamente nel caso del *woikeus* gortinio). Per di più Eumeo, come è noto, è uno schiavo rapito dai pirati e acquistato dal signore di Itaca, così come lo è, con tutta probabilità, la siciliana moglie di Dolio (Od. 24.389). Ma è allora evidente che Eumeo non è inserito in una struttura familiare schiavile, e che il matrimonio fra Dolio e la siciliana si instaura fra uno schiavo e una schiava appartenenti allo stesso padrone. Non troviamo dunque in Omero l'elemento che, almeno a mio parere, è peculiare alla schiavitù gortinia, cioè il matrimonio esogamico degli schiavi. In definitiva non siamo quindi in grado di dire se le strutture familiari schiavili del CdG derivino da un retaggio storico remoto o siano invece una costruzione del legislatore, tendente a preservare delle strutture familiari artificiosamente costruite.

alberto.maffi@unimib.it

BIBLIOGRAFIA

M. Gagarin – P. Perlman, *The Laws of Ancient Crete*, Oxford 2016

S. Hodkinson, *Property and Wealth in Classical Sparta*, London & Swansea 2000

R. Koerner, *Inschriftliche Gesetzestexte der frühen griechischen Polis*, Köln 1993

D.M. Lewis, *Slave marriages in the laws of Gortyn: A matter of rights?*, Historia 62.4, 2013, p. 390–416

[18] Nel suo recente libro sulle manomissioni Zanovello 2021 sostiene che in Od. 14. 61–67 non si tratta di manomissione, ma di privilegi significativi concessi a uno schiavo, "since, legally speaking, slaves were considered objects rather than individuals" (p. 28). Ma lo schiavo che lavora in campagna, come appunto Eumeo, ha un'abitazione annessa al fondo che è tenuto a coltivare per il padrone, e una compagna, che è scelta dal padrone di solito fra le proprie schiave (o, anticipando le disposizioni del CdG, fra le schiave altrui che ritiene più adatte a coadiuvare il proprio schiavo). Il matrimonio non è dunque un privilegio per gli schiavi, ma è funzionale agli interessi del padrone.

D.M. Lewis, *Greek Slave Systems in their Eastern Mediterranean Context, c. 800–146 BC.*, Oxford 2018

M. Lombardo, *Le donne degli Iloti*, in F. Reduzzi Merola e A. Storchi Marino (ed.), *Femmes esclaves*. Atti del XXI Colloquio Girea, Napoli 1999, p. 129–143

N. Luraghi, *Helotic slavery reconsidered*, in A. Powell & S. Hodkinson (eds.), *Sparta: Beyond the Mirage*, London 2002, p. 229–250

A. Maffi, *Il diritto di famiglia nel Codice di Gortina*, Milano 1997

Nomima II = H. Van Effenterre et F. Ruzé, *Nomima II*, Roma 1995

H. H. Schmitt, *Die Staatsverträge des Altertums. 3. Die Verträge der griechisch-römischen Welt von 338 bis 200 v. Chr.*, München, 1969

W. Schmitz, *Dependent rural populations in archaic and classical Greece: free, slave, or between free and slave?* in J. Bischoff & S. Conermann (eds.), *Slavery and Other Strong Forms of Asymmetrical Dependencies*, Berlin & Boston 2022, p. 99–126

Chr. Taubira – A. Castaldo, *Codes noirs*, Paris 2006

K. Vlassopoulos, *Historicizing Ancient Slavery*, Edinburgh 2021

S. Zanovello, *From slave to free. A legal perspective on greek manumission*, Alessandria 2021

S. C. TODD (MANCHESTER)

THE DISCOVERY OF THE GORTYN CODE AND NINETEENTH-CENTURY DEBATES OVER THE UNITY OF GREEK LAW[1]

Abstract: The Gortyn Law Code is a large inscription from the Cretan city of Gortyn, and was discovered in 1884. Rather than focusing on the legal problems of the Code itself, this paper uses the discovery of this text as an opportunity to investigate a research question about trends in nineteenth-century scholarship on ancient Greek legal history, and particularly the debate over the unity of Greek law.

Keywords: Greek law, Gortyn Code, Historiography of law, Nineteenth-century legal scholarship, Nineteenth-century classical scholarship

I. Research Question: a late nineteenth-century paradigm shift

The subject of this paper is not so much the legal history of the ancient Greek world, but an aspect of its historiography. If I may be permitted a mixed metaphor as the price of avoiding false expectations: the Gortyn Code is being used here as a peg on which to hang a research question about nineteenth-century scholarship, rather than as a subject for detailed discussion in its own right.

If we look at any bibliography of nineteenth-century work in the field,[2] we find that until close to the end of that century, the dominant items tend to focus explicitly – in ways that are often clear from the title – not on what is often called Greek law, but specifically on the law of Athens. An obvious example here is the tradition established by Meier & Schömann's systematic and large-scale work *Der attische Process* ("the Athenian trial"), which in its 1824 first edition was physically a

---

[1] This paper has had a long gestation. Previous versions have been delivered to audiences in Cambridge, Manchester, and Glasgow (the latter as a Classical Association branch lecture in honour of our late Symposion colleague Douglas MacDowell). My thanks are due to the successive audiences (especially at Gmunden, and particularly to my respondent Ilias Arnaoutoglou); to my former and current Manchester colleagues Tim Cornell and Peter Liddel, and to Constanze Güthenke, for additional advice on nineteenth-century scholarship; and to Philipp Scheibelreiter, for his patience as volume editor.

[2] A good overall impression, as discussed further at n.15 below, can be gained from Calhoun & Delamere (1927): the title, *A Working Bibliography of Greek Law*, is itself a significant ideological commitment on the part of its senior editor G. M. Calhoun. For the latter's position on the question of Greek law, see e.g. Calhoun (1924: 154, reviewing Vinogradoff 1922a): "At the very outset Professor Vinogradoff renders a distinct service, by emphasizing the essential unity and homogeneity of Greek law".

single volume (albeit a large one), before being revised and expanded by Lipsius as a two-volume re-edition in the 1880s.[3] Indeed, Lipsius' own subsequent four-volume *Das attische Recht und Rechtsverfahren* of 1905–1915 ("Athenian law and legal procedure")[4] follows essentially the same structure with only very minor modifications,[5] and with the title page of this classic work once again explicitly acknowledging the debt to Meier & Schömann, albeit in an often-forgotten subtitle.[6] It would be possible to add other nineteenth-century examples also, on a comparable or even larger scale if not perhaps so widely cited today.[7]

Any argument resting on individual examples does of course run the risk of unrepresentative selection, or in other words that it can be accused of being the product of choices that are designed to support the intended hypothesis. To deal with this point properly would require fuller investigation of earlier works, of the type undertaken much more extensively by my respondent Ilias Arnaoutoglou.[8] But since the aim in this initial section of my paper is primarily to illustrate the scale of the late nineteenth-century change in scholarly terminology from "Athenian law" to "Greek law", rather than to present the latter as something wholly unprecedented,[9] I

---

3 Meier & Schömann (1824), 780 pages excluding indices; (1883–87), 1,023 pages excluding indices.

4 Lipsius (1905–15), 4 vols. but again continuously paginated, in total 977 pages excluding addenda, indices, etc. This is the work for which Lipsius is best known, but also worth mentioning for the purposes of this paper is his short pamphlet *Von der Bedeutung des griechischen Rechts* ("On the Importance of Greek Law": Lipsius 1893): of particular interest here is his introductory comment about its having been only two decades since Hoffmann had lamented the fragmentation of Greek law ("particularistische Zersplitterung", Lipsius 1893: 8–9, quoting at p.8 from Hoffmann 1870: p.v), in a paragraph where Lipsius cites epigraphic discoveries as well as Mitteis in his discussion of subsequent change. Lipsius' own interest in the epigraphic evidence is attested by his subsequent twelve-page article focusing specifically on the law of Gortyn (Lipsius 1909).

5 There is for instance a slightly different ordering of what may be called extraordinary public procedures in Lipsius (1905–15.ii: 263–338), which places *apagōgē* and related procedures after rather than before *phasis* and *apographē*.

6 Subtitled *mit Benutzung des attischen Processes von M. H. E. Meier und G. F. Schömann* ("based on Meier & Schömann's *Attische Process*").

7 E.g. the significantly titled *Histoire du droit privé de la république athénienne* ("History of private law of the Athenian republic") of Beauchet (1897): 4 vols., respectively 535 + 545 + 737 + 536 pages of text (excluding tables of contents, the index, etc.).

8 I am particularly grateful to Arnaoutoglou for drawing attention to a wider variety of national scholarship than I had considered: e.g. his discussion of Pappadoukas and von Maurer (cited at n.10 and n.12 of his response), perhaps indeed with the implication – esp. in Pappadoukas' case (Arnaoutoglou *pers. comm.*) – that their use of "Greek law" terminology at such an early date may have been influenced by motives of national unity within the newly established Kingdom of Greece.

9 Indeed, the existence of additional precedents is in principle something that can in my view readily be accommodated within my phrase about Greek law as "something waiting to happen" (at §I *fin.* below).

will restrict myself here to two points that were discussed in the oral version of this paper as delivered at the Gmunden conference: one of them an additional example, and the other a more general discussion based on analysis of published bibliography.

The first point concerns Thalheim's *Lehrbuch der griechischen Rechtsaltertümer* ("Textbook of Greek legal antiquities"), which in the oral version of this paper I discussed as a possible counter-example, acknowledging that although the successive editions of this work are themselves formally dated in 1884 and 1895, the earlier one traces its origins explicitly as an expanded revision of the final chapter of the third volume of Hermann's *Lehrbuch der griechischen Antiquitäten* ("Textbook of Greek antiquities") as published in 1852. On the face of it, this would certainly suggest a focus on Greek law back in the middle of the century,[10] at least within the pan-Greek context of Hermann's broader project. But on further reflection, it may be better to treat Thalheim's *Lehrbuch* as a cautionary tale about the danger of relying simply on publication titles, because despite the shared title there are in fact significant differences between the successive editions: whereas the earlier one remains in practice – and despite its title – fundamentally an account of Athenian law based on essentially literary evidence (broadly defined, to include sub-literary material such as scholia, lexicographers, etc.), by contrast the later edition acknowledges at the outset the extent to which new discoveries of evidence have made it possible to range more widely, though evidently with some doubts about the feasibility of "Greek law" as a unitary project.[11] It is illuminating also to compare the indexes of the two editions.[12]

---

[10] Specifically in the context of private law (Thalheim 1884: preface, though with page number not recorded), since constitutional law was covered in a different volume of Hermann's *Lehrbuch*.

[11] In the preface to the later edition, Thalheim (1895: p.viii) starts by listing some important recent discoveries both from Gortyn (not just the Code itself but other smaller inscriptions) and also for Athens (the *Ath.Pol.*, and Hypereides' speech *Against Athenogenes*); he acknowledges the call of Mitteis (cf. at n.22 below) for "eine Darstellung des griechischen Rechts" (i.e., a [sc. unitary] description of Greek law), though he himself clearly has reservations about this, emphasising his view of local difference as revealed e.g. by the Gortyn Code.

[12] In the earlier edition (Thalheim 1884), only four of the headings in the two-page *Geographisches Register* have more than five thematic subheadings (Sparta x17, Ephesos x11, Delphi x9, Krete x6), whereas Athens is cited here simply by cross-reference to the (five-page) thematic *Sachregister*. By contrast, the later edition (Thalheim 1895) includes a new entry in the *Geographisches Register* s.v. Gortyn with no fewer than x36 subheadings relating to different points of law (Adoption, Depositum (Tiere), Ehebruch, E[he]scheidung, etc., etc., several of them with multiple page-refs.). Unlike its predecessor, the later edition also introduces a new single-page "Verzeichnis der erklärten Stelle" (i.e., an *index locorum* but restricted to passages that are not simply cited but actively interpreted), with roughly two-fifths of the space devoted to inscriptions as against three-fifths literary passages (but no papyri, which is itself an interesting

That said, the titles of works of scholarship are important symbolically and cumulatively, as a way of illustrating trends over time in scholarly fashion or scholarly self-definition. And there are I think ways in which my opening hypothesis can be defended against the charge of being a circular argument based on prejudicial selection of examples: for instance by adopting temporarily the "big data" (or at least "bigger data") approach familiar to scholars in digital humanities, using this to supplement the tradition of close readings that is more common among classical scholars; and by applying an electronic word-searching approach to an already existing published and digitised bibliography, in this case the 1927 *Working Bibliography of Greek Law* by Calhoun & Delamere. As a choice of corpus, this has several advantages: first, it was designed to find every scrap of material under this heading to which the editors had access,[13] including some pretty obscure items; but perhaps more importantly for present purposes, its senior editor Calhoun was himself a firm believer in the unity of Greek law, and hence is likely to have been on the lookout for earlier items that supported this. Digital analysis that I have conducted of four languages of international scholarship[14] within Calhoun & Delamere's bibliography suggests that there is a strikingly different chronological distribution of items with titles including "Greek / grec / griechish / greco" (in any morphological form) when compared with equivalent items including "Athenian" or "Attic" (in any of the four equivalent languages): the sample is in each case large (200+ items for each of the two terms); but whereas the distribution of items with "Athenian / Attic" in the title remains relatively stable over time, there is a big rise in items with "Greek" in the title during the 1880s–1890s (31%), and even more so after 1900 (55%).[15] This change from Athenian law to Greek law is what I have

statement of focus): this includes eight passages from the Gortyn Code, more than any other text or author except Demosthenes (twenty-five passages).

13 There are likely to have been some areas of systematic under-representation (e.g. the figures for Italian items in the next-but-one footnote seem surprisingly low), but this need not detract from the overall value of the exercise.

14 English, French, German and Italian, as itemised in the following footnote. Any analysis of this type is of course subject to technological and other limitations (e.g. the quality of the digitisation and the efficiency of the word-searching programme, which in this case could only handle items in a western alphabet). The second and third chronological periods used in the following footnote are only loosely equivalent, but since their function is to explore the different distribution over time of the two sets of headline terms, what matters for present purposes is that they are the same for both terms.

15 Raw figures and percentages for chronological distribution, in each case of those bibliographical items in Calhoun & Delamere (1927) where the relevant word appears in the title and where the publication date is reported: **[a] "Greek / grec / griechisch / greco"** (in all morphological forms) (N = 231, made up of 27 items in English, 52 in French, 141 in German, and 11 in Italian): **[a.i] 1879 or earlier @ 13.4%** (= 31 items), **[a.ii] 1880s–1890s @ 31.2%** (= 72 items), **[a.iii] 1900–1924 @ 55.4%** (= 128); as a control experiment, **[b] "Athenian / Attic"** (in any of the four languages) (N = 217, made up of 35 items in English, 56 in French, 123 in German, and 3 in Italian): **[b.i]**

chosen to describe as the first of two paradigm shifts in the history of the subject, and is itself the focus of the present paper.

There is of course a practical reason for the dominance of those earlier Athenocentric works, in that their evidential basis was to a large extent the literary canon, including fragments as mediated by scholia and lexicographers.[16] In part this is obviously a function of the relatively recent (i.e., mid-nineteenth-century) origins of serious epigraphic publication, though I suspect it probably also reflects the fact that Athenian public documentary inscriptions include relatively little of what we would describe as legal statutes, in comparison with e.g. public accounts or honorific decrees: Harrison in 1968–71 is not in this regard much different from Lipsius in 1905–15 (and that is not intended to be taken as a criticism of either Lipsius or Harrison).[17]

If on the other hand we compare a bibliography of twentieth-century and subsequent work,[18] then a very different picture emerges, or rather perhaps two pictures. This can be covered much more briefly, because it is only of indirect relevance to the research question of this paper.

In the first half of the twentieth century, the picture is different but uniform – different, that is, from its nineteenth-century predecessors, but sharing its own dominant paradigm: one in which the subject matter is explicitly "Greek law" rather than "Athenian law". I emphasise the existence of a dominant paradigm, by which I mean that the same emphasis on "Greek law" as the subject was shared not just by the civil-law tradition found throughout continental Europe and perhaps especially in German, but also by much of the relatively limited amount of Anglo-Saxon work

---

1879 or earlier @ 25.8% (= 56 items), **[b.ii] 1880s–1890s @ 41.5%** (= 90 items), **[b.iii] 1900–1924 @ 32.7%** (= 71).

16 The 1824 edn. of Meier & Schoemann has an *index locorum* of 4.5 columns on pp.781–783, restricted to passages which have been emended or clarified, including e.g. 63 passages from the orators, 69 from lexicographers, no inscriptions, and – perhaps surprisingly – only 2 from Plutarch; by contrast, the *index locorum* of the 1883–87 edn. restricts itself to passages which have been emended, in 3.0 columns on pp.1034–1035, with 22 passages from orators, 56 from lexicographers, but for the first time three passages from *CIA*. (Cf. perhaps the discussion of the indexes in Thalheim 1884 and 1895, at n.12 above.)

17 The *index locorum* of Lipsius (1905–15.iv: 1008–1041, formatted in two-col. spread) devotes 60.0 cols. to Greek literary texts (with lexicographers incorporated in the same alphabetic list), a figure which includes 18.1 cols. devoted to Demosthenes alone, compared to a total of 7.5 cols. for Greek inscriptions (catalogued separately). Broadly similar proportions can be found in Harrison (1968–71 vol. i: 321–337 and vol. ii: 249–263: formatted again in two-col. spread, but adding together the *indices locorum* of both vols.): literary texts excluding lexicographers, 47.7 cols., including 18.6 cols. of Demosthenes; lexicographers (catalogued separately), 7.8 cols; inscriptions, 5.5 cols.

18 As has been done by Sundahl, Mirhady & Arnaoutoglou (2011, albeit incorporating earlier material also), with regularly-maintained updates in Mirhady & Arnaoutoglou's online *NOMOI* bibliography at https://www.sfu.ca/nomoi.html.

produced during this period: we may think here of figures like Vinogradoff at Oxford, and Calhoun at Berkeley; while even Bonner & Smith, the authors of what is in large part a study of the development of Athenian legal procedure, advertise it in what are at least implicitly pan-Greek terms (noting the absence of Athens from the title) as *The Administration of Justice from Homer to Aristotle.*[19]

Around the middle of the twentieth century there was a second paradigm-shift, in response to Moses Finley's famous 1951 review-article "Some Problems of Greek Law", which was itself written in response to Pringsheim's *Greek Law of Sale*. Finley's argument here was both epistemological (viz., what does it mean to talk about unity when the statutory rules known from various independent *poleis* appear to have been so different?) and also evidential (how safe is unity as a methodological assumption, given the temptation to use it to fill in the gaps in our knowledge of particular systems?). His anti-unitarian position has been widely though not universally accepted by English-speaking scholars, but much less so among Continental European colleagues.[20] This has given rise to the situation of friendly national disagreement that that can be seen in these Symposion conferences: a world of two competing paradigms that view each other with wonder and astonishment.

It is however my first paradigm shift (the late nineteenth-century shift from "Athenian law" to "Greek law") that furnishes the research question for this paper. The orthodox view, at least within the Anglophone world,[21] is to attribute the invention of Greek law to a single text, viz. Ludwig Mitteis' classic 1891 treatment of the law of the papyri from Graeco-Roman Egypt, which argued for the continuing existence of a local (by which he meant Greek) *Volksrecht* or local legal tradition, being applied at ground level by local courts, in contradistinction to the legal system of the imperial power (i.e. Roman law, which in this context he termed *Reichsrecht*). Now, I certainly do not want to give the impression that I am belittling the intellectual importance of Mitteis, who is a hugely important legal historian, as is emphasised for instance in Vinogradoff's obituary notice, which draws attention to Mitteis having been really the first person to think systematically and juridically about the papyri, and to regard divergences from Roman law as something positive to be explained rather than as incompetent bastardisation.[22]

---

[19] Bonner & Smith (1930–38). For Calhoun and Vinogradoff, see n.2 above.

[20] A useful introduction to the post-Finley debates here is Gagarin (2005), who himself adopts a more nuanced position (anti-unitarian in substantive law, but acknowledging significant shared features in legal procedure).

[21] Todd & Millett (1990: 7); Gagarin (2005: 29).

[22] Vinogradoff (1922b: 258). This of course represents a retrospective view, but the significance of Mitteis' work seems to have been recognised at the outset by a wide consensus of often very thorough reviewers: thus for instance Szanto (*Zeitschrift für die österreichischen Gymnasium*, 43 [1892]: 495–499, at p.495), Wilcken (*Deutsche Literaturzeitung*, 30 [1892]: cols. 886–888, at col. 887) and Swoboda (*Neue philologische Rundschau*, 1892: 188–192, at pp.188–189), each emphasising Mitteis' importance for e.g. historians and

But the thing that has struck me most clearly when looking through some of the early reactions to the 1884 discovery and publication of the Gortyn Code is that what might be termed "Greek law" responses seem very quick-off-the-mark, not just linguistically but also conceptually. On this basis, it cannot in my view be right to continue regarding Mitteis' 1891 monograph as a sufficient explanation for the invention of Greek law.[23] But I should emphasise that I am not simply trying to replace Mitteis with Gortyn. Instead, and more significantly, I suggest that we should view the emphasis on Greek law not so much as a response to either of them, but as something waiting to happen, or perhaps that there are trends in scholarship which have paved the way. Some preliminary thoughts about possible explanatory trends are suggested at the end of this paper.

II. The Gortyn Code: discovery and impact

The story of the discovery of the Gortyn Code is recounted in detail by the earliest editors, with selected elements being summarised more briefly by their more recent successors.[24] Since my interest in this discovery lies in its impact on nineteenth-century legal scholarship and the wider perception of this, the points worth emphasising here are the scale of the text and the speed of its publication. As is well known, the Gortyn Code is a single monumental inscription on a slightly concave wall, covering a wide range of topics in what might now be called private law, and is generally now dated to the second half of the fifth century BC.[25] The total dimensions are 30′ wide by 5′ high,[26] comprising four layers each made up of 7–9 blocks of stone, hence some 30 blocks in total.[27] It is set out in 12 columns, each of them barring the last one containing *c.*55 lines (well preserved barring slight damage in places), and hence an essentially continuous text of some 3,000 words

philologists, i.e. not just for jurists; cf. also Krüger (*Kritische Vierteljahresschrift für Gesetzgebung und Rechtswissenschaft*, 16 [1893]: 31–38, at p.31) alongside Schulthess (*Wochenschrift für klassische Philologie*, 10 [1893]: cols. 257–262, 292–297, 318–323, 339–345, e.g. at col.259), both praising the richness and sophistication of his source-analysis. Note however the reservations expressed in the preface to Thalheim (1895), as discussed at n.11 above.

23 The more so in the light of additional precedents discussed in Arnaoutoglou's response to my paper.

24 Fabricius (1884: 363–373), Comparetti (1885: 233–236); cf. Willetts (1967: 3–4), Gagarin & Perlman (2016: 335).

25 For the epigraphic date as now agreed, see Gagarin & Perlman (2016: 334). The edition by Fabricius (1884: 373 with fig. 20 and fig. 21) includes a facsimile based at least partly on photographs; but many first-generation scholars, lacking good comparative evidence for letter-forms, tended to date the script much earlier: thus Comparetti (1893: 372) suggesting the early decades of the sixth century, and cf. Merriam (1885: 328) proposing "Solonian period".

26 Dimensions as reported by Willetts (1967: 3–4).

27 Cf. the diagram in Willetts (1967: 35). For the total number of stones, see Gagarin & Perlman (2016: 335).

can now be read.[28] Although a couple of the stone blocks had previously received scholarly attention, including one from the top course of col.11 which had been found in 1857 built into the structure of a water mill, and which had been purchased for the Louvre, nevertheless it had taken until 1878 before the Louvre fragment had been sufficiently deciphered for its subject matter (the adoption of children) to be securely determined.[29]

By contrast, the bulk of the inscription was discovered in summer 1884 by an Italian scholar (with the confusingly German surname of Federico Halbherr), who happened to be visiting at a time when the mill-stream had been allowed to run dry, and spotted the remains of inscribed stones in situ. The text below this was then temporarily excavated, transcribed twice and hence separately published by Comparetti (Halbherr's teacher) and by Fabricius (who had done an independent transcription at Halbherr's invitation), before being apparently covered up again at least in the short term.[30] It was not until a decade later that Halbherr managed to secure the purchase of the site by a local archaeological society,[31] leading to the permanent re-excavation of the inscription, though he had apparently been able in the meantime to determine the archaeological context of this inscription.[32]

The size and the novelty of the inscription met with a rapid scale of scholarly response. The bibliography of Willetts' 1967 edition, for instance, cites no fewer than fourteen scholars who published work with "Gortyn" in the title before the end of the 1880s, with an interesting pattern of national languages: three in Italian, five in German, two in French (one of whom also in Dutch), two in English (one USA and one UK), one each in Greek and in Russian.[33] This is of course a bibliography deliberately restricted to items that Willetts considers of long-term importance: these items aside, it is clear that the cultural significance of the discovery was

---

[28] For the structure of the Code, particularly the use of asyndeton and of single-letter *vacat* to indicate what we would regard as paragraph breaks, see Gagarin (1982).

[29] Date of Louvre decipherment: Willetts (1967: 3), who also reports the discovery and transcription of a second fragment (from the top of cols. 8–10) in 1879. A significant factor in delaying decipherment was the unfamiliar nature of the script to nineteenth-century epigraphists (what looks like the western letter "M" is a sigma, what looks like "C" is a pi, and what looks like "S" is in fact an iota).

[30] Edd.prr.: Fabricius (1884), Comparetti (1885). Further details of discovery in Willetts (1967: 3); there are some snippets of contemporary information in e.g. Merriam (1885: 325).

[31] Halbherr's initial reports to his American funders (summarised with extracts in Halbherr 1894: 541) indicate that the original plan had been to remove the inscription and relocate in Candia; his earlier difficulties in negotiation with the villagers, who relied on the mill for irrigation and presumably power, are noted also (Halbherr 1894: 539).

[32] Frothingham (1888: 100–101) reports Halbherr's identification of the building as a Roman-period theatre, and the realisation that each stone was numbered, suggesting that stones had been moved there from an earlier location.

[33] By no means all of these are primarily interested in the subject matter of the Code: e.g. Baunack & Baunack (1885) focus mainly on dialect forms, something which is also a significant interest for Lewy (1885), though the latter comments on legal issues also.

noticed even in the English-speaking world. The Archaeological Institute of America, for instance, funded expeditions to Crete from 1893 onwards by Halbherr,[34] leading to a continuing succession of articles and/or updates in the *American Journal of Archaeology and of the Fine Arts*, as well as some comments in US newspapers.[35]

While on the subject of newspapers and immediate cultural impact, I take the opportunity to mention also the earliest printed UK reference that I have been able to find, which is an article published on 17 October 1885 as the lead item in the weekly supplement to a regional newspaper, the *Leeds Mercury*. Since this is a rather obscure item, as well as being for modern readers a somewhat eccentric one, a full transcript can be found as an appendix to this paper. The author Karl Blind is presumably to be identified with a German revolutionary émigré from the 1848 risings who is himself the subject of an article in the *Oxford Dictionary of National Biography*. Several points are worth noting here: first, the reference both in the subtitle and in the opening paragraph to the "Twelve Tables of Gortyn" (Blind is evidently not the first to use such terminology, but the allusion to early Roman law is clear, as is the implied claim that this is a foundational document);[36] and secondly

---

[34] Initial decision for funding reported in Halbherr (1894: 538); cf. his subsequent expression of gratitude for support received towards this decision from Merriam and from Frothingham (Halbherr 1896: 525–526).

[35] *Boston Daily Advertiser*, 4 August 1893: "A rumor has reached Athens, rather disquieting to the friends of the American school there, that the funds for excavation at Argos and Sparta are next year to be cut down more than half, and that an Italo-German named Halbherr is to have a lot of American money to make diggings with in Crete. It would be very unfortunate thus to divide the scanty funds allocated for American work of this sort. The French and the German governments furnish much larger sums for their schools with which great discoveries are made at Delphi, Athens and elsewhere. The Americans have in Dr. Waldstein an archaeologist of the same rank as Dr. Dörpfeld and M. [H]omolle, and he ought to have money enough and authority enough to carry on the work of excavation at Argos and at Sparta before new work is undertaken in a land controlled by the Turks." Constance Güthenke draws to my attention possible sensitivities regarding the foundation of the AIA and its rôle in promoting US-led classical archaeology, for which cf. Winterer (2002: 157–163). At any rate, a subsequent report in the same newspaper is much less negative in its attitude towards the project (1 June 1895): "Danger threatens the famous Gortyna inscription in Crete. The ground where it stands has been bought by a Greek art committee, but it has been seized by the Turkish military authorities, and it is feared the monument may be seriously damaged."

[36] I have not been able to locate the Munich *Allgemeiner Zeitung* article which Blind cites here as the immediate source of his information (the types of character-recognition software used in nineteenth-century newspaper databases tend often to corrupt the spelling of unfamiliar words like "Gortyn / Gortyna"), but his Twelve Tables allusion is perhaps based ultimately on a phrase in Bücheler & Zitelmann (1885: 41): "Das Gortyner Zwölftafelgesetz ist ein geschlossenes Ganzes, kein Bruchstück" ("The Gortyn Law of the Twelve Tables is a complete whole, not a fragment"); for Blind's knowledge of this volume, cf. the German version of his *Leeds Mercury* article, published a few weeks later in the *Berliner Tageblatt und Handels-Zeitung* of 26 Oct 1885 (p.9). A similar if presumably independent process, i.e. that of drawing out the significance of a

the level of detailed textual knowledge, as well as the (to us) distinctly mad ethnographic theories.

For a broader perspective on scholarly impact, it may be worth looking briefly at successive works of scholarly reference aimed at a more general readership. The great French encyclopaedia by Daremberg & Saglio is interesting in this regard, because the successive publication of successively-lettered volumes means that full discussion is postponed until the FG volume (published 1896), with a 16,000-word article by Caillemer s.v. "Gortyniorum Leges" ("Laws of the Gortynians"), itself drawing attention to the way in which Caillemer's own previous article s.v. "Cretensium Respublica" ("Republic of the Cretans", published 1887) had so rapidly been rendered out-of-date by subsequent epigraphic discoveries.[37] One thing that we do not find in Daremberg & Saglio, however, is any article devoted specifically to "Greek law", though this may reflect the editorial policy decision to use Latin or Latinised Greek terms for its lemmata.[38] By contrast, "Greek law" (alongside Roman law) does form one the of the divisions used in the analytical index produced at the end of the project in 1919, but it is not obvious when the editors started thinking in terms of those categories.[39]

The successive editions of the *Encyclopaedia Britannica* look rather different. There is obviously nothing in the ninth edition, which had already reached vol. 18 out of 24 by 1885. The so-called tenth edition of 1902–03 comprises ten supplementary volumes, intended to be read in conjunction with the ninth, and although the status

---

throw-away phrase, may well account for the similar occurrence of the phrase as the title of the first US translation by Roby, who introduces this with the words "the Twelve Tables of Gortyn (as we may fitly call them)" (Roby 1886: 136), in a work informed by a wide range of scholarship, including Bücheler & Zitelmann. The phrase fairly soon becomes conventional, as in e.g. Caillemer (1896: 1632, col.i): "le législateur auquel nous devons nos Douze Tables" ("the legislator to whom we owe our Twelve Tables").

37 The implication at Caillemer (1896: 1630 col.i) is that his 1887 article s.v. *Cretensium Respublica* had had to be sent for publication in or shortly before 1885. It should however be noted that several of the articles in the 1892 DE volume (e.g. s.vv. "divortium", "donatio", "dos", "epiklēros", "expositio", all cited as cross-references by Caillemer 1896: 1631 col.ii) do each incorporate discussion of material from the Gortyn Code.

38 That said, the only *ius* articles in the 1900 HJ volume are s.v. "jus" and s.v. "jus italicum" (there is e.g. no article s.v. "jus civile", which would be the obvious lemma for a generic article on Roman law).

39 The "Table analytique des matières" (Daremberg & Saglio, vol. 5b [1919], pp.1–22) is set out in seventeen thematic sections. The index entries are themselves in French, with each one supported not by vol. + page numbers, but by a list of the various Latin lemmata that include discussion of relevant information. The sections on "droit grec" (§3, pp.4–5) and "droit romain" (§4, pp.6–8) are broadly comparable in the number of index entries (x145 and x179 respectively), though with the latter having significantly fuller lists of lemmata (§3 takes up 330 lines of three-column text, while §4 takes up 605 lines). It should perhaps be noted that law is one of only two categories that are subdivided into Greek and Roman within this index (the other being "institutions": §§1–2), with the majority of the 17 categories covering both together (e.g. §5 mythology, §6 religion).

of the Gortyn Code as "the most important monument of early law found hitherto in any part of the Greek world" is briefly alluded to in an article s.v. "Crete",[40] nevertheless the focus of Cretan archaeological attention throughout these volumes is much more on the importance of Knossos as validating the historicity of the earliest traditions underlying Homer.[41] But it is the great eleventh edition of 1910/1911 that for the first time takes serious account of the Gortyn Code, in an entirely new, significantly-titled, and highly-regarded article s.v. "Greek Law" by Sir John Sandys,[42] which opens with a series of programmatic claims, including a tricolon that moves in only 50 words from Gortyn via the papyri to the Eastern Roman Empire (i.e., Mitteis).[43]

Perhaps surprisingly, there seems to be no comparable systematic discussion in Pauly-Wissowa's *Realencyclopädie*: i.e., no general overview article either s.v. "Recht" or s.v. "Griechisches Recht", and in practice only the bare minimum by way of a general introduction to the Gortyn Code.[44] That said, specific legal topics even in the alphabetically earliest Pauly-Wissowa volumes are covered from something

---

[40] Bourchier (1902: 273).

[41] A view shared by a range of contributors, e.g. the vol. 27 prefatory essay by Williams (1902: pp.xv–xvii), noting the claim at p.xvi that Greek papyri are not of any great historical significance because they only go back to the Ptolemies. Cf. Giles' article s.v. "writing", where the section on Cretan systems (Giles 1902: 892–894) focuses on the as-yet undeciphered Linear A and Linear B.

[42] Sandys' article is cited for special praise by two reviewers, viz. E. R. Johnson in the *Annals of the American Academy of Political and Social Science*, 37.3 (1911), pp.193–196 at p.195 (nb., writing not specifically for classical readers), and L. Whibley in *Classical Review*, 26.6 (1912) pp.204–205 at p.204 (writing specifically on the Classical articles in the *Encyc. Brit.*).

[43] Sandys' opening paragraph seems worth quoting in full here: "Ancient Greek law is a branch of comparative jurisprudence the importance of which has been long ignored. Jurists have commonly left its study to scholars, who have generally refrained from comparing the institutions of the Greeks with those of other nations. Greek law has, however, been partially compared with Roman law, and has been incidentally illustrated with the aid of the primitive institutions of the Germanic nations. It may now be studied in its earlier stages in the laws of Gortyn; its influence may be traced in legal documents preserved in Egyptian papyri; and it may be recognized as a consistent whole in its ultimate relations to Roman law in the eastern provinces of the Roman empire." In the bibliography of Sandys' article, Mitteis' *Reichsrecht und Volksrecht* is cited as the second of eight items in the "Greek Law" section, with a further seventeen items of secondary literature under the heading "Attic Law", though (perhaps surprisingly) nothing specifically on Gortyn.

[44] Albeit this is perhaps a function of the fact that the article s.v. "Gortyn" (*RE* vol. VII.2, 1912, cols. 1665–1671, by Bürchner) is effectively just an extended bibliography without further comment, which covers "§11 Gesetze" in fewer than 100 words out of *c.*2,400 (albeit plus "§13 Inschriften" in *c.*200 words). Contrast the equivalent "Gortyn" article in *Der Neue Pauly* (*c.*960 words overall, of which *c.*350 words are allocated to Thür's discussion of the Gortyn Code).

approaching a pan-Greek perspective,[45] so it may be simply a question of editorial policy on the balance between broader and more specific articles.

III. The Greek law problem

I have suggested already that I am not simply seeking to substitute Gortyn as a foundational discovery in place of Mitteis as founding father of Greek law, but instead to propose a model which sees both of these as in some sense responding to wider intellectual trends. But that of course raises the question, what trends?

At first sight, an obvious place to look would seem to be Sir Henry Maine's classic and hugely influential 1861 book on *Ancient Law*, subtitled *Its connection with the early history of society and its relation to modern ideas*, which went through sixteen editions by the end of the century, and which put forward a grand theory of comparative legal development drawing on Hindu and to some extent Islamic as well as on Roman and Greek legal thinking. But in fact the first and only use of the phrase "Greek law"[46] that I can find is in the index of Pollock's 1906 revision, where it refers to an appendix discussing recent work on the trial-scene in the Shield of Achilles. And although Maine himself uses the word "Greek" on fifty-odd occasions, nevertheless in context these relate predominantly to Greek philosophical ideas about justice, rather than to substantive or procedural rules;[47] there is discussion of Homer as reflecting an earlier state of societal organisation than in comparable societies,[48] but virtually no interest in the law of the Athenian orators.[49]

---

45 E.g. s.v. "Adoption [1]" (*RE* vol. I.1, 1893, cols.396–398) comprises *c.*1,900 words by Thalheim divided into three paragraphs: an 80-word introduction on "Die Einführung der A. in Griechenland" ("the introduction of adoption in Greece"), mentioning early origins also in Thebes and Sparta, but acknowledging that only Gortyn and Athens are known in detail; plus separate paras. respectively of *c.*190 words on Gortyn and *c.*820 words on Athens. For the development of Thalheim's thinking as reflected in successive editions of his *Rechtsalterthümer*, see n.11 and n.12 above.

46 Maine, rev. Pollock (1906 [1861]: 425), citing Pollock's "note S" at p.406.

47 Maine (1861): e.g. pp.52–54 on the meaning of φύσις / *phusis* and Greek ideas of natural law; pp.58–61 on Greek ideas of ἰσότης / *isotēs* and Roman *aequitas*; pp.340–341 and esp. pp.353–354 on Greek primacy in metaphysics. The nearest he comes to a direct discussion of a Greek legal concept is perhaps on *emphyteusis* (Maine 1861: 299).

48 Maine (1861: 2): "Not a few documentary records exist which profess to give us information concerning the early phenomena of law; but, until philology has effected a complete analysis of the Sanskrit literature, our best sources of knowledge are undoubtedly the Greek Homeric poems, considered of course not as a history of actual occurrences, but as a description, not wholly idealised, of a state of society known to the writer."

49 The only allusion I can find is Maine (1861: 75–76), dismissing the juristic significance of Athenian forensic oratory on the basis that "questions of law were constantly argued on every consideration which could possibly influence the mind of the judges. No durable system of jurisprudence could be produced in this way."

It should perhaps be noted that despite the wide-ranging nature of his interest in comparative legal history,[50] Maine's reading of ancient law was based on a distinction between what he termed "stationary" and "progressive" societies, with the latter being in his view very much the historical exception, but also his focus of interest and the focus of his most influential observations.[51] Rather different approaches, together with more extensive use of "Greek law" terminology, can be found in the work of the founders of historical social theory. So I take as my closing examples two figures that are still (and rightly) highly regarded, especially in terms of their scholarly influence: Fustel de Coulanges and Lewis Henry Morgan.

Admittedly Morgan's notably titled *Ancient Society, or researches in the line of human progress from savagery through barbarism to civilisation*, published in 1877, does not use the phrase "Greek law" any more than Maine does, but his more than 320 uses of "Greek" or "Grecian" include reference to concepts like the "tenure of lands in Grecian tribes",[52] and he is much more ready than Maine to generalise about "the Greeks and Romans" (a phrase found on 17 occasions), and to cross-apply institutional terms, resulting in chapters not just on "The Grecian gens" but also "The Iroquois phratry".[53] Perhaps more significant, however, is Morgan's underlying model of universal evolution,[54] in which all societies are deemed to pass successively

---

50 By far the most frequent of the following phrases to occur within the text of Maine (1861: i.e., excluding the index) is "Roman law" (x77), but there is mention also of "English law" (x10), "German law(s)" (x2), and indeed "Rabbinical Jewish law" (x1); these figures should be regarded as minimum estimates, because they do not include synonyms. His interest in the legal systems of British India ("Hindoo law" x7, and "Mahometan law" x1, the latter in a context discussing rules of princely succession at pp.242–243) is at first sight unsurprising given his period of service as Legal Member of the Governor General's Council, i.e. the senior British law officer in India (1862–1869), though it should be noted that the latter occurred after rather than before the publication of *Ancient Law*, i.e. recognising expertise that he had already demonstrated (Johnson 1991: 376). It is here worth mentioning Maine's interest in what he termed the "Indo-European family of nations" (Maine 1861: 11), to be considered alongside that of Fustel de Coulanges (at n.61 and esp. n.62 below), and in contrast to Morgan (at n.56 below).

51 For the distinction, see e.g. Maine (1861: 22–25, esp. at p.24). Cf. p.168: "[progressive societies as] distinguished by the gradual dissolution of family dependency and the growth of individual obligation in its place"; and p.171: "we may say that the movement of the progressive societies has hitherto been a movement from Status to Contract" (his capitalisation).

52 Morgan (1877: 539).

53 "The Grecian Gens" (Morgan 1877: ch.VIII = pp.215–234); "The Iroquois Phratry" (Morgan 1877: ch.III = pp.88–101).

54 Tim Cornell has suggested to me the possible influence of Darwin on the various scholars discussed in this section of the paper, though if so, any influence is likely to be indirect rather than direct: the only one of them to mention Darwin explicitly seems to be Morgan (1877: 418 with n.1, citing Darwin's 1871 *Descent of Man* rather than his 1859 *Origin of Species*); but it is worth noting Morgan's repeated use of the terms "evolve" and "evolution" (x7 hits for the former, and x6 for the latter).

through seven stages on the route from "lower stages of savagery" to "civilisation",[55] in a manner very different from Maine's focus on "progressive societies",[56] or the again very different focus of Fustel, to which I now finally turn.

A notable feature of Fustel de Coulanges' *La cité antique* ("the ancient city"), first published in 1864, is that he refers with comparable frequency both to "droit athénien" ("Athenian law") and also to "droit grec" ("Greek law").[57] There is however some difference in contexts of usage, in that Fustel tends to speak of "Athenian law" when discussing specific regulations,[58] but of "Greek law" when making often sweeping comparative generalisations.[59] The horizon here is broadly similar to that of Maine, though possibly for different reasons,[60] in that the primary comparison with the Graeco-Roman world is framed through an awareness of Sanskrit as an Indo-European language. In those passages where the term "Indo-European" is used, however, Maine is perhaps more cautious, being ready to emphasise not only similarities but also difference.[61] Fustel by contrast, although

55 Morgan (1877: 9–13): "lower / middle / upper stages of savagery" then "lower / middle / upper stages of barbarism" then "civilisation". Cf. e.g. Morgan (1877: 75): "It was customary law in the Grecian and Latin gentes in the Upper Status of barbarism, and remained as written law far into civilization, that the property of a deceased person should remain in the gens".

56 Morgan (1877: 548): "In this respect and in nearly all respects, the Mosaic law agrees with the law of the Twelve Tables. It affords a striking illustration of the uniformity of human experience, and of the growth of the same ideas in parallel lines in different races." The rejection of any argument from diffusion via shared ancestry forms a striking contrast vis-à-vis the Indo-European focus of Maine and of Fustel (discussed respectively at n.61 and at n.62 below).

57 Fustel de Coulanges (1864): "droit athénien" x8, "droit grec" x7. (Nb, these figures are for the specific phrase, so do not include e.g. synonyms like "la législation athénienne" at p.89, or "la loi / les lois d'Athènes" at p.92 and p.110.) For comparison: "droit romain" x21, "droit hindou" x4.

58 Fustel de Coulanges (1864): "droit athénien" used when discussing e.g. written laws of Drakon and Solon (p.408), Solon's introduction of limited will-making (p.95), inheritance via children of only daughter (p.89, p.411), adoptive son losing inheritance rights from natal family (p.93), *hupothēkē* (p.83 n.1).

59 Fustel de Coulanges (1864) uses "droit grec" typically in the form "le droit grec et romain", or synonyms (p.40, p.42, p.84, p.85, p.86); cf. also "le droit grec . . . le droit hindou" (p.98) and "le droit grec, le droit romain, le droit hindou" (p.103).

60 Cf. two points made by Momigliano with regard to Fustel de Coulanges: first that "it is well known that Fustel was writing without knowing Maine" (1990 [1970], p.163; cf. 1984 [1980], p.171); and secondly that for Fustel (but not Maine), an advantage of the Indo-European model was that this allowed him not to have to get involved with ancient Judaism and hence the dangerous territory of the Bible (1984 [1980]: 172).

61 Maine (1861): "Indo-European" x6, which include passages emphasising putatively shared features such as pattern of monarchy giving way to aristocracy (p.11), agnation (p.150), joint ownership of property (p.260); but also some passages emphasising distinctive elements such as suttee (p.193), different patterns of food distribution within patriarchal societies (p.268). Cf. also Maine's emphasis on the restricted range of such

using the language of "Indo-European" with comparable frequency,[62] is much more ready to generalise, repeatedly using it to emphasise the shared antiquity of the beliefs that he hypothesises.[63]

I should emphasise here that I am not seeking to propose that a unitary belief in Greek law is directly inherited from any specific nineteenth-century social theorist. But it does seem to me that the more that the scholarly world was influenced by theories of shared legal development – either universally à la Morgan or as a distinctive inheritance diffused from remote antiquity among Indo-European communities à la Fustel[64] – then that does tend to encourage a thought-world in which unitary Greek law is something that ought to exist, if only we can find evidence for it. That is the point of my phrase about the nineteenth-century Greek law paradigm-shift being "something waiting to happen".

s.c.todd@manchester.ac.uk

APPENDIX

Leeds Mercury, Saturday 17 October, 1885 (weekly supplement), page 1, cols. i–ii.

Krete and Gothland: Remarkable Discovery of the "Twelve Tables" of Gortyn
A discovery has latterly been made in the island of Krete, of which I have seen no mention yet in the English Press – not even in those journals which specially

evidence ("the legal testimony comes nearly exclusively from the institutions of societies belonging to the Indo-European stock", p.123).

62 Fustel de Coulanges (1864): "indo-européen" x6 (five instances of the phrase "la race indo-européenne" and one of "tous les peuples indo-européens"). Potentially relevant also here is his use of the terms "Aryas" (x9) and "la race aryenne" (x4), which is terminology not used in Maine (1861). Given the subsequent history of the word, it is by no means easy now to interpret the nineteenth-century connotations of "Aryan", though it might be interesting in this context to consider the popularisation of Fustel's ideas in English by Barker (1871), *Aryan Civilization: its Religious Origin and its Progress, with an Account of the Religion, Laws, and Institutions, of Greece and Rome, based on the Work of de Coulanges.*

63 Fustel de Coulanges (1864): death perceived as change rather than dissolution of being (p.7), offerings to the dead (p.18), ancestor cult (p.27), sacred marriage (p.51), sacred boundaries (p.78), genius or hero as communal ancestor (p.184).

64 A very strong statement of this view can be found in the work of Kohler & Ziebarth on the Gortyn Code: not simply their frequent insistence on "gemeingriechische Recht" (x4, including as subtitle for the book), but also the programmatic linking of this with Indo-European heritage (Kohler & Ziebarth 1912: p.viii): "Vor allem aber können wir aus dem gortynischen Recht entnehmen, dass es ein gemeingriechisches Recht gibt, auf indogermanischer Grundlage beruhend" ("above all, we can infer from the Law of Gortyn that there existed a common Greek law based on Indo-European principles"). But to discuss this further would take us beyond the nineteenth-century limits of this paper.

discuss archaeological questions. Yet it is a discovery which, so to say, connects the oldest history of Greece with that Scandinavian population whose blood, together with the blood of the Anglo-Saxon and Frisian stock, still runs in the veins of the English people. I refer to the "Twelve Tables," or laws, of the city of Gortyn, in Krete – laws containing a number of provisions so strangely identical with the most ancient laws of the Swedish isle of Gothland, and with other Germanic customs, as to apparently shut out all possibility of a fortuitous coincidence.

Gothland and Krete are, indeed, widely apart. Those who know nothing of Norse traditions may therefore, at a first glance, look upon such connection with a deal of incredulousness. Yet there is a distinct Scandinavian tradition recording the immigration of the "Asic" branch of the Teuton race into Denmark, Sweden, and Norway from the far East, namely, from the regions of the Black Sea, through what at present is Russia and Germany. The details of this saga are, no doubt – as is always the case in like circumstances – semi-mythical, semi-historic. So is the tale of the siege and fall of Troy, which was once held by some learned men to be a mere imaginary story of Cloud-Cuckoo-Home. But, after all, the "Burnt City" *has* been unearthed! And every one judging with an unbiassed mind must know by this time that the *Iliad* had a very solid sub-stratum of fact, overlaid though that fact was afterwards by fanciful and poetical additions.

For many years past, the writer of the present article has endeavoured, in a number of essays published in Germany, England, Italy, and in America, to press two points upon the attention of learned men. The first was: the manifest connection of that Teutonic "Asic" race, of which the Icelandic Heimskringla speaks, with the vast Thrakian nation which once dwelt near the regions of the Black Sea, in a large portion of the present Ottoman Empire on both sides of the Straits, as well as in parts of Greece, and in the islands of the Archipelago.

The second point was: that in Krete – also anciently inhabited by Thrakians – the key would be found one day, by means of excavations, for many a pre-historical riddle referring to Troy, as well as to Mykene and Tiryns, where Dr. Schliemann has already brought such wonders to light.

The "Asic" race, mentioned in Norse tradition, is literally matched, in classic historical lore, by Aspurgian, Asmanic, Asiotic, Jotic (evidently Gothic), and Asic populations near the Black Sea. The very name of Asia (meaning then only Asia Minor) was distinctly claimed by the Lydian Thrakians as belonging to their own speech. In a mass of personal and place names, in the creed, and in the fragments of folk-speech which have reached us from Thrakian history, the Teutonic element is clearly traceable; "Teut" names themselves being frequent on Thrakian ground. Thrakian words for a freeman, for the sword, for war, for the chieftain, for gold, and so forth, have come down to us, which can almost literally, in some cases entirely so, be matched from Norse speech. Foremost among the Thrakians was the Getic or Gothic branch; also called, in classic antiquity, the Gaudic one. Even this peculiar vocalisation of the Gothic name is matched by the Northern Geats and Gauts. Gaut is the legendary ancestor of the Gothic stock.

As to Krete, it is an ancient Greek tradition that the earliest settlers of Troy came from there. The Ida mountain and the Pergamos of their ancestral island home afterwards reappear in the names of the Troad. *Pergam(os)* was the Thrakian name for all hill-forts; and the word shows evident contact with the Old-German *pereg* [nb, not fully legible] (modern German: *Berg*: that is, hill, or mountain). The Mysian Pergam[on], now Bergamo, in Asia Minor, was situated in the province of Teuthrania, whose name is traced from King Teuthras – a very Teutonic appellation indeed!

In the same way, the Ida mountain on Thrakian ground in Krete and Asia Minor has its curious counterpart in the Ida-field of Norse mythology, which is the centre of the abode of the Germanic gods; that is, of the welkin castle, Asgard. Who can fail to remember the similar divine destination of the Ida mountains in Krete and the Troad – or, to go again back to northern Germanic regions, the frequency of Ida names which have their counterpart in Thrakian and Skythian names recorded by Hellenic historians? Who does not think also of Ida the Flame-bearer?

The Peloponnese – so the Greeks themselves say – has its name from a barbarian Thrakian chieftain, who came from Lydia, in Asia Minor, with his warlike retinue. All through the Peloponnese, the Greeks of old pointed to the great prehistorical Phrygian (that is, again, Thrakian) barrows, or houses, where the once conquering foreign clans slept their sleep of death. In these Phrygians of Southern Greece we have the same people as that which sent forth settlers from Krete to Troy.

The similarity of Kretan and Spartan laws has often been explained from the fact of a Common Doric origin; Doric Greeks having settled in Krete. But seeing that the Doric Greeks in the Peloponnese had been preceded there by Teutonic Thrakians, and that the Spartan race consequently was a mixture of Thrakians and Hellenes, we can easily imagine that both in Spartan and in Kretan institutions a trace of this ancient Thrakian element should have been preserved.

Now, a valuable contribution to our knowledge, as regards Kretan institutions, has been made by the discovery of the "Twelve Tables" of the city of Gortyn. The text of this ancient and somewhat archaic town-law is inscribed on a number of freestones which were found in a mill-brook, derived from the Lethaios. The stones apparently formed part of a circular structure, with an inner diameter of 33 meter. No doubt the structure once served as a court of justice, or session-hall. The letters of the inscriptions are painted red. They covered the inner side of the walls in twelve columns of 53 to 55 lines, running alternately from right to left and from left to right ("boustrophedon:" that is, ploughing-wise). They are cut in at a height of 1.72 meter, so that a man could easily read them. The arrangement of these is said to lack order, which in itself speaks for their high antiquity. The form of the sentences is described as a monotonous one; the phraseology as sparing and heavy, though characterised by that directness of aim which is usually met with in the oldest laws.

Very curious coincidences are pointed out, in the Munich *Allgemeiner Zeitung*, between the Gortyn Twelve Tables and Germanic laws – particularly in regard to the right of a wronged husband against an intruder taken in the flagrant act. On this subject there is a string of provisions of a somewhat complicated nature, referring to the announcement to be made to the relations of the adulterer; to the witnesses before whom this is to be done; to the respective number of witnesses to whom the communication is to be made, if the wrongdoer is a free man or a slave; to the space of time within which a settlement may be effected by means of a fine; and to the sanguinary revenge which the wronged husband is entitled to take by his own action, if that space of time has elapsed without the kinsmen of the wrongdoer having ransomed their relation. All this is very distinctly laid down. And, wonderful enough, quite analogous provisions are contained in the ancient law of Gothland, in the Baltic!

In the same way there is a Gortyn law referring to the oath which it was the right and the duty of an accused to swear, and which could be strengthened by oath-helpers or fellow-swearers. This, again, tallies most remarkably with various old Germanic laws. In the light of the Norse tradition above-mentioned, and of the kinship between the Thrakian stock and the Scandinavians – a kinship which the Gothic historian Jornandes already declared in the sixth century to be an undoubted fact – the coincidence between Kretan and Gothlandic law will no longer appear incomprehensible.

I conclude with a remark of the writer in the Munich *Allgemeine Zeitung*, who discusses these notable analogies. He says –
"During the most flourishing period of Greece, Krete lived an isolated life of her own, as regards the great political and intellectual movements. The island has, therefore, in our time, been rather neglected by the inquirers into antiquity. Only in the last years, archaeological finds and the observation of closer relations between Kretan industry and Dr. Schliemann's discoveries in the tombs of Mykenè, have awakened a more lively interest in Krete; and there is good reason to hope that the keys for the solution of the most important questions of the oldest Greek history will be found there."

It is a promising sign that this view should now come to the front. For my part, I am convinced that, by a fuller application of the "science of the spade" in Krete, not only the most important questions of the oldest history of Greece may be cleared up, but that light will at the same time be shed on the early life of that northern race which has contributed to the formation of the English people.

Karl Blind.

BIBLIOGRAPHY

Barker, T. C. (1871), *Aryan Civilization: its Religious Origin and its Progress, with an Account of the Religion, Laws, and Institutions, of Greece and Rome, based on the Work of de Coulanges*. London & Chipping Norton.

Baunack, J. & Baunack, T. (1885), *Die Inschrift von Gortyn*. Leipzig.

Beauchet, L. (1897), *Histoire du droit privé de la république athénienne*. 4 vols. Paris.

Bonner, R. J., & Smith, G. (1930–38), *The Administration of Justice from Homer to Aristotle*. 2 vols. Chicago.

Bourchier, J. D. (1902), s.v. "Crete", in *Encyclopaedia Britannica*, ed.10, vol. 27, pp.271–275.

Bücheler, F., & Zitelmann, E. (1885), *Das Recht von Gortyn, herausgegeben und erläutert*. Frankfurt am Main.

Bürchner, L. (1912), s.v. "Gortyn", in Pauly-Wissowa, *RE*, vol. vii.2, vols. 1665–1671.

Caillemer, E. (1887), s.v. "Cretensium Respublica", in Daremberg & Saglio, *Dictionnaire des antiquités*, vol. 1 part 2 (the vol. covering letter C), pp.1563 col.ii – 1568 col.i

Caillemer, E. (1896), s.v. "Gortyniorum Leges", in Daremberg & Saglio, *Dictionnaire des antiquités*, vol. 2 part 2 (the vol. covering letters F–G), pp.1630 col.i – 1645 col.i.

Calhoun, G. M. (1924), rev. of Vinogradoff (1922a), in *Columbia Law Review*, 24.2: 154–171.

Calhoun, G. M., & Delamere, C. (1927), *A Working Bibliography of Greek Law*. Cambridge, Mass.

Comparetti, D. (1885), "Iscrizioni arcaiche di Gortyna", *Museo italiano di antichità classica*, 1: 233–275; repr. as separate item also in 1885 under the title *Leggi antiche della città di Gortyna in Creta scoperte dai D. F. Halbherr ed E. Fabricius, lette ed illustrate da Domenico Comparetti*. Turin.

Comparetti, D. (1893), *Le leggi di Gortyna e le altre iscrizioni arcaiche Cretesi edite ed illustrate da Domenico Comparetti*. Milan.

Daremberg, Ch., & E. Saglio, eds. (1873–1919), *Dictionnaire des antiquités grecques et romaines d'après les textes et les monuments*. Paris. (Significant dates for this paper are: C vol. 1887; D–E vol. 1892; F–G vol. 1896; index vol. 1919.)

Encyclopaedia Britannica: ed.9, 1875–89 (24 vols. plus an index vol.); ed.10, 1902–03 (10 vols. of supplement, plus 24 vols. of ed.9, plus new index vol.); ed.11 (the famous edition), 1910–11 (28 vols. + index vol.): see also s.vv. Bourchier, Giles, Sandys, and Williams.

Fabricius, E. (1884), "Alterthümer auf Kreta. I. Gesetz von Gortyn (mit zwei Tafeln und einer Beilage)", *Mitteilungen des Deutschen Archäologischen Instituts*, vol. 9: 363–384.

Finley, M. I. (1951), "Some Problems of Greek Law", review-article of Pringsheim 1950, in *Seminar*, 9: 72–91; repr. in part as an appendix to Finley's 1966 article "The Problem of the Unity of Greek Law", in Finley, *Use & Abuse of History* (London, 1975), ch.8, at pp.147–52.

Frothingham, A. L. (1888), "Archaeological News", *The American Journal of Archaeology and of the History of the Fine Arts*, 4.1: 69–125.

Fustel de Coulanges, N. D. (1864), *La cité antique: étude sur le culte, le droit, les institutions de la Grèce et de Rome*. Paris.

Gagarin, M. (1982), "The Organization of the Gortyn law code", *GRBS*, 23.2: 129–46.

Gagarin, M. (2005), "The unity of Greek law", in M. Gagarin & D. Cohen, eds., *The Cambridge Companion to Ancient Greek Law*, pp.29–40. Cambridge.

Gagarin, M., & Perlman, P. (2016), *The Laws of Ancient Crete, c. 650–400 BCE*. Oxford.

Giles, P. (1902), s.v. "Writing", in *Encyclopaedia Britannica*, ed.10, vol. 33, pp.888–903.

Halbherr, F. (1894), "American Expedition to Krete under Professor Halbherr", *American Journal of Archaeology and of the History of the Fine Arts*, 9.4: 538–544.

Halbherr, F. (1896), "Report of the Expedition of the Institute to Krete", *American Journal of Archaeology and of the History of the Fine Arts*, 11.4: 525–538.

Harrison, A. R. W. (1968–71), *The Law of Athens*. 2 vols.: vol. 1, *The family and property*; vol. 2, *Procedure*. Oxford.

Hermann, K. F. (1852), *Lehrbuch der griechischen Privatalterthümer mit Einschluss der Rechtsalterthümer* (= third vol. of second edn. of Hermann's *Lehrbuch der griechischen Antiquitäten*). Heidelberg.

Hoffmann, F. (1870) *Beiträge zur Geschichte des griechischen und römischen Rechts*. Vienna.

Johnson, G. (1991), "India and Henry Maine", in A. Diamond, ed., *The Victorian Achievement of Sir Henry Maine: a centennial reappraisal*. Cambridge.

Kohler, J., & E. Ziebarth (1912), *Das Stadtrecht von Gortyn und seine Beziehungen zum gemeingriechischen Recht*. Göttingen.

Lewy, H. (1885), *Altes Stadtrecht von Gortyn auf Kreta. Nach der von Halbherr und Fabricius aufgefundenen Inschrift. Text, Übersetzung und Anmerkungen nebst einem Wörter-verzeichnis*. Berlin.

Lipsius, J. H. (1893), *Von der Bedeutung des griechischen Rechts*. (Rede zur Feier des Geburtstags Seiner Majestät des Königs Albert am 23. April 1893, in der Aula der Universität Leipzig gehalten.) Leipzig.

Lipsius, J. H. (1905–15), *Das attische Recht und Rechtsverfahren, mit Benutzung des Attischen Processes von M. H. E. Meier und G. F. Schömann*. 4 vols. in 3. Leipzig.

Lipsius, J. H. (1909), "Zum Recht von Gortyns", *Abhandlungen der philologisch-historischen klasse der königl. sächsischen Gesellschaft der Wissenschaften*, vol. 27, no. 11, pp.393–410.

Maine, H. S. (1861), *Ancient Law: its connection with the early history of society and its relation to modern ideas*. London.

Maine, H. S., rev. F. Pollock (1906 [1861]): reprinted edition of Sir Henry Maine's *Ancient Law*, with introduction and notes by Sir Frederick Pollock. London.

Meier, M. H. E., & Schömann, G. F. (1824), *Der attische Process*. Halle. Revised edn., edited by J. H. Lipsius, 2 vols., 1883–87, Berlin.

Merriam, A. C. (1885 and 1886), "Law Code of the Kretan Gortyna", *American Journal of Archaeology and of the History of the Fine Arts*, 1.4: 324–350 and 2.1: 24–45.

Mitteis, L. (1891), *Reichsrecht und Volksrecht in den östlichen Provinzen des römischen Kaiserreichs. Mit Beiträgen zur Kenntniss des griechischen Rechts und der spätrömischen Rechtsentwicklung*. Leipzig. (repr. Hildesheim 1963).

Momigliano, A. D. (1984 [1980]), "Foreword to N. D. Fustel de Coulanges, *The Ancient City*", in Momigliano, *Settimo Contributo alla Storia degli Studi Classici e del Mondo Antico*, pp.171–177. Rome. (repr. of his introduction to the Johns Hopkins University Press reprint, Baltimore, 1980, pp.ix–xv.)

Momigliano, A. D. (1990 [1970]), "The Ancient City of Fustel de Coulanges", in Momigliano, *Studies on Modern Scholarship*, pp.162–178. Berkeley & Los

Angeles. (Eng. trans. by J. Landry, rev. T. J. Cornell, of "La città antica di Fustel de Coulanges", *Rivista Storica Italiana*, 82 [1970], pp.81–98).

Morgan, L. H. (1877), *Ancient Society, or Researches in the Lines of Human Progress from Savagery, through Barbarism to Civilization*. New York.

Pollock, F.: see Maine (1906 [1861]).

Pringsheim, F. (1950), *The Greek Law of Sale*. Weimar.

Roby, H. J. (1886), "The Twelve Tables of Gortyn", *Law Quarterly Review*, 2: 135–52.

Sandys, J. E. (1910), s.v. "Greek Law", in *Encyclopaedia Britannica*, ed.11, vol. 11, pp.501–507.

Sundahl, M., Mirhady, D., & Arnaoutoglou, I. (2011), *A New Working Bibliography of Ancient Greek Law (7th–4th centuries BC)*. Athens.

Thalheim, T. (1884), "Dritte vermehrte und verbesserte Auflage" of Hermann's *Lehrbuch der Griechischen Rechtsalterthümer*. Freiburg & Tübingen.

Thalheim, T. (1893), s.v. "Adoption [1]", in Pauly-Wissowa, *RE*, vol. i.1, cols.396–398.

Thalheim, T. (1895), "Vierte vermehrte und verbesserte Auflage" von Hermanns *Lehrbuch der Griechischen Rechtsaltertümer*. Freiburg & Tübingen.

Todd, S. C., & Millett, P. C. (1990), "Law, Society and Athens", in Cartledge, P. A., Millett, P. C. & Todd, S. C. (1990), eds., *NOMOS: essays in Athenian law, politics and society*, pp.1–18. Cambridge.

Vinogradoff, P. G. (1922a), *The Outlines of Historical Jurisprudence,* vol. 2, *The jurisprudence of the Greek city*. Oxford.

Vinogradoff, P. G. (1922b), "L. Mitteis (1859–1921) [obituary]", *Journal of Egyptian Archaeology*, vol. 8.3–4: 258–259.

Willetts, R. F. (1967), *The Law Code of Gortyn* (= *Kadmos* suppl. 1). Berlin.

Williams, H. S. (1902), "Prefatory essay: the influence of modern research on the scope of world-history", in *Encyclopaedia Britannica*, ed.10, vol. 27, pp.vii–xx.

Winterer, C. (2002), *The Culture of Classicism: Ancient Greece and Rome in American intellectual life, 1780–1910*. Baltimore.

ILIAS N. ARNAOUTOGLOU (ATHEN)

A PROLONGED BIRTH OF A CONCEPT: THE UNITY OF GREEK LAW: RESPONSE TO S. C. TODD

Stephen Todd's paper focuses on the early history of legal meta-history or, to put it in less trendy terms, the early historiography of a key concept in Greek legal history. The paper is organized around two issues. The first one concerns the two chronologically distinct shifts of the dominant paradigm in ancient Greek law: the predominance of the term *Greek law* after the publication of Ludwig Mitteis' epoch-making book[1] and a second shift in the mid-twenty century introduced by the revisionist critique of Moses I. Finley[2]. The second issue concerns the intellectual origins of the usage of the term (ancient) *Greek law* and the role played by the discovery of the Gortynian legislation. The author concludes that "the more people believed in shared legal developments ... then that does tend to encourage a thought-world in which unitary Greek law is something that ought to exist". In the following few pages, I would like to engage with Todd's argument and provide some thoughts on the question of the 'unity of Greek law'.

It should be noticed from the outset that the legislation of Gortyn, preserved in the long inscription *IC* iv 72 [= Gagarin & Perlman (2016: 334–428)] and in a few other inscriptions as in *IC* iv 41–51 [= Gagarin & Perlman (2016: 291–323)], plays only a secondary role in the whole argumentation. I would have expected an exploration of the ways in which the publication of the Gortynian legislation in the last quarter of the nineteenth century – and in general the growing number of properly published inscriptions from various parts of the Greek world – tempered the outspoken Athenocentrism of earlier studies.

---

1 Mitteis (1891: 61–62) "The innumerable individual statutory laws of the Greek cities rested in essence on identical juristic conceptions (*Anschauungen*) and the same institutions developed with only slight nuances" transl. Finley (1966: 134). Mitteis (1891: 61): *Denn das griechische Recht bildet ein grosses Ganzes, und dies ist für die Rezeptionslehre eine Thatsache von weitreichender Bedeutung* (Since Greek law constitutes a large whole, a fact of utmost importance for the Reception theory). Mitteis (1891: 76): *Es wurde schon oben gezeigt dass die Grundzüge des griechischen Familien- und Vermögensrechts überall gleichmäßig wiederkehren* (It has been demonstrated that the fundamentals of the Greek family and property law appear again and again in a similar manner).

2 Finley (1951) and Finley (1966), followed by Triantaphyllopoulos (1968) and (1985), Gagarin (2005) with modifications. Cf. Sealey (1994).

Todd's effort to understand and explain the chronologically earlier shift must be much appreciated, since it attempts to accommodate legal treatment of antiquity into a wider historical horizon. However, Mitteis (and his followers) in using the term (ancient) *Greek law* seemed to have followed a romantic tradition current among the nineteenth-century historians and jurists. There are plentiful attestations of the collocation *ancient Greek law* in the decades before 1891, albeit not in book titles, in publications in English[3], French[4], German[5], and Italian[6]. These usages are not limited to publications focusing on ancient Greece, but they spill over neighbouring disciplines such as Egyptology[7], Roman[8] and comparative law[9]. Traces of the term (ancient) *Greek law* appear also in

i) its contemporary Greek version as Ἀρχαῖον Ἑλληνικὸν Δίκαιον in the title of a book published in 1844 in the island of Syros by N. Pappadoukas[10]. This is not an original work but effectively a translation of the seventeenth-century collection by Samuel Petit[11], into nineteenth-century erudite Greek. Worth noting is the arbitrary rendering of the title, indicative of the equation of Attic, Athenian, and Greek, a choice that unveils the ideological tendencies of its author.

ii) This is not the earliest piece of evidence; we can pin down another one in German (*altgriechische Recht*) this time almost ten years earlier. The term appears in the account of Georg Ludwig von Maurer (member of the Regency Council of the under-age king of Greece Otto), about his legislative activity published in 1835 in Heidelberg[12]. The romantic

---

3 Herrick (1890: 7–11, 33, 55, 62, 68, 72); *Classical Review* 2 (1888) 10–11 (review article of Roberts of the various publications of Gortyn's laws) and *American Journal of Archaeology* 1888, 424 (publication of security-*horoi* inscriptions).

4 See e. g. Fustel de Coulanges (1866: 84, 99, 103); Reinach (1885[3]: 396–7); Fustel de Coulanges (1885: 228 & 240); Greiff (1888: 71, 135).

5 See e. g. Köppen (1818: 11); Platner (1820: xxii); von Schrader (1838: 19); Mähly (1853: 31); Hermann (1855: 16, 55); Schulin (1882: 3–5, 20, 27, 30, 51–52); Leist (1884: 682); Leist (1886: preface); Post (1891: 105).

6 See e. g. Negri (1864: 25); Saredo (1873: 24); Gabba (1880[2]: 445).

7 See e. g. Révillout (1886: xxix, lvi, 78, 92–93, 143, 145, 154, 159, 197, 225, 265, 347, 352, 620); Paturet (1886: xvi, 29, 43).

8 See e. g. de Schryver (1844: 20); LeFort (1850: 25, 73); von Jhering (1886: 237 n. 1, 312).

9 See e.g. Golfavru (1868: xiii).

10 Σόλων. Ἀρχαῖον ἑλληνικὸν δίκαιον περιέχον τοὺς σωζομένους νόμους τῶν Ἀθηναίων καὶ τοὺς ναυτικούς τῶν τε Ῥοδίων καὶ αὐτοκρατόρων τῆς Κωνσταντινουπόλεως, Ἑρμούπολις 1844. Four years later the author, Nikolaos Pappadoukas, a jurist, published the earliest handbook of constitutional law in modern Greece.

11 Petit (1615).

12 von Maurer (1835: II, 347): "*Am allerliebsten hätte ich freilich aus dem alt-griechischen selbst einen Anhaltspunct für die neuen Schöpfungen entlehnt. Allein das altgriechische Recht und Verfahren war auch in Griechenland schon längst zur Antiquität geworden.*

perception of Greek antiquity held by the Bavarian administrators influenced also the nomenclature assigned to law courts; while in the earlier legal charters the Appeal Court was called Ἔκκλητον and the Supreme Court Ἀνώτατον or Ἀκυρωτικόν, the Bavarian judicial administration changed their names to the Athenian-inspired Ἐφετεῖον and Ἄρειος Πάγος respectively[13].

Such various contexts may suggest that the term *ancient Greek law*, with its undoubtedly romantic undertones, reflects the dominant perception and expression of a distant –yet so close– normative universe. The alternating deployment of the terms, *droit grec*, *droit athénien*, *droit attique* is especially prominent in French publications of the period, but not so dominant in the German ones[14]. But even in the anglophone world, in 1755, J. Taylor explicitly stated "The Greek law, I mean that of the Athenians ..."[15]. Obviously, even before Mitteis scholars were aware of the inadequacies in the study of ancient Greek law and of the ambivalence of the term. Therefore, I doubt that L. Mitteis' use of the term *altgriechische Recht* constitutes a shift of paradigm, from Athenian to Greek law. Mitteis' contribution is not simply the official endorsement of a term, but rather an effort, to a large extent successful,

---

Dazu fehlte es den alt Hellenen selbst, gerade in dieser Beziehungen am allermeisten. Denn, wiewohl, –wie man sagt,– das Vaterland der römischen Zwölf Tafeln, so kann Griechenland dennoch nicht als legislatorisches Muster betrachtet werden." (Most of all I would have liked to borrow a point of reference for the new creations from the ancient Greek itself. However, ancient Greek law and procedure had long since become part of archaeology in Greece. Especially in this respect, ancient Greeks lacked both. For although, as they say, Greece was the fatherland of the Roman Twelve Tables, it cannot be regarded as a legislative model."). The difficulties experienced during this process (lack of competent translators, printers, and lack of legal terminology) are pointed out by von Maurer (1835: 342–345). For the legislative oeuvre of G. L. von Maurer in the Greek kingdom see Antoniou (2013). The earliest legislative penal text was published in 1823, *Apanthisma tōn Enklēmatikōn*, written in the vernacular, while von Maurer's *Poinikos Nomos* was composed in erudite nineteenth-century Greek; see Mirasgetzis (1939).

13 Compare the decree on *Civil and criminal procedure, preceded by the decree no. 152 about the organization of lawcourts*, passed in August 1830 (where the former designations of law courts, available in http://srv1-vivl-volou.mag.sch.gr/islandora/object/voDKI%3A203 last visited 12/1/2023) with the *Organization of lawcourts and notaries* (Gerichts- und Notariats Ordnung) published in the Greek Government Gazette 13/1834 (Annex), art. 1 (available in http://srv1-vivl-volou.mag.sch.gr/islandora/object/voDKI%3A234 last visited 12/1/2023). In the same vein, notaries called *mnemon, -es* till 1834, were renamed to *sumbolaiographos, -oi*.

14 Characteristic is the candid explanation in the thesis of Mavrocordato (1847: 22): *Législation grecque ou législation athénienne. Lorsqu'on veut parler de droit grec, on est presque toujours réduit au droit attique. Les lois des petits États qui formaient en si grand nombre l'ancienne Grèce, sauf des rares exceptions, ne nous sont point parvenues*. Similarly, a few years earlier, Koenigswarter (1843: 7).

15 Taylor (1828: 323, 490, 525).

to firmly establish the content of this collocation. With extensive argumentation including family and inheritance law, property and obligations, status, manumissions, procedure, and international law, he provided a fresh context for the study of ancient Greek legal institutions[16]. Mitteis grounded the term on verifiable criteria, moving away from the traditional, largely arbitrary, and ideological, usage of it. In this respect, Mitteis' approach constitutes the culmination of the perception of *poleis*-laws as being interconnected by common legal concepts. What really differentiate Mitteis 'unitary' approach from earlier efforts is the availability of an increasing volume of epigraphical and papyrological testimonia published by that time[17]. Accommodating them into an interpretative scheme of the legal phenomenon in ancient Greece, Mitteis not only saw the diversity of legal rules, but also the often-imperceptible conceptual lines below the surface[18].

Stephen Todd has made abundantly clear that the shift is not a sudden linear development, but it is a product of the intellectual climate in late nineteenth-century Europe. However, there is little trace of that atmosphere in Mitteis (1891); I could count only a couple of references to Fustel de Coulanges' output[19], but none to Maine or Morgan. Much more important was the publication, at an increasing pace, of epigraphic corpora and papyri from the Central and Eastern Mediterranean.

The article of Georges Barrilleau "Des sources du droit grec" published in *Nouvelle Revue d'Histoire du Droit Français et Étranger* 7 (1883) 613–57 encapsulates eloquently the inherent contradictions of the established scholarship. Although he regularly uses the expression *droit grec* (p.1) or *droit hellénique* (p. 2), he explains the scholarly neglect of ancient Greek law(s) stemming from its lack of unity: *D'abord, ce droit n'a jamais eu l'unité puissante du droit romain. À vrai dire, il n'y a pas eu de droit grec; il y a eu le droit de Crète, le droit de Sparte, le droit d'Athènes. Chaque cité avait ses lois propres, les colonies comme les métropoles*. This is the first *expressis verbis* statement about the lack of unity in ancient Greek law, long before Finley. However, Barrilleau was comfortable in employing the expression *Greek law*.

B. The discovery of the slabs containing the Gortynian legislation in two separate occasions in 1857 and in 1880s is explained by the socio-political context of the island. Crete, which was part of the Ottoman empire, ruled by the Egyptians from

---

16 Mitteis (1891: 61–77).

17 See the indexes in Mitteis (1891: 554–556).

18 Mitteis (1891: 62): *Wohl aber soll damit gesagt sein, dass die zahlreichen einzelnen Statutarrechte der griechischen Städte im wesentlichen auf den Gleichen juristischen Anschauungen ruhten und die gleichen Institutionen mit nur geringen Nuancen entwickelten* (But what is meant with it is that the numerous legislations of Greek cities are based on essentially similar legal perceptions and the cities developed similar institutions with slight nuances).

19 Mitteis (1891: 221 and 341).

1830 to 1841, was granted a sort of semi-autonomy in 1868 (in the aftermath of a bloody crush of the 1866–1868 rebellion) leading to the treaty of Chalepa in 1878. These times were not auspicious for archaeological explorations and excavations; that's why the discrepancy between the first discovery of a slab containing the text taken to Louvre in 1857 and the next one in 1884[20].

The publication of the inscriptions containing the Gortynian legislation did not result in challenging the dominant approach. The newly found normative texts were integrated into the discourse of unity as an expression of the normative values of the Dorians[21]. This trend still predominates, despite the critique of Ioannēs Triantaphyllopoulos, a passionate (and lonely) advocate of ancient Greek laws, in his monumental *Das Rechtsdenken der Griechen*, and the programmatic statement therein[22].

C. In the twenty-first century the discussion over the unity of Greek law has not abated. It came to the front invigorated with fresh arguments by Michael Gagarin (2005) who introduced the scheme procedural unity vs. substantive diversity, and counterarguments by Gerhard Thür (2006) on procedure, David D. Phillips (2014) and Edward M. Harris (2018)[23]. While Phillips follows Mitteis' footsteps on the example of *hybris*, Thür and Harris engage with aspects of Gagarin's argumentation. They are both sided with a milder sense of unity, Thür arguing that it is in the eye of the beholder, while Harris speaks of "shared understanding of certain legal concepts" as they appear "in the common legal vocabulary".

---

[20] For the socio-political context see Vasilakis (2017) and Tzōrakis (2018). The circumstances of the find are summarized in Willets (1967: 8–9) and Fiorakis & Peraki (1973: 17–21).

[21] See Typaldos (1887: 4–5); Willets (1967: 3); Fiorakis & Peraki (1973: 26).

[22] Triantaphyllopoulos (1985: 1): *Wegen der Vielzahl des Rechtsordnungen in Griechenland kann zutreffenderweise von 'einem' positiven Recht Griechenlands nicht die Rede sein* (Because of the large number of legal systems in Greece, it is correct that there can be no talk of 'a' positive law in Greece) … *Man müßte von den positiven Rechten Griechenlands oder noch genauer von den positiven Rechten der griechischen Stadtstaaten sprechen. Hier nun ergibt sich die weitere Schwierigkeit, daß nämlich die griechischen Rechtsordnungen in ihrer Gesamtheit unbekannt sind.* (One should speak of the positive rights of Greece, or more precisely of the positive rights of the Greek city-states. This is where the further difficulty arises, namely that the Greek legal systems are unknown in their entirety.) … *Schließlich ist noch eine dritte Rechtsordnung Griechenlands in vollem Umfang bekannt, die im Hinblick auf die eben erwähnten Quellen ein Außenseiter ist: das sogennante große Gesetz von Gortyn … Es ist unter den heute bekannten Quellen des griechischen Rechts so einmalig …* (Finally, a third legal system of Greece is fully known, which is an outsider in relation to the sources just mentioned: the so-called Great Law of Gortyn... It is so unique among the sources of Greek law known today...). See also Triantaphyllopoulos (1968: 1–2). Cf. Adam-Magnissali (2008: 1–2).

[23] Gagarin (2005); Thür (2007); Phillips (2014); Harris (2018).

It is crucial before going to delve further into theory to make clear the fundamental question touched upon by Thür (2006), namely what ancient Greek law is? Usually it is not spelt out, but everybody seems to assume that it is the whole set of legal rules (laws, statutes, bylaws), court decisions, and practices of the Greek *poleis* from 700 BC to AD 212. This untold assumption adopted –implicitly or explicitly– by Mitteis' followers, applied to prove the continuity and unity of the legal-institutional setting, had instigated the vehement reaction of M. I. Finley.

The concept of *ancient Greek law* is a cultural construct of modernity, the result of the reception of Greek antiquity, on a par with ancient Greek language, philosophy, drama, religion, etc. Just like ancient Greek language was made up of various dialects, which, however, display a certain homogeneity or like Greek philosophy which consisted of seven major schools (Pre-Socratics, Sophists, Academy, Peripatetics, Cynics, Epicureans, Stoics), ancient Greek law comprised the various *poleis*-legal orders. However, *ancient Greek law* was compared unfavourably with its younger sibling, Roman law, and therefore remained a 'stepchild' in legal history. Instead of unity, one may speak of legislation and statutes of Greek *poleis* being homologous, therefore a conceptualization of ancient Greek law would have to rely more on analogy rather than on identity. For example, the concept of the sole heiress (*epikleros*) appears in the three best known jurisdictions (Athens, Gortyn, Sparta, and not only in them), but provisions in each of them are not identical[24]. However, a similar approach may have only limited efficacy and heuristic value since such homology may exist with other, non-Greek, legal orders.

If it is to be a meaningful and useful tool of thought and further research, *ancient Greek law* must be understood as a dynamic (therefore subject to historical mutation) concept, including but not absorbing the vast field of *poleis'* legislations. It is not a structured, hierarchical, and fixed system of legal rules and statutes, but an abstract, descriptive, and conventional term that transcends specific legislations. It is devoid of normative power since it describes the contours of the legal experience in the ancient Greek cities. However, it remains a useful tool in promoting a shared understanding and enabling useful comparisons with the legal orders of ancient Rome, Egypt, Middle East, and Anatolia.

iliasarn@academyofathens.gr

REFERENCES

Adam-Magnissali, S. (2008) *Hē aponomē tēs dikaiosynēs stēn archaia Athēna (5os kai 4os ai.)*, Athens.

Antoniou, D. (2013) "Entre doctrine et nécessité: L'œuvre législative de la monarchie absolue en Grèce (1833–1843)" *Études Balcaniques* 19–20, 259–81.

---

[24] See Karabelias (2002) and Karabelias (2004).

Fiorakis, St.I. & Peraki, E.E. (1973) *Hē megalē dōdekadeltos epigraphē tēs Gortynos*, Hērakleion.
Finley, M.I. (1951) "Some problems of Greek law. A consideration of Pringsheim on sale" *Seminar* 9, 72–91.
Finley, M.I. (1966) "The problem of the unity of Greek law" in: *La storia del diritto nel quadro delle scienze storiche* (Atti del primo Congresso Internazionale della Società Italiana di Storia del Diritto, Rome, December 1963), 129–142, Firenze. (= Finley, M. I. (1975) *The use and abuse of history*, 134–152, London)
Fustel de Coulanges, N.D. (1866) *La cité antique; étude sur le culte, le droit, les institutions de la Grèce et de Rome*, Paris.
Fustel de Coulanges, N.D. (1885) *Recherches sur quelques problèmes d'histoire*, Paris.
Gabba, C.F. (1880) *Della condizione giuridica della donne. Studi e confronti*[2], Torino.
Gagarin, M. (2005) "The unity of Greek law" in: Gagarin, M. & Cohen, C. (eds) *The Cambridge companion to ancient Greek law*, 29–40, Cambridge.
Gagarin, M. & Perlman, P. (2016) *The laws of ancient Crete c. 650–400 BCE*, Oxford.
Golfavru, J.-C. (1868) *Du mariage et du contrat de mariage en Angleterre et aux États-Unis. Législation comparée de l'Angleterre, des États-Unis et de la France*, Paris.
Greiff, Fr. (1888) *De l'origine du testament romain. Étude d'antiquités juridiques*, Paris.
Harris, E.M. (2018) "Some recent developments in the study of ancient Greek law" *JAC* 33, 187–266.
Hermann, K.F. (1855) *Über Grundsätze und Anwendung des Strafrechts im griechischen Alterthume*, Göttingen.
Herrick, F.M. (1890) *The Attic law of status, family relations and succession in the fourth century B.C.*, New York
von Jhering, R. (1886) *L'esprit du droit romain dans les diverses phases de son développement*, 2éme éd., tome 1, Paris (= Der Geist des römischen Rechts auf den verschiedenen Stufen seiner Entwicklung, Teil 1, Leipzig 1852).
Karabelias, E. (2002) *L'épiclérat attique*, Athènes.
Karabelias, E. (2004) *Recherches sur la condition juridique et sociale de la fille unique dans le monde grec ancien excepté Athènes*, Athènes.
Koenigswarter, L.J. (1843) *Essai sur la législation des peuples anciens et modernes relative aux enfants nés hors mariage*, Paris.
Köppen, F. (1818) *Politik nach platonischen Grundsätzen mit Anwendung auf unsere Zeit*, Leipzig.
LeFort, C. (1850) *Essai historique sur la tutelle en droit romain*, Genève.
Leist, B.W. (1884) *Graeco-italische Rechtsgeschichte*, Jena.
Leist, G.A. (1886) *Der attische Eigentumsstreit im System der Diadikasien*, Jena.
Mähly, J.A. (1853) *Die Frauen des griechischen Alterthums*, Basel.
von Maurer, G.L. (1835) *Das griechische Volk in öffentlicher, kirchlicher und privatrechtlicher Beziehung, vor und nach dem Freiheitskampfe bis zum 31. Juli, 1834*, Heidelberg.
Mavrocordato, D.-E. (1847) *Essai historique sur les divers ordres de succession ab intestat*, Paris.

Mirasgetzis, D. (1939) "Ho prōtos poinikos kōdix tēs neōteras Hellados (To 'Apanthisma tōn Enklēmatikōn' tou 1823)" *Sōphronistikai Plērophoriai* 4/2–3, 178ff.

Mitteis, L. (1891) *Reichsrecht und Volksrecht in den östlichen Provinzen des römischen Kaiserreichs: mit Beiträgen zur Kenntniss des griechischen Rechts und der spätrömischen Rechtsentwicklung*, Leipzig.

Negri, Chr. (1864) *Memorie storico-politiche sugli antichi Greci e Romani*, Torino.

Paturet, G. (1886) *La condition juridique de la femme dans l'ancienne Égypte*, Paris.

Petit, S. (1615) *Leges Atticae*, Paris.

Phillips, D.D. (2014) "Hubris and the unity of Greek law" in: Gagarin, M. & Lanni, A. (eds) *Symposion 2013. Vorträge zur griechischen und hellenistischen Rechtsgeschichte* (Cambridge MA, 26–29 August 2013), 75–102, Wien (with a reply by Adriaan Lanni).

Platner, E. (1820) *Beitrage zur Kenntniss des attischen Rechts*, Marburg.

Post, A.H. (1891) *Über die Aufgaben einer allgemeinen Rechtswissenschaft*, Oldenburg.

Reinach, S. (1885) *Traité d'épigraphie grecque*[3], Paris.

Révillout, E. (1886) *Les obligations en droit Égyptien comparé aux autres droits de l'antiquité*, Paris.

Saredo, G. (1873) *Saggio sulla storia del diritto internazionale privato*, Firenze.

von Schrader, E. (1838) *Erläuterung des Zwölf-Tafel-Gesetzes mit Rücksicht auf die Bedeutung desselben für das spätere Recht*, Tübingen.

de Schryver, A. (1844) *Commentaire de la loi Rhodia de jactu précedé d'une introduction historique*, Bruxelles.

Schulin, F. (1882) *Das griechische Testament verglichen mit dem römischen*, Basel.

Sealey, R. (1994) *The justice of the Greeks*, Ann Arbor.

Taylor, J. (1828) *Elements of the civil law*[4], London (first edition 1755).

Thür, G. (2007) "Die Einheit des 'Griechischen Rechts'. Gedanken zum Prozessrecht in den griechischen Poleis" *Etica & Politica* 9, 25–54 (= *Dike* 9 (2006) [2008] 23–62).

Triantaphyllopoulos, J. (1968) *Hellēnika Dikaia*, Athēnai.

Triantaphyllopoulos, J. (1985) *Das Rechtsdenken der Griechen*, München.

Typaldos, I. (1887) *Hermēneia tēs en Gortyni tēs Krētēs to 1884 anakaluphtheisēs epigraphēs*, Athēnai.

Tzōrakis, G.A. (2018) «Hē krētikē archaiologia ston tupo tou Hērakleiou stē metabasē ston 20o aiōna. Hē drasē tou Philekpaideutikou Syllogou Hērakleiou kai hē prin apo auton arcaiologikē pragmatikotēta» in: *Praktika tou 11 Diethnous Krētologikou Synedriou* (Rethymno, 21–27 Oktōvriou 2011), A.1/4, 333–360, Rethymno.

Vasilakis, A. (2017) «Hē krētikē archaiologia se epanastatikē periodo, 1878–1913. Archaiologia kai politikē stēn Othōmanokratia kai tēn Krētikē Politeia» (Archaeology in Crete in a revolutionary period, 1878–1913. Archaeological policy in the late Ottoman period and the Cretan State) *Themata Archaiologias* 1/1, 70–81.

Willets, R.F. (1967) *The law code of Gortyn*, Berlin.

SOPHIA ANEZIRI (ATHEN)

STIFTUNGEN IM ANTIKEN GRIECHENLAND: EINE SELBSTÄNDIGE RECHTSINSTITUTION?

Abstract: Altgriechische Schenkungen oder Zuwendungen von Geldern oder Immobilien, deren Erträge einem vom Stifter festgelegten Zweck auf Dauer dienen sollten, sind in der deutschsprachigen Literatur als „Stiftungen" bezeichnet. Diese Wiedergabe – so wie auch die englische "foundation" oder die französische „fondation" – ist jedoch nicht unproblematisch, da sie eine bestimmte Definition der Stiftung als selbständige Rechtsinstitution voraussetzt. Im Rahmen dieses Artikels werde ich mich zunächst mit der Problematik der modernen Terminologie auseinandersetzen und diese Problematik, in einem zweiten Schritt, anhand von konkreten Beispielen altgriechischer Stiftungen weiter vertiefen. Ziel ist es aufzuzeigen, dass die altgriechischen Stiftungen das Fehlen von Formalismus im antiken griechischen Recht bestätigen und dass sie eine fruchtbare Mischung von finanziellen und administrativen Verfahrensweisen darstellen, die in der Welt der griechischen Poleis weit verbreitet waren.

Keywords: Stiftung, foundation, fondation, endowment, Terminologie, Schenkung, Hinterlassenschaft, Vermögensübertragung

In der griechischen Antike gibt es bekanntlich Übertragungen von mobilem oder immobilem Vermögen durch Schenkung oder Hinterlassenschaft, die auf einen konkreten dauerhaften Zweck abzielen. Dieser Zweck sollte – den Wünschen des Schenkenden entsprechend – durch die Einkünfte des investierten Vermögens auf Dauer bedient werden. Der Spender vertraut das mobile oder immobile Vermögen einer Einrichtung an, die dauerhafter als der Mensch ist. Das Wesentliche bei diesen Übertragungen ist nicht die Freigebigkeit, sondern die ewige Last, mit der das übertragene Vermögen einhergeht.[1]

---

[1] Das Thema war in verschiedenen Zusammenhängen Gegenstand wissenschaftlichen Interesses. Ziebarth 1903, 1906, 1940 äußerte sich zu den rechtlichen Aspekten des Themas. Bernhardt Laum veröffentlichte 1914 eine zweibändige Monographie (Laum 1914), die nach wie vor ein Standardwerk ist. Eine Untersuchung der *Stiftungen* in verschiedenen europäischen und außereuropäischen Gesellschaften, einschließlich der griechischen Antike, unternehmen Sitta von Reden in einem Sammelband (von Reden 2015) und Michael Borgolte in einer kürzlich erschienenen Monographie (Borgolte 2020).

Die verbindenden, unverzichtbaren Elemente, aus denen sich solche Übertragungen zusammensetzen, sind folgende:[2] das mobile oder immobile Vermögen, der vom Schenkenden festgelegte Zweck (der aus den dafür vorgesehenen Vermögenswerten oder, genauer gesagt, aus dessen Erträgen erfüllt werden soll), die Dauer der Spende (die nach den Wünschen des Schenkenden und den Regelungen unbegrenzt sein soll) und eine Einrichtung, die mit der Betreuung und Verwaltung der Spende betraut ist. Zu den Zwecken, die durch solche Spenden finanziert werden, gehören unter anderem Feste und Agone, Gymnasien und Schulen, Geld- und Güterverteilungen, Bau oder Renovierung von Gebäuden.

Tatsache ist, dass es in den antiken Quellen keinen eigenen Terminus für diese Art von Eigentumsübertragungen gibt.[3] Die Begriffe, die in der modernen Forschung dafür verwendet werden, sind „Stiftungen", „fondations", „foundations" oder „ἱδρύματα". Diese Begriffe können irreführend sein, zumal sie unterschiedliche Strukturen in verschiedenen historischen Epochen bezeichnen. Genauer gesagt wurden in jüngerer Zeit als „Stiftungen" Schenkungen bezeichnet, deren Vermögensverwaltung und Zweckerfüllung in der Verantwortung einer eigens zu diesem Zweck gegründeten Trägerinstitution liegen. In der Antike hingegen wurden die Verwaltung des Geschäfts und die Bedienung des jeweiligen Zwecks bereits bestehenden Institutionen anvertraut, wie etwa der Polis, dem Rat, der Gerusia, einem Heiligtum oder auch Körperschaften und Vereinen verschiedenster Art. Dieser Widerspruch wurde in der Forschung bereits erkannt und von Ilias Arnaoutoglou eingehend beleuchtet.[4] Die Meinungsverschiedenheiten über die Auffassung, dass Stiftungen im antiken – insbesondere im römischen – Recht juristische Personen waren, werden dargestellt bei Robert Feenstra und Joseph Mélèze-Modrzejewski.[5]

---

[2] Siehe die Definition von Mélèze-Modrzejewski 1963: 89–90: „Le but de la fondation est d'affecter une masse de biens à un service déterminé sans limitation de durée. Le fondateur confie le capital à un organisme plus durable que l'homme. L'essentiel de la fondation n'est pas la libéralité, mais la charge perpétuelle qui la grève". Definitionen auch bei Harter-Uibopuu 2015: 180 Anm. 6.

[3] Lippert 1967: 25: „die damalige griechische Sprache (kannte) den Begriff Stiftung überhaupt nicht".

[4] Arnaoutoglou 2012–2013. Siehe schon Ziebarth 1940: 1236: „Stiftungen ‚im modernen Sinne', d. h. Zweckvermögen, welche niemand als sich selbst angehören, sind dem klassischen Recht durchaus fremd". In ähnlicher Weise spricht Petropoulos 1944: 428–489 von „nicht selbst existierenden Stiftungen" in der Antike.

[5] Feenstra 1956: 245–263; Mélèze-Modrzejewski 1963: 89 Anm. 29. Die Schwierigkeit der modernen Historiker mit den in vorrömischer Zeit weit verbreiteten unselbstständigen, nicht rechtsfähigen oder fiduziarischen Stiftungen zu handeln, bemerkt Feenstra 1956: 247–248; er äußert sogar die Ansicht, dass diese Art von Stiftungen „n'a même pas disparu après le XVIe siècle et, en Angleterre, elle semble toujours la seule construction possible: c'est l'idée du ‚trust' … qui est à la base de cette fondation appelée dédaigneusement ‚dépendante'". Nach Lohse 2014: 173 ist die Situation auch im Mittelalter nicht eindeutig.

Ein alternativer Begriff für diese Schenkungen, der sich in der heutigen Forschung, insbesondere nach den Arbeiten von Joshua Sosin, durchgesetzt hat, stellt der Begriff „endowment" dar.[6] Der Terminus „endowment" ist meines Erachtens für diese besondere Kategorie von Vermögensübertragungen besser geeignet als der Terminus „foundation", weil er zum einen nicht die modernen Konnotationen von Stiftungen/foundations aufweist und zum anderen sehr zutreffend die Übertragung von einer Einzelperson an eine öffentliche Einrichtung entweder zu Lebzeiten durch Schenkung oder nach dem Tod durch Vermächtnis beschreibt. Der Begriff „endowment" wird zu Recht durch den Zusatz „*sub modo*" (in Analogie zur *donatio sub modo*) ergänzt, um die Verpflichtung auszudrücken, das übertragene Vermögen in einer bestimmten Weise und zu einem bestimmten Zweck zu verwenden. Da jedoch, wie Andreas Victor Walser unter Bezugnahme auf das Referat von Kaja Harter-Uibopuu auf dem vorangegangenen Symposium zu Recht feststellte, nicht alle „endowments *sub modo*" verpflichtet waren, dauerhaften Zwecken zu dienen,[7] erweist sich die Formulierung „perpetual endowments *sub modo*" (d. h. permanente Spenden unter Auflagen) als am geeignetsten, um die Schenkungen mit diesen Merkmalen noch genauer zu erfassen.

Wie ich im Folgenden zeigen werde, führt die Untersuchung der einzelnen Elemente, aus denen sich die „permanenten Spenden unter Auflagen" in der Antike zusammensetzen, zu dem Schluss, dass sie keine besondere Kategorie an sich waren, sondern ein Konstrukt, das auf einer Kombination von bekannten und erprobten Praktiken und Verfahren beruhte. Im Anschluss an diese Ausführungen werden wir die Merkmale (rechtlich, verwaltungstechnisch, finanziell) untersuchen, die diese Kategorie von Spenden charakterisieren.

Der rechtliche Rahmen

Im antiken griechischen Recht gibt es keinen spezifischen Rechtsakt, der diese besondere Art der Vermögensübertragung beschreibt.[8] Die Übertragung des Vermögens zu einem konkreten Zweck erfolgte entweder durch eine Schenkung zu Lebzeiten des Schenkenden oder durch ein Vermächtnis (eventuell durch Testament) nach seinem Tod.

---

6 Unter anderem siehe Sosin 2000; Sosin 2014a; Sosin 2014b. Sosin benutzt den Begriff „endowment" sogar in einem erweiterten Sinn; er wendet ihn u. a. auf die Verkäufe von Land an das Heiligtum in Mylasa an, sowie auf die Bildung eines Kapitalstocks durch Subskriptionen in Samos (Sosin 2000, 78–127; vgl. Sosin 2004b: 1–8).

7 Walser 2021.

8 Laum 1914: I 54–60. Mélèze-Modrzejewski 1963: 90: "Ni en Grèce, ni dans le monde hellénistique, ni à Rome il n'existe une forme juridique *sui generis* qui puisse encadrer cette institution. Le mot fondation … n'a pas d'equivalent ni dans le grec ni dans le latin juridiques". Sosin 2000: 16 irrt sich, wenn er behauptet, Epikteta, Diomedon und Poseidonios hätten „a novel legal and economic mechanism, the economic foundation".

Für Vermögensübertragungen zu Lebzeiten des Spenders werden Termini wie etwa δωροῦμαι, χαρίζω, ἀπονέμω, συγχωρῶ, δόσις, (κατὰ) δωρεάν verwendet und für posthume Übertragungen ἀπολείπω, ἀφήκω, ἐπικαταλείπω, καταλείπω, κατὰ διαθήκην, διὰ διαθήκης.[9] Das neutrale Verb δίδωμι wird für beide Arten von Übertragungen verwendet: zu Lebzeiten des Schenkenden im Fall von Aristomenes und Psylla auf Korkyra und *post mortem* im Fall von Epikteta auf Thera.[10] Die Verben ἀνατίθημι, ἀνιερῶ, ἀφιερῶ, καθιερῶ, die die Weihe des Geschenks an eine Gottheit ausdrücken oder einfach die Verbindung zu einem Kult anzeigen, erscheinen in beiden Kategorien von Vermögensübertragungen, d. h. sowohl zu Lebzeiten als auch nach dem Tod des Schenkenden.[11]

Die bisher genannten Begriffe beschränkten sich jedoch nicht auf die „permanenten Spenden unter Auflagen“, sondern wurden für jede Übertragung von Eigentum durch Schenkung oder Erbschaft verwendet. Nur der Kontext kann uns die ergänzenden und differenzierenden Merkmale dieser besonderen Zuweisungen vermitteln. Der Zweck, dem sie dienen sollen (*sub modo*), wird durch ἐφ’ ᾧ, ἵνα, ὅπως, ὡς etc. eingeführt.[12] Ihre ewige Dauer („perpetual“) wird durch die Adjektive und Adverbien ἀίδιος, (εἰς) ἀεί, εἰς (ἅ)παντα χρόνον, ausgedrückt.[13]

---

9 Laum 1914: I 117–126; Arnaoutoglou 2012–2013: 68.

10 Aristomenes und Psylla: *IG* IX 1^2 4, 798 Z. 3, 5. Epikteta: *IG* XII 3, 330 Z. 29. Genau dasselbe gilt für „ἐπιδίδωμι“ (siehe z.B. *I.Vallée Enipeus* 52 Z. 11–12 und *IG* XII 3, 330 Z. 113). „Ἐπίδ[ο]σ̣[ιν πεποίη]ται“ ist auch gesichert in *IG* XII 6, 132 Z. 6–7, wo die Dotierung testamentarisch erfolgt (siehe auch *IG* XII 6 S. 97) und posthume Ehrungen betrifft.

11 *CID* V 128 Z. 1, 10. Vgl. ἀναθέν[τα κατὰ διαθ]ήκην in *I.Pergamon* 260 Z. 12–13 (= Laum 1914: II Nr. 70, 1. Jh. v. Chr – 1. Jh. n. Chr).

12 So z.B. *I.Labraunda* 8 Z. 20; *I.Didyma* 480 Z. 13; *IG* II^2 1325 Z. 23; *IGLS* VII 4028B+C Z. 23; *I.Ptolemaic* 113 Z. 38. Eine Kategorie von Zeugnissen, die viele Ungewissheiten lässt, eben weil der Zweck nicht explizit angegeben wird, sind die Weihungen von Land auf Grenzsteinen: Die kurzen Texte geben uns meistens nur den Namen des Weihenden, das geweihte Grundstück und den Gott (siehe beispielweise *IG* XII 7, 57A = *Syll.*[3] 1189 aus Arkesine/Amorgos, 3. Jh. v. Chr. und *IG* VII 1786, 1788–1790 = *I.Thespies* 68, 58–60 aus Thespiai, 3. Jh. v. Chr.); der Kontext lässt die Vermutung zu, dass das Einkommen des Landes zur Finanzierung der erweiterten Kultbedürfnisse diente, jedoch wissen wir nicht, ob diese Einkünfte mit spezifischen Ausgaben verbunden waren; dies wird nur in ganz wenigen Fällen deutlich, z.B. beim Grenzstein des Landes, das Philetairos dem Hermes zur Finanzierung des Öls für das Gymnasion in Thespiai weihte (*I.Thespies* 61, 267–265 v. Chr.).

13 So z.B. *I.Thespies* 61 Z. 8–9; *Choix Delphes* 168 Z. 9–10; *IG* XII 7, 515 Z. 103; *IG* XII 9, 236 Z. 15–17; *I.Labraunda* 8 Z. 20–21; *I.Mylasa* 829 Z. 6; *I.Ilion* 52 Z. 8–10; *I.Histria* 58 Z. 19–20. In der römischen Kaiserzeit sind Begriffe wie αἰώνιον, εἰς (τὸν) αἰῶνα, διηνεκῶς, εἰς τὸ διηνεκές für solche permanente Zuwendungen sehr gebräuchlich; siehe z.B. *I.Aphrodisias* 2007 11.110 Z. 17–18; *I.Aphrodisias* 2007 12.1002 Z. 10; *TAM* III 109 Z. 12; *I.Tralleis* 146 Z. 7 = Laum 1914: II Nr. 98; *I.Ephesos* 22 Z. 20–21 = Laum 1014: II Nr. 130–131; *IGR* IV 661 Z. 28 = Laum 1914: II Nr. 173.

Ein weiterer Faktor, der bei diesen „permanenten Spenden unter Auflagen“ eine wichtige Rolle spielt, ist die ἐπαγγελία oder ὁμολογία des Schenkenden.[14] Streng genommen haben diese Handlungen keinen Rechtscharakter und berühren nicht das rechtliche Wesen der Vermögensübertragung selbst. Vielmehr handelt es sich um rituelle Handlungen. So ist *epangelia* das Versprechen, das der Geber öffentlich in Form einer feierlichen Erklärung/Ankündigung abgibt. Bei der *homologia*, die ebenfalls öffentlich vorgenommen wird, liegt der Schwerpunkt auf der verbindlichen Zustimmung des Gebers.[15] Die *epangelia* kann auch durch einen Brief des Gebers (Königs oder königlichen Beamten) an die Gemeinschaft erfolgen; das Gleiche gilt für die *homologia.*[16] Die Gemeinschaft, die eine permanente Spende erhielt, musste auch eine gewisse Verantwortung hinsichtlich der Verwaltung und der Aufrechterhaltung des angegebenen Zwecks übernehmen. Die Spende geht daher manchmal mit einer Annahme durch die Empfängergemeinschaft (Polis, Verein oder andere Gemeinde) einher. In mehreren Fällen liegt uns nicht einmal der Akt/die Urkunde der Spende selbst vor, sondern nur das Dekret, mit dem der Empfänger die Spende akzeptiert und die Einzelheiten ihrer Durchführung regelt.[17] Die Praxis der öffentlichen Ankündigung und der Annahme durch die Gemeinde ist natürlich nicht nur auf „permanente Spenden unter Auflagen“ beschränkt, sondern erscheint auch bei Fällen von „normalen“ Schenkungen, *epidoseis*, Darlehen und sonstigen Wohltaten.[18]

Die Bedingungen, die die Zuweisung regeln und die beiden Parteien, Geber und Empfänger, binden, werden durch die Formulierung „ἐπὶ τοῖσδε“ eingeleitet. Diese Formulierung wird zum Beispiel bei der Einleitung des (in der Form einer Weihung erfolgenden) Schenkungsaktes von Agasigratis in Kalaureia und dem Ver-

[14] *epangelia* und *homologia* sind u. a. in folgenden „permanenten Spenden unter Auflagen“ belegt: Jaccottet 2003: II 279–280 Nr. 170 Z. 6–7; *SEG* 33, 1039 Z. 92; *I.Delphinion* 145 Z. 3–4; *I.Mylasa* 421 Z. 8.

[15] Eine umfassende Übersicht über die Ansichten zur *homologia* und ihrer Entwicklung findet sich in Giouni 2000: 221–223. Über *homologia* und *epangelia* siehe auch Velissaropoulos-Karakostas 2011: II 214–218, 222–252.

[16] *Epangelia* durch den Brief eines Königs sehen wir in *I.Labraunda* 8 Z. 10–26; Welles, *RC* 52. Für briefliche *homologia* siehe *F.Delphes* III 3, 239 Z. 4–5.

[17] Beides, d. h. sowohl der Spendeakt als auch das Annahmedekret, ist z.B. in folgenden Fällen belegt: *IG* IV 841; *IG* IX 12 4, 798; Parker 2010: 106 face iii Z. 23–26. Nur die Annahme seitens des Empfängers ist beispielsweise in *Choix Delphes* 168; *IG* XII 4, 79; *IG* XII 5, 595; *I.Mylasa* 421, 829; *I.Rhodische Peraia* 303; *I.Delphinion* 145; *I.Ilion* 52; I.*Lampsakos* 9 erhalten. Das Annahmedekret kann eventuell auch auf den Spendenakt Bezug nehmen (siehe z.B. Jaccottet 2003: II 279–280 Nr. 170, Z. 6–10 wo das Dekret mit einem direkten Verweis auf das Versprechen des Stifters Argea beginnt).

[18] So z.B. Malay 1983: 8–9 Nr. 3 = *SEG* 33: 1041 Z. 2–9; vgl. Velissaropoulos-Karakostas 2011: II 239–240. Im Dekret *I.Iasos* I 22 Z. 22–25 wird die Ankündigung (*epangelia*) eines Wohltäters namens Chares, ein öffentliches Gebäude (*agoranomion*) auf seinen Kosten zu errichten, akzeptiert und die Durführung des Projektes geregelt (vgl. Velissaropoulos-Karakostas 2011: II 237–238). Für *epangelia* in *epidoseis* siehe Migeotte 1992: 325–326 und in Darlehen Migeotte 1984: 319–322 Nr. 102.

mächtnis (ebenfalls in der Form einer Widmung) von Alkesippos in Delphi verwendet.[19] Es handelt sich noch einmal um eine Formulierung, die nicht ausschließlich in den Urkunden von „permanenten Spenden unter Auflagen" vorkommt, sondern auch in anderen Texten wie Pachtverträgen, Freilassungen oder Vereinbarungen zwischen Städten belegt ist.[20]

Die Abfolge der *epangelia/homologia* durch den Geber und die Annahme durch den Empfänger[21] sowie die Existenz von Bedingungen und nicht die Rechtsnatur der „permanenten Spenden unter Auflagen" an sich sind jene Elemente, die Anneliese Mannzmann darauf gebracht haben, die „Stiftungen" als „Verträge" zu interpretieren.[22] Die Meinung von Mannzmann wurde von Rechtshistorikern stark kritisiert.[23] Das Hauptargument dieser Kritik war, dass eine solche Spende zwar auf den ersten Blick einige Merkmale eines Vertrags aufweist (Geben und Empfangen, Versprechen und Annahme, Zeugen), dennoch nicht als Vertrag verstanden werden kann, zumal der Gegenstand (Geld oder Immobilien) geschenkt, vererbt oder geweiht wurde – Handlungen, bei denen ein Vertrag keinen Platz hat.[24] Was in diesen Fällen erfolgte, war lediglich eine verbindliche Vereinbarung zwischen dem Geber und dem Empfänger. Der Empfänger übernahm Pflichten und trug Verantwortung, etwaige Sanktionen gegen Verstöße ergaben sich aber nicht aus einem Vertragsbruch, sondern aus der Verletzung des Willens des Stifters oder der von der Gemeinschaft beschlossenen Regeln. In manchen Fällen erlangen die von der Empfängergemeinschaft genehmigten Vereinbarungen über die Verwaltung der permanenten Spenden sogar Gesetzeskraft. Beispiele hierfür sind: die Dekrete, mit denen Aigiale und Minoa auf Amorgos sowie Teos in Ionien die von Kritolaos, Hegesarete und Polythrous veranlassten Schenkungen annahmen und die im Text selbst als Gesetze bezeichnet werden;[25] die Ehreninschrift für einen Gymnasiarchen, der dem aiolischen

---

19 *IG* IV 840; *CID* V 128 (Alkesippos in Delphi). In keinem der beiden Fälle ist jedoch das Dekret mit dem die Polis das Geschenk akzeptierte, in Stein gemeißelt.

20 So z.B. *IG* II^2 2498 Z. 6; *F.Delphes* III 1, 302 Z. 2; *I.Cret.* IV 179.

21 Ausgehend von dem bekannten Fall des Demosthenes in Oinoanda in römischer Zeit, bietet Wörrle 1988: 23–31 eine gute Analyse der Abfolge *epangelia* – Akzeptanz.

22 Mannzmann 1956: 127–130; Mannzmann 1962: 81–83, 110–117. Im gleichen Sinne R. Dareste, B. Haussoulier und Th. Reinach, die in einigen Testamenten und Schenkungsurkunden einen „caractère contractuel" sehen (*I.jur.gr.* II S. 175–176).

23 Siehe besonders Wolff 1962: 265–275; Latte 1962: 374–376; Triantaphyllopoulos 1962: 567–569; Mélèze-Modrzejewski 1963: 82–92; Hommel 1964: 614–621.

24 Mélèze-Modrzejewski 1963: 90: "L'élément contractuel est donc souvent présent dans les moyens juridiques utilisés pour constituer une fondation. Cela ne veut pas dire pour autant que la fondation soit un contract". Siehe die Betrachtung von Patera 2012: 54 bezüglich der Weihungen: "Remarquons pour commencer que la formule *do-ut-des* ne s'identifie pas au contrat: elle implique une offrande qui a pour but de susciter une réaction, alors que le contrat suppose l'engagement de deux parties".

25 *IG* XII 7, 515 Z. 3–6, 131–134 (Kritolaos in Aigiale); *IG* Suppl. S. 144 Z. 3–7 (Hegesarete in Minoa); Cassayre 2010: 185–189 Nr. 31 Z. 43–45, 48–50, 52, 64–65, 67 (Polythrous in Teos). Ein ähnlicher Fall kommt aus der Welt der Vereine: Das Dekret, mit dem der

Larissa Land vermachte, in der der in den Archiven aufzubewahrende „νόμος“ und die „διαταγή“ erwähnt wird;[26] das Dekret, mit dem die Stadt Korkyra die Schenkung von Aristomenes und Psylla annahm und mit dem beschlossen wurde, das Gesetz, das die Verwaltung der Schenkung regelt, bei einer Korrektur der Stadtgesetze in die Gesetze der Stadt aufzunehmen.[27]

Der Verwaltungsrahmen

Der Empfänger einer solchen „permanenten Spende unter Auflagen“ konnte eine bürgerliche Gemeinschaft (*polis*, *demos*, *koinon*), eine Gottheit oder ein Verein sein. Er existierte meistens bereits vor der Spende und verfügte über bestimmte Strukturen und spezifische rechtliche und verwaltungstechnische Instrumente. Die jeweilige Schenkung ging genau in dieses bereits existierende Netzwerk ein.[28]

Wichtig war die Rolle des Stadtrates bei der Verwaltung der Schenkung von Aristomenes and Psylla auf Korkyra und von Kritolaos auf Amorgos.[29] Auch Magistrate der jeweiligen Empfängergemeinde spielten eine wichtige Rolle, zumal sie mit der Investition des übertragenen Vermögens oder der Erfüllung des Schenkungszwecks betraut wurden; so wurde z. B. bei der Schenkung des Theopompos für das Gymnasion in Eretria der Kauf des Öls und die Anlage des Kapitals städtischen Beamten übertragen.[30] Bei der Eintreibung von Bußgeldern von denjenigen, die gegen die Regeln der Spenden verstießen, oder von Beamten, die ihre Aufgaben bei der Verwaltung der Spenden nicht erfüllt hatten, wurden auch die Rechtsmechanismen der Städte genutzt; dies ist der Fall bei den *euthynoi* in der Schenkung des Polythrous in Teos[31] oder beim *boulomenos* in der Schenkung des Kritolaos in Aigiale auf Amorgos.[32]

Die Poleis, die solche Spenden erhielten, konnten bestehende Gesetze für ihre Verwaltung nutzen. Beispielsweise setzte die Stadt Milet seine Markt- und Erziehungsgesetze in Kraft, um Angelegenheiten zu regeln, die die permanente Spende des Eudemos für die Erziehung der Kinder betrafen[33], und Delphi nutzte das *mastrikos*-

---

von Epikteta gegründete Familienverband ihr Testament annimmt und bestimmte Fragen regelt, wird auch als „νόμος“ bezeichnet (*IG* XII 3, 330 Z. 212, 243, 246, 274, 282).

26 *I.Kyme* 102 Z. 8.

27 *IG* IX 1² 4, 798 Z. 137–140.

28 Harter-Uibopuu 2011: 119: „...foundations required relatively complex procedures of investment and management of the capital in order to produce a regular income...“.

29 *IG* IX 1² 4, 798 Z. 8–12, 42–44, 94–98, 140; *IG* XII 7, 515 Z. 18–19, 30–31, 34, 38, 99, 108, 111–112.

30 *IG* XII 9, 236 Z. 60–65.

31 Cassayre 2010: 185–189 Nr. 31 Z. 59–60.

32 *IG* XII 7, 515 Z. 119–120, 125–130. *Boulomenos* war jeder, der eine Anzeige wegen eines Verstoßes vorbringen wollte, wobei die übliche Belohnung ein Teil der Geldstrafe war (siehe Rubinstein 2003: 87–113).

33 *I.Delphinion* 145 Z. 61–64. Um die Gesetze der Erziehung (*paidonomikos*) und des Gymnasions (*gymnasiarchikos*) handelt es sich vermutlich bei den Gesetzen (ohne nähere

Gesetz gegen diejenigen, die die Dauerschenkung von Attalos II. für die Erziehung der Kinder und das Fest der Attaleia missbrauchten und die damit verbundenen Riten nicht durchführten.[34] Die permanente Spende von Aristomenes und Psylla bezieht sich hingegen auf das Gesetz des Agonotheten, während die des Kritolaos das gymnasiarchische Gesetz zur Grundlage nimmt.[35] Möglich war auch, dass die Angelegenheiten solcher permanenten Spenden ähnlich wie bei anderen Fällen behandelt wurden; so folgte die Zahlung der Zinsen für die Darlehen aus dem Kritolaos-Kapital in Aigiale von Amorgos beispielsweise den Regeln für die heiligen Gelder.[36]

Zwei weitere Instrumente, die in der Verwaltung allgemein üblich und hilfreich waren, nämlich der Eid und die Rechenschaftsablegung der Magistrate, wurden auch auf permanente Spenden angewandt, um Verstöße gegen ihre Regeln zu verhindern. An dieser Stelle seien nur zwei Fälle aufgeführt: Die Epimeleten, die die Geschenke der Attaliden an Delphi verwalteten, mussten zu Beginn ihrer Amtszeit einen Eid leisten,[37] während bei den Geschenken von Agasikles und Nikagora sowie von Agasigratis in Kalaureia der Eid der Epimeleten mit der Rechenschaftsablegung am Ende ihrer Amtszeit verbunden war.[38]

Aus verwaltungstechnischer Sicht gibt es also kein Element, von dem man sagen könnte, dass es den „permanenten Spenden unter Auflagen“ eigen ist und ihnen ein besonderes Merkmal verleiht. Die Empfänger dieser Spenden bedienten sich vertrauter Verwaltungsmechanismen.

Der finanzielle Rahmen

Bei „permanenten Spenden unter Auflagen“ geht es darum, den gestifteten oder vererbten Vermögenswert (Geld oder Immobilien) zu bewahren und ihn so anzulegen, dass er Erträge abwirft, mit denen der angegebene Zweck auf Dauer unterstützt werden kann.

Im Wesentlichen war die Verknüpfung von Einnahmen und Ausgaben eine gängige Praxis, die in verschiedenen Bereichen der antiken griechischen Wirtschaft angewandt wurde. Im Interesse größerer Effizienz und einer besseren langfristigen Kontrolle ihrer Finanzen verpflichteten sich die Städte, bestimmte Einnahmen zu verwenden, um bestimmte Ausgaben regelmäßig zu bedienen.[39] Ein charakteristisches

---

Angaben), die im Dekret von Teos über die Zuwendung des Polythrous genannt werden (Cassayre 2010: 185–189 Nr. 31 Z. 27–30).

[34] *Choix Delphes* 168 Z. 48–53. Das Gleiche gilt für das Geschenk von Eumenes II (*F.Delphes* III 3, 238 Z. 2–5).

[35] *IG* IX 1^2 4, 798 Z. 15–16, 22–23, 80–81, 86–87, 93–95; *IG* XII 7, 515 Z. 81–83.

[36] *IG* XII 7, 515 Z. 19, 31–32.

[37] *F.Delphes* III 3, 238 Z. 1; *Choix Delphes* 168 Z. 38–39.

[38] *IG* IV 841 Z. 28–31 und 840 Z. 15–16.

[39] Migeotte 2014: 175–204, 444–449. Siehe auch Harter-Uibopuu 2013: 51–66: „Wenn auch für die hellenistischen und kaiserzeitlichen Städte kein detaillierter Haushaltsplan oder Budgetvoranschlag nachgewiesen werden kann, zeigen die erhaltenen Quellen doch

Beispiel ist das Athener Getreidegesetz, mit dem die Stadt festlegte, dass die Beträge aus der Getreideproduktion der in Lemnos, Imbros und Skyros installierten Athener für Militärausgaben aufgebracht werden sollten.[40] Ein samisches Gesetz über die Einfuhr von Getreide verknüpft die Zinseinnahmen aus bestimmten Darlehen mit dem Kauf von Getreide.[41] Die Pflege zur dauerhaften Verbindung der Grundbedürfnisse einer Gemeinde mit einem stabilen Einkommen wird klar in der Haushaltsplanung zweier neuer Gemeinden der hellenistischen Zeit: Im Synoikismos von Teos und Lebedos um 303 v. Chr. schlagen die Lebedier vor, 1400 Goldstatere aus den Einnahmen zur Getreideversorgung beiseite zu legen, so dass jeder, der es wünschte, mit diesem Geld gegen Hinterlegung von Sicherheiten Getreide in die Stadt einführen konnte.[42] Als die Gemeinde von Toriaion (oder Tyriaion) in Phrygien nach 188 v. Chr. zur Stadt erhoben wurde, wies Eumenes II. die vom Agoranomos erhobenen Steuereinnahmen dem Kauf von Öl für das Gymnasion zu, bis Land oder Felder oder andere zinspflichtige Güter zur Finanzierung diesen Zweckes gefunden wurden.[43]

Die „permanenten Spenden unter Auflagen", so wie wir sie definiert haben, folgen also im Wesentlichen einer finanziellen Standardpraxis und beruhen auf einem Standard-Wirtschaftsmodell.[44] Gleichzeitig weisen sie aber Merkmale auf, die eine Verwechslung mit anderen Fällen von Staatsfinanzen ausschließen.

1) In den „permanenten Spenden unter Auflagen" sind die Immobilien oder Gelder, aus denen die Mittel zur Finanzierung des jeweiligen Zwecks stammen, solange privates Eigentum, bis sie (durch Schenkung oder Vermächtnis) in den Besitz der Gemeinde übergehen.[45] Im Umkehrschluss bedeutet dies, dass die Widmung von anderem als privatem Eigentum zur Finanzierung eines bestimmten Zweckes keine „permanente Spende unter Auflagen" ist.

---

deutlich, dass die Verwendung von Geldern aus den städtischen Kassen oftmals an einen bestimmten Zweck gebunden war" (S. 52).

[40] Stroud 1998: S. 5 Z. 53–55, 374/3 v. Chr.

[41] *IG* XII 6, 172, um 250 v. Chr.

[42] Welles, *RC* 3-4, um 303 v. Chr.

[43] *I.Sultan Daği* I 393 Z. 42–47 = *SEG* 47, 1745, nach 188 v. Chr.

[44] Meines Erachtens verwendet Migeotte gerade aus diesem Grund den Begriff „fondations" für alle Einnahmen, die, ohne notwendigerweise aus einer Schenkung oder einem Vermächtnis hervorgegangen zu sein, über einen langen Zeitraum an bestimmte Ausgaben gebunden waren (Migeotte 2014: 183–204). Eine feste Bindung an bestimmte Ausgaben ist nach Migeotte auch ein Merkmal dessen, was er „fonds de roulement" nennt (Migeotte 2014: 176–183).

[45] Dies gilt auch für königliche Liegenschaften, die von hellenistischen Königen den Heiligtümern zur permanenten Finanzierung kultischer Aktivitäten überlassen wurden. Siehe z.B. das syrische Dorf Baitokaike, das von einem seleukidischen König namens Antiochos dem Zeus von Baitokaike geschenkt wurde (*IGLS* VII 4028B+C) und die Ländereien, die Antiochos I. von Kommagene den Heiligtümern seines Reiches anbot (Dörner – Goell 1963: 40–59; Dörner – Young 1996: 206–217, vielleicht 70/69–38 v. Chr.).

Zwei Fälle können nach dem zuvor Ausgeführten nicht als „permanente Spenden unter Auflagen" verstanden werden, auch wenn Laum beide Fälle zu den „Stiftungen" zählt.[46] In Oropos weiht Sulla im 1. Jh. v. Chr. Land von 1000 Fuß Länge und Breite sowie die Einkünfte aus Stadt, Land und den Häfen dem Heiligtum des Amphiaraos; dadurch wurden diese Einkünfte von den durch die Römer auferlegten Steuern befreit und für Opfer und Spiele (besonders das Fest der Amphiaraieia und Romaia) verwendet.[47] Es handelt sich zwar um Land, dessen Einkommen für einen konkreten Zweck bestimmt werden, aber diese Zuwendung kann nicht als Schenkung im engeren Sinne betrachtet werden, und schon gar nicht als Schenkung von Privateigentum: Sulla überträgt dem Heiligtum Ländereien und Einkommen, die früher der Stadt gehörten.

Im Ägypten des 3. Jhs. v. Chr. widmeten die *Synbasilistai* and *Dioskouriastai* zusammen mit ihrem Priester Theoros die Mieten bestimmter Grundstücke, die offensichtlich ihrem Verein gehörten, zur Finanzierung von Opfern für das Königspaar und die Götter – die höchstwahrscheinlich im Rahmen des Vereins begangen wurden.[48] Es handelt sich um keine „Stiftung" bzw. „Rentenstiftung", denn es gibt kein Vermögen bzw. Einkommen, das den Eigentümer wechselt. Es handelt sich vielmehr um eine einfache interne Regelung, bei der bestimmte Einnahmen des Vereins mit einer bestimmten Ausgabe desselben Vereins verbunden waren.

2) In den „permanenten Spenden unter Auflagen" sind die Personen, die ihr Vermögen übertragen, diejenigen, die die Verwendung des übertragenen Eigentums (mit)bestimmen. Im Umkehrschluss bedeutet dies, dass Erträge aus einem Kapital, beispielsweise aus einer *epidosis* mehrerer Personen, dessen Verwaltungsregeln durch die Polis festgelegt wurden, nicht als Beleg für eine „permanente Spende unter Auflagen" betrachtet werden können. Ein solcher Fall ist z. B. der Fond, der aus den Beiträgen der Bürger von Samos gebildet wurde, um mit den Zinsen daraus den Kauf von Getreide zur kostenlosen Verteilung an das Volk zu finanzieren.[49]

Zusammenfassend kann festgestellt werden, dass „permanente Spenden unter Auflagen" ein Patch-Work aus bestehenden rechtlichen, wirtschaftlichen und administrativen Instrumenten und Praktiken waren, das das Fehlen von jeglichem Formalismus im antiken griechischen Recht bestätigt. Diese Kategorie von Vermögensübertragungen unterscheidet sich dank ihrer besonderen Merkmale deutlich von

[46] Laum 1914: Nr. 26 und 207.

[47] *I.Oropos* 308 = Manieri 2009: 237–241 Nr. 14. Siehe auch Sherk, *RDGE* 23 und Rigsby 1996: 77–81.

[48] *I.Mus. Varsovie* 44, ca. 246–241 v. Chr.

[49] *IG* XII 6, 172, um 250 v. Chr. Trotzdem zählen Sosin 2000: 78–109 und Migeotte 2014: 185–187 diesen Fall zu ihren „fondations" und „endowments" (es sei hier jedoch daran erinnert, dass beide Autoren die Termini „fondations" und „endowments" in einem erweiterten Sinn benutzen, siehe oben Anm. 6 und 44).

anderen Formen der dauerhaften, bedingten Finanzierung. Wie bei den meisten Definitions- und Kategorisierungsversuchen gibt es dennoch auch hier Fälle, die nicht mit Sicherheit zugeordnet werden können.

Zusammenfassung

„Permanente Spenden unter Auflagen" sind Schenkungen oder Zuwendungen von Geldern oder Immobilien, deren Erträge einem vom Stifter festgelegten Zweck auf Dauer dienen sollten. Diese Spenden stellen eine fruchtbare Mischung von rechtlichen, administrativen und finanziellen Verfahrensweisen dar, die in der Welt der griechischen Poleis weit geläufig waren.

sanez@arch.uoa.gr

BIBLIOGRAPHIE

Die Abkürzungen der Inschriften-Corpora folgen den *Abbreviations of Editions and Works of Reference for Alphabetic Greek Epigraphy* auf der Website der *International Association of Greek and Latin Epigraphy* (AIEGL).

Arnaoutoglou, I.N. 2012–2013. „Δωρεές, κληροδοτήματα και ιδρύματα στην ελληνορωμαϊκή αρχαιότητα. Προβλήματα ορολογίας", *Epetiris tou Kentrou Ereunis tis Historias tou Ellinikou Dikaiou* 44: 59–85

Borgolte, M. 2020. *World History as the History of Foundations, 3000 BCE to 1500 CE*. Leiden/Boston

Cassayre, A. 2010. *La justice sur les pierres. Recueil d'inscriptions à caractère juridique des cités grecques à l'époque hellénistique*. Rennes

Dörner, F.K. – Goell, T. 1963. *Arsameia am Nymphaios*. Istanbuler Forschungen 23. Berlin

Dörner, F.K. – Young, J.H. 1996. „Sculpture and Inscription Catalogue", in D.H. Sanders (Hrsg.), *Nemurd Daği: The Hierothesion of Antiochus I of Commagene*. 2 Bde. Winona Lake: 175–360

Feenstra, R. 1956. "Le concept de fondation du droit romain classique jusqu'à nos jours: théorie et pratique", *Revue Internationale du Droit de l'Antiquité*, 3ème sér., 3: 245–263

Giouni, M. 2000. *Provincia Macedonia: θεσμοί ιδιωτικού δικαίου στη Μακεδονία*. Athen

Harter-Uibopuu, K. 2011. „Money for the *polis*. Public administration of private donations in Hellenistic Greece", in O.M. van Nijf – R. Alston (Hrsg.), *Political culture in the Greek city after the Classical Age*. Leuven: 119–139

Harter-Uibopuu, K. 2013. „Bestandklauseln und Abänderungsverbote: Der Schutz zweckgebundener Gelder in der späthellenistischen und kaiserzeitlichen Polis", *Tyche* 28: 51–96

Harter-Uibopuu, K. 2015. „Stadt und Stifter: Rechtshistorische Einblicke in die Struktur und Verwaltung hellenistischer und kaiserzeitlicher Stiftungen", in S. von Reden (Hrsg.), *Stiftungen zwischen Politik und Wirtschaft: Geschichte und Gegenwart im Dialog*. Historische Zeitschrift. Beiheft 66. Berlin: 177–204

Harter-Uibopuu, K. 2021. „Die diatheke des Epikrates aus Nakrason. Ein Beitrag zur Verwaltung privater *donationes sub modo*", in K. Harter-Uibopuu – W. Riess (Hrsg.), *Symposion 2019. Vorträge zur griechischen und hellenistischen Rechtsgeschichte.* Hamburg, 26.–28. August 2019. Hamburg: 367–402

Hommel, H. 1964. „Rez. A. Mannzmann, Griechische Stiftungsurkunden", *Gnomon* 36: 614–621

Jaccottet, F. 2003. *Choisir Dionysos: les associations dionysiaques ou la face cachée du dionysisme*. 2 Bde. Kilchberg

Latte, K. 1962. „Rez. A. Mannzmann, Griechische Stiftungsurkunden", *Zeitschrift der Savigny–Stiftung für Rechtsgeschichte: Romanistische Abteilung* 79: 374–376

Laum, B. 1914. *Stiftungen in der griechischen und römischen Antike. Ein Beitrag zur antiken Kulturgeschichte*. 2 Bde. Leipzig/Berlin

Lippert, G. 1967. *Über die Rechtsformen altgriechischer Stiftungen*. Diss. Nürnberg

Lohse, T. 2014. „Lateinische Christen", in M. Borgolte (Hrsg.), *Enzyklopädie des Stiftungswesens in mittelalterlichen Gesellschaften* 1: *Grundlagen*. Berlin: 167–182

Malay, H. 1983. „Three Decrees from Kyme", *Epigraphica Anatolica* 2: 1–20

Manieri, A. 2009. *Agoni poetico-musicali nella Grecia antica* 1. Beozia, Pisa/Rom

Mannzmann, A. 1956. „Die Rechtsform der griechischen Stiftung", *Revue Internationale du Droit de l'Antiquité*, 3ème sér., 3: 119–134

Mannzmann, A. 1962. *Griechische Stiftungsurkunden: Studie zu Inhalt und Rechtsform.* Münster

Mélèze-Modrzejewski, J. 1963. „A propos des fondations en droit grec. Rezension zu A. Mannzmann, Griechische Stiftungsurkunden (Studie zu Inhalt und Rechtsform), Münster 1962", *Revue historique de droit francais et étranger* 41: 82–92

Migeotte, L. 1984. *L'emprunt public dans les cités grecques. Recueil des documents et analyse critique*. Québec/Paris

Migeotte, L. 1992. *Les souscriptions publiques dans les cités grecques*. Hautes études du monde gréco-romain 17. Genf/Québec

Migeotte, L. 2010. „Pratiques financières dans un dème attique à la période classique: l'inscription de Plôtheia *IG* I^3 258", in G. Thür (Hrsg.), *Symposion 2009. Vorträge zur griechischen und hellenistischen Rechtsgeschichte*. Wien: 53–72

Migeotte, L. 2014. *Les finances des cités grecques aux périodes classique et hellénistique*. Paris

Miller, S.G. 1974. „A family of Halikarnassian in North-Central Greece", *American Journal of Archaeology* 78: 151–152

Papazarkadas, N. 2011. *Sacred and Public Land in Ancient Athens*. Oxford

Parker, R. 2010. „A funerary foundation from Hellenistic Lycia", *Chiron* 40: 103–121

Patera, I. 2012. *Offrir en Grèce ancienne. Gestes et contextes*. Stuttgart

Petropoulos, G. 1944. *Ἱστορία καὶ εἰσηγήσεις τοῦ ρωμαϊκοῦ δικαίου ὡς εἰσαγωγὴ εἰς τὸν Ἀστικὸν Κώδικα καὶ εἰς προϊσχύσαν αὐτοῦ ἀστικὸν δίκαιον*. Athen (2. Auflage 2008)

Rigsby, K.J. 1996. „Craton's Legacy“, *Epigraphica Anatolica* 26, 137–139

Rubinstein, L. 2003. „Volunteer Prosecutors in the Greek World“, *Dike* 6: 87–113

Sosin, J.D. 2000. *Perpetual Endowments in the Hellenistic World: A Case-Study in Economic Rationalism*. Diss. Duke

Sosin, J.D. 2014a. „Endowments and Taxation in the Hellenistic Period“, *Ancient Society* 44: 43–89

Sosin, J.D. 2014b. „Endowed Eponymous Festivals on Delos“, *Kérnos* 27: 127–157

Stroud, R.S. 1998. *The Athenian Grain-Tax Law of 374/3 B.C.* Princeton

Triantaphyllopoulos, I. 1962. „Rez. A. Mannzmann, Griechische Stiftungsurkunden“, *Deutsche Literaturzeitung* 84: 567-569

Velissaropoulos-Karakostas, J. 2011. *Droit grec d'Alexandre à Auguste (323 av. J.-C. – 14 ap. J.-C.)*. Meletemata 66. 2 Bde. Athen

von Reden, S. 2015. *Stiftungen zwischen Politik und Wirtschaft: Geschichte und Gegenwart im Dialog*. Historische Zeitschrift. Beiheft 66. Berlin

Walser, A.V. 2021. „Menschen und Götter. Zu den Rechtsgrundlagen griechischer Stiftungen. Antwort auf Kaja Harter-Uibopuu“, in K. Harter-Uibopuu – W. Riess (Hrsg.), *Symposion 2019. Vorträge zur griechischen und hellenistischen Rechtsgeschichte. Hamburg, 26.–28. August 2019*. Hamburg: 403–418

Wörrle, M. 1988. *Stadt und Fest im kaiserzeitlichen Kleinasien: Studien zu einer agonistischen Stiftung aus Oinoanda*. Vestigia 39. München

Wolff, H.J. 1962. „Rez. A. Mannzmann, Griechische Stiftungsurkunden“, *Iura* 13: 265–275

Ziebarth, E. 1903. „Beiträge zum griechischen Recht I. Die Stiftung nach griechischem Recht“, *Zeitschrift für vergleichende Rechtswissenschaft* 16: 249–315

Ziebarth, E. 1906. „Beiträge zum griechischen Recht II. Juristisches aus griechischen Inschriften“, *Zeitschrift für vergleichende Rechtswissenschaft* 19: 269–312

Ziebarth, E. 1940. „Stiftungen“, *RE* Suppl. VII: 1236–1240

ANDREAS VICTOR WALSER (ZÜRICH)

ZUR REALEN SICHERHEIT IM GRIECHISCHEN RECHT: *SUBSTITUTIVE VS. COLLATERAL*

Abstract: War die reale Sicherheit im griechischen Recht ein Ersatzpfand, das im Falle der Zahlungsunfähigkeit substitutiv an die Stelle des Darlehens trat und unabhängig vom genauen Verhältnis zur Schuldsumme an den Gläubiger verfiel? Oder war sie ein Verkaufspfand, das als kollaterale Sicherheit diente, wobei der Schuldner Anspruch auf einen allfälligen Mehrwert hatte und ein Mindererlös auszugleichen war? In dem Beitrag wird die Evidenz zu diesem kontroversen Problem systematisch geprüft und im Ergebnis dafür plädiert, dass grundsätzlich vom Ersatzprinzip auszugehen ist, von dem aber in den individuellen Darlehensverträgen abgewichen werden konnte.

Schlagwörter: Darlehen – reale Sicherheit – Ersatzpfand – Verkaufspfand

1. Grundlagen

Der vorliegende Beitrag greift ein Problem auf, das die Forschung zum Recht der griechischen Poleis seit ihren Anfängen bis in die jüngste Zeit vielfach beschäftigt hat. Auch beim Symposion für griechische und hellenistische Rechtsgeschichte wurde es wiederholt diskutiert, so im Jahre 2007 und in knapperer Form erneut 2013. Zwei Gründe rechtfertigen, erneut darauf zurückzukommen: Zum einen handelt es sich, wie zu zeigen ist, um ein Problem, das auch jenseits seiner im engeren Sinne rechtshistorischen Dimensionen von keineswegs unerheblicher sozial- und wirtschaftsgeschichtlicher Relevanz ist, zum andern herrscht über seine Lösung nach wie vor keine Einigkeit und es stehen sich gegensätzliche Auffassungen gegenüber. Vorwegzunehmen ist, dass dieser Beitrag keine neu erschlossene Evidenz beitragen kann, der das Problem in ungeahnter Weise erhellen könnte, sondern im Wesentlichen von Quellen ausgehen muss, die bereits in früheren Diskussionen aufgegriffen wurden.

Bevor ich zu der im Titel angedeuteten Frage komme, ist es hilfreich, einige grundsätzliche Beobachtungen zu Darlehen zu rekapitulieren.[1] Unter einem Darlehen können wir ausgehend von Definitionen im geltenden Recht die Überlassung vertretbarer Sachen zum wirtschaftlichen Verbrauch verstehen, wobei sich der Empfänger zur Rückgabe in gleicher Qualität und Quantität nach Ablauf

[1] Vgl. meine früheren Ausführungen in Walser 2008, 105–109.

einer vereinbarten Frist verpflichtet. Wer als Gläubiger ein solches Darlehen vergibt, erbringt zunächst eine Vorleistung, für die er nicht unmittelbar entschädigt wird und die für ihn mit einem Risiko verbunden ist. Bei einer Leihgabe wird dieses Risiko dadurch abgemildert, dass der Leihgeber Eigentümer an der übertragenen Sache bleibt, notfalls auf diese zurückgreifen und sie zurückholen kann, falls der Empfänger die vereinbarten Leistungen nicht erbringt. Im Unterschied dazu ist die Position des Gläubigers bei der Vergabe eines Darlehens insofern schwächer, als er dem Borger eine vertretbare Sache überlässt, auf die er keinen Anspruch mehr erheben kann: Das Saatgut wird gesät, das Mehl gegessen, das Geld verbraucht. Der Borger verpflichtet sich lediglich dazu, die Sache zu einem vereinbarten Zeitpunkt gleichwertig zurückzuerstatten. Da der Gläubiger im Gegensatz zum Leihgeber nicht die Möglichkeit hat, auf die überlassene Sache zurückzugreifen, ist sein Risiko entsprechend höher.[2]

Dieses Risiko des Gläubigers kann vermindert werden, indem schon bei der Darlehensvergabe dem Gläubiger das Recht eingeräumt wird, sich vor einem Verlust durch den Zugriff auf eine Sicherheit zu schützen. Bei dieser Sicherheit kann es sich um eine Drittperson handeln, die sich als Bürge verpflichtet, für die Rückerstattung des Darlehens notfalls selbst zu sorgen. Alternativ kann bei der Darlehensvergabe eine Sache aus dem Eigentum des Schuldners als Sicherheit definiert werden, auf die der Gläubiger dann zurückgreifen und die er verwerten kann, wenn der Schuldner zur Rückerstattung des Darlehens nicht willens oder nicht fähig ist. Diese Form des Darlehens, in der der Schuldner eine Sache als dingliche Sicherheit stellt, ist Gegenstand der folgenden Überlegungen.

Die vorangehende Darstellung versucht, möglichst von allen rechtlichen Formen, in die das Geschäft in einer gegebenen Rechtsordnung gebracht werden muss, zu abstrahieren. Das Recht der griechischen Poleis kannte verschiedene rechtliche Gestaltungen, in denen ein solches Geschäft konzipiert und vollzogen werden konnte, und verwendete verschiedene Begriffe – von der πρᾶσις ἐπὶ λύσει zur ὑποθήκη zum ἀποτίμημα –, um es terminologisch zu fassen. Edward M. Harris hat vor rund 25 Jahren in klassisch gewordenen Beiträgen den Nachweis zu erbringen versucht, dass die Unterschiede zwischen den unterschiedlichen Darlehensformen im Wesentlichen nur die Terminologie, nicht aber die Substanz des Geschäfts betreffen.[3] Diese Auffassung hat weite Zustimmung gefunden, ist zuletzt aber auch wieder grundsätzlich angezweifelt worden.[4]

---

2 Siehe auch schon Harris 2006b, 228f., der mit Blick auf die terminologische Differenz von Hypothek und ἀποτίμημα Darlehen und Miete vergleicht.

3 Die ursprünglich 1988 und 1993 publizierten Beiträge werden im Folgenden nach dem Wiederabdruck in Harris 2006a und 2006b zitiert.

4 Vgl. Faguer 2020 und 2021a.

2. *substitutive vs. collateral*

Die Frage, auf die ich mich im Folgenden konzentrieren möchte, ist die, was mit der dinglichen Sicherheit zu geschehen hat, falls der Schuldner zahlungsunfähig ist und der Gläubiger die Vollstreckung vollzieht, mithin also die ihm zugestandenen Ansprüche auf die Sicherheit durchsetzt. In der Forschung zum griechischen Recht stehen sich seit langer Zeit grundsätzlich zwei Auffassungen gegenüber:

a) Gemäß der einen ist die reale Sicherheit im griechischen Darlehensgeschäft ein sogenanntes Verfalls- oder Ersatzpfand. Sie dient als eigentlicher Ersatz für das schuldig gebliebene Darlehen und verfällt an den Gläubiger. Die Frage, welchen genauen Wert die Sicherheit, etwa eine als Hypothek gestellte Immobilie, hatte, spielt dabei keine Rolle, da sie substitutiv an die Stelle des Darlehens tritt, auch dann, wenn ihr genauer Wert höher oder niedriger als der des Darlehens ist.

b) Nach der zweiten Auffassung ist die reale Sicherheit ein Sicherungs- bzw. Verkaufspfand, das den Gläubiger nur kollateral gegen Verluste absichert. Kommt es zur Vollstreckung, wird die Sicherheit verwertet, in der Regel durch Verkauf. Den dabei erzielten Verkaufserlös kann der Gläubiger dazu nutzen, die ausstehende Schuld – die Darlehenssumme zuzüglich allfälliger Zinszahlungen – zu kassieren, einen allfälligen Rest hingegen hat er an den Schuldner zurückzuzahlen. Reicht der erzielte Erlös aus dem Verkauf der Sicherheit nicht aus, um die Schuld zu decken, kann sich der Gläubiger in anderer Weise am Schuldner schadlos halten.

Die Frage nach der Funktion der realen Sicherheit – ob sie nach der englischen Terminologie „substitutive“ oder „collateral“ wirkt – scheint zunächst ein Problem der Rechtsdogmatik zu sein, das jenseits davon von geringer Relevanz ist. Das dem keineswegs so ist, wird deutlich, sobald konkrete Darlehensgeschäfte in den Blick genommen werden. Wie sich auf Basis verstreuter Quellenzeugnisse zeigen lässt, lag der Geldwert der realen Sicherheit bei Darlehensgeschäften nicht nur ausnahmsweise, sondern vielmehr in der Regel erheblich über der gesicherten Darlehenssumme, etwa beim Eineinhalbfachen oder Doppelten der Darlehenssumme.[5] Der Verlust, der dem Schuldner bei Zahlungsunfähigkeit drohte, war mithin ungleich größer, wenn die Differenz zwischen dem Wert der Sicherheit und der Darlehenssumme nicht an ihn zurückerstattet werden musste. Der Verlust dieses Mehrwertes traf den Schuldner wie eine zusätzliche Strafe, falls er die Rückzahlung versäumt hatte. Umgekehrt war es aus Sicht des Gläubigers von Vorteil, wenn das Ersatzprinzip galt und er zu keiner Herausgabe eines solchen Mehrwertes verpflichtet war. Die Sicherheit garantierte dann nicht nur, dass er keinen Verlust erlitt und für das Darlehen entschädigt wurde, sondern eröffnete in der Form des Mehrwertes eine Gewinnmöglichkeit. Mit Blick auf die möglichen ökonomischen Konsequenzen für Schuldner und Gläubiger stellten folglich Kredite, die auf dem Prinzip des Verfallspfandes beruhen, und solche, die den Verkauf der Sicherheit vorsehen, ganz unterschiedliche Geschäfte dar. Aus gesamtwirtschaftlicher Perspektive ist das

[5] Für die Nachweise vgl. Walser 2008, 128–131.

Darlehen mit Verkaufspfand wesentlich effizienter, weil die Hürden zur Aufnahme eines Darlehens wesentlich tiefer liegen und somit eine wirkungsvolle Ressourcenallokation erleichtert wird. Da nach dem Quellenbefund die Sicherheit die Schuldsumme in der Regel mehr als nur deckte, fiel die mit dem kollateralen Sicherungsprinzip verbundene Verpflichtung des Schuldners, eine nach Verwertung der Sicherheit noch vorhandene Restschuld anderweitig zu decken, in der Praxis weniger ins Gewicht.

3. Die Positionen der Forschung

Wie erwähnt haben in der Forschungsgeschichte beide Auffassungen ihre Vertreter und Vertreterinnen gefunden, und es kann an dieser Stelle genügen, die Forschungsgeschichte knapp – und notwendigerweise lückenhaft – zu skizzieren. Der Zürcher Rechtshistoriker Hermann F. Hitzig war in seiner wegweisenden Studie zum griechischen Pfandrecht als erster darum bemüht, exakt nachzuweisen, dass der Gläubiger im Falle der Vollstreckung „Eigentum am ganzen Pfandobjekt" erhält, denn „er ist nicht verpflichtet, die Differenz zwischen dem Forderungsbetrag und dem Wert des Pfandes herauszugeben".[6] Diese Sicht blieb nicht lange unangefochten: Demetrius Pappulias, ein Schüler Ludwig Mitteis', unterschied in seiner Studie zum altgriechischen Pfandrecht von 1909 die Hypothek einerseits, die seiner Auffassung nach Verkaufspfand war, und das Apotimema andererseits, das als Verfallspfand zur Sicherung von Mündelvermögen und der Mitgift zur Anwendung kam.[7] In Replik bemühte sich Leo Raape in einer dem „Verfall des griechischen Pfandes" gewidmeten Monographie noch einmal grundsätzlich den Nachweis zu erbringen, dass die Sicherheit im griechischen Recht von Anfang an Verfallspfand war und dies auch im Laufe der Rechtsentwicklung im Wesentlichen blieb.[8] Eine unangefochtene *communis opinio* vermochte auch Raape nicht zu etablieren.

Moses I. Finley verteidigte in seiner Studie zu den athenischen Horoi von 1951 die Sicht von Hitzig und Raape erneut gegen Einwände, jedenfalls für die Verhältnisse in Athen. Während sich die Diskussion bis dahin ganz auf die rechtlichen Fragen konzentriert hatte, unterstrich nun Finley besonders auch die wirtschaftshistorischen Dimensionen des Problems. Gleichzeit versuchte John Fine in seiner parallel entstandenen Studie zu den Horoi ähnlich wie schon Pappulias zwischen unterschiedlichen Darlehensformen zu unterscheiden und den Nachweis zu erbringen, dass nur beim Verkauf auf Lösung, der πρᾶσις ἐπὶ λύσει, ein Verfallspfand vorlag, die Hypothek hingegen ein Verkaufspfand sei. Hans J. Wolff lehnte in seiner

[6] Hitzig 1895, 85.

[7] Pappulias 1909, 141–174 §20–22.

[8] Raape 1912. Die ebenso ausgewogene wir scharfsichtige Besprechung von Bruck 1912 bietet eine hervorragende Bestandsaufnahme der älteren Forschung.

Besprechung der beiden Bücher Fines Sicht zwar ab, aber nicht ohne auf Probleme in Finleys Darstellung hinzuweisen.[9]

In seinen wichtigen Beiträgen zur realen Sicherheit hat sich Edward M. Harris 1988 und 1993 nicht nur gegen die Unterscheidung verschiedener Darlehenstypen ausgesprochen, sondern noch einmal klar die Sicht vertreten, dass die Sicherheit Verfallspfand war.[10] Mir schien die Frage damit geklärt und ein hinreichender Konsens zu bestehen, so dass ich in meiner Studie zum ephesischen Schuldentilgungsgesetz vor rund 15 Jahren von der Auffassung, dass die Sicherheit in Athen und wohl auch darüber hinaus in aller Regel Verfallspfand war, ohne vertiefte Diskussion ausging.[11]

Schon beim Wiederabdruck seiner beiden Beiträge im Jahr 2006 brachte Harris jedoch Zweifel an seiner älteren Auffassung an. Er nutzte dann seine Response zu einem Beitrag von Gerhard Thür beim Symposion 2007, um seine Sicht grundsätzlich zu revidieren und sich mit Vehemenz für die konträre Auffassung auszusprechen, dass die Sicherheit im griechischen Recht kollateral wirkte und stets als Verkaufspfand diente.[12] Entlang der beim Symposion dargelegten Argumentation präsentierte Harris seine neue Sicht in den folgenden Jahren noch mehrmals.[13] Als Mark Sundahl beim Symposion 2013 dafür plädierte, die Debatte über „Secured Credit in Athens“ wiederzueröffnen, schien ihm die Frage, ob die Sicherheit „substitutive“ oder „collateral“ ist, von geringem Interesse. Die Evidenz sei nicht klar, würde aber insgesamt für die kollaterale Sicherungsfunktion sprechen.[14] Gerhard Thür ging in seiner Response nur knapp auf das Problem ein, hielt indes daran fest, dass die Sicherheit – jedenfalls in dogmatischer Perspektive – Verfallspfand sei, dass der Vertrag jedoch Abweichungen möglich mache.[15]

In mehreren kürzlich veröffentlichten Beiträgen griff Julien Faguer das Problem erneut auf, wobei sein Ausgangspunkt die Verkaufsregister und -urkunden von Tenos und von der Chalkidike bildeten. Nach Faguer ist die Auffassung, dass die reale Sicherheit grundsätzlich kollateral als Sicherungspfand dient – seiner Meinung nach die herrschende *communis opinio* –, nicht haltbar, vielmehr sei zwischen der πρᾶσις ἐπὶ λύσει und dem Darlehen auf eine Hypothek zu unterscheiden. Erstere würde einen abgeschlossenen Verkauf darstellen, bei dem das Eigentum an den Kreditgeber übertragen wird, und folglich substitutiv wirken. Bei der Sicherung durch eine Hypothek würde eine solche Eigentumsübertragung nicht stattfinden, was daran ersichtlich wäre, dass eine mit einer Hypothek belastete Immobilie verkauft werden könne, so dass hier ein kollaterales Sicherungsgeschäft vorliegen

---

9 Finley 1951; Fine 1951; Wolff 1953. Zur Studie von Fine besonders auch Harris 2006a, 165–170.

10 Harris 2006a; 2006b.

11 Walser 2008, 127.

12 Harris 2008. Zur Position von Harris vgl. auch Millett 2016, 54–56.

13 Harris 2013, 137–142; 2016, 128–131.

14 Sundahl 2014, 232f.

15 Thür 2014, 239.

würde.[16] Damit plädiert Faguer indirekt für eine Rückkehr zur Position, die Fine 1951 ausgehend von den attischen Horoi entwickelte.

Dies ist im Wesentlichen der Forschungsstand, an den die folgenden Ausführungen anknüpfen. Mit der Ausnahme von Finley, der seine Untersuchung explizit auf das attische Material beschränkte, bezogen die früheren Autoren stets auch Quellen, insbesondere epigraphische Zeugnisse, aus anderen Poleis der griechischen Welt der klassischen und hellenistischen Zeit in die Diskussion mit ein. Dieses Vorgehen, dem ich mich anschließe, setzt methodisch die Einheit des griechischen Rechts voraus – eine Einheit, die aber eben nicht auf einem gemeinsamen Gesetzescorpus, sondern auf geteilten Rechtsprinzipien beruht.[17] Dass eine Einheit des griechischen Rechts, die auf geteilten Grundvorstellungen beruht, keineswegs ausschließt, dass deren Ausformungen im positiven Recht der verschiedenen Poleis sehr unterschiedlich ausfallen mag, hat Hans J. Wolff schon beim allerersten Symposion natürlich mit vollem Recht betont.[18] Das papyrologische Material bleibt im Folgenden aus pragmatischen Gründen ausgeschlossen, wobei ich explizit offen lassen möchte, ob dies sachlich geboten ist oder der Einbezug vielmehr nötig und erhellend wäre.[19]

Die folgenden Ausführungen stellen in wesentlichen Punkten eine kritische Auseinandersetzung mit den Positionen von Harris dar, der sich zuletzt systematisch mit der hier verfolgten Fragestellung befasst hat. Gerade weil ich dabei wiederholt zu abweichenden Schlussfolgerungen gelange, ist hier explizit zu betonen, wie viel ich seinen Darlegungen verdanke.

4. Die ökonomischen Voraussetzungen der Darlehensgeschäfte

Wie schon angedeutet, stellt die Frage nach der Funktion der Sicherheit als Verfalls- oder Sicherheitspfand zunächst zwar ein rechtliches Problem dar, das aber nicht nur gewichtige ökonomische Konsequenzen hat, sondern auch an spezifische ökonomische Voraussetzungen gebunden ist. Harris wies auf einer fundamentalen Ebene mit Recht darauf hin, dass bei Finley die Überzeugung, dass die Sicherheit Verfallspfand war, eng an seine Auffassung vom Charakter der antiken Wirtschaft

---

[16] Faguer 2021a, bes. 14–18, mit Verweis auf die Untersuchungen zu Tenos in Faguer 2020. Siehe auch hier S. 325–326.

[17] Die Diskussion ist hier nicht aufzugreifen, und ich beschränke mich auf den Verweis auf Thür 2008, 174, dem die hier verwendete Formulierung zu verdanken ist. Umfassend und die älteren Stellungnahmen aufgreifend Thür 2006 und Thür 2008.

[18] Wolff 1975, 20–22. Finleys Position, „dass die allgemein anerkannte Meinung, allen griechischen Poleis sei *eine* Rechtsordnung gemeinsam gewesen, bestenfalls eine Arbeitshypothese ist, die durch eine exakte Analyse einzelner Einrichtungen in den verschiedenen Poleis noch sorgfältiger untersucht werden muß" (so nur e.g. Finley 1968, 544 Anm. 16 mit der Hervorhebung im Original), scheint mir davon weniger weit entfernt zu sein, als bisweilen angenommen wird.

[19] Gerne verweise ich auf die Response zu diesem Beitrag von Thomas Kruse, die explizit dem papyrologischen Material gewidmet ist.

geknüpft ist.[20] Nach der von Finley programmatisch in seiner späteren Monographie über die „Ancient Economy“ dargelegten Auffassung, die man gern als die neoprimitivistische Sicht der antiken Wirtschaft bezeichnet, unterschied sich diese grundsätzlich von modernen Volkswirtschaften. Insbesondere war Finley der Auffassung, dass es in der Antike im Allgemeinen und in der griechischen Welt im Besonderen kaum preisbildende Märkte gab, jedenfalls kein die gesamte Wirtschaft umfassendes Konglomerat interdependenter Märkte. Da es insbesondere einen eigentlichen Immobilienmarkt nicht gab, konnte – so Finley jedenfalls nach Harris – die Sicherheit gar nichts anderes sein als ein Verfallspfand. Die Möglichkeit, die Sicherheit als Verkaufspfand auf dem Markt zu Geld zu machen, stand nämlich gar nicht offen: „In Athens, the very idea of collateral is to all intents and purposes unknown even in the fourth and third centuries B.C.“[21]

Schon in diesen grundsätzlichen Fragen ging Harris von ganz anderen Grundlagen aus. Seiner Auffassung nach waren in Athen – und darüber hinaus – sehr wohl die ökonomischen Voraussetzungen dafür gegeben, dass ein intensiver Güteraustausch auf lokalen und regionalen Märkten stattfinden konnten: „*Pace* Finley this meant that creditors did have a permanent market available where they could readily convert securities into cash and were therefore capable of thinking in market terms. The obstacle that Finley claimed was responsible for preventing the emergence of the collateral idea did not in fact exist.“[22]

In der Tat hat sich die Forschung zur Wirtschaft der griechischen Welt seit gut 25 Jahren auch Dank Harris’ eigenen Beiträgen etwa zur Spezialisierung in den Herstellungsprozessen erheblich von den – lange noch als Orthodoxie bezeichneten – Vorstellungen Finleys entfernt. Die Existenz von Marktsystemen, die durch flexible und von Angebot und Nachfrage bestimmten Preisen koordiniert wurden, wird – bei allen Differenzen im Einzelnen – heute kaum mehr bestritten. Ebenso herrscht weitgehender Konsens darüber, dass Finley die Rolle der Handwerksgüter und landwirtschaftlichen Produkte auf lokalen und regionalen Märkten unterschätzte.[23]

Dennoch bleiben Schwierigkeiten auf mehreren Ebenen. Während die Bedeutung von Marktransaktionen von mobilen Gütern heute kaum mehr bezweifelt wird, ist gerade die Frage danach, inwieweit in Athen oder in anderen griechischen Poleis ein funktionierender Immobilienmarkt existierte, weit weniger geklärt, und da die Sicherheiten in der Regel eben Immobilien waren, ist gerade dies die entscheidende Frage. Nicht zu bestreiten ist, dass sich auch Käufe und Verkäufe von Grund und

---

[20] Harris 2008, 191f. Zum ökonomischen Kontext vertieft Harris 2013 und 2016. Ich beschränke mich im Folgenden auf Verweise auf Harris 2008, sofern in den späteren Beiträgen keine substanziell neuen Argumente eingebracht werden.

[21] Finley 1951, 117. Zur Rolle der „Studies in Land and Credit“ im Gesamtwerk Finleys, auch mit Blick auf das besonders in Finley 1973 gezeichnete Bild der antiken Wirtschaft vgl. neben Harris 2013 besonders Millett 2016.

[22] Harris 2008, 191f.

[23] Die beste umfassende Synthese zur griechischen Wirtschaft bietet heute Bresson 2016.

Boden nachweisen lassen, und dass es auch Personen gab, die im modernen Sinne in Immobilien investierten.[24] Zu Recht hat man sich auch längst von der These verabschiedet, dass das Land in der griechischen Polis grundsätzlich unveräußerbar war. Hinzuweisen ist dennoch auch darauf, dass rechtliche Schranken wie die *enktesis* als Voraussetzung zum Immobilienerwerb die Entstehung eines effizienten Immobilienmarktes zweifellos erschwerten, da gerade den finanzkräftigen Fremden der Zugang zu einem solchen Markt verwehrt blieb.[25] Die Nachrichten darüber, dass Plinius der Jüngere in Bithynien ebenso wie eine öffentliche Kommission in Sinuri beim Versuch, Geld durch den Ankauf von Land anzulegen, scheiterten, sind oft zitierte Hinweise auf den prekären Charakter des Immobilienmarktes, die als anekdotische Evidenz freilich kaum mehr Aussagekraft haben als vereinzelte Hinweise auf Landverkäufe.[26] Wer Land verkaufen musste – insbesondere kurzfristig –, dürfte vermutlich zwar einen Käufer gefunden haben, aber ob dies heißt, dass ein gut funktionierender Immobilienmarkt existierte und dass Gläubiger „could readily convert securities into cash" bleibt noch immer fraglich.

Ohnehin genügt der Nachweis, dass ein Immobilienmarkt existierte, nicht, um zu beweisen, dass die Sicherheit kollateral wirkte und Verkaufspfand war. Wie Finley richtig sah, setzt die Existenz der Institution des Verkaufspfand zwingend voraus, dass es möglich war, die Sicherheit zu einem erwartbaren Marktpreis zu verkaufen. Das heißt im Umkehrschluss jedoch nicht, dass die Sicherheit ebenso zwingend den Status eines Verkaufspfandes hatte, wenn die Möglichkeit zum Verkauf gegeben war. Harris schien dies jedoch zu implizieren, wenn er festhielt: „There can be no question that the Athenians in particular and the citizens of the Greek poleis in general viewed land as an asset that could be exchanged on the market *and therefore* adopted the collateral form of security".[27] Zwar sind die rechtlichen Verhältnisse und Entwicklungen an ökonomische Voraussetzungen gebunden, doch werden sie nicht durch die wirtschaftlichen Verhältnisse determiniert.[28] In diesem Kontext ist auch in Erinnerung zu rufen, dass die Auffassung, die Sicherheit

[24] Bresson 2016, 153f., der von existierenden Immobilienmärkten ausgeht, stellt die spärliche Evidenz zusammen. Zum Stand der Diskussion vgl. aus jeweils unterschiedlichen Blickwinkeln etwa Faguer 2021b; Game 2008; Nevett 2000.

[25] Vgl. auch die Studie von Faguer 2021b zur ökonomischen (In-)Signifikanz der Enktesis-Verleihung in Athen und seine daran anschliessenden weiterführenden wirtschaftlichen Überlegungen.

[26] Plin. Epist. 10, 54; I.Sinuri 50, Z. 8–14.

[27] Harris 2016, 128 (meine Hervorhebung).

[28] Wolff 1953, 416 hat in seiner Besprechung von Finleys Studie mit Recht vor einer „gewissen Einseitigkeit" gewarnt, die „das Privatrecht ausschließlich als eine Funktion der jeweils vorherrschenden wirtschaftlichen Bedürfnisse faßt und daher diese bei der Erklärung und konstruktiven Erfassung rechtlicher Gestaltungen über Gebühr in den Vordergrund schiebt, unter Vernachlässigung sowohl des rein gedanklichen Gehalts der Rechtsfiguren wie auch anderer rechtsbildender Faktoren, wie politischer und prozessualer Bedingungen oder auch einfach der Macht des Herkommens."

sei Verfallspfand, zunächst in rechtshistorischen Studien und weitgehend unabhängig von Überlegungen zu den sozio-ökonomischen Verhältnissen etabliert wurde und von Finley nur zusätzlich mit ökonomischen Argumenten gestützt wurde.

Dabei ging schon Finley keineswegs davon aus, dass sich Gläubiger und Schuldner keinerlei Gedanken zum potenziellen „Marktwert" der Sicherheit und dessen Verhältnis zur Darlehenssumme machten. Auch wenn die Sicherheit ein Verfallspfand ist, besteht durchaus ein Interesse an dem in Geld auszudrückenden Wert einer Hypothek, unabhängig davon, ob ein Gläubiger die Sicherheit nun langfristig in sein Eigentum übernehmen wollte oder nicht. Entscheidend schien Finley – und ich meine mit Recht –, dass die strategischen Abwägungen von Schuldner und Gläubiger eben ganz andere sind, je nach dem, ob wir es mit einem Verfalls- oder einem Verkaufspfand zu tun haben.[29]

5. Belege für kollaterale Sicherungsgeschäfte?

Harris diskutierte in seinen Beiträgen eine Reihe von Quellenstellen, die seiner Auffassung nach eindeutig belegen, dass die Sicherheit nicht Verfallspfand war, sondern kollateral wirkte. Die Interpretation dieser Stellen sowie ihre Aussagekraft soll systematisch überprüft werden.[30]

a) Um 250 v. Chr. äufneten die Bürger von Samos einen Fonds, aus dessen Anlageerträgen Getreidekäufe getätigt werden sollten.[31] Das Getreidegesetz, das die Verwaltung des Fonds und die Käufe regelte, sah dabei vor, dass Verwaltungsbeamte, die aus den Untereinheiten der Bürgerschaft zu bestimmen waren, die Gelder als Darlehen gegen Zins vergeben sollten. Zur Sicherung waren sowohl eine dingliche Sicherheit wie auch ein Bürge zu stellen. Das Gesetz sah schließlich vor (Z. 64-68):

> ἐὰν δέ τις τῶν
> δανεισαμένων μὴ ἀποδιδῶι τὸ ἀργύριον ἢ πᾶν ἢ μέρος τι, τὸ ὑ-
> πόθεμα ἀποδόσθω ἡ χιλιαστύς, καὶ ἐάν τις ὑπεροχὴ γένητα[ι],
> ἀποδότω τῶι τὸ ὑπόθεμα δόντι· ἐὰν δέ τι ἐνλίπῃ, τὴν πρᾶξιν
> ποιησάσθω ἐκ τοῦ ἐγγύου.

„Wenn einer der Darlehensnehmer das Geld nicht zurückzahlt, ob ganz oder zum Teil, so soll die Tausendschaft die dingliche Sicherheit verkaufen, und wenn dabei

[29] Finley 1951, 116f.: „It would be absurd to suggest that the value of the debt on the one hand and of the encumbered property on the other bore no relationship whatever. Certainly an Athenian had a pretty good idea of the value of the security he was offered before he agreed to make a loan. But what he would look for in value would be something different from what his modern counterpart would seek."

[30] Dieselben Belege wurden auch schon von Biscardi 1983 systmatisch diskutiert und häufig auch schon in den älteren Studien aufgegriffen.

[31] IG XII 6, 1, 172.

ein Überschuss entsteht, ihn dem Besteller der Sicherheit geben; wenn aber etwas fehlt, soll sie die Vollstreckung beim Bürgen durchführen."[32]

Das Text lässt keinen Zweifel daran aufkommen, dass die dingliche Sicherheit hier als Verkaufspfand dienen soll. Die Chiliastys – wohl in der Person des sie vertretenden Amtsträgers – soll vollstrecken, indem die Sicherheit verkauft wird. Ein allfälliger Überschuss ist an den Darlehensnehmer rückzuerstatten. Deckt der Verkaufserlös die geschuldete Summe nicht, haftet der Bürge.[33] Eine Übernahme der Sicherheit selbst in das Eigentum der Chiliastys ist im Text noch nicht einmal angedeutet.

Die entscheidende Frage ist, wie weit sich aus dieser Stelle zu verallgemeinernde Schlussfolgerungen ziehen lassen. Die Situation ist augenscheinlich in mehrfacher Hinsicht eine unübliche: Ausgangspunkt der Darlehensgeschäfte sind nicht die Bedürfnisse der Kreditnehmer, sondern das Bestreben der Polis, durch die Anlage der Fondsgelder ein kontinuierliches Zinseinkommen zu generieren. Sie hat dabei ein hohes Sicherheitsbedürfnis, ist aber auch darauf angewiesen, dass die Darlehen überhaupt angenommen werden. Die Sicherheiten zu übernehmen, wäre für die Chiliastyen nicht nur praktisch schwierig, sondern auch nicht sinnvoll. Wie Christian Koch und Gerhard Thür in ihrem Kommentar klar gesehen haben, braucht der Getreidefonds das Kapital in Form von Geld, denn nur dieses kann wie vorgesehen weiterhin angelegt werden.[34] Dass der Mehrwert gegebenenfalls an den Schuldner fiel, war sicherlich ein Zugeständnis an die Kreditnehmer, das diese sich mit der Verpflichtung für die Haftung für einen Minderertrag gewissermaßen erkauften. Selbst wenn man die Auffassung von Koch und Thür nicht teilt, dass der Grundgedanke des Prinzips des Verfallspfandes in der Bestimmung noch spürbar bleibt, ist doch der besondere Charakter der Darlehensgeschäfte nicht zu bestreiten.

Diese Überlegungen zu den Spezifika, die den vorliegenden Fall prägen, scheinen mir bedeutsamer als ein grundsätzlicher Einwand, der sich gegen alle vergleichbaren Zeugnisse erheben ließe: Weshalb wird die Vollstreckung in dieser Form so ausführlich beschrieben, wenn sie dem Normalfall entsprach? Grundsätzlich lassen sich primär deklaratorische Wiederholungen der an sich bekannten Verfahren nicht ausschließen. Im vorliegenden Fall gab es zudem genügend Besonderheiten – Vollstreckung durch die Chiliastys, Haftung des Bürgen –, die eine ausführliche Darlegung rechtfertigten.[35]

---

32 Übersetzung K. Hallof.

33 Nach der Übersetzung von Harris (2008, 193) geht der Mehrwert „to the person who gave the security", haftbar für den Minderwert ist „the person who provides the security". Anders als diese Übersetzung unterscheidet der griechische Text indes präzise zwischen demjenigen, der die Sicherheit stellt, und dem damit nicht identischen Bürgen.

34 Koch – Thür 1981, 87f.

35 Zum Problem der Bürgschaft vgl. unten.

b) Dem Getreidegesetz aus Samos stellt Harris eine Passage aus einem delphischen Beschluss zur Seite, mit dem die Delpher die Verwaltung einer Schenkung *sub modo* des Königs Attalos II. im Jahr 160/59 v. Chr. regelten.[36] Wie in Samos ging es auch hier darum, die erhaltenen Gelder durch die Vergabe als Kredite gewinnbringend anzulegen. Und ebenso wie die Samier versuchten sich auch die Delpher vor Verlusten durch die Stellung von Sicherheiten, in die gegebenenfalls vollstreckt werden konnte, zu schützen (Z. 63-72):[37]

ἀποδιδόντω δὲ οἱ δανεισάμενοι τὸ ἀργύριον πᾶν
τᾶι πόλει ἐν τῶι πέμπτωι ἐνιαυτῶι. εἰ δέ κα μὴ ἀποδι-
δῶντι καθὼς γέγραπται, τὰ ἐνέχυρα αὐτῶν τᾶς πό-
λιος ἔστω, καὶ οἱ ἐπιμεληταὶ ἀεὶ οἱ ἐγδανείζοντες κύρ[ι]-
οι ἔστωσαν πωλέοντες· εἰ δὲ πωλείμενα τὰ ἐνέ-
χυρα μὴ εὑρίσκοι τὸ ἀργύριον ποθ' ὃ ὑπέκειτο τᾶι πόλει, πρά-
κτιμοι ἔστωσαν τοῖς ἐπιμεληταῖς ἀεὶ τοῖς ἐνάρχοις τοῦ
ἐλλείποντος ἀργυρίου αὐτός τε ὁ δανεισάμενος καὶ
οἱ γενόμενοι ἔγγυοι, τρόπωι ὧι θέλοιεν πράσσειν, καθὼς
καὶ τἆλ[λ]α δαμόσια καὶ ποθίερα πράσσονται.

„Die Darlehensnehmer sollen das ganze Geld an die Polis zurückzahlen im 5. Jahr. Falls sie (sc. die Darlehensnehmer) nicht zurückzahlen, wie es vorgeschrieben ist, sollen ihre Sicherheiten der Polis gehören, und die jeweils für die Verleihung zuständigen Funktionäre sollen ermächtigt sein, sie zu verkaufen. Wenn aber die Sicherheiten beim Verkauf nicht das Geld einbringen, für das sie der Polis als Sicherheit gestellt wurden, dann sollen gegenüber den jeweils amtierenden Funktionären für das fehlende Geld sowohl der Darlehensnehmer selbst als auch die gestellten Bürgen haftbar sein; die Vollstreckung sollen sie (sc. die Funktionäre) vollziehen, wie sie wollen, so wie sie auch andere öffentliche und heilige (Schulden) eintreiben."

Harris kommentierte: „As in the law from Samos, the security is not viewed as a substitute for the loan, but as providing cash from its sale. The debtor has the right to the excess."[38] Richtig ist, dass auch in Delphi die Sicherheiten durch Funktionäre der Polis im Falle der Vollstreckung verkauft werden sollten. Ganz genauso wie Samos konnten auch die Delpher nur durch den Verkauf der Hypotheken sicherstellen, dass die von Attalos geschenkte Summe weiterhin vollumfänglich als Anlagevermögen zur Verfügung stand. Und genauso wie die Samier behielten sich auch die Delpher das Recht vor, eine Restschuld, die durch den Verkaufserlös nicht

---

36 Syll.[3] 672.

37 Einen scharfsichtigen Kommentar der rechtlichen Aspekte dieser Inschrift, der sich mit den hier vertretenen weitgehend deckt, bietet Dimopoulou 2007, bes. 444–447; vgl. zur Stelle ausserdem Migeotte 2015, 322–226 (2009/2010, 212–217).

38 Harris 2008, 193.

gedeckt wurde, anderweitig beim Schuldner oder dessen Bürgen durch Vollstreckungsmaßnahmen einzutreiben.

Bemerkenswert ist allerdings, dass die Sicherheit insofern nicht als kollaterales Sicherheitspfand diente, als die Erstattung eines allfällig erzielten Mehrwerts an den Schuldner nicht vorgesehen war. Jedenfalls ist dies im Beschluss, entgegen der Aussage von Harris, gerade nicht gesagt. Nur dann, wenn man davon ausgeht, dass die Erstattung des Mehrwertes stillschweigend im Dekret impliziert ist,[39] kann man hier von einem echten Verkaufspfand, das als kollaterale Sicherung diente, sprechen. Schon Raape wies freilich darauf hin, dass in der delphischen Urkunde – im Gegensatz zum Getreidegesetz aus Samos – schon vor der Bestimmung über den Verkauf ausdrücklich festgehalten wird, dass die Sicherheiten der Polis gehören sollen (Z. 65f.: τὰ ἐνέχυρα αὐτῶν τᾶς πόλιος ἔστω): „Wenn die Gemeinde das Pfand veräußert, so veräußert sie ihre Sache, nicht die des Schuldners.“[40] Insofern ist auch folgerichtig, dass an eine Rückerstattung des Mehrwertes an die Schuldner nicht gedacht ist.

Raape sprach sich grundsätzlich entschieden dagegen aus, dass aus einer Bestimmung über die Haftung für einen allenfalls durch die Sicherheit nicht gedeckten Restschuld automatisch darauf zu schließen sei, dass auch ein entsprechender Mehrwert vom Gläubiger an den Schuldner zu erstatten wäre. Allein aus der Haftung für die Restschuld folgt nach seiner Auffassung nicht, dass ein Verkaufs- oder Sicherungspfand vorliegt. Da sich der Gläubiger in der Regel in einer stärkeren Position befindet, muss es nach Raape nicht erstaunen, dass er sich gegenüber dem Schuldner vor Verlusten zu schützen vermag, ohne zwingend auch den Anspruch auf den Mehrwert aufzugeben.[41]

Selbst wenn man für die delphische Urkunde daran festhalten möchte, dass die Erstattung des Mehrwertes impliziert ist und tatsächlich das kollaterale Sicherungsprinzip gilt, bleibt auch hier die grundsätzliche Beobachtung bestehen, dass es sich wie in Samos um ein besonderes Geschäft handelt, das kaum allgemeingültige Schlussfolgerungen stützen kann.

c) In der zweiten Rede gegen Aphobos richtete Demosthenes einen emphatischen Appell an die Richter, um klarzumachen, dass er bankrott wäre, wenn das Urteil gegen ihn ausfallen würde (D. 28, 18):

> ποῖ δ' ἂν τραποίμεθα, εἴ τι ἄλλο ψηφίσαισθ' ὑμεῖς περὶ αὐτῶν; εἰς τὰ ὑποκείμενα τοῖς δανείσασιν; ἀλλὰ τῶν ὑποθεμένων ἐστίν. ἀλλ' εἰς τὰ περιόντ' αὐτῶν; ἀλλὰ τούτου γίγνεται, τὴν ἐπωβελίαν ἐὰν ὄφλωμεν.

---

[39] Davon ging vor Harris auch Biscardi 1983, 54 aus.

[40] Raape 1912, 6.

[41] Raape 1912, 23f. Die Erstattung des Mehrwertes ist demnach das Ergebnis einer späteren Rechtsentwicklung.

„Wohin sollten wir uns wenden, wenn ihr über sie ein anderes Urteil fällt? Zu dem, was den Kreditgebern als Sicherheiten dient? Aber das gehört den Kreditgebern. Dann aber zu dem Überschuss von diesen? Aber der geht an diesen (sc. Aphobos), wenn ich die *epobelia* schulde."

Harris übersetzte die Passage wie folgt:[42]
„To where would we turn if you should vote for any other verdict? To the property pledged as security to our creditors? But that belongs to them. To the excess (resulting from the sale of the security)? But that belongs to him if we owe the *epobelia*."

Harris verstand die Stelle so, dass Demosthenes angebe, dass er den größten Teil seines Vermögens als Sicherheit für Darlehen eingesetzt habe. Außerdem würde Demosthenes davon ausgehen, dass er im Fall, dass die Gläubiger seine Güter bei der Vollstreckung beschlagnahmen und verkaufen würden, Anrecht auf den Mehrwert (περιόντα) hätte, mit dem er dann allerdings an Aphobos fällig werdende Strafzahlungen, *epobelia*, zu zahlen hätte. Wenn Demosthenes davon ausgehen kann, dass er die Differenz zwischen dem Verkaufspreis der Sicherheit und der geschuldeten Summe erhalten wird, bedeutet das selbstverständlich, dass das Prinzip des Verkaufspfandes vorausgesetzt ist, das ihm – wenn auch nur vorerst – den Mehrwert garantiert hätte.

Der eigentlich kritische Punkt liegt nicht in dieser Analyse, sondern bereits in der Übersetzung der Passage, auf die Harris nicht weiter einging. Was ist mit εἰς τὰ περιόντ' αὐτῶν gemeint? Douglas M. MacDowell blieb in seiner Übersetzung ganz unspezifisch: „To what is left over?" Augustus T. Murray legte sich stärker fest und übersetzte: „To what is left after the creditors are paid?". Spezifisch war Rodolphe Dareste, der schrieb: „Est-ce dans l'excédant de valeur de ces biens?"[43]

Ugo E. Paoli wies dies zurück und plädierte für ein freies Verständnis der Stelle – „ciò che mi resta" –, und Finley ist ihm darin gefolgt.[44] Sprachlich führt aber nichts daran vorbei, τὰ περιόντα auf τὰ ὑποκείμενα zu beziehen, wie dies Dareste und dann wieder Harris in ihren Übersetzungen getan haben.[45] Zwar ist auch nicht von der Hand zu weisen ist, dass die Passage rhetorisch stark gestaltet ist,[46] doch bleibt dennoch der Befund, dass Demosthenes' Argumentation hier die Funktion der Sicherheiten als Verkaufspfand voraussetzt.

d) In späteren Beiträgen zog Harris zwei weitere Passagen aus Reden des Demosthenes in die Betrachtung mit ein, bei denen einmal der Ertrag, der beim

[42] Harris 2008, 192.
[43] MacDowell 2008, 46; Murray 1936, 75; Dareste 1875, 39. Vgl. auch Pappulias 1909, 144f.
[44] Paoli 1930, 160f., zustimmend Finley 1951, 203 n. 7.
[45] So schon Raape 1912, 32; auch Biscardi 1983, 46.
[46] Anders als für die Ungenauigkeiten am Ende der Rede, auf die Raape 1912, 32 verweist und die dem Argument des Redners entgegenkommen, ist für diese Passage eine rhetorische Motivation nicht erkennbar.

Verkauf der Sicherheiten erzielt wurde, die Schuldsumme nicht deckte, ein andermal diese Möglichkeit zumindest in Betracht gezogen wurde.[47] Grundsätzlich gilt auch in diesen Passagen wiederum, dass die Haftung für eine etwaige Restschuld nach der Verwertung der Sicherheit thematisiert wird, ein allfälliger Übertrag aber gar nicht zur Sprache kommt.[48] Noch wichtiger scheint mir freilich, dass wir es in beiden Fällen mit Seedarlehen zu tun haben, die mit herkömmlichen, durch Immobilien gesicherten Darlehensgeschäften nur bedingt vergleichbar sind. Beim Seedarlehen ist der Verkauf der Ladung, die als Sicherheit dient, immer schon vorgesehen, da die Schuld anders nicht beglichen werden kann. Folglich liegt es nahe, dass der Umgang mit Fehlbeträgen geregelt wird.[49]

Harris ist zuzustimmen, dass sich die bis hierher diskutierten Zeugnisse recht problemlos deuten lassen, wenn vom Prinzip des Verkaufspfandes ausgegangen wird. Gleichzeitig sehe ich aber in keinem – und auch nicht in ihrer kumulativen Evidenz – einen zwingenden Grund, von der Auffassung abzuweichen, dass die Sicherheit normalerweise Verfallspfand war.

6. Das Phänomen der „Mehrfachhypotheken"

Im Quellenmaterial erscheinen jenseits der bis hierhin diskutierten Zeugnisse zwei Phänomene, denen in der Debatte über Verfalls- oder Verkaufspfand besondere Bedeutung zukommt: Zum einen die sogenannten Mehrfachhypotheken, zum anderen die Bürgschaft bei real gesicherten Darlehen.

Harris verwies in seinem Beitrag auf zwei athenische Horoi mit weitgehend analogen Inschriften, deren besondere Bedeutung auch Finley bereits erkannt hatte. Exemplarisch sei an dieser Stelle der eine der beiden Texte zitiert:[50]

ὅρος χωρίο προικὸς
Ἱπποκλείαι Δημοχά-
[ρ]ος Λευκονοιῶς Τ·
[ὅσ]ωι πλείονος ἄξι-
[ον], Κεκροπίδαις
[ὑπό]κειται καὶ Λυκ-
[ομί]δαις καὶ Φλυεῦ-
[σι]. *vac.*

---

[47] Harris 2013, 139f. zu D. 33, 10; Harris 2016, 129 ausserdem zu D. 32, 30.

[48] Auch im vieldiskutierten Seedarlehensvertrag, der in der Rede gegen Lakritos überliefert ist, wird D. 35, 12 nur der Fall geregelt, dass der Verkaufserlös aus der Ladung das Darlehen nicht deckt und ein ἐλλεῖπον verbleibt.

[49] Vgl. schon Finley 1968, 545 Anm. 18. Zum Seedarlehen vgl. als Übersicht etwa Schuster 2005.

[50] IG II^2 2670 (Finley 1951, Nr. 146); ganz analog Hesperia Suppl. 7, 1943, 1 (Finley, Studies, 147) Z. 5f.: ὅσωι πλέονος ἀξία ἐ[τιμήθ]η Ἀγλαοτίμει ὑπόκε[ιται].

„Horos eines Brautgutes für Hippokleia, Tochter des Demochares, aus Leukonoion, 1 Talent; um was es mehr wert ist, dient es den Kekropidai als Hypothek sowie den Lykomidai und Phlyeis."

In einer ganz üblichen Form ist auf diesem und dem analogen Stein zunächst angegeben, dass der Horos eine Immobilie markiert, die als reale Sicherheit dient, um die allfällige Rückgabe einer Mitgift zu sichern. Für diesen Typ von Sicherungsgeschäften gibt es zahlreiche weitere Beispiele. Besonderheit erlangt die besondere Gruppe von Horoi dadurch, dass auf beiden im Anschluss an den ersten Teil des Textes festgehalten ist, dass das, um was die Immobilie mehr wert ist und mithin ihr „Mehrwert", als Hypothek in einem anderen Darlehensgeschäft dient.

Dasselbe Phänomen wird durch weitere Quellen anderen Typs dokumentiert: Finley lenkte den Blick auf einen Bericht der athenischen Poletai aus dem Jahr 367/66 v. Chr., in dessen ersten Teil die Versteigerung eines konfiszierten Hauses dokumentiert ist.[51] Von Anfang an stand fest, dass das Haus für eine Summe von 150 Drachmen als Hypothek diente, und *de facto* wurde das Haus abzüglich dieser Summe versteigert, die der Käufer sogleich dem Gläubiger zu erstatten hatte. Im Laufe des Versteigerungsverfahrens stellte es sich heraus, dass das Haus noch in drei weiteren Geschäften als Sicherheit eingesetzt war, nämlich zum einen in zwei Darlehensgeschäften mit Kultgemeinschaften in Höhe von 100 bzw. 24 Drachmen, zum anderen zur Sicherung einer Schuldforderung in Höhe von 30 Drachmen wegen einer ausstehenden Begleichung von Begräbniskosten. Wann und wie diese Forderungen – deren Berechtigung der Bericht der Poleten explizit feststellt – zu begleichen waren, geht aus der Inschrift nicht hervor. Sowohl im Falle der durch den Horos dokumentierten Kredite wie auch im Falle der von den Poleten verkauften Immobilie steht jedenfalls fest, dass eine Immobilie gleichzeitig in mehreren Schuldgeschäften als Sicherheit eingesetzt war.[52]

Das Verständnis dieser Fälle erhellt ein Abschnitt aus einem Gesetz aus Ephesos aus den ersten Jahren des 3. Jh. v. Chr., das die Tilgung von Schulden in einer Krisensituation regelt. Das Gesetz definiert ein Verfahren, das es Schuldnern ermöglichen sollte, nach Ende eines Krieges Schulden zu begleichen, für deren Rückzahlung man für die Dauer der als „Bundeskrieg" bezeichneten Auseinandersetzung ein Moratorium verfügt hatte. Zu den komplexen Bestimmungen gehören auch Anordnungen, die den Umgang mit mehrfach belasteten Hypotheken betreffen und auf die auch Harris verwies (Z. 32–42):[53]

---

[51] SEG 12, 100 Z. 1–39. Vgl. Finley 1968, dem ich jedenfalls in der Deutung der Tatbestände folge.

[52] Vgl. zum Text auch Harris 2006a, 168f. und 184 (mit Anm. 62). An letzterer Stelle stellt Harris fest „that three successive loans were made on the same security in this case". Im Gegensatz zu Finley sah Harris in dieser Inschrift seinerzeit kein Indiz für eine kollaterale Sicherung.

[53] I.Ephesos 4 (Syll.^{3} 364; Walser 2008). Die von Harris 2008, 193f. (mit entstelltem griechischen Text) und ders. 2013, 141 jeweils gegebenen Übersetzungen sind nicht präzise.

– ὅσοι δὲ ἐπὶ
τοῖς ὑπερέχουσι δεδανείκασιν, εἶναι τὴγ κομιδὴν αὐτοῖς ἐκ το περιόντος μέρους τῶι
γεωργῶι, κἂν εἷς κἂμ πλείους ὦσι, τοῖς πρώτοις πρώτοις καὶ τοῖς ἄλλοις ἐπεξῆς, τὸν δὲ
[μερισ]ṃὸν εἶναι καί τούτοις καθάπερ καὶ τοῖς πρώτοις δανείσασιν. – εἰ δέ τινες
[ὑποθέ]ντες ἄλλοις κτήματα δεδανεισμένοι εἰσὶμ παρ’ ἑτέρων ὡς ἐπ’ ἐλευθέροις
[τοῖς κ]τήμασιν ἐξαπατήσαντες τοὺς ὑστέρους δανειστάς, ἐξεῖναι τοῖς ὑστέροις
[δανεισ]ταῖς ἐξαλλάξασι τοὺς πρότερον δανειστὰς ḳατὰ τὸν συλλογισμὸν τοῦ κοινοῦ πο-
[λέμου] ἔχειν τὰ κτήματα· ἐὰν δὲ ἐνοφείληταί τι αὐτοῖς ἔτι, εἶναι τὴγ κομιδὴν τοῖς
[δανειστ]αῖς ἐκ τῆς ἄλλης οὐσίας τοῦ χρείστου πασῆς τρ̣ό̣πωι ὧι ἂν δύνωνται ἀζημίοις
[ἁπάση]ς ζημίας· ἂν δὲ καὶ ἔγγυος ἦι, εἶναι τὴν ἐκ τοῦ ἐγγύου κομιδὴν καθάπερ ἐκ τῶν
[τὰ μετέ]ωρα ἐγγυωμένων.

„Die, die auf den Rest (eines bereits belasteten Grundstücks) geliehen haben, denen soll die Befriedigung (der Schuldforderung) aus den dem Bauern übrig gebliebenen Teilen erfolgen, sei es dass es einer oder mehrere (Gläubiger) sind, den ersten zuerst und dann der Reihe nach, das Teilungsverfahren soll dasselbe sein auch für diese wie für die ersten Kreditgeber. – Wenn irgendwelche aber auf Besitz, der bereits anderen als Sicherheit gegeben worden war, bei anderen Anleihen machten, so als ob der Besitz noch frei wäre und (sie) so die späteren Gläubiger betrogen haben, dann steht es den späteren Gläubigern frei, die ersten Gläubiger gemäß der Berechnung für den Bundeskrieg zu entschädigen und den Besitz zu übernehmen. Wenn noch ein Teil der Schuld unbefriedigt bleibt, können es die Kreditgeber wiedererlangen aus allem übrigen Vermögen, auf jede Art, die sie wollen, ohne jede Strafe. Wenn es aber auch noch einen Bürgen gibt, erfolgt die Entschädigung durch den Bürgen so wie bei den Bürgen von normalen hängigen Schulden.“

Ich habe das ephesische Gesetz und diese Passage an anderer Stelle im Detail analysiert,[54] so dass ich mich darauf beschränke, die für das hier diskutierte Problem wichtigsten Beobachtungen zu rekapitulieren:

Auch das ephesische Gesetz bezeugt zweifelsfrei, dass es Darlehen gab, die gegen eine Hypothek gewährt wurden, die bereits in einem früheren Sicherheitsgeschäft als Sicherheit eingesetzt war. Sofern der Schuldner den Gläubiger über die frühere Belastung in Unkenntnis ließ und suggerierte, dass die Sicherheit noch

[54] Walser 2008, 135–142.

gänzlich unbelastet war, handelte er widerrechtlich, so dass die Darlehen illegal waren, mit der Konsequenz, dass er mit seinem übrigen Vermögen zu haften hatte.[55] Allerdings gab es auch Darlehensgeschäfte, bei denen eine Sicherheit völlig legal mehrfach belastet wurde. In diesen Fällen waren die späteren Kreditgeber über die bereits bestehenden Belastungen informiert, und spätere Darlehen wurden explizit nur auf jenen Teil der ursprünglichen Hypothek gewährt, um den die Immobilie mehr wert war als das ursprüngliche Darlehen. Das ephesische Gesetz spricht dabei vom „Übriggebliebenen" (τὰ ὑπερέχοντα), und gemeint ist damit offenbar eben das, was die athenischen Horoi und der angeführte Bericht der Poleten mit der Wendung ὅσωι πλείονος ἄξιον (vel sim.) umschrieben: Die Differenz zwischen Darlehenssumme und dem geschätzten Wert der Sicherheit.

In Ephesos wie in Athen gab es folglich die Möglichkeit, nach dem Abschluss eines ersten Sicherungsgeschäftes ein weiteres Darlehensgeschäft abzuschließen, bei dem dieselbe Sicherheit als Hypothek diente, allerdings nur in dem Umfang, in dem ihr Wert die erste Kreditsumme überstieg.

Es ist schon vor langer Zeit erkannt worden, dass die Existenz solcher Mehrfachhypotheken – die Bezeichnung Zusatzhypotheken wäre vielleicht präziser – das eigentliche *pièce de resistance* darstellt, wenn die Geltung des Ersatzpfandprinzips behauptet werden soll. Wie ist es denkbar, dass auf den „Mehrwert" einer Hypothek ein weiteres Darlehen vergeben wurde, wenn das Ersatzprinzip doch gerade darauf beruhte, dass die Sicherheit unabhängig von ihrem exakten Wert zur Gänze an den Gläubiger verfiel? Oder eben anders gewendet: Diese Zusatzhypotheken stellen überhaupt kein Problem dar, wenn das Verkaufspfandprinzip galt und der Gläubiger ohnehin stets nur einen begrenzten Anspruch auf die Hypothek erwarb. Wenn die Hypothek bei der Vollstreckung verkauft werden musste und der Mehrwert an den Schuldner zurückfiel, dann war es wohl auch möglich, diesen Mehrwert schon vorher in einem weiteren Geschäft als Hypothek einzusetzen.

In einem sorgfältig argumentierenden Beitrag unternahm Arnaldo Biscardi 1983 den Versuch, dieses Phänomen der „pluralité hypothécaire" dogmatisch zu erklären, ohne grundsätzlich vom Grundsatz abzuweichen, dass die hypothekarische Sicherheit ein Verfallspfand war. Biscardi ging davon aus, dass die Gläubiger auf Basis einer am Grundsatz von *prior tempore potior iure* orientierten Rangfolge Anspruch auf die Hypothek erwarben. Im Range schlechter gestellte Gläubiger – also die, die auf den Mehrwert Kredit gaben – hatten die Möglichkeit, einen früheren Gläubiger durch die Zahlung seines jeweiligen Darlehens abzulösen und nun ihrerseits die Sicherheit als Ersatzpfand zu übernehmen. Dieses Erklärungsmodell erscheint mir nach wie vor in dogmatischer Hinsicht bemerkenswert schlüssig. Das Prinzip einer Rangfolge zwischen den Schuldnern bei mehrfacher

[55] Das ephesische Gesetz belegt dies nur für den Sonderfall der Regelungen, die für die Schuldentilgung nach dem Bundeskrieg galten, man wird es aber zuversichtlich auf die normalen Verhältnisse übertragen können.

Belastung ist durch das ephesische Gesetz tatsächlich bezeugt, wenn auch streng genommen nur für das dort definierte besondere Tilgungsverfahren. Ansonsten kann sich Biscardis Vorschlag indes auf keine direkten Zeugnisse stützen. Zweifel an Biscardis Lösung ergeben sich weniger aus dogmatischen, sondern vielmehr aufgrund praktischer Überlegungen, wenn den wirtschaftlichen Konsequenzen Rechnung getragen wird. Im Fall, den der oben rekapitulierte Bericht der Poleten dokumentiert, müsste etwa der Gläubiger, dessen Forderung auf die Zahlung von 30 Drachmen an Bestattungskosten durch die Immobilie gesichert ist, zunächst Forderungen besser gestellter Gläubiger im Umfang von insgesamt 250 Drachmen begleichen, bevor er selbst die Immobilie übernehmen könnte – wobei ihn freilich die zweite, im Rang nachgestellte Kultvereinigung, deren Schuld lediglich 24 Drachmen betrug, noch ablösen könnte. Wie hier deutlich wird, müssten nachgestellte Gläubiger über beträchtlich finanzielle Mittel verfügen, um besser gestellte Gläubiger abzulösen, denen in der Regel wesentlich größere Summen geschuldet wurden.

Eine aus dogmatischer Perspektive sicherlich weniger konsequente Erklärung hatte Finley vorgeschlagen:[56] Nach seiner Ansicht bestand für Gläubiger und Schuldner grundsätzlich die Möglichkeit, in der Übereinkunft beim Abschluss eines Darlehensgeschäfts festzuhalten, dass die Sicherheit nicht als Ganzes an den Gläubiger verfällt, sondern „soweit sie mehr wert ist" und im Vollstreckungsfall dem Schuldner verbleibt. Dies würde also bedeuten, dass die Möglichkeit grundsätzlich bestand, in konkreten Darlehensverträgen vom Ersatzprinzip der Sicherung abzurücken und stattdessen die Hypothek als kollaterale Sicherheit einzusetzen und mithin den Verkauf der Sicherheit vorzusehen. Unter dieser Voraussetzung würde auch der Belastung des Mehrwertes in weiteren Kreditgeschäften nichts entgegenstehen.

Tatsächlich scheint ein vor einigen Jahren neu entdeckter athenischer Horos, der bislang kaum Beachtung fand, eben diese Sicht zu stützen:[57]

ἐπὶ Γλαυκίππου ἄρχοντο<ς>
ὅρος χωρίου καὶ οἰκίας προι-
κὸς Πυθύππει Μνησάρχου
Ἁλαέως θυγατρὶ ΧΗ
τοῦτο ἀποτιμᾶι ὅσωι πλ-
έονος ἄξιόν ἐστιν ἢ τοῖ-
ς χρείσταις ὑπόκειται

„Unter dem Archonten Glaukippos. Horos des die Mitgift sichernden Gutes und Hauses für Pythippe, Tochter des Mnesarchos aus Halai, 1100 Drachmen; dies schätze ich höher ein, als (die Summe, für die) es den Gläubigern als Sicherheit dient."

[56] Finley 1968, 346f.
[57] SEG 44, 82. Vgl. Oikonomakou 1993.

In der Inschrift ist zunächst in ganz üblicher Weise festgehalten, dass der Horos ein Landgut und ein Haus als Sicherheit markiert, die eine Mitgift im Wert von 1100 Drachmen garantiert. Hierauf folgt eine Angabe, die bislang ohne Parallele ist: τοῦτο ἀποτιμᾶι ὅσωι πλέονος ἄξιόν ἐστιν ἢ τοῖς χρείσταις ὑπόκειται. Dies lässt sich wohl nur so verstehen, dass der Steller der Hypothek festhält, dass die Immobilie mehr wert ist, als die Summe, für die sie den Gläubigern als Sicherheit gestellt wird. Damit scheint sich der Schuldner die Möglichkeit offen halten zu wollen, die Sicherheit gegebenenfalls in einem weiteren Darlehensgeschäft zu belasten. Zu vermuten ist, dass die Angabe auf dem Horos einer ebenso expliziten Klausel im Vertrag über das Sicherungsgeschäft entspricht. Es ist wenig wahrscheinlich, dass dies auf dem Horos in dieser Form festgehalten worden wäre, wenn dies ohnehin der gängigen Praxis entsprochen hätte. Vielmehr dürften wir hier einen Fall fassen, in dem sich Gläubiger und Schuldner darauf geeinigt hatten, vom üblichen Ersatzprinzip abzuweichen, indem dem Mitgiftgeber der Mehrwert vorbehalten bleibt.

Dass dies eben keineswegs selbstverständlich war, verdeutlicht die ps.-demosthenische Rede gegen Nikostratos ([D.] 53, 10). Wie der Sprecher berichtet, versuchte Nikostratos verzweifelt an Geld zu kommen, blieb dabei aber erfolglos. Niemand wollte sein Landgut kaufen oder ihm gegen das Landgut als Hypothek ein Darlehen gewähren, weil sein Bruder Arethousias weder das eine noch das andere erlauben würde, da ihm darauf schon Geld geschuldet würde.[58] Ob Nikostratos sein Landgut mehrfach als Sicherheit belasten konnte, hing mithin ganz vom Willen des Erstgläubigers ab, der dies in seinem Falle nicht erlaubte.[59]

Eine Form der mehrfachen Belastung von Grundstücken wird nach den jüngst entwickelten Analysen von Julien Faguer auch in dem Kaufregister von Tenos und in Verkaufsurkunden aus Nordgriechenland sichtbar.[60] Faguer meint nachweisen zu können, dass in Tenos und auch in Nordgriechenland unterschiedliche real gesicherte Darlehensformen nebeneinander existierten. Die πρᾶσις ἐπὶ λύσει, der Verkauf mit Möglichkeit des Rückkaufes, war grundsätzlich ein vollwertiger Verkauf („une vente véritable“) und ging folglich mit einer sofortigen Übertragung des Eigentums – wenn wohl auch nicht des Besitzes – an den als Käufer auftretenden Darlehensgeber einher. Die Rückzahlung des Darlehens konnte nur in Form eines vollwertigen Rückkaufs der Immobilie zum Preis der Darlehenssumme geschehen. Erfolgte dieser Rückkauf nicht, blieb die (gesamte) Immobilie beim Käufer/Gläubiger,

[58] [D.] 53, 10: ἔλεγεν (*sc.* Nikostratos) … ὅτι τὸ χωρίον τὸ ἐν γειτόνων μοι τοῦτο οὐδεὶς ἐθέλοι οὔτε πρίασθαι οὔτε θέσθαι· ὁ γὰρ ἀδελφὸς ὁ Ἀρεθούσιος, οὗ τἀνδράποδ᾽ ἐστὶ ταῦτα ἃ νῦν ἀπογέγραπται, οὐδένα ἐᾴη οὔτε ὠνεῖσθαι οὔτε τίθεσθαι, ὡς ἐνοφειλομένου αὐτῷ ἀργυρίου.

[59] So auch Harris 2006a, 166. Es ist an dieser Stelle nicht möglich, auf die demosthenischen Rede gegen Pantainetos (D. 37) einzugehen. Harris ging bei seinem Versuch, die komplexen Transaktionen zu entschlüsseln (2006a, 190–199), von Voraussetzungen aus, die er selbst heute nur noch teilweise teilt.

[60] Faguer 2020, bes. 175–188; ders. 2021, bes. 16–18.

stellte also *de facto* ein Verfallspfand dar. Daneben existierten nach Faguer aber andere Formen real gesicherter Darlehen, die mit keiner Eigentumsübertragung verbunden waren, sondern nur einen Anspruch auf die Sicherheit konstituierten, der auf den dem Darlehen entsprechenden Wert beschränkt blieb. Es handelte sich demnach um eine kollaterale Sicherung, was nach Faguer insbesondere daran ersichtlich wird, dass eine in dieser Form als Hypothek dienende Sicherheit in einer πρᾶσις ἐπὶ λύσει „verkauft" bzw. erneut belastet werden konnte. Der nach Faguer oft unerwartet niedrige „Verkaufspreis" hätte dabei der Tatsache Rechnung getragen, dass die Immobilie bereits belastet war.

Eine vertiefte Auseinandersetzung mit Faguers interessanten, aber auch nicht unproblematischen Überlegungen ist an dieser Stelle nicht möglich.[61] Selbst wenn man seiner Interpretation insbesondere der Transaktionen im Register von Tenos folgt, geht daraus, so weit ich sehe, nicht eindeutig hervor, welchen Charakter die Sicherheit hatte: Faguers Interpretation setzt grundsätzlich nur voraus, dass der Verkauf einer hypothekarisch belasteten Sicherheit – ob auf Lösung oder nicht – zulässig war, wobei der Käufer in diesem Fall die Schuld, die weiterhin auf der Immobilie lastete, in seinem Kaufpreis berücksichtigte. Ob das bestehende Darlehen dabei kollateral oder substitutiv gesichert war, machte aus Sicht des Käufers, der den ursprünglichen Gläubiger wohl zu entschädigen beabsichtigte, keinen Unterschied.

Festzuhalten bleibt, dass jedenfalls in Ephesos, wo das Schuldentilgungsgesetz die Existenz von mehrfachen hypothekarischen Belastungen am klarsten dokumentiert, keine terminologische Unterscheidung verschiedener klar definierter Darlehensformen, von denen die eine substitutiv nach dem Verfalls-, die andere kollateral nach dem Verkaufspfandprinzip gesichert gewesen wäre, fassbar wird.

7. Bürgschaften bei Hypotheken

Auch ein weiteres signifikantes Phänomen, das bislang wenig Beachtung fand, zeigt sich zwar nicht nur, aber ebenfalls in besonderer Klarheit im ephesischen Schuldentilgungsgesetz.[62] Nachdem schon mit Blick auf die illegale Belastung einer Sicherheit die Haftung eines eventuell vorhandenen Bürgen bekräftigt wurde, folgt gleich im Anschluss ein längerer Abschnitt, der – wie ein Zwischentitel festhält – diejenigen betrifft, die für Hypotheken Bürgschaften leisten (Z.42–48).

---

[61] Vgl. vorerst Harris 2023, der ebd. 101 Anm. 34 eine kritische Auseinandersetzung mit Faguers Thesen zur realen Sicherheit ankündigt. Faguer 2021a, 17 Anm. 50 unterstreicht zu Recht, dass eine umfassende Analyse auch das Material aus Delos berücksichtigen müsste.

[62] Vgl. Walser 2008, 142–148.

– ὑπὲρ τῶν ἐγγύων τῶν ἐγγυωμένων πρὸς
[αὐτὰ] τὰ κτήματα· – ἐὰμ μὲν ἴση ἧι ἡ τιμὴ τοῦ κτήματος τῶι δανείωι, πρὸς ὃ
44 [ἂν ἧι ἔ]γγυος, τῆι τιμήσει τῆι πρὸ τοῦ πολέμου γεγενημένηι, ἀπηλλάχθαι τὸν ἔγγ-
[υον τῆ]ς ἐγγύης· ἐὰν δὲ πλέον ἧι τὸ ὀφείλημα τῆς τιμῆς τοῦ κτήματος, τὸ πλ̣έον ὀφεί-
[λημα τῆς] τ̣ιμῆς ὁ ἔγγυος ἀποτινέτω κατὰ λόγον ὥσπερ οἱ ἄλλοι οἱ τὰ μετέωρα ἐγγυώ-
[μενοι, ἐὰμ] μὴ ἐπιτετοκισμένον ἧι εἰς πλείω χρόνον τῆς ἐν τῆι πράξει γεγενημένης
48 [ἐγγύη]ς̣·

„– Über Bürgen, die für diese Besitztümer Bürgschaft leisten: – Wenn der Schätzwert des Besitzes gleich dem Darlehen ist, für das der Bürge bürgt, nach der Schätzung, die (für den Wert) vor dem Krieg gemacht wurde, ist der Bürge von der Bürgschaft befreit. Wenn das Darlehen den Schätzwert des Besitzes übersteigt, soll der Bürge das, was den Schätzwert übersteigt, abzahlen, im Verhältnis wie die Übrigen, die für hängige Schulden Bürgschaft leisten, wenn nicht Zins über längere Zeit angehäuft wurde, als im Bürgschaftsvertrag ausgemacht war."

Sieht man von den Besonderheiten ab, die sich im Zusammenhang mit dem Tilgungsverfahren ergeben und die ich an anderer Stelle diskutiert habe,[63] so lautet die Kernaussage der Bestimmung, dass ein Bürge für den Fehlbetrag haftbar ist, falls der Wert der Hypothek die Darlehenssumme nicht vollumfänglich zu decken vermag. Der Bürge haftet explizit nur subsidiär, nachdem die Hypothek bereits verwertet wurde. Ganz analog sahen auch das samische Getreidegesetz sowie die Urkunde über die Attalos-Schenkung aus Delphi jeweils eine subsidiäre Haftung von Bürgen für allfällige Fehlbeträge nach der Verwertung der realen Sicherheiten vor.[64]

Es liegt auf der Hand, dass die subsidiäre Haftung eines Bürgen nicht mit dem Grundprinzip des Ersatzpfandes in Reinform vereinbar ist. Definitionsgemäß kann sich kein Fehlbetrag, ἐλλεῖπον, ergeben, wenn die Sicherheit als einfacher Ersatz für den Darlehensbetrag dienen soll. Vielmehr scheint vorausgesetzt, dass die Sicherheit bei der Vollstreckung monetär verwertet oder zumindest geschätzt wird. Allerdings geht aus den Bestimmungen im ephesischen Gesetz sowie in der delphischen Urkunde nur hervor, dass Bürgen für Fehlbeträge haften. Ob dies impliziert, dass auch ein Mehrwert an den Schuldner zu erstatten ist, bleibt im ephesischen Fall offen und ist im delphischen, wie oben festgestellt wurde, nicht wahrscheinlich.

8. Fazit

Überblickt man die diskutierten Zeugnisse, ist zweifellos festzuhalten, dass man sich beim Abschluss von Kreditgeschäften häufig darüber Gedanken machte, ob der Wert einer Immobilie, der bei einem Verkauf realisiert werden konnte, die Darlehenssumme, die sie sicherte, deckte oder ob sich ein Fehlbetrag oder ein Überschuss ergab. Von der simplen Vorstellung, dass die Sicherheit einfach als Ersatz an Stelle

63 Walser 2008, 142–148 mit der früheren Literatur.
64 Vgl. oben 5. a) und b).

des geliehenen Kapitals an den Gläubiger fallen sollte, war man damit weit entfernt. Es muss deshalb auch nicht erstaunen, dass es Darlehensgeschäfte gab, in denen eine Hypothek – wie im samischen Getreidegesetz – ein Darlehen nicht als Ersatzpfand, sondern kollateral sicherte und als Verkaufspfand diente. Will man alle Darlehensgeschäfte konsequent auf ein allgemeingültiges Sicherungsprinzip zurückführen, dann ist daraus mit Harris zu folgern, dass die reale Sicherheit im Recht der klassischen und hellenistischen Polis nicht Ersatzpfand, sondern ein kollateral wirkendes Verkaufspfand war.

Diese Verallgemeinerung scheint mir jedoch weder zwingend noch gerechtfertigt: Die Anzahl der Zeugnisse, die das Verkaufspfandprinzip eindeutig belegen, bleibt sehr klein, und zwar auch dann, wenn man davon ausgeht, dass „Mehrfachhypotheken", wie sie in Athen und Ephesos existiert haben, das Verkaufspfandprinzip voraussetzen. Bei aller Problematik von Aussagen, die auf dem Fehlen von Belegen abstützten, scheint dies doch signifikant. Auch im ephesischen Schuldentilgungsgesetz, in dem sowohl Zusatzhypotheken als auch die subsidiäre Haftung von Bürgen problematisiert wird, ist die allgemeine Geltung des Verkaufspfandprinzips keineswegs zwingend und, wie ich meine, unwahrscheinlich. Die Möglichkeit, dass eine Sicherheit die Darlehenssumme nicht zu decken vermochte, wird überhaupt nur im Kontext von Bürgschaften in Betracht gezogen.

Die Zeugnisse erlauben es meiner Auffassung nach nicht, eine allgemeingültige Entscheidung darüber zu treffen, ob im Allgemeinen das substitutive oder das kollaterale Sicherungsprinzip galt. Sie legen vielmehr nahe, dass das Ersatzpfandprinzip und das Prinzip der kollateralen Sicherung durch ein Verkaufspfand nebeneinander existierten. Ermöglicht wurde dieses Nebeneinander durch die Freiheit in der Ausgestaltung der Darlehensverträge. In der Regel dürften sich diese Verträge am Ersatzpfandprinzip orientiert haben.

Zur Illustration kann man noch einmal auf das ephesische Schuldentilgungsgesetz verweisen. Dort heißt es mit Bezug auf Vollstreckungsmaßnahmen, die erfolgt waren, bevor man im Monat Posideon in der Prytanie des Demagoras den Kriegszustand verhängte, der für Darlehensgeschäfte Sonderregelungen mit sich brachte (Z. 75–77):

ὅσοι μὲμ πρὸ μηνὸς Ποσιδεῶνος
76 τοῦ ἐπὶ Δη[μ]αγόρου ἐμβάντες εἰς κτήματα κατὰ πράξεις ἔχουσιν τὰ κτήματα καὶ νέμον-
ται, εἶναι [αὐ]τοῖς κυρίας τὰς ἐμβάσεις, εἰ μή τι ἄλλο ἑκόντες πρὸς αὑτοὺς ὡμολογήκασιν. περὶ
δὲ τῆς π[αγ]κτησίας ἄν τινες ἀμφισβητῶσιν, κρίσιν αὐτοῖς εἶναι κατὰ τοὺς νόμους.

„Für jene, die vor dem Monat Posideon und der Prytanie des Demagoras in den Besitz vollstreckt haben entsprechend den Verträgen, den Landbesitz (nun) besitzen und bewirtschaften, soll die Besitznahme rechtskräftig sein, wenn sie (*sc.* der Schuldner und der Gläubiger) nicht freiwillig zu einer anderen Übereinkunft miteinander gekommen sind."

Das Gesetz scheint hier als Normalfall vorauszusetzen, dass die Vollstreckung aufgrund einer Zahlungsunfähigkeit durch eine ἐμβάσις erfolgt ist, in deren Folge der Gläubiger Eigentümer und Besitzer der Sicherheit geworden ist. Mit dem Verweis darauf, dass die ἐμβάσις ausdrücklich κατὰ τὰς πράξεις erfolgte, und dem expliziten Vorbehalt, dass sich die Parteien auch anders einigen konnten, wird aber auch hier betont, dass von dem üblichen Verfahren abgewichen werden konnte.

Anderslautende Abmachungen, die explizit festlegten, dass nur ein Teil der Sicherheit Gegenstand einer Vollstreckung sein können, waren im Rahmen eines Vertrages möglich, wohl eben vorausgesetzt, dass beide Parteien einer entsprechenden Regelung zustimmten. Der neu hinzugezogene Horos aus Athen zeigt, dass solche Bestimmungen bezüglich des Mehrwertes in der Tat wohl schon Gegenstand des ursprünglichen Vertrages sein konnten und nicht erst später vereinbart wurden. Solche Verträge, die aus unserer Sicht moderner erscheinen, machten dann auch Phänomene wie die mehrfache Belastung von Hypotheken möglich. In der Tatsache, dass wir häufiger Bestimmungen über einen allfälligen Fehlbetrag ohne zugleich Regelungen zu einem allfälligen Mehrwert finden, dürfte sich ein Verhandlungsprozess spiegeln, in dem sich die Gläubiger häufig in einer stärkeren Position befanden als die auf Kredit angewiesenen Darlehensnehmer. Das Ergebnis war ein Darlehensvertrag, der zum Nachteil des Schuldners zwischen dem Ersatz- und dem Verkaufspfandprinzip stand und sich gegen eine eindeutige dogmatische Einordnung sträubt.

Keine Aussage lässt sich, über die relative Häufigkeit treffen, mit der das substitutive oder das kollaterale Sicherungsprinzip zur Anwendung kam, und wir sollten auch nicht von einer progressiven zeitlichen Entwicklung von der substitutiven zur kollateralen Sicherung ausgehen.[65] Es ist keineswegs auszuschließen, dass mancherorts und zu mancher Zeit Verträge, die dem Verkaufspfandprinzip folgten, sehr häufig, vielleicht sogar häufiger waren als andere. Welches Prinzip zur Anwendung kam, dürfte einerseits auf die Stärke der jeweiligen Verhandlungsposition von Gläubiger und Schuldner zurückzuführen sein, andererseits aber von den spezifischen ökonomischen Rahmenbedingungen in einer bestimmten Zeit und an einem bestimmten Ort abhängen. In Erinnerung zu rufen ist dann auch, dass die Mehrzahl der Poleis in der griechischen Welt nicht aussahen wie Athen, auch nicht wie Ephesos, sondern kleine Gemeinden waren, in denen der Verkauf von Immobilien weit schwieriger gewesen sein dürfte. Damit entfernen wir uns aber endgültig von den primär rechtshistorischen Problemen und gelangen zu wirtschaftsgeschichtlichen Fragestellungen, die hier nicht mehr zu behandeln sind.

victor.walser@hist.uzh.ch

---

[65] Vgl. schon treffen Bruck 1912, 564: „Es ist recht unwahrscheinlich, daß eine ausdrückliche Verdrängung des Ersatzprinzips auf gesetzlichem Wege je stattgefunden hat, daß so gesetzlich festgelegt worden sei: ‚von heut ab ist der Pfandschuldner zur Nachzahlung des Elleipon verpflichtet, andererseits darf er die Hyperocha fordern.'" Grundsätzlich zur Problematik, eine zeitliche Entwicklung unterschiedlicher Darlehensformen nachzuweisen vgl. schon Harris 2006a169f.

BIBLIOGRAPHIE

Biscardi 1983: A. Biscardi, Le régime de la pluralité hypothécaire en droit grec et romain, JJP 19, 1983, 41–59 (ders., Scritti di diritto Greco, 1999, 173–198).

Bresson 2016: A. Bresson, The Making of the Ancient Greek Economy, 2016.

Bruck 1912: E.F. Bruck, Rez. L. Raape, Der Verfall des griechischen Pfandes, besonders des griechisch–ägyptischen, ZRG Rom 33, 1912, 551–569.

Dareste 1875: R. Dareste, Les plaidoyers civils de Démosthène, tome premier, 1875.

Dimopoulou-Piliouni 2007: Dimopoulou-Piliouni, Les garanties des dettes envers und fondation: le cas de Syll.[3] 672, RIDA 85, 2007, 437–453.

Faguer 2020: J. Faguer, Ventes immobilières et sûretés réelles à Ténos et Paros, BCH 144, 2020, 155–207.

Faguer 2021a: J. Faguer, Le marché du crédit à Olynthe et le calendrier des Chalcidiens de Thrace, REG 134, 2021, 1–32

Faguer 2021b: J. Faguer, Status et propriété foncière dans l'Athènes des IIIe et IIe siècles av. J.-C.: la question de l'*enktesis*, in: S. Maillot – J. Zurbach (Hg.), Status personnels et main-d'oeuvre en Méditterranée hellénistique, 2021, 61–91.

Fine 1951: J.V.A. Fine, Horoi. Studies in Mortgage, Real Security and Land Tenure in Ancient Athens, 1951.

Finley 1951: M.I. Finley, Studies in Land and Credit in Ancient Athens, 500–200 B.C., 1951, erg. Neuausgabe, 1985.

Finley 1968: M.I. Finley, Mehrfache Belastung von Grundstücken im attischen Recht. Neues Beweismaterial aus einer auf der Agora gefundenen Inschrift, in: E. Berneker (Hg.), Zur griechischen Rechtsgeschichte, 1968, 534–558 (ursprünglich Multiple Charges on Real Property in Athenian Law: New Evidence from an Agora Inscription, in: Studi in onore die Vincenzo Arangio–Ruiz, 1953, 473–491).

Finley 1973: M.I. Finley, The Ancient Economy, 1973, 2. erw. Aufl., 1985.

Game 2008: J. Game, Actes de vente dans le monde grecque: témoignages épigraphiques des ventes immobilières, 2008.

Harris 2006a: E.M. Harris, When Is a Sale Not a Sale? The Riddle of Athenian Terminology for Real Security Revisited, in: ders. Democracy and the Rule of Law in Classical Athens, 2006, 163–206 (ursprünglich CQ 38, 1988, 351–381).

Harris 2006b: E.M. Harris, Apotimema: Athenian Terminology for Real Security in Leases and Dowry Agreements, in: ders. Democracy and the Rule of Law in Classical Athens, 2006, 207–239 (ursprünglich CQ 43, 1993, 73–95).

Harris 2008: E.M. Harris, Response to Gerhard Thür, in: G. Thür – E.M. Harris (Hg.), Symposion 2007, 2008, 189–200.

Harris 2013: E.M. Harris, Finley's Studies in Land and Credit Sixty Years Later', Dike 16, 2013, 123–146.

Harris 2016: E.M. Harris 2016, The Legal Foundations of Economic Growth in Ancient Greece. The Role of Property Records, in: E.M. Harris – D.M. Lewis – M. Wohler (Hg.), The Ancient Greek Economy: Markets, Households and City-States, 2016, 116–146.

Harris 2023: E.M. Harris, The Language of Sale in Documents about Property from Northern Greece, ZPE 225, 2023, 93–102.

Hitzig 1895: H.F. Hitzig, Das griechische Pfandrecht, 1895.

Koch – Thür 1981: Chr. Koch – G. Thür, Prozessrechtlicher Kommentar zum „Getreidegesetz" aus Samos. Prozeßrechtliche Inschriften der griechischen Poleis, Sonderheft B, 1981.

MacDowell 2004: D.M. MacDowell, Demosthenes, Speeches 27–38 (The Oratory of Classical Greece, Vol. 8), 2004.

Migeotte 2015: L. Migeotte, La fondation d'Attale II à Delphes: dispositions administratives et financières, in: ders., Économie et finances publiques des cités grecques. Volume II. Choix d'articles publiés de 2002 à 2014, 2015, 315–326 (ursprünglich Dike 12/13, 2009/2010, 203–217).

Millett 2016: P. Millett, The Impact of Studies in Land and Credit, in: D. Jew – R. Osborne – M. Scott (ed.), M.I. Finley: An Ancient Historian and his Impact, 2016, 31–57.

Murray 1936: A.T. Murray, Demosthenes. Private Orations, Vol. I., 1936.

Nevett 2000: L. Nevett, A Real Estate 'Market' in Classical Greece? The Example of Town Housing, ABSA 95, 2000, 329–343.

Pappulias 1909: D.P. Pappulias, Η εμπράγματος ασφάλεια κατά το ελληνικόν και το ρωμαϊκόν δίκαιον. Τόμος πρώτος (Das Pfandrecht nach dem griechischen und römischen Recht), 1909.

Oikonomakou 1993: M. Oikonomakou, Ὅρος προικώου ἀποτμήματος, AEph 132, 1993, 211–214.

Paoli 1930: U.E. Paoli, Ipoteca e ἀποτίμημα nel diritto attico. In: Studi di diritto attico, Firenze 1930, 141–194.

Raapc 1912: L. Raapc, Dcr Vcrfall des griechischen Pfandes besonders des griechisch-ägyptischen. Eine Studie, 1912.

Schuster 2005: S. Schuster, Das Seedarlehen in den Gerichtsreden des Demosthenes. Mit einem Ausblick auf die weitere historische Entwicklung des Rechtsinstitutes: dáneion nautikón, fenus nauticum und Bodmerei, 2005.

Sundahl 2014: M.J. Sundahl, Secured Credit in Athens: Reopening the Debate, in: M. Gagarin – A. Lanni (Hg.), Symposion 2013, 2014, 223–238.

Thür 2006: G. Thür, Die Einheit des „Griechischen Rechts". Gedanken zum Prozessrecht in den griechischen Poleis, Dike 9, 2006 [2008], 23–62.

Thür 2008: G. Thür, Ownership and Security in Macedonia Sale Documents, in: Ders. – E.M. Harris (Hg.), Symposion 2007, 2008, 173–187.

Thür 2014: G. Thür, Ownership and Secured Credit in Athens, in: M. Gagarin – A. Lanni (ed.), Symposion 2013, 2014, 239–238.

Walser 2008: A.V. Walser, Bauern und Zinsnehmer. Politik, Recht und Wirtschaft im frühhellenistischen Ephesos, 2008.
Weiss 1923: E. Weiss, Griechisches Privatrecht auf rechtsvergleichender Grundlage, 1923.
Wolff 1953: H.J. Wolff, Rez. Fine 1951 und Finley 1951, ZRG Rom 70, 1953, 411–425.
Wolff 1975: H.J. Wolff, Juristische Gräzistik – Aufgaben, Probleme, Möglichkeiten, in: ders. (Hg.), Symposion 1971. Vorträge zur griechischen und hellenistischen Rechtsgeschichte, 1975, 1–22.

THOMAS KRUSE (WIEN)

SUBSTITUTIVE UND KOLLATERALE SICHERHEIT IN DARLEHENSURKUNDEN AUS DEM HELLENISTISCHEN UND RÖMISCHEN ÄGYPTEN: ANTWORT AUF ANDREAS VICTOR WALSER*

Die folgenden Ausführungen sollen die Frage, ob das Darlehenspfand Verfallspfand war oder lediglich der kollateralen Absicherung des Gläubigers diente, anhand der griechischen Quellen aus Ägypten beleuchten. Sie verstehen sich eher als Ergänzung, denn als explizite Gegenposition zu den Ausführungen von Victor Walser, zumal diese ja auch auf die Behandlung des papyrologischen Materials ausdrücklich verzichten. Dabei wird der Zeithorizont bis in die römische Kaiserzeit hinein ausgedehnt, was dem Verfasser insofern legitim erscheint, als auch die aus römischer Zeit überlieferten Darlehensverträge in den griechisch-hellenistischen Rechtsprinzipien der früheren Zeit wurzeln.

Auch in Ägypten kann mitunter die Besicherung eines Darlehens durch eine Hypothek auf Immobilienbesitz (Land, Häuser, Baugrundstücke) des Schuldners zugunsten des Gläubigers erfolgen; auch wenn dies ausweislich unserer Quellen in ptolemäischer Zeit im Gegensatz zur römischen Epoche nicht eben häufig vorgekommen zu sein scheint. Ein Beispiel hierfür ist ein im Agoranomeion der arsinoitischen Gaumetropole Krokodilopolis errichteter Vertrag zwischen zwei jüdischen Vertragsparteien vom 4. November 182 v.Chr. (P.Tebt. III.1 817)[1]: Apollonios, Sohn des Protogenes, gibt dem Sostratos, Sohn des Neoptolemos, ein zinsloses Darlehen in Höhe von 15.000 Bronzedrachmen für ein Jahr.[2] Das Darlehen wird mit einer Hypothek auf ein dem Schuldner gehörendes Haus im Dorf Apias

* Die Verwendung von Siglen für Editionen von Papyri, Ostraka und papyrologischen Reihenwerken erfolgt gemäß der „Checklist of Editions of Greek, Latin, Demotic and Coptic Papyri, Ostraca and Tablets" zugänglich unter: https://papyri.info/docs/checklist.

1 = SB I 4232 = C.Pap.Jud. I 23.

2 Das Darlehen wird zwar ausdrücklich als ἄτοκος bezeichnet, jedoch könnte der übliche Zins in der Darlehenssumme inkludiert sein; falls ja, dann betrüge die Darlehenssumme, legt man den damals üblichen Zinssatz von 2% pro Monat zugrunde, 12.500 Dr. Trotz des Zinsverbotes im jüdischen Religionsgesetz, konnte ein Darlehenszins auch zwischen jüdischen Vertragsparteien in der ägyptischen Diaspora durchaus stipuliert werden, siehe etwa P.Polit. Iud. 8,16 (siehe zu diesem Text auch sogleich im Folgenden; siehe allgemein auch Rupprecht 1967, 79–81.

besichert.[3] Wenn der Schuldner nicht zurückzahlt, soll der Gläubiger den Zugriff auf das Pfand haben, gemäß dem Diagramma des Königs: ἐπικα|[τ]αβολὴν ποιήσασθαι τῆς ὑποθήκης ἀκολούθως τῶι διαγράμματι (Z. 19–20).[4] Der Schuldner garantiert ferner, daß die Hypothek frei von sonstigen Belastungen ist; falls dies nicht der Fall sein sollte und falls Sostratos das Darlehen nicht fristgerecht zurückzahlt, kommt zur Rückzahlung ein Aufschlag von 50% auf die Darlehenssumme (das ἡμιόλιον) sowie ein Strafzins von 24% je Monat hinzu.[5]

Bei der ἐπικαταβολή handelt es sich offenbar um einen durch ein königliches Edikt geregelten Zugriffsakt des Gläubigers auf die Hypothek, mit dem Ziel, sich in den Besitz der betreffenden Sache zu setzen. In einem Text aus dem Archiv des jüdischen Politeuma von Herakleopolis von 133 v.Chr. (P.Polit. Iud. 8), der einen Rechtsstreit über ein hypothekarisch besichertes Darlehen betrifft, sagt der Petent: τὴν ἐπικατα|βολὴν π̣[οιη]σ̣α̣μ̣ε̣νου [μ]ο̣υ ἐκυρίευσα | τῆς κτήσε̣ω̣ς.[6] Rechtsfolge der ἐπικαταβολή war also eindeutig das κυριεύειν, die volle Verfügungsgewalt über die verpfändete Sache. Die rechtliche Natur der Epikatabole, welche auch in römischen Darlehensverträgen mit Hypothekenbestellung als Recht des Gläubigers bei Nichtbezahlung erscheint[7], ist indes nach wie vor weitgehend ungeklärt. Sie hat aber sicher die Zahlung von Steuern seitens des Gläubigers beinhaltet sowie wahrscheinlich auch eine staatliche Registrierung (möglicherweise des Gläubigers als des neuen Besitzers der Immobilie). Ludwig Mitteis bezeichnete die ἐπικαταβολή einmal als den „dunkelsten Punkt bei der Hypothekenrealisation“[8], und wesentlich heller ist es seitdem anscheinend nicht geworden.[9]

Wir können den genannten Texten jedoch leider keine Informationen darüber entnehmen, ob im Falle der Nichtbezahlung der Darlehensschuld die verpfändete Immobilie zur Gänze an den Gläubiger überging oder dieser im Falle eines Verkaufs einen etwaigen die Darlehenssumme übersteigenden Mehrwert an den Schuldner herausgeben musste, denn darüber treffen die Vertragsparteien keine Vereinbarungen. Man könnte allenfalls aus dem Schweigen der Texte darüber den Schluss ziehen, dass die Parteien davon ausgingen, dass es sich bei der Hypothek um ein Verfallspfand handelt bzw. unterstellen, dass sie im Falle einer beabsichtigten bloßen kollateralen Sicherung des Darlehens Verabredungen hierüber in den Vertrag aufgenommen hätten.

---

3 Z. 12–14: ἐπὶ ὑποθήκηι τῆι | ὑπαρχούσηι αὐτῶι οἰκίαι καὶ αὐλῆι καὶ τοῖς συγκυροῦσι πᾶσι τοῖς | οὖσιν ἐν Ἀπιάδι τῆς Θεμίστου μερίδος.

4 P.Tebt. III.1 817,19–20; siehe auch Rupprecht 1967, 92.

5 Siehe hierzu auch Rupprecht 1997, 872.

6 P.Polit. Iud. 8,20–22; siehe aus ptolemäischer Zeit zur ἐπικαταβολή noch P.Enteux. 14,4 (Magdola, 222 v.Chr.); 15,9 (Magdola, 218 v.Chr.); P.Tebt. III.2 970,17 (Tebtynis, frühes 2. Jh. n.Chr.).

7 Siehe P.Flor. I 1,7 (Hermupolis, 103 n.Chr.); P.Bas. I 7,19–20 (Arsinoites, 117–138 n.Chr.); BGU VII 1651,4 (Philadelphia, 2. Jh. n.Chr.).

8 Mitteis 1912 I, 163.

9 Siehe auch Alonso 2008, 23 Anm. 16.

Indes bietet ein auf einem Genueser Papyrus erhaltene Darlehensvertrag vom 29. Oktober 98 n.Chr. aus Oxyrhynchos (PUG II 62) vielleicht doch einige Anhaltspunkte für die kollaterale Sicherung eines Darlehens durch ein Verkaufspfand. Dieser Text wurde anläßlich des 4. Symposions 1979 in Ägina erstmals von Mario Amelotti und Livia Migliardi-Zingale der Öffentlichkeit präsentiert.[10] Mit diesem Vertrag gibt der Freigelassene Epaphroditos dem Theon – bei dem er offensichtlich bereits mehrfach anderweitig verschuldet ist – für ein von diesem empfangenes Darlehen von 356 Drachmen mit monatlicher Zinszahlung und einer Frist von sechs Monaten, als Sicherheit – πρὸς δὲ τὴν τούτων ἀσφάλειαν ὑποτιθέναι σοί heißt es im Text – 24 Artaben „hellenisches Natron" (νίτρον ἑλληνικόν), das er selbst verwahrt, sowie „anderes Natron" im Gewicht von 4 Talenten, welches in dem Haus der Taarpaesis verwahrt wird. Der Raum, in welchem das Natron lagert, ist vom Schuldner und vom Gläubiger versiegelt worden. Bei nicht fristgerechter Rückzahlung des Darlehens hat der Gläubiger das Recht, den Raum zu öffnen, das Natron zu dem geltenden Marktpreis zu verkaufen und aus dem Erlös die Darlehenssumme zu empfangen: ἐὰν δὲ μὴ ἀποδῶ καθὰ γέγρ(απται) |[20] ἐξεῖναι σοὶ διὰ σεαυτοῦ ἀνοῖξαι τὸν οἶκον καὶ πωλεῖν | τὸ νίτρον κατὰ τὴν πολιτευομένην τούτου τιμ[ὴν καὶ] | μεταλαβ̣ε̣ῖ̣σ̣θα̣ι̣ τὸ προκείμενον κεφάλαιον.[11] Falls dabei ein λοιπόν entstehen sollte – der Erlös aus dem Verkauf des Natrons die Darlehenssumme also nicht decken sollte – wird Epaphroditos den ausstehenden Rest ohne Verzögerung, zuzüglich des Aufschlags von 50% und der Verzugszinsen bezahlen, wobei dem Gläubiger das Recht der Vollstreckung unbeschadet anderer bereits bestehender Schulden zugestanden wird.[12]

Der Text wurde in dem auf seine Vorstellung auf dem Symposion folgenden Jahr 1980 im zweiten Band der Genueser Papyri von Livia Migliardi-Zingale publiziert.[13] In seiner im darauffolgenden Jahr in der Savigny-Zeitschrift erschienenen Rezension des Bandes äußerte Hans Julius Wolff Zweifel, „ob die von den Parteien getroffene Regelung wirklich eine 'Hypothek' im technischen Sinne des in jener Zeit in Ägypten herrschenden Rechtsverhältnisses zustande bringen konnte oder auch nur sollte, d.h. die Einräumung eines dinglichen … Zugriffsrechts des Gläubigers. Ich möchte eher meinen, ihre Absicht sei in Wahrheit nicht weiter gegangen, als die Position des Gläubigers dadurch zu stärken, dass man ihm die Möglichkeit bot, sich eine Ersatzbefriedigung zu verschaffen, bevor er auf die normalen, vielleicht wegen Vermögenslosigkeit des Schuldners faktisch für ihn

---

10 Siehe Amelotti – Migliardi-Zingale 1983.

11 PUG II 62,19–22. Es folgt in Z. 22–24 eine verstümmelte Klausel über die Gefahrtragung für die Hypothek.

12 PUG II 62,24–29: τὸ |[25] λοιπὸν ἀποδώσω σοὶ χωρὶς ὑπερθέσεως ἢ εὑρησιλογ(ίας), | μεθ' ἡμιολίας σὺν τοῖς τοῦ ὑπερπεσόντος χρόνου τόκοις, | τῆς πράξεω[ς σ]οὶ οὔσης ἔκ τε ἐμοῦ καὶ τῶν ὑπαρχόντων μοι | πάντων καθάπερ ἐκ δίκης, μὴ ἐλαττουμένου ἐν τῇ πράξει | ὧν ἄλλων ὀφείλω σοὶ κ.τ.λ.

13 PUG II 62.

wertlosen Verzugsfolgen zurückgreifen musste. War das der Fall, so wirft die Tatsache, dass die anscheinend nicht ganz rechtsunkundigen Parteien [bzw. ihre Berater] vermutlich unbewusst ihr Arrangement als Bestellung einer 'Hypothek' formulierten, ein interessantes Schlaglicht auf den Stand des damaligen juristischen Denkens in der Chora, dem feinere begriffliche Unterscheidungen unzugänglich gewesen sein werden."[14] Soweit Wolff. Eine Art von „unbewusster" Bestellung einer Hypothek also, die aber keine sein soll, obwohl die Parteien dies mit πρὸς δὲ τὴν τούτων ἀσφάλειαν ὑποτιθέναι σοί[15] zum Ausdruck bringen und ihnen von Wolff doch immerhin konzediert wird „nicht ganz rechtsunkundig" zu sein. Das ist schon eine recht eigentümliche Volte, die mich nicht recht überzeugt. Ist es nicht vielmehr so, dass hier jemand, der ein Darlehen benötigt, aber womöglich über keinen Grund- und Immobilienbesitz verfügt, das Darlehen hypothekarisch eben mit dem besichert, was er besitzt, nämlich eine nicht unbeträchtliche Menge an Natron? Eine von Epaphroditos ausgebeutete Saline ist ja laut Z. 29–30 bereits als Sicherheit für ein früheres Darlehen gegeben worden. Was im Übrigen wohl impliziert, dass jener nicht ganz so vermögenslos gewesen sein kann, wie Wolff vermutet. Hierfür spricht wohl auch, dass sein Gläubiger Theon ihn offenbar nach wie vor als kreditwürdig erachtete, denn obwohl Epaphroditos bei diesem bereits mehrfach verschuldet war, gewährt Theon ihn ein weiteres Darlehen in Höhe von 356 Silberdrachmen.

Aus der Klausel, in welcher die Parteien des oben zitierten Darlehensvertrags stipulieren, dass der Erlös aus dem Verkauf des Darlehenspfandes die Darlehensschuld nicht deckt und den Schuldner zu einer Zahlung des Restes verpflichtet, ergibt sich, dass es sich um ein Verkaufspfand handelt. Darf man nun aber, im Umkehrschluß implizit davon ausgehen, dass im Falle eines erzielten Verkauferlöses, welcher die Darlehenssumme übersteigt, der Gläubiger zur Herausgabe des Mehrwerts verpflichtet war? Victor Walser hat anlässlich seiner Behandlung des delphischen Beschlusses zur Verwaltung einer Schenkung Attalos' II. aus dem Jahr 160/159 v.Chr. (Syll. II^3 672), wo zwar ebenfalls der Fall einer Restschuld nach dem Verkauf des Pfandes des Kreditnehmers geregelt ist, der Fall der Herausgabe eines etwaigen Mehrwertes an diesen jedoch nicht, im Anschluss an Leo Raape dargelegt, dass man hieraus (im Gegensatz zu anderen Gelehrten) in diesem Fall gerade kein *argumentum e silentio* für eine Erstattung des Mehrwerts ableiten kann, weil der Beschluss explizit festhält, dass die Pfänder der Polis gehören und mithin diese lediglich ihr Eigentum verkauft, weshalb konsequenterweise eine Rückerstattung des Mehrwertes an den Schuldner nicht geregelt wird.[16] Generell

---

14 Wolff 1981, 388.

15 Den von einigen Gelehrten (siehe etwa Rupprecht 1995, 427 m. Anm. 21) thematisierten Umstand, dass die Besicherung des Darlehens hier nicht mit dem Substantiv ὑποθήκη, sondern verbal mit ὑποτιθέναι zum Ausdruck gebracht wird, erachte ich als für die rechtliche Bewertung des Textes nicht relevant.

16 Siehe im Beitrag Walsers in diesem Band S. 317–318.

neigt Walser zu der Auffassung, dass im Recht der klassischen und hellenistischen Polis das Rechtsprinzip des Verfallspfandes vorrangig wirkte, dass jedoch Darlehensverträge individuell so ausgestaltet werden konnten, dass die Parteien sich auf ein Verkaufspfand einigten und beide Prinzipien daher im Laufe der Zeit nebeneinander existierten. Dabei weist Walser auf den interessanten Umstand hin, dass im Falle der Einigung auf ein Verfallspfand sich „häufiger Bestimmungen über einen allfälligen Fehlbetrag ohne zugleich Regelungen zu einem allfälligen Mehrwert finden" und sieht hierin das Ergebnis eines Verhandlungsprozesses, „in dem sich die Gläubiger häufig in einer stärkeren Position befanden als die auf Kredit angewiesenen Darlehensnehmer. Das Ergebnis war ein Darlehensvertrag, der zum Nachteil des Schuldners zwischen dem Ersatz- und dem Verkaufspfandprinzip stand und sich gegen eine eindeutige dogmatische Einordnung sträubt."[17] Demgegenüber sind nach Walser die wenigen Zeugnisse, welche nach dem Verkauf des Pfandes auch die Herausgabe eines Mehrwertes durch den Gläubiger an den Schuldner regeln eher als sehr begrenzte Ausnahmen für recht spezifische Rechtsgeschäfte anzusehen, in welchen auch der Darlehensschuldner eine – sonst ja in der Regel nicht gegebene – bessere Verhandlungsposition gegenüber dem Gläubiger hat, so etwa im Falle der aus dem Getreidefonds von Samos ausgegebenen Darlehen, die in einem um 250 v.Chr. erlassenen Gesetz geregelt werden.[18]

Folgt man dieser Auffassung Walsers, dann stünde also auch der oben behandelte Darlehensvertrag zwischen Epaphroditos und Theon mit Besicherung durch im Besitz des Epaphroditos befindliches Natron als im Falle der unterbleibenden Rückzahlung des Darlehens zu verkaufendes Pfand zwischen dem substitutiven und dem kollateralen Sicherungsprinzip im Sinne Walsers, da auch in ihm nur der Fall einer Restschuld nach dem Verkauf des Pfandes geregelt wird, nicht hingegen der eines Überschusses. Man könnte auch argumentieren, dass es sich bei diesem Vertrag insofern um einen Sonderfall gegenüber den herkömmlichen durch Immobilien besicherten Darlehen handelt, der mit diesen nicht so ohne weiteres vergleichbar ist, weil hier ein Mobilienpfand vorliegt, welches nur durch seinen Verkauf für die Deckung der Darlehensschuld verwertet werden konnte, wohingegen das Immobilienpfand (Haus- oder Landbesitz) vom Gläubiger auch anderweitig gewinnbringend genutzt werden konnte, vor allem durch Vermietung oder Verpachtung. Das als Sicherheit verpfändete Natron im Darlehensvertrag zwischen Epaphroditos und Theon wäre damit den Seedarlehen an die Seite zu stellen, weil (wie Walser zutreffend bemerkt) auch bei diesen immer schon *a priori* an den Verkauf der als Sicherheit dienenden Schiffsladung gedacht ist, da auch hier die Darlehensschuld nicht anderweitig gedeckt werden kann, weshalb in solchen Darlehen naheliegenderweise auch der Fall von etwaigen Fehlbeträgen geregelt

---

[17] Siehe im Beitrag von Walser in diesem Band S. 329.

[18] IG XII 6, 1, 172, Z. 64–68, behandelt im Beitrag von Walser in diesem Band S. 315–316.

wird.[19] Eine solche Regelung findet sich etwa in dem von Demosthenes in der Rede gegen Lakritos zitierten Vertrag über ein Seedarlehen (Dem. 35,10–13) von 3000 Drachmen, welches mit 3000 Krügen Wein im Wert von 6000 Dr. hypothekarisch besichert ist, welchen die Darlehensgeber im Falle der Nichtbezahlung der Schuld entweder selbst als Sicherheit einsetzen oder aber zum dann geltenden Preis verkaufen können. Sollte der Verkaufserlös die Darlehenssumme nicht decken, dann haben die Gläubiger das Recht, für diesen Rest gegen den Schuldner zu vollstrecken.[20] Walser weist darauf hin, dass auch in diesem Darlehen nur der Fall eines etwaigen Fehlbetrags (ἔλλειπον) geregelt ist, nicht hingegen der eines eventuellen Mehrertrags, der an den Schuldner herauszugeben wäre.[21] Das ist zweifellos der Fall, jedoch geht die Mehrheit der Gelehrten (und mit ihnen auch Stephan Schuster in seiner ausführlichen Monographie über die bei Demosthenes überlieferten Seedarlehen) davon aus, dass sich dies im Falle der Seedarlehen (zumindest zur Zeit der griechischen Redner) von selbst versteht, denn „es wäre zumindest merkwürdig (wenn nicht sogar ein Verstoß gegen das auch im griechischen Seehandel bedeutsame Prinzip von Treu und Glauben), wenn der Schuldner einerseits für den Mindererlös haften würde, andererseits aber keinen Anspruch auf die Herausgabe des beim Verkauf des Pfandes erzielten Überschusses hätte."[22] Im Falle der in der Rede gegen Lakritos erwähnten συγγραφή über ein Seedarlehen spricht hierfür insbesondere auch der dort genannte Wert des Pfandes von 6000 Drachmen, also des Doppelten der Darlehenssumme, die sich auf lediglich 3000 Drachmen (zzgl. Zinsen) beläuft. Schuster ist deshalb darin zuzustimmen, dass „die zusätzliche Sicherheit i.H. v. 3000 Drachmen lediglich dazu [diente], den Darlehensgebern auch bei einem massiven Preisverfall Sicherheiten in ausreichender Höhe zu gewährleisten"[23] und dass ansonsten der Mehrwert nach dem Verkauf des Pfandes dem Darlehensnehmer zu erstatten war. Ich neige daher auch im Falle des Darlehensvertrags zwischen Epaphroditos und Theon zu der Annahme, dass die Vereinbarung über die Haftung des Epaphroditos für eine etwaige nach dem Verkauf des verpfändeten Natrons verbleibende Restschuld, impliziert, dass der Gläubiger Theon auch einen eventuell verbleibenden Mehrwert an Epaphroditos zu erstatten hatte. Es wird im Übrigen weiter unten auch noch zu zeigen sein, daß die Frage eines Übergewinns nach dem Verkauf der Pfandsache durchaus auch explizit geregelt werden konnte.

[19] Siehe im Beitrag von Walser in diesem Band S. 319–320.

[20] Dem. 35,12: ἐὰν δὲ μὴ ἀποδῶσιν ἐν τῷ συγκειμένῳ χρόνῳ, τὰ ὑποκείμενα τοῖς δανείσασιν ἐξέστω ὑποθεῖναι καὶ ἀποδόσθαι τῆς ὑπαρχούσης τιμῆς· καὶ ἐὰν τι ἐλλείπῃ τοῦ ἀργυρίου, ὃ δεῖ γενέσθαι τοῖς δανείσασι κατὰ τὴν συγγραφὴν, παρὰ Ἀρτέμωνος καὶ Ἀπολλοδώρου ἔστω ἡ πρᾶξις τοῖς δανείσασι καὶ ἐκ τῶν τούτων ἁπάντων.

[21] Siehe im Beitrag von Walser in diesem Band S. 320 mit Anm. 48.

[22] Schuster 2005, 116.

[23] Schuster 2005, 116; siehe auch *ibid.* 96–98.

Zunächst möchte ich aber noch kurz auf zwei weitere ägyptische Darlehensverträge zu sprechen kommen, in denen auch im Falle eines herkömmlichen – im Sinne Walsers also durch verpfändete Immobilien besicherten – Darlehens eine kollaterale Sicherung durch die Hypothek vereinbart wird.

Der erste Text ist ein vielleicht in Alexandria abgeschlossener Darlehensvertrag zwischen zwei römischen Soldaten vom 14. September 143 n.Chr. (BGU III 741).[24] L. Valerius Ammonianos gewährt dem Q. Gellius Valens ein Darlehen in Höhe von 800 Drachmen, welches durch diverse Grundstücke Ackerlandes im Besitz des Schuldners hypothekarisch besichert wird. Für den Fall, dass Gellius Valens das Darlehen nicht fristgerecht zurückzahlt, ist Valerius Ammonianos berechtigt, die Hypothek zu realisieren, „im Hinblick darauf, was diese (*sc.* zur Deckung der Darlehensschuld) trägt“; zur Deckung einer etwaigen nach dem Verkauf verbleibenden Restschuld steht dem Gläubiger das Recht der Vollstreckung gegen das sonstige Vermögen des Schuldners zu.[25] Wie im Falle des oben behandelten Darlehensvertrags zwischen Epaphroditos und Theon wird also auch hier nur der Fall eines Mindererträgs aus dem Verkauf des Pfandes ausdrücklich geregelt, nicht hingegen der der Herausgabe eines etwaigen Übergewinns aus dem Verkauferlös an den Schuldner und man könnte allenfalls vermuten, daß eine solche Regelung deshalb unterblieb, weil sie sich von selbst verstand.

Jedoch konnte ein solcher Fall offensichtlich auch ausdrücklich geregelt werden, denn ein Fragment eines Darlehensvertrags mit Hypothekenbestellung aus dem 2. Jh. n.Chr. in der Giessener Papyrussammlung (SB VI 9254)[26] lässt trotz der starken Zerstörungen des Textes erkennen, dass sich in diesem Vertrag eine Gläubigerin namens Aphrodous verpflichtet, den Mehrertrag nach dem Verkauf der Darlehenshypothek an ihren Schuldner herauszugeben: καὶ ἔστω ἡ πρᾶξις Ἀφροδοῦτι ὡς προγέγραπται, τὰ δ' ἄλλα ἐκ [τῶν ὑπε]ρ̣όχων | ἀπεδότ̣[ω. -ca.?-].[27]

---

[24] = M.Chr. 244 = FIRA III 119.

[25] BGU III 741,27–31: ἐὰν δὲ μὴ [ἀ]ποδοῖ (l. ἀποδῶ), [ἐ]ξῖναι (l. ἐξεῖναι) τῷ Λουκίῳ Οὐαλε|ρίῳ Ἀμμωνιανῷ ἐπι[τ]ελεῖν τὰ κατὰ τῆς ὑ|ποθήκης νόμιμα πρ[ὸ]ς οὗ τι ἂν βαστάζ[η̣] καὶ |[30] τοῦ ἐνλείψοντος γείνεσ[θ]αι αὐτῷ τὴν πρᾶξιν — | ἐκ τῶν ἄλλων τοῦ ὑ[πο]χρέου ὑπαρχό[ν]των κ.τ.λ., siehe hierzu auch Weiß 1909, 14–15. Dieselbe Klausel findet sich auch in dem Fragment eines Darlehensvertrags BGU VII 1651,3–5 (Philadelphia, 2. Jh. n.Chr.).

[26] P.Giss.Bibl. inv. 132 (*editio princeps*: Kalbfleisch 1953 [= SB VI 9254]).

[27] SB VI 9254,6–7. Kalbfleisch 1953 hat darauf hingewiesen, daß der *terminus technicus* τὰ ὑπέροχα (bzw. ἡ ὑπεροχή, τὸ ὑπερεχές) zur Bezeichnung des Mehrwerts der Pfandsache gegenüber der Darlehensschuld, der zuvor nur inschriftlich belegt war, hier zum ersten Mal in den Papyrusurkunden aus Ägypten bezeugt ist. Ausweislich einer Suche auf papyri.info (3.6.2023) ist seitdem nur ein einziges Zeugnis hinzugekommen, nämlich: P.Oxy. XXIV 2411,40.51 (Oxyrhynchos, ca. 173/174 n.Chr.): Petition mit inkorporierten Abschriften amtlicher Korrespondenz über die Versteigerung von Hypotheken, wo die Herausgabe des Mehrwerts (ὑπεροχή) an die Schuldner verfügt wird (siehe auch den Kommentar des Hg. zu Z. 40).

Eine ausdrückliche Bestimmung über die Erstattung eines etwaigen Mehrwertes aus dem Verkauf eines Darlehenspfandes findet sich auch im berühmten Wiener 'Muziris-Papyrus' (SB XVIII 13167)[28] über einen Darlehensvertrag zur Absicherung eines Transports von importierten Luxusgütern aus Südindien vom Roten Meer nach Alexandria aus dem 2. Jh. n.Chr., welchen Gerhard Thür vor nunmehr 36 erstmals Jahren juristisch kommentiert hat.[29] Dieses Darlehen ist durch verpfändete Waren hypothekarisch besichert, die der Gläubiger im Fall der Nichterfüllung an Dritte verkaufen oder etwa auch zum dann geltenden Tagespreis auf eigene Rechnung erwerben kann: ὠνεῖσθαι τῆς ἐπὶ \τοῦ/ | καιροῦ φανησομένης τιμῆς.[30] Ferner wird festgesetzt, daß sowohl ein beim Verkauf des Pfandes erzielter Mindererertrag als auch ein etwaiger Übergewinn auf Rechnung des Darlehensnehmers geht: τοῦ δὲ περ̣ὶ τὴ̣ν ἐνθήκην ἐνλείμματός | [τ]ε καὶ πλεονάσματος πρὸς ἐμὲ τὸν δεδανεισμένον κα̣ὶ̣ ὑποτεθει|[μένον ὄντος[31], d.h. für ein etwaiges ἔλλειμα haftet der Schuldner, ein etwaiger πλεονασμός ist ihm hingegen vom Gläubiger herauszugeben.

Als (zumindest vorläufiges) Fazit ließe sich also abschließend vielleicht festhalten, dass – ebenso wie es Walser in seinem Beitrag für das hellenistische Griechenland und Kleinasien festgestellt hat – auch für das Ägypten der Ptolemäerzeit und der römischen Kaiserzeit ein Nebeneinander von substitutivem und kollateralen Sicherungsprinzip zu beobachten ist. Hier genauso wie dort war es von den Präferenzen und insbesondere der jeweiligen Position von Schuldner und Gläubiger in ihrem jeweiligen Gegenüber bei einem spezifischen Darlehensgeschäft abhängig, welches der beiden Prinzipien bei der Pfandbestellung zur Anwendung kam.

Stephan Schuster hat zu Recht bemerkt, dass die Regelungen des 'Muziris-Papyrus' aus der Mitte des 2. Jh. n.Chr. –„von wenigen Modifikationen abgesehen

---

28 P.Vindob. G 40.882 (*editio princeps*: Harrauer – Sijpesteijn 1985 [= SB XVIII 13167]).

29 Thür 1987; auf die Frage, welcher Natur die Urkunde auf dem Rekto des Papyrus ist (auf dem Verso findet sich eine Liste der transportierten Waren mit Angabe ihres Wertes) ist, kann hier nicht näher eingegangen werden. Die Herausgeber hielten sie für den Seedarlehensvertrag für eine Reise nach Muziris in Südindien, was nicht richtig ist (siehe Thür 1987; 1988; Casson 1986). Thür 1987 (siehe auch Thür 1988) vertrat hingegen die These, dass es sich bei der Urkunde auf dem Rekto um „eine selbständige Hypothekenurkunde" zur Absicherung des Geschäftes handelt (zustimmend Schuster 2005, 119 u. 173), wofür es indes keine Parallele gibt und woran mittlerweile begründete Zweifel geäußert wurden, siehe bereits Casson 1990, 203 und dann vor allem Morelli 2011, 199–206, der präzise herausarbeitet, dass dieser Vertrag lediglich die Absicherung des Warentransportes per Karawane über Land vom Roten Meer nach Alexandria betrifft, und nicht die vorhergehende Reise vom Roten Meer nach Muziris und zurück. Diese war Gegenstand eines früheren Vertrags, auf dessen Typus in den Z. 12–13 mit der Wendung κατὰ Μουζεῖριν τοῦ δανείου συγγραφαί Bezug genommen wird. Der Auffassung Morellis schließe ich mich an. Für weitere Literatur zu diesem vieldiskutierten Text siehe unter trismegistos.org, Trismegistos-Nr. 2766.

30 SB XVIII 13167 Rekto Z. 23.

31 SB XVIII 13167 Rekto Z. 25–27 (zur Lesung siehe auch Morelli 2011, 200 Anm. 3).

– aus der Zeit des Demosthenes stammen [könnten]. Diese Kontinuität über einen Zeitraum von fünf Jahrhunderten ist – gerade vor dem Hintergrund der zahlreichen historischen Umwälzungen, die der hellenistische Rechtsraum in diesem Zeitraum erlebte – bemerkenswert.“[32]

Diesen Worten, die man wohl auch als ein Plädoyer für die – ebenfalls von Victor Walser in seinem Beitrag vertretene – Einheit des griechischen Rechts im Sinne geteilter rechtlicher Grundvorstellungen verstehen darf, hat der Autor des vorliegenden Beitrags nichts hinzuzufügen.

thomas.kruse@oeaw.ac.at

LITERATUR

Alonso 2008 = J.L. Alonso, The Alfa and Omega of *Hypallagma*, JJP 38, 2008, 19–51.

Amelotti – Migliardi Zingale 1983 = M. Amelotti – L. Migliardi-Zingale, Un mutuo ipotecario di diritto ellenistico in un papiro di età Traianea, in: P. Dimakis (Hg.), Symposion 1979. Vorträge zur griechischen und hellenistischen Rechtsgeschichte (Ägina, 3.–7. September 1979) (Akten der Gesellschaft für griechische und hellenistische Rechtsgeschichte, Band 4), Köln – Wien 1983, 75–81.

Casson 1986 = L. Casson, P.Vindob. G 40822 and the Shipping of Goods from India, BASP 23, 1986, 73–79.

Casson 1990 = L. Casson, New Light on Maritime Loans: P.Vindob. G 40822, ZPE 84, 1990, 195–206.

Harrauer – Sijpesteijn 1985 = H. Harrauer – P.J. Sijpesteijn, Ein neues Dokument zu Roms Indienhandel. P.Vindob. G 40822, Anzeiger der phil.-hist. Klasse der Österreichischen Akademie der Wissenschaften 122, 1985, 124–155.

Kalbfleisch 1953 = K. Kalbfleisch, Hyperocha, APF 15, 1953, 106–107.

Mitteis 1912 I u. Mitteis 1912 II = Grundzüge und Chrestomathie der Papyruskunde von Ulrich Wilcken und Ludwig Mitteis, Zweiter Band: Juristischer Teil, Erste Hälfte: Grundzüge, Zweite Hälfte: Chrestomathie, von Ludwig Mitteis, Leipzig – Berlin 1912.

---

[32] Das hieße dann wohl auch, dass man für Regelungen über den Verkauf des Pfandes in den ägyptischen Urkunden der römischen Kaiserzeit nicht unbedingt einen Einfluss des römischen Rechts verantwortlich machen muss, wie dies gelegentlich in der älteren Forschung geschehen ist (siehe etwa die Bemerkung von Mitteis 1912 II, 276 zu dem oben besprochenen BGU III 741); dafür wirken die Urkunden (selbst wenn sie unter römischen Bürgern abgeschlossen werden) dann doch zu griechisch. Zum Verkauf des Pfandes im römischen Recht siehe etwa D. 13.7.4 (Ulp. 41 ad Sab.); zur Erstattung eines Überschusses aus dem Verkauf des Pfandes an den Schuldner bzw. zur diesbezüglichen Klage siehe D. 13.7.24.2 (Ulp. 30 ad ed.) u. die kaiserliche Konstitution C. 8.27.20 (Diokletian und Maximian, a. 294).

Morelli 2011 = F. Morelli, Dal Mar Rosso ad Alessandria. Il *verso* (ma anche il *recto*) del 'papiro di Muziris' (SB XVIII 13167), Tyche 26, 2011, 199–233.

Rupprecht 1967 = H.-A. Rupprecht, Untersuchungen zum Darlehen im Recht der graeco-aegyptischen Papyri der Ptolemäerzeit (Münchener Beiträge zur Papyrusforschung und antiken Rechtsgeschichte 51), München 1967.

Rupprecht 1995 = H.-A. Rupprecht, Die dinglichen Sicherungsrechte nach der Praxis der Papyri – Eine Übersicht über den urkundlichen Befund, in: R. Feenstra et al. (Hg.), Collatio Iuris Romani. Études dédiées à Hans Ankum à l'occasion de son 65e anniversaire, Amsterdam 1995, 425–436.

Rupprecht 1997 = H.-A. Rupprecht, Veräußerungsverbot und Gewährleistung in pfandrechtlichen Geschäften, in: B. Kramer et al. (Hg.), Akten des 21. Internationalen Papyrologenkongresses, Berlin, 13.–19.8.1995 (Archiv für Papyrusforschung, Beiheft 3) II, Stuttgart – Leipzig 1997, 870–880.

Schuster 2005 = S. Schuster, Das Seedarlehen in den Gerichtsreden des Demosthenes. Mit einem Ausblick auf die weitere historische Entwicklung des Rechtsinstitutes: dáneion nautikón, fenus nauticum und Bodmerei (Freiburger Rechtsgeschichtliche Abhandlungen, Neue Folge, Band 49), Berlin 2005.

Thür 1987 = G. Thür, Hypotheken-Urkunde eines Seedarlehens für eine Reise nach Muziris und Apographe für die Tetarte in Alexandreia (zu P.Vindob. G 40.822), Tyche 2, 1987, 229–245.

Thür 1988 = G. Thür, Zum Seedarlehen κατὰ Μουζεῖριν P.Vindob. G 40822, Tyche 3, 1988, 229–233.

Weiß 1909 = E. Weiß, Pfandrechtliche Untersuchungen I. Abteilung: Beiträge zum römischen und hellenistischen Pfandrecht enthaltend, Weimar 1909.

Wolff 1981 = H.J. Wolff, Rezension von: Livia Migliardi-Zingale, Papiri dell'Università di Genova (PUG. II) (Papyrologica Florentina a cura die Rosario Pintaudi, vol. VI), Florenz 1980, ZRG-RA 98, 1981, 386–389.

CARLOS M[A] SÁNCHEZ-MORENO ELLART (VALENCIA)

DER VERKAUF DER GERAUBTEN KALLIRHOE (CHAR. II 14 2–3): GRIECHISCHES RECHT UND RÖMISCHES RECHT IM ROMAN *CHAIREAS UND KALLIRHOE* VON CHARITON VON APHRODISIAS*

Abstract: This chapter deals with an episode from Callirhoe, the novel by Chariton of Aphrodisias (II.14 2-3) in which the protagonist, a free woman of noble birth, is sold into slavery by the pirate who has kidnapped her. This episode provides a means to study the transmission of property, especially that of slaves, and to compare the Greek system with the Roman one. The text follows the Greek system, where traditio is not given prominence and katagraphe (registration) is required and where the contract is not conceived in the same way. Nevertheless, the influence of the Greek system can be seen later in Justinian's Institutiones.

Key words: Greek law; Roman law; traditio, katagraphe, transfer of ownership

1. Einleitung

Ich habe eine Episode des Romans *Chaireas und Kallirhoe* (Τὰ περὶ Χαιρέαν καὶ Καλλιρρόην)[1] von Chariton von Aphrodisias als Thema für meinen Beitrag zu diesem Symposion gewählt, weil ich mich für literarische Quellen interessiere, Quellen, die – wie wir alle wissen – eine grundlegende Rolle für die Kenntnis des griechischen Rechts spielen, mehr noch als im römischen Recht, die aber auch gewisse Probleme

* Ich bedanke mich bei Katja Krell, Prof. Dr. Christoph Schäfer (Universität Trier) und Prof. Dr. Philipp Scheibelreiter (Universität Wien) für das Korrekturlesen des deutschen Textes. Ich möchte auch meiner Kollegin Prof. Dr. María Paz López (Universität Alicante), an deren Forschungsprojekten über den griechisch-römischen Roman ich mitarbeite, für ihre Informationen zu bestimmten Aspekten des griechischen Romans und ihre wertvollen Hinweise danken. Ich schulde Prof. Dr. Eftychia Stavrianopoulou (Universität Heidelberg) Dank für ihre Hilfe bei den Milet-Inschriften und ich möchte auch Prof. Dr. Matthias Armgardt meinen Dank dafür aussprechen, dass er mich als Gast an der Universität Hamburg aufgenommen hat, wo ich diese Arbeit vorbereiten konnte.

1 Der Originaltitel des Romans lautete ursprünglich einfach *Kallirhoe*. Zu diesem Punkt, siehe. e. g. Ruiz Montero (2006) 77. Die Grundlage für diese Behauptung sind der P. Michaelides aus dem 2. Jahrhundert n. Chr. und die letzten Worte des Romans, in denen Chariton seinen Roman als *Kallirhoe* bezeichnet. Die Nennung beider Protagonisten im Titel ist wahrscheinlich eine Folge des Einflusses anderer Romane mit solchen Titeln. So nennt das byzantinische Manuskript (13. Jahrhundert), das den Roman enthält (*Cod. Laurentinianus Conventi Soppresi* 627), beide Protagonisten im Titel. Zu diesem Thema siehe Perry (1967) 344.

für ihre Interpretation bieten. Ich möchte auf die berühmte Episode des Verkaufs von Kallirhoe als Sklavin in Milet eingehen.

Der Titel, den ich gewählt habe, könnte auch irreführend sein[2], denn eine Untersuchung der griechischen und römischen Elemente in den Verweisen auf das Recht in diesem Roman wäre eine viel umfassendere Studie, die neben Problemen wie dem Verkauf eines Sklaven auch Fragen des Ehe- und Strafrechts abdeckt. Das war unsere erste Absicht, aber als wir merkten, dass der Verkauf von Kallirhoe als Sklavin komplex genug war, um eine eigene Betrachtung zu rechtfertigen, haben wir uns darauf beschränkt. Im Rahmen des gewählten Themas werden wir uns diesbezüglich auch mit den Lösungen des römischen Rechts beschäftigen. Wir werden beispielsweise sehen können, wie die Bedeutung, die das griechische Recht der vollständigen Zahlung des Preises beimisst, die römischen Vorstellungen aus der Zeit Justinians beeinflusst. In diesem Sinne ist der Titel, den wir für unseren Vortrag gewählt hatten, immer noch gültig.

Die Studien über den griechischen Roman und das Recht haben in den letzten Jahren große Fortschritte gemacht und daher sehr nützliche Elemente für die Rekonstruktion verschiedener Institutionen aufgezeigt. Wie wir bereits an anderer Stelle dargelegt haben[3], ist die Frage nach dem Wert bestimmter Informationen, die uns literarische Quellen über juristische Institutionen bieten, aus unterschiedlichen Gründen manchmal schwer zu beantworten. Bei dieser Gelegenheit haben wir uns diesbezüglich jedoch noch nicht näher mit dieser Frage hinsichtlich des griechischen Romans befasst.

Wenn es, wie wir eben festgestellt haben, in den letzten Jahren Studien über das Recht im griechischen Roman gegeben hat, so werden wir sehen, dass die *Kallirhoe* und dieses besondere Kapitel zum Sklavenkauf hier keine Ausnahme sind. Was uns jetzt interessiert, ist, dass die griechischen Romane Elemente der zeitgenössischen Realität, nämlich der des Römischen Reiches[4], auf viel unkonkretere Weise enthüllen als die lateinischen Romane. Dies wurde insbesondere von Fergus Millar in seinem berühmten Artikel über den Goldenen Esel festgestellt[5]. Im vorliegenden Fall ist *Kallirhoe* nicht nur ein griechischer Roman, sondern auch ein Roman, der im 5. Jahrhundert v. Chr. spielt, bei dem es jedoch eine Spannung zwischen dem Schauplatz und den zeitgenössischen Elementen zu konstatieren

2 Unsere erste Absicht war es, den Beitrag von Karabélias (1990) im *Symposion* 1988 zu bewerten, siehe dazu infra. Darin befasst er sich mit verschiedenen rechtlichen Problemen, die in diesem Roman auftauchen.

3 Sánchez-Moreno Ellart (2013) 3952–3957.

4 Bowie / Harrison (1993) 159–178.

5 Millar (1981) 63–75, bes. 63: "Rather than in Wuthering Heights, the remarkable and fantastic goings-on in Apuleius' novel take place in a solidly realistic background (...). Indeed, I am going to suggest that the realism of tone in the novel may extend beyond purely physical descriptions, to realistic images of social and economic relations, the framework of communal life in a Roman province and even, here and there, to the wider concept of what it meant to be a subject of the Roman empire".

gibt[6]. Die Wahl der historischen Epoche, während der die Handlung angesetzt ist, ist nicht zufällig und wirkt sich direkt auf unsere Arbeit aus. Wahrscheinlich wollte der Autor mit der Entscheidung für eine Zeit, in der die klassische Polis auf ihrem Höhepunkt war, seine nostalgische Grundhaltung vor dem Hintergrund der hellenistischen Welt und der römischen Eroberung zum Ausdruck bringen[7].

2. Die Perspektive des griechischen Rechts im griechischen Roman

Zunächst ist es notwendig, eine eventuell vorhandene juristische Ausbildung des Erzählers in Betracht zu ziehen, da in der Literatur vertreten wurde, dass es Chariton von Aphrodisias nicht an ihr mangelte[8]. Von seiner tatsächlichen Kenntnis der Rechtspraxis wird die Zuverlässigkeit der Nachrichten abhängen, die er uns übermittelt. Aber wir müssen uns immer vor Augen halten, dass wir von der deutlich griechischen Sichtweise des Autors auf rechtliche Probleme ausgehen. Im Fall des Sklavenverkaufs ist es von größerer Bedeutung, dass bestimmte Aspekte des griechischen Rechts das römische Recht in späterer Zeit beeinflusst haben, insbesondere das der justinianischen Kodifikationen.

Es geht nicht darum, in der Analyse des Falles nach römischen Elementen in diesem Verkauf zu suchen, sondern darum, aufzuzeigen, welche davon teilweise Einfluss auf das spätere römische Recht hatten. Zusammenfassend lässt sich sagen, dass die Existenz von Elementen des römischen Rechts in diesem Roman nicht ausgeschlossen werden kann. In der Tat wurde kürzlich für den Roman Kallirhoe nach solchen Elementen gesucht – zum Beispiel anhand von Fragen bezüglich der Ehe[9]. In der hier zu untersuchenden Episode vom Verkauf der Protagonistin als Sklavin hingegen scheinen sie nicht zu finden zu sein, außer – wie oben erwähnt – in Bezug auf ihren späteren Einfluss.

Zweitens – und das ist nicht so sekundär, wie es auf den ersten Blick scheinen könnte –, müssen wir die Rolle berücksichtigen, die diese rechtlichen Bezüge innerhalb der Handlung des Romans spielen; in dem Maße nämlich, in dem das Auftreten einer solchen Rechtsinstitution für die Handlung des Romans produktiv ist,

---

6 Perry (1967) 115; De Temmerman (2002) 161–188. Dieser Autor versucht, die verschiedenen Schichten innerhalb des Werkes zu unterscheiden.

7 Holzberg (1986) 54–56.

8 Es muss unterschieden werden zwischen dem juristischen Wissen des Autors und den wenigen Informationen, die er selbst im Rahmen des Romans über sein Leben gibt. Der Autor sagt zu Beginn des Romans (I.1), dass er selbst „Schreiber des Redners Athenagoras“ war (Ἀθηναγόρου τοῦ ῥήτορος ὑπογραφεύς), aber gerade das wurde z.B. von Rhode (1914) 523 in Frage gestellt: „Er schreibt eben einen echten, ‚historischen' Roman, dergleichen zumeist auf sehr naive Leser berechnet zu sein pflegen“. Wie wir sehen werden, bezieht sich Chariton auf Fragen, die mit dem Recht zu tun haben (z.B. I.12.1). Die Diskussion aber seiner Biografie ist, wie Rohde sagt, ein Rätsel. Zur Übersetzung des Wortes ῥήτωρ als Anwalt, vid. Zamarou (2017) 232 und zu diesem Thema im Allgemeinen, vid. Baumbach / Sanz Morales (2021) 66–68.

9 Schwartz (2016) 35–39.

wird ihre Rolle hervorgehoben, und das vielleicht zum Nachteil der Rechtswirklichkeit jener Zeit, in der dieser Roman geschrieben wurde. Diese Überlegung gilt es hinsichtlich aller Informationen, welche der Erzähler über rechtliche Institutionen gibt, stets mitzuberücksichtigen. Sein Hauptaugenmerk liegt immer auf der Erzählung selbst, und man kann davon ausgehen, dass er auch das Recht betreffende Angaben als Element der Erzähltechnik einsetzt. Und das ist, wie wir bei Gelegenheit sehen werden, im Fall des Verkaufs von Kallirhoe sehr offensichtlich, denn die rechtlichen Anforderungen spielen eine sehr wichtige Rolle im Verlauf der Handlung. Und sogar einige der ideologischen Vorurteile des griechischen Romans werden in Bezug auf diesen Verkauf deutlicher akzentuiert, zum Beispiel die Vorstellung, dass die extreme Schönheit der Protagonistin ein Zeichen für ihren Status als freie Frau ist, was ihren möglichen Verkauf als Sklavin von vornherein ausschließen würde[10].

Wie oben bereits erwähnt, wurde der Beitrag auf den wir uns maßgeblich beziehen, im Rahmen des Symposions zu Fragen der hellenistischen und griechischen Rechtsgeschichte 1988 gehalten und später in dessen Akten publiziert. Es handelt sich um einen sehr allgemeinen Beitrag von Evangelós Karabélias: „Le roman de Chariton d'Aphrodisias et le droit“. Wie der Titel zeigt, hat Karabélias nicht nur das komplexe Thema des Kaufs der Kallirhoe, sondern auch andere juristische Aspekte des Romans behandelt[11].

Der Autor stützt sich, vor allem in Bezug auf das vorliegende Thema, auf zwei grundlegende Studien von Franz Zimmermann[12], wobei sich dieser vor allem in der zweiten speziell mit unserem Thema beschäftigt. Bei Zimmermann und Karabélias findet sich die frühere Literatur, die in einigen Fällen sehr bemerkenswert ist, weil sie grundlegende Studien zum griechischen Recht enthält wie jene von Fritz Pringsheim zum Kaufrecht oder zum Prinzip des Forderungsübergangs[13]. Sowohl bei Karabélias als auch bei Zimmermann sind wir jedoch der Meinung, dass es Ungenauigkeiten gibt, die geklärt werden sollten, und das ist hier unser Ziel.

Was die Datierung dieses Romans angeht, so ist sie ein entscheidender Punkt für seine Interpretation. Obwohl keine Einigkeit darüber besteht, wann genau er geschrieben wurde, besteht doch Konsens darüber, dass dies im 1. oder 2. nachchristlichen Jahrhundert geschehen sein muss[14]. Der Handlung aber spielt, wie wir wissen,

---

[10] Redondo Moyano (2007) 691–706, bes. 693–694. *Kallirhoes* Hauptrolle hat auch mit ihrer höheren sozialen Stellung im Vergleich zu ihrem Mann zu tun, vid. Lalanne (2019) 221–251.

[11] Karabélias (1990) 369–396, bes. 382–386.

[12] Zimmermann (1936) und (1957).

[13] Pringsheim (1916) und (1950).

[14] Ein Großteil der von uns zitierten Literatur – zum Beispiel Pringsheim (1950) 240 – siedelt diesen Roman um das 2. Jahrhundert nach Christus an. Heute wird ein etwas früheres Datum, im letzten Viertel des 1. Jahrhunderts, angenommen, vid. e. g. Reardon (2021) 309–338, bes. 311–317; Ruiz Montero (2006) 77.

im 5. Jahrhundert v. Chr., da die Protagonistin die Tochter des Hermokrates von Syrakus ist, einem berühmten Feldherrn jener Zeit. Für die Lehre war es daher schon immer interessant, zu überlegen, ob der Autor in seiner Darstellung rechtlich relevanter Sachverhalte auf Beispiele aus seiner eigenen Zeit zurückgreift, die ihm aufgrund seiner Position als Sekretär eines Rechtsanwalts bekannt gewesen sein mögen.

In der Folge werden wir uns – wie angekündigt – auf eine Episode von Chariton von Aphrodisias konzentrieren, in der dies deutlich wird. Wir beziehen uns auf den Verkauf der Protagonistin, der *Kallirhoe*, als Sklavin durch den Piraten Theron an Leonas, den Verwalter von Dionysios. Die Literatur zu dieser Episode ist relativ alt und reicht mehr als dreißig Jahre zurück, abgesehen von den allgemeinen Kommentaren zu dem Roman, die in den letzten Jahren veröffentlicht wurden, nämlich von Rena Zamarou[15] und, noch jünger, im Jahr 2021, von Manuel Baumbach und Manuel Sanz Morales[16]. Weder diese Kommentare noch der weitaus ältere von Karl Plepelits[17] befassen sich eingehend mit dem eigentlichen juristischen Problem der Stelle.

Da sich der vorliegende Beitrag als ein rechtswissenschaftlicher Kommentar zu diesem Text des Chariton versteht, wollen wir uns diesem nun direkt zuwenden. Viele Elemente scheinen hier bedeutsam, angefangen von der Erzählung selbst bis hin zu der von Chariton verwendeten Terminologie. So haben zum Beispiel sowohl Pringsheim als auch Zimmermann darauf hingewiesen, dass in der Geschichte immer wieder die Heimlichkeit des Verkaufs betont wird: Er wird absichtlich im Geheimen durchgeführt[18].

3. Die Episode vom Verkauf der Kallirhoe

William M. Owens argumentiert zu Recht, dass Romanleser in dieser Zeit nicht immer mit der im Reich herrschenden Elite ident sind. Es sind Leser, die zu einer bestimmten intellektuellen Schicht gehören, gebildete Menschen, zu denen aber in vielen Fällen z.B. auch ehemalige Sklaven zu zählen sind. Dies erklärt das Interesse an dem Fall, bei dem Mitglieder der Elite (der Ehemann und die Frau der Protagonisten gehören dazu) in die Sklaverei geraten und an der Wiedererlangung ihres früheren Status. Der Roman behandelt somit ein Thema, das sowohl die herrschende Elite als auch insbesondere die hellenisierte kulturelle Oberschicht ansprach[19].

Dies steht meiner Meinung nach nicht im Widerspruch zu dem, was ich oben über die Rolle der Rhetorik bei der Verherrlichung des freien Menschen als tugendhaften und schönen Menschen gesagt habe. Tatsächlich ist sich der ehemalige

[15] Zamarou (2017) 320–321.
[16] Baumbach / Sanz Morales (2021) 134–139.
[17] Plepelits (1976) 166–169.
[18] Pringsheim (1950) 69.
[19] Owens (2019) 37–54.

Sklave seines sozialen Aufstiegs bewusst, und der freie Mensch, der kein Sklave war, freut sich über die Wiedererlangung des Status der Protagonisten[20].

In Kapitel Kall. I.14 finden wir die detaillierten Angaben zum Verkauf und Kauf von Kallirhoe:

> Θήρων δὲ τῆς δεξιᾶς λαβόμενος τοῦ Λεωνᾶ "τὰ μὲν παρ' ἐμοῦ σοι" φησὶ "πιστῶς πεπλήρωται, σὺ δὲ ἔχε μὲν ἤδη τὴν γυναῖκα (φίλος γὰρ εἶ λοιπόν), ἧκε δὲ εἰς ἄστυ καὶ λάμβανε τὰς καταγραφὰς καὶ τότε μοι τιμὴν ἣν θέλεις ἀποδώσεις." (4) ἀμείψασθαι δὲ θέλων [ὁ] Λεωνᾶς "οὐ μὲν οὖν" φησίν, "ἀλλὰ καὶ ἐγώ σοι τὸ ἀργύριον ἤδη πιστεύω πρὸ τῆς καταγραφῆς," ἅμα δὲ καὶ προκαταλαβεῖν ἤθελε, δεδιὼς μὴ ἄρα μετάθηται· πολλοὺς γὰρ <ἂν> ἐν τῇ πόλει γενέσθαι τοὺς ἐθέλοντας ὠνεῖσθαι. (5) τάλαντον οὖν ἀργυρίου προκομίσας ἠνάγκαζε λαβεῖν, ὁ δὲ Θήρων ἀκκισάμενος λαμβάνει.

Ehe wir darauf näher eingehen, ist es notwendig, die ganze Szene zu kontextualisieren. Fassen wir zunächst die vorhergehenden Ereignisse zusammen. Nach einem Treffen der Piraten, bei dem Theron durchsetzt, dass *Kallirhoe* verkauft werden soll, vermeidet Theron die Reise nach Athen, weil er glaubt, dass die sprichwörtliche Neugierde der Einwohner sein Vorhaben, eine freie Frau als Sklavin zu verkaufen, gefährden könnte (Kall. I.6). Er zieht Ionien vor, und so landen sie etwa achtzig Stadien vor Milet. Dort angekommen, geht Theron in die Stadt, aber ohne offen nach einem Käufer zu suchen, denn das könnte seine Absichten verraten (Kall. I.12). Hier entdeckt Theron, dass seine Situation komplizierter ist, als er zunächst dachte: Die Ware, die er verkaufen will, ist für sehr mächtige Leute geeignet – sie ist sogar eines Königs würdig, und an solche Leute traut er sich nicht heran. Da der Pirat sich des Risikos bewusst ist, beschließt er, *Kallirhoe* zu töten, da sie als Beweis gegen ihn verwendet werden könnte. Er hält sie für eine nutzlose und unverkäufliche Ware (Kall. I.12.4). Doch in der Nacht sieht er eine Prozession. Er erfragt die Identität eines traurig aussehenden, schwarz gekleideten Teilnehmers daran und erfährt, dass es Dionysios ist, ein sehr reicher Mann aus Milet und ein Freund des Königs von Persien, der in Trauer sei, weil er gerade Witwer geworden ist.

Diese Information erhält Theron von Leonas, dem Verwalter von Dionysos, der sich seinerseits um Dionysios' halb-verwaiste Tochter kümmert. Auch hier werden erzählerische Mittel mit rechtlichen Elementen kombiniert, um der Szene einen Impuls zu geben. Theron, so kommentiert der Erzähler, ist daran interessiert, das Gespräch mit Dionysios' Verwalter zu verlängern, weil er einen potenziellen Kunden gefunden hat. Er erzählt ihm, dass er ein Kaufmann aus Italien sei, wo er gerade eine schöne Sklavin gekauft habe, die ihr Besitzer aus Eifersucht verkauft

[20] Owens (2019) 40 erkennt, dass ".. in the explicit narrative, Callirhoe is not a 'real' slave. Not according to the law: her sale was illegal and lacked proper documentation. Not according to her nature: Callirhoe's beauty and character mark her out as noble".

hatte. Da die Sklavin gebildet ist, könnte sie Leonas bei der Erziehung von Dionysios' Tochter behilflich sein: Es wäre nämlich für ihn auf jeden Fall besser, eine schöne Sklavin zu haben, als wieder zu heiraten und seiner Tochter eine Stiefmutter zu geben. Leonas nimmt das Angebot mit Begeisterung an, und beeilt sich, Theron als Gast zu einzuladen; er selbst will den Wert der Sklavin beurteilen, welche ihm dieser anbietet.

Auch in Leonas' Haus behält Theron seine Verstellung bei und versucht, Leonas' Vertrauen zu gewinnen, indem er auf seinem Vorschlag beharrt. Er versäumt es nicht, die Qualitäten der Sklavin, die er verkaufen will, auf die raffinierteste Weise hervorzuheben: Er lobt *Kallirhoes* Ausbildung, um sie als Erzieherin von Dionysios' Tochter anzupreisen. Der Pirat, so der Autor, weiß, dass *Kallirhoes* Schönheit sofort ins Auge fällt und nicht angepriesen und beurteilt werden muss. Deshalb verweist er auf andere Eigenschaften, die nicht so offensichtlich sind.

Als Zeichen seiner Loyalität ergreift Theron Leonas' rechte Hand (τῆς δεξιᾶς λαβόμενος) und sagt zu ihm: „Meine Rolle ist nun treu erfüllt. Du bist bereits der Herr der Frau (denn außerdem bist du mein Freund). Geh zur Stadt und nimm die καταγραφή (er benutzt den Plural: λάμβανε τὰς καταγραφάς) an, und dann gibst du mir den Preis, den du möchtest (καὶ τότε μοι τιμὴν ἣν θέλεις ἀποδώσεις)."

Leonas, der sich bedanken will, antwortet: „Nein, in der Tat, aber ich gebe dir das Geld bereits vor der καταγραφή."

So – fährt nun der Erzähler fort – möchte der Verwalter von Dionysios den Verkauf sicherstellen. Vor allem aber befürchtet er auch, dass der Verkäufer es sich vielleicht anders überlegen würde, im Bewusstsein, dass es viele in der Stadt geben würde, die eine solche Sklavin kaufen wollten.

Also fordert Leonas den Theron auf, das Talent Silber anzunehmen, welches er bei sich hat, und Theron nimmt es mit gespielter Bescheidenheit an: Er hätte eigentlich gar kein besonderes Interesse daran (ἀκκισάμενος)[21].

---

[21] Zimmermann (1957) 72–81, bes. 76. In diesem Text nimmt sich Zimmermann die Zeit, Therons geschicktes Verhalten zu analysieren: „Die Suche nach dem Agoranomos in der Stadt scheint weder Gegenstand der Aufmerksamkeit des großen Herrn Theron zu sein, noch scheint sie für ihn von irgendeinem Wert zu sein. Er spielt seine Rolle weiterhin mit Bravour. Komm in die Stadt", fährt er fort, „nimm die Katagraphen in Empfang und zahle mir dann den Preis, den du willst, nach deinem Belieben". So krönt sich der Betrüger mit seiner vorgetäuschten Großzügigkeit. Über den Preis wird nicht gesprochen: Theron weiß, dass Leonas ihn mit Würde zahlen wird. Das Ergebnis kommt schnell. Theron hat Leonas' Seele berührt. Parallelität: Leonas möchte Therons Vertrauen erwidern (...). Für Leonas gilt „Loyalität für Loyalität": Da Theron ihm die Frau vor der καταγραφή gibt, gibt er ihm auch vorher das Geld. Von *Kalirrhoes* Schönheit beeindruckt, befürchtet er, dass der Verkäufer es sich wieder überlegen könnte.

4. Juristische Fragen im Zusammenhang mit dem Verkauf von *Kallirhoe*: der Kaufvertrag

Es gibt zwei wesentliche Aspekte in der Schilderung des Verkaufs von *Kallirhoe*: die Natur des Vertrags und die Rolle, welche die καταγραφαί spielt. Hinzu kommen weitere Fragen, die direkt mit den rechtlichen Aspekten der gesamten Szene zu tun haben, wie zum Beispiel, ob der Preis für den Sklaven der Gesamtpreis ist, oder, ob es sich um eine Anzahlung handelt. Mit anderen Worten: Was ist die Funktion des Silbertalents? Ist es die Zahlung des vollen Preises oder nur die Entrichtung einer Anzahlung?

Wir beginnen mit der Feststellung, dass die Natur von *Kallirhoes* Kaufvertrag als Sklavin nicht strittig zu sein scheint und Pringsheims Theorie bestätigt, die bekanntlich besagt, dass der Eigentumsübergang im griechischen und hellenistischen Recht von der vollständigen Zahlung des Preises abhängt; ohne diese verbleibt das Eigentum im Besitz des Verkäufers. Hans-Albert Rupprecht fasst zusammen: „Der griechische Vertrag im griechischen Recht kommt auf der Grundlage einer Realität zustande, die durch den Konsens der Parteien bestimmt wird“[22]. Mit anderen Worten: Der Konsens hat die Funktion, den Inhalt des Vertrags festzulegen, aber er erzeugt an sich keine vertragliche Bindung; diese wird erst durch das eigentliche Element, nämlich die Zahlung des Preises, geschaffen[23].

Es erscheint notwendig, diese Theorie zu berücksichtigen, weil sie in der griechischen Sphäre bis in die Spätzeit so entscheidend ist. So scheint sie auch in Dokumenten der späten Kaiserzeit auf wie in P.Oxy XII 1470, 12 (Oxyrhynchites, 336 n. Chr.): μεταβαλ{ε}όμεωος τὴν συμφωνη[θεῖ]σαν τιμήν, und so hatte sie auch einen Einfluss auf das römische justinianische Recht (I.2.41)[24]:

[22] Rupprecht (2017) 10.

[23] Pringsheim (1950) 191–192; 220 stellt fest, dass im attischen Recht die Übergabe nie als Voraussetzung für die Übertragung des Eigentums an einer Sache erwähnt wird. Er rekurriert dafür z.B. auf Dem. XXXII.14 und 18 *In Zenothemin* und Hyp. III.9 *contra Athenogenem*. Im ersten Fall wird das Vorhandensein der *traditio* der Sache (ein Getreideimport) nicht als Argument für den Eigentumserwerb herangezogen. Dass die Fracht in Besitz genommen worden war, geht aus §14 hervor (ἐπειδὴ τοίνουν ἀφικετο δεῦρο τὸ πλοῖον, γνόντων τῶν Κεφαλλήνων ἀντιπράττοντος τούτου, ὅθεν ἐξέπλευσε τὸ πλοῖον ἐνταυθα καὶ καταπλεῖν αὐτό, τὴν μὲν ναῦν οἱ ἐπὶ τῇ νηὶ δεδενεικότες ἐνθενδ᾽ εὐθέως εἶχον, τὸν δὲ σῖτον ὁ ἠγορακὼς εἶχεν). Im zweiten Fall wird das Fehlen der *traditio* auch nicht dazu benutzt, um zu bestreiten, dass die Eigentumsübertragung stattgefunden hat. Es ist bedeutsam, dass der Autor die Zahlung des Preises als den entscheidenden Moment bezeichnet, in dem das Eigentum an der Parfümerie (und damit die hiermit verbundenen Schulden) als übertragen angesehen werden kann: τὰς δὲ τετταράκοντα μνᾶς εγὼ καταλαβὼν τὴν ὠνὴν ἐποιησάμην. τούτου δὲ γενομένου προσήεσάν μοι. Vgl. dazu vor allem Pringsheim (1950) 191 n.6.

[24] Pringsheim (1916) 54; Biscardi (1953) 275; vgl. dazu auch PSI IV 313, 5 (Oxyrhynchites, 3.–4. Jh.n. Chr.).

Sed si quidem ex causa donationis aut dotis aut qualibet alia ex causa tradantur, sine dubio transferentur: venditae vero et traditae non aliter emptori adquiruntur, quam si is venditori pretium solverit vel alio modo ei satisfecerit, veluti expromissore aut pignore dato. quod cavetur quidem etiam lege duodecim tabularum: tamen recte dicitur et iure gentium, id est iure naturali, id effici. sed et si is qui vendidit fidem emptoris secutus fuerit, dicendum est, statim rem emptoris fieri.

Der Text ist nicht einfach zu interpretieren: Erfolgt die Übergabe einer Sache aufgrund einer Schenkung, einer Mitgift oder eines anderen gerechtfertigten Erwerbsgrundes, besteht kein Zweifel, dass das Eigentum übertragen wird. Anders liege der Fall bei der *emptio-venditio.* Nach dem hier besprochenen Text nämlich gehen die verkauften und gelieferten Dinge erst dann in das Eigentum des Käufers über, wenn er den Verkäufer bezahlt oder ihn auf andere Weise befriedigt hat, z.B. indem er ihm ein Pfand oder einen Bürgen bestellte. Probleme wie die schwer zuzuordnende Erwähnung des Rechts der XII-Tafeln, die in der umfassenden Literatur zu diesem Text diskutiert werden[25], müssen hier ebenso unberücksichtigt bleiben wie die Interpretation der Wortfolge *fidem emptoris sequi*[26].

Dass die Wirksamkeit der *traditio* in diesem Fall von der Zahlung des Preises abhängt, kommt im Text klar zum Ausdruck[27]: [s.c. *ex causa*] *venditae vero et traditae non aliter emptori adquiruntur, quam si is venditori pretium solverit vel alio modo ei satisfecerit, veluti expromissore aut pignore dato.* In jedem Fall bedarf der Ansatz Biscardis einer Klarstellung: Während im justinianischen Recht die Wirksamkeit der *traditio venditionis causa* von der vollständigen Zahlung des Preises abhängig gewesen ist, war im griechischen Recht das Erfordernis der *traditio* der Sache – anders als von Biscardi behauptet – für den Erwerb des Eigentums daran nicht vorausgesetzt[28].

---

25 Vid. z.B. Kaser (1971) 418 und n. 43.

26 Es ist bezeichnend, dass der Text der Institutionen denselben Ausdruck verwendet wie D. 18.1.19 (Pomp. 31 ad Quint. Muc.): *Quod vendidi non aliter fit accipientis, quam si aut pretium nobis solutum sit aut satis eo nomine factum vel etiam fidem habuerimus emptori sine ulla satisfactione.*

27 Feenstra (1950) 455–465.

28 Biscardi (1953) 271–284, bes. 251. Zu der Behauptung, dass die Übergabe der Sache notwendig war, um das Eigentum an ihr zu übertragen, vid. Biscardi (1982) 151: „La vendita (πρᾶσις-ὠνή) presuppone il consenso delle parti. Essa si perfeziona tuttavia con il pagamento del prezzo e la contestuale consegna della cosa". Die letztgenannte Bedingung besteht nicht, vid. Pringsheim (1950) 219: "In Greece and in Hellenistic Egypt as elsewhere it is unusual for a purchaser to pay the price unless he receives the goods. But in systems in which ownership is acquired by the payment such a practice, though commendable, has not the same importance as in systems in which ownership passes with *traditio*".

Andererseits kann nach den Quellen ausgeschlossen werden, dass die Zahlung des Preises im römischen klassischen Recht notwendig war. Auch Biscardi hat dies erkannt und sich dabei auf Autoren wie Pringsheim und Arangio-Ruiz[29] gestützt[30].

Obwohl wir dieses Thema hier nicht vertiefen können, sei gesagt, dass die Frage der Bedeutung der Kaufpreiszahlung für den Eigentumserwerb im römischen Recht immer noch umstritten ist[31]. Hier mag es genügen, zu erwähnen, dass in den uns erhaltenen vorjustinianischen Quellen kein Hinweis für das Erfordernis der Zahlung des Preises für den Eigentumsübergang zu finden ist[32]. Und auch viele Texte, die in Justinians Kompilation enthalten sind, belegen das gleiche sachenrechtliche Modell[33]. Biscardi hebt einige Texte hervor, in denen dem gutgläubigen Käufer die *actio Publiciana* gewährt wird, ohne die Zahlung des Preises zu erwähnen[34]. In diesem Zusammenhang ist es wichtig, den zweiten Text (D. 6.2.8 Gai 7 *ed. prov.*) hervorzuheben, in dem es eindeutig heißt, dass die Zahlung des Preises bei der Übertragung des Eigentums keine Rolle spielt (*de pretio vero soluto nihil exprimitur*)[35]. Der dritte Text, der von Biscardi zitiert wird, würde unserer Meinung nach eine genauere Analyse verdienen. Im vorliegenden Kontext mag es genügen, zu erwähnen, dass er verdeutlicht, dass die Zahlung des Preises für die Übertragung des Eigentums nicht erforderlich ist; dabei gibt uns der Text die Information, dass diese Lösung aus der Zeit des Marcus Antistius Labeo (gestorben um 10/11 n. Chr.) stammt. Wir werden uns mit dieser Frage später befassen, da sie uns hilft, die Unterschiede zwischen den beiden Rechtskreisen (dem griechischen und dem römischen) historisch in jene Epoche einzuordnen, in welche dieser Roman datiert werden kann.

---

29 Biscardi (1953) 273 zitiert im Wesentlichen Pringsheim (1916) 50–89, Pringsheim (1950) 79–82 und z.B. Arangio-Ruiz (1952) 341 und n. 1; später Arangio-Ruiz (1956) 276–278.

30 Biscardi (1953) 275: „La irrelevanza della *numeratio pretii* per il trasferimento della proprietà *ex causa venditionis* armonizza perfettamente con la chiara distinzione concepita e rigorosamente applicata in ogni campi della scienza giuridica romana, fra negozi obbligatorii e traslazioni, mentre sarebbe un controsenso che l'esecuzione di un obbligo derivante da un contratto già perfetto condizionasse istituzionalmente la manifestazione di volontà in cui si concreta l' atto di alienazione che ha per base la compravendita, ma che è del tutto indipendente nella sua struttura di essa“. Zu dieser Kontroverse siehe e.g. Honoré (1983) 56–57.

31 Zimmerman (1990) 272–275.

32 Vid. dazu etwa Gai. 2.19–20; *Tit. ex Corp. Ulp.* 19.7; *Paul. Sent.* 2.17.14; 2.17.15.

33 Vid. z. B. D.6.1.41.1 (Ulp. 17 *ad ed.)*; D.6.1.50 pr. Call. 2 *ed. mon.*; D.13.7.2 Pomp. 6 *ad Sab.*

34 Biscardi (1953) 275 verweist auf D.6.2.7.16 (Ulp. 16 *ad ed.*); D.6.2.8 (Gai 7 *ed. prov.*); D.19.1.50 (Lab 4 *post a Iav. epit.*). Die ersten beiden Texte wurden bereits von Pringsheim (1916) 74–75 kommentiert.

35 Pringsheim (1916) 74 sagt zu diesen beiden Texten: „Aus diesen Stellen zieht die herrschende Meinung mit Recht den Schluß, das Edikt und die Praxis habe das Erfordernis der Preiszahlung für die *Publiciana* nicht aufgestellt“.

Ein weiteres entscheidendes Argument ist, dass einige kaiserliche *rescripta* des dritten und vierten Jahrhunderts[36] zugrunde legen, dass die Übertragung des Eigentums einfach durch Kauf und *traditio* vollzogen wird[37]. Es ist bezeichnend, dass die Griechen, an die die Antwort der kaiserlichen Kanzleien jeweils gerichtet ist, von unterschiedlichen sachenrechtlichen Konzepten ausgehen: So meinen die Empfänger der *rescripta* oftmals, dass sie, weil sie den Preis nicht erhalten haben, immer noch Eigentümer der verkauften Sache sind[38]. Die Reichskanzleien aber vertreten das Modell des klassischen römischen Rechts.

Andererseits – und deshalb glauben wir, dass das Thema für einige Autoren immer noch nicht abschließend geklärt ist –, gibt es in den Digesten einige Fragmente klassischer Juristen[39], die beim Eigentumserwerb auf die Kaufpreiszahlung abstellen könnten und daher vielfach zum Ergebnis einer Interpolation erklärt werden[40]. Wir werden uns hier nicht mit diesen Texten befassen, sondern nur vermerken, dass es nicht bei allen von ihnen notwendig ist, an eine Interpolation zu denken[41], um ihre Lösung mit dem Text der justinianischen Institutionen in Einklang zu bringen. Bei einigen Texten kann man z.B. sagen, dass es sich um Ausnahmefälle handelt: So behandelt D. 49.14.5.1 (Ulp. 16 *ad ed.*) einen Fall, bei dem es um den kaiserlichen *fiscus* ging.

Es bleibt festzuhalten: Während beim Eigentumserwerb nach griechischem Recht der Fokus auf der Zahlung des Kaufpreises liegt, wird bei Justinian die Gültigkeit der *traditio* von einer solchen Zahlung abhängig gemacht. Dies ist zwar

---

36 Z.B. C.3.32.12; C.3.32.27; C.4.54.6; C.4.38.8; C.4.38.9; C.4.38.12; C.4.49.1; C.4.49.6. Honoré (1983) 58 betont, dass diese *rescripta* aus dem *Codex Gregorianus* oder dem *Codex Hermogenianus* stammen.

37 Die Theorie der Eigentumsübertragung durch Verkauf und *traditio* ist die allgemein akzeptierte, aber manchmal ist auch der Preis von Bedeutung oder, ähnlich, in gewissem Sinn wie beim ‚Subrogationprinzip', die Tatsache, von wem das Geld stammt, z.B. im Fall der Mitgift (D.23.3.54 Gai *ad ed. prov.*).

38 Pringsheim (1916) 50–53; Biscardi (1953) 275.

39 Z.B. D.7.1.12.5 (Ulp. 17 *ad Sab.*; D.7.1.25.1 (Ulp. 18 *ad Sab.*); D.14.4.5.18 (Ulp. 29 *ad ed.*); D.18.1.53 (Gai. 29 *ad ed prov.*); D.19.1.11.2 (Ulp. 32 *ad ed.*); D.40.12.38.2 (Paul. 15 *resp.*); D.49.14.5.1 (Ulp. 16 *ad ed.*).

40 Möglicherweise ergibt die Lösung, die auf der Annahme beruht, dass diese Texte interpoliert wurden, wenig Sinn – denn in diesem Fall wären die oben zitierten kaiserlichen *rescripta*, die die Irrelevanz der Zahlung des Preises belegen, nicht erhalten geblieben. Honoré (1983) 60–72 schlägt eine andere und vielleicht sinnvollere Lösung vor: die Interpolationen sind, seiner Meinung nach, immer gering und begrenzt, aber die Arbeitsmethode von Tribonianus und seiner Kommission beinhaltet die Verwendung von Texten, die zwar ihren ursprünglichen Wortlaut beibehalten, aber zu sehr unterschiedlichen Kontexten gehören. Für Honoré (1983), um seine These kurz zusammenzufassen, beziehen sich die Texte (z.B. D.18.1.19 Pomp *ad Quint. Muc.*; D.18.1.58 Gai. *ad ed. prov.*), die von der Zahlung des Preises sprechen, im ursprünglichen Kontext auf die *mancipatio*, nicht auf die *traditio*.

41 Pringsheim (1916) 54–64 und Pringsheim (1950) 190–195 ist der Ansicht, dass es sich hierbei lediglich um eine Interpolation handelt.

eine Zwischenlösung, die auf griechischen Einfluss zurückgehen könnte, die aber nicht genau dem von Pringsheim rekonstruierten System folgt. Wir wissen, dass in der Praxis das Erfordernis der vollständigen Zahlung des Preises durch eine fingierte Zahlung umgangen wurde, wobei eine weitere Vereinbarung über ein – ebenfalls fingiertes – Darlehen (zuzüglich Zinsen) dokumentiert und hinzugefügt wurde[42].

Es ist wichtig zu betonen, dass Pringsheim selbst ausschließt, dass die *traditio* (παράδοσις)[43] nach griechischem Recht eine Voraussetzung für die Übertragung von Eigentum war. Darin stimmt er mit der bisherigen Literatur überein, wie er selbst betont[44].

Der Unterschied zwischen dem römischen, konsensualen Kauf und dem griechischen, realen Kauf wurde hier etwas ausführlicher behandelt, weil es sich um ein Element handelt, das hinsichtlich der Abfassungszeit des Romans zu beurteilen ist. Und in diesem Zusammenhang ergibt die Preiszahlungspflicht Sinn. Man geht heute im Allgemeinen davon aus, dass das Entstehen des Romans, so umstritten die Datierung auch sein mag, in das späte erste oder frühe zweite Jahrhundert nach Christus fällt[45].

Aus Sicht eines juristischen Laien ist es ein weit verbreiteter Glaube, dass die Zahlung des Preises konstitutive Wirkung für den Kaufvertrag und damit auch für den Eigentumserwerb habe. Diese Vorstellung ist nicht nur typisch für das griechische Recht und andere antike Rechtskulturen wie das babylonische Recht[46], wo sie ja auch umgesetzt worden war, sondern findet sich vielleicht auch in Rom, wo die doktrinäre Entwicklung des Konsensualvertrags die breite Wahrnehmung und rechtliche Fehlbewertung der Bedeutung der Kaufpreiszahlung wohl nicht so schnell ändern konnte. Dies erklärt, warum etwa auch bei Varro[47] die Zahlung des Preises als Voraussetzung für die Eigentumsübertragung aufscheint. Das lässt uns vorsichtig sein: Vielleicht wäre ein römischer Autor ohne juristische Ausbildung auch nicht in der Lage gewesen, den bindenden Charakter bloß eines Konsensual-

---

[42] Biscardi (1982) 52.

[43] Pringsheim (1950) 220–222 stellt zu Recht fest, dass es in den Papyri keine Übergabe als Voraussetzung für die Übertragung des Eigentums gibt.

[44] Pringsheim (1950) 219, n. 4. erwähnt auch klassische Abhandlungen zum attischen Recht, z.B. Lipsius (1908) 742: „Erst mit Erlegung des Kaufpreises erfolgt der Übergang des Eigentums, ohne daß zu ihm eine förmliche Tradition erfordert wurde"; vgl. dazu auch n. 241. Pringsheim verweist auch auf Beauchet (1897) 105, welcher den Kauf jedoch als Konsensualvertrag darstellt und die Meinung vertritt, dass sich die Eigentumsübertragung aus dem Vertrag ergibt: „D' un autre côté la tradition qui joue un si grand rôle à Rome comme mode de translation de la proprieté n' a, dans le droit attique, que la valeur d'un simple fait; elle y est dépourvue de toute qualité translative et n' apparait que comme un simple moyen d' exécution des obligations, l' acquisition de la proprieté étant déjà anterieurment réalisée par l'effet de la convention".

[45] Vid. z.B. Reardon (2021) 311–317; Ruiz Montero (2006) 77.

[46] Vid. zu einem Überblick über die Literatur Scheibelreiter (2020) 47–49.

[47] Varro, *de re rust.* II.1.15; II.2.5.

vertrags zu erkennen. Und in Charitons Fall ist sein Wissen über die Rechtspraxis auf den griechischen Kontext beschränkt.

Wie wir bereits erwähnt haben, lässt die Tatsache, dass in einem der Digesten-Texte, welche der Zahlung keine konstitutive Wirkung beimessen, Labeo zentral zitiert wird, den Schluss zu, dass diese Theorie des konsensualen Kaufs zum Zeitpunkt der Abfassung des Romans bereits weit verbreitet war[48]. Mit anderen Worten: Der Kauf und Verkauf auf der Grundlage des Konsenses und die Übertragung des Eigentums unabhängig von der Zahlung des Preises sind bereits im Recht des frühen Prinzipats etabliert. Sowohl im griechischen Milieu als auch im täglichen Leben der Römer, die mit der Theorie nicht vertraut waren, wurde aber weiterhin die Zahlung des Preises als wesentlich angesehen.

Es sollte nicht unerwähnt bleiben, dass Karabélias, abgesehen von den hier behandelten Problemen, einen weiteren Aspekt in die Diskussion einführt, der unserer Meinung nach nichts Relevantes zur Interpretation des Kaufvertrags über *Kallirhoe* beiträgt, sondern das Panorama eher noch mehr verwirrt. Wir beziehen uns auf das, was er „promesse de vente“ nennt. Damit meint er das eine vorbereitende Phase für die Willensübereinstimmung über die Kaufsache und ihren Preis. Es ist bezeichnend, dass sowohl das Konzept, welches Karabélias hier behandelt, als auch der Begriff die Folge einer Analogie zum Artikel 1589 des Code Napoléon („La promesse de vente vaut vente, lorsqu'il y a consentement réciproque des deux parties sur la chose et sur le prix“) zu sein scheint. Da die Lehre vom Vorvertrag zu Recht als eine der komplexesten Materien des französischen Kaufrechts bezeichnet wird, sind wir der Meinung, dass die Verwendung dieser Kategorie zur Erklärung des Kallirhoe-Verkaufs nichts Nützliches beiträgt[49].

Gelegentlich kommt es – wie im Roman von Chariton – vor, dass der Vertrag nicht sofort endgültig geschlossen werden kann, entweder, weil dem ein aktuelles, faktisches Hindernis im Wege steht, oder, weil es einige materielle oder rechtliche Schwierigkeiten gibt, die dem bindenden Vertragsschluss abträglich sind. So besteht etwa zuweilen aus Gründen der Kosten einer Vertragserrichtung noch kein Wunsch, einen Vertrag zu schließen, weshalb eine Vereinbarung geschlossen wird, welche die Lehre als „Vorvertrag“, „Vertragsversprechen“ oder „vorbereitenden Vertrag“ bezeichnet. Diese Idee passt theoretisch ja auch auf die vorliegende Erzählung, insofern als es formale Dokumentations- und Registrierungsanforderungen gibt, die noch nicht erfüllt sind. Da diese den Verkauf auf dem Markt

---

48 Cf. D.19.1.50 (Lab 4 *post a Iav. epit.*). Obwohl dieser Text zu einer Überarbeitung von Iavolenus gehört, ist die Struktur des Textes klassisch und unterscheidet in unserem Fall die Meinung von Labeo von der des Iavolenus, vid. Schulz (1961) 257–261. Der Text stammt aus dem vierten Buch der Labeo-epitome Iavolens, und die Ausgabe, zu der die Kompilatoren Zugang hatten, unterscheidet sich deutlich von dem, was Labeo behauptete (258).

49 De Castro y Bravo (1950) 1134–1186, bes. 1135: “El tema del precontrato ha sido considerado, y no sin alguna razón, como un engendro del conceptualismo jurídico”.

voraussetzen, lässt sich dies im Haus des Leonas nicht durchführen. Daneben gibt es auch formale Anforderungen wie die καταγραφή. Dies verdeutlicht jedoch nicht die Merkmale des betrachteten Verkaufs, sondern beinhaltet eine Perspektive, die in der Mentalität des Autors nicht vorhanden zu sein scheint.

Es stimmt – und Pringsheim hat das bemerkt –, dass der Erzähler betont, dass Verkauf und Kauf im Verborgenen und nicht in der Öffentlichkeit stattfinden. Das Lexikon gibt diese Tatsache durch die Kontraposition[50] φανερῶς / κρύφα wieder. In den griechischen Quellen gibt es noch andere Möglichkeiten, diesen Gegensatz auszudrücken, aber Chariton verwendet die von uns erwähnte, um darauf hinzuweisen, dass der scheinbare Vertragsschluss es dem Theron ermöglichen wird, die Erfüllung der Verpflichtungen, die er in Bezug auf die καταγραφή übernommen hat, zu unterlassen.

Der Erzähler schildert nämlich die Absichten des Piraten (Kall. I.12.32):

> φανερῶς μὲν οὐκ ἐβούλετο ζητεῖν τὸν ὠνητὴν οὐδὲ περιβόητον τὸ πρᾶγμα ποιεῖν. κρύφα δὲ καὶ διὰ χειρὸς ἔσπευδε τὴν πρᾶσιν.

Diese Absichten bestehen darin, den Verkauf heimlich auf der Agora abzuwickeln[51]. Wie wir wissen, wird der Begriff πρᾶσις, der in den Papyri häufig vorkommt, in römischer Zeit allgemein im Sinne von Verkauf verwendet, was in hellenistischer Zeit durch den Begriff ὠνή ausgedrückt wurde[52]. In diesem Zusammenhang interpretiert Pringsheim διὰ χειρός als Verkauf „ohne Öffentlichkeit": der Verkauf von *Kallirhoe*[53] ist eine πρᾶσις διὰ χειρός. Aber wir sollten nicht vergessen, dass der Ausdruck im Text auch auf die tatsächliche Zahlung des Preises anspielt[54]. In einem anderen Kapitel (Kall. I.13.16) lautet die Kontraposition, die sich auf diesen Verkauf bezieht, οὐκ ἐν ἀγορᾷ ἀλλ' ἐν ἐρημίᾳ, d.h. ohne Zeugen und ohne die (erforderliche) Publizität[55], welche nach Ansicht des Autors eine καταγραφή implizierte.

Für Karabélias beinhalten die vorvertraglichen Formalitäten eine Verhandlung zwischen Leonas und Theron und werden mit einem Handschlag, dem Symbol der Einigung, abgeschlossen. Das ist zwar faktisch richtig, aber in einem System, in dem der Konsens ein sekundäres Element ist, weil er an sich keine Bindungswirkung entfaltet, rechtlich von geringer Bedeutung. Karabélias selbst räumt ein,

---

50 Pringsheim (1950) 68–69. Der Autor verweist zum Beispiel auf den Gegensatz zwischen φανερὰ οὐσία und ἀφανὴς οὐσία (Dem. 38,7) oder φανερὰ οὐσία und ὀφειλόμενα (And. 1. 118).

51 Karabélias (1990) 382–383,

52 Pringsheim (1950) 117; 122.

53 Pringsheim (1950) 69, n. 5.

54 In Übereinstimmung mit Zimmermann (1957) 73, der ebenfalls den Kontrast zwischen διὰ χειρός und περιβόητον hervorhebt.

55 Pringsheim (1950) 76.

dass sich aus dem Text nicht ableiten lässt, dass bereits irgendeine Art von Verpflichtung begründet wird.

Beseler befasste sich in diesem Kontext mit der Frage nach der Bedeutung des Händedrucks und kam zu dem Schluss, dass dieser eine Geste von moralischem Wert, aber irrelevant für die Sphäre des Rechts gewesen sei. Auch Beseler beruft sich in der Folge auf das Konzept des Vorvertrags – ein Konzept, das, wie wir gezeigt haben, nichts zur Erklärung dieses Problems beiträgt[56].

Abgesehen davon muss man aber jedenfalls anerkennen, dass Karabélias eine im Wesentlichen korrekte Analyse des Kaufs vornimmt: So stellt er fest, dass der Kauf nur durch die Zahlung des Preises perfektioniert wird. Wenn er der Übergabe der Sache, in diesem Fall der Sklavin, die gleiche Bedeutung beimisst, so stellt dies eine falsche Interpretation von Pringsheims Theorie dar, wie sie auch – wie bereits erwähnt – Biscardi vertreten hat. Pringsheim wiederholte ja mehrfach, dass die *traditio* für die Eigentumsübertragung im griechischen Recht keine Rolle spielt[57].

5. Anzahlung oder Vollpreis?

Wenden wir uns nun der Frage danach zu, wie das Talent Silber zu bewerten ist. Hans Julius Wolff erklärt, dass die Frage, ob es sich bei dem von Leonas gezahlten Silbertalent um eine Anzahlung oder den vollen Preis handelt, von geringer Bedeutung ist[58]. Das Einzige, was man mit Sicherheit über diesen Sklavenverkauf sagen kann, ist, dass der Käufer, Leonas, versucht, eine Verpflichtung zu schaffen, wobei er davon ausgeht, dass diese ohne Geldzahlung nicht begründet werden könnte. Dabei ist es unerheblich, ob die Zahlung auf den Preis (als Anzahlung) oder als der volle Preis geleistet wurde. Es wird deutlich, dass der Erzähler und die Figuren davon ausgehen, dass der Verkauf real und nicht konsensual konzipiert ist.

Es stellt sich dann die Frage, welchen Unterschied es für die Position des Verkäufers machen würde, wenn die Sklavin nicht geliefert würde. Möglicherweise nur, dass bei vollständiger Zahlung des Preises die Verpflichtung zur *traditio* entsteht, zumindest *inter partes*. Wir wissen, dass die Position des nicht zahlenden Verkäufers im Falle der Anzahlung nicht so eindeutig ist wie die des nicht zahlenden Käufers. Theophrastus informiert uns in dem berühmten Fragment, das uns von Stobaeus überliefert wurde (*Florilegium* 44.6), über die Bestimmungen der Stadt Thurioi, gibt uns aber keine allgemeine Antwort. In dieser Stadt musste der volle Preis gezahlt werden, und er erzählt uns, dass in anderen Städten der Betrag der *arrha* zum Gesamtpreis hinzugerechnet wurde. Das aber hilft uns nicht zu entscheiden, inwiefern Theron aus der Sicht von Leonas verpflichtet war, dem nachzukommen.

---

56 Beseler (1925) 396–455, bes. 400–401.

57 Biscardi (1953) 251.

58 Wolff (1947) 61, n. 3.

Nach Talamanca ist im griechischen Recht die Leistung eines Angeldes ein eigenständiger Vertrag, der dem Verkauf vorausgeht, während sie im römischen Recht, wo sie einen Vertragsbeweis darstellt[59], eine Ergänzung zum Vertrag ist[60]. Aus diesem Grund erklärt Gaius (Gai. 3.139), dass der römische Kauf unabhängig von der Zahlung des Preises oder der Leistung einer Anzahlung abgeschlossen wird[61].

Talamanca vertritt für das griechische Kaufrecht die Theorie von Partsch, wonach der Kaufvertrag mittels einer „condizione sospensiva negativa della penalità“ gestaltet würde, die den Vertrag über die Zahlung einer Strafsumme vorsieht. Da die Parteien – außer, wie wir nochmals unterstreichen wollen, durch die Zahlung des Preises – einander nicht verpflichtet werden können, wird auf eine bilaterale Garantie zurückgegriffen[62]. Mit anderen Worten: Das griechische Recht konzentriert sich auf die Vertragsstrafe, das römische Recht aber auf die Erfüllung des Vertrages[63].

Doch dies ist für den Kauf der *Kallirhoe* ist bisher ebenso wenig zufriedenstellend geklärt worden wie die Tatsache, dass einige Autoren hier mehrfach ihre Meinung geändert haben:

Pringsheim ist 1916 – in Übereinstimmung mit Rhode[64] – der Meinung, dass es sich um eine Anzahlung handelt[65]; 1950 jedoch ändert er seine Meinung, ohne die

---

[59] Mayer-Maly (1964) 603–604: „Die Klassiker sehen in der a. nur die Bestätigung eines schon anders, beim Kauf durch Konsens zustande gekommenen Vertragsabschlusses (D.18.1.35 pr.). War die a. Geld, wurde sie nach Übergabe der Ware auf den Kaufpreis angerechnet, war sie ein Ring, konnte man mit der *actio empti* zurückfordern. Dies setze sich jedoch im Bereich der hellenistischen Volksrechte nicht durch“. Dennoch gibt es in den römischen Texten komplexe Fälle, in denen die Anzahlung eine ähnliche Rolle spielen könnte wie im hellenistischen Recht, aber eine Untersuchung dieser Texte lässt daran zweifeln, dass dies etwas mit der griechischen Reichshälfte zu tun hat. Wie Jakab (2002) 210 argumentiert, ist eine solche traditionelle These zwar denkbar, aber nicht notwendig: „Derartige Entscheidungen beziehen sich aber ausnahmslos auf die sogenannte Ring-*arrha* (Sachhingabe) und diese kann (...) auch nur dann zurückverlangt werden, wenn das Schuldverhältnis durch Leistung des Käufers oder durch einvernehmliche Auflösung erloschen ist (D.19.1.11.6, Ulp.32 ed.; D.14.3.5.15, Ulp.28 ed.). Die Funktion der *arrha* beschränkt sich nur dann auf den Beweis des Konsenses, wenn keine weitere Nebenabreden getroffen wurden“.

[60] Talamanca (1953) 11.

[61] Gai.3.139: *Emptio et uenditio contrahitur, cum de pretio conuenerit, quamuis nondum pretium numeratum sit ac ne arra quidem data fuerit.* Vid. Kommentar in Nelson / Manthe (1999) 249–253. Dieser Jurist drückt sich in D.18.1.35 pr. (Gai. 10 ad ed. prov.) noch deutlicher au, vid. Peters (1973) 62–63.

[62] Talamanca (1953) 12 zitiert z.B. die Suda (Ἀρραβῶν ἡ ἐν ὠναῖς περὶ τοῦ ὠνουμένου δεδομένη πρώτη καταβολὴ ὑπὲρ ἀσφαλείας) oder das *Ethymologicum Magnum* 31, ähnlich formuliert.

[63] Pringsheim (1950) 334; 376 fasst den Vergleich kurz zusammen: „In Rome the agreement of the parties, in their word, suffices. In Greece legal consequences result from the payment of money of arra in the first, of the residue in the second stage“; Talamanca (1953) 73: Talamanca (1990) 583.

[64] Rhode (1914) 485.

Gründe dafür zu nennen. Freundt, der sich, wie wir sehen werden, mehr auf das formale Erfordernis der καταγραφή konzentriert, begreift die Bedeutung der Zahlung des Preises, bevor Pringsheim seine Theorie formulierte, und stellt auch die Irrelevanz der *traditio* der Sache fest. Wenn es aber um die Frage geht, ob es sich um eine vollständige oder teilweise Zahlung handelt, ist seine Darstellung widersprüchlich.

In seinem Buch von 1916 konzentrierte sich Pringsheim auf seine These vom Prinzip des Forderungsübergangs und interessierte sich daher für die Tatsache, dass der von Leonas mit Dionysios' Geld getätigte Kauf automatisch für diesen getätigt worden sei: Der Pakt zwischen den Parteien (Theron und Leonas) sieht vor, dass der Verkauf in der Stadt abgeschlossen wird. Um die Transaktion abzusichern, zahlt Leonas ein Talent an Theron. Da das Geld aus dem Vermögen des Dionysios stammt, wird dieser von nun an wie der Eigentümer der Sklavin behandelt[66].

Aber Pringsheim, der von der Hypothese ausgeht, dass es sich um eine Anzahlung handelt, schränkt ein und behauptet, dass Dionysios durch seinen Verwalter den vollen Preis bezahlt haben hätte müssen, um der Eigentümer der Sklavin zu werden. Nur auf diese Weise wäre das Prinzip der Subrogation verwirklicht, wodurch er direkt Eigentum an dem mit seinem Geld bezahlten Kaufsachen erwerben würde. In diesem Sinne würde sich Pringsheims These bestätigen, wonach derjenige, der mit dem Geld anderer Leute kauft, im Namen desjenigen kauft, der das Geld zur Verfügung gestellt hat. Pringsheim vermutet jedoch, dass es sich bei der Zahlung des Leonas um ein Angeld (*arrha*) handelt, so dass der Abschluss des Barkaufs zwar unmittelbar bevorstand, aber, da der Preis noch nicht vollständig bezahlt worden war, noch nicht vollzogen worden ist. Pringsheim fährt ausführlich fort, dass wir in Kall. II.1.3 sehen können, dass ein Unterschied zwischen einem de-facto-Verkauf und einem Verkauf besteht, bei dem auch die καταγραφή bereits stattgefunden hat[67].

Leonas erklärt ja auch dem Dionysios, dass er einen Kaufmann getroffen hat, der auf der Flucht vor den Steuereintreibern (διὰ δὲ τοὺς τελῶνας) weit vor der Stadt gelandet war und er von diesem eine schöne Sklavin gekauft habe[68]. Er berichtet, dass der Verkauf in der Tat (ἔργῳ) in seinem Haus stattgefunden habe. Leonas teilt ihm mit, dass er für sie ein Talent bezahlt hat, dass aber aus rechtlicher Sicht (νομίμως) die καταγραφή fehlt. Wir wollen noch einmal zum Text zurückkehren (Kall. II.1.4):

---

65 Pringsheim (1916) 39.

66 Pringsheim (1916) 39: „Trotzdem scheint der Herr im weiteren Verlaufe sich als Eigentümer der *Kallirhoe* zu betrachten. Es könnte scheinen, als ob nach dem Satze von der Surrogation der Verwalter hier Eigentum erwerben musste. "

67 Pringsheim, (1916) 39, n. 3.

68 Wie Plepelits (1976) 16 feststellt, waren die Zölle in den griechischen Städten in hellenistischer und römischer Zeit sehr wichtige Finanzierungsquellen, da die Bürger keine direkten Steuern zahlten. Sie lagen bei 2% des Warenwerts.

καγὼ συνταξάμενος ἀπῆλθον εἰς ταγόν. ἐκεῖ δὲ συμβαλόντες ἀλλήλοις ἔργῳ μὲν τὴν πρᾶσιν ἀπηρτίκαμεν ἐγώ τε γὰρ ἐκείνῳ τάλαντον δέδωκα δεῖ δὲ ἐνταῦθα γενέσθαι νομίμως τὴν καταγραφήν.

Diese Passage lässt sich als die Sicht eines Griechen auf den Verkauf bewerten, der die Rechtswirkungen des Verkaufs von der vollständigen Zahlung des Preises abhängig macht[69]. Pringsheim, der sich auf diesen Text stützt, um seine Theorie zu belegen, interpretiert im Jahre 1916 das Talent nur als Anzahlung. Vielleicht stützt er sich dabei auf Rhode, die zu Pringsheims Zeit führende Autorität für den griechischen Roman. Rhode schrieb den Roman noch einer viel späteren Zeit zu, und vielleicht hielt er angesichts der Inflation ein Talent Silber für einen Sklaven, dessen Tugenden so hoch geschätzt wurden, für einen sehr niedrigen Preis. Das ließ Pringsheim zunächst zweifeln und er interpretierte die Zahlung aufgrund der Höhe der Summe bloß als Angeld[70].

Pringsheim aber führt dies auf die Tatsache zurück, dass der Preis noch nicht vollständig gezahlt worden ist und dass das Talent ohnehin nur den bisher gezahlten Anteil des Kaufpreises darstellt. Deshalb sagt er, dass es sich noch um eine Anzahlung handeln könnte[71]. Der Rest der Fakten – so betont er – lege nahe, dass das Talent bezahlt wird und das Mädchen im Voraus erhalten wird, nur um zu verhindern, dass der Verkäufer die Sklavin an jemand anderen verkauft. Dieser Umstand wird zwar vom Erzähler auch ausgeführt, indem er darauf hinweist, dass Leonas an die Möglichkeit denkt, dass es noch mehr Käufer in der Stadt gibt und den Kauf absichern will. Doch das bedeutet nicht unbedingt, dass die Zahlung deswegen notwendiger Weise als teilweise erfolgt zu verstehen ist. Da wir uns in einer improvisierten Situation befinden, könnte man auch annehmen, dass das silberne Talent das einzige Geld ist, das der Verwalter zu diesem Zeitpunkt hatte; dagegen aber spricht wiederum, dass die gesamte Szene in Dionysios' Haus spielt.

Ein weiteres Argument, das Pringsheim anführt, um zu verteidigen, dass das silberne Talent als Anzahlung geleistet wird, ist das verwendete Vokabular. Er betrachtet die Verwendung des Verbs προκαταλαβεῖν in Kall. I.14.4 (προκαταλαβεῖν ἤθελεν) und leitet daraus ab, dass es sich um eine Vorauszahlung handelt[72], basierend auf

[69] Pringsheim (1950) 242: "The true conception of Greek sale becomes apparent in Leonas' report to his master".

[70] Auch andere Autoren haben eher an eine *arrha* als an den vollen Preis gedacht: Wieacker (1932) 93. Dagegen Partsch (1916) 1–46, bes. 15, n. 2; Felgenträger (1933) 69 und n. 20.

[71] Pringsheim (1916) 39–40 mit n. 3.

[72] Pringsheim (1916) 39 n. 3: „Aber da der ganze Kauf nicht vollzogen ist, das Talent jedenfalls den bisher gezahlten Kaufpreis darstellt, kann es doch eine Anzahlung sein. Der ganze übrige Sachverhalt läßt darauf schließen; nur um den Verkäufer vom Verkauf an einen anderen abzuhalten, wird das Talent bezahlt, und das Mädchen vorausempfangen".

der Präposition προ, die von Partsch als „voraus" interpretiert wird[73]. Das Verb mit dieser Präposition beinhaltet die Vorstellung, etwas im Voraus einzunehmen, z.B. eine Stadt im Krieg präventiv zu besetzen[74]. In einem solchen Kontext könnte man die Übergabe des silbernen Talents als Anzahlung interpretieren.

Auch dieses Argument scheint nicht ausschlaggebend zu sein, denn Chariton ist daran interessiert, zu betonen, dass sowohl die Übergabe des Sklaven als auch die Zahlung des (vollen) Preises in aller Eile erfolgen: Theron will weglaufen und Leonas will nicht, dass ihm ein anderer Käufer zuvorkommt[75]. Die Verwendung dieser Präposition lässt sich unserer Meinung nach auch so erklären: Der volle Preis wird vorweg bezahlt, um den Verkäufer zu binden. Pringsheim selbst unterstreicht diesen Gedanken, unter Anführung und Kommentierung unterschiedlicher Quellen[76] (darunter auch der vorliegenden): „Der Käufer, obwohl nicht zahlungspflichtig, ist am meisten darauf bedacht, sie anzubieten und auf diese Weise das Eigentum an den verkauften Waren zu erwerben". Tatsächlich gibt es keine „Haftung", weil wir uns in einem System befinden, in dem es, wie der Autor selbst feststellt, die Vereinbarung, die dem Barkauf vorausgeht, nicht wie ein Konsensualvertrag des römischen Rechts verstanden werden kann und daher keine Bindungswirkung entfaltet – somit wird hiermit keine Haftung, sondern lediglich eine Schuld begründet[77].

Anders als Pringsheim hatte etwa Freundt festgestellt, dass *Kallirhoe*, als sie Dionysios bittet, dieser möge sie ihrem Vater zurückgeben (Kall. II.5.11), jenem versichert, er werde den von ihm gezahlten Preis nicht verlieren, weil ihr Vater ihn zurückgeben werde, den Begriff τιμή verwendet, welcher sich durchaus auf den vollen Preis beziehen könnte[78]:

> μικρὸν ἐστί σοι πλουτοῦντι σῶμα ἕν καὶ τὴν τιμὴν οὐκ ἀπολέσεις, ἐὰν ἀποδῷς με τῷ πατρί.

---

[73] Partsch (1909) 367 und n. 1: „Es ist die Bedeutung von πρό als des zeitlichen 'voraus', wie sonst πρόδοσις oder πρόδομα".

[74] Vgl. dazu auch die Formulierung in Syll.^{3} 742, 7 (Ephesos, 85 v. Chr.).

[75] Beseler (1925) 400–401.

[76] So z.B. Plat. *leg.* 849e; Dem. 20.27 *in Leptinem*; Is. 5.4–5 *de Dicaecogenis hereditate*; P.Hal I 257–259; vgl. dazu Pringsheim (1950) 241: „Leonas entrusts the money to Theron because he does not acquire ownership as long as the *katagraphe* is missing. By this act of trust before the *katagraphe* he does not bind the vendor in any legal way. He hopes that Theron will be less likely to change his mind if he receives the price".

[77] Pringsheim (1950) 91: "Although no binding contract of sale exists some agreement must obviously precede each cash sale, especially if valuable goods have to be sold. The Greeks called it ὠνή-πρᾶσις; or simply ὠνή. But no liability (Haftung) arose; it was merely a duty (Schuld). No 'obligatio', only a 'debitum' was created. No actions were available. This agreement is only the first step, an introduction to the real, the cash sale. This agreement is only the first step, an introduction to the real, the cash sale".

[78] Kall. II. 5.7: Auch vor dem Großkönig wird dieser Begriff gebraucht, wenn er sagt, dass man den Verkauf als Heirat und den Preis als Mitgift betrachten solle (γάμον ὀνομάζε τὴν πρᾶσιν προῖκα τὴν τιμήν).

Ein Aspekt des Problems ist also die Frage, ob der Preis (ein Talent Silber) ausreichend ist für einen wertvollen Sklaven. Jüngste Forschungen lassen vermuten, dass dies der Fall ist[79], und interessanter Weise finden wir eine Parallele in einem anderen Fragment des nicht vollständig überlieferten Romans *Parthenope*. Wir beziehen uns auf den Verkauf und den Kauf des Sklaven, der in P.Oxy 435, Kol. I, ll. 4–5 erscheint[80].

1950 änderte Pringsheim seine Meinung und verstand das Talent Silber als den vollen Preis[81]. Pringsheim stützt sich dabei nun nicht mehr auf Rhode, sondern betrachtet auch den Dialog zwischen Leonas und Dionysios: Als Leonas Dionysios erklärt, dass Theron verschwunden ist, sagt er ihm, dass er ein Talent verloren habe, das ihm als seinem Herren gehörte (Kall. II.1.8): ἀπολώκεκα σου, ὦ δέσποτα, τάλαντον.

Dies allein sagt, unserer Meinung nach, noch nichts über die Natur der Zahlung aus: Es kann sich um eine Anzahlung oder den vollen Preis handeln. Der Verlust des Geldes kann darauf zurückgeführt werden, dass der Sklave, wie Dionysios zu Recht vermutet, in Wirklichkeit frei ist. Ab hier ist Pringsheims Argumentation nicht mehr ganz klar. Er geht davon aus, dass der gesamte Kauf noch nicht abgeschlossen ist: Dies trifft zu, da die καταγραφή fehlt[82].

In Hinblick auf die Natur der Anzahlung und des Kaufs und Verkaufs im griechischen Recht können wir bestätigen, dass nur die vollständige Zahlung des Preises Theron dazu verpflichtet hätte, den angeblichen Sklaven zu übergeben. Ein Autor, welcher älter ist als Pringsheim, Carl Freundt, ist sich in seinem Kommentar zu dem fraglichen Text bewusst[83], dass nur die Zahlung des Preises relevant ist und nicht die *traditio*: Durch die Zahlung des vollen Preises (Freundt hat, wie wir gesehen haben, diese Tatsache bereits erkannt) perfektioniert der Käufer den Vertragsabschluss und hindert so den Verkäufer daran, seine Meinung zu ändern, da dadurch bereits die Verpflichtungen aus dem Kaufvertrag entstehen[84]. Pringsheim be-

---

79 Ruffing / Drexhage, (2008) 321–351.

80 Zimmermann (1936) 62–63; Kussl (1991) 165–167; Stephens / Winkler (1995) 95–100; López Martínez (1998) 121–144 [133–134]; López Martínez / Ruiz Montero (2016) 479–490. Nur Stephens / Winkler (1995) bezweifeln, dass das Fragment zu dem Roman Parthenope gehört.

81 Pringsheim (1950) 240–241.

82 Pringsheim (1950) 241.

83 Freundt (1901) 44.

84 Freundt (1901) 44–45: „Aus diesen charakteristischen Äußerungen beider Parteien ergibt sich zunächst, dass die Übergabe der Kaufsache für die Perfektion des Kaufgeschäfts ein völlig indifferenter Vorgang ist, sodann dass die Zahlung des Kaufpreises vor Empfang des Kaufbriefes zwar die Folge hat, einen Rücktritt (μετατίθεσθαι) des Verkäufers auszuschließen, nicht aber dem Käufer die κτῆσις des Kaufobjektes verschafft, denn der Käufer selber bezeichnet eine solche Zahlung als ein Anvertrauen (πιστεύειν) des Kaufpreises.“

streitet jedoch diese Idee. Für ihn[85] hat die Vereinbarung nur moralischen Wert und würde Theron daher nicht binden.

6. Der Kontext der Piraterie

Bevor wir uns nun dem Problem der καταγραφή zuwenden, halten wir es für notwendig, den Verkauf als Sklavenverkauf zu behandeln, denn dieses Registrierungsverfahren als solches wurde in vielen Fällen, die wir etwas genauer kennen, wie etwa im hellenistischen und römischen Ägypten, in Zusammenhang mit Sklaven- und Immobilienhandel eingeführt[86]. Aber wir werden diesen Punkt für den nächsten Abschnitt aufheben und uns darauf beschränken, den Verkauf und Kauf von Sklaven nur als Teil des historischen Kontextes zu behandeln, der sich im Roman widerspiegelt, d.h. die Anfänge des Prinzipats.

In diesem Sinne waren der Verkauf eines freien Menschen als Sklave (wie bei *Kallirhoe*) oder der Verkauf des Sklaven eines anderen (beides sind Fälle, für welche das Katagraphenverfahren als Erschwernis eingeführt worden sein könnte) wahrscheinlich häufiger, als wir vielleicht denken[87]. Obwohl der Roman im 5. Jahrhundert v. Chr. spielt, gehört er in den Kontext der frühen Kaiserzeit, und trotz der Kontrolle der Piraterie durch Pompejus' Intervention haben einige der Bedingungen, die in den Inschriften von Milet, wo *Kallirhoes* Verkauf als Sklavin spielt, offenbar werden, immer noch Bestand[88]. Obwohl Pompejus und später Augustus

---

[85] Pringsheim (1950) 41.

[86] Über den Sklavenhandel in der römischen Zeit, vid. e.g. Harris (1980) 117–140.

[87] Boswell (1988) 96–97: Die Fälle von Versklavung durch Piratenentführung erscheinen uns unplausibel, weil wir den historischen Kontext nicht berücksichtigen, trotz aller Übertreibungen der romanhaften Plots. Dieser Autor weist darauf hin, dass selbst in Romanen, in denen Piraten keine Rolle spielen, auf sie Bezug genommen wird (z.B. Longos, Daphnis und Chloe II. 32). In anderen literarischen Quellen finden sich Hinweise auf vermisste Personen und darauf, dass sich diese Personen in Sklavengefängnissen (*ergastula*) befinden könnten (z.B. Plin. *Ep.* VI.25; Suet. *Aug.* 32; *Tiber.* 8; Ap. *Bellum Civile* V. 132)., vid. Bradley (1994) 37–39. Natürlich finden wir das Problem des Abfalls in die Sklaverei und die Gerichtsverfahren zum Nachweis des freien Status (*causae liberales*) in mehreren Rechtstexten, z.B. D.40.12.3 (Ulp. 54 *ad ed.*). Der Fall der von Banditen entführten Sklavin des Cocceius Firmus ist ebenfalls dokumentiert: Ihre Besitzer konnte sie vom Sklavenmarkt zurückholen, vid. Birley (1936) 363–377.

[88] Harris (1980) 121: In den literarischen Quellen taucht die Piraterie weiterhin als Ursache für die Sklaverei auf. Ein Autor nach der Zeit des Augustus, Dio Chrysostomos (XV.25), sagt noch, dass die häufigsten Ursachen für Sklaverei Krieg und Räuberei auf See oder an Land sind. Bei mehreren späteren Autoren, vor allem im Roman (e. g. Apul. *Met.* VII.9; Philostr. V; Xen. Eph. I.13–14), ist das Thema der Seeräuber allgegenwärtig. Wie Fitzgerald (2000) 93 erklärt: „The motifs of exposure, kidnapping and abduction by pirates are among the most maligned or literary plot devices, but ancient comedy and the novel".

die Piraterie einschränkten, gab es dieses Problem im Römischen Reich in gewissem Umfang immer[89].

Wir wissen, dass Milet eines der Handelszentren des Mittelmeers und damit auch eines der Zentren des Sklavenhandels war.[90] Die als *I.Delphinion* 140 A–C identifizierten Inschriften verzeichnen Verträge mit drei Städten auf Kreta (Gortys, Knosos und Phaistos), die den Verkauf von freien Menschen als Sklaven oder den Verkauf von Sklaven anderer Leute regeln. Vielleicht ist daher auch dieser Aspekt der Geschichte vom Verkauf der *Kallirhoe* nicht so ungewöhnlich und fiktional, wie sie uns auf den ersten Blick erscheinen mag[91].

7. Die καταγραφή

Leonas würde ihm das Geld auch als Vertrauensbeweis geben, da das Eigentum erst nach Fertigstellung der καταγραφή erworben werden würde. Dies hängt – so glauben wir – von dem Wert ab, welcher der καταγραφή beigemessen wird. Pringsheim votiert nicht dafür, dass Theron, nachdem er den vollen Preis erhalten hat, verpflichtet wäre, die Sklavin auszuhändigen, da erst die καταγραφή den Abschluss des Kaufvertrags bewirke. Wenn die καταγραφή konstitutiven Wert hätte, wie Pringsheim meint, gäbe es ohne sie keine Eigentumsübertragung, aber wenn sie nur ein Erfordernis der Publizität wäre, gäbe es zumindest zwischen den Parteien eine Verpflichtung zur Übertragung der Sache. Wir sind der Meinung, dass nur das Fehlen der καταγραφή den Verkauf unvollständig macht, aber nur unter dem Gesichtspunkt der Publizität, nicht in Bezug auf die bereits erfolgte Zahlung des Preises. Es stimmt, dass Theron die angebliche Sklavin mittels der καταγραφή an einen Dritten übereignen könnte, aber das würde wahrscheinlich einen größeren wirtschaftlichen Schaden nach sich ziehen als der Verlust des an ihn gezahlten Silbertalents. Mit anderen Worten: Das Eigentum wäre bereits übertragen worden, wenn nicht die Erfordernisse der Öffentlichkeit und der Archivierung – auf beides weist der Begriff καταγραφή hin – gegeben wären; natürlich immer aus der Sicht desjenigen, der nicht weiß, dass das Mädchen frei und keine Sklavin ist.

Pringsheim erörtert auch das Wesen der καταγραφή auf Grundlage der Deutung von Freundt, einem der Vertreter für die Theorie der dispositiven Urkunde[92]. Wir versuchen die Bedeutung von καταγραφή in diesem Zusammenhang zu erklären. Die Sätze ἧκε δὲ εἰς ἄστυ καὶ λάμβανε τὰς καταγραφάς[93] und ἐγώ σοι τὸ ἀργύριον

89 Bradley (1994) 39: Cic. *pro Flacco* 29–37; Cass. Dio XXXVI 20.1.

90 Harris (1980) 124: In der Nähe von Milet gibt es Hinweise auf die Existenz eines Sklavenhändlers, Aeschines Flavius (*FIRA* III 134= *CPL* 193= *SB* III 6304), obwohl nicht bewiesen ist, dass er in der Stadt Milet selbst tätig war.

91 Kawerau / Rehm (1914) 307–312; Felgenträger (1933) 63–65; Brulé (1978) 612; Bielman (1994) 311–313.

92 Freundt (1901) 44; zur Theorie vgl. Wolff (1978) 141–153.

93 Char. Kall. I.13.3.

ἤδη πιστεύω πρὸ τῆς καταγραφῆς[94] sind nicht einfach zu interpretieren. Wenn wir keine genaue Datierung des Romans haben, so ist es aus den Untersuchungen zur καταγραφή offensichtlich, dass es schwierig ist, zu verstehen, was der Erzähler meint. Aber vielleicht können wir durch die Auswertung der Quellen genauer bestimmen, was mit dem Begriff καταγραφή in diesem speziellen Kontext gemeint ist.

Seit Wolffs berühmtem Artikel über die Registrierung von Übertragungen von Immobilien[95] und Sklaven sind uns Funktion und Wesen der καταγραφή in hellenistischer Zeit und ihre Denaturalisierung in römischer Zeit klarer geworden. In diesem Artikel geht Wolff auch kurz auf Chariton ein. Wolff selbst kommt auch in seinem einflussreichen Band von 1978 auf die καταγραφή zurück, kommentiert Charitons Text[96] dort aber nicht weiter. Unabhängig davon, ob man annimmt, dass Chariton seinen Roman am Ende des ersten oder in der ersten Hälfte des zweiten Jahrhunderts geschrieben hat, ist es offensichtlich, dass die καταγραφαί nicht dieselben Funktionen wie in der hellenistischen Welt gehabt haben konnten, sodass die Bedeutung, welche die Figuren diesem Begriff geben, eine kurze Untersuchung verdient.

Die καταγραφή bedeutet im Allgemeinen „das Eintragen in Listen“. Bereits 1934 befasste sich Rabel mit der καταγραφή in nicht-ägyptischen Zusammenhängen[97]. Eine der Quellen, die Rabel diskutiert, ist aber auch der Roman des Chariton. In den literarischen Quellen taucht der Begriff καταγραφή im Sinne einer Liste auf, die von der Staats wegen erstellt werden, etwa in Zusammenhang mit der Rekrutierung von Soldaten[98] oder in Zusammenhang mit gesellschaftlicher oder politischer Ächtung[99]. Auch in den Inschriften haben wir einen Beleg dafür[100] .

Es gibt Fälle, die der καταγραφή als Vertragsregister näherstehen, wie bei den Erbpachtverträgen von Mylasa (*Rec. Inscr. Iur.* I 246,5; 244,12). In der griechischen Welt gibt es eine Tradition der Aufzeichnung von Verträgen, für die wir in den uns bekannten Quellen Belege finden, wie die bereits erwähnte Inschrift von Tenos (*IG* XII.5.872)[101]. In diesem Register der Immobilienkäufe und -verkäufe wird der Begriff ἀναγραφή verwendet, aber Rabel selbst weist darauf hin, dass seine Verwendung auf lokale Besonderheiten der Sprache zurückzuführen sein könnte. Anders als etwa noch wie Ludwig Mitteis differenziert Rabel nicht zwischen den Begriffen ἀναγραφή und καταγραφή, da beide den Eintrag in eine Liste bedeuten würden[102].

---

[94] Char. Kall. I.13.4.

[95] Wolff (1947) 17–96, esp. 89–96.

[96] Wolff (1978) 184–221, bes. 197–221. Wolff (1998) 110 spricht das Thema, aber noch prägnanter an.

[97] Rabel (1934) 189–232, bes. 205–209.

[98] Pol 6.19.5.

[99] Plut. *Cic*. 46.2.

[100] z.B. Syll.[3] 731und 1157

[101] Faraguna (2000) bes. 88–92.

[102] Mitteis (1912) 177. Die Dokumente über die Registrierung von Sklaven aus der frühen Kaiserzeit vermitteln ein sehr kompliziertes Verfahren (Straus 1981 753–754), und wir müssen bedenken, dass der Kauf und Verkauf in Charitons Roman nicht in Ägypten statt-

Wir haben festgestellt, dass Pringsheims Erklärung auf einer Interpretation der καταγραφή als konstitutives Erfordernis des Verkaufs zu beruhen scheint, wie sie auch Schönbauer vertreten hat[103]. Aus diesem Grund hielt er die durch die Zahlung des Preises entstandene vertragliche Bindung nicht für ausreichend, um die Parteien zu binden. Doch hier ist nicht der Ort, um sich umfassend mit der komplizierten Frage zu beschäftigen, welche Bedeutung der καταγραφή insgesamt zugeschrieben wurde, sondern vielmehr um konkret darüber nachzudenken, was die im Roman handelnden Figuren – Leonas und Theron – meinen, wenn sie sich darauf beziehen.

Ich glaube, dass die oben genannten Studien von Wolff weiterhin die maßgebliche Interpretation bieten, vor allem, wenn die Ergebnisse dieser Studien in dem betreffenden Fall mit der inneren Logik jener Szene übereinstimmen, die wir gerade besprechen. In Wirklichkeit läuft das ganze Problem darauf hinaus, zu entscheiden, welche Bedeutung wir dem Verhalten von Theron und Leonas beimessen sollen. Was genau ist der Zweck ihrer Vorgehensweise? Ist es die Schaffung eines Vertrauensverhältnisses, das keine rechtlichen Konsequenzen nach sich zog und daher auch keine einklagbare Verpflichtung? Oder richten die Figuren ihr Verhalten – insbesondere Leonas, der den Preis bezahlt – jeweils nach dem rechtlich Gebotenen aus, um auf diese Weise Verpflichtungen zwischen den Parteien zu begründen?

Die Tatsache, dass Theron sich auf die καταγραφή im Plural bezieht, kann zu dem seltsamen Effekt führen, dass jemand die Bedeutung dieser Anforderung im Vergleich zu der Treue, die er anscheinend anbietet, herunterspielt, aber es kann auch auf ein Formular oder eine Reihe von Formularen anspielen, mit denen man zum für die Eintragung zuständigen Beamten gehen würde. In jedem Fall ist es

---

findet, so dass wir die Papyri möglicherweise als ungeeigneten Vergleichswert heranziehen. Eigentlich ist es meiner Meinung nach sehr schwierig zu erraten, welche Art von Verfahren oder Dokument sich hinter dem Wort καταγραφή verbirgt, denn es gibt keine Dokumente, die der Form nach als solche bezeichnet werden, sondern nur indirekte Verweise auf dieses Substantiv oder das entsprechende Verb (Biezunska-Malowist [1974] 96 An. 49). Dies ist ein schwieriger Punkt, denn beide Verben (καταγράφειν und ἀναγράφειν) sind zweifellos miteinander verwandt und ihre Verwendung (noch mehr in einem literarischen Text) kann verzerrt sein. Es stimmt, dass in beiden Fällen die Existenz einer Liste vorausgesetzt wird, ungeachtet der Bedeutung, welche Mitteis dem Verb καταγράφειν beimisst, was eigentlich „hin oder niederschreiben" bedeutet. Mitteis ([1912] 177) schließt die Bedeutung von „registrieren" für das Verb καταγράφειν aus, da er diese Bedeutung eher für das Verb ἀναγράφειν hält, aber er erkennt an dass, „καταγράφειν heißt eigentlich ‚hin' oder ‚niederschreiben' und wird daher zunächst von der Verfassung der Urkunde selbst gebraucht". Doch der Gegensatz zum ἀναγράφειν ist nicht so eindeutig, denn Mitteis selbst warnt, dass „in diesem Sinne berührt es sich mit ἀναγράφειν, das ja auch den Beurkundungsakt selbst bedeuten kann". Tatsächlich relativiert Rabel ([1934] 205–209) den scheinbar radikalen Gegensatz von Mitteis.

103 Schönbauer (1924) 16–17, wo er feststellt, dass in ptolemäischer Zeit die καταγραφή für die Perfektionierung des Vertrags notwendig war. Ab dem 2. Jahrhundert n.Chr. erkennt dieser Autor den Einfluss des römischen Rechts und des Konsensualvertrags.

schwierig, den Inhalt der καταγραφαί in allen Teilen der griechischen Welt während des Römischen Reiches anhand der Belege aus Ägypten zu definieren, aber einige Daten sind relevant, um daraus abzuleiten, worin ihre Funktion bestanden hat. Dennoch müssen wir auch bedenken, dass der Begriff in der Kaiserzeit zunehmend in Zusammenhang mit dem Vertrag, genauer gesagt mit der Übertragung von Eigentum durch Kauf und Verkauf, verwendet wird. Vielleicht gebraucht Theron diesen Begriff daher bewusst und in einem technischen Sinn[104].

Wir wissen aus der papyrologischen Evidenz mit Sicherheit, dass die Registrierung für Grundbesitz und Sklaven notwendig gewesen ist; zur Zeit der Niederschrift des Romans aber waren die Dinge auch in Ägypten im Umbruch. Vergessen wir nicht, dass die Rolle der ptolemäischen καταγραφή durch die römische Neuorganisation der Verwaltung stark verändert worden ist, insbesondere durch die Schaffung der βιβλιοθήκη ἐγκθήσεων, welche jedoch nicht auf die καταγραφαί zurückgehen: So stellt Wolff[105] für das 1. Jahrhundert das Fortbestehen einiger Merkmale der ptolemäischen καταγραφή bei der Übertragung von Sklavenbesitz fest, allerdings in Fällen wie ἐνεχυρασία (im griechischen Recht die Vollstreckung einer Forderung nach Geld oder die Herausgabe von Waren) oder προσβολή (in Vollstreckung einer zuvor eingetragenen Belastung)[106].

Wir haben bereits darauf hingewiesen, dass die ptolemäische καταγραφή, eine bloße Aufzeichnung des Agoranomos war, welche – wie Wolff argumentiert und Rabel behauptet hatte –, keine konstitutive Wirkung zeitigte, sodass der Verkauf von *Kallirhoe* (wenn sie unfrei gewesen wäre) im Gegensatz zu dem, was Pringsheim sagt, möglicherweise durch die bloße Zahlung des Preises *inter partes* Verpflichtungen geschaffen hätte. Die Argumente sind stichhaltig: Wenn man zugeben will, dass die καταγραφή eine Voraussetzung für die Gültigkeit des Verkaufs war, versteht man die Funktion der βεβαίωσις-Klausel in den registrierten Verträgen nicht. Mit anderen Worten, wenn dieser Schutz, den die καταγραφή als konstitutives Erfordernis impliziert, für den gutgläubigen Erwerber bestünde, würden diese Klauseln nicht in die Kaufverträge aufgenommen werden müssen[107]. Diese letzten Beobachtungen legen tatsächlich nahe, dass wir es bei der καταγραφή aus dem Roman mit einer Institution zu tun haben, welche mit der ptolemäischen vergleichbar ist. Doch dies bleibt eine Vermutung: Wie wir ja bereits bemerkt haben, ist davor zu warnen, den Begriff und dessen Bedeutung in der *Kallirhoe* aus dem Verständnis der καταγραφή im ptolemäischen Ägypten zu übernehmen.

---

[104] Wolff (1947) 91–92.

[105] Wolff (1947) 62, und. n. 1.

[106] Wolff (1947) 68–69; Wolff (1978) 211–213: In Oxyrhynchus gibt es auch einige Dokumente über den Verkauf von Sklaven, die nach dem alten Formular der καταγραφή verfasst wurden (P.Oxy II 375; P.Oxy IV 809).

[107] Rabel (1934) 218; Wolff (1947) 62.

Schlussfolgerungen

Trotz der Tatsache, dass die Erzählung im 5. Jh. v. Chr. spielt, lassen sich viele Aspekte aus Charitons Zeit (1./2. Jh. n. Chr.) in dem Roman erkennen, und die Szene des Verkaufs von *Kallirhoe* als Sklavin ist keine Ausnahme.

Die im Roman geschilderten Fakten, nämlich die Entführung durch Piraten und der Verkauf von freien Menschen in die Sklaverei als Folge solcher Entführungen, sind gut dokumentiert, und speziell im Fall von Milet, dem Schauplatz der Erzählung, ist dies auch durch die oben zitierten Inschriften gut belegbar.

Obwohl, wie wir festgestellt haben, einige Autoren auf Elemente des römischen Rechts in diesem Roman hingewiesen haben, wird der Verkauf von *Kallirhoe* rein nach griechischen Parametern beschrieben. In diesem Fall ist unsere Erwähnung des römischen Rechts nur als Kontrast nützlich.

Der Roman wurde zu einer Zeit geschrieben, in der das Konzept des konsensualen Kaufvertrags und die damit einhergehende Irrelevanz der Zahlung des Preises für die Entstehung von Verpflichtungen und zur Übergabe der Ware bereits etabliert war. Dennoch folgt die Darstellung des Verkaufs von *Kallirrhoe* als Sklavin dem Konzept des griechischen Vorbilds.

Die Frage, ob es sich bei der geleisteten Zahlung um eine Anzahlung oder um den vollen Preis handelt, kann auf der Grundlage der jüngsten wirtschaftshistorischen Studien vielleicht zugunsten des vollen Preises entschieden werden. Maßgeblich ist jedoch, dass beide Möglichkeiten (Anzahlung oder vollständige Zahlung des Preises) aus Sicht des griechischen Rechts, im Gegensatz zum römischen Recht, gerechtfertigt sind, da eine Verpflichtung der Parteien nicht *consensu* begründet und einklagbar gemacht worden sein kann.

Die Anwendung der Vorvertragstheorie scheint keine weitere Erklärung für diesen Verkauf zu bieten. Diese Theorie beruht, unserer Meinung nach, auf der Rückprojektion zivilrechtlicher Kategorien in das griechische Recht, die dem des Code Napoléon entstammen und gerade dort in einem Kontext stehen, wonach – anders als beim griechischen Kaufvertrag – der Konsens der Parteien vorausgesetzt wird.

Zusätzlich ist für den Kontext des antiken Sklavenhandels mit formalen Voraussetzungen des Kaufgeschehens wie einer Registrierungs- und Dokumentationspflicht zu rechnen; aufgrund der knappen Hinweise, die der Autor des Romans vor allem durch die Erwähnung des Begriffs καταγραφή gibt, ist es freilich schwierig, den Umfang dieser Anforderungen zu bestimmen.

Die Zeit der Niederschrift des Romans fällt merkwürdigerweise mit einer Änderung der Bedeutung der καταγραφή im Recht der Papyri zusammen, was freilich nicht für den Sklavenkauf gilt. Es ist daher insgesamt schwierig zu entscheiden, ob diese Tatsache dazu verwendet werden kann, den Verkauf eines Sklaven in einem anderen Kontext zu interpretieren. Was die Romanfiguren über die καταγραφή sagen wollten, scheint auch nicht die Theorie zu rechtfertigen, wonach der Errichtung der Urkunde eine konstitutive Wirkung zuerkannt werden soll, denn allem Anschein nach sind die Verpflichtungen bereits ab jenem Zeitpunkt vollstreckbar geworden, zu dem die Zahlung des Preises stattgefunden hat.

carlos.sanchez-moreno@uv.es

BIBLIOGRAPHIE

Arangio-Ruiz (1952): V. Arangio-Ruiz *Istituzioni di Diritto romano*[11], Napoli 1952.

Arangio-Ruiz (1956): V. Arangio-Ruiz, *La compravendita in Diritto romano*[2], Napoli 1956.

Baumbach / Sanz Morales (2021): M. Baumbach / M. Sanz Morales, *Chariton von Aphrodisias Kallirhoe. Kommentar zu den Büchern 1–4*, Heidelberg 2021.

Beauchet (1897): L. Beauchet, *Histoire du droit privé de la république athénienne* III, Paris 1897.

Beseler (1925): G. Beseler, „Bildung und Lösung", *Zeitschrift der Savigny-Stiftung* (Rom. Abt.) 45 (1925) 396–455.

Bielman (1994): A. Bielman, *Retour à la liberté. Libération et sauvetage des prisionniers en Grèce ancienne*, Paris 1994.

Biezunska-Malowist (1974): I. Biezunska-Malowist, *L'esclavage dans l'Égypte gréco-romaine*, Warsaw 1974.

Birley (1936): E. Birley, "Marcus Cocceius Firmus: An Epigraphic Study", *Proceedings of the Society of Antiquaries of Scotland* 70 (1936) 363–377.

Biscardi (1953): A. Biscardi, "Sulla genesi della norma giustinianea in materia di trasferimento della cosa venduta" *Revue Internationale des Droits de l'Antiquité* 2 (1953) 271–284.

Biscardi (1982): A. Biscardi, *Diritto greco antico*, Milano 1982.

Boswell (1988): J. Boswell, *The Kindness of Strangers*, Chicago 1988.

Bowie / Harrison (1993): E. L. Bowie & S. J. Harrison, "The Roman of the Novel", *Journal of Roman Studies* 83 (1993) 159–178.

Bradley (1994): K. Bradley, *Slavery and Society at Rome*, Cambridge 1994.

Brulé (1978): P. Brulé, *La piraterie cretoise héllenistique*, Paris 1978.

De Castro y Bravo (1950): F. de Castro y Bravo, "La promesa de contrato", *Anuario de Derecho Civil* 4 (1950) 1134–1186.

Faraguna (2000): M. Faraguna, "A proposito degli archivi nel mondo greco", *Chiron* 30 (2000) 65–115.

Feenstra (1950): R. Feenstra, "Inst. 2.1.41 et les origines de la revendication du vendeur non payé", *Revue d'Histoire des Droits de l'Antiquité* 4 (1950) 455–465.

Felgenträger (1933): W. Felgenträger, *Antikes Lösungsrecht*, Berlin-Leipzig 1933.

Fitzgerald (2000): *Slavery and the Roman literary imagination*, Cambridge 2000.

Freundt (1901): C. Freundt, *Wertpapiere im antiken und frühmittelartigen Rechte* I, Leipzig 1901.

Harris (1980): W. V. Harris, "Towards a Study of the Roman Slave Trade", *Memoirs of the American Academy in Rome* 36 (1980) 117–140.

Holzberg (1986): N. Holzberg, *Der antike Roman: eine Einführung*, München 1986.

Honoré (1983): T. [A. M.] Honoré, "Sale and Transfer of Ownership: The Compilers' Point of View", in P. G. Stein / A. D. E. Lewis (eds.) *Studies in Justinian Institutes in the Memory of J. A. C. Thomas*, London 1983, 56–72.

Jakab (2002). É. Jakab, „*Ein fundus cum instrumento legatus* und der verbliebene Wein: Scaevola D. 33.7.27.3 zum Kauf mit Anzahlung", *Zeitschrift der Savigny Stiftung (Rom.* Abt.) 119 (2002) 176–211.

Karabélias (1990): E. Karabélias, "Le roman de Chariton d'Aphrodisias et le droit. Renversements de situation et exploitation des ambiguïtés juridiques", in G. Nenci / G. Thür (Hg.) *Symposion 1988: Vorträge zur griechischen und hellenistischen Rechtsgeschichte*, Wien – Köln 1990, 369–396.

Kaser (1971): M. Kaser, *Das römische Privatrecht* I, München ²1971.

Kawerau / Rehm (1914): G. Kawerau / A. Rehm (Hg.) *Milet. Ergebnisse der Ausgrabungen* III.2, Berlin 1914.

Kussl (1991): R. Kussl, *Papyrusfragmente griechischer Romane*, Tübingen 1991.

Lalanne (2019): S. Lalanne, "Les femmes du roman Grecque entre réalités et répresentations", in S. Lalanne (Hg.) *Femmes grecques dans l' orient romain*, Bésançon 2019, 221–251.

Lipsius (1908): J. Lipsius, *Das attische Recht und Rechtsverfahren* II, Leipzig 1908.

López Martínez (1998): M. P. López Martínez, *Fragmentos papiráceos de novela griega*, Alicante 1998.

López Martínez / Ruiz Montero (2016): M. P. López Martínez / C. Ruiz Montero, "Parthenope's Novel: P.Oxy. 435 Revisited", *Fronteras entre el verso y la prosa*, Bari 2016, 479–490.

Mayer-Maly (1964): Th. Mayer-Maly, s. v. 'Arra', in *Der kleine Pauly* I, Stuttgart 1964, col. 603–604.

Millar (1981): F. Millar, "The World of the Golden Ass", *Journal of Roman Studies* 71 (1981) 63–75.

Mitteis (1912): L. Mitteis / U. Wilcken, *Grundzüge und Chrestomathie der Papyrusurkunde* II.1 *Juristischer Teil*, Leipzig 1912 (Nachdruck Hildesheim 1963).

Nelson / Manthe (1999): H. L. W. Nelson / U. Manthe, *Studia Gaiana VIII. Gai. Inst. III 88–181*, Berlin 1999.

Owens (2019): W. M. Owens, "Callirhoe: A Therapeutic Slave Narrative", in S. Panayotatis / M. Paschalis, *Slaves and Masters in the Ancient Novel*, Groningen 2019, 37–54.

Partsch (1909): J. Partsch. *Griechisches Bürgschaftsrecht* I, Leipzig – Berlin 1909.

Partsch (1916): J. Partsch, „Mitteilungen aus der Freiburger Papyrussammlung: Juristische Texte der römischen Zeit“, *Sitzungsberichte der Heidelberger Akademie der Wissenschaften, Philosophisch-Historische Klasse* 10 (1916) 1–46.

Perry (1967): B. E. Perry, *The Ancient Romances*, Berkeley – Los Angeles 1967.

Peters (1973): F. Peters, *Die Rücktrittsvorbehalte des römischen Rechts*, Köln 1973.

Plepetis (1976): K. Plepelits, *Chariton von Aphrodisias, Kallirhoe. Eingeleitet, übersetzt und erläutert*, Stuttgart 1976.

Pringsheim (1916): F. Pringsheim, *Der Kauf mit fremdem Geld*, Leipzig 1916 (Nachdruck New York 1979)

Pringsheim (1950): F. Pringsheim, *The Greek Law of Sale*, Weimar 1950.

Rabel (1934): E. Rabel, „*Katagraphe*“, *Zeitschrift der Savigny-Stiftung (Rom. Abt.)* 54 (1934) 189–232.

Reardon (2021): B. P. Reardon, “Chariton”, in G. L. Schmeling (Hg.) *The Novel in the Ancient World*, Leiden 2021, 309–338.

Redondo Moyano (2007): E. Redondo Moyano, “Aspecto físico y retórica en la novela griega antigua”, in F. Alonso Aldama et alii (Hg.) ΣΤΙΣ ΑΜΜΟΥΔΙΕΣ ΤΟΥ ΟΜΗΡΟΥ *Homenaje a la Profesora Olga Omatos*, Vitoria 2007, 691–706.

Rhode (1914): E. Rhode, *Der griechische Roman*, Leipzig 1914.

Ruffing / Drexhage (2008): K. Ruffing / H.-J. Drexhage, „Antike Sklavenpreise“, in P. Mauritsch et al. *Antike Lebenswelten. Konstanz-Wandel- Wirkungsmacht: Festschrift für Ingomar Weiler*, Marburg 2008, 321–351.

Ruiz Montero (2006): C. Ruiz-Montero, *La novela griega*, Madrid 2006.

Rupprecht (2017): H.-A. Rupprecht, „Zu Entwicklung, Stand und Aufgaben der juristischen Papyrologie“, in *Beiträge zur juristischen Papyrologie. Kleine Schriften*, Stuttgart 2017, 1–114.

Sánchez-Moreno Ellart (2013): C. Sánchez-Moreno Ellart, s.v. “Law: Literary Sources for (Greek and Roman)”, in R. S. Bagnall et alii, *Encyclopedia of Ancient History*, New York 2013, 3952–3957.

Scheibelreiter (2020): Ph. Scheibelreiter, *Die sachenrechtliche Konzeption des Darlehens nach römischem und griechischem Recht: Zwischen „Surrogationsprinzip“ und wirtschaftlichem Eigentum*, *Dike* 23 (2020) 43–81.

Schulz (1961): F. Schulz, *Geschichte der römischen Rechtswissenschaft*, Weimar 1961.

Schönbauer (1924): E. Schönbauer, Beiträge zur Geschichte des Liegenschaftsrechtes im Altertum, Leipzig–Graz.

Schwartz (2016): S. Schwartz, *From Bedroom to Courtroom. Law and Justice in the Greek Novel*, Groningen 2016.

Stephens / Winkler (1995): A. Stephens / J. J. Winkler, *Ancient Greek Novels: The Fragments*, Princeton 1995

Straus (1981): J. Straus, „P.Oxy. II 336 descr : enregistrement de la vente d’une esclave“. in L’Antiquité Classique 50 (1981) 753–758.

Talamanca (1953): M. Talamanca, *L' arra della compravendita in diritto greco e in diritto romano*, Milano 1953.

Talamanca (1990): M. Talamanca, *Istituzioni di diritto romano*, Roma 1990.

De Temmerman (2002): K. De Temmerman, "Institutional *Realia* in Chariton", *Humanitas* 54 (2002) 161–188.

Wieacker (1932): F. Wieacker, *Lex commissoria*, Berlin 1932.

Wolff (1947): H.-J. Wolff, "Registration of Conveyances in Ptolemaic Egypt", *Aegyptus* 27 (1947) 17–96.

Wolff (1978): H.-J. Wolff, *Das Recht der griechischen Papyri Ägyptens in der Zeit der Ptolemäer und des Prinzipats* II, München 1978.

Wolff (1998): H.-J Wolff, *Vorlesungen über juristische Papyrusurkunde* (hg. von J.G. Wolf), Berlin 1998.

Zamarou (2017): R. Zamarou, Χαριτωνος Αφροδισιεως. Τα περι Καλλιρροην ερωτικα διηγηματα, Athen 2017.

Zimmermann (1936): F. Zimmermann, *Griechische Roman-Papyri und verwandte Texte*, Heidelberg 1936.

Zimmermann (1957): F. Zimmermann, „Kallirhoes Verkauf durch Theron. Eine juristisch-philologische Betrachtung zu Chariton", *Aus der byzantinischen Arbeit der DDR* I, Berlin 1957, 72–81.

Zimmermann (1990): R. Zimmermann, *The Law of Obligations: Roman Foundations of the Civilian Tradition*, Oxford 1990.

PATRICK SÄNGER (MÜNSTER)

DAS PROBLEM DER *KATAGRAPHE* IN CHARITONS KALLIRHOE: ANTWORT AUF CARLOS SÁNCHEZ-MORENO ELLART

Dieser Beitrag setzt gleich dort an, wo Carlos Sánchez-Moreno Ellart geendet hat: bei der Auseinandersetzung mit dem Begriff *katagraphe*, dessen terminologische Interpretation erhellen mag, welchen Charakter Chariton dem geschilderten Kaufgeschäft zuschreiben möchte. Die Lösung, die im Folgenden angeboten wird, wird dabei weniger auf die rechtshistorische Ausdeutung des Kaufvorganges und dessen etwaige Bestandteile als vielmehr auf urkundentechnische Realitäten abzielen, die ein solches Geschäft bei ordentlicher Dokumentation nach sich zieht.

Bevor auf die Semantik des Begriffs *katagraphe* eingegangen wird, sollen zunächst alle Stellen, an denen von *katagraphe* bzw. *katagraphai* im Roman von Chariton die Rede ist, zusammengestellt werden. Drei der insgesamt fünf Belegstellen haben wir zuvor bereits kennengelernt. Die ersten beiden gehören in den unmittelbaren Kontext der den Kauf von Kallirhoe betreffenden Erzählung. Nachdem der Pirat Theron die vorgebliche Sklavin Kallirhoe dem Kaufinteressenten Leonas ausgehändigt hatte, sagte er (1,14,3):[1]

> τὰ μὲν παῤ ἐμοῦ σοι ... πιστῶς πεπλήρωται, σὺ δὲ ἔχε μὲν ἤδη τὴν γυναῖκα· φίλος γὰρ εἶ λοιπόν, ἧκε δὲ εἰς ἄστυ καὶ λάμβανε τὰς καταγραφὰς καὶ τότε μοι τιμὴν.

> „Mein Teil (...) ist gewissenhaft erfüllt, du aber behalte inzwischen schon die Frau; du bist ja jetzt mein Freund. Doch komm in die Stadt, nimm die *katagraphai* entgegen und dann bezahle mir so viel du willst!“

Darauf erwiderte Leonas – offenbar auf Erwiderung der vor dem Kauf erfolgten vertrauenswürdigen Überlassung Kallirhoes bedacht (1,14,4):

> οὐ μὲν οὖν ... ἀλλὰ καὶ ἐγώ σοι τὸ ἀργύριον ἤδη πιστεύω πρὸ τῆς καταγραφῆς.

[1] Die Wiedergabe des griechischen Textes sowie die hier und im Folgenden angeführten Übersetzungen orientieren sich an: Chariton 2006.

„Nein, auf keinen Fall (…), auch ich vertraue dir das Geld bereits vor der *katagraphe* an.“

Als dann Leonas seinem Herren Dionysios von dem Erwerb der Kallirhoe – welcher ja zugunsten des Dionysios erfolgt war – berichtete, bemerkte er einschränkend (2,1,4):

δεῖ δὲ ἐνταῦθα γενέσθαι νομίμως τὴν καταγραφήν.

„Hier muss nun rechtmäßig noch die *katagraphe* vollzogen werden.“

Im darauffolgenden Romantext wird auf *katagraphe* bzw. *katagraphai* noch an zwei weiteren Stellen verwiesen. Einmal ist es der hinsichtlich des Erwerbs einer weiblichen Sklavin noch zögerliche Dionysios, der Leonas anwies (2,1,6):

ἀλλ᾽ ἐπείπερ ἐπρίω, βάδιζε εἰς τὴν ἀγοράν· Ἄδραστος δὲ ὁ ἐμπειρότατος τῶν νόμων διοικήσει τὰς καταγραφάς.

„Aber da du sie nun einmal gekauft hast, geh nur zum Marktplatz! Adrastos, der sich mit den Gesetzen bestens auskennt, soll die *katagraphai* verwalten.“

Besonders interessant ist der letzte Beleg, der in den Rahmen eines nächtlichen Selbstgesprächs gehört, das Dionysios mit sich führt, nachdem er Kallirhoe das erste Mal begegnet war und sich sofort in sie verliebt hatte. Eingedenk des Umstandes, dass er erst unmittelbar vor der Bekanntschaft mit Kallirhoe seine Frau zu Grabe tragen musste, entwich ihm – auf seinem Landsitz vor den Toren Milets verweilend, wo die Transaktion zwischen Theron und Leonas stattgefunden hatte – folgender Gedanke (2,4,5):

τούτου γε ‹ἕνεκεν› ἧκες εἰς ἀγρόν, ἵνα μελανείμων γάμους θύσῃς, καὶ γάμους δούλης, τάχα δὲ καὶ ἀλλοτρίας; οὐκ ἔχεις γὰρ αὐτῆς οὐδὲ τὴν καταγραφήν.

„Bist du dazu aufs Land gekommen, um in Trauerkleidung Hochzeit zu feiern, noch dazu Hochzeit mit einer Sklavin, vielleicht sogar der eines anderen? Du hast ja noch nicht einmal ihre *katagraphe*.“

Anders als in den anderen Belegstellen ist der Kontext, in dem der Begriff *katagraphe* in 2,4,5 verwendet wird, mit Bezug auf den Erwerb der Kallirhoe ein negativer: Leonas musste unmittelbar nach der Unterredung mit Dionysios – in welcher Adrastos zur Verwaltung der *katagraphai* bestimmt wurde – nämlich erfahren, dass es sich bei dem Verkäufer Theron um keinen redlichen Kaufmann, sondern einen Sklavenräuber handelte, und gab diese Information natürlich unverzüglich an seinen Herren weiter. Die von Dionysios gedanklich angesprochene Konsequenz aus dieser Situation ist ein Schlüssel zum semantischen Verständnis des Begriffs in der Erzählung des Chariton. Die Formulierung οὐκ ἔχεις γὰρ αὐτῆς οὐδὲ τὴν καταγραφήν zwingt dazu, unter der *katagraphe* etwas Dingliches zu verstehen, das Dionysios in Empfang nehmen, in Händen halten konnte und das wohl auch ursächlich für ihn bestimmt war. Ein Zusammenhang mit einer zu einem allgemeinen administrativen Zweck hergestellten „Liste" oder einem amtlichen „Vertragsregister" – Bedeutungsinhalte, die von Sánchez-Moreno Ellart ins Spiel gebracht wurden – liegt hier also nicht auf der Hand.[2] Vielmehr scheint es äußerst attraktiv, *katagraphe* gemäß einer unlängst herausgegebenen Übersetzung zum Roman mit „Übereignungsurkunde" wiederzugeben.[3]

In diesem Kontext soll zunächst Hans-Julius Wolff zu Wort kommen, der in seiner bislang maßgebenden Untersuchung des vorliegenden Gegenstandes einleitend folgendes festhielt:

> „Im Schrifttum unbestritten, da durch so gut wie alle Papyri [...], die die Worte in juristischer Verwendung zeigen, bezeugt, ist die spezifische Verknüpfung der mehrmals in ptolemäischen Quellen und zahlreich in solchen des Prinzipats und Dominats erscheinenden Ausdrücke καταγράφειν und καταγραφή mit dem Erwerb des Eigentums an Liegenschaften und Sklaven.[4]"

Entscheidend ist nun, in welcher Zeit die Begrifflichkeiten in ihrem juristischen Kontext begegnen, und darauf hat bereits Sánchez-Moreno Ellart hingewiesen. In hellenistischer Zeit gibt es in Ägypten das konkrete Institut der *katagraphe*, mit der ein von den Agoranomenämtern verwaltetes Sonderregister bezeichnet wird, das Grundeigentum und Sklaven betraf und in das Eigentumsübergänge und Freilassungen eingetragen wurden.[5] In römischer Zeit veränderte sich das Verständnis des Begriffs in der Urkundensprache aufgrund des allmählichen Absterbens des ptolemäischen Instituts der *katagraphe*, was mit der Einführung der Dorfgrapheia und der in den Gauhauptstädten angesiedelten *bibliotheke enkteseon* als Behörde zur Kontrolle des privaten Grundstücks- und vielleicht auch Sklavenverkehrs zu verknüpfen sein dürfte – folgenschwere Entwicklungen, die hier nicht näher beleuchtet werden können.[6] Nach Ausweis der Urkundensprache scheinen sich die Begrifflichkeiten *katagraphe* bzw. *katagraphein* mit dem Beginn der Kaiserzeit jedenfalls recht rasch von ihrem alten Bezugspunkt – besagtem Sonderregister bzw. dem entsprechenden auf die Eigentumsübertragung bezogenen Akt des Registrierens durch den Agoranomen – gelöst und eine neue Semantik ausgebildet zu haben. In dieser wird

---

2 Zu zwei weiteren abzulehnenden Verständnismöglichkeit siehe weiter unten in Anm. 10 und 11.

3 Chariton 2006, 49.

4 Wolff 1978, 184.

5 Zur ptolemäischen *katagraphe* siehe Wolff 1978, 188–197 und 213–220; vgl. auch Straus 2004, 45–47; Yiftach 2014, 314–321 und 325.

6 Zum Verständnis der römischen *katagraphe* siehe Wolff 1978, 197–213 und 221; vgl. auch Straus 2004, 47–52; Yiftach 2014, 320–325.

der ursprünglich terminologisch-technische, mithin spezifische Zusammenhang mit der ptolemäischen Institut insofern aufgeweicht, als der Sinngehalt im Kontext der Eigentumsübertragung nicht mehr allein aus dem agoranomischen Akt des Registrierens gespeist werden kann, sondern dazu übergeht, *katagraphe* bzw. *katagraphein* auch mit der Übereignungsurkunde an sich oder deren Aufsetzung in Verbindung zu bringen, ohne hier aber von technischer Bedeutung zu sein oder als Selbstbezeichnung der die Transaktion festhaltenden Urkunden aufzutreten.[7] Insgesamt war der Semantik von *katagraphe* im alltäglichen Sprachgebrauch demgemäß „nur noch in allgemeiner Weise ein nicht weiter qualifiziertes „Verschreiben" zu Eigentum"[8] inhärent. Dabei war der Aspekt der öffentlichen Beurkundung so lange entscheidend, bis im 3. Jahrhundert n.Chr. die als Cheirographon stilisierte Übereignungsurkunde – nun durchaus auch in technischem Sinne – als *katagraphe* bezeichnet werden konnte.[9]

Kommen wir zurück zu Chariton und dem Kauf der schönen Kallirhoe. Nach den vorangehenden Ausführungen scheint es sinngemäß, unter dem Wort *katagraphe* den Hinweis auf eine Urkunde zu verstehen, in der der auf Kallirhoe bezogene Eigentumsübergang auf Leonas in Vertretung von Dionysios verbrieft wurde; das wäre mithin der Kaufvertrag – eine semantische Interpretation, die bei Sánchez-Moreno Ellart durchaus anklingt, bei ihm aber offenbar von untergeordneter Bedeutung bleibt.[10] Das Verständnis im Sinn von „Urkunde/Kaufvertrag" funktioniert an allen Stellen, an denen der Begriff im Singular verwendet wird. Den Gebrauch im Plural könnte man sich damit erklären, dass einerseits Theron damit vorgeben wollte, weitere Urkunden zu besitzen, welche die vorangehende Übereignungen der Kallirhoe dokumentieren konnten;[11] in 1,12,8 hatte er – um seine tatsächliche Identität und jene Kallirhoes zu verschleiern – vorgegeben, er habe als reisender Kaufmann Kallirhoe im italischen Sybaris von einer Frau gekauft. Dass es eine Mehrzahl an Kaufdokumenten – hier vielleicht auch schon inklusive des künftigen Vertrages zwischen Theron und Leonas – zu verwalten gab, mag dann andererseits in der diesbezüglichen Bemerkung des Dionysios mitschwingen. Man müsste jetzt verstärkt in die Materie der Sklavenkäufe eintauchen, um plausibel untermauern zu können, dass beim rechtmäßigen Sklavenkauf die Erwerbsgeschichte des betreffenden

---

7 Siehe Wolff 1978, 208–210; vgl. Yiftach 2014, 325.

8 Wolff 1978, 210.

9 Siehe Wolff 1978, 209 und 211 mit Bezug auf P.Oxy. XIV 1636, 42–43 (249 n.Chr.) und 1704, 25 (298 n.Chr.).

10 Das kurz davor von Sánchez-Moreno Ellart im Kontext von 1,14,3 eher beiläufig angedachte Verständnis der *katagraphai* im Sinn von „Formularen" ist demgegenüber ohne weitere Erläuterungen schwer nachvollziehbar.

11 Auf jeden Fall scheint der pluralische Gebrauch auch dagegen zu sprechen, *katagraphe* die Bedeutung „Registrierung" oder „Eintragen/Eintragung" (letzteres fand ebenfalls bei Sánchez-Moreno Ellart Erwähnung) zuzusprechen; die Sinnhaftigkeit der in 1,14,3 und 2,1,6 begegnenden Formulierung wäre dann äußerst erklärungsbedürftig (vgl. Anm. 10).

Sklaven zu dokumentieren war, aber zumindest für die Zeit ab dem Ende des 2. Jahrhunderts n.Chr. scheint sich ein derartiger Befund recht deutlich abzuzeichnen.[12]

Schlussendlich ist zu konstatieren, dass aufgrund der dem Begriff *katagraphe* zuzuweisenden Bedeutung ein Zusammenhang mit der römischen Zeit unumgänglich ist – das entspricht auch der Entstehungszeit des Romans. Als Konsequenz folgt, dass der Kauf der Kallirhoe mit einem Vertrag abgeschlossen werden soll, der aber nicht zustande kam. Dionysios konnte letztlich also nicht beweisen, dass Kallirhoe sein Eigentum war. Ob dies für die Erzählung von eigentlicher Bedeutung ist, ist aber eher zweifelhaft. Denn kaum jemand mag in der Lage gewesen sein, einem einflussreichen Mann wie Dionysios aufgrund der diesem zukommenden Machtstellung die Verfügungsgewalt über Kallirhoe streitig zu machen, zumal sich diese in seinem *oikos* befand, der Preis für sie unter Beisein von Zeugen bezahlt wurde und der Verkäufer über alle Berge war.[13] Dennoch gilt es zu beachten, dass der widrige Ausgang des Kaufgeschäfts, der fast schon emblematisch für dessen windigen, von Betrug geprägten – also unmoralischen – Charakter zu sein scheint, implizit einen runden Übergang zu dem weiteren Handlungsverlauf herstellt. Musste Dionysios zuvor, als noch mit dem Zustandekommen des Vertrags gerechnet wurde, aufgrund seines hohen Standes und der ihm zugeschriebenen Vorbildfunktion noch eine Liebesbeziehung zu einer Sklavin ablehnen (2,1,5), gab es nach dem Scheitern des Vertragsabschlusses keinen aktenkundigen Nachweis für den – gleichwohl fälschlichen – Sklavenstatus der Kallirhoe. Wenn also im Verlauf des zweiten Buches deren wahre Identität herauskommt und der Erzählstrang weiter auf die Hochzeit von Kallirhoe und Dionysios zuläuft, kann dies folglich ohne juristische Vorbelastung geschehen. Tatsächlich scheint es nach der Kaufepisode im Roman nur mehr darum zu gehen, wie man Kallirhoe als fremde und eigentlich freie und vornehme Frau im Haus des Dionysios – im Hinblick auf eine moralische Verpflichtung – zu behandeln habe.[14] Das lässt die juristischen Sachverhalte

---

[12] Zu dem hier angesprochenen Institut der *anakrisis* siehe Wolff 1978, 255–260; Straus 2004, 62–71; Straus 2014, 456–457.

[13] Demgemäß Kallirhoe zu Dionysios (2,5,11): μικρόν ἐστί σοι πλουτοῦντι σῶμα ἐᾶσαι. τὴν τιμὴν οὐκ ἀπολέσεις, ἐὰν ἀποδῷς με τῷ πατρί· Ἑρμοκράτης οὐκ ἔστιν ἀχάριστος („Für einen reichen Mann wie dich ist es eine Kleinigkeit, einen Sklaven freizulassen. Das Geld wirst du nicht verlieren, wenn du mich meinem Vater zurückgibst: Hermokrates ist nicht undankbar“); vgl. auch Leonas zu Dionysios (2,6,2): κύριος γὰρ εἶ καὶ τὴν ἐξουσίαν ἔχεις αὐτῆς, ὥστε καὶ ἑκοῦσα καὶ ἄκουσα ποιήσει τὸ σοὶ δοκοῦν· ταλάντου γὰρ αὐτὴν ἐπριάμην („Du bist doch der Herr und hast die Gewalt über sie. Daher wird sie, ob sie will oder nicht, das tun müssen, was du für richtig hältst. Ich habe sie ja schließlich für ein Talent gekauft“).

[14] So Dionysios (2,5,12): ἐν δὲ τῷ μεταξὺ θεραπείαν ἕξεις παρ’ ἡμῖν δεσποίνης μᾶλλον ἢ δούλης („In der Zwischenzeit sollst du bei uns behandelt werden wie eine Herrin, nicht wie eine Sklavin“); Dionysios zu Leonas (2, 6, 3): ἐπρίω σύ, τρισάθλιε, τὴν εὐγενῆ … ἐγὼ τυραννήσω σώματος ἐλευθέρου καὶ Διονύσιος, ὁ ἐπὶ σωφροσύνῃ περιβόητος, ἄκουσαν ὑβριῶ, ἣν οὐκ ἂν ὕβρισεν οὐδὲ Θήρων ὁ λῃστής („Gekauft hast du sie, Unseliger? Eine Frau von vornehmer Abstammung? […] Ich soll mich zum Tyrannen

zurücktreten und setzt den Fokus auf die sozialen Implikationen des Ereignisverlaufs.

saengerp@uni-muenster.de

LITERATUR

Chariton 2006: Chariton, Kallirhoe, herausgegeben, übersetzt und kommentiert von Ch. Meckelnborg, K.-H. Schäfer, Darmstadt 2006.

Straus 2004: J.A. Straus, L'achat et la vente des esclaves dans l'Égypte romaine. Contribution papyrologique à l'étude de l'esclavage dans une province orientale de l'empire romaine (ArchivBeih. 14), Leipzig 2004.

Straus 2014: J.A. Straus, Slaves and slavery in the Roman period, in: Kennan, Manning, Yiftach-Firanko (Hrsg.), Law and Legal Practice in Egypt from Alexander to the Arab Conquest. A Selection of Papyrological Sources in Translation, with Introductions and Commentary, Cambridge 2014, 452–461.

Wolff 1978: H.J. Wolff, Das Recht der griechischen Papyri Ägyptens in der Zeit der Ptolemaeer und des Prinzipats, Zweiter Band: Organisation und Kontrolle des privaten Rechtsverkehrs (HdAW X 5, 2), München 1978.

Yiftach 2014: U. Yiftach-Firanko, State registration of sales: the katagraphê, in: J. G. Kennan, J. G. Manning, U. Yiftach-Firanko (Hrsg.), Law and Legal Practice in Egypt from Alexander to the Arab Conquest. A Selection of Papyrological Sources in Translation, with Introductions and Commentary, Cambridge 2014, 314–325.

über einen freien Menschen aufwerfen und ich, Dionysios, dessen Sittsamkeit weithin berühmt ist, soll einer Frau gegen ihren Willen Gewalt antun, der nicht einmal der Räuber Theron Gewalt angetan hätte?"); und Kallirhoe selbst (3,1,6): εἰ μὲν οὖν ὡς παλλακὴν θέλει με Διονύσιος ἔχειν καὶ τῆς ἰδίας ἀπολαύειν ἐπιθυμίας, ἀπάγξομαι μᾶλλον ἢ ὕβρει δουλικῇ παραδώσω τὸ σῶμα, εἰ δὲ γαμετὴν κατὰ νόμους, κἀγὼ γενέσθαι θέλω μήτηρ, ἵνα διάδοχον ἔχῃ τὸ Ἑρμοκράτους γένος („Wenn mich Dionysios also zur Geliebten haben und nur seine eigene Lust befriedigen will, dann erhänge ich mich lieber, als mich wie eine Sklavin missbrauchen zu lassen; will er mich jedoch zur rechtmäßigen Gattin, dann bin ich meinerseits bereit, Mutter zu werden, damit das Geschlecht des Hermokrates einen Nachfolger hat").

CHRISTEL MÜLLER (PARIS)

THE USES OF *TRIGONIA*: DESCENT, CITIZENSHIP AND FREEBORN STATUS IN GREEK CITIES FROM PERICLES TO MARCUS AURELIUS*

Abstract: The rule of *trigonia*, which shows a desire to filter the civic body, consists in ensuring that the grandparents' generation is involved in a process of recognition. It appears in a letter of Marcus Aurelius to the Athenians about the access to the Areopagus for grandsons of freeborn people. It reinterprets a classical rule applied to future archons who had to prove their civic status over three generations according to Aristotle. This rule is known in other cities in the Hellenistic period.

Keywords: Trigonia; citizenship; freeborn status; archonship; Marcus Aurelius.

The importance of filiation and patronymic to establish one's status in Greek societies is a commonplace well known to legal historians. The notion of *trigonia*, on the other hand, which implies not two but three generational levels, is less studied, even if it is part of an essential tendency of Greek cities, in both anthropological and ideological terms, to seek the purity of the group and its blood. The term, to quote the Souda (*s.v.* T 964 [Adler], τριγονία: ἡ τρίτη γενεά), can be defined as the implementation of a third γενεά, "generation", whatever its subsequent use for access to office in particular.

This notion, which is expressed variously on the lexical and grammatical level, is therefore of deep interest to those who take a long-term interest, as I do, in questions of citizenship[1]. Its complex and nuanced articulation with *politeia* thus forms the backdrop to this research. The *trigonia* raises the following questions about its uses, which are simple in themselves but rarely admit of an easy answer: How does it work? What purposes does it serve? What difficulties did it encounter when being implemented?

I will look here, very concretely, at several case-studies, starting from the Imperial period and then going back to the Classical and Hellenistic periods. The reign of Marcus Aurelius, as evidenced by a letter from the emperor to the Athenians

* This article benefited from comments made by a well-informed audience at the conference, especially Kostas Buraselis, Mirko Canevaro, David Lewis, Lina Girdvainyte, and Anna Magnetto, as well as from lengthy discussions with Claudia Moatti and (*per ep.*) Sara Forsdyke. Finally, Graham J. Oliver has accepted to read and emend the text. I would like to thank them all warmly.

1 See Müller 2023.

dated 174/5 AD, constitutes a moment when the term crystallizes, at least in the current state of our sources, and invites us to reflect on the reception of the Classical rules considered at the time as an inheritance to which one could only aspire to return. This will be followed by several dossiers from the Hellenistic period, in Massalia, Halicarnassus and Cos, which do not claim to exhaust the subject matter, but simply to shed light on "tri-generational" practices in a world undergoing profound changes.

I. Marcus Aurelius' letter to the Athenians: *GC* 184

1. Presentation of the document

The letter of Marcus Aurelius to the Athenians that serves here as a starting point is an exceptional epigraphic document, discovered between 1936 and 1939 during the American excavations of the Greek and Roman Agorai in Athens and published only in 1970 by James H. Oliver[2]. It consists of two white marble slabs now in six fragments (A to F). Plate II, "reused as a paving slab in the Roman Agora (...) is now in the Epigraphical Museum (EM 13366), after being mended from over 200 small pieces"[3]. It bears fragment E, the longest and most interesting in terms of institutional arrangements. Several readings have been made of it which have contributed to the significant improvement of the text after 1970. I present here[4] two passages that combine corrections made by Simone Follet and others proposed by James H. Oliver himself after the *editio princeps*. The latter included the inscription (under no. 184) in his collection of *Greek Constitutions*, published posthumously in 1989.

The letter deals with problems concerning the city of Athens and several of its citizens who appeal to the emperor against the decisions of various bodies on diverse matters. It also deals with the relationship between Herodes Atticus and the Athenians and gives information on the organisation of the Panhellenion[5]. But the two passages that interest us most, taken from fragment E, are a paragraph entirely devoted to the question of *trigonia* (**l. 57–81**) and, in a secondary but enlightening way, a decision of the emperor concerning the civic status of a certain Popilius Pius (**l. 30–35**). The documentary wealth of the letter has given rise to an abundant bibliography, oriented for a large part towards the nature of the document (letter or edict) and judicial issues, in particular appeals, with an important article by Kaja Harter-Uibopuu in 2008[6], followed in 2009 by a book by Veronika Wankerl[7] and, in 2010, the numerous pages devoted to the functions of the Areopagus and the role of the emperor in Julien Fournier's fine opus on judicial administration in the Eastern

---

[2] Oliver 1970.

[3] *SEG* 29, 127 (lemma), which reproduces Simone Follet's text (Follet 1979).

[4] See the Annex.

[5] On the Panhellenion, see *inter alia* Jones 1996 and Ferrary 2017 [2011].

[6] Harter-Uibopuu 2008.

[7] Wankerl 2009.

provinces[8]. On the other hand, as far as the *trigonia* itself is concerned, only James H. Oliver has really examined this question in some detail, and the topic has subsequently become somewhat lost in the sands.

2. The *trigonia* and the provisions of the letter

How is *trigonia* defined in 174/5 AD by the emperor, and what purpose does it serve in this paragraph (**l. 57–81**), which might have been originally a separate piece? The *trigonia* appears to be based on the status of a freeborn man (*eugenēs*/*ingenuus*) from the grandfather's generation included, a condition supposedly indispensable at some point for access to the Areopagus. Marcus Aurelius repeatedly refers to an earlier letter, in which he had tried (**l. 59**: ἐπειράθην) to renew this principle. This first letter has been identified by J.H. Oliver as the joint letter addressed by the same emperor and Lucius Verus to the Areopagus in AD 165 (*GC* 173), but its lacunose state makes it impossible to judge exactly what it contained, even if it did indeed concern this Council. The initial provisions did not have the desired effect and, some ten years later, the emperor, who had been ruling alone since 169, decided to partially renounce them, as they seemed untenable to the Athenians (**l. 60–63**). As Follet brilliantly showed in 1979[9], three stages can be distinguished, with partial exceptions[10]: before the first letter, between the two letters and since the second letter. I will present them here, trying to amend and clarify Follet's reconstruction.

In phase one (before the first letter), considered 'the past' (**l. 64**: ἐπὶ μὲν τοῦ παρεληλυθότος χρόνου), Athenians could enter the Areopagus with merely a freeborn father (**l. 64–65**). The emperor therefore consents here to rehabilitate (**l. 65–66**) those who, having entered before 165, had since been expelled on the grounds of *trigonia*, thus the grandsons of freedmen, by virtue of the non-retroactivity of the provision, it is assumed. For this phase one, we must also look in the letter for the sons of freedmen who would have entered the Areopagus before this first letter (**l. 68–69**: τις πρὸ τῆς ἐπιστολῆς ἀπελευθέρου πατρὸς γεγονὼς): they should not have been able to get in since a free–born father was required, but if they were not expelled by the decision of a court, they will be able to stay. This is the first exception, due to the fact that the emperor had not yet intervened by imposing a precise rule.

Phase three (from the second and present letter onwards) poses no problem of interpretation: it is now sufficient to have both parents of free birth (**l. 66**: μετὰ ταῦτα δὲ τὸ ἐξ ἀμφοῖν τῶν γονέων εἶναί τινα εὖ γεγονότων ἀρκέσει). Therefore, the last clause, **l. 74–76,** must be placed here: if some people persist in contravening the two free-born parents rule (μετὰ τὰ ἀπηγορευμένα διατελέσηι μένω̣[ν]) or fraudulently

[8] Fournier 2010.

[9] Follet 1979, 38–39.

[10] The right word would be the French "prescriptions", which has no exact equivalent in English.

introduce themselves (contravening the same rule: παρὰ τὰ προγεγραμμένα εἰσδύηται) from the second letter onwards, then not only will they be excluded, but they will be exposed to sanctions regarding less prestigious offices.

For **phase two** (that is for people who entered between the two letters), when *trigonia* was theoretically *de rigueur*, the emperor establishes several distinctions, not all of which have been fully elucidated:

–**l. 66–68**: if, after the first letter of 165, some sons of freedmen entered because of ignorance, it is time to put an end to their *agnoia* (**l. 67**: τῆς ἀγν[οίας] ὥρα πεπαῦσθαι), which announces the exclusion to come later[11]. From now on, they can no longer be ignorant as the current document spells out the various situations, starting with the grandsons of freedmen.

–thus, **l. 69–71**: if, after the first letter, some grandsons of freedmen were excluded by a court or withdrew of their own accord, they will remain excluded (because the decision was legal at the time). **L. 71–72**: if (in the future tense this time), some (belonging to the latter category, grandsons of freedmen) decide to leave the Areopagus now of their own accord on the grounds mentioned (τούς γε μὴν ὑπεξστησομένους διὰ προειρημένα ἐκ τοῦ συνεδρίου), then they shall not incur any additional penalty for the exercise of other charges.

–**l. 72–74**: if, after the first letter, some were recruited in contradiction to the rule laid down before (thus *trigonia*) and are at the same time in contradiction to the rule laid down by the second letter (two free-born parents: οἷς οὐδὲ μετὰ τὴν νῦν ἐξενεχθεῖσαν γνῶσιν οἷόν τὲ ἐστιν ἐν Ἀρείωι π[άγωι] καθῆσθαι), then they are given one year to get out of the Areopagus. This is, in my opinion, a double category which includes both grandsons and sons of freedmen who would, in both cases, have been enlisted after the first letter and would therefore all have violated the *trigonia*: indeed, whoever does not have an *ingenuus* father is by definition violating the three-generation provision. What is their fate? Only the sons of freedmen will be in fact excluded because they also violate the provisions of the second letter (having free-born parents). These sons of freedmen, who must settle their situation within one year, are the sons of freedmen referred to earlier, who entered the system out of ignorance and must be informed. On the other hand, and even if it is not explicitly stated, one must deduce that the grandsons of freedmen who also have two free-born parents are allowed to stay, even if they initially violated the *trigonia*. This is the second exception, but it is in accordance with the rule contained in the second letter. However, this is not the case for the grandsons of freedmen whose mother is not free-born: they are not allowed to stay.

In short, even if the style and order of clauses are not always transparent, the text is perfectly consistent in its provisions. Its interest, from my perspective, lies in the threefold statutory hierarchy it sets out: one can simply be born free oneself, the

[11] Follet 1979, 38: "il est temps qu'il soit mis fin à cette ignorance. Ils seront exclus, mais n'encourront aucune sanction supplémentaire".

condition eventually retained for another Council, that of the Five-Hundred (**l. 80–81**); one can have a free-born father or two freeborn parents: that was the condition required before 165 (father), and this is the condition required for the Areopagus from the present letter onwards (father and mother); one can, finally, have a free-born grandfather and thus satisfy the *trigonia*, a condition retained in the future for the Panhellenion alone, with a third and final exception concerning the Panhellenes grandchildren of freedmen entered before the present provision (**l. 76–79**).

3. What is the aim of *trigonia*?

Trigonia aims at ensuring that the grandparents' generation (the third generation in the Greek count) is fully or partially (but explicitly) involved in a recognition process, whatever it is. The considering of three generations is, in my view, that of the possibly living members of real families: looking back are the *progonoi*, a term that refers to the grandparents' generation and also to ancestors in general; looking ahead are the *epigonoi*, the "successors". *Trigonia* is used only in a negative way, to sort out and eliminate potential candidates for this or that status or office. It reflects a Greek desire for purity of *genos* (paralleled with a Roman repulsion for *infamia*), manifested in a great distrust of people perceived as having an insufficiently established —foreign or enfranchised, status.

From the emperor's statement concerning "the past" (that is before AD 165), we have deduced that, for this period, the official rule of access to the Areopagus was that of the "free-born father", introduced at a date unknown to us. But it is clear that even this rule was not respected, since there were sons of freedmen in the Council. Marcus Aurelius' provisions are here explicitly aimed at freedmen and their descendants, in other words more or less recent Roman citizens, or individuals of unclear condition and status with regard to local provisions. An echo of this situation can be found, as J.H. Oliver has shown[12], in Lucian's delightful and satirical short dialogue, *The Assembly of the Gods*, composed precisely in 165 or 166, after the author's return to Athens. This dialogue is devoted to the question of who among the gods deserves his seat, when some of them are half-human, and even of servile descent. Returning to Marcus Aurelius, the emperor produced in his letter a hybrid provision, so to speak, between Greek and Roman statutory systems. The expulsion of freedmen's descendants from the Areopagus was a very severe provision for the Romans, which seems to respond to a Greek practice: in theory, freedmen in Greek cities never became citizens, unlike *liberti*, and the presence of their offspring in local institutions must have shocked more than one native Athenian under the Empire. In view of this, perhaps we should assume that in 165 Marcus Aurelius, together with Lucius Verus, had responded to a request from the Athenians themselves to "clean up" the Areopagus.

[12] Oliver 1983 [1980]; see also Kennell 1997, 355–356.

But like all rules, *trigonia* was subject to a wide range of applications and circumventions followed by readjustments, to which Marcus Aurelius' letter is ample evidence. The Athenians, who ten years later would have found themselves unable to meet the established criterion, for lack of citizens able to sit (**l. 60**: *endoxa genē* are missing), would then have resisted its application and asked the emperor for a relaxation. This kind of request is generally the result of challenging historical circumstances, which in the 160s included the Antonine plague, and are referred to at **l. 61** (τὰ συμβάντα διὰ τὴν τύχην)[13]. These circumstances, which the text shows affected many cities (**l. 62**), were responsible for the scarcity of candidates endowed both with *eugeneia* and the funds necessary for the exercise of the highest offices, and they forced the emperor to reduce his own claims.

II. *Trigonia* and the return to tradition: looking back towards Aristotle and the Classical period

1. The "old custom"

The emperor presents the *trigonia* provisions as a return to "the old custom" (**l. 59**: τὸ παλαιὸν ἔθος). This way of introducing a novelty by invoking *ta patria* is usual in the ancient world, where revolutions are often returns to bygone times. But what ancient custom is involved here? Undoubtedly, Marcus Aurelius is referring to the three-generation rule as mentioned by Aristotle about archons. In the *AP* (55.3[14]), the archons, once drawn by lot, undergo a double *dokimasia* by the *boulē* and by a *dikastērion*. It is difficult to say whether the nine archons were really all concerned by the total set of questions that may have been put to them according to their field of competence[15]. In any case, the following four questions were asked: Who is your

[13] On the Antonine plague, see Duncan-Jones 1996 and the contributions in Lo Cascio 2012.

[14] Arist., *AP* 55.3: ἐπερωτῶσιν δ’ὅταν δοκιμάζωσιν, πρῶτον μὲν "τίς σοι πατὴρ καὶ πόθεν τῶν δήμων, καὶ τίς πατρὸς πατήρ, καὶ τίς μήτηρ, καὶ τίς μητρὸς πατὴρ καὶ πόθεν τῶν δήμων;" μετὰ δὲ ταῦτα εἰ ἔστιν αὐτῷ Ἀπόλλων Πατρῷος καὶ Ζεὺς Ἑρκεῖος, καὶ ποῦ ταῦτα τὰ ἱερά ἐστιν, εἶτα ἠρία εἰ ἔστιν καὶ ποῦ ταῦτα, ἔπειτα γονέας εἰ εὖ ποιεῖ, καὶ τὰ τέλη <εἰ> τελεῖ, καὶ τὰς στρατείας εἰ ἐστράτευται· ταῦτα δ’ ἀνερωτήσας, "κάλει" φησὶν "τούτων τοὺς μάρτυρας", "The questions put in examining qualifications are, first, 'Who is your father and to what deme does he belong, and who is your father's father, and who your mother, and who her father and what his deme?', then whether he has a Patrōos Apollo and Herkeios Zeus, and where these shrines are; then whether he has family tombs and where they are; then whether he treats his parents well, and whether he pays his taxes, and whether he has done his military service. And after putting these questions the officer says, 'Call your witnesses to these statements'" (text and tr. H. Rackham, The Loeb Classical Library, London, 1935). See the excellent commentary, by Blok 2017, 124–125, on the religious dimension of this scrutiny, which shows "the fundamental role of descent anchored in cult as the persistent criterion of citizenship; (…) the prospective archons were asked about their *active* sharing in *hiera kai hosia*".

[15] On this complex procedure, see Feyel 2009, 171–181.

father and from which deme? Who is your father's father? Who is your mother? Who is your mother's father and from which deme?. In other words, the *trigonia* here concerns Athenian *politeia* over three generations. And the text is explicit: the questions systematically and symmetrically mention both grandfathers, paternal and maternal. The father of the father appears here as fundamental, exactly as for the provisions of the Areopagus between AD 165 and 175. The imperial reception allows us, I believe, to better understand the case of the classical archons.

Yet the validity of this particular classical procedure has been challenged by institutional historians, as it seems to clash with the Periclean rule of "dual descent"[16], necessary for access to citizenship and therefore office in Athens. Although Pollux in his gloss of the *AP* (*Onomasticon* 8, 85–87[17]) confirms (in fact quotes and comments) Aristotle, Peter J. Rhodes thinks he (Pollux not Aristotle) is totally mistaken about the archons. Pollux' statement "should be seen not as a sign of a stricter requirement of third-generation Athenian citizenship but as an inaccurate summary of the questions about ancestry listed by *A.P.* (…) The proof that a man was a citizen was that his name was entered on the register of his deme; women were not registered, and the proof that a woman was a πολῖτις was that her father was registered as a citizen. Thus, candidates were asked their father's name, deme and paternity (the last was not strictly necessary […]), and their mother's name, paternity and her father's deme" [18]. The historian puts great emphasis on the question about the mother and the maternal grandfather, because the latter was recorded in the deme lists and the former was not. But if the sole identity of this *pappos* had been needed, no question would have been asked about the paternal grandfather, since the father himself was obviously recorded on demes' lists. Rhodes sidesteps the problem by saying that "the last [i.e. the paternal grandfather]

---

16 On this rule (both parents *astoi*), see now Blok 2017, *passim*.

17 Poll., *Onom.* 8, 85: ἀρχόντων δὲ τῶν Ἀθήνησιν ὀνόματα οἱ ἐννέα ἄρχοντες· εἰσὶ δὲ ἄρχων, βασιλεύς, πολέμαρχος καὶ θεσμοθέται ἕξ· ἐκ τούτων γὰρ οἱ ἐννέα συμπληροῦνται. ἐκαλεῖτο δέ τις θεσμοθετῶν ἀνάκρισις, εἰ Ἀθηναῖοί εἰσιν ἑκατέρωθεν ἐκ τριγονίας καὶ τὸν δῆμον πόθεν κτλ. (ed. E. Bethe, *Lexicographi Graeci* 9.2., Teubner, Leipzig 1931), "the archons in Athens have for names the nine archons; they are the archon (i.e. eponymous), the king, the polemarch and the six thesmothetes; it is indeed thanks to the latter that the number of nine is reached; an examination was claimed relating to the thesmothetes: if they were Athenians on each side since three generations and from which deme they were originating etc". The only divergence between the text of Aristotle and that of Pollux lies in the fact that the examination would relate only to the thesmothetes and not to the whole of the archons. Also known is a gloss of Aristotle from Photius (fragment 414, V. Rose, *Aristotelis qui ferebantur librorum fragmenta*, Teubner, Leipzig, 1886), which refers to the examination of the thesmothetes who are asked who "their fathers" (πατέρες) are, who are to be understood as "paternal ancestors".

18 See Rhodes 1981, 617.

was not strictly necessary"[19]. Another argument against this *trigonia* would be the fact that Pollux would first and foremost reflect the situation of the imperial period: the rule would even be an invention of this period and the author would reinterpret here the classical situation according to the one created by Marcus Aurelius[20]. However, the recent studies carried out on book VIII of Pollux by historians of classical Attic law, for example on the Athenian *boulē* and Assembly, show on the contrary, to quote Paolo Tuci, "that a diligent and careful Pollux emerges, concerned not only in lexical peculiarities (…), but also in providing more accurate descriptions (…) in comparison with those provided by Aristotle's *Athenaion Politeia*"[21]. What about Aristotle, Pollux' main source in book VIII, sometimes quoted quasi *verbatim* by the lexicographer as is the case here?

In my opinion, Aristotle either cannot be dismissed that easily, and I will use here as a counter-argument for my demonstration what can be called the Plataean case, which is precisely the argument used by the opponents of the archons' *trigonia*. According to several passages of the speech *Against Neaira* ([Dem.] 59. 92; 106), there was a *nomos* regulating the status of the children of naturalized citizens, as can be seen in the case of the Plataeans in 427, who took refuge in Athens when their city was destroyed by the Thebans[22]. So, what does the plaintiff Apollodorus say? He explains that access to the archonship and priesthoods was strictly forbidden to the naturalized citizen, but allowed to his sons under the condition that the mother was an *astē*[23]. We would be dealing here with two generations and not

---

19 P.J. Rhodes is followed by Sarah Forsdyke (*per ep.*): "While the name and deme of the paternal grandfather was not strictly necessary, questions about the paternal grandfather provided further confirmation of citizen status on the father's side, as well as a satisfying symmetry (I underline) with the (necessary) questions about maternal paternity. It is important to emphasize that these questions about grandfathers were asked not because three generations of citizenship were required, but in order to determine that the candidate for citizenship was descended from citizens on both sides (the two-generation rule). There was technically a two-generation rule but practically a three-generation rule, especially as concerned the status of the mother".

20 As suggested by Sarah Forsdyke.

21 Tuci 2007, 102. If Pollux finds his main source for book VIII in Aristotle's *AP*, he probably also drew from the tradition of the Scholiasts and from the Atthidographers (p. 101).

22 Mirko Canevaro has brilliantly shown that the Plataean decree, as formulated in the speech, is a fake and that "in order to reconstruct the conditions of the grant to the Plataeans it is safer therefore to rely on Apollodorus' account and to dismiss the document": Canevaro 2010, 369.

23 Dem., 59 [*Neair.*] 92 (same stipulations in 106): ὅσους γὰρ ἂν ποιήσηται ὁ δῆμος ὁ Ἀθηναίων πολίτας, ὁ νόμος ἀπαγορεύει διαρρήδην μὴ ἐξεῖναι αὐτοῖς τῶν ἐννέα ἀρχόντων γενέσθαι, μηδὲ ἱερωσύνης μηδεμιᾶς μετασχεῖν· τοῖς δ' ἐκ τούτων μετέδωκεν ἤδη ὁ δῆμος ἁπάντων, καὶ προσέθηκεν 'ἐὰν ὦσιν ἐκ γυναικὸς ἀστῆς καὶ ἐγγυητῆς κατὰ τὸν νόμον, "for in the case of all those whom the Athenian people may make citizens, the law expressly forbids that they should be eligible to the office of the nine archons or to hold any priesthood; but their descendants are allowed by the people to share in all

three (the naturalized father and his son). The speech against Neaira would thus contradict and even invalidate that of the *AP*, as one would only need a father and not a grandfather citizen to be an archon. How can the problem be solved?

The problem can be solved in the following way. For the naturalized man, as Josine Blok points out with great institutional accuracy and subtlety, by granting *politeia*, the *dēmos* acts as if the person were born ἐξ ἀμφοῖν ἀστοῖν[24]. So, it is a construction, a legal fiction, as she writes. But one can go further and say that this fiction is replicated in the next generation: if the naturalized person has a fictitious ancestry (the *Dēmos*), he is, as it were, fictitiously placed in the second generation; his son is then placed in turn, again fictitiously, in the third generation. It is therefore he who can exercise the archonship, in the same way as a lambda citizen can be an archon according to the *trigonia* rule. But, another element is added here, the necessity to have an *astē* mother, if one wants to access the archonship with a naturalized father. Blok has made it clear that "the actual birth from an *astē* was decisive for transmitting real Athenian-ness". This introduces a discrepancy between the Athenian *astē* and her Plataean husband who has become an Athenian. The latter does not need to be an *astos* by birth to hold the ordinary offices and his son does not need to be born of an *astos* to hold the archonship. The most important for us is that, in the end, the two cases —native or naturalized citizen— are therefore aligned in legal terms and, in both cases, it is a symmetrical *trigonia* that is at stake in the access to the archonship.

If one rejects this interpretation, then one must find an explanation for the following two exceptions: on the one hand, why naturalized citizens, who were considered lambda citizens through the fiction evoked, would have access to other offices but not to the archonship? And, on the other hand, why would the Athenians bother to carry out such a *dokimasia* for the archons if archonship was really a standard *archē*? A mistake of Aristotle doesn't do, when the set of questions asked in the examination is so clear, nor an alleged taste for symmetry. In both cases, the archonship appears indeed to be a special case: This is not surprising given the ongoing importance of this office in the 4th c. BC.[25]

In short, the two texts (Aristotle and Demosthenes) not only do not contradict each other, but they're in agreement and can be understood one through the other, since they introduce in both cases a generation gap: they are the two sides of the same coin and both proceed from the same legal principle. The conclusion is the

---

privileges, though the proviso is added: if they are born from an Athenian woman who was betrothed according to the law" (text and tr. modified A.T. Murray, The Loeb Classical Library, London, 1939).

[24] Blok 2017, 254, who explains that "in the decrees, *Athenaion einai* operated as a speech act", and p. 262–263: "for an Athenian-by-decree, his status was recognized as a legal fiction, *as if* he were a born Athenian, which was not the equivalent of real Athenian birth".

[25] Feyel 2009, 179–181.

following: neither Apollodoros, nor Aristotle and Pollux are wrong, and it is reassuring if I dare say: it seems obvious there was indeed a real legal principle of symmetrical *trigonia* here, in the case of future archons. Its actual implementation was, however, another matter.

2. Displacements of *trigonia* and chronology

The imperial letter is therefore a wonderful case of reception of an old law: the emperor "is making creative use of the past to respond to new concerns"[26]. Doing this, Marcus Aurelius operated three successive shifts, already identified by James H. Oliver.

The first is the shift from inherited *politeia* (citizen-status) to inherited *eugeneia* (freeborn status). In the case of the Classical archons, there is no mention of freedom. In fact, it is implicit when the archon was drawn by lot, because one couldn't become a citizen at the age of 18 without being recognised as free by the deme, and in case of appeal, by a court (*AP*, 42.1). In this sense, *eleutheria* being included in *politeia*, it is indeed possible to say with J.H. Oliver that Marcus Aurelius "has subsumed both types [of *trigonia*] under the phrase παλαιὸν ἔθος of line 59"[27], rather than erased the difference between the two. The second shift from the traditional use of *trigonia* concerns the fact that it is now a condition of entry to the Areopagus rather than one imposed on the archons themselves. In Classical times, although the Areopagus was made up of the archons who had left office, they were subject to a new *dokimasia*[28]. But it had nothing to do with the spectacular *dokimasia*, and most well-known for a Greek city, undergone by the future archons. If there was any fraud, it must have taken place during the latter, which also involved checking whether they belonged to the first two census categories, and then from 457/6 also to the *zeugitai*. Aristotle (*AP*, 26.2) considers, for example, the possibility that even before this date some *zeugitai* could have reached the archonship, "the provisions of the laws" being neglected. He even mentions the fact that, in practice, some thetes also had access to it (*AP*, 7.4). The third and last shift is that, in the *trigonia* as understood by the emperor, only the paternal grandfather was concerned, while for the archons both grandfathers were.

James H. Oliver questioned the timing of these moves. In his view, this "great constitutional alteration"[29] might be traced back to the time of Hadrian in AD 125, and maybe to the time of Augustus and his visit to Athens in 21 BC, during which he had, according to Cassius Dio (54.7), banned the sale of citizenship[30]. He also likens the great statutory purge in the Areopagus to that carried out by Octavian in

---

26 To quote Sara Forsdyke (*per ep.*).
27 Oliver 1970, 48.
28 Wallace 1989, 94–95; Feyel 2009, 181–184.
29 Oliver 1970, 48.
30 Müller 2016, 282–284.

29 BC within the Senate according to the same author (52.42 and 54.13–14)[31]. He even mentions the possibility that this reform took place in the 2nd c. BC, but without formally supporting any of these three hypotheses. The idea that the development of local citizenship was responsible for the change in the conditions of access to the Areopagus seems to lie underneath here. It is therefore interesting to look at the evolution of the local *politeia* by observing first how this criterion, rather than *eugeneia* alone, is considered in the letter itself and then, going back to the Hellenistic period, what are the elements of an evolution of citizenship in Athens until the Empire.

III. The *politeia* question under Marcus Aurelius and backwards

1. The case of Popilius Pius

The first pending point is the place of the local *politeia* in Marcus Aurelius' provisions. In the long paragraph devoted to *trigonia*, there is no mention of Athenian citizenship status. The *politeia* appears in the letter only in connection with the case of Popilius Pius (**l. 30–35**), because his status was contested under circumstances that we know nothing about: it has been suggested that entry to the Panhellenion was at stake, but nowhere does it say so[32]. According to J. Fournier[33], there is no question of an appeal, but simply of an investigation and a decision by the Areopagites. The latter, in fact, by virtue of their ancient role as guardians of the constitution, are also, so to speak, the "guardians of citizenship". The case of Pius was submitted to the Areopagites, at a time when he could no longer prove his citizenship, and he is compared here to those citizens who could keep it although their family grave had been destroyed. This remark again directly reminds of *AP* 55.3 and the question asked to the future archon as to whether he has ἠρία[34], the old Homeric term for the ancestors' tombs, and where they are located. This is also the term used in Demosthenes' speech *Against Euboulidēs* (57.67) by the litigant Euxitheos to prove his citizenship through the existence of ancestral graves[35]. Marcus Aurelius finally asks, in a perfectly Classical style that could apply to the Athenian 4th c. BC, that *nomoi* and *patria* be respected for the *dokimasia* of new citizens: δοκιμασθήσεται εἴ τις ἐκ γένους [Ἀθηναῖ]ός ἐστιν (**l. 34–35**), *genos* here having the meaning of "birth". These "ancestral laws and customs" can only refer, in my view, to the provisions prevailing in the Classical period and especially Aristotle's time again, given what we have observed before about archons. The emperor confirms, following the Areopagites, the maintaining of Popilius Pius in

---

31 Oliver 1970, 48.

32 Oliver 1989 (*GC*), 383.

33 Fournier 2010, 155.

34 *AP*, 55, 3.

35 The witnesses include οἷς ἠρία ταὐτά, "those who have the right to the same places of burial". See also Din., *Aristog.* 17.

Athenian citizenship. This gesture appears as a return to the stability of status, βεβαιότης [τῆς στά]σεως, which is claimed by the emperor in a quite remarkable phrase, which to my knowledge knows no parallel, but for which I can hardly see how else one can fill the lacuna: here, stability has priority over material proof as reminded by Wankerl[36]. Whatever Pius' actual situation was, this call to order by the emperor is essential for two reasons: it shows that there could have been frauds in access to citizenship, which is no surprise if one remembers the problems raised by the recruitment of Areopagites; it also shows that the Athenian *politeia* still played (or again?) an essential role in its traditional configuration, which was not necessarily expected after the evolution of the Hellenistic period. In what purpose? We don't know, but it did matter a lot.

2. Access to the Athenian *politeia* in the Hellenistic period

There were of course still a large number of "native citizens" under the Empire, able to prove their legitimate descent for participation in political affairs. But there had been some developments during the Hellenistic period. Firstly, it has been noted that, from 229 BC, the granting of *politeia* concerned simply the *honorandus* himself and not his offspring[37]. It was rightly concluded that this procedure was no longer necessary because the sons acquired it automatically even with a foreign mother. Also, the count of intermarriages established by Maria Niku and Graham J. Oliver[38] from funerary stelae seems to prove not only that the prohibition of such marriages no longer took place, but also that the Periclean rule of admission to citizenship must have fallen into disuse. The number of mixed marriages increased from the 2nd c. BC onwards and especially from the 120's, maybe partly due to the possibilities of *epigamia* (right of intermarriage) offered between cities. It was thus possible to become a *politēs* even though only one's father was himself an Athenian citizen. We find ourselves here in exactly the same situation as in Rome, where Roman citizens could marry peregrines and have Roman citizen children, as long as the wife enjoyed *conubium*. Those recent Athenians who owed their citizenship to this type of provision, while they could justify their ancestry on the male side, could not on the female side, but it didn't matter anymore. One could also be granted Athenian citizenship, the granting of which was still parsimonious and not at all devalued. It is still well attested at the time of Cicero, as shown by the case of his friend Atticus who had earned it through his merit, although he had to refuse it[39].

[36] Wankerl 2009, 44.

[37] Osborne 1981–1983, IV, 152–153.

[38] Niku 2007, 18–19; Oliver 2010, 156–159 and 162–163.

[39] Nep., *Att.* 3, 1–2: *Hic autem sic se gerebat, ut communis infimis, par principibus videretur. Quo factum est ut huic omnes honores, quos possent, publice haberent civemque facere studerent; quo beneficio ille uti noluit quod nonnulli ita interpretantur, eum civitatem Romanam amittere noluisse*, "and he behaved in a way to appear without height with the humble ones and without baseness with the elite. Also, one bestowed on him all the

3. Foreigners in local institutions

In short, the means of access to the *politeia* were undoubtedly more varied than in the Classical period, which explains why there were "foreigners" in local institutions. The presence of many *xenoi* among Athenian ephebes, though, must be disconnected from the subsequent acquisition of the *politeia*: on this point, J.H. Oliver's 1970 commentary is no longer valid, as shown by Eric Perrin-Saminadayar[40]. On the other hand, we will agree with the former that the presence of prominent foreigners among the archons might show a different access to the archonship: to take several examples at the beginning of the Principate, one can mention the Spartan C. Julius Lakōn *ca* AD 4/5 AD, the Thracian Kotys between AD 14 and 19, another Thracian king Rhoimetalkes III in AD 37/8, the Roman G. Carrinas Secundus (*major*) in AD 39/40 or Mithridates VIII king of the Bosporus before AD 45[41].

These cases lead to two questions concerning the recruitment of archons at the time: first, that of the abandonment of the drawing of lots; second, that of the necessity (or not) of being an Athenian citizen for the exercise of the archonship. On the first point, the rule of drawing lots, which had prevailed for the archonship between 487/6 and the time of Sylla, seems to have been abolished with this office becoming elective again, as Daniel J. Geagan has shown[42], probably in connection with the financial necessities linked to it. The archonship had always involved significant personal expenditure, an aristocratic or more broadly plutocratic social dimension. Even during the period when its members were chosen by lot, the archons had to ensure important personal expenses. But more than ever during the imperial period, access to the archonship depended on individual or family wealth, as shown by the predominance of a few large families and the expenses incurred by some archons who took office and proceeded to distributions: one thinks for instance of Tiberius Claudius Hierophantēs who, at the beginning of the 2nd c. AD, offered a *medimnos* of grain and 15 drachmas to each of his fellow citizens. The sources do not explicitly mention any census criteria, but the kind of expenditure just mentioned reminds *ob honorem* type payments, in the absence of a formal *summa honoraria* as such[43]. The second point, that of local *politeia*, is highly debated: it must be assumed that (at least part of) the foreigners previously mentioned did not accede, at least for the end of the Republic, to the archonship and

possible public honours and one wanted to make him citizen of Athens. But he refused this privilege, what some explain by saying that he did not want to give up the title of Roman citizen". Atticus had, indeed, to give up the Athenian *politeia*, because of the impossibility in Rome of the double citizenship, principle which knew a relaxation only in the years 40–30 BC: see Ferrary 2005, 68–70 and n. 57 and Müller 2016, 283.

40 Perrin-Saminadayar 2007, 470–475; Oliver 2010, 156.

41 See the list of archons established, for Augustan and Julio-Claudian Athens, by Schmalz 2008, 319–325.

42 Geagan 1967, 17.

43 Fournier 2010, 141.

Areopagus without having obtained Athenian citizenship. This is evidenced by a famous passage in Cicero's *Pro Balbo* (30) in 56 BC[44], where the author recalls the incompatibility (in his time) of Roman and local citizenship, underlining the errors committed by some of his fellow-citizens who shamelessly sat in the Areopagus, among others, "in a regular tribe" (*certa tribu*), in other words after registration of their Athenian citizen-status.

Then comes the case of the Areopagus in imperial times. We have seen already that probably some people in this Council might have sat there without freeborn parents or grandparents, in a way that escapes us. That would be the reason for the big cleansing of the Council. Under the empire, *adlectio* was a specific way to be admitted without necessarily having been an archon beforehand. The letter of Marcus Aurelius (**l. 28**) bears witness to this procedure through the verb προσγραφῆναι, also used elsewhere in the letter about the appeal of a certain Nostimos (**l. 28**): in this case, as Fournier has suggested[45], it was no doubt necessary to pay a sum of money "analogous to the *summa honoraria* paid by the *adlecti* of the local *curia*". James H. Oliver himself distinguishes between the people he perceives as real members (the ancient archons) and those who are simply honorary members[46]. The phrase "honorary membership" has been used because of several later honorific inscriptions in which the status of Areopagite appears as a title, in the same way as that of *euergetes* for example (*IG* II^2 13263 and *IG* II^2 13264[47]). The Areopagus, which probably had about a hundred members, was not a local though prestigious equivalent of the Roman Senate, but presented yet all the characteristics of an *ordo*, as Geagan has pointed out[48]. In short, "the post-Syllanian and imperial Areopagus appears to be an elite body, plutocratic if not always aristocratic, where the representatives of the most influential and ancient

---

44 Cic., *Balb.* 30: *itaque in Graecis civitatibus videmus Atheniensis, Rhodios, Lacedaemonios, ceteros undique adscribi multarumque esse eosdem homines civitatum. Quo errore ductos vidi egomet non nullos imperitos homines, nostros cives, Athenis in numero iudicum atque Areopagitarum, certa tribu, certo numero, cum ignorarent, si illam civitatem essent adepti, hanc se perdidisse, nisi postliminio reciperassent. Peritus vero nostri moris ac iuris nemo umquam, qui hanc civitatem retinere vellet, in aliam se civitatem dicavit*, "Thus we see that citizens in Athens, Rhodes, Sparta, and of other cities far and wide, are enrolled, and that the same persons are citizens of many cities. And I myself have seen certain ignorant men, citizens of ours, misled by this, sitting at Athens amongst jurymen and members of the Areopagus, in a definite tribe, under a definite number, since they did not know that if they had acquired citizenship there, they had forfeited it here, unless they should recover it 'by right of subsequent return' (*postliminium*). But no one who understands our custom and our law has ever, if he wished to retain the citizenship of Rome, formally attached himself to another city" (text and transl. modified R. Gardner, The Loeb Classical Library, London, 1958).

45 Fournier 2010, 142, n. 784.

46 Oliver 1970, 56.

47 Honorific inscriptions for the proconsul Claudius Illyrius, AD 270–290.

48 Geagan 1974.

Athenian families rubbed shoulders with citizens of recent date, but with significant wealth"[49]. This sentence implies for Fournier that all members were also *politai*, which is not obvious at all for Marcus Aurelius time. Can one, indeed, totally exclude that some foreigners could, at this date, have sat in the Council without going through the local *politeia*, simply because of the prestige of their name or their wealth? Probably not. The citizenship criterion, let alone that of civic descent by going back to the grandfather, had probably disappeared as a formal requirement for the Areopagus, as the emperor would not have failed to state it if this condition had to be respected: that also could be a reason why the emperor focuses on *eleutheria* rather than *politeia.*

4. The role of mothers and women in *politeia* and *eugeneia*

First point: the role of the mother in both systems. This position was first contested in relation to Marcus Aurelius' text by James H. Oliver, since he saw in the *goneis* of l. 66 "the father and the grandfather" and not the parents, in the sense of "the father and the mother". Other commentators, including Follet, have corrected the mistake and restored the presence of the mother here. Other elements can be added to their arguments. As already said, the expression ἐξ ἀμφοῖν τῶν γονέων is directly imitated from Aristotle's passage in the *AP* on the reform of Perikles (26.3): there it is stipulated that nobody would be a citizen ὃς ἂν μὴ ἐξ ἀμφοῖν ἀστοῖν ᾖ γεγονώς, "one who is not born of two *astoi*"[50]. The dual ἀμφοῖν can be applied only to a couple and the notion of *trigonia* cannot be expressed in Greek through number two. The argument that made the mother disappear had served James H. Oliver[51] — at first, for he later changed his point of view— to consider that the mention of the παλαιὸν ἔθος could signify a desire to return to the Athens of Solon, or at any rate before Cleisthenes, where an Alcmaeonides like him could perfectly well have been the son of a well-born woman from another city, in this case Agaristē of Sicyon[52]. Indeed, *eugeneia* then lay in something other than pure, native ancestry. In fact, the role of the mother, explicitly stated in the letter, implies, it seems to me, that the reference to ancient custom definitely points back to the Classical period and in particular to the reading of the *AP*. In both cases, however, the importance of women stops at the generation of the parents as there is no mention of the grandmother(s) as there is of the grandfather(s): the paternal grandfather in Marcus

---

[49] Fournier 2010, 142.

[50] Arist., *AP* 26.3: καὶ τρίτῳ μετὰ τοῦτον ἐπὶ Ἀντιδότου διὰ τὸ πλῆθος τῶν πολιτῶν Περικλέους εἰπόντος ἔγνωσαν μὴ μετέχειν τῆς πόλεως, ὃς ἂν μὴ ἐξ ἀμφοῖν ἀστοῖν ᾖ γεγονώς, "And in the third year after this, when Antidotos was archon, they decided owing to the large number of citizens on the proposal of Pericles that no one who was not born from both *astos* parents would participate (*metechein*) in the *polis*." (text H. Rackham, The Loeb Classical Library, London, 1935; tr. Blok 2017, 1, n. 2).

[51] Oliver 1970, 20–21.

[52] Oliver 1970, 57.

Aurelius' *trigonia*, both paternal and maternal grandfathers in Aristotle's definition of the archons.

5. Displacement of the *trigonia* and evolution of the *politeia*

How can we conclude on the shift from one *trigonia* to another, in connection with the evolution of the *politeia*? One can, indeed, wonder if the opening of the *politeia* did not lead to value other criteria than citizenship for being a member of the Areopagus. But the question has no simple answer. There was certainly a more pronounced opening of the citizenship towards foreigners from the 2nd c. BC, with a relaxation of the "dual descent" criterion and an acceptance of *metroxenia*. For the imperial period, and in our case in the 2nd c. AD, it remains to understand which were the exact ways, at this time, to become a citizen, apart from strict filiation, consequence of *epigamia* and the granting by the city. The insistence of Marcus Aurelius who pleads, in connection with Pius, for a return to an examination of the potential citizen according to the ancestral methods (l. 33–35) suggests that the access to the *politeia* was far from conforming to the old requirements. A highly plausible hypothesis is that one must have been able to pay for *politeia*. But, and this is pretty complex here, these circumstances did not devalue citizenship neither at the time of Cicero, nor even in the 2nd c. AD: the case of Pius makes us understand it was still essential in some circumstances.

There is thus a dissociation, at least in Athens, between institutions accessible through the quality of local *politēs*, such as the Panhellenion, and those like the Areopagus, where entry was made at that time on other criteria, including that of *eugeneia*/*ingenuitas* over two or three generations. There is therefore no obvious link between the opening of the *politeia* at a local level and the shift of *trigonia* towards the criterion of free birth at the expense of citizen-descent. It seems more a question of an interference between Greek and Roman institutions. In terms of chronology, this shift was certainly later than the late Hellenistic period and even than Augustus' time, as there is no reason to attribute it with certainty to the first Princeps. I would suggest it might have been an invention of Marcus Aurelius.

IV. Other cases of Classical and Hellenistic *trigonia*

Let us now return to the uses of *trigonia* between the 4th and 1st c. BC.

1. 4th c. Athens

The term is already found in Demosthenes in the speech *Against Theocrines* (17): the debtor, whose debt goes back to the time of his grandfather, is accused of being a πονηρὸς ἐκ τριγονίας, "a scoundrel of the third generation"! Similarly, in Hyperides' *Against Athēnogenēs* (19), the plaintiff attacks the eponymous character of the speech, who is an Egyptian residing in Athens and ἐκ τριγονίας ὢν μυροπώλης, a man with "two generations of perfume sellers behind him", with another case of debts at stake. These expressions show that the term was perfectly accepted and understood, and we might have expected to see it used in Aristotle's *AP* or *Politics*. It is however found, as we have seen, in Pollux (*Onomast.* 8, 85–87), when he glosses the controversial passage of the *AP* on the ancestors of the archons.

2. Massalia in Strabo

We come back to Aristotle again by reading Strabo and his description of the pyramidal system of government in Massalia. As Strabo explains (4.1.5)[53], there is a *synedrion* of 600 *timouchoi*, meaning the ones "holding the *timē/timai*"; "no one can become a *timouchos* who has not children, and who has not been a citizen for three generations", τιμοῦχος δ' οὐ γίνεται μὴ τέκνα ἔχων μηδὲ διὰ τριγονίας ἐκ πολιτῶν γεγονώς (4.1.5). The situation is given by the geographer in the present tense as being that of his time, which must have been so. But this sentence seems to refer to some works of Aristotle, since there is an allusion in the *Politics* (1321a), where the Stagirite explains that ἐν Μασσαλίᾳ κρίσιν ποιουμένους τῶν ἀξίων ἐν τῷ πολιτεύματι καὶ τῶν ἔξωθεν, "one operates a division in the citizen body between the ones who deserve it and those outside it". This group of 600 certainly, in reality, formed the *politeuma* of the city, in other words its civic body and not a simple Council[54]. An interesting remark concerns the nature of the regime thus described: πάντων εὐνομώτατα, "the best ordered" of aristocratic constitutions, which corresponds perfectly to the idea of a regime based on three generations of well-born people. The perspective of Marcus Aurelius in AD 174/5, for whom the Areopagus implicitly constitutes the aristocratic element of government in Athens, is exactly the same.

3. Halicarnassus and Cos' priesthoods

Going down into the Hellenistic period, the provision of *trigonia* appears through "the thing without the word" about priesthoods. Thus, in Asia Minor, the city of Halicarnassus has provided the most spectacular testimony that can exist, concerning the sale of the priesthood of Artemis Pergaia between 250 and 200 BC (*CGRN* 118[55]). The priestess had to be an *astē*, thus a "local citizen", herself ἐξ ἀστῶν ἀμφοτέρων ἐπὶ | [τρε]ῖς γενεὰς γεγενημένην καὶ πρὸς πατρὸς καὶ πρὸς | [μη]τρός, "a descendant of *astoi* over three generations on both her paternal and maternal sides". This particular requirement, according to the commentators of the *CGRN*, "may perhaps be attributed to the *prytaneis* and their oversight over this matter: the integration of the new cult into the city and community of Halicarnassus is to be ensured by a woman who is a true Halicarnassian"[56]. But it seems to have been the standard provision in this city for any priesthood, as evidenced by the

---

53 Strab. 4.1.5.

54 As convincingly shown by Giangiulio 2018, 287–288.

55 Halicarnassus, decree containing the contract of sale for the priesthood of Artemis Pergaia, *CGRN* 118 (= *LSAM* 73, 250–200 BC), http://cgrn.ulg.ac.be/file/118/, l. 4–8.

56 *CGRN* 118: http://cgrn.ulg.ac.be/file/118/.

recent publication of the sale of a priesthood of Nikē also from the 3rd c. BC (2nd quarter?), under the same conditions (*SEG* 64, 911[57]).

In other cases of priesthood sales, which are numerous on the island of Cos for instance, it is a standard requirement that the priest or priestess be *holoklaros* or *holoklara*, "intact", which in my view could refer not to physical integrity, but to statutory "completeness". One may hesitate, however, because the adjective is usually accompanied by two other indispensable qualifications, which relate to the body: the incumbent must be "healthy", *hygiēs*, and, in the case of the priestess of Aphrodite Pandamos at the beginning of the 2nd c. BC (after 198), "adult": ἁ πριαμένα ἔστω ὑγιὴς καὶ ὁλόκλαρος καὶ τελέα (*IG* XII, 4, 302, l. 6–7). If *holoklaros* refers to statutory integrity, the adjective can be understood as *gnēsios*, which implies a legitimate birth, in other words generally a dual civic descent with a legitimate marriage between the parents.

4. Cos' lists of cult membership

In Cos again, but for another matter, some lists of citizens display names that may be intriguing. One thinks in particular of a decree of the tribes in the Halasarna deme taken around 180 BC, which organises the registration of the participants in the cult of the patron deities Apollo and Herakles (*IG* XII, 4, 103–104)[58]. The precise instructions it provides on the procedure are very instructive and distinguishes three categories of citizens: residents, absentees and, finally, naturalized citizens. Because they live abroad or temporarily reside outside the city, the absentees, *apodamoi*, must be declared by their representative on the spot or provide their full identity by themselves on their return: they then give their name, their patronymic, the name of their tribe, the name of their mother and the name of the citizen from whom she was born. In the list of names that follows, a certain "Agepolis son of Aristaichmos and whose mother is Halias daughter of Agepolis" is for instance recorded[59].

How can one explain such a denomination in Cos? The first explanation might be the desire to avoid ambiguities due to potential homonyms. But it does not account for the absence of the paternal grandfather. A second explanation could be whether the need to provide the identity of the maternal grandfather should not be

57 The *SEG* reproduces the (good) edition by Parker and Thonemann 2015, with l. 5–8: [ὁ] | πριάμενος τὴν ἱερητείαν τ̣[ῆς Νί]κ̣η[ς ἔσ]|τω μὲν ἀστὸς ἐξ ἀστῶν ἐπὶ [τρεῖς γενεὰς] | γεγενημένος, "the purchaser of the priesthood of Nikē will be a citizen descendant of citizens for three generations" (the *trigonia* principle is restored here on safe bases).

58 *IG* XII, 4, 103, l. 29–37: ἀπογραφέσθων αὐ|τοὶ ἐπεί κα παραγένη|ται ἐν τριμήνωι τὸ ὄνο|μα πατριαστὶ ποτὶ τὸς | ναποίας, ἐξαγευμέ|νος καὶ τὰν φυλὰν καὶ | τᾶς ματρὸς τὸ ὄνομα | καὶ τίνος τ̣ῶν πολιτᾶν | θυγάτηρ ὑ̣πάρχει, "they will have to register themselves when they get home within three months, presenting their name with their patronymic before the *napoiai*, producing also their tribe, the name of their mother, and that of the citizen whose daughter she is".

59 *IG* XII, 4, 104, l. 34–37: Ἀγέπολις Ἀρι|σταίχμου ματρὸς δὲ Ἁ̣|λιάδος τᾶς Ἀγεπόλι|ος.

seen as actually more drastic conditions for the recognition of citizenship than elsewhere[60]. Yet, the asymmetry between the father and the mother remains difficult to understand, since the name of the paternal grandfather does not seem to be necessary. One should in this case assume that there were more irregularities on the maternal than on the paternal side in Cos, with the need for greater control. On the contrary, in the Imperial period, there are many cases where the sole name of the paternal grandfather is mentioned after that of the father, as for example in Delphi for "Lamenēs, son of Lamenēs, grandson of Lamenēs" in an act of enfranchisement[61]. But, rather than the legal provision, the prestige of the family's seniority plays here a fundamental role. Unsurprisingly, the purpose of naming is always an essential parameter in the evaluation of onomastic formulas.

The third, and most plausible explanation, is that a woman could only establish her citizenship by giving her own father's name, no more and no less than in Athens, where an *astē* of legitimate birth was also and primarily a "daughter of". Even if, in the Athenian material, the immense majority of the onomastic formulas rested on the couple "personal name-patronymic", we know that, in one of the phratries, it was necessary for the phratriarch to have engraved, so that all would know the future members, τὸ ὄνομα πατρόθεγ καὶ τοῦ δήμου καὶ τῆ|ς μητρὸς πατρόθεν καὶ τοῦ δήμου, "their name with their patronymic and their demotic, and their mother's name with her patronymic and her father's demotic", though probably only for temporary exhibition (*IG* II^2, 1237, l. 119–120[62]). The two cases would then amount to the same thing, so to speak, and all systems in which a citizen is said to be a "son of a citizen and of a daughter of a citizen" would introduce a form of asymmetrical *trigonia*, which is the equivalent of the "dual descent" in the form ἐξ ἀμφοῖν ἀστοῖν.

In this case, what should be avoided in Cos (as elsewhere)? First and foremost, as Julie Vélissaropoulos has pointed out[63], children born to foreign mothers, *metroxenoi*, outside the legal framework of *epigamia*, the right of intermarriage. This hypothesis is strengthened by the fact that, in the same Coan inscription, naturalized citizens also are obliged to give the name of their maternal grandfather. Problems could come, in this case, from wives possibly originating from a third city other than Cos and their husband's city. However, I now wonder, after analysing Marcus Aurelius' letter, whether it is not also a question of avoiding forms of civic infiltration by families formerly of servile status, thus with mothers who were themselves freed. This is an interesting hypothesis, but it remains difficult to verify.

---

60 This is the interpretation given by Sherwin-White 1978, 153–154, who considers this to be a genuine case of *trigonia*.

61 *CID* V, 1191, l. 3–5: βουλευόντ[ων δὲ Λαμ]έ|νους τοῦ Λα̣[μένους τοῦ] | Λαμένου[ς] etc. (first quarter of 1st c. AD, D. Mulliez *per ep.*)

62 *IG* II^2, 1237 (396/5 BC). See the excellent commentary by Scafuro 1994, 162 and n. 59. I thank S. Forsdyke for drawing my attention to this document.

63 Vélissaropoulos-Karakostas 2011, 138.

It should be remembered, however, that one of the great problems for the cities was to identify the families of the former *apeleutheroi*, who must have tried to blend in with the rest of the population without being distinguishable except in the immediate aftermath of the emancipation. Athina Dimopoulou-Piliouni has remarkably shown that, like the *nothoi*, they belonged to a statutory "grey zone", "between metics and foreigners" and this, "both in Athens and other cities"[64]. Their main characteristic was "the lack of citizenship" and thus a kind of apolitical status wherever they were, which they had to try to conceal as much as possible by settling, for example, elsewhere than in their place of origin. Their only means of becoming proper *politai* was if they were granted *politeia*, as the former Athenian slave-banker Pasiōn had been granted, a rare occurrence.

In any case, civic descent was still important on the island of Cos in the early Empire, albeit with developments: probably in AD 21, a religious regulation of the deme of Halasarna (*IG* XII, 4, 365) asks for the erasure of the inscriptions engraved without authorisation in order to reinstall a new stele with the exact list of the holders of the priesthood of Apollo in chronological display from 27 BC, with the obligation to name them πατριαστεί, "by the name of the father", this time without the name of the mother.

Conclusion

In its legal uses, *trigonia* is based either on citizenship (*politeia*) or freedom at birth (*eugeneia*). In both cases, the aim is to ensure that the grandparents' generation (the third generation in the Greek count) is explicitly involved in a given recognition process. This norm, relatively little explored by historians, knows an unexpected resurgence in the letter addressed by Marcus Aurelius in AD 174/5 to the Athenians and intended, *inter alia*, to specify the rules of access to the Areopagus. These rules are relaxed here after nearly ten years of unsuccessful practice of the trigenerational system, where potential candidates had to be able to establish their *eugeneia* from their paternal grandfather's generation included. The implementation of *trigonia* represents a reinterpretation and a shift of an ancient rule applied by the Athenians of the classical period when recruiting archons, who had to be able to prove their *politeia* over three generations as well, as explained by Aristotle and Pollux, whom we follow here. But the *trigonia* exists in different versions. It can be perfectly symmetrical (the two grandfathers being concerned, as in the case of classical archons) or asymmetrical (the sole maternal or paternal grandfather being concerned). In the case of asymmetrical *trigonia*, if the maternal grandfather is mentioned alone, as in Cos or Athens in some contexts, the system implies only dual descent "ἐξ ἀμφοῖν parents", for women existed in legal terms primarily through their father. But, when the sole paternal grandfather is mentioned as in

64 Dimopoulou-Piliouni 2008, 50.

Marcus Aurelius' letter, then the necessity of a three-generation descent weighs much more heavily.

This norm forms what can be called a horizon of expectation, which must be interpreted as a desire of purifying the social body in some of its organs, insofar as it is always used in a negative way in order to eliminate all kinds of unwelcome people, never native enough or, as here, never free enough. But, like any legal provision of this kind, it is contradicted by practices where the categories fixed by the law turn out to be more permeable than expected. This is generally due in ancient times, and it's the case here, to historical circumstances leading to a lack of capable citizens, i.e. oliganthropy, the terror of Greeks as Romans, which forces them to open the floodgates of admission and therefore change the rules.

To conclude this presentation with a hint of provocation, I would like to quote, again, Aristotle this time in the *Politics* (1275b[65]), who casts doubts on descent rules in Greek cities, especially the *trigonia*, and confirms doing so the implementation of the latter in Greek cities. In this magnificent passage, he questions the possibility of imposing such a rule of origin for certain totally incongruous cases and wonders how far up one can go: "In practice citizenship is limited to the child of citizens on both sides (…); but, other people carry this requirement further back, for example to the second or the third preceding generation or further. But given this is a practical and hasty definition, some people raise the difficulty: how will that ancestor three or four generations back have been a citizen?", especially among the founders of cities. This is an excellent question

[65] Arist., *Pol.* 1275b : ὁρίζονται δὲ πρὸς τὴν χρῆσιν πολίτην τὸν ἐξ ἀμφοτέρων πολιτῶν καὶ μὴ θατέρου μόνον, οἷον πατρὸς ἢ μητρός, οἱ δὲ καὶ τοῦτ᾽ ἐπὶ πλέον ζητοῦσιν, οἷον ἐπὶ πάππους δύο ἢ τρεῖς ἢ πλείους. [25] οὕτω δὲ ὁριζομένων πολιτικῶς καὶ ταχέως, ἀποροῦσί τινες τὸν τρίτον ἐκεῖνον ἢ τέταρτον, πῶς ἔσται πολίτης. Γοργίας μὲν οὖν ὁ Λεοντῖνος, τὰ μὲν ἴσως ἀπορῶν τὰ δ᾽ εἰρωνευόμενος, ἔφη, καθάπερ ὅλμους εἶναι τοὺς ὑπὸ τῶν ὁλμοποιῶν πεποιημένους, οὕτω καὶ Λαρισαίους τοὺς ὑπὸ τῶν δημιουργῶν πεποιημένους: [30] εἶναι γάρ τινας λαρισοποιούς. ἔστι δ᾽ ἁπλοῦν. εἰ γὰρ μετεῖχον κατὰ τὸν ῥηθέντα διορισμὸν τῆς πολιτείας, ἦσαν πολῖται: καὶ γὰρ οὐδὲ δυνατὸν ἐφαρμόττειν τὸ ἐκ πολίτου ἢ ἐκ πολίτιδος ἐπὶ τῶν πρώτων οἰκησάντων ἢ κτισάντων, "In practice citizenship is limited to the child of citizens on both sides, not on one side only, that is, the child of a citizen father or of a citizen mother; but, other people carry this requirement further back, for example to the second or the third preceding generation or further. But given this is a practical and hasty definition, some people raise the difficulty: How will that ancestor three or four generations back have been a citizen? Gorgias of Leontini therefore, partly perhaps in genuine perplexity but partly in jest, said that just as the vessels made by mortar-makers were mortars, so the citizens made by the magistrates were Larisaeans, since some of the magistrates were actually Larisa-makers. But it is really a simple matter; for if they were partaking in citizenship in the manner stated in our definition of a citizen, they were citizens—since it is clearly impossible to apply the qualification of descent from a citizen father or mother to the original colonizers or founders of a city" (text J. Aubonnet, CUF, Paris; tr. modified from H. Rackham, The Loeb Classical Library, London, 1932). See Blok 2017, 16.

that pushes reasoning to the point of absurdity and, *mutatis mutandis*, also concerns contemporary societies: what proof of identity can we ask of an individual before granting him a place in the city?

christel.muller@parisnanterre.fr

ANNEX

Letter of Marcus Aurelius to the Athenians, 174/5 AD.
SEG 29, 127: the text used here is the one given by Follet 1979 after corrections, apart from specific indications referring to the text finally given by J.H. Oliver in the collection of the *Greek Constitutions* (*GC*). Oliver's translation has been faithfully respected here, which may therefore differ from that used in the article.

§7. On Popilius Pius

Ποπίλι[ος Πεῖος ἐπὶ]
τ̣ῶι δικαίωι τῆς πολειτείας τῆς Ἀθηναίων μενεῖ, καθὰ ἐπέγνωσαν οἱ Ἀρεοπαγεῖται· χ̣ρ̣ὴ [γὰρ τῆς στά]-
σεω̣ς̣ α̣ὐ̣τ̣ῶ̣ι̣ τὴν βεβαιότητα ὑπάρχειν καὶ τοῖς ἄλλοις ὅσοι, τῆι δοθείσηι ἐξο̣υσίαι ὑποφθ̣ο̣[ρὰν παθόν]-
τι τ̣άφου ἐπακολουθοῦντες, τοῖς Ἀρεοπαγείταις τὰ ἑ̣αυτῶν δίκαια παρέσχοντο· εἰς δ̣ὲ̣ τὸ μέλλο[ν κατὰ]
34 τοὺς νόμους καὶ κατὰ τὰ πάτρια ἔθη παραφυλαχθήσεται καὶ δοκιμασθήσεται εἴ τις ἐκ γένους [Ἀθηναῖ]-
ός ἐστιν.

"Popilius Pius shall remain [in possession] of the right to Athenian citizenship as the Areopagites ruled. [For] it is necessary that there be security [of sta]tus for him and for all the others who, pursuing the option granted to [one who suffers] ruin of a burial site, presented their claims to the Areopagites. For the future, a close watch and a test according to both the laws and ancestral custom shall be made as to whether one is eligible by birth".

L. 32/33, I admit J.H. Oliver's correction rather than Follet 1979: ὑπὸ φθ̣ο̣[ρᾶς τινος ἀν]|τιγρ̣άφου.

§10.

Ὅσην εἰσφέρομαι σπουδὴν ὑπὲρ τῆς δόξης τῶν Ἀθηνῶν, ὡς τῆς παλαιᾶς αὐτὴ[ν ἐ]-

58 πικρατεῖν σεμνό̣τητος, ἱκανῶς δεδηλωκέναι νομίζω, καὶ ἡνίκα τὸ παρ' αὐτοῖς ἔκκριτον συνέδριο̣[ν]

ἐπαναγαγεῖν ἐπειράθην πρὸς τὸ παλαιὸν ἔθος, καθ' ὅ τούτους μόνους εἰς Ἄρειον πάγον εἰσεδέχον[το]

τοὺς ἀπὸ τῆς **τριγονίας** ἐξετασθέντας· καὶ εἴθε ἦν περιουσία τῶν ἐνδόξων γενῶν, ἵν' ἐξῆι μο̣ι κα̣[ὶ νῦν]

ἔτι τὴν γνώμην τὴν ἡμετέραν φυλάξαι, ἀλλ' ἐπειδὴ τὰ συμβάντα διὰ τὴν τύχην ὑπολογιζομένου̣[ς, ἐ]-

62 φ' οἷς πολλ̣ὰς καὶ ἄλλας πόλεις οἶδα θεραπείας εἰς τὰ μάλιστα ἐπιδικασαμένας, τὰ μὲν ἐπανειέναι δε̣ῖ [τῆι]

πρὸς τὸ παρεληλυθὸς φιλανθρωπίαι, τὰ δὲ τῆ̣ι πρὸς τὸ μέλλον αὐτάρκως ἱδρῦσαι, μέχρι τοσούτου συν[θέ]-

μενος Ἀθηναίοις ἐνδώσω ὡς ἐπὶ μὲν τοῦ παρεληλυθότος χρόνου πρὸς τοῦτο μόνον ἀφορᾶν ε̣ἴ τ[ινι πα]-

τὴρ εὐγενής, κἄν τις τῶν ἐξ Ἀρείου πάγου διὰ τὸν κανόνα τῆς **τριγονίας** ἐξεῶσθαι φαίνηται τὸ ἀξίωμα ἀ[να]-

66 κομιεῖται, μετὰ ταῦτα δὲ τὸ ἐξ ἀμφοῖν τῶν γονέων εἶναί τινα εὖ γεγονότων ἀρκέσει. Τοῖς μετὰ τὴν ἐπ[ιστο]-

λ̣ὴ̣ν̣ τὴν ἡμετέραν ἀπελευθέρου πατρὸς οὖσιν καὶ εἰς Ἄρειον πάγον ἑαυτοὺς ἐνβεβληκόσιν τῆς ἀγν[οίας]

ὥρα πεπ̣α̣ῦ̣σ̣θαι· εἰ μέντοι τις πρὸ τῆς ἐπιστολῆς ἀπελευθέρου πατρὸς γεγονὼς ὑπ' οὐδενὸς δικαστηρ[ίου]

τῶν ἐπὶ τούτο[ι]ς ἀποδ̣οθῆναι δυναμένων ἐξεώσθη, μενεῖ. Ὅσοι μετὰ τὰ ἡμέτερα γράμματα διὰ τὸ τὸν [πάπ]-

70 πον ἀπηλευθερῶσθαι ἢ ὑπεξήχθησαν τῆς ἐν Ἀρείωι πάγωι βουλῆς ἢ ἑκόντες ὑπεξῆλθον τὴν τιμήν, ἔ[τι]

ἀ̣π̣ε̣ί̣ρ̣γο̣ν̣ται· τούς γε μὴν ὑπεξστησομένους διὰ τὰ προειρημένα ἐκ τοῦ συνεδρίου χρὴ μηδὲν ἐκ τοῦ τοι[ού]-

του π[α]ραλυπεῖσθαι πρὸς τὸ τὰς ἄλλας τιμὰς καὶ τάξεις μετιέναι. Εἴ τινες εἶεν ὑπεναντίον τοῖς ὑφ' ἡμῶν ἐ[πε]-

σταλμένοις κατειλεγμένοι, οἷς οὐδὲ μετὰ τὴν νῦν ἐξενεχθεῖσαν γνῶσιν οἷόν τὲ ἐστιν ἐν Ἀρείωι π[άγωι]

74 καθῆσθαι, ἀπαλλαττέσθωσαν ἐντὸς ἐνιαυτοῦ· ὃς δ' ἂν καὶ μετὰ τὰ ἀπηγορευμένα διατελέσηι μένω̣[ν ἢ καὶ]

παρὰ τὰ προγεγραμμένα εἰσδύηται, ἐν ἴσωι ταχθήσεται τοῖς ὑπεξαχθεῖσιν διὰ τοῦ δικαστηρίου ἐλάττοσι̣[ν τε]

ἐκ τούτου καὶ ἐν τῶι μετιέναι τὰς καταδεεστέρας τάξεις κ[α]ὶ τιμάς. // Ἐάν τινες ἐξ Ἀρεοπαγειτῶν ἐν τοῖς [Πανέλ]-

λησιν ὄντες τήμερον καταλημφθῶσιν τὴν **τριγονίαν** παρασχεῖν μὴ δυνάμενοι, οὐ διὰ τοῦτο ἀπ[εω]-
78 σθήσονται τοῦ συνεδρίου· πρὸς δὲ τὸ μέλλον οὐδεὶς ἄλλος ἐξ Ἀρεοπαγειτῶν τοῖς Πανέλλησιν ἐνγρα̣[φή]-
σεται ἢ ὅσοι πρὸς τὰς χειροτονίας ἀφικνεῖσθαι δύνανται τὴν **τριγονίαν** ἔχοντες. // Τὸ πρὸς τὴν βου[λὴν]
τῶν Πεντακοσίων φέρον [ἀ]ποχρώντως ἔχει ταύτηι τετάχθαι ὥστε αὐτοὺς τοὺς καταλεγομένους ε[ὖ γε]-
γονένα̣ι.

"[*Regulations for eligibility to the Areopagus (l. 57–76)*]
How much concern I have for the glory of Athens, that she continue to preserve her ancient dignity, had, I think, been sufficiently shown, especially when I tried to lead their select *synedrion* back to the ancient custom whereby they received into the Areopagus only those who had passed the test of three generations (*trigonia*). And would there were an abundance of the notable families, so that it might be possible for me even [now] to stand by our decision. But since, counting the disasters which have befallen them through the intervention of chance, because of which many other cities have, I know, made special claims for relief, they have partly to retreat in kindness toward the past and to make in other respects a viable settlement for the future, I compromise and grant to the Athenians, that in respect to the past[66] they consider only this, whether a man has a father of good birth, and if anyone appears to have been expelled from the Areopagus on account of the rule concerning three generations (*trigonia*), he shall recover his rank; after this it will suffice for both parents of a man to have been born free. As for those of freedman fathers who have inserted themselves into the Areopagus after our epistle, it is high time for their ignorant disobedience to have been stopped. However, a man who has been born from a freedman father shall remain, if (having entered) before the epistle he was not expelled by any court of those which could be assigned for these cases. All who after our letter because of the grandfather's manumission either were removed from the Council on the Areopagus or willingly renounced this honor are still debarred. However, those who will get out of the *synedrion* on account of the aforesaid rules must not, as a result of such compliance, be made to feel unpleasant side effects in respect to the pursuit of the other honors and posts. If any have been enrolled contrary to the instruction given by us, any for whom even after the ruling now made public it is illegal to sit in the Areopagus, let them withdraw within a year. Whoever continues to remain even after the prohibitions [or indeed] surreptitiously enters in defiance of the published rules shall be placed in the same condition as those expelled through the action of a court and, diminished as a result in status, be ineligible for the minor posts and honors.

[*Regulations for eligibility to the Panhellenion and boulē (l. 76–81)*]
If it is discovered that there are today among the Panhellenes Areopagites who cannot show the three-generation qualification (*trigonia*), they shall not for this reason be expelled from the *synedrion*, but in respect to the future no other

[66] Here Oliver writes: "(family's) past", but this is obviously an erroneous translation. The past is an allusion to the time preceding the first letter.

Areopagite shall be enrolled in the Panhellenes apart from those who can come to the elections in possession of the three-generation qualification (*trigonia*). As for what concerns the Council of the Five-Hundred it suffices that rules have been established for it so that those who each time are enrolled have themselves been [free]born".

BIBLIOGRAPHY

Abbreviations

CGRN: J.-M. Carbon, S. Peels-Matthey, V. Pirenne-Delforge, *Collection of Greek Ritual Norms* 2017-, http://cgrn.ulg.ac.be

GC: *Greek Constitutions of Early Roman Emperors* = Oliver 1989.

LSAM: F. Sokolowski, *Lois sacrées de l'Asie Mineure*, Paris 1955

Blok (2017): J. Blok, *Citizenship in classical Athens*, Cambridge 2017

Canevaro (2010): M. Canevaro, "The Decree Awarding Citizenship to the Plataeans ([Dem.] 59.104)", *GRBS* 50 (2010) 337–369

Dimopoulou-Piliouni (2008): A. Dimopoulou-Piliouni, Apeleutheroi: metics or foreigners?, *Dikē* 11 (2008) 27–50

Duncan-Jones (1996): R. P. Duncan-Jones, "The Impact of the Antonine Plague", *JRA* 9 (1996) 108–36

Ferrary (2005): J.-L. Ferrary, "Les Grecs des cités et l'obtention de la *civitas Romana*", in P. Fröhlich and C. Müller, eds, *Citoyenneté et participation à la basse époque hellénistique*, Geneva 2005, 51–75

Ferrary (2017 [2011]): J.-L. Ferrary, "La géographie de l'hellénisme sous domination romaine", in *Rome et le monde grec: choix d'écrits*, Paris 2017, 497–518

Feyel (2009): C. Feyel, ΔΟΚΙΜΑΣΙΑ. *La place et le rôle de l'examen préliminaire dans les institutions des cités grecques*, Nancy 2009

Follet (1979): S. Follet, "Lettre de Marc-Aurèle aux Athéniens (*EM* 13366): Nouvelles lectures et interprétations", *RPh* 53 (1979) 29–43

Fournier (2010): J. Fournier, *Entre tutelle romaine et autonomie civique. L'administration judiciaire dans les provinces hellénophones de l'empire romain (129 av. J.-C.–235 ap. J.-C.)*, Athens 2010

Geagan (1967): D.J. Geagan, *The Athenian Constitution after Sylla*, Princeton 1967

Geagan (1974): D.J. Geagan, "Ordo Areopagitarum Atheniensium", in D.W. Bradeen and M.F. McGregor eds, ΦΟΡΟΣ. *Tribute to Benjamin Dean Meritt*, New-York 1974, 51–56

Giangiulio (2018): M. Giangiulio, "Oligarchies of 'Fixed Number' or Citizen Bodies in the Making?", in A. Duplouy and R. Brock, eds, *Defining Citizenship in Archaic Greece*, Oxford 2018, 275–293

Harter-Uibopuu (2008): K. Harter-Uibopuu, "Die Anlassverfahren für die Appellationen an Mark Aurel (Athen, *EM* 13366), *ZRG-RA* 125 (2008) 214–250

Jones (1996): C.P. Jones, "The Panhellenion", *Chiron* 26 (1996) 29–56

Kennell (1997): N.M. Kennell, "Herodes Atticus and the Rhetoric of Tyranny", *CPh* 92 (1997) 346–362

Lo Cascio (2012): E. Lo Cascio, ed., *L'impatto della peste antonina*, Bari 2012

Müller (2016): C. Müller, "Le prestige peut-il s'acheter? Réflexions sur la vente de la citoyenneté et des honneurs dans les cités grecques aux époques hellénistique et romaine", in R. Baudry and F. Hurlet, eds, *Le Prestige à Rome à la fin de la République et au début du Principat*, Paris 2016, 281–294

Müller, C. (2023): "The making of the citizen in Hellenistic cities", in J. Filonik, Ch. Plastow and R. Zelnick-Abramovitz, eds., *Citizenship in antiquity: Civic communities in the ancient Mediterranean*, London 2023, 466–481

Niku (2007): M. Niku, *The Official Status of the Foreign Residents in Athens 322–120 B.C.*, Helsinki 2007

Oliver (1970): J.H. Oliver, *Marcus Aurelius. Aspects of Civic and Cultural Policy in the East*, Princeton 1970

Oliver (1983 [1980]): J.H. Oliver, "The actuality of Lucian's Assembly of the Gods", in *The Civic Tradition and Roman Athens*, Baltimore-London, 76–84

Oliver (1989): J.H. Oliver, Greek Constitutions of Early Roman Emperors from Inscriptions and Papyri, Philadelphia 1989

Oliver (2010): G.J. Oliver, "Foreign Names, Inter-Marriage and Citizenship in Hellenistic Athens", in R.W.V. Catling and F. Marchand, eds, Onomatologos: *studies in Greek personal names presented to Elaine Matthews*, Oxford 2010, 158–167

Osborne (1981–1983): *Naturalization in Athens*, 4 vol., Brussels 1981–1983

Parker and Thonemann (2015): R. Parker and P. Thonemann, "A Hellenistic Sale of a Priesthood from Halikarnassos", *ZPE* 194 (2015) 132–134

Perrin-Saminadayar (2007): E. Perrin-Saminadayar, *Éducation, culture et société à Athènes*, Paris 2007

Rhodes (1981): P.J. Rhodes, *A Commentary on the Aristotelian Athenaion Politeia*, Oxford 1981

Scafuro (1994): A.C. Scafuro, "Witnessing and False Witnessing: Proving Citizenship and Kin Identity in Fourth-Century Athens", in A.L. Boegehold and A.C. Scafuro, eds, *Athenian Identity and Civic Ideology*, Baltimore 1994, 156–198

Schmalz (2008): G. Schmalz, *Augustan and Julio-Claudian Athens: A New Epigraphy and Prosopography*, Leiden 2009

Sherwin-White (1978): S. Sherwin-White, *Ancient Cos: an historical study from the Dorian settlement to the imperial period*, Göttingen 1978

Tuci (2007): P.A. Tuci, "*Boulé* e assemblea ateniesi in Polluce, Onomasticon VIII", in C. Bearzot, F. Landucci and G. Zecchini, eds, *L'Onomasticon du Giulio Polluce. Tra lessicografia e antiquaria*, Milan 2007, 69–102

Vélissaropoulos-Karakostas (2011): J. Vélissaropoulos-Karakostas, *Droit grec d'Alexandre à Auguste*, Athens 2011

Wallace (1989): R.W. Wallace, *The Areopagos Council to 307 B.C.*, Baltimore–London 1989

Wankerl (2009): V. Wankerl, Appello ad principem. *Urteilstechnik in kaiserlichen Berufungsentscheidungen (Augustus bis Caracalla)*, Munich 2009

JOSÉ LUIS ALONSO (ZÜRICH)

AGRAPHOS GAMOS: MARRIAGE, FAMILY AND INHERITANCE IN ROMAN EGYPT[1]

Abstract: For over a century, the discussion of marriage law and practice in Hellenistic and Roman Egypt has been dominated by the mysterious distinction between written and unwritten marriages and the strange consequences associated with it. This paper is a new attempt at solving a puzzle that has perplexed generations of papyrologists and legal historians.

Kewords: legal pluralism, paternal power, dowry-loan, panprasion/proprasis, family katoche

I. Problem, Sources and Method

The mysterious distinction between written and unwritten marriage – *engraphos* and *agraphos gamos* – and its strange legal consequences have been known for over a century, since the publication of the first volume of CPR and the second volume of the Oxyrhynchos papyri in 1895 and 1899. With it, three documents came to light that have shaped the discussion ever since and will also be at the centre of this paper: *P. Oxy*. II 267 = *MChr*. 281 (37 CE), the marriage loan between Tryphon and Saraeus, the inheritance trial in CPR I 18 (124 CE Arsinoites) and *P. Oxy*. II 237 (after June 27th, 186 CE), the famous petition of Dionysia against her father Chairemon.[2]

---

1 Research financed by the National Science Centre of the Republic of Poland (Narodowe Centrum Nauki, Opus 14, nr. 2017/27/B/HS3/01350: How to Apply Law in Egypt? A Practical Guide for the Roman Judge: A Case-study of *P. Oxy*. II 237 and Other Papyrological Evidence on Legal Pluralism in the Roman Times). I am thankful to the Symposion organisers and most especially to Gerhard Thür for a most fruitful dialogue. These pages have greatly benefited from the work on the Dionysia papyrus with Jakub Urbanik and his team at the University of Warsaw.

2 A new commented edition of *P. Oxy*. II 237, which will include the columns left unpublished by Grenfell and Hunt (col. 1–3 and 9), is in course of preparation by Jakub Urbanik, Constantinos Balamoshev, Kacper Zochowski and myself. Since its publication, the papyrus has attracted much attention in great part due to the legal materials appended to the petition proper, in Col. 7, l. 19 onwards: the 89 CE Edict of Mettius Rufus on the correct functioning of the property record offices, the 109 CE Edict of Sulpicius Similis on the registration of marriage *syngraphai* and the ensuing *katochai* (*infra* VII), and the 142 CE Edict of Valerius Eudaimon on debtors' protests against the authenticity of credit deeds; the opinion of a *nomikos* on paternal *exousia* (*infra* II), a

Ever since the publication of these documents, the distinction itself and its consequences have remained one of the most puzzling mysteries in the whole legal history of Greco-Roman Egypt. Properly addressing or even summarising the many theories proposed to solve it would exceed the limits assigned to this paper.[3] I will therefore limit myself to presenting an outline of my own take on the problem, which builds on important connections between the Greek and the Demotic marriage practice detected by Traianos Gagos and others in 1992[4] and first linked to our problem by Uri Yiftach in his 2003 reference work on marriage and marital arrangements in the Greek papyri from Egypt.[5]

In building the hypothesis I outline here, I have observed an important methodological caution kept also by Uri Yiftach in his careful and balanced treatment of the topic: namely, respecting the terminology of the sources, limiting the attestations of the phenomenon to those documents where the terms themselves, *agraphos* or *engraphos*, are actually used, avoiding unwarranted assumptions that marriage deeds where the terminology does not occur refer to one or the other category.[6]

---

second part of which will come now to light as part of the newly edited col. 9; and a whole series of court precedents – to the five we already knew at least two more must be added, in the fragmentary col. 9. The petition itself has been studied mostly from the point of view of Chairemon's attempt against Dionysia's marriage: lit. *infra* in n. 24. Their financial conflict, obscured by the fragmentary preservation of col. 4–5, remains to be clarified: this is one of the main purposes of the new commented edition, aided by the publication of what remains of col. 1–3.

3 Among the vast literature: Mitteis 1901: 343–351; Wilcken 1901: 487–490; Brassloff 1902: 70–71; Nietzold 1903: 1–12; De Ruggiero 1903; Révillout 1903: 1120, 1139–1142 passim; Bortolucci 1904; Spiegelberg 1906: 190–195; Wilcken 1906: 507–508; De Ruggiero 1908; Frese 1909: 38–51; Mitteis 1912a: 200–213; Mitteis 1912b: 313–317; Marci 1915; Taubenschlag 1916: 188–189 = Taubenschlag 1959: 274–275; Möller 1918; Sethe 1918: 376–378; Spiegelberg-Partsch 1918; Kreller 1919: 155–156, 167–168; Meyer 1920: 40–43; Sethe-Partsch 1920: 578–590; Jüncker 1921: 47–52; Spiegelberg 1923: 36–37; Partsch-Wilcken 1927: 15–25, 60–61; Wilcken 1927: 578–584; Wenger 1928: 66–81; Kunkel 1928: 664–668; Arangio-Ruiz 1930: 61–84; Edgerton 1931; Petropoulos 1931; Huwardas 1931: 46–57; Bozza 1934: 205–228; Thompson 1934: XXIII; Montevecchi 1936; Schönbauer 1938: 42–60; Erdmann 1939; Wolff 1939; Erdmann 1940: 165–169; Erdmann 1941: 54–57; Wolff 1952: 164–181; Taubenschlag 1955: 112–119, 141, 184–185; Mélèze Modrzejewski 1956; Préaux 1959: 150–153; Lüddeckens 1960: 347; Pestman 1961: 30, 42; Seidl 1962: 170; Häge 1968: 111–116, 182–183 passim; Seidl 1973: 213–217; Wolff 1973: 68–71; Πανταζόπουλος 1984; Cotton-Yardeni 1997: 227–229; Cotton 1998: 117; Wolff 1998: 79–83; Yiftach-Firanko 2003: 81–104; Oudshoorn 2007: 427–432; Kreuzsaler-Urbanik 2008: 135–138; Lippert 2008: 120; Platschek 2015: 157–160; Czajkowski 2017: 44.

4 Gagos-Koenen-McNellen 1992.

5 Yiftach-Firanko 2003: 81–104.

6 This leaves out documents traditionally understood as transformations of an *agraphos* into an *engraphos gamos*, but where the terms themselves are not used, like *PSI* I 36a

The first effect of this methodological caution is a drastic reduction of the material, not only in quantity (20 papyri in all) but also in its temporal arch, that starts as late as 12 BCE and ends in the late 4th cent. CE.[7] This means, whatever roots the phenomenon may have in institutions and practices that go back to the Ptolemaic period and even beyond, to pre-Ptolemaic law, Greek or Egyptian (on this, *infra* V–VII), it cannot be assumed (also in this respect Yiftach's treatment of the subject is exemplary) that the distinction as such had any relevance before the beginning of the Roman Era. This unwarranted assumption contaminates much of the 20th century literature on the subject.

Paying attention to the actual terminology of the sources yields yet another important insight. Since the publication of the Dionysia papyrus, it has been assumed that *engraphos gamos* was the technical denomination of the type of marriage to which the peculiar regime of the *agraphos gamos* did not apply. This is indeed what Dionysia claims in a crucial part of her argumentation.[8] And yet, the term *engraphos gamos* is attested only in Dionysia and in an improvised argumentation *ex parte* in the trial recorded in *CPR* I 18 (infra VIII). Most

(11–13 CE Arsinoites), *P. Mich.* V 339 (46 CE Tebtynis), *CPR* I 28 = *MChr.* 312 (110 CE Ptolemais Evergetis), or *P. Oxy.* XLIX 3491 (157–8 CE Oxyrhynchos)

7 Chronologically: *SB* XXIV 16073 (12 BCE Alexandria) l. 7 (and l. 5 of the verso); *P. Oxy.* II 267 = *MChr.* 281 (36–43 CE Oxyrhynchos) l. 19; *P. Mich.* V 322 a (46 CE Tebtynis) l.2; *APF* 60 (2014) 123 Nr. 1 (83 CE Antaiopolites?) l. 14; *PSI* VII 777 (96 CE Hermopolis?) l. 11; *P. Fam. Tebt.* 20 (120–1 CE Tebtynis) l. 12; *CPR* I 18 = *SPP* XX 4 = *MChr.* 84 = *Jur. Pap.* 89 (124 CE Arsinoites) ll. 10 and 26; *PSI* XII 1223 (131 CE Alexandria) l. 11; *P. Kron.* 52 = *P. Mil. Vogl.* II 85 = *C. Pap. Hengstl* 79 (138 CE Tebtynis) l. 10; *SB* III 7239 (141 CE Alexandria) l. 19; *PSI* VIII 921 R (143–4 CE Arsinoites) l. 28; *BGU* IV 1045 = *MChr.* 282 (154 CE Alabanthis) l. 10; *PSI* XII 1224 (156–157 CE Alexandria) l. 10; *P.Mil. Vogl.* II 71 = SB VI 9264 (172–5 CE Ptolemais Evergetis) l. 4; *P. Oxy.* II 237 (186 CE Oxyrhnychos) Col. 7, l. 13, Col. 8, ll. 4–6; *P. Dura* 31 (204 CE Dura Europos) l. 6; *BGU* IV 1084 = *WChr.* 146 (222 CE Arsinoites) ll. 24–25; *SB* XVI 12527 (224 CE unknown provenance) l. 17; *P. Flor.* I 24 = *MChr.* 187 (3rd cent. CE Ptolemais Evergetis) l. 7; *P. Lips.* I 41 = *MChr.* 300 (late 4th cent. CE Hermopolis) l. 5. Pure conjecture is the term ἀγράφως in *P. Hamb.* III 220 (223–4 CE Arsinoites) l. 3, and also, entirely arbitrary, in *P. Strasb.* VII 668 (2nd cent. CE unknown provenance) ll. 1–2. To the list, *P. Oxy.* LXXIII 4961 (223 CE Oxyrhynchos) must be added: a copy of a petition to the prefect, presented by a woman regarding the testament of her father –with whom there had been previous litigation– and some property registered to her name; in l. 26 an expression until now unattested is used, *asyngraphos gamos* (καὶ μὴ εἶναί με ἐξ ἀσυνγράφων γάμων), in a way that suggests that descending from such marriage would have been an obstacle for her petition; whether the expression is synonymous with *agraphos gamos* remains an open question.

8 Col. 7, l. 12–13: οὐδεὶς μὲν γὰρ νόμος ἀκούσας γυναῖκας ἀπ᾽ ἀνδρῶν ἀποσπᾶν ἐφείησιν, εἰ δὲ καὶ ἔστιν τις, ἀλλ᾽ οὐ πρὸς τὰς | ἐξ ἐνγράφων γάμων γεγενημένας καὶ ἐνγράφως γεγενημένας: For no law permits to drag wives away from their husbands against their will; and if there is any such one, then not against those | who come from written marriages and have become (wives) in written form.

significantly, the learned opinion on which Dionysia bases her assertion (*infra* III) does not use it, and the *ephebeia* certificates that disclose the form of the parents' marriage do not ever refer to those which are not *agraphos*[9] as *engraphos*, but merely as existing καθ' ὁμολογίαν.[10] This advises caution in treating *engraphos gamos* as a technical term – Dionysia's petition is particularly adept at bending the formulation of the law to better serve her interests– and will be quite relevant for us later.

Important for our hypothesis will also be another peculiarity of the temporal arch traced by the material: the evidence for the peculiar legal consequences associated with the 'unwritten' character of the marriage is limited to two 2nd century sources: the 124 CE trial record in *CPR* I 18 (*infra* III) and Dionysia's petition, *P. Oxy.* II 237, dated to 186 CE. In both cases, as we will see, the only sources available both to the judges and to the parties in conflict regarding the practical relevance of the 'unwritten' nature of the marriage are legal experts, *nomikoi*. This imposes caution in assuming that such practical consequences were already in place when the term *agraphos* is first attested in our sources and remained in place throughout until the last attestation. Certain is only that *agraphia* was decisive in second century Egypt, but it could well be that its consequences were only at that time first associated with it. A confirmation that this warning is to be taken seriously: although the legal consequences that *CPR* I 18 and *P. Oxy.* II 237 associate to *agraphia* belong to the 'laws of the Egyptians' (*infra* n. 19), understood as the law applicable to all inhabitants of the Roman province of Egypt who lacked citizen status (*infra* III), the notion of *agraphos gamos* itself is attested outside of Egypt, in *P. Dura* 31 (204 CE Dura Europos), where it could hardly have had the same consequences, and also in late 4th century Hermopolis (*P. Lips.* I 41 = *MChr.* 300), long after 'Egyptians' in that sense of non-citizens had ceased to exist.

II. *Agraphos*

Why the topic is so puzzling can be easily summarised. The first surprise comes with the meaning of *agraphos* in this context: for convenience, I will often speak of 'unwritten' marriages, but *agraphos* does not seem to mean unwritten in the ordinary sense of the term. Not every marriage document was enough, it seems, for a

9 Even though the total number of certificates containing the indication is too small to allow statistical inferences, *agraphos* marriages seem notably more frequent – six out of eight: *APF* 60 (2014) 123 Nr. 1 (83 CE Antaiopolites?) l. 14; *PSI* VII 777 (96 CE Hermopolis?) l. 11; *SB* III 7239 (141 CE Alexandria) l. 19; *PSI* XII 1224 (156–157 CE Alexandria) l. 10; *BGU* IV 1084 = *WChr.* 146 (222 CE Arsinoites) l. 24–25; *SB* XVI 12527 (224 CE unknown provenance) l. 17.

10 So, most significantly, in *PSI* XII 1223 (131 CE Alexandria), where the marriage was initially *agraphos*, then καθ' ὁμολογίαν (ll. 10–12: φάμενοι συνεῖναι | ἑαυτοῖς πρότερον μὲν ἀγράφως, νυν|εὶ δὲ καθ' ὁμολογίαν), and in *P. Bodl.* I 66 (225 CE) ll. 13–14: φάμενοι συνεῖ]|ναι ἑαυτοῖς καθ' ὁμ̣[ολογίαν].

marriage to cease being considered *agraphos*: a marriage based on a written document could be still deemed 'unwritten'. Of this we are aware since the problem first came to light in 1899: in the second volume of the Oxyrhynchos papyri, a text that will be crucial for us was first published: *P. Oxy.* II 267 = *MChr.* 281 = *Biscottini* 12 (37 CE Oxyrhynchos), an agreement between a certain Tryphon and the woman who would be his wife for at least 15 years, Saraeus.[11]

Tryphon was a weaver in mid first century Oxyrhynchos. Of him we have a substantial archive of 44 documents, spanning from year 11 to 66 CE,[12] that present the picture of a family of modest means even if in the privileged class of the *metropolitai.*[13] On May 22nd 37 CE Tryphon, following a turbulent separation with his first wife Demetrous,[14] concluded this agreement with Saraeus, who seven weeks later appears in another document[15] as pregnant. It can well be that she was

---

[11] For a detailed analysis, cf. in particular, together with those quoted *supra* in n. 1, Whitehorne 1984, Yiftach-Firanko 2003: 91–94, with further lit., and *infra* V.

[12] Biscottini 1966; Vandoni 1975; Whitehorne 1984; Pestman 1989: 74–80; Gagos-Koenen-McNellen 1992: 189–192; Rowlandson 1998: 112–118; Piccolo 2003: 197–213; Kelly 2011: 131–133, 313–315; Waebens 2019: 206–208. Trismegistos (https://www.trismegistos.org) archive number: TM Arch 249.

[13] Cf. the reduced rate of twelve drachmas for the poll tax in *P. Oxy.* II 288 = *Biscottini* 9 (25 CE Oxyrhynchos) and *SB* X 10243 = *P. Oxy. descr.* II 308 = *Biscottini* 25 (50 CE Oxyrhynchos). About the family's ethnic and cultural background nothing can be said, neither regarding Tryphon nor Saraeus: regarding the latter, Rowlandson's suggestion that in the trial recorded in *P. Oxy.* I 37 = *MChr.* 79 = Jur. Pap. 90 = *Biscottini* 23 (49 CE Oxyrhynchos), her child was identified as hers by the *strategos* because he may have seemed to him 'Egyptian rather than Greek' is unwarranted.

[14] Cf. Tryphon's petition against Demetrous upon her alleged desertion in *P. Oxy.* II 282 = *MChr.* 117 = *Biscottini* 10 (29–37 CE Oxyrhynchos): the date of the petition being lost, there is no certainty about the temporal distance between Demetrous' departure and Saraeus' pregnancy and marriage to Tryphon. Yet, the attack on Saraeus by Demetrous and her mother (*infra* n. 15) weeks after our document was executed, and the fact that Saraeus was then pregnant, strongly suggests that her pregnancy, Demetrous departure and Tryphon's new marriage are all related in a full-fledged family drama. Vandoni further supposes, on the basis of a new reading of *SB* XIV 11415 = *SB* X 10235 = *P. Oxy.* II 321 descr. = *CPGr* I 16 = *Biscottini* 207, that Saraeus was employed as wetnurse for a daughter of Tryphon and Demetrous when the whole situation exploded: but her reading is highly conjectural and not free from problems (Whitehorne 1984: 1268–1269) and, crucially, the date of the document is lost – it could well be a document related to Saraeus' (well attested) occupation as wetnurse after her marriage.

[15] *SB* X 10239 = *P. Oxy.* II 315 *descr.* = *Biscottini* 17 (37 CE Oxyrhynchos), a petition of Tryphon to the *strategos* dated to July 37 CE, regarding an aggression suffered by Saraeus at the hands of his former wife Demetrous and of the latter's mother. The attack happened on Epeiph 10th of the first year of Caius Caesar, July 4th 37 CE (our marriage deed is dated May 22nd 37 CE), and at that point Saraeus was pregnant: [ἄ]λόγον ταύτης ἠṿέγκạντο | [καὶ συν]εστήσαντο ἔνκυον | [οὖ]σαν καὶ π̣ .[. . . .] . . . . ||[. . .]πει δẹκο[. .]ν πληγῶν | [. . .] . .[. .] .[.] .[. .] . [. . .] .ρ̣ω̣( ) (ll. 13–17, corrections by M. Vandoni, *BL* VII 217). The text is usually understood in the sense that the blows did not

already pregnant when our deed was executed, and that this is precisely the reason why it was executed – and possibly the reason for the separation from Demetrous. In any case, Tryphon agrees to pay her a sum of money on account of childbirth expenses, should they separate in pregnancy:

> ἐπεὶ δὲ σύνεσμεν |19 ἀλλήλοις ἀγράφω[ς] προσομολογῶι (l. προσομολογῶ) ἐὰν ὡσαύτως ἐκ διαφορᾶς |20 ἀπ[αλλαγ]ῶμεν ἀπ' ἀλλήλ[ων] ἐνκύου σ[ο]ῦ οὔση[ς] δώσειν σοι (Whitehorne; prev. ed.: ἕως ἄν σοι̣) |21 [εἰς λόγον δ]απάν[ης λ]ο̣χ[είας δραχμάς - ca.17 -][16]

This arrangement regarding a possible future separation in pregnancy, we read, is necessary <u>because</u> Tryphon and Saraeus live together in an unwritten manner.[17] This clearly implies that the present contract is not enough to change the nature of their union in that respect; it also seems to imply that otherwise wife and children would be somehow protected without the need for such explicit arrangement. We will later (*infra* VIII) come back to the possible reasons why.

Important for us is the fact itself that the term *agraphos* is not used here in its ordinary sense, as often in the papyri, simply referred to an undocumented transaction,[18] but has acquired a highly artificial, technical sense – whether the specific rules associated with it in the 2nd century were already here in place or not (*supra* I). As we will see (*infra* VIII), this artificial sense is present already in the first attestation of the term, in *SB* XXIV 16073 (12 BCE Alexandria). It does not seem farfetched to assume that also in later documents the term tended to keep in marriage contexts this technical meaning – as it is certainly the case in the two crucial 2nd century texts where the specificities of *agraphos gamos* come to light, *CPR* I 18 and *P. Oxy*. II 237 –, but an absolute certainty is not always possible: the atechnical meaning remains a distinct possibility particularly in the latest 4th century attestation (*P. Lips*. I 41 = *MChr*. 300, Hermopolis) and in that of Dura Europos (*P. Dura* 31, 204 CE).

---

just risk a miscarriage but actually caused one: Vandoni 1975: 336; Rowlandson 1998: 115–116. Saraeus' firstborn, in fact, seems to be Apion, born almost a decade later: cf. the Solomon-like trial against Saraeus in *P. Oxy*. I 37 = *MChr*. 79 = *Jur. Pap*. 90 = *Biscottini* 23, dated 49 CE, when Apion must still have been a baby, and Rowlandson 1998: 114.

16 *P. Oxy*. II 267 (37 CE Oxyrhynchos), ll. 18–21: since we live | together in an unwritten way, I further agree if as aforesaid owing to a quarrel | we separate from each other while you are in a state of pregnancy, I will give you | on account of childbirth expenses [the sum of ... drachmas ...]. Cf. Whitehorne 1984: 1271 and n. 14.

17 Rightly emphasised by Yiftach-Firanko 2003: 92: "it is precisely in the framework of that *locheia* provision that the couple is said to be living together *agraphos*".

18 Particularly frequent in clauses like the ubiquitous "ηδὲ περὶ ἑτέρου ἁπλῶς πράγματος ἐγγράπτου ἀγράφου" or "κατ' ἔγγραπτον ἀσφάλειαν".

III. *Agraphos gamos* and paternal *exousia*

Even more perplexing than this peculiar meaning of *agraphos* are the legal consequences of the *agraphia* itself, as they result from *CPR* I 18 and *P. Oxy*. II 237. The very position of the father in the family, his power over his children and their property, seems to have depended on it, under the so-called 'laws of the Egyptians'.[19]

A small *excursus* regarding these 'laws of the Egyptians' is perhaps here necessary.[20] Crucial for us is the following: in Roman Egypt, the laws of the Egyptians are not necessarily native Egyptian laws. Egyptians, *Aigyptioi*, are in fact for the Roman administration all those who are nothing else than inhabitants of the province. All those, that is, who have no citizenship: neither the Roman nor that of any of the *poleis* of pre-Severan Egypt, namely Naukratis, Alexandria, Ptolemais and later Antinoopolis.[21] The category thus comprises the immense majority of the population of Egypt: all the inhabitants of the *chora* who, for Rome, are *apolides*, *peregrini nullius civitatis*, and precisely for that reason cannot be referred to with any other denomination than 'Egyptians'. This means: not just ethnic Egyptians, but also the Greeks of the *chora*, including the *metropolitai* and the gymnasial elite, together with those of mixed descent, the Jewish communities of the *chora* and all others, at least as far as they were not organised in *politeumata*. This has for us an important consequence: all legal traditions that the Romans find in Egypt, and in particular both the Egyptian and the Greek, fall now, with the only exception of the *politikoi nomoi* of the *poleis*, under the category of the 'laws of the Egyptians' and

---

[19] *CPR* I 18 refers generically to "the law" or "the laws": ll. 9–10, τοῦ νόμου καλοῦντος τοὺς πατέρας ἐπ[ὶ] τὰ[ς] κληρονομίας | τῶν ἐξ ἀγράφων παίδων; ll. 11–13, ἔχοντος ἐκεί|νου ἀπὸ τῶν νόμων ἐξουσίαν περιόντος πατρὸς εἰς ἄλλον τινὰ | γράφειν δ[ια]θήκην. *P. Oxy*. II 237 confirms that these are indeed the "laws of the Egyptians", cf. in particular: (a) Col. 7, ll. 40–42: τὰ πρόσωπα Αἰγ[ύ]πτια ὄ̣ν̣τ̣α̣ παρ' οἷς ἄκρατός ἐστιν ἡ τῶν ν[ό]μων ἀποτομ̣[ί]α·| διοριζόμενος γάρ σοι λέγω [ὅ]τι Α̣ἰ̣γ[ύ]π̣τ̣ιοι οὐ μόνον τοῦ ἀφελέσθαι τὰς [θυγατ]έρ[ας ὧ]ν ἔδωκαν ἐξουσίαν, ἔχουσιν δὲ καὶ ὧν ἐὰν κ̣α̣ὶ̣ ἴδια | κτήσωνται, clearly related to the same paternal power on the children's property behind the decision in *CPR* I 18; (b) Col. 7, ll. 31–33, referred to the alleged paternal right to take the daughter away from her husband against her will: Ἰσίδωρος ῥήτωρ ὑπὲρ Φλαυήσιος εἶπεν, τ̣ὸ̣ν οὖν α̣ἰ̣τ̣ι̣ώ̣μενον | ἀποσπάσαι βουλόμενον τ[ὴ]ν θυγατέρα αὐτοῦ συνοικοῦσαν τῷ ἀντιδίκῳ δεδικάσθαι ὑπογύως πρὸς αὐτὸν ἐπὶ τοῦ ἐ̣[πι]σ̣τ̣ρ̣α̣τ̣ήγου | καὶ ὑπερτεθεῖσθαι τὴν δίκην ὑ̣μ̣εῖ̣ν̣ ἵνα ἀναγνωσθῇ ὁ τῶν Αἰγυπτίω[ν νό]μος; (c) now also, in Col. IX l. 20, τὰ τ̣ῶ̣ν̣ Αἰγυπτίων νόμ̣ιμα, in the previously unpublished second half of the opinion of the *nomikos* Ulpius Dioskourides (on him, *infra* n. 30).

[20] On the notion, Alonso 2023, with sources and literature.

[21] Cf. Jördens 2012. This purely administrative meaning of Egyptians as non-citizens, as opposed to Romans, Alexandrians, and all others with a *status civitatis* is especially clear in the *Gnomon of the Idios Logos*: cf. in particular the rules concerning marriage and inheritance in §§ 38 – 56.

are in principle applicable to everyone who is not a citizen, no matter their ethnic origin or their culture.[22]

It is to this common normative mass that the rules associated with the *agraphos gamos* belong, according to our sources. And yet, *agraphos gamos* is not a category that we find in the previous Greek or Egyptian legal traditions. In second-century Egypt, instead, as it results from *CPR* I 18 and *P. Oxy.* II 237, it seems to be decisive for the power of the father within the family, in the most peculiar, counter-intuitive way. Fathers married *agraphos*, in fact, had under the 'laws of the Egyptians' an enormous power, *exousia*, over their children and their children's belongings. It seems to follow that they would entirely lack such power when their

22 Mélèze Modrzejewski 2014: 259–271 greatly underestimates the Egyptian component in these 'laws of the Egyptians' and assumes all too readily a Greek origin for the institutions attested as part of them. Nevertheless, despite Platschek 2015: 148–149, he is quite right in rejecting Wolff's identification of the '*nomoi ton Aigyption*' of Roman Egypt with the Ptolemaic '*nomoi tes choras*', i.e. with the native Egyptian law *tout court* (Wolff 1953: 42–44), as we find it compiled in the so-called *codex Hermopolis*. As explained above, 'Egyptian' in the Roman administrative parlance of the 2nd century is every *peregrinus nullius civitatis* of the province, including the Greeks. Platschek's assumption that the majority of the population in the *chora* lived under native Egyptian law is hardly compatible with our sources – already when one considers the dominance of Greek in the documentary practice, despite the fact that the Egyptian tradition had at the time of Alexander's conquest embraced written documentation more thoroughly than the Greek. It is true that the native Egyptian tradition remained vital even after the Roman annexation, but the dominant culture since the establishment of the Ptolemaic monarchy was and remained the Greek: native Egyptians had no chance of social ascent beyond the priestly milieu without Hellenisation, which paved the way to intermarriage; likewise, Egyptian legal traditions could only survive the disappearance of the *laokritai* with the fall of the Ptolemies and the gradual extinction of the Demotic notarial practice thereafter only in the measure in which they had found an *interpretatio graeca*, a Greek documentary expression. The autochthonous developments of Greek culture in the *chora* already under the Ptolemies (often strikingly new: cf. the *ekdosis* of the mother already in *P. Eleph.* 1), the Greek form that the Egyptian legal tradition started adopting in the late Ptolemaic period (most visible for us through the activity of the bilingual *agoranomoi* of Pathyris, giving Greek notarial form to native Egyptian practices: Alonso 2016: 137–139, with lit.), and the interaction between both, facilitated by the Roman annexation, as both Egyptians and Greeks became administratively '*Aegyptioi*', all subjected to the same jurisdiction, so that the formal barrier between both legal cultures fell down: all this is what falls now under the category of the 'laws of the Egyptians'. Remarkably, when Sulpicius Similis and Mettius Rufus characterise the family *katoche*, which most certainly (*infra* VII) had native Egyptian roots, they use, instead of the usual *nomoi ton Aigyption*, the expression *enchoria nomima* (*P. Oxy.* II 237, Col. 8, l 22) or *epichorios nomos* (*P. Oxy.* II 237, Col. 8, l. 34), echoing the Ptolemaic '*nomoi tes choras*' – one wonders if consciously, to refer to institutions that they knew or suspected were of native Egyptian origin.

marriages were not *agraphos* or had ceased being *agraphos*,[23] although such assertion we find only in the petition of Dionysia (*P. Oxy*. II 237). If we are to trust Dionysia – on this, later – whatever it was that made a marriage not be *agraphos*, or not anymore, it also deprived the father of his power over the children and their property.[24]

The aspect of the paternal power that Dionysia fights against is the supposed right of the fathers, under the laws of the Egyptians, to take their daughters away from their husbands, the so-called *apospasis*.[25] Dionysia's father, Chairemon, an ex-gymnasiarch and therefore – whatever his ethnic origin – part of the Greek elite of the *metropolis*, after a long financial conflict with his daughter, invokes the laws of the Egyptians against her in order to separate her from her husband,[26] either

---

[23] That marriages could cease being *agraphos* is confirmed by the *ephebeia* certificate in *PSI* XII 1223 (131 CE Alexandria) ll. 10–12: φάμενοι συνεῖναι | ἑαυτοῖς πρότερον μὲν ἀγράφως, νυν|εὶ δὲ καθ' ὁμολογίαν. The marriage of the parents in P. Bodl. i 66 (225 CE), instead, seems to have been ab initio *kath'homologian*: ll. 13–14, [φάμενοι συνεῖ]|ναι ἑαυτοῖς καθ' ὁμ̣[ολογίαν]. Uncertain remains whether this would change the legal position of the children, since both *P. Oxy*. II 237 col. VII, I. 13, col. VIII, I. 5. and *CPR* I 18, I. 26 refer to those ἐξ ἀγράφων γάμων γενόμενοι.

[24] Among the recent literature on Dionysia's petition: Lewis 1970; Katzoff 1972: 257–268; Katzoff 1982; Anagnostou-Cañas 1984: 351–353; Urbanik 2002: 316–322; Kreuzsaler 2008; Kreuzsaler-Urbanik 2008; Urbanik 2008; Yiftach-Firanko 2009: 550–552; Bryen 2013: 143–150, 191–199; Platschek 2014; Platschek 2015; Urbanik 2016: 1063–1067; Dolganov 2019: 42–58; Urbanik 2019: 318–327; Besson 2020: 209–215; Alonso 2023: 250–253 (§§ 63–68), with further lit. From the earliest literature, particularly valuable Gradenwitz 1901.

[25] The substantive *apospasis* for this 'taking back' of the daughter, frequent in the literature, is our own neologism; Dionysia uses only the verb ἀποσπάω: (a) in the decision of the deputy *strategos* Harpokration who presided over a hearing of the case in Oxyrhynchos upon Chairemon's second petition against Dionysia, authorising her to present the present petition, Col. 7, ll. 4–5: ἐπεὶ δὲ | ὁ Χ[αιρ]ήμων δι' ἧς καὶ νῦν πεπο[ίη]ται παρὰ τῷ [λ]αμπροτάτῳ ἡγεμόνι ἐντυχίας ἠξίωσεν τὴν θυγατέραν ἄκ̣[ο]υ̣σ̣α̣ν̣ ἀποσπᾶν; (b) in her *petitum*, where she denies its existence (probably because the court precedents she presents could support the idea that it had been overridden by the Roman jurisdiction), Col. 7, l. 12: οὐδεὶς μὲν γὰρ νόμος ἀκούσας γυναῖκας ἀπ' ἀνδρῶν ἀποσπᾶν ἐφείησιν; (c) in her second court precedent, dated 133 CE, col. 7, ll. 31–32: τ̣ὸν οὖν α̣ἰ̣τ̣ι̣ώ̣μενον | ἀποσπάσαι βουλόμενον τ[ὴ]ν θυγατέρα αὐτοῦ συνοικοῦσαν τῷ ἀντιδίκῳ δεδικάσθαι ὑπογύως πρὸς αὐτὸν ἐπὶ τοῦ ἐ̣[πι]σ̣τ̣ρ̣α̣τ̣ήγου. The verb does not seem to be used in any technical sense, though. Indeed, in Dionysia's first court precedent, dated 128 CE, the verb is ἀποζευχθῆναι: col. 7, l. 25, αἰτ̣ε̣ῖσθ̣α̣ι̣ ο̣ὖ̣ν̣ ἐὰν δοκῇ μὴ ἀποζευχθῆναι γυναικὸς οἰκείως πρὸς αὐτὸν ἐχούσης; in her third court precedent, which is also the earliest, dated to 87 CE, ἀφαιρεῖσθαι: col. 7, l. 43, χεῖρόν ἐστι ἀνδρὸς ἀφαι[ρεῖσθαι]. Moot seems the discussion whether we are dealing with a forced divorce or with the mere factual 'taking away' of the wife by the father (Platschek 2015: 146: "Die Quellenlage gestattet es nicht, dieses Recht als ein originäres 'Eheauflösungsrecht' zu qualifizieren"): marriage being understood as marital cohabitation, the dissolution of the latter necessarily ends the marriage.

[26] Much discussed is the origin of this paternal *exousia*. Mélèze Modrzejewski 2014: 261–262, following Lewis 1972, argued for a Greek origin, related to the Athenian *aphairesis*, and deemed unlikely that a member of the Greek elite like Chairemon (a fair characterisation

because he sees him as responsible for her behaviour or because in this way he expects to regain control over it.[27]

When Dionysia, after a long summary of the conflict, comes to her *petitum* (Col. 7, ll. 8–19), her main argument against his father's attempt is that the law he invokes does not exist (indeed, as the court precedents she appends show, its application had been at least twice rejected by the Roman courts)[28] and, if it does exist (since those specific cases of rejection may not yet mean abrogation) it does not apply to wives who – as she claims to be – come from a written marriage (*engraphos gamos*) and are themselves married in a written form:

---

for an ex-gymnasiarch, regardless of how purely Greek his ancestry may have been) would appeal to native Egyptian law. The hypothesis, while not incompatible with the characterisation of the *exousia* as part of the 'laws of the Egyptians' (understanding 'Egyptians' not ethnically or culturally, but in its Roman administrative sense, as the *peregrini* of the *chora*, Greeks included: *supra* n. 21), is in view of the sources (problematic even for the supposed Greek *aphairesis*) highly conjectural and the argumentation inconclusive, cf. Wolff 2002: 75 n. 18. For our purposes, the question is less relevant: suffice to say that, whatever its origin, this *exousia* was invoked both by the Greek elite and by Egyptians so uncontaminated by Greek culture that they needed an interpreter in court (*P. Oxy*. II 237, col. 7, l. 37–38, in the 133 CE case before Paconius Felix). Against the idea that Chairemon articulates his petition on the basis of the Roman *interdictum de liberis exhibendis vel ducendis* (Dolganov 2019: 42–58), cf. Alonso 2023: 251 n. 155. On the Greek *aphairesis*, the incidence of the Roman *patria potestas* on the marriage of the *potestate subiecti*, the *interdictum de liberis exhibendis*, and Dionysia's *apospasis*, cf., most extensively, Urbanik 2002 and Urbanik 2016.

27 Lit. *supra* in n. 24.

28 *P. Oxy*. II 237 (186 CE Oxyrhynchos), col. 7, ll. 19–29 and ll. 29–38. Both cases were quite close in time: the first arrived to the court of the prefect Flavius Titianus in 128 CE after being tried by the *epistrategos* M. Aemilius Bassus (for the identification, Thomas 1982: 194–195); the second, in 133 CE, was judged by the *epistrategos* Paconius Felix, following explicitly the precedent set by Titianus five years earlier. Whether these two decisions sufficed as abrogation of the paternal *apospasis*, we would be in a better position to decide if we had Chairemon's court materials, and not only Dionysia's; but her own argumentation – no law permits to drag wives away from their husbands … and if there is any such one, then not against those who come from written marriages – strongly suggests that this was far from certain even for her. Contrary to what sometimes assumed (cf. for instance Kreuzsaler-Urbanik 2008: 141 n. 38; Mélèze Modrzejewski 2014: 262 n. 17), the paternal *apospasis* does not seem to be the *thema decidendi* in the 87 CE trial before the *iuridicus* Umbrius (*P. Oxy*. II 237, col. 7, ll. 39–43), where the plaintiff seems to be the daughter and what she claims against her father is to effectively deliver the dowry he granted her; the *iuridicus*' assertion 'It is worse to take her away from her husband' (l. 43, χεῖρόν ἐστι ἀνδρὸς | ἀφαι[ρεῖσθαι]), unfortunately interrupted by the broken papyrus, is no conclusive evidence of him overruling the paternal *apospasis*.

ἐντυγχάνω σοι καὶ νῦν πάντα παρατιθεμένη τὰ ἐν τῷ πράγματι, $|_{10}$ καθὼς καὶ ὁ βασιλικὸς διαδεχόμενος καὶ τὴν στρατηγίαν ἠθέλησεν, καὶ δέομαι κελεῦσαι γραφῆναι τῇ στρατηγίᾳ τάς τε χορηγίας $|_{11}$ ἀποδίδοσθαί μοι κατὰ καιρόν, ἐπισχεῖν τε (*corr. ex* δε) αὐτὸν ἤδη ποτὲ ἐπειόντα (*l.* ἐπιόντα) μοι, πρότερον μὲν ὡς ἀνόμου κατοχῆς χάριν, νῦν δὲ προφάσει νό$|_{12}$μου οὐδὲν αὐτῷ προσήκοντος· οὐδεὶς μὲν γὰρ νόμος ἀκούσας γυναῖκας ἀπ᾽ ἀνδρῶν ἀποσπᾶν ἐφείησιν, εἰ δὲ καὶ ἔστιν τις, ἀλλ᾽ οὐ πρὸς τὰς $|_{13}$ ἐξ ἐνγράφων (*l.* ἐγγράφων) γάμων γεγενημένας καὶ ἐνγράφως (*l.* ἐγγράφως) γεγενημένας.[29]

To prove her point, Dionysia reproduces the opinion of a legal expert, the *nomikos* Ulpius Dioskourides,[30] dated some decades earlier, to 138 CE, regarding an unrelated Dionysia. According to Dioskourides, in fact (Col. 8, ll. 2–7), only fathers married *agraphos* have such power (and even these not anymore if they have given their daughters in *ekdosis*: an important caveat that I will leave aside for the purposes of this paper):[31]

---

[29] *P. Oxy.* II 237 (186 CE Oxyrhynchos), col. 7, ll. 9–13: I now once more make my petition to you, giving a full account of the case, | as also the royal scribe and deputy-strategus has wished, and beseech you to give orders that written instructions be sent to the office of the *strategos* so that the provisions | are paid to me at the proper time, and he finally stops his attacks upon me, previously on account of an allegedly unlawful lien and now under the pretext of a | law which does not apply to him. For no law permits to drag wives away from their husbands against their will; and if there is any such one, then not against those | who come from written marriages and have become (wives) in written form. The text above, that of our new edition (supra n. 2), corrects in l. 11 the inf. pres. ἐπίσχειν by the likelier aor. ἐπισχεῖν, and reintegrates in l. 12 the clearly readable μὲν.

[30] The *nomikos*' name results from a correction of our new edition: (*supra* n. 2): in *P. Oxy.* II, Grenfell and Hunt had read Ulpius Dionysodoros, and it is under such name that our *nomikos* appears in the literature so far. The correction is not only palaeographically sound: prosopographically also, it is supported by the fact that Dioskourides is well-known for his activity as *nomikos* in the thirties and forties of the 2nd century: *SB* XX 15147 (ca. 138 CE Oxyrhynchos) l. 8; *PSI* V 450 col. 2 (2nd cent. CE Oxyrhynchos) l. 37, l. 45; *BGU* XX 2863 (133–137 CE Arsinoites?) l. 19; *P. Fouad* I 25 (144–149 CE Arsinoites) verso, l. 4–5.

[31] An interesting attempt at solving the riddle of the relation between *ekdosis*-marriage and paternal *exousia* in Lewis 1970. In the light of Dioskourides' answer, two observations on the role of the *ekdosis*' seem to me important: (i) the *nomikos*' opinion in this respect is anticipated (Yiftach-Firanko 2003: 47–48) by a similar argument made by an advocate in one of the precedents appended by Dionysia (Col. 7, ll. 28–29); (ii) the text presupposes that not every marriage contracted in the lifetime of the wife's father required the latter's *ekdosis*; (iii) the answer is best understood not as a fiction (so Platschek 2015: 154–157), in the sense that *ekdosis* wives are dealt with as if they came from a 'written marriage' (notice that the *nomikos* does not use the latter term: on this, *supra* I and *infra* VIII), but rather in the sense that the *ekdosis* severs the daughter's connection to her parents' marriage: it does not change, not even as far as the daughter is

ἀντίγραφον προσφων̣[ήσεως νομ]ικοῦ. Οὔλπιος Δ[ι]οσ[κ]ο̣υ̣[ρίδης] τῶν ἠγορανομηκό|$_{3}$των νομικὸς Σαλουιστ[ίῳ Ἀφ]ρικανῷ ἐπάρχῳ στόλου καὶ [ἐπὶ τῶ]ν κεκριμένων τῷ τειμιω[τά]τῳ (*l.* τιμιωτάτῳ) χαίρειν. Δ̣[ιον]υ̣σ̣ί̣α |$_{4}$ ὑπὸ τοῦ πατρὸς ἐκδοθεῖσα [πρ]ὸς γάμον ἐν τῇ τοῦ π[α]τρὸς ἐξουσ[ί̣α̣ οὐ]κέτι γεΐνεται (*l.* γίνεται). καὶ γὰρ ε̣ἰ̣ ἡ μήτηρ̣ α̣ὐ̣τ̣ῆ̣ς τῷ πατρὶ ἀγράφως |$_{5}$ συνῴκησε̣ [κ]αὶ διὰ τοῦτο αὐτὴ δοκεῖ ἐξ ἀγράφων γάμων γεγενῆσθαι, τῷ ὑπὸ τοῦ πατρὸς αὐτὴν ἐκδόσθαι πρὸς γά̣μ̣ο̣ν οὐκέτι |$_{6}$ ἐξ ἀγράφων γάμων ἐστίν. πρὸς τοῦτο ἴσως γράφεις, τειμιώτα[τε] (*l.* τιμιώτατε)· καὶ δι' ὑπομνηματισμῶν ἠσφά̣[λι]σται περὶ τῆς πρ[οι]κὸς ἡ παῖς |$_{7}$ ὑπὸ τοῦ πατρός, καὶ τοῦτο αὐτῇ̣ βοηθεῖν δύναται. vac. (ἔτους) κβ θεοῦ Ἁδριανοῦ, Μεχεὶρ κ. vac.[32]

The unwritten quality of the marriage was therefore decisive – even if, according to Dioskourides not the only relevant factor – for the power of the fathers over their daughters' marriage. But this is not all. Another link between paternal power and *agraphia* was already known before the publication of the petition of Dionysia, through *CPR* I 18 = *SPP* XX 4 = *MChr.* 84 = *Jur. Pap.* 89 (124 CE Arsinoites):[33] fathers married *agraphos* were called to the inheritance of their children, so that these could not make testament in favour of someone else as long as their father lived. So we read in the plaintiff' plead:

τοῦ Ἀ[φ]ροδεισίου διὰ Σωτηρί|^{7}χου ῥήτορος εἰπόντος [σ]υνελθόντα ἑαυτὸν ἀγράφως Σαραποῦτί |$_{8}$ τιν̣ι̣ ἐσχηκέναι ἐξ αὐ[τ]ῆς Ὠριγένην ὃς ἐτελεύτησεν καὶ |$_{9}$ ἄλλους· τοῦ νόμου καλοῦντος τοὺς πατέρας ἐπ[ὶ] τὰ[ς] κληρονομίας |$_{10}$ τῶν ἐξ ἀγράφων παίδων τὸν ἀντίδ[ι]κον θέλειν κατὰ δια|$_{11}$θή[κ]ην κληρονόμειν ε[ἶ]ναι τοῦ Ὠριγένους, οὐκ ἔχοντος ἐκεί|$_{12}$νου ἀπὸ τῶν νόμων ἐξουσίαν περιόντος πατρὸς εἰς ἄλλον τινὰ |$_{13}$ γράφειν δ[ια]θήκην, παραξίου [π]αρ[α]νόμο[υ] οὔσης [τ]ῆς εἰς τὸν ἀντί|$_{14}$δικον δι[α]θήκης ἀντιποιεῖσθ[α]ι τῶν ὑπὸ τοῦ υἱοῦ καταλειφθέν|$_{15}$[των·] [34]

---

concerned, the nature of her parents' marriage, but merely results in her not 'coming from it' in a legally relevant sense any more (notice the emphatic ἐξ ἀγράφων γάμων ἐστίν).

[32] *P. Oxy.* II 237 (186 CE Oxyrhynchos), col. 8, ll. 2–7: Copy of the opinion of a legal expert. Ulpius Dioskourides, former *agoranomos*, | legal expert, to his most esteemed Salvistius Africanus, commander of the fleet and (appointed) for judicial matters, greetings. Since Dionysia | has been given away in marriage by her father, she is no longer under the father's power. For even though her mother lived with her father in an unwritten way, | and for this reason seems to be issue of an unwritten marriage, by the fact of her having been given away in marriage by her father, she is no longer | from an unwritten marriage. It is probably about this issue that you write to me, my good friend. Moreover, there are minutes of trials which regarding the dowry protect the girl | against her father, and this too can help her. (*vacat*) 22nd year of the deified Hadrian, Mecheir 20th. (*vacat*)

[33] Purpura 2005.

[34] *CPR* I 18 (124 CE Arsinoites), ll. 6–15: Aphrodisios through Soteri|chos, rhetor, declares that he joined in an unwritten manner a certain Sarapous | and had from her Origenes, who

The judge, Blaesius Marianus, a *praefectus cohortis* acting by delegation of the prefect (ll. 1–3), who presides over the case (as often in 2nd cent. Egypt when the intricacies of local family law were involved) with the aid of a legal expert, the *nomikos* Claudius Artemidoros, accepts that the law is indeed as described by the plaintiff:

> Βλαίσιος Μαριανὸς |$_{23}$ ἔπαρχος σπε[ί]ρη]ς πρώτης Φλα[υ]ία[ς Κι]λίκων ἱππικῆς συ<λ>λαλήσας |$_{24}$ Ἀρτε[μι]δ[ώρῳ τ]ῷ νομ[ι]κῷ [π]ε[ρὶ το]ῦ πράγματος ὑ[πη]γόρευσεν ἀπό|$_{25}$[φ]α[σιν ἣ καὶ ἀν]εγνώσθη κατὰ λέξ[ιν ο]ὕτως· ὁ τελευτήσας Ὡρι|$_{26}$[γένης ἐξ ἀγρά]φ[ω]ν [γάμων γε]νόμ[ε]ν[ος τῷ πα]τ̣ρ̣ὶ φαίνετα̣ι̣ κ̣α̣τ̣[α]|$_{27}$[λείπειν τὰ ἴδια δι]α̣θήκη[ς] ἐξουσία[ν] μὴ ἐσχ̣[η]κὼς τ[οῦ] πατρ[ὸς αὐτ]οῦ |$_{28}$ [ζ]ῶν[τ]ος [35]

Here, the father's power refers to the property of the children and not to their person, but in truth, also the *apospasis* in Dionysia's petition has a patrimonial side. In the legal materials she appends, in fact, the father's power to take back his daughter is presented together with his power to take back the dowry, as two sides of the same coin. In the first court precedent she quotes on her behalf, for instance, a case tried directly before the prefect Flavius Titianus in 128 CE (Col. 7, ll. 19–29), the defence argues against a father who wishes to take his daughter back from the husband in the following terms:

> Προκ̣λ̣ηιανὸς ὑπὲρ Ἀντωνίου προσέθηκεν: ἐὰν ἀπερίλυτος ἦν ὁ γάμος, τὸν πατέρα μήτε τῆς προικὸς μηδὲ τῆς παιδὸς τῆς ἐκδεδο|$_{29}$μένης ἐξουσίαν ἔχειν. [36]

---

died, and | others: (although) the law calls the fathers to the inheritances | of the children from unwritten (marriages); (that) the adversary wishes | according to the testament to be the heir of Origenes, (although) he has | according to the laws no faculty, living the father, to write a testament | in favour of anyone else, (that) the testament in favour of the adversary being inequitable and illegal | he lays claim to what was left by the | son.

[35] *CPR* I 18 (124 CE Arsinoites), ll. 22–28: Blaesius Marianus | praefect of the first equestrian cohort Flavia of the Cilicians, having consulted | Artemidoros the legal expert about the case, dictated on the question a de|cree which was also read, word for word in these terms: the deceased Ori|genes, conceived in an unwritten marriage, seems to have left his property | to his father, since he did not have the faculty to write a testament while his father | was alive. — The situation of such children, who, despite being owners, cannot bestow their inheritance on anyone but their fathers is akin to that of the *latini Iuniani*, whose property, despite being their own, returns upon their death to their patrons *iure peculii*: Gai. 3.56.

[36] *P. Oxy.* II 237 (186 CE Oxyrhynchos), col. 7, ll. 28–29: Prokleianos on behalf of Antonius added that if the marriage was not cancelled the father had no power over the dowry any more than over the daughter whom he had | given in marriage. For the advocate's name, Προκληιανός instead of Grenfell and Hunt's Προβατιανός, see our new edition of the text (*supra* n. 2).

And, in Dionysia's third court precedent (Col. 7, ll. 39–43 – Col. 8, ll. 1–2), in the context of an 87 CE trial before the *iuridicus* regarding an apparently undelivered dowry, the father's advocate argues that Egyptian fathers have power to deprive their daughers not only of what they have given them, but also of whathever they may acquire as their own:

> διοριζόμενος γάρ σοι λέγω [ὅ]τι Ạἰγ̣[ύ]π̣τ̣ιοι οὐ μόνον τοῦ ἀφελέσθαι τὰς [θυγατ]έρ[ας ὧ]ν ἔδωκαν ἐξουσίαν, ἔχουσιν δὲ καὶ ὧν ἐὰν κ̣α̣ὶ̣ ἴδια |42 κτήσωνται [37]

IV. Written law and legal expertise

Two central questions raised by the sources must be kept separate from each other: (a) where does this power come from, what is its source? (b) why is it linked to the form, written or unwritten, of the marriage?

Concerning the source: through Dionysia's petition we know that the paternal *exousia* was a part of the laws of the Egyptians that could be read in court.[38] The information comes from the second court precedent she appends in her defence (Col. 7, ll. 29–38), a case tried in 133 CE before the *epistrategos* Paconius Felix, where the hearing had been adjourned so that the law could be presented in court:

> Ἰσίδωρος ῥήτωρ ὑπὲρ Φλαυήσιος εἶπεν, "τ̣ὸ̣ν οὖν α̣ἰ̣τ̣ιώ̣μενον |32 ἀποσπάσαι βουλόμενον τ[ὴ]ν θυγατέρα αὐτοῦ συνοικοῦσαν τῷ̣ ἀντιδίκῳ̣ δεδικάσθαι ὑπογύως πρὸς αὐτὸν ἐπὶ τοῦ ἐ̣[πι]σ̣τ̣ρ̣α̣τ̣ή̣γου |33 καὶ ὑπερτεθεῖσθαι τὴν δίκην ὐ̣μ̣ε̣ῖ̣ν̣ (*l.* ὑμῖν) ἵνα ἀναγνωσθῇ ὁ τῶν Αἰγυπτίω[ν νό]μος. [39]

---

[37] *P. Oxy.* II 237 (186 CE Oxyrhynchos), col. 7, ll. 41–42: For I declare to you that the Egyptians have power to deprive their daughters not only of what they have given them, but also of whatever they may | acquire as their own.

[38] That this particular law could be read in court does not mean, as often assumed, that the 'laws of the Egyptians' had been object of a compilation. Such compilations existed for the native Egyptian law: cf. the so-called *Zivilprozessordnung* (*P. Berlin P* 13621 r., *P. Cairo CG* 50108a–b, *P. Giessen* UB 101), *P. Berlin P.* 23890 r., *P. Carlsberg* 236, and especially the so-called *codex Hermopolis* (*P. Matha*), conjectured by Lippert 2008: 85 to be fragments from the codification ordered soon after the Persian conquest by Darius I, according to the so-called Demotic chronicle (*P. Bibl. Nat.* 215 *verso*, c 6–16). That such compilations remained in circulation in Roman times, in the Greek versions we also know existed, would not be surprising: and indeed, it may well be that the law was read in our case from one of them. That the 'laws of the Egyptians' in the 2nd cent. sense of the term, comprising all legal traditions present in the *chora*, could have been compiled, is instead hardly thinkable – and our text does not require it either.

[39] *P. Oxy.* II 237 (186 CE Oxyrhynchos), col. 7, ll, 31–33: Isidorus, advocate for Phlauesis, said that the plaintiff therefore, wishing | to take away his daughter who was living with

And in fact, the continuation of the court record confirms that the law was indeed presented in court and read before the *epistrategos*:

> Πακώνιος Φῆλιξ· ἀναγνωσθητο (*l.* ἀναγνωσθήτω) ὁ ν[ό]μ[ος. Ἀ]να|36γνωσθέντος Πακώνιος [Φῆ]λιξ· ἀνάγνωται (*l.* ἀνάγνωτε) καὶ τὸν Τειτιανοῦ ὑπομ[ν]ηματισμόν. [40]

The paternal *exousia* itself, therefore, was written law. For the link between the *exousia* and the form of the marriage, instead, Dionysia cannot quote any law, but merely (Col. 8, ll. 2–7) the opinion of the *nomikos* Dioskourides reproduced *supra sub* III.[41] Also for the link between *testamenti factio* of the children and the form of the father's marriage the plaintiff in *CPR* I 18 does not produce any written law, and the judge himself seeks instead confirmation through a legal expert (see *supra* in III).

If our sources do not mislead us, therefore, the power of the father was written law; its connection to the form of the marriage, instead, resulted from the interpretation of the legal experts. This means: it is not the remnant of a remote tradition or of old laws the purpose of which might have become obscure with time, but arises in the 2nd century from a certain legal logic that was still then very much alive and which therefore we can aspire to reconstruct. There must have been something in the difference between *agraphos* and *engraphos gamos* that led the 2nd century *nomikoi* to link them to the paternal *exousia*. This logic, I believe, can be reconstructed going back to Tryphon's unwritten marriage, *P. Oxy.* II 267 = *MChr.* 281 (36 CE).

V. The loan-dowry tradition

Two aspects of Tryphon's document will be particularly significant for us: it is a non-notarial document, a *cheirographon*; and it is not fashioned as a marriage deed, documenting the marriage itself and the duties of the spouses, but as a bank-confirmed receipt, in the typical Oxyrhnchite form of a *cheirographon kai diagraphe*:[42]

---

the defendant, had recently brought an action against him before the *epistrategos* | and the case had been deferred in order that the Egyptian law might be read.

40 *P. Oxy.* II 237 (186 CE Oxyrhynchos), col. 7, ll. 35–36: Paconius Felix said, 'Let the law be read.' When it had | been read Paconius Felix said, 'Read also the minute of Titianus.'

41 In the same sense, Platschek 2015: 158: "Dass das Gesetz beide von Dionysia genannten Negativbedingungen für das Heimholrecht des V aters formulieren würde, ist zu bezweifeln".

42 The equation of bank-*diagraphai* to public documents occurred only with the advent of the so-called 'independent' *diagraphe* – no longer mere confirming of payment regarding a transaction otherwise documented, v.gr. through *cheirographon* as in our case, but execution of the entire document through the bank – and only regarding the latter, not earlier than the turn of the 1st to the 2nd century CE: Wolff 1978: 95–105. There is, therefore, little doubt that Tryphon's document, as all the other *cheirographa kai diagraphai* that we

> ὁμολογῶι (l. ὁμολογῶ) ἔχειν |3 παρὰ σοῦ ἐπὶ τοῦ πρὸς Ὀξυρύγχων πόλει Σαραπιείου διὰ τῆς |4 Σαραπίωνος τοῦ Κλεάνδρου τραπέζης ἀργυρίου Σεβαστοῦ |5 καὶ Πτολεμαικοῦ νομίσματος δραχμὰς τεσσαράκοντα καὶ |6 τιμῆς ἐνωτίων χρυσῶν ζεύγους ἑνὸς ἀργυρίου δραχμὰς (corr. ex δραχμαι) |7 εἴκοσι καὶ χιτῶνος γαλακτίνου ἀργυρίου δραχμὰς δέκα δύο, |8 ὥστ' εἶναι ἐπὶ τὸ αὐτὸ ἀργυρίου δραχμὰς ἑβδομήκοντα δύο |9 κεφαλαίου αἷς οὐδὲν τῶι καθόλου προσῆκται, ὑπὲρ ὧν καὶ |10 συνπέπεισμαι. τὰς δὲ τοῦ ἀργυρίου δραχμὰς ἑβδομήκον|11τα δύο ἀποδώσω σοι τῇ τριακάδι τοῦ Φαῶφι τοῦ ἰσιόντος (l. εἰσιόντος) |12 δευτέρου ἔτους Γαίου Καίσαρος Γερμανικοῦ Νέου Σεβαστοῦ |13 Αὐτοκράτορος, χωρὶς πάσης ὑπερθέσεως.[43]

Tryphon acknowledges to Saraeus that he has received from her through a bank at the Serapeum 40 silver drachmas – with the bank's subscription in ll. 32–34 – and, in addition, a pair of gold earrings and a robe, typical dotal objets, given, as it is typical for dowries, under estimation: 20 and 12 drachmas respectively. All in all, 72 drachmas, which he promises to repay. Remarkably, not in case of separation, but in roughly 5 months: the document was executed on May 22nd (i.e. Pachon 27th of the first year of Caligula, l. 22) and the sum must be repaid on October 27th (Phaophi 30th of Caligula's second year, ll. 11–13). Why this exact term we do not know, but it might be related to Saraeus pregnancy (*supra* II).

Together with this general obligation to return the entire sum in five months, Tryphon promises: in ll. 18–21, as we have seen (*supra* II), to pay a sum on account of childbirth, should they separate during her pregnancy; and in general in case of separation (l. 17–18), to return the earrings:

> ἐὰν δὲ |[17] ἀπαλλαγῶμεν ἀπ' ἀλλήλων ἐξέσται σοι ἔχειν τὸ τῶν ἐνω|[18]τίων ζεῦγος ἐν τῆι ἴσῃ διατιμ[ή]σει. ἐπεὶ δὲ σύνεσμεν |[19] ἀλλήλοις ἀγράφω[ς] προσομολογῶι (l. προσομολογῶ) ἐὰν ὡσαύτως ἐκ διαφορᾶς |[20] ἀπ[αλλαγ]ῶμεν ἀπ' ἀλλήλ[ων] ἐνκύου σ[ο]ῦ οὔσῃ[ς] δώσειν σοι (Whitehorne; prev. ed.: ἕως ἄν σοι) |[21] [εἰς λόγον δ]απάν[ης λ]οχ[είας δραχμάς - ca.17 -][44]

---

will review in this section, were yet purely private documents and would not have been recognised at the time of their execution as *demosioi chrematismoi.*

[43] *P. Oxy.* II 267 (37 CE Oxyrhynchos), ll. 2–13: I acknowledge the receipt | from you at the Serapeum at Oxyrhynchus through the bank of | Sarapion, son of Kleandrus, of 40 silver drachmae of the Imperial | and Ptolemaic coinage, and | for the value of one pair of gold earrings, 20 drachmae of silver, | and for a milk-white robe, 12 drachmae of silver, | making a total sum of 72 drachmae of silver, | to which nothing at all has been added, in consideration of which | I have consented. And I will repay you the 72 drachmae of silver | on the 30th of Phaophi in the coming | second year of Gaius Caesar Germanicus Novus Augustus | Imperator (Oct. 27th. 37 CE) without any delay.

[44] *P. Oxy.* II 267 (37 CE Oxyrhynchos), ll. 16–21: If | we separate from each other, you shall be empowered to have the pair of | earrings at their present value. And since we are

The earrings clause is best understood in the sense that Tryphon needs to return them immediately if a separation occurs before the established 5-month term, the rest becoming due only then.[45] In any case, both the earrings and the pregnancy clause show that this is indeed a marriage document of some sort, with the earrings and probably also the robe and the money functioning as a dowry. A dowry articulated in such a way, though, that both espouses are free to depart from each other, if they so wish, after five months: Saraeus by claiming back the sum, Tryphon by giving it back to her – with the only addition of childbirth expenses if the pregnancy progresses without problems and he nevertheless repudiates her. And yet, the term dowry is avoided, and the entire agreement is articulated as a loan would be.

This is not the only case known to us of a dowry given as a loan. In the early nineties, Traianos Gagos, Ludwig Koenen and Brad McNellen[46] called attention to a series of marital loans in the archive of Pausiris – like Tryphon, a weaver in 1st century Oxyrhynchos.[47] These are, like in Tryphon's case, loans granted by a wife to her husband through a bank at the Serapeum of Oxyrynchos; again, by non-notarial document; and just like for Tryphon and Saraeus, they clearly function as a dowry. Unlike Tryphon's, the loans in Pausiris' archive do not always include a preestablished term for payment: most are open ended, to be returned only if the wife requests them, and then within thirty days.

As an example, let us consider *P. Mich. inv.* 92: three hundred drachmas are here documented as received through a bank at the Serapeum of Oxyrhynchos – although the sum in truth arises from the estimation of typical dotal objects like earrings and a chain, granted to Pausiris by his wife Tauris. The document was given in Tybi of Vespasian's sixth year, December 73 CE to January 74 CE, as we learn through its repayment in *P. Mich. inv.* 89, despite which the marriage continued:[48]

---

living | together in an unwritten way, I further agree if as aforesaid owing to a quarrel | we separate from each other while you are in a state of pregnancy, I will give you | on account of childbirth expenses ...

45 So, convincingly, Whitehorne 1984: 1272, and Yiftach-Firanko 2003: 92, with further lit., against Wolff's interpretation, that Saraeus would be entitled to the sum only if the couple remains together, while in case of separation she would lose everything except the earrings.

46 Gagos-Koenen-McNellen 1992.

47 Pauriris' archive, in the Michigan collection, and Gagos' work on it, remain unfortunately unpublished.

48 *P. Mich. inv.* 92 was Published as Appendix I in Gagos-Koenen-McNellen 1992; in their document list (ibid.: 202–204), the loan is nr. 13, its likely repayment in P. Mich. inv. 89, nr. 18; for a detailed analysis of both and of the complex financial situation of Pausiris, Gagos-Koenen-McNellen 1992: 184–187.

ὁμολογῶι (l. ὁμολογῶ) |6 ἀπ[έχε]ι̣ν̣ παρὰ σ̣ο̣ῦ [ἐπὶ] τοῦ πρὸς Ὀξυρύγχων πόλει Σαραπιείου |7 διὰ τῆς Ἀμμ[ωνίου κα]ὶ Σαραπίωνος καὶ τῶν μετόχων τρα|8πέζης ἀργυρ[ίου Σεβασ]τοῦ νομίσματο[ς δραχμὰς] τριακο|9σίας, (γίνονται) [ἀρ]γ̣[υ(ρίου)] (δραχμαὶ) [τ̅, κεφαλα]ί̣ου, ἐ̣ν αἷς ἐστιν ἐν[ω]τίων χρ[υ]σῶν ζεῦ|10γος ἓν ἐν συντειμήσει δραχμῶν τε̣[σσαρ]άκον̣τ̣α [κ]αὶ ἅλυ|11σιν ἀργυρίου ὁλκῆς ἀσήμου δραχμῶν τ̣ρ̣ιάκο̣[ν]τ̣α̣ κ̣[α]ὶ ... |12 ἐν συντειμήσ̣ε̣ι̣ δραχμῶν ἑκατὸν [ἑξ]ήκοντα καὶ κ̣α̣.|13[. . .]ενα δραχμῶν ὀγδοήκοντα. τὸ δὲ προκείμενον |[14] κ[ε]φ̣[άλ]α̣ιον ἀποδώσω σοι ἐν ἡμέραις τριάκοντα ἀφ' ἧς ἐὰν |15 ἀπαιτηθῇ. π̣ροσομολογῶ δὲ καὶ ἐὰ̣[ν] ἀ̣παλλ̣αγὴ γένη|16ταί σου ἐνκύ̣ο̣υ̣ οὔσης ἀποδώσειν σοι χωρὶς τοῦ προκειμένου |17 κεφαλαίου εἰς τὴν τῆς λοχείας δαπάνην ἄλλας <ἀ>ργ(υρίου) δ̣ρ̣[αχ]μ̣[ὰ]ς̣ ρ̣.[49]

Like Pausiris' and Tryphon's, most of the preserved dowry-loans from Oxyrhynchos and their repayments are executed as *cheirographon kai diagraphe* through the banks at the Serapeum,[50] suggesting that this was a model kept alive particularly in their scribal tradition. In any case, as Gagos realised,[51] these dowry-loans are related to a well-known Demotic practice. One of the best pieces of evidence for this is a Demotic papyrus, of which only the Greek subscription has been published, as *P. Tebt.* II 386 = *MChr.* 298 (12 BCE Hiera, Arsinoites):

[49] *P. Mich. inv.* 92 (73–74 CE Oxyrhynchos): I acknowledge | that I have received from you at the Serapeum in the city of Oxyrhynchos | through the bank of Ammonios, Sarapion and Co, | [the capital sum of] three hundred [drachmas] | of Augustan silver coinage, [that is 300 drachmai of silver], which includes one pair of gold | earrings, forty drachmas in value and a | chain of a weight of thirty drachmas of uncoined silver and [...] | one hundred and sixty drachmas in value, and [...] | [...] worth eighty drachmas. The aforesaid | capital I shall repay to you within thirty days of | request. I further acknowledge that if there is a separation | while you are pregnant, I shall pay you, aside from the aforesaid | capital, another 100 drachmas of silver for the expense of childbirth.

[50] Linked to the Serapeum banks are, in Pausiris' archive (document numbers after Gagos-Koenen-McNellen: 202–204): nr. 18 (*P. Mich. inv.* 89, 74 CE), the repayment by Pausiris of the loan above; nr. 6 (*P. Mich. inv.* 79, 60 CE), a 20 dr. two-month loan granted to Pausiris' older brother Dioskous by his wife Thermouthion, and its repayment in nr. 10 (*P. Mich. inv.* 77, 60 CE). Also through the Serapeum banks had been executed the loan repaid by a certain Sarapion to his wife Taÿsoreus in *P. Oxy.* XLIX 3487 (65 CE Oxyrhynchos). Agoranomic are instead a second loan granted to Pausiris' brother Dioskous by his wife Thermouthion (nr. 9, *P. Mich.* III 191–192 *dupl.* 60 CE) and its repayment a year later (nr. 11, *P. Mich.* III 194, 61 CE); a draft of an agoranomic loan is also *P. Yale* I 64 (75–76 CE Oxyrhynchos), granted by Thaesis to her husband Aperos. A pure *cheirographon* instead is *P. Lund.* VI 3 = *SB* VI 9353 (139 CE? unknown provenance), cf. Gagos-Koenen-McNellen 1992: 196–199.

[51] Gagos-Koenen-McNellen 1992: 198–199.

> |$_{12}$ ἔτους ιη Καίσαρος Παῦνι ιβ, κεχρη(μάτισται) |$_{13}$ διὰ Ἡρώδου συναλλαγ(ματογράφου) .α̣. .( ) |$_{14}$ (hand 2) Πακῆμις Πακήμιος τῶν ἀπὸ Εἱερα|$_{15}$ν (l. Ἱερα|ς) τῆς Πολέμων[ο]ς μερίδος Πέρσης τῆς |$_{16}$ ἐπιγονῆς ἔχω τὸ δάνηον (l. δάνειον) παρὰ Ταμεισ̣|$_{17}$χε̣[ως] τῆ[ς Σ]οκ[ο]νώπιος τῆς γυναικός μ[ου] |$_{18}$ φερνὴν σὺν ἱματισμῷ ἀργυρίου δραχμ|$_{19}$ὰς εἴκοσι τέσσαρ[α]ς ἃ[ς] καὶ ἀπο[δ]ώσ[ω]. |$_{20}$ ἐὰν δὲ χωρισμὸς γένηται ἀπ' [ἀ]λλή|$_{21}$λων ἐκτ<ε>ίσω ἐν ἡμέραις τριάκοντα ἀ|$_{22}$φ' ἧς ἐάν μοι παρανγ<ε>ίλῃ ἄνευ πάση[ς] |$_{23}$ ὑπερθέσεως καὶ εὑρησολογία<ς> καθότι |$_{24}$ προγέγραπται [52]

Crucial for us here is the explicit assimilation of the estimated dowry to a loan – ἔχω τὸ δάνηον παρὰ Ταμεισ̣|χε̣[ως] … τῆς γυναικός μ[ου] | φερνὴν σὺν ἱματισμῷ ἀργυρίου δραχμ|ὰς εἴκοσι τέσσαρ[α]ς ἃ[ς] καὶ ἀπο[δ]ώσ[ω]. The text confirms beyond any doubt the Demotic roots of this loan-dowry practice, typically articulated as open-term loans to be returned within thirty days of being claimed by the wife. It is the exact same legal structure that we find in Pausiris' archive, and indeed it corresponds to a well attested Demotic practice, that Pieter Pestman, in his ground-breaking study on marriage and marital property in Egyptian law, classified as type B.[53] An example of this Demotic type B is *P. Cairo* 50129 = *P. Eheverträge* 51 = *Spiegelberg, Demotische Denkmäler* III, p. 93 = *Acta Orientalia* 23, p. 119 = *Pasek, Urkunde Hawara* 46 = *SB* vi 9297 (86 BCE Hawara, Arsinoites), the central clauses of which read as follows:

> (a) You have given to me 500 (deben) of money, half of it is 225 (deben) of money, is 500 (deben) of money again, by which 24 (obols) of copper (go into a stater) as your money to become a wife to me (*ḥḏ n ỉr ḥm.t*), which you have given to me (in) Hawara (and) Nablu, the villages the Pharaoh has made (into) a place of oath; I [have received] it from your hand, my heart is content with it, (for) it is complete and without any remainder; I have nothing, not a single claim in the world on you on the grounds thereof from this day and afterwards; I cannot [impose] on you an oath before a God or before (the) Pharaoh from this day and afterwards; you have a right to it, at my charge;
> (b) I shall give you emmer, 27 artabas of 40 hin, is barley 18 artabas of 40 hin, is emmer 27 artabas of 40 hin again and 200 (deben) of money, half of it is 100

---

52 *P. Tebt.* II 386 = *MChr.* 298 (12 BCE Hiera, Arsinoites): Year 18 of Caesar, Pauni 12th, executed | through Herod the notary (…) | (hand 2) I, Pakemis son of Pakemis, of those from Hiera | of the division of Polemon, Persian of the | descent, have the loan from my wife Tameis|chis daughter of Soknopis, | a dowry with clothing (to the value) of twenty-four drachm|as of silver, which I will also return. | If a separation from each | other shall take place, I shall pay it within thirty days | after she will claim it from me, without any | delay or pretext, in accordance with | what is written above.

53 Pestman 1961: 32–37. In *P. Tebt.* II 386, the husband's duty to pay the sum back upon divorce clearly points to model B rather than C: *infra* VI and Pestman 1961: 36.

> (deben) of money, is 200 (deben) of money again, (by which) 24 obols of copper (go into a stater) as your maintenance (*ʿḳ ḥbs*), annually.
> (c) On your day you demand from my hand the above 500 (deben) of money, I shall give it to you thereupon, on a day within 30 days after it being claimed from my hand which you will do; if I do not give you (back) the above 500 (deben) of money within the above 30 days, from [my] hand [(then) I shall] give you maintenance in accordance with the maintenance as written above: the (same) emmer and copper-money above described, till I give you the above 500 (deben) of money (back);

Central to the model is the clause (a) where the husband acknowledges that the bride has given him the so-called 'money to become a wife' (*ḥḏ n ỉr ḥm.t*), and the clause (c) where he promises to give it back within 30 days of being required - thus securing the right of the wife to recover the sum upon separation. Having accepted the sum and, with it, the woman as his wife, the husband untertakes to provide for her maintenance, at a carefully specified annual rate.

Not only the legal structure of the *ḥḏ n ỉr ḥm.t* as open debt, to be returned whenever demanded, rendered in Greek subscriptions like *P. Tebt.* II 386 = *MChr.* 298 simultaneously as *pherne* and *daneion*, finds a clear echo in Pausiris (thirty-day term included) and Tryphon. Noteworthy also, as underlined by Gagos,[54] is the clause ὑπὲρ ὧν καὶ | συνπέπεισμαι in Tryphon (*P. Oxy.* II 267, l.9–10), lit. 'by which I am persuaded', referred to the amount of the dowry. Such clause is not attested in Greek loan or dowry models, and indeed, would not make much sense there, considering that the party receiving the sum does not have any claim to it – but rather takes on a debt – and that her consent is already expressed by taking the sum. Instead, συμπείθω, as Gagos observed, was routinely used in the early Roman time to translate the standard Egyptian consent locution 'my heart is content with it',[55] precisely the expression we find in model B when the husband receives the *ḥḏ n ỉr ḥm.t*: a further trace, even in the formulation of the clauses, of the Egyptian origin of these Greek dowry-loans.

VI. The Demotic 'universal sale' marriage tradition

In the Demotic tradition there was yet another form, deeply different, to create a wife's right to an annuity: the so-called "endowment document" (*sẖ n sʿnḫ*), which Pestman

[54] Gagos-Koenen-McNellen 1992: 190.

[55] Cf. already Biscottini 1966: 201 n. 2 i.f. Gagos' example is *SB* I 5231 = *Jur. Pap.* 28 (11 CE Psinachis, Arsinoites), a Demotic 'document for silver' translated into Greek, 'as far as possible', as such translations routinely warn – [ἀν]τί[γ]ρ[αφ]ον Αἰγυπτίας π[ρά]σεως Ἑ[λ]ληνιστὶ μεθηρμηνε[υ]μένης [κα]τὰ [τὸ δ]υνατόν (l. 1); the clause 'my heart is satisfied with the silver, the price of my house' is there rendered πέπε[ι]κάς με ἀργυρίωι | τῆι τι[μῆι] τῆς ὑπαρχού[σ]ης μοι οἰκία[ς]. Yet a better example may be *CPR* XV 1 = *SB* I 5246 (3 BCE Arsinoites), from the archive of Satabous, a Greek translation of a Demotic *apostasion* (ll. 1–20) and its equally Demotic subscriptions, the first of which reads: [ἀντίγραφον ὑπογραφῆς Αἰγυπτίας Ἑλληνιστὶ μεθηρμηνευμένης κατὰ τὸ δυνατόν. Σαταβοῦς] Πετεσο[ύ]χου . . [. . . . .]ασω καὶ [ὁμολογῶ συμ]πεπεῖσθαι (l. 18).

labelled as model C.[56] As an example, *P. Bibl. Nat.* 224 = *P. Eheverträge* 10 D = *Rev. Ég. 2,* p. 92 = *SB* I 2 = *UPZ* I 137 = *P. Précis* p. 1007 n. 1 (69 BCE Memphis), the central clauses of which are articulated thus:

> (a) You have caused my heart to be satisfied by giving to me 21 (deben) of pure silver from the treasury of Ptah, is 20 (deben) of silver and 9 kite 2/3 1/6 1/10 1/30 1/60 1/60, is 21 (deben) of pure silver from the treasury of Ptah again, as your endowment (*sꜥnḫ*).
> (b) To the god's seal-bearer Peteesis, son of Hereius, my eldest son, your eldest son, and of the same status to Petosiris, son of Hereius, my son, your son, both, my children, your children that you have born to me, and to the children that you will bear to me, belongs everything and all that belongs to me and that I shall acquire.
> (c) I shall give you emmer, 37 artabas of 40 hin, is barley 24 artabas of 40 hin, is emmer 37 artabas of 40 hin again, and 2 (deben) 4 kite of pure silver from the treasure of Ptah, is 2 (deben) 3 Kite 2/3 1/6 1/10 1/30 1/60 1/60, is 2 (deben) 4 kite of pure silver from the treasure of Ptah again, for your food (and) clothing (and) money, annually in the house, as you wish.

Here, the sum received by the husband (a) did not serve to turn the woman into a wife, but directly to establish his duty (c) to provide alimonies. Called *sꜥnḫ*, lit. 'what enables to live', often translated as endowment, this sum and the ensuing arrangement could indeed be granted also in non-marital contexts and its repayment did not depend on divorce but exclusively on the will of the woman.[57] Unlike in model B, the sum does not seem to have depended on the specifics of the situation and the bride's possessions, but was determined at a stereotype rate, most often of 21 deben of silver.[58] That the sum could at least in some cases have been not just stereotype

---

[56] Pestman 1961: 37–50; Lippert 2008: 167–169.

[57] Pestman 1961: 69–71. Procedural solutions and documentary models regarding some of the possible conflicts arising from such endowment arrangements can be found in a long section of codex Hermopolis col. 4, l. 6 – col. 5, l. 31.

[58] 21 deben are equivalent to 420 drachmas. This is the sum in practically every preserved endowment contract from the 2nd and 1st cent. BCE: *P. Mich.* 4526 A1/AII = *P. Eheverträge* 4D/Z (199 BCE Philadelphia); *P. Mich.* 4244/4a = *P. Eheverträge* 6Z (142 BCE Heliopolis), wrongly labelled by Lüddeckens as a document for silver; *P. Hamb. dem.* 14 = *Urk. Hawara* VIII a (129 BCE Hawara); *P. Kairo* 30607 = *P. Eheverträge* 7D (128 BCE); *P. Kairo* 30608–30609 = *P. Eheverträge* 8D–Z (123 BCE); *P. Kairo* 30616b–a = *P. Eheverträge* 9D–Z (78 BCE Tebtynis); and *P. Bibl. Nat.* 224–225 = *P. Eheverträge* 10D–Z (68 BCE Memphis), used above as example. The 21-deben tradition seems to have solidified only in the 2nd. century BCE: previous endowment deeds were given at 30 (*P. Chic.* 17481 = *P. Eheverträge* 1D, 365 BCE Arsinoites) and 6 deben (*P. Bibl. Nat.* 219 = *P. Eheverträge* 2D, 316 BCE Memphis); at 50 deben still in the early 2nd century (*P. BM* 10591B VI 21–VII 5 = *P. Eheverträge* 5D, 181 BCE Siut). Significantly, when in later Ptolemaic and early Roman times the sum oscillates again, it does not return to round numbers but insists on adding one: not 50 but 51 deben in *P. Heid. Aeg.* 10–11 = *P. Eheverträge* 11D–Z (late Ptolemaic, Karara), not 10 but 11 in *P. Mich.* 347 = *P. Eheverträge* 12D (21 CE Tebtynis); also in the early Roman examples

but also fictitious, rather than actually received by the husband, is suggested by the famous episode of Tabubu in Setne's cycle (*infra* in this same section).[59]

Two further differences between this model C and model B will be crucial for us:[60]

(i) In model C, the acknowledgement that the sum has been paid (clause a) leads to the recognition of the – future or already born – common children as heirs (clause b). This is never the case in model B, where no inheritance rights whatsoever are bestowed on the children, who are not even mentioned. Securing the inheritance rights of the common children seems therefore one of the main specific goals of model C.

(ii) In model C, the entire property of the husband, present and future, is sold to the wife – without her paying any actual price.[61] This is done in a separate document, a so-called "document for silver" (*sẖ ḏbꜣ-ḥḏ*), the standard form of the Demotic sale, labelled in Greek simply as *prasis*. As illustration, the counterpart of the previous document, concluded by the same parties on the same day – Mesore 29th of the 13th year of Ptolemy XII Auletes –, *P. Bibl. Nat.* 225 = *P. Eheverträge* 10Z = *Rev. Ég.* 2, p. 93 = *UPZ* I 138 (69 BCE Memphis) will suffice. Its central clauses are the following:

> (a) You have satisfied my heart with the money, the price of everything that belongs to me and that I shall acquire, house, field, yard, land, wall, square, garden, vineyard, male servant, female servant (…) all household goods, every prebend, and of all things, all writings, all documents, agreements with any free person (…) of everything on earth. They belong to you from today onwards. I have no claim in the world against you in their regard.
> (b) Whoever comes against you because of them I will cause to be far from you with regard to them necessarily without delay. And I will make them be clear for you from every document (…) everything on earth.

---

from the *grapheion* of Tebtynis the sum is 21 or 11, now not in silver deben but in gold pieces, proving that decisive in these endowment documents is less the currency value than the number symbolism – which again suggests that the sum may often have been fictitious. Behind this tradition of adding one to a round number there is probably no other reason than the imperative to avoid illiberality at least when marrying: to the round sum one is added, for the exact same reason that makes imperative in modern discount sale practice to detract one, even if it is only one cent, from the round price, leaving 20 at 19.99.

59 In the regime outlined in Codex Hermopolis, though, lawsuit can be brought by the part owing the alimonies, claiming not to have actually received the *sꜥnḫ* documented in the endowment deed: should his adversary refuse to swear under oath that the sum was given, the document will be torn up: col. 5, ll. 7–11.

60 Cf., in extenso, Pestman 1961: 48–50.

61 Pestman 1961: 39–41. Unlike the symbolic (and probably often fictitious) sum of the *sꜥnḫ*, which constitutes the core of the endowment document and is thus never omitted, no sum is ever mentioned as price in the 'document for silver' when executed in a marriage context.

(c) To you belongs every document that has been made concerning them, and every document that has been made for me concerning them, and every document due to which I have a right with regard to them. They and their rights belong to you. To you belongs all on the basis of which I have rights regarding them.

Unlike Greek sales, Demotic 'documents for silver' are not enough to deprive the seller –here the husband– of ownership. This would have required a deed of surrender called 'document of being far' (*sẖ n wꜣy*), *apostasion* in Greek, which of course is not granted in marriage contexts. Without it, the husband remains owner, but the wife becomes owner as well, in a form of functionally divided ownership.[62] In

[62] The careful fashioning of the clauses in the 'document for silver' and in the 'document of being far' clearly shows that the buyer acquired already through the former. The core clause of the document for silver reads (*P. BM* 262 + *MChr.* 181 = *P. Dime* III 5, 11 CE Soknopaiu Nesos, right column, l. 3): "you have satisfied my heart with the money, the price of my house …"; and, after the description of the object (ll. 5–6), "they belong to you | from today onwards". In actual sales, where a 'document of being far' is also granted, usually on the exact same day, the core clause reads (in the same *P. BM* 262 + *MChr.* 181 = *P. Dime* III 5, 11 CE Soknopaiu Nesos, left column, l. 3): "I am far from you concerning your house …"; and, after a description of the object, identical to that of the first document (ll. 5–6), "I do not have any claim at all on you concerning them | from today onwards". The quite deliberate form (Zauzich 1968:152–153) in which the 'my' of the first document gives way to the 'your' in the second speaks for itself: when the latter document is executed, the house belongs already to the buyer, by virtue of the former. It would be a mistake, though, to consider the 'document of being far' – with Depauw 2014: 56–57 – as 'secondary' and 'mere confirmation' of the sale. It is true that the sale version of the 'document of being far' belongs to a wider genre used for many other purposes, like quitclaims after judgment, after payment or among heirs. But it is far from obvious that such quitclaims merely confirm an existing situation, as often held: the assumption that, without explicit quitclaim, no lawsuit would be possible after a first trial, a payment or a distribution of inheritance, is, in fact, an unwarranted *petitio principii*; it rather seems that the 'document of being far' is the actual way in which a claim that otherwise would remain possible is excluded. Regarding sales, law historians have tended – as Depauw does, cf. also Lippert 2008: 153–154 – to unreflectedly use the modern paradigm of 'transfer of rights', and ask themselves when ownership is transferred, which obviously can only happen once, either with the document of silver (as Depauw holds) or with the document of being far. But the idea of something called 'ownership' being 'transferred' is a rather artificial, ontologising view of subjective rights as substantial realities passing from alienor to acquirer; even in Roman law, this idea arose comparatively late – to the point that in the early 20th century the idea itself of a '*dominium transferre*' came to be dismissed as a later Byzantine interpolation in the classical sources, cf. De Francisci 1924, and now Stagl 2009: 1191–1206. If, instead of thinking in terms of 'transfer of ownership', we consider the situation of the two individuals involved, a buyer who will acquire something and a seller who will lose it, it is no longer a logical necessity for the seller's loss to be simultaneous with the buyer's acquisition. This is precisely what the Demotic two-step model allows the parties to decide for themselves, depending on their aims: the document for silver is, as we have seen, sufficient for the buyer to acquire; for the seller to lose his right, his actual surrender through the document of being far is nevertheless necessary. When the parties

practice, this means that no alienation by the husband without her consent can be opposed to her: a limitation of the husband's alienation power that the Greek sources (*infra* VII) will construct as a 'hold' or 'lien' (German: 'Verfangenschaft'), a *katoche*. Only in case of divorce, if the husband is not in the position to return the endowment sum (*sꜥnḫ*), will he have to forfeit his entire estate to the wife through a 'document of being far'.[63] Securing the wife's right to the *sꜥnḫ* is the first function of this 'universal sale' that the Greek sources (*infra* VII) call *panprasion* (since it refers to his entire property) or *proprasis* (since it is not a definitive sale with loss of ownership).[64]

The two peculiarities of model C, the veto arising from the *panprasion*, and the inheritance rights of the children, are related. It is, in fact, not only to secure her *sꜥnḫ* but also the future inheritance for the common children that the wife acquires a veto right. The most effective illustration can be found in a famous Demotic novel, the story of Prince Setne Khaemwaset, son of Ramses II, preserved in the part relevant for us in *P. Cair.* 30646 (probably 3rd century BCE).[65] The story, and particularly the episode of Tabubu that will interest us, has fascinated readers since the late nineteenth century, when Gaston Maspero included it in his 'Contes populaires de l'Égypte ancienne'.[66]

---

aim at an actual sale, both documents are executed immediately one after the other, as in the above mentioned *pBM* 262 + *MChr.* 181 = *P. Dime* III 5 (11 CE Soknopaiu Nesos). When they aim instead at securing a debt, the same two-step model allows them to do so by just postponing the second step, the *apostasion*, to the moment of the debtor's default: cf. *P. Hauswaldt* 18 = *Berlin Äg. Mus.* inv. 11337 (212–211 BCE Edfu), where land is given as security for a loan, and the document of being far is written a year later than the document of silver, on the same papyrus; in the meantime, the debtor does not lose the land, even though the creditor is also already owner (what other position could he acquire as security in a system that unlike the Roman does not know the category of the 'limited real rights'?), with the result that the debtor, who will typically retain possession, use and enjoyment, will not be able to alienate without his consent – exactly the same practical effect that this truncated sale without 'document of being far' had in the marriage context that interest us, see *infra* in text. On 'functionally divided ownership', Alonso 2016: 123 n. 11.

63 An example, in *P. Louvre* 2428 (277 BCE), cf. Pestman 1961: 40–41.

64 On this function of the *panprasion*, Pestman 1961: 133–136.

65 This is the so-called 'first Setne papyrus', Setne I. For an English translation, Lichtheim 1980: 125-138; Ritner 2003. Another part of Setne's saga is preserved in *P. BM* 10822, the so-called Setne II. On the historical figure of Ramses' son Khaemwaset, Fischer 2001; Ray 2002: 78–96. Fist detailed studies: Révillout 1887 and Griffith 1900. Even if the legendary stories associated with Setne may go back to the Saitic time or even beyond, the legal practice used as narrative device in the Tabubu episode is anchored in the Demotic tradition of the Persian and Ptolemaic period: the earliest preserved *sḫ n sꜥnḫ* is dated 365 BCE (*P. Chic.* 17481 = *P. Eheverträge* 1D (Arsinoites); the earliest example of a 'type B' marriage agreement comes from just a few years after the Persian conquest (*P. BM* 10120 A = *P. Eheverträge* 6 = *P. Tsenhor* 3, 517 BCE Thebes).

66 Maspero 1911: 123–182, first edition 1882; the episode of Tabubu (144–150) captured immediately the imagination of its time, as a new Judith, Dalila or Salome. As soon as 1892,

As the story goes (col. 4, l. 38 – col. 5, l. 30), prince Setne sees one day in Memphis the most fascinating woman, covered in jewels, followed by servants, and proceeds to make one of the most appalling advances in literature history, offering ten pieces of gold for one hour with her. She, by name Tabubu, is horrified and haughtily rejects him: "I am pure, I am not a nobody. If you desire to do what you wish with me, you must come to Bubastis, to my house". Tabubu is in fact the daughter of the prophet of Bastet, the cat goddess of domestic life, but also, in her dual manifestation as Sekhmet, the blood-thirsty lion goddess of war and destruction: both 'nurturing mother' and 'mistress of dread'. As Setne, after long search, finds her splendid house, she presents her conditions: "I am pure, I am not a nobody. If you desire to do what you wish with me, you will make for a me a endowment document (*sẖ n sꜥnḫ*) and a document for silver (*sẖ ḏbꜣ-ḥḏ*) for everything you own". In other words: in exchange for the hour that Setne wishes, Tabubu requests a marriage arrangement of Pestman's C type. Setne consents, but Tabubu has a further demand: "I am pure, I am not a nobody. If you desire to do what you wish with me, you must make your children subscribe to my deed. Do not leave them to contend with my children over your property". The children, who magically happen to be present, confirm the sale, but Tabubu is still not satisfied: she wants them dead. Setne, full of desire, consents. The children are killed in his presence and thrown from the window to be devoured by the dogs and cats on the street. As he approaches Tabubu to finally embrace her, her mouth opens in a horrifying cry … and Setne wakes up, on the street, naked, just on time for his father, the pharaoh, to pass by and find him in such state.

Tabubu's preoccupation with Setne's children, and their terrible fate in his dream, illustrate quite effectively the function of the veto right acquired by the wife in Pestman's model C: it served, as Tabubu proclaims, to protect the entitlement of the common children (the future children that Tabubu's marital demands imagine) to the paternal inheritance. When the children come of age, it is their consent – typically the consent of the eldest son – that is required: it is for this reason that Tabubu wants to have her documents subscribed by Setne's children; she assumes that Setne had concluded a similar arrangement with the children's mother and therefore no alienation – and certainly no new universal sale – would prevail over their right without their consent. So much is confirmed by one of the legal rules quoted in the famous lawsuit before the *laokritai* of Siut, in *P. BM* 10591 (170 BCE Siut) *recto*, col. 10, ll. 7–9:

> If a man draws up an endowment document (*sẖ n sꜥnḫ*), for a woman and he gives goods of his to another person, without the woman or her eldest son having approved of said deed: If the woman or her eldest son brings an action against the man to

an adaptation entitled "Taboubou" was published by J.-H. Rosny (pseudonym of the borthers Boex), lavishly republished in the thirties with Art Déco illustrations by Maurice Lalau.

whom the goods are given, they (the goods) will not be pure for him and he shall not be allowed to be full of them.[67]

Notice that the acquisition of the buyer yields only to a claim of the beneficiaries of the universal sale: it is in this sense that the goods are 'not pure' for him – he does acquire, and his right prevails over third parties, but is outmatched by that of wife and children, in a form of relative ownership. Properly speaking, therefore, it is not so much that the assets become inalienable, but rather that without the consent of wife or eldest son the alienation does not prevail over their right.

If this position of wife and children is in the Siut rule associated with the endowment document, it is certainly because – aside from cementing by itself the latter's inheritance rights – the practice linking it to the universal sale was so constant that it could be assumed the former would not be granted without the latter. How common this practice remained in later Ptolemaic and early Roman Egypt is illustrated by the invariable mention of the wife's or eldest son's consent in sale documents, whenever the selling party is Egyptian. In such universal-sale marriages, the husband's property becomes family property, secured as inheritance for the common children, and no longer disposable for him without their consent.

VII. Loan-marriages and Sale-marriages in Early Roman Egypt

In early Roman times, as it became increasingly clear how unpractical Demotic had become – with the eradication of the Egyptian *laokritai* – for deeds needed in court,[68] a Greek version of Pestman's model B became widespread, as we have seen through the cases of Tryphon and Pausiris, and many other examples attest well into the 2nd century, in Oxyrhynchos[69] and elsewhere.[70] Onomastics are

---

67 Cf. also, in the same *P. BM* 10591 (170 BCE Siut) recto, the previous rule, regarding precisely the case feared by Tabubu, namely a man who after divorce from a type C marriage, concluded yet another one of the same kind: "If a man marries a woman and he draws up a deed for her concerning a *sꜥnh* and he has a child by her and he divorces her and he marries another woman and he draws up a deed concerning a *sꜥnh* for her and he has a child by her and said man dies: his possessions shall be given to the children of the first wife for whom he first drew up a deed concerning a *sꜥnh*." This exclusion of the children of the second marriage by those of the first can only be avoided if the latter waive their rights by consenting to the new universal sale.

68 Demotic execution of model B, like the Demotic documentary practice in general, does not seem to have survived beyond the first century CE: the latest attestations of model B in its Demotic original are the unpublished Demotic part of *P. Tebt.* 386 (12 BCE Tebtynis), and three documents from Soknopaiu Nesos: *P. Dime* III 39 (11–10 BCE), 40 (28 CE) and 41 (53 CE).

69 In Oxyrhynchos, Greek dowry-loans like those of Tryphon and Pausiris we find also, twice, between Pausiris' older brother Dioskous and his wife Thermouthion: nr. 6 and 9 in the list of Gagos-Koenen-McNellen 1992: 202–204, namely *P. Mich. inv. 79 (60 CE)* and *P. Mich.* III 191–192 *dupl.* (60 CE), repaid in *P. Mich. inv.* 77 (60 CE) and *P. Mich.* III 194 (61 CE), respectively. Beyond Pausiris' archive, between a certain Sarapion and

notoriously unreliable, more so as we advance in time, but the frequent presence of Greek names in this material, alongside others with Egyptian roots, suggests that the practice was not confined to purely Egyptian circles. Indeed, now that in the *chora* both Egyptians and Greeks are equally *Aigyptioi* in front of the administration, no formal barrier is left between their legal traditions that would prevent them from freely using the forms that best suit their interests, no matter their ethnic or cultural background.

Even better attested is the success of model C in the first two centuries of our Era. At the beginning of the 1st century, multiple examples appear among the records of the *grapheion* of Tebtynis. These belong still to a clear Egyptian milieu, are executed in Demotic, with the preceptive Greek subscription, and registered at the *grapheion* as *syngraphe trophitis* – the endowment deed – and *proprasis* – the

---

his wife Taÿsoreus in *P. Oxy.* XLIX 3487 (65 CE); between a certain Aperos and his wife Thaesis in *P. Yale* I 64 (75–76 CE Oxyrhynchos); and in *P. Lund.* VI 3 = *SB* VI 9353 (139 CE unknown provenance), preserved only in its final part, where a man receives from his father-in-law a loan to be returned within 60 days from being requested – and at the latest in ca. 4 months, within which the husband undertakes to have notarial *syngraphe gamou* executed for his wife. For a detailed analysis of these documents, Gagos-Koenen-McNellen 1992: 192–199. Nothing indicates, instead, that the 'chirographarian *syngraphe*' predating the notarial one in *P. Oxy.* XLIX 3491 (157–158 CE Oxyrhynchos), had the form of a loan; on the document, Gagos-Koenen-McNellen 1992: 195.

70 The Fayumic *P. Mich.* V 339 (46 CE Arsinoites) seems another example of dowry-loan: when this deed was executed, dowry and *parapherna* had already been documented in a previous one, not through a marriage *syngraphe*, but through an alimentary contract (*syngraphe trophitis*) referred to an amount of money secured by the husband's parents: μέν<ε>ιν ταί σοι τῇ Ταορσενοῦφι ἣν ἔχ<ε>ις <παρά> μου | μεδενκοίων (l. μετεγγύω) τῶν γωιναίων (l. γονέων) μου συνγραφὴν τροφῖτην (l. τροφῖτιν) ἑτέρας ἀργυρικῆς φερνῆς καὶ παραφέρνọụ | {ἣν καὶ μένιν} κοιρίαν (l. κυρίαν) καὶ των (l. τὰ) διὰ αὐτῆς δεδηιλωμενων (l. δεδηλωμένα) διαστωλων (l. διάστολα) πασων (l. πάντα) κοιριων (l. κυρία), καὶ ἕκα|στα ποήσωι (l. ποιήσω) καθὼς πρόκιται. Both the security, unusual otherwise in dotal context, and the fact that no actual dotal or paraphernal items were given but a sum of money, suggest that the whole had been treated as a loan. Also the addition to that previous dowry brought to the present document, even if not explicitly labelled as *daneion* but merely as *pherne*, is articulated following the standard loan model: ὁμολογῶι (l. ὁμολογῶ) ἔχ<ε>ιν παρὰ τῆς προούσις (l. προούσης) καὶ σοινούσης (l. συνούσης) γυναικὸς | Ταορσενοῦφις (l. Ταορσενούφεως) τῆς Ἀφροδισίου παραχρῆμα διὰ χ<ε>ιρὸς ἐξ ὕκου (l. οἴκου) ἐν προσδόσ<ε>ι ἐφ' αὐτης (l. αὐτῇ) φερνὴν ἀργυρίου | ἐπισήιμου (l. ἐπισήμου) δραχμὰς ἑκατὸν καὶ χρήσωιμαι (l. χρήσομαι) ὡ<ς> γυναικὶ γαμετῆι καὶ ἂν χ<ω>ρισμὸς ἀπ' ἀλλήλων γένηιτα(ι) (l. γένητα(ι)) | ἀποδώσωι (l. ἀποδώσω) τὰς προκιμένας ἀργυρίου δραχμὰς ἑκατόν. Gagos-Koenen-McNellen 1992: 194 mention also *P. Mich.* II 121 IV 7 (42 CE Tebtynis) and *SB* XII 10924 (114 CE Theadelphia), but only the former could be a case of dowry-loan, and also there the question must remain open, since the clauses regarding devolution – would shed light on the legal articulation of the document – are left out of the abstract.

universal sale –.[71] In the turn from the 1st to the 2nd century, despite the extinction of the Demotic notarial practice, the universal sale marriage model remained alive – necessarily in Greek form – and became widespread enough that it arrived repeatedly to the attention of the prefect. Through a collection of Roman court decisions on peregrine testamentary freedom preserved in *P. Oxy.* XLII 3015 (after 117 CE Oxyrhynchos) we learn that one such case reached the court of Sulpicius Similis, prefect of Egypt between 113/4 and 117 CE. He seems to have deemed the institution important, because, despite the consistent prefectural practice of delegating cases of pure private law[72], he decided on the case personally, in deliberation with his *consilium* and consulting a *nomikos*:

> [(ἔτους) . .] θεοῦ Τρα[ι]αν[ο]ῦ Τῦβι κ̣ ἐπὶ τῶν κατὰ Τρύφωνα |$_{14}$ [πρὸ]ς Διδ̣[. . . . .] μεθ' ἕ[τερα]· Σουλ[πίκι]ος Σίμιλις |$_{15}$ [συνλ]α̣λή̣[σας τοῖ]ς συνβ[ούλοις] καὶ ἀνα[κοιν]ωσαμέν̣[ος] |$_{16}$ [Ἀρ]τ̣εμιδώ̣ρ̣ῳ̣ ν̣ομικῷ̣ ἔ[φη·λ]έγεται .[. . .] .ονε .[. . . .] |$_{17}$ [. .] . . οὔτε ἡ γυνὴ ἐφ' ἧς καινότερόν τι συνεφώνη̣[σεν] |$_{18}$ ὁ πατὴρ τοῦ γαμοῦντος οὔτε οἱ υἱοὶ αὐτῆς περίεισι |$_{19}$ οἷ̣ς ἐδύνατο κατέχεσθαι τὰ κατὰ τὴν συμφωνίαν, |$_{20}$ ἄκυρόν ἐστιν ἤδη τοῦτο τὸ γράμμα. ὁ δὲ νόμος ὡς λέ|$_{21}$γεται δίδωσιν ἐξουσίαν τῶι τὸ

[71] Six in total are the examples from the Tebtynis *grapheion*: a Demotic endowment contract with Greek subscription with indication that a universal sale (*proprasis*) was also concluded, dated 21 CE (*P. Eheverträge* 12D + *P. Mich.* V 347), and five Greek abstracts of *syngraphe trophitis* and *proprasis* from the *grapheion* records of 42 CE: *P. Mich.* II 121 r. col. 2 ii; col. 3 i, vii and xii; col. 4 iv, first edited in Boak 1926. Curiously, they all refer to the *apostasion* as already executed – a clear indication that certain aspects of the legal logic behind the Demotic tradition were no longer properly understood. The contracting espouses are not in their first youth (in 3 i, forty and twenty-six; in 3 vii forty-six and thirty-six; in 3 xii, thirty-eight and thirty; in 4 iv, fifty-six and fifty), and the husband often refers to all or some of the property he 'sells' to his wife as inherited (3 i, vii and xii), suggesting that the document was typically executed not upon marriage but after inheriting; the only exception is 2 ii, a deed executed not by the husband but by his parents, securing their son's future inheritance; despite the *apostasion*, they do not lose the listed assets but merely bestow on their son and daughter in law a right on them – the right that the Roman administration will articulate as a *katoche* (so, rightly, Arangio-Ruiz 1930: 51–53): in fact, 2 ii begins by explicitly underlining that the property will devolve upon the son only after the death of his parents, μετὰ τὴν ἡμῶν τελευτὴν (l. 1).

[72] Cf., in *SB* XII 10929 (133–137 CE unknown provenance), the Edict of Petronius Mamertinus restricting the cases he will adjudge personally to criminal offenses and the behaviour of children and freedmen: Seidl 1972, Lewis 1972, Lewis 1973, Jördens 2011. The restriction seems to have been kept in place throughout the 2nd century, cf. in the petition of Dionysia, *P. Oxy.* II 237 (186 CE Oxyrhynchos) col. 6, ll. 6–7: καὶ σοῦ τοῦ κυρίου πάλιν καθ' ὁμοιότητα τῶν ἄλλων ἡγεμόνων ὑπογύως διαταξαμένου περὶ ἰδιωτι|κῶν ζητήσεων ἐπιστολάς σοι μὴ γράφειν: and although you, my Lord, in the same way as the other governors, recently again proclaimed that | letters concerning private lawsuits are not to be written to you.

> πανπράσιον \οἰ/κονομή|$_{22}$σαντι καὶ κ̣ατασχόντ̣α̣ τοῖς τέκνοις τὰ ἴδια ἐκλέ|$_{23}$ξασθαι ἐξ α̣ὐ̣τῶν ἕνα καὶ κληρονόμων ποιῆσαι. οὔκου̣ν |$_{24}$ παραπ̣εσούσης τῆς δευτέρας ἀσφαλείας εἰς τὴν προ|$_{25}$τέραν ἀνέκαμψεν τὸ δίκαιον. ἐξῆν αὐτῷ ὡς ἐβούλετο |$_{26}$ διαθέσθαι κληρονόμου̣ς καταλιπόντι τοὺς παῖδας αὐ|$_{27}$τοῦ ἐφ' οἷς ἐποιήσατο τὸ πανπράσιον.[73]

A *panprasion*, a general sale, made in the context of a marriage (cf. ὁ πατὴρ τοῦ γαμοῦντος, l. 18) through a written agreement (*symphonia*, *gramma*, *asphaleia*) out of which a hold, a *katoche*, arises for the children on their father's property, can only be the universal sale of Pestman's C model. This is indeed one of the main sources that show how the Roman jurisdiction, likely following Ptolemaic precedents, had articulated the effects of the Egyptian universal sale as a lien on the father's property: instead of functionally divided ownership of father and children, a hold of the latter on the former's property. The practical effect remains the same: no alienation without the consent of wife and children can be opposed to them. There is no need to underline how deeply un-Greek this notion is, that a man needs the consent of his wife or children to dispose of his own property. True to its Egyptian origins remains also the function of the institution: like in Tabubu's story four centuries earlier, the *katoche* serves to protect the inheritance rights of the common children: as we learn from our text, so long the *panprasion* remains in force, it is among them that the father must choose an heir.[74]

---

[73] *P. Oxy.* XLII 3015 (after 117 CE) ll. 13–27: [Year …] of the deified Trajan, Tybi 20. In the case of Tryphon | against Did[...] After other questions. Sulpicius Similis, | after talking with his advisers and referring the case | of Artemidoros the legal expert, said: "I am told [...] | […] neither the wife, over whom the father of the groom | made a new agreement, nor her sons, are alive, | for whom it was possible to have the (property) under lien according to the agreement – | this document is now without force. The law, I am | told, gives to a man who has negotiated | a 'general sale' (*panprasion*) and granted a lien (*katochê*) over his property to his children, the power | to choose out one of them and make this one his heir. It is therefore the case | that, with the disappearance of the second bond, the right | reverts to the first one. It was lawful for him to make his will on whatever terms he wished, | (provided that?) he left as heirs those children of | his on whose behalf he made the 'general sale'."

[74] In the case submitted to Similis, the wife and children for whom the *panprasion* had been made – not by the groom but by his father – have all died, but the father had granted a previous *panprasion*. The later one falling out of force, "the right" – as we read – "reverts to the first one", so that the (father's) heirs must be chosen among its beneficiaries: or rather, should have been chosen, since the question is clearly posed after his death, regarding the validity of the testament he left. The *katoche*, as it seems, would allow the children to claim the inheritance against a testament where none of them is made heir. Two hypothesis are possible regarding the earlier *panprasion*: (a) it may have referred to a previous marriage of the grantor's son; in such case, since the text makes clear that the later *panprasion* would have prevailed if its beneficiaries were alive, we would have to assume that the son's first family had waived their rights by

The text not only confirms that the practice remained common in the early 2nd century, but also that the rules derived from it had become 'the law', applicable, it seems, to all peregrines of the *chora*, no matter their ethnic origin or cultural background: the rights arising from the *panprasion* are in fact, in the words of Similis, ὁ νόμος. Of course, such *nomos* would apply only to those who concluded a *panprasion*. In the early 1st century, if the *grapheion* of Tebtynis is any indication, these were mostly Egyptians. It would be vain to speculate on the basis of the – rather Greek – names of the parties in Similis' case, Tryphon and Did[…]. But it is enough to remember that Dionysia's conflict with her father, the ex-gymnasiarch Chairemon, in *P. Oxy.* II 237, had arisen from a *katoche* over part of his property that she obtained from her mother's marriage *syngraphe*, in order to realise how widespread the institution had become also among the Greek elite of the *metropoleis*.[75]

By far the most striking confirmation of the importance that the family *katoche* had gained in early Roman Egypt are the two prefectural Edicts concerning its registration, preserved to us among the materials appended by Dionysia to her petition: the famous 89 CE Edict of Mettius Rufus regarding the correct functioning of the property record offices (*bibliothekai enkteseon*) and a 109 CE Edict of (again!) Sulpicius Similis on the registration therein of our *katochai*. Let us start with the latter:

> Σέρουιος Σουλπίκιος Σίμιλις ἔπαρ[χος] Αἰγύπτου λέγει· διαζη|$_{22}$τοῦντί μοι μαθεῖν ἐκ τίνος ὑποθέσεως ἐτελεῖτο τὰς Αἰγυπτιακὰς γυναῖκ̣α̣ς̣ κατὰ ἐνχώριον (l. τὰ ἐγχώρια) νόμ̣ι̣μ̣α κατέχειν τ̣ὰ̣ ὑπάρχ̣ο̣ν̣τ̣α̣ τ̣ῶ̣ν̣ |$_{23}$ ἀνδρῶν διὰ τῶν γαμικῶν συνγραφῶν (l. συγγραφῶν) ἑαυταῖς τε̣ κ̣α̣ὶ̣ τοῖς τέ̣κ̣νοις,

consenting to the later deed; a surrender that – as it would seem – would hold only as long as the deed they had consented to; (b) a second, much simpler and hence likelier hypothesis, is that the earlier *panprasion* had been given by the father for his own wife and children; nobody's consent was therefore needed to make a second one in favour of one of the sons, in the occasion of his marriage; and, after the demise of the latter's family, the right reverts to that of the father, namely to his own children – including, unless he had also died – the one for whose family he had executed the later deed.

75 In Dionysia's case, the *katoche* referred to an '*ousia*' (Col. 6, ll. 21–22, κατοχην̣ τ̣ῆ̣ς̣ οὐσίας) described as 'maternal' (Col. 6, l. 24: ἐπὶ τ̣ῆ̣ς̣ μ[η]τρῴας οὐσίας). It was created for Dionysia (Col. 6, l. 40: ἡ κατοχὴ γέγονέ̣ν̣ μ̣[οι]) by the marriage *syngraphe* of her mother (on which Chairemon's contestation of the *katoche* centers in the yet unpublished col. 2, but cf. also col. 7, ll. 16–18: ἀλλὰ | δὴ καὶ ὅτι τὰς συνγραφὰς πα[ρα]τίθεσθαι τοῖς βιβλιοφυλακίοις νόμιμον καὶ τὰς ἐκ τούτων γενομένας κατοχὰς πάντες ἡγεμόνες | καὶ αὐτοκράτορες κυρίας [εἶν]αι καὶ βεβαίας τεθελήκασι), quite likely by Dionysia's (maternal) grandfather (repeatedly mentioned in col. 2), who would have bestowed the ownership on Chairemon with *katoche* for the common children: for a parallel, cf. *P. Oxy.* XLIX 3491 (157 – 158 CE Oxyrhynchos) ll. 15–17. The '*ousia*' was 'maternal' because it was part of what was given to Chairemon on behalf of Dionysia's mother when marrying her.

> πλειστάκ̣ι̣ς̣ δ̣ὲ ἐ̣κ̣ τ̣ο̣ύ̣του ἀμφισβη̣τ̣ήσεων γενομένων, |$_{24}$ ἐπὶ (l. ἐπεὶ) ἐδ̣ύ̣ν̣αντο ἀγνοεῖν ο<ί> τοῖς γεγαμηκόσι συναλλά̣σ̣σ̣οντε̣ς̣ ε̣ἰ̣ τ̣ούτ̣ῳ̣ [τ]ῷ̣ δ̣ι̣κα̣ί̣ῳ̣ κ̣ατέχε̣τ̣α̣ι̣ τ̣ὰ ὑπ̣ά̣ρ̣χ̣ο[ντ]α̣ α̣ὐ̣τ̣ῶ̣ν̣ ταῖς γυναιξὶ |$_{25}$ διὰ τ̣ὸ̣ κ̣α̣ὶ̣ ἑτέροις βιβλιοφυλακίοις τὰς συνγραφὰς (l. συγγραφάς) καταχωρίζεσθαι, [κ]ε̣κελευκ̣έ̣ναι Μέ[τ]τιον Ῥοῦφον τὸ[ν] γενόμενον ε̣π̣ι̣ . . . ν̣ |$_{26}$ ἔπαρχον τὰ ἀντίγραφα τῶν συνγραφῶν (l. συγγραφῶν) ταῖς τῶν ἀνδρῶν ὑπο̣σ̣τ̣άσεσ̣ι̣ π̣α̣ρ̣α̣τίθ̣ε̣σ̣θ̣αι καὶ τοῦτο διατά[γ]ματι προ̣σ̣τ̣ε̣τ̣α̣χ̣έ̣ν̣α̣ι̣ ο̣ὗ̣ κ̣α̣ὶ̣ |$_{27}$ ἀντίγραφον ὑπέταξα, φανερὸν ποιῶν κατακολουθεῖν το̣ῖ̣ς ὑπὸ Μεττίου Ῥούφου . . θ̣ε̣ι̣σι̣ [.] . vac. (ἔτους) κ̣γ, Ἁθὺρ ι̣β.[76]

The Edict confirms, once more, that the source of the family *katoche* was the parents' marriage contract – γαμικὴ συγγραφή – and that out of it the *katoche* arose both for the wife and for the common children. At least since Mettius Rufus (*infra*), such *katochai* had to be registered in the *bibliotheke enkteseon*, an annotation (*parathesis*) being made in the property record of the husbands "so that those who enter into agreements (with them) may not be defrauded by their ignorance". Our Edict concerns a rather specific problem in this regard: marriage deeds registered in one nome, despite the husband owning property elsewhere. That such a specific constellation had become enough of a problem to require a specific edict shows how widespread family *katochai* had become. Since such partial registration violated Rufus' Edict not just in its aims but, strictly understood, also in its text, which ordered copies of the marriage deeds to be attached to the property returns of the husbands – as many of these as there may be –, Similis merely reiterates Rufus' command and appends the latter's Edict. In the part relevant for us it reads thus:

> παρατιθέτωσαν δὲ καὶ αἱ γυναῖκες τ̣α̣ῖ̣ς ὑποστάσεσι τῶν ἀνδρῶν α̣ἷ̣ς κατά τινα ἐπιχώριον νόμον κρατεῖται (l. κρατῆται) τὰ ὑπάρ|$_{35}$χοντα, ὁμοίως δὲ καὶ τὰ τέκνα ταῖς τῶν γονέων οἷς ἡ μὲν χρῆσεις (l. χρῆσις) διὰ δημοσίων

[76] *P. Oxy.* II 237 (186 CE Oxyrhynchos), col. 8, ll. 21–27: Servius Sulpicius Similis, prefect of Egypt, proclaims: When I | wished to know on what grounds it was established that Egyptian wives according to the tradition of the land have a lien upon their | husbands' property through their written marriage agreements both for themselves and for their children, since disputes were often arising from this, | because those who contract with married people could ignore if due to such right their property is under lien for their wives, | due to the written (marriage) agreements being registered at other record-offices, Mettius Rufus, the former […] | prefect, ordered copies of the written agreements be attached to the property-statements of the husbands, and established this through an edict, a | copy of which I have appended to make clear that I am following what Mettius Rufus had ordered. 23rd year, Hathyr 12th. The edict is preserved also, rather fragmentarily, in *P.Merton* III 101 (after 109 CE unknown provenance): there, in ll. 6–7, <τὰ> ἐνχώρια νόμ̣ιμα, brought above as correction to l. 22. New (*supra* n. 2) is here in l. 23 δ̣ὲ ἐ̣κ̣ τ̣ο̣ύ̣του instead of δ̣ι̣' ἐ̣ν̣ι̣α̣υ̣τ̣οῦ (ed. pr.); Grenfell and Hunt's correction νόμι<σ>μα in l. 22 is unnecessary.

τετήρηται χρηματισμῶν, ἡ δὲ κτῆ|36σις μετὰ θάνατον τοῖς τέκνοις κεκράτηται, ἵνα οἱ συναλλάσσοντες μὴ κατ' ἄγνοιαν ἐνεδρεύονται (l. ἐνεδρεύωνται).[77]

Rufus' Edict was issued to address the deficient functioning of the property record office of the Oxyrhynchites, but in ordering everyone to present fully comprehensive property returns anew, it explicitly lists the rights that must be brought to registration: not only those of landowners, but also of hypothecarian creditors and holders of family *katochai*.[78] Rufus' presentation of the latter – wives who have a hold on their husbands property by virtue of some *epichorios nomos*, and children for whom their parents' property has been reserved through public instruments – might suggest, if we were not better informed, that we are in front of two different situations, articulated differently and arising from different sources, one *ex lege* and the other *ex contractu*. We know – also thanks to Similis' Edict – that this is not the case: the false impression arises from Rufus' need to list separate categories of people and describe each of their rights, and from the fact that although both wives' and children's right consists in their immunity to alienations made without their consent, this serves now exclusively to secure the children's inheritance – *panprasion/katoche* being now evidently independent from any endowment arrangement of the kind that the *katoche* once also secured.[79] Remarkable is the *interpretatio romana* of the right of the children: not as mere veto securing the inalienability of items destined to them but not theirs yet, but as

[77] *P. Oxy.* II 237 (186 CE Oxyrhynchos), col. 8, ll. 34–36: Also wives for whom by virtue of some law of the land the property (of their husbands) is under hold shall add (it) for registration to the property returns of their husbands, | and likewise children to those of their parents, if through public instruments these retain the enjoyment but the possession | after their death has been put under hold for the children, so that those who enter into agreements (regarding such properties) may not be defrauded by their ignorance.

[78] Unlike the rights of owners and of hypothecarian creditors, *katochai* are in truth not registered as rights of the *katoche*-holders, in their own *folium*, but in that of the owners, through marginal annotation (the literature often wrongly reserves the term '*parathesis*' for this marginal annotation: so Wolff 1978: 238–239; contra, Alonso 2010: 20 n. 36, with lit.), as a limitation of their freedom to dispose. This neatly corresponds to the nature of the *katoche* as a lien or hold that binds the owner, rather than a right. Yet, since the *katoche*-holders can oppose the *katoche* against third party acquirors, as the Edict of Rufus and Similis confirm, it was inevitable that it would come to be seen as a right: and indeed in Similis' Edict the *katoche* is described as existing by virtue of a right (l. 24: ε̣ἰ̣ τ̣ούτ̣ῳ̣ [τ]ῷ̣ δ̣ικα̣ίῳ̣ κ̣ατέχ̣ετα̣ι̣ τ̣ὰ ὑπ̣άρ̣χο[ντ]α̣ α̣ὐ̣τ̣ῶ̣ν̣) and the *katoche* itself is characterised as a source or bundle of rights by Dionysia: τα περὶ τῆς κατοχῆς δίκαια (col. 4, l. 32; cf. also δίκαια and δίκαιον in col. 4, l. 23, col. 5, ll. 5, 22, 34, 38, 40, 43, col. 6, l. 23).

[79] Not only in the Demotic practice of the Persian and Ptolemaic time (*supra* VI) but quite likely still in the Demotic deeds registered at the *grapheion* of Tebtynis in the mid-first century CE: *supra* n. 71.

latent ownership over them, the father retaining only the usufruct (*chresis*), the possession (*ktesis*) reserved for them *meta thanaton*.[80]

Regarding this right of children and wife Mettius Rufus merely imposes a registration duty, so that third parties who conclude contracts regarding items affected by it are informed of its existence; registration seems therefore mere means of publicity, not constitutive. In fact, the *katoche* is explicitly presented as arising, by virtue of an *epichorios nomos,* from public deeds, *demosioi chrematismoi* – described more precisely by Similis as marriage deeds, *gamikai syngraphai*. Unlike other *katochai*, like those created through *hypallagma* or hypothec, family *katochai* therefore do not arise from registration, but from the marriage deed itself, which suffices for them to be opposable to third parties: precisely the risk that Rufus' Edict addresses in their regard. Indeed, if this were not the case, if unrecorded *katochai* could not be opposed to third parties, the problem addressed by Similis in his Edict would not have existed.

As the mechanics of the property record office are usually understood, registration should have had added to the *katoche* more than just publicity: it is generally assumed that items under registered *katoche* were denied the *epistalma* necessary for any notarised alienation or hypothecation[81] and therefore registration would effectively block any such attempt, at least through public document.[82]

---

80 On this articulation *chresis* – *ktesis* and the possible parallel of Gai. 2, 7 (*possessio vel ususufructus*), Kreller 1933. Remarkably, it is the exact same articulation that Constantine introduces for the *bona materna*, the property inherited from their mother by children still under *patria potestas*, which should therefore devolve to their fathers: the latter, since Constantine, acquire merely the usufruct, so that he cannot alienate, the ownership being reserved for the children. The parallel (precisely because with a notoriously Roman inflected articulation of the *katoche* by a Roman prefect) is completely independent from any speculation about Hellenistic influence on the Constantinian *bona materna*, starting with Mitteis 1891; Lit. in Kaser 1975: 217 n. 25, cf. also Castelli 1917. That Rufus speaks of *ktesis* instead of *kyreia* is perfectly in line with the denomination of the *bibliotheke* as *enkteseon*; instead, the fact that, unlike Similis, he avoids the language of the *katoche*, preferring *κρατέω* to *κατέχω*, may be yet another light Romanising trait.

81 On this so-called *epistalma*-system, Mitteis 1912a: 97–103; von Woess 1924: 107–201; Wolff 1978: 247–253. The *epistalma* denial is explicit in some 2nd cent. CE *hypallagmata* contracted directly through the *bibliotheke* (*P. Wisc*. II 54, 116 CE Arsinoites; *P. Kron*. 18, 143 CE Tebtynis; *P. Vars*. 10 col. 3, 156 CE Arsinoites), following a model that forces the debtor to request from the *bibliophylakes* "not to cooperate with me in anything whatsoever until I present the receipts of the payment of everything", thus securing for their creditors that no *epistalma* will be issued until they receive their due.

82 This still leaves open the possibility of alienation or hypothecation through *cheirographon*: the obstacle that prevented the registration of such purely private documents in the *bibliotheke* could be overcome through their notarisation by *ekmartyresis* or *demosiosis* (Wolff 1978: 129–135). Whether in these procedures possible registered *katochai* were checked remains an open question: in the abundant evidence there are no traces of any kind of scrutiny of the legal situation (Wolff 1978: 132 and n. 120) or of the

Regarding family *katochai*, instead, Similis and Rufus' language suggests that registration did not serve to formally preclude alienations but to ensure that interested third parties act knowing that rights exist that will prevail over their own[83] – even if this should in most cases suffice to dissuade them. If this interpretation is correct, it would show a remarkable accuracy and respect regarding the original articulation of the institution, which, indeed, under Egyptian law, did not entail objective inalienability, but rather immunity of the katoche holder regarding non-consented alienations.

The marriage deed from which the family *katoche* arises, γαμικὴ συγγραφή in Similis' Edict and variously called πανπράσιον, συμφωνία, γράμμα and ἀσφαλεία in *P. Oxy.* XLII 3015, is here explicitly presented as δημόσιος χρηματισμός, public – i.e. notarised – document. This notarial character of the document does not seem decreed by Rufus, but rather taken by him for granted. This is not surprising, when one considers the regulations under which these documents were executed, both in Ptolemaic and in Roman times. From the mid-second century BCE, Demotic documents required notarial registration through the *grapheion*, the so-called *anagraphe*: without it, as we know through Hermias' trial record, they would have no validity in court (τὰ μὴ ἀναγεγραμμένα Αἰγύπτια | συναλλάγματα ἄκυρα εἶ̣ν̣α̣ι).[84] Thus, for two hundred years, until the Demotic notarial practice dries out around the mid-first cent. CE, as long as the universal sale was concluded in Demotic among Egyptians it was necessarily through notarised deed (as indeed still at the *grapheion* of Tebtynis: *supra* n. 71). When in the course of the first century CE a Greek documentary form started replacing the Demotic one, not only the example of the latter but also the Roman institutional logic would have pushed in the same direction: a marriage document that secures the inheritance for the common children is in substance an inheritance contract, and therefore should require notarial form, as *diathekai* did.[85]

In fact, in our best example for the actual registration of a family *katoche* in the property record office, *P. Oxy.* IV 713 = *MChr.* 314 (97 CE Oxyrhynchos), the

---

involvement of the local *bibliothekai*, where the possible *katochai* would be recorded: Wolff 1978: 175–176. In any case, items other than land and – sometimes – slaves remain outside of the *bibliotheke* and therefore of the *epistalma* system.

83 On the possibility that also other *katochai* functioned not by preventing the sale but by making third party buyers aware of their existence and explicitly accept their priority, Alonso 2010: 21–54.

84 *P. Tor. Choach.* 12 = *MChr.* 31 = *Jur. Pap.* 80 = *UPZ* II 162, 117 BCE Thebes, col. 4, l. 14–15. Cf. also *UPZ* I p. 596 = *P. Par.* 65 = *Sel. Pap.* II 415 (145 BCE Memphis). On this registration procedure, which seems to have been introduced around 146 BCE, Kraus 1967; Wolff 1978: 36–40, 169–173; Rupprecht 1995. On the *anagraphe* of Greek documents from the late 2nd cent. BCE, Yiftach-Firanko 2008.

85 Cf. the *Gnomon of the Idios Logos*, *BGU* V 1210 = *Jur. Pap.* 93 (after 149 CE Theadelphia) ll. 33–34: ζ δ[ι]αθῆκαι, ὅσαι μὴ κατὰ δημοσίους χρηματισμοὺς γείνων|ται, ἄκυροί εἰσι: §7 Testaments which are not executed as public documents | are not valid.

marriage deed that established the *katoche* had been executed in 52 CE, in Oxyrhynchos, as an agoranomic *syngraphe gamou*:

> καθ' ἣν οἱ γονεῖς μου Διόδωρος Δι[ο]|$_{8}$δώρου τοῦ Ἀγαθείνου καὶ Σαραεῦς |$_{9}$ Λεωνίδου τοῦ Ἀλεξάνδρου μη|$_{10}$τρὸς Ἰσιδώρας Κάλα ἀπ[ὸ] τῆς αὐτῆς |$_{11}$ πόλεως πεποίηνται πρὸς ἀλ|$_{12}$λήλους τοῦ γάμου συγγραφὴν διὰ |$_{13}$ τοῦ ἐν Ὀξυρύγχων πόλει ἀγορανο|$_{14}$μείου τῷ δωδεκάτῳ ἔτει θεοῦ |$_{15}$ Κλαυδίου μηνὶ Σεβαστῷ κατέσ|$_{16}$χον τῇ ἐξ ἀλλήλων γενεᾷ τὰ |$_{17}$ ἑαυτῶν πάντα πρὸς τὸ μετὰ τὴν |$_{18}$ τελευτὴν αὐτῶν βεβαίως καὶ |$_{19}$ ἀναφαιρέτως εἶναι τῶν τέκνων [86]

Quite explicit is here, once more, the genetic link between *katoche* and marriage deed, and the former's effect and function. Through their marriage deed, the couple, in fact, "placed under arrest for their common children the whole of their property, in order that after their death, secure and inalienable, it may be their children's". New instead is the fact that the *katoche* does not affect merely the paternal property but that of both spouses.[87] The institution, poured into new Greek documentary forms and expanding beyond its original native Egyptian milieu, was bound to become increasingly detached from the old Demotic models, to evolve and diversify. And thus, together with the unilateral *panprasion*, attested still in Similis, we find here a reciprocal *katoche* of the spouses, probably not contracted any more in the form of a general sale, but through a mere documentary clause. And yet, despite all differences, function and effect remain true to the original: securing through an encumbrance the inheritance of the common children.

In casu, the paternal inheritance has already devolved on the children upon the father's death, and although the mother still lives, the petitioner's brother and sister have equally received in advance their portions of the maternal inheritance through their own marriage deeds (ll. 20–34).[88] Thus, only the petitioner's *katoche* on his

---

[86] P. Oxy. 713 = MChr. 314 (97 CE Oxyrhynchos) ll. 7–19: My parents Diodorus son of | Diodorus, son of Agathinus, and Saraeus | daughter of Leonides, son of Alexander, her | mother being Isidora, daughter of Kalas, from the same | city, according to the contract | of marriage made between them through | the notarial office in the city of Oxyrhynchos | in the 12th year of the divine | Claudius, in the month Sebastos (July–August 52 CE), placed | under arrest for their common children | the whole of their property, in order that after their | death, secure and | inalienable, it may be their children's.

[87] In truth, also in Rufus' Edict the children's *katoche* is referred generically to the parents' property (τῶν γονέων, l. 35), even if between spouses only as held by the wife on the property of the husband.

[88] *P. Oxy*. 713 = *MChr*. 314 (97 CE Oxyrhynchos) ll. 20–34: ἐπεὶ δὲ ὁ πατὴρ ἐτελεύτησεν ἐπ' ἐ|μοὶ καὶ ἀδελφοῖς μου Διοδώρῳ | καὶ Θαίδι καὶ τὰ αὐτοῦ εἰς ἡμᾶς | κατήντησε, ἡ δὲ μήτηρ ἀφ' ὧν | ἔχει περὶ μὲν Νέσλα ἀρουρῶν | ἐννέα ἡμίσους περὶ δὲ {περὶ δὲ} | Πεẹννὼ ἐκ τῆς Θρασυμάχου παρ|ειμένης ἀρουρῶν δύο ἡμίσους | τῶν ἐπὶ τὸ αὐτὸ ἀρουρῶν δεκα|δύο ἐμέρισε τοῖς προγεγραμμέ|νοις μου ἀδελφο[ῖ]ς ἀπὸ τῶν πε|ρὶ Νέσλα ἑκατέρῳ

share of the maternal estate remains: it is this *katoche* that, abiding by Mettius Rufus' Edict, he brings for registration to the property record office of the Oxyrhynchites.[89]

About the ethnic background of the parties nothing can be said, but their onomastic pratice – Diodoros, Agathinos, Saraeus, Leonidas, Alexander, Isidora, Kalas, Thais – points to a fully hellenised family. When Mettius Rufus and Sulpicius Similis refer this practice to an *epichorios nomos* or to the *enchoria nomima*, one could imagine that these expressions, in Ptolemaic Egypt unequivocally referred to the native Egyptian law, are consciously preferred by them to the usual *nomoi ton Aigyption* precisely because they are seen as less neutral, perhaps because it was for them manifest – as one would expect – that the institution had no Greek roots. But whatever their impression about the institution's possible origins, our evidence, starting with the present text, strongly suggests that they could not have associated its use exclusively with the native Egyptian population: that by the second century the practice had expanded in its multiple new Greek forms up to the Greek metropolitan elite is obvious on the example of Dionysia's *katoche* (*supra* n. 75).

VIII. *Agraphos gamos*: A hypothesis

In a nutshell, the last sections (V–VII) boil down to the following: in first and second century Egypt we find, in addition to the earlier Greek marriage documentary forms, two strongly contrasting ones that originated in the Demotic practice and now spread, in Greek form, beyond their original Egyptian milieu: *daneion*-based marriages, like those of Tryphon and Pausiris, and *katoche*-based marriages, with or without *panprasion*, of the sort that Mettius Rufus and Sulpicius Similis address in the Edicts and decisions reviewed *supra* in VII. Among the differences between these two Egyptian-inspired models, one is crucial for us: in

ἀρούρας τέσσα|ρας διὰ τῆς περὶ γάμου αὐτοῦ συγγρα|[φῆς] αἵ εἰσι τὸ τρίτον τῶν προκειμέ|νων ἀρουρῶν δεκαδύο: and whereas my father died leaving as heirs | me and my brother and sister Diodoros | and Thais, and his property devolved | upon us, and whereas our mother | owns at Nesla nine | and a half arouras | and at Peenno, from the concessional land | of Thrasymachos, two and a half arouras, | together making twelve arouras | and bestowed upon my aforesaid | brother and sister from the arouras at | Nesla to each of them four arouras | through their written marriage agreement, | that is, one third of the aforementioned | twelve arouras

89 *P. Oxy*. 713 = *MChr*. 314 (97 CE Oxyrhynchos) ll. 34–45: ἀπογρά|φομαι καὶ αὐτὸς πρὸς παράθεσιν | κατοχὴν τῶν λοιπῶν τῆς μη|τρὸς ἀρουρῶν τεσσάρων. ἡ δὲ προ|κειμένη τῶν γονέων μου συγγρα|φή ἐστιν ἔνθεσμος καὶ ἀπερί|λυτος εἰς τὴν ἐνεστῶσαν ἡμέραν. | (ἔτους) α Αὐτοκρά[τ]ορος Νερ[ού]α [Καίσαρος] | Σεβαστοῦ [H1] Φαμενὼθ ιθ. | Δημήτριος σεση(μείωμαι). ἔτους πρώτου | Αὐτοκράτορος Νερούα Καίσαρος | Σεβαστοῦ Φαμενὼθ ιθ.: I too | declare for registration | my hold on the remaining | four arouras of my mother. And the | aforesaid contract of my parents | remains in force and uncancelled | to the present day. Year 1 of Emperor Nerva Caesar | Augustus [H1] Phamenoth 19th. | [H3] Demetrios has signed. First year | of Emperor Nerva Caesar | Augustus, Phamenoth 19th.

katoche-based marriages the father is bound, has no autonomous power over his own property: not *inter vivos*, since he is no longer free to alienate without the consent of his wife or children, nor *mortis causa*, since the children are entitled to his inheritance, and he is thus bound to leave it among them. In a *daneion*-based marriage, instead, the father preserves full power over all his belongings, and neither wife nor children have on them any rights whatsoever: precisely for this reason, both Tryphon's and Pausiris' deeds include a clause covering child expenses if the wife is repudiated while pregnant (*supra* II and V).

How does this relate to our problem? The difference between *agraphos* and *engraphos gamos* (*supra* III) concerns the fathers' rights over their children's person and property; here, instead, the difference concerns the fathers' rights over their own property. I suspect that these could be two sides of the same coin: *daneion*-fathers, like Tryphon or Pausiris, would have been deemed as preserving all rights on the family property, both on their own and on that of their future children; *katoche*-fathers, instead, had no such power on their own property, let alone on that of their children. This postulates a conception of the property as family property, either fully in the father's hands, who then keeps a right over the children's acquisitions – to inherit them upon their death (*CPR* I 18, *supra* III) and, if he so wishes, to reclaim them in their lifetime, their own as well as those coming from him, like the dowry (*P. Oxy*. II 237, col. 7, ll. 28–29, ll. 41–42, *supra* III and nn. 36–37) – or not any more fully in the hands of the father, so that, conversely, it is the children who have a right over his property, which he cannot alienate without their (or his wife's) consent nor bestow *mortis causa* if not to among them.

The Egyptian marriage practice that Pestman labelled as model C, as its Greek offspring in Roman times, the family-*katoche*, lead by itself to the second construction, of a father who has entirely abdicated his autonomous power. The first construction instead, the autocratic paternal position linked in the 2nd cent. to the *agraphos gamos*, could be derived from the logic behind the inherited Demotic practice only through induction: from the *katoche* system, a conception of the father's property as family property could be quite naturally induced; generalised, this conception could be used to explain the paternal *exousia* over the children contained in the circulating versions of the *nomoi ton Aigyption*; that this was the case is evident in the fact that the *exousia* was understood as a power not just over their persons but also and foremost over their dowry and their own belongings; again a construction of the property as family property, this time entirely under the father's control: the mirror image of the position of the *katoche*-father, applicable therefore only to fathers who unlike these had not surrendered authority over their own property – *daneion*-fathers like Tryphon or Pausiris, but also all others, whatever marriage tradition they may have followed, who had not given to wife and children power over their belongings. Such construction could only have arisen inductively through interpretation of the *nomoi ton Aigyption* and of the actual marriage practice: and, in fact, as we know (*supra* IV), it is through the work of the

2nd century *nomikoi* that the paternal power came to be linked to the form of the marriage; whether they were further influenced in their construction by the Roman *patria potestas* must remain an open question.

A difficulty remains, though. What does this distinction between non-*katoche* and *katoche* fathers have to do with the written or unwritten form of the marriage? Also for this an answer is, I believe, possible. In the first decades of Roman rule, the two main marriage models inherited from the Demotic tradition that survived and found their way into the Greek practice were, as we have seen, the *daneion*-marriage and the *panprasion*-marriage. From the point of view of the Roman administration, there was a crucial difference between them: for a loan-based marriage, like for any loan, a non-notarial document, a *cheirographon*, was perfectly sufficient – and indeed, both Tryphon's and Pausiris' documents, as most other preserved loan-marriage deeds, are *cheirographa* (*supra* IV and nn. 42 and 50); a marriage deed, instead, that binds the husband to leave the inheritance to the common children is in essence an inheritance contract and therefore would have required notarial form, as we know *diathekai* did (*supra* n. 85) – and indeed, not only was the *katoche* marriage deed in *P. Oxy.* IV 713 an agoranomic *syngraphe gamou*, but, crucially, for Mettius Rufus in his Edict it is self-evident that *katochai* can only be established through *demosios chrematismos*.

This means: a *panprasion*-marriage and indeed any *katoche*-marriage would be impossible through non-notarial document. Here lies, in my opinion, the key to decipher the meaning of the expression *agraphos gamos*: as we have known for over a century, *agraphos* is not necessarily an undocumented marriage; it is simply – I submit – a non-notarised one (*LSJ* s.v. III; *DGE* s.v. I 2), a marriage for which no notarial document has been produced –whether no document at all or a non-notarial one changes nothing. Thus, the reason why the 2nd century *nomikoi* came to the conclusion that *agraphos* fathers preserved their full *exousia* becomes also obvious: since *katoche*-marriages require notarisation, fathers married without notarial document necessarily have preserved their whole power their own belongings and those of his children.

The hypothesis presented here has yet an important consequence: if it holds true, a specific uniform legal regime crystalised in the 2nd century only for *agraphos gamos*: only in the absence of a *demosios chrematismos* – *agraphia* in technical sense – is there certainty that the husband has not surrendered his power over property and family. No general legal framework could be predicated, instead, for marriages based on a *demosios chrematismos*: their legal regime depended, in fact, on the specific content of the document, which may or may not contain limitations to the husband's power.[90] The most invasive of such limitations at least,

[90] Even within the realm of the models inherited from the Demotic tradition, the execution of a *demosios chrematismos* did not imply a *katoche*, as the *daneion* marriage deeds executed through an *agoranomos* prove: *supra* n. 50.

namely a general *katoche* on all present and future belongings, would lead him to lose not only the power to decide autonomously over his own property but also over that of his children and over their persons. Whether less invasive limitations – partial *katochai*, on specific items or on part of the property, as in Dionysia's case in *P. Oxy*. II 237 – led to the same result, must remain an open question, even though an affirmative answer seems to me unlikely, despite Dionysia's protestations to the contrary.

This is consistent with the fact that in *CPR* I 18 (l. 32) it is not the *engraphia* but the *agraphia* that needs to be proven in order to ascertain the validity of the testament. Revealingly – and this seems to me a litmus test of the hypothesis here presented – it is only here and in Dionysia that we find the term *engraphos gamos*. Here not in the words of the judge, of the assisting *nomikos* or of the parties' advocates, but (ll. 28–29) in an improvised intervention of the defendant himself, whose advocate's initial strategy, claiming unrestricted testamentary freedom for the *Aigyptioi*, had collapsed, confronted with the fact that *agraphos* children have no such freedom. Otherwise, the term is used only by Dionysia, in her attempt to argue that not being born *agraphos* she is free from parternal *exousia*. Not even the *nomikos'* opinion that she appends as her only substantiation of her claim that *engraphos* fathers necessarily lack such *exousia* contains the expression. It is not only that the term is otherwise unattested: when the rest of the sources refer to marriages that are not *agraphos*, they do not label them as *engraphos*, but as existing καθ' ὁμολογίαν (*supra* n. 10). The nuance is important: not only because it makes Dionysia's argumentation, around a category practically invented by her lawyers, suspicious, but also because it seems to confirm that indeed, as predicted by the hypothesis here presented, written marriages did not exist as a definite legal category, associated with a specific legal regime.[91]

[91] This is the crucial difference between the hypothesis presented here and the one proposed some years ago by Johannes Platschek 2015: 146, 157–160, also linking *agraphia* and *katoche*. Platschek identifies *engraphos gamos* with the *katoche*-marriage of the Egyptian tradition; in my opinion, instead, it is not the presence of a *katoche* that made a marriage *engraphos*, but rather the impossibility – due to lack of notarisation – of its presence, that made it *agraphos*. Platschek's theory consists of three equations: (a) the laws of the Egyptians are to be identified with native Egyptian law; (b) Egyptian law marriages are *katoche*-based; (c) such *katoche*-based marriages are what our sources call *engraphos gamos*. My disagreement with 'a' (*supra* n. 22) is here irrelevant: although the technical meaning of 'Egyptian' in the Roman administrative parlance of the 2nd century precludes identifying the 'laws of the Egyptians' *tout court* with the native Egyptian law, there is no doubt that the family *katoche* had indeed Demotic roots, as abundantly shown in sections VI and VII *supra*. These same sections, together with V, are enough to discard 'b': *katoche* marriages were by no means the only possibility within the Demotic tradition nor the only one to find continuity in the later Greek practice: crucial is here the survival in the *daneion* marriages of the first and second centuries of Pestman's model B. Regarding 'c': in the present state of our sources, Dionysia's *engraphos gamos* is a *hapax*, and multiple reasons suggest (see above), not

A final piece of evidence can still be added to the puzzle. In the mid-nineties, a marriage *synchoresis* dated 12 BCE, and on the verso a draft of the same text, were published by W. M. Brashear:[92] *SB* XXIV 16073 and *SB* XXIV 16072 respectively. Before the specific stipulations that the spouses bring to the *synchoresis*, and immediately after the address, we read the following (SB XXIV 16073):

> ἐ]|$_{6}$πεὶ σύν<ε>ισιν ἀλλήλοις ἥ τε Θαυ̣[βάριον καὶ] |$_{7}$ Ἑρμίας ἔτι πάλαι ἀγράφ̣[ης οὔσης] |$_{8}$ [τ]ῆ̣ς συ̣μβιώσεως γε̣ν̣ο̣[μένης Ἑρ|$_{9}$μίας] πεπο<ι>ημένος <ε>ἰς τ̣ὴ̣ν̣ [Θαυβάριον] |$_{10}$ η̣ν̣ διέχουσι̣ν δ̣ι̣κ̣α̣[στηρίῳ̣ . . . . . . |$_{11}$ τ]ὴν χιραν (l. χεῖρα) τὰ δὲ νῦν β̣ο̣υ̣λ̣[όμενοι τὰ] |$_{12}$ κ̣ατ' ἑ̣αυτῶν ἐξασφαλίσ[ασθαι . . . . .] |$_{13}$ τ̣ῷ χρηματισμῷ̣ συγχω[ροῦσιν πρὸς] |$_{14}$ ἀλλήλους …

Hermias and Thaubarion wish through the present *synchoresis* to make their affairs more secure: they have lived together for a long time, but their living arrangements were hitherto unwritten. This is, to date, the earliest attestation of *agraphos* in our context: its publication pushed the term's *terminus a quo* half a century earlier than Tryphon's document. Some help with the difficult lines 10–11 may be found in the draft, at this point better preserved and more detailed:

> |$_{5}$ [ἐπ]εὶ σ̣ύ̣ν(εισιν) ἀλλήλοις ἥ τε Θαυβάριον καὶ Ἑρμίας̣ ἔτι π(άλαι) ἀγράφης |$_{6}$ [οὔ]σ̣(ης) [τ]\ῆ/ς συνβιω (l. συμβιώσεως) δι' ἑ̣τ̣ε̣ρ συνθεσει (l.

by coincidence: it is to be suspected, in fact, that 'written marriage' did not exist as a category that could be associated with a specific legal framework. Platschek's theory results from a close reading of some sections of the Dionysia petition, rather isolated from the rest of the sources. His point of the departure (p. 157) is a correction of Grenfell and Hunt's – indeed implausible – interpretation of 'often' (πλειστάκις) in the Edict of Sulpicius Similis (Col. 8, l. 23: *supra* VII); as Platschek argues, the word most likely refers in Similis' Edict to 'disputes were arising' (ἀμφισβητ̣ήσεων γενομένων) and not to the wives' *katoche*; yet, this does not entail that every Egyptian wife had a *katoche* on her husband's property. The conclusion is logically unwarranted ('often' would have made such interpretation impossible but its removal does not make it necessary: we do not need to assume that when Similis asked on what grounds Egyptian wives had a *katoche* he believed that each and every one of them had one) and historically false: both if we understand 'Egyptian' in ethnic-cultural sense, as Platschek does, since we know that the native Egyptian tradition knew non-*katoche* marriages and that *katoche* marriages had spread also among the Greek and Hellenised; and also if we understand 'Egyptian', as in my opinion we should, in its pure Roman administrative sense, since *katoche* marriages were far from the only possibility open to the non-citizens of the *chora*.

92 Brashear 1996. On the document, Sánchez-Moreno Ellart 2006; Rodríguez Martín 2020, with lit.

ἑτέρας συνθέσεως) – Ἑρμίας πεπο<ι>ημέν(ος) |7 [<εἰ>ς τὴν Θα]υβάριο(ν) τὴν διέχουσιν δικαστηρί`ῳ´ χεῖρα{ν}

The couple's previous joint life, we read, had been established "through other kind of arrangement" (δι' ἑτέρας συνθέσεως, l. 6). This suggests a written arrangement and, indeed, it is in this sense that χεῖρα must be understood in both the document (l. 11) and the draft (l. 7): the term is here shorthand for *cheirographon*,[93] in contrast with the notarial document now executed in form of *synchoresis gamou*.[94]

Important for us here is not just that the technical, artificial use of *agraphos* for a marriage based on a written document is already in place fifty years before Tryphon; but rather the fact that, as our theory predicts and Tryphon's case confirms, a marriage based on a *cheirographon*, a purely private document, no matter its content, remains *agraphos*. Together with Tryphon, the papyrus also shows that, although we must wait until the 2nd century to find a source associating paternal *exousia* to *agraphia*, and the link seems indeed – at the present state of our sources – a product of the *interpretatio iuris* of the 2nd century *nomikoi*, their construction relied on a technical meaning of *agraphos gamos* that can be traced back at least to the earliest years of Roman rule.

joseluis.alonso@ius.uzh.ch

LITERATURE

Alonso, J.L 2010. 'The bibliotheke enkteseon and the alienation of real securities in Roman Egypt', The Journal of Juristic Papyrology 40: 11–54.

Alonso, J. L. 2016. 'One en pistei, guarantee sales, and title-transfer security in the papyri', in D. F. Leão, G. Thür (eds.), Symposion 2015. Conferências sobre a História do Direito grego e helenístico (Coimbra, 1 – 4 Setembro 2015). Wien: ÖAW, 121–192.

---

93 The draft, where τὴν διέχουσιν δικαστηρί`ῳ´ χεῖρα{ν} clearly is the object of πεπο<ι>ημέν(ος), excludes an interpretation in the sense (Preisigke 1925–1931: 726 l. 5 ss.) of the mere giving of the hand as pledge. For χεῖρ as *cheirographon*, Preisigke 1925–1931: 728 l. 42 ss. In this sense, also Brashear in the edition. [Ἑρ|μίας] πεποημένος ἰς τ̣ὴν̣ [Θαυβάριον] | ην̣ διέχουσ̣ιν δ̣ι̣κ̣α̣[στηρίῳ̣ . . . . . . | τ]ὴν χιραν (ll. 8–11) is translated by Brashear 'Hermias forfeiting in court the document he had made with Thaubarion'; van Minnen in his online publication of the Alexandrian *synchoreseis* suggests 'Hermias having made for Thaubarion the document they have separate from a ... court'. This is best understood as referred to the fact that unlike *synchoreseis*, *cheirographa* are executed outside of the court.

94 Our *synchoresis* labels itself on l. 1 of the draft συμβ[ιώ(σεως)], document of 'joint life'; the term is used also in *BGU* IV 1103 ll. 1–30 (13 BCE Alexandria), a self-described synchoresis gamou (l. 8, συμ|βιώσεως κατὰ συγχώρησιν; l. 15, τὴν τοῦ γάμου συνχώρησιν).

Alonso, J. L. 2023. 'Papyrologische Quellen', in U. Babusiaux et al. (eds.), Handbuch des römischen Privatrechts I. Tübingen: Mohr Siebeck, 224–275.

Anagnostou-Cañas, B. 1984. 'La femme devant la justice provinciale dans l'Égypte romaine', Revue historique de droit français et étranger 62: 337–360.

Anagnostou-Cañas, B. 1991. Juge et sentence dans l'Egypte romaine, Paris: L'Harmattan.

Arangio-Ruiz, V. 1930. Persone e famiglia nel diritto dei papiri. Milano: Vita e Pensiero.

Besson, A. 2020. Constitutio Antoniniana. L'universalisation de la citoyenneté romaine au 3e siècle. Basel: Schwabe.

Biscottini, M.V. 1966. L'archivio di Tryphon tessitore di Oxyrhynchos, Aegyptus 46: 186–292.

Boak, A.E.R. 1926. 'Alimentary Contracts from Tebtunis', Journal of Egyptian Archaeology 12: 100–109.

Bortolucci, G. 1904. 'Il matrimonio nell'Egitto greco-romano', Archivio Giuridico Filippo Serafini 72: 164–156.

Bozza, F. 1934. 'Il matrimonio nel diritto dei papiri dell'epoca tolemaica', Aegyptus 14: 205–244,

Brashear, W. M. 1996. 'An Alexandrian Marriage Contract', in R. Katzoff (ed.), Classical Studies in Honor of D. Sohlberg, Ramat Gan: Bar-Ilan University Press, 367–384.

Brassloff, S. 1902. Zur Kenntnis des Volksrechtes in den romanisierten Ostprovinzen des römischen Kaiserreiches. Weimar: Böhlau.

Bryen, A.Z. 2013. Violence in Roman Egypt. A Study in Legal Interpretation. Philadelphia: University of Pennsylvania Press.

Castelli, G. 1917. 'I bona materna nei papiri greco-egizî', Studi della Scuola Papirologica 2: 77–79.

Cotton, H.M., Yardeni, A. 1997. Aramaic, Hebrew and Greek Documentary Texts from Nahal Hever and Other Sites (P. Hever). Oxford: University Press.

Cotton, H.M. 1998. 'The Law of Succession in the Documents from the Judaean Desert Again', Scripta Classica Israelica 17: 115–123.

Czajkowski, K. 2017. Localized Law. The Babatha and Salome Komaise Archives. Oxford: University Press.

Depauw, M. 2014. 'Demotic cessions', in J. G. Keenan, J. G. Manning, U. Yiftach Firanko (eds.), Law and Legal Practice in Egypt from Alexander to the Arab Conquest. Cambridge: University Press, 56–57.

Dolganov, A. 2019. 'Reichsrecht and Volksrecht in Theory and Practice: Roman Justice in the Province of Egypt (P.Oxy. II 237, P.Oxy. IV 706, SB XII 10929)', Tyche 34: 27–60.

Edgerton, W.F. 1931. Notes on Egyptian Marriage chiefly in the Ptolemaic Period. Chicago: University of Chicago Press.

Erdmann, W. 1939. 'Zum gamos agraphos der gräco-ägyptischen Papyri', in Festschrift P. Koschaker III. Weimar: Böhlau, 224–240.

Erdmann, W. 1940. 'Die Eheschließung im Rechte der graeco-aegyptischen Papyri von der Besetzung bis in die Kaiserzeit', Zeitschrift der Savigny-Stiftung für Rechtsgeschichte: Romanistische Abteilung, 60: 151–184.

Erdmann, W. 1941. 'Die Ehescheidung im Rechte der graeco-aegyptischen Papyri', Zeitschrift der Savigny-Stiftung für Rechtsgeschichte: Romanistische Abteilung, 61: 44–57.

Fischer, M. 2001. The sons of Ramesses II. Wiesbaden: Harrasowitz.

De Francisci, P. 1924. Il trasferimento della proprietà. Padova: Editrice Universitaria.

Frese, B. 1909. Aus dem gräko-ägyptischen Rechtsleben: eine papyrologische Studie. Halle: Niemeyer.

Gagos, T., Koenen, L., McNellen, B. E. 1992. 'A First Century Archive from Oxyrhynchos or Oxyrhynchite Loan Contracts and Egyptian Marriage', in: J. Johnson (ed.), Life in a multi-cultural society: Egypt from Cambyses to Constantine and beyond. Chicago: Oriental Institute, 181–205.

Gradenwitz, O. 1901. 'Zur "Petition of Dionysia"', Archiv für Papyrusforschung und verwandte Gebiete 1: 328–335.

Griffith, F.L. 1900. Stories of the High Priests of Memphis: The Sethon of Herodotus and the Demotic Tales of Khamuas. Oxford: University Press

Häge, G. 1968. Ehegüterrechtliche Verhältnisse in den griechischen Papyri bis Diokletian. Köln–Graz: Böhlau.

Huwardas S. G. 1931. Beiträge zum griechischen und gräkoägyptischen Eherecht der Ptolemäer- und frühen Kaiserzeit. Leipzig: Weicher.

Jördens, A. 2011. 'Eine kaiserliche Konstitution zu den Rechtsprechungskompetenzen der Statthalter', Chiron 41: 327–356.

Jördens, A. 2012. 'Status and Citizenship', in Ch. Riggs (ed.), Oxford Handbook of Roman Egypt. Oxford: University Press, 247–259.

Jüncker, H. 1921, Papyrus Lonsdorfer I. Ein Ehepakt aus der Zeit des Nektanebos. Wien: Akademie der Wissenschaften.

Kaser, M. 1975: Das römische Privatrecht. Zweiter Abschnitt: Nachklassische Entwicklungen, 2. Aufl. München: Beck.

Katzoff, R. 1972. 'Precedents in the Courts of Roman Egypt', Zeitschrift der Savigny-Stiftung für Rechtsgeschichte: Romanistische Abteilung 89: 256–292.

Katzoff, R. 1982. '"Responsa prudentium" in Roman Egypt', in Studi in onore di A. Biscardi II. Milano: Cisalpino La Goliardica, 523–535.

Kelly, B. 2011. Petitions, litigation and social control in Roman Egypt. Oxford.

Kraus, H. W. 1967. Ἀναγραφή und ἀναγράφειν im Ägypten der Ptolemäer und Römer. Köln: Sülz.

Kreller, H. 1919. Erbrechtliche Untersuchungen auf Grund der Gräko-Ägyptischen Papyrusurkunden, Leipzig: Teubner.

Kreller, H. 1933. 'Spuren römischer Jurisprudenz in der ägyptischen Praxis', Aegyptus 13: 260–274.

Kreuzsaler, C. 2008. 'Dionysia vs. Chairemon: Ein Rechtsstreit aus dem römischen Ägypten', in U. Falk, M. Luminati, M. Schmoeckel (eds.), Fälle aus der Rechtsgeschichte. Beck: München, 1–13.

Kreuzsaler, C., Urbanik, J. 2008. 'Humanity and Inhumanity of Law. The Case of Dionysia', The Journal of Juristic Papyrology 38: 119–155.

Kunkel, W. 1928. Review of J. Partsch, U. Wilcken, Juristische Urkunden der Ptolemäerzeit, Gnomon 4: 659–669.

Lewis, N. 1970. 'On paternal authority in Roman Egypt', Revue Internationale des Droits de l'Antiquité 17: 251–258 = Lewis 1995: 120–127.

Lewis, N. 1972. 'Un nouveau texte sur la juridiction du préfet d'Égypte', Revue historique de droit français et étranger 50: 5–12 = Lewis 1995: 157–164.

Lewis, N. 1973. 'Un nouveau texte sur la juridiction du préfet d'Égypte (Complément)', Revue historique de droit français et étranger 51: 5–7 = Lewis 1995: 165–167.

Lewis, N. 1982. ''Αφαίρεσις in Athenian law and custom', in J. Modrzejewski, D. Liebs (eds.), Symposion 1977. Vorträge zur griechischen und hellenistischen Rechtsgeschichte, Köln: Böhlau, 161–178.

Lewis, N. 1995. On Government and Law in Roman Egypt. Collected papers of Naphtali Lewis. Atlanta: Scholars Press.

Lichtheim, M. 1980. Ancient Egyptian Literature III. The Late Period. Berkeley: University of California Press.

Lippert, S. 2008. Einführung in die altägyptische Rechtsgeschichte. Berlin: Hopf.

Lüddeckens, E. 1960. Ägyptische Eheverträge. Wiesbaden: Harrassowitz.

Marci, F. 1915. 'Un caratteristico documento di ἔγγραφος γάμος per la storia del matrimonio nell'Egitto Greco-Romano', Bullettino dell'Istituto di Diritto Romano 28: 97–130.

Maspero, G. 1911. Les contes populaires de l'Egypte ancienne, 4th ed. Paris: E. Guilmoto.

Meyer, P.M. 1920. Juristische Papyri. Berlin: Weidmann.

Mitteis, L. 1891. Reichsrecht und Volksrecht in den östlichen Provinzen des römischen Kaiserreichs. Leipzig: Teubner

Mitteis, L. 1901. 'Neue Rechtsurkunden aus Oxyrhynchus', Archiv für Papyrusforschung und verwandte Gebiete 1: 178–199, 343–354.

Mitteis, L. 1912a. Grundzüge und Chrestomathie der Papyruskunde II. Juristischer Teil I. Grundzüge. Leipzig: Teubner.

Mitteis, L. 1912b. Grundzüge und Chrestomathie der Papyruskunde II. Juristischer Teil II. Chrestomathie. Leipzig: Teubner.

Möller, G. 1918. Zwei ägyptische Eheverträge aus vorsaïtischer Zeit. Berlin: Akademie der Wissenschaften.

Mélèze Modrzejewski, J. 1956. 'Note sur P. Strasb. 237. Une contribution au problème de l'agraphos et engraphos gamos', Eos 48, 3 (Symbolae R. Taubenschlag III): 139–154.

Mélèze Modrzejewski, J. 2014. Loi et coutume dans l'Égypte grecque et romaine, Warszawa: Fundacja im. Rafala Taubenschlaga.

Montevecchi, O. 1936. 'Richerche di sociologia nei documenti dell'Egitto greco-romano II. I contratti di matrimonio e gli atti di divorzio', Aegyptus 16: 3–83.
Nietzold, J. 1903. Die Ehe in Ägypten zur ptolemäisch-römischen Zeit nach den griechischen Heiratskontrakten und verwandten Urkunden. Leipzig: von Veit.
Oudshoorn, J.G. 2007. The Relationship between Roman and Local Law in the Babatha and Salome Komaise Archives. Leiden: Brill.
Πανταζόπουλος, N. 1984. 'Ἄγραφος γάμος – Παλλακεία. Συμβολή εις την έρευναν του δικαίου των μικτών γάμων κατά την ελληνιστική και την βυζαντινήν περίοδον', in Π.Δ. Δημάκης (ed.), Μνήμη Γ. Α. Πετρόπουλου II. Ἀθήνα: Αντ. Ν. Σάκκουλας, 153–193.
Partsch, J., Wilcken, U. 1927. Juristische Urkunden der Ptolemäerzeit (P. Freib. III). Heidelberg: Carl Winter.
Pestman, P.W. 1961. Marriage and Matrimonial Property in Ancient Egypt. Leiden: Brill.
Pestman, P. W. 1989. Familiearchieven uit het land van Pharao, Zutphen: Terra.
Petropoulos, G. 1931. 'Τινὰ μερὶ γάμου ἐν Αἰγύπτῳ κατὰ τοὺς ἑλληνο-αἰγυπτιακοὺς παπύρους', Πρακτικά της Ακαδημίας Αθηνών 6: 115–129.
Piccolo, M. 2003. 'Osservazioni ad alcuni papiri dell'archivio di Tryphon', Aegyptus 83: 197–213.
Platschek, J. 2014. '"My Lord, save me from my father!" Paternal power and Roman imperial state', in B. Sirks (ed.), Nova Ratione: Change of Paradigms in Roman Law, Wiesbaden: Harrassowitz, 51–61.
Platschek, J. 2015. 'Nochmals zur Petition der Dionysia', The Journal of Juristic Papyrology 45: 145–163.
Préaux, C. 1959. 'Le statut de la femme à l'époque hellénistique, principalement en Égypte', Recueils de la societé Jean Bodin 11: 127–175.
Preisigke, F. 1925–1931. Wörterbuch der griechischen Papyrusurkunden mit Einschluß der griechischen Inschriften, Aufschriften, Ostraka, Mumienschilder usw. aus Ägypten I–III, Göttingen: Hubert & co.
Purpura, G. 2005. 'Il giurista e l'avvocato. Nomikoi e rhetores in CPR I, 18', Minima Epigraphica et Papyrologica 9–10: 269–278.
Ray, J. 2002. Reflections of Osiris: Lives from Ancient Egypt. Oxford: University Press.
Révillout, E. 1877. Le Roman de Setna. Étude philologique et critique avec traduction mot à mot du texte démotique, introduction historique et commentaire grammatical. Paris: Leroux.
Révillout, E. 1880. Rituel funéraire de Pamonth en démotique: avec les textes hiéroglyphiques et hiératiques correspondants. Paris: Leroux.
Révillout, E. 1903. Précis du droit Égyptien comparé aux autres droits de l'Antiquité II. Paris: Giard & Brière.
Ritner, R. 2003. 'The Romance of Setna Khaemuas and the Mummies (Setna I)', in W.K. Simpson (ed.), The Literature of Ancient Egypt: An Anthology of Instructions, Stelae, Autobiographies and Poetry, 3rd ed. New Haven: Yale University Press, 453–469.

Rowlandson, J. 1998. Women and Society in Greek and Roman Egypt. A Sourcebook. Cambridge: University Press.

De Ruggiero, R. 1903. 'Studi papirologici sul matrimonio e sul divorzio nell'Egitto greco-romano', Bullettino dell'Istituto di diritto romano 15: 179–282.

De Ruggiero, R. 1908. 'Nuovi documenti per la storia del matrimonio e del divorzio nell'Egitto greco romano', Studi storici per l'antichità classica 1: 161–198.

Rupprecht, H.-A. 1995. 'Sechs-Zeugenurkunde und Registrierung', Aegyptus 75: 37–53 = Rupprecht 2017, 266–278.

Rupprecht, H.-A. 2017. Beiträge zur Juristischen Papyrologie. Kleine Schriften (ed. A. Jördens), Stuttgart: Franz Steiner.

Sánchez-Moreno Ellart, C. 2006. '"Pherne" and "parapherna" in the documents of Augustus' reign: on the subject of P.Ryl. II 125 once again', Aegyptus 86: 177–193.

Rodríguez-Martín, J.D. 2020. 'Textual Evidences of the Executive Legal Effects of a "καθάπερ ἐκ δίκης" Formula in Early Roman Egypt', in Neue Grenzen – New Frontiers. Sonderheft der Zeitschrift des Humboldt-Vereins Ungarn 39: 89–104.

Schönbauer, E. 1938. 'Untersuchungen zum Publizitäts-Rechte im ptolemäischen und römischen Ägypten', Archiv für Papyrusforschung und verwandte Gebiete 13: 39–60.

Seidl, E. 1962. Ptolemäische Rechtsgeschichte, 2nd ed. Glückstadt-Hamburg–New York: J.J. Augustin.

Seidl, E. 1972. 'Eine neue kaiserliche Konstitution über die Appellation', Studia et Documenta Historiae et Iuris 38: 319–320.

Seidl, E. 1973. Rechtsgeschichte Ägyptens als römischer Provinz. Sankt Augustin: H. Richarz.

Sethe, K. 1918. Review of Möller, G. 1918. Zwei ägyptische Eheverträge aus vorsaïtischer Zeit, Göttingische gelehrte Anzeigen 180: 362–378.

Sethe, K., Partsch, J. 1920. Demotische Urkunden zum ägyptischen Bürgschaftsrechte vorzüglich der Ptolemäerzeit. Leipzig: Teubner.

Spiegelberg, W. 1906. 'Demotische Miszellen', Recueil de travaux relatifs à la philologie et à l'archéologie égyptiennes et assyriennes 27: 187–204.

Spiegelberg, W., J. Partsch 1918. 'Der demotische Papyrus der Stadtbibliothek Frankfurt a. M. (Ein Ehevertrag.)', Zeitschrift für Ägyptische Sprache und Altertumskunde 54: 93–98.

Spiegelberg, W. 1923. Demotische Papyri. Veröffentlichungen aus den Badischen Papyrus Sammlungen (P. Bad. I). Heidelberg: Carl Winter.

Stagl, J. F. 2009. 'Zur translativen Struktur des derivativen Eigentumserwerbs', in W. Ernst et al. (eds.) Festschrift für R. Knütel zum 70. Geburtstag. Heildelberg: C. F. Müller, 1191–1206.

Taubenschlag, R. 1916. 'Die patria potestas im Recht der Papyri', Zeitschrift der Savigny-Stiftung für Rechtsgeschichte: Romanistische Abteilung 37: 177–230 = Taubenschlag 1959 II: 261–321.

Taubenschlag, R. 1955. The Law of Greco-Roman Egypt in the Light of the Papyri, 2nd ed. Warszawa: Państwowe Wydawnictwo Naukowe.

Taubenschlag, R. 1959. Opera Minora I–II. Warszawa: Państwowe Wydawnictwo Naukowe.

Thomas, J.D. 1982. The Epistrategos in Ptolemaic and Roman Egypt II. The Roman Epistrategos. Köln: Westdeutscher Verlag.

Thompson, H. 1934. A Family Archive from Siut. Oxford: University Press.

Urbanik, J. 2002. 'D. 24.2.4: … Pater tamen eius nuntium mittere posse: l'influsso della volontà del padre sul divorzio dei sottoposti', in T. Derda, J. Urbanik, M. Węcowski (eds.), Εὐεργεσίας χάριν. Studies Presented to Benedetto Bravo and Ewa Wipszycka by Their Disciples. Warszawa: Fundacja im. Rafala Taubenschlaga, 293–336.

Urbanik, J. 2008. 'Un padre inhumano y la humanidad del derecho: el caso de Dionisia', in J. A. Tamayo (ed.), De la humanidad en el Derecho a los derechos humanos: de Roma a los tiempos actuales, Bilbao: Universidad del País Vasco, 59–72.

Urbanik, J. 2016. 'Dissolubility and Indissolubility of Marriage in the Greek and Roman Tradition', in Z. Benincasa, J. Urbanik (eds.), Mater Familias. Scritti romanistici per Maria Zabłocka. Warszawa: Fundacja im. Rafala Taubenschlaga, 1039–1068.

Urbanik, J. 2019. 'Józef inter gentes. On status and law between the centre and periphery', The Journal of Juristic Papyrology 49: 289–345.

Vandoni, M. 1975. 'Dall'archivio del tessitore Trifone', in Proceedings of the XIV International Congress of Papyrologists. Oxford, 24–31 July 1974. London: English Exploration Society, 331–336.

Waebens, S. 2019. 'Life Portraits: People and their Everyday Papers in a Bureaucratic Society', in K. Vandorpe (ed.), A Companion to Greco-Roman and Late Antique Egypt. Hoboken: Wiley & Sons, 199–213.

Wenger, L. 1928. 'ἄγραφος in der Rechtssprache', in Id., Aus Novellenindex und Papyruswörterbuch. München: Akademie der Wissenschaften, 15–102.

Whitehorne, J. E. G. 1984. 'Tryphon's second marriage (P. Oxy. II 267)', in Atti del XVII Congresso Internazionale di Papirologia III. Napoli: Centro Internazionale per lo studio dei papiri ercolanesi, 1267–1274.

Wilcken, U. 1901. 'Zu den griechischen Papyri der königlich bayerischen Hof- und Staatsbibliothek zu München', Archiv für Papyrusforschung und verwandte Gebiete 1: 468–491.

Wilcken, U. 1906. 'Papyrus-Urkunden', Archiv für Papyrusforschung und verwandte Gebiete 3: 502–569.

Wilcken, U. 1927. Urkunden der Ptolemäerzeit I. Berlin–Leipzig: De Gruyter.

von Woess, F. 1924: Untersuchungen über das Urkundenwesen und den Publizitätsschutz im römischen Ägypten. München: Beck.

Wolff H. J. 1939. Written and Unwritten Marriages in Hellenistic and Postclassical Roman Law. Haverford: American Philological Association.

Wolff, H. J. 1952. 'Die Grundlagen Des Griechischen Eherechts', Tijdschrift voor Rechtsgeschiedenis 20: 1–29, 157–163.

Wolff, H. J. 1953. 'Faktoren der Rechtsbildung im hellenistisch-römischen Ägypten', Zeitschrift der Savigny-Stiftung für Rechtsgeschichte: Romanistische Abteilung 70: 20–57.

Wolff, H.J. 1973. 'Hellenistisches Privatrecht', Zeitschrift der Savigny-Stiftung für Rechtsgeschichte: Romanistische Abteilung 90: 63–90.

Wolff, H.J. 1978: Das Recht der griechischen Papyri Ägyptens in der Zeit der Ptolemäer und des Prinzipats. Band 2. München: Beck.

Wolff, H.J. 1998. Vorlesungen über juristische Papyruskunde. Berlin: Duncker & Humblot.

Wolff, H.J. 2002. Das Recht der griechischen Papyri Ägyptens in der Zeit der Ptolemäer und des Prinzipats. Band 1 (hrsg. von Hans-Alber Rupprecht). München: Beck.

Yiftach-Firanko, U. 2003. Marriage and Marital Arrangements. A History of the Greek Marriage Document in Egypt. 4th century BCE – 4th century CE. München: Beck.

Yiftach-Firanko, U. 2008. 'Who Killed the Double Document in Ptolemaic Egypt?', Archiv für Papyrusforschung und verwandte Gebiete 54: 2013–2218.

Yiftach-Firanko, U. 2009. 'Law in Greco-Roman Egypt: Hellenization, Fusion, Romanization', in R. Bagnall (ed.), The Oxford handbook of papyrology. Oxford: 541–560.

Zauzich, K. Th. 1968. Die ägyptische Schreibertradition in Aufbau, Sprache und Schrift der demotischen Kaufverträge aus ptolemäischer Zeit. Wiesbaden: Harrassowitz.

GERHARD THÜR (WIEN)

UNGESCHRIEBENES IN P.OXY. II 267: ANTWORT AUF JOSÉ LUIS ALONSO

Das Thema bietet die Gelegenheit, an den Gründer unseres Symposion zu erinnern, Hans Julius Wolff. Geboren 1902, nach Assessorexamen 1929 als Richter im Kammergerichtsbezirk Berlin tätig, 1933 in den Ruhestand versetzt, dann (finanziert von der Rockefeller-Stiftung) am Thesaurus Linguae Latinae in München beschäftigt, emigrierte er 1935 nach Panama. An der dortigen Universidad Nacional lehrte er Römisches Recht und beendete seine „inoffizielle Habilitationsschrift", *Written and Unwritten Marriages*, die 1939 von der American Philological Association gedruckt wurde. In diesem Jahr wagte er auch den Sprung in eine ungewisse Zukunft in die Vereinigten Staaten. 1952 wurde er an die Universität Mainz berufen, 1955 nach Freiburg. Er starb 1983.[1] Die *Marriages* sind mit jugendlichem Elan geschrieben und nach gründlicher Ausbildung in Berlin durch Eduard Meyer, Ulrich Wilcken, Wilhelm Schubart, Josef Partsch und Ernst Rabel. Sie führen zu dem heutigen Thema.

Alonso ist bereits durch eine Reihe bahnbrechender Arbeiten im Bereich der juristischen Papyrologie bekannt, vor allem zur dinglichen Sicherung von Ansprüchen. So hat er 2008 das *hypallagma* entzaubert und 2016 dem Phantom der ὠνὴ ἐν πίστει den Todesstoß versetzt.[2] Nun versucht er mit Elan den *agraphos gamos* neu zu erklären.[3] Alonso hat erkannt, dass neben der viel behandelten *sedes materiae*, dem „Dionysia-Papyrus" (P.Oxy. II 237, 186 n.Chr.), vor allem der zwischen Tryphon und der Saraëus abgeschlossene Ehevertrag (P.Oxy. II 267, 37 n.Chr.) von Bedeutung ist. Der Ausdruck *agraphos* wird im Vertragstext rein deskriptiv gebraucht, während die Eingaben Dionysias mit *gamos agraphos* und *engraphos* bestimmte Rechtsfolgen zu suggerieren trachten. Abgesehen davon, dass der Dionysia-Papyrus derzeit einer umfassenden Revision unterzogen wird, kann auch dessen Inhalt nicht in einer kurzen ‚Antwort' abgehandelt werden. Zu Recht klammert Alonso den

---

[1] S. den Nachruf von Thür, *OpOm* 055 (1984).

[2] Alonso 2008 und 2016 [zum letzten s. Thür, *OpOm* 335 (2016)].

[3] Sein Vortrag wurde nach guter Gelehrtentradition erst in letzter Minute fertig. Er teilte mir als Respondenten allerdings vorweg seine Grundtendenz und die wichtigsten Quellen samt Literatur mit, nicht aber das Resultat seiner Arbeit. Aus seinen Angaben formte ich mir mein eigenes Bild, das ich anstatt einer förmlichen ‚Antwort' im Symposion vortrug. Die gegenwärtige Fassung weicht davon wesentlich ab.

angeblich nur dort, als *hapax*, auftretenden Ausdruck ἔνγραφος γάμος als ungebräuchlich aus seiner Untersuchung aus.[4]

Ἄγραφος.

Das Wortfeld von γράφειν und seiner Komposita umfasst einen weiten Bedeutungskreis. In rechtlichem Zusammenhang kann man nicht von einer strikten Terminologie sprechen. Vielmehr hatten Hörer oder Leser je nach dem Sinnzusammenhang die richtigen Bezüge herzustellen. So wird zum Beispiel in der jüngst publizierten Strafstele aus Epidauros genau zwischen ἐπιγράφειν (in die Schuldnerliste eintragen) und ἀναγράφειν (öffentlich, auf einer Stele publizieren) unterschieden (Z. 33–25; ca. 360 v.Chr.), ohne dass die Schriftträger genannt würden.[5] Die einfachste Erklärung der Wendung in der Tryphon-Urkunde ἐπεὶ δὲ σύνεσμεν | ἀλλήλοις ἀγράφω[ς], προσομολογῶι … (P. Oxy. II 267, 18–19) wäre, dass das Paar ohne schriftlichen Ehevertrag — unbeurkundet — zusammengelebt oder von einer demotischen auf die nun vorliegende griechische Eheform gewechselt habe. Doch das Dokument selbst ist die Eheurkunde, nach Alonso die griechische Version eines demotischen Formulars, die Ehe ist also demotisch. Richtig schließt er daraus, dass der Schlüssel zur Erklärung von *agraphos* in der unterschiedlichen Beurkundung verschiedener demotischer Eheformen liege.

Etwas Geschriebenes als „ungeschrieben“ zu bezeichnen, ist nicht neu. Als sprachliche Parallele zu erwähnen wäre der ἄγραφος νόμος. Der Rechtsphilosoph denkt sofort an den Gebrauch dieses Wortes in Sophokles’ Antigone und Perikles’ Leichenrede im Sinne von „natürlichen, ungeschriebenen Rechtsgrundsätzen“.[6] Anders ist jedoch die Vorschrift ἀγράφῳ δὲ νόμῳ τὰς ἀρχὰς μὴ χρῆσθαι zu verstehen.[7] Hier geht es nicht um „ungeschriebenes“ Recht, sondern sehr wohl um publizierte Vorschriften, die aber im Zuge der Rechtsbereinigung durch die *anagrapheis* (410–400 v.Chr.) als undemokratisch nicht neu publiziert, also ausgemerzt wurden. Es handelt sich also nicht um νόμοι ἄγραφοι. Technisch korrekt (allerdings sprachlich unmöglich) müsste man von νόμοι ἀν-ανάγραπτοι sprechen, also von nicht „*wieder*-aufgeschriebenen“ Gesetzen.[8]

Νόμος Αἰγυπτίων.

Neben dem demotischen Hintergrund und den hierdurch begründeten unterschiedlichen Beurkundungsformen ist in Alonsos Beweisführung eine neue Deutung des

---

4 Auch das Problem der *eiskrisis* der Epheben in den „Griechen“-*poleis* Alexandria und Ptolemais wird nicht berührt. Dort wird eine „formlose“, durch *synchoresis* geschlossene Ehe von der durch die *hierothytai* dokumentierten unterschieden, letztere wird vielleicht als ἔνγρ]αφος bezeichnet (P.Flor. I 57, 82, Hermopolis, 166 n.Chr.; s. Wolff 1939, 41).

5 Ed. Ch. Kritzas, S. Prignitz, 2020, [s. dazu Thür, *OpOm* 364 (2020)].

6 Thuk. 2, 37, 2; Sophokl. Ant. 454.

7 Andok. 1, 85.

8 Thür, *OpOm* 172 (2000) 92.

nomos Aigyption (relevant vor allem im Dionysia-Prozess) ein tragendes Element.[9] Seine These ist, vom Standpunkt der römischen Verwaltung seien vor der Severerzeit alle Einwohner Ägyptens als Αἰγυπτίοι bezeichnet worden, soweit sie nicht als römische Bürger oder als solche der Poleis Naukratis, Alexandria, Ptolemais oder später Antinoopolis privilegiert waren. Sie seien einheitlich, je nach den vorgelegten Urkunden behandelt worden. Im zweiten Jahrhundert habe die ethnische Herkunft als „Ägypter" keine Rolle mehr gespielt. Unabhängig von der Ethnie seien jedem (und jeder) alle Formen der Rechtsgeschäfte offen gestanden[10]. Griechische Eigennamen seien als Kriterium der Zuordnung irrelevant geworden. Diese ansprechende These hat weitreichende Folgen für die Lehre vom ‚Rechtspluralismus', worauf hier nur hingewiesen sei.

Ἄγραφος γάμος.

Alonso knüpft seine Lösung, abgesichert durch zahlreiche Parallelstellen, an einen ‚Leitfall' an, an die Ehe zwischen Tryphon und der Saraëus (P. Oxy. II 267). Wie er in seinem Abschnitt V ausführt, handelt es sich um eine Privaturkunde, ein *cheirographon* in Form einer Bank-*diagraphe*, im Grunde eine bloße Quittung, womit der Mann bestätigt, von der Frau als Darlehen einen Geldbetrag und Gegenstände (typisch für eine Mitgift) erhalten zu haben, was er zu einem fixen Termin (in fünf Monaten) zurückzuerstatten verspricht; da sie „ungeschrieben" in Ehe leben, verspricht er außerdem bei Trennung während einer Schwangerschaft Entbindungskosten zu zahlen. Mit Ausnahme des fixen Termins und der Entbindungskosten findet Alonso hier — in griechischer Sprache — die typischen Klauseln einer demotischen „Darlehen-Mitgift-Urkunde", von Pestman (1961) in seiner grundlegenden Untersuchung der ägyptischen Ehe als „Modell B" klassifiziert. Dieses Ehemodell entspricht der für Griechen und Römer (und auch für uns) leicht eingängigen agnatischen Familienverfassung, zumal der Mann väterliche Gewalt über seine Kinder hat. „Ungeschrieben zusammenleben" ist aus dieser Variante allein nicht zu erklären.[11]

Kühn geht Alonso den Weg in die demotische Praxis weiter. Er sieht den Gegensatz „ungeschrieben – geschrieben" nicht in der Sprache der Urkunden, sondern in unterschiedlichen demotischen Eheformen, die in römischer Zeit weiter-

---

[9] Alonso / Babusiaux (2023) 253–254.

[10] Nach neueren Forschungen gilt das übrigens auch weitgehend für römische Bürger, s. Jakab 2021.

[11] Es sei denn, man legt (mit Thür im mündlichen Vortrag) der Sprache der Urkunde rechtliche Bedeutung bei: Griechisch wäre „schriftlich", demotisch vom Standpunkt der römischen Verwaltung „nichtschriftlich". Trotz „griechisch" würden Tryphon und Saraëus demotisch zusammenleben wollen. Doch die Sprache der Urkunde ist mit dem Ende der Laokriten-Gerichte schon in ptolemäischer Zeit irrelevant geworden. Römische Gerichte akzeptieren de facto nur griechische Dokumente. Demotische Notariatsurkunden sind nur bis zur Mitte des 1. Jh. n.Chr. in Gebrauch.

leben. Pestman beschreibt als Modell C die „Gesamtverkauf-(*panprasion*)-Urkunde". Hier bringt die Frau keine Mitgift ein (auch nicht in Darlehensform), sondern „kauft" (nominell) das gesamte Vermögen des Mannes, der überdies die Verpflichtung übernimmt, sie zu unterhalten (deshalb auch „Unterhalt-Urkunde"). Der Mann verliert hiermit seine Verfügungsmacht über all sein Vermögen zu Lebzeiten und von Todes wegen und hat keine väterliche Gewalt über die gemeinsamen Kinder. Welches Ehemodell dahinter steht, verrät uns Alonso nicht. Überzeugend ist aber seine Erklärung der „Schriftlichkeit". Die vom Mann eingebrachte Vermögensmasse wird nämlich in dieser Eheform zum ‚Familienvermögen'. Der Mann kann nichts ohne die Zustimmung der Frau und Kinder veräußern. Und diese familienrechtliche Bindung, κατοχή, wird im Grundbesitzregister (βιβλιοθήκη ἐγκτήσεων) unter seinem Namen zugunsten der Berechtigten vermerkt. Zur *katoche* gibt es Edikte mehrerer Statthalter, was indirekt beweist, dass die römische Verwaltung das Güterrecht der griechisch beurkundeten demotischen *panprasion*-Eheform voll anerkennt.[12]

Die „Schriftlichkeit" dieser Eheform — vom römisch/griechischen Standpunkt aus gesehen — findet Alonso in einem nicht ganz einfachen Gedankengang. Die *bibliotheke enkteseon* ist im Personalfolien-System angelegt und verzeichnet die der jeweiligen Person gehörigen Grundstücke. In *parenthesis* angemerkt (παρατιθέναι) werden dort auch die Belastungen durch Pfand- oder Verfangenschaftsrechte. Diese Publizitätsform soll künftige Erwerber warnen, ist aber nicht konstitutiv. Um solche Belastungen eintragen zu lassen (durch ἀπογραφή), bedarf es einer notariellen Urkunde, eines δημόσιος χρηματισμός. Und nur auf diese Weise hätten auch die im *panprasion*-Modell (C) vorgesehenen erbrechtlichen Verfügungen wirksam getroffen werden können. „Schriftlichkeit" der Ehe (im Sinne von Dionysias Ausführungen vor Gericht) erblickt Alonso in der notariellen *syngraphe* mit ihren vermögens- und erbrechtlichen Bestimmungen, sei sie nun in der *bibliotheke* registriert oder nicht. Im Gegensatz dazu konnte die Darlehen-Mitgift-Ehe (Modell B) bequem durch *cheirographon-diagraphe* privat beurkundet werden. Dies habe zur zusammenfassenden Bezeichnung als „nichtschriftlich" geführt.[13] Damit hat Alonso eine denkbare Lösung einer jahrhundertalten Streitfrage vorgetragen. Jeder Kenner des römischen Rechts stieß sich daran, dass Kinder einer (vermutlich minderen)

[12] Edikte des Mettius Rufus, (erlassen 89 n.Chr., P. Oxy. II 237 col. VIII 27–43, „Dionysia-Papyrus" 186 n.Chr.) und des Sulpicius Similis (erlassen 109 n.Chr., ebenda col. VIII 21–27). — Ob die *katoche* als „Verfangenschaft" zu definieren ist oder als „funktionell geteiltes Eigentum", wird nicht immer klar (bei Anm. 62). Dies wird auch erst bei der Arbeit am Dionysia-Papyrus aktuell: Haben Ehefrau oder Kinder neben dem Ehemann selbständige (von der Zustimmung des Mannes abhängige) Veräußerungsrechte oder sind sie auf die bloße Zustimmung zu Verfügungen des Mannes beschränkt?

[13] In Diskussion mit Alonso wurde erwogen, dass derartige Urkunden nicht in einem *grapheion* notariell durch *anagraphe* registriert werden mussten (dazu Wolff 1978, 178), also ähnlich wie eingangs erwähnt wären diese Ehen ἄγραφοι im Sinne von ἀν-ανάγραπτοι.

„nichtschriftlichen" Ehe unter einer Art *patria potestas* standen, solche aus einer (wohl bevorzugten) „schriftlichen" aber nicht. Mit den Eigenarten der von Alonso herangezogenen notariell dokumentierten *panprasion*-Ehe ist das Bild nun zurechtgerückt.[14]

Familienverfassung.
Voll befriedigt ist der Leser mit dem von Alonso umsichtig begründeten Beitrags freilich nicht. Das Modell der Darlehen-Mitgift-Ehe passt gut in das Bild der agnatisch-patrilokalen Familienform der griechisch-römischen Antike. Doch welche Familienstruktur steht hinter der *panprasion*-Ehe? Es sei hier ein Denkanstoß versucht. Wenn der Ehemann alle seine Vermögensrechte aufgibt, besteht die Vermutung, dass er in das Haus der Frau eintritt. Das könnte nötig sein, wenn der Vater der Braut keinen männlichen Nachkommen hat. Die Griechen lösen das Problem durch Adoption oder, nach dem Tod des Vaters der „alleinigen Tochter", mit der Institution der „Erbtochter". Wer sie zur Heirat zugesprochen bekommt, ist zwar *kyrios* des Vermögens, doch muss es im *oikos* erhalten bleiben. Darüber wachen in Athen die Mitbürger, vor allem die Seitenverwandten, denen eine Popularklage wegen Misshandlung der Erbtochter zusteht (γραφὴ κακώσεως ἐπικλήρου). Dieses Problem wäre in der demotischen *panprasion*-Ehe durch das Erfordernis gelöst, dass die Frau zu Veräußerungen zustimmen muss. Doch wer hat die Familengewalt in solchen Ehen? Der Brautvater, solange er lebt? Und nach dessen Tod? Die Ehefrau? Der Ehemann ist ja ausgeschlossen. Derartige Fragen könnten bei der Neuedition des Dionysia-Payrus geklärt werden, allerdings wohl aus weiteren demotischen Dokumenten. In der *agraphos*-Frage hat Alonso jedenfalls bereits einen festen Boden bereitet.

Nochmals zu Tryphon.
Die Ehe mit Saraëus war bereits seine zweite. Auffällig ist die fixe Laufzeit des „Darlehens" (also der Ehe) von fünf Monaten. Üblicherweise kann die Frau das „Darlehen" (die Mitgift) zu dem ungewissen Zeitpunkt der Eheauflösung zurückverlangen. In Verbindung mit den ebenfalls unüblich versprochenen Entbindungskosten[15] drängt sich folgender Schluss auf: Die Ehe wurde zunächst „auf Probe" geschlossen. Gebar die vermutlich schwangere Saraëus in jenen fünf Monaten einen Sohn, lief das „Darlehen" unbefristet weiter. In der Tat wurde es erst sechs Jahre später zurückbezahlt (und vermutlich durch ein anderes ersetzt). Tryphon war diesmal zufrieden.

---

[14] Erwägenswert wäre auch der Gedanke, dass die Darlehen-Mitgift-Ehe deswegen als „nichtschriftlich" bezeichnet wurde, weil sie keine *katoche* bewirkte und diese auch nicht durch *apographe* in der *bibliotheke enkteseon* registriert wurde.

[15] Zum Fall s. Gagos et al. 1992, 189–192; zu den Entbindungskosten s. dort S. 191 mit Verweis auf den Parallelfall Pausiris, S. 187 (P. Mich. inv. no. 92, Ox. 73–74 n.Chr., Taf. 19.1).

Der Wunsch nach einem männlichen Leibeserben ist oft hinter den Regeln des antiken Ehe- und Erbrechts unausgesprochen greifbar, selten jedoch so brutal auf den Punkt gebracht wie in einer Grabinschrift aus Aphrodisias (MAMA 8, 576, 3–13, Anf. 3. Jh. n.Chr.): εἰς ἣν σορὸν | κηδευθήσονται αὐτός τε Πο|[5]λυχρόνιος καὶ Αὐρ(ηλία) Μελτίνη ἡ | γυνὴ αὐτοῦ ἡ πρότερον Μελ|τίνη Ἀντιόχου τοῦ Ζήνωνος | ἐὰν μείνῃ γυνὴ τοῦ Πολυχρο|νίου καὶ ἐὰν γένηται τῷ Πο|[10]λυχρονίῳ ἀρρενικὸν τέκνον | καὶ Αὐρ(ηλία) Ζωσίμη ἡ πρότερον | Ζωσίμη Ἀπολλωνίου τοῦ Ἀρ|χελάου οὐδεὶς δὲ ἕτερος...[16]

Polychronios schämt sich nicht, auf seinem Sarkophag seiner Ehefrau Meltine das Grabrecht neben ihm unter der Bedingung einzuräumen, dass sie ihm einen Sohn gebiert. Andernfalls droht er ihr — indirekt — mit der Scheidung. Vielleicht ist mit der hierauf genannten Zosime bereits die potenzielle Nachfolgerin eingeführt. Die öffentliche Meinung war offenbar auf Polychronios' Seite. Eine ähnliche Mentalität könnte auch hinter dem zwischen Tryphon und Saraëus geschlossenen Ehevertrag stehen, was aber einen glücklichen Ausgang nicht verhinderte.

gerhard.thuer@oeaw.ac.at

LITERATUR

Alonso, José Luis (2008): The alpha and omega of *'hypallagma'*, *JJP* 38, 19–51.

Alonso, José Luis (2016): One en pistei, Guarantee Sales, and Title-Transfer Security in the Papyri, in: Delfim Leão, Gerhard Thür (Hgg.), *Symposion 2015*, 121–192.

Alonso, José Luis /Babusiaux, Ulrike (2023): Papyrologische und epigraphische Quellen, in: Babusiaux, Ulrike / Baldus, Christian / Ernst, Wolfgang / Meissel, Franz-Stefan / Platschek, Johannes / Rüfner, Thomas (Hgg.), *Handbuch des römischen Privatrechts I*, Tübingen, 222–317.

Gagos, Traianos / Koenen, Ludwig / McNellen, Brad E. (1992): A First Century Archive from Oxyrhynchos or Oxyrhynchite Loan Contracts and Egyptian Marriage, in: Janet H. Johnson (Hg.), *Life in a multi-cultural society: Egypt from Cambyses to Constantine and beyond.* Chicago: Oriental Institute, 181–205.

Jakab, Éva (2021): Some Thoughts on Succession in Provincial Context, in: Mario Capasso et al. (Hgg.), *Proceedings of the 29th International Congress of Papyrology*, Salento, 584–598.

Kritzas Charalampos, Sebastian Prignitz (2020): The 'Stele of Punishments'. A New Inscription from Epidauros, *AEphem* 159, 1–61.

[16] MAMA 8, 576, 3–13: ... in welchen Sarkophag bestattet werden Polychronios selbst und Aurelia Meltine, seine Ehefrau, früher Meltine, Tochter des Antiochos, Sohn des Zenon, wenn sie Ehefrau des Polychronios bleibt und dem Polychronios ein männliches Kind gebiert, und Aurelia Zosime, früher Zosime, Tochter des Apollonios, Sohn des Archelaos, niemand aber sonst ... Zur Inschrift s. Praust, Wiedergut 2019, 71.

Pestman, Pieter W. (1961): *Marriage and Matrimonial Property in Ancient Egypt*, Leiden.

Praust Karl, Karin Wiedergut (2019): I.Milet VI 2, 570. Rekonstruktion und Interpretation einer bemerkenswerten Grabinschrift, *Chiron* 49, 69–92.

Thür, Gerhard (*OpOm*): *Opera Omnia*, https://epub.oeaw.ac.at/gerhard-thuer

Thür, Gerhard (1984): Hans Julius Wolff zum Gedenken, *ZRG RA* 101, 476–491. (*OpOm* 055)

Thür, Gerhard (2000): Rechtsvorschriften und Rechtsanwendung in Athen (5./4. Jh. v. Chr.), in: Ant. N. Sakkoula (ed.), *Timai Ioannou Triantaphyllopoulou*, 89–100. (*OpOm* 172)

Thür, Gerhard (2016): Zu den Sicherungsrechten in den Papyri in: Delfim Leão, Gerhard Thür (Hgg.), *Symposion 2015*, 193–198. (*OpOm* 335)

Thür, Gerhard (2020): Prozessrechtlicher Kommentar zur „Strafstele“ aus Epidauros, *Geistes-, sozial- und kulturwissenschaftlicher Anzeiger* (*AnzÖAW*) 155/1+2, 29–62. (*OpOm* 364)

Wolff, Hans Julius (1939): *Written and Unwritten Marriages in Hellenistic and Postclassical Roman Law*, Haverford PA.

Wolff, Hans Julius (1978): *Das Recht der griechischen Papyri Ägyptens* II, München.

URI YIFTACH-FIRANKO (TEL AVIV)

THE IMPACT OF THE *STIPULATIO*: ON THE RECEPTION OF DIGEST 19.2.54.1 IN BYZANTINE OXYRHYNCHOS[1]

Abstract: The impact of the *stipulatio* on the shape and language of Greek legal documents after the *constitutio Antoniniana* has long been acknowledged. At the same time, past studies of that impact have focused first and foremost on the stipulation-clause that was incorporated into Greek legal documents immediately after 212 CE to render their contents actionable in Roman courts of law. In the present paper, I wish to propose a different approach. Documents from the late Roman and Byzantine periods exhibit multiple innovations in terminology, syntax, and content, that, I suggest, derive from a Roman legal language and institutions engendered, in the classical period, in the context of the *stipulatio*. In one particular case, that of contracts of labour from mid and late sixth century Oxyrhynchos, a clause legitimizing the 'warranted' expulsion of the lessee by the lessor in the duration of the contract, may derive from the text of the fifth book of Paul's *responsa* as incorporated in Justinian's Digest 19.2.54.1.

Keywords: *stipulatio*, Roman law (reception), late Roman documentary practice, Byzantine Oxyrhynchos, contracts of lease and labour, *expulsio*.

Introduction

Soon after that grant of Roman citizenship by the *Constitutio Antoniniana* of 212 CE, new citizens began to insert at the end of their contracts the text ἐπερωτηθεὶς ὡμολόγησα, the subject being, routinely, the obligor. With very few exceptions, scholars have seen in this clause a Greek translation of the Roman *stipulatio*, consisting of an *interrogatio* by the prospective obligee and a *responsio* by the prospective obligor. The clause was meant, it has been argued, to accord actionability in Roman courts of law to contracts executed by the new citizens, which otherwise remained unaltered. Accordingly, studies dedicated to the institution of the *stipulatio* as recorded in the papyrological source material have entirely focused on the contents and structure of the above mentioned clause.[2]

In the following paper I would like to offer a different approach. In Rome, the *stipulatio* was the key form of contracting, introducing obligation to perform a

[1] I thank the organizers of Symposion 2022 for inviting me to deliver this paper, and to the respondent for her stimulating and innovative thoughts as well as to Johannes Platschek for his attentive reading and suggestions.

[2] Wolff 2003, 131–133. See in particular Simon 1964.

future act, in particular that of delivery and payment.[3] While the contract of the *stipulatio* was *per se* chiefly incorporated into Greek legal documents in the framework of the above mentioned clause,[4] the terminology that developed in the context of the *stipulatio* has infiltrated into, and transformed the text of the legal document as a whole. In the present paper I wish (1) to discuss how the syntax of a clause enables us to trace back its origin in the 'world of the *stipulatio*'. I will then (2) focus on a test case, that of Digest 19.2.54.1. In that text, Paul, the early third-century jurist, discusses two *stipulationes* that enjoined penalties on both parties to a land lease for prematurely dissolving the contract. In that case, I will argue for an outright reception of the text of the 'Pauline *stipulatio*' into Greek documents drawn up in Oxyrhynchos in the sixth and seventh centuries CE. (3) In the third section I will contextualize the Oxyrhynchite evidence. I will argue that while the Pauline *stipulatio* has only been introduced into documents from Oxyrhynchos after the promulgation of Justinian's Digest, a penalty for dissolving contracts of lease and labour *per se* was much older, first recorded in a document from the early fourth century CE. Outside the Oxyrhynchite nome the clause remained largely unaltered throughout the Byzantine period. (4) A methodological post-script will end this short contribution.

A: Modalities of Change

In the Classical and Hellenistic periods, the act of contracting is commonly reported 'objectively'. The document records the act that has elicited the creation of the contract, using the indicative of the aorist tense. Gradually, in a process that is well underway at the beginning of the Roman period, the objective style is superseded by the subjective formulation, introduced through the verb ὁμολογέω. The subject of ὁμολογέω ('say the same things, agree') is the obligor, and its object is an infinitive signifying or implying the past performance of the act of contracting.[5] When the *stipulatio* is introduced into the language of the Greek legal document from Egypt at the beginning of the third century CE, the verb ὁμολογέω is used in much the same way. In the clause that has established itself in sale documents composed at the third-century *agoranomeia* of the Herakleopolite and Oxyrhynchite nomes, the text of the *stipulatio* is used to acknowledge the performance of past acts: the receipt of the consideration and the due performance of the act of

---

[3] *Digest* 45.1.5.1 (Pomp. 26 ad Sabinum): *stipulatio autem est verborum conceptio, quibus is qui interrogatur daturum facturumve se quod interrogatus est responderit.* and Yiftach 2021, 169–187, at 172 n. 10, and most recently, Finkenauer 2023, 564–624.

[4] See also, however, the *stipulatio Aquiliana*: e.g., P.Mich. XIII 677.19–23 (mid VI CE, Aphrodite): εἰ δὲ ἐπιχειρήσειέν τις ἐξ ἡμῶν | [20] παραβῆναι καὶ μὴ ἐμμεῖναι ταύτῃ τῇ αἰωνίᾳ καὶ ἐγγράφῳ ὁμολογίᾳ | [21] παρέξει ὁ μὴ ἐμμένον μέρος τῷ ἐμμένοντι μέρει λόγῳ προστίμου | [22] ἐξ ἐπερωτήσεως καὶ παραβάσεως χρυσοῦ ὀγγίας τρῖς ἔργῳ καὶ δυνάμει | [23] ἀπαιδούμενα (l. ἀπαιτούμενα) and Simon 1964, 36–40.

[5] Wolf 1957, 26–72, at 53–61.

contracting itself. In both cases, the past performance is conveyed through the infinitive of the perfect tense.[6]

The tenets of the Roman *stipulatio* are completely different. The verbs *spondeo* and *fideipromitto*, both introducing infinitive, are used by the respondent to promise the performance of a future act. When the text of the *stipulatio* is translated into Greek, *promitto* is also conveyed through ὁμολογέω, but the verb does not take the perfect, but the future, present, and most conspicuously, the infinitive of the aorist tense. In Leo's *basilika*, the verb ὁμολογέω is most notably used in that sense with verbs denoting delivery: διδόναι, καταβαλεῖν and παρασχεῖν.[7] It is precisely in that sense that the syntax of the *stipulatio* is introduced into the language of Greek legal documents in sixth and seventh century Egypt.

Clauses stipulating the delivery of cash and fungibles have always been routinely introduced into a wide variety of documents, in particular in the context of contracts recording loan, sale on delivery, and lease.[8] Before the Byzantine period, the verb denoting that delivery was ἀποδίδωμι. As soon as the verb ὁμολογέω, that is the 'old', Greek ὁμολογέω, has been introduced to denote the act of contracting, the account of the duty of payment was integrated into the flow of the same text. So, in P.Hamb. I 21.4–8 (315 CE, Oxyrhynchos), recording sale on delivery, the vendor acknowledges the receipt of the consideration (ὁμολογῶ ἐσχηκέναι) for the commodity, which stands in the genitive (τιμὴν πλήρη λινοκαλάμης ὠμῆς) and antecedes the relative pronoun ἥνπερ. In its turn, the said pronoun serves in the relative clause as the direct object of ἐπάναγκες ἀποδώσω.[9]

Similar structure is evident in the six-century loan contract P.Oxy. XVII 1970 (554 CE, Oxyrhynchos):[10] the borrower acknowledges the receipt of the loan, and professes his duty to repay it. But whereas the clause recording the act of lending

---

6 Cf., e.g., *P.Coll.Youtie* II 71.35–36 (281 CE, Panopolis): καὶ ἐπερωτηθεὶς περὶ τοῦ ταῦτα οὕτως | [36] ὀρθῶς καλῶς γεγενῆσθαι ὡμολόγησα; *P.Oxy.* XX 2270.3–4 (V/VI CE, Oxyrhynchos): π̣ε̣ρὶ ἧς ἀ̣ρι[θ]μ̣[ή]σ̣ε̣ω̣ς τ̣ῆ[ς] ὁ̣λοκλήρου τιμῆς ἐ[π]ερ̣ωτη|[4]θέντ̣ε̣[ς ὑπὸ] σ̣ο̣ῦ̣ [π]επ̣λ̣η[ρ]ῶσθαι ὡμολογήσαμεν and Yiftach 2021, 175–177.

7 Cf., e.g., *Bas.* 29.1.83 = *Cod.Just.* 5.11.3 (διδόναι); *Bas.* 52.1.49 = *Digest* 44.7.50 (παρασχεῖν); *Bas.* 23.2.4.7 = *Nov.Just.* 134.8 (καταβαλεῖν).

8 See in particular Weber 1932, 102–135.

9 P.Hamb. I 21.4–8 (315 CE, Oxyrhynchos): ὁμολογῶ ἐσχηκέναι παρά σου ἐντεῦθεν τιμὴν πλήρη λινο|[5]καλάμης ὠμῆς μαντ̣ακίων (l. μανδακίων) ἕξ, ἥμπερ λινοκαλάμ[ην] | [6] καθαρὰν ἐπάνα̣γκες ἀποδώσω σοι ἐν ἀγροῖς τῷ Παῦνι μη̣ν̣ὶ̣ | [7] τοῦ ἐνεστῶτος ἐνάτου ζ (ἔτους) ἄνευ πάσης ὑπερθέσεως | [8] καὶ εὑρ̣ησιλογίας.

10 P.Oxy. XVII 1970.16–28 (554 CE, Oxyrhynchos): ὁμολογοῦμεν ἐσχηκέναι παρὰ | [17] τῆς ὑμῶν μεγαλοπρ(επείας) ἐξ ἡμετέρας | [18] παρακλήσεως ἐν χρήσει διὰ χειρὸς | [19] ἐξ οἴκου αὐτῆς εἰς ἰδίας ἡμῶν καὶ | [20] ἀναγ'καίας χρείας χρυσοῦ νομισμάτια | [21] τέσσερ[α] ἰδ(ιωτικῷ) ζυγῷ νομ(ιτευόμενα), γί(νονται) χρ(υσοῦ) νο(μισμάτια) δ | [22] νομ(ιτευόμενα), καὶ ὁμολογοῦμεν ταῦτα ἀπο|[23]δοῦναι τῇ ὑμῶν μεγαλοπρ(επείᾳ) μετ̣ὰ̣ π̣άσης | [24] εὐχα̣ρ̣ι̣[σ]τ̣ί[α]ς ἐν τῇ πρώτῃ δόσει τοῦ | [25] ἡμ̣ῶ̣ν̣ [μ]ι̣σ̣θ(οῦ) τοῦ ἐνδόξ(ου) οἴκου ἐν τῷ Ἁθὺρ | [26] μην[ὶ] τῆς εἰσιούσης τρ[ί]της ἐπινεμ(ήσεως) | [27] ἀνυ̣π̣ε̣ρ̣θ̣(έτως) κινδύνῳ̣ τῶν ἡμῖν ὑπαρχ(όντων) | [28] ὑποκειμ(ένων) εἰς τοῦτο.

exhibits the same text as in the preceding document (ὁμολογοῦμεν ἐσχηκέναι κτλ.), the clause stipulating repayment is completely different, reflecting, I believe, reception of the phrasing of the *stipulatio*: (1) The clause is independent, not relative.[11] (2) The duty of repayment is rendered through ὁμολογέω which is followed by the infinitive aorist ἀποδοῦναι ('I promise to repay'). Within the same short text of P.Oxy. XVII 1970, then, the verb ὁμολογέω is used twice in two different renderings: once (l. 16), in the old Greek sense, meaning 'acknowledge', and once (l. 22) meaning 'promise' as a Greek rendering of the Roman *promissio*. The practical consequences of the said change seem, *prima facie*, marginal: the contents of the documents remained unaltered, only the form of expression changed.[12] But there are cases in which the language of the Roman *stipulatio* has a pervasive impact also on the substance of the contract.

B: Digest 19.2.54.1 and the Roman *Expulsio*

In contracts of labour and lease, the existence of the contract is predicated upon the physical attachment of the employee/lessee to the premises of the employer/lessor. Such is the case in a contract brought before the jurist Paul, recorded in the fifth book of his *responsa*, and then incorporated by Justinian's compilators in the nineteenth book of the Digest (19.2.54.1).[13] Let us first read the beginning of the text:

> Inter locatorem fundi et conductorem convenit, ne intra tempora locationis Seius conductor de fundo invitus repelleretur et, si pulsatus esset, poenam decem praestet Titius locator Seio conductori: vel Seius conductor Titio, si intra tempora locationis discedere vellet, aeque decem Titio locatori praestare vellet: quod invicem de se stipulati sunt.

> "It was agreed by the lessor and the lessee of a tract of land that the tenant, Seius, should not be ejected against his will during the term of the lease, and if he was ejected, the lessor, Titius, should pay him a penalty of ten; or, if the lessee, Seius, should desire to withdraw during the term of the lease, he should be compelled to pay ten to the lessor, Titius, and the parties reciprocally stipulated with reference to this".[14]

Paul's text records two independent *stipulationes*, one by the lessor and another by the lessee. Both presuppose the existence of a lease for a set duration, which was

[11] Compare *T.P.Sulp.* 51.11–12, 52.15–18 (37 CE, Pompei): *et ea sestertia ... dari stipulatus.*

[12] To assess the impact of the said change, we have to study, both seperately and in conjointly, the following phenomena: (1) The expression of duties of future performance through the aorist infinitive. (2) Their introduction by the verb ὁμολογέω. (3) Further indications of Romanization in the contents of the clause. All three elements are evident in PSI VI 709.23–25 (566 CE, Oxyrhynchos): καὶ ὁπόταν βουληθείης ὁμολογῶ | [24] τὴν ν̣[ο]μὴν τῆς αὐτῆς οἰκίας ἄτρωτον | [25] ἀβλαβῆ παραδοῦναι ὡς καὶ παρείληφ(α) and Wolff 1974, 54–105, at 83–89.

[13] Among the plethora of studies dedicated to this passage, see in particular Cruz 1962, 240–243.

[14] Transl. Scott 1932, vol. 3, p. 97.

recorded elsewhere, presumably in the contract of lease. According to the lessor's *stipulatio*, he shall be prohibited from evicting the lessee against his will. Should he do so, he shall pay to the lessee as penalty ten units of unnamed currency, presumably *aurei*. The rules regarding the lessee are not formulated as injunction, but as a conditional clause, recording the consequence of his departure in the course of the contract. The lessee will have to pay ten *aurei* as well.[15]

In Egypt, while the duty of stay (*paramonê*) is normally recorded in the contract,[16] sanctions against departure by the employee/lessee or expulsion by the employer/lessor are first attested in the fourth century and become common in the sixth and seventh centuries, i.e., in the period for which we generally witness extensive Romanization of the language of legal documents from Egypt.[17] Such chronological coincidence is not in itself sufficient ground to assume any relation between Paul's text and its Egyptian younger counterparts in their entirety. In fact, as I will later show, while the introduction of the clause itself may be attributed to some Roman influence, the suggested impact of the 'Pauline *stipulatio*' was restricted to the city of Oxyrhynchos, and set in only in the sixth century CE. At the same time, focusing on Oxyrhynchite evidence alone, I claim that such a connection becomes ever more plausible as we discuss the following points: (1) The origin of the Oxyrhynchite clause in the language and syntax of the *stipulatio*. (2) The text in the Oxyrhynchite documents as a follow-up on Paul's interpretation of the *stipulatio*. Let us now address these two questions.

(1) The Egyptian Clause and the Roman *Stipulatio*

As suggested earlier, whenever we encounter in legal documents from Egypt the combination ὁμολογέω with the present, and most conspicuously, the infinitive of the aorist tense of verbs denoting delivery, we assume origin in the *stipulatio*. Among the documents recorded in the chart below this is not always, or even predominately the case. However, if we consider the evidence from Oxyrhynchos, the picture changes. In ten cases (7 dating to the sixth and seventh centuries), the document records penalty clauses dealing with termination of the contract both by the declarant, who is always the employee/lessee,[18] and in six by the 'tacit (i.e. non-

[15] Du Plessis 2012, 144–145, 150–153; Frier 1980, 70–105; Mayer-Maly 1956, 215–223.

[16] In lease contracts from Egypt, the most common formulation is BGU I 197.15–16 (17 CE, Dionysias): μὴ ἐξέστωι [τοῖς μεμισ]|[16]θωμένοις προλιπεῖν τὴν μίσθωσιν ἐ[ν]τὸς τοῦ χρόν[ου. Cf. Herrmann 1958, 169.

[17] Among the 47 texts listed in the appended chart, one text, CPR V 11.11–14, dates to the early fourth century CE, and another, P.Haun. III 56.6–12, approximately dated to the fourth or fifth century CE. P.Köln II 102.9–12 (418 CE, Oxyrhynchites) and P.Rein. II 105.4–7 (432 CE, Oxyrhynchos) are both early texts from the Oxyrhynchite nome.

[18] P.Heid. V 345.6–12 (early VI CE, Oxyrhynchos); P.Herm. 30.11–14 (552 CE, Oxyrhynchites); P.Köln II 102.9–12 (418, Oxyrhynchites); P.Mil. I 48.14–17 (549 CE, Oxyrhynchos?); P.Oxy. I 140.23–29 (550 CE, Oxyrhynchos); LI 3641.15–19 (544 CE, Oxyrhynchos);

acknowledging) party', who is the employer/lessor.[19] Among the seven documents that treat the premature departure of the lessee and date to the sixth or seventh centuries, in four the penalty clause is formulated along the lines set out earlier in this paper for clauses that may derive from the vocabulary of the *stipulatio*—ὁμολογῶ διδόναι in P.Heid. V 345.7–8 (early VI CE, Oxyrhynchos) as well as in P.Mil. I 48.15 (549 CE, Oxyrhynchos?), ὁμολογῶ ἀποκαταστῆσαι in P.Oxy. I 140.25–26 (550 CE, Oxyrhynchos), and ὁμολογῶ ζημιοῦσθαι in P.Oxy. LXXIII 4967.12 (late VI/ early VII CE, Oxyrhynchos)—in all cases but the last with the penalty as the direct object.

An expulsion by the lessor/employer is dealt with differently. As we recall, in the case of Digest 19.2.54.1 the sanction against dissolution by both parties was created through two, independent *stipulationes*. In the clause recorded in the papyri this is not the case: the sanctions against dissolution by the acknowledging party are integrated into a text formulated as an acknowledgement (ὁμολογέω in the Greek sense), as was always the case in the documents under discussion. In this case, the clause recording the 'Roman' ὁμολογέω—that creating a bond for future performance by the acknowledging party—is fully integrable, just as it was in the cases discussed in the preceding section. But those anticipating activity by the 'silent party' are not; a change to the second person, ὁμολογεῖς, is unsustainable.[20] For this reason, in all six contracts recording penalty of the silent party, one uses a different formulation. In P.Heid. V 345.12 (early VI CE, Oxyrhynchos), P.Mil. I 48.17 (549 CE, Oxyrhynchos?), and P.Oxy. LI 3641.19 (544 CE, Oxyrhynchos) one uses the formula ὑποκεῖσθαί σε (name of the violator, in the accusative) τῷ ἴσῳ προστίμῳ. In P.Oxy. I 140.28 (550 CE, Oxyrhynchos), LVIII 3933.26 (588 CE, Oxyrhynchos), the scribe employs ἐπὶ τῷ καὶ αὐτὴν (i.e., the silent party) ζημιοῦσθαι followed by the extent of the penalty. P.Oxy. LXXIII 4967.14–15 (late VI/early VII CE, Oxyrhynchos) the text runs ἐπὶ τὸ (l. τῷ) πληρῶσαι. All these forms, I suggest, were used to integrate the text of the stipulation made by the silent party into the context of an *homologia*.

LVIII 3933.19–27 (588 CE, Oxyrhynchos); LXXIII 4967.7–15 (late VI/early VII CE, Oxyrhynchos); P.Rein. II 105.4–7 (432 CE, Oxyrhynchos).

[19] P.Heid. V 345.6–12 (early VI CE, Oxyrhynchos); P.Mil. I 48.14–17 (549 CE, Oxyrhynchos?); P.Oxy. I 140.23–29 (550 CE, Oxyrhynchos); P.Oxy. LI 3641.15–19 (544 CE, Oxyrhynchos); LVIII 3933.19–27 (588 CE, Oxyrhynchos); LXXIII 4967.7–15 (VI^{l}/VIIe CE, Oxyrhynchos).

[20] This point is made clear in a scrutiny of the document of sale as created at the beginning of the Roman period. The body of the document is introduced through the verb ὁμολογέω followed by infinitives of verbs denoting activities of the declarant: sale, receipt of the consideration and his duty to warrant the buyer's title. But when the document records the buyer's right of disposal, the construction is impersonal. Cf., e.g., P.Stras. III 144.9–10 (244 CE, Hermopolites): καὶ εἶναι περὶ σ̣ὲ [κ]α̣ὶ̣ τοὺς παρὰ σοῦ τὴν τοῦ [πεπραμέν]ο̣υ ὡς π[ρό]κ̣ε̣[ι]τα̣ι κατοικικοῦ ἀρο̣ύ̣[ρ]ης [ἡμίσους] | [10] κυ[ρία]ν καὶ κράτησιν χρωμ[έν]ους κα[ὶ] οἰκο̣νομοῦν[τ]α̣ς̣ κτλ. and Schwarz 1920, 170–184.

It can however be objected that the use of ὁμολογέω to denote a pledge to pay penalty is by no means universal, even in the case of the declaring party. It is never attested in this context outside the Oxyrhynchite nome,[21] and even in that nome it is not a rule without exception. In two sixth-century Oxyrhynchite documents one uses the ἐπὶ τῷ construct to denote payment by the acknowledging party as the tacit party. So, in particular, in P.Oxy. LI 3641.16–17 (544 CE, Oxyrhynchos): εἰ δὲ [τοῦ]το ποιήσω, ἐπὶ τῷ με δοῦναι |[17] τῇ ὑμετέρᾳ ὑπερφυείᾳ λόγῳ προστίμου χρυσοῦ νομισμάτια εἴκοσι τέσσαρα.[22] Offhand, therefore, one could assume that the said clause evolved in the papyrus uninfluenced by the Roman penalty clause, or that if it is originally Roman it did not derive from the Pauline *stipulatio*.[23] This may well be the case outside Oxyrhynchos, but the connection between Paul's text and the clause as evidenced in the Oxyrhynchite papyri lies not only in the very attestation of the same form of remedy, but also in the way it is interpreted in both settings.

(2) The Pauline Background of the Egyptian Clause

Digest 19.2.54.1 has been included by Paulus in his *liber responsorum* because the practice of introducing through *stipulatio* penalty on disruption of contracts became common in his days.[24] The same state of affairs has motivated the authors of Justinian's Digest to incorporate the text in their compilation as well: A *stipulatio* enjoining penalty for the disruption of contracts of labour and lease was a widely employed institution in the third and in the sixth centuries CE alike. Moreover, the text of the clause inserted in Greek documents from Egypt shows much affinity with, and continuity from, Paul's text. This continuity can be most plausibly explained in terms of reception of its contents.

In contracts of lease and labour, the lessee and employee were required to undertake two key duties. First, they had to undertake all the tasks essential for the performance of the contract, viz. in the case of land leases, the cultivation of the land.[25] The lessee was also required to pay the rent. At the same time, while both cultivation and payment of the rent are routinely regulated in lease contracts of all periods, a penalty for non-payment of the rent is only recorded in documents from

---

[21] P.Ant. II 91 (VI CE?, Antinoites). The restoration [ὁμολογῶ] at the beginning of line 8 should, in view of the provenance, be reconsidered.

[22] Cf. also P.Oxy. LVIII 3933.19–27 (588 CE, Oxyrhynchos): ἐπὶ τῷ ἐμὲ μηδὲν δέξασθαι in the case of the employee; ἐπὶ τῷ καὶ αὐτὴν ζημιοῦσθαι, in that of the employer.

[23] Penalty deriving not from a *stipulatio* but from the *locatio-conductio* itself, is implied in C. 4.65.15.pr. (259 CE): *Si fundo a locatore expulsa es, agere ex conducto potes poenamque, quam praestari rupta conventionis fide placuit, exigere ac retinere potes.*

[24] See, in general, on possible cases of reception of jurisprudential literature in Egypt, Taubenschlag 1940/1, 280–295; Steinwenter 1952, 131–137.

[25] Widely attested in the early Roman Arsinoites is the formulation evident in P.Mert. III 107.17–19 (II CE, Arsinoites): καὶ ἐπιτελ̣έ̣σομ̣ε̣ν τὰ κατ' ἔτος ἔ̣[ργα π]ά̣ν|[18][τα ὅσα καθήκει ἐκ τοῦ ἰδίου τ]οῖς δέο̣υ̣σι καιροῖς βλάβος μηδὲν ποιο̣ῦ̣ν|[19][τες σπείροντες οἷς ἐὰν αἱρ]ῴ̣μ̣α̣ιθα (l. [αἱρ]ώμεθα) γέ̣νεσι πλὴν γνήκου (l. κνήκου) and Henning 1972, 111–131.

the Ptolemaic period and early Roman Oxyrhynchos.[26] Similarly, no direct sanction is regularly anticipated if the lessee has not duly cultivated the land.[27] Digest 19.2.54.1 offers remedy.

Paul, we recall, discusses in that passage the case of disruption of the lease by both the lessee and the lessor. In both cases, the party in breach becomes subject, through *stipulatio*, to penalty. In addition, according to the wording of the *stipulatio* that was brought before the jurist, the penalty for disruption is unconditional. The lessor will be subject to penalty regardless of the conduct of the lessee. But should this really be the case? Following the presentation of the details, Paul addresses that very issue:

> quaero, cum Seius conductor biennii continui pensionem non solveret, an sine metu poenae expelli possit. Paulus respondit, quamvis nihil expressum sit in stipulatione poenali de solutione pensionum, tamen verisimile esse ita convenisse de non expellendo colono intra tempora praefinita, si pensionibus paruerit et ut oportet coleret: et ideo, si poenam petere coeperit is qui pensionibus satis non fecit, profuturam locatori doli exceptionem.
>
> "I ask, as the lessee, Seius, did not pay the rent for two consecutive years, whether he could be ejected without Titius fearing to incur the penalty. Paulus answered that although nothing was stated in the penal stipulation with reference to the payment of the rent, still, it is probable that it was agreed that the tenant should not be ejected during the term of the lease, if he paid the rent, and cultivated the land, as he should do; so that if he understood to bring suit for the penalty, and had not paid the rent, the lessor could avail himself of an exception of fraud."[28]

The lessor has decided to prematurely terminate the contract. He did so for a good cause. The lessee has not paid the rent for two years. However, the text of the *stipulatio* did not give any terms that would warrant the lessor's casting the lessee out of the estate. Formally, non-payment would not warrant eviction. Accordingly, the lessor was concerned that even under these circumstances an eviction of the lessee would entail the payment of the prescribed penalty. Paulus came to his aid. Even though the issue was not addressed in the *stipulatio*, it should be interpreted, he argued, as if it was undertaken under the presumption that the lessee shall not fail in these two fundamental duties. On that premise, since the lessee has not paid the rent for a period of two years, the lessor could remove him from the estate *sine*

---

[26] A clause anticipating the consequences of a failure to duly pay the rent is better attested, recorded in 72 documents, but is routinely applied only in documents from the Ptolemaic period and from Roman Oxyrhynchos. I discuss this clause, in detail, in Yiftach forthcoming 3.19.

[27] Among the 1,816 lease contracts that record the duty of the lessee to cultivate the land, 23 documents only introduce sanction. See also Yiftach forthcoming 6.34.

[28] Transl. Scott 1932, 97 with minor corrections.

metu poenae. Put in procedural terms, should the lessee introduce a suit on account of a *stipulatio*, the lessor could object through the *exceptio doli.*

Greek documentary texts from sixth and seventh-century Oxyrhynchos pick up the discussion in the same point. In Digest 19.2.54.1 the right of the lessee to claim remedy on account of the text of the *stipulatio* was *a priori* unreserved. It was only checked in Paul's advisory. In Byzantine Egypt, the same issue has already been settled in the text of the clause itself. In every Oxyrhynchite document that subjects the lessor to a penalty for ejecting the lessee, the penalty can only be enforced if the lessor has acted without good cause (δίχα εὐλόγου αἰτίας *vel sim.*).[29]

What could constitute 'a good cause' for ejecting the lessee is a question not directly addressed in the document. We may assume that the lessee's failure to pay the rent and to cultivate the land—the two violations explicitly addressed in Digest 19.2.54.1—would warrant eviction. But, even if the lessee were to formally comply with these two terms, he could still be removed for ‚showing contempt towards the performance of his duties properly.[30] But what would be regarded as contempt? The text does not answer this question. Most importantly, as the document does not tell who should establish contempt, this privilege seems to fall to the share of the lessor. Should this be the case, by means of the new clause, the lessor would get unprecedented power: to expel the lessee, and terminate the contract, at all times, by will.

III. The Regional Factor

As stated earlier, in Greek translations of the Roman *stipulatio*, *promitto* is conveyed through ὁμολογέω, which takes the infinitive of the present and the aorist tense. The verbs commonly denote delivery. According to the argument enfolded in the preceding sections, the text of the *stipulatio* recorded in Digest 19.2.54.1 was introduced into Egypt in the Byzantine period. I have also noted, however, that as far as the wording was concerned ὁμολογέω was not always used. It is not used if the document records the penalty of the 'silent party'. In this case, I suggested, the

[29] δίχα εὐλόγου αἰτίας: P.Oxy. LXXIII 4967.14 (late VI/early VII CE, Oxyrhynchos); P.Select. 4.7 (VI/VII CE, Unknown Provenance, but probably Oxyrhynchite); δίχα αἰτίας τινός: P.Heid. V 345.11 (early VI, Oxyrhynchos); ἄνευ αἰτίας τινός: P.Mil. I 48.16 (549, Oxyrhynchos?); P.Oxy. I 140.28 (550 CE, Oxyrhynchos); LVIII 3933.25 (588 CE, Oxyrhynchos). ἐκτὸς καταγνώσεως | ἢ ῥ̣αθυμία‹ς ἢ› ο̣ἱασδήποτε αἰτίας: P.Oxy. LI 3641.18–19 (544 CE, Oxyrhynchos) and Jördens 1990, 160–162.

[30] A flexible standard of conduct by the lessee is already addressed in C. 4.65.3pr. (214 CE), where the lessor is entitled to expel the lessee if the latter *in re locata versatus est.* In P.Ross.Georg. III 51.22–25 (630 CE, Arsinoiton Polis), the lessor is allowed to remove the lessee from the leased land if the latter shows contempt towards his work or is found responsible for damage: εἰ δ]ὲ π̣ερ̣[ι]φρονήσω εἰς τὴν | [23] ἀπεργασίαν τ̣ο̣ῦ̣ αὐτοῦ χ[ωρίου] ἢ [κατ]α̣γνώσθω εἰς βλάβη(ν) | [24] καρποῦ αὐτοῦ ἐπὶ τῷ̣ σε ἀ̣π̣α̣γ̣αγέσθαι με ἐξ αὐτοῦ δίχα̣ | [25] γεωργί[ας] καὶ κ̣ὰ̣ν̣ (l. ἐὰν) φθάσω τὸ̣ν [καιρὸν τ]ῆς τρ[ύ]γης.

scribe used an alternative text, introducing the clause through alternative constructions, ἐπὶ τῷ, or simple infinitive.

At the same time, the picture portrayed here obtains just for the Oxyrhynchite evidence, and just from the sixth and seventh century. One of the earliest document that features the clause, P.Köln II 102, of 418 Oxyrhynchites, exhibits one element whose existence was noted in connection with the Roman *stipulatio*, the infinitive παρασχεῖν, but also others that have already been typical in Greek contracts before the fifth century and will disappear from the clause in its later manifestations: the adverbs ἐπάναγκες and ἀνυπερθέτως and the *praxis* clause.[31] Later documents from different parts of Egypt exhibit a mixture of syntax and vocabulary that can not be aligned with the Pauline paradigm either: in P.Köln II 104, for example, composed in the village of Aphrodite in the sixth century CE the act of delivery is denoted through the indicative form παρέξω.[32] When one does use the aorist infinitive, it is never introduced outside the Oxyrhynchite nome by ὁμολογέω. In the Arsinoite nome, for example, one commonly uses ὥστε or ἐπὶ τῷ ἀναδοῦναι.[33] Also in terms of substance, the non-Oxyrhynchite documentation does not keep pace with its Oxyrhynchite counterpart. Whenever the document prohibits the employer from expelling the employee, the prohibition is just as unconditional as it was in the case brought before Paul in Digest 19.2.54.1. The employer can not justify his action by reverting to 'just cause'.[34]

In accordance with the above description, we may reach the following conclusions: (1) At the beginning of the fourth century a clause was introduced into contracts of labour and lease throughout Egypt, which prohibited the physical dissolution of the contract. The clause was introduced throughout Egypt. Its exact source is unknown, but the use of new terminology (cf., e.g., the form παρασχεῖν) allows us to believe external, viz. Roman influence. (2) Following the promulgation of the Digest, scribes in the Oxyrhynchite nome started to apply the wording of the *stipulatio* documented in 19.2.54.1. They have also updated the text, introducing into the clause the exception conceived by Paul in his advisory: the lessor shall not

---

[31] P.Köln II 102.9–12 (418 CE, Oxyrhynchites): καὶ ὁπότ̣[αν βο]υληθῶ ἀν[αχω]ρεῖν | [10] ἀπὸ σοῦ ἢ ὁπηνίκα ἂν αὐτὸς ἐθέλοις, ἐπάναγ[κέ]ς με π[α]ρ[α]σχεῖν σοι ἄ[ν]ε̣υ δια|[11]φόρου τὰ προκείμενα τοῦ χρυσοῦ νομισμάτια [δ]ύο ἀνυπερθέτως, γιγνομένης | [12] σοι τῆς πράξεως παρά τε μ̣ου καὶ ἐκ τῶν ὑπαρχόντων μοι πάντων.

[32] P.Köln II 104.21, 23 (VI CE, Aphrodite), P.Cair.Masp. II 67164.8–10 (569 CE, Antinoopolis); P.Hamb. I 23.35–37 (569 CE, Antinoopolis) SB XX 15043 (VI/VII CE, Hermopolis).

[33] SB I 4490.27 (646/656 CE, Arsinoiton Polis); 4739.19 (VI/VII CE, Arsinoites); XVIII 13962.8 (630–645 CE, Arsinoites). Also restored in SB XVIII 13960.19 (VI/VII CE, Hermopolis).

[34] P.Cair.Masp. III 67305.21–23 (568 CE, Antinoopolis); P.Köln II 104.19-24 (VI CE, Aphrodite); PSI IX 1056.16-21 (VII CE, Arsinoites); SB I 4503.24–30 (605/607 CE, This). See however BGU I 310.20–23 = SB I 5330 (663 CE?, Arsinoiton Polis): εἰ δὲ [καὶ σὺ ἀ]π̣ο̣βάλῃς με | [21] [ἄνευ καταγνώσ]εως καὶ π[α]ραφρονήσεως | [22] [ἐπὶ τῷ λαβεῖν με] τ̣ὸν μισθὸν τοῦ ἐνιαυτοῦ | [23] [εἰς πλῆρες.

pay penalty for evicting the lessee if he can provide justification for his act. For all that we know, the Pauline version of the clause did not catch on in any other nome. Elsewhere the older version of the text was still applied as it was since the early fourth century. This is yet another case of regional peculiarity in Greco-Roman Egypt.[35]

A Methodological Postscript

Following my recent studies of the clauses of the legal document in Ptolemaic, Roman and Byzantine Egypt, I would like to propose tentative guidelines for studying the penetration of Roman law and and legal terminology into papyri in Roman and Byzantine Egypt. I intend to develop them in future studies.

1) The form ὁμολογέω, followed by the aorist or present denoting delivery is Roman, and probably derives from the text of a *stipulatio.*
2) The constructs ὥστε or ἐπὶ τῷ followed by an aorist infinitive are not *a priori* Roman, unless they are followed by a verb which is not common before the fifth century CE. See, e.g., διδόναι (praes.!), καταβαλεῖν and παρασχεῖν.
3) The use of the said verbs *per se* may denote a Roman origin, but not necessarily derives from a *stipulatio.*

uiftach@tauex.tau.ac.il

APPENDIX

Negative *Paramonê* Clauses in Byzantine Egypt

	Document and Date	Type of Clause[36]	Type of Contract	Unilateral/ Bilateral
1.	BGU I 3.20–24 (605 CE, Arsinoiton Polis)	Pen.Anach	Labour	Unilateral
	εἰ δὲ ἀφ᾽ ἧς εσεαυτοῦ (l. σεαυτοῦ) ἐθελή|[21]σῃς ἀναχωρῆσαι ἐκ τοῦ αὐτοῦ τόπου | [22] μηδέν σε λαβεῖν ὑπὲρ τῶν αὐτῶν | [23] ἀναλωμάτων τῶν γεναμένων παρὰ | [24] σοῦ ἐν τῇ αὐτῇ ἐπαύλει.			
2.	BGU I 310.20–23 = SB I 5330 (663 CE?, Arsinoiton Polis)	Pen.Ekb.	Labour	Unilateral
	εἰ δὲ [καὶ σὺ ἀ]ποβάλῃς με | [21] [ἄνευ καταγνώσ]εως καὶ π[α]ραφρονήσεως | [22] [ἐπὶ τῷ λαβεῖν με] τὸν μισθὸν τοῦ ἐνιαυτοῦ | [23] [εἰς πλῆρες.			

[35] I have already discussed that theme, with regard to an entirely different timeframe, in Yiftach-Firanko (2003), 347–365.

[36] Anach. = Anachoresis; Aposp. = Apospasis; Apost. = Apostasis; Ekb. = Ekballein; Pen. = Penalty.

3.	BGU XII 2186.10–13 (514 CE?, Hermopolis)	Pen.Apost.	Lease	Unilateral
	παρ[έ]ξω δὲ καὶ ε[- -]| 11 [- -] ἁπαλῶν ἀρτάβης ἥμισυ, καὶ μὴ δύνασθαί μ[ε ἀποστῆναι - -] | 12 [. . . εἰ] δὲ τοῦτο τολμήσαιμι ποιεῖν, ἐξεῖναί σοι [- -] | 13 [. . . . .]πελου·			
4.	CPR V 11.11–14 (early IV CE, Unknown Provenance)	Pen.Apost.	Labour	Unilateral
	ἐὰν δὲ θελήσω ἀποστῆναι .[- ca.12 -] | 12 σου ἢ καὶ χωρὶς γραμμάτων μ[- ca.10 -] | 13 ρου τυχάνιν (l. τυγχάνειν) δῆθεν ἐγὼ τῆς δια .[- ca.10 -] | 14 λα λαικῆς κοινωνίας μεταξιω .[- ca.10 -]			
5.	CPR VIII 82.7–9 (699/700 CE, Arsinoites)	Anach., Pen.Anach.	Labour	Unilateral
	καὶ μὴ δύνασθαί με ἀπελ[θεῖν εἰς ἕτερον τόπον - -] | 8 ἀλλὰ κοιμηθῆναί με πρὸς τὰ αὐτὰ ἀμπελικὰ ἄχρις οὗ ταῦτα ἀποτρ[υγῶ [- -. εἰ δὲ μή,] | 9 ἐξουσίαν ὑμᾶς ἔχειν πρὸς τὸ παριστάμενον ὑμῖν κελεῦσαι γενέσθαι [- -]			
6.	CPR XIX 33.15–19 (591 CE, Arsinoiton Polis)	Pen.Anach.	Labour	Unilateral
	(hand 2) εἰ δὲ ἀναχωρῆσαι (l. ἀναχωρήσω) τῆς πρὸς σὲ | 16 παραμονῆς πρὸ{ς} συμπλη| 17 ρώσεως (hand 3) τοῦ ἐνιαυτοῦ ἐπὶ τῷ (hand 2) ἄμισθον | 18 ἀναχωρῆσαι ἀναμφιβόλως | 19 ἐξ ὑπαρχόντων μου πάντων			
7.	P.Ant. II 91.2–10 (VI CE?, Antinoites)	Aposp., Pen.Aposp.	Labour	Unilateral
	καὶ] μὴ [δ]ύνασθαί με τοῦτον | 3 [ἀποσπᾶν πρὸ συμπλη]ρώσεως τοῦ αὐτοῦ ἑνὸς ἐνιαυτοῦ | 4 [. . . .] . ασαι . . . [. .] . οἱαδήποτε ἡμέρ\α/ δίχα κακώσ(εως(?)) | 5 [καὶ τῆς] ἁγίας κυρι[ακῆ]ς καὶ τῶν μεγάλων ἑορτῶν· εἰ δὲ | 6 [συμβαίν]ειν ἀποσπᾶν αὐτου (l. αὐτόν) ἀπὸ σοῦ ἢ αὐτὸν δι' ἑαυτοῦ | 7 [ἀποστῆ]ναι πρὸ συμπληρώσεως τοῦ αὐτοῦ ἑνὸς ἐνιαυτοῦ | 8 [ὁμολογῶ] παρασχεῖν σοι λόγῳ προστίμου χρυσοῦ κεράτια | 9 ἐ[νν]έα μετὰ \καὶ/ τοῦ εἴ τι ἂν ὀφθείην λαβὼν ἀπὸ σο\ῦ/ ἀπὸ τοῦ μισθο\ῦ/ ἀργ(υρίου) | 10 χωρίς τινος ἀντιλογίας καὶ ὑπερθέσεως			
8.	P.Cair.Masp. II 67158.21–23 (568 CE, Antinoopolis)	Pen.Apost.	Labour	Unilateral
	ο[ὐ]δὲν ἧττον, εἰ ἐθελήσοιμεν ἀποστῆ[ν]αι τῆς κοινῆς μετ' ἀλλήλων ἐργασίας, | 22 [ἑτοίμως ἔχειν τ]ὰ δάνια (l. δάνεια) το(ῦ) ὄπιθεν χρόνο(υ), [τ]ὰ γενάμενα ἡμῖν κοινῶς πραγματευομένοις, ἐπιγνῶναι κατὰ τὸ αὐτὸ ἥμισυ μέρος | 23 [ἐξ ἰσομοιρίας], ἐφ' ὅ τε ἐν μιᾷ ἐργασίᾳ καὶ εὐζωΐᾳ κοινῇ μετ' ἀλλήλων διήξαμεν τὸν κατ' ἐκεῖνο καιρο(ῦ) χρόνον·			
9.	P.Cair.Masp. II 67159.34–33 (568 CE, Antinoopolis)	Apost., Pen.Apost.	Labour	Unilateral
	μὴ δυναμένου τινὸς ἡμῶν μήτε δυνησομένο(υ) | 35 ἀποστῆναι τῆς ἐμπιπτούσῃ[ς ἡ]μῖν ἐργ[α]σίας | 36 καθ' οἷον δήπο[τε χ]ρόνον ἢ καιρὸν ἢ ἡμέραν, καὶ ὑπερ| 37 θέ[σ]θαι καὶ προφάσεις ἐπανατεῖναι καὶ τοῦ ἔργου καταφρονήσιν (l. καταφρονήσειν) | 38 κα[ὶ εἰ] ἀποσταινη (l. ἀποσταίη) τις παρὰ ταῦτα τὰ συντεταγμένα σύμφωνα ὑπερ| 39 βῆ[ναι], καὶ μὴ δικ[αί]ως ἐξακολουθῆσαι τῷ ἐπίοντι ἔργῳ καθ' | 40 ἑκάστην Θεοῦ βουλομένου, δίχα νοσήματος, παρέξει τὸ παρα| 41 βαῖ[ν]ον μέρος ὑπὲ[ρ ἀμ]ελείας χρυσοῦ [νομ]ίσμ(ατα) τέσσαρα . καὶ εἰ ἀπο| 42 σταίη τοῦ ἔργου πρὸ συμπληρώσεως το[ῦ ἐ]νιαυτοῦ, τὸ αὐτὸ πρόστιμον | 43 ἐπιγινώσκειν δίχα κρίσεως καὶ δίκης καὶ οἵας δήποτε εὑρεσιλογίας (l. εὑρησιλογίας) | 44 καὶ παραγραφῆς νόμο[υ]			

10.	P.Cair.Masp. II 67164.8–10 (569 CE, Antinoopolis)	Pen.Apost.	Loan	Unilateral
	καὶ εἰ ἀποσταίην τῆς πόλ(εως) τῆσδε πρὶν ἤ με | 9 ἀπολογήσασθαί σοι αὐτά, παρέξω σοι δίχα κρίσεως κ(αὶ) δίκης χρυσο(ῦ) νομισμ(άτιον) ἓν παρὰ κερ(άτια) | 10 ἓξ τῷ αὐτῷ ζυγ(ῷ), κινδύνῳ πάσης μο(υ) εὐπορίας, διὰ το(ῦ) προσφέροντός \μοι/ το(ῦ)το τὸ ἀσφαλές.			
11.	P.Cair.Masp. III 67305 (568 CE, Antinoopolis)	Pen.Ekb.	Labour	Unilateral
	εἰ τὲ (l. δὲ) | 22 κἀγὼ (l. καὶ ἐγὼ) βουληθείη[ν] ἐκβαλεῖν σε π[α]ρὰ τὰ εἰρημ[(ένα) σύμφωνα, . .]εν . ε . ταλματα τῆς ἀταξίας, ἑτοίμως | 23 ἔχω παρασχεῖν σοι [χρυ]σο(ῦ) νομίσμα(τα) ἕ[ξ]			
12.	P.Erl. 74.4–11 (VI CE, Unknown Provenance)	Pen.Apost., Pen.Ekb.	Lease	Bilateral
	[- - μι]σθός με καταφρονῆσαι ἔν τιν[ι - -] | 5 [- -]μην ἐπαναχωρῆσαι ἀπ[ὸ - -] | 6 [- -] κομπρο(μίσσου) πρὸ συμπληρώσεως | 7 [- -] τοῦ ἑνὸς ἐνιαυ[τοῦ]. εἰ δὲ τοῦτο ποιή[σω] | 8 [- - ὁμολ]ογῶ ζημιοῦ[σθ]αι τὸν ἐμὸν | 9 [- -] . . κ[αὶ ἐὰν ἐ]κ[βλ]ηθῶ ἀπ' αὐτῆς | 10 [- - ἐ]πὶ τῷ καὶ αὐτὴν | 11 [ζημιοῦσθαι - -] μισθόν			
13.	P.Gascou 30.22–27 (565–579 CE, Aphrodite)	Apost.	Labour	Unilateral
	καὶ μὴ δύνασθαί με ἀποστῆναι τῆς ὁμονοίας τῶν ἐμῶν | 23 ὁμογνησίων ἀδελφῶν καὶ τῆς ἐμῆς μητρὸς ἄχρι τῆς | 24 αὐτῶν, ὡς εἴρη[ται], ἐ[ν]νόμου ἡλικίας μήτε τούτων | 25 καταφρ[ονεῖν ἀλλὰ μ]εῖναι ὡς ἐν ταυτότητι . . . . μένου [-1-2-]υ | 26 ἐν μιᾷ εὐζωίᾳ καὶ οἰκήσει κἂν [.] γαμήσαντά με κἂν | 27 μὴ γαμήσαντα·			
14.	P.Giss. I 56.22–24 (VI CE, Hermopolites)	Apost.	Lease	Unilateral
	μὴ δύνασθαί με ἀποστῆναι | 23 [τ]ῆ[ς - ca.12 -]ς χρείας πρὸ συμπληρώ(σεως) το(ῦ) αὐτ(οῦ) δεκα‹ε›τοῦς | 24 [χρόνου - ca.12 -			
15.	P.Hamb. I 23.35–37 (569 CE, Antinoopolis)	Apost., Pen.Apost.	Lease	Unilateral
	οὐ δυνατὸν [ἡ]μῖν ἀποστῆναι τῆς τούτου ἐργασίας πρὸ περαιώσεως τοῦ | 36 χρόνου ὡς ἂν εἰ νόμων βοηθείας [ὑ]περειδομ[ε]νοι (l. ὑπερειδομένοι<ς>), καὶ εἰ τοῦτο ποιήσοιμεν, παρέξωμεν (l. παρέξομεν) λόγῳ προστίμου | 37 χρυσίου νομισμα (l. νομίσμα<τα>) δώδ[ε]κα ἀναμφιλόγως.			
16.	P.Haun. III 56.17–18 (IV/V CE, Unknown Provenance)	Anach., Pen.Anach.	Loan	Unilateral?
	ἀπὸ τῆς οἰκίας οὐκ ἐξέστω [- -] | 18 μην θελησο (l. θελήσω) ἀναχωρῖν (l. ἀναχωρεῖν) ε[- -]			
17.	P.Heid. V 345.6–12 (early VI CE, Oxyrhynchos)	Anach., Pen.Anach., Pen.Ekb.	Labour	Bilateral
	καὶ μὴ | 7 ἐξεῖναί μοι ἐντὸς τοῦ χρόνου ἀναχωρεῖν | 8 ἀπὸ σοῦ. εἰ δὲ τοῦτο ποιήσω, ὁμολογῶ | 9 διδόναι σοι λ[όγῳ π]ροστίμου χρυσοῦ | 10 νομ[ισ]μ[ά]τιον ἕν , καὶ σὲ δὲ ἐκβάλλοντά | 11 με πρὸ τοῦ χρόνου δίχα αἰτίας τινὸς | 12 ὑποκεῖσθαι μοι τῷ ἴσῳ προστίμῳ.			
18.	P.Heid. V 350.35–40 (612 CE, Arsinoiton Polis)	Pen.Anach.	Labour	Unilateral
	καὶ εἰ | 36 ὑπαναχωρήσω πρὸ τοῦ | 37 ἐνιαυτοῦ συμπληρώσεως, | 38 ἄμισθον ἀναχωρῆσαι, | 39 εἰ δὲ καὶ σοι (l. σὺ) ἀποβάλῃς με, | 40 λαβεῖν με εἰς πλήρης τὰ τέσ|σαρα νομ(ισμάτια).			

<table>
<tr><td>19.</td><td>P.Herm. 30.11–14 (552 CE, Oxyrhynchites)</td><td>Anach., Pen.Anach.</td><td>Labour</td><td rowspan="2">Unilateral</td></tr>
<tr><td></td><td colspan="3">[- -]τοῦ αὐτοῦ διετοῦς χρόνου ἀναχωρῆσαι τῆς | [12] [- -]νώσει γεν[έ]σθαι, οὐκ ἔστιν τῶν προγεγραμμ(ένων) | [13] [- - εἰ δ' ἀναχω]ρήσω τῆσδε τῆς μισθώσεως ὑπεύθυνόν με | [14] [- -]εως καὶ παραβάσεως τὰ μεταξὺ ἡμῶν συναρέσαντα</td></tr>
<tr><td>20.</td><td>P.Köln II 102.9–12 (418 CE, Oxyrhynchites)</td><td>Pen.Anach.</td><td>Loan</td><td rowspan="2">Unilateral</td></tr>
<tr><td></td><td colspan="3">καὶ ὁπότ[αν βο]υληθῶ ἀν[αχω]ρεῖν | [10] ἀπὸ σοῦ ἢ ὁπηνίκα ἂν αὐτὸς ἐθέλοις, ἐπάναγ[κέ]ς με π[α]ρ[α]σχεῖν σοι ἄ[ν]ευ δια|[11]φόρου τὰ προκείμενα τοῦ χρυσοῦ νομισμάτια [δ]ύο ἀνυπερθέτως, γιγνομένης | [12] σοι τῆς πράξεως παρά τε μου καὶ ἐκ τῶν ὑπαρχόντων μοι πάντων</td></tr>
<tr><td>21.</td><td>P.Köln II 104 (VI CE, Aphrodite)</td><td>Pen.Apost., Pen.Ekb.</td><td>Lease</td><td rowspan="2">Bilateral</td></tr>
<tr><td></td><td colspan="3">εἰ δὲ θελήσω ἀποστῆναι τῆς γεωργίας τοῦ προκ(ειμένου) | [20] κτήματος πρὸ περαιώσεως τοῦ χρόνου ταύτης τῆς μισθώσεως, | [21] παρέξω χρυσοῦ νομίσματα δώδεκα, εἰ δὲ καὶ ὑμε[ῖς] βο[υ]ληθείητε | [22] ἐκβαλεῖν με ἐκ τῆς τού[του] γεωργείας (l. γεωργίας) πρὸ πελεσεως (l. περαιώσεως) τοῦ αὐτοῦ χρόνου, | [23] παρέξετέ μοι τὸ ἴσον τοῦ αὐτοῦ προστίμου τῶν αὐτῶν δ[ώ]δ[ε]κα | [24] νομισμάτων.</td></tr>
<tr><td>22.</td><td>P.Michael. 34.8–10 (VI CE, UP)</td><td>Apost.</td><td>Lease</td><td rowspan="2">Unilateral</td></tr>
<tr><td></td><td colspan="3">καὶ μὴ ἐξεῖναι ἡμῖν πρὸς ὑμ[ᾶς] | [9] [- - ἀπο]στῆναι ἐκ τῆς γεωργίας καὶ μισθώσεως τῶν αὐτῶν ἀρουρῶν δύο . εἰ δὲ [. .] | [10] [- -] . . νη τῶν φόρων τῶν αὐτῶν δώδεκα ἐνιαυτῶν</td></tr>
<tr><td>23.</td><td>P.Mil. I 48.14–17 (549 CE, Oxyrhynchos?)</td><td>Anach., Pen.Anach., Pen.Ekb.</td><td>Labour</td><td rowspan="2">Bilateral</td></tr>
<tr><td></td><td colspan="3">μήτε μὴν ἀναχ[ω]ρῆσαι ἀπὸ σοῦ πρὸ τέλους τοῦ αὐτοῦ χρόνου. | [15] εἰ δὲ τοῦτο ποιήσ[ω, ὁ]μολογῶ διδόναι σοι λόγῳ προστίμου χρυσ(οῦ) νομισμάτια | [16] τριάκοντα ἕξ, [ε]ἰ δὲ καί σε ἐκβάλλοντά με ἄνευ αἰτίας τινὸς καὶ καταγνώσεως | [17] ὑποκεῖσθαι καί σε τῷ ἴσῳ προστίμῳ</td></tr>
<tr><td>24.</td><td>P.Oxy. I 140.23–29 (550 CE, Oxyrhynchos)</td><td>Anach., Pen.Anach.; Pen.Ekb.</td><td>Labour</td><td rowspan="2">Bilateral</td></tr>
<tr><td></td><td colspan="3">ομολογῶ δὲ ἐσχηκέναι παρὰ τῆς ὑμῶν μεγαλοπρ(επείας) ἐντεῦθεν ἤδη λόγῳ ἀρραβῶνος | [24] χρυσοῦ νομίσματα τέσσαρα ἥμισυ, καὶ μὴ ἐξεῖν[αί] μοι ἐντὸς τοῦ αὐτοῦ ἑνὸς ἐνιαυτοῦ | [25] ὑπαναχωρῆσαι ἀπὸ [τ]ῆς ὑμῶν χρείας καὶ παραμονῆς. εἰ δὲ τοῦτο ποιήσω, ὁμολογῶ τὰ | [26] αὐτὰ τέσσαρα ἥμισυ νομίσματα ἐν [τ]ῷ διπλῷ ἀποκαταστῆσαι αὐτῇ. εἰ δὲ ἡ [ὑμῶν] | [27] μεγαλοπρ(έπεια) ἐθελήσῃ ἐκβαλεῖν με ἐκ τῆς χρείας τοῦ σταβλίτου πρὸ συμπληρώσεως τ[οῦ] | [28] αὐτοῦ ἑνὸς ἐνιαυτοῦ ἄνευ αἰτίας τινός, ἐπὶ τῷ καὶ αὐτὴν ζημιοῦσθαι τὰ αὐτὰ τέσσαρα ἥμισυ | [29] νομίσματα τοῦ ἀρραβῶνος.</td></tr>
<tr><td>25.</td><td>P.Oxy. LI 3641.15–19 (544 CE, Oxyrhynchos)</td><td>Apost., Pen.Apost., Pen.Ekb.</td><td>Lease</td><td rowspan="2">Bilateral</td></tr>
<tr><td></td><td colspan="3">καὶ μη[- ca.10 -] . . ἀποστῆναι ἀπὸ τῆς ὑμετέρας [χρείας] | [16] ἢ ἀπὸ τῶν ὀφειλόντων γενέ[σθα]ι [ἔ]ργων. εἰ δὲ [τοῦ]το ποιήσω, ἐπὶ τῷ με δοῦναι | [17] τῇ ὑμετέρᾳ ὑπερφυείᾳ λόγῳ προστίμου χρυσοῦ νομισμάτια εἴκοσι τέσ'σαρα. εἰ δὲ | [18] ἡ ὑμετέρα ὑπερφυεία διὰ τῶν αὐτῆς διοικητῶν ἐκβάλῃ με ἐκτὸς καταγνώσεως | [19] ἢ ῥαθυμία‹ς ἢ› οἱασδήποτε αἰτίας, ὑποκεῖσθαι καὶ αὐτῇ τῷ ἴσῳ προστίμῳ.</td></tr>
</table>

26.	P.Oxy. LVIII 3933.19–27 (588 CE, Oxyrhynchos)	Apost., Pen.Apost., Pen.Ekb.	Labour	Bilateral
	καὶ μὴ δύνασθαι | [20] με ἀποστῆναι ἀπὸ τῆς σῆς θαυμασι(ότητος) | [21] καὶ ἀπὸ τῆς αὐτῆς χρείας πρὸ τέλους | [22] τοῦ εἰρημένου ἐνιαυτοῦ, εἰ δὲ τοῦτο ποιήσω, | [23] ἐπὶ τῷ ἐμὲ μηδὲν δέξασθαι παντελῶς | [24] ἐκ τοῦ παντός μου μισθοῦ, εἰ δὲ καὶ αὐτὴν | [25] ἐκβάλλουσάν με ἄνευ αἰτίας τινός, | [26] ἐπὶ τῷ καὶ αὐτὴν ζημιοῦσθαι τὸν πάντα | [27] μου μισθόν.			
27.	P.Oxy. LXXIII 4967.7–15 (late VI/early VII CE, Oxyrhynchos)	Anach., Pen.Anach.; Pen.Lab.	Labour	Bilateral
	ὁμολογῶ δὲ | [8] ἐσχηκέναι παρ' ὑμῶν τὴν ῥάβδον τοῦ κηρυκτοῦ μετὰ τῶν | [9] αὐτοῦ κωδονίων (l. κωδωνίων) καὶ μὴ δύνασθαί με ἐπαναχωρῆσαι | [10] τῆς αὐτῆς λειτουργίας πρὸ τέλους τοῦ ἑνὸς ἐνιαυτοῦ | [11] δίχα ἀρωστείας (l. ἀρρωστίας) καὶ πόνου τινός. εἰ δὲ τοῦτο ποιήσω, | [12] ὁμολογῶ ζημιοῦσθαι τοὺς ἐμοὺς μισθούς. εἰ δὲ | [13] κἀγὼ ἐκβληθῶ παρ' ὑμῶν πρὸ τέλους τοῦ ἑνὸς | [14] ἐνιαυτοῦ δίχα εὐλόγου αἰτίας, ἐπὶ τὸ (l. τῷ) καὶ ὑμᾶς | [15] πληρῶσαι τὸν ἐμὸν μισθόν.			
28.	P.Prag. II 160.4–9 (mid VI CE, Hermopolis)	Apost., Pen.Apost.	Lease	Unilateral
	[- - κ]αὶ μετεμεληθῆναι (l. μεταμεληθῆναι) | [5] [- -] πρὸ συμπληρ]ώσεως μελέτην ἀποστῆναι | [6] [- -] ἄχρι συμπληρ]ώσεως τοῦ αὐτοῦ διετοῦς | [7] [χρόνου - - βοη]θείᾳ νόμων βοηθῆσαί μοι | [8] [- - πρὸ συ]μπληρώσεως τοῦ εἰρ[η]|[9][μένου χρόνου - - παρέξω λ]όγῳ προστίμου χρυσοῦ | [10] [νομισμάτια - - κ]ινδύνῳ ἐμῷ καὶ πόρῳ | [11] [τῆς ἐμῆς παντοίας ὑποστάσεως.			
29.	P.Rein. II 105.4–7 (432 CE, Oxyrhynchos)	Anach., Pen.Anach. (?)	Loan	Unilateral
	καὶ μὴ ἐξεῖ[ναί μ]οι | [5] [μήτ' ἐντὸς τοῦ] ἐνιαυτοῦ ὑπαναχωρεῖ[ν] μήτε ἐνεδρεῦσαι τῇ παρ[ὰ σ]οὶ | [6] [- ca.9 -] . . καὶ ἐπάναγκες ἐκ τ[ῆς] προχρίας (l. προχρείας) διδόναι ς . . . . | [7] [- ca.9 -] . . . [. .] .μην καί σου ν[ο]μισμάτιον ἕν ·			
30.	P.Ross.Georg. III 40.24–26 (588 CE, Sesiy)	Apost.	Lease	Unilateral
	[- ca.56 - μοι τῷ γεω]ργῷ ἀποστῆναι | [25] [- ca.56 - πρὸ τῆς συμπ]ληρώσεως το(ῦ) | [26] [εἰρημένου ἑξαετοῦς χρόνου - ca.16 -			
31.	P.Ross.Georg. V 42.20–22 (602 CE, Hermopolites)	Apost.	Lease	Unilateral
	καὶ μὴ δύνασθαί με [ἀποστῆναι - -] | [21] [- - πρὸ συμπ]ληρώσεω[ς τοῦ αὐτοῦ] δεκαετοῦς χρόνου ἀποταττόμενος τη .[- -] | [22] [- - π]ρῶτον ἐνιαυτὸν ἀλλ' ἢ [ὁ]μολογία [- -]			
32.	P.Select. 4.5–8 (VI/VII CE, Unknown Provenance)	Anach., Pen.Anach., Pen.Ekb.	Labour	Bilateral
	μὴ ἐξεῖν[αι δ]έ μοι ἐντὸς τοῦ χρόνου ἀναχωρεῖν ἀπὸ σοῦ | [6] [ἄνευ αἰτίας τινὸς - ca.32 - ἐὰν δέ ἀπαλλ]άξωμαι δώσω σοι λόγῳ προστίμου χρυσοῦ νομι[σμάτια - -] | [7] [- ca.14 - ἐὰν δὲ βούλῃ ἐκβαλεῖν με ἐκ τῆς χρείας πρὸ συμπληρώσ]εως τοῦ χρόνου δίχα εὐλόγου αἰτίας [ὑ]ποκεῖσθαι τῷ ἴ[σῳ] | [8] [προστίμῳ.			
33.	P.Stras. I 40.34–38 (569 CE, Antinoopolis)	Apost.	Labour	Unilateral
	καὶ μ[η]δαμῷ[ς] ἀποστῆναι τῆς δουλικῆς α[ὐ]τοῦ | [35] προστασί[ας καταλαμβανό(?)]μενον ἐπὶ τετραετῆ χρ[όνο]ν λογιζόμ(ενον) | [36] [ἀ]πὸ [ν]εομην[ν]ία[ς τ]οῦ ε[ἰ]σιόντος μηνὸς Φαῶφι τῆ[ς] ἀρτίως ἐλαυνομένης(?) | [37] [δ]ευτ[έρα]ς ἐπινεμήσεως καὶ αὐ[τ]ῆς καὶ τοῦ ἑξῆς χρόνου καθ' (l. κατ') ἔτος μέχρι | [38] υπεραιώσεως (l. περαιώσεως) τοῦ αὐτοῦ τετραετοῦς χρόνου			

34.	P.Stras. V 489.2–4 (VI CE, Hermopolites)	Pen.Apost.	Lease	Unilateral
	[- -] ἀποστῆναι ἐκ τῆς τούτω]ν γε[ωρ]γίας καὶ | 3 [μισθώσεως - -] . . ἀποδώσω αὐτῇ | 4 [- -]			
35.	PSI IX 1056.16–21 (VII CE, Arsinoites)	Ekb., Pen.Ekb.	Lease	Unilateral
	καὶ μ[ὴ ἐξεῖναι] ὑμᾶς ἐκβληθῆναί με ἐκ | 17 τῶν [. . . . . . ἀ]ρουρῶν ἕως συμπληρώσεως | 18 τῆς ἑξαετί[ας]· εἰ δὲ τοῦ[το] ποιήσομεν ὥστε ὑμᾶς | 19 δοῦναί μοι νομίσματα ἕξ · μη[.]ε ημ . . . χωρῆσ[αι] | 20 ἐξ αὐτῶν · εἰ δὲ τοῦτο ποιήσ[ε]τε [. . . . .]παρ[.]χ[.] . . . | 21 τεισατων ἓξ νομισμάτων.			
36.	SB I 4490.24–29 (646/656 CE, Arsinoiton Polis)	Pen.Anach.	Labour	Unilateral
	ἐὰν πρὸ | 25 τῆς τοῦ ἐνιαυτοῦ συμπληρ[ώσεως] | 26 ζητήσω ἀναχωρῆσαι ἐκ τῆς παραμονῆς, | 27 ὥστε με ἀναδοῦναι ὑμῖν εἴ τι ἔσχον | 28 παρ' αὐτῆς ὑπὲρ [μισ]θοῦ καὶ ἄμισθόν με | 29 ἀναχωρῆσαι.			
37.	SB I 4503.24–30 (605/607 CE, This)	Pen.Apost., Pen.Ekb.	Labour	Bilateral
	εἰ δὲ συμβαίη, ὅπερ ἀπεί[η, ἐμὲ] | 25 [ἀπ]οστῆναι ἀπὸ τοῦ σου οἴκου ἕως πληρουμέ(νων) τ[ῶν]δε τῶν δύο | 26 ἐνιαυτῶν, ἐπὶ τῷ ἐμὲ παρασχ(εῖν) σοι ὑπὲρ λ[όγ]ῳ προστίμου | 27 χρυσ(ίου) ν[ο(μισμάτιον)] α, εἰ δὲ καὶ ἐμὲ τοῦ προκε(ιμένου) Παχυμ[ίο]υ βουληθῇ | 28 ἐκβαλεῖν σοι (l. σε) ἐκ τῆς αὐτῆς τέχνης ἄχρις [πλη]ρουμ(ένου) τοῦ | 29 αὐτοῦ χρόνου, ἐπὶ τῷ ἐμὲ παρασχεῖν σοι [τὸν] μισθόν | 30 σου εἰς πλῆρες			
38.	SB I 4739.15–21 (VI/VII CE, Arsinoites)	Anach., Pen.Anach.	Labour	Unilateral
	[καὶ μὴ ἐξεῖ]ναί μοι ὑπ[αναχωρῆ]|16[σαι ἀπὸ τῆ]ς σε . . [. . . . . πρὸ] | 17 [συμπληρ]ώσεω[ς τοῦ ἐνιαυτοῦ.] | 18 [εἰ δὲ ἀναχ]ωρήσω, [ἐπὶ τῷ με] | 19 [ἀναδοῦνα]ί σοι εἴ τ[ι ἔσχον] | 20 [παρὰ σοῦ] καὶ ἄνευ μ[ισθοῦ] | 21 [ἀναχωρῆσ]αι.			
39.	SB VI 9151.2–5 (ca. 600 CE, Hermopolis)	Apost., Pen.Apost.	Lease	Unilateral
	κα]ὶ [οὐ δυνατόν μοι ἀπο]|2[στῆναι] τῆς τοια[ύ]της ἀμπελουργικῆς χρείας πρὸ συπληρ[ώσεω]ς | 3 [διετοῦ]ς χρόνου. ἀποτάττομαι γὰρ πάσῃ βοηθείᾳ νόμων | 4 [τῇ παρ]εχούσῃ παντὶ μισθωτῇ ἀποστῆναι μετὰ τὸν | 5 [πρῶτ(ον) ἐνι]αυτόν			
40.	SB XVIII 13585.1–5 (VI/VII CE, Hermopolis)	Anach., Pen.Anach.	Lease	Unilateral
	κ[α]ὶ μ[ὴ δύν]ασθαι ἡμᾶς | 2 ἀναχωρῆσαι ἐκ [τῆς ἀπεργασί]ας τῶν αὐτῶν ἀρουρῶν ἄχρι συμπληρώσεως | 3 τοῦ αὐτοῦ ὀκταετοῦς χρονους (l. χρόνου)· εἰ δὲ τοῦτο ποιήσομ(εν) παρέξομεν ὑμῖν ὅλον τὸν | 4 φόρον τῶν αὐτῶν ὀκτὼ ἐτῶν ἀποταττόμενοι πάσῃ νόμου βοηθείᾳ βουηθοῦσι (l. βοηθούσῃ) | 5 ἡμῖν περὶ τούτου.			
41.	SB XVIII 13960.15–21 (VI/VII CE, Hermopolis)	Anach., Pen.Anach.	Labour	Unilateral
	[καὶ μὴ ἐξεῖ]ναί μοι ὑπ[αναχωρῆ]|16[σαι ἀπὸ τῆ]ς σε . . [. . . . . πρὸ] | 17 [συμπληρ]ώσεω[ς τοῦ ἐνιαυτοῦ.] | 18 [εἰ δὲ ἀναχ]ωρήσω, [ἐπὶ τῷ με] | 19 [ἀναδοῦνα]ί σοι εἴ τ[ι ἔσχον] | 20 [παρὰ σοῦ] καὶ ἄνευ μ[ισθοῦ] | 21 [ἀναχωρῆσ]αι.			
42.	SB XVIII 13962.6–10 (630–645 CE, Arsinoites)	Pen.Anach.	Labour	Unilateral
	[εἰ δὲ ἀναχωρήσω πρ]ὸ συμπληρώσεως | 7 τῶν αὐτ[ῶν πέντε] μηνῶν, ἐπὶ τῷ με | 8 ἀναδοῦν[αι αὐ]τῇ εἴ τι ἔσχον παρ' αὐτῆς | 9 ὑπὲρ μισθοῦ ὅλου τ[οῦ] ἐνιαυτοῦ . . | 10 [- ca.13 -]ω[.]			

<table>
<tr><td>43.</td><td>SB XVIII 13963.6–8 (VI/VII CE, Arsinoites)</td><td>Pen.Anach.</td><td>Labour</td><td rowspan="2">Unilateral</td></tr>
<tr><td></td><td colspan="3">εἰ δ[ὲ ἀναχωρήσω πρὸ] | 7 [συμπληρώσεως] τοῦ ἐνιαυτοῦ, ὥστε με ἐν [διπλῷ παρασχεῖν σοι] | 8 [τὸ αὐτό. Αὐρήλι]ος ἄπα [. . . .] . . σθ( ) τὸ χάρισμα [- ca.15 -]</td></tr>
<tr><td>44.</td><td>SB XVIII 13964.2–8 (early VII CE, Arsinoites)</td><td>Pen.Anach.</td><td>Loan</td><td rowspan="2">Unilateral</td></tr>
<tr><td></td><td colspan="3">εἰ δὲ] | 3 ὑπαναχωρήσω [ἐκ τῆς παραμονῆς] | 4 πρὸ συμπληρώσ[εως τοῦ ὑπὲρ τῆς] | 5 αὐτῆς προχρείας [συμπεφωνημ(ένου)] | 6 ἔργου, ἐπὶ τῷ με αὐτ[ῇ παρασχεῖν] | 7 ἐν διπλῷ τὴν αὐτὴν προχρήαν (l. προχρείαν) | 8 ἐξ ὑπαρχόντων μου πάντων,</td></tr>
<tr><td>45.</td><td>SB XX 14969.3–6 (VI/VII CE, Hermopolis)</td><td>Apost., Pen.Apost.</td><td>Labour</td><td rowspan="2">Unilateral</td></tr>
<tr><td></td><td colspan="3">μὴ δύνασθαί με | 4 [- ca.29 - ἀφίσ]τασθαι τῆς ὑμετέρας παραμονῆς. | 5 [εἰ δὲ ἀποστήσω τῆς παραμονῆς, ἐπὶ τῷ με ὑ]μας (l. [ὑ]μῖν) παρασχεῖν λόγῳ ποινῆς χρυσοῦ{ς} | 6 [νο(μισμάτια) τόσα, κινδύνῳ ἐμῷ καὶ τῆς ἐμῆς παντο]ίας ὑποστάσεως.</td></tr>
<tr><td>46.</td><td>SB XX 15043.4–8 (VI/VII CE, Hermopolis)</td><td>Pen.Apost.</td><td>Labour</td><td rowspan="2">Unilateral</td></tr>
<tr><td></td><td colspan="3">ἅπερ παρέξω σοι ἡνίκ[α (?)] | 5 ἀποσταίην τῆς ἀρδείας τοῦ αὐτοῦ χωρίου ἀμπελικοῦ ἐν χρυσῷ χαρά[γματι] | 6 ὡς παρέλαβον, χωρίς τινος ὑπερθέσεως καὶ ἀντιλογίας καὶ κρίσεως | 7 καὶ δίκης, ὑποκειμένων σοι εἰς τοῦτο τὸ χρέος πάντων μοι τῶν ὑπαρχ[όντων] | 8 κ[αὶ] ὑπαρξ[ό]ντων πραγμάτων καθάπερ [ἐ]κ δίκης.</td></tr>
<tr><td>47.</td><td>SPP XX 218.33–35 (early VII CE?, Hermopolites)</td><td>Apost., Pen.Apost.</td><td>Lease</td><td rowspan="2">Unilateral</td></tr>
<tr><td></td><td colspan="3">καὶ μὴ δύνασθαί με | 34 ἀποστῆναι τῆς τούτων ἀμπελουργιγῆς (l. ἀμπελουργικῆς) χρείας πρὸ | 35 συμπληρώσεως τοῦ εἰρημένου τριετοῦς χρονους (l. χρόνου)·| 36 ἀποτάττομαι γὰρ πάσῃ βοηθ‹ε›ίᾳ νόμων βοηθούσῃ με | 37 περὶ τού[το]υ</td></tr>
</table>

BIBLIOGRAPHY

Cruz 1964: S. CRUZ, *Da «Solutio»: terminologia, concieto e caracterîsticas e anälise de värios institutos afins. 1, Épocas arcaica e classica*, Coimbra 1962.

Du Plessis 2012: P.J. DU PLESSIS, *Letting and Hiring in Roman Legal Thought: 27BCE – 284CE*, Leiden–Boston 2012.

Finkenauer 2023: TH. FINKENAUER, 'Stipulatio (Verbalkontrakt)', in: U. Babusiaux /Ch. Baldus/W. Ernst/F.-St. Meissel/J. Platschek/Th. Rüfner (eds.), *Handbuch des römischen Privatrechts I*, Tübingen 2023, 564–643.

Frier 1980: B.W. FRIER, *Landlords and Tenants in Imperial Ro*me, Princeton, NJ. 1980.

Henning 1972: D. HENNIG, 'Die Arbeitsverpflichtungen der Pächter in Landpachtverträgen aus dem Faijum', *ZPE* 9 (1972), 111–131.

Herrmann 1958: J. Herrmann, *Studien zur Bodenpacht im Recht der gräco-ägyptischen Papyri* (MBPR 41), Munich 1958.

Jördens 1990: A. JÖRDENS, *Vertragliche Regelungen von Arbeiten im späten griechischsprachigen Ägypten, mit Editionen von Texten der Heidelberger Papyrus-Sammlung, des Istituto Papirologico "G. Vitelli", des Ägyptischen Museums zu Kairo und des*

British Museum, London (P. Heid. V). (Veröffentlichungen aus der Heidelberger Papyrus-Sammlung, N.F. 6), Heidelberg 1990.

Mayer-Maly 1956: TH. MAYER-MALY, *Locatio conductio: Eine Untersuchung zum klassischen römischen Recht*, Vienna–Munich 1956.

Schwarz 1920: A.B. SCHWARZ, *Die öffentliche und private Urkunde im römischen Ägypten*; Studien zum hellenistischen Privatrecht, Leipzig 1920.

Scott 1932: S.P. SCOTT, *The Civil Law*, New York 1932.

Steinwenter 1952: A. STEINWENTER, 'Was beweisen die Papyri für die praktische Geltung des justinianischen Gesetzgebungswerkes?', *Aegyptus 32 = Raccolta di scritti in onore di Girolamo Vitelli*. II (1952), 131–137.

Simon 1964: D. SIMON, *Studien zur Praxis der Stipulationsklausel* (MBPR 48), Munich 1964.

Taubenschlag 1940/1: R. TAUBENSCHLAG, 'The legislation of Justinian in the light of the papyri', *Byzantion* 15 (1940/1), 280–295 (= *Opera Minora*. II. Warsaw 1959, 69–89).

Weber 1932: F. WEBER, *Untersuchungen zum gräko-ägyptischen Obligationenrecht* (MBPR 5), Munich 1932.

Wolff 1957: H.J. WOLFF, 'Die Grundlagen des griechischen Vertragsrechts', *ZSav RA* 74 (1957), 26–72.

Wolff 1974: H.J. WOLFF, 'Das Vulgarrechtsproblem und die Papyri', *ZSav RA* 91 (1974), 54–105.

Wolff 2003: H.J. WOLFF, *Das Recht der griechischen Papyri Ägyptens in der Zeit der Ptolemaeer und des Prinzipats. Erster Band. Bedingungen und Triebkräfte der Rechtsentwicklung*, H.-A. RUPPRECHT (ed.) (HaW 10.5.1), Munich 2003.

Yiftach-Firanko 2003: U. YIFTACH-FIRANKO, 'Regionalism and Legal Documents: The Case of Oxyrhynchos', in: H.-A. RUPPRECHT (ed.), *Symposion 2003. Vorträge zur griechischen und hellenistischen Rechtsgeschichte* (Rauischholzhausen, 30. September – 3. Oktober 2003) (Akten der Gesellschaft für griechische und hellenistische Rechtsgeschichte, 17), Vienna 2006.

Yiftach 2021: U. YIFTACH, 'Olim tradita fuerunt? On the obsoleteness of the *sollemnia verba* in Inst. 3.15pr.', *JJP* 51 (2021), 169–187.

Yiftach forthcoming: U. YIFTACH, *The Taxonomy of the Legal Document: an account of the Language and Terminology of Clauses in Greek Legal Documents from Ptolemaic, Roman and Byzantine Egypt* (Liége forthcoming).

ÉVA JAKAB (BUDAPEST)

ZUR PROBLEMATIK DER STIPULATION IN DER URKUNDENPRAXIS: ANTWORT AUF URI YIFTACH

Die Romanisierung des Rechts in den Provinzen des Imperium Romanum ist ein beliebtes Thema, das seit der bahnbrechenden Studie von Ludwig Mitteis[1] immer wieder zur Diskussion steht. Mitteis legte wertvolle Ergebnisse vor, die auf die Notwendigkeit einer komplexen, vielschichtigen Betrachtung des ‚Rechts' im Imperium Romanum aufmerksam machten. Seinen Spuren folgend sind zahlreiche Studien entstanden, die eine „fortschreitende Romanisierung" in den Provinzen feststellen.[2] Die Autoren sind dabei überwiegend fest überzeugt von der führenden Rolle, vom Primat des römischen Rechts. Im jüngeren Schrifttum ist jedoch eine Tendenz zu beobachten, die dem Rechtsleben der Provinzen, dem Fortbestehen der ‚lokalen Rechte' mehr Bedeutung zumisst. Einzelstudien haben nachgewiesen, dass die notarielle Praxis in den östlichen Provinzen der hellenischen Tradition fest verbunden blieb. Man kann sogar Belege dafür finden, dass manche römische Bürger, die in einer ‚griechischen Umgebung' lebten, sich den griechischen Rechtsvorstellungen angepasst haben: Sie beurkundeten ihre Rechtsgeschäfte *inter vivos* oder *mortis causa* nach den Formularen der örtlichen ‚Rechtskundigen'.[3]

Uri Yiftach packt das Thema aus dem Blickwinkel der Stipulation an. Seine Untersuchung konzentriert sich – dem alten Pfad folgend – auf die ‚Romanisierung' der Urkundengestaltung in den griechisch-sprachigen Provinzen. Die andere Seite, die Möglichkeit von wechselseitigen Einwirkungen, bleibt dabei unberücksichtigt. Sein Beitrag zitiert eine reiche Fülle an Urkunden – in meiner ‚Antwort' kann ich nur auf wenige davon eingehen.

I. *Verbis contrahere*

Die Stipulation der Römer ist ein mündliches, an eine feste Frage- und-Antwortform gebundenes Leistungsversprechen.[4] Sie erzeugt durch einen einseitig verpflichtenden Formalakt eine *obligatio unilateralis*. Auf die Frage des Gläubigers sichert der Schuldner zu, dass er eine Leistung (*dare* oder *facere*) erbringen werde (Gai. 3,92):

---

1 Mitteis, Reichsrecht.

2 Mitteis, Reichsrecht 5–6 und 8; zu der Problematik s. vor kurzem Alonso, Constitutio Antoniniana 49–50.

3 Jakab, Prozess 493; Jakab, Parakatatheke 340–344; Jakab, Kaiserliche Rechtspflege 105–106. S. vor kurzem auch Czajkowski, Eckhardt, Strothmann, Introduction 3–5.

4 Kaser, Knütel, Lohsse, Römisches Privatrecht 296–300.

Verbis obligatio fit ex interrogatione et responsione, velut Dari spondes? Spondeo. – Dabis? Dabo. – Promittis? Promitto.[5] Die Wirksamkeit der Stipulation war also an den Formzwang der übereinstimmenden, mündlichen Frage und Antwort gebunden.

Im klassischen Recht wurden jedoch die Erwartungen gegenüber dem Wortlaut weitgehend gelockert: *Interrogatio* und *responsum* konnten sowohl von römischen Bürgern (mit *spondere*) als auch von Peregrinen (mit *promittere*, aber auch in Fremdsprachen) relativ frei formuliert werden.[6] Ein großer Vorteil war weiterhin, dass der Vertrag abstrakt oder auch kausal abgefasst werden konnte. Die Stipulation diente dem Interesse des Gläubigers: Es entstand dadurch gegen den Schuldner eine *actio stricti iuris* mit objektiver Haftungsgrundlage, welche die Durchsetzung des Anspruchs mit einem leichten Beweisprogramm ermöglichte.[7] Andererseits war das Kontrahieren dadurch erschwert, dass der Formzwang die Anwesenheit beider Vertragspartner verlangte.[8]

II. Wozu die Stipulation in den Provinzen?

Yiftach geht davon aus, dass die ‚römische' Stipulationsklausel in der notariellen Praxis der Provinzen unmittelbar nach der *Constitutio Antoniniana* übernommen und mechanisch angewendet wurde. Damit baut er auf alte Thesen.[9] Die Neubürger hätten die Stipulation dem althergebrachtem (griechischem) Formular einfach angehängt, um den vertraglichen Inhalt vor einem römischen Gericht überhaupt klagbar zu machen.[10] Diese alte These wurde von Yiftach ohne Kritik übernommen.[11] Sein neuer Aspekt besteht darin, dass er linguistische Argumente ins Spiel bringt. Er sieht in der Formulierung der Stipulationsklausel der griechischen Urkunden im 6. Jh. einen

---

5 Gai. 3,92. Ähnlich in Gaius D. 44,7,1,7 (2 *aureorum*) und in den Pauli Sententiae; PS 2,3: *Stipulatio est verborum conceptio, ad quam quis congrue interrogatus respondet: velut Spondes? Spondeo, Dabis? Dabo, Promittis? Promitto* ... Die Quellen unterstreichen die Unentbehrlichkeit der mündlichen Frage-Antwort-Form.

6 Nelson, Manthe, Gaius 103–111; zu den Stipulationen in Fremdsprachen s. Gai. 3,93; vgl. Nelson, Manthe, Gaius 112–113.

7 Bei *certa res* eine *condictio certae pecuniae creditae, condictio certae rei,* bei *incertum* eine *actio ex stipulatu*, vgl. Kaser, Knütel, Lohsse, Römisches Privatrecht 296 und 272.

8 PS 2,3: *Interpretatio: Stipulatio est inter praesentes haec verba, quibus se invicem partes obligari possunt* ... Finkenauer, Wie formal 87–108.

9 Dabei scheint Yiftach Wolffs Aussage missverstanden zu haben. Wolff hat die Const. Antoniniana nicht als große Zäsur betrachtet. Ganz im Gegenteil, er stellte fest, dass „römische Einflüsse gelegentlich schon vor der Const. Antoniniana" feststellbar seien, und nach der Constitutio Antoniniana keine „vollständige Rezeption des römischen Rechts" erfolgt sei; vgl. Wolff, Romanisierung 1.

10 S. etwa Yiftach in diesem Band S. 463.

11 Die jüngere Forschung geht inzwischen andere Wege, vgl. etwa Czajkowski, Eckhardt, Strothmann, Introduction 2–3. Ein präziseres Bild über die Verwendung der Stipulation in den Papyri Ägyptens zeichnet Alonso, Constitutio Antoniniana 57–58.

Wandel, wodurch – seiner Meinung nach – erst die Einführung der „future oriented contents of the Roman stipulation“ durchgeführt wurde.[12]

Seine Arbeitshypothese und die angeführte statistische Auswertung zahlreicher Dokumente beeindrucken den Leser. Der Rechtshistoriker sieht trotzdem Bedarf, seine juristischen Aussagen an mehreren Punkten zu präzisieren bzw. zu korrigieren. Die vorliegende Antwort muss sich – notgedrungen – auf wenige Aspekte beschränken.

Es keimt vor allem die methodologische Frage auf: Kann eine statistische Auswertung des Vorkommens gewisser sprachlicher Wendungen als Grundlage juristischer Schlüsse dienen? Kann man dokumentarische Quellen rechtlichen Inhalts ohne fundierte Sachverhaltsanalysen relevant erklären? Diese und ähnliche Bedenken drängen sich bei der Betrachtung der Urkundenpraxis der Stipulation besonders stark auf, weil die obligierende Wirkung der förmlichen Frage und Antwort für vielerlei Zwecke eingesetzt werden konnte. In der kontraktuellen Alltagspraxis kann die Stipulation in verschiedenen Rollen beobachtet werden. Sie konnte einerseits als Verbalkontrakt *sui generis* die primäre Leistungspflicht des Schuldners in eine Obligation *stricti iuris* kleiden.[13] Andererseits konnte sie die Erfüllung einer Hauptobligation durch die Festlegung von Vertragsstrafen für den Fall von Leistungsstörungen sichern.[14]

III. Pachtvertrag und Stipulation

Yiftach wählt ein Zitat aus der Gutachterpraxis des Iulius Paulus (eines prominenten Vertreters der Spätklassik) zum Kardinaltext seiner Untersuchung. Es wäre hilfreich gewesen, den Sachverhalt in der üblichen Methode einer juristischen Exegese kurz darzustellen[15] (D. 19,2,54,1 Paulus 3 resp.):

> *Inter locatorem fundi et conductorem convenit, ne intra tempora locationis Seius conductor de fundo invitus repelleretur et, si pulsatus esset, poenam decem praestet Titius locator Seio conductori: vel Seius conductor Titio, si intra tempora locationis discedere vellet, aeque decem Titio locatori praestare vellet: quod invicem de se stipulati sunt. Quaero, cum Seius conductor biennii continui pensionem non solveret, an sine metu poenae expelli possit. Paulus respondit, quamvis nihil expressum sit in stipulatione poenali de solutione pensionum, tamen verisimile esse ita convenisse de non expellendo colono intra tempora praefinita, si pensionibus paruerit et ut oportet coleret: et ideo, si poenam petere coeperit is qui pensionibus satis non fecit, profuturam locatori doli exceptionem.*

---

[12] Zu Recht hat P. Sänger in der Diskussion zum Vortrags von Yiftach am 24.08.2022 dagegen eingebracht, dass sich die Urkundenformulare im 6. Jh. allgemein verändert haben.

[13] Vgl. etwa die Anwendung der Stipulation in den Rechtsurkunden des Sulpicius-Archivs.

[14] Zu den Vertragsstrafen s. vor allem Knütel, Stipulatio poenae 10–16.

[15] In der Druckfassung hat der Autor (ohne darauf zu verweisen) meine Exegese des Falles weitgehend übernommen.

Titius hat ein Landstück dem Seius zur entgeltlichen Bebauung überlassen. Durch übereinstimmende, formlose Willenserklärung (*convenit*) kam zwischen ihnen ein Pachtvertrag (*locatio conductio rei,* Konsensualvertrag) zustande. Der Jurist geht auf den eigentlichen Vertragsinhalt gar nicht ein. Landpachtverträge wurden in Rom üblicherweise in Form von Versteigerungen vergeben; der Verpächter fasste seine allgemeinen Bedingungen in den sog. *leges locationis* zusammen.[16] Solche *leges* richteten sich nach allgemein gebräuchlichen Formularbüchern, und die dort empfohlenen Klauseln konnten im individuellen Fall mit eigenen ergänzt werden. Die *leges locationis* enthielten eigentlich die ‚Willenserklärung' einer der Parteien; sie verkörpern das Angebot des Verpächters. Die potentiellen Pächter studierten diese *leges* und nahmen sie zur Kenntnis; die Auswahl des Vertragspartners (des kontrahierenden Pächters) erfolgte dann durch ein Lizitationsverfahren.[17]

Im Paulus' Fall legen die Parteien zusätzlich noch Vertragsstrafen in Form von gegenseitigen Stipulationen fest: Der Verpächter solle zehn zahlen, wenn er den Pächter während der Pachtzeit vertreibt, und ebenso solle der Pächter zehn zahlen, wenn er vorzeitig wegzieht. Daraufhin bezahlte der Pächter zwei Jahre lang keinen Pachtzins. Der Vertragsbruch des *conductor* hat dem Verpächter Schaden zugefügt, deshalb wollte er den Vertrag einseitig auflösen. Er befürchtete jedoch, dass er wegen des Vertreibens des Pächters aus der Strafstipulation belangt werden könne.

War es eine reale Gefahr? Wenn ja, warum? Für die Antwort müssen wir die Rechtsverhältnisse zwischen den Parteien aus der juristisch-dogmatischen Perspektive skizzieren. Es ist zu betonen, dass zwischen den Parteien zwei, voneinander unabhängige Rechtsverhältnisse entstanden sind: der formfreie, konsensuale Pachtvertrag (*locatio conductio rei*) und der förmliche Verbalvertrag (*stipulatio*). Aus dem Pachtvertrag steht dem Verpächter die *actio locati* auf Erfüllung bzw. Schadensersatz zu, wobei sein Schaden und die Haftung des Pächters nach dem Maßstab der *bona fides* bemessen werden; über die Höhe des Schadens müssen Beweise vorgelegt werden.

Im Paulus' Fall haben jedoch die Parteien auch Vertragsstrafen in Form von Stipulationen für den Fall von einseitiger Auflösung festgelegt. Daraus haftet jede von ihnen auf einen bestimmten Betrag (zehn), wenn er den Vertrag vor dem Ende der Laufzeit einseitig beendet. Die zwei Schuldverhältnisse existieren nebeneinander, ohne miteinander (synallagmatisch?) verbunden zu sein. Streng genommen verfällt die Stipulation unabhängig von einem eventuellen sonstigen Vertragsbruch des Betroffenen. Deshalb ist es nach dem *ius strictum* eine reale Gefahr, dass der säumige Pächter den hart durchgreifenden (ihn vertreibenden) Verpächter aufgrund der *stipulatio poenae* auf zehn belangen könnte. Theoretisch müsste der Pächter bloß die erfolgte Stipulation und die Tatsache der Vertreibung nachweisen, weil den Verpächter eine

[16] Vgl. etwa Cato agr. 156 (*Oleam pendentem hac lege venire oportet*); 153 (*lex oleae legendae*); 154 (*lex oleae faciundae*); 155 (*lex oleae pendentis*); und insbesonders Cato agr. 158 (*lex pabulo*). Zu dem Ausschreibungsverfahren s. etwa Thielmann, Privatauktion 43–48.

[17] Vgl. Frier, Landlords and Tenants 34–39.

objektive, verschuldensunabhängige Haftung trifft. Der Vertragsbruch des Pächters spielt dabei – nach den formellen Kriterien des *ius civile* – keine Rolle. Der klassische Jurist, Paulus, stellt trotzdem darauf ab, dass derjenige, der vertragsbrüchig handelt, von seinem Gegner keine Vertragstreue erwarten kann. Paulus greift hier auf die Pflichten der Parteien aus dem konsensualen Pachtvertrag zurück, um den Verpächter vor der stipulierten Vertragsstrafe zu schützen. Nur mit dieser dogmatisch nicht sauberen Lösung konnte er dem Verpächter gegen die *condictio certae pecuniae* des Pächters die *exceptio doli* zusprechen.

Im lateinischen Text wird auf die Vereinbarung zwischen den Parteien hingewiesen: *Inter locatorem fundi et conductorem convenit, ne intra tempora locationis Seius conductor de fundo invitus repelleretur* … Das Verbum *convenit* bezeichnet hier das formlose Übereinkommen der Parteien und nicht die Stipulation. Pächter und Verpächter haben zunächst im Rahmen der *locatio conductio* vereinbart, dass im Falle einer einseitigen Auflösung des Vertrags beide jeweils auf zehn haften würden. Wäre es bei dieser *conventio* geblieben, hätte der Pächter wegen seiner Vertreibung nur mit der *actio conducti* aus der *bonae fidei obligatio* klagen können. Damit hätte er jedoch keine Chance, weil er sich mit seinem Vertragsbruch (unterlassene Pachtzinszahlung) schuldig gemacht hat.[18]

Aber die Parteien haben diesen Teil des Pachtvertrags zusätzlich auch in Form einer Strafstipulation bekräftigt: *quod invicem de se stipulati sunt.* Paulus zitiert also den Wortlaut der Strafstipulation überhaupt nicht, er verweist bloß darauf, dass gegenseitige Stipulationen abgeschlossen wurden. Die für uns relevante Stipulation hätte etwa so lauten können: S*i intra tempora locationis pulsatus sum, mihi decem dari spondesne? Spondeo.*

Nachdem Paulus darauf verzichtet hat, den Wortlaut der Stipulation wörtlich zu zitieren, kann der Text für linguistische Vergleiche nicht – wie es Yiftach gemacht hat – herangezogen werden.[19] Man muss weiterhin unterstreichen, dass die *stipulatio poenae* (Festlegung einer Vertragsstrafe) nur eine der denkbaren Anwendungsfälle der Stipulation war. Yiftach sieht darin aber „die typisch-römische" Formulierung.

IV. Parallelen?

Anschließend werden mehrere Papyri angeführt, in denen ‚Paulus' Stipulationsfassung' belegt seien.[20] Zweifelsohne enthalten Yiftach's Texte irgendeine Form von Versprechen.

---

[18] Die Klageformel enthält die Wendung *quidquid dare facere oportet ex fide bona* … Gai. 4,136; s. dazu Kaser, Knütel, Lohsse, Römische Privatrecht 296.

[19] In Yiftachs Vortrag: "Then, in the text of the stipulatio itself, a conditional clause describes the violation, and the apodosis introduces the sanction, a payment of a fine of ten currency units. We do not know, if the text of the stipulation was incorporated, in the case brought forward before Paulus, in a broader agreement of the type well attested in the papyri from Egypt …"

[20] S. etwa Yiftach in diesem Band S. 464: "… an outright reception of the text of the 'Pauline stipulatio' into Greek documents …"

Vom juristischen Inhalt her findet sich jedoch kein einziger, welcher die vorzeitige Kündigung in einer *stipulatio poenae* geregelt hätte. Wurde eine Vertragsstrafe vereinbart, ist die Klausel im Vertragstext integriert, ohne dass eine explizite *stipulatio poenae* angehängt worden wäre.

Nach Yiftach seien aus der byzantinischen Epoche insgesamt nur vier Dokumente überliefert, in denen für die unterlassene Pachtzinszahlung eine Vertragsstrafe vereinbart wurde: P.Flor. III 384 (Verpachtung einer Badeanlage); P.Michael. 43 (Verpachtung von Land und Darlehen); BGU XIX 2828 (Erntekauf oder Arbeitsvertrag) und BGU II 366 (Lieferung von Webwaren). Unter dem Gesichtspunkt einer funktionell und linguistisch vergleichenden Analyse scheint es äußerst problematisch, dass aus den vier Urkunden zwei (50%) gar keine Pachtverträge überliefern. Es ist weiterhin bedenklich, dass die Anwendung der Verben ἐπερωθητείς bzw. ὡμολόγησα nur linguistisch untersucht, aber der inhaltliche Kontext (wofür die Wendungen in dem jeweiligen Text stehen) nicht berücksichtigt wird.

Um die Bedenken gegenüber einer solchen, rein äußerlichen Untersuchung zu demonstrieren, soll eine der genannten Urkunden näher (obwohl nur paraphrasiert) betrachtet werden (P.Michael 43, Aphrodites Kome, 8. Juni 526):

> (4) ἐξεμίσ̣θωσά σοι̣ πρὸς ὀκτωέτη χρόνον … | (11) παραέξεις δ̣ὲ μοι … | (12)προσομολογ̣ῶ δε ἐσχηκέναι παρά σου σήμερον λόγῳ̣ | [… χ̣ρ̣έ̣ο̣υ̣ς̣] χρυσο̣ῦ ν̣ο̣μ̣ισμά̣τια δέκα ὀκτὼ … | (20) παρελθούσης δὲ τῆς προ̣κ̣(ειμένης) ἡ̣μ̣έ̣ρ̣α̣ς κατ᾿ ἔτος κα̣ὶ <εἰ> μὴ ἀποδοίην σοι τῆς προκ(ειμένης) προχρείας, ἐξουσίαν ἔχεις τὸ αὐτὸ γ̣εώργιον ἐπὶ τὸν ἐπίοντα κύκλον <ἔχειν> καὶ γ[ε]ω̣ργεῖν | … (21) ἡ̣] ἀ̣ν̣τιμίσθ(ωσις) κυρία καὶ βεβαία καὶ ἐπερωτηθ̣[---.[21]

P.Michael. 43 enthält einen mit Darlehen kombinierten Pachtvertrag: Der Pachtzins für acht Jahre wurde vorgeschossen und als Darlehen quittiert. Im ersten Teil (Z. 4–13) sind die Pflichten der Parteien beschrieben: Laufzeit, Bebauungsvorschriften, Pachtzins *in natura* und Geldzahlung, Risikoverteilung usw. Davon getrennt folgt die Quittierung des Pachtzins-Darlehens in Homologie-Form (Z. 13–21): Der Verpächter anerkennt (*proshomologo*), dass er am Tag der Urkundenerrichtung 18 *nomismata* bar (und dazu noch eine bestimmte Menge Getreide) erhalten hat – und er verspricht das Empfangene zurückzuzahlen, wenn der Pächter das Land verlässt. In den Zeilen 20–21 wird vom Verpächter (und nicht vom Pächter!) zugesichert, dass er das Land dem Pächter ein Jahr länger überlässt, falls er mit der Rückzahlung in Verzug geraten sollte. Anschließend folgen die Kyria- und die Stipulationsklausel

---

[21] P. Michael 43: "I have let to you for eight year … | I also acknowledge that I have received from you as a loan eighteen nomismata … | (20)If the afore-said day passes each year and I have not repaid the afore-said loan, you have the power to (hold) and cultivate the afore-said farm and --- | (21)The lease is valid and operative. And having been asked the formal question (I agreed)…" (Übersetzung des Editors; "each year"?).

(letzte fragmentarisch) – die den Pachtvertrag bekräftigen. Fazit: Es geht bei der Strafe für die unterlassene Zahlung nicht um den Pachtzins, sondern um die Rückzahlung der Vorleistung von der Seite des Verpächters. Es liegt also ein Sachverhalt vor, der mit dem des Paulus nichts zu tun hat. Die abweichende Rollenverteilung wird von Yiftach nicht erkannt.

Auch P.Flor. III 384 (Verpachtung einer Badeanlage, Alexandria, 489) zeigt in seiner Struktur oder Formulierung keine Verwandtschaft mit dem Text des Paulus. Betrachtet man BGU XIX 2828 (Hermopolis, Anfang 7. Jh., vom Editor als Erntekauf oder Arbeitsvertrag eingestuft) näher, scheint das dreifache Vorkommen des Verbum *homologein* juristisch keine Besonderheiten auszudrücken. Aurelios Viktor, der Schuldner, anerkennt in einer Homologie-Urkunde, dass er sich um die Bebauung eines Stückchen Landes für eine Erntephase kümmern werde: Er wird die Erde dreimal pflügen, dreimal bewässern und die Früchte bis zum Abtransport bewahren.[22] In Z. 5 (ὁμολογῶ ... πεπληρῶσθαι) erklärt der sich Verpflichtende, dass er dafür den vollen Arbeitslohn erhalten habe. Dieser Teil der Urkunde ist also eine ganz normale Quittung.[23] Dann folgt in der Tat eine Strafklausel (Z. 9: ὁμολογῶ διδόναι σοι ...):[24] Aurelios Viktor erklärt, dass er im Fall eines vertragsbrüchigen Verhaltens seinem Partner 18 Keratien als pauschalen Schadensersatz zahlen werde. Obwohl hier eine künftige Leistung festgehalten wird, kann man darin keine Stipulation sehen, weil die Frage-Antwort-Form fehlt.[25] Es handelt sich um eine einseitige Willenserklärung. Die ungewöhnliche Höhe der Vertragsstrafe könnte nicht nur mit dem unterstellten hohen Wert der Früchte zusammenhängen.[26] Es geht eher darum, dass die 18 Keratien sowohl die Rückzahlung des vorgeleisteten ‚Arbeitslohns' als auch den pauschalen Schadensersatz mit enthalten.[27] Eine Stipulation ist in der Urkunde nur in der gekürzten Schlussklausel zu erkennen, Z. 11–12: ἡ παροῦσα μησθαποχὴ κυρία καὶ βεβαία καὶ ἐπερ(ωτηθεὶς) ὡμολ(όγησα). Es handelt sich um eine typische angehängte Stipulationsklausel, die für das Untersuchungsfeld von Yiftach eigentlich irrelevant ist.

Als weitere Parallele zu Paulus' Fall wird P.Köln II 102a präsentiert (Ox., 418), ein Chirographum, das als Homologie beurkundet wurde. Das Dokument ist aber

---

22 Die Verpflichtung der Bewahrung erinnert an die *custodia*-Haftung des römischen Rechts; diese Möglichkeit ist dem Editor (und auch Yiftach) entgangen.

23 Ganz im Sinne der Wolff'schen Zweckverfügung ... vgl. Wolff, Grundlagen 39–44.

24 Ähnlich ist der Wortlaut in P.Mil. II 48 (SB VI 9011), ein Arbeitsvertrag aus Oxyrhynchos, aus dem Jahre 549, der von Yiftach ebenfalls als Parallele mit herangezogen wird. Es gibt keine Anhaltspunkte dafür, die Wendung ὁμολογῶ διδόναι im Vertragstext als Stipulation zu deuten.

25 Zum Vergleich möchte ich darauf hinweisen, dass die Vertragstrafen wegen Leistungsstörungen auch in den lateinischen Urkunden oft ohne Stipulation erscheinen, vgl. etwa FIRA 150 (Dacia, 164 n.Chr.); FIRA III 157 (Dacia, 167 n.Chr.). Es ist überhaupt bedauerlich, dass Yiftach die lateinischen Urkunden nicht berücksichtigt hat.

26 So der Editor von BGU XIX 2828 auf S. 151.

27 Weder der Editor noch Yiftach erwägen diese Möglichkeit.

kein Pachtvertrag, sondern ein Arbeitsvertrag mit *paramone*-Klausel. Eine gewisse Asenneth (Tochter eines Paulus) anerkennt, dass sie zwei Goldsolidi als Kapital (als Darlehen beurkundet) erhalten hat. Der Betrag ist eine Vorleistung des Arbeitgebers, der das Dienstmädchen anstellt. Die Angestellte verspricht, bei dem Arbeitgeber zu bleiben, und nicht frühzeitig fortzugehen. Für den Fall ihres vorzeitigen Weglaufens oder eines Entlassens durch den Arbeitgeber verspricht sie das Empfangene (ohne Zinsen) zurückzugeben. Es handelt sich hier keineswegs um eine Strafstipulation. Die Geldzahlung des Arbeitgebers ist seine Vorleistung, wodurch das Mädchen überhaupt verpflichtet wird.[28] In den letzten Zeilen der Urkunde wird zwar eine Stipulation angehängt, aber sie hat mit der *stipulatio poenae* des Paulus nichts gemeinsam.

V. Geänderte Auffassung in der Spätantike?

Die Förmlichkeit der übereinstimmenden Frage und Antwort wurde durch die Jahrhunderte beibehalten. Zweifelsohne gibt es Kaiserkonstitutionen, die – auf der Ebene der Höchstgerichtsbarkeit – für Einzelfälle Ausnahmen zulassen. Dieser Prozess setzt jedoch nicht erst im 5. Jahrhundert (wie von Yiftach betont), sondern bereits in der Spätklassik ein. Als Beleg dafür kann C. 8,37,1, eine Konstitution von Septimus Severus aus dem Jahre 200 n.Chr. zitiert werden:

> *Licet epistolae, quam libello inseruisti, additum non sit stipulatum esse eum, cui cavebatur, tamen si res inter praesentes gesta est, credendum est praecedentem stipulationem vocem spondentis secutam.*

Es handelt sich um ein kaiserliches Reskript, das auf die Anfrage eines gewissen Aurelius Secundus erlassen wurde. Offenbar hat Secundus als Kläger eine Klageschrift/Petition (*libellus*) eingereicht; als Gerichtsherr kann ein Statthalter vermutet werden. Als Beilage hat er in seine Petition auch eine *epistula* kopiert; man kann darin eine Urkunde in Briefform sehen, die als Beweis seiner Forderung diente.[29] Aus der Antwort der Kaiser kann man darauf schließen, dass der Kläger aus einer Stipulation klagen wollte. Die Gegenpartei dürfte die Beweiskraft der Urkunde angezweifelt haben, weil darin die Frage-Antwort-Form nicht präzise festgehalten wurde. Darauf hat das Reskript Bezug genommen: Wurde ein Rechtsgeschäft unter Anwesenden abgeschlossen, aber in der ausgestellten Urkunde nur die Zusicherung (*promissio*) des Schuldners dokumentiert (ohne die Wendung, dass der Empfänger „sich versprechen ließ“, *stipulatum esse)*, soll die Vermutung gelten, dass die Stimme des Versprechenden (*vox spondentis*) auf eine vorangehende Frage (*interrogatio*)

---

[28] Zur Zweckverfügung am Beispiel der *misthosis* s. Wolff, Grundlagen 39–44; vgl. Scheibelreiter, Der ungetreue Verwalter 36–41 mit weiterführender Literatur.

[29] Zur verbreiteten Anwendung dieser Urkundenform s. etwa Jakab, Urkunden in Briefform 219; Kovarik, Briefform in spätantiken Verträgen 201.

folgte.[30] Es handelt sich also um eine Ausnahme-Entscheidung im Einzelfall. Die Stelle bestätigt keineswegs, dass jedes *promittere* oder *homologein* als Stipulation zu deuten wäre.[31] Das Reskript betrifft allein die Frage, ob der Kläger mit einer unvollständigen Urkunde die formgerechte Vornahme einer Stipulation beweisen, d.h. seinen Anspruch mit einer *stricti iuris* Klage durchsetzen kann.

Das allgemeine Festhalten am Formzwang bestätigen auch die dokumentarischen Texte, die lateinischen Urkunden aus dem 5.–6. Jh. Diese sprechen dafür, dass die Stipulation auch in dieser Periode konsequent als Frage und Antwort beurkundet wurde (und damit sprechen sie gegen die These von Yiftach). Es reicht hier auf einige Beispiele hinzuweisen: FIRA III 139 (= TA IV, *emptio fundi Africana*, 439/494); FIRA III 140 (*instrumentum emptionis ex Ravenna*, 591); FIRA III 141 (*instrumentum venditionis Bavaricum*, 7.–8. Jh.). Aber auch weitere Dokumente in den Tablets Albertini und in den (noch zum Teil unveröffentlichten) ‚North African tablets' aus dem 5. Jh. bestätigen die überraschend korrekte Anwendung der Stipulation.

Dieser Befund wird auch durch eine zeitgenössische Quelle bestätigt, die hier kurz dargestellt werden soll. Der Kirchenvater Augustinus (354–430), der aufgrund seines Rhetorikstudiums und seiner richterlichen Tätigkeit als Bischof von Hippo umfassende Rechtskenntnisse hatte, bezieht sich auf das verbreitete Urkunden-Modell in einem schönen Gleichnis (Aug. serm. 110,4):

> *Promissorum suorum nobis chirographum fecit. Non debendo enim sed promittendo debitorem se Deus fecit, id est non mutuo accipiendo ... Non possumus dicere ei, Redde quod accepisti, sed plane dicimus, Redde quod promisisti.*[32]

Augustinus greift auf die juristische Begriffswelt zurück, um seinem Publikum die Verlässlichkeit der göttlichen Gnade einzuprägen. So wie ein *chirographum* und eine *promissio* sicherstellen, dass man künftig etwas erhält – ebenso sicher ist die vom Gott versprochene Erlösung.[33] Für unser Thema ist die Gegenüberstellung von *debere* und *promittere* von Bedeutung: Aus dem *chirographum* (das in der griechischen Welt als Homologie beurkundet wurde) entsteht die Verpflichtung, das Empfangene zurückzuzahlen; aus der *promissio* (Stipulation) hingegen die Ver-

[30] Auch Albers, Versprechen als Verpflichtungsgrund 341–342 und 345–347 hebt hervor: „Geschäftsurkunden, die den Hergang genau dokumentieren sollen, berichten über das Geschäft nicht als Einheit, sondern trennen die bewirkenden Akte … Die Juristen hingegen geben den Wortlaut meistens nur mit einem Verbum wieder: *si stipulor, stipulatus sum* – oder, seltener, von der Schuldnerseite her mit der *promissio*."

[31] In diesem Sinne etwa Yiftach in diesem Band S. 468.

[32] Ähnlich in Aug. serm. 16,7: *Dignatus est se ipsum facere debitorem, et qualem debitorem? Chirographum fecit, pignus dedit. Chirographum eius est scriptura divina, pignus euis est mors Christi, promissio eius est mors Christi.*

[33] Zu der Quelle s. vor kurzem ausführlich Albers, Versprechen als Verpflichtungsgrund 347–350 mit weiterer Literatur.

bindlichkeit, eine für die Zukunft zugesicherte Leistung zu erbringen. Augustinus' Interpretation schildert die Rechtsauffassung des 5. Jahrhunderts – und zeigt, wie die Homologie-Urkunden, die uns Yiftach vorgeführt hat, damals verstanden wurden. Bezieht sich das Verbum *homologein* auf die Rückgabepflicht von etwas Empfangenem (s. etwa P.Michael. 43), ist es als *debere* zu deuten, während mit der *promissio* ein künftiges Leistenmüssen, ohne vorher etwas empfangen zu haben, zugesichert wird.

Zweifelsohne, eine kaiserliche Konstitution aus dem Jahre 472 scheint den Formzwang erheblich aufgelockert zu haben (C. 8,37,10, Imperator Leo A. Erythrio): *Omnes stipulationes, etiamsi non sollemnibus vel directis, sed quibuscumque verbis consensu contrahentium compositae sint, legibus cognitae suam habeant firmitatem.*[34] Diese Anordnung, die aus der Kanzlei von Kaiser Leo erging, scheint die Formerfordernisse der Stipulation grundsätzlich abschaffen zu wollen. Sie betrifft jedoch nicht die Beurkundung des Formalaktes, sondern versucht die Grenzen der *pacta* (Vereinbarungen, die dem Typenzwang nicht folgen und deshalb keine Klagbarkeit haben) aufzuweichen.

VI. Kurz zum Schluss

Die Stipulation des klassischen Rechts geht von der aktiven, anfänglichen Tätigkeit des Gläubigers aus, dem Sich-Versprechen-Lassen (*stipulari*). Die Urkunden aus dem 1.–2. Jh. berichten über das Rechtsgeschäft, indem sie meistens beide Akten nennen: *interrogatio – promissio* (der geschäftliche Inhalt wird in der Frage des Gläubigers resümiert). Übereinstimmende Frage und Antwort bilden eine Einheit (*sollemnia verba, conceptio verborum*), wodurch das Leisten-Müssen entsteht.

Die Stipulation wird in den Formularen typischerweise mit weiteren Verpflichtungsgrundlagen kombiniert. Diese Eigentümlichkeit kann etwa schon im Archiv der Sulpicii beobachtet werden. Es reicht hier ein Textbeispiel zu zitieren, in dem *chirographum, mutuum* und *stipulatio* ineinander verschmelzen (TPSulp. 51, Puteoli, 18. Juni 37):

> *C(aius) Novius Eunus scripsi me accepisse mutua ab Euno | Ti(berii) Caesaris Augusti liberto Primiano apsente per | Hesychum servum eius et debere ei sestertium | decem millia nummum, quae ei reddam cum petierit | et ea HS X m(illia) n(ummum), q(uae) s(upra) s(cripta) s(unt), p(roba) r(ecte) d(ari) stipulatus est | Hesychus Eueni Ti(berii) Caesaris Augusti l(iberti) Primianis | servus, spopondi ego C(aius) Novius Eunus ...*

Es fällt auf, dass im Urkundentext römische und griechische Elemente geschickt kombiniert werden. Die Wendung *scripsi me debere* ist ein Schuldschein nach

[34] Eine weitere Entwicklung zeigt in Inst. Just. 3,15,1 (533): ... *sed haec sollemnia verba olim quidem in usu fuerunt: postea autem Leoniana constitutio lata est, quae, sollemnitate verborum sublata, sensum et consonantem intellectum ab utraque parte solum desiderat, licet quibuscumque verbis expressus est.*

griechischem Muster, der als *chirographum* bereits früh in das römische Vertragssystem integriert wurde.[35] *Mutua accepi* nennt die *causa* des Rechtsgeschäfts, das Darlehen; durch den Empfang der Valuta entstand die Verpflichtung zur Rückerstattung (*reddere*) der gleichen Menge. Angehängt ist noch eine Stipulation, die eine weitere Klagemöglichkeit erzeugt. Dem Gläubiger stehen – im klassischen Formularprozess – wahlweise drei Klagen zur Verfügung, aber das jeweilige Beweisprogramm fällt sehr unterschiedlich aus: Klagt er aus dem *chirographum*, muss er das Schriftstück vorlegen; klagt er aus dem *mutuum,* muss er die Valutierung des Geldes (*numeratio*) nachweisen; klagt er aus der Stipulation, muss er die mündliche Frage und Antwort beweisen. Die klare Trennung zwischen den obligierenden *causae* und den dadurch entstandenen Klagemöglichkeiten sollte man sich vor Augen halten, auch wenn man die Rolle der Stipulation in der notariellen Praxis der Spätantike untersucht.

All dies sollte man berücksichtigen, wenn man die Stipulation rechtshistorisch bewerten will. Yiftach wählt jedoch den Weg einer rein linguistischen Argumentation. Konfrontiert man seine Thesen mit juristischen und literarischen Quellen, bekommt man Zweifel. Weder die interpretierenden, theoretischen Schriften, noch die Notare scheinen den Begriff der Stipulation so weit aufgelockert zu haben, dass es uns erlaubt wäre jedes *homologein* als eine Stipulation zu deuten. Abschließend sei bemerkt, dass nach der Untersuchung von Yiftach die für den Rechtshistoriker wichtigsten Fragen unbeantwortet blieben (bzw. nicht einmal gestellt wurden): Hatte die in der griechischen notariellen Praxis oft angehängte ἐπερωθητεὶς ὡμολόγησα Klausel überhaupt juristische Relevanz? Hat die Klausel etwa die Haftungslage aus dem Vertrag modifiziert? Hat sie eine neue Klagemöglichkeit erzeugt? Hat sie das Beweisprogramm in einem eventuellen Prozess verändert? Oder handelt es sich angesichts des in der Spätantike geänderten Prozessrechts um eine bloße Floskel?

jakab.eva@kre.hu

BIBLIOGRAPHIE

Albers G., Zum Versprechen als Verpflichtungsgrund in der Spätantike: Urkundenpraxis, Kirchenlehrer und der westgotische Gaius, ZRG RA 135, 2018, 334–363.

Alonso J.-L., The Constitutio Antoniniana and Private Legal Practice in the Eastern Empire, in Czajkowski K., Eckhardt B., Strothmann M. (Hgg.), Law in the Roman Provinces (Oxford Studies in Roman Law and Society), Oxford 2020, 44–64.

Czajkowski K., Eckhardt B., Strothmann M. (Hgg.), Law in the Roman Provinces (Oxford Studies in Roman Law and Society), Oxford 2020.

[35] Platschek, Pecunia constituta 253–262.

Du Plessis P., Letting and Hiring in Roman Legal Thought: 27 BCE – 284 CE, Leiden – Boston 2012.

Finkenauer Th., Wie formal war die römische Stipulation? in Piro I. (Hg.), Scritti per Alessandro Corbino, Tricase 2017, 87–108.

Frier B., Landlords and Tenants in Imperial Rome, Princeton 1980.

Jakab É., Urkunden in Briefform: Chirographum und Epistula im römischen Privatrecht, in Yiftach-Firanko U. (Hg.), The Letter. Law, State and the Epistolary Format in the Ancient World, Wiesbaden 2013, 219–238.

Jakab É., Prozess um eine entlaufene Sklavin: P.Cair.Preis 1^2. Prozess in der provinzialen Rechtskultur, in ZRG RA 135, 2018, 474–526.

Jakab É., Parakatatheke und letztwillige Verfügungen: Zum Hintergrund von D. 32,37,5, in ZRG RA 138, 2021, 338–378.

Jakab É., Kaiserliche Rechtspflege und provinziale Praxis. Überlegungen zu C. 3.42.8 pr.-1, in Isola L. (Hg.), Testamentsgestaltungen in Römischen Testamenten (= Akten einer Internationalen Tagung zum Römischen Testamentsrecht), Berlin 2022, 95–128.

Kaser M., Knütel R., Lohsse S., Römisches Privatrecht, München 2021^{22}.

Kovarik S., Der Brief in der Urkunde: Zur Briefform in spätantiken Verträgen, in Yiftach-Firanko U. (Hg.), The Letter. Law, State and the Epistolary Format in the Ancient World, Wiesbaden 2013, 201–218.

Knütel R., Stipulatio Poenae. Studien zur römischen Vertragsstrafe, Köln-Wien 1976.

Mitteis L., Reichsrecht und Volksrecht in den östlichen Provinzen des römischen Kaiserreichs, Leipzig 1891.

Nelson H.L.W., Manthe U., Gai institutiones III 88-181. Die Kontraktobligationen. Text und Kommentar, Berlin 1999.

Platschek J., Das Edikt de pecunia constituta. Die römische Erfüllungszusage und ihre Einbettung in den hellenistischen Kreditverkehr, München 2013.

Scheibelreiter Ph., Der ‚ungetreue' Verwahrer. Eine Studie zur Haftungsbegründung im griechischen und frühen römischen Depositenrecht, München 2020.

Rupprecht H.-A., Griechen und Ägypter – Vielfalt des Rechtslebens nach den Papyri, in Thür G. (Hg.), Antike Rechtsgeschichte – Einheit und Vielfalt, Wien 2005, 17–25.

Thielmann G., Die römische Privatauktion, Berlin 1961.

Wolf J.G., Neue Rechtsurkunden aus Pompeji. Tabulae Pompeianae Novae, Darmstadt 2010.

Wolff H.J., Zur Romanisierung des Vertragsrechts der Papyri, ZRG RA 73, 1956, 1–28.

Wolff H.J., Die Grundlagen des griechischen Vertragsrechts, ZRG RA 74, 1957, 26–72.

Yiftach U., Olim tradita fuerunt? On the Obsoletness oft he Sollemnia Verba in Inst. 3.15 pr., JJP 51 (2021) 169–187.

KOSTAS BURASELIS (ATHEN)

CONSTITUTIO ANTONINIANA: IMPERIAL WHIMS AND SCHOLARLY ASSUMPTIONS

Abstract: The epochal Edict of Caracalla (212 AD), the Constitutio Antoniniana, remains a vexed subject of modern scholarship. One of its most tantalizing aspects is how to correlate the scanty literary evidence on it with the famous P.Giss. 40 I, most probably containing a fragmentary form of that edict. The restoration and understanding of the latter (and its grantees) are here brought into closer connection with the important Tabula Banasitana.

Keywords: Constitutio Antoniniana, Caracalla, Cassius Dio, Ulpian, Tabula Banasitana.

I.Introduction

Few epoch-making measures in history have remained so meagerly covered by contemporary (or later) sources and so long controversial in modern scholarship as Caracalla's famous edict dated to 212 (less probably 213) AD, which we have come to know as the *Constitutio Antoniniana* (: CA). It is perhaps telling that even the latter term is a modern creation, a Latin name retroactively coined for this imperial act. However, the development of Roman citizenship policy, that is the gradual extension of the *civitas Romana* to the various subject populations of the Roman empire, truly and dramatically culminates at that point, and appears in a new context from then on.

For the needs of this contribution I have thought it useful to begin with an overview of ancient data and the main modern opinions on the CA, in the latter case especially those published after my own monographic treatment of many relevant problems (first in Greek, 1989, and finally in German, 2007). After this, I am going to offer a new proposal for the restoration of a crucial passage in the basic piece of direct evidence for the CA, P.Giss. 40 I, and to conclude with a concise overall interpretation of Caracalla's decision which follows these thoughts and restoration.

II. Ancient sources on the CA are neatly divided into two main categories: some pieces of literary evidence and an excruciatingly fragmentary papyrus. The former include:[1] (a) a passage of the contemporary (but declaredly hostile to Caracalla) senatorial historian Cassius Dio (77 (78). 9. 5) who mentions the emperor's doubling the inheritance tax owed by Roman citizens, and appends the following remark: οὗ (: τῆς δεκάτης τῶν κληρονομιῶν) ἕνεκα καὶ Ῥωμαίους *πάντας τοὺς ἐν*

[1] For citations of this and the following literary sources see Buraselis 2007, 2–4.

τῇ ἀρχῇ αὐτοῦ, λόγῳ μὲν τιμῶν, ἔργῳ δὲ ὅπως πλείω αὐτῷ καὶ ἐκ τοῦ τοιούτου προσίῃ διὰ τὸ τοὺς ξένους τὰ πολλὰ αὐτῶν μὴ συντελεῖν, ἀπέδειξεν (It was therefore that he also made all his subjects Roman citizens, honouring them in words, but really in order to raise his revenues from that further source [: the –now doubled- *vicesima hereditatum*, thus practically reformed as *decima hereditatum*], for non-Romans were largely free from that obligation). With that note Dio ascribes a purely fiscal motive to the measure, while he himself admits that it was presented (that is, it could also be perceived by contemporaries) as an honour. After all, it was still under Septimius Severus that a decree of the Athenian sacred *gerousia* mentioned Roman citizenship as the highest distinction previously achieved by a specific honorand, who was also variously important in local cult and society (*IG* II^2. 3658: ...τιμηθέντα δὲ ὑπὸ θεοῦ Κομμόδου τῇ Ῥωμαίων πολιτείᾳ).

Another point of Dio's quoted testimony proves to be a constant element of all further literary passages on the CA: Caracalla's decision concerned '*all* his subjects' (πάντας τοὺς ἐν τῇ ἀρχῇ αὐτοῦ). It is thus (b) that the great Severan jurist Ulpian (*Dig.* I 5. 17) epigrammatically touches on it : « *In orbe Romano qui sunt* ex constitutione imperatoris Antonini cives Romani effecti sunt » (All people resident in the Roman world were turned into Roman citizens after a decision of the emperor Antoninus). To note: Antoninus was indeed the official name of Caracalla, which he received due to the effort of Severus' house to appear as the continuation of Marcus Aurelius' family line by adopting the respected *nomen Antoninorum*.

Later authors invariably repeat the general character of the grant and amusingly prefer a 'better' emperor as its intellectual father: thus, (c) Aurelius Victor ascribes it to Marcus Aurelius (in every sense a proper Antoninus), while (d) John Chrysostom refers it back to Hadrian and (e) Justinian himself mentions it as a measure of Antoninus Pius. Other later praises of Roman power and political wisdom like Augustinus' comment in the *De civitate Dei* make no specific mention of the CA and of the emperor behind it but speak unmistakably of a move that provided "a share in citizenship to all inhabitants of the Roman empire (*ad Romanum imperium pertinentes*, ib. 5. 17), thus awarding to all what previously belonged to few".

The dearth of the evidence has already become clear, and is further accentuated by the grave silence of the second important historiographical source on the Severan age, Herodian, who apparently saw no reason to make any mention at all of the CA. There is also no certain hint at the grant in the collection of imperial biographies from late antiquity known as the *Historia Augusta.*

One had then the problematic fortune to see this short catalogue of testimonies enriched by the papyrus already alluded to. This sheet of papyrus, published as P.Giss. 40, was found and sold in Egypt (more precisely, in the area of Upper Egypt) in the beginning of the previous century. It was acquired by the *Oberhessischer Geschichtsverein*, and subsequently kept in the University Library of Giessen. It proved to contain the promulgation of three edicts by Caracalla, identified as such on the basis of other measures of this emperor known from Cassius Dio. The first of these edicts (40 I), with gaps almost ironically gazing at our curiosity, was recognised to contain the CA. Some serious scholars (mainly Elias Bickerman and later Hartmut Wolff) contested this but their doubts seem now to have gone too far.[2]

The preserved words of this text, the basic sense of which emerges with some clarity, mainly testify that: (a) Caracalla himself attributed a religious rationale to his act: he wishes to involve all people of his empire in the cult of the gods of Rome, thus showing the piety corresponding to the effective divine protection of his rule and safety. He then (b) certainly awards Roman citizenship to "all people in the world (*oikoumene*)", precisely: Δίδωμ̣ι τοί[ν]υν ἅπα[σιν τοῖς κατοικοῦσιν τ]ὴ̣ν οἰκουμένη̣ν π[ολιτ]είαν Ῥωμαίων... He proceeds by adding a tantalizingly ill-preserved clause, stating that some status (?) should remain untouched (the participle [μ]ένοντος is certain at this point) with a named exception introduced by the preposition χωρίς. Already the first editor of the papyrus, P. Meyer, restored the latter passage as χωρ[ὶς] τῶν [δε]δ̣ειτ̣ικίων, that is in the sense of involving the exclusion of a category of people from the universal grant of Roman citizenship. Later scholarship has thus embarked on an arduous discussion of the content of this (restored!) term [δε]δ̣ειτ̣ικίων in the Edict of Caracalla on the basis of its meaning in other sources. However these *dediticii* of Caracalla's age should be understood (more on this below), some sort of exception from the grant of citizenship is still the prevalent interpretation of the papyrus at this point, and of the actual decree in respect to its extent. It is thus clear, and significant, that the admittedly scanty but unanimous literary evidence concerning the extent of the imperial measure still contradicts the testimony of the papyrus at this point as restored and interpreted by the majority of scholars so far. The nagging question then remains: if any exception from the grant was so important as to be mentioned specifically in its official pronouncement by the emperor himself, why should this have been constantly absent from its literary echo?

III. The methodical way out of the impasse could only be to look for specific evidence on the results of the edict, above all the eventual existence of free persons of non-Roman status in the empire after the CA or any other signs of a limited range in its application. To begin from the latter issue, the evidence we possess and its repeated and systematic evaluation, also in the format of a detailed statistical analysis by areas of the empire undertaken by Janken Kracker and Markus Scholz (in: Pferdehirt – Kracker – Scholz 2012, 67–75), has decidedly shown that the opposite is the case. The gentilicium of Caracalla, Aurelius, which has been naturally adopted by all new citizens after the grant, has a really overwhelming presence thereafter. This is especially the case, of course, in areas that had remained largely outside the spread of Roman citizenship and at least political Romanization until the CA (as in

2 Cf. now also in this sense all other recent studies on the subject: Imrie 2018; Thür 2021; Besson 2020; Jördens 2022, with further interesting remarks on the whole content of P.Giss. I 40 and the correlation of its documents.

many Greek-speaking provinces of the East). There, apart from the omnipresent Aurelii we find also name formulas which point to the CA as an onomastic landmark, after which the new, Roman form of name, including that gentilicium, was meticulously distinguished from the older onomastic norm in 'Greek style' comprising personal and father's name. The flood of Aurelii repeatedly forced these new Romans themselves to append in official documents as a sort of clarification of identity their old name form or at least elements of it (e.g. by stating that someone appearing now as 'Aurelius X' used to appear as 'X son of Y', especially in accordance with the Greek onomastic tradition).[3]

Do we have then any signs of exclusion of free persons in the empire from Roman citizenship after Caracalla's grant? There are some such indications but their precise interpretation is not as simple as it might at first appear.[4] In fact, we know of cases after the CA where e.g. auxiliary army units proudly added the label *c.R.* (:*civium Romanorum*) after their official title, whereas we find also dedications of persons still self-styled as *peregrini*, e.g. on an inscription of 232 AD from Belgica[5]: 'genio pagi Dervete(nsis) peregrini qui pos(uerunt) vico Soliciae'. Does this mean that the old distinctions were still, at least partially, in force? Concerning the former case, the bombastic projection of the Roman identity certainly does not signify a parallel retention of the old status by other soldiers of the empire. Persons appearing as *peregrini* on the Roman periphery, on the other hand, may still ascribe themselves to an older-style official identity, which they had no compelling reason to abandon; nor need they become conscious of their new identity soon after the enactment of the CA.

Furthermore, the Roman state itself seems sometimes to have continued the practice of distinguishing in general between 'Romans' and 'provincials' (or specific regional populations) within the Roman empire, thus not encouraging any deeper or conscious integration of these provincials into a common *Romanitas*. Two examples of such a practice may illustrate the point. Herodian (7.7.5) relates that the Roman senate tried in 238 AD to oppose Maximinus Thrax and gain the support of the provinces with letters sent to them in which the old distinction was pointedly used: 'Romans' are there understood as the residents and administrators of the imperial centre in the interest of the whole empire while the populations of the provinces are perceived simply and expressly as their traditionally loyal subjects. For reasons of actual politics the status of full legal Roman citizens as possessed by all (or even

---

3 Detailed study of these onomastic formulas: Buraselis 2007, 108–118.

4 The most systematic older studies of the evidence on people of foreign status (*peregrini*) in the Roman Empire after the CA and the relevant hypothetical category of 'peregrini dediticii'(cf. below) after Caracalla's Edict remain those by Sasse 1958, 68–124 and then Wolff 1976, 35–62, 210–238; cf. recently also Thür 2021. A detailed examination of data, scope and results of the CA in the context of a systematic juristic interpretation of Roman citizenship policy in the imperial period has been provided by Marotta 2009, 101–151.

5 CIL XIII. I,2, 4679 (area of Solicia, mod. Soulosse). Cf. Sherwin-White 1973^2, 388.

almost all on the above assumption) free provincials after the CA could apparently be overlooked.[6] Still much later, in a precious document (*SEG* 9. 356) from Ptolemais in Cyrenaica under Anastasius I (501 AD) one finds again such an explicit distinction made between 'Romans' and 'Egyptians' in the regulations of life and contact with their barbarian neighbours that were imposed on the inhabitants of that garrison-city: neither 'Romans' nor 'Egyptians' nor anyone else should have free access to the barbarian territory without a specific order, for obvious reasons of security. It should be clear that the distinction between 'Romans' and 'Egyptians' cannot have had any strictly legal sense here. Most probably, it refers to the provenience of the persons concerned: residents from other Roman areas are distinguished from 'local' people, and in practice this takes on the form of describing the former as 'Romans' and the latter as 'Egyptians'. Therefore even new efforts[7] to recognize here supporting evidence for a large exclusion of local populations from Roman citizenship after the CA carry no conviction.

Of course, the status of free persons, especially barbarian soldiers, who had entered and served the Roman Empire after the CA constitutes a further problem. The traditional view in relevant scholarship has been that they too only gradually attained the award of Roman citizenship, while at first, quite naturally, they were seen as *peregrini.* The remark of Sidonius Apollinaris in the second half of the fifth century AD that "(Rome is) the one community of the whole world in which only slaves and barbarians are foreigners (*peregrinantur*)"[8] at least indicates a non-automatic integration of barbarians into a common *Romanitas*. However, a penetrating study by Ralph W. Mathisen (2012) has shown that curiously we do not possess any explicit evidence on citizenship grants subsequent to the CA. Military diplomas providing discharged auxiliaries with the *civitas Romana* even some years after 212 should rather be attributed to a sort of 'bureaucratic inertia'.[9]Mathisen's conclusion was that the CA had in later periods acquired retrospective force and thus built the basis for the implicit integration of further non-Romans into a common Roman identity after a certain process of assimilation. One could best formulate realities by

6 In more detail: Buraselis 2001.

7 Purpura 2013. This is partly a return to old reserves on the inclusion of especially rural populations of the empire in the beneficiaries of the CA, which have already been aptly refuted by Wolff 1976, 35–62.

8 Sid. Apoll., *Epist.* I. 6. 2 (where Sidonius doubts the sense of peregrination if used for a Roman of the periphery travelling to Rome): '...si tamen senatorii seminis homo, qui cotidie trabeatis proavorum imaginibus ingeritur, iuste dicere potest semet peregrinatum, si semel et in iuventa viderit domicilium legum, gymnasium litterarum, curiam dignitatum,verticem mundi, patriam libertatis, *in qua unica totius orbis civitate soli barbari et servi peregrinantur*' (ca. 459 AD). Cf. Sherwin-White 1973², 386–7. The English translation in the text is that by W.B. Anderson in the LCL volume.

9 Thus Mathisen 2012, 746, 756 (n. 19). The objections to such a view by (i.a.) Wolff 1976, 48 cannot convince if one allows for an understandable transitional period of administrative adjustment to such a universal change.

saying that all inhabitants of the Roman Empire had become potential Romans due to Caracalla's edict. Thus besides its role as forming an immediate measure to regulate some status problems of its age, the CA seems to have created a sort of weighty precedent or even an administrative maxim with far-reaching consequences for the continuation of imperial policy versus new demographic injections.

IV. If we were then to understand, on the basis of these research results, that even after its issue the CA meant not only the end of the previous selective Roman citizenship policy, mainly on the basis of specific merits already presented by new citizens, but also the beginning of a similarly 'all-inclusive' imperial strategy vis-à-vis new settlers in the Roman world, the question as to who the *dediticii* of 212 might have been returns in a more acute form. It has already been correctly observed that the term cannot refer to barbarians surrendering themselves to the Romans and installed on Roman soil. Why should Rome have excluded them from citizenship now whereas already in the Republican period the *deditio* of enemies of Rome carried no impediment to their acquisition of citizenship if that had indeed been constantly perceived as in the Roman interest? Kuhlmann 2011 has aptly pointed to the explicit award of the *civitas Romana* to such a form of *dediticii* already in the age of Cinna as reported by Granius Licinianus (lib. 35). As historians we could add the whole dramatic and characteristic piece of Roman policy concluding the Social War through the lex Plautia Papiria in 89 BC: Rome did not then deny even its recent enemies in Italy the benefit of Roman citizenship.

Therefore the only way discovered to save the existence of the (restored!) *dediticii* of 212 has been to fill their apparently important but elusive entity with life borrowed from the jurist's Gaius description of them in his *Institutiones*. For the great jurist of the second century AD mentions there (1.13–14), according to the Lex Aelia Sentia of Augustus (4 AD), a class of freedmen who had been liberated despite various forms of ignominious conduct but who had been given only the status of 'peregrini dediticii', that is of previous enemies of the Roman people subjected to Rome through a final *deditio*. These 'we shall never call citizens', declares Gaius categorically. However, it should be clear that the retention of this exclusion did not entail in Gaius' time any such retrospective parallel status of the original foreign enemies of Rome, and their natural or practical successors. The exclusion was in force only in regard to freedmen who had been severely punished before the time of their manumission, and thus they were verbally or ideally stigmatized. Why should then Caracalla in an edict concerned with the inclusion of many new *free* men into the civitas Romana have specifically referred to this (most probably very limited) subcategory of *freedmen* whose status was already clearly defined? Such a juristic meticulous precision does not seem to match the panegyric and general character of the emperor's act and style.

Gerhard Thür has recently considered the possibility of fresh evidence on these problematic *dediticii*. In an original and careful study, he evaluated in this respect the epigraphic dossier of the manumissions from the Sanctuary of the Μήτηρ Θεῶν Αὐτόχθων at Leukopetra (near Beroia) in the Roman Province of Macedonia as testimonies for the existence of such an important category of possible claimants to the civitas Romana after 212 whose final status would have necessitated an extra mention in Caracalla's Edict, and consequent further administrative care. Specifically, he proposed to understand a decree of the governor of Macedonia, M. Ulpius Tertullianus Aquila, just alluded to in these inscriptions and dated in the year of the *Constitutio Antoniniana,* as stemming from the need to define the status of manumitted slaves who would have belonged to the category of *peregrini dediticii* (after Gaius, see above) and would have thus remained juristically and socially barred from the euergetic measure of Caracalla.

However, this interpretation is not necessary. It seems more natural to understand Aquila's decision rather as having regulated identity problems that had arisen from the former and new (after the CA) official nomenclature of the numerous Roman citizens now appearing and possessing a new official Roman name (Aurelius+cognomen instead of the old Greek form 'X son of Y', cf. above). Why should the detail of manumitted *dediticii* have been such a pressing problem in Macedonia –as far as we know, only there!– to have caused the local governor's clearing intervention?

After all these considerations, it seems to me inescapable to conclude that the hypothetical *dediticii* of the CA simply do not fit into any reasonable pattern within that measure on the basis of the existing evidence.[10]

V. A precious new access to the rationale of Roman imperial grants of citizenship was opened up through the publication of an inscription (its text already easily accessible as *An.Ép.* 1971, 534) from Banasa in Mauretania Tingitana (modern Morocco), which has come now to be generally known as the *Tabula Banasitana.*[11] This is a bronze tablet inscribed with official texts concerning the grant of citizenship and concomitant privileges under M. Aurelius and Commodus to the chief of a local tribe (the Zegrenses) and to members of his family. The tablet includes first two imperial letters on the subject: from M. Aurelius and L. Verus and then from Marcus and Commodus as co-emperors, directed to the Roman provincial governors involved, and announcing the award of the new status. Both texts mention the grant of citizenship in connection with a clause guaranteeing the parallel continuation of the local legal status of the grantees through the formula: *salvo iure gentis* ('while local rights remain untouched'). A specific analysis of a part of this retained local status then appears in the third document of the *Tabula.* Now, this document copies a relevant entry from the central archive of such

---

[10] The possibility of a reference to the status of the dediticii in the CA and its reasoning as announced by Caracalla in P.Giss. 40 I has now also been rejected in detail by Besson 2020, 284–88.

[11] Seston – Euzennat 1972.

citizenship grants (*commentarius civitate Romana donatorum*) kept at Rome by the imperial administration, and concludes with the expanded formula: "…his civitatem Romanam dedimus, salvo iure gentis, *sine diminutione tributorum et vect[i]galium populi et fisci*". It is evident that the preservation of 'local rights' entailed here also the further obligation to pay the tributes and taxes owed by provincials to Rome. In other words, Roman citizenship was now granted without any financial loss to the imperial budget. This does not seem to have been so from the beginning of the imperial period (although Augustus' third Cyrenaean Edict already pointed to such a direction of policy!) but the considerably aggravated conditions of the later second century AD had obviously imposed by now a spirit of fiscal austerity.

The affinity, even the similarity, of the latter formula with the wording of the CA even as it appears in fragmentary form in the P. Giss. 40 I occurred to scholars quite early on. The *doyen* of Roman citizenship specialists in the 20th century, A.N. Sherwin White, devoted a special article (Sherwin-White 1973) to this shortly after the publication of the *Tabula Banasitana*. He also recognized the repetition of the same phrasal structure, that is: grant plus condition of continuing local rights/obligations. However, he still adhered to the existing interpretation and tried somehow to integrate the notion of the *dediticii* within this pattern since he believed that some group of persons who were excepted from the grant of Caracalla and not a restrictive clause concerning the Roman rights of new Roman citizens should fit the meaning of the context.

Others were more daring. The great American scholar, and real specialist on edicts of Roman emperors, James H. Oliver believed that Caracalla's edict revived the spirit of the condition lately and wisely appended to the citizenship awards as now revealed by the *Tabula Banasitana*. He tried therefore (Oliver 1972) to offer an alternative restoration in the papyrus disposing of the 'mysterious' (so Sherwin White himself!) and evidently very problematic *dediticii*. Instead he proposed reading: [ἀδ]δ̣ειτ̣ικίων, that is to substitute the Hellenized Latin term *dediticii,* as a mention of a group of people not benefiting from the CA, with *additicia,* being here in effect the genitive plural of a Latin term transliterated into Greek. He interpreted this as referring to 'additional rights', meaning additional privileges which were not accorded the new citizens of Caracalla's age. In other words, 'citizenship without extras'. Although Oliver's proposal has recently also been adopted by Kuhlmann (without further discussion) and Imrie,[12] it still seems to me difficult to accept. It is clear that we should think here of a Latin-Greek term that fits the context; the fact, therefore, that we do not have any parallels for a Greek term ἀδδειτίκιος/-α is not the real problem. Nonetheless, the mention of 'additional privileges' that should not be further enjoyed seems to me too vague and imprecise as an administrative caveat if only the fiscal interests of the Roman state were under consideration here. The nature of these 'additions' would remain confusingly unspecified. Various privileges

---

12 Imrie 2018, esp. 150.

of local communities and individuals in the provinces might be misunderstood (or misrepresented) as also covered by such a clumsily general formula. This appears also in e.g. Kuhlmann's effort to understand its sense in the following, rather unsatisfactory way: "..die Formel...garantiert dagegen Vorteile und Privilegien gegenüber den Heimatgemeinden und -provinzen"[13]. This does not correspond to the administrative-fiscal logic of the Tabula Banasitana: there the preservation of the local status (*ius gentis*) is carefully distinguished from the sense of any further (and denied!) privileges concerning Roman revenues. The same should also be the case in the CA.

Therefore, I would finally think of reading here simply [ῥε]δειτικίων, that is to restore again a Greek-Latin term (*rediticia*). Admittedly, this too is not so far attested in the extant ancient texts, but here it would summarily, and most sensibly, refer to the revenues, the *reditus* of the Roman state. That the latter term might generally comprise all tributes and taxes flowing into the state treasuries (both the *aerarium* and the *fiscus*) emerges clearly from various literary and epigraphic passages: e.g. in Suetonius (*Cal.* 41. 1) we find an epigrammatic mention of "Caesaris reditus", while Velleius Paterculus (2. 39.2) mentions that Augustus presented to the state treasury the income from various provinces: "... in aerarium reditus contulit".[14] Thus the creation of such a derivative of *reditus* as a generic term would easily occur to contemporaries.[15] A relevant clause would then apply through one comprehensive word the same idea of fiscal austerity to the Aurelii of Caracalla as had already been the norm under his genuine Antonine forerunners.

VI. Some conclusions may be sketched here. On the basis of all the above considerations an alternative restoration of l. 8/9 of Pap. Giss. 40 I would run: ...π[ολιτ]είαν Ῥωμαίων [μ]ένοντος/ [παντὸς γένους δικαιωμ]άτων χωρὶς τῶν [ῥε]δειτικίων. The sense would then be: "(I offer) the Roman citizenship, while any sort of (other) rights are retained, apart from those concerning state revenues". The correspondence between the wording of the sober maxim of Roman administration presented in the *Tabula Banasitana* and Caracalla's new measure would be a perfect fit.

Such a view then cuts here an old 'Gordian knot' as the restored and notorious *dediticii* of P.Giss. 40 I have never been fully understood as a clear and unique category of exception from the grant of Caracalla, which appears unanimously as a

---

13 Kuhlmann 2011, 272.

14 Cf. also the similar use of *reditus* in Tac., *Ann.* 15. 18.3 and later the title of CJ 11.70: 'De diversis praediis urbanis et rusticis templorum et civitatum et *omni reditu civili'*. Epigraphic examples collected in *Oxford Latin Dictionary* (1968), s.v. reditus, 3 (p. 1592).

15 Although it represents a later, medieval usage, one could also consider here the generic terms *reddita*, *red(d)ituarius*, *redditualis* to describe the financial obligations of tenants/ the tenants themselves in respect to their lord: Du Cange, *Glossarium mediae et infimae latinitatis*, VI, repr. 1954 s.vv.; *Lexicon Latinitatis Nederlandicae Medii Aevi*, VII (2002), s.vv.

universal award in all literary sources. What else we have come to study in detail and understand of the extension of the citizenship to barbarians (also after the CA) contradicts the idea of such an original personal exclusion.

In the end, Caracalla's decision appears to be both conservative (in its administrative logic) and innovative (in its extent), the act of a paradoxical ´conservative revolutionary` as Gerhard Thür has aptly remarked.[16] Its separation from any idea of financial privilege for the new citizens may thus better explain both the absence of any widespread popular positive reactions to it as also the understandable suspicion of the contemporaries, echoed by Cassius Dio, that its secret aim was merely to raise the state revenues through subjecting the new citizens also to the taxes to date owed only by *cives Romani*. It facilitated social mobility and cohesion inside the Roman empire, especially in a long perspective,[17] but without immediate financial gains for the new citizens, rather the opposite.[18] On the other hand, its ideological Severan background, the climate of 'l'Empire égalitaire' as it has aptly been called already by A. Piganiol (and studied by later scholars in detail),[19] should not be underestimated. The genesis of imperial 'whims' may finally be no less intriguing (but retraceable) than that of scholarly assumptions.[20]

kburasel@arch.uoa.gr

BIBLIOGRAPHY

Besson, A., Constitutio Antoniniana. *L'universalisation de la citoyenneté romaine au 3e siècle* (Schweizerische Beiträge zur Altertumswissenschaft, 52), Basel 2020.

Buraselis, K., "Πείθεσθαι Ρωμαίοις. Considerations on the Official Relation of Rome to the provinces before and after the Constitutio Antoniniana", in: A. Barzanò et al. (eds.), *Identità e valori. Fattori di aggregazione e fattori di crisi nell`esperienza politica antica*, Roma 2001, 183–193.

[16] Thür 2021, 10.

[17] Humfress 2013 has tried to devalue the CA as a turning-point in the development of Roman law and its more general application in the empire. However, local and social factors may have been inextricably connected with this impact of Roman legal thought and practice on the life of all the empire's inhabitants even before the CA but the change after 212 AD did remain big enough.

[18] The fiscal aspects of the CA as its proper and main interpretive background have now been re-emphasized by both Imrie 2018 and Besson 2020 (though mitigated as esp. 376). However, I still think it would be misguided to attribute to these aspects a preponderant position in the historical reasoning of Caracalla's decision. We should not remain eternal victims of Cassius Dio's distinctly prejudiced authority.

[19] An analytical treatment of this aspect: Buraselis 2007, 14–87.

[20] I thank Dorothy Thompson for a generous revision of my original English text; of course, all remaining errors are mine.

Buraselis, K., ΘΕΙΑ ΔΩΡΕΑ, *das göttlich-kaiserliche Geschenk. Studien zur Politik der Severer und zur* Constitutio Antoniniana, Wien 2007.

Humfress, C., 'Laws' Empire: Roman Universalism and Legal Practice', in: P.J. du Plessis (ed.), *New Frontiers. Law and Society in the Roman World*, Edinburgh 2013, 73–101.

Imrie, Al., *The Antonine Constitution. An Edict for the Caracallan Empire*, Leiden 2018.

Jördens, A., 'P.Giss. I 40: der *status quaestionis*', *Quaderni Lupiensi di Storia e Diritto*, 12 (2022), 305–335.

Kuhlmann, P., 'Papyrologie – Philologie – Alte Geschichte', in: Egelhaaf-Gaiser, Ul., et al. (eds.), *Kultur der Antike. Transdisziplinäres Arbeiten in den Altertumswissenschaften*, Berlin 2011, 257–277.

Marotta, V., *La cittadinanza romana in età imperiale (secoli I–III). Una sintesi*, Torino 2009.

Mathisen, R.W., 'Concepts of Citizenship', in: Johnson, S.F. (ed.), *The Oxford Handbook of Late Antiquity*, Oxford 2012, 744–63.

Oliver, J.H., 'Text of the Tabula Banasitana, A.D. 177', *AJPh* 93 (1972), 336–40.

Oliver, J.H., *Greek Constitutions of Early Roman Emperors from Inscriptions and Papyri*, Philadelphia 1989.

Pferdehirt, B. – Kracker, J. – Scholz, M., 'Neubürger mit Beisterung? Die Auswirkungen der *Constitutio Antoniniana* auf das Indiviuum', in: Pferdehirt – Scholz (2012), 59–75.

Pferdehirt, B. – Scholz, M. (eds.), *Bürgerrecht und Krise. Die* Constitutio Antoniniana *212 n. Chr. und ihre innenpolitischen Folgen*, Mainz 2012.

Purpura, G., 'Il P. Giss. 40, I', *Iuris Antiqui Historia* 5 (2013), 73–85.

Seston, W. – Euzennat, M., 'Un dossier de la chancellerie romaine, la *Tabula Banasitana*, étude de diplomatique', *CRAI* 1971 (publ. 1972), 468–490.

Sherwin-White, A.N., *The Roman Citizenship*, Oxford 1973^2.

Sherwin-White, A.N., 'The *Tabula* of Banasa and the *Constitutio Antoniniana*', JRS 63 (1973), 86–98.

Sasse, C., *Die Constitutio Antoniniana. Eine Untersuchung über den Umfang der Bürgerrechtsverleihung auf Grund des Papyrus Giss. 40 I*, Wiesbaden 1958.

Swain, S. – Harrison, St. – Elsner, J. (eds.), *Severan Culture*, Cambridge 2007.

Thür, G., The *dediticii* in *P.Giss.* 40 I 7–9, in: K. Harter-Uibopuu – W. Riess (Hrsg.), *Symposion 2019,* Wien 2021, 501–516.

Wolff, H. 1976, *Die Constitutio Antoniniana und Papyrus Gissensis 40 I*, (Diss.), Köln 1976.

LINA GIRDVAINYTE (EDINBURGH)

RIGHTS, OBLIGATIONS, AND THE ANTONINE CONSTITUTION: RESPONSE TO KOSTAS BURASELIS

Just when you think there cannot possibly be anything new to add to the existing debates concerning the 'divine gift' of citizenship by the emperor Caracalla in 212 CE—the fragmentary record of which has arguably received more scholarly attention than any other surviving documentary papyrus[1]—professor Kostas Buraselis proposes a new reading of one of the most problematic and widely debated lacunas in the text. In his thought-provoking paper, Buraselis revisits the famous citizenship papyrus (*P.Giss.* 40, col. I), and suggests a new reconstruction of lines 8–9, one which claims to align Caracalla's measure more closely with "the wording of the maxim of Roman administration presented in the *Tabula Banasitana*" of 177 CE (p. 9), thus better fitting the immediate context as well as the subsequent reception of the enactment.

I start by evaluating the current *status quo* with regards to the reading of the lines in question. I then turn to Buraselis' arguments in favour of rejecting the prevailing [δε]δ̣ειτ̣ικίων restoration in line 9, and present some additional reasons as to why this reading has been criticised in some of the most recent scholarship on the *Constitutio Antoniniana* (henceforth, the *CA*). Then, turning to Buraselis' proposed restoration, I share some of my concerns, particularly with regards to the beginning of line 9. Finally, I highlight some avenues of research which may perhaps be more productive in estimating the overall impact of the *CA*, irrespective of how we choose to interpret the much debated lacuna in the papyrus.

Despite some diverging restorations over the years,[2] lines 7 to 9 of *P.Giss.* 40, col. I, have been read and understood as follows:

> δίδωμ̣ι τοῖ]ς σ]υνάπα||[σιν τοῖς κατοικοῦσιν? τ]ὴν οἰκουμέν̣ην π[ολει]τ̣είαν Ῥωμαίων μ̣έ̣νοντος | [τοῦ δικαίου τῶν πολιτευμ]άτων̣ χωρ[ὶς] τῶν [..]δ̣ειτ̣ικίων (Kuhlmann 1994, 222)

> "Ich verleihe allen [… im] Reich das Römische Bürgerrecht. Dabei behalten [die Rechtsansprüche der Gemeinwesen] ihre Gültigkeit abgesehen von den [..]" (Kuhlmann 1994, 223)

[1] Bryen 2016, 29.

[2] Compare, e.g., Meyer 1920, Wilhelm 1934, Magie 1950, and van Minnen 2016, among others.

In English, this could be translated as:

> "I bestow upon everyone inhabiting the (Roman) world the citizenship of the Romans, the rights of the communities remaining intact, except … (?)"

Alternatively, given that χωρίς in Greek can also have the meaning of 'besides' or 'independently of', the phrase might also be understood as:

> "I bestow upon everyone inhabiting the (Roman) world the citizenship of the Romans, the rights of the communities remaining intact, independently of … (?)"

I will come back to this point later. The earliest and most widely accepted restoration of [..]δ̣ειτ̣ικίων at the end of the clause is the genitive plural of a Hellenised version of the Latin *dediticius*:

> δίδωμ̣ι τοῖ[ς σ]υνάπα|[σιν τοῖς κατοικοῦσιν? τ]ὴ̣ν οἰκουμέν̣ην π[ολει]τ̣είαν Ῥωμαίων μ̣έ̣νοντος | [τοῦ δικαίου τῶν πολιτευμ]άτων̣ χωρ[ὶς] τῶν [δε]δ̣ειτ̣ικίων

> "I bestow upon everyone inhabiting the (Roman) world the citizenship of the Romans, the rights of the communities remaining intact, except for the *dediticii*."

More recently, an alternative restoration was proposed by Gerhard Thür, who maintained the [δε]δ̣ειτ̣ικίων, but modified the reading of the preceding lacunas in lines 8 and 9:[3]

> δίδωμ̣ι τοῖ[ς σ]υνάπα|[σιν ἐλευθέροις καθ' ὅλην τ]ὴ̣ν οἰκουμέν̣ην π[ολει]τ̣είαν Ῥωμαίων μ̣έ̣νοντος | [οὐδενὸς ἄνευ τῶν δικαιωμ]άτων̣ χωρ[ὶς] τῶν [δε]δ̣ειτ̣ικίων.

> "I donate every free person all over the (Roman) world Roman citizenship so that nobody shall remain without the privileges except dishonourable freedmen."[4]

The precise identity of this category of people has been much debated in modern scholarship. While some have argued that this refers to Rome's conquered external enemies,[5] others suggested this should rather be taken to mean slaves who had been severely punished by their masters prior to their manumission.[6] Others yet, suggested the term should be read in a general sense to mean all those deemed unworthy of

---

[3] Thür 2021, 513–514, partly based on Magie 1950, vol. II, 1555–1556; for a sound critique of this restoration: Sänger 2021.

[4] Thür 2021, 514 n. 60.

[5] Buraselis 2007, 7; van Minnen 2016, 219.

[6] Bickermann 1926, Kunkel 1935, and now Thür 2021, on the basis of Gaius *Inst.* 1.15 & 25–26.

Roman citizenship.[7] Regardless of its precise meaning, the restoration [δε]δ̣ειτ̣ικίων has been accepted by most scholars who discuss the impact of the *CA* more generally.[8] In other words, the *communis opinio* still holds that "the *dediticii* (whoever they may be) are excluded from the gift of Roman citizenship".[9]

However, with the recent upsurge in the studies of Roman citizenship, including the consequences of its universal extension, there has also been an upsurge in scholarly treatments that are considerably more cautious in accepting the original restoration in question. Buraselis' own rationale behind rejecting [δε]δ̣ειτ̣ικίων is two-fold. First, he rightly points out that no exception to the extension of citizenship is ever alluded to in any of the literary sources which mention the grant, all of which unanimously present it as universal. Secondly, he argues that the exclusion of "this (most probably very limited) subcategory of freedmen whose status was already clearly defined … does not seem to match the panegyric and general character of the emperor's act and style" (p. 6). Further, equally convincing arguments can be added to these.

For an argument that a particular type of freedmen, i.e. *dediticii* or *qui dediticiorum numero sunt* were excluded from the *CA* one must assume that other types of freed slaves were not. Thus, in his discussion of the very same lacunae in the citizenship papyrus, Gerhard Thür maintained that the *CA* extended Roman citizenship "also to peregrine freedmen", such as those manumitted in Greek sanctuaries.[10] In light of this argument, it might be worth briefly exploring the potential impact of the *CA* on freed slaves, more generally. Let us start with the so-called Junian Latins, or informally manumitted slaves of Roman citizens, who acquired Latin status, but were nonetheless barred from immediate access to full citizenship.[11] In his discussion of Junian Latins, Egbert Koops pointed out that, in the municipal context, a Latin patron who manumitted his slave, thereby creating a Junian Latin, retained his patronal rights over the freedman even if the latter acquired full citizenship subsequently (*Lex Irn.* 97.27–28). In view of this and similar traditions, Koops argued that "it is highly unlikely that the biggest imperial grant of citizenship of all, the *constitutio Antoniniana*, brought any real difference in status to Junian Latins living at the time"; otherwise, he rightly adds, "patrons would have been in uproar".[12] The same, by extension, should apply to peregrine freedmen: if they were 'transformed' to Roman citizens by the very same imperial enactment as their former masters, they too would have been required to maintain their freedmen obligations. Otherwise, the *CA* would have placed the freedmen and their former

7 Sänger 2021, in response to Thür 2021.

8 Thus, e.g., Blanco-Pérez 2019.

9 Thür 2019, 508.

10 Thür 2021, 511–513, with particular reference to 'sacred' manumissions from Leukopetra in Macedonia, to which I will come back shortly.

11 For ways in which they could eventually accede to it, see, e.g. Sirks 1983 and Koops 2014.

12 Koops 2014, 124.

masters on the same legal footing, which is hardly conceivable. Furthermore, on the assumption that peregrine freedmen were included in Caracalla's grant, they would have nonetheless remained barred from local citizenships, which would have led to a situation parallel to that of formally manumitted slaves of Roman citizens in the provinces prior to 212 CE.[13]

As Arnaud Besson pointed out in his very recent monograph on the *CA*, from the point of view of the legal consistency of the text, it seems odd that the enactment would specifically address the status of *dediticii*, but say nothing of the other freed statuses or conditions which continued to exist following the grant.[14] Admittedly, given the fragmentary state of the papyrus, we cannot be certain that the condition of Junian Latins was not dealt with elsewhere in the text. However, the technical part of the edict seemingly ends here and another clause begins, which makes it less likely that other categories of freed slaves were returned to later on.[15] Ultimately, since the conditions of Junian Latins as well as the *dediticii* were only formally abrogated by Justinian (*Inst. Just.* 1.5.3; *CJ* 7.5-6), it seems reasonable enough to assume that the Antonine Constitution left these two freedmen statuses unchanged. As noted recently by Rose MacLean, the *CA* "did nothing to alter the legal conditions under which ex-slaves gained Roman citizenship or were barred from the rewards that it offered".[16] Given that the freedmen *dediticiorum numero* were, in any case, already excluded from ever obtaining Roman citizenship, whether by law, *senatus consultum* or an imperial constitution (Gai. *Inst.* 1.15 & 26, cf. Ulp. *Epitome* I,14), their exclusion from the universal citizenship grant would have hardly required an explicit mention in Caracalla's enactment.

Though Thür's proposal to see the *CA* as "harmonizing Roman and peregrine, primarily Greek, ways of manumission" is perhaps going a step too far, some sort of harmonisation of Roman and peregrine manumission practices was, indeed, attempted at regional level, by one Tertullianus Aquila, the governor of Macedonia in 212/3 CE. Discarding Thür's arguments that Aquila's regulation, referred to as *keleusis*, first, and then as *apophasis* in a series of manumission records from Leukopetra was meant to ensure that "no dishonorable freedman, no person *dediticiorum numero*, should become Roman citizen",[17] Buraselis proposes to understand Aquila's measure "as having regulated identity problems that had arisen from the former and new (after the *CA*) official nomenclature of the numerous

---

13 That formally freed slaves of Roman citizens did not automatically become citizens of the *poleis* is evident from an inscription from Sillyon in Pamphylia, where the two categories of freedmen—*vindictarii* and *apeleutheroi*—appear side by side: *IGR* III, 801, second c. CE.

14 Besson 2020, 42–43; this point was already raised by Marotta 2017, 467.

15 Cf. Besson 2020, 42.

16 MacLean 2021, 168.

17 Thür 2021, 511, cf. p. 512. For the Leukopetran manumission inscriptions: Petsas et al. 2000, with a summary of their main findings in *SEG* 50–597.

Roman citizens now appearing and possessing a new official Roman name" (p. 7). Since the slaves in these records are traditionally identified by their servile name, origin, and mode of acquisition (before as well as after 212 CE), the said identity problems would have primarily concerned slave owners, present and former.[18]

However, upon manumission, the slaves freed at the sanctuary by Roman citizens would assume the status of Junian Latins and, as such, would acquire the right to use the *tria nomina*, which would make them particularly difficult to distinguish from Roman citizens. Nomenclature aside, Junian Latins were subject to a particular set of Roman legal regulations concerning property (which was to return to their former masters upon their death: Gai. *Inst.* 1.22–24; 3.56) as well as potential ways for them to acquire full Roman citizenship in the future (Gai. *Inst.* 1.28–35, 1.80). Might claims related to this particular status have been what was at stake? Granted, a substantial proportion of sacred manumissions recorded at the sanctuary of Leukopetra prior to 212 CE were already performed by Roman citizens.[19] In that sense, potential issues concerning the status of informally manumitted slaves of Roman citizens in the provinces was nothing new. But the sheer number of claimants to the Junian Latin status would have exploded following the universal extension of Roman citizenship, which may have warranted more stringent regulations on ground level.

Be that as it may, the ordinance of the governor of 212/3 CE seemingly regulated the way that sacred manumissions in Macedonia were performed by prescribing one or more specific procedures to be followed.[20] One provision that most likely emanated from Aquila's regulation is the publication of a letter of intent, referred to as πιττάκιον or γραμματεῖον, together with any other relevant documents, either at the temple itself or at the Kaisareion at Beroia, for a period of thirty days before the manumission could take place.[21] The thirty-day window allowed to bring opposing claims is attested in a number of Roman ordinances.[22] From the point of view of provincial administration, ensuring maximum publicity of any legal act or transaction served the practical purpose of allowing any opposing claims to arise right away, thus preventing any later disputes. Though

[18] Note, however, that not all people consecrating their slaves by way of reference to Aquila's regulation are Aurelii: see, e.g., *I.Leukopetra* 76, 230 CE.

[19] Namely, twenty-three out of fifty-two: Meyer 2002, 138, cf. Thür 2021, 504.

[20] See, e.g., *I.Leukopetra* 87 (238 CE), where the dedicator's mother and the original owner of the slave girl is said to have performed all the νόμιμα in accordance with Aquila's ordinance (ll. 9–12): ποι|ήσασα τὰ νόμιμα πάντα κα|τὰ τὴν ἀπόφασιν τὴν Τερτυλ|λιανοῦ Ἀκύλα·

[21] Youni 2010, 331–332.

[22] See, e.g., Hadrian's letter to the council of the Macedonians, stipulating that the potential successors to their offices should be informed thirty days in advance (*SEG* 37.593, ll. 8–13), or the edict of the governor of Asia in 136 CE, granting the locals' petition for the right to hold a market, but allowing a period of thirty days to bring any opposing claims (*SEG* 44.977b/d).

only directly attested at Leukopetra, Aquila's regulation may have applied to sacred manumissions throughout the province, as some manumission records from other locales refer to the publication of a πιττάκιον or γραμματεῖον using almost identical phrasing.[23] A more substantial change in procedure would also explain why Aquila's regulation was still referred to decades later, when the issues related to nomenclature or 'identity' were no longer of immediate concern. In any case, the issue dealt with by Aquila's apophasis, whatever its nature may be, was understood to be primarily of local rather than empire-wide concern. Aquila's ἀπόφασις regulated and, in so doing, authorised the continuation of this particular type of local manumission after the universal extension of Roman citizenship, without making any fundamental changes to the practice.

The second and, in my view, more serious issue with reading [δε]δ̣ειτ̣ικίων at the end of line 9 has to do with syntax. That is, syntactically, the χωρίς clause should depend on μ̣έ̣νοντος rather than δίδωμ̣ι, unless one envisages a rather clumsy translation of Latin into Greek, which is unlikely for an imperial edict of such paramount importance. In this sense, somewhat ironically, if the χωρίς clause did, in fact, concern a certain group of people, this would have had to be a privileged rather than a disadvantaged group: that is, they would have been the ones exempt from submitting to the thereby expressly preserved continuation of local obligations.[24]

So much for the *dediticii*. This, however, is not the only possible restoration. An alternative one was proposed by James H. Oliver, who suggested reading [ἀδ]δ̣ειτ̣ικίων, from Latin *additicia*, instead:[25]

> δίδωμ̣ι τοῖ[ς σ]υνάπα|[σιν ἐν τῇ ἀρχῇ μου κατὰ τ]ῆ̣ν οἰκουμένη̣ν π[ολει]τ̣είαν Ῥωμαίων μ̣έ̣νοντος | [τοῦ δικαίου τῶν πολιτευμ]άτων̣ χωρ[ὶς] τῶν [ἀδ]δ̣ειτ̣ικίων

Oliver translated this as follows:

> "I grant to all those [who throughout] the world [are under my rule] Roman citizenship without the [extras], with [the claim of communities] (on the services of their members) remaining unimpaired."[26]

The lack of comparable attestations in Greek need not immediately discard this restoration: Oliver had every reason to point out that "the Latin word *additicia* from Caracalla is no more difficult than *asp<e>ratura* from Hadrian".[27] However, as

---

[23] Thus, e.g., *EKM* II, 156 (247 CE) from Edessa, or *I.Beroia* 53–54 & 56 (248 CE) from Beroia. Cf. Youni 2010, 335.

[24] Cf. Kuhlmann 1994, 236.

[25] Oliver 1972, cf. *id.* 1989, 500.

[26] Oliver 1989, 500.

[27] Oliver 1989, 504, referring to line 25 of *OGIS* II, 484.

rightly noted by Peter van Minnen, Oliver's reading of [ἀδ]δ̣ειṭικίων, taken to mean "Roman citizenship without the [extras]", in the sense of any additional privileges which sometimes accompanied the earlier grants of Roman citizenship, is also dependent on δίδωμι rather than on μ̣ένοντος, which leaves this restoration syntactically flawed as well.[28]

Pointing out that Oliver's restoration was recently adopted by Peter Kuhlmann, Buraselis rejects [ἀδ]δ̣ειṭικίων as "too vague and imprecise as an administrative caveat", which leaves the nature of these additional privileges "confusingly unspecified" (p. 8). Nonetheless, rather than blindly accepting Oliver's interpretation, Kuhlmann suggested that *additicia* might refer not to some privileges attached to Roman citizenship and excluded from Caracalla's grant, but rather to any additional privileges (*iura*, greek: τὰ δίκαια) attached to local communities.[29] In other words, what follows χωρίς might be understood as supplementary to rather than directly opposing the μ̣ένοντος clause, and could thus be read in the sense of any fiscal privileges and immunities preceding the *CA*, which were to continue, in addition to the continued existence of local obligations.[30] A tentative translation of the clause could perhaps read along the lines of "preserving the rights of the communities", i.e. to impose fiscal dues and liturgies on their newly enfranchised members, "except where additional rights exist", e.g. individual immunities from taxes and liturgies, such as those routinely granted by cities to their ambassadors.

In fact, Kuhlmann was not the only one to adopt Oliver's restoration: [ἀδ]δ̣ειṭικίων is now accepted by an increasing number of scholars, including Clifford Ando, Valerio Marotta, Alex Imrie and, most recently, Arnaud Besson.[31] The latter built on Kuhlmann's interpretation and suggested to read the clause as a Greek translation of *salvo iure civitatum praeter additicia*, translated by the author as either "est préservé le droit des communautés, outre les adjonctions" or "est préservé l'ordre juridique des communautés, outre ce qu'il faut y ajouter".[32] This way, according to Besson, the clause can be read as generally protecting the legal relationships between communities, individuals, and imperial authorities, while also allowing for future adaptations, whether at the fiscal level or elsewhere.[33]

Be that as it may, Buraselis discards both earlier readings and proposes, instead, a brand new restoration of the lines in question (p. 9):

> δίδωμι τοῖ[ς σ]υάπα|[ιν τοῖς κατοικῦσιν? τ]ὴν οἰκουμένη̣ν π[ολι]είαν Ῥωμαίων [μ]ένοντος | [παντὸς γένους δικαιωμ]άτων χωρὶς τῶν [ῥε]δειτικίων

---

[28] van Minnen 2016, 219 n. 67.

[29] Kuhlmann 1994, 233–237.

[30] Kuhlmann 1994, 232–233, pointing out the more flexible meaning of χωρίς; cf. Besson 2020, 43.

[31] Ando 2016, Marotta 2016, Imrie 2018, 70–72, Besson 2020, 162–164.

[32] Besson 2020, 163.

[33] Besson 2020, 163.

The author translates this as follows:

> "… (I offer) the Roman citizenship, while any sort of (other) rights are retained, apart from those concerning state revenues"

As Buraselis himself admits, [ῥε]δειτικίων, as derived from Latin *reditus*, is not otherwise attested in Greek. Then again, neither is [ἀδ]δειτικίων or, for that matter [δε]δειτικίων, so this in itself is no particular cause for concern. The fact that such a derivative is unattested in Latin, on the other hand, is considerably more challenging. But my main problem with Buraselis' proposed restoration lies elsewhere: namely, in his reading δικαιωμ]άτων instead of πολιτευμ]άτων. As rightly stressed by Patrick Sänger in his response to Gerhard Thür, the communities were the administrative backbone of the empire.[34] In a similar vein, I cannot imagine that the emperor would set out to preserve "any sort of rights" (παντός γένους δικαιωμ]άτων) without specifying whose rights were at stake.

Buraselis himself argues for interpreting lines 8 to 9 of *P.Giss.* 40, col. I, as corresponding to the so-called reservation clause preserved in the *Tabula Banasitana* of 177 CE, which records the grants of Roman citizenship to the two Juliani, father and son, chieftains of the Zegrenses tribe (*gens Zegrensium*), together with their wives and children (*AE* 1971, 534 = *IAM* II 94, l. 35-37):[35]

> *his civitatem Romanam dedimus, salvo iure gentis, sine diminutione tributorum et vect[i]galium populi et fisci*
>
> "We grant to them Roman citizenship, the right(s) of their tribe remaining intact, without reduction of the tributes and taxes payable to the (Roman) people and the imperial treasury."

If we were to press the analogy with the *Tabula Banasitana* and look for a Greek equivalent of the *salvo iure gentis* clause in the citizenship papyrus, I am not convinced that the term δικαίωμα (pl. δικαιώματα) is a better alternative to either νόμος or δίκαιον suggested in the earlier reconstructions.[36] The rights and privileges of certain communities confirmed by imperial correspondence are routinely referred to as τὰ δίκαια: see, for instance, the letter of Septimius Severus and Caracalla to Aphrodisias, confirming the existing rights of the city (Reynolds 1982, no. 17 (198 CE), l. 11-12: τὰ ὑπάρχοντα δίκα[ια τῇ πόλει ὑμῶν μεμενηκότα μέχρι τῆς] | *vac.* ἡμετέρας ἀρχῆς ἀσάλευτα καὶ ἡμεῖς φυλάττομεν). The reference to δικαιώματα in the petition of the Antinoites in 254 CE, referred to by David Magie

[34] Sänger 2021, 519: "das administrative Rückgrat des römischen Reiches".

[35] The parallel between the two was already drawn by Sherwin-White 1973.

[36] Note also a comparable phrase attested in a mid-first c. BCE petition: BGU VIII, 1827, l. 24–25: μενουσης (= μένοντος) αὐτῆι τοῦ | ἀπὸ τῆς συγγραφῆς δικαί[ου].

and Gerhard Thür in support of their restoration, is considerably less common (*P.Oxy*. 8.1119, l. 15: τῶν ἐξαιρέτων τῆς ἡμετέρας πατρίδος δικαιωμάτων). Note also that, elsewhere in the same papyrus, the rights connected to the Antinoite citizenship are, indeed, referred to as τὰ δίκαια Ἀντινοειτικά.[37]

Rather than preserving 'the local status' (so Buraselis on p. 8), the *salvo iure gentis* clause in the *Tabula Banasitana* was meant to ensure that the beneficiaries' obligations towards the community remained intact by the grant of Roman citizenship.[38] It therefore seems reasonable to assume that the *CA*, which created a comparable situation in all political communities at once, sought to clarify the same point: namely, it is not just *any* rights that were to remain intact following the citizenship grant, but rather the rights of the communities to continuous obligations (liturgies, *munera*) of their members, which may well have differed from one place to another. Thus, for instance, the sophist Philiscus, long-term resident at Athens, was successfully sued by the Macedonian community of Heordaioi over liturgies they considered due to them since Philiscus' mother was a citizen of their community, and they traditionally traced such obligations through maternal lineage (Philostr. *VS* II, 30, cf. Ulpian in *Dig*. 50.1.1.2, who speaks of the right of Delphi and Ilium to trace their citizenships through maternal lineage as *privilegium*). Likewise, in the aforementioned petition, dating to 254 CE, two citizens of Antinoopolis successfully claimed immunity from being subject to liturgies in Alexandria due to the right "to bear office and burdens" (ἄρχειν καὶ λειτουργεῖν) nowhere else except in Antinoopolis, guaranteed to the Antinoites since the foundation of their city by Hadrian.

Gerhard Thür, among others, rightly warned against drawing too close a parallel between the *Tabula Banasitana* and the *CA*, since the former was an individual and the latter a universal grant.[39] However, albeit universal, the grant of Roman citizenship concerned individuals: to quote François Jacques and John Scheid, "la constitution de 212 concernait les personnes, non les cités".[40] But for such a major grant to take effect without causing administrative and legal havoc, it was necessary to specify the beneficiaries' subsequent relationship to their native communities, which continued to form "the administrative backbone of the empire". It was, indeed, a divine gift, and one which implied no loss of revenues or existing privileges for the empire's communities.

Now, as regards specifically Roman revenues: Buraselis notes how, in the *Tabula Banasitana*, "the preservation of the local status (*ius gentis*) is carefully distinguished from the sense of any further (and denied!) privileges concerning Roman revenues" (p. 8). However, as some have rightly pointed out, the *sine*

---

37 *P.Oxy*. 8.1119, l. 28: ἐπισκεψάμενος οὖν εὗρον αὐ]τοὺς ἔχειν δίκαια Ἀντινοειτικὰ ἐκ πατρό[ς].

38 See, most recently, Lavan 2021, 119–120, estimating the formula as "merely a new shorthand for what was by this point normal practice" (p. 120).

39 Thür 2021, 508–509, cf. Sänger 2021, 520.

40 Jacques & Scheid 1990, 281.

diminutione clause in the *Tabula Banasitana* explains or supplements the *salvo iure gentis* clause, rather than opposes it.[41] To quote Peter Kuhlmann: "aus dem Weiterbestehen des Rechts der *gens* resultiert das Fortbestehen von Steuer- oder Abgabeverpflichtungen".[42] In her brilliant treatment of the fiscal semantics of the second century CE, Lisa Eberle convincingly argued that the idea that no Roman citizen should pay the *tributum capitis* had disappeared by the late second century CE.[43] Under the Severans, taxation and liturgies at any given community were ideologically linked with enjoying that community's benefits: this kind of fiscal thought, according to Eberle, "allowed the payment of taxes to constitute communities".[44] This way, taxation could be framed as a form of participation rather than a mark of subjection. By the later second century CE, such participation in one's local community implied, by extension, participation in the empire. In that sense, a separate clause denying the beneficiaries of the citizenship grant any privileges with regards to Roman revenues, which Buraselis suggests to restore in *P.Giss*. 40, col. I, was no longer deemed necessary.[45] It is possible, then, that the universal extension of Roman citizenship encouraged thinking of the empire as a community, with shared rights as well as obligations.[46]

Caracalla's own concern for the well-being of civic communities is evident in his third edict, preserved on the same papyrus, which concerns expulsion of Egyptian farmers from Alexandria (*P.Giss*. 40, col. III, 215 CE). Likewise, imperial confirmations of the rights and privileges of some communities continue well into the later third century CE: letters of Severus Alexander and of Gordian III to Aphrodisias, confirming the continuity of the city's δίκαια, are a case in point (Reynolds 1982, nos. 19, 224 CE, and 20, 239 CE).[47] These δίκαια, continuously upheld by the emperors, were directly tied to local citizenships, which remained essential in claims concerned with local rights and obligations: think again of the

41 Cf. van Minnen 2016, 217 n. 58, though wrongly assuming that the grant covered the entire *gens*.

42 Kuhlmann 1994, 234.

43 Eberle 2021.

44 Eberle 2021, 97.

45 Note, also, that what we have in *P.Giss*. 40, col. I, is the emperor's pronouncement, in all its rhetorical flare, and not an extract from an official register, as is the case with the *Tabula Banasitana*: in fact, the full reservation clause which includes *sine diminutione tributorum et vect[i]galium populi et fisci* only appears in the extract from the *commentarius civitate Romana donatorum*, and not in the imperial letters conferring Roman citizenship on the two African chieftains and their families. Cf. Thür 2021, 508 n. 31. Likewise, Paulus' remark that the colonial status was granted by Caracalla to Antioch *salvis tributis* (*Dig*. 50.15.8.5) had more to do with the status of Roman colonies than with Roman citizenship.

46 Eberle 2021, 97–99.

47 See also Kantor 2016.

δίκαια Ἀντινοειτικά, referred to in the Antinoite petition of 254 CE (*P.Oxy.* 8.1119, l. 28), among similar examples.[48]

Indeed, one of the most interesting questions, to my mind, which might still prove more productive in estimating the overall impact of the *CA*, is that of the relationship between local and Roman citizenships following the universal grant. Even prior to the Antonine Constitution, for the majority of Roman citizens in the provinces it was their local citizenships which carried the most weight in their daily life, actively performed and celebrated in a plethora of political, social, and religious contexts.[49] Rather than disappearing into thin air, this celebration and assertion of local civic identities was arguably endowed with additional significance precisely due to the homogenisation of legal status in 212 CE.[50] The intention behind Caracalla's constitution was never to rid the empire of its regional diversity—which, in itself, was grounded in the variety of 'ancestral' rights of the empire's constituent communities, and of obligations due to those communities (and, by extension, to Rome) by their individual members.

lina.girdvainyte@ed.ac.uk

BIBLIOGRAPHY:

Ando, C., ed. 2016. *Citizenship and empire in Europe 200-1900: The Antonine Constitution after 1800 years. Potsdamer altertumswissenschaftliche Beiträge 54*. Stuttgart.

Besson, A. 2020. *Constitutio Antoniniana, L'universalisation de la citoyenneté romaine au 3ᵉ siècle*. Basel.

Bickermann, E. 1926. *Das Edikt des Kaisers Caracalla in P.Giss. 40*. Berlin.

Blanco-Pérez, A. 2019. "*Salvo iure gentium*: Roman citizenship and civic life before and after the Constitutio Antoniniana", *Al-Masāq* 32:1, 4–17.

Brélaz, C. 2021a. "Experiencing Roman citizenship in the Greek East during the second century CE: Local contexts for a global phenomenon", in *Roman and Local Citizenship in the Long Second Century CE*, ed. M. Lavan and C. Ando, 255–282. New York.

Brélaz, C. 2021b. "Democracy, citizenship(s), and 'patriotism': Civic practices and discourses in the Greek cities under Roman rule', in *Civic identity and civic participation in Late Antiquity and the early Middle Ages*, ed. C. Brélaz and E. Rose, 65–90. Turnhout.

---

[48] Cf. Blanco-Pérez 2019, 17: "What remained unaltered after the CA, however, was the attachment of these new Roman citizens to their fatherlands in the Greek East and the continuing requirement to contribute to their wellbeing through liturgies. <...> the preservation of civic structures actually fortified the survival of the imperial power."

[49] See, especially, Brélaz 2021a.

[50] Brélaz 2021b: 80.

Bryen, A.Z. 2016. "Reading the citizenship papyrus (P.Giss. 40)", in *Citizenship and Empire in Europe 200-1900: The Antonine Constitution after 1800 Years*, ed. C. Ando, 29–43. Stuttgart.

Buraselis, K. 2007. ΘΕΙΑ ΔΩΡΕΑ: *Das göttlich-kaiserliche Geschenk. Studien zur Politik der Severer und zur Constitutio Antoniniana*. Vienna.

Eberle, L.P. 2021. "Fiscal semantics in the long second century: Citizenship, taxation, and the *Constitutio Antoniniana*", in *Roman and Local Citizenship in the Long Second Century* CE, ed. M. Lavan and C. Ando, 69–100. New York.

Imrie, A. 2018. *The Antonine Constitution. An Edict for the Caracallan Empire*. Leiden.

Jacques, F., Scheid, J. 1990. *Rome et l'intégration de l'Empire: 44 av. J.-C.–260 apr. J.-C.* Paris.

Kantor, G. 2016. "Local law in Asia Minor after the *Constitutio Antoniniana*", in *Citizenship and empire in Europe 200-1900: The Antonine Constitution after 1800 years*, ed. C. Ando, 45–62. Stuttgart.

Koops, E. 2014. "Masters and freedmen: Junian Latins and the struggle for citizenship", in *Integration in Rome and in the Roman World*, ed. G. de Kleijn and S. Benoist, 105–126. Leiden.

Kuhlmann, P.A. 1994. *Die Giessener literarischen Papyri und die Caracalla-Erlasse*. Giessen.

Kunkel, W. 1935. *Römisches Recht*. Berlin.

Lavan, M. 2021. "Roman citizenship, marriage, and family networks", in *Roman and Local Citizenship in the Long Second Century CE*, ed. M. Lavan and C. Ando, 103–139. New York.

Magie, D. 1950. *Roman rule in Asia Minor: To the end of the third century after Christ*. Princeton.

MacLean, R. 2021. "Manumission, citizenship, and inheritance: Epigraphic evidence from the Danube", in *Roman and Local Citizenship in the Long Second Century CE*, ed. M. Lavan and C. Ando, 140–164. New York.

Marotta, V. 2016. "Doppia cittadinanza e pluralità degli ordinamenti. La Tabula Banasitana e le linee 7–9 del papiro di Giessen 40 Col. 1", *Archivio Giuridico*, 236, 3-4: 461–491.

Meyer, E.A. 2002. "Review of Petsas et al.", *The American Journal of Philology 123/1*: 136–40.

Meyer, P. 1920. *Juristische Papyri. Erklärung von Urkunden zur Einführung in die juristische Papyruskunde*. Berlin.

Oliver, J.H. 1972. "Text of the Tabula Banasitana, A.D. 177", *The American Journal of Philology* 93: 336–340.

Oliver, J.H. 1989. *Greek constitutions of early Roman emperors from inscriptions and papyri*. Philadelphia.

Petsas, P.M., Hatzopoulos, M.B., Gounaropoulou, L., and P. Paschidis, eds. 2000. *Inscriptions du sanctuaire de la Mère des Dieux autochtone de Leukopétra (Macédoine)*. *Meletemata* 28. Athens.

Reynolds, J. 1982. *Aphrodisias and Rome*. London.

Sänger, P. 2021. "Das Problem der „Schutzklausel" in P.Giss. I 40 Kol. I, 8–9. Antwort auf Gerhard Thür", in *Symposion 2019. Vorträge zur griechischen und hellenistischen Rechtsgeschichte* (Hamburg, 26.–28. August 2019), ed. K. Harter-Uibopuu and W. Rieß, 517–524. Vienna.

Sirks, A.J.B. 1983. "The lex Junia and the effects of informal manumission and iteration", *Revue Internationale des Droits de l'Antiquité* 30: 216–227.

Sherwin-White, A.N. 1973. "The Tabula of Banasa and the *Constitutio Antoniniana*", *The Journal of Roman Studies* 63: 86–98.

Thür, G. 2021. "The dediticii in P.Giss. 40 I 7–9", in *Symposion 2019. Vorträge zur griechischen und hellenistischen Rechtsgeschichte* (Hamburg, 26.–28. August 2019), ed. K. Harter-Uibopuu and W. Rieß, 501–516. Vienna.

van Minnen, P. 2016. "Three edicts of Caracalla? A new reading of P.Giess. 40", *Chiron* 46: 206–221.

Wilhelm, A. 1934. "Die *Constitutio Antoniniana*", The American Journal of Archaeology, 38: 178–180.

Wolff, H. 1976. *Die* Constitutio Antoniniana *und Papyrus Gissensis 40, I* (Diss.), Köln.

Youni, M.S. 2010. "Transforming Greek practice into Roman law: Manumission in Roman Macedonia", *The Legal History Review* 78: 311–340.

INDEX LOCORUM

erstellt von Susanne Lorenz (Wien)

1. Griechische und lateinische Autoren
2. Lexika
3. Biblische Texte
4. Juristische Quellen
5. Inschriften
6. Papyri

1. Griechische und lateinische Autoren

2. Lexika

3. Biblische Quellen

4. Römisches Recht

5. Inschriften

6. Papyri

TEILNEHMERINNEN UND TEILNEHMER

José Luis Alonso, Professor für Römisches Recht, Juristische Papyrologie und Privatrecht, Rechtswissenschaftliche Fakultät der Universität Zürich
joseluis.alonso@rwi.uzh.ch

Sophia Aneziri, Associate Professor für Alte Geschichte, Ἐθνικόν και Καποδιστριακόν Πανεπιστήμιον Ἀθηνῶν (Nationale und Kapodistrias-Universität Athen)
sanez@arch.uoa.gr

Ilias N. Arnaoutoglou, Research Director am Forschungszentrum für Griechische Rechtsgeschichte, Ἀκαδημία Ἀθηνῶν (Akademie von Athen)
iliasarn@academyofathens.gr

Kostas Buraselis, Professor em. für Alte Geschichte und ehemaliger Vizerektor, Ἐθνικόν και Καποδιστριακόν Πανεπιστήμιον Ἀθηνῶν (Nationale und Kapodistrias-Universität Athen)
kburasel@arch.uoa.gr

Mirko Canevaro, Professor for Greek History, School of History, Classics and Archaeology, The University of Edinburgh
Mirko.Canevaro@ed.ac.uk

Athina Dimopoulou, Professorin für Rechtsgeschichte, Law School, Ἐθνικόν και Καποδιστριακόν Πανεπιστήμιον Ἀθηνῶν (Nationale und Kapodistrias-Universität Athen)
adimopoul@law.uoa.gr

Martin Dreher, em. Professor für die Geschichte des Altertums, Universität Magdeburg
martin.dreher@ovgu.de

Michael Gagarin, James R. Dougherty, Jr. Centennial Professor of Classics, Emeritus, University of Texas at Austin
gagarin@austin.utexas.edu

Lina Girdvainyte, Lecturer in Ancient History, School of History, Classics and Archaeology, The University of Edinburgh
lina.girdvainyte@ed.ac.uk

Kaja Harter-Uibopuu, Professorin für Alte Geschichte, Fachbereich Geschichte, Universität Hamburg
kaja.harter@uni-hamburg.de

Éva Jakab, Professorin für Römisches Recht, Rechtswissenschaftliche Fakultät, Károli Gáspár Református Egyetem (Károli Gáspár Universität), Budapest
jakab.eva@kre.hu

Thomas Kruse, Senior Scientist, Österreichische Akademie der Wissenschaften, Österreichisches Archäologisches Institut, Wien
thomas.kruse@oeaw.ac.at

David Lewis, Senior Lecturer in Greek History and Culture, School of History, Classics and Archaeology, The University of Edinburgh
david.lewis@ed.ac.uk

Alberto Maffi, Professore di diritto romano e diritti dell´antichità, Dipartimento di giurisprudenza, Università degli Studi Milano-Bicocca
alberto.maffi@unimib.it

Anna Magnetto, Professore Associato di storia Greca, Scuola normale Superiore, Pisa
anna.magnetto@sns.it

Christel Müller, Professeur d`Histoire grecque, Membre senior de l'IUF, Université Paris Nanterre
christel.muller@parisnanterre.fr

Bernhard Palme, Professor für Alte Geschichte und Papyrologie, Institut für Alte Geschichte und Altertumskunde, Papyrologie und Epigraphik, Universität Wien
bernhard.palme@univie.ac.at

Werner Riess, Professor für Alte Geschichte, Fachbereich Geschichte, Universität Hamburg
werner.riess@uni-hamburg.de

Mariagrazia Rizzi, Ricercatrice di diritto romano e diritti dell´antichità, Dipartimento di giurisprudenza, Università degli Studi Milano-Bicocca
mariagrazia.rizzi@unimib.it

Lene Rubinstein, Professor of Ancient History, Royal Holloway, University of London
l.rubinstein@rhul.ac.uk

Patrick Sänger, Professor für Alte Geschichte, Seminar für Alte Geschichte Westfälische Wilhelms-Universität in Münster
saengerp@uni-muenster.de

Carlos M[a] Sánchez-Moreno Ellart, Titular de Derecho Romano, Facultad de Derecho, Universidad de Valencia
carlos.sanchez-moreno@uv.es

Adele C. Scafuro, Professor of Classics, Brown University
adele_scafuro@brown.edu

Philipp Scheibelreiter, Professor für Antike Rechtsgeschichte und Römisches Recht, Institut für Römisches Recht und Antike Rechtsgeschichte, Universität Wien
philipp.scheibelreiter@univie.ac.at

Winfried Schmitz, Professor für Alte Geschichte, Rheinische Friedrich-Wilhelms-Universität Bonn
winfried.schmitz@uni-bonn.de

Gerhard Thür, em. Professor für Römisches Recht an der Universität Graz; Mitglied der Österreichischen Akademie der Wissenschaften, Wien
gerhard.thuer@oeaw.ac.at

S. C. Todd, Professor of Ancient History, University of Manchester
stephen.todd@manchester.ac.uk

Robert W. Wallace, Professor of Classics, Northwestern University
rwallace@northwestern.edu

Andreas Victor Walser, Professor der Geschichte der Alten Kulturen vom östlichen Mittelmeer bis zum Mittleren Osten, Historisches Seminar, Universität Zürich
victor.walser@hist.uzh.ch

Uri Yiftach-Firanko, Professor, Head of the Department of Classics, Faculty of Humanities, Tel Aviv University
uiftach@tauex.tau.ac.il